INTERNATIONAL MILITARY AND DEFENSE ENCYCLOPEDIA

INTERNATIONAL MILITARY AND DEFENSE ENCYCLOPEDIA

Volume 1

A–B

Editor-in-Chief
Col. Trevor N. Dupuy, USA (Ret.)

Executive Editor
Col. Franklin D. Margiotta, USAF (Ret.), Ph.D.

Managing Editors
Mr. Curt Johnson
Col. James B. Motley, USA (Ret.), Ph.D.

Associate Managing Editor
Mr. David L. Bongard

Brassey's (US), Inc.
A Division of Maxwell Macmillan, Inc.
Washington · New York

Brassey's (US), Inc.

Editorial Offices	*Order Department*
Brassey's (US), Inc.	Brassey's Book Orders
8000 Westpark Drive	% Macmillan Publishing Co.
First Floor	100 Front Street, Box 500
McLean, Virginia 22102	Riverside, New Jersey 08075

LIBRARY OF CONGRESS CATALOGING-IN-PUBLICATION DATA

International military and defense encyclopedia / editor-in-chief,
Trevor N. Dupuy . . . [et al.].
p. cm.
Includes index.
ISBN 0-02-881011-2 (set)
1. Military art and science—Encyclopedias. I. Dupuy, Trevor
Nevitt, 1916–
U24.I58 1993
355′.003—dc20 92-33750
CIP

ISBN 0-02-881061-9 (vol. 1)

10 9 8 7 6 5 4 3 2 1

PRINTED IN THE UNITED STATES OF AMERICA

DEDICATION

The *International Military and Defense Encyclopedia* is dedicated to the memory of Morris Janowitz (1919–1988), the Distinguished Service Professor of Sociology, University of Chicago. Morris would have been pleased that the world finally has a comprehensive codification of knowledge about the military and defense, international in scope and authorship. For almost half a century, he focused his intellectual life on organizing the study of the military and issues of defense. Through his scholarship, his Inter-University Seminar on Armed Forces and Society, and his scholarly journal, Morris expanded the study of the military and society to all parts of the globe. He was brilliant at opening windows into defense establishments and let us all understand them better. Our only regret is that Morris Janowitz is no longer here to provide the scorching criticism and generous encouragement we always expected. It is only fitting that we remember him upon the publication of this *International Military and Defense Encyclopedia*.

INTERNATIONAL HONORARY ADVISORY BOARD

CONTENTS

Preface xiii

Acknowledgments xxi

List of Articles xxiii

List of Articles by Subject Area xli

Contributors li

Abbreviations and Acronyms lxvii

International Military and Defense Encyclopedia

Volume 1: A–B *1*

Volume 2: C–F *436*

Volume 3: G–L *1041*

Volume 4: M–O *1587*

Volume 5: P–S *2083*

Volume 6: T–Z *2657*

Index *(Volume 6)* *2985*

PREFACE

The *International Military and Defense Encyclopedia* (*IMADE*) is the first and only definitive and comprehensive English-language encyclopedia of international military and defense information. It contains 786 alphabetically organized articles presented in six volumes. This Preface explains how Brassey's (US) determined there was a need for this encyclopedia, how *IMADE* was defined and developed, and what aids the publisher has built in to help the reader find information.

The Need for *IMADE*

War, defense, the military, budgets, force structures, external threats, arms control, and peace are clearly subjects that must concern people of virtually every political persuasion. Yet if one went to a "good library" in search of information on these subjects, one would have to consult numerous sources, and still the result would be a very incomplete picture of the primary issues and information on the military, defense, and security. Further investigation would reveal that the general public had little access to detailed information about many military and defense subjects. Some of the most important military and defense information is arcane and has little parallel in civilian life and society. A commercial jet airliner relies upon the same physical principles as a modern jet fighter, but the similarities end quickly. The uses of these two marvelous machines, their internal equipment, and the training of the crews differ significantly. One could draw the same distinctions between naval forces and merchant shipping and many other areas of defense and civilian activity. Moreover, governments classify military and defense information, thereby restricting public knowledge. Even in the most open societies, details about the military and defense are normally contained within the relatively closed systems of the armed forces and within those research, development, and manufacturing entities that provide the weapons of war.

Brassey's (US) first explored and then undertook the difficult and lengthy task of developing a comprehensive and international encyclopedia on the military and defense because the societies that provide the funds and the young men and women to the military and the defense industries have a right to understand these subjects. Thus, we decided to address the most fundamental issues that have faced humanity since humans first started taking up weapons.

We were confident enough to explore the daunting task of compiling this encyclopedia for three reasons: (1) we are the oldest book publisher in these fields; (2) we have published the largest collection of books and authors in these fields; and (3) we are one of the few commercial publishing houses managed by former military officers with operational and combat experience, advanced academic and research experience, and worldwide contacts.

Intuitive feelings about the need for *IMADE* were reinforced by research. I visited major U.S. military libraries with large collections to ascertain the availability of comprehensive works. Telephone calls were made to heads of similar libraries. One would have to collect 25 to 30 books to have only a portion of the material that logically belonged in a military and defense encyclopedia. The heads and staffs of these libraries noted that the mere collection of this information would make such a work valuable, particularly to smaller libraries, which had a difficult time finding the right books and budgeting for them every year.

To test further these initial impressions about the need for *IMADE*, Brassey's (US) convened a two-day international conference of distinguished librarians, journalists, scholars, and active and former government and military officials. Strong expressions of support emerged from Mr. John Barry (Senior National Security Correspondent, *Newsweek*); Col. John Collins, USA (Ret.), Ph.D. (Senior Defense Analyst, U.S. Library of Congress); Col. Trevor N. Dupuy, USA (Ret.) (author and eventually Editor-in-Chief of *IMADE*); Jacques Gansler, Ph.D. (Vice President, The Analytic Sciences Corp.); Gen. Paul Gorman, USA (Ret.) (former Commander, U.S. Southern Command); Prof. William Kaufmann, Ph.D. (author; former DoD official; faculty member, MIT and Harvard University); Mr. John Keegan (author; Defence Editor, *Daily Telegraph*, London; faculty member, Oxford University); Col. Fred Kiley, USAF (Ret.) (Director of Research and Press, National Defense University); Prof. Charles C. Moskos (faculty member, Northwestern University; Chairman, Inter-University Seminar on Armed Forces and Society); Mr. Thomas Russell (Director, National Defense University Library); and Mr. Steven Shaker (author; former Navy program analyst). Based upon this group's preliminary suggestions about content, we then began to define more precisely the purpose and scope of *IMADE*. The first step was to assess more carefully the potential audiences.

Defining and Developing *IMADE*

Audiences for IMADE

A wide range of potential users was identified. They included faculty and students in civilian high schools, universities, and educational institutions; private and government academies and military colleges, universities, and training organizations; active, reserve, and retired officers and enlisted personnel of armed forces; and all levels of defense and military personnel in government agencies concerned with security and foreign policy issues. Researchers and staff of research institutes and organizations devoted to the study of security, foreign policy, defense, and the military would also find *IMADE* valuable, as would all those involved in defense industries or areas affected by defense spending and procurement, including journalists. Finally, the encyclopedia would serve as a ready reference guide for the knowledgeable, informed citizen needing information about the military and defense. *IMADE* should be a major vehicle for informing and educating.

IMADE was basically defined by the end of 1987. I early decided that *IMADE* must be international; we should strive to cover the world's experience and knowledge about the military and defense, with as little ethnic or cultural bias as possible. How we moved toward this goal is described later in this Preface. The extraordinary media coverage of the 1991 Gulf War and the breakup of the Soviet empire seemingly validated my 1987 conclusion that improvements in transportation and communication systems would make issues of war and peace almost anywhere on the globe of interest and concern worldwide.

At this point, the project was discussed with the reference experts at Pergamon Press in Oxford and received the substantial financial investment necessary after personal approval by Robert Maxwell. Later, *IMADE* would receive the bulk of its support from Macmillan Publishing Company, New York, after Macmillan was purchased by Maxwell Communications Corporation and Brassey's (US) became part of this fine publishing company.

The Advisory and Editorial Boards

In mid-1987, an agreement was reached with Col. Trevor N. Dupuy, USA (Ret.), to become the Editor-in-Chief and for his research group to help organize and manage the development of the encyclopedia. Colonel Dupuy's international scholarly reputation was unparalleled—among his more than 60 books were a well-known military dictionary, a book on world power measurements, the *Encyclopedia of Military History*, and a forthcoming *Encyclopedia of Military Biography*. Our Editor-in-Chief later became even more internationally known through his book and media analyses of the Gulf War.

Brassey's (US) then formed two distinguished boards. The Honorary Advisory Board included British and Indian Field Marshals, a former Chairman of the U.S. Joint Chiefs of Staff, a senior General from the People's Republic of China, and three leading civilian scholars from Germany, Japan, and the United States. Later, we added the former Chairman of the Republic of Korea Joint Chiefs of Staff, the former Commandant of the United States Marine Corps, an Admiral of the Fleet from the United Kingdom, and an internationally known scholarly leader in the study of the military and society.

Based primarily on the suggestions of our Editor-in-Chief, we named an impressive editorial board of seventeen subject editors, each responsible for a subject area. They were experienced, prominent experts from three continents and seven countries. Selecting people of reputation and experience from around the world was a start toward making *IMADE* international in scope and approach. We brought the Editorial Board to Virginia for a week of debate, discussion, and decision. This was a lively, stimulating experience because of the quality of the individuals involved, their broad range of backgrounds, and the level at which most of them had actively participated in or studied the military and defense. The multicultural basis of *IMADE* later was enhanced further by the selection of authors from seventeen countries and the richness of examples used in their articles. Depending on the subject, we sometimes found it essential to select board members and authors who were active-duty or retired senior military officers, particularly those who had both operational and academic experiences.

The Editor-in-Chief, Colonel Dupuy, had prepared a master list of topics, and each subject editor brought his own. Trevor did a masterful job of leading twenty determined and knowledgeable personalities in lively debate and discussion for four days. He skillfully closed in and sharpened the group's focus over the next two days. At the end we had a virtual consensus on responsibilities, scope, weight of effort in each subject area, and on more than 90 percent of the final topics. Any user of this encyclopedia owes Colonel Dupuy a debt of gratitude: it is virtually impossible to look for a major military or defense topic that is not covered and indexed in this comprehensive encyclopedia.

Because of the range of subjects and audiences for *IMADE*, our editorial meeting decided that the articles must be at times simple, at times very complex. Younger students should be able to find summary histories of major wars or biographies of leading military figures. Graduate students in a defined scientific field should be able to find a definitive exposition on esoteric or advanced technological subjects. Young military cadets in a developing nation should find information about their region and neighboring countries, plus primary definitions, explanations, and histories dealing with the art and science of warfare. The encyclopedia would codify the world's knowledge about the military and defense to provide a sound departure point for further research. But we also realized that this must be a unique encyclopedia. Because of the relative dearth of public literature, we determined that this encyclopedia should also *create* primary *public* knowledge. Also, when possible, the articles should preview future developments, particularly where technology and world events were changing rapidly. This would give *IMADE* lasting relevance and, again, make it unique.

As we defined the subject areas and article list, we concluded that only in brief definitions of very discrete subjects could one separate an article completely from other aspects of the military and defense. For instance, armor (the subject of one article) is about armored fighting vehicles, which incorporates several elements of advanced technology. Armor is used under strategies, tactics, and doctrines that seek to integrate artillery, infantry, support, and airpower with tank use. Tanks are affected by terrain and are organized and led differently than are other military elements. Armor in battles and wars has created history, has made leaders famous, and has been used to further political objectives and outcomes that depended upon and affected budgets, policies, training, morale, diplomacy, and negotiation.

We thus determined that *IMADE* articles would often be multidisciplinary, including disciplines that were rarely treated publicly and never collected in one comprehensive English-language reference work. *IMADE* would cross in a major way into traditional academic areas: political science, regional studies, and international affairs; sociology; military history and biography; psychiatry; psychology; engineering and technology; law; military science/ROTC; and operations research. *IMADE* would touch on many more disciplines and on subsets of the above-listed disciplines. Although for management and intellectual purposes we separated *IMADE* into seventeen discrete subject areas, there was never doubt that there must be significant overlap between subjects and articles. We thus decided in the Editorial Board meeting upon a strategy of developing fewer but longer articles and of encouraging the authors to integrate the information necessary from other, related subjects.

In defining the scope of the encyclopedia, we agreed that, except for very important historical treatments, the encyclopedia would focus on events and developments since the end of World War II in 1945. The reader will find a substantial, but not detailed, history of three to four pages on the French Revolutionary–Napoleonic Wars and the American Civil War: both are covered elsewhere by a considerable body of literature that the reader can consult further. A student being introduced to these subjects will have enough material to make a good report; an expert looking for subtle nuances would not likely turn to this encyclopedia on those subjects. We spent more words on creating *new public* information, yet still have good coverage of material available in great depth elsewhere.

We had a lively debate, but then ruled out of the encyclopedia major world figures such as Prime Minister Winston Churchill, President Franklin D. Roosevelt, and others who made their mark as political leaders and were not directly engaged in the military and defense. We decided that *IMADE* obviously could not compare every country of the world in every article; thus we chose to contrast American, Soviet, British, and French systems in comparisons because so many countries of the world have adopted these nations' armaments, strategies, tactics, and doctrine.

We encouraged authors, where appropriate, to present competing perspectives or views. Country articles would be standardized and provide statistical data and information on the country's military history, politico-military background and policy, force structure, and future security issues.

The Contributors: Opportunities and Constraints

The subject editors and Colonel Dupuy were instrumental in finding authors for the articles. Many articles were written by people who have both lived and studied the military and defense subjects of which they wrote. Many of the authors have participated in combat operations. Their unique insights are not normally available to those outside military and defense establishments. Most authors have advanced degrees and academic and/or operational credentials. Collectively, they represent a distinguished international group of practitioners, warriors, scientists and engineers, former high-level commanders, researchers, and scholars.

IMADE is thus both a scholarly and an "expert" work. Because some subjects have little public literature, some articles are based primarily upon personal knowledge, plus unclassified government manuals, documents, studies, memos, and education and training materials from military academies, schools, and training sites.

We recognized the bias that could emerge from *IMADE*'s publication in American English, management by Colonel Dupuy and me, and the weight of America in the military and defense worlds. The possibility of an unbalanced focus on things American was resisted in many ways. We have almost 60 articles from authors from the United Kingdom; more than 60 by German authors; and 30 from Egyptian flag ranks. The Advisory Board, Editorial Board, and author list contain experts from seventeen countries and four continents. Our non-American subject editors also insisted on an international approach in articles. During editorial review, articles were returned to authors for examples beyond American or British experience.

This struggle to keep *IMADE* multicultural created significant editorial issues. Articles were written by authors whose English was their second language. At times, we paid for translations into English. Some articles were revised or rewritten by English-capable associate editors, resulting in team authorship. Sometimes new authors replaced non-Americans if agreement could not be reached. We generally respected the author's spelling of non-English words, especially those in Chinese and Russian. Although international mail flows more quickly than it once did, development time was stretched by having articles written in the People's Republic of China, Japan, Egypt, and India.

Revising IMADE: The Second Review, Evaluation, and Revision

Eventually, a major consideration became the very length and complexity of *IMADE*. Articles written promptly became dated, especially when, to the great joy of most of the world, the cold war ended symbolically with the Berlin Wall's collapse. Suddenly there was one Germany, not two. The article on the Soviet Union became a historical one, while the fledgling Soviet republics had not yet completed their military and defense apparatus. A major article on the Warsaw Pact also was turned into a history. The 1991 Gulf War erupted, with startling results in alliance building, military technology, tactics, and the weight of airpower. In early 1991, I decided to re-evaluate every article, then rewrite, reject, or recommission as necessary. Fortunately, I was able to draw upon colleagues met during my more than three decades of experience and education in air combat and operations, advanced academic study and teaching at the Air Force Academy and Air Command and Staff College (ACSC), research and publication, and management of large academic research organizations at ACSC and National Defense University.

Associate and contract editors were added to speed this approach; authors were asked to revise and update; all 129 country and regional articles were revised with the latest data from three prestigious annuals: *The Military Balance*, *The Statesman's Yearbook*, and *The World Factbook*.

We rewrote articles that dealt with the turmoil in the Soviet Union and Yugoslavia and the creation of numerous new states whose futures appear uncertain. The reader may find yearly updates of this material in the annuals noted above.

The world's gain in peace and freedom created editorial difficulties, but this added level of review and revision significantly improved *IMADE*'s currency, value, and quality.

Structure, Organization, and Use of *IMADE*

As noted earlier, *IMADE* was developed within seventeen major subject areas; this greatly facilitated assigning responsibility, workload, and weight of effort given to particular subjects. The encyclopedia was completed in 786 articles, presented herein alphabetically, after intellectual development under the following areas:

- Aerospace Forces and Warfare
- Combat Theory and Operations
- Leadership, Command, and Management
- Countries, Regions, and Organizations
- Armed Forces and Society
- History and Biography
- Land Forces and Warfare
- Logistics
- Manpower and Personnel
- Materiel and Weapons
- Naval Forces and Warfare
- Technology, Research, and Development
- Military Theory and Operations Research
- Defense and International Security Policy
- Military and International Security Law
- Military Intelligence
- General Military

The length of the articles ranges from 100 to more than 10,000 words. Most of the articles should help the general interested reader gain an understanding of the topic. Narrower and more technical articles (such as those on advanced technologies or on research and development) can help the knowledgeable specialist, but some may prove difficult for the general reader.

Using IMADE

IMADE is presented alphabetically for the convenience of the reader, and a detailed index is presented in Volume 6. There are approximately 7–10 index entries per encyclopedia page and a total of nearly 25,000 index terms. As noted earlier, because of the complexity and interrelationships of defense information, we guided authors to write broad articles and to identify key words or phrases in their articles. These terms formed an initial base that was extended considerably by a professional encyclopedia indexer.

The smart users of *IMADE* will find it a rich source of information but will be most successful if they take time at the beginning to use the many aids we have put in Volumes 1 and 6. Readers looking for information on a particular area should begin by looking up key words in the index and then scanning the entries to which they are referred. They can also use the significant cross-indexing, which details specialized areas that might be covered in other articles. Another aid is the detailed cross-referencing system to be found at the end of each article, the "See Also" section. This refers the reader to related articles recommended by the author and editors. Almost all articles conclude with a bibliography which sends the reader to primary source material or to longer, sometimes "classic," treatments of the subject.

Volume 1 is another valuable source of information; it includes lists of names and affiliations of *IMADE*'s Honorary Advisory Board, Subject Editors/Editorial Board, Associate Editors, and authors. The alphabetical list of entries lists each article with its author's name. The classified list of entries outlines the basic organizing structure used in commissioning and managing articles and lists all articles on related topics under the seventeen general subject headings. A list of acronyms and abbreviations is also contained in each volume.

These aids should help the reader find solid, objective information on virtually any major topic dealing with international defense and military information.

Franklin D. Margiotta, Ph.D.
Colonel, USAF (Ret.)
Executive Editor and Publisher
Washington, D.C.
United States of America

ACKNOWLEDGMENTS

Hundreds of people are responsible for the development, quality, and publication of Brassey's (US) *International Military and Defense Encyclopedia* (*IMADE*).

The first general recognition must go to the distinguished international group of military leaders, scholars, research and library experts (identified in the Preface) who strongly suggested in an exploratory meeting that *IMADE* would be a significant contribution to public information and education about the military and defense. They also emphasized that the mere collection of this material into one major work would be of great benefit. Their encouragement, preliminary advice on content, and suggestions on potential contributors sustained us through the next long six years.

We also must thank the International Honorary Advisory Board, which includes seven of the most senior military leaders in the world and four of the most prominent scholars of military and defense matters. Their faith in and support of Brassey's and this project from the earliest days permitted us to attract experts from seventeen countries whose work is displayed in the articles. Their advice on the selection of the editorial board and authors was especially helpful in broadening the international basis of the work.

The subject editors who formed the Editorial Board must be acknowledged for their diligence, their positive approach to *IMADE*, and their significant contributions to a better understanding of the military and defense. After helping to define the encyclopedia's scope, weight of effort, responsibilities, and topics, these subject editors signed up author-experts from around the world. They then reviewed and edited the articles, sometimes translating them into English. Without their efforts, this reference work would not exist. We must also recognize those brought on board late as Associate Editors who pitched in when deadlines neared and we needed to reevaluate and rewrite dozens of articles because of translation problems, late or incomplete work, or monumental changes in the world.

Most important, of course, are the more than 400 authors who generously wrote the expert articles, sometimes receiving a modest honorarium, sometimes prohibited by their governments from accepting any compensation. We hope that they will feel that this final product is worthy of their efforts. In addition, there are those who made a special contribution to the intellectual richness of *IMADE* by stimulating some of the final articles: Bassam Al Assaly, Ali Gamal El-Din Barekat, Donald R. Baucom, Kenneth W. Bushell, Thomas A. Cardwell III, Hellmut O. K. Goos, Alan Gropman, Charles A. Hawkins, Jr., Fred Holmes, Manfred Kühr, James Murphy, Peter K. O'Globlin, Meir Pa'il, Thomas L. Saaty, Hartmut Schmedt, Hartmut Schmidt-Petri, Jürgen Singer, Charles R. Smith, Dietmar Schössler, Eugene Tighe, Richard Trainor, Haluk Unaldi, Gerhard Wettig.

The Brassey's and Macmillan staffs, too, deserve special mention. As Associate Director of Publishing for Reference Works, Deirdre Murphy spent more than three years of her life working with authors and with senior subject editors while managing an impossibly large and complex encyclopedia project. Toward the middle stages, she was joined in these tasks by a first-class contract editor,

Jack Hopper; Martha E. Rothenberg completed the contract editorial team and added her substantial skills in computers and database management to our effort. At different times during the six-year gestation period, we were helped by Christine E. Williams and Anne Stockdell. Carrie Burkett helped me start it all, and Elizabeth Ashley helped us finish. At Macmillan in New York, book production was managed with great professionalism by John Ball, Terry Dieli, and Benjamin Barros. I could not have spent the time I did on *IMADE* without our fine book publishing staff who stepped up their efforts and kept the book program alive and well: Don McKeon, Associate Director of Publishing for Books; Vicki Chamlee, Editor; and Kim Borchard, Director of Marketing and Public Relations.

Special recognition goes to Colonel James B. Motley, USA (Ret.) who particularly assisted *IMADE* during the last six months of manuscript completion. Jim helped us smooth articles, chased authors and editors, rewrote certain articles, and assisted us all with his management and organizational skills. He applied well the skills and knowledge he learned in his combat, leadership, and academic assignments. We could not have finished on schedule without him.

Finally, we acknowledge the cooperation of the International Institute for Strategic Studies and St. Martin's Press for giving us permission to use their data on the countries of the world collected annually in the internationally known *Military Balance* and *The Statesman's Yearbook*. Their generous assistance moved us well toward the goal of excellence that we applied to the development of this *International Military and Defense Encyclopedia*.

LIST OF ARTICLES

Academies, Military	Charles F. Hawkins
Accession Standards	Patricia Insley Hutzler
Administration, Military	J. H. Skinner
Aerial Mining	Stephen P. Randolph
Aerial Refueling	Thomas D. Phillips Gregory M. Shaka Kim Lott
Afghanistan	John G. Merriam
Afghanistan, Soviet Invasion of	James B. Motley
Air Assault	Friedrich K. Jeschonnek
Air Interdiction	Jasjit Singh
Air Reconnaissance	Yossef Bodansky
Airborne Land Forces	Reinhard Uhle-Wettler
Aircraft Carrier	Ronald O'Rourke
Aircraft, Military	Perry M. Smith
Aircraft, Short Take-off and Landing	Perry M. Smith
Aircraft Technology Applications	P. W. Liddell Bryan Young
Aircraft, Unmanned	Michael Armitage
Air-land Battle	Franz Uhle-Wettler
Airlift	Charles J. Jernigan
Airman	John R. Brinkerhoff
Airpower	Clifford R. Krieger
Airpower, History of	Michael Armitage
Airpower, Strategic	Thomas M. Kearney
Airpower, Tactical	Daniel R. Mortensen
Airspace Control, Military	Perry M. Smith
Alexander, Harold Rupert Leofric George	Harold E. Raugh, Jr.
Alexander the Great	Janice J. Gabbert
Algeria	David L. Bongard
Allenby, Edmund Henry Hynman	Arnold C. Dupuy
Alliance, Military and Political	Terry L. Deibel
American Revolutionary War	Max R. Williams
Ammunition	Charles Q. Cutshaw
Amphibious Forces	Thomas L. Wilkerson
Amphibious Ships and Craft	William L. Eldred
Amphibious Vehicle	Moustafa Aly Morsy Aly
Amphibious Warfare	Joseph H. Alexander
Angola	David L. Bongard Trevor N. Dupuy
Antisubmarine Warfare	Jan S. Breemer
Antitactical Ballistic Missile Policy	Thomas Enders
Arab Conquests	Lawrence D. Higgins
Arab-Israeli Wars	James J. Bloom
Arab League	David L. Bongard
Archives, Military	Jeffrey C. Barlow

Arctic Warfare	Gerhard Schepe Alexander Hartinger
Ardant du Picq, Charles J. J. J.	David L. Bongard
Argentina	Nora Stewart
Armed Forces and Society	Gwyn Harries-Jenkins
Armenia	[Executive Editor]
Armor	Paul-Werner Krapke
Armor Technology	Robert J. Eichelberger
Armored Ground Vehicle	Moustafa Aly Morsy Aly
Armored Land Vehicle Technology Applications	Ernest N. Petrick
Arms Control and Disarmament	Peter R. Weilemann
Arms Control and Disarmament: Mathematical Models	Reiner K. Huber
Arms Trade and Military Assistance	Stephanie G. Neuman
Army Aviation	Arno Möhl
Arnold, H. H. ("Hap")	Albert D. McJoynt
Art of War	John I. Alger
Artillery	Manfred Kühr
Artillery, Antiaircraft	Kheidr K. El Dahrawy
Artillery, Rocket and Missile	Alaa El Din Abdel Meguid Darwish
Artillery, Tube	Alaa El Din Abdel Meguid Darwish
Assistance, Military	N. T. P. Murphy
Assistance, Mutual	N. T. P. Murphy
Association of Southeast Asian Nations	Donald S. Marshall
Assyria, Military History of	Lawrence D. Higgins
Atlantic-Mediterranean Area	Paul C. Davis
Attaché, Military	Scott A. Koch
Attack	Axel von Netzer
Attila the Hun	Szabolcs M. de Gyürky
Attrition: Personnel Casualties	Trevor N. Dupuy
Auftragstaktik	Daniel J. Hughes
Australia	David L. Bongard Trevor N. Dupuy
Austria	David L. Bongard Trevor N. Dupuy
Automatic Weapon	Samir H. Shalaby
Aviation, Military	Peter R. Faber
Azerbaijan	[Executive Editor]
Balkan Wars	Trevor N. Dupuy
Ballistic Missile Defense	William A. Davis, Jr.
Ballistics	Abraham Flatau
Bangladesh	David L. Bongard Trevor N. Dupuy
Battleship	Paul Stillwell
Belarus (formerly Byelorussia)	[Executive Editor]
Belgium	David L. Bongard Trevor N. Dupuy
Biological Warfare	Benjamin C. Garrett
Biological Warfare Technology	David W. Einsel, Jr.
Blitzkrieg	Daniel J. Hughes
Blockade and Maritime Exclusion	Roger W. Barnett
Boer Wars	Trevor N. Dupuy
Bolívar, Simón	Walter P. White
Bolivia	David L. Bongard Trevor N. Dupuy

Bombardment, Strategic	Thomas D. Philips
	William G. Kuller
	Raymond E. Franck, Jr.
	Michael J. Kaiser
	Jeffrey A. Neal
Border Guard	Manfred Obst
Bosnia-Hercegovina	[Executive Editor]
Bradley, Omar Nelson	Kevin J. Weddle
Branches, Military	James B. Motley
Brauchitsch, Walther von	Szabolcs M. de Gyürky
Brazil	John Hoyt Williams
Briefings	John Hemsley
Brooke, Alan Francis, 1st Viscount Alanbrooke	Robert Calvert, Jr.
Budget and Finance, Military	Charles Q. Cutshaw
	Dianne M. Cutshaw
Budget, Defense	Alice C. Maroni
Bulgaria	David L. Bongard
	Trevor N. Dupuy
Burial, Military	Wilfred L. Ebel
Burma	Charles F. Hawkins
	Donald S. Marshall
Byzantine Empire	Lawrence D. Higgins
Cadet	John R. Brinkerhoff
Cadre	John R. Brinkerhoff
Caesar, Julius	Arther Ferrill
Cambodia	Charles F. Hawkins
	Donald S. Marshall
Canada	David L. Bongard
	Trevor N. Dupuy
Canteen and Shopping Services	J. H. Skinner
Casualties: Evacuation and Treatment	N. T. P. Murphy
Cavalry	Johannes Gerber
Censorship	W. Stanford Smith
Central America and the Caribbean	David L. Bongard
Central and East Asia	David L. Bongard
Ceremonies and Displays	Susan M. Watson
Chad	David L. Bongard
	Trevor N. Dupuy
Chaff	Ibrahim Ahmed Salem
Chaplaincy, Military	Daniel B. Jorgensen
Charlemagne	John F. Sloan
Charles XII, King of Sweden	David L. Bongard
Chemical Warfare	Benjamin C. Garrett
Chemical Warfare Technology	David W. Einsel, Jr.
Chiang Kai-shek	Edward C. O'Dowd
Chile	James D. Boggs
China, People's Republic of	David L. Bongard
	Donald S. Marshall
Chu-Teh	Suen Fu-tian
Civil Affairs	J. H. Skinner
Civil Emergency Planning	Leon Goure
Civil-Military Cooperation	Hans Höster
Civil-Military Relations	Claude E. Welch, Jr.
Civil War	Dieter Bangert
Civil War, American	Ralph M. Mitchell

Civil War, Russian	Dianne L. Smith
Civil War, Spanish	R. Dan Richardson
Civilian Substitution	John R. Brinkerhoff
Clausewitz, Karl von	John E. Tashjean
Close Air Support	Timothy E. Kline
Coalition Warfare	Albert D. McJoynt
Coast Defense	Johannes Gerber
Cold War	Charles R. Smith
Colombia	David L. Bongard Trevor N. Dupuy
Colonial Empires, European	Phillip E. Koerper
Combat Effectiveness	Trevor N. Dupuy
Combat Motivation	Anthony Kellett
Combat Power and Potential	Donald S. Marshall
Combat Service Support	J. H. Skinner
Combat Stress	Reuven Gal
Combat Support	Klaus Kleffner
Combined Arms	Sturmhard Eisenkeil
Combined Operations	Albert D. McJoynt
Command	Roger H. Nye
Command, Control, Communications, and Intelligence	Arie Mizrachi
Command Post	Keith E. Bonn
Commonwealth of Independent States	[Executive Editor]
Commonwealth of Nations	David L. Bongard
Communications Equipment Trends	Richard J. Roca
Communications, Signal	Ulrich Stork
Compensation, Military	James B. Motley
Computer Security	E. Edward Bassett
Computers, Military Use of	Jay R. Sculley
Condé, Louis II de Bourbon, Prince de	Curt Johnson
Conditions of Military Service	James Murphy
Conflict Termination	Stephen J. Cimbala
Conscientious Objection	David A. Smith
Conscription	John Whiteclay Chambers II
Consumption Rates, Battlefield	N. T. P. Murphy
Conventional War	Heinz Kozak
Convoy and Protection of Shipping	Stuart D. Landersman
Coordination	Henry Alan Staley
Correlation of Forces	Franz Uhle-Wettler
Cost Analysis	John G. Honig
Costa Rica	David L. Bongard Trevor N. Dupuy
Counterintelligence	James H. Hansen
Coup d'état	Claude E. Welch, Jr.
Covert Action	Abram N. Shulsky
Crimean War	Trevor N. Dupuy
Crisis Management	Dieter Ruloff
Croatia	[Executive Editor]
Cromwell, Oliver	David L. Bongard
Cross-servicing	N. T. P. Murphy
Crusades	John F. Sloan
Cuba	John Hoyt Williams
Cuban Missile Crisis	Graham T. Allison, Jr.
Cunningham, Sir Alan G.	David John Fitzpatrick
Customs and Etiquette	John F. Geraci

Cybernetics, Soviet Concepts of Military	Allan S. Rehm
Czechoslovakia	David L. Bongard
Deception	Franz Uhle-Wettler
Decorations, Honorary Orders, and Awards	Raymond Oliver
Defeat	James B. Motley
Defense	Johannes Gerber
Defense, Aerospace	Jasjit Singh
Defense Decision Making: Analysis and Models	Reiner K. Huber
De Lattre de Tassigny, Jean	E. C. Kiesling
Delaying Action	Hermann Büschleb
Demilitarized Zone	Karl Liko
Demonstration	Alessandro Politi
Denial Measure	Heinrich Quaden
Denmark	David L. Bongard Trevor N. Dupuy
Deployment	Rolf Bergmeier
Depth Charge	Omar El Farouk Amin Omar Yousri Kandil
Desert Warfare	Donn Starry
Desertion	James D. Blundell
Deterrence	Ulrich Weisser
Diplomacy, Aerospace	Robert R. Haffa, Jr.
Directives, Orders, and Instructions	John Hemsley
Discipline	Larry H. Ingraham
Disinformation	Roy Godson
Diversion, Operational	Friedrich K. Jeschonnek
Doctrine	Donald S. Marshall
Doenitz, Karl	Vincent B. Hawkins
Dominican Republic	David L. Bongard Trevor N. Dupuy
Dominican Republic: 1965 Crisis	James B. Motley
Douhet, Giulio	I. B. Holley, Jr.
Dual Capability	Heinrich Quaden
Eastern Europe	David L. Bongard
Echelon	Christian Meyer-Plath
Economics, Defense	Lutz Köllner
Ecuador	David L. Bongard Trevor N. Dupuy
Education, Military	W. Stanford Smith
Edward I	David L. Bongard
Edward III	David L. Bongard
Egypt	John G. Merriam
Eisenhower, Dwight David	Brian R. Bader
Electronic Warfare, Air	Donald J. Alberts
Electronic Warfare Technology Applications	George F. Steeg
El Salvador	David L. Bongard Trevor N. Dupuy
Encounter Battle	Joachim W. K. Böethling
Engine Technology, Aircraft	William H. Heiser
Engine Technology, Ground Vehicle	Albert M. Karaba
Engineering, Constructional	J. H. Skinner
Engineering Equipment, Combat	Charles M. Bussey

Engineering, Military	Ulrich Kreuzfeld
Engineering, Naval	Charles J. Smith
Enlisted Personnel	Robert F. Lockman
Envelopment	Charles E. White
Environmental Impact of Armed Forces	Bonnie Ram
Escalation	Ulrich Weisser
Espionage, Legal Aspects of	Juan C. Marrero
Estonia	[Executive Editor]
Ethics, Professional Military	Kenneth W. Kemp
Ethiopia	David L. Bongard Trevor N. Dupuy
Ethnicity and the Armed Forces	Cynthia H. Enloe
Eugene, Prince of Savoy-Carignan	David L. Bongard
European Communities	Paul C. Davis
Exercises	Samuel Gardiner
Exercises, Naval	Frederick D. Thompson
Exploitation	Alessandro Politi
Explosives Technology, Conventional	Nikolaus Fiederling Axel Homburg
Family Dependent Programs	Ruth Ann O'Keefe
Farragut, David Glasgow	Bruce W. Watson
Feudalism	Dianne L. Smith
Field Service Regulations	Bruce I. Gudmundsson
Fifth Column	Mark G. McLaughlin
Finland	Fielding Dupuy
Fire and Movement	Carl-Gero von Ilsemann Erhard Drews
Firepower	Trevor N. Dupuy
Fisher, John Arbuthnot, 1st Baron Fisher of Kilverstone	Jon Tetsuro Sumida
Flags and Symbols	Mark G. McLaughlin
Flamethrower	Mamdouh H. Attiah
Fleet	James Alden Barber, Jr.
Fleet Air Defense	Charles D. Allen, Jr.
Flexible Response	Dov S. Zakheim
Foch, Ferdinand	Robert E. Knotts
Fog of War	Donald C. Snedeker
Follow-on Forces Attack	Franz Uhle-Wettler
Food and Catering Services, Military	J. H. Skinner
Force de Frappe	Walter Rudolf Schutze
Force Multiplier	Robert McQuie
Force Ratio	Robert McQuie
Force Structure	John R. Brinkerhoff
Force Structure, Personnel	James F. Murphy
Formation	J. H. Skinner John F. Geraci
Fortification	Hansjörg Schwalm
Forward Defense	Axel Bürgener
France	Theresa Lennon Conroy
France, Military Hegemony of	Curt Johnson
Franco-Prussian War	Trevor N. Dupuy
Fratricide	Curt Johnson
Fratricide of Nuclear Warheads	K. Gerhard Locke
Frederick the Great	Vincent B. Hawkins
French Foreign Legion	Howard R. Simpson
French Revolutionary–Napoleonic Wars	James K. Kieswetter

Friction	John E. Tashjean
Front	Hermann Büschleb
Fuller, J. F. C.	A. J. Trythall
Fuze	Charles Q. Cutshaw
Gendarmerie	Stephan Link
	Karlheinz Böckle
General War	Rudolf Hecht
Generalship	K. E. Hamburger
Geneva Conventions	George H. Aldrich
Genghis Khan	Lawrence D. Higgins
Geography, Military	John R. Brinkerhoff
Georgia	[Executive Editor]
Germany	Edwina S. Campbell
Ghana	Lee A. Sweetapple
Giap, Vo Nguyen	Donald S. Marshall
Gonzalo de Córdoba	Paul Stewart
Government, Military	Bruce W. Watson
Graeco-Persian Wars	Janice J. Gabbert
Grant, Ulysses Simpson	Brian R. Bader
Greece	David L. Bongard
	Trevor N. Dupuy
Grenada, U.S. Intervention in	James B. Motley
Grenade	Samir H. Shalaby
Ground Defense of Air Bases	Yossef Bodansky
Ground Reconnaissance	Rod Paschall
Guatemala	David L. Bongard
	Trevor N. Dupuy
Guderian, Heinz	Vincent B. Hawkins
Gulf War, 1991	Anthony H. Cordesman
Gun, Aerial	Kheidr K. El Dahrawy
Gun, Antitank	Alaa El Din Abdel Meguid Darwish
Gun Technology Applications	Ingo Wolfgang Weise
Gunboat Diplomacy	James Cable
Gustavas Adolphus	Albert D. McJoynt
Hague Conventions	John W. Hopper
Haiti	David L. Bongard
	Trevor N. Dupuy
Halsey, William F. ("Bull")	Bruce W. Watson
Hannibal Barca	Lee A. Sweetapple
Helicopter	Gabr Ali Gabr
Helicopter, Battlefield	Gabr Ali Gabr
Helicopter: Military Missions	Philip D. Stinson
Helicopter, Naval	Gabr Ali Gabr
Hierarchy of Combat	David L. Bongard
Hindenburg, Paul von	Timothy T. Lupfer
History, Ancient Military	Arther Ferrill
History, Early Modern Military	Mark G. McLaughlin
History, Medieval Military	David L. Bongard
History, Military	James J. Bloom
History, Modern Military	Eloise Paananen
	Dwayne Anderson
Ho Chi Minh	Donald S. Marshall
Honduras	Lee A. Sweetapple
Host Nation Support	N. T. P. Murphy
Hostage	Lee A. Sweetapple
Hundred Years' War	David L. Bongard

Article	Contributor
Hungary	Szabolcs M. de Gyürky
	Cheryl de Gyürky
Identification Friend or Foe Technology	Michael I. Keller
India	David L. Bongard
Indirect Fire	Trevor N. Dupuy
Indonesia	Charles F. Hawkins
	Donald S. Marshall
Indo-Pacific Area	Donald S. Marshall
Infantry	Peter Bolte
Information Fusion	William August Sander III
	David William Hilsop
Infrastructure, Military	J. H. Skinner
Initiative in War	Virgilio Ilari
Inspection and Supervision	Susan M. Watson
Installations, Military	James Toth
Intelligence Analysis, Military	John R. Bondanella
Intelligence Collection	James H. Hansen
	Edmund R. Thompson
Intelligence Cycle	Susan M. Watson
Intelligence Establishment	John Prados
Intelligence, General	Abram N. Shulsky
Intelligence, Human	Kenneth J. Campbell
Intelligence, Imagery	Dino A. Brugioni
Intelligence: Indications and Warning	Cynthia M. Grabo
Intelligence, Military	Lloyd Hoffman
Intelligence, Naval	Prescott Palmer
Intelligence, Signal	Uzal W. Ent
Intelligence, Strategic	Dennis J. Quinn
Intelligence, Tactical	Uzal W. Ent
Interior and Exterior Lines of Operation	Virgilio Ilari
Internal Security and Armed Forces	Henry Axel Krigsman, Jr.
Internal Security Forces	W. Stanford Smith
Iran	David L. Bongard
	Trevor N. Dupuy
Iraq	Walter P. White
Ireland	Desmond Dinan
Israel	David L. Bongard
	Trevor N. Dupuy
Italian Unification Wars	Arnold C. Dupuy
Italian Wars	Max George Kellner
Italy	James D. Boggs
Jackson, Thomas Jonathan ("Stonewall")	Uzal W. Ent
Japan	Tsuneo Akaha
Japan, Modernization and Expansion of	Lawrence D. Higgins
Jellicoe, John Rushworth, 1st Earl	Harold E. Raugh, Jr.
Joint Operations	Albert D. McJoynt
Jomini, Antoine Henri	Max R. Williams
Jordan	David L. Bongard
	Trevor N. Dupuy
Jungle Warfare	Donn Starry
Kazakhstan	[Executive Editor]
Kemal, Mustafa Pasha (Atatürk)	J. E. Wade
Kenya	David L. Bongard
	Trevor N. Dupuy
Kesselring, Albert	Harold E. Raugh, Jr.
Khalid ibn al-Walid	James J. Bloom

King, Ernest J.	Grace Person Hayes
Kirgizstan	[Executive Editor]
Konev, Ivan Stepanovich	Dianne L. Smith
Korea, North	James F. Dunnigan
Korea, South	James F. Dunnigan
Korean War	David L. Bongard Trevor N. Dupuy
Labor, Military	J. H. Skinner
Lanchester Equations	Maurice Bresson
Land Forces, Effectiveness and Efficiency of	Hans W. Hofman
Land Warfare	James D. Blundell
Laos	Charles F. Hawkins Donald S. Marshall
Latin American Wars of Independence	Jack Child
Latvia	[Executive Editor]
Law, Military	Peter Rowe
Law of the Sea and Piracy	William L. Schacte, Jr.
Leadership	Kevin Donohue Leonard Wong Steven M. Jones
Leahy, William Daniel	Bruce W. Watson
Leave, Military	W. Stanford Smith
Lebanon	David L. Bongard Trevor N. Dupuy
Lee, Robert Edward	Uzal W. Ent
Legal Assistance	Stephen C. Glassman
Libya	David L. Bongard
Limited War	Heinz Kozak
Lines of Communication	N. T. P. Murphy
Lin-Piao	Jiang Feng-bo
Lithuania	[Executive Editor]
Logistic Movement	J. H. Skinner
Logistics: A General Survey	J. H. Skinner
Logistics, Air Force	Ted Kluz
Logistics, Limited War	John E. Murray
Logistics, NATO	N. T. P. Murphy
Logistics, Naval	Wayne P. Hughes, Jr. Mark L. Mitchell
Logistics, Soviet and Warsaw Pact	Charles Blandy
Low-intensity Conflict: The Military Dimension	William P. Yarborough
Low-intensity Conflict: Theory and Concept	Heinz Vetschera
Ludendorff, Erich	Timothy T. Lupfer
MacArthur, Douglas	Vincent B. Hawkins
Machine Gun	Samir H. Shalaby
Madagascar	David L. Bongard
Mahan, Alfred Thayer	Bruce W. Watson
Maintenance	J. H. Skinner
Malaysia	Charles F. Hawkins Donald S. Marshall
Management	Jeffrey A. McNally
Manchu (Ch'ing) Empire	Zhou Shi-chang
Maneuver	William S. Lind
Man-Machine Interface	M. F. Allnutt

Manpower Policies in the U.S. and NATO	John R. Brinkerhoff Joseph E. Nation James N. Dertouzos
Manstein, Erich von	Vincent B. Hawkins
Mao Tse-tung	Edward J. Marolda
Mapping, Charting, and Geodesy	L. Sam Thompson
Maps, Charts, and Symbols, Military	Charles Q. Cutshaw
Marine	John R. Brinkerhoff
Maritime Logistics	Wayne P. Hughes, Jr. Mark L. Mitchell
Maritime Strategy	Colin S. Gray
Marlborough, John Churchill, Duke of	Albert D. McJoynt
Marshall, George Catlett, Jr.	Albert D. McJoynt
Materials Technology	Maurice de Morton
Mathematical Modeling and Forecasting	Robert H. Kupperman Harvey A. Smith
Mathematics and the Military	Jagdish Chandra
Mauritania	David L. Bongard Trevor N. Dupuy
Measures of Effectiveness	John G. Honig
Mechanized Warfare	Donn Starry
Medical Research and Technology	C. Fred Tyner
Medical Service	Ernst Rebentisch
Medicine, Military	James W. Kirkpatrick
Mercenary	Gerry S. Thomas
Merchant Fleet	Horace G. Davy
Meterology, Military	Nicholas H. Chavasse
Mexico	Roger Anderson
Middle East	David L. Bongard Trevor N. Dupuy
Militarism	Edward W. Walker
Military	Charles C. Moskos
Military Aid to the Civil Power—A U.S. Model	Charles Doyle
Military Police	John R. Brinkerhoff
Mine	Donald E. Bennett Steven M. Kosiak
Mine Warfare, Land	Ulrich Kreuzfeld
Mine Warfare, Naval	J. Jan W. van Waning
Missile, Air-launched Cruise	Thomas D. Phillips Robert A. Frye Alan P. Williams Michael M. Eller
Missile, Air-to-air	Kheidr K. El Dahrawy
Missile, Air-to-surface	Kheidr K. El Dahrawy
Missile, Antitank Guided	Alaa El Din Abdel Meguid Darwish
Missile, Ballistic	William A. Davis, Jr.
Missile, Cruise	Kheidr K. El Dahrawy
Missile, Guided	Kheidr K. El Dahrawy
Missile, Intercontinental Ballistic	Frank B. Horton
Missile Propulsion Technology	Geoffrey I. Evans Peter D. Penny
Missile, Strategic Ballistic	Alaa El Din Abdel Meguid Darwish
Missile, Surface-to-air	Kheidr K. El Dahrawy
Missile Technology Applications	Robert F. Jackson
Mobility	David L. Bongard

Mobilization	J. H. Skinner
Models, Simulations, and War Games	Francis B. Kapper
Moghul Empire	Lawrence D. Higgins
Moldova (formerly Moldavia)	[Executive Editor]
Moltke the Elder	David A. Niedringhaus
Mongol Conquests	Lawrence D. Higgins
Mongolia	Charles F. Hawkins Donald S. Marshall
Montgomery, Bernard Law	Harold E. Raugh, Jr.
Moral Guidance	Mohammed Gamal-Aldin Mahfouz
Morale	Frederick M. Manning
Morality and War	Kenneth W. Kemp
Morocco	Barry O'Connor
Mortar	Samir H. Shalaby
Mountain Warfare	Alexander Hartinger Gerhard Schepe
Mozambique	David L. Bongard Trevor N. Dupuy
Munitions, Aerial	Kenneth H. Bell
Munitions and Explosives: Engineering and Handling	J. H. Skinner
Munitions and Explosives Technology Applications	Manfred Held
Musashi, Miyamoto	Donald S. Marshall
Music, Military	John Taylor
Napoleon I	James K. Kieswetter
National Guard of the United States	William Thralls
National Guards: International Concepts	W. Stanford Smith
NATO (North Atlantic Treaty Organization)	Rolf Schumacher Rolf Braband
NATO Policy and Strategy	Hans-Heinrich Weise
Naval Auxiliary and Support Ships	James L. George
Naval Forces	David Foxwell
Naval Propulsion Technology	Reuven Leopold
Naval Warfare	Robert S. Wood
Navy	Roger W. Barnett
Nelson, Lord Horatio	Bruce W. Watson
Netherlands	David L. Bongard Trevor N. Dupuy
New Zealand	David L. Bongard Trevor N. Dupuy
Nicaragua	David L. Bongard
Nigeria	David L. Bongard Trevor N. Dupuy
Night Vision Technology Applications	Lawrence J. Acchione
Nimitz, Chester William	Vincent B. Hawkins
Nonattacking Capabilities	Reinhard Meyers
Noncommissioned Officer	Francis M. Rush, Jr.
Normans	Walter P. White
North Africa	Walter P. White
North America	David L. Bongard
Norway	David L. Bongard Trevor N. Dupuy
Nuclear Employment Policy and Planning	John M. Weinstein
Nuclear Nonproliferation/Proliferation	George H. Quester

Article	Author(s)
Nuclear Powers (China, United Kingdom, France)	Jacquelyn K. Davis Robert L. Pfaltzgraff, Jr.
Nuclear Propulsion	Jacques Chevallier
Nuclear Theory and Policy (United States, USSR)	Robert A. Levine Rose E. Gottemoeller
Oceania	Donald S. Marshall
Oceanography, Military	John R. Seesholtz Julian M. Wright, Jr.
Offense	Carlo Jean
Officer	Francis M. Rush, Jr.
Operational Art	Edward B. Atkeson
Operational Maneuver Group	Franz Uhle-Wettler
Operations Research, Military	John G. Honig
Operations Research, Soviet and Western Military	Allan S. Rehm
Operations Security	Arion Pattakos
Ordnance Corps	Günter Pauleit
Organization, Air Force	Kenneth H. Bell
Organization, Army	John R. Brinkerhoff
Organization, Military	J. H. Skinner
Organization, Naval	Hideo Sekino Sadao Seno
Organization of African Unity	David L. Bongard
Organization of American States	David L. Bongard Trevor N. Dupuy
Osipov Equations	Robert L. Helmbold
Ottoman Empire	Lawrence D. Higgins
Pacifism	L. William Yolton
Pakistan	Edward S. Shea
Panama	David L. Bongard Trevor N. Dupuy
Panama, U.S. Invasion of	James B. Motley
Paraguay	John Hoyt Williams
Paramilitary Forces	Rod Paschall
Patton, George Smith, Jr.	Arnold C. Dupuy
Peace Movements	Ulrike C. Wasmuht
Peacekeeping	Gunther G. Greindl
Peloponnesian Wars	John F. Sloan
Pershing, John Joseph	John Kennedy Ohl
Persian Empire	Lawrence D. Higgins
Personnel	John R. Brinkerhoff
Peru	David L. Bongard Trevor N. Dupuy
Peter the Great	Dianne L. Smith
Philippines	David L. Bongard Trevor N. Dupuy
Physics and the Military	George A. Keyworth II
Planning, Defense	Frank Rosa Peter L. Hayes Lynn M. Hollerbach
Planning, Military	Keith E. Bonn
Poland	David L. Bongard Trevor N. Dupuy
Policy, Defense	Adrian von Oër
Policy, Military	Bruce W. Watson
Political Control of Armed Forces	Claude E. Welch, Jr.

Article	Author(s)
Portugal	David L. Bongard Trevor N. Dupuy
Postal and Courier Services	J. H. Skinner
Precision-guided Munitions	Robert F. Jackson
Preventive War	Dieter Bangert
Principles of War	Gertmann Sude
Prisoner of War	Howard S. Levie
Procurement, Military	Charles Q. Cutshaw Dianne M. Cutshaw
Professionalism, Military	Sam C. Sarkesian
Promotion	John R. Brinkerhoff James Murphy
Propulsion	Charles H. Church Kenneth A. Evans
Prussia and Germany, Rise of	Franz Uhle-Wettler
Psychological Warfare	Ortwin Buchbender
Psychology, Military	James E. Driskell Eduardo Salas
Public Relations	Robert B. Sims
Publications, Regulations, and Manuals	Bruce I. Gudmundsson
Punic Wars	Phillip E. Koerper
Quartering, Military	J. H. Skinner
Radar	Ibrahim Ahmed Salem
Radar Technology Applications	H. A. D'Assumpçao D. H. Sinnott
Rank and Insignia of Rank	Bruce W. Watson
Rapid Reaction Force	Walter Jablonsky
Reassignment and Rotation	John R. Brinkerhoff
Reconnaissance and Surveillance	Dino A. Brugioni
Records, Military	Susan M. Watson
Refugees	J. H. Skinner
Reinforcements	J. H. Skinner
Replacements: Personnel and Materiel	J. H. Skinner
Reports, Liaison, and Feedback	Susan M. Watson
Research and Development Establishments and Policies	James E. Spates
Reserve Components	David A. Smith
Reserve Forces, Naval	Floyd D. Kennedy, Jr.
Reserves	Dieter Bangert
Resource Management	John Hemsley
Retirement, Military	Hardy L. Merritt
Retrograde Movement	Hermann Büschleb
Riverine Warfare	Frank Uhlig, Jr.
Robotics, Military (Land Systems)	Frank D. Verderame
Rocket, Antiarmor	Alaa El Din Abdel Meguid Darwish
Rokossovskii, Konstantin Konstantinovich	Dianne L. Smith
Roman Empire	Arther Ferrill
Romania	David L. Bongard
Rommel, Erwin	Vincent B. Hawkins
Rotary-wing Aircraft Technology	Daniel P. Schrage
Rules of Engagement	Rolf Bergmeier
Ruses and Stratagems	Everett L. Wheeler
Russia	[Executive Editor]
Russia, Expansion of	Dianne L. Smith

Russo-Japanese War — Franklin D. Margiotta
Sailor — John R. Brinkerhoff
Saladin — Phillip E. Koerper
San Martín, José de — Jack Child
Satellite Technology — Marshall H. Kaplan
Satellite Technology Applications — Neil R. Helm
Saudi Arabia — David L. Bongard, Trevor N. Dupuy
Saxe, Herman Maurice, Comte de — David L. Bongard
Scharnhorst, Gerhard Johann David von — Charles E. White
Scheer, Reinhard — Gary E. Weir
Schlieffen, Alfred, Count von — David A. Niedringhaus
Schwerpunkt — Daniel J. Hughes
Science of War — John I. Alger
Scipio Africanus — John F. Sloan
Scott, Winfield — Brian R. Bader
Sea Control and Denial — Geoffrey Till
Seapower — John B. Hattendorf
Seapower, British — David L. Bongard
Search Theory and Applications — Maurice Bresson
Security Classification — Susan M. Watson
Security Clearance — Charles F. Hawkins
Sensor Technology — Robert Moore
Seven Years' War — Szabolcs M. de Gyürky
Sherman, William Tecumseh — Gregory Forster
Ship and Naval Technology Applications — Albert J. Baciocco, James A. Carney
Ship Design and Construction — James W. Kehoe, Kenneth S. Brower
Ship Protective Systems — James W. Kehoe, Kenneth S. Brower
Siege — Gert Bode
Signals Processing Technology — J. B. G. Roberts, R. A. Evans
Simulator — James T. Westwood
Singapore — Charles F. Hawkins, Donald S. Marshall
Slim, William Joseph, Viscount — Harold E. Raugh, Jr.
Slovenia — [Executive Editor]
Small Arms — Samir H. Shalaby
Sniper — James D. Blundell
Social Defense — Jan Surotchak
Social Science Research and Development, Military — Edgar M. Johnson
Sociology, Military — David R. Segal, Mady Wechsler Segal
Soldier — John R. Brinkerhoff
Somalia — David L. Bongard
South Africa — Arnold C. Dupuy
South America — David L. Bongard, Trevor N. Dupuy
South and Southeast Asia — Donald S. Marshall
Soviet Military Doctrine — Bruce W. Watson
Soviet Union — Charles F. Hawkins
Spaatz, Carl A. — Arnold C. Dupuy
Space Law — Kenneth Schwetje

Space, Military Aspects of	David Messner
Space Warfare	George Reed
Space Weapons	Kheidr K. El Dahrawy
Spain	David L. Bongard
	Trevor N. Dupuy
Span of Control: Military Organizations and Operations	Oswald Hahn
Span of Control: Theories and Concepts	Jeffrey A. McNally
Spanish Empire	Lawrence D. Higgins
Spanish Foreign Legion	Trevor N. Dupuy
Special Operations	William P. Yarborough
Special Operations Forces	James T. Westwood
Spectrum of Conflict	Donald S. Marshall
Spruance, Raymond Ames	David L. Bongard
Sri Lanka	Lee A. Sweetapple
Staff	J. H. Skinner
Standardization and Interoperability	Rod Paschall
Standing Operating Procedure	Charles Q. Cutshaw
Status of Forces Agreements	Lawrence B. Brennan
Stealth and Counterstealth Technology	Jay H. Goldberg
Stilwell, Joseph Warren	Brian R. Bader
Stockpiles	N. T. P. Murphy
Strategic Defense Initiative	Julian Davidson
Strategic Defense Initiative: Policy Implications	Jacquelyn K. Davis
	Robert L. Pfaltzgraff, Jr.
Strategic Stability	Dov S. Zakheim
Strategic Warfare, Operations Research in	Barry O'Neill
Strategy	Gertmann Sude
Strategy, National Security	Terry L. Deibel
Sub-Saharan Africa	David L. Bongard
	John F. Geraci
Submarine	John L. Byron
Submarine and Antisubmarine Technology Applications	Bernard M. Kauderer
Submarine Silencing and Detection	Jay H. Goldberg
Submarine Warfare	William J. Ruhe
Subversion	Frederic N. Smith
Sudan	David L. Bongard
	Trevor N. Dupuy
Suffren de St. Tropez, Pierre André de	David L. Bongard
Sun Tzu	Donald S. Marshall
Supply	J. H. Skinner
Surrender	James T. Westwood
Surveillance and Target Acquisition Equipment	Ibrahim Ahmed Salem
Surveillance, Ocean	Robert B. Shields, Jr.
Survivability	Lutz Unterseher
Sustainability and Viability	N. T. P. Murphy
	Charles W. Blandy
	J. H. Skinner
Suvorov, Aleksandr Vasil'evich	Dianne L. Smith
Sweden	David L. Bongard
	Trevor N. Dupuy
Switzerland	Arnold C. Dupuy

Syria	David L. Bongard Trevor N. Dupuy
Systems Analysis	John G. Honig
Tactics	Timothy T. Lupfer
Taiwan	Charles F. Hawkins Donald S. Marshall
Tajikistan	[Executive Editor]
Tamerlane	David L. Bongard Trevor N. Dupuy
Tank	Moustafa Aly Morsy Aly
Tanzania	David L. Bongard
Task Force	Donald C. Snedeker
Technology Acquisition and Development	Jacques S. Gansler
Technology and Arms Control	Robert L. Maust
Technology and the Military	Timothy Garden
Technology and Warfare	Zeev Bonen
Technology Transfer	Jacquelyn K. Davis Robert L. Pfaltzgraff, Jr.
Territorial Army	Gottfried Greiner
Terrorism	Robert H. Kupperman Debra van Opstal
Terrorism, Legal Aspects of	James P. Terry
Test and Evaluation, Materiel	Walter W. Hollis
Thailand	Charles F. Hawkins Donald S. Marshall
Theater of War	Franz Uhle-Wettler
Theory of Combat	Trevor N. Dupuy
Thirty Years' War	Curt Johnson
Tirpitz, Alfred von	Spencer C. Tucker
Togo, Heihachiro	Malcolm Muir, Jr.
Tooth-to-Tail: Land Forces	David L. Bongard
Torpedo	Mohamed Gamal Al Shanawani
Total War	Rudolf Hecht
Training	G. Thomas Sicilia
Training Technology	Paul F. Gorman
Transportation	J. H. Skinner
Transportation Corps	Günther Nagel
Trench Warfare	Friedrich K. Jeschonnek
Trenchard, Sir Hugh Montague	Robert Calvert Jr.
Trotsky, Leon	Brian R. Bader
Tukhachevsky, Mikhail Nikolaevich	Jacob W. Kipp
Tunisia	David L. Bongard Trevor N. Dupuy
Turenne, Henri de La Tour d'Auvergne, Vicomte de	David L. Bongard
Turkey	David L. Bongard Trevor N. Dupuy
Turkic Empire	Lawrence D. Higgins
Turkmenistan	[Executive Editor]
Tuthmosis III	Michael A. Mabe
Ukraine	[Executive Editor]
Unconventional War	William P. Yarborough
Underwater Management	Richard R. Pariseau
Uniforms and Accouterments	Raymond Oliver
Unit Cohesion	Reuven Gal
Unit, Military	John R. Brinkerhoff

United Kingdom of Great Britain and Northern Ireland	David L. Bongard Trevor N. Dupuy
United Nations	Martin Ganderson
United States	James B. Motley
Urban Warfare	Lutz Unterseher
Uruguay	David L. Bongard
Uzbekistan	[Executive Editor]
Vasilevskii, Aleksandr Mikhailovich	Dianne L. Smith
Vauban, Sebastien Le Prestre de	David L. Bongard
Venezuela	David L. Bongard
Veteran	Wilfred L. Ebel
Victory	James B. Motley
Vietnam	Charles F. Hawkins Donald S. Marshall
Vietnam and Indochina Wars	Donald S. Marshall
Vikings	Rose-Marie Oster
War	Franz Uhle-Wettler
War Crimes	Howard S. Levie
War of Attrition	Dermot Bradley
War: The Soviet View	James Sherr
Warrant Officer	Francis M. Rush, Jr.
Warsaw Pact	Manfred Backerra
Warship	John C. Reilly, Jr.
Washington, George	Albert D. McJoynt
Wavell, Archibald Percival (1st Earl)	Robert Calvert, Jr.
Wei Li-huang	Edward C. O'Dowd
Western Europe	Charles F. Hawkins
Women in the Armed Forces	Sandra Carson Stanley Mady Wechsler Segal
World War I	Timothy T. Lupfer
World War II	James F. Dunnigan
Yamamoto, Isoroku	Curt Johnson
Yamashita, Tomoyuki	Carl Boyd
Yemen	Charles F. Hawkins
Yugoslavia	David L. Bongard Trevor N. Dupuy
Zaire	David L. Bongard
Zambia	David L. Bongard Trevor N. Dupuy
Zhukov, Georgii Konstantinovich	William J. Spahr
Zimbabwe	David L. Bongard
Zone of Operations	Bernd Weber

LIST OF ARTICLES BY SUBJECT AREA

Aerospace Forces and Warfare

Aerial Mining
Aerial Refueling
Air Interdiction
Air Reconnaissance
Aircraft, Military
Aircraft, Short Take-off and Landing
Aircraft, Unmanned
Airlift
Airpower
Airpower, History of
Airpower, Strategic
Airpower, Tactical
Airspace Control, Military
Aviation, Military
Ballistic Missile Defense
Bombardment, Strategic
Close Air Support
Defense, Aerospace
Diplomacy, Aerospace
Electronic Warfare, Air
Ground Defense of Air Bases
Helicopter: Military Missions
Logistics, Air Force
Missile, Air-launched Cruise (ALCM)
Missile, Intercontinental Ballistic
Organization, Air Force
Space, Military Aspects of
Space Warfare

Combat Theory and Operations

Attrition: Personnel Casualties
Auftragstaktik
Biological Warfare
Blitzkrieg
Chemical Warfare
Civil War
Coalition Warfare
Combat Effectiveness
Combat Power and Potential
Combined Operations
Conventional War
Correlation of Forces
Deception
Demilitarized Zone
Demonstration
Denial Measure
Deployment
Diversion, Operational
Doctrine
Dual Capability
Echelon
Envelopment
Exploitation
Firepower
Fog of War
Forward Defense
Fratricide of Nuclear Warheads
Friction
General War
Hierarchy of Combat
Initiative in War
Interior and Exterior Lines of Operation
Joint Operations
Limited War
Low-intensity Conflict: The Military Dimension
Low-intensity Conflict: Theory and Concept
Maneuver
Mobility
Nuclear Employment Policy and Planning
Offense
Operational Art
Preventive War
Principles of War
Psychological Warfare
Rapid Reaction Force
Reserves

Rules of Engagement
Ruses and Stratagems
Schwerpunkt (Center of Gravity)
Soviet Military Doctrine
Special Operations
Standardization and Interoperability
Strategy
Tactics
Task Force
Terrorism
Theater of War
Theory of Combat
Total War
Unconventional War
War
War of Attrition
War: The Soviet View

Leadership, Command, and Management

Briefings
Combat Motivation
Combat Stress
Command
Command, Control, Communications and Intelligence
Command Post
Coordination
Desertion
Directives, Orders, and Instructions
Discipline
Generalship
Inspection and Supervision
Leadership
Management
Morale
Planning, Military
Reports, Liaison, and Feedback
Span of Control: Theories and Concepts
Standing (Standard) Operating Procedure (SOP)
Unit Cohesion

Countries, Regions, and Organizations

Afghanistan, Republic of
Algeria, Democratic and Popular Republic of
Angola, People's Republic of
Arab League
Argentina (Argentine Republic)
Armenia
Association of Southeast Asian Nations (ASEAN)
Atlantic-Mediterranean Area
Australia, Commonwealth of
Austria, Republic of
Azerbaijan
Bangladesh, People's Republic of
Belarus (formerly Byelorussia)
Belgium, Kingdom of
Bolivia, Republic of
Bosnia-Hercegovina
Brazil, Federative Republic of
Bulgaria, Republic of
Burma (Union of Myanmar)
Cambodia (State of Cambodia)
Canada
Central America and the Caribbean
Central and East Asia
Chad, Republic of
Chile, Republic of
China, People's Republic of
Colombia, Republic of
Commonwealth of Independent States
Commonwealth of Nations
Costa Rica, Republic of
Croatia
Cuba, Republic of
Czechoslovakia (Czech and Slovak Federal Republic)
Denmark, Kingdom of
Dominican Republic
Eastern Europe
Ecuador, Republic of
Egypt (Arab Republic of Egypt)
El Salvador, Republic of
Estonia
Ethiopia, People's Democratic Republic of
European Communities
Finland, Republic of

France (French Republic)
Georgia
Germany, Federal Republic of
Ghana, Republic of
Greece (Hellenic Republic)
Guatemala, Republic of
Haiti, Republic of
Honduras, Republic of
Hungary, Republic of
India, Republic of
Indo-Pacific Area
Indonesia, Republic of
Iran, Islamic Republic of
Iraq (Republic of Iraq)
Ireland (Irish Republic)
Israel, State of
Italy (Italian Republic)
Japan
Jordan, Hashemite Kingdom of
Kazakhstan
Kenya, Republic of
Kirgizstan (formerly Kirghizia)
Korea, North (People's Democratic Republic of Korea)
Korea, South (Republic of Korea)
Laos (Lao People's Democratic Republic)
Latvia
Lebanon, Republic of
Libya (Socialist People's Libyan Arab *Jamahiriya*)
Lithuania
Madagascar, Democratic Republic of (formerly Malagasy Republic)
Malaysia, Federation of
Mauritania, Islamic Republic of
Mexico (United Mexican States)
Middle East
Moldova (formerly Moldavia)
Mongolia (Mongolian People's Republic)
Morocco, Kingdom of
Mozambique, Republic of
Netherlands, Kingdom of
New Zealand
Nicaragua, Republic of
Nigeria, Federal Republic of
North Africa
North America
Norway, Kingdom of
Oceania
Organization of African Unity (OAU)
Organization of American States (OAS)
Pakistan, Islamic Republic of
Panama, Republic of
Paraguay, Republic of
Peru, Republic of
Philippines, Republic of the
Poland, Republic of
Portugal (Portuguese Republic)
Romania
Russia
Saudi Arabia, Kingdom of
Singapore, Republic of
Slovenia
Somalia (Somali Democratic Republic)
South Africa, Republic of
South America
South and Southeast Asia
Soviet Union (Union of Soviet Socialist Republics)
Spain, Kingdom of
Sri Lanka, Democratic Socialist Republic of
Sub-Saharan Africa
Sudan, Republic of the
Sweden, Kingdom of
Switzerland (Swiss Confederation)
Syria (Syrian Arab Republic)
Taiwan (Republic of China)
Tajikistan
Tanzania, United Republic of
Thailand, Kingdom of
Tunisia, Republic of
Turkey, Republic of
Turkmenistan
Ukraine
United Kingdom of Great Britain and Northern Ireland
United Nations (UN)
United States of America
Uruguay
Uzbekistan
Venezuela, Republic of
Vietnam, Socialist Republic of
Western Europe
Yemen, Republic of
Yugoslavia, Socialist Federal Republic of
Zaire, Republic of
Zambia, Republic of
Zimbabwe, Republic of

Armed Forces and Society

Armed Forces and Society
Civil-Military Relations
Coup d'état
Economics, Defense
Environmental Impact of Armed Forces
Ethics, Professional Military
Ethnicity and the Armed Forces
Internal Security and Armed Forces
Militarism
Moral Guidance
Morality and War
Pacifism
Political Control of Armed Forces
Professionalism, Military
Psychology, Military
Public Relations
Social Defense
Sociology, Military
Women in the Armed Forces

History and Biography

Afghanistan, Soviet Invasion of
Alexander, Harold Rupert Leofric George
Alexander the Great (Alexander III)
Allenby, Edmund Henry Hynman
American Revolutionary War
Arab Conquests
Arab-Israeli Wars
Ardant du Picq, Charles J. J. J.
Arnold, H. H. ("Hap")
Assyria, Military History of
Attila the Hun
Balkan Wars
Boer Wars
Bolívar, Simón
Bradley, Omar Nelson
Brauchitsch, Walther von
Brooke, Alan Francis, 1st Viscount Alanbrooke
Byzantine Empire
Caesar, Julius
Charlemagne
Charles XII, King of Sweden
Chiang Kai-shek
Chu-Teh
Civil War, American
Civil War, Russian
Civil War, Spanish
Clausewitz, Karl von
Colonial Empires, European
Condé, Louis II de Bourbon, Prince de
Crimean War
Cromwell, Oliver
Crusades
Cunningham, Sir Alan G.
De Lattre de Tassigny, Jean
Doenitz, Karl
Dominican Republic: 1965 Crisis
Douhet, Giulio
Edward I
Edward III
Eisenhower, Dwight David
Eugene, Prince of Savoy-Carignan
Farragut, David Glasgow
Feudalism
Fisher, John Arbuthnot, 1st Baron Fisher of Kilverstone
Foch, Ferdinand
France, Military Hegemony of
Franco-Prussian War
Frederick the Great (Frederick II)
French Revolutionary–Napoleonic Wars
Fuller, J. F. C.
Genghis Khan
Giap, Vo Nguyen
Gonzalo de Córdoba
Graeco-Persian Wars
Grant, Ulysses Simpson
Grenada, U.S. Intervention in
Guderian, Heinz
Gulf War, 1991
Gustavas Adolphus (Gustavus II)
Halsey, William F. ("Bull")
Hannibal Barca
Hindenburg, Paul von
History, Ancient Military [Prehistory–A.D. 476]
History, Early Modern Military [1453–1789]
History, Medieval Military [ca. A.D. 45–145]

History, Modern Military [1792–present]
Ho Chi Minh
Hundred Years' War
Italian Unification Wars
Italian Wars
Jackson, Thomas Jonathan ("Stonewall")
Japan, Modernization and Expansion of
Jellicoe, John Rushworth (1st Earl)
Jomini, Antoine Henri
Kemal, Mustafa Pasha (Atatürk)
Kesselring, Albert
Khalid ibn al-Walid
King, Ernest J.
Konev, Ivan Stepanovich
Korean War
Latin American Wars of Independence
Leahy, William Daniel
Lee, Robert Edward
Lin-Piao
Ludendorff, Erich
MacArthur, Douglas
Mahan, Alfred Thayer
Manchu Empire (Qing, or Ch'ing Empire)
Manstein, Erich von
Mao Tse-tung
Marlborough, John Churchill, Duke of
Marshall, George Catlett, Jr.
Moghul Empire
Moltke the Elder (Helmuth Karl Bernard, Graf von)
Mongol Conquests
Montgomery, Bernard Law
Musashi, Miyamoto
Napoleon I
Nelson, Lord Horatio
Nimitz, Chester William
Normans
Ottoman Empire
Panama, U.S. Invasion of
Patton, George Smith, Jr.
Peloponnesian Wars
Pershing, John Joseph
Persian Empire
Peter the Great (Peter I)
Prussia and Germany, Rise of
Punic Wars
Rokossovskii, Konstantin Konstantinovich
Roman Empire
Rommel, Erwin
Russia, Expansion of
Russo-Japanese War
Saladin
San Martín, José de
Saxe, Herman Maurice, Comte de
Scharnhorst, Gerhard Johann David von
Scheer, Reinhard
Schlieffen, Alfred, Count üon
Scipio Africanus
Scott, Winfield
Seapower, British
Seven Years' War
Sherman, William Tecumseh
Slim, William Joseph (Viscount)
Spaatz, Carl A.
Spanish Empire
Spruance, Raymond Ames
Stilwell, Joseph Warren
Suffren de St. Tropez, Pierre André de
Sun Tzu
Suvorov, Aleksandr Vasil'evich
Tamerlane
Thirty Years' War
Tirpitz, Alfred von
Togo, Heihachiro
Trenchard, Sir Hugh Montague
Trotsky, Leon
Tukhachevsky, Mikhail Nikolaevich
Turenne, Henri de La Tour d'Auvergne, Vicomte de
Turkic Empire
Tuthmosis III
Vasilevskii, Aleksandr Mikhailovich
Vauban, Sebastien Le Prestre de
Vietnam and Indochina Wars
Vikings
Washington, George
Wavell, Archibald Percival (1st Earl)
Wei Li-huang
World War I
World War II
Yamamoto, Isoroku
Yamashita, Tomoyuki
Zhukov, Georgii Konstantinovich

Land Forces and Warfare

Air Assault
Airborne Land Forces
Arctic Warfare
Armor
Army Aviation
Artillery
Attack
Border Guard
Branches, Military
Cavalry
Coast Defense
Combat Support
Combined Arms
Communications, Signal
Defense
Delaying Action
Desert Warfare
Encounter Battle
Engineering, Military
Field Service Regulations
Fire and Movement
Force Structure
Fortification
Front
Gendarmerie
Ground Reconnaissance
Infantry
Jungle Warfare
Land Forces, Effectiveness and Efficiency of
Land Warfare
Mechanized Warfare
Medical Service
Mine Warfare, Land
Mountain Warfare
Nonattacking Capabilities
Ordnance Corps
Retrograde Movement
Siege
Span of Control: Military Organizations and Operations
Survivability
Territorial Army
Tooth-to-Tail: Land Forces
Transportation Corps
Trench Warfare
Urban Warfare
Zone of Operations

Logistics

Administration, Military
Assistance, Military
Assistance, Mutual
Budget and Finance, Military
Canteen and Shopping Services
Casualties: Evacuation and Treatment
Combat Service Support
Consumption Rates, Battlefield
Cross-servicing
Engineering, Constructional
Food and Catering Services, Military
Host Nation Support
Infrastructure, Military
Labor, Military
Lines of Communication
Logistic Movement
Logistics: A General Survey
Logistics, Limited War
Logistics, NATO
Logistics, Naval
Logistics, Soviet and Warsaw Pact
Maintenance
Maritime Logistics
Munitions and Explosives: Engineering and Handling
Postal and Courier Services
Procurement, Military
Quartering, Military
Refugees
Reinforcements
Replacements: Personnel and Materiel
Resource Management
Stockpiles
Supply
Sustainability and Viability
Transportation

Manpower and Personnel

Accession Standards
Airman
Burial, Military
Cadet
Cadre
Chaplaincy, Military
Civilian Substitution
Compensation, Military
Conditions of Military Service
Conscientious Objection
Conscription
Decoration, Honorary Orders, and Awards
Education, Military
Enlisted Personnel
Family Dependent Programs
Force Structure, Personnel
Internal Security Forces
Leave, Military
Manpower, Military
Manpower Policies in the U.S. and NATO
Marine
Medicine, Military
Mercenary
National Guard of the United States
National Guards: International Concepts
Noncommissioned Officer
Officer
Personnel
Promotion
Rank and Insignia of Rank
Reassignment and Rotation
Reserve Components
Retirement, Military
Sailor
Soldier
Training
Uniforms and Accouterments
Veteran
Warrant Officer

Materiel and Weapons

Ammunition
Amphibious Vehicle
Armored Ground Vehicle
Artillery, Antiaircraft
Artillery, Rocket and Missile
Artillery, Tube
Automatic Weapon
Chaff
Depth Charge
Engineering Equipment, Combat
Flamethrower
Fuze
Grenade
Gun, Aerial
Gun, Antitank
Helicopter
Helicopter, Battlefield
Helicopter, Naval
Machine Gun
Mine
Missile, Air-to-air
Missile, Air-to-surface (ASM)
Missile, Antitank Guided (ATGM)
Missile, Ballistic
Missile, Cruise
Missile, Guided
Missile, Strategic Ballistic
Missile, Surface-to-air (SAM)
Mortar
Munitions, Aerial
Radar
Rocket, Antiarmor
Small Arms
Space Weapons
Surveillance and Target Acquisition Equipment
Tank
Torpedo

Naval Forces and Warfare

Aircraft Carrier
Amphibious Forces
Amphibious Ships and Craft
Amphibious Warfare
Antisubmarine Warfare
Battleship
Blockade and Maritime Exclusion
Convoy and Protection of Shipping

Engineering, Naval
Exercises, Naval
Fleet
Fleet Air Defense
Gunboat Diplomacy
Maritime Strategy
Merchant Fleet
Mine Warfare, Naval
Naval Auxiliary and Support Ships
Naval Forces
Naval Warfare
Navy
Oceanography, Military
Organization, Naval
Reserve Forces, Naval
Riverine Warfare
Sea Control and Denial
Seapower
Ship Design and Construction
Ship Protective Systems
Submarine
Submarine Warfare
Surveillance, Ocean
Underwater Management
Warship

Technology, Research, and Development

Aircraft Technology Applications
Armor Technology
Armored Land Vehicle Technology Applications
Ballistics
Biological Warfare Technology
Chemical Warfare Technology
Communications Equipment Trends
Computers, Military Use of
Electronic Warfare Technology Applications
Engine Technology, Aircraft
Engine Technology, Ground Vehicle
Explosives Technology, Conventional
Gun Technology Applications
Identification Friend or Foe (IFF) Technology
Information Fusion
Man-Machine Interface
Materials Technology
Mathematics and the Military
Medical Research and Technology
Missile Propulsion Technology
Missile Technology Applications
Munitions and Explosives Technology Applications
Naval Propulsion Technology
Night Vision Technology Applications
Nuclear Propulsion
Physics and the Military
Precision-guided Munitions (PGMs)
Propulsion
Radar Technology Applications
Research and Development Establishments and Policies
Robotics, Military (Land Systems)
Rotary-wing Aircraft Technology
Satellite Technology
Satellite Technology Applications
Sensor Technology
Ship and Naval Technology Applications
Signals Processing Technology
Social Science Research and Development, Military
Stealth and Counterstealth Technology
Strategic Defense Initiative (SDI)
Submarine and Antisubmarine Technology Applications
Submarine Silencing and Detection
Technology Acquisition and Development
Technology and Arms Control
Technology and the Military
Technology and Warfare
Test and Evaluation, Materiel
Training Technology

Military Theory and Operations Research

Cost Analysis
Cybernetics, Soviet Concepts of Military
Force Multiplier
Force Ratio
Lanchester Equations
Mathematical Modeling and Forecasting
Measures of Effectiveness
Models, Simulations, and War Games
Operations Research (OR), Military
Operations Research, Soviet and Western Military
Osipov Equations
Search Theory and Applications
Strategic Warfare, Operations Research in
Systems Analysis

Defense and International Security Policy

Alliance, Military and Political
Antitactical Ballistic Missile (ATBM) Policy
Arms Control and Disarmament
Arms Control and Disarmament: Mathematical Models
Arms Trade and Military Assistance
Budget, Defense
Civil Emergency Planning
Civil-Military Cooperation (CIMIC)
Cold War
Conflict Termination
Crisis Management
Cuban Missile Crisis
Defense Decision Making: Analysis and Models
Deterrence
Escalation
Flexible Response
Force de Frappe
NATO (North Atlantic Treaty Organization)
NATO Policy and Strategy
Nuclear Nonproliferation/Proliferation
Nuclear Powers (China, United Kingdom, France)
Nuclear Theory and Policy (United States, Soviet Union)
Peace Movements
Peacekeeping
Planning, Defense
Policy, Defense
Spectrum of Conflict
Strategic Defense Initiative: Policy Implications
Strategic Stability
Strategy, National Security
Technology Transfer
Warsaw Pact

Military and International Security Law

Espionage, Legal Aspects of
Geneva Conventions
Hague Conventions
Law, Military
Law of the Sea and Piracy
Legal Assistance
Military Aid to the Civil Power—A U.S. Model
Prisoner of War
Security Clearance
Space Law
Status of Forces Agreements
Terrorism, Legal Aspects of
War Crimes

Military Intelligence

Attaché, Military
Computer Security
Counterintelligence
Covert Action
Disinformation
Intelligence Analysis, Military
Intelligence Collection
Intelligence Cycle
Intelligence Establishment
Intelligence, General
Intelligence, Human (HUMINT)
Intelligence, Imagery
Intelligence: Indications and Warning
Intelligence, Military
Intelligence, Naval
Intelligence, Signal (SIGINT)
Intelligence, Strategic
Intelligence, Tactical
Mapping, Charting, and Geodesy (MC&G)
Operations Security (OPSEC)
Reconnaissance and Surveillance
Security Classification

General Military

Academies, Military
Air-land Battle
Archives, Military
Art of War
Censorship
Ceremonies and Displays
Civil Affairs
Customs and Etiquette
Defeat
Exercises
Fifth Column
Flags and Symbols
Follow-on Forces Attack (FOFA)
Formation
Fratricide
French Foreign Legion
Geography, Military
Government, Military
History, Military
Hostage
Indirect Fire
Installations, Military
Maps, Charts, and Symbols, Military
Meteorology, Military
Military
Military Police
Mobilization
Music, Military
Operational Maneuver Group
Organization, Army
Organization, Military
Paramilitary Forces
Policy, Military
Publications, Regulations, and Manuals
Records, Military
Science of War
Simulator
Sniper
Spanish Foreign Legion
Special Operations Forces (SOF)
Staff
Subversion
Surrender
Unit, Military
Victory

CONTRIBUTORS

Mr. Lawrence J. Acchione
President, SENSCI Corporation
United States

Prof. Tsuneo Akaha, Ph.D.
Director, Center for East Asian Studies, Monterey Institute of International Studies
United States

Col. Donald J. Alberts
United States

Mr. George H. Aldrich, Ph.D.
Judge, Iran–U.S. Claims Tribunal
United States

Col. Joseph H. Alexander, USMC (Ret.)
United States

Col. John I. Alger, USA (Ret.), Ph.D.
Former Faculty, National War College
United States

Capt. Charles D. Allen, Jr., USN (Ret.)
United States

Prof. Graham T. Allison, Jr., Ph.D.
JFK School of Government, Harvard U.
United States

Mr. M. F. Allnut, Ph.D.
Royal Aircraft Establishment, Ministry of Defence
United Kingdom

Mr. Dwayne Anderson
Author
United States

Mr. Roger Anderson
United States

Air Chief Marshal Sir Michael Armitage, KCB, CBE, RAF (Ret.)
MGA Associates
United Kingdom

Maj. Gen. Edward B. Atkeson, USA (Ret.)
United States

Maj. Gen. Mamdouh H. Attiah
Egypt

Vice Adm. Albert J. Baciocco, USN (Ret.)
United States

Col. Manfred Backerra
Führüngsakademie der Bundeswehr
Germany

Mr. Brian R. Bader
Director of Research, Historical Evaluation and Research Organization
United States

Lt. Col. Dieter Bangert (Ret.), Ph.D.
Germany

Capt. James Alden Barber, Jr., USN (Ret.)
Executive Director, U.S. Naval Institute
United States

Mr. Jeffrey C. Barlow, Ph.D.
United States

Capt. Roger W. Barnett, USN (Ret.), Ph.D.
The National Institute for Public Policy
United States

Mr. E. Edward Bassett
United States

Brig. Gen. Kenneth H. Bell, USAF (Ret.)
Author
United States

Capt. Donald E. Bennett, Jr., USA
United States

Col. Rolf Bergmeier (Ret.)
NATO Headquarters Situation Center
Germany

Lt. Col. Charles W. Blandy (Ret.)
United Kingdom

Mr. James J. Bloom
JB Historical Research Consultants Ltd
United States

Col. James D. Blundell, USA (Ret.)
Institute of Land Warfare, Association of the U.S. Army
United States

Mr. Karlheinz Böckle
Germany

Mr. Yossef Bodansky
Military Analyst
United States

Lt. Col. Gert Bode
Germany

Mr. James D. Boggs
United States

Lt. Col. Peter Bolte
Germany

Lt. Col. John R. Bondanella, USA (Ret.)
Defense Analyst
United States

Mr. Zeev Bonen, Ph.D.
Senior Research Fellow, The Neaman Institute
Israel

Mr. David L. Bongard
Military Historian
United States

Maj. Keith E. Bonn, USA
United States

Lt. Col. Joachim W. K. Böthling (Ret.)
Germany

Prof. Carl Boyd, Ph.D.
Director, Graduate Program of History, Old Dominion U.
United States

Mr. Rolf Braband
Germany

Mr. Dermot Bradley, Ph.D.
Military Historian
United States

Prof. Jan S. Breemer, Ph.D.
U.S. Naval Postgraduate School
United States

Cdr. Lawrence B. Brennan, USNR
United States

Col. Maurice Bresson (Ret.)
France

Col. John R. Brinkerhoff, USA (Ret.)
Former Deputy Assistant Secretary of Defense for Reserve Affairs
United States

Mr. Kenneth S. Brower
President, Spectrum Associates, Inc.
United States

Mr. Dino A. Brugioni
Former Senior Reconnaissance Analyst, CIA
United States

Col. Ortwin Buchbender
Germany

Col. Axel Bürgener
Army Staff, Ministry of Defense
Germany

Maj. Gen. Hermann Büschleb (Ret.)
Germany

Lt. Col. Charles M. Bussey, USA (Ret.)
Author
United States

Capt. John L. Byron, USN
United States

Sir James Cable, KCVO, CMG
United Kingdom

Mr. Robert Calvert, Jr.
Publisher, Garrett Park Press
United States

Ms. Edwina S. Campbell, Ph.D.
Senior Analyst, Eagle Research Group, Inc.
United States

Mr. Kenneth J. Campbell, Ph.D.
Executive Director, National Historical Intelligence Museum
United States

Capt. James A. Carney, USN (Ret.)
United States

Prof. John Whiteclay Chambers II, Ph.D.
Dept. of History, Rutgers U.
United States

Mr. Jagdish Chandra, Ph.D.
Director, Mathematical Sciences Division, U.S. Army Research Office
United States

Col. Nicholas H. Chavasse, USAF (Ret.)
United States

Mr. Jacques Chevallier
Ministry of Defense
France

Prof. Jack Child, Ph.D.
American U.
United States

Mr. Charles H. Church, Ph.D.
Director, Advanced Concepts & Tech. Assessment Office of the Assistant Secretary of the Army
United States

Prof. Stephen J. Cimbala, Ph.D.
Dept. of Political Science, Pennsylvania State U.
United States

Prof. Theresa Lennon Conroy, Ph.D.
Dept. of Political Science, Marymount U.
United States

Mr. Anthony H. Cordesman, Ph.D.
U.S. Senate Staff; ABC News Military Analyst; Prof. of National Security Studies, Georgetown U.
United States

Mr. Charles Q. Cutshaw
Senior Scientific Technical Intelligence Analyst, USMC
United States

Ms. Dianne M. Cutshaw
United States

Prof. H. A. d'Assumpçao, Ph.D.
Chief Defence Scientist, Microwave Radar Division, Surveillance Research Laboratory, Dept. of Defence
Australia

Maj. Gen. Kheidr K. El Dahrawy (Ret.)
Professor, Nasser Higher Military Academy
Egypt

Maj. Gen. Alaa El Din Abdel Meguid Darwish (Ret.), Ph.D.
Defense Analyst
Egypt

Mr. Julian Davidson, Ph.D.
Senior Vice President, Booz-Allen & Hamilton
United States

Ms. Jacquelyn K. Davis, Ph.D.
Executive Vice President, Institute for Foreign Policy Analysis
United States

Col. Paul C. Davis, USA (Ret.), Ph.D.
United States

Mr. William A. Davis, Jr., Ph.D.
Former Director, Ballistic Missile Defense Advanced Technology Program
United States

Mr. Horace G. Davy, MBE, FICS
Director, Lowline Ltd
United Kingdom

Ms. Cheryl de Gyürky
United States

Maj. Szabolcs M. de Gyürky, USA (Ret.)
United States

Mr. Maurice E. de Morton, Ph.D.
Chief, Ship Structures & Materials Division, Dept. of Defence
United Kingdom

Prof. Terry L. Deibel, Ph.D.
National War College
United States

Mr. James N. Dertouzos
Resident Scholar in Economics, Rand Corp.
United States

Prof. Desmond Dinan, Ph.D.
George Mason U.
United States

Capt. Kevin Donohue, USA
Faculty, U.S. Military Academy
United States

Mr. Charles Doyle
Congressional Research Service
United States

Lt. Gen. Erhard Drews (Ret.)
Germany

Mr. James E. Driskell, Ph.D.
President, Florida Maxima Corporation
United States

Mr. James F. Dunnigan
Author
United States

Mr. Arnold C. Dupuy
United States

Mr. Fielding Dupuy
United States

Col. Trevor N. Dupuy, USA (Ret.)
Author and Media Military Analyst
United States

Col. Wilfred L. Ebel, USA (Ret.)
Dept. of Veterans Affairs
United States

Mr. Robert J. Eichelberger, Ph.D.
Defense Analyst
United States

Maj. Gen. David W. Einsel, Jr., USA (Ret.)
United States

Lt. Col. Sturmhard Eisenkeil
German Military Attache, Hungary
Germany

Cdr. William L. Eldred, USN
United States

Maj. Michael M. Eller, USAF
United States

Mr. Thomas Enders, Ph.D.
German Society for Foreign Affairs
Germany

Prof. Cynthia H. Enloe, Ph.D.
Chairman, Dept. of Government, Clark U.
United States

Brig. Gen. Uzal W. Ent, USA (Ret.)
United States

Mr. Geoffrey I. Evans
Technical Director, Royal Ordnance PLC, Rocket Motors Division
United Kingdom

Col. Kenneth A. Evans, USA (Ret.), Ph.D.
Vice President, System Planning Corporation
United States

Mr. R. A. Evans, Ph.D.
Royal Signals and Radar Establishment
United Kingdom

Maj. Peter R. Faber, USAF
Former Faculty, U.S. Air Force Academy
United States

Prof. Jiang Feng-bo
Military Science Academy
China

Prof. Arther Ferrill, Ph.D.
Dept. of History, U. of Washington
United States

Mr. Nikolaus Fiederling, Ph.D.
Dynamit Nobel
Germany

Maj. David John Fitzpatrick, USA
Faculty, U.S. Military Academy
United States

Mr. Abraham Flatau
United States

Mr. Gregory F. Forster
United States

Mr. David Foxwell
United Kingdom

Col. Raymond E. Franck, Jr., USAF
Strategic Air Command
United States

Col. Robert A. Frye, USAF
United States

Prof. Suen Fu-tian
Military Science Academy
China

Prof. Janice J. Gabbert, Ph.D.
Chair, Dept. of Classics, Wright State U.
United States

Air Vice Marshal Gabr Ali Gabr (Ret.)
Egypt

Mr. Reuven Gal, Ph.D.
Director, Israeli Institute for Military Studies
Israel

Col. Martin Ganderson, USA
United States

Mr. Jacques S. Gansler, Ph.D.
Senior Vice President, The Analytic Sciences Corp.
United States

Air Vice Marshal Timothy Garden, RAF
Assistant Chief of the Air Staff
United Kingdom

Col. Samuel Gardiner, USAF (Ret.)
Former Faculty, National War College
United States

Mr. Benjamin C. Garrett, Ph.D.
United States

Mr. James L. George, Ph.D.
Center for Naval Analyses
United States

Col. John F. Geraci, USA (Ret.)
United States

Maj. Gen. Johannes Gerber (Ret.)
Germany

Capt. Stephen C. Glassman, USNR
United States

Prof. Roy Godson, Ph.D.
Dept. of Government, Georgetown U.
United States

Mr. Jay H. Goldberg
Author and Defense Analyst
United States

Gen. Paul F. Gorman, USA (Ret.)
Former Commander in Chief, U.S. Southern Command
United States

Ms. Rose Gottemoeller
Senior Defense Analyst, Rand Corp.
United States

Mr. Leon Goure, Ph.D.
Science Applications International Corp.
United States

Ms. Cynthia M. Grabo
Former Intelligence Analyst, Defense Intelligence Agency
United States

Mr. Colin S. Gray, Ph.D.
Chairman, National Institute for Public Policy
United States

Maj. Gen. Gunther G. Greindl
Osterreicheische Botschaft Verteidigungsattache
Austria

Maj. Gen. Gottfried Greiner (Ret.), Ph.D.
Germany

Capt. Bruce I. Gudmundsson, USMC
Faculty, Marine Corps Command and Staff College
United States

Mr. Robert P. Haffa, Jr.
United States

Col. Oswald Hahn (Ret.), Ph.D.
Dept. of Economics, U. Erlangen-Nuernberg
Germany

Col. K. E. Hamburger, USA
Faculty, U.S. Military Academy
United States

Mr. James H. Hansen
Author
United States

Mr. Gwyn Harries-Jenkins, Ph.D.
Dean, U. of Hull
United Kingdom

Capt. Alexander Hartinger
1st Mountain Division
Germany

Prof. John B. Hattendorf, Ph.D.
U.S. Naval War College
United States

Maj. Charles F. Hawkins, USAR
President, Data Memory Systems, Inc./Historical Evaluation and Research Organization
United States

Mr. Vincent B. Hawkins
Military Historian
United States

Ms. Grace Person Hayes
Author
United States

Capt. Peter L. Hayes, USAF
Air Force Institute of Technology
United States

Mr. Rudolf Hecht, Ph.D.
Austrian Defense Academy
Austria

Prof. William H. Heiser, Ph.D.
Massachusetts Institute of Technology and U.S. Air Force Academy
United States

Prof. Manfred Held, Ph.D.
Messerschmitt-Bölkow-Blohm GmbH
Germany

Mr. Neil R. Helm
President, Helm Communications
United States

Mr. Robert L. Helmbold, Ph.D.
United States

Brig. John Hemsley (Ret.)
Author
United Kingdom

Maj. Clyde R. Henderson, USAF
Strategic Air Command
United States

Mr. Lawrence D. Higgins
Author
United States

Mr. David William Hilsop, Ph.D.
Former Staff Member, U.S. Army Research Office
United States

Mr. Lloyd Hoffman
United States

Prof. Hans W. Hofman, Ph.D.
Universität der Bundeswehr
Germany

Mr. Lynn M. Hollerbach, USAF
United States

Prof. I. B. Holley, Jr., Ph.D.
Dept. of History, Duke U.
United States

Hon. Walter W. Hollis
Deputy Under Secretary of the Army (Operations Research)
United States

Mr. Axel Homburg, Ph.D.
Chairman, Dynamit Nobel
Germany

Mr. John G. Honig, Ph.D.
Former Deputy Director, Weapon Systems Analysis, Office of the Army Chief of Staff
United States

Mr. John W. Hopper
Author
United States

Maj. Gen. Frank B. Horton III, USAF, Ph.D.
Strategic Air Command
United States

Maj. Gen. Hans Höster
Befelshaber, Territorialkommando Nord
Germany

Prof. Reiner K. Huber, Ph.D.
Universität der Bundeswehr
Germany

Mr. Daniel J. Hughes
United States

Capt. Wayne P. Hughes, Jr., USN (Ret.)
Naval Postgraduate School
United States

Ms. Patricia Insley Hutzler
United States

Prof. Virgilio Ilari, Ph.D.
Dept. of History, Catholic U.
Italy

Col. Larry H. Ingraham, USA, M.S.
Neuropsychiatry, Walter Reed Army Institute of Research
United States

Capt. Walter Jablonsky, German Navy
Germany

Mr. Robert F. Jackson
Engineering Director, British Aerospace Dynamics Ltd
United Kingdom

Maj. Gen. Carlo Jean, Italian Army
Ministry of Defense
Italy

Col. Charles J. Jernigan, USAF
C-141 Management Directorate, Robins AFB, Georgia
United States

Lt. Col. Friedrich K. Jeschonnek, German Army
Germany

Mr. Curt Johnson
Military Historian
United States

Mr. Edgar M. Johnson, Ph.D.
Technical Director, U.S. Army Research Institute
United States

Capt. Steven M. Jones, USA
Faculty, U.S. Military Academy
United States

Chaplain Col. Daniel B. Jorgensen, USAF (Ret.), Ph.D.
Professor, Chapman College
United States

Capt. Michael J. Kaiser, USAF
Strategic Air Command
United States

Rear Adm. Mohamed Yousri Kandil (Ret.)
Egypt

Mr. Marshall H. Kaplan, Ph.D.
Executive Director, Space Research Institute, Florida Institute of Technology
United States

Mr. Francis B. Kapper, Ph.D.
United States

Mr. Albert M. Karaba
Director of Engineering, Combat Vehicle Operations, Cadillac Gage Textron
United States

Vice Adm. Bernard M. Kauderer, USN (Ret.)
United States

Lt. Col. Thomas M. Kearny, USAF
United States

Capt. James W. Kehoe, USN (Ret.)
United States

Mr. Michael I. Keller
President, Michael I. Keller Enterprises, Inc.
United States

Mr. Anthony Kellet
Analyst, Dept. of National Defence
Canada

Mr. Max George Kellner
Military Historian
Germany

Prof. Kenneth W. Kemp, Ph.D.
Dept. of Philosophy, College of St. Thomas
United States

Capt. Floyd D. Kennedy, Jr., USNR
United States

Mr. George A. Keyworth II, Ph.D.
Former Science Advisor to the President
United States

Prof. E. C. Kiesling, Ph.D.
Dept. of History, U. of Alabama
United States

Mr. James K. Kieswetter, Ph.D.
Dept. of History, Eastern Washington U.
United States

Mr. Jacob W. Kipp, Ph.D.
Soviet Army Studies Office, Fort Leavenworth, Kansas
United States

Col. James W. Kirkpatrick, USA, M.D., MPH
Commandant, Uniformed Services U. of the Health Sciences
United States

Col. Klaus Kleffner
Operations Division, SHAPE—Belgium
Germany

Col. Timothy E. Kline, USAF (Ret.)
United States

Mr. Ted Kluz
Faculty, Air War College
United States

Mr. Robert E. Knotts
Faculty, U.S. Military Academy
United States

Mr. Scott A. Koch, Ph.D.
United States

Prof. Phillip E. Koerper, Ph.D.
Dept. of History, Jacksonville State U.
United States

Mr. Lutz Köllner, Ph.D.
Director of Sciences, Institute of the Social Sciences in the German Armed Forces
Germany

Mr. Steven M. Kosiak
United States

Brig. Gen. Heinz Kozak
National Defense Academy
Austria

Mr. Paul-Werner Krapke
Germany

Capt. Ulrich F. J. Kreuzfeld
Germany

Col. Clifford R. Krieger, USAF
United States

Maj. Henry Axel Krigsman, Jr., USA
Faculty, U.S. Military Academy
United States

Lt. Col. Manfred Kühr, German Army
Germany

Col. William G. Kuller, USAF
Strategic Air Command
United States

Mr. Robert H. Kupperman, Ph.D.
Center for Strategic and International Studies
United States

Capt. Stuart D. Landersman, USN (Ret.)
United States

Mr. Reuven Leopold, Ph.D.
United States

Prof. Howard S. Levie, Ph.D.
Naval War College
United States

Mr. Robert A. Levine
Director, National Security Strategies Program, Rand Corp.
United States

Mr. P. W. Liddell
Head of Advanced Studies, British Aerospace Ltd
United Kingdom

Lt. Gen. Karl Liko (Ret.)
Austria

Mr. William S. Lind
Director, Center for Cultural Conservatism, Free Congress Foundation
United States

Mr. Stephan Link
Germany

Mr. K. Gerhard Locke, Ph.D.
Senior Scientist
Germany

Prof. Robert F. Lockman, Ph.D.
Economics Dept., U.S. Naval Academy
United States

Capt. Kim Lott, USAF
Strategic Air Command
United States

Lt. Col. Timothy T. Lupfer, USA
United States

Mr. Michael A. Mabe
Major Works, Pergamon Press
United Kingdom

Maj. Gen. Mohammed Gamal-Aldin Mahfouz (Ret.)
Egypt

Lt. Col. Frederick M. Manning, USA
Division of Neuropsychiatry, Walter Reed Army Inst. of Research
United States

Col. Franklin D. Margiotta, USAF (Ret.), Ph.D.
President and Publisher, Brassey's (US)
United States

Mr. Edward J. Marolda, Ph.D.
U.S. Naval Historical Center
United States

Ms. Alice C. Maroni, Ph.D.
Congressional Research Service
United States

Mr. Juan C. Marrero
International Security Section, Criminal Division, Dept. of Justice
United States

Col. Donald S. Marshall, USA (Ret.), Ph.D.
Peabody Museum
United States

Mr. John L. Martin
Chief, Internal Security Section, Criminal Division, Dept. of Justice
United States

Mr. Robert L. Maust
United States

Lt. Col. Albert D. McJoynt, USA (Ret.)
United States

Mr. Mark G. McLaughlin
Journalist
United States

Lt. Col. Jeffrey A. McNally, USA (Ret.), Ph.D.
Faculty, U.S. Military Academy
United States

Mr. Robert McQuie
United States

Mr. John G. Merriman, Ph.D.
Dept. of Political Science, Bowling Green State U.
United States

Capt. Hardy L. Merritt, USNR, Ph.D.
United States

Mr. David Messner, Ph.D.
Vice President, E-Systems, Garland Division
United States

Col. Christian Meyer-Plath, German Army
Commander, 30th Mechanized Infantry Brigade
Germany

Prof. Reinhard Meyers, Ph.D.
U. of Munster
Germany

Cdr. Mark L. Mitchell, USN
Faculty, Naval Postgraduate School
United States

Col. Ralph M. Mitchell, USA (Ret.)
Former Faculty, National War College
United States

Brig. Gen. Arie Mizrachi (Ret.)
President, Armaz Consulting, Ltd
Israel

Maj. Arno Möhl
Germany

Mr. Robert Moore
United States

Prof. Moustafa Aly Morsy Aly, Ph.D.
Egypt

Mr. Daniel R. Mortensen, Ph.D.
Office of Air Force History
United States

Prof. Charles C. Moskos, Ph.D.
Dept. of Sociology, Northwestern U.
United States

Col. James B. Motley, USA (Ret.), Ph.D.
Author and Defense Analyst
United States

Prof. Malcolm Muir, Jr., Ph.D.
Chairman, Dept. of History and Philosophy, Austin Peay State U.
United States

Capt. James Murphy, USN (Ret.)
United States

Lt. Col. N. T. P. Murphy (Ret.)
United Kingdom

Maj. Gen. John E. Murray, USA (Ret.)
Former First Principal Deputy Assistant Secretary, Special Operations and Low-intensity Conflict, Dept. of Defense
United States

Lt. Col. Günther Nagel
Germany

Mr. Joseph E. Nation
Rand Corp.
United States

Capt. Jeffrey A. Neal, USAF
Strategic Air Command
United States

Prof. Stephanie G. Neuman, Ph.D.
Columbia U.
United States

Capt. David A. Niedringhaus, USA
Faculty, U.S. Military Academy
United States

Col. Roger H. Nye, USA (Ret.)
Former Faculty, U.S. Military Academy
United States

Prof. Barry O'Connor, Ph.D.
Marymount U.
United States

Lt. Col. Edward C. O'Dowd, USA
Mesa Community College
United States

Ms. Ruth Ann O'Keefe, Ph.D.
Former Director, Navy Family Support Programs, Dept. of Navy
United States

Prof. Barry O'Neill, Ph.D.
Yale School of Organization and Management, Dept. of Political Science, Yale U.
Canada

Mr. Ronald O'Rourke
Congressional Research Service
United States

Mr. Manfred Obst
Germany

Mr. John Kennedy Ohl, Ph.D.
United States

Mr. Raymond Oliver
United States

Cmdr. Omar El Farouk Amin Omar (Ret.)
Ministry of Emigration and Expatriates' Affairs; General Director for Information and Research
Egypt

Ms. Rose-Marie Oster, Ph.D.
United States

Mrs. Eloise Paananen
Author
United States

Mr. Prescott Palmer
United States

Capt. Richard R. Pariseau, USN (Ret.)
United States

Col. Rod Paschall, USA (Ret.)
Former Commander, Delta Force
United States

Col. Arion Pattakos, USA (Ret.)
United States

Lt. Col. Günter Pauleit
Ministry of Defense
Germany

Mr. Peter D. Penny, Ph.D.
Manager, Design Services, Royal Ordnance PLC, Rocket Motors Division
United Kingdom

Mr. Ernest N. Petrick, Ph.D.
Consultant, General Dynamics Land Systems Division
United States

Mr. Robert L. Pfaltzgraff, Jr., Ph.D.
President, Institute for Foreign Policy Analysis
United States

Col. Thomas D. Phillips, USAF
Former Special Assistant to the Commander in Chief, Strategic Air Command
United States

Mr. Alessandro Politi, Ph.D.
Defense Analyst
Italy

Mr. John Prados
Author
United States

Col. Heinrich Quaden
Germany

Prof. George H. Quester, Ph.D.
U. of Maryland
United States

Col. Dennis J. Quinn, USA
United States

Ms. Bonnie Ram
Advanced Sciences, Inc.
United States

Maj. Stephen P. Randolph, USAF
United States

Maj. Harold E. Raugh, Jr., USA
Faculty, U.S. Military Academy
United States

Lt. Gen. Ernst Rebentisch, Medical Corps (Ret.)
Germany

Mr. George A. Reed
U.S. Mission to NATO
United States

Mr. Allan S. Rehm
Mitre Corporation
United States

Mr. John C. Reilly, Jr.
United States

Prof. R. Dan Richardson, Ph.D.
Roanoke College
United States

Mr. J. B. G. Roberts, Ph.D.
Royal Signals and Radar Establishment
United Kingdom

Mr. Richard J. Roca
Executive Director, AT&T Bell Laboratories
United States

Lt. Col. Frank Rosa, USAF
Faculty, U.S. Air Force Academy
United States

Prof. Peter J. Rowe, Ph.D.
U. of Liverpool
United Kingdom

Capt. William J. Ruhe, USN (Ret.)
United States

Prof. Dieter Ruloff, Ph.D.
U. of Zurich
Switzerland

Col. Francis M. Rush, Jr., USAF (Ret.)
Former Director, Sixth Quadrennial Review of Military Compensation
United States

Mr. Eduardo Salas, Ph.D.
United States

Maj. Gen. Ibrahim Ahmed Salem
Egypt

Mr. William August Sander III, Ph.D.
C^3I Manager, Electronics Division, Army Research Office
United States

Prof. Sam C. Sarkesian, Ph.D.
Loyola U. of Chicago
United States

Rear Adm. William L. Schachte, Jr., USN
Former DOD/JCS Representative for Ocean Policy Affairs
United States

Lt. Col. Gerhard Schepe
Policy Division, SHAPE—Belgium
Germany

Mr. Victor P. Schmit, Ph.D.
Assistant Director, Army Personnel Research Establishment, Ministry of Defence
United Kingdom

Prof. Daniel P. Schrage, Ph.D.
Georgia Institute of Technology
United States

Mr. Rolf Schumacher
Germany

Mr. Walter Rudolf Schütze, Ph.D.
Secretaire-General of French-German Relations Studies, French International Relations Institute
Germany

Mr. Hansjörg Schwalm
Federal College of Public Administration
Germany

Lt. Col. F. Kenneth Schwetje, USAF
United States

Mr. Jay R. Sculley, Ph.D.
United States

Rear Adm. John R. Seesholtz, USN
U.S. Naval Observatory
United States

Prof. David R. Segal, Ph.D.
U. of Maryland
United States

Prof. Mady Wechsler Segal, Ph.D.
U. of Maryland
United States

Cdr. Hideo Sekino, IJN (Ret.)
Director, Institute for Historical Research
Japan

Cdr. Sadao Seno, JMSDF (Ret.)
Japan

Maj. Gregory M. Shaka, USAF
Strategic Air Command
United States

Gen. Samir Hassan Mohammed Shalaby (Ret.), Ph.D.
Egypt

Adm. Mohamed Gamal Al Shanawani
Chief, High Dam Port Authority—Aswan, Egypt
Egypt

Mr. Edward S. Shea
Defense Analyst
United States

Mr. James Sherr
Soviet Studies Research Centre, Sandhurst Royal Military Academy
United Kingdom

Mr. Zhou Shi-chang
Military Science Academy
China

Cdr. Robert B. Shields, Jr., USN
United States

Mr. Abram N. Shulsky
Author
United States

Mr. G. Thomas Sicilia, Ph.D.
Former Director, Defense Training and Performance Data Center
United States

Mr. Howard R. Simpson
Author
United States

Mr. Robert B. Sims
Former Assistant Secretary of Defense, Public Affairs
United States

Air Cmdr. Jasjit Singh, Indian Air Force (Ret.)
Director, Institute for Defence Studies and Analyses
India

Mr. D. H. Sinnott
Chief, Microwave Radar Division, Surveillance Research Laboratory, Defence Science and Technology Organisation, Dept. of Defence
Australia

Brig. J. H. Skinner, U.K. (Ret.)
United Kingdom

Lt. Col. John F. Sloan, USA (Ret.)
Faculty, Defense Intelligence College
United States

Capt. Charles J. Smith, USN (Ret.)
Executive Director, American Society of Naval Engineers
United States

Mr. Charles R. Smith, Ph.D.
Marymount U.
United States

Col. David A. Smith, USAF (Ret.)
United States

Maj. Dianne L. Smith, USA, Ph.D.
United States

Lt. Cdr. Frederic N. Smith, USN (Ret.)
Former Soviet Bloc Editor, *Defense and Foreign Affairs Magazine*
United States

Mr. Harvey A. Smith
Mathematics Dept., Arizona State U.
United States

Maj. Gen. Perry M. Smith, USAF (Ret.), Ph.D.
Former Commandant, National War College; Author; Military Analyst, Cable Network News
United States

Maj. Gen. W. Stanford Smith, USA (Ret.)
Military Analyst
United States

Lt. Col. Donald C. Snedeker, USA
United States

Mr. William J. Spahr, Ph.D.
United States

Mr. James E. Spates
United States

Mr. Henry Alan Staley
Former Faculty, Air Command and Staff College
United States

Prof. Sandra Carson Stanley, Ph.D.
Dept. of Sociology, Towson State U.
United States

Gen. Donn A. Starry, USA (Ret.)
Former Commander, U.S. Army Training and Doctrine Command
United States

Mr. George F. Steeg, Prof. Eng.
Former Vice President, Systems Analysis, United Technologies Corp.
United States

Mr. Donald Stewart, Ph.D.
Former Staff Member, Organization of American Studies
United States

Ms. Nora Stewart, Ph.D.
Author
United States

Mr. Paul Stewart, Ph.D.
Southern Connecticut State U.
United States

Mr. Paul Stillwell
Director of Oral History, U.S. Naval Institute
United States

Lt. Col. Philip D. Stinson, USAF (Ret.)
Former Vice Commandant, Air Force Special Operations School
United States

Lt. Col. Ulrich Stork
Federal Armed Forces Office for Studies and Exercises
Germany

Lt. Col. Gertmann Sude
Germany

Prof. Jon Tetsuro Sumida, Ph.D.
U. of Maryland
United States

Mr. Jan Surotchak, Ph.D.
Institute for Foreign Policy Analysis
United States

Mr. Lee A. Sweetapple
Military Analyst
United States

Mr. John E. Tashjean, Ph.D.
President, Conflict Morphology, Inc.
United States

Master Sgt. John Taylor, USA (Ret.)
United States

Col. James P. Terry, USMC
Deputy Legal Counsel to the Chairman, JCS
United States

Cdr. Gerry S. Thomas, USN
United States

Mr. Edmund R. Thompson
United States

Mr. Frederick D. Thompson
Center for Naval Analyses
United States

Col. L. Sam Thompson, USA (Ret.)
Former Faculty, U.S. Military Academy
United States

Capt. William Thralls, Air National Guard
United States

Prof. Geoffrey Till, Ph.D.
Professor, Dept. of History & International Affairs, Royal Naval College, Greenwich
United Kingdom

Col. James Toth, USMC (Ret.)
Faculty, Industrial College of the Armed Forces, Fort Lesley J. McNair
United States

Maj. Gen. A. J. Trythall, CB (Ret.)
Managing Director, Brassey's (UK)
United Kingdom

Prof. Spencer C. Tucker, Ph.D.
Texas Christian U.
United States

Col. C. Fred Tyner, USA, M.D.
Walter Reed Army Medical Center
United States

Lt. Gen. Franz Uhle-Wettler (Ret.), Ph.D.
Former Commandant, NATO Defense College
Germany

Brig. Gen. Reinhard Uhle-Wettler
Germany

Mr. Frank Uhlig, Jr.
Editor, *Naval War College Review*
United States

Mr. Lutz Unterseher, Ph.D.
Independent Analyst, Studiengruppe Alternative Sicherheitspolitik
Germany

Mr. Alexander Uschakow, Ph.D.
Institüt für Östrecht der Universität in Köln
Germany

Ms. Debra van Opstal
Center for Strategic and International Studies
United States

Capt. J. Jan W. van Waning, Netherlands Navy (Ret.)
Netherlands

Mr. Frank D. Verderame, Ph.D.
Former Assistant Director of Army Research
United States

Lt. Col. Heinz Vetschera, Ph.D.
Federal Ministry of Defense
Austria

Lt. Gen. Carl-Gero von Ilsemann (Ret.)
Germany

Lt. Col. Axel von Netzer
Federal Armed Forces Office for Studies and Exercises
Germany

Brig. Gen. Adrian Frhr. von Oër (Ret.), Ph.D.
Germany

Mr. J. E. Wade
Jacksonville State U.
United States

Mr. Edward W. Walker
Columbia U.
United States

Mr. Ulrike C. Wasmuht, Ph.D.
Peace Researcher, Free U. of Berlin
Germany

Cdr. Bruce W. Watson, USN (Ret.), Ph.D.
Adjunct Faculty, Defense Intelligence College
United States

Ms. Susan M. Watson
Author
United States

Lt. Col. Bernd Weber
Germany

Capt. Kevin J. Weddle, USA
United States

Mr. Peter R. Weilemann, Ph.D.
United States

Mr. John M. Weinstein, Ph.D.
Chief of Policy and Programs, U.S. Nuclear Command and Control Systems Support Staff
United States

Mr. Gary E. Weir, Ph.D.
U.S. Naval Historical Center
United States

Prof. Hans-Heinrich Weise, Ph.D.
German Federal Ministry of Defense
Germany

Mr. Ingo Wolfgang Weise, Ph.D.
General Director, Rheinmetall GmbH
Germany

Capt. Ulrich Weisser, German Navy
Germany

Prof. Claude E. Welch, Jr., Ph.D.
SUNY Buffalo; Former Editor, *Armed Forces and Society*
United States

Lt. Cdr. James T. Westwood, USN (Ret.)
Defense Analyst
United States

Prof. Everett L. Wheeler, Ph.D.
Dept. of Classical Studies, Duke U.
United States

Mr. Charles E. White, Ph.D.
United States

Mr. Walter P. White
United States

Col. Thomas L. Wilkerson, USMC
United States

Maj. Alan P. Williams, USAF
United States

Prof. John Hoyt Williams, Ph.D.
Indiana State U.
United States

Prof. Max R. Williams, Ph.D.
Western Carolina U.
United States

Capt. Leonard Wong, USA
Faculty, U.S. Military Academy
United States

Mr. Robert S. Wood, Ph.D.
Dean, Center for Naval Warfare Studies, Naval War College
United States

Capt. Julian M. Wright, Jr., USN
U.S. Naval Observatory
United States

Lt. Gen. William P. Yarborough, USA (Ret.)
Former Commander, U.S. Army Special Warfare Center
United States

Mr. L. William Yolton
Executive Director, National Interreligious Service Board for Conscientious Objectors
United States

Mr. Bryan Young
Director of Strategic Projects, British Aerospace Ltd
United Kingdom

Mr. Dov S. Zakheim, Ph.D.
Former Deputy Under Secretary of Defense for Planning and Resources
Chief Executive Officer, SPC International, Inc.
United States

ABBREVIATIONS AND ACRONYMS

AA	antiaircraft
AAA	antiaircraft artillery
AASR	advanced airborne surveillance radar
AAM	air-to-air missile
AAW	antiair warfare
AB	airborne
ABD	airborne division (Sov)
ABM	antiballistic missile(s)
about	the total could be higher
ac	aircraft
ACDA	Arms Control and Disarmament Agency
ACE	Allied Command, Europe
ACM	advanced cruise missile
ACV	air cushion vehicle/vessel
AD	air defense
adj	adjusted
AE	auxiliary(ies), ammunition carrier
AEF	auxiliary(ies), explosives and stores
AEW	airborne early warning
AF	stores ship(s) with RAS capability
AFB	air force base
AFV	armored fighting vehicle
AFR	Air Force Reserve (US)
AGHS	hydrographic survey vessel(s)
AGI	intelligence collection vessel(s)
AGM	air-to-ground missile
AGOR	oceanographic research vessel(s)
AGOS	ocean surveillance vessel(s)
AH	hospital ship(s)
AI	artificial intelligence
AIFV	armored infantry fighting vehicle
AIP	air-independent propulsion
AK	cargo ship(s)
ALCM	air-launched cruise missile(s)
amph	amphibious/amphibian(s)
AMRAAM	advanced medium-range air-to-air missile
ANG	Air National Guard (US)
AO	tanker(s) with RAS capability; area of operations
AOE	auxiliary(ies), fuel and ammunition, RAS capability
AOT	tanker(s) without RAS capability
AP	passenger ship(s); armor piercing
APC	armored personnel carrier(s)
APDS	armor piercing, discarding sabot missile
API	armor piercing, incendiary
APO	army post office
AR	Army Reserve (US)
AR	repair ship(s)
Arg	Argentina
ARM	antiradiation (antiradar) missile
armd	armored
ARNG	Army National Guard (US)
arty	artillery
AS	submarine depot-ship(s)
ASAT	antisatellite weapon
aslt	assault
ASM	air-to-surface missile(s)
ASRAAM	advanced short-range air-to-air missile
ASROC	antisubmarine rocket
ASTT	antisubmarine TT
ASUW	antisurface-unit warfare
ASW	antisubmarine warfare
AT	tug(s)
ATBM	antitactical ballistic missile
ATF	advanced tactical fighter
ATGW	antitank guided weapon(s)
ATK	antitank
ATTU	Atlantic to the Urals
Aust	Australia
avn	aviation
AVT	aviation training ship
AWACS	airborne warning and control system
BA	Budget Authority
BB	battleship
bbr	bomber(s)
bde	brigade(s)
bdgt	budget(s)
Be	Belgium
BMD	ballistic missile defense
BMEWS	ballistic missile early warning system
bn	battalion(s)/billion(s)
BSAG	battleship surface attack group
bty	battery(ies)
Bu	Bulgaria
BVR	beyond visual range
CAD	computer-aided design
CAP	combat air patrol; civil air patrol
CAS	close air support
Cat	Category
cav	cavalry
cbt	combat

CBW	chemical and biological warfare
CC	cruiser(s)
CCM	counter-countermeasures
Cdn	Canada
CCP	Chinese Communist Party
CD	civil defense
cdo	commando
CEP	circular error probable
CG	SAM cruiser(s)
CGF	Central Group of Forces (Sov)
CGH	CG with helicopters
CGN	nuclear-fueled CG
cgo	freight aircraft
Ch	China (PRC)
C^3I	command, control, communications, and intelligence
CINC	commander in chief
CLOS	command line-of-sight
COIN	counterinsurgency
comb	combined/combination
comd	command
COMINT	communications intelligence
comms	communications
CONUS	Continental United States
coy	company(ies)
CP	command post
CPSU	Communist Party of the Soviet Union
CV	aircraft carrier(s)
CVBG	carrier battle group
CVN	nuclear-fueled CV
CVV	V/STOL and hel CV
CW	chemical warfare
CY	current year
Cz	Czechoslovakia
DD	destroyer(s)
D Day	day operation begins
DDG	destroyer(s) with area SAM; destroyer(s) with hel
def	defense
defn	definition
det	detachment(s)
DEW	directed-energy weapon; distant early warning
div	division(s)
Dk	Denmark
ECM	electronic countermeasures
ECR	Electronic combat and reconnaissance
ELINT	electronic intelligence
elm	element(s)
EMP	electromagnetic pulse
engr	engineer(s)
EOD	explosive ordnance disposal
eqpt	equipment
ESM	electronic support measures
est	estimate(d)
EW	electronic warfare
excl	excludes/excluding
exp	expenditure
FAC	forward air control
FAE	fuel-air explosive
fd	field
FEBA	forward edge of the battle area
FF	frigate(s)
FFG	frigate(s) with area SAM
FGA	fighter(s), ground-attack
FH	frigate(s) with helicopter
FLIR	forward-looking infrared radar
flt	flight(s)
FMA	foreign military assistance
Fr	France
ftr	fighter(s) (aircraft)
FW	fixed-wing
FY	fiscal year
GA	Chinese Integrated Group Army
GB	Sarin (chemical agent)
GBU	guided bomb unit
GCI	ground control intercept
GD	Soman (chemical agent)
GDP	gross domestic product
Ge	Germany
GLCM	ground-launched cruise missile
GNP	gross national product
gp	group(s)
GP	general purpose
GPS	global positioning system
Gr	Greece
GW	guided weapon(s)
hel	helicopter(s)
HARM	high-speed antiradiation missile
HQ	headquarters
Hu	Hungary
HWT	heavy-weight torpedo(es)
hy	heavy
ICBM	intercontinental ballistic missile(s)
IFF	identification friend or foe
IFS	International Financial Statistics
IG	inspector general
IMF	International Monetary Fund
imp	improved
incl	includes/including
indep	independent
Indon	Indonesia
inf	infantry
INF	intermediate-range nuclear forces
IR	infrared
IRBM	intermediate-range ballistic missile(s)
Is	Israel
It	Italy
k	kilobyte
KE	kinetic energy
kg	kilogram(s)
kHz	kilohertz

km	kilometer(s)
KT	kiloton(s)
LAMPS	Light airborne multipurpose system
LAW	light antitank weapon
LCA	landing craft, assault
LCAC	landing craft, air cushion
LCM	landing craft, mechanized
LCT	landing craft, tank
LCU	landing craft, utility
LCVP	landing craft, vehicles and personnel
LHA	landing ship(s), assault
LHX	light helicopter, experimental
LKA	assault cargo ship(s)
log	logistic
LORAN	long-range air navigation system
LPD	landing platform(s), dock
LPH	landing platform(s), helicopter
LSD	landing ship(s), dock
LSM	landing ship(s), medium
LST	landing ship(s), tank
lt	light
LWT	light-weight torpedo(es)
m	million(s)
MAC	Military Airlift Command (US)
MAAG	military assistance and advisory group
MAD	mutual assured destruction; magnetic anomaly detection
maint	maintenance
MBT	main battle tank(s)
MC&G	mapping, charting, and geodesy
MCC/I/O	mine countermeasures vessel(s), coastal/inshore, offshore
MCMV	mine countermeasures vessel(s)
MCR	Marine Corps Reserve (US)
MD	Military District(s)
M Day	mobilization day
mech	mechanized
med	medium
medevac	casualty transport/air ambulance
MEF/B/U	Marine Expeditionary Force(s)/Brigade(s)/Unit(s) (US)
MFO	Multinational Force and Observers
MG	machine gun
MHC/I/O	minehunter(s), coastal/inshore/offshore
MHz	megahertz
MICV	mechanized infantry combat vehicle(s)
mil	military
MINURSO	UN Mission for the Referendum in Western Sahara
MIRV	multiple independently targetable re-entry vehicle(s)
misc	miscellaneous
Mk	mark (model number)
ML	minelayer
MLRS	multiple-launch rocket system
MMW	millimeter-wave radar
mob	mobilization
mod	modified/modification
mor	mortar(s)
mot	motorized
MPS	marine pre-positioning squadron(s)
MR	maritime reconnaissance/motor rifle
MRASM	medium-range air-to-surface missile(s)
MRBM	medium-range ballistic missile(s)
PSC	principal surface combatants
psi	pounds per square inch
PSYOPS	psychological operations
R&D	research and development
RAS	replenishment at sea
RCL	recoilless launcher(s)
RCS	radar cross-section
RDF	rapid deployment force
recce	reconnaissance
regt	regiment(s)
RF	radio frequency
RL	rocket launchers
Ro	Romania
ROM	read-only memory
ro-ro	roll-on, roll-off
RPG	rocket-propelled grenade
RPV	remotely piloted vehicle(s)
RV	re-entry vehicle(s)
SAC	Strategic Air Command (US)
SACEUR	Supreme Allied Commander, Europe
SACLANT	Supreme Allied Commander, Atlantic
SAH	semi-active homing
SALT	Strategic Arms Limitation Treaty
SAM	surface-to-air missile(s)
SAR	search and rescue; synthetic aperture radar
SDI	Strategic Defense Initiative
SES	surface-effect ship(s)
SF	Special Forces
SGF	Southern Group of Forces (Sov)
SHAPE	Supreme Headquarters Allied Powers, Europe
SIGINT	signals intelligence
sigs	signals
SLAR	side-looking airborne radar
SLBM	sea- or submarine-launched ballistic missile(s)
SLCM	sea- or submarine-launched cruise missile(s)
SLEP	service life extension program
SLOC	sea line of communication
some	up to
SOP	standard operating procedure
Sov	Soviet
Sp	Spain
SP	self-propelled
spt	support
SQ	superquick fuze

sqn	squadron
SRAM	short-range attack missile(s)
SRBM	short-range ballistic missile(s)
SS(C/I)	submarine(s) (coastal/inshore)
SSB	ballistic-missile submarine(s)
SSBN	nuclear-fueled SSB
SSGN	SSN with dedicated nonballistic missile launchers
SSM	surface-to-surface missile(s)
SSN	nuclear-fueled submarine(s)
START	Strategic Arms Reduction Talks
STOL	short take-off and landing
STOVL	short takeoff, vertical landing
SUGW	surface-to-underwater GW
Sw	Sweden
Switz	Switzerland
sy	security
t	tons
TA	Territorial Army (UK)
tac	tactical
TAC	Tactical Air Command (US)
TADS	target acquisition and designation system
TASM	tactical air-to-surface missile
TD	tank division
T&E	test and evaluation
TERCOM	terrain contour-matching guidance
tk	tank(s)
tkr	tanker(s)
TLE	treaty-limited equipment
TOE	table of organization and equipment
TOW	tube-launched, optically tracked, wire-guided antitank missile
tps	troop(s)
tpt	transport(s)
trg	training
TT	torpedo tube(s)
Tu	Turkey
UHF	ultra-high frequency
UN	United Nations
UNAVEM	UN Angolan Verification Mission
UNDOF	UN Disengagement Observer Force
UNFICYP	UN Force in Cyprus
UNIFIL	UN Interim Force in Lebanon
UNIKOM	UN Iraq/Kuwait Observer Mission
UNMOGIP	UN Military Observer Group in India and Pakistan
UNTSO	UN Truce Supervisory Organization
URG	underway replenishment group(s)
USGW	underwater-to-surface GW
USMC	US Marine Corps
UUGW	underwater-to-underwater GW
UV	ultraviolet
veh	vehicle(s)
VERTREP	vertical replenishment
VHF	very high frequency
VIP	very important person(s)
VLS	vertical launch system(s)
V(/S)TOL	vertical(/short) takeoff and landing
WGF	Western Group of Force (Sov)
WP	Warsaw Pact
wpn	weapon
Yug	Yugoslavia

Designations of Aircraft and Helicopters listed in Country Articles

Type	Name/designation	Origin	Maker
AIRCRAFT			
A-3	Skywarrior	U.S.	Douglas
A-4	Skyhawk	U.S.	MD
A-5	Fantan	China	Nanchang
A-6	Intruder	U.S.	Grumman
A-7	Corsair II	U.S.	LTV
A-10	Thunderbolt	U.S.	Fairchild
A-36	Halcón (C-101)		
A-37	Dragonfly	U.S.	Cessna
AC-130	(C-130)		
AC-47	(C-47)		
Airtourer		NZ	Victa
AJ-37	(J-37)		
Ajeet	(Folland Gnat)	India/U.K.	HAL
Alizé		France	Breguet
AlphaJet		France/Ge	Dassault/ Breguet/ Dornier
AM-3	Bosbok (C-4M)	Italy	Aermacchi
An-2	"Colt"	USSR	Antonov
An-12	"Cub"	USSR	Antonov
An-14	"Clod"	USSR	Antonov
An-22	"Cock"	USSR	Antonov
An-24	"Coke"	USSR	Antonov
An-26	"Curl"	USSR	Antonov
An-30	"Clank"	USSR	Antonov
An-32	"Cline"	USSR	Antonov
An-124	"Condor" (Ruslan)	USSR	Antonov
Andover	[HS-748]		
Atlantic	(Atlantique)	France	Dassault/ Breguet
AS-202	Bravo	Switz	FFA
AT-3		Taiwan	AIDC
AT-6	(T-6)		
AT-11		U.S.	Beech
AT-26	EMB-326		
AT-33	(T-33)		
AU-23	Peacemaker [PC-6B)	U.S.	Fairchild
AV-8	Harrier II	U.S./U.K.	MD/BAe
Aztec	PA-23	U.S.	Piper
B-1		U.S.	Rockwell
B-52	Stratofortress	U.S.	Boeing
BAC-111		U.K.	BAe
BAC-167	Strikemaster	U.K.	BAe

TYPE	NAME/DESIGNATION	ORIGIN	MAKER
BAe-146		U.K.	BAe
BAe-748	(HS-748)		
Baron	(T-42)		
Be-6	"Madge"	USSR	Beriev
Be-12	"Mail' (Tchaika)	USSR	Beriev
Beech 50	Twin Bonanza	U.S.	Beech
Beech 95	Travel Air	U.S.	Beech
BN-2	Islander, Defender, Trislander	U.K.	Britten-Norman
Boeing 707		U.S.	Boeing
Boeing 727		U.S.	Boeing
Boeing 737		U.S.	Boeing
Boeing 747		U.S.	Boeing
Bonanza		U.S.	Beech
Bronco	(OV-10)		
Buccaneer		U.K.	BAe
Bulldog		U.K.	BAe
C-1		Japan	Kawasaki
C-2	Greyhound	U.S.	Grumman
C-4M	Kudu (AM-3)	S. Africa	Atlas
C-5	Galaxy	U.S.	Lockheed
C-7	DHC-7		
C-9	Nightingale (DC-9)		
C-12	Super King Air (Huron)	U.S.	Beech
C-18	[Boeing 707]		
C-20	(Gulfstream III)		
C-21	(Learjet)		
C-22	(Boeing 727)		
C-23	(Sherpa)	U.K.	Short
C-42	(Neiva Regente)	Brazil	Embraer
C-45	Expeditor	U.S.	Beech
C-46	Commando	U.S.	Curtis
C-47	DC-3 (Dakota) (C-117 Skytrain)	U.S.	Douglas
C-54	Skymaster (DC-4)	U.S.	Douglas
C-91	HS-748		
C-93	HS-125		
C-95	EMB-110		
C-97	EMB-121		
C-101	Aviojet	Spain	CASA
C-115	DHC-5	Canada	De Havilland
C-117	(C-47)		
C-118	Liftmaster (DC-6)		
C-119	Packet	U.S.	Fairchild
C-123	Provider	U.S.	Fairchild
C-127	(Do-27)	Spain	CASA
C-130	Hercules (L-100)	U.S.	Lockheed
C-131	Convair 440	U.S.	Convair
C-135	[Boeing 707]		
C-137	[Boeing 707]		
C-140	(Jetstar)	U.S.	Lockheed
C-141	Starlifter	U.S.	Douglas
C-160		Fr/Ge	Transall
C-212	Aviocar	Spain	CASA
C-235		Spain	CASA
CA-25	Winjeel	Aust	Common-wealth
Canberra	(B-57)	U.K.	BAe

TYPE	NAME/DESIGNATION	ORIGIN	MAKER
CAP-10		France	Mudry
CAP-20		France	Mudry
CAP-230		France	Mudry
Caravelle	SE-210	France	Aérospatiale
CC-109	(Convair 440)	U.S.	Convair
CC-115	DHC-15		
CC-117	(Falcon 20)		
CC-132	(DHC-7)		
CC-137	(Boeing 707)		
CC-138	(DHC-6)		
CC-144	CL-600/-601	Canada	Canadair
CC-18	F/A-18		
CF-116	F-5		
Cheetah	[Mirage III]	S. Africa	Atlas
Cherokee	PA-28	U.S.	Piper
Cheyenne	PA-31T [Navajo]	U.S.	Piper
Chieftain	PA-31-350 [Navajo]	U.S.	Piper
Chipmunk	DHC-1		
Citabria		U.S.	Champion
Citation	(T-47)	U.S.	Cessna
CJ-5	[Yak-18]	China	
CL-215		Canada	Canadair
CL-44		Canada	Canadair
CL-601	Challenger	Canada	Canadair
CM-170	Magister [Tzukit]	France	Aérospatiale
CM-175	Zéphyr	France	Aérospatiale
CN-235		Sp/Indon	CASA/ IPTN
Cochise	T-42		
Comanche	PA-24	U.S.	Piper
Commander	Aero-/Turbo-Commander	U.S.	Rockwell
Commodore	MS-893	France	Aérospatiale
Corvette	SN-601	France	Aérospatiale
CP-3	P-3 Orion		
CP-121	S-2		
CP-140	Aurora (P-3 Orion)	U.S.	Lockheed
CT-4	Airtrainer	NZ	Victa
CT-39	Sabreliner	U.S.	Rockwell
CT-114	CL-41 Tutor	Canada	Canadair
CT-133	Silver Star [T-33]	Canada	Canadair
CT-134	Musketeer		
Dagger	(Nesher)		
Dakota		U.S.	Piper
Dakota	(C-47)		
DC-3	(C-47)	U.S.	Douglas
DC-4	(C-54)	U.S.	Douglas
DC-6	(C-118)	U.S.	Douglas
DC-7		U.S.	Douglas
DC-8		U.S.	Douglas
DC-9		U.S.	MD
Deepak	(HT-32)		
Defender	BN-2		
DH-100	Vampire	U.K.	De Havilland
DHC-1	Chipmunk	Canada	DHC
DHC-2	Beaver	Canada	DHC
DHC-3	Otter	Canada	DHC
DHC-4	Caribou	Canada	DHC
DHC-5	Buffalo	Canada	DHC
DHC-6	Twin Otter	Canada	DHC
DHC-7	Dash-7 (Ranger, CC-132)	Canada	DHC
DHC-8		Canada	DHC

Type	Name/designation	Origin	Maker
Dimona	H-36	Ge	Hoffman
Do-27	(C-127)	Ge	Dornier
Do-28	Skyservant	Ge	Dornier
Do-128		Ge	Dornier
Do-228		Ge	Dornier
E-2	Hawkeye	U.S.	Grumman
E-3	Sentry	U.S.	Boeing
E-4	[Boeing 747]	U.S.	Boeing
E-6	[Boeing 707]		
EA-3	[A-3]		
EA-6	Prowler [A-6]		
Electra	(L-188)		
EC-130	[C-130]		
EC-135	[Boeing 707]		
EMB-110	Bandeirante	Brazil	Embraer
EMB-111	Maritime Bandeirante	Brazil	Embraer
EMB-120	Brasilia	Brazil	Embraer
EMB-121	Xingu	Brazil	Embraer
EMB-312	Tucano	Brazil	Embraer
EMB-326	Xavante (MB-326)	Brazil	Embraer
EMB-810	[Seneca]	Brazil	Embraer
EP-3	(P-3 Orion)		
Etendard		France	Dassault
EV-1	(OV-1)		
F-1	[T-2]	Japan	Mitsubishi
F-4	Phantom	U.S.	MD
F-5	-A/-B: Freedom Fighter; -E/-F: Tiger II	U.S.	Northrop
F-6	J-6		
F-7	J-7		
F-8	J-8		
F-8	Crusader	U.S.	Republic
F-14	Tomcat	U.S.	Grumman
F-15	Eagle	U.S.	MD
F-16	Fighting Falcon	U.S.	GD
F-18	[F/A-18]		
F-21	Kfir	Israel	IAI
F-27	Friendship	Nl	Fokker
F-28	Fellowship	Nl	Fokker
F-35	Draken	Sweden	SAAB
F-84	Thunderstreak	U.S.	Lockheed
F-86	Sabre	U.S.	N. American
F-100	Super Sabre	U.S.	N. American
F-104	Starfighter	U.S.	Lockheed
F-106	Delta Dart	U.S.	Convair
F-111		U.S.	GD
F-172	(Cessna 172)	France/ U.S.	Reims-Cessna
F/A-18	Hornet	U.S.	MD
Falcon	Mystère-Falcon		
FB-111	(F-111)		
FH-227	(F-27)	U.S.	Fairchild/ Hiller
Flamingo	MBB-233	Ge	MBB
FT-5	JJ-5	China	CAC
FT-6	JJ-6		
FTB-337	[Cessna 337]		
G-91		Italy	Aeritalia
G-222		Italy	Aeritalia
Galaxy	C-5		
Galeb		Yug	SOKO
Gardian	(Falcon 20)		
Genet	SF-260W		
GU-25	(Falcon 20)		
Guerrier	R-235		
Gulstream		U.S.	Gulfstream Aviation
Gumhuria	(Bücker 181)	Egypt	Heliopolis Ac
H-5	[Il-28]	China	Harbin
H-6	[Tu-16]	China	Xian
H-36	Dimona		
Halcón	[C-101]		
Harrier	(AV-8)	U.K.	BAe
Harvard	(T-6)		
Hawk		U.K.	BAe
HC-130	(C-130)		
HF-24	Marut	India	HAL
HFB-320	Hansajet	Ge	Hamburger FB
HJ-5	(H-5)		
HJT-16	Kiran	India	HAL
HPT-32	Deepak	India	HAL
HS-125	(Dominie)	U.K.	BAe
HS-748	[Andover]	U.K.	BAe
HT-2		India	HAL
HU-16	Albatross	U.S.	Grumman
HU-25	(Falcon 20)		
Hunter		U.K.	BAe
HZ-5	(H-5)		
IA-35	Huanquero	Arg	FMA
IA-50	Guaraní	Arg	FMA
IA-58	Pucará	Arg	FMA
IA-63	Pampa	Arg	FMA
IAI-201/-202	Arava	Israel	IAI
IAI-1124	Westwind, Seascan	Israel	IAI
IAR-28		Ro	IAR
IAR-93	Orao	Yug/Ro	SOKO/ IAR
Il-14	"Crate"	USSR	Ilyushin
Il-18	"Coot"	USSR	Ilyushin
Il-20	(Il-18)		
Il-28	"Beagle"	USSR	Ilyushin
Il-38	"May"	USSR	Ilyushin
Il-62	"Classic"	USSR	Ilyushin
Il-76	"Candid" (tpt) "Mainstay" (AEW) "Midas" (tkr)	USSR	Ilyushin
Impala	[MB-326]	S. Africa	Atlas
Islander	BN-2		
J-2	[MiG-15]	China	
J-5	[MiG-17F]	China	Shenyang
J-6	[MiG-19]	China	Shenyang
J-7	[MiG-21]	China	Xian
J-8	[Sov Ye-142]	China	Shenyang
J-32	Lansen	Sweden	SAAB
J-35	Draken	Sweden	SAAB
J-37	Viggen	Sweden	SAAB
JA-37	(J-37)		
Jaguar		Fr/U.K.	SEPECAT
JAS-39	Gripen	Sweden	SAAB
Jastreb		Yug	SOKO
Jet Provost		U.K.	BAe

TYPE	NAME/DESIGNATION	ORIGIN	MAKER
Jetstream		U.K.	BAe
JJ-6	(J-6)		
JZ-6	(J-6)		
KA-3	[A-3]		
KA-6	[A-6]		
KC-10	Extender [DC-10]	U.S.	MD
KC-130	[C-130]		
KC-135	[Boeing 707]		
KE-3	[E-3]		
Kfir		Israel	IAI
King Air		U.S.	Beech
Kiran	HJT-16		
Kraguj		Yug	SOKO
Kudu	C-4M		
LIM-6	[MiG-17]	Poland	
L-4	Cub		
L-18	Super Cub	U.S.	Piper
L-19	O-1		
L-21	Super Cub	U.S.	Piper
L-29	Delfin	Cz	Aero
L-39	Albatros	Cz	Aero
L-70	Vinka	Finland	Valmet
L-100	C-130 (civil version)		
L-188	Electra (P-3 Orion)	U.S.	Lockheed
L-410	Turbolet	Cz	LET
L-1011	Tristar	U.S.	Lockheed
Learjet	(C-21)	U.S.	Gates
Li-2	[DC-3]	USSR	Lisunov
LR-1	(MU-2)		
Magister	CM-170		
Marut	HF-24		
Mashshaq	MFI-17	Pakistan/ Sweden	PAC/ SAAB
Matador	(AV-8)		
MB-326		Italy	Aermacchi
MB-339	(Veltro)	Italy	Aermacchi
MBB-233	Flamingo		
MC-130	(C-130)		
Mercurius	(HS-125)		
Merlin		U.S.	Fairchild
Mescalero	T-41		
Metro		U.S.	Fairchild
MFI-15	Safari	Sweden	SAAB
MFI-17	Supporter (T-17)	Sweden	SAAB
MH-1521	Broussard	France	Max Holste
MiG-15	"Midget" trg	USSR	MiG
MiG-17	"Fresco"	USSR	MiG
MiG-19	"Farmer"	USSR	MiG
MiG-21	"Fishbed"	USSR	MiG
MiG-23	"Flogger"	USSR	MiG
MiG-25	"Foxbat"	USSR	MiG
MiG-27	"Flogger D"	USSR	MiG
MiG-29	"Fulcrum"	USSR	MiG
MiG-31	"Foxhound"	USSR	MiG
Mirage		France	Dassault
Mission-master	N-22		
Mohawk	OV-1		
MS-760	Paris	France	Aérospatiale
MS-893	Commodore		
MU-2		Japan	Mitsubishi
Musketeer	Beech 24	U.S.	Beech
Mya-4	"Bison"	USSR	Myasishchev
Mystère-Falcon		France	Dassault
N-22	Floatmaster, Missionmaster	Aust	GAF
N-24	Searchmaster B/L	Aust	GAF
N-262	Frégate	France	Aérospatiale
N-2501	Noratlas	France	Aérospatiale
Navajo	PA-31	U.S.	Piper
NC-212	C-212	Sp/Indon	CASA/ Nurtanio
NC-235	C-235	Sp/Indon	CASA/ Nurtanio
Nesher	[Mirage III]	Israel	IAI
NF-5	(F-5)		
Nightingale	(DC-9)		
Nimrod		U.K.	BAe
O-1	Bird Dog	U.S.	Cessna
O-2	(Cessna 337, Skymaster)	U.S.	Cessna
OA-4	(A-4)		
OA-37	Dragonfly		
Orao	IAR-93		
Ouragan		France	Dassault
OV-1	Mohawk	U.S.	Rockwell
OV-10	Bronco	U.S.	Rockwell
P-2J	[SP-2]	Japan	Kawasaki
P-3		Switz	Pilatus
P-3	Orion	U.S.	Lockheed
P-95	EMB-110		
P-149		Italy	Piaggio
P-166		Italy	Piaggio
PA-18	Super Cub	U.S.	Piper
PA-23	Aztec		
PA-24	Comanche	U.S.	Piper
PA-28	Cherokee	U.S.	Piper
PA-31	Navajo	U.S.	Piper
PA-34	Seneca	U.S.	Piper
PA-44	Seminole	U.S.	Piper
PBY-5	Catalina	U.S.	Consolidated
PC-6	Porter	Switz	Pilatus
PC-6A/B	Turbo Porter	Switz	Pilatus
PC-7	Turbo Trainer	Switz	Pilatus
PC-9		Switz	Pilatus
PD-808		Italy	Piaggio
Pembroke		U.K.	BAe
Pillán	T-35		
PL-1	Chien Shou	Taiwan	AIDC
Porter	PC-6		
PZL-104	Wilga	Poland	PZL
PZL-130	Orlik	Poland	PZL
Q-5	"Fantan" [MiG-19]	China	Nanchang
Queen Air	(U-8)		
R-160		France	Socata
R-235	Guerrier	France	Socata
RC-21	(C-21)		
RC-47	(C-47)		
RC-95	(EMB-110)		
RC-135	[Boeing 707]		
RF-4	(F-4)		
RF-5	(F-5)		
RF-35	(F-35)		
RF-84	(F-84)		
RF-104	(F-104)		
RF-172	(Cessna 172)	France	Reims-Cessna

Type	Name/designation	Origin	Maker
RT-26	(EMB-326)		
RT-33	(T-33)		
RU-21	(King Air)		
RV-1	(OV-1)		
S-2	Tracker	U.S.	Grumman
S-3	Viking	U.S.	Lockheed
S-208		Italy	SIAI
S-211		Italy	SIAI
Sabreliner	(CT-39)	U.S.	Rockwell
Safari	MFI-15		
Safir	Skyvan	U.K.	Short
SC-7	SAAB-91 (SK-50)	Sweden	SAAB
SE-210	Caravelle		
Sea Harrier	(Harrier)		
Seascan	IAI-1124		
Searchmaster B/L	N-24		
Seneca	PA-34 (EMB-810)	U.S.	Piper
Sentry	(O-2)	U.S.	Summit
SF-37	(J-37)		
SF-260	(SF-260W Warrior)	Italy	SIAI
SH-37	(J-37)		
Shackleton		U.K.	BAe
Sherpa	Short 330, C-23		
Short 330		U.K.	Short
Sierra 200	(Musketeer)		
SK-35	(J-35)	Sweden	SAAB
SK-37	(J-37)		
SK-50	(Safir)		
SK-60	(SAAB-105)	Sweden	SAAB
SK-61	(Bulldog)		
Skyvan		U.K.	Short
SM-1019		Italy	SIAI
SM-601	Corvette		
SNJ	T-6 (Navy)		
SP-2H	Neptune	U.S.	Lockheed
SR-71	Blackbird	U.S.	Lockheed
Su-7	"Fitter A"	USSR	Sukhoi
Su-15	"Flagon"	USSR	Sukhoi
Su-17/-20/-22	"Fitter"	USSR	Sukhoi
Su-24	"Fencer"	USSR	Sukhoi
Su-25	"Frogfoot"	USSR	Sukhoi
Su-27	"Flanker"	USSR	Sukhoi
Super Etendard		France	Dassault
Super Galeb		Yug	SOKO
Super Mystère		France	Dassault
T-1		Japan	Fuji
T-2	Buckeye	U.S.	Rockwell
T-2		Japan	Mitsubishi
T-3		Japan	Fuji
T-6	Texan	U.S.	N. American
T-17	(Supporter, MFI-17)	Sweden	SAAB
T-23	Uirapurú	Brazil	Aerotec
T-25	Neiva Universal	Brazil	Embraer
T-26	EMB-326		
T-27	Tucano	Brazil	Embraer
T-28	Trojan	U.S.	N. American
T-33	Shooting Star	U.S.	Lockheed
T-34	Mentor	U.S.	Beech
T-35	Pillán [PA-28]	Chile	Enaer
T-36	(C-101)		
T-37	(A-37)		
T-38	Talon	U.S.	Northrop
T-39	(Sabreliner)	U.S.	Rockwell
T-41	Mescalero (Cessna 172)	U.S.	Cessna
T-42	Cochise (Baron)	U.S.	Beech
T-43	(Boeing 737)		
T-44	(King Air)		
T-47	(Citation)		
TB-20	Trinidad	France	Aérospatiale
TB-30	Epsilon	France	Aérospatiale
TC-45	(C-45, trg)		
T-CH-1		Taiwan	AIDC
Texan	T-6		
TL-1	(KM-2)	Japan	Fuji
Tornado		U.K./Ge/Italy	Panavia
TR-1	[U-2]	U.S.	Lockheed
Travel Air	Beech 95		
Trident		U.K.	BAe
Trislander	BN-2		
Tristar	L-1011		
TS-8	Bies	Poland	PZL
TS-11	Iskra	Poland	PZL
Tu-16	"Badger"	USSR	Tupolev
Tu-22	"Blinder"	USSR	Tupolev
Tu-26 (Tu-22M)	"Backfire"	USSR	Tupolev
Tu-28	"Fiddler"	USSR	Tupolev
Tu-95	"Bear"	USSR	Tupolev
Tu-126	"Moss"	USSR	Tupolev
Tu-134	"Crusty"	USSR	Tupolev
Tu-142	"Bear F"	USSR	Tupolev
Tu-154	"Careless"	USSR	Tupolev
Tu-160	"Blackjack"	USSR	Tupolev
Turbo Porter	PC-6A/B		
Twin Bonanza	Beech 50		
Twin Otter	DHC-6		
Tzukit	[CM-170]	Israel	IAI
U-2		U.S.	Lockheed
U-3	(Cessna 310)	U.S.	Cessna
U-7	(L-18)		
U-8	(Twin Bonanza/ Queen Air)	U.S.	Beech
U-9	(EMB-121)		
U-10	Super Courier	U.S.	Helio
U-17	(Cessna 180, 185)	U.S.	Cessna
U-21	(King Air)		
U-36	(Learjet)		
U-42	(C-42)		
U-93	(HS-125)		
UC-12	(King Air)		
UP-2J	(P-2J)		
US-1		Japan	Shin Meiwa
US-2A	(S-2A, tpt)		
US-3	(S-3, tpt)		

Type	Name/designation	Origin	Maker
UTVA-66		Yug	UTVA
UTVA-75		Yug	UTVA
UV-18	(DHC-6)		
V-400	Fantrainer 400	Ge	VFW
V-600	Fantrainer 600	Ge	VFW
Vampire	DH-100		
VC-4	Gulfstream I		
VC-10		U.K.	BAe
VC-11	Gulfstream II		
VC-91	(HS-748)		
VC-93	(HS-125)		
VC-97	(EMB-120)		
VC-130	(C-130)		
VFW-614		Ge	VFW
Victor		U.K.	BAe
Vinka	L-70		
Viscount		U.K.	BAe
VU-9	(EMB-121)		
VU-93	(HS-125)		
WC-130	[C-130]		
WC-135	[Boeing 707]	U.S.	Boeing
Westwind	IAI-1124		
Winjeel	CA-25		
Xavante	EMB-326		
Xingu	EMB-121		
Y-5	[An-2]	China	Hua Bei
Y-7	[An-24]	China	Xian
Y-8	[An-12]	China	Shaanxi
Y-12		China	Harbin
Yak-11	"Moose"	USSR	Yakovlev
Yak-18	"Max"	USSR	Yakovlev
Yak-28	"Firebar" ("Brewer")	USSR	Yakovlev
Yak-38	"Forger"	USSR	Yakovlev
Yak-40	"Codling"	USSR	Yakovlev
YS-11		Japan	Nihon
Z-43		Cz	Zlin
Z-226		Cz	Zlin
Z-326		Cz	Zlin
Z-526		Cz	Zlin
Zéphyr	CM-175		

HELICOPTERS

Type	Name/designation	Origin	Maker
A-109	Hirundo	Italy	Agusta
A-129	Mangusta	Italy	Agusta
AB-. . .	(Bell 204/205/206/ 212/214/etc.)	Italy/U.S.	Agusta/ Bell
AH-1	Cobra/Sea Cobra	U.S.	Bell
AH-6	(Hughes 500/530)	U.S.	MD
AH-64	Apache	U.S.	Hughes
Alouette II	SE-3130, SA-318	France	Aéro- spatiale
Alouette III	SA-316, SA-319	France	Aéro- spatiale
AS-61	(SH-3)	U.S./Italy	Sikorsky/ Agusta
AS-332	SuperPuma	France	Aéro- spatiale
AS-350	Ecureuil	France	Aérospatiale
AS-355	Ecureuil II		
ASH-3	(Sea King)	Italy/U.S.	Agusta/ Sikorsky
AUH-76	(S-76)		
Bell 47		U.S.	Bell
Bell 204		U.S.	Bell
Bell 205		U.S.	Bell
Bell 206		U.S.	Bell
Bell 212		U.S.	Bell
Bell 214		U.S.	Bell
Bell 406		U.S.	Bell
Bell 412		U.S.	Bell
Bo-105	(NBo-105)	Ge	MBB
CH-3	(SH-3)		
CH-34	Choctaw	U.S.	Sikorsky
CH-46	Sea Knight	U.S.	Boeing- Vertol
CH-47	Chinook	U.S.	Boeing- Vertol
CH-53	Stallion (Sea Stallion)	U.S.	Sikorsky
CH-54	Tarhe	U.S.	Sikorsky
CH-113	(CH-46)		
CH-118	Bell 205		
CH-124	SH-3		
CH-135	Bell 212		
CH-136	OH-58		
CH-139	Bell 206		
CH-147	CH-47		
Cheetah	[SA-315]	India	HAL
Chetak	[SA-319]	India	HAL
Commando	(SH-3)	U.K./U.S.	Westland/ Sikorsky
EH-60	(UH-60)		
EH-101		U.K./Italy	Westland/ Agusta
FH-1100	(OH-5)	U.S.	Fairchild- Hiller
Gazela	(SA-342)	France/ Yug	Aérospatiale/ SOKO
Gazelle	SA-341/-342		
H-34	(S-58)		
H-76	S-76		
HA-15	Bo-105		
HB-315	Gavião (SA-315)	Brazil/ France	Helibras/ Aérospatiale
HB-350	Esquilo (AS-350)	Brazil/ France	Helibras/ Aérospatiale
HD-16	SA-319		
HH-3	(SH-3)		
HH-34	(CH-34)		
HH-53	(CH-53)		
Hkp-2	Alouette II/SE-3130		
Hkp-3	AB-204		
Hkp-4	KV-107		
Hkp-5	Hughes 300		
Hkp-6	AB-206		
Hkp-9	Bo-105		
Hkp-10	AS-332		
HR-12	OH-58		
HSS-1	(S-58)		
HSS-2	(SH-3)		
HT-17	CH-47		
HT-21	AS-332		
HU-1	(UH-1)	Japan/U.S.	Fuji/Bell
HU-8	UH-1B		
HU-10	UH-1H		
HU-18	AB-212		
Hughes 269		U.S.	MD
Hughes 300		U.S.	MD
Hughes 369		U.S.	MD

TYPE	NAME/DESIGNATION	ORIGIN	MAKER
IAR-316/-330	(SA-316/-330)	Ro/France	IAR/ Aérospatiale
Ka-25	"Hormone"	USSR	Kamov
Ka-27	"Helix"	USSR	Kamov
KH-4	(Bell 47)	Japan/U.S.	Kawasaki/ Bell
KH-300	(Hughes 269)	Japan/U.S.	Kawasaki/ MD
KH-500	(Hughes 369)	Japan/U.S.	Kawasaki/ MD
Kiowa	OH-58		
KV-107	[CH-46]	Japan/U.S.	Kawasaki/ Vertol
Lynx		U.K.	Westland
MH-6	(AH-6)		
MH-53	(CH-53)		
Mi-1	"Hare"	USSR	Mil
Mi-2	"Hoplite"	USSR	Mil
Mi-4	"Hound"	USSR	Mil
Mi-6	"Hook"	USSR	Mil
Mi-8	"Hip"	USSR	Mil
Mi-14	"Haze"	USSR	Mil
Mi-17	"Hip"	USSR	Mil
Mi-24	"Hind"	USSR	Mil
Mi-25	"Hind"	USSR	Mil
Mi-26	"Halo"	USSR	Mil
Mi-28	"Havoc"	USSR	Mil
Mi-35	(Mi-25)		
NAS-332	AS-332	Indon/ France	Nurtanio/ Aérospatiale
NB-412	Bell 412	Indon/ U.S.	Nurtanio/ Bell
NBo-105	Bo-105	Indon/Ge	Nurtanio/ MBB
NH-300	(Hughes-300)	Italy/U.S.	Nardi/MD
NSA-330	(SA-330)	Indon/ France	Nurtanio/ Aérospatiale
OH-6	Cayuse (Hughes 369)	U.S.	MD
OH-13	(Bell 47G)		
OH-23	Raven	U.S.	Hiller
OH-58	Kiowa (Bell 206)		
OH-58D	(Bell 406)		
PAH-1	(Bo-105)		
Partizan	(Gazela, armed)		
RH-53	(CH-53)		
S-55	(Whirlwind)	U.S.	Sikorsky
S-58	(Wessex)	U.S.	Sikorsky
S-61	SH-3		
S-65	CH-53		
S-70	UH-60		
S-76		U.S.	Sikorsky
S-80	CH-53		
SA-315	Lama [Alouette II]	France	Aérospatiale
SA-316	Alouette III (SA-319)	France	Aérospatiale
SA-318	Alouette II (SE-3130)	France	Aérospatiale
SA-319	Alouette III (SA-316)	France	Aérospatiale
SA-321	Super Frelon	France	Aérospatiale
SA-330	Puma	France	Aérospatiale
SA-341/-342	Gazelle	France	Aérospatiale
SA-360	Dauphin	France	Aérospatiale
SA-365	Dauphin II (SA-360)		
Scout	(Wasp)	U.K.	Westland
SE-3130	(SA-318)		
SE-316	(SA-316)		
Sea King	[SH-3]	U.K.	Westland
SH-2	Sea Sprite	U.S.	Kaman
SH-3	(Sea King)	U.S.	Sikorsky
SH-34	(S-58)		
SH-57	Bell 206		
SH-60	Sea Hawk (UH-60)		
Sioux	(Bell 47)	U.K.	Westland
TH-55	Hughes 269		
TH-57	SeaRanger (Bell 206)		
UH-1	Iroquois (Bell 204/ 205)		
UH-12	(OH-23)	U.S.	Hiller
UH-13	(Bell 47J)		
UH-19	(S-55)		
UH-34T	(S-58T)		
UH-46	(CH-46)		
UH-60	Black Hawk (SH-60)	U.S.	Sikorsky
VH-4	(Bell 206)		
Wasp	(Scout)	U.K.	Westland
Wessex	(S-58)	U.S./U.K.	Sikorsky/ Westland
Whirlwind	(S-55)	U.S./U.K.	Sikorsky/ Westland
Z-5	[Mi-4]	China	Harbin
Z-6	[Z-5]	China	Harbin
Z-8	[SA-321]	China	Changhe
Z-9	[SA-365]	China	Harbin

Source: International Institute for Strategic Studies. 1991. *The Military Balance, 1991–1992*. London: Brassey's.

Note: The use of [square brackets] shows the type from which a variant was derived. "Q-5 . . . [MiG-19]" indicates that the design of the Q-5 was based on that of the MiG-19.

(Parentheses) indicate an alternative name by which an aircraft is known—sometimes in another version. "L-188 . . . Electra (P-3 Orion)" shows that in another version the Lockheed Type 188 Electra is known as the P-3 Orion.

Names given in "quotation marks" are NATO reporting names (e.g., "Su-27 . . . "Flanker").

When no information is listed under "Origin" or "Maker," take the primary reference given under "Name/designation" and look it up under "Type."

A

ACADEMIES, MILITARY

Military academies have been institutionalized in most nations of the world. Their purpose is to provide instruction to young members of the society so that they can perform effectively as junior officers upon graduation and commissioning. Military academies date to the late seventeenth century in Europe when standing armies and navies had become permanent national fixtures with the consequent need to generate a cadre of trained officers to lead them—a need that was only gradually recognized and fulfilled. Feudal military systems had been dominated by the nobility, and there was no skilled middle class from which to recruit new leaders. At the beginning of the eighteenth century, however, social and economic progress began to create enough skilled middle class workers so that the military could draw from them without risk to national economic production. Consequently, the founding of military academies did not begin until the latter half of the eighteenth and early nineteenth centuries.

Before the industrial revolution greatly contributed to the complexity of warfare with better weapons and munitions, with steam (and later, internal combustion) engines, and with electronic communications, military academies trained officer cadets in handling weapons, drilling and management of men, tactics and strategy, and, for naval cadets, navigation, sailing, and naval doctrine. As the contribution of science and technology to warfare increased, the subject matter of the academies broadened, entrance standards became tougher, and academic requirements for graduation became more stringent, becoming equivalent to that needed to graduate from a college or university. In the twentieth century, some countries established air force academies. By that time, cadets had come to represent an ever-broader cross section of society, and most were educated at the state's expense in exchange for their commitment to military service.

Canada

The Royal Military College (RMC) of Canada was founded in 1875 at Kingston, Ontario. It was reorganized in 1948 to provide naval and air force training, in addition to training for army cadets. The RMC has constituent institutions of Royal Roads in British Columbia (1942) and the Collège Militaire Royal de Saint Jean at St. Jean, Quebec (1952).

Belgium

Army, navy, air force, and *gendarmerie nationale* officers are trained at the Brussels Ecole Royale Militaire in Brussels. Candidates must be at least 17 and no older than 25. Two divisions comprise the academy: one, the Polytechnique, features a five-year curriculum; the other, the Toutes Armes is a three-year school. After two years cadets receive a commission and stay on as officers until graduation.

United States

The United States has four military academies: the U.S. Military Academy (USMA), West Point, New York (see Fig. 1); the U.S. Air Force Academy (USAFA), Colorado Springs, Colorado; the U.S. Naval Academy (USNA), Annapolis, Maryland; and the U.S. Coast Guard Academy (USCGA), New London, Connecticut.

Applicants to the U.S. military academies must be at least 17 years of age but not have reached the age of 22 prior to 1 July of the year they enter the academy. Those who complete the four-year program receive a bachelor of science degree in a major or field of study of their choice and are commissioned as a second lieutenant in the U.S. Army, Air Force, or Marine Corps (from the USMA, USAFA, and USNA, respectively), or an ensign in the Navy or Coast Guard (from the USNA and USCGA). As of

Figure 1. A graduation ceremony on the parade field at the U.S. Military Academy, West Point, New York. (Source: U.S. Army)

1992, each graduate is required to spend six years on active duty in his or her respective service.

U.S.S.R.

In 1698, Peter the Great founded a so-called military academy in Russia, but in the modern sense, the first academy, a naval academy, was founded in 1827; followed by a military academy in 1855. A communist military academy was formed in Moscow in 1918, and in 1924 its director was the brilliant Red Army commander, Mikhail Vasilievich Frunze. Frunze died the following year, and the academy was renamed the Frunze Academy in his honor. The Soviet Union also established naval, air, engineering, and military political academies. Admission to these academies is limited to officers who have already completed specialized schools and who have already served in the armed forces. In this regard, the Soviet academies differ from academies in the West; they relate more closely to the service schools and war colleges of Western armed forces. The so-called schools and junior schools in the Soviet Union are similar to the military academies in the West; their focus is on training young cadets to become officers. There are about 30 junior military schools dating to 1943, and two naval junior schools created in 1944. Instruction is entirely at the expense of the state.

With the demise of the Soviet Union (1989–91), the future status of former Soviet military institutions is uncertain. It is likely, however, that military education will be retained in some form.

Conclusion

Military academies will continue in service throughout the world. Their course content will adapt to consider changes in technology and the application of military force through doctrine, tactics, and operational art. Present differences and similarities between countries are likely to remain, and the effect of the end of the cold war may reduce funding and enrollment somewhat in the 1990s.

CHARLES F. HAWKINS

SEE ALSO: Command; Education, Military; Leadership; Officer; Professionalism, Military.

Bibliography

Encyclopaedia Britannica. 1966. Vol. 15. Chicago: Encyclopaedia Britannica Ed.

Jones, D. 1978. Academies, military. In *The Military-Naval Encyclopedia of Russia and the Soviet Union*. Gulf Breeze, Fla.: Academic International Press.

ACCESSION STANDARDS

Accession standards identify the individuals in the eligible population who may serve in a nation's armed forces. They are the means by which a nation manages the number and quality of new recruits or conscripts entering military service. While the general goal is to secure the best manpower available to defend the national interests, the standards actually applied vary according to the nature of the armed forces, the urgency of the situation, and the number and kinds of people available for military service. In the twentieth century, many nations have codified their accession standards into formal rules for determining the acceptability of an individual for military service.

Accession standards define the basic physical, mental, and moral qualifications a person must have to become a member of a nation's armed forces. They also assist in defining any limitations on this membership. The information gathered during the initial evaluation of a new entrant is also used to assign those who qualify for entrance to jobs and training.

Accession standards usually apply to military personnel only. Standards for civilian employees of the armed forces tend to be less rigorous than military standards and are applied on an individual basis.

Factors Affecting Accession Standards

The standards for membership in a nation's armed forces are driven by the needs of the nation for military personnel. The rigor of standards may vary greatly depending on the criticality of the need for military manpower. Other variables affecting accession standards include the technological sophistication of weapons and equipment used by the armed forces, the source of those weapons and equipment (domestic or foreign), and the demographic composition of the nation.

PEACETIME VERSUS WARTIME

The most important factor in determining the capabilities required to enter a country's armed forces is whether the nation is actually involved in a conflict. Wartime accession standards tend to be much less stringent than those used in peacetime. Nations actively involved in armed conflicts tend to be less selective about the personnel allowed or required to enter military service. Although initially the rules for wartime accession may be as selective as in peacetime, as losses are incurred in combat, nations usually must delve more deeply into their populations to maintain adequate fighting forces.

Nations experiencing long periods of peace, conversely, may enjoy the luxury of very rigorous accession standards, as well as shorter periods of enlistment. Peacetime accession standards tend to emphasize the admission of physically fit, mentally acute, and morally upright youth. Wartime standards are usually lower because of the gradual reduction in the supply of high-quality people.

Countries engaged in protracted conflicts usually expand the qualifying age range for military service, taking both younger and older recruits than in peacetime. They also lower the standards for acceptable physical condition.

While wartime mobilization planning starts with the idea of "only the best will do," by war's end people with varying levels of capability and limitations are found acceptable.

The prospect of armed conflict also determines whether military service is voluntary or mandatory and establishes the length of the term of enlistment. Nations experiencing protracted periods of conflict or having chronically hostile neighbors tend to require involuntary military service—conscription. Those who meet the general accession standards are required to serve in the military for a set length of time. An eligible person usually begins this mandatory military service after completing the level of training or schooling generally expected of the majority of the population. Advanced training or education, such as attendance at a college or university, may be deferred until completion of required military service, or military service may be deferred until completion of the advanced training. This policy is based on the specific demands of the nation in a given conflict.

The prospect of war is not the only reason for conscription, however. A nation not actively engaged in an armed conflict may mandate military service as a mechanism to ensure equitable participation by the population in national service, to maintain military preparedness, and to demonstrate national loyalty.

The term of enlistment can vary substantially, from twelve months to six years, depending on the country and the branch of service. The term of enlistment is driven by such factors as the time it takes to provide adequate training, the size of the available population, and the overall needs of the armed forces for experienced personnel. Generally, nations adopt shorter enlistment periods when:

- A large manpower pool exists from which to draw personnel
- The country is not actively engaged in an armed conflict and therefore is not losing sizeable portions of its military personnel as casualties
- The emphasis during the initial enlistment is on training rather than employing personnel
- Sufficient experienced personnel are available through means other than new enlistments.

Impact of Mission and Technology

The actual military mission is a prime consideration in determining the accession standards for members of the armed forces. Aspects of a military mission that can influence the physical, mental, and moral standards for enlistees include whether the forces are to be deployed outside the national borders, the expected duration of the deployment (e.g., 1 month, 1 year, 10 years), and whether the mission is to maintain a military presence or to actually participate in an armed conflict. These factors may affect standards regulating the enlistment age range, physical condition, eligibility for special training, and personal behavior.

Technology also plays an important role in determining accession standards. It is particularly important in establishing standards for mental capabilities. Modern armed forces may employ a mixture of high-technology weapons and equipment with low-technology tactics employing large numbers of soldiers in the field. The proportion of high-technology weapons and equipment varies by country, and with it the portion of personnel who must be capable of operating and maintaining that technology. This is particularly true for armed forces that acquire weapons and equipment from another, more industrialized, nation. In these cases, the local population may be poorly prepared to operate and maintain high-technology equipment, and the nation may not have the infrastructure to provide adequate material support. Instead, technicians and other highly trained personnel may need to be imported, in which case enlistees may not be required or expected to have the appropriate mental capability to receive training in operation of high-technology weapons and equipment.

Types of Accession Standards

Accession standards focus on determining a person's capabilities in three major areas: physical condition, mental capability, and moral behavior. In addition, many nations also determine eligibility for military service by applying demographic criteria such as age, gender, race or ethnic group, religion, and social status.

There is usually a distinction between standards for officers and standards for enlisted personnel. Officers are expected to have higher mental capabilities and more extensive education than enlisted personnel. Officers are often drawn from different social or ethnic groups than the majority of the enlisted personnel. Generally, training for officers is different from that provided enlisted personnel. In the United States, enlisted personnel are expected to enter military service with a high school education and with little or no preexisting technical training. The armed forces provide both basic and specialized training to new enlisted personnel, based on aptitudes identified during entrance processing. New enlisted personnel with preexisting skills are also identified during entrance processing, and are often assigned to specific jobs to take advantage of their knowledge. Officers are expected to enter military service with a college education to serve as the basis for professional military education. Many officers, such as doctors, lawyers, and chaplains, enter military service already trained in their specialties, and require only initial military training. The training enlistees receive is largely determined through the military job classification process.

The primary focus of this article is on the accession standards applied to enlisted personnel, who comprise the bulk of a nation's military population.

Physical Standards

Physical condition is a prime consideration in determining an individual's suitability for membership in the armed forces. Physical condition is evaluated upon initial processing, and those failing to meet the physical standards are denied entry. Physical condition is also evaluated periodically during military service to ensure that members remain physically qualified. Physical standards are usually driven by the duties a soldier can be expected to perform. Most nations have developed general physical criteria that are appropriate for all personnel entering any branch of military service—army, navy, or air force. In many nations, each service then develops more discrete criteria for determining physical eligibility. These service-specific standards may be different during peacetime and wartime. Physical standards for certain jobs, such as pilots or divers, are usually more rigorous than the general standards.

Physical examination. An individual's overall health and performance potential is determined by a standardized physical (medical) examination. Existing physical conditions are identified or verified, and their impact on the person's capability to perform fundamental tasks is evaluated. The rigor and sophistication of this examination is largely determined by the overall character of the military service and the urgency of need for manpower. The depth of physical examinations may range from a cursory check to ensure that the individual has adequate sensory capability and mobility to a full battery of complex medical tests. The physical examination identifies disqualifying physical conditions, assesses how well an individual meets specific health and physical standards of performance for particular assignments, and determines if the individual has a temporary or correctable physical condition requiring delay in admission or a special assignment.

Philosophically, the major distinction between peacetime and wartime physical standards usually concerns the potential of the individual for a career in the military. In peacetime, physical standards are designed to minimize long-term medical workload and disability retirements over the course of a 20- to 30-year military career. In wartime, the standards are designed to admit personnel in good enough physical condition to be fully deployable and to perform an adequate range of military duties, including combat.

Physical disqualification. A primary goal of the physical examination is to identify physical conditions that categorically disqualify a person for military service. Generally, the armed forces of the industrialized nations disqualify those with conditions that may impair job performance and involve extensive treatment or care. Some of the usual disqualifying conditions are: illness requiring continuous medication or treatment, such as epilepsy or diabetes melitis; sensory limitations such as blindness or deafness; missing limbs; mobility limitations such as paralysis; heart conditions; diseases of the blood such as leukemia; and certain neurological conditions such as convulsive disorders and multiple sclerosis.

Physical standards are applied flexibly depending on the need for military personnel. Waivers for particular physical conditions may be granted on a case-by-case basis; more rarely, a blanket waiver is granted for all occurrences of a single condition. Blanket waivers are used instead of actual modifications to the physical standards in order to retain flexibility in applying the standards. Modifications and waivers may occur in both peacetime and wartime, either to make previously unacceptable degrees of physical condition acceptable, or to make the standards more rigorous. On occasion, a nation may adopt a policy of categorizing an individual as not acceptable physically at the time of evaluation but subject to recall should the need for manpower increase (usually a wartime strategy).

Physical profiles. The United States has developed the PULHES Profile, a composite profile of the major physical functions and systems that is used to summarize the physical condition of enlistees and members of the U.S. Army. The PULHES Profile categorizes body functions (i.e., functions of the organs, systems, and integral parts of the body) and considers the full physical, mental, and medical status of the individual. Functions are assigned to one of the following six areas: Physical capacity or stamina, Upper extremities, Lower extremities, Hearing and ears, Eyes, and pSychiatric. A person's status in each of these areas is graded on the following four-point scale:

1. The person possesses a high level of medical fitness and is medically fit for military assignment.
2. The person possesses some medical conditions or physical defects that may impose some limitations on classification and assignment.
3. The person has one or more medical conditions or physical defects that require certain restrictions in assignment within which the individual is physically capable of performing military duty.
4. The person has one or more medical conditions or physical defects of such severity that performance of military duty must be drastically limited.

Each individual in the U.S. Army is assigned a PULHES profile. A person in good condition would have a profile of "111111." An individual with some problems but who would be retained in military service with some assignment limitations could have a profile of "122111." An individual not qualified for military service might have a profile of "412341." As the member undergoes periodic physical examinations during military service, the PULHES profile is adjusted to reflect the current physical condition. The degree to which category 3 or 4 conditions affect the acceptability of an individual for military service usually is determined by the needs of the service at the time.

Mental Standards

Evaluation of a person's mental capability includes evaluation of aptitude for particular jobs and training; consideration of previous education, training, and experience; and estimation of overall intellectual capability. Each enlistee is given a set or battery of tests during initial processing. The results are used to deny entry to individuals with low mental capability and to assign those admitted to jobs and related training. The mental capability scores are also used by personnel managers to ensure an appropriate distribution of personnel among and within the armed forces of a nation.

Aptitude testing. Evaluation of people's aptitudes in particular areas is vital to determining their desirability for acceptance into military service and their assignment thereafter. Modern armed forces need large numbers of highly skilled personnel in critical specialties. Most of these highly skilled personnel receive their training in the military. Individuals entering military service are given specialized training based on the results of their initial mental tests, which indicate their aptitude for particular kinds of jobs.

Most of the industrialized nations use a standardized battery of tests designed to assess broad areas of knowledge. Minimum scores in each of the aptitude areas are set by each service for each entry-level occupation and are used as the basis for determining the applicant's qualifications for training in specific occupations. The actual aptitudes required for occupations vary by nation and service, even for very similar occupations.

In the U.S. armed forces, each new enlistee is given the Armed Services Vocational Aptitude Battery (ASVAB). The ASVAB consists of ten subtests in the following areas: general science, arithmetic reasoning, word knowledge, paragraph comprehension, numerical operations, coding speed, auto and shop information, mathematics knowledge, mechanical comprehension, and electronics information. The tests scores are used as the basis for assignment to schools for particular jobs, such as computer operator, automotive mechanic, or heavy weapons infantryman.

Education, training, and experience. Special consideration is given to persons with skills acquired in civilian life. Individuals with training or experience in critical specialties are identified in the initial enlistment processing. While the armed forces plan to provide most enlistees with all of the training they need to accomplish their responsibilities, they also try to make good use of previous training. Since training for some specialties would take longer than a conventional enlistment period, individuals with previous training in specialties such as engineering, computer sciences, and health fields are actively sought by military recruiters. Depending on the circumstances, individuals with previous training or experience may be waived from further skill training, paid occupational bonuses, or advanced in rank ahead of their contemporaries.

Mental capability. Mental or intellectual capability is a major factor in determining what military jobs a person can do and what military training he or she can absorb. Experience has shown that mental capability is an indicator of the potential success the person may achieve in the military. It is also an indicator of the probability that he or she will be able to successfully complete training in a particular specialty.

An indicator of intellectual capability is derived from the aptitude tests by computing a composite score. Persons with composite scores below the current accession standard will be denied entry into military service. Persons with high composite scores will be earmarked for demanding schools or for officer training.

The measure of mental capability used in the United States is the Armed Forces Qualification Test (AFQT) score. The AFQT score is a composite score obtained from the arithmetic reasoning, word knowledge, paragraph comprehension, and mathematics knowledge subtests of the ASVAB. The range of AFQT scores is from 1 to 99. Enlistees are assigned to one of five mental categories according to their AFQT scores. The five mental categories and the corresponding AFQT scores are shown below:

Mental category	AFQT scores
I	93–99
II	65–92
III	31–64
IV	10–30
V	1–9

The U.S. armed forces are prohibited by law from accepting a person in Mental Category V. There are also restrictions on the proportion of accessions who may be in Mental Category IV. Emphasis is on recruiting enlistees in the top three mental categories, and particularly in Categories I and II.

Personnel quality management. Evaluation of mental capability provides a means to manage the overall quality of personnel in the armed forces of a nation. *Quality* is the term used by personnel managers to describe the aggregate mental capability of a group of military personnel. Personnel quality is managed by limiting the proportion of people in the lower mental categories who may enter military service and by maintaining an equitable distribution of mental capability among the services. This ensures that there is not a disproportionately large percentage of personnel in the lower mental categories at any given time in a single service and to ensure that each service has an appropriate proportion of higher quality personnel. As with the other types of accession standards, the limits placed on the percentage of personnel falling into the lower mental categories who may join the armed forces are subject to change during wartime.

Most nations have more than one armed force. Experience has shown that it is important to have a mix of personnel with varying degrees of mental capability in each armed force, reflecting the mixture of occupations in the armed force. The distribution of high-quality personnel among the armed forces frequently becomes an issue, particularly in wartime. Conscription facilitates a system of assignment to the armed forces that ensures that no one branch of service will be disproportionately populated by a certain quality of personnel—high or low. A policy of voluntary service, on the other hand, makes it more difficult to ensure a balanced mix of intelligence because the armed forces vary in their attractiveness for volunteers. The United States, which has a mixed wartime manpower accession policy of voluntary enlistment and conscription, has established a policy limiting the proportion in each armed force of personnel in the lower mental categories.

Moral Standards

An evaluation of an individual's moral behavior is the third major kind of accession standard. Unlike the physical and mental standards, which establish degrees or levels of acceptability, the moral behavior standard is intended to identify and exclude absolutely those individuals who are unacceptable for military service on the basis of their previous behavior. The moral behavior standard is designed to bar entry by people with known antisocial or antimilitary inclinations. Historically, this has included people with mental illness, people convicted of felonies, and conscientious objectors. As with the other types of accession standards, the strictures placed on an enlistee's moral behavior are less rigorous in wartime than in peacetime.

Mental illness. While mental illness and psychological problems are now categorized as physical conditions in some countries, at times these conditions have been considered indicators of a person's moral behavior and have been the basis for exclusion from military service.

Criminal history. Individuals with a history of breaking laws are usually excluded from military service. Policies generally exclude from the military people who have demonstrated strong antisocial behavior, as indicated by conviction for felonies or capital offenses. A person's social behavior is evaluated in this context to determine if the individual is capable of fitting into the disciplined atmosphere of military service without abusing the opportunity to have access to weapons. In some cases, a nation may state explicit prohibitions regarding behavior that makes a person unacceptable. However, the bulk of the determination will be based on evaluating the overall pattern of individual behavior with respect to upholding the law.

The rules on criminal history have been modified to a remarkable degree in wartime. Although the prison population is normally not part of the pool of eligible manpower, reductions of prison sentences have been used during times of extreme manpower shortages as an inducement to enter military service. More frequently, waivers have been granted allowing a person with relatively minor offenses to enter military service, as an exception to the normal standards.

Conscientious objection. Another element of moral behavior is the individual's belief in the morality of bearing arms. Conscientious objection to participating in the conduct of war has been a position taken by many individuals throughout history. Accession standards for many nations allow for the determination of an individual's belief in this position, as part of the overall application of the moral standards. Conscientious objectors may choose to perform alternative service outside of the armed forces or to serve in the armed forces in positions that do not involve bearing arms. In earlier times, conscientious objection was stigmatized as antisocial behavior, but more recently it has been viewed in many countries (including all the Western democracies) as a legitimate expression of individual self-determination.

Homosexuality. The U.S. Department of Defense currently excludes homosexuals from membership in the armed forces. New accessions who are homosexuals are denied entry, and current members who are identified as homosexuals are discharged. Prior to 1982, persons who committed or were suspected of committing homosexual acts were court-martialed and/or discharged as unfit for military service. Homosexual members of the armed forces were treated the same as others as long as they did not commit or stand accused of a crime or admit their sexual preference. Those accused of homosexual acts were given discharges.

In 1982 the U.S. Department of Defense adopted the policy that merely being a homosexual was grounds for separation from military service. Internationally, most nations bar homosexuals from serving in their armed forces, including several nations that consider homosexual acts between consenting adults to be legal. Several other countries, however, do permit homosexuals to serve. Brazil and Spain permit homosexuals to serve, although they treat as criminal certain homosexual acts. Homosexuals are allowed to serve in Israel and Germany, with some constraints on assignment and promotion. Sweden and the Netherlands have allowed homosexuals to serve in their armed forces since the mid-1970s.

Demographic Standards

In addition to the three major categories of standards discussed above, many nations place restrictions on individuals entering military service based on demographic characteristics. The most common restrictions are age, gender, race or ethnic group, religion, and social status.

Age. Age is one of the key factors in determining the eligibility of an individual for military service. The minimum acceptable age varies among nations, ranging from 18 in many Western industrialized nations to 20 in the Middle East. The maximum age is determined primarily by the need for military manpower. In wartime, the eligible age of the manpower pool is usually extended. Men from 17 to 50, or older, may be eligible for conscription in wartime.

Gender. Gender has been a major criteria for military service throughout history. Men have tended to dominate the warrior groups, with women providing various types of support and generally maintaining families and social continuity. Demographic shifts in the proportion of men and women in the eligible population, as well as losses of males in protracted conflicts, have caused increases in the percentage of women in military service in modern wars. Recent social developments and the problems of obtaining sufficient volunteers have also increased the percentage of women in many armed forces, including those of the United States and the United Kingdom. Despite the greater numbers of women in service, however, most nations continue to prohibit women from assignment to combat units.

Race, ethnic group, or religion. Membership in a particular race, ethnic group, or religion has been an important element in accession policies for centuries. Members of certain groups have often been excluded from military service entirely because they were thought unworthy or unreliable. Sometimes members of these groups were allowed to perform military service but were limited to certain assignments or training. The use of these characteristics to decide assignments, training, or membership in the armed forces occurs most often in nonhomogeneous societies; the prohibitions are applied to groups with only limited political influence. These policies tend to be controversial when employed to restrict opportunities or to isolate similar people in special units. Special ethnically homogeneous units, however, have been used effectively in wartime to avoid trouble arising from ethnic animosity. Inserting a unit with a neutral ethnic composition between warring factions often increases security and reduces friction. In some cases, military members of a specific ethnic group are required to be stationed outside of their home areas or provinces to improve internal security. Accession standards or limitations based on race, ethnic group, or religion are still used extensively today.

Social status. Social status has also long been used as the basis for discriminatory decisions regarding membership or assignment. Most often social status, or membership in a selected economic class, provides distinct privileges. For example, officers were drawn almost entirely from the upper classes or nobility until recently. In many nations, there is a ruling group that dominates the leadership positions of the armed forces as a means of ensuring their continued social and economic dominance.

Waivers and Deferments

The interests of a nation may not be best served by accepting into military service all who are eligible without considering civil needs for particular skills and aptitudes. This is particularly true in wartime, when high-quality men and women are needed to work in the factories and workshops in a civilian capacity. The accession screening process identifies not only individuals who are eligible for military service, but also those who have special knowledge or aptitude. If these people are needed elsewhere to support the national war effort, they may not be taken into the armed forces. On the other hand, excluding some high-quality people from military service may require taking more people of lesser quality into military service. Waivers of selected accession standards and deferments from military service are the mechanisms for balancing the needs of the armed forces for manpower with the needs of the rest of the nation.

Waivers

Waivers allow entry into military service on a selective basis for individuals who otherwise would not qualify. Accession standards are intended primarily to identify individuals who do not meet the minimum standards for membership in the armed forces of a nation. The screening process does, however, identify those who have certain skills or aptitudes that make them desirable for military service despite a usually disqualifying condition. In those cases, an exception may be made waiving the normal minimum standards for an individual. Waivers are usually granted on a case-by-case basis, and may be permanent or conditional, pending confirmation of test results or depending on success of the individual in a job. Exceptions can be made for any of the accession criteria, but waivers are granted for exceptions to the physical and moral standards more often than to the mental standards.

During the major wars of the twentieth century, it became apparent that nations would have to make rational use of all of the available population to sustain the war effort. To do this, many nations used a temporary limited-duty or limited-assignment mechanism for military personnel who did not meet the general standards. Under the limited-assignment approach, the granting of a waiver for a temporary, correctable minor physical condition would mean that the individual would have limitations placed upon future job assignments, locations, or permissible physical activity until the condition was corrected. Limited-duty personnel have permanent physical conditions that would normally make them unacceptable for membership in the armed forces, but waivers may be granted to allow them to perform necessary but less-demanding work. Limited-duty personnel can perform a variety of service and support functions, freeing able-bodied personnel for combat duties.

DEFERMENTS

Wartime creates the need to balance the demand for military personnel with the demand for workers in industry and other fields of endeavor. Deferments are the mechanism by which exceptions are made for military service, allowing individuals to continue their civilian training or occupations in wartime, rather than being drafted for the armed forces.

The particular needs of a nation determine deferment policy. Deferments have been granted to ministers and teachers in order to maintain social continuity; to workers with critical production skills to support the defense industrial base; to farm workers to ensure production of food; to students to ensure that the nation's populace continues to receive necessary training and education; and to fathers and sole surviving sons to protect the family structure of the nation. Deferment policies have frequently been criticized as being discriminatory—a device for protecting members of one group from being exposed to the dangers and disruption of combat, while conversely exposing members of less privileged groups to these dangers. As a social management device, it is extremely difficult to ensure an equitable policy of deferment from wartime military service.

Deferments are different from exemptions; a deferment explicitly states that the individual is being excused from military service only temporarily, conditional upon retaining the status for which the deferment was granted. An exemption, on the other hand, implies permanent relief from military service.

Summary

Accession standards are an important element of national manpower policy because they define the kinds of men and women who are allowed to serve in the nation's armed forces during peace and war. As society becomes more complicated, the standards become more controversial. While there is not much controversy in peacetime, when the tendency in most nations is to recruit or draft a relatively small proportion of eligible persons for military service, the situation is different in wartime. In a major war, it will be necessary to find a satisfactory way to apply the entire population of a nation to the war effort. Usually this means that conscription will be used to obtain new recruits for the armed forces. Sound accession standards for entry into military service, accompanied by rational waiver and deferment policies, are necessary to implement a rational wartime manpower policy.

PATRICIA INSLEY HUTZLER

SEE ALSO: Conscientious Objection; Conscription; Education, Military; Ethnicity and the Armed Forces; Force Structure, Personnel; Manpower, Military; Mobilization; Personnel; Psychology, Military; Social Science Research and Development, Military; Sociology, Military; Women in the Armed Forces.

Bibliography

Anderson, R. S., and C. M. Wiltse, eds. 1967. *Physical standards in World War II.* Washington, D.C.: U.S. Army Medical Department.

Austrian Government. 1977. *Guidelines for the military medical examination and classification in the new induction method.* Washington, D.C.: U.S. Army Medical Intelligence and Information Agency.

Brunner, E. 1981. *Soviet demographic trends and the ethnic composition of draft age males.* Santa Monica, Calif.: Rand Corp.

Curran, S. L., and D. Ponomaroff. 1982. *Managing the ethnic factor in the Russian and Soviet armed forces.* Santa Monica, Calif.: Rand Corp.

Chu, D. S. C., and E. Norrblom. 1974. *Physical standards in an all-volunteer force.* Santa Monica, Calif.: Rand Corp.

Davis, J. S. 1991. Military policy toward homosexuals: Scientific, historical, and legal perspective. *Military Law Review* 131:55–108.

Eitelberg, M. J., et al. 1984. *Screening for service: Aptitude and education criteria for military entry.* Alexandria, Va.: Human Resources Research Organization.

Kan T'Ang, trans. 1979. *An analysis of the Communist revampment of the conscription system.* Wright-Patterson Air Force Base, Ohio: Foreign Technology Division.

Orkand Corp. 1984. *Manpower (to include women) and the military establishments in the Middle East and North Africa.* Silver Spring, Md.

Means, B. 1983. *Moral standards for military enlistment: Screening procedures and impact.* Alexandria, Va.: Human Resources Research Organization.

Minkler, R., R. N. Ginsburgh, and G. Rebh. 1977. *Soviet defense manpower: A summary on the proceedings and results of a seminar.* Washington, D.C.: TEMPO General Electric Center for Advanced Studies.

Pickett, D., et al. 1990. *Expanded use of draftees.* Bethesda, Md.: Logistics Management Institute.

Saunders, P. L., E. J. Celentana, and J. W. Nottredt. 1982. *Canadian forces occupational physical selection standards study, phase 1.* Downsview, Ontario: Defense and Civil Institute of Environmental Standards.

Sohlberg, R. 1980. *Defense manpower policies in northern and central Europe.* Santa Monica, Calif.: Rand Corp.

U.S. Department of the Army. 1965. *Marginal man and military service: A review.* Washington, D.C.: Dept. of the Army.

U.S. Department of the Army. 1987. *Army regulation 40-501: Standards of medical fitness.* Washington, D.C.: Dept. of the Army.

U.S. Department of Defense. 1986. Instruction 6130.3, *Physical standards for enlistment, appointment, and induction.* Washington, D.C.: Dept. of the Army.

ADMINISTRATION, MILITARY

The Oxford dictionary defines *administration* as the management of public affairs. It is more difficult, however, to suggest a brief definition of *military administration* that is both up-to-date and used generally by different armed forces.

Military administration may describe the running of the internal affairs of a unit. The term also refers to the high-level, politico-military conduct of national and, if applicable, multinational military and defense affairs. Yet both these functions are *management* in its modern meaning and application. Moreover, the direction and positive supervision of these activities, in units and high-level headquarters, are more appropriately termed *control*.

Some armed forces define *administration* as the management and execution of all military matters not included in strategy and tactics; primarily they include logistics and personnel under this wider, longer-standing heading. Others specify manpower and personnel as administration and treat logistics as a separate, autonomous military function.

Napoleon meant by *logis* the provision of quarters and lodgings—the responsibility of his *maréchal général des logis*—although logistics had existed for as long as armed men had looked to others for that variety of support. During the last half century or so, the scope, content, doctrine, and practice of logistics have developed swiftly and extensively, propagating a term that has rapidly gained currency and popularity not just in the military environment in which it was originally conceived. As the relative importance and impact of logistics *per se* has grown, so its former inclusion as part of military administration has been increasingly challenged.

Strategy, tactics, and logistics are now widely accepted as inseparable and interdependent functions of command that should be integrated at every operational level. Yet people are the most vital military resource in both peace and war. By nature of activity, rather than by some artificial figment of terminology, the separation of military administration and logistics is regarded as logical and practical. If military administration primarily concerns manpower and personnel (people), then it must remain an indispensable command function. Together with logistics, it forms a crucial part of the operational and nonoperational support of armed forces.

A definition, therefore, that would seem to have a current and general application is: Military administration describes the organization, management, and execution of all military affairs not included in strategy, tactics, and logistics; primarily the term applies to manpower and personnel.

The following are the main constituents of military administration.

Manpower planning, both operational and nonoperational, is performed in peace and war, mainly by staffs in higher level headquarters and national ministries of defense, on a single or joint service basis. Operational manpower planning, for instance, is a general staff (G1) function.

Personnel management is also performed continually in peace and war in all military units, and in central organizations such as personnel management centers. The significance and extent of certain activities may diminish during active operations. Personnel management includes such activities as: recruitment, selection, qualification, career planning, promotion, appointment, posting, records and information, conditions of service, morale, discipline, appeal, military law and regulations, discharge, retirement and conditions of retirement, reserve liability, and mobilization.

Personnel services differ considerably among armed forces. The wide range of services that may be provided within larger organizations include: individual basic and advanced training, education, sports and physical training, leisure and welfare, medical and associated services, veterinary service, pay and finance, records, audit, chaplaincy or equivalent, burial and graves, military police, military detention service, military legal, advocacy, and judicial services, military trades unions, military commissioner or ombudsman service, and political commissar or commissioner service. Most services are provided in some form in wartime as well as peacetime, and a number are organized on a joint basis: for example, medical and associated services may support the army, navy, and air force collectively.

Peacetime superintendence is a term that incorporates a miscellany of external-to-unit functions. Although they concern nonoperational activities, some may well continue after hostilities have started. These include the inspection of

- Personnel management efficiency and records
- Military establishments (tables of organization and equipment); application, as necessary, of such techniques as work study and work measurement
- Provisioning, upkeep, management, and administration of garrison or barrack accommodation, facilities, and amenities
- Health and safety arrangements, fire prevention measures, and other auxiliary services
- Unit management efficiency and economy (including responsibility budgets)

Also included with the realm of peacetime superintendence is the audit of financial, materiel, and other accounts, and monitoring of accounting practices; and any action taken by a military commissioner (ombudsman), trade union, or political commissioner, in armed forces that employ them, in response to a representation made from within the unit.

Civil affairs concerns the issues, questions, and problems that may arise between a foreign armed force and the local government and people in wartime. They are the affairs that concern the force's relations, either with a host nation that has invited the military presence, or with the appropriate civil authorities when a force has mounted intervention operations within another country. In the

North Atlantic Treaty Organization, the term *civil and military cooperation* (CIMIC) denotes similar tasks to those described as civil affairs, but CIMIC applies to both peace and war.

Refuges and prisoners of war are additional subjects included within the function of military administration.

J. H. SKINNER

SEE ALSO: Command; Logistics: A General Survey; Management; Manpower, Military; Organization, Military; Personnel; Staff.

Bibliography

U.S. Department of the Army. Headquarters. 1953. FM 101-10: *Staff officers' field manual: Organizational, technical, and logistical data.* Washington, D.C.: Government Printing Office.

———. 1977. *Field manual 100-5: Operations.* Washington, D.C.: Government Printing Office.

AERIAL MINING

Aerial mining is the delivery of mines by aircraft. Aerial delivery of mines, coupled with advances in mine technology, has transformed mine warfare on land and in maritime combat. Traditionally, mines have been associated with static, positional warfare, and have been used primarily in a defensive role. Aerial delivery has enabled combatants to employ mines in areas under enemy control, and with a flexibility and responsiveness previously impossible.

Aerial Mining in Naval Warfare

Naval mines may be employed either as defensive weapons to protect friendly ports and waterways against enemy action, or as offensive weapons to menace an adversary's military and commercial shipping. Offensive mining operations may be conducted against ports, anchorages, or waterways, or in sea-lanes removed from the adversary's harbor areas. Aircraft-laid mines are normally employed in offensive operations to establish a threat against shipping in enemy-held waters; they also provide the capability to replenish minefields without danger from previously laid mines, and permit mines to be laid in shallow bodies of water that cannot be transited by submarines or surface minelayers.

Naval mines may be placed by cargo aircraft, helicopters, or nearly any aircraft that can carry bombs. Most air-laid mines use some sort of flight gear, usually a parachute, to decrease water-impact velocity, and incorporate a tail fin to provide stability during free-fall.

PAST EMPLOYMENT

Both the British and the Germans developed proximity-fuzed mines for aerial delivery between the world wars. The Germans placed great hopes on the effectiveness of these weapons to interdict English shipping, and employed them as early as October 1939. However, these systems, while effective, were not employed with sufficient density to have a significant effect, and weapons mistakenly delivered on shore enabled the British to develop and field effective countermeasures.

The British first employed a comparable system in April 1940. From that point aerial delivery of naval mines was widely and frequently used by Allied forces in Europe and in the Mediterranean—against ports and shipping routes throughout German-occupied Europe, against U-boat operations, to interdict shipping through chokepoints such as the Kiel Canal, and to interdict inland waterway traffic on the Danube River. The latter operation still represents the most efficient naval mining operation ever recorded, with one of every six mines deployed damaging or destroying an enemy vessel.

The Germans continued to develop aerial mining techniques and fuze technology throughout the war. Notable campaigns included an attempt to close the Suez Canal in 1941 and an effort aimed at isolating the Normandy battlefields through mining operations after the Allied invasion. The latter operation, in which the Germans employed pressure-sensing mines for the first time, enjoyed some success, sinking about 30 ships. The employment of Luftwaffe heavy bombers in this mining operation had the further advantage that, at this stage of the war, mining was one of the few missions the Luftwaffe bomber force could conduct with satisfactory survivability.

German magnetic and acoustic fuzes recovered by the British were delivered to the U.S. Navy Ordnance Laboratory early in 1940. These demonstrated the degree to which U.S. capabilities lagged behind those of the warring European powers, and provided the technical basis upon which developmental work could begin. The U.S. Navy accelerated research on mines with proximity fuzes, and by the time the United States entered the war in December 1941, had some limited operational capability.

Shortages of aircraft and mines delayed employment of aerial mines by the Allies in the Pacific theater until early 1943. From that point until the end of the Pacific war, aerial mines were employed frequently, widely, and with remarkable success in a variety of roles. Operational objectives included the disruption of reinforcements to land campaigns (Solomons 1943 and Rangoon 1943); denial of anchorages to surface fleets (Eniwetok 1943–44) and submarines (Penang 1944); and entrapment of surface combatants for destruction at leisure by other means (Palau 1944). In addition, mines delivered in the Yangtze River were highly effective in interdicting Japanese supplies along that important river route.

The Pacific war's most strategically significant employment of aerial mines, however, occurred in the aerial blockade of Japan, code-named Operation Starvation. This operation opened on 27 March 1945 and continued until the end of the war. At a cost of fifteen B-29s and 12,308 mines, and with an employment of about 10 percent of the total B-29 force committed to operations in the Pacific, this operation sank or damaged about 650 Japanese vessels. What was more significant was that it forced extensive rerouting and delay of shipping. This combination reduced effective deliveries by about 77 percent. In conjunction with the simultaneous bombing campaign conducted by the 20th Air Force, the mine campaign destroyed the Japanese economy and warmaking potential, and eventually that nation's ability to subsist.

During the Vietnam conflict, the U.S. Navy employed the Destructor mine series—general-purpose bombs modified with influence fuzes—to interdict travel on inland waterways. This mining, while providing some harassment, had little impact on the flow of supplies within North Vietnam or to the forces operating in the South, due to the lack of time-urgency in movement of supplies and the existence of alternate routes.

Far more effective was the mining operation that closed the port of Haiphong on the night of 8 May 1972. This mining, conducted without losses, probably achieved more than the aerial interdiction campaigns conducted at great expense over the previous seven years. The North Vietnamese were unable to reopen the harbors, which remained closed for eight months. The U.S. Navy cleared the mines as one condition of the peace settlement, which ended direct U.S. military involvement in that war.

Current Naval Mine Capabilities and Doctrine

Technological developments in sensors, warhead effectiveness, command and control capabilities, ability to discriminate among targets, and effective range have increased the operational utility of naval mines. Their employment in the Persian Gulf in the 1980s and 1990s reinforced this trend, demonstrating the capability of even the relatively unsophisticated mines employed in that region.

Aerial mining received a great deal of emphasis in Western naval planning as operators contemplated a large-scale naval conflict with the Soviet Union. During the cold war, mining offered the United States and its allies a means of closing off Soviet access to the shipping lanes in a superpower conflict by shutting off the straits through which Soviet vessels had to pass to reach the high seas; this was an especially important capability in antisubmarine warfare.

The Destructor mine series employed in Southeast Asia remains in the U.S. inventory, supplemented by newer series of air-deliverable influence mines. The major capability developed since that war is represented by the Captor mine, essentially a Mk46 acoustic torpedo, launched by a mine employing passive acoustic sensors for detection and an active sonar for ranging prior to employment of the torpedo. This system is normally optimized for antisubmarine operations.

The Soviet Union fielded air-deliverable naval mines of various types. These include both bottom mines, with a variety of influence fuzes, and moored rocket-propelled rising mines similar in concept to the Captor. These systems have been deployed for over a decade and remain operational with the naval forces of the Commonwealth of Independent States. As is normally the case with Soviet systems, information on frontline weapons is lacking. Soviet operational doctrine called for submarine delivery of offensive mines, with aircraft used primarily for reseeding operations and reactive mining.

Aerial Mining in Land Warfare

As in naval warfare, traditional employment of mines on land emphasized use in static, positional warfare, with minefields emplaced by hand and covered by defensive fire. The development of scatterable mines in the early 1970s revolutionized mine warfare on land; it allowed for a dramatic increase in the operational flexibility of that weapon.

These mines, deliverable by artillery, helicopters, or fixed-wing aircraft, play their traditional role in the close combat arena by reinforcing terrain obstacles. In addition, they have great potential to delay and disrupt follow-on forces, to channel the flow of reinforcing units into close combat, and to counter thrusts by mechanized forces. They stress the command and control capabilities of adversary maneuver elements and provide the psychological advantages inherent in rear-area operations. They also offer tactical aircraft a means of limiting exposure to enemy organic air defenses, and reduce the delivery accuracy necessary for tactical aircraft to gain a kill.

The area-denial capabilities of scatterable mines offer a high payoff in operations against fixed facilities. This payoff is especially high when the installation under attack has urgent mission requirements.

These weapons may be used to protect forces engaged in raids or amphibious assaults; on a far larger scale, they permit the rapid construction of barriers against large-scale armored attacks across a wide front. This capability had particular applications for the North Atlantic Treaty Organization (NATO).

Past Employment

The Luftwaffe adapted naval mines for the bombing campaigns against British cities, and employed these weapons for the first time on 16 September 1940 in the air assault on London. The following October the Luftwaffe began delivering antipersonnel mines in attacks on British cities to hinder recovery from air attacks. These weapons, and Italian "thermos" bombs, were later used for the same purpose in Malta, and against troops in the field in Africa and on the eastern front.

The American military employed aerial delivery of land mines extensively in Southeast Asia, with limited effectiveness. Mines were delivered primarily against the adversary's logistics systems, in areas otherwise inaccessible to American forces. These mines were somewhat effective in harassing the movement of supplies, but because time was not a critical factor in the infiltration and logistics movements, mining operations had no serious disruptive effect on the flow of materiel or personnel.

The Destructor mine series, previously discussed in connection with naval operations, was employed as an antivehicle mine, but with limited success. This weapon suffered from a mismatch between seeker sensitivity and warhead destructiveness; it created an easily recognizable signature when delivered; and because the typical ordnance load of tactical aircraft was only ten mines, it was difficult to create minefields with the proper density and distribution.

The experimental Wide Area Antipersonnel Mine, delivered in a canister carrying 540 tripwire-actuated mines, was employed successfully despite a restricted delivery profile and an unreliable self-destruct mechanism.

The Soviets employed helicopter-delivered mines extensively in Afghanistan. As with the American use in Vietnam, antipersonnel mines were more successfully employed than antivehicle ordnance, with PFM-1 "butterfly bombs" apparently having been the most widely employed. Afghan resistance forces employed Western scatterable antivehicle and antipersonnel mines with some success. The Soviet withdrawal from Afghanistan underscored one inherent limitation of aerial-delivered mines: the difficulty of clearing minefields which, by the nature of delivery techniques, could not be accurately charted.

During the 1991 Gulf War, coalition forces employed aerial mines for airfield attacks, and for restricting the mobility of Iraqi field forces. Most notably, American tactical aircraft employed mines to cut off the retreat from Kuwait of the Iraqi army, creating a "kill zone" of stationary vehicles on the roads north of Kuwait City.

Current and Future Capabilities in Land Warfare

As with naval mines, advances in warhead; sensor; and command, control, and communications technology are fueling a proliferation of land mine development efforts. Again as with naval mines, these have been undertaken by both major and minor military powers.

The American experience with mining operations in Southeast Asia encouraged development of scatterable mines. In the early 1970s, the U.S. Army deployed the M56 scatterable mine system for delivery from UH-1 helicopters, and began development of the Family of Scatterable Mines (FASCAM) program. This family of systems employs common subsystems in a series of munitions and dispensers for delivery by vehicles, artillery, helicopters, and fixed-wing aircraft. A follow-on system for deployment of mines from helicopters, the Volcano, is scheduled to reach operational status in the early 1990s.

The U.S. Air Force fielded the CBU-89A Gator system in 1985. (Another member of the Gator system is shown in Figure 1.) This system corrects many of the deficiencies of the aerial mines in the Vietnam era. It incorporates both antipersonnel and antivehicle mines in a single canister, complicating clearing operations; it permits an essentially unrestricted attack profile; and it has proven more reliable than earlier systems. This system was employed with great effect during Operation Desert Storm.

The MW-1 weapons delivery system developed in West Germany uses an alternative approach to delivering aerial mines—that is, from a dispenser mounted on the belly of a Tornado attack aircraft. The MW-1 carries a mixture of bomblets in tubes that eject submunitions laterally. The mixture of submunitions may be varied depending on the target set. This system offers an improvement over canister-delivered munitions in permitting better-controlled distribution of the ordnance, and in permitting lateral displacement of the weapons from the aircraft flight path. Like the Gator, however, this system requires overflight by the attack aircraft. Developmental efforts, such as the Modular Stand-off Weapon, are focused on fielding systems with a stand-off delivery capability.

The Soviet Union appears to have followed a pattern in mine development similar to that traditional in the West. For decades after World War II, the Soviets fielded mines with roughly the technological capability of those employed in that conflict. Combat experience in Afghanistan reemphasized the utility of this weapon, and accelerated efforts at developing influence-fuzed scatterable mines for both antipersonnel and antivehicle operations. Through the decade of the 1980s the Soviet Union fielded such weapons and employed them, as noted above, in warfare in Afghanistan. Normal operational practice in that war was to deliver these mines primarily with mobile rocket launchers. Aerial delivery would be employed when the field to be laid was beyond the range of artillery or rocket units.

Finally, aerial mines have been incorporated into airfield attack weapons fielded by Germany (MW-2) and

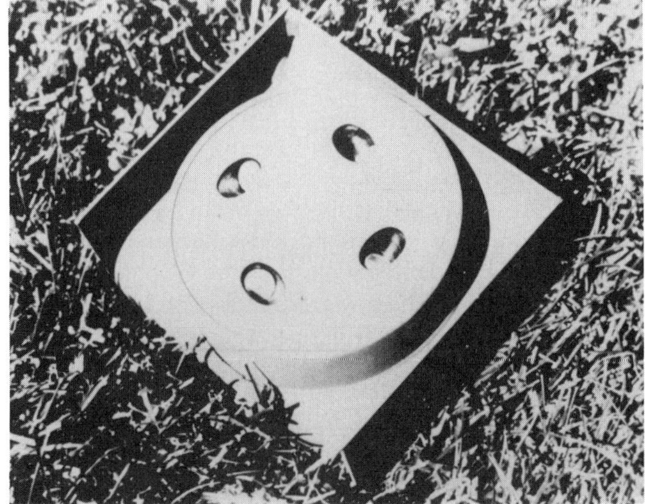

Figure 1. A CBU-89/B Gator mine. (Source: U.S. Air Force)

Great Britain (JP-233). Both systems include a mix of runway-cratering munitions and area-denial mines that are designed to suppress runway repair operations and airfield activities long after the actual attack. The JP-233 was employed effectively by the British Tornados during the Gulf War, but the low-level overflight delivery profile required by that munition contributed to the comparatively high loss rate among Tornado units. The United States is in the process of developing a similar capability expected to become operational in the mid-1990s. These and similar systems clearly offer high payoff in disruption and attrition of theater air operations. The Soviet Union, similarly, addressed the incorporation of mining in airfield attacks as one aspect of a general emphasis on countering NATO's air forces through airfield attack.

STEPHEN P. RANDOLPH

SEE ALSO: Airpower; Engineering Equipment, Combat; Mine; Mine Warfare, Land; Mine Warfare, Naval.

Bibliography

Cowie, J. S. 1949. *Mines, minelayers and minelaying*. London: Oxford Univ. Press.

Griffiths, M. 1981. *The hidden menace*. Greenwich, U.K.: Conway Maritime Press.

Hartmann, G. K. 1979. *Weapons that wait: Mine warfare in the U.S. Navy*. Annapolis, Md.: U.S. Naval Institute Press.

Isby, D. C. 1987. *Weapons and tactics of the Soviet army*. 2d ed. London: Jane's.

Sloan, C. E. E. 1986. *Mine warfare on land*. London: Brassey's.

AERIAL REFUELING

Aerial refueling is the in-flight provision of fuel to one aircraft by another aircraft known as a tanker. Aerial refueling can increase the effectiveness of the refueled aircraft by expanding the following capabilities:

- Range: allows deeper penetration of enemy territory, or operations from remote bases that are less susceptible to enemy attack.
- Endurance: increases aircraft endurance to the point where crew endurance becomes the critical factor.
- Survivability: allows penetration of the enemy's territory using a more advantageous speed, altitude, and approach path to decrease airplane vulnerability.
- Tonnage: increases the payloads or combat weapons loads an aircraft can carry to the objective and decreases the tradeoff of fuel versus payload.
- Mobility: allows combat aircraft to operate from smaller, less developed fields.

Growth of the Concept of Aerial Refueling

The need to keep the flying machine aloft and in action longer was identified as early as World War I. However, no experiments were conducted during that war.

Aerial refueling experiments had a "daredevil" beginning in 1921. An American, Wesley May, with a 5-gallon can of aviation gasoline strapped to his back, climbed from the wing of a Lincoln Standard up to the wing skid of a JN-4 Jenny flying above. He maneuvered to the Jenny's engine, unstrapped the can and poured the gasoline into the fuel tank, thus completing the first successful aerial refueling attempt.

Attempts during the interwar period emphasized only one of the fundamental benefits associated with aerial refueling, that is, aircraft could remain airborne for long periods of time. The interwar air forces saw little practical advantage in air refueling.

After World War II, aerial refueling emerged as an accepted requirement. In 1947 the new Strategic Air Command (SAC) concluded that air refueling was necessary if U.S. bombers were to conduct global operations. Since then, air refueling has become an integral part of U.S. air operations and forms the backbone of aerial force projection efforts by major powers throughout the world.

EARLY MILITARY AND PRIVATE AERIAL REFUELING

Most aircraft histories acknowledge that the first serious attempt at aerial refueling occurred in 1923 at Rockwell Field, California. A single-engine U.S. Army DH-4B was refueled in flight. Two refuelings (25 and 50 gal., respectively) were made by hose from another DH-4B using gravity flow. In August 1923, the same U.S. Army team set an endurance record of 37 hours and 15 minutes with the aid of aerial refueling.

A milestone in aerial refueling occurred on New Year's Day, 1929. Two Douglas C-1s, the tankers in this experiment, were equipped with two 150-gallon fuel tanks each. A 50-foot length of metal-lined hose with a lead weight attached to the lower end was let down through a trap door in the bottom of the fuselage. The receiver aircraft, a Fokker C-2A named the *Question Mark* was outfitted with additional fuel tanks and other special equipment. The aircraft was piloted by Maj. Carl Spaatz; also on board was Capt. Ira Eaker.

The *Question Mark* took off from Metropolitan Airport, Los Angeles, at 7:27 A.M. on 1 January 1929. For a week, the two tankers made refueling and resupplying contacts. About 40 tons of supplies were passed during the operation, including 36,000 pounds of gasoline. On the seventh day, Major Spaatz terminated the mission after the aircraft's left engine had become useless and its right engine was losing power. The *Question Mark*, powered by the nose engine, coasted home on 7 January 1929, touching down at 2:07 P.M. When the *Question Mark* finally landed, the record was 150 hours, 40 minutes, and 15 seconds of continuous flying. This record stood until 1930, when Dale Jackson and Forest O'Brine established an endurance record of more than 25 days in their monoplane, the *Greater St. Louis*.

Commercial Aerial Refueling Ventures

In 1934 Alan J. Cobham of Great Britain formed Flight Refueling, Ltd., and in conjunction with Imperial Airways of England began the commercial exploitation of aerial refueling. By 1938 Imperial Airways had agreed to a series of trials with an Empire flying boat as the receiver aircraft. These successful trials led to an agreement to operate a series of air-refueled trans-Atlantic crossings. Two Empire boats were to be "souped up" so they could be flown at a maximum take-off gross weight of 53,000 pounds. Once airborne, the flying boats' weight could be increased to 64,000 pounds. Four Handley Page Harrows were obtained and modified as tankers so that they could pass nearly 1,000 gallons of fuel each.

The contact mechanism and procedures—called the "looped hose" method—were somewhat complicated. The tanker would fly alongside and a few feet below the receiver. It would then fire a harpoonlike projectile across the receiver's trailing line and grapnel hook. Once snared, the line would be drawn into the tanker and the fuel hose attached and returned to the receiver. Subsequently the tanker would climb slightly and gravity refueling would commence. During 1939 eight successful westbound refuelings were made and seven eastbound. Britain's entry into World War II brought an end to the venture.

Post–World War II Aerial Refueling

After World War II, the British continued to experiment with aerial refueling for commercial applications on numerous refueling flights between London and Bermuda and between London and Montreal. These experiments proved successful and validated the aerial refueling concept; however, the program was not pursued to full operational status because of possible dangers to passengers.

The need for greater range became imperative in the years following World War II. New technology and global politics had changed the dimensions of conflict. There was a clear need for a heavy bomber with intercontinental range. The newly formed Strategic Air Command took the lead in projecting global power for the United States.

On 22 July 1948 three U.S. 43d Bomb Group Boeing B-29s departed Davis-Monthan Air Force Base (AFB), Arizona, on a round-the-world flight attempt. The flight was scheduled for fourteen days but required one extra day due to the crash of one B-29 into the Arabian Sea. The other two aircraft made eight en-route stops and completed the 32,187-kilometer (20,000-mi.) flight in 103 hours and 50 minutes of actual flight time.

On 2 March 1949 *Lucky Lady II*, a Boeing B-50 bomber, landed at Carswell AFB, Texas, after having flown 37,742 kilometers (23,452 mi.) around the world in 94 hours and 1 minute. In this record flight, B-29s were used as tankers, and refueling was accomplished by using a hose-and-drogue system allowing fuel to be transferred by gravity feed.

On 16 January 1957 five Boeing B-52B aircraft lifted off from Castle AFB, California, and headed east for an around-the-world flight. One of the primary aircraft and one spare departed the formation and landed in Goose Bay, Labrador, and in England. The remaining three bombers headed across Africa, Saudi Arabia, and the Persian Gulf. They simulated a bomb run on a railway crossing in Malaya and then crossed the Pacific on their way back to California. All three B-52s landed at March AFB, California, on the morning of 18 January. Their flight time—45 hours, 19 minutes—was less than half that required by *Lucky Lady II* just eight years before.

This feat was made possible by the 98 KC-97s that had taken part. Twenty tankers provided refuelings over eastern Canada, 22 over north Africa, and eighteen over the Persian Gulf. A brief refueling by twelve tankers over the Philippines got the bombers to Guam, where 26 KC-97s provided the final air refuelings.

Refueling Equipment

Through 1950 all operations had used the "looped-hose" method. This required an operator in the tanker and one in the receiver to complete the refueling. When the United States became involved in the Korean War, its air force needed a method that would enable single-seat fighters to reach targets beyond their normal range. The looped-hose method proved unworkable for fighters. Furthermore, fuel transfer time was too long for large receiver aircraft.

There were two parallel efforts to resolve the complexity of the looped-hose-refueling technology. One effort developed by the British resulted in a simple "probe-and-drogue" system that proved well suited to the refueling needs of fighter aircraft. Using the probe-and-drogue system, the tanker trails a hose terminating in a reception coupling and a cone-shaped drogue. The receiver has a matching nozzle fitted to a probe, mounted on the fuselage or the leading edge of the wing, or, in some instances, on wingtip tanks. To make contact, the receiver flies the probe into the conical drogue while overtaking at 2 to 5 knots. Valves in the nozzle and the drogue are automatically opened on contact. The tanker then pumps fuel to the receiver. When refueling is complete, the receiver pilot closes his throttles slightly and drops back until he has a disconnect. Both fuel valves close automatically to minimize spillage. Throughout the operation, the tanker flies straight and level or makes gradual turns. Maneuvering is the responsibility of the receiver.

The other effort pursued by the Boeing company in the United States sought a means to provide the maximum refueling capability to large receiver aircraft. A system with a long flexible pipe and high-capacity pumps was proposed to transfer large amounts of fuel rapidly. The Boeing effort led to the retractable flying boom which extends from the tanker's tail and plugs into a receptacle socket on the receiver aircraft. Boom refueling requires a boom operator to "fly" the boom to the receptacle of the receiver which is flying in formation just under and behind the tanker on centerline (see Fig. 1). The boom operator can give voice command to the receiver or, during radio-silent operations, can signal the receiver through a combination of director lights on the tanker belly.

The boom proved to be a highly successful means to refuel the bombers of the U.S. Strategic Air Command. The first production Boeing flying boom tanker was a propeller-driven, converted bomber, the Boeing KB-29P, delivered to the U.S. Air Force in March 1950. In July 1950, an RB-45C reconnaissance bomber and an F-86 fighter were refueled by a KB-29P tanker for the first time by boom refueling.

Air Refueling Fleets

Nations throughout the world have realized the importance of air refueling. Outside the United States, the Boeing 707, modified for probe-and-drogue refueling, is by far the most prevalent tanker aircraft. Currently Australia, Brazil, Canada, France, Israel, Morocco, Italy, Saudi Arabia, and South Africa maintain 707 tankers in their inventories. Great Britain operates Victor tankers and the Soviet Union is building a new Midas (modified Il-76) tanker fleet to eventually replace its fleet of Bison tankers.

The United States operates the largest fleet of tankers, the majority in the U.S. Air Force. The U.S. fleet of boom-equipped Boeing KC-135 tankers supports bombers, transports, and fighters. If drogue refueling for the fighters is required, an add-on hose-and-drogue assembly must be attached to the boom before takeoff and left installed for the duration of the flight.

Figure 1. View from boom operator's position of the refueling boom and receiver receptacle. Note steerable wings on boom and open receptacle doors. (SOURCE: USAF)

Figure 2. RAF's newest tanker Tristar refueling Tornado. (SOURCE: RAF)

Several countries currently practice "buddy refueling" to augment their tanker capability: a tactical aircraft with a special fuel tank unwinds a hose and drogue to transfer fuel to another tactical aircraft. This practice reduces the need for a large standing fleet of dedicated tanker aircraft. It also permits refueling aircraft to penetrate deeper with the strike force. Buddy tankers can carry armament, so the concept can reduce the stand-off refueling required with larger, unprotected tankers.

WIDE-BODY TANKERS

In many situations, large-capacity tankers are more cost-effective than smaller tankers. The United States achieved the flexibility offered by a wide-body tanker when it acquired the first of 60 KC-10s in 1981. The KC-10, a modified Douglas DC-10, carries up to 345,000 pounds of fuel or 169,000 pounds of cargo. The large-capacity KC-10 is equivalent to approximately three of the smaller KC-135As. All fuel is transferable, and the KC-10 is itself capable of being refueled in flight. Unlike the KC-135, the KC-10 is permanently equipped with both flying boom and probe-and-drogue systems. The fleet is also being modified to carry removable underwing refueling pods, adding system redundancy as well as additional refueling stations. The modification also includes a closed-circuit TV camera and viewing screen for the boom operator's use.

The United Kingdom has added a wide body, the Lockheed L-1011 Tristar, to its tanker inventory (Fig. 2). The L-1011 augments the U.K. fleet of British Aerospace VC-10s and Victors. It is now equipped with a single centerline drogue; however, MK 32 underwing pods are being pursued. Like the VC-10, the L-1011 has no boom and is receiver-capable. In addition, the Tristar is equipped with a cargo door and cargo handling system, and the aircraft has been built to withstand large cargo loads. Neither the VC-10 nor the Tristar carry a boom operator. The flight engineer handles the refueling role from controls in the cockpit, aided by a camera under the fuselage.

Tanker Employment in Combat

Aerial refueling is used to extend the range and endurance of combat aircraft. Generally, deep strike aircraft and transports require extended range; air superiority fighters, airborne warning and control systems (AWACS), and command and control aircraft require endurance on station; and close-air-support aircraft require both range and endurance.

Tankers in Korea

During the Korean War a U.S. Air Force KB-29M conducted the first air refueling operation over enemy territory under combat conditions. On 6 July 1951, operating out of Yokota Air Base, Japan, the tanker refueled four RF-80 aircraft flying a reconnaissance mission over North Korea. On 14 July 1951 a KB-29P (equipped with a flying boom) refueled an RB-45C on a combat mission over North Korea. Overall there were fewer than 50 combat refueling sorties during this war.

Tankers in Vietnam

The Vietnam War demonstrated the importance of air refueling to all aspects of air combat operations. Reconnaissance, air superiority, search and rescue, command and control, and deep interdiction aircraft, as well as long-range B-52 bombers, were dependent on air refueling. To support air operations, extensive air-refueling areas and "tracks" were developed for pre- and poststrike refueling. These refueling tracks were positioned as close as possible to enemy territory to give strike aircraft maximum range and endurance. Multiple refueling formations were frequently separated only by altitude. This permitted refueling of large attack formations in a small area.

Tankers operated in support of the Vietnam conflict from June 1964 to August 1973—110 months of air-refueling support. They flew 194,687 sorties, provided 813,878 aerial refuelings, transferred a total of 9 billion pounds of fuel, and flew a total of 911,364 hours. As many as 172 USAF KC-135s were committed to this theater.

Falkland Islands/Islas Malvinas Campaign

In the Falklands/Malvinas, the lack of adequate aerial refueling spurred the Royal Air Force (RAF) to make rapid improvisations. Two squadrons of Victor tankers were available at the outset to support a fighting force 12,875 kilometers (8,000 mi.) away. Even though tankers were based on Ascension Island, 6,437 kilometers (4,000 mi.) closer to the front, ten Victor tankers (see Fig. 3) were required to support one Vulcan bomber mission. Consequently some Vulcan bombers were converted to tankers to give additional temporary refueling capacity. Also, the RAF's Nimrod MR-2s were given refueling probes to add needed loiter time to maritime patrol missions in the South Atlantic. The modification was completed in 21 days. Without aerial refueling, the projection of British airpower into the Falklands/Malvinas campaign would have been severely limited.

Figure 3. British Victor tanker refueling RAF Buccaneer fighters. (Source: RAF)

Libya Strike, April 1986

Tankers were indispensable in the support of U.S. air strikes against Libya. Strike aircraft flying from England were denied overflight rights by France, Spain, and Portugal. This forced a 2,800-nautical-mile circuitous route south from England along the European Atlantic coast and through the Strait of Gibraltar to the Libyan coast. Strike aircraft received eight refuelings—four prestrike and four poststrike. All air refuelings were completed as scheduled, demonstrating the reliability of air refueling equipment. The Libyan strike further illustrated the importance of air refueling in the success of difficult, complex air operations.

A composite force of nineteen KC-10s and ten KC-135s supported the U.S. air strike. The KC-135s refueled the KC-10s to maximum in-flight capacity. The KC-10s then provided prestrike and poststrike refuelings for the attacking force (see Fig. 4).

Persian Gulf War, 1991

Large-scale aerial refueling played a significant role in rapid, long-range deployment of troops and equipment in the Gulf War. During the buildup phase (Operation Desert Shield), U.S. Air Force tankers supported 4,967 sorties, refueled 14,588 airplanes, and off-loaded 68.2 million gallons of fuel. During combat operations (Operation Desert Storm), tankers supported 15,434 sorties, refueled 45,955 airplaines, and transferred 110.2 million gallons of aviation fuel to receiver aircraft. Three-quarters of the U.S. Air Force's KC-10 fleet and nearly half of the KC-135 fleet were committed to the Gulf crisis.

Single Integrated Operations Plan (SIOP)

The SIOP is the United States' retaliatory plan for nuclear war should deterrence fail. Tankers are key to bomber employment in the SIOP. Prestrike and poststrike refuelings are planned to give maximum effectiveness to the bomber force. When military tensions increase and bombers assume alert status, tankers respond in kind. Without refueling support, bombers would have to trade weapon load for fuel and thereby limit bomber effectiveness.

Mobility Support

Airlift is closely tied to rapid force deployment and the initial resupply of deployed forces. Basically, the first 30 days of deployment require airlift support for timely force supply. Aerial refueling is the essential element without which rapid deployment of forces would be impractical.

The importance of tankers to strategic airlift was made clear by the Middle East War in 1973. Following the outbreak of fighting, European nations initially refused landing rights to U.S. cargo planes carrying supplies to Israel. At that time, none of the U.S. Military Airlift Command C-141 transports could be refueled in flight and could not fly nonstop from the United States to Israel. Eventually, Portugal relented, and supplies for Israel were flown through the Azores. The vulnerability of airlift to foreign approval of basing or overflight rights was a principal reason for adding air-refueling receptacles to C-141s. This relieved the need for ground-refueling stops while greatly increasing the air-refueling requirement for airlift missions.

The Falklands/Malvinas campaign also illustrated the requirement for aerial refuelable airlift. The air line of communication (ALOC) to deliver men and materiel to the Falklands/Malvinas ran from Great Britain to Ascension Island in the South Atlantic (4,300 naut. mi.), and from Ascension to the task force around the Falklands/Malvinas (4,000 naut. mi.). ALOC resupply was necessary because merchant ships from Great Britain needed three to four weeks to reach the Falklands/Malvinas. C-130 transports were modified with refueling probes to enable them to make the 25-hour flight nonstop. C-130 transports and British Airways VC-10 airliners flew over 600 sorties to Ascension, delivering 5,000 troops and 6,000 tons of supplies. An additional 44 C-130 sorties were flown to the British fleet in the Falklands/Malvinas area where their loads were parachuted for sea recovery.

During the 1991 Persian Gulf War, tankers supported cargo aircraft in delivering 17 million ton-miles of cargo daily at the height of the Operation Desert Shield buildup. Landings of cargo aircraft peaked at 127 per day, an average of one landing every 11 minutes, during Desert Storm combat operations.

Aircraft Carrier Operations

Aerial refueling has become an integral part of aircraft carrier operations. Tankers based aboard aircraft carriers

Figure 4. Overhead view of SAC's newest tanker, the KC-10, refueling B1-B bomber. (Source: USAF)

are dedicated, permanently configured aircraft or "buddy" aircraft, outfitted with removable drogue pods. Tankers add endurance to defensive air cover and range to strike aircraft. In addition, they provide increased safety to recovery operations when the aircraft carrier is deployed far from land bases. Recovery tankers orbiting near the carrier can save aircraft that initially miss carrier landings.

The lack of sufficient Argentinian aerial tankers and the British fleet's defense in depth were factors that allowed Britain to control the sky in the Falklands/Malvinas war. However, the entire campaign might have been lost by the British had the Argentines used tanker refuelings to extend the combat range of their fighters. The success of the Etendard aircraft using Exocet missiles against HMS *Sheffield* forced the British fleet to operate at extended distances to stay outside the range of land-based air strikes.

Tanker Improvements

The United States, along with several nations, is attempting to revitalize its aging KC-135 fleet through re-engining. In many cases the original Pratt and Whitney J57 engines installed on the KC-135A will not supply sufficient power for the aircraft to take off at maximum gross weight. The U.S. Air National Guard (ANG) and Air Force Reserve (AFRes) KC-135s were the first re-engined with refurbished Pratt and Whitney TF33 (JT3D-3P) turbofan engines. These engines offer better specific fuel consumption and are more powerful and quieter than the older engines. A TF-33-equipped KC-135, designated KC-135E, is equivalent in capability to approximately 1.2 aircraft equipped with the older J57 engines. The U.S. Air Force is also re-engining its fleet of KC-135s, using the CFM 56-2B-1 and designating this re-engined model KC-135R. The maker of the engine, CFM International, is a consortium of General Electric of the United States and

SNECMA of France. France is re-engining its C-135 tanker fleet in a parallel program. One KC-135R is equal to about 1.5 KC-135As. Eventually both ANG and AFRes aircraft will also receive the CFM 56 engine.

Future Tankers

The United States. As a result of increasing air-refueling requirements, the U.S. Air Force is considering plans to acquire a new tanker, the KC-X. This next-generation tanker will augment its fleet of KC-135s and KC-10s. The aircraft type has not yet been determined.

Russia. The former Soviet Union augmented its fleet of Bison tankers with the Midas. The Midas, a modified Il-76, enables Russian receiver-capable combat aircraft to greatly extend their ranges.

North Atlantic Treaty Organization (NATO). It has been proposed that NATO acquire a dedicated fleet of tankers. Experts argue that a NATO tanker force with an international command structure and international crews would increase interoperability and expand military cooperation. Although Great Britain, France, and the United States possess tankers, these assets are primarily dedicated to national, rather than NATO, missions. A NATO tanker force would also provide a much needed force-multiplying effect in Europe since NATO lacks dedicated tanker support. The value of a NATO tanker fleet has often been discussed; however, to date, no plans exist to actually acquire it.

Future Technologies

Aerial refueling technology is apparently nearing maturity. While no major breakthroughs appear imminent, there are ongoing technological upgrades in development which include automatic fuel management and automatic hook-up systems.

Automatic fuel management. An automatic fuel management system allows the tanker to supply large amounts of fuel rapidly to receiver aircraft while maintaining the best center of gravity or balance for the airframe and flight conditions. An on-board computer would calculate the opening and closing of fuel valves and pumps to maintain a trimmed or balanced airplane, presently a manual job. Automatic fuel management has already been incorporated into the plans for the McDonnell Douglas MD-87 and C-17.

Automatic hookup. An automatic hook-up system eliminates the need for a boom operator. The receiver pilot positions his aircraft in a capture zone behind the tanker. The tanker's system automatically locks on the receiver's system and effects a hookup. It then tracks receiver position and responds accordingly. A tanker crew member in the cockpit would monitor the system for safety purposes.

Changing World Situation

Increasing restrictions on the use of foreign ports and airfields for military purposes have decreased the utility of numerous venues. As nations assert their independence more forcefully, prohibitions are placed on military hardware based in or transported through their countries. These restrictions have limited the number of forward bases from which combat operations can be conducted and caused lines of communication to be stretched through often costly and circuitous routing. Both denied base-siting privileges and routing difficulties have greatly increased the requirement for aerial refueling. As the movement to the Persian Gulf in 1990 and the Gulf War in 1991 illustrated, aerial refueling has become the *sine qua non* of global airpower.

Thomas D. Phillips
Clyde Henderson
Gregg Shaka
Kim Lott

See Also: Aircraft, Military; Airpower; Airpower, Strategic.

Bibliography

Berent, M. 1983. Air refueling in NATO. *NATO's Sixteen Nations* 28:52.

Dorr, R. 1987. *Boeing KC-135 stratotanker.* London: Ian Allan.

Garden, T. 1986. *Technology lessons of the Falklands conflict.* Low Intensity Conflict and Modern Technology, Maxwell A.F.B., Ala.: Air Univ. Press.

Hopkins, C. [1979] 1987. *SAC tanker operations in the southeast Asia war.* Reprint. Office of the Historian, Strategic Air Command. Washington, D.C.: Government Printing Office.

Hopkins, J., and S. Goldberg. 1987. *The development of strategic air command, 1946–1986.* Office of the Historian, Headquarters, Strategic Air Command. Washington, D.C.: Government Printing Office.

Hornung, R. 1986a. Aerial tankers: Running low. *United States Military Forum* 2 (April):28–31.

———. 1986b. Air tankers aid in raid on Libya. *United States Military Logistics Forum* 2 (June):11.

Morgery, R. 1986. Tankers for a thirsty fleet. *Air Force Magazine* 69 (June):74–80.

Nix, B. 1986. *Long-range air power and standoff weapons in low-intensity conflict.* Low Intensity Conflict and Modern Technology. Maxwell A.F.B., Ala.: Air Univ. Press.

Peek, K. 1986. *Air refueling: Keystone to global deterrence. Combat Crew* 27 (September):2.

Schoch, B. 1986. Logistics of the Falklands War. *United States Army Logistician* 18:2–7.

Ulsamer, E. 1982. Air Lift: Key to modern military mobility. *Air Force Magazine* 65 (September):174–76.

U.S. Department of the Air Force. 1991. *Reaching globally, reaching powerfully: The United States Air Force in the Gulf War.* Washington, D.C.: Government Printing Office.

Additional Sources: *Armed Forces Journal International; Aviation Week and Space Technology.*

AFGHANISTAN, REPUBLIC OF

Afghanistan is an extremely poor, landlocked country highly dependent on farming and raising livestock. Economic considerations, however, are secondary to the political and military upheavals that have occurred within the country, including the nine-year Soviet military occupation that ended on 15 February 1989, and the continuing bloody civil war between the Kabul government and the guerrillas (the mujaheddin). A deeply divided government and divisions within the antigovernment mujaheddin has to date prevented a negotiated settlement.

Power Potential Statistics

Area: 647,500 square kilometers (250,000 sq. mi.)
Population: 16,922,000 est.
Total Active Armed Forces: 45,000 (0.216% of pop.)
Gross Domestic Product: US$3 billion (1989 est.)
Annual Defense Expenditure: US$450 million (15% of GDP, 1990 est.)
Iron and Steel Production: none
Fuel Production:
  Coal: 0.145 million metric tons (1983–84)
  Crude oil: 0.008 million metric tons (1985)
  Natural gas: 2,400 million cubic meters (1985)
Electrical Power Output: 1,470 million kwh (1989)
Merchant Marine: none
Civil Air Fleet: 8 major transport aircraft; 36 usable airfields (9 with permanent-surface runways); none with runways over 3,659 meters (12,000 ft.); 10 with runways 2,440–3,659 meters (8,000–12,000 ft.); 17 with runways 1,220–2,440 meters (4,000–8,000 ft.).

For the most recent information, the reader may refer to the following annual publications:
The Military Balance. International Institute for Strategic Studies. London: Brassey's (UK).
The Statesman's Year-Book. New York: St. Martin's Press.
The World Factbook. Central Intelligence Agency. Washington, D.C.: Brassey's (US).

History

Zahir Shah, the last king (now in exile), reigned from 1933 to 1973. Afghanistan was neutral during both world wars. In 1953, the king's cousin, Daud Khan, became prime minister and obtained aid from the Soviet Union, thus opening the door to Soviet penetration. His successor, Dr. Mohammad Yusuf, introduced a new, democratic constitution, but the king did not allow political parties to operate.

In July 1973 General Daud overthrew the monarchy while the king was in Italy, abolished the 1964 constitution, and proclaimed a republic with himself as head of state. A *Loya Jirgah* (national assembly) adopted a new constitution. Discontent ensued, and in April 1978 the Saur revolution resulted in the overthrow and death of the president.

Nur Mohammad Taraki, leader of the banned People's Democratic Party of Afghanistan (PDPA), took power, and the country was renamed the Democratic Republic of Afghanistan. The constitution was abolished and only the PDPA was permitted. While ties to the Soviet Union were strengthened, opposition grew to the alien regime, and thousands sought refuge in Pakistan and Iran. In an increasingly intolerable political climate, Taraki was ousted in September 1979 by Hafizullah Amin, who imposed highly unpopular Marxist policies.

In December 1979, invading Soviet troops killed Amin, replacing him with Babrak Karmal. In May 1986 the Soviets installed Najibullah, former head of the state security service (KHAD, now KAM), as president.

Politico-Military Background

The April 1978 Saur revolution placed power in the hands of the tiny and unrepresentative Khalqi-dominated PDPA. Center-periphery relations between Kabul and the countryside were sorely tested by local uprisings in outlying provinces; nevertheless, they were manageable and did not create a viable military threat. The Afghan army, apparently intact, possessed relatively sophisticated Soviet-supplied weaponry.

Continued uprisings and even mutinies sapped the army's confidence. Losses to guerrilla warfare and an embarrassingly high number of desertions indicated low morale and questionable military effectiveness. Strongly nationalist officers were troubled by growing Soviet military influence through 1979, while conscripts and noncommissioned officers faced harsh military discipline, meager pay, and the prospect of grisly death at the hands of fierce tribal resistance.

Soviet military and financial involvement was already considerable by the summer of 1979. Successive purges by Hafizullah Amin, who had taken control of military operations, failed to quash the opposition of nationalist officers objecting to the army's support of a hated, Soviet-supported regime. An attempted coup (5 August 1979) against the Taraki-Amin cabinet, led by junior officers acting together with guerrilla forces, raised questions about the reliability of the armed forces and the police. In September, Taraki was murdered and Amin assumed power.

Although a Marxist, Amin was also undoubtedly a nationalist. His brief rule saw a Soviet buildup of combat troops and advisers in response to the guerrilla war and internecine party strife. Soviet control of the Bagram air base and part of Kabul airport and the presence of Soviet officers down to the company level indicated the extent of penetration. Amin unconvincingly promised an end to repression, but he believed that, through his faction of the Khalq party, he could muster sufficient commitment of key armed forces elements to maintain control. Meanwhile, the Soviets continued to plan their military operation of December 1979, which terminated Amin's unpopular rule and installed Babrak Karmal.

Politico-Military Policy

The Soviet invasion, with an initial force of 85,000 troops, has been interpreted as an implementation of the Brezhnev doctrine, which justified armed suppression in order to deal with forces "hostile to socialism." Amin, faced with internecine conflict within the Marxist-Leninist PDPA and strong, rural-based Islamic opposition, had failed to consolidate Communist rule. Soviet leaders feared that rejection of Taraki and Amin by urban as well as rural constituencies, heightened by the sheer brutality of the Marxist rulers and their zealous cadres, would lead to anti-Communist chaos and even collapse. Another interpretation holds that the Soviets' primary aim was to be within striking distance of the Persian Gulf. The most credible theory is that they feared that Islamic militancy would affect Soviet Central Asians.

In any case, the Soviets pursued a politico-military policy of establishing control through pacification and proselytization, using at the outset ethnically similar Soviet troops of Central Asian origin (which had disastrous results). The installation of Babrak Karmal was to provide a mantle of legitimacy for the Soviet presence. Under heavy Soviet pressure, Karmal declared an amnesty and released political prisoners, including prominent PDPA members, and hastened to form an ostensibly broad-based, popular cabinet of Parchamis and Khalqis. In foreign affairs he made concilatory gestures to revolutionary Iran and Pakistan while provocatively calling for self-determination of Pakistani-based Pushtuns and the Baluch.

The Karmal regime failed to win widespared popular support, despite the convocation of a *Loya Jirgah* and the use of Islamic symbols. In May 1986, Major-General Najib (Najibullah, the former head of the KHAD or state security service) replaced Karmal as PDPA General Secretary, once again touching off internecine party rivalries. He has been no more successful in consolidating power.

Strategic Problems

Soviet troops were ill prepared to wage a non-European campaign, despite their expectations of a blitzkrieg victory along well-established planned access routes. The flat plains of Europe, the site of the 1941–45 Great Patriotic War and therefore the principal model for Soviet training, contrasted with Afghanistan's rugged terrain, with its mountainous topography, deserts, climatic extremes, and considerable impediments to dependable all-weather communications.

Heavy armor, artillery, and antiaircraft units were unsuitable for fighting the mujaheddin resistance operating in almost perfect guerrilla terrain. The Soviet-DRA forces faced an enemy lightly armed with traditional (although highly accurate) bolt-action .303 Lee-Enfield rifles, and with no air support or even modern communications. But DRA and Soviet army conscripts lacked combat effectiveness and essential troop morale. In contrast, the highly motivated mujaheddin, who began activities after the 1978 Saur coup, effectively employed hit-and-run attacks in classic guerrilla style and valued fearlessness and seemingly reckless regard for personal safety over preservation of personnel. The net result was a stalemate, with the Soviet-DRA forces controlling urban areas and strategic outposts while the resistance occupied much of the countryside and continued to threaten urban areas.

The Soviets adjusted to the guerrillas over time by using the more suitable and highly effective Mi-24 attack helicopters and special *spetznaz* commando forces. At the same time, the resistance forces improved and modernized their training and equipment while learning to safeguard trained fighters. They also acquired more modern weapons, such as AK-47 Kalashnikov rifles and the newer, high-velocity AK-74 assault rifles (from deserting DRA and Soviet soldiers), as well as RPG-7 antitank grenade launchers from Egyptian and Chinese sources funded by the United States and Gulf Arabs.

Despite the presence of as many as 120,000 Soviet troops plus the DRA forces, the stalemate continued. Shipments of foreign military supplies to the resistance, begun in early 1980, had risen dramatically so that in 1987 the United States alone was providing US$600 million worth (up from $300 million in 1986). More sophisticated weapons such as the Stinger antiaircraft missile, while ending the West's pretense of "plausible deniability" provided by the cover of Soviet-style weapons supplied through the Pakistani conduit, markedly reduced the Soviet airpower advantage and contributed to the impasse.

After years of seemingly fruitless "proximity talks" sponsored by the United Nations, Soviet leader Mikhail Gorbachev, on 8 February 1988, signaled a breakthrough with a nine-month withdrawal timetable (to begin May 15). Ultimately, this led to the April 14 Geneva Accords, with the governments of Afghanistan and Pakistan as signatories and the United States and Soviet Union as guarantors but without the seven members of the Peshawar-based mujaheddin alliance. The earlier Soviet removal of Babrak Karmal and his replacement with Najibullah, erroneously thought to be more pliant, contributed to the breakthrough.

The U.S. insistence on continuing aid to the Afghan resistance unless Moscow terminated aid to the Kabul regime was labeled "positive symmetry." Although embarrassingly severe mujaheddin attacks on withdrawing Soviet forces—and on Kabul itself—provoked Soviet protests and military counterstrikes, the withdrawal continued consistent with the 15 February 1989 deadline. The accords called for mutual noninterference and nonintervention and the voluntary return of the refugees, but did not actually provide for a cease-fire.

With a stable, Kabul Communist government still elusive, the Soviet Union at this juncture, was willing to settle for a neutral regime that would be cognizant of its geographical propinquity and security interests.

Military Assistance

Afghanistan has received military assistance directed toward both the government and the guerrilla opposition. Soviet military assistance to the Kabul regime has been massive but difficult to calculate. Shortly before the accords went into effect, Moscow let it be known that it had transferred US$1 billion in aid to the Kabul regime. To forestall the regime's collapse during the withdrawal phase, the Soviets employed SS-1 Scud long-range missiles, MiG-27 high-performance aircraft, and Backfire bombers.

The Carter and Reagan administrations funneled US$2.1 billion in military supplies to the mujaheddin; an additional US$2 billion came from Saudi Arabia, China, and the Gulf states. Under an agreement announced on 13 September 1991, the Soviet Union and the United States pledged to end all military assistance to their respective allies (the leftist government of President Najibullah in Afghanistan and a loose alliance of Islamic rebel groups based in Pakistan) by early 1992.

Defense Industry

Neither the government of Afghanistan nor the mujaheddin has more than rudimentary manufacturing capability, and both must rely on foreign suppliers.

Alliances

Afghanistan is a member of several international organizations, including the United Nations and most of its specialized agencies, the World Bank, the International Monetary Fund (IMF), the Asian Development Bank, INTELSAT, the Nonaligned Movement, the Colombo Plan, and the Group of 77.

A direct, formal Soviet role dates from the 1921 Soviet-Afghan Friendship Treaty. On 5 December 1978, the Soviet Union and Afghanistan signed a "Treaty of Friendship, Good-neighborliness, and Cooperation" to justify a military role for a "limited military contingent" in a nonaligned sovereign state. Joint announcements in Kabul and Moscow on 4 April 1980 of a signed agreement retroactively validated conditions for a "temporary stay" of Soviet units.

By the end of 1988, the Amu Darya (formerly the Oxus River), which forms the northern boundary between the Soviet Union and Afghanistan, was the scene of returning Soviet troops. The pullback was in keeping with the schedule set by the UN-negotiated Geneva Accords of 14 April 1988 under which withdrawal was to begin May 15 and to end 15 February 1989. In his December 1988 address to the UN General Assembly, Mikhail Gorbachev reaffirmed his country's commitment to the planned withdrawal, which was completed as scheduled.

Nevertheless, the Soviets left behind US$1 billion worth of weapons and continued providing military supplies to the Kabul regime. However, the Kabul regime withdrew from indefensible outposts to reinforce the major cities and key positions. Reports varied with regard to mujaheddin strikes at the departing Soviets and at Kabul itself (against American advice) and informal truce agreements between the besiegers and the besieged. Not in doubt was the ability of the Soviets to mount air strikes from bases inside the Soviet Union even after departure.

The overriding aim of the Soviet Union was to effect a withdrawal in good order and, if practicable, to leave behind a viable coalition government. Secret talks took place in December 1988 in Saudi Arabia between a Soviet team led by Moscow's ambassador to Kabul, Yuli Vorontsov, and resistance leaders, who had ruled out any thought of a post-Soviet coalition government in Kabul. (Two of the seven Peshawar resistance leaders had met earlier in Islamabad: Professor Burhanuddin Rabbani, head of Jamiat-e-Islami and leader at that time of the Alliance, and Gulbuddin Hekmatyar, who was rumored to have cultivated earlier contacts through Bonn and Vienna with the Soviets.)

The key to settlement that retained some modicum of Soviet influence lay with the field commanders, Ahmad Shah Massoud in the north, Isma'il Khan in the west, Amin Wardak in the southeast, and Abdul Haq in the east. It was significant that hardline Afghan Interior Minister Sayed Mohammad Gulabzoi had been removed from Kabul and posted to Moscow as ambassador. Massoud apparently agreed not to interfere with the Soviet departure.

Center-periphery relations have historically always been tenuous. Most commanders are unlikely to relinquish authority to any future central government regardless of its makeup, whether led entirely by the resistance or comprising some form of coalition. The more visible Peshawar-based mujaheddin leaders were scorned as being out of touch.

PDPA officials were not ready to concede defeat in the event of a total Soviet departure—and with a claimed membership of 200,000, high levels of discipline, and substantial military hardware, it might have to be taken into account. However, some observers thought it would shrink to one-tenth of its size in the wake of Soviet withdrawal. But even at a tenth of its present size, PDPA's stranglehold over the country's security, police, and military structures could make it a force to be reckoned with. Nevertheless, Soviet officials themselves openly admitted that the PDPA had no popular support.

The resistance desire for full control contrasted with the Soviet desire to safeguard its geostrategic interests. Mohammad Hassan Sharq, prime minister at the end of 1988 and officially a non-Communist, was viewed by the Soviets as a future coalition leader. Guerrilla support was thought unlikely. The continued presence of Najibullah was unacceptable, and it was thought that Soviet acquiescence would have to be courted with assurances of neutrality and cooperation.

Afghan public opinion regarding an acceptable future leader was difficult to ascertain. According to one Afghan trader, perhaps 50 percent of the public favored the return of deposed King Zahir Shah, 30 percent were for Ahmad Shah Massoud, 10 percent for Rabbani, less than 10 percent for Hekmatyar, and only 1 percent for Najibullah.

The 16 November 1988 elections in Pakistan and the subsequent appointment of Benazir Bhutto as prime minister raised questions about Pakistan's commitment to President Zia's pro-American policy on Afghanistan. Dialogues with the military, and particularly with the army's powerful ISI (Inter-Services Intelligence), through which the downed president conducted the Afghan policy, nevertheless indicated a continued flow of weapons to the guerrillas through Pakistan.

For the refugees, returning to a land with three-quarters of its 22,000 villages destroyed, the widespread threat of more than 3 million antipersonnel land mines, and the danger of being caught up in conflict, survival was the first priority.

Prince Sadruddin Aga Khan was appointed UN coordinator for Humanitarian and Economic Assistance in Afghanistan. The United Nations established monitoring teams in Kabul and elsewhere. UN Under Secretary General Diego Cordovez continued to promote a dialogue among the Afghan parties.

(For an explanation of the abbreviations and symbols used in the following section of military statistics, see the list of Abbreviations and Acronyms in each volume.)

Total Armed Forces

Active: 45,000. Terms of service: Males 15–40: conscription 2 years followed by a break of 3 years, then another 2 years.
Reserves: No formal force identified; call-up from ex-servicemen, Youth League, and tribesmen from age 20 to age 40.

ARMY: 40,000 (mostly conscripts): actual strength suspect; divisions reported to average 2,500—about quarter strength; desertion common.
5 corps HQ.
16 inf div.
3 armd bde.
5 Special Guard bde.
1 mech inf div/bde.
5 cdo bde.
1 arty bde.
Equipment:
MBT: 800: 500 T-54/-55, 300 T-62.
Light tanks: 60 PT-76.
Recce: 75 BRDM-1/-2.
AIFV: 400 BMP-1/-2.
APC: 850 BTR-40/-60/-70/-80/-152.
Towed arty: 2,000+: 76mm: M-1938, M-1942; 85mm: D-48; 100mm: M-1944; 122mm: M-30, D-30; 130mm: M-46; 152mm: D-1, D-20, M-1937 (ML-20).
MRL: 122mm: BM-21; 140mm: BM-14; 220mm: BM-22.
Mortars: 1,000+: 82mm: M-37; 107mm; 120mm: 100 M-43.
SSM: 10 Scud, 12 FROG-7 launchers.
ATGW: AT-1 Snapper, AT-3 Sagger.
RCL: 73mm: SPG-9; 82mm: B-10.
AD guns: 600+ 14.5mm; 23mm: ZU-23, 20 ZSU-23-4 SP; 37mm: M-1939; 57mm: S-60; 85mm: KS-12; 100mm: KS-19.
SAM: SA-7.

AIR FORCE: est. 5,000 (incl AD comd); 253 cbt ac, 90 armed hel.†
FGA: 9 sqn: 2 with 30 MiG-23; 7 with 80 Su-7/-17/-22.
Fighter: 7 sqn with 100 MiG-21F.
Attack helicopters: 8 sqn with 25 Mi-8, 35 Mi-17, 30 Mi-25.
Recce: 1 An-30.
Transport:
Aircraft: 1 VIP sqn with 2 Il-18D; 2 sqn with 10 An-2, 10 An-12, 20 An-26, some An-32.
Helicopters: 12 Mi-4.
Training: 25* L-39, 18* MiG-21.
Missiles: AAM: AA-2.
AD: 1 div: 2 SAM bde (each 3 bn) with 115 SA-2, 110 SA-3; 1 AD arty bde (2 bn) with 37mm, 85mm, 100mm guns; 1 radar bde (3 bn).

PARAMILITARY
Border Guard (under Army): some 3,000; 10 'bde'.
Wad (Khad) (Ministry of State Security): est. 12,000.
Tribal Militias: 60,000+.
Sarandoy (Ministry of Interior): est. 12,000.

OPPOSITION: Afghan resistance is a broad national movement. The military elements, mujaheddin fighters, comprise numerous groups affiliated to either one of the seven parties of the Peshawar-based Resistance Alliance or one of the predominantly Shi'a groups based in Iran, plus a few indep groups. It is not possible to give accurate strengths; however, of the Peshawar groups some 40,000 are reported to be active, supported by a further 120,000.
Peshawar groups: leaders' names follow strengths.
Traditionalist Moderate:
National Liberation Front (Jabhāt-Nijāt-Milli): est. 15,000. Sibghatullah Modjaddi.
National Islamic Front (Mahaz-Millin Islāmi): est. 15,000. Sayyed Amhad Gailani.
Islamic Revolutionary Movement (Harakāt-Inqilāb-Islāmi): est. 25,000. Mohammed Nabi Mohammed.
Islamic Fundamentalist:
Islamic Party (Hizbi-Islāmi-Khālis): est. 40,000. Yūnis Khālis
Islamic Party (Hizbi-Islāmi-Gulbaddin): est. 50,000. Gulbaddin Hekmatyar.
Islamic Union (Ittihād-Islāmi): est. 18,000. Abdul Rasul Sayyaf.
Islamic Society (Jamiāt Islāmi): est. 60,000. Burhanuddin Rabāni.
Iran-based:
Sazman-e-Nasr (some 50,000).
Harakat-e-Islami (20,000).
Pasdaran-e-Jehad (8,000).
Hezbollah (4,000).
Nehzat (4,000).
Shoora-e-Ittefaq (some 30,000+).
Equipment: (predominantly captured): T-34, T-55 MBT; BMP MICV, BTR-40/-60 APC; 76mm guns; 122mm D-30 how; 107mm, 122mm MRL; 82mm M-41, 120mm mor; Milan ATGW; RPG-7 RL; 12.7mm, 14.5mm, 20mm AA guns; Blowpipe, Stinger, SA-7 SAM.

Future

The story of Afghanistan's most recent civil strife is far from over. Afghan rebels, quarreling among themselves, are united in their unwillingness to include President Najibullah in talks about a future government. Najibullah's creation of a new political party, the Hezb-e-Wattan (Homeland party), in June 1990 marked a futile attempt to attract support. Confronted with economic collapse and ethnic and sectarian conflict, Afghanistan faces increased instability. The collapse of the Soviet Union may create a power vacuum in the region and encourage unpredictable initiatives from Afghanistan's neighbors, Iran and Pakistan.

JOHN G. MERRIAM

SEE ALSO: Afghanistan, Soviet Invasion of; Low-intensity Conflict: The Military Dimension.

Bibliography

Bradsher, H. S. 1985. *Afghanistan and the Soviet Union.* Durham, N.C.: Duke Univ. Press.

Farr, G. M., and J. G. Merriam, eds. 1987. *Afghan resistance: The politics of survival.* Boulder, Colo.: Westview Press.

Girardet, E. R. 1985. *Afghanistan: The Soviet war.* New York: St. Martin's Press.

Harrison, S. S. 1988. Inside the Afghan talks. *Foreign Policy* 72(fall):31–60.

Hunter, B., ed. 1991. *The statesman's year-book, 1991–92.* New York: St. Martin's Press.

Klass, R. 1988. Afghanistan: The accords. *Foreign Affairs* 5(summer):922–45.

Majrooh, N., ed. Monthly. *Afghan information centre monthly bulletin.* Peshawar, Pakistan: Afghan Information Centre.

Mark, U. 1988. *War in Afghanistan.* New York: St. Martin's Press.

U.S. Central Intelligence Agency. 1991. *The world factbook, 1991–92.* Washington, D.C.: Brassey's.

AFGHANISTAN, SOVIET INVASION OF

The December 1979 Soviet invasion of Afghanistan marked a development unparalleled in Soviet international behavior outside the Warsaw Pact since the end of World War II. The invasion signaled a dramatic and dangerous change in the Soviet approach to resolving international problems. Many countries viewed the invasion as inherent proof of an expansionist tendency in Soviet foreign policy. It shocked the West, especially the United States, which felt a sense of betrayal in light of the sustained efforts of the Carter administration to maintain a policy of detente with the USSR.

The invasion alarmed China, which perceived the Soviet action as part of an elaborate plan to encircle it, especially in light of the Soviet-backed Vietnamese 1978 invasion of Kampuchea (Cambodia). Many developing nations viewed the Soviet use of military force as an atheist assault on their wider religious interests. For the main regional actors (Pakistan, Iran, and India), the Soviet invasion seriously changed the regional balance of power, placing them in the position of having to respond to this action and to cope with its consequences. Pakistan chose to pursue active opposition to the invasion; Iran, although condemning Soviet actions, took a much lower profile. India made no public condemnation of the invasion.

This article provides a historical summary of Soviet-Afghan relations, examines some of the events leading up to the Soviet invasion of Afghanistan, presents some of the most important features of the invasion, and discusses Soviet military strategy. It concludes with comments regarding the significance of the Soviets' withdrawal from Afghanistan.

Historical Summary: Soviet-Afghan Relations

Soviet-Afghan relations followed fairly closely the phases of Soviet policy toward developing nations. Stalin avoided direct involvement and was satisfied with Afghan neutrality. Khrushchev took advantage of mutual hostility toward Pakistan to foster cooperation with the Afghan government during Mohammad Daoud's premiership and in 1955 began providing military aid to Afghanistan. It was not until Brezhnev's phase of activism in developing countries in the early-to-mid-1970s that substantial Soviet involvement in Afghanistan's internal affairs began. The seizure of power by the Marxist-Leninist People's Democratic Party of Afghanistan in April 1978 was the culmination of the increasing Soviet influence in Afghan political and military life.

Prelude to Invasion

April 1978 marks the start of a series of events that led the Soviets, in fewer than twenty months, from providing assistance to Afghanistan to mounting an invasion. Three of these events stand out: the assassination of Mir Akbar Khyber, the kidnapping and death of the U.S. ambassador Adolph ("Spike") Dubs, and the Herat Massacre.

On 17 April 1978, Mir Akbar Khyber, a former police official and a Parcham ideologue, was assassinated by unknown assailants. (Afghanistan has one political party—the People's Democratic Party of Afghanistan, or PDPA. The PDPA has two factions: the Parchami faction, which has been in power since December 1979; and members of the deposed Khalqi faction, which continues to hold some important posts in the military and the ministry of interior.) Shortly thereafter, a massive demonstration by approximately 15,000 people occurred in Kabul. On 26 April the Afghan government began to arrest Khalq and Parcham leaders. Early the next morning Afghan armed forces, some supporting the PDPA and others loyal to Prime Minister Daoud, began fighting. Approximately 1,000 people died including Daoud, his brother Naim, most of their families, and about half of the 2,000-man

Republican Guard who defended the presidential palace. By 28 April, PDPA forces had captured the palace, the Kabul airport, Radio Kabul, and the central jail. Two days later, Nur Mohammed Taraki was named head of the Military Revolutionary Command (MRC) and prime minister. His two deputy prime ministers, who would assume prominence in the following months, were Hafizullah Amin and Babrak Karmal. That same day the Soviet Union recognized the new People's Democratic Republic of Afghanistan (PDRA).

The New Government

In Taraki's initial cabinet, the Khalqi faction had eleven seats, the Parchami faction ten. The new government repeatedly denied that the PDRA was a communist party. Between April and August 1978 the government issued a series of decrees that abolished the MRC, abrogated the 1977 constitution, declared racial and ethnic equality, eliminated all pre-1973 debts and diminished payments on subsequent loans (which disrupted the rural economy of the country), and declared a land reform that met with widespread resistance from both landowners and peasants.

On 5 December 1978 the Soviet Union and Afghanistan signed a Treaty of Friendship, Good-Neighborliness, and Cooperation, which was to run for a term of twenty years. Although there were few specifics in the treaty, Article 4 contained an implicit security commitment that would be used in December 1979 to justify the Soviet invasion.

The United States was hesitant to classify the Taraki regime as communist. Thus, it followed a constructive-engagement policy toward the Taraki government until 6 May 1978, at which time the United States recognized the Democratic Republic of Afghanistan (DRA). Beginning in midsummer, other more pressing foreign policy problems confronted the United States: On 29 July 1978, riots in thirteen Iranian cities drew U.S. attention to the problems of the Pahlavi dynasty. The following month, the Camp David meetings began. During the first six months of the Taraki regime, the NATO long-term defense program, the final outline of the Strategic Arms Limitation Talks (SALT) II agreement, and the normalization of relations with the People's Republic of China were all negotiated or finalized. Up until February 1979, the United States continued to watch the situation in Kabul closely while continuing to provide Afghanistan with economic assistance.

Ambassador Dubs' Death

On 14 February 1979, the same day the U.S. embassy was temporarily seized in Teheran and a few days before the Sino-Vietnamese war began, U.S. Ambassador Dubs was kidnapped off the streets of Kabul and taken to a hotel. He and the kidnappers were subsequently killed when the Afghan police, in the presence of several Soviet advisers, stormed the hotel room where Dubs was being held.

As a result of this incident, the United States announced on 22 February that it was terminating further aid to Afghanistan and that, henceforth, U.S. interests in Kabul would be handled by a chargé d'affaires. In addition, the Peace Corps ended its twenty-year program in Afghanistan, and U.S. dependents and most of the embassy staff left the country.

The Herat Massacre

In March, the Afghan Islam resistance forces (the mujaheddin) who opposed the PDPA attacked the city of Herat. The attack, coupled with a local army mutiny, resulted in the capture of Herat and the massacre of the local Soviet advisory group, which included approximately fifty Soviet soldiers and their dependents. In reprisal, an Afghan army unit with Soviet advisers sacked the town of Kerala and killed 640 of its male inhabitants. In April 1979 the United States began a modest program to aid the mujaheddin. During that summer the Soviets provided an increase in military aid and advisers to the Afghan government.

Shortly after the Herat massacre, Amin engineered his own appointment as prime minister. Although the media continued to pay homage to Taraki, increasing power came to rest with Amin. In the following months, however, personal relations between Amin and the Soviet staff in Kabul became increasingly strained.

From September to December 1979 the military situation in Afghanistan continued to deteriorate, prompting the Soviets to decide to: (1) unseat Amin; (2) install Karmal as the leader of a new Khalq-Parcham coalition; and (3) use Soviet troops to gain time for the new regime to restore order and rebuild the Afghan army.

Invasion

The Soviets' invasion of Afghanistan was modeled after their 1968 invasion of Czechoslovakia. Both operations featured elaborate deception, subversion of an "unreliable" communist government, the introduction of airborne troops to seize key objectives in the capital, the movement of motorized rifle troops to link up with airlanded elements, and the replacement of a government with more "reliable" comrades.

On Christmas Eve 1979 the Soviets began landing elements of an airborne division and a *spetsnaz* (commando unit) at the Kabul airport. On 27 December a few hundred spetsnaz troops deployed to the Darulaman Palace outside Kabul and killed President Amin and his bodyguards. Also on the 27th, Soviet troops blew up the main telephone exchange, seized Radio Kabul, and captured most of the central government facilities in Kabul. Serious fighting in the city ended by dawn of 28 December. Karmal was proclaimed president of the Revolutionary Council, general secretary of the PDPA, and prime minister. In the following months the Karmal regime was beset with internal conflict; rather than becoming a puppet, it became a virtual Soviet prisoner with nearly every ministry openly under Soviet control. In May 1986, Karmal—a despised and ineffectual figure—was removed from office and replaced by Mohammad Najibullah, former head of the Afghan secret police, who had better relations with Moscow.

By the end of the first week of January 1980, Soviet troops in Afghanistan totaled 50,000. This number increased to approximately 85,000 by the end of March, equivalent to six Soviet divisions.

International Reaction to the Invasion

In January 1980 the United Nations General Assembly voted 104 to 18 (with 30 absences or abstentions) to "deplore the recent armed intervention in Afghanistan." And in May, although not mentioning the Soviet Union by name, the General Assembly called for "the immediate, unconditional and total withdrawal of foreign troops from Afghanistan."

The significance of the General Assembly vote was that more than two-thirds of the nonaligned nations voted against the USSR. Even some socialist states or fraternal parties either voted against (Yugoslavia) or criticized (Romania) the Soviet Union. China added the removal of Soviet troops from Afghanistan to its demands required prior to a renormalization of Sino-Soviet relations.

The U.S. reaction to the invasion was one of the strongest actions ever taken by the United States in response to a specific Soviet act. Claiming that the implications of the Soviet invasion "could pose the most serious threat to peace since the Second World War," President Carter announced six measures that affected the Soviet Union: (1) blocking the U.S. export of 17 million metric tons of grain; (2) stopping the sale of U.S. computers and high-technology equipment; (3) reducing the allowable catch of the Soviet fishing fleet in U.S. waters from 350,000 tons to 75,000 tons; (4) delaying the opening of the new Soviet consulate in New York; (5) postponing a renegotiation of the U.S.–Soviet Union cultural agreement that was under consideration; and (6) boycotting U.S. participation in the Moscow Olympics, an action later joined by 55 other countries.

The Soviets were surprised by the severity of the international reaction. They attempted through diplomatic measures to shift blame for the conflict to the United States and China and to reassure nations in the area that the USSR had no designs on their territory, resources, or interests. Soviet efforts to develop a favorable peace agreement began in February 1980, but the USSR was unsuccessful in its search for regional allies and its initial efforts to gain a favorable peace were unsuccessful.

Military Occupation and Withdrawal

Over the next nine years, Soviet troops became increasingly bogged down in a bloody occupation of Afghanistan. Soviet strategy was to hold the major centers of communication, limit infiltration, and destroy local strongholds with the minimum risk to its own forces. The use of helicopters, chemical weapons, and terror tactics, key instruments in the Soviet strategy, resulted in hundreds of thousands of Afghan casualties and forced one-third of the population into exile. According to conservative estimates, approximately 1 million of Afghanistan's 12.5 million people had been killed by the time the last Soviet troops left Afghanistan (15 February 1989) and about 5 million had fled as refugees to neighboring Pakistan or Iran. Another million had been displaced from their homes within the country. Most of the deaths were civilians; however, close to 100,000 resistance fighters were also among the dead. The Soviet emphasis on attacking the civilian population from which the mujaheddin drew support eventually led to the deployment of expensive Soviet weapon systems such as the Mi-24 (Hind) helicopter gunship to Afghanistan.

In April 1986, President Reagan ordered the U.S. Central Intelligence Agency to provide the Afghan resistance forces with Stinger antiaircraft missiles—a decision that would dramatically affect the course of the war. With these weapons, the mujaheddin were able to destroy Hind gunships, disrupt Soviet air resupply operations, and reduce the close air support provided by Soviet and Afghan air forces to Soviet ground forces. The Soviet leadership, faced with either increasing its military forces or seeing their effectiveness decline further, decided to withdraw Soviet forces from Afghanistan.

On 8 February 1988, President Gorbachev announced that Soviet troops would begin withdrawing from Afghanistan on 15 May; the withdrawal was completed on 15 February 1989.

The Geneva Accords on Afghanistan of 14 April 1988, concluded under the auspices of the United Nations between the PDPA and the government of Pakistan and jointly guaranteed by the Soviet Union and the United States, provided the overall framework for the Soviet withdrawal. Although the accords met with widespread international approval and were a diplomatic triumph for the United Nations, they did not provide for the transition to a legitimate government in Afghanistan based on the claims of Afghans to determine their own future free of outside interference. They did, however, prompt Soviet leadership to commence direct talks with the mujaheddin.

Conclusion

The war in Afghanistan was never popular with the post-Brezhnev Soviet leadership, and the growing number of Soviet dead played a significant role in shaping the Soviet public's attitude toward the war. The official Soviet Defense Ministry figure for Soviet military deaths was 13,831, justifying Gorbachev's description of Afghanistan as a "bleeding wound." This figure includes only those killed in action; a more comprehensive estimate of Soviet war deaths from all causes is 36,000.

The decision to withdraw from Afghanistan was one of the most important of the Gorbachev era. It was consistent with the overall thrust of Gorbachev's leadership as embodied in the proceedings of the 27th Congress of the Soviet Communist Party—specifically, reducing East-West tensions and eliminating unsuccessful Soviet commitments in the developing world. Indications are that the Soviets' withdrawal was a turning point in Moscow's foreign policy. These indications have been reinforced by the priority that the Soviet leadership later placed on domestic reform under the rubric of *perestroika* and *glasnost*.

JAMES B. MOTLEY

SEE ALSO: Airborne Land Forces; Chemical Warfare; Helicopter, Battlefield; Helicopter: Military Missions; Logistics, Limited War; Low-intensity Conflict: The Military Dimension; Missile, Surface-to-air; Moral Guidance; Refugees; Unconventional Warfare.

Bibliography

Collins, J. J. 1986. *The Soviet invasion of Afghanistan: A study in the use of force in Soviet foreign policy.* Lexington, Mass.: D.C. Heath.

Hammond, T. T. 1984. *Red flag over Afghanistan: The communist coup, the Soviet invasion, and the consequences.* Boulder, Colo.: Westview Press.

Oberdorfer, D. 1991. *The turn: From the cold war to a new era.* New York: Poseidon Press.

Saikal, A., and W. Maley, eds. 1989. *The Soviet withdrawal from Afghanistan.* New York: Cambridge Univ. Press.

AIR ASSAULT

An air assault is an attack against a terrain feature or other objective held by enemy forces executed by a force carried to the place of attack by aircraft. Related terms are:

Airborne/airmobile/airlift operations: An air assault is a special type of airborne, airmobile, or airlift operation characterized by an assault on enemy forces immediately after the respective dedicated troops have landed from aircraft.

Raid: An air assault is a special type of raid in which the assault forces approach through the air.

Special operations: An air assault can be a special operation if conducted in line with, or as part of, unconventional warfare operations of operational or strategic importance.

Air attack: This is an attack against an objective by aircraft in order to destroy or to incapacitate it without taking permanent or temporary control of it. An air assault can be supported by an air attack.

Characteristics as a Special Form in Modern Warfare

After gaining the capability of exploiting the third dimension for fast movements, the old idea to launch a fast surprise attack unexpectedly through the air into the objective area became feasible. This led to air attacks and, later, air assaults. An air assault is the combination of a fast surprise approach through the air with a classic assault into or against an objective of significance in order to seize it—at least temporarily. Therefore, an air assault is a special form of attack characterized by speed, surprise, and approach through the air.

An air assault is seldom an autonomous or independent operation. It is usually carried out in support of major ground attacks or offensive operations by ground, air, or naval forces. It requires the close cooperation of air and ground elements. This cooperation makes it a complex matter with specific rules and principles. An air assault requires more coordination and preparation than ground-based operations or sea maneuvers. Its intensive organizational and material efforts will be undertaken only if the value of the objective justifies an air assault and cannot be achieved by a classic attack on the ground.

The objectives of an air assault can be to:

- take enemy positions, terrain features, or other targets in the front line behind natural or artificial obstacles (e.g., field and/or permanent fortifications, rivers);
- take protected/guarded objectives in the enemy's rear such as artillery, air defense or missile sites, nuclear or chemical assets, logistic installations, command posts, key terrain, and river crossings;
- hold seized terrain or objectives until relieved by ground forces or destroy these objectives;
- form an airhead/bridgehead after the initial assault and hold it until relieved by ground forces;
- divert the enemy's attention from other sectors of the front or theater of war.

Depending on the intention and the level of employment, an air assault can be of tactical, operational, or strategic importance for the conduct of an operation, battle, campaign, or war. Principally, the following interrelations can be assumed between level, range of insertion, size of objective (including enemy strength), and assault force (Table 1).

An air assault is carried out in three major phases (see Fig. 1):

1. approach to the objective through the air and landing near, on, or inside the objective;
2. final approach or assault to defeat the enemy and to carry out destruction or denial measures;
3. relief by ground forces or extraction/withdrawal from the objective.

TABLE 1. *Interrelations Between Level, Range of Insertion, Objectives of Air Assault, and Size of Force*

LEVEL	RANGE OF INSERTION	OBJECTIVES	ASSAULT FORCE SIZE
Tactical	Frontline	Strong points	Platoon/company
		Bridges, sites	Platoon/company
		Fortifications, small	Platoon/company
		Fortifications, major	Battalion
	Enemy's rear up to 50 km (always in the area of responsibility of the tasking level)	Command post	Platoon/company
		Artillery sites	Company
		Communication sites	Squad/platoon
		EW sites	Squad/platoon
		Missile sites	Platoon/company
		Logistic installations	Company
Operational	Frontline	Bridgeheads	Battalion/brigade
		Fortifications	Company/battalion
	Enemy's rear up to 150 km (always in the area of responsibility of the tasking level giving consideration to the range of airlift assets)	Airheads	Battalion
		Major command posts	Company/battalion
		Major logistic installations	Battalion
		Airfields	Battalion/regiment
		River crossings/passes	Battalion/regiment
		Key terrain	Battalion/regiment
		Nuclear assets	Platoon/company
		Islands	Battalion/regiment/brigade
*Strategic**	Theater of war (maximum global war) (considering the range of air assets)	Government installations of strategic importance Strategic nuclear asssets, POW camps, lock-ups of hostages	Platoon to brigade-size level (depending on identified size of enemy strength in/around the objective)

* In conjunction with conventional offensive or unconventional operations.

Principles

During all phases of an air assault the assault force and the transporting elements are vulnerable to enemy reaction, especially to air defense. The high likelihood of contact with an unexpected enemy makes the air assault an extremely risky operation. This requires the consideration of special principles in preparation and execution.

Preparations for assaults are often executed in a clandestine manner in order to make the assault fast, dynamic, unpredictable, and successful. Intelligence about the objective must be gathered with priority and analyzed in detail (e.g., enemy strength and available reserves, characteristics of the objective and its environment, landing sites, obstacles, weak points, weather, air defense). Permanent intelligence watch on the objective should be established until the end of the operation.

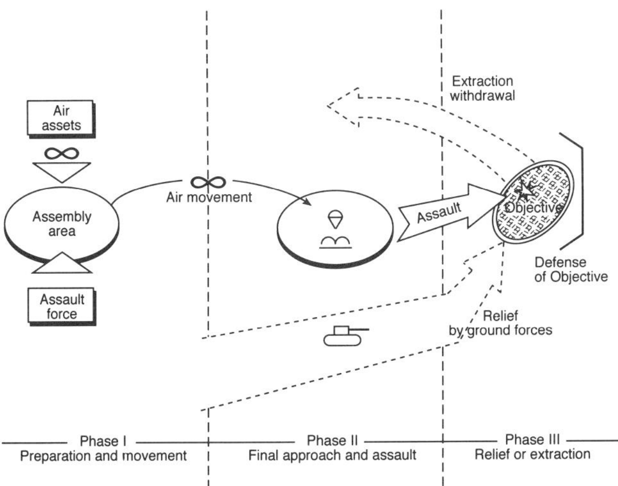

Figure 1. Major phases of an air assault.

The selection of the assault force takes into consideration

- strength of force in comparison with the enemy inside and around the objective
- own combat experience and morale
- requirement for experts such as artillery observers, ground liaison officers, engineers, intelligence experts
- appropriate air assets (one or more types of aircraft) for insertion
- logistic and medical support
- task organization, consideration of the objective and possible subobjectives.

The selection of the air assets considers the air situation, distance, weather, available air resources, qualifications of the aircrews, and available aircraft. Special emphasis is placed on support measures such as air escort, suppression of enemy air defense, electronic warfare (EW) support, and fire support from the ground or air.

The responsibility for the execution and support of the air assault should be clearly defined. All elements involved should be controlled by the same commander who is responsible for the air assault.

Operation plans for air assaults are more detailed than those for classic ground assaults and include detailed task organization down to the individual level, loading plans, ammunition and special equipment allocation, code words, alternate and emergency operations, target lists, communication rules, procedures to link up with ground forces or for exfiltration, evasion, and escape. In many armed forces, standing operating procedures (SOPs) for airborne/air assault/airmobile/airlift operations have been developed. Whenever and wherever possible air assault troops should be briefed in more detail about the assault than normal troops before an attack. In many cases it has proven worthwhile to build models of objectives and execute rehearsals before the assault.

Air Assault Forces

Suitable forces for the execution of the assault are specially trained air assault infantry; paratroopers (e.g., commando, special forces, and rangers); infantry; and mountain infantry. They might be reinforced by elements or individual members of the artillery, communications, engineer, technical, intelligence, medical, and/or reconnaissance forces, and staff personnel. The amount of preparation necessary to carry out an air assault depends on the experience and the training of the forces.

Air Support

The transport assets might be tactical transport aircraft for assault landings or parachute insertion, helicopters for assault landings, gliders (these have generally been replaced by helicopters), and ultralight aircraft (for small assault teams only).

Additional support can be provided by a ground attack by mechanized forces, air escort by interceptor aircraft, EW support for air defense suppression, attack helicopters, attack aircraft and gunships, and long-range artillery or missile fire.

Defense Against Air Assaults

Since the first air assaults in history caught most defenders by surprise and proved a successful and effective method, most defense plans incorporate measures against air assaults and air landings.

Preventive measures against air assaults include the following:

- maintenance of reserves for counterattacks
- air observers at important objectives and at key points
- surveillance of possible landing sites
- allocation of air defense assets for area defense
- combat air patrols over key terrain or threatened areas
- electronic intelligence watch on enemy airborne forces and their air assets in the depth of the enemy area.

When an air assault is undertaken and in process, the defenders' air assets are employed to counter the transport and support elements in the air. Quick-reaction forces are used to attack the ground elements before or just after they have taken the objective, because air-landed assault troops are most vulnerable immediately after landing and debarkation.

History

In military history, the idea of air assault was born long before appropriate air assets were available. When Napoleon was massing his barges at Boulogne, it was quite seriously suggested that he should use balloons to carry his assault troops, or at least some of them, across the channel. One idea was for 2,500 balloons, each carrying four men, to be launched before the invasion by sea and to land in England a few hours in advance of the main body to cause confusion, if not complete surrender. The operation could not be carried out due to the lack of balloons, and the whole invasion was canceled because of other politico-military events on the continent.

Toward the end of World War I, U.S. general William Mitchell proposed a large-scale air assault behind the German front by the 1st U.S. Infantry Division to take the fortification of Metz. The plan was not executed because it was forestalled by the Armistice.

After the First World War, the development of mobile and mechanized warfare in Russia, Germany, and other nations was accompanied by the creation of parachute and glider formations, mainly to carry out air assaults. The first successful trials were executed in France, Poland, Germany, Italy, Japan, and the Soviet Union before the outbreak of World War II.

Along with the new tactics and operation of mechanized warfare, the Germans were the first to employ airborne assault forces in northern and western Europe. They did so with great surprise, shock to the defenders, and success for their own strategic intentions.

The circumstances under which the first operations were carried out gained the fascination of the public and the press. Other nations, especially those who lost the battles, copied the air assault posture and redeveloped it for their own purposes. These types of operations remain an extraordinary issue for the media and public whenever they occur.

The initial and most shocking air assault was launched in May 1940 against Belgium's modern fortification of Eben Emael by a glider-borne force of 100 men. Outnumbered six to one by the forces deployed around and inside the fort, the paratroopers proved able to blind and destroy part of the artillery systems. Within 48 hours the air assault force was reinforced by ground forces, and the commander of the fort—caught by surprise—agreed to surrender. The fall of Eben Emael was a shock to the Belgian army, which soon surrendered to the broad German ground attack.

Other major airborne attacks during the Second World War, such as those on Rotterdam, Corinth, Crete, Sicily,

Normandy, Arnhem, and others in Southeast Asia, were combinations of air assaults and air landings. The heavy losses among the paratroopers and glider forces during the air assaults on Crete in 1941 clearly showed the risks inherent in airborne/air assault operations, especially if the assault is launched against a more-or-less prepared enemy on the ground. Therefore, the principle was established that air assault directly into the enemy should be avoided wherever possible and that, instead, airborne forces should be inserted behind the enemy lines into areas not controlled by major forces. If, however, it is impossible to avoid launching an air assault, the enemy must be totally suppressed during the landing and advance-to-attack phases.

After World War II, nearly all nations activated airborne, air assault, commando, and infantry units that were trained to execute air assaults. During this period forces of the colonial powers carried out air assaults against indigenous forces and so-called liberation armies.

During the Korean War (1950–53), the French Indochina War (1945–54), and the Arab-Israeli Wars (1956 and 1967), air assault operations were carried out by parachute insertion. During the Vietnam War (1965–73), the Israeli October War (1973), and the Rhodesian War (1968–79), helicopters were used for insertion of air assault forces. The tactics on the ground remained unchanged.

Two of these operations received wide publicity. One was an air assault launched to free U.S. prisoners of war from a camp near Hanoi in 1970 (Schemmer 1976). The other was an operation to free U.S. hostages held by Irani revolutionary guards in 1980 (Beckwith and Knox 1983). Both operations failed; the first, because the POWs had been moved to another camp, the latter because of deficiencies in air transport capabilities and aircrew skills. As a consequence, various improvements, especially in the United States, but also in other armed forces, were made that have enhanced the capability for air assaults.

The Israeli air assault against Entebbe, Uganda, in 1976 to free Israeli hostages in the hands of international terrorists proved the advantages of air assaults if the basic principles are considered and if surprise can be maintained until the final assault.

Soviet special forces and airborne forces executed various air assaults in Afghanistan.

Regardless of the difficulties and high risks involved, air assaults remain tactical, operational, and strategic (unconventional) warfare options for many armed forces today.

Major powers like the United States, the former USSR, the United Kingdom, France, Poland, India, Pakistan, Brazil, and Korea maintain major units whose elements are primarily dedicated to carry out air assaults or airborne operations.

The United States maintains ranger and airborne units including two airborne/airmobile divisions and one ranger regiment. Nearly all of the U.S. Marines combat units can be employed in air assault missions by helicopter.

In the former Soviet Union, each division had a motorized rifle battalion, specially trained for tactical air assaults, and each army had a motorized rifle regiment for executing tactical air assaults. At front level, air assault brigades consisting of air-mechanized parachute battalions and additional combat support were envisaged for conducting air assaults of operational importance. For strategic purposes, elements of eight Soviet airborne divisions and other special forces brigades (*Spetsnaz*) were capable of making air assaults. The composition of these forces varied.

Other countries have developed similar air assault concepts tailored to their tactical, operational, and strategic requirements. Wherever suitable they are already implemented in the war plans. NATO, in particular (when the Warsaw Pact was intact) expected various air assaults on tactical, operational, and strategic levels by Warsaw Pact airborne forces. This threat led to the development of rear area defense concepts and the employment of major combat formations in the rear echelons.

Air assault forces also have been identified in nearly all of the smaller developing countries. Their capabilities seem to be limited to only independent companies or battalions due to a shortage of air assets and limited strength.

Future Prospects

In the future, the air assault option will continue to play an important role for crisis management. Air assault elements might belong to intervention forces or to rapid deployment forces. Air assault options also might become part of Western defense strategy to threaten the potential aggressor's rear areas and force him to commit major forces to his own rear areas, thus preventing their use in frontline assaults. Small assault forces will be inserted by parachute or ultralight aircraft; major formations are likely to be inserted by landing helicopters or aircraft.

Air assault will not be limited to major conflicts, but also might be executed during low-intensity conflicts as well as against terrorists and criminal organizations. For the latter purpose, some nations have already formed airmobile police reaction forces.

FRIEDRICH K. JESCHONNEK

SEE ALSO: Airborne Land Forces; Army Aviation; Crisis Management; Helicopter; Special Operations; Special Operations Forces.

Bibliography

Beckwith, C. E., and D. Knox. 1983. *Delta Force*. San Diego, New York, London: Harcourt-Brace-Jovanovich.

Gavin, J. 1963. *War and peace in the space age*. New York: Harper and Row.

Merglen, A. 1968. *Histoire et avenir des troupes aéroportées*. Grenoble: Arthaud.

Morzik, F. 1965. *German air force airlift operations*. New York: Amo Papers.

Morzek, J. 1972. *The fall of Eben Emael.* New York, London: Hyde.
Otway, B. H., trans. 1951. *Airborne forces.* London: War Office.
Schemmer, B. F. 1976. *The raid.* New York, London: Harper and Row.
Tugwell, M. A. J. 1971. *Airborne to battle.* London: Kimber.
Weeks, J. 1976. *Airborne equipment: A history of its development.* Newton Abbott, UK: David and Charles.
———. 1982. *The airborne soldier.* Poole, Dorset: Blandford Press.

AIR INTERDICTION

Among the many missions of airpower, with their inevitably overlapping roles, the air interdiction mission is very important, in spite of debates and controversies related to its effectiveness in the past. As the term implies, *air interdiction* involves efforts by an air force to deny an enemy the material and human resources needed to carry on the war. Air interdiction uses air combat operations to attack material and human resources at the source, en route to the battlefield, and in assembly areas. *Air interdiction*, therefore, may be defined as the airpower mission that involves systematic air attack on the enemy's logistics organization, route network, and forces and resources that are being moved, with the purpose of destroying, restricting, disrupting, and/or delaying his military potential (men and materiel) before it can be brought to bear effectively against friendly forces.

Interdiction strikes may span the distance from close to the immediate battlefield to areas well inside the enemy's heartland. In the past some strikes have also extended into third countries. The objective is to isolate the military potential of the enemy from the battlefield.

Varying Definition of Air Interdiction

The above narrow definition of *air interdiction* is generally accepted by the air forces and airpower experts of the United States and most Western countries. Other Western air force theorists, officers, and scholars, however, adhere to a broader, more inclusive definition that is espoused in some developing nations, including the author's native India. As this article will demonstrate, the primary difference involves where the line is drawn between the intellectual and doctrinal categories of "air interdiction" and "strategic bombing." Much of this debate about definitions results from the fact that air attack missions may achieve both strategic bombing and air interdiction objectives, and because the distinctions between these types of attack are not well defined, somewhat subjective, and dependent upon the assumptions made.

The traditional view of air interdiction since World War II maintained a distinction between "strategic" and "tactical" operations in air interdiction missions. Various criteria, singly or in combination, were employed to make this distinction. Of these, the most notable has been the criterion of target location. Tactical interdiction by definition was confined to areas and targets close to the battlefield. Strategic interdiction, involving much of the strategic bombing offensive, meant penetration deeper into hostile territory. This distinction arose from two factors: the delivery vehicle with its concomitant classification as strategic or tactical, and the nature of the target. Fighter and fighter-bomber aircraft in World War II (and for more than a decade later) possessed limited weapon payload and range, especially for a strike mission against surface targets. Even in the Korean War, U.S. fighter-bombers (F-51, F-80, and F-84) were capable of carrying average weapon loads of 200 to 450 kilograms per aircraft per sortie. The weapons were all unguided. Whenever heavier bombloads were required, even in the battle zone, medium and heavy bombers (B-26 and B-29) were used. Otherwise, traditionally, interdiction with bombers came to be associated with strategic operations, and tactical interdiction implied the use of fighters and fighter-bombers. This in turn created the interrelationship of the target criteria with interdiction missions. The type of delivery vehicle, the quality and quantity of its weapon load, and the implied effects of weapon delivery accuracies created the distinction based on target criteria. Vehicles, troops, supplies, and lines of communications were targets that could be engaged with success by fighter-bombers due to the inherent superiority of these aircraft over bombers of the day in achieving the pinpoint accuracy required against such targets. Since movement of troops and logistics support elements was not as rapid as today, the important clusters of maneuver forces and logistics support were fairly close to the battlefield. Such factors resulted in the introduction of terms and concepts like *short-range* interdiction being associated with tactical interdiction by tactical combat airpower.

The enemy's industrial potential and other sources of war-making, on the other hand, could be attacked only with the long-range bomber, the premier air vehicle for strategic air offensive. Strategic air offensive, in turn, included two types of missions, one directed against the will of the enemy nation and the other against its means and resources for waging war. The former implied operations against population centers, economic targets, and the like, and thus remained in the category of strategic air offensive. Attacks on industrial targets like oil refineries, armaments factories, logistics infrastructures, and military installations could be considered as falling under the category of air interdiction.

Transportation networks and systems (routes, bridges, marshaling yards, rolling stock, etc.) are central to interdiction operations and can be tactical or strategic targets. Transportation targets illustrate the overlapping nature of interdiction missions. Target criteria, therefore, cannot be used as an unqualified factor for classification of interdiction missions. Similarly, the distinction between strategic and tactical interdiction based on the air vehicle criteria is not always reliable. In World War II (Operations Strangle and Overlord), Korea, and Vietnam, heavy and medium bombers were employed in the tactical interdiction role. On the other hand, because of the increasing capabilities of fighter-bombers, the air interdiction campaign in North Vietnam, which involved 41,653 sorties (mostly by fighter-bombers such as the F-4s, F-105s, and F-111s) and dropped 155,548 tons of bombs during Operation Linebacker between May and October 1972, would have been classified as purely strategic three decades earlier. Such dichotomies have also led to the emergence of terms like *deep* interdiction, leaving *shallow* or *short-range* interdiction as a tactical mission. The semantic complexities of interdiction missions also include terms like *long-term* and *short-term,* indicative of the relationship of the mission to the time taken for the results to demonstrate their effectiveness.

Historical Perspective

It was only in World War II that air interdiction started being recognized as a distinct mission of airpower. Although significant refinement of the concept and its application occurred during the campaigns in North Africa, operations in Italy and France during 1943 and 1944 placed air interdiction in its proper perspective. At the same time, significant air interdiction was undertaken under the Allied strategic bombing offensive against the Axis powers, especially in the campaign against POL (petroleum, oil, and lubricant) targets.

Aviation Industry and POL

During World War II, a concerted air interdiction campaign under the generic term *strategic bombing* was conducted by the Allies against aircraft industry and POL targets both in Germany (including Austria, Sudetenland, West Poland, Alsace-Lorraine, and prewar Germany) and in Japan. During the "Big Week" of 20–26 February 1944, the Allies carried out coordinated strikes against Germany's aircraft and antiaircraft weapons factories and assembly plants. The Luftwaffe attempted to meet the challenge, but it lost 692 airplanes in the air alone, followed by another 2,442 fighters lost in action and 1,500 to accidents and other causes in the following three months. While the industry recovered remarkably quickly, the loss of trained pilots was irreparable. The Allies' air superiority was thereafter not seriously challenged. In a concentrated air interdiction campaign, the Allies' airpower delivered a total of 207,305 tons of bombs against German POL targets between May 1944 and May 1945. This represented 14 percent of the total tonnage dropped during the strategic bombing offensive. The object of the initial phase of this campaign was to reduce drastically POL available to the German armed forces and thereby impose severe restrictions on operations by those forces, especially armored and mechanized forces, in the context of the impending landing in Europe by the Allies. The bombing reduced the German aviation fuel output (among other items) to 12 percent of the average pre-POL campaign production. The impact of the aircraft and POL interdiction campaign had such a deleterious effect on the fighting ability of the German armed forces that Germany had to concede air superiority to the Allies over Europe, and Reichminister Albert Speer affirmed that the POL attacks of 1944 essentially decided the outcome of the war.

In the Pacific theater, U.S. Army air forces undertook a similar interdiction campaign against the Japanese POL systems during May–August 1945, when 10,613 tons of bombs were dropped against thirteen POL plants. Oil stocks amounting to 470,000 barrels and storage capacity of 7.5 million barrels were destroyed. The large scale of the air effort in both POL campaigns (68,790 sorties) was necessitated by the problems of accurate bombing from high altitudes. In fact, only a little over 2 percent of the bombs dropped actually hit POL plant structures. Better accuracy would have led to greater effectiveness with less effort.

Operation Strangle

The first full-scale, consciously planned air interdiction campaign of World War II was conducted under Operation Strangle. In January 1944, Allied forces conducted a successful, surprise amphibious landing at Anzio. The U.S. VI Corps failed to move quickly inland and the Germans were able to move up reinforcements and pin down the U.S. forces. To alleviate this enemy pressure, and force a German withdrawal by denying the Germans essential supplies, Allied air forces began Operation Strangle on 15 March. This was a two-month air interdiction campaign conducted by the air force against the enemy's supply and transportation system in northern and central Italy. Flying more than 50,000 sorties and dropping some 26,000 tons of bombs, these air forces destroyed or damaged large numbers of Italian rail, road, and port facilities. Despite these bombing attacks, the German armies continued to receive sufficient supplies and war materiel to keep pressing the U.S. VI Corps on the beaches at Anzio and the U.S. Fifth Army farther south near Cassino. By itself, the interdiction of supplies failed to achieve the objective since the enemy transportation system had a capacity of nearly 90,000 tons per day, and its military requirement—without major ground combat action—did not exceed 5,000 tons per day. The stocks of some critical items, such as fuel and ammunition, remained fairly level or actually increased during the pure interdiction phase when no ground offensive was launched. Among major factors responsible for the failure of the interdiction campaign were the redundant capacity of the enemy's transport network, German recuperative capabilities, periods of bad weather that hampered air operations, and the absence of night attack capability.

By mid-May, the Allies were sufficiently reinforced and resupplied to effect a breakout on the Cassino front, led by the British Eighth Army and the U.S. Fifth Army, pushing up from south of Rome (this was called Operation Diadem). When the Allied ground offensive started on 11 May 1944, tangible effects of the interdiction became evident. Within three weeks the German army was pushed back 300 kilometers (186 mi.) sustaining 30 percent casualties. During this stage, the interdiction campaign contributed immeasurably to the defeat of the German army by denying it the supplies and the tactical mobility that were so essential. Aggressive ground action forced the enemy to expend men and materiel in battle at a faster rate than they could be replaced. At the same time, systematic interdiction strikes limited German capacity for force redeployment, especially in time-critical situations. Thus air interdiction was a decisive success in Operation Diadem because it was coordinated with a ground offensive.

Allied Invasion of Europe

The air interdiction campaign to support the Allies' invasion of Europe, in the context of the "strategic" bombing of military industrial and POL target systems, included the preparatory phase and the operations on D-Day (6 June 1944) and afterward. The object of the initial and preparatory phase was to reduce the supplies available to the German military forces so drastically that they would be unable to contain a landing by the Allies, and severely limit the possibility and scope of a German counteroffensive. Specifically, it was planned to divert the total air effort, including strategic bombers, for the last three months before the invasion, to the destruction of the transportation system in northern France. A detailed interdiction plan was drawn up, covering about 80 targets along the Seine and Loire rivers and in the Orléans Gap spread out in an arc 150 to 250 kilometers (93–155 mi.) from the beachhead. Access to bridges on the rivers and the railway line through Orléans was vital for German reserves to move up against the Allies' landings.

These targets were attacked from March 1944 onward by the Royal Air Force Second Tactical Air Force and the U.S. Ninth Air Force, joined by the strategic bombing forces of the Allies. Roads, bridges, tunnels, vehicles, railway networks, rolling stock, and all possible transportation targets were attacked with persistent frequency day and night. All air bases in France within a 200-kilometer (124-mi.) radius from the assault beaches in Normandy were neutralized. The bridges over the Loire and Seine rivers were destroyed, isolating the beachhead. This was one of the most elaborate and interconnected road and railway networks in the world, where an average of 275 trains moved per day in northeast France and Belgium during the first quarter of 1944. The average movement dropped to 210 by 30 April and came down to an average of 125 per day by mid-May 1944, a week before D-Day. The end result was that during the first four weeks after D-Day, the Germans were able to dispatch to the Normandy bridgehead an average of only four troop trains per day, many of them failing to reach their destination. By 6 June Normandy and Brittany were in effect isolated from the remainder of France. In all, some 4 million tons of bombs had been dropped in the interdiction campaign.

As part of Operation Overlord, on D-Day, 6 June, U.S. Army air forces sent 8,772 aircraft and the Royal Air Force launched another 4,115 aircraft over France on a vast variety of missions, including interdiction. The Allies' air forces dominated the skies, and by the end of the day 150,000 Allied troops had landed on European soil. Less than a week after D-Day, Field Marshal Erwin Rommel recorded:

> Our operations in Normandy are tremendously hampered, and in some places even rendered impossible, by the following factors: the immensely powerful, at times overwhelming, superiority of the enemy air force. As I and the officers of my staff have repeatedly experienced . . . the enemy has total command of the air over the battle area up to a point some 60 miles (96 km) behind the front. During the day, practically our entire traffic—on roads, tracks, and in open country—is pinned down by powerful fighter-bombers and bomber formations, with the result that the movement of our troops on the battlefield is almost completely paralysed, while the enemy can manoeuvre freely. (Liddell Hart 1953, pp. 476–77)

Because of the air interdiction campaign before and during Operation Overlord, the Germans were unable to move sufficient troops to overwhelm the Allies' landings. The reserves that did arrive were inadequate or weakened, and sufficient equipment to refit and prepare them for battle was not available. Field Marshal Karl Von Rundstedt, Commander of the German Western Front, was to later state his assessment of the causes of German collapse in the face of the Allies' invasion of Europe as:

> It was all a question of air force, air force and again air force. The main difficulties that arose for us at the time of the invasion were the systematic preparations by your air force; the smashing of the main lines of communications, particularly the railway junctions. We had prepared for various eventualities[;] . . . that all came to nothing or was rendered impossible by the destruction of railway communications, railway stations, etc. The second thing was the attack on the roads, on marching columns, etc., so that it was impossible to move anyone at all by day, whether a column or an individual, that is to say, carry fuel or ammunition. That also meant that the bringing up of the armoured divisions was also

> out of the question, quite impossible. And the third thing was this carpet bombing. (Tedder 1966, p. 113)

During the period June 1944–May 1945 over 51 percent of the Allied tactical air effort, amounting to 249,200 sorties, was devoted to air interdiction. The experiences of World War II and lessons learned from them led to development of the following concepts of air interdiction (Momyer 1986):

1. Strike the source of war materiel.
2. Concentrate the attacks against the weak elements of the logistical system.
3. Continually attack, night and day, the major lines of communication supporting the army in the field.
4. Inflict heavy losses on enemy logistics and forces before they approach the battlefield where the difficulty to successful interdiction is greatest.
5. Keep continuous ground pressure on the enemy to force him to consume large quantities of logistics.

Korea

During the first year of the war in Korea, which started on 25 June 1950, air interdiction was claimed to have provided significant payoffs. While some modest delays and shortages may have been achieved through supply interdiction, however, these appear to have been mainly the result of force interdiction. In the achievement of these results the factor of surprise was dominant: the North Korean army was totally unprepared for (and did not appreciate the significance of) air strikes and their effects. Later in the war when the situation had stabilized and the United Nations (UN) forces were on the defensive, supply interdiction was the objective of several extended campaigns: Operations Strangle I and II, and Saturate. This was probably the most adverse battle environment for a successful interdiction campaign. Supplies continued to flow despite the 220,168 interdiction sorties flown between June 1950 and July 1953 by the U.S. Far East Air Force alone, expending 218,448 tons of bombs, 3,815 tons of napalm, 97,885 rockets, and over 73 million rounds of ammunition. Despite the magnitude of the UN air effort, which included 87,552 interdiction sorties by the U.S. Far East Air Force alone (resulting in over 19,000 rail cuts and the destruction of 34,211 vehicles, 276 locomotives, and 3,820 rail cars), the communists were able to supply their frontline troops and even build logistics dumps in the forward areas.

During the war as a whole, 55 percent of U.S. Far East Air Force (and nearly 50% of U.S. Navy and Marine Corps) air effort was devoted to air interdiction. By far the largest fraction of the effort was aimed at limiting or cutting off enemy supply movement. Supply interdiction sorties were flown in every phase of the war and outnumbered force interdiction sorties in every phase except possibly the first. The overall effectiveness of supply interdiction in Korea, however, must, at best, be regarded as doubtful. Communist forces were not only able to meet their daily consumption needs, but also built up substantial stocks in forward areas. In July 1951, before the beginning of Strangle II and Saturate, communist troops fired only 8,000 artillery and mortar rounds. In May 1952, after ten months of supply interdiction, they were able to fire over 102,000 rounds.

Although each of the interdiction campaigns met with initial success, the successes were of a transient nature. The North Korean rail and road transport network was the main target. The flexibility of the enemy's logistics system, the ability of the enemy to effect rapid repairs, and the extremely low supply requirements resulting from the low scale of ground combat activity and the low supply demands of communist troops militated against any tangible or lasting success.

The war in Korea clearly established that, for air interdiction to be successful:

1. the best time was when the ground situation was fluid, fighting intensity was high, and the enemy's logistic needs, therefore, were high;
2. operations had to be well planned and persistently sustained; and
3. all-weather, day-and-night air interdiction capabilities were necessary to apply continual pressure.

War in Vietnam

The air interdiction campaign in Southeast Asia commenced in the spring of 1965 across the lower regions of North Vietnam. In 1967 the weight of effort shifted farther north into the North Vietnamese heartland, and continued until 1 November 1968 when bombing of North Vietnam was halted. As a result of a contingent agreement with North Vietnam prohibiting movement of men and materiel directly through the demilitarized zone, attention shifted to what came to be known as the Ho Chi Minh Trail.

The U.S. interdiction campaign against the trail needs to be seen in the context of three factors. First, the mountainous jungle terrain placed constraints on supply movement, but it also provided cover from observation, detection, and attack. Second, the cyclic monsoon weather forced a seasonal pattern of resupply, with the communists concentrating their logistics effort during the comparatively dry periods forcing interdiction response accordingly. The third factor was the route structure itself: the network was operated and maintained by 40,000 to 50,000 personnel organized on geographical area units, movements taking place mostly at night and the network being defended by 600 to 700 antiaircraft guns.

The United States used modern technology to devise and deploy seismic, acoustic, and electronic sensors delivered by fighter aircraft alongside known routes. Sensor inputs were received by an orbiting aircraft and relayed to an infiltration surveillance center where they were analyzed and translated into truck movements. The information was used on a real-time basis to analyze trends; compute enemy input and throughput supply tonnages; and assist in location of truck parks, storage areas, and new routes so that air interdiction strikes could be planned effectively. At the same time specialized systems for night interdiction attacks with advanced gunships were developed to enable the interdiction campaign to continue around the clock.

There was a close relationship between trail interdiction and the air war against North Vietnam (which included interdiction among its objectives). The two operations competed for aircraft resources, the perennial problem of interdiction planners. The scale of air effort against the trail may be gauged by the average fighter-bomber sorties flown per day against it: during 1966–67, there were 125 sorties daily; this increased over 1968–69 to 220 sorties, falling to 175 sorties per day in 1970–71. Sorties during the peak interdiction seasons (November–April) were higher. From 1966 through 1971, U.S. fighter-bombers flew a total of 388,000 interdiction sorties against the trail.

The statistics might suggest that the interdiction campaign was very effective, but the communist invasion of South Vietnam in 1972 raised doubts about the overall effectiveness of the interdiction effort in Southeast Asia. There are conflicting and controversial assessments. While the aggregate supply tonnage available to communist forces may have been adequate for an offensive, its mobility and distribution no doubt came under heavy strain, which in turn contributed in large measure to the blunting of communist offensives. While no firm quantitative conclusion on the viability of interdiction in Southeast Asia can be drawn, the resemblance to Operation Strangle in Italy (World War II) is notable. German aggregate supply tonnage during Strangle was sufficient for operations, although constrained after Allies' ground offensive; the Allies' interdiction had the primary effect of seriously curtailing mobility of men and materiel for timely repositioning. Mobility denial, even more than supply denial, had been the key to the Allies' success. Historical evidence of other campaigns reinforces the view that by itself supply denial has seldom, if ever, proved to be decisive.

High-Technology Environment

The war in Vietnam witnessed the introduction of precision-guided munitions and use of electronic warfare (EW) on a significant scale. In particular, surface-to-air missiles integrated into an effective air defense system on the one hand, and laser-guided bombs on the other, were to prove their efficacy. A combination of precision-guided munitions and electronic warfare became a necessity to carry out air interdiction in the more sophisticated air defense environment. This in turn led to changes in tactics, placing a higher premium on the precision of a smaller strike force with unprecedented weapon delivery accuracies. At the same time, the strike force had to be heavily supported by missions enhancing its survivability in the new and more lethal air defense environment. In the high-risk environment over North Vietnam, a typical operation required a sixteen-aircraft strike force to be supported by a force of 250 aircraft on a variety of missions including EW, defense suppression, air refueling, and combat air patrols. Air interdiction became highly structured and precisely timed as the ratio of the combat support forces to the attack force increased dramatically in response to the lethality of the air defense environment. The role of unmanned aircraft (drones and remotely piloted vehicles) increased significantly. The overriding need for air superiority, both in time and space, which had been a prerequisite of earlier air interdiction campaigns, was reinforced.

Israeli air operations against Syrian forces in the Bekaa Valley in June 1982 demonstrated the complexities and sophistication of high-technology warfare. Concerted and coordinated operations to gain air superiority were rapidly followed by air interdiction, which prevented the 3d Syrian Armored Division from being brought to bear at the battlefield in time to reinforce the frontline forces. As much as attainment of air superiority made air interdiction feasible, air interdiction itself had a profound impact on the ground battle, opening up opportunitites for Israeli success beyond original conceptions. A vast range of technologies, combat support systems (including reconnaissance, surveillance, target acquisition, and EW), and missions were used to increase the effectiveness and survivability of air interdiction strike forces. The operation was also a typical example of force and mobility interdiction highlighting the payoffs in interdiction of mechanized maneuver forces.

Air Interdiction Missions

By its very definition and the nature of operations involved in air interdiction, this mission of airpower spans tactical and strategic roles, and overlaps other classical airpower missions. (For example, counterair operations involving air-to-ground strikes to neutralize airfields/aircraft on the ground could be also classified as air interdiction.) In terms of level of warfare, therefore, air interdiction as a component of operations belongs more appropriately to the operational level of war.

Air interdiction missions are best classified according to objectives, rather than to other criteria such as target or air vehicle. A nation's war-making potential and capabilities rest on a triad of its industrial capability, the logistics organization and network, and the combat forces with their implied capabilities in terms of mobility and firepower. These three elements present varying targeting problems that demand different solutions although the overall aim in each case would remain unchanged—that is, to degrade the enemy's military capability for successful prosecution of war. Air interdiction missions, therefore, can be classified by objectives under three heads: *force* interdiction, that is, mobility interdiction; *supply* or logistics interdiction; and *source*, including industrial, interdiction.

Force Interdiction

Force interdiction is directed against enemy maneuver units including armored and soft vehicles and tracked and wheeled vehicles. Interdiction of enemy forces might be directed against units in assembly areas, while moving en route, or when stationary between moves.

Greater payoffs in force interdiction are seen at ever-increasing distances in future wars because of the increased mobility of forces and support formations, which also increases their vulnerability to air interdiction. The U.S. doctrine called AirLand Battle 2000 and the NATO concept of FOFA (Follow-on Forces Attack) are structured on this premise. Taking into account the projected Soviet capability for mobility by the turn of the century, U.S. doctrine envisioned force interdiction as much as 400 to 450 kilometers (248–79 mi.) away from the forward line of battle. From these distances, second-echelon division-size Soviet forces would have been able to deploy for engagement in the battle zone within 16 to 48 hours. Not many armies in the world may be able to achieve such mobility in the foreseeable future. The AirLand Battle 2000 concept does emphasize the changing nature of air interdiction needs in the future. Interdiction, to be successful in such scenarios, will need to rely heavily on accurate and up-to-date intelligence and target acquisition. Air interdiction based on long-range sensors, advanced information management systems, reliable communications, and appropriate weapons to disrupt the buildup of enemy frontline strength through "surgical" air interdiction can alter the force ratios significantly.

Supply Interdiction

Supply interdiction is concerned with the interdiction of logistics networks, organizations, and means. Supply interdiction incorporates two facets of logistics support: the route structure and transport capabilities. Route structure relates to fixed assets like roads, railway lines and marshaling yards, bridges, tunnels and other chokepoints, and fixed sources of power such as railway electric power grids. Transport capabilities cover the supplies themselves and the means of transporting them, such as vehicles and their support equipment.

Greater mechanization and mobility of land forces place greater demand on logistics support, and enhanced firepower has in practice generated consumption and increasing demands on resupply. For example, in the Korean War, a communist division (10,000 men) required 48 tons of supplies per day. An American division (16,000 men), on the other hand, had to be resupplied at a rate of 500 tons per day. With increasing demand for resupply, the requirement of logistics support for the transportation system itself increases, multiplying the total requirement of supplies needing movement. In the past a great deal of resupply took place under the comparative security of darkness or bad weather, but with the development of advanced sensors like low-light television, infrared, and thermal imagery, significant movements at night or bad weather are becoming more and more difficult to conceal and increasingly vulnerable to air attacks.

Source Interdiction

Source interdiction covers a wider field, and a large number of targets could be classified as objectives in this category. Of these, oil is perhaps the most important. It is in the area of source interdiction that the duration of war plays an important role, since, in many cases, more time and greater effort become necessary before significant results are achieved. During World War II these missions came under the generic term of *strategic bombing* and their efficacy later came under serious scrutiny and question. In subsequent conflicts, source interdiction has been applied with greater selectivity. An extreme example is the Israeli air strike against Iraq's Osirak nuclear facility in June 1981. Aerial attacks on economic targets in the Iran-Iraq war (1980–88) have also played a significant role in shaping the course of war and war-making capabilities.

Past experience in interdiction campaigns indicates that mobility interdiction provides greater payoffs than supply interdiction. Mobility of ground forces, however, may rest either on mechanized capability as in the case of modern armies, or be the type inherently associated with guerrilla-type forces. Air interdiction payoffs with the latter would be low. Physical vulnerability of mechanized forces to interdiction attacks is enhanced if the mechanized elements can be detected and attacked efficiently. This implies availability of suitable weapons with the interdictor as well as a night (and, if possible, all-weather) interdiction capability. Terrain and weather, with implied impact on mobility, would naturally affect interdiction strategy and results.

Time and timing are extremely important for the success of an interdiction campaign. The operational situation in a ground war is favorable for interdiction when the enemy has an urgent need for movement for deployment or supply, is highly mechanized, and relies mainly on vehicular movement. The same is true if the enemy is a naturally high consumer with few supplies forward when interdiction begins. An interdiction campaign, therefore, calls for integrated mutually supportive air and ground operations. Such operations would be easier to plan for and achieve when the interdicting side is strong and has the initiative both in the air and on the ground.

Air interdiction needs to be seen in the context of the overall plans for cost-effective application of airpower. Factors like air defense environment and defense suppression have to be noted. Although a great deal will depend on specific operational scenarios, generally the air defense environment around interdiction targets would tend to be less lethal and dense than around combat elements already deployed or in contact. This factor should help keep the interdictor's own attrition low, permitting generation of high sortie rates. This is borne out by historical evidence. During World War II, the First Tactical Air Force suffered an attrition rate of 0.65 aircraft lost per hundred sorties in the last seven months of the war. U.S. Air Force known losses in the interdiction campaign against the Ho Chi Minh Trail averaged 0.05 aircraft lost per hundred sorties flown from January 1970 through April 1971. Against these figures, the attrition during close air support missions has revolved around a figure of four aircraft lost per hundred sorties in most wars for which data are available.

Almost all successful air interdiction campaigns are characterized by the interdictor possessing air superiority. There are few instances in which interdiction has been attempted without it. This may explain Egypt's hesitancy in 1973 and Syria's lack of attempt at interdicting during the Israeli thrust into Lebanon in 1982. The increasing emphasis on air superiority, both in doctrine and in the means of achieving it, would only help to emphasize its impact on other air operations, especially air interdiction. This was certainly the case in the 1991 Persian Gulf War where the forces of the United Nations quickly established air superiority, were almost never challenged by Iraq's air force, and lost very few planes to ground fire.

Future

The 1991 Gulf War and the extraordinary developments in military technology and the world political and military situation suggest that the concept and definition of air interdiction will encroach further into the airpower missions once defined as strategic bombing. Since the danger of global nuclear war has been dramatically reduced with the breakup of the Soviet Union and the apparent end to the cold war, it is highly likely that war planning will focus primarily on regional and local conflicts. In these cases, as in the Gulf War, both fighter and bomber aircraft can reach all targets; both aircraft types can attack targets in the enemy's homeland and disrupt supplies and troops heading to the battlefield area. Definitions and concepts of air interdiction are bound to shift as fewer distinctions can be made based upon aircraft type, weapon loads, and long distances. The combining of the U.S. Air Force's Strategic Air Command into one command with the U.S. Tactical Air Force may be the most visible symbol of the change in doctrine and definition required by a rapidly changing world.

Jasjit Singh

See Also: Air-land Battle; Airpower; Airpower, History of; Airpower, Strategic; Airpower, Tactical; Bombardment, Strategic; Close Air Support; Combined Operations; Follow-on Forces Attack; Gulf War, 1991; Korean War; Logistic Movement; Logistics: A General Survey; Munitions, Aerial; Precision-guided Munitions; Vietnam and Indochina Wars; World War II.

Bibliography

Futrell, R. F. 1983. *United States Air Force in Korea: 1950–1953*. Washington, D.C.: Government Printing Office.

Kohn, R. H., and J. P. Harahan, eds. 1986. *Air interdiction in World War II, Korea, and Vietnam*. Washington, D.C.: Office of Air Force History.

Liddell Hart, B. H. 1953. *The Rommel papers*. New York: Harcourt, Brace.

MacIsaac, D. 1976. *Strategic bombing in World War II: The story of the United States strategic bombing survey*. New York: Garland.

Mason, R. A. 1987. *Air power: An overview of roles*. London: Pergamon-Brassey's.

Momyer, W. W. 1986. *Airpower in three wars: World War II, Korea, and Vietnam*. Washington, D.C.: Office of Air Force History.

Singh, J. 1985. *Air power in modern warfare*. New Delhi: Lancers.

Tedder, A. W. 1966. *With prejudice*. Boston: Little, Brown.

AIR RECONNAISSANCE

Air reconnaissance is an outgrowth of man's aspiration to see the enemy behind the hill, anticipate his moves, and avoid surprise. From the beginning, air reconnaissance was intended to collect intelligence data beyond the constraints of traditional capabilities.

Air reconnaissance technology has been aimed at expanding human capabilities by extending the range of collection (provided by the altitude of the collecting system), the point of collection (provided by the speed and depth of penetration of the collecting system), and the type and quality of the acquired data (provided by the resolution of the collecting mechanism and by special collecting facilities such as ELINT/SIGINT [electronic intelligence and signal intelligence] receivers, infrared sensors). Air reconnaissance is categorized by the scope of intelligence data provided and the timeliness of their use. There is a marked difference between the reconnaissance data used for the identification of potential targets for strategic bombing and the reconnaissance data exploited immediately by the tactical commander in order to hit the enemy behind the hill.

This analysis covers only aerial means and methods of reconnaissance and excludes space-based systems. As a direct result of the introduction of industrialized technology into military affairs, the intensity of warfare has grown, the spatial scope of the battlefield and theater have expanded, and the rates of advance and lethality of nonnuclear forces have increased in an unprecedented manner. Consequently, it has become crucial for the commander to have a better overall picture, that is, to be able to see farther, faster, and more accurately. Air reconnaissance is the primary means to provide the commander with this intelligence, facilitating expansion of the battlefield.

A revolution in the relationship between air reconnaissance and the military decision maker has taken place in recent years. In the past, air reconnaissance had to struggle to expand the scope of collection and data acquired on a timely basis in order to quench the commander's thirst for intelligence. Today's technology breaks all past barriers and introduces the potential for an unprecedented increase in volume, data acquisition, management, and storage. Consequently, the user is being overwhelmed by the available and the obtainable. He is seduced into collecting data for the sake of having it rather than understanding, comprehending, and effectively using what intelligence he really needs.

In the West, on the one hand, the available information-gathering technologies and data storage and management capacities seem to have made the acquisition of quantities of detail the end objective rather than the means toward better understanding and using reconnaissance and intelligence data. Indeed, all the futuristic air reconnaissance systems contemplated and forecast in the West are aimed at a further increase (dramatic at times) of the volume and scope of data collected.

The Russians, on the other hand, use the single term *razvedka* (reconnaissance-intelligence) to cover the entire scope of intelligence-related activities ranging from collecting data (by any means from reconnaissance to raids) to analysis and the capitalizing on this data (in attacks by special forces or tactical aircraft on choice objectives). To them air reconnaissance is but one of many resources geared toward the timely and effective use of collected data to further policy objectives. The scope of reconnaissance-intelligence data collected at any level of command is determined primarily by the abilities of the customer to analyze, comprehend, and capitalize on the acquired intelligence.

History

Air reconnaissance is the oldest form of air power. The first employment of balloons for aerial reconnaissance over the battlefield took place on 26 June 1794 in Belgium. The French sent Capt. Jean M. J. Coutelle up in an observation balloon to observe Austrian deployments during the battle of Fleurus. However, Napoleon rejected further development of balloon reconnaissance because launch and recovery units could not cope with the fast rate of advance of the French forces.

A balloon reconnaissance unit, the Army Aeronautics Corps, was organized by the Federal forces in June 1861 during the American Civil War. Its creator and commander, T. S. C. Lowe, launched his balloons from horse-drawn vans which could keep up with the army. He was the first to use the telegraph for real-time reporting including target identification and the directing of long-range artillery fire. The first aerial pictures for military use were taken from Lowe's balloon.

Fixed-wing aircraft were first used for reconnaissance during the Italian-Turkish war. In October 1911, Captain Piazza began a systematic reconnaissance of the Turkish lines in Tripolitania in a Bleriot monoplane. The Italian forces were able to advance through the Turkish lines on the basis of Piazza's information. In February 1912, Captain Piazza took the first aerial pictures of enemy positions from an aircraft.

A most important breakthrough in aerial reconnaissance took place in early 1914 when the British introduced a chemical process that enabled the developing of photographic negatives in the air so that they were ready for printing and use by commanders at the front by the time the aircraft landed. In a concluding test, two British officers took a series of aerial photographs in one day of the entire defenses of the Isle of Wight and Solent, delivering developed negatives to the headquarters as they landed.

World War I

During World War I, aerial reconnaissance was the primary source of intelligence on enemy activities and dispositions. Real-time tactical data was provided by fixed observation balloons along the front. Aircraft were used primarily for long-range photographic reconnaissance, determination of the enemy situation, target identification, and damage assessment. The bulk of early aerial fighting took place in repeated attempts to cover or prevent the operations of reconnaissance aircraft. Both sides used hand-held and turret-mounted oblique cameras as well as vertical cameras attached to the side of the aircraft.

The development of air reconnaissance during World War I went beyond the improvements in aerial camera technology. An institutionalized intelligence system was established to cope with, and exploit the data in, the growing volumes of pictures. The foundations for such prerequisites as on-site speedy processing, and especially photo-interpretation techniques and knowledge, were laid during World War I.

The bane of reconnaissance was also created during World War I as commanders were overwhelmed with useless as well as usable data just because it existed. Aerial reconnaissance identified tactical objectives, but the sheer volume of data, in addition to difficulty with the control and accuracy of firepower, precluded full exploitation of the accurate and detailed information available. Strategic objectives, major offensives, and breakthrough attempts were largely beyond the range of reconnaissance aircraft, except when a few attempts were made to use bombers for deep reconnaissance. Therefore, despite the vast improvements in the quality and accuracy of aerial reconnaissance during World War I, it had only marginal impact on the carnage or on the conduct of the war, primarily because the senior commanders either did not know how to utilize it or were incapable of exploiting it.

Interwar Years

Between the wars, developments in camera technology continued. There were major successes in the reduction of size and weight, increases in altitudes from which pictures could be taken, the introduction of continued and flexible films rather than fragile plates, major improvements in lens quality and ensuing picture resolution, enhancement of the stability of cameras in aircraft, and the development of night photography with flares and special films. Increases in the range and performance of aircraft permitted coverage of new areas far behind enemy lines. There were significant improvements in photo interpretation, data management, and storage capabilities which permitted better use of available pictures. Most important, however, was the integration of air reconnaissance products into a comprehensive strategic and technological intelligence process whereby interpreted photographs were used in concert with other inputs from intercepts of communication, SIGINT, technical data, and classical espionage. The growing significance of strategic air reconnaissance was demonstrated in the covert collection efforts of Sir Sidney Cotton (U.K.) and Senior Lieutenant (later Colonel) T. Rowehl (Germany) on the eve of World War II.

World War II

World War II saw the expansion and institutionalization of air reconnaissance leading to the emergence of organizational and analytic methods which are still valid. Aircraft collected more than just diversified imagery data. The first efforts to identify and record enemy radar signals from the air took place during World War II. Air reconnaissance was the most important source of intelligence for both the Soviets and the Germans during the war. For the Allies, air reconnaissance was the second most important source of strategic intelligence (after the Ultra intercepts), and the single most important source of tactical intelligence.

All aircraft types used by the major powers were also employed in aerial reconnaissance, mainly via modifications in existing combat aircraft. There were specialized reconnaissance versions of virtually all fighters, attack aircraft, and bombers. Dedicated light aircraft for observation and fire direction along the front lines were developed and widely used. Reconnaissance versions of heavy bombers collected strike results and SIGINT during strikes (flying inside the regular bomber formations), and performed long-range maritime reconnaissance that included coverage of remote islands in the Pacific. Most effective were the specialized modifications of the "hottest" aircraft of the day. These aircraft relied on speed and range, as well as pilot excellence and audacity, to get to their objectives and return with the photographs. The several models of the British-developed Mosquito and Spitfire were the best and most versatile reconnaissance aircraft of World War II. Dedicated high-performance reconnaissance aircraft were developed during the war but never adopted for operational use.

Instruments for the collection of data improved considerably during the Second World War. There were great innovations in camera technology, especially the development of the fully automatic, electrically operated camera and the shutterless camera for high-speed photo reconnaissance. Diversified techniques for night collection with artificial illumination (flares, flash bombs) were introduced. Airborne collection of signal intelligence, that is, the recording of enemy radar signals and tactical communication was introduced during World War II. Of great tactical significance was the development of a standard reconnaissance pod with several cameras that could be installed on all combat aircraft with proper (and simple) wiring. Consequently, it was possible to collect aerial photographs without dedicated reconnaissance aircraft. In places where only a limited number of aircraft was available, such as on aircraft carriers, this pod had direct impact on both the air combat and air reconnaissance capabilities of the units in question.

The most significant contributions of aerial reconnaissance to the war effort were the tremendous advances in the interpretation and analysis process which enabled the extraction of extensive military and technical data from the collected imagery. Key technical aids, ranging from high-quality automated film processing and picture printing to stereoscopes and other picture-reading aids, assisted greatly in photo interpretation. So, too, did intensive training for interpreters and analysts. Data bases and photo intelligence archives were established to permit better analysis of available photographs. The data bases included background material on established and recognizable patterns of enemy functioning, repetitions of shapes and forms of buildings and their meaning, identification of key installations and encampments, and identification of weapon systems and related (supporting) pieces of equipment. Relying on these data bases, photo interpreters were able to better comprehend what they were seeing in a photograph.

Postwar Technology

Postwar reconnaissance continued to develop according to principles proven during World War II. Reconnaissance versions of the latest jet fighters were developed. Photo reconnaissance capabilities of converted bombers, especially regarding night photography, were significantly improved. The cold war introduced new challenges which required technological breakthroughs. The closing of Soviet bloc borders demanded better and deeper penetration, which led to development of a new generation of strategic reconnaissance aircraft such the Lockheed U-2. With the nuclear age came specialized collectors of radioactive air samples to analyze the nuclear capabilities of the other side. The electronic age brought a growing emphasis on ELINT/SIGINT/COMINT (communications intelligence) and, subsequently, the development of specialized collection platforms. Such platforms were converted transports and bombers loaded with electronic equipment and specialists.

The introduction of space-based reconnaissance and intelligence gathering systems did not reduce demand for airborne collection of comprehensive intelligence and reconnaissance data. Trends in military affairs, such as the intensity and rapidity of major combat actions and the expansion of theaters to a global scope, have introduced demand not only for a real-time supply of unprecedented quantities of diversified intelligence but also for the quick collection of such data in unfolding crises. Only manned and man-controlled platforms have the flexibility for such collection efforts.

The performance and capabilities of contemporary air reconnaissance systems are determined primarily by technological progress in electronic and electro-optical systems. Aviation technology has become sufficiently flexible to provide appropriate platforms to carry the required equipment to the collection point. Aerial refueling stretches the limited range of some reconnaissance aircraft. Present-day air reconnaissance technology covers developments since the mid-1960s when introduction of the unified weapon system approach to design permitted effective integration of diversified developments in aviation technology and electronics.

Collection Methods and Technology

The camera remains the main source of air reconnaissance with the trend continuing to reduce the camera's size and weight. The major forms of aerial photograph are:

1. Vertical—coverage of a limited area (per frame) directly below the aircraft providing a maplike, uniform photograph of the area in question which can also be studied with stereoscopes to obtain a three-dimensional (height) effect.
2. Oblique—coverage of a limited area (per frame) to the side (or ahead) of the aircraft which is ideal for covert collection of pictures when the flight path does not cross the photographed object and for acquiring photographs of weapon installations from safe stand-off ranges. Oblique take provides a distorted image on the photograph which can be corrected through calculations or computer-aided analysis.
3. Horizon-to-horizon panoramic—comprehensive coverage of a narrow stretch of land (per frame) with the quality of each take ranging from vertical in the middle to distorted large-angle oblique at the edges, used to quickly photograph large areas in a single sortie. Such coverage is achieved by a quick run of a shutterless camera or by building a mosaic of frames photographed either by a swinging lens or by multiple (usually 3 or 4) lenses.

Visible Light

A significant improvement in aerial photography is achieved through integration of diversified support systems into aerial cameras. Automatic focus and light sensors ensure a uniform quality of imprint despite changes in light, shadows, or terrain features. A camera's automatic stabilization and guidance systems ensure that both it and the photograph quality are less influenced by sudden movements of the carrying platform and by changes in speed and altitude. Automatic correction systems are introduced in order to reduce optical distortions of multiple-lens panoramic coverage by individually controlling each lens.

Since the quality and sensitivity of film affect the quality of the aerial photograph, improvements in black-and-white film sensitivity permit far better resolution despite shorter exposure time. High-quality color film, especially for highly detailed vertical takes, has been introduced to service. There are also improvements in the sensitivity of false-color film which, when exposed through a special pale yellow filter, can distinguish between foliage and camouflage.

Infrared

Heat sources in the infrared (IR) spectrum are the second most important source of intelligence collected through aerial reconnaissance. Mapping of heat sources can provide extensive data that cannot be obtained by visual coverage alone. The use of the IR spectrum enables one to see great details of activity at night without a visual source of light, either by recording the heat radiation of the photographed objective or by illuminating it with invisible IR light. Examination of the heat signature of a military installation can provide details on the rate of activity in the installation by identifying, for example, hot (cold) engines which point to current or recent use (or lack of it), heated garrisons which point to current occupancy, and cooler spots in parking areas which indicate where weapon systems stood until shortly before the photograph was taken.

Early IR takes were achieved by installing an IR filter on regular cameras and using extremely sensitive film. Because of the growing importance of IR coverage, dedicated collection systems—the infrared line scan (IRLS)—were developed for high-quality vertical coverage. The IRLS is based on a highly sensitive and always cooled sensor which rotates at great speed along an axis vertical to the axis of flight. The IR photograph is recorded electronically in narrow strips so that the resulting picture looks very much like a black-and-white TV picture. Modern IRLS systems are the same size as modern cameras and can be fitted into most reconnaissance aircraft and dedicated reconnaissance pods.

Radar

Current improvements in electronics and computers have resulted in significant upgrading of radar technology for aerial reconnaissance. The use of radar enables the reconnaissance platform to "see" in the dark and through clouds and smoke. The veteran side-looking aircraft radar (SLAR) has been significantly improved with the integration of moving-target indication (MTI) systems which enable SLAR to identify activities on the ground. The major deficiency of SLAR is that it has oblique coverage on both sides of the aircraft; moreover, in early models, the platform had to fly low, slow, and along straight lines. Later models permitted high speeds.

With the introduction of high-speed miniaturized computers, a new era in the use of radar for aerial reconnaissance opened. In synthetic aperture radar (SAR) systems, computers are used to process the reflected radar signals so that a very clear artificial picture, usually a clean vertical view or the pilot's view, is created on a screen in the cockpit and is recorded. In the Doppler beam-sharpening (DBS) systems, the computer is used to provide a sharp visual presentation and to record moving objects in the covered area. The ASARS (Advanced Synthetic-Aperture Radar System) installed in the Lockheed TR-1 is the first operational next-generation SAR.

Electronic Collection of Visual Reconnaissance

A new era in air reconnaissance is emerging with development of highly sensitive electro-optical recording systems (super-TV cameras) and miniaturized high-performance computers. These permit electronic collection of visual reconnaissance. Moreover, it is possible to integrate the platform's computer, which provides data on the exact location and performance of the platform at any given moment, with computers controlling the recording of the various sources of radiation (visual, IR, and radar). Through the computers, it is possible to superimpose the data on a single multiple-source artificial presentation which has a far greater clarity than any single-source coverage. Computerized electronic recording and storage also permit speedier handling, analysis, and comparison of larger quantities of collected reconnaissance and intelligence data, giving the customer a single comprehensive presentation.

Others

The proliferation of electronic radiation in military affairs, and its growing significance to their conduct, has resulted in the emergence of highly specialized airborne platforms for the collection, storage, and initial analysis of electronic data. There are now specialized fields of electronic radiation collection such as ELINT, SIGINT, and COMINT with corresponding dedicated collection platforms. Also in operation are specialized platforms for high-performance SLAR coverage of vast areas, as well as antisubmarine warfare (ASW) and naval reconnaissance over extensive and remote areas. Highly specialized collection systems have been developed for specific tasks such as tracking ICBM testing and the reentry and splash of MIRVs. The Boeing RC-135 and E-3 family serves as the U.S. Air Force's standard platform for most of these specialized and dedicated airborne reconnaissance and intelligence systems. The Tupolev Tu-20/Tu-95/Tu-142 Bear family and Tu-126 Moss serve as the main Russian platforms. Specialized models of the Ilyushin Il-76 (Candid and Mainstay) are also in operational service in Russia.

The Vietnam War saw the emergence of a new type of air reconnaissance, namely, the collection and analysis of data emitted by fields of sensors. This system was pioneered in the Igloo White project, which sought to provide a detailed survey of traffic along the enemy's infiltration route through the use of sensor fields and airborne monitoring of their automatic reporting. Recent developments in electronics have contributed to the emergence of more sensitive and accurate sensors. However, the primary challenges of dispersing the sensors onto the area to be covered and the close monitoring of their emission still need to be conducted from the air.

Emerging Technologies

In the West the most important emerging technology is the further integration of data from several collection sources (visual, IR, radar, etc.) into a uniform and detailed enhancement image. The availability of electronically managed and stored data will permit the real-time reporting of data collected by the reconnaissance aircraft to any rear headquarters. Electronic management and reconstruction of collected reconnaissance with computers make it possible to reshape the available data electronically, which in turn permits faster and more accurate computerized scanning of the raw material before the data reaches human analysts. Electronically treated images could simulate combat missions, as viewed through the pilot's eye, for training purposes.

In the East, the emphasis is also on greater flexibility of collection and analysis systems so that senior commanders can use collected reconnaissance intelligence in a more timely fashion. The Soviet commitment to speedy development of offensive military operations far behind enemy lines was followed by the introduction of desktop computers to forward headquarters for the transfer of the data, including intelligence, from senior commanders to subordinates. The most significant technological development was the further extension of this computer-communication system to transmitting visual images, that is, maps and aerial photographs.

Reconnaissance Aircraft

Despite growing reliance on space-based systems for collection of intelligence, reconnaissance aircraft continue to play a major role. Aircraft are still more flexible than satellites, can react to crises, and can be called back if circumstances demand. The quest for the optimal penetrability of the reconnaissance aircraft led to unprecedented technological breakthroughs. The U.S. Air Force's Lockheed SR-71, which first flew on 26 April 1962 (the A-11 prototype), can collect large quantities of aerial reconnaissance faster and higher than any other operational aircraft (Fig. 1).

As in past wars, the aircraft most frequently used for air reconnaissance are specialized modifications of fighters and attack aircraft. Radar and weapon systems in the nose of the aircraft are replaced by reconnaissance systems, cameras, or ELINT systems. Leading Russian-made reconnaissance aircraft are the MiG-25 Foxbat, the Su-24 Fencer, and, most likely, the Su-27 Flanker. In the West, the McDonnell RF-4 Phantom remains the primary reconnaissance workhorse. Improvements in technology permit installation of highly capable reconnaissance pods on high-performance fighters, using the fighters for both combat and reconnaissance missions. In the West, the Panavia Tornado and Grumman F-14 Tomcat are pod-carrying reconnaissance platforms while in the East the ubiquitous MiG-21 Fishbed performs this role.

Changing battlefield scenarios have led to a demand for a new class of reconnaissance platforms with staying capabilities in extremely high altitudes for battlefield coverage and battle management in high-intensity theaters, as well as for deep penetration in areas of lesser threat. In the West, the U.S. Air Force's Lockheed U-2/TR-1 family performs this mission. In Russia, the venerable Yak-25 Mandrake, repeatedly modified and upgraded, is reportedly about to be replaced by a new Myasishchev design M-17 designated Mystic in the West.

Technological progress made it possible in the late 1960s to introduce yet another class of reconnaissance platforms—the unmanned remotely piloted vehicles (RPVs). At present, it is possible to commit these planes to deep penetration missions with a degree of control and relative flexibility close to those of a manned platform but without danger to pilots and political reputation. The U.S. Teledyne Ryan family of Firebee RPVs derived from the original Model 147 is the most versatile and effective unmanned air reconnaissance platform. The Soviets developed the *Yastreb*, an extremely high performance hybrid rocket plane based on the principles of the German Sanger-plane project, for high-risk strategic missions.

Figure 1. The Lockheed SR-71 is the world's most advanced strategic reconnaissance aircraft and one of the U.S. Air Force's most sophisticated aircraft. (Source: U.S. Department of Defense)

The growing need for real-time reconnaissance data for commanders in the field even in the most saturated environment has resulted in development of the expandable mini-RPV. Using TV cameras and related sensors (such as forward-looking infrared, or FLIR), the mini-RPV transmits images to mobile ground stations attached to the ground unit headquarters. Thus the mini-RPV is the first air reconnaissance platform to have the true ability to look "behind the hill"—the reason air reconnaissance started. The first operational mini-RPV, the IAI (Israeli Aircraft Industries) Scout, was developed in Israel and proven in combat during the 1982 Israeli incursion into Lebanon. A new generation of vastly improved mini-RPVs has since been developed, the Israeli Mazlat Pioneer being the first combat-proven second-generation mini-RPV.

Modern Doctrine

In the West, there is a revival of the World War I bane of reconnaissance, namely, saturation of data. The demand for air reconnaissance products is a reflection of, and is conditioned by, technological performance and availability. Commanders claim a need for exceedingly large quantities of real-time and raw intelligence and reconnaissance data to the point of saturating the system and preventing study of the acquired reconnaissance. To cope with the growing quantities of collected material, early examination of the material and selection of material for further study is conducted by computers. Consequently, all meaningful interpretation and analysis by humans depends on the computer's judgment.

In the East, the quest for timely and on-site air reconnaissance has resulted in the return to reliance on human (aircrew) observation without cameras. A leading pilot is sent to identify the objective so that he can guide strikes capitalizing on the discovered data, or at least provide last-minute instructions to the strike leader. Helicopter pilots land near the ground subunit commander to deliver reports. This is the essence of *razvedka*—collecting reconnaissance-intelligence and acting upon it. At the same time, there is a dramatic progress in classic air reconnaissance as a new generation of aircraft and collection systems is introduced into operational service. The new computerized data management system significantly expands the ability of the senior commanders to use and exploit results of air reconnaissance on a timely basis. Yet, the Soviets were extremely careful not to overwhelm their commanders with excessive data that they cannot use or that would slow down their conduct of combat operations.

YOSSEF BODANSKY

SEE ALSO: Electronic Warfare, Air; Intelligence Analysis, Military; Intelligence Collection; Intelligence, General; Intelligence, Imagery; Intelligence, Military; Intelligence, Signal; Intelligence, Strategic; Reconnaissance and Surveillance.

Bibliography

Burrows, W. E. 1986. *Deep black: Space espionage and national security*. New York: Random House.
Goddard, G. W., with D. W. S. Copp. 1969. *Overview: A life-long adventure in aerial photography*. New York: Doubleday.
Krasnov, A. B. 1987. *Bar'yery vozdushnoy razvedki* [Barriers of Air Reconnaissance]. Moscow: Voenizdat.
Stanley, R. M., II. 1981. *World War II photo intelligence*. New York: Scribner's.
Streetly, M. 1983. *World electronic warfare aircraft*. London: Jane's.
———. 1988. *Airborne electronic warfare*. London: Jane's.
Taylor, J. W. R., and D. Mondey. 1972. *Spies in the sky*. London: Ian Allan.

AIRBORNE LAND FORCES

Airborne land forces are army combat forces that use the third dimension for airborne, airlanding, and air assault operations. For air movement and for combat support they depend on air force or army aviation aircraft. They have tactical, operational, or strategic missions. Regardless of terrain characteristics, they will quickly deploy over great distances and, to the extent possible, be committed in surprise operations.

Their missions may include raids, security and surveillance, air assault, containment of enemy penetrations and breakthroughs, reinforcement or relief of committed forces, closing of gaps, and employment as operational and strategic reserve.

During aerial deployment airborne land forces require effective protection against the enemy's air force, attack helicopters, and air defense. Their limited ground mobility is increased by tactical vehicles carried with the deploying force and by organic or attached helicopters. Their special training and equipment make such forces particularly well-suited for close combat operations in urban areas, woods, jungle, and other difficult terrain. The development of airborne land forces began before World War II and is still going on. At present, there are three types of airborne land forces: airborne, airmobile, and air assault forces.

Airborne Forces

Airborne forces specialize in parachute assault and airlanding operations. Air mobility is provided by transport aircraft, by gliders, or by helicopters. Combat and combat service support is provided by the air force or by organic or attached army aviation assets.

Organization, arms, and equipment are tailored to the requirements of airborne operations. The air transport capacities available limit the size, weight, and number of items that may be airlifted. Often air transport must be accomplished in several waves. If possible, the force will be organized into an air echelon transported by air and a ground echelon following the air echelon by land marches. The air echelon will primarily comprise the combat/fire-support elements, while the ground echelon primarily comprises the service-support elements.

Airborne forces have a high proportion of infantry. Weapons and equipment are mostly light and man-portable. Shoulder-fixed guided antitank and antiaircraft missiles are standard armament. Air-transportable light artillery as well as light armored and unarmored vehicles provide additional firepower and mobility in operations after the airlanding but require air transport space.

AIRBORNE OPERATIONS

Airborne forces will normally be committed only if time and environment leave no other choice and when no other forces can carry out that mission. Another prerequisite is comprehensive and up-to-date intelligence. Operational security (OPSEC), deception, ruses, and surprise are other aspects critically important to success. Airborne forces will try to avoid frontal assaults and, instead, attempt to hit the enemy's weak spots in surprise operations, leaving him no time for preparation; they try to cut off the enemy's communications and disrupt the synchronization of his operations. This is done by attacks against the enemy flanks and rear, or by airlanding/airdrop directly atop the objective.

Coup de main. A coup de main operation is executed by task-organized forces. It is an operation of very limited duration and should be accomplished by the time the enemy can institute effective countermeasures. A coup de main operation is conducted to seize or destroy key objectives, eliminate an adversary's command and control structure, or disrupt enemy defenses. It is often the opening phase of a major operation.

Tactical and operational missions. Forces from battalion to division size and larger conduct tactical and operational missions, such as preliminary attacks, flanking attacks, or deep attacks, or seize and hold key terrain. The decisive success must be achieved before the airborne operation turns into a regular battle fought in accordance with the principles applicable for all ground forces. The light armament and limited ground mobility of airborne forces are highly limiting. Airborne forces may also be retained as reserves to reinforce committed forces in critical situations or relieve them in position or by rearward passage of lines. They may also be employed as a gapfiller, or to seal off enemy breakthroughs and to protect threatened flanks.

The limited mobility of airborne forces after airlandings and the mostly light arms available in the initial battle frequently call for the seizure of airfields or the establishment of expedient airstrips to land vehicles, heavy weapons, supplies, and reserves. Apart from this, heavy loads are routinely dropped by cargo chutes. Another option is unassisted low-level flight delivery of resilient bulk supplies like food and ammunition. Heavy loads may also be transported by helicopter as external loads. Once on the ground, the mobility of airborne forces should be increased by providing them with helicopter assets.

PRINCIPLES

Thorough and detailed preparation is essential for these operations. Also indispensable, at least for a limited period of time and in local areas, are air superiority and the suppression of enemy air defenses along the air avenues of approach and in the landing zone. Effective and continuous air combat support, good communications, and, in most cases, cooperation with the ground forces will be required. Only an orchestrated combined-arms effort will ensure success. To prevent losses by friendly defensive fire while the force is airborne, clear airspace management and rapid identification of friendly elements are needed. If the landing takes place far from enemy forces, initial losses will be avoided, but this means giving up surprise and the crucial headstart. It is usually more promising to attack the enemy directly, leaving him no time for a concerted response. Airborne operations against a well-prepared and strong enemy have little chance of success and bring especially great losses.

AIRBORNE FORCES AND FLYING UNITS

Some believe the necessary close cooperation between flying units and airborne forces can be achieved only if both elements belong to the same branch of service. Whether or not airborne forces and flying units are integrated, it is logical that the airborne force should be stationed in the vicinity of airfields. Such stationing will decisively enhance coordination, training, and organization and improve responsiveness. The elements conducting the ground battle must know that they can rely on "their" pilots under enemy fire. They should develop an understanding for the technical aspects of the aircraft and flight conditions and understand the influence of weather conditions on airborne operations. Conversely, the personnel of the flying units should have a thorough knowledge and understanding of the conditions and tactical doctrine of the ground battle.

Airmobile Forces

Airmobile forces may be committed in support of airborne forces but may also operate independently. These forces are normally light division-size army forces. They are air-transportable with air force or army aviation assets. Frequently, their task is to expand successes and complete the mission of commandos or initial tactical/operational successes achieved by airborne forces. They specialize in airlandings but they may also be used in a traditional role in the ground battle if required. Their equipment and doctrine are similar to that of light infantry with emphasis placed on antitank capability. Their heavy weapons and tactical vehicles require an extensive air transport effort by the air force or army aviation.

Air Assault Forces

Air assault units are combined-arms units of brigade and division size. All assets and forces required for airborne/air assault landings are organic to these units, and aviation assets are an integral part. This gives them high mobility. They conduct all types of offensive and defensive operations and are well-suited for operations in urbanized terrain, woods, jungles, and mountains, and for operations in extreme climates. They are capable of seizing and holding objectives or airheads. Only under extremely favorable conditions can they attack without support against armored or mechanized forces. They are primarily employed at the operational or strategic level. They can conduct independent operations, but are normally employed as elements of a larger force. The most prominent aspect of their operations is that they can concentrate forces with great firepower and momentum over great distances rapidly.

Historical Example: Operation Merkur (Scorcher)

The first operational airborne operation in military history was the capture of the island of Crete by the German Wehrmacht in World War II. Numerous tactical airlandings in the campaigns in Scandinavia and the West in April and May 1940 had preceded it. In these actions, the Germans successfully seized important airfields, bridges, forts, and government institutions in Denmark, Holland, and Belgium and held them until the link-up with follow-on forces.

At the end of the Balkan campaign, on 20 May 1941, Crete was attacked by paratroopers of the 7th Air Division and mountain infantry of the 5th Mountain Division, under control of Gen. Kurt Student's XI Air Corps. The defenders—from Australia, Great Britain, Greece, and New Zealand—were superior in numbers, but short of equipment. The German attackers suffered high losses but seized the island within twelve days. Three methods of invasion were used: parachute jumping, glider assault landing, and airlanding with transport aircraft. All of this took place by day. Tactically, it was a deliberate attack against a prepared defense. The parachute drops and glider landings were mostly atop or in the immediate vicinity of the objectives.

Additional naval transport had been planned. Naval

support, however, was prevented by British naval superiority. Therefore, personnel, combat support, resupply, and medical support came almost exclusively by air.

PROBLEMS

The preparation and execution of airlandings suffered from the following problems:

Great pressure of time. The beginning of the offensive against the Soviet Union (Operation Barbarossa) had been set for 22 June 1941, and that operation was to take precedence over all others.

Improvisation. Elements of the Luftwaffe's VIII Air Corps had been assigned other missions or had already been redeployed in preparation for the Russian campaign; as a result, the Luftwaffe ground elements for flight operations, air traffic control, maintenance, repair, refueling operations, and communications were inadequate.

Inadequate infrastructure. The only feasible airfields were mostly unprepared agricultural areas. At best they could be called improvised or expedient airfields, and were suited only to a limited degree for such an operation. The clouds of dust caused by landing and takeoff of aircraft consequently upset the schedule of the operation and resulted in piecemeal commitment of the second wave in the afternoon of the first day of combat.

Logistical deployment problems and lack of service support forces. Most supplies, especially ammunition, POL, food, and gliders and transport vehicles, had to be moved over some 2,500 kilometers (1,550 mi.) from Germany to southern Greece by rail, ship, or air, with several transshipments; XI Air Corps had no organic logistics component and, therefore, had to organize a supply element from other units within one week.

Inadequate communications. Essential elements of the signal troops of the Fourth Air Force, assigned overall responsibility for Operation Merkur, had already been redeployed for the Russian invasion; as a result, the force had to rely primarily on wire communications, which were often disrupted by actions of resistance groups.

Deficiencies of the parachute force organization. During the past year the force had been expanded from five battalions, several companies, and the training establishment to four regiments plus corps and divisional units, and the buildup was not yet completed. Previous wartime experience had been limited to the aforementioned tactical operations in Denmark, Norway, Belgium, and Holland, but the troops had no experience in operational-level employment. Battalion, regimental, and division tactics, combined-arms operations, and cooperation with the air force for close air support had not been sufficiently practiced.

The technical development of the parachute corps was still in the early stages. Individual soldiers carried only a pistol, hand grenades, and explosives during the jump. Rifles and machine guns were stowed in special weapons containers and dropped separately. The parachutes and cargo platforms as well as the procedures for delivery of weapons, equipment, and heavy loads were sometimes inadequate—particularly in difficult terrain. Many of the radios and heavy weapons were damaged in the airdrop and rendered inoperational.

Deficiencies of air transportation forces. Air transport forces were unable to keep up with the development of the parachute forces. Only a small portion of available air transport was permanently assigned to XI Air Corps. Additional planes and crews were assembled from units from all corners of the Reich and few had experience in cooperation with, and airdropping of, parachute troops. The total capacity was just sufficient to transport in one wave half of the force that was to be airdropped. A Junkers Ju 52 aircraft could carry only twelve fully equipped and armed paratroopers. Large transport aircraft were not available.

Unclear picture of the enemy situation. Crete's defenders had excellent camouflage and fire discipline. Their location on the island permitted only aerial reconnaissance, the results of which were inadequate. Information on the enemy was hardly available; thus, the enemy was underestimated.

Failure to achieve surprise. The British had succeeded in deciphering the German radio code. They monitored the Luftwaffe's radio traffic and knew the German intentions and plans.

Moreover, it was impossible to keep the preparations for an airlanding of such scale secret because they took place in occupied enemy territory. The well-functioning British intelligence service provided a steady input of information. The Luftwaffe first defeated the British air elements stationed on the island in a preparatory air battle that lasted about one week and thus gained absolute air superiority. Although this was essential, it further confirmed the intended German attack. The enemy knew the day and hour of the attack as well as did the German task organization.

British dominance of the sea. Since the British navy dominated the sea around Crete, seizure of one or more airfields on the island was essential for the success of the planned German attack. The commander of the British defense, New Zealand general Bernard C. Freyberg, was aware of this fact. He therefore concentrated on defending the airfields at Maleme, Rethymon, and Heraklion, Suda Bay with the village of Suda (important for his lines of naval communications), and the capital of Chania. This meant that defense efforts were concentrated exactly in the areas of the attacker's points of main effort.

Outcome

Despite these serious problems, Operation Merkur was a success. The well-prepared defenders, assisted by the Greek civilian population, and armed and motivated by the British secret service, fought a battle that inflicted high losses on the Germans. Still, the defenders were forced to evacuate the island. The deciding factors included:

- Organizational skills and initiative of the troops and staff in the preparation of the airlanding;
- Readiness to take risks on the part of the flying units of the Luftwaffe to provide good and continuous combat support;
- Flexible command and control of the XI Air Corps in battle; shifting of the main effort to Maleme and the airlanding of the 5th Mountain Division while the airfield was still under enemy fire; commitment of liaison teams, resupply and reserves;
- Courage, fighting spirit, battle experience, and endurance of the parachute troops and the mountain infantry, and the initiative of the individual soldier in battle;
- Shortages of equipment and the inexperience of the defenders.

The victory of the airlanded force definitely was attributable in part to superior leadership. The Germans call it "mission-oriented leadership." It means that any leader must know the intent of the higher command. Unit leaders to a large extent then act at their own discretion in accordance with this intent and within the framework of the mission, which delineates the objective and the means available. This enables them to react flexibly, to exploit favorable situations without delay, and to respond quickly to contingencies without waiting for orders. From the German point of view, the British system of "leading by orders" responded without flexibility and gave the landed paratroopers ample time. Counterattacks, though they were conducted methodically, normally came too late. Because airlandings are always characterized by a greater extent of imponderables than normal ground operations, "mission-oriented leadership" seems the most effective means of control for airborne forces.

The island of Crete was captured in only twelve days by numerically inferior parachute and mountain infantry forces—some 22,000 versus 42,000 men—with heavy and continuous air support rendered under unfavorable conditions. The losses were high compared with the previous battles of the "Blitz," and even disastrous for some parachute units, but justifiable in relation to the overall success; losses were low in comparison with the subsequent Russian campaign. Operation Merkur showed the operational-level capabilities of airborne forces and opened a new chapter in the history of war.

Battle Experiences and Lessons Learned

Following Operation Merkur, German evaluation of the battle led to changes and new actions, such as the following:

1. reconstitution of the depleted parachute units
2. activation of new parachute units, including a Parachute School Battalion
3. activation of logistics units
4. improvement of in-service gliders, including installation of dive brake flaps and drag chutes for pinpoint landing after a dive. General Student coined the term "assault glider"
5. development and introduction of new transport gliders for greater loads, to include tanks and artillery pieces
6. improvement of cooperation with the Luftwaffe, especially for training and employment of special airborne observers for locating the planned drop zones and eliminating drop errors
7. training and employment of direction-finding teams to jump in first and then guide the follow-up transports to the drop zones
8. expedient communications procedures to make up for disrupted radio communications (e.g., black cloth strips with white letters some 70 cm high that could be photographed and read from the air)
9. upgrading of small arms and ammunition
10. improvement of jump procedure, to make the soldiers combat ready immediately after removing their parachutes
11. development of special foods for arctic, temperate, and tropical climates

By the spring of 1942, more than 30,000 fully trained paratroopers and some 1,200 modern gliders were available for new operational airlandings, despite the fact that elements of the force had been employed in current operations in Russia and Africa and suffered further losses. In addition, two Italian divisions (an airborne division and the parachute division "Folgore") had been activated with German assistance and they would later give proof of superior bravery and true comradeship in arms.

Experience of the Allies in World War II

The American and the British armies carefully evaluated the German experiences and doctrine, and especially captured German documents, and immediately began to expand their small forces significantly. By 1942 they had strong and well-trained parachute forces for tactical and operational missions. They proved their value on the battlefields of North Africa, Sicily, Italy, in the Far East, and in France. The first major operation in which the new force was successfully employed at the operational level took place the night of 5–6 June 1944 in Normandy as part of Operation Overlord. The 101st and 82d U.S.

Airborne Divisions and the 6th British Airborne Division, employed to secure the flanks of the invasion zone north of Carentan and east of Caen, accomplished their missions and made an essential contribution to the success of the landing.

Post–World War II Developments

The French army developed the parachute assault tactics of its airborne forces to perfection during the War in Indochina from 1945 to 1954. In more than 150 airborne operations of forces from platoon to regiment size, the "Paras" gained legendary fame. In the Algerian War from 1954 to 1962, they were the first to prepare the way to modern airmobility with the use of helicopters for airlandings.

U.S. forces developed the concept of the airmobile division in the Vietnam War from 1964 to 1973 with the 1st Cavalry Division (Airmobile), using massive helicopter operations for transportation and armed helicopters for combat support operations. This marked the birth of the attack helicopter and the air assault concept.

The Soviet Union carefully evaluated these wartime experiences and subsequently built a strong, efficient airborne force belonging to the Guard Forces (an elite unit of the Soviet army) that was capable of power projections worldwide. After the Vietnam War, the USSR developed an attack helicopter fleet that rivaled its American counterpart. In the Afghanistan War from 1979 to 1988, the Soviets took numerous losses of helicopters in the battle against the freedom fighters, who initially had only light arms but later received Stinger man-portable air defense missiles.

The Present

As of early 1991, the situation is characterized by rapid development of the airborne land forces of almost all large nations. Rapid technological progress in aeronautics has contributed to the use of the helicopter as an airborne weapons platform, and there is an emerging capability of airborne land forces to conduct independent operations.

The Soviet Union

The Soviet Union, in early 1990, had eight airborne divisions, eight separate air assault brigades at front level, and a great number of battalion-size airborne forces at army level. The ground force divisions were assigned organic attack helicopter assets. The Mi-26 HALO transport helicopter has a capacity of 20 tons or 100 soldiers. New attack and antihelicopter helicopters were under development or awaiting introduction.

The Soviet Union also had a large air transport capacity in the air force, which could be augmented by civilian air transport assets (Aeroflot) when required. An example of the capability of the Soviet air transport fleet was the Antonov 124, a large, four-engine transport jet with a speed of 834 km/h (517 mph) and a capacity of 150 tons.

Tactical, operational, and strategic airlandings, close air support with attack helicopters, and the employment of air/ground assault groups were elements of the offensive-oriented Soviet doctrine. Mixed helicopter units, including attack, multiple-purpose, and transport helicopters, supported by ground-attack aircraft and radio-electronic warfare assets played an important role. Helicopters were to conduct all kinds of offensive and defensive operations; and also operate over enemy-occupied territory and within the range of threat weapon systems. Soviet helicopter protective measures included the use of armor, system redundancy, IR protection, a mix of weapons, and electronic countermeasures (ECM) and counter-countermeasures (ECCM).

With the concept of air/ground assault groups the Soviet Union also explored new methods. Attack helicopters, fighter-bombers, and airmobile infantry of at least regimental size were grouped together with mechanized ground forces under the direct control of the ground force commander to execute missions typical of advance forces, such as seizure of key terrain and attacks against the flanks and the rear.

The following options were considered for antihelicopter defense:

- proper siting of radar
- man-portable air defense missiles
- artillery-firing procedures to engage helicopters
- helicopters in an air-to-air combat role
- fighters in an antihelicopter role
- new munitions with proximity fuzes and large fragmentation radii fired from tanks and antitank guns

The operations of the Soviet land forces were developed into an integrated air-land battle.

The United States

The U.S. Army has the 101st Airborne Division (Air Assault) as a mixed major unit, integrating under central control all ground forces and aviation units needed for independent operations. The units include three infantry brigades, one aviation brigade, one artillery brigade, and one support command. The organization is flexible enough to form mixed major air assault task forces tailored to a given mission. In addition, the army has the 82d Airborne Division for the traditional spectrum of operations (Fig. 1).

The integration of an aviation brigade into U.S. corps and divisions has resulted in a significant increase in combat power. The aviation brigade has attack, reconnaissance, multiple-purpose, and transport helicopters. The divisional aviation brigade has its own reconnaissance battalion, in which armored cavalry and its aviation elements are combined. This gives the brigade the necessary footing on the ground during separate operations and prevents unplanned clashes of the attack helicopters with enemy ground force defenses.

Figure 1. Paratroopers of the 82d Airborne Division, shown at Fort Bragg, N.C., in August 1990, make up the only fully airborne force still in service in the United States. (SOURCE: Robert F. Dorr Archives)

The main tasks of the aviation brigade are:

1. air attack in cooperation with ground forces, but also independently (this also includes combat operations in the depth of the area),
2. air assault of infantry additionally supported by attack helicopters,
3. air-to-air engagement of enemy helicopters to protect the friendly operations, and
4. air transport of troops and aerial supply.

FRANCE

Similar to the American concept of rapid deployment forces, the French army has created the Force d'Action Rapide as a ready-reaction force consisting of five air-transportable divisions, with missions both overseas and in central Europe. An innovative development is the 4th Airmobile Division, which includes three attack helicopter regiments, one airborne regiment, and one aviation transport regiment. Employed as an operational reserve moved forward from the depth, this division can contain enemy breakthroughs and destroy them in close cooperation with other forces. Operations are conducted by combined reconnaissance, antitank, and attack-helicopter assets.

GERMANY

The German army in World War II had been the role model and lead example for operational-level employment of airborne forces. It has now developed, after years of hesitation, a concept for concentrating its airmobile forces and for their future development, with the long-term goal of establishing two airmechanized divisions as operational reserve.

WEAKNESSES OF AIRBORNE LAND FORCES

Airborne land forces still suffer from several weaknesses. The all-weather capability and night-flying capability of the inservice aircraft and the duration of operations are still limited. Aircraft vulnerability remains a serious operational concern and can be reduced only to a limited extent by the application of new materials for the airframe, electronic countermeasures (ECM) and ECCM, and active suppression of enemy air defenses. Friend-foe identification still poses a problem; the systems currently in use require further development. Organizing a continuous and up-to-date airspace management remains complicated and time-consuming. The ground element—the soldier fighting on foot—is still too vulnerable and immobile.

The Future of Airmobile Land Forces

AERONAUTICAL ENGINEERING

While the possibilities of improving ground vehicles are mostly exhausted, significant innovations appear in the aeronautical sector. As a result of research, new materials such as fiber compound materials and titanium will significantly reduce aircraft vulnerability. The use of "stealth" technology complicates identification, location, and engagement by reducing the radar, infrared, and laser as well as the acoustic and visual signature. By means of electronic countermeasures enemy reconnaissance and air defenses can be jammed, deceived, or neutralized. For example, advanced sensor missiles can lock on the radar emissions of enemy air defenses and destroy the emitting system. Electromagnetic pulse and electromagnetic interference protection will be part of new concepts. Survivability in a nuclear-biological-chemical (NBC) environment will be improved by an overpressure atmosphere inside the aircraft and protective suits for the pilots, as well as by other measures.

A combination of VSTOL and tilt-rotor technology for aircraft can exploit the advantages of the fixed wing and the rotary wing in one aircraft. This would mean high speed and acceleration with independence from large and, thus, vulnerable runways. Use of satellites will revolutionize navigation. Electronic data and image transmission and digital map displays will improve command and control and significantly enhance the responsiveness of flying units. By means of image intensification and thermal imaging devices and use of terrain-avoidance/terrain-following radar, flight operations will be possible at night and with limited visibility. Identification systems not susceptible to interference will solve the problem of friend-foe identification. Mast-mounted sights for helicopters allow better use of cover during observation and engagement. Counter-rotating rotors give more lift and speed and eliminate the tail rotor. Better crash resistance will improve the chances of crew survival. Intelligent camouflage by a digital camouflage screen will improve protection of aircraft on the ground. Aerial refueling greatly expands the radius of action.

It will always be important to establish the right balance of armor protection and weight and to keep maintenance and repair performance and resources as low as possible. Only the large industrial nations can afford the high costs of aeronautic research and development. Smaller nations wishing to keep up will have to work cooperatively with each other or with the larger countries.

The Helicopter as a Weapon System

Lasers and optical waveguide technology will likely be used for target location and engagement. Armament will consist of air-to-ground and air-to-air rockets and missiles as well as automatic guns with a variety of ammunition. Stand-off weapons with submunitions and intelligent ammunition will complement the helicopter's offensive and defensive capabilities.

Air Transport Aircraft

The variety of transport aircraft is wide-ranging and continually developing. On the one hand are propeller aircraft with a weight-carrying capacity of some tons and extremely short landing and take-off ability, which can be used as assault transport aircraft and can take off and land also on makeshift airstrips. On the other hand are large jet-engine transport aircraft that can carry 100 tons or more, refuel in flight, and operate at speeds just below the speed of sound. The Soviet Antonov 225, developed from the Antonov 124, will have a payload capacity of 250 tons, with 6 engines and a speed of 800 km/h (500 mph).

A recent development is the American V-22 Osprey, a tilt-rotor aircraft that combines the efficient flight characteristics of a modern turboprop aircraft with the vertical take-off and landing capabilities of a conventional helicopter. It will cruise at 275 knots (510 kph), carry combat payloads more than 1,000 nautical miles (1,852 km), and—with a flight ferry range of 2,100 nautical miles (3,889 km)—will be capable of self-deploying worldwide without aerial refueling.

The V-22 Osprey can supplement or replace the helicopter in many roles. It will be used for basic troop and cargo transport missions as well as for combat rescue, special warfare, assault support, medical evacuation, and the special requirements of the navy.

Parachutes

The rectangular ram air parachute with its cell design is an example of the possibilities for development of parachutes. Safe and quick release at both extremely high and extremely low drop altitudes, and controllability of the parachutes expand and improve the spectrum of operational use.

Land Warfare in the Future

The intensive use of the third dimension by land forces redistributes the classical elements of battle: fire and movement. The battle becomes highly dynamic. The time needed to move is reduced. Large forces with great firepower can be moved over great distances, concentrated, and dispersed again within a short time. The friendly area is better used and covered completely irrespective of tactical boundaries. Points of main effort can be established and shifted rapidly, gaps can be accepted without great risk, surveyed, and closed as required. Enemy breakthroughs can be contained more rapidly and destroyed by counterattacks. It is possible to attack the enemy on his own territory by overflying obstacles and barriers in surprise attacks. The third dimension will likely gain increased importance. The two-dimensional battlefield will be turned into three-dimensional battlespace. Land warfare will assume a wholly different nature.

Airborne land forces and army aviation can be integrated into an air/land combat branch that will fight the air-land battle in the air, from the air, and on the ground. Units of this air-land combat branch will complement the battle of armored forces. They will conduct all kinds of offensive and defensive operations, normally in cooperation with other operational forces.

The battle in and from the air requires a main battle air vehicle (MBAV) whose different versions will be able to fulfill all tasks of the combined-arms combat. Its development might lead to "air mechanization." Maximum effectiveness can be obtained by concentrating the MBAV as an independent force. Parceling out the valuable MBAV to army divisions would repeat the mistake made in some nations at the beginning of World War II of parceling out tanks to infantry divisions. Success was finally achieved then by the creation of armored divisions.

Particular attention should be given to those elements of the force that are to fight the ground battle. Similar to mechanized infantry, a "heliborne infantry" force will dismount only if so dictated by the combat situation. Its operations might be continually supported by attack helicopters. The force will need new and effective weapons and armament that provide it with the necessary combat power, and it will need modern equipment for field fortifications and barriers. Reconnaissance, combat support, and resupply will be effected by air. For movements, these forces will mount their "laagered" aircraft. The primary weapon system of heliborne infantry will likely be the main battle air vehicle.

Reinhard Uhle-Wettler

See Also: Air Assault; Airlift; Army Aviation; Auftragstaktik; Helicopter; Special Operations; Special Operations Forces.

Bibliography

Bellamy, C. H. 1987. *The future of land warfare.* London and Sydney: Croom Helm.

Galvin, J. R. 1969. *Air assault: The development of airmobile warfare.* New York: Hawthorn Books.

Glantz, D. M. 1984. *The Soviet airborne experience.* Research Survey no. 4. Combat Studies Institute. U. S. Army Command and General Staff College. Washington, D.C.: Government Printing Office.

Merglen, A. 1968. *Histoire et avenir des troupes aéroportées.* Grenoble: B. Arthaud.

Mrazek, J. 1975. *The glider war.* London: Robert Hale; New York: St. Martin's Press.
v. Senger und Etterlin, F. 1983. New operational dimensions. *Journal of the Royal United Service Institute for Defence Studies,* June.
Simpkin, R. E. 1985. *Race to the swift.* London: Brassey's.
Winterbotham, F. 1975. *The ultra secret.* New York: Dell Books.

AIRCRAFT CARRIER

Aircraft carriers are warships designed primarily to carry and operate aircraft at sea. Developed to give surface naval forces integral airpower, they brought about a revolution in seapower. The development of the aircraft carrier began prior to World War I, and carriers played a major role in naval warfare in World War II, particularly in the Pacific theater. For a period of about twenty years beginning in the early 1940s, they were the world's undisputed capital ships. In the post–World War II era, they have figured prominently in navy organization, maritime strategy, gunboat diplomacy, and international politics. They remain the most operationally flexible of warships and among the most expensive and controversial.

An aircraft carrier (*carrier* for short) is a warship designed or modified primarily to carry, launch, and recover aircraft at sea, with the embarked group of aircraft constituting the ship's main battery. An aircraft carrier's most distinguishing visual feature is its flight deck—a large platform elevated some distance above the water that is used to launch and recover aircraft. Aircraft carriers can operate and support aircraft over extended periods in mid-ocean waters. Carriers are thus also distinguished from other warships by their flight control facilities, large aircraft hangars (usually below the flight deck), extensive aviation maintenance facilities, and sizable storage space for aircraft fuel, munitions, and spare parts.

Aircraft carriers typically carry and operate groups of at least ten aircraft; the largest carry 80 or more. The term *aircraft carrier* thus generally excludes surface combatants or other ships equipped to carry and operate a very small number of aircraft (typically helicopters) as one of several installed capabilities. The distinction between aircraft carriers and other aircraft-capable surface warships, however, is not a clean one. Some ships with an intermediate aircraft capability—including today's amphibious dock landing ships, the Soviet Moskva-class cruisers, the French cruiser *Jeanne d'Arc,* and the Italian cruiser *Vittorio Veneto*—occupy a gray zone in between. The Soviet, French, and Italian ships are sometimes called helicopter cruisers.

Somewhat larger gray-zone ships, such as the British Invincible-class and Soviet Kiev-class vessels, are called either aircraft carriers, through-deck cruisers, or (because of their mission orientation) antisubmarine warfare cruisers or carriers. In the case of the Kiev-class ships, constructed in a Black Sea shipyard, the ambiguous nomenclature took on international legal and political significance due to the carrier-related sections of the 1936 Montreux Convention regulating the passage of warships through the Turkish Straits.

Smaller aircraft carriers have been given a variety of names, including light carrier, escort carrier, and more recently sea control ship. Carriers that operate helicopters or fixed-wing vertical/short take-off and landing (VSTOL) aircraft are sometimes called helicopter or VSTOL carriers; carriers oriented toward amphibious warfare are sometimes called amphibious assault ships or commando carriers.

The term *air-capable ship* refers to any ship with a capability to operate at least a few aircraft. *Sea-based air* and *naval aviation* can refer to the broad range of naval aircraft operations, including those involving not just carrier-based aircraft but also surface combatant–based helicopters, seaplanes, unmanned aircraft, and (in the case of *naval aviation*) land-based aircraft and airships as well.

The *air wing* is the carrier's embarked group of aircraft and the personnel who fly and maintain them. An *aircraft carrier battle group* (CVBG or CBG) is a naval grouping including the carrier and associated combatant and naval auxiliary and support ships. A *carrier task force* is either a CVBG or a naval grouping including more than one carrier or CVBG.

Why Aircraft Carriers?

The aircraft carrier exists because: (1) controlling and using the airspace in the area of battle is critical to success in modern naval warfare; (2) land-based aircraft cannot in all circumstances sufficiently control or use the airspace in the area of a naval battle; (3) seaplanes, airships, unmanned aircraft, and missiles cannot in all circumstances adequately substitute for manned, wheeled aircraft; and (4) to reduce costs and improve effectiveness, at least some of a naval force's sea-based aircraft must be deployed together in a group on a single platform.

1. Aircraft perform a variety of important functions in modern warfare, whether on land or at sea. A modern naval force can operate without airpower if need be, but a naval force with insufficient or inferior airpower generally suffers an important and potentially decisive disadvantage.

2. Naval forces operating in areas far from friendly airfields may be beyond the operating radii of friendly land-based aircraft. Even if friendly land-based aircraft are within range they may have to reduce their payloads to reach the area of battle, may have insufficient endurance (time on station) in the area, or may not be able to reach the area in a timely manner. Friendly airfields may be attacked or overrun. Moreover, coordinating operations

between naval forces and distantly located land-based aircraft can be problematic.

3. Seaplanes do not require flight decks but suffer range, payload, and speed disadvantages compared with wheeled aircraft, and they can be used only in calmer waters. Airships (blimps) have great airborne endurance but are much slower than fixed-wing aircraft. Unmanned aircraft are smaller and less expensive than manned aircraft, but for the same mission their payloads can be smaller. Unmanned aircraft lack the operational flexibility and on-scene adaptability that a pilot offers, and they can present greater command and control problems at extended ranges. Missiles are smaller, less expensive, and as fast or faster than manned aircraft, but a given missile can be used only once, and missiles also lack the operational flexibility and adaptability of manned aircraft.

4. Conventional take-off and landing (CTOL) aircraft require a large flight deck and airspace around the ship that is free of missiles and gunfire. These requirements limit the ability of the ship to carry and use many kinds of weapons. Dispersing CTOL aircraft to many ships in a naval force spreads these costs. Helicopters and VSTOL aircraft do not require equally large flight decks and can be dispersed with less of a penalty. Dispersing aircraft, however, also means dispersing flight control and maintenance facilities and personnel. Concentrating aircraft on a single ship makes possible economies of scale in these facilities and personnel, and basing the aircraft on a single ship improves command and control of the aircraft.

Roles, Missions, and Importance

The aircraft carrier is a uniquely flexible warship. Its aircraft have inherent mission flexibility, and the carrier can embark different mixes of aircraft at different times. Carriers are thus useful in a wide variety of naval roles and missions ranging from peacetime presence and crisis response to major war at sea and strategic nuclear deterrence. Carriers and CVBGs are used mostly in operations aimed at establishing control of the sea for one's own use (sea control) and attacking the land from a position at sea (naval power projection).

During World War II, engagements between opposing U.S. and Japanese carrier task forces played a major role in determining which side exercised sea control over broad regions of the Pacific. Carriers were also used heavily in naval power projection operations either to suppress enemy defenses prior to amphibious landings, to support friendly forces in ongoing land battles, or to assist in strategic bombing campaigns.

Since the end of World War II, carriers have participated primarily in strategic nuclear deterrence and in operations oriented toward situations on land. The strategic nuclear role of carriers was particularly important in the 1950s and early 1960s. It then became less important with the deployment of submarine-launched ballistic missiles (SLBMs).

Carrier operations oriented toward situations on land have included participation in wars (e.g., the Korean and Vietnam wars, and the 1982 Falklands/Malvinas conflict) but have more often involved regional deterrence and responses to political crises. To many, the carrier has become the principal instrument of "great power" gunboat diplomacy of the post–World War II era. Concomitantly, movements of carriers have become important as a means to signal resolve and intent, and thus can have an important influence on international politics.

The addition of aircraft as integral elements of surface naval forces greatly increased the area over which surface naval forces could carry out sea-control operations, enhanced their ability to support amphibious operations, and enabled them to project power from the sea directly against deep-inland targets for the first time. By expanding the battle space for surface naval forces by an order of magnitude and by greatly increasing the ability of naval forces to affect land operations, the aircraft carrier brought about a revolution in seapower.

The carrier also revolutionized naval warfare by making the air dimension of battle important even in mid-ocean areas. Moreover, because carrier aircraft frequently operate (or approach at great speed) from beyond visual range, carriers made radio communication and radar detection more critical in naval warfare.

By demonstrating an ability to sink battleships at a range far beyond where battleships could attack it and an ability (with the help of escorts) to fend off attacks from other warships, the aircraft carrier succeeded the battleship early in World War II as the capital ship of the world's navies. It retained this title without dispute until the 1960s, when nuclear propulsion and the SLBM transformed the capabilities of the submarine.

Historical Development

The first milestone in the development of the aircraft carrier occurred in 1910, when a U.S. naval officer made the first takeoff from a ship. Over the next several years, U.S. and British naval officers spearheaded efforts to bring aircraft to sea, but other countries in Europe and elsewhere were also interested in the concept. The first prototype seaplane tenders and aircraft carriers appeared in the British fleet during World War I. Still largely experimental, however, naval aviation played only a small role in that conflict.

Carrier design and development in the 1920s and 1930s featured much experimentation and were influenced by the displacement limits of the interwar naval limitation treaties (Fig. 1). Japan, with early aid from the British (especially in aircraft design), emerged during this time as a third major center of carrier development and operations. In the early interwar period, the principal role envisioned for carriers was to provide reconnaissance for and otherwise support the operations of battleships. By the

Figure 1. Aerial view of an early aircraft carrier, the USS Saratoga; *a T4M-1 airplane with tail hook extended is above (January 1929).* (SOURCE: U.S. Navy)

1930s, however, naval exercises demonstrated that carrier task forces could operate as powerful, independent naval formations.

This capacity was confirmed early in World War II by the late-1940 British carrier raid on the Taranto, Italy, naval base and by the late-1941/early-1942 Japanese carrier-led attacks on Pearl Harbor and other sites in the Pacific. The U.S.-Japanese carrier task force battles in the Coral Sea and off Midway in mid-1942 were the first in the history of naval warfare in which ships from opposing sides never came within visual range of one another. Carrier task force sea control and power-projection operations were central to the U.S. effort in 1943–45 to capture Japanese-held islands, destroy Japan's military, and strangle the Japanese war effort at home. At the end of the war in 1945, the United States had a force of about 100 aircraft carriers (20 large-deck carriers, 9 light carriers, and about 70 smaller escort carriers), about 41,000 carrier-based planes, and about 61,000 carrier-qualified pilots.

British carriers during World War II participated in the early defense of Norway but operated more extensively in the Mediterranean and the North Atlantic, where they escorted convoys and surface combatants and supported the invasions of North Africa, Italy, and southern France. Late in the war, British carriers operated in the South Pacific as well, where they carried out land-attack operations. Britain ended the war with a force of about 50 carriers, most of them of the smaller escort type and many built in the United States.

The post–World War II period has featured a decline in the total number of carriers in the world's navies, the emergence of additional countries as carrier operators, and four important developments in carrier design and use: (1) the atomic bomb, which gave carriers a strategic nuclear role; (2) the appearance of jet aircraft, which prompted the adoption of the angled deck, the steam catapult, and the mirror landing system; (3) the development of naval nuclear propulsion, which gave carriers and CVBGs greater endurance; and (4) the advent of the helicopter and fixed-wing VSTOL aircraft, which led to the development of the amphibious assault ship, the concept of vertical envelopment in amphibious landings, the VSTOL carrier, and the helicopter-equipped surface combatant.

Key Technical Features

The key technical features of the carrier are those that help its aircraft take off and land with maximum efficiency and those involved with aircraft storage and upkeep. The angled deck, the steam catapult, the mirror landing system, and the "ski jump" ramp were all originally British conceptions.

The angled- or canted-deck design, developed in the early 1950s, enables the carrier to support take-off and landing operations simultaneously or (if no aircraft are landing) to launch a larger number of aircraft in a given time. The angled deck thus increases the tempo at which the carrier can conduct air operations. It also improves safety: pilots overshooting a landing attempt run much less risk of crashing into parked aircraft and can return for another landing attempt.

Catapults enable heavier CTOL aircraft to take off from carriers, allow aircraft to take off with reduced wind over deck or in a crosswind, shorten take-off rolls and thus allow more aircraft to be parked on deck, permit night takeoffs without deck lights, and make possible takeoffs even with some level of flight deck damage. Early catapults were operated by compressed air and hydraulics; the current steam-driven type was developed in the early 1950s.

The upward-sloping ski jump ramp has emerged within the last several years as a simple yet important advance in VSTOL carrier operations. The ramp enables a VSTOL jet plane to make a rolling takeoff, which increases range and payload capacity substantially compared with vertical operation.

Prior to the jet age, CTOL aircraft were guided to their landings by landing signal officers. Jet aircraft prompted the development of the mirror landing system, which used lights and mirrors to provide a landing path for the pilot and could aid approaching pilots farther out and provide them with more rapid, continuous feedback. The mirror system has been succeeded by a Fresnel lens system and by carrier-controlled approach, in which the carrier tracks the position of the approaching aircraft by radar and controls its approach by radio command.

A landing CTOL airplane is brought to a halt by a system of transverse arresting wires that catch a hook on the tail of the airplane. Arresting-wire systems shorten the landing roll, permit higher landing speeds, and allow landings with greater degrees of ship roll and pitch.

The hangar takes up much of the internal volume of a carrier. The hangar and the elevators that connect it to the flight deck together limit the number and size of aircraft that can be embarked and influence the cycle of operations on the flight deck. Maintenance facilities, located in or adjoining the hangar, are critical for supporting aircraft operations for extended periods of time. Aircraft carriers are very personnel-intensive warships—the largest U.S. carriers have a total complement of more than 5,500—in large part because of the number of people required to maintain the ship's aircraft.

Current Issues and Future Prospects

Two important issues regarding the aircraft carrier today are (1) the extent to which nations will continue to include carriers as part of their navies and (2) the extent to which CTOL carrier aviation will survive as VSTOL aircraft and alternatives to manned aircraft are developed.

Prominence of Carriers

Few nations today believe they must maintain an ability to control the seas away from their coastal zone or carry out distant power-projection operations; fewer still can afford to maintain such a capability in the form of carriers and CVBGs. Advances in technologies for long-range, precision-guided weapons, unmanned aircraft, and submarines, moreover, have led some to question the wartime survivability and cost-effectiveness of carriers relative to the alternatives. Carrier supporters, however, strongly demur, and the issue has been extensively debated, particularly in the United States.

Today, only the United States, with a force of more than a dozen large, angled-deck carriers and several additional amphibious assault ships, remains a major operator of aircraft carriers. Given its investment and experience in carriers, the United States will likely remain a major carrier operator into the next century. The former Soviet Union, with a force of two helicopter cruisers, four through-deck cruisers, and plans for at least three large, angled-deck carriers, appeared to stand the best chance of joining the United States in this category. More likely, however, they will remain a member of a second tier of carrier-operating nations that also includes Great Britain, France, and India, which currently operate two or three carriers each. Japan (which has not operated carriers since World War II) and China are often mentioned as candidates to join this second tier over the next ten or twenty years.

CTOL and VSTOL Carrier Aviation

Sea-based aviation was once dominated by the CTOL carrier, but helicopters and VSTOL jet planes now play a much more prominent role. Although CTOL aircraft are still more capable in most respects than VSTOL aircraft, the technology for VSTOL aircraft is improving, and VSTOL aircraft can be operated off smaller, less expensive carriers. Given these factors, as well as limits of national budgets and on perceived needs for sea control and naval power-projection capabilities, most carrier navies in the future will probably operate VSTOL rather than CTOL carriers.

Aircraft carriers in the future may thus constitute a smaller portion of global naval aviation than at times in the past, and CTOL carriers will likely be operated by only a small portion of all carrier operators. Nevertheless, carriers have proved to be enduring and valuable elements of naval power for countries that need and can afford them, and countries that operate carriers, particularly those with CTOL aircraft, will continue to rank among the top naval powers.

Ronald O'Rourke

See Also: Aircraft, Short Take-off and Landing; Fleet; Fleet Air Defense; Gunboat Diplomacy; Halsey, William F.; Nimitz, Chester William; Organization, Naval; Vietnam and Indochina Wars; World War II; Yamamoto, Isoroku.

Bibliography

Beaver, P. 1987. *The British aircraft carrier.* 3d ed. New York and Wellingborough, Northamptonshire: P. Stephens.

Belote, J. H. 1975. *Titans of the seas: The development and operations of Japanese and American carrier task forces during World War II.* New York: Harper and Row.

Chesneau, R. 1984. *Aircraft carriers of the world, 1914 to the present: An illustrated encyclopedia.* Annapolis, Md.: U.S. Naval Institute Press.

Friedman, N. 1981. *Carrier air power.* Greenwich, U.K.: Conway Maritime.

———. 1983. *U.S. aircraft carriers: An illustrated design history.* Annapolis, Md.: U.S. Naval Institute Press.

———. 1989. *British carrier aviation: The evolution of the ships and their aircraft.* Annapolis, Md.: U.S. Naval Institute Press.

Jordan, J. 1983. *An illustrated guide to modern naval aviation and aircraft carriers.* New York: Arco.

Lehman, J. F. 1978. *Aircraft carriers: The real choices.* Beverly Hills, Calif.: Sage.

Melhorn, C. M. 1974. *Two-block fox: The rise of the aircraft carrier, 1911–1929.* Annapolis, Md.: U.S. Naval Institute Press.

Polmar, N., et al. 1969. *Aircraft carriers: A graphic history of carrier aviation and its influence on world events.* Garden City, N.Y.: Doubleday.

Poolman, K. 1988. *Allied escort carriers of World War Two in action.* Annapolis, Md.: U.S. Naval Institute Press.

Preston, A. 1979. *Aircraft carriers.* London and New York: Hamlyn.

Reynolds, C. G. 1978. *The fast carriers: The forging of an air navy.* Huntington, N.Y.: R. E. Krieger.

Terzibaschitsch, S. 1989. *Aircraft carriers of the U.S. Navy.* 2d ed. Annapolis, Md.: U.S. Naval Institute Press.

Y'Blood, W. T. 1983. *Hunter-killer: U.S. escort carriers in the battle of the Atlantic.* Annapolis, Md.: U.S. Naval Institute Press.

———. 1987. *The little giants: U.S. escort carriers against Japan.* Annapolis, Md.: U.S. Naval Institute Press.

AIRCRAFT, MILITARY

The twentieth century has been the century of the airplane, as the development of military aircraft led the way to a technological and social revolution. Even more than the automobile, the airplane has dramatically changed the lifestyles of individuals and businesses and the relationships among nations in war and peace. Airplanes have literally shrunk the planet Earth.

The first practical applications of aircraft were military. First there was observation, then reconnaissance, then air-to-ground bombardment, then air-to-air combat. Other combat missions such as air transport and electronic warfare developed rapidly. In fact, most military uses of aircraft had been conceived, developed, and utilized by the time World War I ended, just fifteen years after the first flight of a fixed-wing aircraft.

The principles of physics and aerodynamics that permit an airplane to fly are the same in civilian and military aircraft, but military aircraft differ in several ways from those used by civilians for commercial passengers, freight transportation, pleasure, and rescue. Military aircraft are used for these same purposes, but the most distinct uses are in the defense of a government and country against its enemies, or the posturing of military aircraft to prevent attack by an enemy. In almost all cases, military aircraft are owned and operated by a national government and used for national purposes.

Military aircraft, therefore, may be armored and are designed with more sophisticated technology to permit the effective delivery of a wide range of weapons. The research and development of military aircraft components is often more elaborate than that devoted to civilian aircraft. Military aircraft may be designed to stretch performance envelopes to develop longer range, greater lift capacity, shorter takeoffs and landings, higher air speeds, the ability to refuel in the air, and so forth. These developments enhance the capabilities of the air force's aircraft, but eventually may also be used to improve the capabilities of aircraft used in civilian pursuits.

When considering the enormous variety of military aircraft that are available to the nations of the world at the end of the twentieth century, it is useful to establish categories or mission areas. It should be kept in mind, however, that any categorization is arbitrary and many military aircraft perform two or more types of missions. It is also useful to remember that many civil aircraft can support military missions, especially in military transportation and observation.

Observation

Although almost all military aircraft can accomplish the observation mission, it is secondary for all but a few types of light aircraft. There are a few aircraft, notably light observation helicopters, whose principal mission is observation. The mission is not only to observe and report back the disposition of enemy forces but also to observe and report on terrain, refugees, and other relevant military information. Many modern military forces possess observation helicopters controlled and flown by army officers and noncommissioned officers. In addition to observation helicopters, light, fixed-winged aircraft are dedicated to observation. These observation aircraft provide army commanders with up-to-date, almost minute-by-minute, analysis of the battlefield as well as the area immediately to the rear of the battlefield.

The most serious deficiencies of observation aircraft are their short range, their vulnerability to enemy ground fire, and their general inability to accomplish effective observation in very bad weather and at night. In fact, it is genuinely accepted doctrine throughout the world that observation aircraft should not fly over heavily defended enemy territory if they are to avoid unacceptable attrition. A good example of a modern observation aircraft is the British Optica Scout. To maximize observation, pilot and observers have marvelous visibility downward, to each side, upward, and to the rear. This 2,000-pound aircraft, very inexpensive to fly and to maintain, takes off and lands in less than 300 meters (1,000 ft.), and has an eight-hour endurance capability.

Reconnaissance

When aircraft are equipped with sensors such as cameras, radar, and infrared detectors, they usually are designated reconnaissance aircraft. Dedicated reconnaissance aircraft that use speed and low-altitude penetration to avoid being shot down are normally called tactical reconnaissance aircraft. The best example of a dedicated tactical reconnaissance aircraft in the Western world in the 1970s, 80s, and 90s is the RF-4 Phantom. First used in combat during the Vietnam War by the United States, it has been modified many times to incorporate more and more sophisticated sensors, a number of which can downlink information directly to analysis centers on the ground.

There is a strong trend in the 1980s and 1990s away from dedicated reconnaissance aircraft and toward the use of reconnaissance pods that are hung on fighter aircraft whenever the reconnaissance mission is of vital importance. Another strong trend in the area of tactical reconnaissance in the 1980s and 1990s is the development and deployment of reconnaissance drones or remotely piloted vehicles. Israel has led the way, having developed sophisticated remotely piloted vehicles and having used them in combat, but a number of other nations have such programs. Their great advantage is that no aircrew is lost if one is shot down or lost over enemy territory. Also, unmanned vehicles can be sent into areas and at altitudes that would be extremely daunting to a pilot flying a reconnaissance aircraft.

Another important trend in recent years in the area of tactical reconnaissance is the rapid analysis of raw reconnaissance information into intelligence that can be useful to the commanders in the field. This is a real challenge since reconnaissance aircraft with many sensors can collect an enormous amount of information on a single sortie.

Military aircraft that fly at very high altitudes and that have sensors that can reach out many hundreds of miles to collect information are normally labeled strategic reconnaissance aircraft. Only the more powerful nations of the world have aircraft dedicated to strategic reconnaissance. Examples of strategic reconnaissance aircraft are the U.S. SR-71 and RC-135, both of which have served with the Strategic Air Command. The SR-71 (now retired) is a Mach-three aircraft, while the RC-135 is a large four-engine subsonic aircraft.

Close Air Support

In the years since World War II, few nations have developed aircraft like the wartime German Stuka, that was dedicated to the specific role of close air support of ground forces in combat. However, the American A-10 aircraft and various armed helicopters (the American Cobra and Apache and the Soviet Hind) have provided fire support and close air support to ground forces as their primary mission. Close air support is an especially challenging mission for manned aircraft since they are vulnerable when they maneuver over the combat area. In addition, they must be careful not to attack friendly forces. Hence, precise target identification is quite important, yet attempts to be absolutely sure that the target is an enemy target often mean even more vulnerability to enemy ground fire. Aircraft that are especially effective for this mission are the A-10, the Alpha jet, the A-4, the Forger, the Harrier, and the A-7, as well as helicopters such as the Hind and the Apache.

Air Interdiction

Interdiction is a natural and appropriate mission for fighter and attack aircraft. Unlike close air support, interdiction is conducted far enough behind enemy territory that all military targets may be considered enemy. The key to interdiction is the selection of targets that will make a real difference in the overall campaign plan. If the intensity of combat is high and the enemy needs a resupply, if lines of communication are fragile, and if there are no major sanctuaries that interdicting aircraft are not authorized to attack (e.g., Cambodia during the Vietnam War) then interdiction can be highly effective and at times decisive to the battle. Military aircraft engaged in the interdiction mission must have the ability to hit targets with precision and persistence; these include bridges, command and control centers, roads and railroads that pass through mountain passes, and major supply areas. These attacks can seriously disrupt the ability of the enemy to support and resupply frontline troops. Precision-guided weapons, long range, and heavy ordnance loads are helpful in ensuring that each interdiction sortie is of high value. It is also very helpful if a significant number of interdiction aircraft can find and destroy targets in inclement weather and at night.

There are two subelements of the interdiction mission: battlefield air interdiction and deep interdiction. Battlefield air interdiction is conducted close enough to the front lines that fairly close coordination is needed with ground forces, although the degree of close control is not as strict as that required for close air support because in battlefield air interdiction friendly troops are not normally endangered by friendly aircraft. Deep interdiction is conducted hundreds of miles deep into enemy territory. It is designed to impede the movement of follow-on forces that might be moving forward to support the immediate battle area. Aircraft that are especially adept at the interdiction mission include the West European Tornado; the Italian Alpha jet; the Soviet MiG-27 Fencer; the U.S. F-117A, F-16, A-7, and F-18; and the new Indian light combat aircraft.

Offensive Counterair

One of the most important roles for military aircraft is the establishment and maintenance of air superiority. One way to ensure this is the destruction of enemy air bases so the ability of the enemy to produce combat sorties is seriously degraded. The classic success story was the Israeli attack on Arab airfields during the 1967 Arab-Israeli war. Within a few hours, the Israeli air force destroyed so many aircraft on the ground that for the rest of the war Israel had not only air superiority, but air supremacy.

Aircraft engaged in the offensive counterair mission must have the range, the payload, the types of ordnance, and the persistence to knock out the key enemy airfields and keep them largely unserviceable throughout the duration of the war. This is a difficult mission if the enemy has a large number of airfields, the airfields are heavily defended by air defense systems, and they have large numbers of hardened shelters to protect aircraft, maintenance, supply, and command and control facilities. This is clearly the case in both Western and Eastern Europe since the mid-1970s. The development in air-to-ground munitions, which will allow an attacking aircraft to do significant long-term damage to runways, taxiways, and shelters, has made the attacking of airfields a feasible mission. Aircraft that are especially useful in this mission are the Fencer, the F-111, the F-15E, and the Tornado since all can carry a large ordnance load and have very long combat radii at low altitude.

Defensive Counterair

Shooting enemy aircraft down in air-to-air combat has been an important and exciting mission ever since World War I. Very high performance aircraft with superb maneuverability, a good mix of air-to-air munitions, and highly trained and aggressive pilots are all required if this mission is to be accomplished successfully. Aircraft that are particularly well designed for the air-to-air mission include the Spitfire and P-51 of World War II, the MiG-15 and the F-86 of the Korean War in the early 1950s, the F-4 and the MiG-21 of the Vietnam War, and the MiG-23, Mirage, Kfir, F-16, and F-15 of the Middle East wars of the 1960s, 70s, 80s, and 90s.

The F-15 aircraft, which was specifically designed for the air-to-air mission, is worth examining in some detail since it has been the best defensive counterair aircraft of the 1970s, 80s and the early 90s (see Fig. 1). With two powerful afterburning engines, it is the first fighter capable of accelerating while climbing straight up, since the thrust of its engines is greater than its weight. It has superb cockpit visibility and the best long-range radar of any fighter aircraft. The head-up display in the cockpit allows the pilot to spend the majority of his time looking outside the aircraft rather than having to look into the cockpit many times each minute. Critical information is displayed on the windscreen in such a way that the pilot can quickly gain radar, attitude, weapons systems firing parameters, and other information without looking into the cockpit.

Figure 1. Air-to-air front view of two F-15 Eagle aircraft, one directly behind the other. (SOURCE: Courtesy of the U.S. Air Force)

Soviet developments in defensive counterair aircraft were quite impressive in the 1970s and 1980s. These decades saw the deployment of large numbers of MiG-23 Floggers, MiG-25 Foxbats, MiG-29 Fulcrums, Su-27 Flankers, and MiG-31 Foxhounds. Some of the most modern Soviet fighters are equipped with infrared search and track systems. The French Mirage 2000 is also an impressive air-to-air fighter as are the Swedish Viggen and Grippen and the new Taiwanese Indigenous Fighter.

One of the disappointments in fighter developments in the 1980s was the cancellation of the Israeli Lavi. There is a useful lesson here. The design, development, and procurement of the best in air-to-air fighters is very expensive and difficult. Even an advanced nation, Israel, was not able to design, build, and market overseas a fighter appreciably better than the F-16.

Missile development has also been very impressive and the better defensive counterair aircraft have heat-seeking and radar-homing missiles as well as cannon. Developments to be expected in the 1990s are antiradiation missiles that will allow air-to-air missiles to home in on the radar energy of enemy fighters, attack aircraft, and bombers.

Strategic Bombardment

This is the classic mission for military aircraft. It was the Italian, Giulio Douhet, a prophet of airpower, who saw strategic bombardment as the means by which airpower would be decisive in warfare. The idea of air forces, separate and distinct from armies and navies, came about because of the belief in the independent and potentially decisive role of the strategic bomber in warfare. In modern times, a strategic bomber has a combat radius of at least 4,800 kilometers (3,000 mi.) and is normally able to fly much farther as a result of a capability to be refueled while airborne.

The B-17, B-24, B-29, and Lancaster of World War II and the Bear, Bison, Blackjack, Vulcan, B-52, and B-1 in the postwar period have been classic long-range strategic bombardment aircraft. Strategic bombers carry nuclear weapons (in many cases up to 20) or conventional bombs. These bombers can penetrate enemy territory at low altitudes to avoid detection and interception. They often are equipped with terrain-following radar which allows them to fly at altitudes of 60 meters (200 ft.) or less even in bad weather and at night. Most modern bombers can deliver a mix of weapons including freefall bombs, glide bombs, short-range attack missiles, and long-range cruise missiles. Older bombers normally are relegated to the standoff role in nuclear war since they are so likely to be shot down if they try to penetrate. In the standoff role, they launch long-range cruise missiles that have the capability to reach their targets on their own. The latest bombers use stealth technology. The American B-2 is radical in design; it maximizes the uses of airframe and engine geometries, radar absorptive materials, and other techniques and devices to make it very difficult to observe by sensors such as radars and infrared detectors. Large stealthy bombers are extremely expensive and it remains to be seen if they will be built in large numbers, even by the major world powers.

Airlift

Aircraft designed to carry troops or military cargo are called airlift aircraft. The short-range aircraft that can get in and out of small airfields near the battlefield are called tactical airlifters, those that fly long distances and deliver their cargo at airfields to the rear of the combat zone are called strategic airlift aircraft. Examples of strategic airlift aircraft are the American C-141, the C-5; and the Soviet Il-76 Candid, the An-22 Cock, the An-124, and the new six-engine An-225. Examples of tactical airlift aircraft are the U.S. C-130 Hercules, the Casa 235, the Transall C-160, the Kawasaki C-1, and the An-12 Cub. A new airplane slated for operational use in the early 1990s should span both of these missions quite nicely. The C-17, manufactured by McDonnell Douglas, is designed to fly intercontinental distances, carry oversize and outsize cargo, yet land on short runways near the combat zone. Nations that possess this type of aircraft will have a great advantage over those that do not for there will be no need to offload cargo and troops at a major base and transport them to the battlefield.

Warning and Surveillance

One of the most fascinating developments in military aircraft has been the placement of radar on an aircraft that can look out in all directions. The United States was first to produce an operational system and there are two American aircraft now operational. The E-3 airborne warning and control system (AWACS) aircraft is a Boeing 707 with a large rotating antenna anchored to its top. Aboard the aircraft are a dozen or so radar controllers who have access to all the radar information that the AWACS collects and are in radio communications with friendly fighters. Using air-to-air radios, these controllers direct interceptors toward enemy aircraft. Hence, they control the air battle and make the air-to-air environment over friendly territory much more favorable to the defense. The United States has more than 30 of these aircraft. The North Atlantic Treaty Organization (NATO) alliance has purchased eighteen of the large American AWACS and Britain, France, and Saudi Arabia a few.

There is a fascinating organizational aspect to AWACS aircraft operated by NATO. For the first time in history, an alliance owns a weapon. These aircraft, which have their main operating base in Geilenkirchen, West Germany, are manned by airmen from eleven NATO nations. Since the aircraft support air defense throughout the alliance, they serve a useful purpose in helping to standardize air defense procedures from one NATO tactical air force to another. The U.S. Navy also has an aircraft that serves the same purpose—the E-2C. These aircraft are based on aircraft carriers and although they have smaller radars and fewer on-board controllers than the larger AWACS, they play a vital role in controlling the air war at sea. Israel also uses a few E-2Cs. The Soviets developed an AWACS capability with their Tupolev 126 Moss and Ilyushin 76 Mainstay.

Aerial Refueling

Although the capability to transfer aviation fuel from one aircraft to another was demonstrated as early as the 1920s, it was not until the 1950s that dedicated air-refueling aircraft began to appear in large numbers. The U.S. Air Force, immediately after World War II, realized that if it was to carry out its global responsibilities it would need large numbers of air-refueling aircraft deployed around the world to support bomber and fighter aircraft. KB-50s and KC-97s in large numbers supported the Strategic Air Command during the 1950s. These were large, propeller-driven aircraft that offloaded fuel while maintaining a speed of about 200 knots at an altitude of 6,100 meters (20,000 ft.). With the deployment of the B-47, B-52, F-100, and F-105 in the mid-1950s, a high speed, jet-powered air-refueling aircraft was needed. The KC-135 was the answer and in the late 1950s and early 1960s more than 800 KC-135s were manufactured by Boeing and deployed throughout the world. In the 1980s and the 1990s these aircraft have been reskinned and reengined and given an additional 30,000 hours of airframe time. As a result the KC-135 could become the first 100-year-old aircraft, since some may still be in service past the middle of the twenty-first century. In the 1980s, the U.S. Air Force purchased 60 KC-10s from McDonnell Douglas. These large tankers not only provide a great deal of jet fuel to various receivers but also have a huge cargo capacity. The KC-10 is a favorite for fighter deployments because it can carry much of a maintenance support team and the team's equipment for its fighter aircraft.

Another innovation of the 1970s and 80s in air refueling is the ability to transfer fuel to other aircraft besides fighters and bombers. For instance, every strategic airlift aircraft in the U.S. Air Force (C-5 and C-141) can receive fuel through air-to-air refueling. Hence, en-route stops of the past are no longer necessary because American airlift aircraft can be topped off with fuel half-way across the Atlantic or Pacific. With the growing uncertainty about overseas bases, every major power can benefit from a significant air-refueling capability. Russia, the United Kingdom, and Israel also have an air-refueling capability. The United States, however, is so dominant in this area of military airpower that it possesses more air-refueling capability than all other nations combined.

Electronic Combat Aircraft

Those aircraft, whose primary role is electronic combat, are jamming aircraft and hunter-killer aircraft. During the Vietnam War the Americans used "wild weasel" aircraft, which were able to detect enemy radars, lock on to those radars, and launch antiradiation missiles to attack and destroy these radars. The main targets were the radars of North Vietnamese surface-to-air missile sites. A deadly cat-and-mouse game would often take place. The North Vietnamese radars would come on the air in order to locate, lock on, and engage the American attack aircraft. The American wild weasel aircraft would detect the radar signal, lock on to it, and launch antiradiation missiles. The sites would often turn off their radars in order to avoid being destroyed by the American missiles. If the sites turned off their radars, they were unable to guide missiles proceeding toward the American attack aircraft.

Also used extensively during the Vietnam War were jamming aircraft. Aircraft such as the EB-66 flew off the coast of North Vietnam and sent out strong electronic jamming signals aimed at the North Vietnamese radars in order to reduce their effectiveness against attacking American fighters and fighter bombers.

Airborne Command Posts

Starting in the 1950s, there has been development of a new type of military aircraft, the airborne command post. In the era of the nuclear weapon it is terribly important that essential command and control nodes be able to survive the initial nuclear attack so that appropriate retaliation can take place. Airborne command posts serve a deterrent and warfighting purpose in this regard. If nation A knows that nation B can orchestrate nuclear retaliation even after nation A launches a first strike, nation A will be much less likely to launch an attack in the first place. The United States had a command post airborne twenty-four hours a day, 365 days per year, for many decades. The aircraft was a modified KC-135 (code word "Looking Glass") with a general officer on board and sophisticated communications and command-and-control equipment. In addition, the Americans have a larger and more sophisticated command post, the E-4 (a modified Boeing 747) designed to carry the president. There are carefully developed procedures for getting the president into the command post in the case of a nuclear crisis. This aircraft, using air-refueling, can remain airborne for a number of days.

There are also tactical airborne command posts, which were used extensively during the Vietnam War. They were C-130 Hercules, which carried a large, self-contained pod. Inside the pod were controllers who gave mission direction to the attack aircraft going to their targets. They also received bomb damage assessment reports. These airborne command posts flew over friendly territory and helped senior commanders manage the air campaign on a minute-by-minute basis.

Special Operations Aircraft

The special operations mission is a fascinating one and has received great interest in recent years. The ability to insert troops deep into the territory of another nation, to keep them supplied, and to extract them on short notice is a particularly demanding mission. This mission is accomplished by three distinct types of military aircraft: specialized helicopters, fixed-wing aircraft such as the C-130, and tiltrotor aircraft such as the V-22 Osprey. Since special operations will become a more important mission in the future, trends in this mission area will be important. This mission area is particularly important to the Soviet Union, the United States, Israel, and Britain and most of the technological and doctrinal developments come from these nations.

Training Aircraft

There are a large number of aircraft used throughout the world to train military aviators. In fact, the greatest amount of sales competition occurs in this area because so many nations have designed and built training aircraft that they hope to sell to others. With the U.S. Air Force and Navy looking for new trainers in the 1990s, the competition for these big markets is very high, indeed. The Argentine Pampa, the Spanish CASA C-101, the Belgian Squalus, and the British Hawk are all jet powered; the Swiss PC-9 Pilatus and the Brazilian Tucano are powered by turboprop engines. These are just a few of the excellent two-seat military training aircraft that came to the fore in the 1980s.

Trends for the Future

The early part of the next century will be a time of radical change for military aircraft. There will be a strong move toward remotely piloted vehicles, drones, and autonomous vehicles. These will be military aircraft performing military missions; however, the introduction of these aircraft into the inventories of the air forces, armies, and navies of the world will be traumatic for leaders who have been pilots and navigators of manned aircraft. The trend toward autonomous vehicles will result from a number of important factors. First, explosive changes in technology will permit the marriage of very small, efficient engines, light and inexpensive composite materials, and very sophisticated sensors. Second, political factors will encourage national decisionmakers to build vehicles that are stealthy and unmanned, so that if one is lost, there is not the embarrassment of having a downed aviator captured.

Third, cost factors will be at play and it will be cheaper to build and maintain autonomous systems. Not having to fly these vehicles on a regular basis to keep the aircrews trained will reduce costs. Autonomous vehicles will be able to take over a major portion of the tactical reconnaissance, close air support, interdiction, and offensive counterair missions. Autonomous vehicles will have less of an impact on the defensive counterair, airlift, strategic reconnaissance, and observation missions. In other words, those missions that require flying over enemy territory will be most significantly affected by autonomous vehicles. Unmanned autonomous military aircraft will also be quite useful in "softening up" the enemy before manned aircraft penetrate enemy airspace. By attacking radar sites, command, control and communications nodes, surface-to-air missile sites, and gun positions, they can reduce losses of manned penetrating aircraft.

Another significant trend for the future will be the impact of low-observable technology on military aircraft, both manned and unmanned. Stealthy military aircraft, particularly those that are stealthy in many dimensions (hard to detect on radar screens, on infrared detection devices, to the human eye, to photonic systems), will be able to operate over enemy territory for extended periods of time (hours and, in some cases, days) with relative impunity. Most stealthy aircraft will have the capability to make themselves nonstealthy, so they can be picked up on radar in peacetime for air traffic control purposes. This ability to quickly move from visible to invisible (and vice versa) will also have some tactical applications. For instance, a penetrating aircraft may wish to be nonstealthy in order to flush out the interceptors and then become stealthy before being intercepted. This would be an especially useful technique if the stealthy penetrating aircraft were followed by nonstealthy vehicles. If the enemy interceptor force was out of fuel and having to recover for refueling purposes, penetration by nonstealthy aircraft could then be more effective.

Summary

The evolution of military aircraft in the past century has gone through a number of phases. There have been times when developments have been evolutionary and other times of radical change in a short period. Those who wish to plan for the future must study the past while remaining extremely open minded to new ideas, technical developments, and doctrinal innovation. The best military aircraft of the future will be developed by those who can combine doctrinal flexibility, a keen awareness of technological possibilities, and the ability to cut through bureaucratic barriers to creative innovation. In addition, reliability and maintainability must be weighed carefully in the design bureaus of the world. Since airpower may soon become the dominant force in military operations, the nations that stay in the forefront of the development of military aircraft will have disproportionate influence in world affairs in the twenty-first century.

Perry M. Smith

See Also: Air Interdiction; Air Reconnaissance; Aircraft, Short Take-off and Landing; Aircraft Technology Applications; Aircraft, Unmanned; Airpower; Army Aviation; Aviation, Military; Close Air Support; Combined Arms; Electronic Warfare, Air; Engine Technology, Aircraft; Helicopter; Stealth and Counterstealth Technology.

Bibliography

Jane's all the world's aircraft, 1987–1988. 1987. London: Jane's.

Jane's all the world's aircraft, 1988–1989. 1988. London: Jane's.

Mason, R. A. 1987. *Air power: An overview of roles.* London: Brassey's.

Singh, J. 1985. *Air power in modern warfare.* New Delhi: Lancer International.

Shaker, S. M., and A. R. Wolf. 1988. *War without men: Robots on the future battlefield.* Washington, D.C.: Pergamon-Brassey's.

AIRCRAFT, SHORT TAKE-OFF AND LANDING (STOL)

One of the most fascinating phenomena of the post-World War II era has been the development of fixed-wing aircraft that can take off and land vertically or in very short distances. If a high percentage of a nation's combat or combat support aircraft can take off and land in about 100 meters (or approx. 330 ft.), the need for expensive and vulnerable airfields diminishes enormously. This article explains technological and doctrinal aspects of short-take-off-and-landing aircraft and reviews possible future trends that could have a major impact on military aircraft, on major air bases, and on warfare itself.

Types of Aircraft

In their purest form, vertical/short take-off and landing aircraft are able to take off and land vertically. V/STOL is the common acronym for these fixed-wing aircraft that can take off and land either vertically or in a short distance (approx. 100m, or 328 ft.). Since helicopters are a separate category they are discussed elsewhere in this encyclopedia.

The Harrier

The classic example of a vertical take-off and landing combat aircraft is the Harrier. A very versatile aircraft, it has served as a fighter, attack, and reconnaissance aircraft and has been used by the British, American, and Spanish air services. Designed and developed by the British, it was a truly revolutionary airplane when it first appeared in the 1960s, and was probably the most important technological breakthrough in combat aviation in the decade of the

1960s, since for the first time, an operational fighter had a true vertical take-off and vertical landing capability. In combat, and combat training, however, the aircraft usually takes off horizontally and lands vertically. During these missions, its take-off roll is very short, usually only 120–150 meters (400–500 ft.). By taking off horizontally, the aircraft can carry a larger payload and the operation is safer since, in the event of an engine problem immediately after takeoff, the aircraft can descend quickly and land on the remaining portion of the runway or road service. In normal, peacetime, day-to-day operations the landing is also made horizontally since a vertical landing is always a bit more hazardous than a horizontal landing. If engine failure should occur in the hover during a vertical landing, the potential for a serious crash landing is high.

The British Royal Air Force has been the primary force for technological, doctrinal, and logistic support concepts for this radical new capability. In fact, one of the primary advocates of the Harrier concepts in the Royal Air Force, Air Chief Marshal Paddy Hine, became the head of the Royal Air Force in the late 1980s. The U.S. Marine Corps has also made significant contributions to the development of V/STOL doctrine and has become the major institutional supporter of V/STOL aircraft within the U.S. Department of Defense.

The Harrier is also the major fighter aircraft of the Royal Navy's Fleet Air Arm, and it performed very effectively in the 1982 Falklands/Malvinas conflict between Great Britain and Argentina.

In the late 1980s an updated version of the Harrier began to come off the production line. The AV-8B has a greater payload, range, and performance than the AV-8A, the original Harrier. The AV-8B has become a major element in the air combat capability of the U.S. Marine Corps. The Royal Air Force has also introduced a new and better version of the Harrier into its inventory, the Gr-5, which has about double the range and payload of the earlier model of the Harrier, the Gr-3. The Soviets have also developed a vertical take-off fighter aircraft, the Yakolev 36 Forger, which is similar to the Harrier and employed much like U.S. Marine Corps Harriers, that is, from small carriers.

The Osprey

Another breakthrough in V/STOL technology is the American V-22 Osprey (Fig. 1). This is also a fixed-wing aircraft, but the engines, located at the extremities of each wing, can rotate 90 degrees so the aircraft can take off and land on extremely short runways or landing pads. The ability to rotate the engines throughout the full range from horizontal to vertical provides an extraordinary capability to the pilot. For instance, he may rotate the engines to about 45 percent of the vertical for a very short takeoff that will minimize the use of runway while still providing a margin of safety in case of engine problems.

In 1989 the U.S. Secretary of Defense, Richard Cheney, decided during a severe budgetary crisis to cancel development of this aircraft. There is strong support for the Osprey in the U.S. Congress, however, especially among those who feel that the United States must develop a capability to deal with low-intensity warfare in the future.

Figure 1. V-22 aircraft. (SOURCE: Bell Helicopter Textron Inc.)

If the Osprey is built, it will be able to accomplish the special operations mission; that is, it will be able to insert and pick up small teams of troops deep inside unfriendly territory, and it will also be able to fly from aircraft carriers (small and large) to insert Marine Corps or naval infantry forces and perform combat rescue missions since it will be able to fly into small clearings to pick up downed airmen. Even if the Cheney decision is sustained in the U.S. Congress and the program is canceled, it is quite likely that an aircraft of a similar capability will be developed by one or more of the technologically advanced nations sometime in the 1990s or in the first decade of the twenty-first century.

Disadvantages of V/STOL Aircraft

The major disadvantage of STOL and VTOL aircraft of the past has been a deficiency in range and payload when compared with that of fixed-engine (or fixed-thrust-vector) aircraft. These deficiencies are being corrected by better engines and lightweight composite materials for airframes, while the development of smaller precision weapons will ease the payload problem.

Advocates for V/STOL have argued for decades that lack of imagination and vision on the part of political, business, and military leaders has caused developments to move so slowly. There is some truth in this criticism. On the other hand, V/STOL technology clearly involves a heavy price to pay in terms of weight, aircraft range, and the ability to carry heavy loads of fuel, ordnance, and/or combat soldiers. The debate will surely continue, particularly in nations with advanced technological capabilities. Nations lower on the technological ladder will probably have to wait many years before they can design and build V/STOL aircraft.

Doctrinal Aspects

Doctrinally, V/STOL aircraft have great significance because they are not tied to fixed airfields but can operate from a wide variety of surfaces, such as secondary roads, grassy fields, sections of paved parking lots, and the like. Although operating in these field locations provides logistic and maintenance challenges, particularly if the V/STOL unit changes location every day or two, there are many advantages. The primary advantage of such flexibility is that it is more difficult for the enemy to locate and destroy these units on the ground than it is to locate and destroy aircraft that are tied to large fixed main operating bases.

Many investigations were performed in the 1980s on the issue of air base survivability, and most objective students have concluded that, over time, it will become more and more difficult to operate from, and defend, large, fixed airfields. This will be particularly true in the twenty-first century when stealthy, autonomous systems should be able to deliver surprise attacks that destroy the key elements of these bases (command and control nodes, major maintenance facilities, sheltered and unsheltered aircraft, and aircrew headquarters).

The airmen, who for years have enjoyed the luxury of clean sheets, restful sleep between sorties, and a psychological break from warfare, on occasion may well have to return to the mud, dirt, noise, and inconvenience of a battlefield environment as they move from place to place in their V/STOL aircraft in order to survive as an effective element of the air-ground team. The lessons of the World War I airmen who had to operate out of very austere bases may have considerable relevance for the combat aviator of the twenty-first century.

Secondary Missions of V/STOL Aircraft

An important aspect of V/STOL fighter aircraft is the potential they provide in secondary missions. Whereas these aircraft are primarily designed for air-to-ground missions, the ability to vector their thrust can be quite useful in the air-to-air arena. The British proved this in the Falklands/Malvinas war. In the air-to-air environment, the aviator who can maneuver his aircraft to a firing position by pointing the nose of his aircraft at the enemy aircraft before the enemy can do the same to him can usually win the battle. This has been true since the first air-to-air engagements in World War I and is likely to remain true for many years to come. An aircraft that can vector the thrust of his engine in a way that allows the aircraft to turn very quickly has a great advantage. Hence, vectored thrust not only helps reduce take-off and landing distances but also helps in air-to-air engagements.

Vectoring an engine thrust in flight or vectoring in forward flight (VFF) should become a more important consideration in combat aircraft design than it has been in the past. Until weapons can be fired (or laser beams directed) in all directions, the ability to point an aircraft's nose rapidly will remain terribly important. If the lift vector can be enhanced by vectoring of thrust without putting undue stress on the aviator, fighter pilots will want to have that additional edge.

Commercial Applications

Commercial applications for short take-off and landing aircraft have considerable potential. If, for instance, an aircraft like the Osprey could carry 30 or 40 passengers into a very small airfield in the central city of any large metropolitan area, it could be extremely attractive commercially. This would be especially true if the cost per seat- mile were low and the safety aspects of flying passenger airplanes close to large buildings and large accumulations of people could be fully satisfied. If an aircraft could be designed, developed, and procured that would serve both military and commercial purposes, the cost savings for both the civilian and military communities would be considerable. There was, for instance, great hope that the airline industry would be willing to share the development costs of the Osprey and produce enough aircraft to reduce production costs.

Future of V/STOL Aircraft

There is little question that the future of short take-off and landing aircraft is interesting. This impressive potential will, however, test the imagination and persistence of leaders in both the military and commercial sectors. They must ensure that research, development, and procurement are based on sound analysis and a realistic appraisal of the technological challenges. These leaders must also be prepared to react to changing world conditions. For example, if deterrence and arms control in the future make the likelihood of nuclear war (and of large conventional war) among nuclear powers less likely, there should be an even greater shift in emphasis to low-intensity conflict, special operations, and antiterrorist activity than there has been in the first four decades after World War II. This shift should favor V/STOL aircraft. Further trends in more efficient and lightweight engines and airframes are also favorable. On the other hand, the development of unmanned vehicles may mean that these systems replace the V/STOL aircraft in the fighter, attack, and reconnaissance roles. Support aircraft of the Osprey type, however, are likely to be useful for many years into the future.

PERRY M. SMITH

SEE ALSO: Aircraft, Military; Airpower; Airpower, Tactical; Close Air Support; Helicopters.

Bibliography

Ethell, J., and A. Price. 1986. *Air war South Atlantic*. New York: Berkeley Publishing Group.

Mason, R. A. 1987. *Air power: An overview of roles*. London: Brassey's.

Myles, B. 1986. *Jump jet: The revolutionary V/STOL fighter*. 2d ed. London: Brassey's.

Paschall, R. 1990. *LIC 2010: Special operations and unconventional warfare in the next century*. Washington, D.C.: Brassey's.

Singh, J. 1985. *Air power in modern warfare*. New Delhi: Lancer International.

Walker, J. R. 1987. *Air-to-ground operations*. London: Brassey's.

AIRCRAFT TECHNOLOGY APPLICATIONS

Aircraft development and production processes have traditionally been subject to a high rate of technological development. The stimulus in these processes has long been the need to maintain a competitive edge, both commercially and militarily. In the military field, the dynamics of this competition are clear, with obvious pressure to establish and maintain superiority in all facets of air operations—attack, defense, transport, and training. The drive for superiority remains, but increasingly national defense establishments are emphasizing technologies that reduce the cost of owning advanced military systems.

The application of technology to future aircraft systems requires a thorough understanding and careful consideration of the technology acquisition process. Increasingly, commercial constraints such as fixed-price contracting are imposed on the potentially risky design and development phases of advanced military systems. These constraints demand a sound and largely risk-free definition of the product at the commencement of the process. This definition will have to be sound regarding not only the technical standard of the proposed product but also its technological standard. A definition based on technological goals that have yet to be realized is clearly problematic. Any necessary technological advance must be identified well before the product definition point to allow time for research, development, and demonstration of the new technology before commitment to a full-scale program. Whether the technology foreseen is specific to the application or is subject to transfer from an alternative field, judgments about technological feasibility have to be made long before product requirements are finally determined. Therefore, establishing a long-term view for a new product's requirements is crucial to both contractor and customer alike.

Technology Development and Application Time Scales

Time spans for the development and production of military systems can vary considerably, both with the nature of the system and with the procurement process adopted. A complex weapon system developed to meet a demanding air defense role could certainly take longer to develop and introduce into service than a new basic trainer. As to the procurement process, overall time scales can be extended by the introduction of a competitive fly-off phase, even though the fly off might provide a sounder base for later phases of the program. As a result of variability, it may take as long as ten years to develop an effective airborne weapon system and introduce it into service.

In today's circumstances, airborne systems are expected to remain in service, with system upgrades as appropriate, for 35 years or more. Therefore, when in-flight demonstration of essential technologies is deemed necessary so as to reduce risk at program launch, work in the research and technology development fields directly applicable could be initiated ten years or more in advance of authorizing full-scale development. An overall weapon system program including all these necessary phases could easily span a total of 55 years or more.

The implications of these time scales for the prediction, identification of appropriate technology, and technology development processes can perhaps be better appreciated by using hindsight as a comparative yardstick. Effective airborne military systems first appeared during World War I, just over 70 years ago. High-performance monoplane fighters and effective long-range bombers with significant payload capacity emerged primarily during World War II, some 45 to 50 years ago. Supersonic flight was first achieved a little over 40 years ago, with true supersonic systems entering service about 30 years ago.

Systems for aiming a weapon developed progressively through the fixed-sighting arrangements of World War I, and gyroscopic gun sights of World War II, to radar-aimed systems. With the proliferation of more sophisticated weapons, both in terms of capability and variety, weapon-aiming systems developed into complete avionic systems, encompassing such other functions as navigation, electronic warfare, flight control, and so on. True avionic systems, as opposed to discreet electronic subsystems, began to see service 20 to 25 years ago.

In the propulsion field, the gas-turbine engine has displaced the previously dominant piston engine as the prime mover of military air vehicles. This process took place over a period of 45 years, from the end of World War II. Over that period, the capabilities and characteristics of gas-turbine engines have undergone dramatic development, both in terms of their specific weight (engine weight per unit of thrust or power) and specific fuel consumption (fuel burned per unit of thrust or power).

The above represent but a few examples of the rate of technology growth in the field of military aviation. The fact that particular technologies have grown at high rates, however, does not mean that they will continue to do so. There are many examples of such growth rates that show progressively diminishing returns on development efforts.

But there are also many examples of the emergence of fundamentally new technologies or technology applications that sustain the overall growth rate of system capability.

The foregoing historical analysis indicates how difficult it is to predict the nature of a product whose development may not be initiated for ten years or more but which demand the initiation of specific research and technology development today.

Technology Trends

Similar historical analysis, but of a more quantitative nature, can be used to identify trends in technology that have dominated the design of military systems and are likely to continue their dominance for some time to come. One difficulty with this type of analysis is ensuring that the examples used to establish a trend are actually equivalent. For example, if one attempts to study trends in fighter developments one quickly discovers that *fighter* is a general term applied to aircraft that serve in a variety of roles—interceptor, air superiority fighter, and attack fighter. Furthermore, the role emphasized for aircraft varies with time. This can change the list of aircraft that are generically classed as fighters over the period under analysis.

An examination of a series of fighter aircraft that entered service or might enter service from 1950 to 2010 in terms of their weight breakdown reveals a progressive reduction in fighter basic mass empty (BME) as a proportion of all up weight (AUW). The difference between BME and AUW is essentially the payload and fuel carried by the fighter. Even with the substantially increased capabilities of fighter weapons (advanced air-to-air missiles as opposed to cannon) and improved power-plant fuel efficiency, the increased proportion of weight allocated to weapons and fuel indicates the much increased payload/range capability expected of the modern fighter. This trend, however, could not have been sustained were it not for corresponding reductions of weight in other airframe and system areas.

Despite increasing design demand, notably the extension of the flight envelope to supersonic speed and higher levels of maneuverability, structural mass as a proportion of AUW has steadily declined from about 35 to 30 percent or below. This trend is as much a product of improved design technique, including more comprehensive computer-based analysis, as of advances in material standards.

Similarly, despite substantial increases in aircraft thrust-to-weight ratio, engine weight as a proportion of AUW has declined. This indicates that engine specific weight has also improved dramatically.

In addition to these advances, the weight of mechanical systems (e.g., controls, air-conditioning, fuel, hydraulics) has been reduced as a result of improvements in systems technology, such as increasing hydraulic system pressure. These mechanical systems were more than 15 percent of all up weights in 1950, but are expected to be closer to 10 percent in 2010.

The weight of avionics systems has, however, increased as a proportion of AUW, even with the dramatic miniaturization that has been typical of electronics and computing technologies. The proportion of AUW devoted to avionics is now more than twice the 2 percent that was common in the 1950s. The steady growth in avionics weight thus represents orders of magnitude expansion of the capability of avionic systems.

Analysis of such trends can form one basis for predicting the probable form future equivalent systems might take. One further trend, however, must be considered—cost, which seems to be escalating at an exponential rate. For the United Kingdom (U.K.), the costs per aircraft have increased from less than US$50,000 each in 1910–18 to well over US$15 million each in the 1980s. Suffice it to say that this trend implies a quite unacceptable reduction in fleet size. Thus historical trends can indicate not just the possible forms that future systems might take but also specific areas where fundamental changes in approach could well prove essential. Although this analysis has concentrated on fighter-type aircraft, the principles are generally applicable to all classes of military aircraft.

Technology Identification and Acquisition—An Example

It has been suggested that analysis of trends in military systems and their design could point to the potentially key technologies for future systems. The technology identification and acquisition process can perhaps be best illustrated by a detailed examination of one area of technology.

Assessments of the escalating threats to air operations suggest that in the event of war it would be unwise to plan for the use of large, well-designed main air bases that are within reach of an enemy's offensive counterair (OCA) capabilities. For one thing, these analyses indicate that main bases do not provide adequate protection for aircraft on the ground. They also show that the use of main runways is likely to be impaired by enemy attacks.

Responses to these findings involve such things as the construction of hardened shelter facilities for aircraft. One could also choose to locate main bases outside the range of an enemy's OCA forces. This, however, would be extremely difficult given the range of cruise and ballistic missiles. If main bases are to be maintained where they can be attacked, an air force must develop operational capabilities such as rapid runway repair to cope with likely damage to these bases.

Another possible response to this situation would be to develop aircraft that do not require large, fixed bases to support their operations. This is the purpose behind efforts to develop vertical take-off and landing aircraft (VTOL). Such aircraft would require a new form of propulsion system. In Great Britain, such a propulsion system was developed for use with the proposed Hawker Siddeley P1154 supersonic fighter and was initially exercised in the P1127 demonstrator. For a number of reasons, essentially political, the P1154 program did not proceed, but the progressive development of the P1127 technology base led to the Harrier subsonic VTOL fighter and ground-attack aircraft.

From its initial entry into service with the Royal Air Force in 1969, the Harrier has undergone considerable development to meet the operational requirements of its users, the Royal Air Force, Royal Navy, Indian Navy, and U.S. Marine Corps. Through this development, Harrier performance, notably in payload/range, has been substantially enhanced. In parallel with air vehicle performance improvements, its weapons systems have been, and will continue to be, similarly developed.

Many lessons have been learned in the course of this development, not the least of these being the restrictive consequences, particularly in terms of payload/range, that result from design for pure VTOL. In Harrier operations, payload/range has been enhanced through the use of a short take-off (STO) roll, augmented in the case of naval operations through the development of the ski jump principle, now seen as standard on Harrier-capable ships in the Royal Navy and also certain other naval fleets.

With the passage of time, the threats against large, fixed airfields have become progressively more severe. Yet the operational demands being made on modern aircraft in terms of range, payload, and maneuverability are also increasing. Under these conditions, the challenge becomes to develop high-performance aircraft that can operate from surfaces that are considerably shorter and narrower than those that aircraft have traditionally used. These operational requirements would affect future aircraft development in the following ways.

To begin with, consideration would be given to the choice between a short take-off and landing (STOL), VTOL, or a short take-off and vertical landing (STOVL) system design strategy. In this consideration, recognition of operational and hence technological synergies would soon become apparent, for example, in terms of the new system's ultimate role. If operational flexibility is to be at least part of the aim, it is then probable that very high levels of maneuverability would be demanded of the system, even if its prime role were to be air-to-ground attack. With the levels of thrust-to-weight ratio and wing loading that result from the need for maneuverability, an extremely short take-off capability would in any event be inherent in the design. Unfortunately, landing performance would remain problematic. To land safely on a short, narrow strip, quite possibly with a turbulent crosswind, demands the solution of a number of reasonably obvious operational problems, soluble perhaps through the adoption of a range of advanced technologies, such as powered lift to enhance low-speed flight and control capabilities. Adoption of a vertical landing strategy avoids many of these problems but introduces others, such as the potentially adverse environmental effects produced by the high-energy jets of the engines required for vertical landing. Both approaches are alternative means of achieving a dispersed operational capability. Both demand solutions to the many problems generated by its particular mode of operation to include logistics, base flexibility, and maintenance.

Still, in the context of this specific example, positive commitment to a particular technology development and demonstration program should apparently await the properly researched choice between the short or vertical landing route, a choice subject to all the risks of long-distance military judgment and of unexpected developments in military or political posture. In this as in many other cases, however, it will be found that technological need is not totally dependent on the choice of a single strategy (short or vertical landing). Although apparently very different in nature, the technology demands to enable either short or vertical landing are in many respects common. Thus, given confidence at least in perceptions of the threat, positive and valuable progress can be made in developing the enabling technologies that would be common to both forms of landing and would, therefore, be important regardless of the option selected. These basic technologies can be pursued while detailed and thorough comparisons of the operational alternatives are being made. Powered lift is one example of such an enabling technology. Both short and vertical landing aircraft will be dependent to some degree on powered lift, with the propulsion and control system complexities it implies. Research in these areas will not be wasted, even with a late final choice of strategy. Indeed, a technology development process culminating in the demonstration of a full vertical landing capability can be seen now as an essential step in achieving an operational ability to land vertically and as an important step in determining the real difference between the short and vertical landing options that must be understood before a choice can be finally and properly made.

Within a generic area of interest, such as "dispersed operating capability," several other enabling technology developments can be identified, if at least a broad operational scenario can be reliably established. After a scenario is established, a core research and demonstration program can be initiated, subject perhaps to the later, but timely, addition of any specific activities that may be appropriate to particular planned products. The identification of these specific activities is potentially a greater problem than establishing a sensible core research and development (R&D) program, simply because it demands the timely resolution of long-term predictive issues to a large degree irrelevant to the core activity. Examples of this would be technology enablers that are unique to vertical landing aircraft but which would have no applicability if the short-landing approach were adopted.

In this way the technological demands, and hence research investment and ultimately the cost to provide the landing capability necessary to enable dispersed operation, can be evaluated. In parallel, effectiveness studies would be carried out to determine the ultimate worth of such a landing capability. Confident perceptions of a positive balance between cost and value would support the funding and initiation of the detailed programs necessary to develop technologies in support of the overall objective.

Future System Technology Base

The process described above is but one example of the range of issues that must be thoroughly reviewed in planning a technology acquisition program for a particular product or range of products. Because the resources available to support such an investment would in all probability be limited, careful judgments would be needed about the many technology fields appropriate to future systems.

The development of future system technology base(s) must take into account candidate technologies applicable to many system elements, including structures, mechanical systems, propulsion systems, avionics, sensors, acquisition cost, and cost of ownership.

In some areas, it is possible that the value of candidate technologies can be identified regardless of the intended application. Others may be application-specific. The breadth of investment necessary to support such technology development could lead to the establishment of collaborative arrangements to attract the necessary investment. Such collaborations could involve industry, government establishments, and educational organizations in one country or in several working collectively toward a common goal. While international collaboration in development and production is now commonplace, having been practiced in Europe for well over twenty years, similar collaboration in research and technology development is in comparison unusual, particularly in the military field.

As a proportion of overall system development and acquisition cost, the costs of technology development and even demonstration are typically quite small. Thus the financial pressures leading to development and production collaboration apply less to the earlier research phases of the programs. As costs increase with the increasing technical complexity of modern systems, however, this balance could change. Almost inevitably, significant attention will be paid to achieving substantial reductions in acquisition cost and cost of ownership. As noted above, achievement of such reductions will probably lead to the identification and development of cost-reducing technologies such as advanced design and manufacturing techniques, improved reliability, and easier maintainability. Such necessary improvements, therefore, can only be realized through increased investment in research and technology development ahead of full program initiation. This increased relative level of "up front" investment could well lead to the need for international collaboration in these earlier program phases.

The possibility of such collaborations at the technology level prompts consideration of their implications. Such a review generally indicates a number of difficulties centered on, for example, intellectual property rights. Nevertheless, through negotiations such as those completed by the U.K. and U.S. governments in establishing their agreement jointly to develop the technologies applicable to future advanced STOVL systems, these problems have been, and will continue to be, identifiable and solvable.

P. W. LIDDELL
BRYAN YOUNG

SEE ALSO: Aircraft, Military; Aircraft, Short Take-off and Landing; Engine Technology, Aircraft.

Bibliography

Seldon, M. R. 1979. *Life-cycle costing: A better method of government procurement.* Boulder, Colo.: Westview Press.

Spinney, F. C. 1985. *Defense facts of life: Plans/reality mismatch.* Boulder, Colo.: Westview Press.

U.S. Congress, Senate. 1985. *Defense organization: The need for change.* Staff Report 99-86, prepared for the Senate Armed Services Committee. Washington, D.C.: Government Printing Office.

U.S. Department of Defense. 1987. Department of Defense Directive 5000.1, "Major and non-major acquisition programs." Washington, D.C.: Government Printing Office.

———. 1987. Department of Defense Directive 5000.2, "Defense acquisition program procedures." Washington, D.C.: Government Printing Office.

AIRCRAFT, UNMANNED

Unmanned aircraft are machines sustained in flight by aerodynamic lift and guided without an on-board crew. The terminology in this branch of air vehicles is, however, loosely applied, and the dividing line between aircraft and missiles is often blurred. Cruise missiles, for example, are not missiles in the strict definition of the term; they are, in fact, unmanned aircraft.

The two most common types of unmanned aircraft are remotely piloted vehicles (RPVs) and drones. An RPV is a pilotless machine that transmits mission-related data to a remote controller and reacts to his commands and to other control inputs. A drone, on the other hand, is an autonomous pilotless machine programmed to fly a preset course, which can include the automatic acceptance of data inputs. In practice, many unmanned aircraft are basically drones, but also carry remotely controlled override facilities.

Like manned aviation, the history of unmanned aircraft

has its beginnings in the early years of the twentieth century. It is a history marked, again like that of aviation in general, by the interplay between operational requirements and available technology. This analysis will stress those aspects, rather than offer a comprehensive and international history, and it will discuss the potential of unmanned systems in general. It is not proposed to analyze specific current projects, since the entire field of unmanned aircraft is one in which proposals and developments change and quickly become dated.

Earliest Unmanned Aircraft

Aircraft, as distinct from balloons, became feasible once the technologies of aerodynamic structures and lightweight engines were combined by the Wright brothers in their successful experiments of 1903. Only six years earlier, the first crude radios had been demonstrated, and the technologies of gyroscopes and of aneroid barometers were already well known. It was therefore not long before the notion emerged of aircraft remotely controlled by radio signals.

But it remained only a notion until the First World War. During that war, the British, the French, the Germans, and the Americans experimented with unmanned aircraft, but none of these experiments was marked by conspicuous success.

With the Armistice of 1918 much of the interest in unmanned aircraft fell away, but it did not altogether evaporate. The fact was that no clear operational requirement had existed for unmanned aircraft. By the standards of the time, other weapons systems were functioning well enough, and where unmanned aircraft might have had some utility, the technology to provide the necessary reliability and accuracy was simply not available. These same factors were to become familiar in later stages of the development of unmanned aircraft for war.

Interwar Years

During the interwar years there was sporadic interest in using unmanned aircraft as weapons systems in Britain and in the United States. In Britain, early experiments resulted in development of the radio-controlled RAE (Royal Aeronautical Establishment) 1921 Target, and led to an aircraft called the Larynx with a 200-horsepower Armstrong-Siddeley Lynx motor. Twelve Larynxes were built. In trials they proved capable of carrying a warhead of 250 pounds over a distance of 480 kilometers (300 mi.), and they could maintain with reasonable accuracy a preset flight path.

The next British venture was inspired by an interservice dispute about the alleged vulnerability of warships to attack from the air. In the resulting demonstrations, Fairey IIIF floatplanes, known as Fairey Queens, were modified to accept radio controls and to fly attack patterns against Royal Navy ships. Two of the aircraft crashed soon after launch, but the third came unscathed through more than two hours of naval antiaircraft gunfire before being landed safely back on the water. This success led to the development of an expendable radio-controlled version of the Tiger Moth biplane trainer, known as the Queen Bee. Some 420 of these target aircraft were built between 1934 and 1943 and they rendered good service in training antiaircraft gunners of that era.

During those same interwar years, the United States' interest in unmanned aircraft continued at a similarly modest level, while in Germany low-key experimental work went on into technologies relevant to aviation, including that of simple, inexpensive aircraft engines. One of these was the Schmidtrohr impulse duct jet engine.

First Operational Cruise Missile

The value of the Schmidtrohr engine as a power unit was recognized, and by 1942 the engine had been incorporated into the design of the world's first cruise missile, the V-1 (*Vergeltungswaffe Eins*), or Flying Bomb, for use against Britain. This unmanned aircraft was a monoplane of simple and rugged thin sheet-steel construction weighing just over 2,270 kilograms (5,000 lb.) at launch, including a standard warhead of 455 kilograms (1,000 lb.) of high explosive. The machine had a wingspan of about 5.8 meters (19 ft.) and a fuselage of just over 7.3 meters (24 ft.) in length, above which was mounted the Schmidtrohr engine, giving a total length of almost 7.9 meters (26 ft.).

The German offensive against England with these missiles began in earnest on 16 June 1944 when 244 missiles were launched; 144 reached the coast and 73 fell into the Greater London area. Despite Allied air attacks on the production facilities, the logistic support network, and the firing sites, the German bombardment continued until March 1945 with a total of 8,892 missiles being launched from their ramps in France and Belgium.

Another 1,600 or so of these first-generation cruise missiles were air-launched from specially modified Heinkel He-111s, a stratagem that offered greater flexibility in the choice of launch point and thus in target selection. The result was that not only London, but cities such as Southampton, Gloucester, and Manchester came under attack—though on a much lesser scale than that directed against the capital.

Altogether, 1,847 of the missiles were destroyed by gunfire, 1,878 by fighters, and 232 by barrage balloons. No fewer than 2,419 reached the London Civil Defence region, killing 6,184 people and seriously injuring another 17,981. (For comparison, German conventional bombing against the United Kingdom killed 51,509 and seriously injured another 61,423 citizens during the course of the war.)

The United States also entered the field of unmanned aircraft during the Second World War, using time-expired bomber aircraft. Under the code name Aphrodite, a number of B-17s were modified to give an open cockpit and stripped of all nonessential equipment. They were then loaded with 20,000 pounds of high explosive and used as flying bombs.

Raids using this weapon were carried out between 4 August 1944 and 1 January 1945 but Aphrodite proved to be unreliable (several exploded prematurely), inaccurate, and vulnerable to both enemy defenses and unfavorable weather. The project was therefore abandoned. Aphrodite had not been created to fill any particular pressing operational requirement; rather, it was at worst an expedient and at best a less-than-wholehearted attempt to mitigate the losses being sustained by American daylight bombers over Europe.

Other U.S. efforts included a plan in 1941 to convert 100 obsolescent Navy torpedo bombers into attack drones, and a later proposal to procure up to 1,000 specially designed attack drones. This program eventually resulted in the production of 388 weapons, 46 of which were actually launched at Japanese secondary naval targets and 29 of which seem to have been successful in hitting the target.

Finally, to link wartime experience with postwar development, there was the U.S. Army Air Corps effort to copy the German V-1 Flying Bomb. The result was an RPV rather than a drone, since the JB-2, as it was known, carried not only a radar beacon to indicate its position, but also a radio control system giving guidance over a range of about 160 kilometers (approx. 100 mi.). About 1,400 JB-2s were produced before the end of the war, and although they were never employed operationally, some were acquired by the U.S. Navy and given the code name "Loon." These weapons were tested and then fitted to the submarine USS *Cusk* (SSG-348) in 1947, thus starting the postwar U.S. program in unmanned aircraft.

Postwar U.S. Developments

Postwar programs created a second generation of cruise missiles, beginning with the Northrop Snark. This was an intercontinental weapon designed to meet a 1945 operational requirement for a system to carry a 2,000-pound warhead over a maximum range of 8,046 kilometers (5,000 mi.). Snark in its original form was an 18-meter (60-ft.) long aircraft with a wingspan of over 12.5 meters (42 ft.) and an all-up weight of 12,700 kilograms (28,000 lb.). This huge system was accelerated from launch by two solid-fuel booster motors, but then flew under the power of a J33 jet engine. Navigation was effected by means of an inertial guidance system updated (because of the inherent inaccuracy of that period's inertial navigation systems) by observations of preselected stars by an on-board automatic sextant. Snark was thus an automatic unmanned system, in other words, a drone.

Following many failures in test flights, a second version, the N-69, was produced, but proved to be as unreliable as its predecessor. These failures led to a dispute about the value of unmanned aircraft that was to become familiar in the years that followed. Proponents of Snark were able to point out that it cost only about 5 percent of the price of a B-52 bomber, and that it did not put at risk the lives of valuable aircrew. The opponents of Snark emphasized the one-shot nature of its operational profile, the fact that it carried no self-defense systems and was therefore more vulnerable than a bomber, and, very tellingly, the fact that over a range of 3,218 kilometers (2,000 mi.) Snark had produced average circular errors of probability (CEPs) of 32 kilometers (20 mi.). Nor was the system at all reliable. In trials, only one in three launches had been successful and only one in ten missiles flew the planned distance to its simulated target. Surrounded by controversy about these weaknesses and its growing cost, Snark finally entered service in the spring of 1957, but it was deactivated and withdrawn after only four years.

A second ambitious strategic system of this era was the North American Navajo. This huge system (the booster alone weighed 76,900 kg., or 169,500 lb., and the total weight was 131,550 kg., or 290,000 lb.) was vertically launched, and intended to accelerate to a cruise speed of Mach 3.25 to fly over a range of 8,850 kilometers (5,500 mi.) at an altitude of 13,720 meters (45,000 ft.). A series of failures marked the trial launches in 1956 and 1957, leading to very serious doubts about the viability of the system. But the final blow to this and to ideas of similar cruise missiles had already been struck in 1954 when it was realized that the successful work on reducing the size of nuclear warheads made feasible their delivery over intercontinental ranges by ballistic missiles rather than by cruise missiles.

Meanwhile, development had been proceeding in the United States with what would later be known as theater weapon systems, weapons with less than intercontinental (strategic) ranges. These were Matador, Mace, and Regulus. Matador (Fig. 1) was the result of a 1945 operational requirement calling for a surface-to-surface attack cruise missile with a range of 805 kilometers (500 mi.). Its size was about that of a contemporary fighter-bomber, almost 12.2 meters (40 ft.) long and with a wingspan of less than 9.1 meters (30 ft.). It carried a warhead of 3,000 pounds and flew a maximum range of 1,000 kilometers (620 mi.) at a speed of 1,050 kilometers per hour (650 mph).

The main weakness of the Matador was to become a familiar one—the lack of accuracy over the full operational range. In a forerunner of later and much more advanced automatic navigation methods, a radar map–matching system was added to the basic Matador. This version was designated the Mace. Mace was fitted with an inertial navigation system and deployed with U.S. Air Force units in Germany from 1955 until the mid-1960s when it was withdrawn.

The U.S. Navy also had ambitions for a theater-range cruise missile and made proposals in 1947 for a system that was to become the Chance Vought Regulus. This was

Figure 1. The U.S. Matador. (SOURCE: Martin Marietta Corp. photo)

a submarine-launched weapon not unlike Matador in size and carrying a similar hyperbolic grid navigation system. Regulus entered service in 1955 and was eventually deployed not only on submarines but also on cruisers and aircraft carriers. It could carry a small nuclear warhead over a range of almost 965 kilometers (600 mi.) at subsonic speed, but its critical weakness again was the lack of any reliable system to give the accuracy demanded by operational conditions. Because of its unreliability and inaccuracy this system, too, was abandoned in favor of conventional aircraft and ballistic missiles.

Bombers offered reasonable accuracy as well as flexibility in operation. Ballistic missiles had the overwhelming advantage that they were invulnerable to opposing defenses.

Smaller Systems

During these same postwar years, developments had been progressing in two other fields for the use of unmanned aircraft—as decoy aircraft and as standoff air-to-surface missiles. The most prominent U.S. decoy system was the Quail, a drone designed to simulate the radar image of a U.S. Air Force bomber. Four Quails could be carried by a B-52, and two by a B-47. Quail was a turbojet-powered aircraft 2.7 meters (9 ft.) long with a wingspan of 1.5 meters (5 ft.). The decoy could operate at an altitude of up to 15,240 meters (50,000 ft.) at speeds as high as Mach 0.9, and could be programmed to make two changes of heading and one change in airspeed after release, thus adding to the realism of its bomberlike performance. Quail entered service in late 1960, but by that time Soviet radars had advanced beyond the levels that Quail was designed to counter, and trials confirmed that it was a relatively simple matter to distinguish Quails from bombers on radar. The system was therefore withdrawn after only a few years. Technology had again failed to match operational requirements.

Improvements in Soviet radars were matched by advances in Soviet air defenses as a whole, and as early as the mid-1950s trials were being made by the U.S. Air Force with airborne weapons such as the Hound Dog, which could be launched from outside dense enemy terminal defenses. But the Hound Dog proved to be of only moderate reliability. Because it was carried externally on a B-52, the bomber's air speed was reduced to an unacceptable degree. The Hound Dog was withdrawn in 1976 after sixteen years' service to be replaced by the Short Range Attack Missile (SRAM), a small, light, and fast air-to-surface attack weapon.

A more successful venture was the AGM-84 Harpoon, a sea-skimming antiship cruise missile powered by a J402 turbojet. This is a small tactical weapon with an all-up weight of 522 kilograms (1,150 lb.) and a range of about 64 kilometers (40 mi.). It was developed in three variants, but its real significance was that the technologies employed led eventually to more advanced systems. By the early 1970s, the U.S. armory thus included only two short-range cruise missiles, the SRAM and the Harpoon.

Third-Generation Cruise Missiles

This state of affairs was shortly to be transformed by two related factors. The first was growing concern over the cost and performance of the B-1 bomber, the successor to the B-52. The second factor was the prospect that new technologies might make possible a weapon that would eliminate the need for the B-1 altogether. These technologies were, first, miniaturized engines with remarkably high power-to-weight ratios; second, miniaturized nuclear warheads; and third, new and very accurate techniques for navigation and for terminal guidance.

These last were particularly significant, for they overcame one of the principal and hitherto insurmountable problems with drones—their gross lack of accuracy. Two techniques were involved, terrain contour matching (TERCOM) for long-range navigation, and digital scene matching area correlation (DSMAC) for shorter ranges and for terminal guidance. TERCOM employs a digitized contour map of the route to be followed; the system "reads" the ground over which it flies, makes periodic comparisons with the map stored in its computer, and calculates the necessary corrections, which are then fed by computer to the controls of the carrying vehicle. DSMAC employs a similar principle but uses comparative photographic techniques instead of altitude comparisons. The accuracies resulting from a combination of TERCOM and DSMAC are reported to be as close as a few feet.

The combination of the new technologies in propulsion, warheads, and navigation made possible a third generation of U.S. cruise missiles. The U.S. Navy developed the submarine-launched cruise missile (SLCM), while the U.S. Air Force went ahead with a program for an air-launched cruise missile (ALCM) and a ground-launched cruise missile (GLCM). After various disputes, fly-offs, and other trials, ALCM went into service with B-52s in late 1982. The SLCM, now known as the Tomahawk, was accepted in three versions by the U.S. Navy—a tactical antiship missile (TASM), a tactical land-attack version fitted with a conventional warhead (TLAM/C), and a tactical land-attack version carrying a nuclear warhead (TLAM/N). All three versions can be fired from a standard torpedo tube. TASM is reported to have a range of 250 nautical miles; TLAM/C a range of 675 nautical miles and an accuracy of less than 31 meters (100 ft.). GLCM is essentially the same weapon as TLAM/N, but it is mounted on 45-ton transport erector launchers (TELs), each carrying four cruise missiles housed in launching canisters.

Finally, in addition to these five cruise missiles, another and more advanced air-launched surface attack missile was developed using many of the same new technologies. This was the medium-range air-to-surface missile (MRASM) of the U.S. Air Force, which is similar in appearance to the Tomahawk, but carries a warhead of submunitions designed primarily for airfield attack.

These third-generation cruise missiles were designed to operate at high speed and at very low altitude so as to fly under the lobes of opposing radar systems. Their range and (in the case of SLCMs and ALCMs) the flexibility they provide in the choice of launching area, together with their capacity to accept widely varying automatic route profiles, meant that the new cruise missiles could be programmed to avoid opposing defenses. To penetrate terminal defenses, the missiles relied again on high speed and low altitude and on their remarkably small size to avoid acquisition and engagement. Thus, for the second time (the first had been the German V-1 offensive), an unmanned aircraft had been produced that successfully matched a specific and viable operational requirement.

Unmanned Reconnaissance Vehicles

A third area of activity in which operational requirements were successfully met, although not without difficulty or combat losses, was the employment by the United States of unmanned reconnaissance aircraft in Southeast Asia from 1964 to 1975. Most of the machines employed were from the Teledyne-Ryan series of drones and RPVs derived from the Firebee target drone of the early 1950s. The program had its origins in the need to monitor surveillance of certain overseas areas during the gap between the loss of two U.S. manned reconnaissance aircraft in early 1960 with the resulting halt to these flights, and the advent of reconnaissance satellites.

With the start of the U.S. involvement in Vietnam in August 1964, Ryan 147 drones were soon operating over North Vietnam and China, and indeed as early as 15 November 1964 Beijing reported the combat loss of a U.S. drone over China. By April of the following year, five drones had been destroyed by Chinese defenses. Although these losses illustrated the vulnerable nature of drones with their steady flight paths and total lack of protection, they also demonstrated the political advantage of employing systems that did not risk the death or capture of a crew and the propaganda that would certainly follow from any such incident.

As the war developed, so did the extent of the drone program both in quantity and quality. From the basic 147 preprogrammed photographic drone, remotely piloted versions were developed for very high-level photographic work, for very low-altitude photography, and for electronic intelligence collection. Other models were fitted out as decoys, while still more were employed in night reconnaissance, in dispensing chaff, and in electronic jamming of North Vietnamese SA-2 missiles.

Refinements to the original 147 concept led to sophisticated control by C-130 mother ships, and to the midair retrieval system (MARS), by parachute and wire or net, of returning drones so as to prevent their loss in the sea or damage to them as they came down on land. Between 1964 and 1973, it was reported that 3,435 sorties had been flown by drones over Vietnam, China, and other parts of the Far East, with a loss rate as low as 4 percent (Wagner 1983). It was a remarkable achievement in a combat environment that posed serious challenges to conventional manned aircraft.

A fourth instance of technology matching operational requirement, although in even more limited scope, has been seen in the Israeli employment of drones and RPVs. The Israelis have employed very small RPVs since at least 1973. The Mastiff, Scout, and Pioneer are all similar machines able to carry cameras or TV equipment for tactical surveillance purposes. A particularly successful employment by the Israelis of various unmanned aircraft was seen in the Bekaa Valley operation of 1982. For many months before the operation, reconnaissance drones had been collecting intelligence on Syrian positions, and at least five were admitted to have been lost.

During the operation itself, small air-launched gliders simulated attacking Israeli F-4 fighters so as to draw Syrian surface-to-air missile fire, while other unmanned aircraft were monitoring Syrian air defense airfields. It seems likely that Israeli harassment drones were used against the fire-control radars of Syrian antiaircraft guns. Successful though the operation was, unmanned aircraft played only one part in an extremely complex series of engagements, and surprise was not the least of the factors in favor of the Israelis. It would not be easy to sustain or to repeat so decisive a superiority in technology and tactics.

Unmanned Aircraft in the 1990s

Apart from cruise missiles, many of which are being withdrawn under the INF (Intermediate Nuclear Forces) Treaty, interest in unmanned aircraft seems now to be almost entirely confined to support roles. This includes decoys, short-range reconnaissance and surveillance systems, electronic warfare systems of various types, and defense suppression. The notion, once prevalent, that unmanned systems would one day replace manned aircraft has receded. Ballistic missiles have utility only in certain inflexible roles, while cruise missiles have some disadvantages that can often outweigh their positive attributes.

An advantage of dispensing with a crew is that crew support equipment is not necessary. This includes cockpit and canopy structures together with environmental control, oxygen equipment, interface mechanisms such as the connections and instruments between systems and crew, lighting, intercommunication and other radio equipment, manual controls, parachutes and other survival gear, and ejection seats. The space and weight saved, in addition to that of the crew members themselves, is considerable, and enables a designer not only to reduce the size of the airframe, but also to make resulting use of smaller power plants and to make provision for less fuel.

If the resulting aircraft is simple and therefore cheap enough, it may no longer be cost-effective to include in its design any active or passive self-defense features. A supersonic dash capability is almost certainly redundant, making possible further simplification of airframe and particularly of the power plant. Defensive weapons, radar warning equipment, and indeed anything beyond a rudimentary facility for dispensing chaff or infrared flares can also be dispensed with, and the aircraft is now, figuratively speaking, in a downward spiral of very rapidly falling complexity and cost.

Such simple and relatively inexpensive machines can be equipped with a lightweight automatic pilot set before takeoff to fly a predetermined route, including, if needed, variations in altitude, heading, and airspeed. If the mission has a two-way profile, then several roles suggest themselves. The principal ones, because of the lightweight characteristics of the equipment needed, will be photographic or electronic reconnaissance. An electronic countermeasures role in jamming hostile radars and radios will also be attractive, although the necessary power source will entail some weight penalty.

If the mission is to be one-way only, then at least two possibilities suggest themselves. One is attack against a predetermined target. The other is to fit automatic target-seeking equipment to the aircraft, possibly including, in the case of the radar attack role, an automatic loitering and homing facility so that the aircraft can delay its dive onto an emitting target until the emitter is radiating. More complexity in the aircraft is involved, but the result will still be a small and inexpensive machine.

The high accuracies of radar-homing drones can also be made available against other targets by the use of matching TV, or by employing infrared or thermal imagery devices. Complexity and cost will rise again in such a drone, and the homing capability of the aircraft could be affected by weather, dust, and smoke. Nevertheless, against high-value targets, drones with conventional warheads may be cost-effective weapons systems, and with nuclear warheads their utility is already recognized by the deployment of third-generation cruise missiles such as GLCM and ALCM.

Automatic systems of that kind are of course inflexible in operation, and they can be very vulnerable to enemy countermeasures. Their steady flight path and their inability to sense threats mean that they can be intercepted by air and by ground-based defenses, and it may even be possible to jam or to interrupt the automatic system by means of electronic countermeasures activity.

Both flexibility and a useful degree of reaction to threats can be provided to unmanned aircraft by adding remote control. RPVs generally require at least four essential characteristics to operate in a combat environment. First, they need on-board sensors, including some degree of the visual capability that would be provided by a crew. Second, reliable communications will be needed to transmit the information from these sensors back to a distant controller. Third, a skilled operator will be necessary to exploit the characteristics of the RPV. Fourth, reliable communications must be available that can carry the operator's instructions back to the controls of aircraft.

Those links, if they are indeed reliable, will enable an operator to monitor and to direct the progress of an RPV, maneuvering as and when necessary to maintain the required flight profile. But those same links will be limited in effectiveness by range, by intervening terrain, and, perhaps most crucially, by enemy countermeasures. If the opponent can interrupt or even distort a critical part of the whole complex control cycle, then he may well be able to seduce the RPV into a self-destructive spiral of inappropriate reactions.

It must be stressed that this option would not be available to the defense against manned aircraft. An on-board crew can bring to bear their situational awareness, and a crew would be able to recognize malfunctions, and often either to correct them or circumvent them by improvisation. An RPV is only a weapon or a platform for weapons; a manned aircraft is a fighting platform. In this balance between survival and destruction, it is important to bear in mind that RPVs operating in hostile airspace will be moving progressively away from the controller who is attempting to apply his judgment to the safe progress of the machine, and moving progressively more deeply into the airspace where the opponent will be applying his judgment to ensure its destruction. The RPV is operating in the opponent's tactical arena.

Future

In the future, unmanned aircraft will continue to make a valuable contribution to air operations. The operational requirement for unmanned surveillance platforms that can provide visual or electronic intelligence is an important one in combat, and a vital one in crises short of war.

Other roles seem likely to be less pervasive, but there will be operational circumstances when a range of possibilities may be brought to bear. These will include decoys, antiradar homing drones, and other attack vehicles, including cruise missiles armed with submunitions. On the whole these seem likely to be shorter range systems, whether drones or RPVs. For longer range operations, the place of nuclear-tipped cruise missiles seems secure, but it is difficult to envisage the use of such expensive vehicles over long ranges armed only with conventional warheads.

With exceptions, therefore, unmanned aircraft are likely to supplement combat aviation rather than offer a viable alternative to manned machines. Their main impact will probably be an enhancement of the manned aircraft in operations by providing passive protection in the form of decoys and active protection in defense suppression. There is also interest in support roles such as those mentioned. But in terms of systems in operation or even in the development stage, most unmanned aircraft—as distinct from missiles—are intended as target aircraft or as surveillance platforms of one kind or another.

MICHAEL ARMITAGE

SEE ALSO: Air Reconnaissance; Intelligence Collection; Missile, Air-launched Cruise; Missile, Cruise; Missile, Guided; Missile, Surface-to-air; Radar.

Bibliography

Armitage, M. J. 1988. *Unmanned aircraft*. Vol. 3 of *Air power: Aircraft, weapons systems and technology series*, ed. R. A. Mason. London: Brassey's.

O'Brien, T. H. 1975. *Civil defence*. London: Her Majesty's Stationery Office.

Wagner, W. 1983. *Lightning bugs and other reconnaissance drones*. Fallbrook, Calif.: Aero.

Werrel, K. P. 1985. *The evolution of the cruise missile*. Maxwell AFB, Ala.: Air Univ. Press.

Young, R. A. 1978. *The flying bomb*. London: Ian Allan.

AIR-LAND BATTLE

The United States Army's basic operational concept is called the air-land battle doctrine (ALB), a doctrine based on securing or retaining the initiative and exercising it aggressively to defeat the enemy. It was presented in *Field Manual (FM) 100–5: Operations* published on 20 August 1982. This manual established the rules for waging war at the operational level (division and army corps). For the purpose of this discussion, the author addresses the August 1982 version of *FM 100–5*. Since its initial introduction in 1976, *FM 100–5* has been revised about every five years. Revisions to the May 1986 version are now under way by the U.S. Army Training and Doctrine Command. Almost simultaneously with *FM 100–5*, the U.S. Army Training and Doctrine Command (TRADOC) published a paper entitled *Air-land Battle 2000*. Encompassing the period 1995–2015, this effort was intended to distinguish it as a future-oriented concept while referring to its roots in the ALB doctrine of the 1980s. Air-land battle 2000 was envisioned as a concept that would be the starting point for all future weapon acquisition, as well as future doctrine, force design, and training requirements. To eliminate the resulting confusion between the army's ALB doctrine and the air-land battle 2000 concept, in November 1983, TRADOC retitled the warfighting concept for the twenty-first century *Army 21*.

To assess properly the 1982 *FM 100–5*, it is useful to note its predecessor's characteristics. The 1976 version, titled *Active Defense*, came under sharp criticism almost from the moment it was published. A group of American military thinkers known as the Military Reform Movement, both inside and outside of the armed forces, accused the manual and its doctrine of being tied to positional warfare; that is, being firepower-oriented to the detriment of mobile tactics, reactive to enemy action instead of emphasizing initiative, relying primarily on attrition through firepower exchange, and neglecting the teachings of the art of war.

This dissatisfaction with the army's operational doctrine led to the concepts of the *integrated battlefield*, which tried to combine nuclear and conventional operations, and the *extended battlefield*, which advocated an extension of operations far and deep into enemy territory. Both concepts depended heavily on the use of nuclear weapons for military purposes, thus causing considerable criticism.

In the late 1970s and early 1980s, the effect of emerging technologies became apparent, promising weapon delivery of remarkably increased accuracy and lethality, not only against point targets such as bridges and armored vehicles, but also against area targets such as armored formations. The effects of all these weapons were viewed by many as a substitute for low-yield nuclear weapons, thus reducing the emphasis on the use of nuclear weapons for tactical, military purposes.

Responsible authorities must have considered some of

the dissatisfaction with the 1976 operational doctrine as justified, because a new *FM 100–5*, titled *Operations*, was issued six years later. It described how the army must conduct campaigns and battles in order to win; explained U.S. Army operational doctrine involving maneuver, firepower, movement, combined arms warfare, and cooperative actions with sister services and allies; and emphasized tactical flexibility and speed as well as mission orders, initiative among subordinates, and the spirit of the offense.

The thrust of the 1982 edition of *FM 100–5* is best captured by a quotation from chapter 2, "Combat Fundamentals":

> Army units will fight all types of operations to preserve and to exploit the initiative. They will attack the enemy in depth with fire and maneuver and synchronize all efforts to attain the objective. They will maintain the agility necessary to shift forces and fires to the point of enemy weakness. Our operations must be rapid, unpredictable, violent and disorienting to the enemy.

Success on the modern battlefield will depend on the basic tenets of Air-land Battle doctrine: initiative, depth, agility and synchronization.

It is significant that *FM 100–5* placed the principles of war, and their application to classical and modern theory, at the foundation of the army's ALB doctrine. ALB was a return to the tried and true principles of experience in war.

In remarks to a group of TRADOC historians, one of the principal authors of the ALB doctrine, Gen. Donn A. Starry, U.S. Army (Retired) said:

> In a very broad sense, AirLand Battle is a grand offensive defense—one on the style fought so successfully by General George Washington in the revolution, with great skill and initial success by Lee and Jackson in the Civil War, and with striking success by MacArthur in World War II.

In addition to the examples identified by General Starry can now be added the brilliantly conceived and professionally executed multinational Persian Gulf ground campaign against Saddam Hussein.

In sum, it is important to remember that military doctrine is a set of attitudes about war conditioned by historical experience. Therefore, doctrine cannot promise too much, nor suggest too little.

Franz Uhle-Wettler

See Also: Doctrine; Fire and Movement; Initiative in War; Joint Operations; Mobility; Offense; Principles of War.

Bibliography

Starry, D. A. 1989. A perspective on American military thought. *Military Review*, July, pp. 9–10.

Romjue, J. L. 1984. *From active defense to airland battle: The development of U.S. Army doctrine, 1973–1982.* Ft. Monroe, Va.: U.S. Army Training and Doctrine Command (TRADOC).

U.S. Department of the Army. 1982. *Field manual 100–5: Operations.* Washington, D.C.: Government Printing Office.

AIRLIFT

Airlift forces deploy, employ, and sustain other military forces and provide resources, military assistance, and humanitarian relief as directed by national authorities. Airlift capability can be considered both a military and diplomatic instrument of national policy. In support of military operations, airlift fulfills both a combat and a combat support function. As a combat mission, airlift forces project power through air-land, airdrop, or extraction delivery into combat. Airlift provides the field commander with a unique maneuver capability for his fighting forces which enables him to exploit an enemy's weakness. In the combat support role, airlift forces provide logistic support by transporting personnel and equipment. Airlift support may be provided for either strategic or tactical purposes and can be flown by fixed- or rotary-wing aircraft. Depending on the airlift air order of battle, support can be provided over continental or intercontinental ranges.

History Perspective

Airlift has perhaps the shortest history of any major air power mission. In the United States, it officially dates from 1941 and can be traced to the same period globally. Unofficially, airlift heritage, like the heritage of other air power missions, dates from the 1920s. The history of airlift can be divided into four major periods: the prewar years, World War II, the postwar era, and the modern era.

Pre–World War II

Before World War II, thinking about the role of airlift as either a military or diplomatic instrument was limited, abstract, and generally restricted to thinking about how air transportation could support other airpower missions such as bombardment, pursuit, observation, and attack. During the 1920s, early advocates of airpower such as Douhet, Mitchell, and Trenchard were eager to define airpower as an entity in and of itself. The close relationship seen today between airlift and ground forces, therefore, was not a particularly attractive area of intellectual pursuit.

This is not to say that air transportation was totally ignored in the prewar era; in fact, over 80 types of transport aircraft were purchased or tested by the U.S. air service. What was missing, unlike the development of other types of aircraft during this period, was any real theory for employment. Before World War II, what occurred or failed to occur concerning air transportation should be understood in relationship to the development of early airpower doctrine. Throughout this period, the debate over the mission of airpower focused on strategic bombardment and pursuit aviation. While some interest was indicated in air transportation, employment concepts concentrated on how air transportation could support the mobility of an air force. In the United States, for example, the use of air transportation to support air corps maneuvers was exercised in 1927 and 1928 at the suggestion of the U.S. Air Corps Tactical School.

These tests demonstrated the ability to move air corps units using air transportation; however, this capability was considered practical only for moving aviation units supporting coastal defense. Despite initial success in using airlift to deploy and sustain air corps units in exercises and despite suggestions contained in U.S. Army War College studies during 1932–33 on the need for further study and standardization of air transport procedures, no significant airlift doctrine was developed during the prewar years.

World War II

In contrast to the prewar years, the World War II era was an exceptionally productive period for the evolution of airlift. In the United States, in response to global demands for the delivery of aircraft and critically needed supplies, the chief of the U.S. Army Air Corps formed the Air Transport Command as a separate entity on 20 June 1942. His decision to make the Air Transport Command a separate command resulted from the mismanagement of transport aircraft by theater commanders early in the war. Under the new arrangement the Air Transport Command, flying primarily C-46, C-47, and C-54 aircraft, was responsible for strategic airlift to the entire military community, not just to the air corps.

The advantage of this new arrangement was soon evident. The China-Burma-India theater, before and after the establishment of the Air Transport Command, produced particularly telling results. In this theater alone, by implementing a single-manager concept, the Air Transport Command increased deliveries from 85 tons per month in July 1942 to a maximum of 53,000 tons in August 1945. During the same period, the number of aircraft available increased from 45 to 367. The increase in tons delivered was primarily attributable to Air Transport Command's single-manager concept. Similar gains were evident in other theaters of operation. While not involved in strategic airlift per se, Germany and the Soviet Union also adopted centrally controlled and managed airlift resupply and air mobile operations.

Tactical airlift history also dates from World War II. Before the United States became involved in the war, both the Germans and Soviets experimented with the three major tactical airlift missions—airdrop, air assault, and tactical resupply. While their experience in tactical resupply missions was not particularly promising, airborne assault operations were sufficiently successful to offer battlefield commanders new maneuver options.

In the United States, creation of the 82d and 101st Airborne Divisions initiated an airlift evolution leading to the formation of the Troop Carrier Command. This command provided transportation support for the airborne infantry and theater airlift as directed by the theater commander. Throughout the war, the primary focus of the Troop Carrier Command in Europe continued to be airborne operations. The tactics and techniques required to employ airborne forces were developed during maneuvers in the United States during 1942 and 1943. Thereafter, large-scale employment of Anglo-American airborne units in Northwest Africa, Sicily, Italy, France, and Germany demonstrated the combat value of an air assault capability. This capability helped Western Allied commanders and their planning staffs achieve high degrees of tactical and strategic surprise. Early examples of airborne operations include the German capture of Crete in May 1941 and Allied operations including "Torch" (Morocco and Algeria, November 1942), "Husky" (Sicily, July 1943), and "Avalanche" (Salerno, September 1943). Perhaps the most notable Western Allied airborne operation was "Market Garden" in September 1944. The airborne portion, code-named "Market," involved over 35,000 men and their equipment. This force parachuted or rode gliders into battle in the Netherlands over a three-day period. Current doctrinal principles for airborne operations stem from the lessons learned during "Market Garden" and other airborne operations conducted in the European theater.

If the Troop Carrier Command in Europe can be considered the focus for airborne doctrinal development, the Pacific Troop Carrier Command was the proving ground for theater logistics doctrine. The war in the Pacific was different from the Mediterranean and European theaters in both execution and geography and required a much different logistical approach. Early in the Pacific campaign, the need for a systems approach to airlift was recognized and implemented. In the Pacific, the early recognition and subsequent use of theater airlift was deemed an essential element supporting General MacArthur's indirect campaign strategy. In the southwest Pacific the following observations applied: air transportation provided the principal logistical support for land and air operations in both Darwin, Australia, and Papua, New Guinea; air transportation was essential for island warfare; and troop carrier aviation had far greater effect when used for air logistics support than when used for troop movements.

The enduring theater airlift lessons from World War II can be learned only by observing operations in the European, Pacific, and China-Burma-India theaters collectively. Unfortunately, the combined lessons of how tactical airlift could best be employed did not form a clear and integrated picture in the United States. Not until the tactical airlift mission was absorbed by the Military Airlift Command over 30 years later, were many combat lessons from World War II reflected in U.S. Air Force doctrine.

Postwar Era

The postwar era between 1945 and 1965 was the third historical airlift phase. Three events characterize the period. First, the Berlin Airlift established airlift forces as a diplomatic instrument of national power. Second, the austere military funding during the 1950s, coupled with legislative action by Congress following a lobbying effort by the airline industry, clarified the relationship between the airline industry and military airlift forces. Third, a shift in military strategy by the United States signaled an increase in the importance of an airlift force projection capability.

Of the three events, the Berlin Airlift was the most significant. Operation "Vittles," the Berlin resupply operation, represents the single most important example of how airlift forces can influence international events. This aerial resupply effort lasted from 26 June 1948 until 1 August 1949 and provided supplies, food, and fuel to the 2,500,000 civilian and military residents of West Berlin following a Soviet blockade (Fig. 1). During the thirteen months the airlift operation was in effect, airlift forces completed 266,600 flights and delivered over 2,223,000 tons of cargo. The combined efforts of the United States, Great Britain, and France thwarted the Soviet attempt to force Western powers out of West Berlin. Operation "Vittles" also demonstrated that large-scale operations could be sustained indefinitely using massive amounts of airlift. The Berlin Airlift provided Western powers with a diplomatic solution to a hostile military act.

The second aspect affecting airlift operations during the postwar era was the evolving relationship between the civil and military airlift communities. During the 1950s, the U.S. civilian airline industry was rapidly expanding and began to consider the postwar military air transport service as a direct competitor. Indeed, the airlines' fear was well-founded because the U.S. Military Air Transport Service provided the Department of Defense passenger service. As a result of its lobbying efforts, the U.S. airline industry succeeded in narrowing the focus of air force airlift activity to flights in support of military operations or combat training missions. Any airlift support necessary above this level was to be provided by the civil sector. Over time, this new relationship proved effective and ultimately resulted in a civil reserve air fleet arrangement that contributes to the United States' total airlift capability. Today similar arrangements exist in all major industrialized nations and, the United States and the former USSR excluded, civilian assets provide most, if not all, strategic airlift capability.

Figure 1. During the Soviet blockade, coal-hauling USAF C-54s are unloaded at Gatow Air Terminal in the British sector of Berlin. (Source: U.S. Air Force)

The shift in military strategy by the United States during the late 1950s and early 1960s was the third significant aspect of this era. This shift had a significant impact on airlift demand and fit conveniently with increased capability provided by civilian augmentation. Under the new strategy, conventional capability and a flexible response would precede a strategic nuclear exchange. Recognition of the fact that, under the new strategy, not only was a force projection required, but also that a shortfall existed, led to an airlift modernization.

During this era, the U.S. C-130 and C-141 were developed and entered the air force inventory. In addition, in 1963 the operational design and concept for the C-5 was approved. By the close of the postwar era in 1965, the force structure, roles and missions, and organizational structure governing airlift operations had been significantly altered. On 1 January 1966 the U.S. Military Air Transport Service was redesignated as the Military Airlift Command and became the single manager of long-range airlift for the U.S. Department of Defense.

Modern Era

The modern era is the era since 1965 and is characterized by the growing use of helicopters for tactical mobility and the use of airlift support as a form of military aid to foreign countries. In addition, both the United States and former Soviet Union each adopted airlift principles recognized by the other during a previous historical phase.

Beginning in the early 1970s, the Soviets expanded their airlift concepts to include strategic airlift. During the 1970s and 1980s, the Soviet air order of battle changed to include large jet transports useful in strategic force projection. For example, the Il-76, the most common Soviet jet transport, was introduced in the 1970s and the An-124, the world's largest cargo carrier, was developed in the 1980s.

Western airlift thought, as reflected in U.S. doctrine, also changed during the modern era. For the West, the change was mostly organizational and involved accepting principles adopted much earlier in the Eastern bloc. In the early 1970s the United States recognized that the single-manager concept should be extended to include all airlift aircraft under a single command. In 1975 tactical airlift aircraft previously assigned to the U.S. Tactical Air command and to theater commanders were consolidated under the Military Airlift Command, the U.S. Department of Defense executive agent for fixed-wing airlift support. This change was significant. For the first time, all U.S. airlift forces were commanded by a single specified commander reporting directly to the Joint Chiefs of Staff rather than to an individual service chief.

Technological change also characterizes the modern era. In the United States, large airlift aircraft capable of moving the majority of the army's equipment were acquired and helicopter technology progressed at a rate equal to fixed-wing development. These efforts resulted in the acquisition of large, fixed-wing aircraft such as the C-5 Galaxy and heavy lift, rotary-wing aircraft capable of transporting loads exceeding twenty tons. During this period, the use of rotary-wing aircraft to provide battlefield mobility became commonplace for both East and West military forces.

Airlift Doctrine

The preceding brief history demonstrates the change in airlift doctrine during the past 60 years. Over time, policy makers have expanded their view of air transportation from one of logistic support between air depots to a recognition that airlift forces are the *sine qua non* in a mobility triad that enables insular nations to pursue a military strategy of forward defense. In addition, the nonmilitary diplomatic use of airlift support has contributed increasingly to the foreign policy process.

Current airlift doctrine is expressed from both the intertheater and intratheater perspective. However, this approach is changing to one more clearly reflecting the systematic and combined nature of airlift support. An integrated approach recognizing the combined effort required to move units and cargo from their point of origin to their final destination is beginning to emerge. Airlift doctrine is categorized by the following principles:

1. A single airlift manager should be responsible for directing airlift operations throughout the conflict spectrum.
2. Theater commanders should establish airlift priorities within their area of responsibility.
3. Airlift apportionment decisions should be made by the national command authority. Theater apportionment should reflect the relative priority of competing theaters and support the national military strategy.
4. The operational management of airlift forces within an area of operations should be exercised by a commander of airlift forces. This individual will work with both intertheater and intratheater airlift issues for the theater commander.

Ultimately, there is only one airlift mission—the delivery of what is needed, where it is needed, when it is needed. Existing airlift doctrine, based upon a rich history, helps resolve the complex organizational and resource issues affecting this task.

Airlift Planning Factors

Airlift planning involves the systematic balancing of interrelated factors to achieve the desired transportation effect. These factors fall into four categories: the number of air lift aircraft apportioned; the type of force to be moved and its closure requirement; route support capability; and throughput considerations. Each factor and its relationship to the others must be understood when planning an airlift operation.

Force Apportionment

The most apparent factor influencing airlift support is the size of the airlift force apportioned to the task. Apportionment levels are determined by the priority associated with the task and the priority of competing demands on the same resources. Apportioned support can range from zero to 100 percent of the available capability and is determined by the national command authority. With the exception of the United States and the former Soviet Union, the majority of contemporary nation-states are regional powers who can devote all of their airlift support to a single theater. However, airlift planning for the United States, and previously for the former Soviet Union, is more complicated in that they had to anticipate the need to support multiple theaters simultaneously. For these superpowers, force apportionment depends on strategic warning available, the distance to the objective, and closure time for alternative means of transportation. The relationship between each factor is unique and must be considered when planning theater apportionment.

Force Closure Considerations

Force closure is the ability to move a unit from one location to another in a specific time. Airlift capability will always provide the best closure window. However, the actual closure capability will be based on four interrelated variables: the type of unit being moved, the amount of pre-positioned equipment, simultaneous access to other modes of transportation, and the efficient use of the available infrastructure. The joint efforts of the airlift manager, the theater commander, and the national command authority are required to minimize the effect of these variables and maximize combat capability. The following actions will improve force closure capability:

1. Forward-deploy units that require a significant amount of airlift, and leave in the home country lighter, more mobile units.
2. For home-based units with exceptionally heavy equipment, such as an armored division or brigade, preposition as much of the very large equipment as possible.

3. Use maximum strategic warning consistent with diplomatic efforts. Once deployment begins, in concert with the theater commander's campaign plan, move units with large quantities of heavy equipment late in the deployment flow. This phasing will generally result in the bimodal movement of the deploying unit with a decrease in the time required to achieve "closure."
4. To the maximum extent possible, apply the principle of mass to deployment operations. Force closure windows are minimized when the supporting infrastructure is fully used.

The preceding recommendations represent ideal solutions to a theater commander's force closure requirements. Sound planning well before hostilities begin is the only way to accomplish most of the preceding recommendations. National planners should seriously consider the deterrent value of forward defense, pre-positioning, and appropriately sized airlift fleets when developing military budgets. The balance between airlift, pre-positioning, and surface transportation depends on a nation's strategy and geostrategic position.

Route Support Requirements

Balancing route support capability to the apportioned airlift force is the next planning step. Once the air line of communication has been determined and the airlift force apportioned to a specific theater is known, the airlift manager can determine the maintenance and aerial port support required to support the airlift operation. The size of the support structure is set to minimize the aircraft's time on the ground. By rapidly refueling, maintaining, loading, or unloading the aircraft dedicated to the airlift flow, the total airlift capacity of the air line of communication is increased. Decreasing ground time increases daily utilization rates, which has the same effect as providing additional aircraft. If the utilization rate can be increased by changing the level of support, this option should be exercised before assigning additional aircraft.

Throughput Considerations

The last step in the planning process is to consider the effect of throughput constraints on the airlift operation. Throughput is the amount of transported equipment or personnel that can be processed through a location over a specific amount of time. When considering airlift apportionment, the airlift planner should balance the force structure committed with the available infrastructure. During the operation, the efficient use of the available infrastructure must be monitored to ensure that it does not become saturated. If saturation occurs, the supporting infrastructure should be increased or, if more than one theater is being supported, the excess aircraft should be reapportioned to support another theater. Either option will increase total airlift capability.

The Airlift Planning Process

Airlift planning involves two distinct processes—the deliberate planning process and the execution planning process. Both require the interaction of three principal parties: the national command authority, the theater commanders, and the commander of airlift forces. While the parties involved are usually the same in both planning situations, the process is clearly more demanding during the execution phase due to the friction and fog of war. In addition to providing all interested parties with an initial estimate of combat capabilities, the deliberate planning process provides the national command authority with an assessment of risk.

Deliberate Planning

Deliberate planning involves the preliminary apportionment of military resources in support of a national military strategy. Once the theater commander has been apportioned his combat force (land, air, and naval units), he develops a campaign strategy and arrays his forces to best support his concept of operation and scheme of maneuver. Airlift forces are important in this process for two reasons: first, with the exception of the simplest of theaters, the peacetime garrison of forces rarely mirrors a theater commander's wartime force disposition; and second, airlift support provides the maneuver and resupply capability needed during combat.

A commander must address two questions during the deliberate planning process: what is the closure window required for those forces not in the theater, and how can airlift forces shorten the internal lines of communication?

The theater commander and supporting airlift commander jointly address the time phasing of the deploying units, the theater throughput capability, the interrelationship between airlift forces and other means of transportation, and the requirement to deploy supporting airlift personnel and equipment to establish and use an air line of communication. This planning process is the same for any nation employing airlift forces, but it is more difficult and dynamic for nations supporting multiple theaters from external lines of communication. Typically, the results of the airlift planning process are contained in a transportation annex to the theater war plan.

Employment Planning

Airlift employment planning involves three distinct types of airlift support: first, force projection to one or more theaters; second, theater airlift support for resupply operations; and third, the use of theater-assigned and temporarily apportioned airlift to execute maneuver options in support of the campaign strategy.

A theater commander's first airlift consideration should be whether or not his apportioned airlift force will support his force closure goal. Generally, the projected closure time will not meet the commander's desired goal unless his total combat force is in place before hostilities begin. Since this condition will rarely exist, the theater commander will attempt to improve his situation by increasing his airlift support. Subsequent reapportionment may be possible depending on the relative priority of his theater and the competing demands of other theater commanders. This apportionment issue amounts to a mass/economy-of-force trade-off decision by the national command authority. Some factors influencing the apportionment decision are the distances involved to each theater, the enemy order of battle, allied support, the closure time for alternate modes of transportation, and the consequence of defeat. Since each factor is likely to be different than was assumed during the deliberate planning process, reapportionment should be considered for the existing conditions.

The second type of wartime airlift support, resupply, will demand most of the theater airlift capability. The majority is provided by airlift forces deployed in the theater. Theater airlift forces are managed by the theater commander of airlift forces who provides an interface between the national commander of airlift forces and the theater commander. Determining the support priority for theater-assigned forces rests with the theater commander and is based on his campaign plan.

The level of airlift support provided to specific units is determined by factors such as the security of ground lines of communication, the intensity of combat activity, and the time available and priority of the supported unit. Theater airlift forces shorten lines of communication by increasing logistics velocity and provide a method for resupplying units temporarily cut off from their normal supply depots. Depending on the priority of deploying forces, airlift aircraft committed to force projection missions and strategic resupply may be temporarily used in the theater to augment theater-assigned airlift forces. This type of augmentation would be coordinated by the theater commander of airlift forces and approved by the national airlift manager and the national command authority.

The third type of airlift support involves the redeployment of a unit from one location to another as part of a theater maneuver scheme. When contemplating redeployment of forces, a commander should consider whether airfields will support his concept of maneuver. Specifically, will the on-load and off-load sites proposed by his strategy support the throughput necessary to close the transported unit when required? Computations of this nature are quite complicated and are normally the responsibility of the airlift planner.

Assuming airfields are adequate, the commander should determine if forced entry will be required at the off-load airfield(s). This will not be a problem for airlift operations from one corps' rear area to another corps' rear area. But for the envelopment, the objective airfield may well be in enemy hands and, therefore, require a forced entry before airlift begins. This will require the use of a small ground unit maneuvering in depth, an air assault force, or the air drop of a combat force at the objective airfield to secure the site.

Once the objective airfield issues are resolved, the theater commander should consider force phasing and follow-on logistics support. Phasing of deployed forces should be planned so as to concentrate the maximum number of combat units in the shortest period of time. Therefore, the airlift flow should deploy combat units first, combat support units second, and combat service support elements last. As a general rule, the suggested loading sequence will concentrate the maximum combat capability in the shortest period of time. This type of phasing will be particularly effective for maneuver operations in which an existing combat support and combat service support structure assist the deploying combat force until its support arrives. For units employed in deep operations, this technique will be somewhat less useful since immediate support will not be available. In the latter instance, the early deployment of combat and combat support units will primarily benefit the overall operation by helping defend the off-load airfield and adjacent marshaling area.

The Future

Airlift will become increasingly important in the future. The force projection flexibility provided by airlift aircraft will increasingly act as a force multiplier for nations possessing airlift capability. Airlift forces used in combination with pre-positioning will decrease forward basing requirements and will become the preferred diplomatic and political solution to military strategy options.

Future airlift aircraft will be designed to optimize the airlift system and will be specifically matched to the type of equipment used by the transported unit. They will be designed to minimize the en-route support and infrastructure requirements. The U.S. C-17 may become a model for the major powers since its design is better suited to both the force projection and theater airlift mission than are other contemporary airlift aircraft.

In the future, theater airlift will be characterized by an increase in the number of aircraft used to support maneuver warfare. Theater airlift forces will contain a mix of fixed-wing, tilt-rotor, and rotary-wing aircraft capable of supporting mobile operations. The emerging trend in land warfare doctrine with its increased reliance on maneuver, speed, timing, and tempo will dictate a commensurate increase in the reliance on airlift for its combat mobility.

CHARLES J. JERNIGAN

SEE ALSO: Logistics: A General Survey; Logistics, Air Force; Organization, Air Force.

Bibliography

Burkhard, D. J. 1984. *Military airlift command: Historical handbook, 1941–1981*. Scott AFB, Ill.: Military Airlift Command.

Cassidy, D. H. 1988. An interview with the commander-in-chief, U.S. Transportation Command and Commander-in-

Chief, Military Airlift Command. *Armed Forces Journal International*, January, pp. 49–54.
———. 1988. Putting the pieces together. *Military Forum*, September, pp. 26–36.
Davis, R. G. 1987. *The 31 initiatives: A study in airforce-army cooperation*. Washington, D.C.: Office of Air Force History.
Harvey, J. 1988. Carrying the cord. *Airlift*, Fall, pp. 6–9.
Kitfield, J., and F. Elliot. 1988. The defense transportation dilemma. *Military Forum*, September, pp. 16–28.
Leary, W. M. 1986. Strategic airlift: Past, present, and future. *Air University Review*, September–October, pp. 74–85.
Lesser, I. D. 1986. The mobility trend—Airlift, sealift and prepositioning in American strategy. *RUSI*, March, pp. 31–35.
Miller, C. E. 1988. *Airlift doctrine*. Maxwell Air Force Base, Ala.: Air Univ. Press.
Nguyen, H. P. 1985. Soviet thinking on the next land war. *Parameters*, Winter, pp. 41–47.
Patterson, D. J. 1988. The C-17 in an Iran scenario: A perspective beyond 66 million ton-miles per day. *Armed Forces Journal International*, January, pp. 42–48.
Ross, J. D. 1987. Jointness receives major emphasis in logistics planning. *Army*, October, pp. 148–59.
Saw, D. 1987. Trends in military air transport. *Military Technology Miltech*, November, pp. 32–42.
Trainor, R. E. 1988. The evolution of an air force logistics concept of operations. *Air Force Journal of Logistics*, Winter, pp. 1–4.
Wadstalm, B., and M. Lambert. Military airlifters: More than just camouflaged commuters. *Interavia*, July, pp. 731–35.
Welch, J. 1984. Strategic mobility: A tale of four SecDefs. *Armed Forces Journal International*, July, pp. 75–91.

AIRMAN

The term *airman* is used for an enlisted member of an air force or of the aviation element of a navy. It applies primarily to enlisted personnel, including noncommissioned officers. It may be applied in a general sense also to air force officers, but this usage is rare. Airman is an enlisted grade in the U.S. Air Force corresponding to private in the army and seaman or fireman in the navy. In the Royal Air Force, the term *aircraftman* is used to denote the four lowest enlisted ranks. The equivalent French term *aviateur* is used in the most general sense of an airman being a person who flies. The term *airman* also may be used in English to mean an aviator or pilot who actually operates an aircraft.

JOHN R. BRINKERHOFF

SEE ALSO: Enlisted Personnel.

AIRPOWER

Airpower has generally been understood as a nation's ability to exploit the air for national security purposes—a traditional view that dates from World War I. Some, such as Gen. H. H. Arnold of the United States Army Air Force, expanded airpower to include the total aviation community, both military and civilian. In fact, it was the exploitation of the civilian side of aviation that allowed Germany to subvert the limitations of the Versailles Treaty and prepare for a massive expansion of the Luftwaffe, which they did beginning in 1934.

Technology and the Characteristics of Airpower

The key to understanding airpower is understanding that it is radically dependent on technology. Airpower exists because technology has advanced to the point where man can move a payload, including a pilot or a crew, from one point to another in a relatively short period of time, free from contact with the earth's surface. The exploitation of this technology results in three attributes that distinguish airpower systems: speed, range, and flexibility. The terms, however, are relative. *Speed*, in this context, is the ability to respond to requirements in a timely manner, rather than an ability to take off quickly or fly fast. *Range* is the ability to go where the system's capabilities are needed. *Flexibility* is the ability to meet one of several different requirements with minimum effort. None of the three terms, standing alone, defines an air system. A bullet can have tremendous speed, but it lacks the range and flexibility to be classified as an air system. The same applies to an artillery shell, although it has greater range and, due to its size, the potential for much greater flexibility, including terminal homing. Yet the artillery shell's range and flexibility are still limited.

The Need for Effective Control

Airpower systems are those which, due to their speed, range, and flexibility, can meet a variety of needs, albeit not all at the same time. The flexibility of airpower means that it can be assigned a number of different potential tasks, while the speed and range allow it to quickly meet the needs of a number of different potential requesters, often in disparate locations. This ability to satisfy different requirements, but not all requirements at once, results in another fundamental aspect of airpower, the need for an effective control regime to allow full exploitation of potential.

Weight, Consistency, and Duration

While airpower has the characteristics of speed, range, and flexibility, its application is limited by the need for weight, consistency, and duration. Operational requirements, both commercial and military, center upon delivering a required amount of material, and doing so in a repetitive manner.

For airlines, the ability to fill a certain percentage of passenger seats and to do so consistently is fundamental to financial success. Airline operations have defined a minimum load factor below which an operation is financially unsupportable and above which a profit is made.

For a military application, the ability to achieve an objective depends upon the ability to deliver combat power against a coherent set of targets and to do so until the objective is obtained. When airpower is dissipated in its application, in "penny packets" in the words of Air Chief Marshal Sir Arthur Tedder, the result will be failure of the air effort, and failure of any accompanying land or naval effort.

To ensure the effective use of airpower, several principles should be followed. First, when an objective is assigned, a proper target set must be determined to allow airpower to achieve that objective. Once the target set is in hand, sufficient airpower must be applied against the set to ensure the desired results. This means weight in terms of the numbers of aircraft assigned as well as ordnance load.

A single attack on a target is usually not sufficient to achieve a long-term objective. The opposing side will react and create a new set of circumstances. Thus, airpower must be applied in a consistent manner against the target set, either in its original form or as it has been modified. There is often the temptation to take advantage of the flexibility of airpower to switch from one target set to another. Normally, this temptation must be resisted or the opposing side will overcome the effects of airpower and rebound.

If airpower is applied with sufficient weight and consistency it will begin to have a telling effect on the opposing side. This is when duration becomes an important factor. As a rule, an air campaign is only effective after a long period of time. If the effort is ended too soon it will allow the opposing side to recover.

A major danger in the application of airpower is to continue using the mathematical exactness that is needed to design and produce weapon systems in the concepts for their employment. In actual operational experience, especially in combat, such precise measurements are often misleading. The confusion of battle and the inability to fully know all the strengths and weaknesses of an enemy will result in gross errors when overprecise calculations are used to determine force application. The effective application of airpower demands weight, or mass, to cope with problems caused by inaccurate or missing data. Often a lack of accurate data can be overcome by the judicious application of a reserve capability.

Strategic, Operational, or Tactical Application

Experts disagree on the proper focus for the application of airpower. Following World War I, such airpower advocates as Gen. Giulio Douhet (Italy) and Gen. William Mitchell (U.S.) placed emphasis on the use of airpower to achieve strategic objectives. In light of the tremendous cost of World War I in lives and treasure, they looked to airpower to reduce the price of waging war. Using the somewhat limited wartime air operations as a basis, they concluded that the use of airpower to destroy a modern nation's population or economic or industrial base would result in defeat of that nation. During the interwar period, all air forces considered strategic bombing and made efforts to procure the capability. Only in the Royal Air Force and the U.S. Army Air Corps, however, was strategic airpower dominant.

Strategic bombardment was given impetus by the development of the fast, all-metal monoplane bomber, which could outrun the standard fighter aircraft of the day. In U.S. Army Air Corps maneuvers in 1933, fighter aircraft failed to stop penetrating bombers. The appearance of four-engined heavy bombers in the mid-1930s, particularly the Boeing B-17, convinced strategic airpower advocates of the correctness of their thinking, but it would take World War II to test the theories. Lessons drawn from that war are still subject to argument.

Another view of airpower emphasizes its role at the operational-strategic level. This view dominated thinking in both the German and Soviet air forces at the beginning of World War II, and remained strong in the Soviet Union, except for the special case of transpolar nuclear warfare. It is also the view of the North Atlantic Treaty Organization (NATO) since the adoption of the strategy of flexible response, which saw confronting aggression with three possible responses: direct defense, theater nuclear response, and massive retaliation. The two things critical to the operational-strategic view of airpower are the gaining of air superiority and the use of airpower to master the time dimension in support of surface, usually land, operations. This view of airpower was effectively demonstrated by the Luftwaffe in Poland in 1939 and in France in 1940. It was also used effectively by the Allies in the Mediterranean theater. Although the Germans attempted to exploit airpower at the operational level in their campaigns against the Soviet Union, the Luftwaffe lacked the strength to complete the necessary tasks. Eventually, the Soviet Union turned the tables on the Germans and began their own effective operational air effort.

When employed at the operational level, airpower must first gain freedom of action for itself and for surface forces. This requires a concentration of the air effort during the first days of a battle to gain control of the air. In Soviet terms, this meant a theater-independent air operation, aimed not only at air supremacy but also at the elimination of an opponent's nuclear-capable forces. The freedom of action gained by achieving air superiority is then employed to support surface forces. This usually means support of land forces, but it can also mean support of naval forces.

The main objective of the operations, normally termed *air interdiction*, is to expand further the surface forces' freedom of action. To do this, air forces attack the enemy to delay, disrupt, divert, and destroy his forces. Given the very limited ability of airpower to hold territory, or even destroy or capture forces, the emphasis in air interdiction is on delay, disruption, and diversion. Destruction is normally a beneficial outcome of air operations. Fundamental to obtaining air superiority and conducting air interdiction are effective reconnaissance and surveillance operations to provide accurate information for land and air forces.

The final concept governing the application of air assets stresses tactical purposes. This view, held by a number of land and naval theorists, is exemplified by France's employment of its force in World War II and by the doctrine of the U.S. Army as espoused in a 9 April 1942 document, *Aviation in Support of Ground Forces*. This view holds that aircraft should be used to meet the needs of individual ground commanders.

During the invasion of North Africa and the subsequent campaign until just before the Battle of Kasserine Pass, this view prevailed and resulted in the subordination of the U.S. Twelfth Air Force to the Army's II Corps. As a result, opportunities to deal decisive strikes were missed and Allied forces were punished unnecessarily when they encountered determined German resistance.

All of this changed with the consolidation of the Mediterranean theater under General Eisenhower and the appointment of Air Chief Marshal Tedder as the air component commander. A major reorganization was undertaken and completed on 18 February 1943, the day before the Battle of Kasserine Pass. Subsequent air and land operations prospered under the new command arrangement that centralized control of air forces. This principle was used during operations in Italy and for the Normandy invasion.

The application of airpower at the tactical level can provide major benefits. If air superiority is achieved, or obtained by default, and if sufficient air assets are available, airpower can increase the effectiveness of land and sea operations and thus reduce the required size of the land and naval forces. Examples of such application include the Allied efforts subsequent to the breakout from Normandy and the wars in Korea and Vietnam. It was again demonstrated during the 1991 Gulf War.

Air Superiority

Whether a nation believes that the principal use of airpower should be at the strategic, operational, or tactical level, air superiority is fundamental to success in modern war. In the words of Sir Arthur Tedder, "Air superiority is the prerequisite to all war-winning operations, whether at sea, on land, or in the air."

The exact meaning of *air superiority*, or its companion term *air supremacy*, has varied according to the time and the air force. Soviet military thought concentrated on air supremacy, which the Soviets defined as the decisive superiority by one of the combatant sides in the air space of a theater or on a major axis.

Before the dissolution of the Soviet Union as many as 7,000 aircraft, ranging from fighters to medium bombers, would be employed in the Soviet western theater of operations to attack enemy airfields, critical command and control facilities, and nuclear-capable systems and storage sites. At the same time, defensive forces would be employed to prevent the enemy from conducting similar operations.

In Western usage, there is a difference between air superiority and air supremacy. The former refers to a degree of dominance in the air battle at a given time and location. The latter refers to a general dominance over an opposing air force, making that air force incapable of interfering with "friendly" operations. The attainment of air supremacy normally follows from a prolonged period of air superiority.

Generally, Western doctrine provides for the same preemptive offensive operation as Soviet doctrine. The best example of a preemptive operation to achieve air superiority since World War II is the Israeli attack on Egyptian and Syrian air forces during the Arab-Israeli War of 1967. The United States obtained air superiority in Korea, after the entry of the Chinese into the war, by air-to-air combat, since airfields in China were off limits and Chinese aircraft could not be destroyed on the ground. The Israeli air force obtained an enviable exchange ratio against the Syrian air force in the 1982 air battles over the Bekaa Valley. These air battles, which resulted in the Syrians losing 86 aircraft and 24 missile sites, were conducted using a sophisticated combination of aircraft and electronic warfare. Using multinational air, land, and sea forces to achieve quick and decisive air supremacy was demonstrated by Coalition forces liberating Kuwait in early 1991.

Gaining air superiority is never an end in itself. Its purpose is to provide air, land, and sea forces with freedom of action, which includes freedom from surveillance and reconnaissance as well as from air attack. The attainment of air superiority, while nominally an air concern, is achieved by some combination of the efforts of air, land, and sea forces. The Arab-Israeli War of 1973 provides an example; land forces moved into Egypt to help achieve air superiority, with a reciprocal benefit to the land forces when that air superiority had been achieved. The World War II Pacific amphibious campaigns are an example of naval forces contributing to extension of air superiority, which in turn allowed airpower to contribute to the success of the landing operation.

Command and Control

It has been stated that each weapon system seeks its natural level of command and control. Because of the speed, range, flexibility, and expense of airpower systems, they require centralized control to ensure that their use best meets the needs of all who might need their support. The theater command level is where control of air forces is normally centralized. In the West, the concept of co-equal air, land, and sea component commanders, subordinate to a joint (or combined) theater commander in chief, has been dominant since World War II. In the former Soviet Union, the emphasis was on combined arms and the predominance of the land commander. In both cases, the theater commander is the agent for bringing together air, land, and naval forces.

Centralized command is normally coupled with decentralized execution. Decentralized execution allows subordinate commanders, once assigned a task, to execute their missions in a manner they find best suits their situation. While there are many advantages to decentralized execution, this principle becomes more difficult to follow as defenses become stronger, for the increasing strength of defenses forces airpower systems to become more specialized to deal with those defenses. Thus, as defense suppression forces and dedicated electronic combat aircraft become a major part of any large operation, the ability to decentralize becomes more restricted. The options available to the air commander are to decentralize the limited number of specialized aircraft or to retain a more centralized control on operations, risking delays and dissipation of effort due to wartime command, control, and communications problems.

One form of decentralization is most undesirable for effective employment of airpower. When airpower is used in support of surface forces, there is a tendency on the part of the supported commander to want maximum control over the air operation. If not resisted, this desire can result in major inefficiencies. In the past, control of air forces by supported ground commanders has resulted in the fragmentation of the air effort. An example of such fragmentation was the U.S. decision to allow control of B-52 aircraft in Southeast Asia to be shared between the commander in chief, Strategic Air Command, and the commander, Military Assistance Command Vietnam. Thus, rational choices by a single commander regarding the best mix of forces to achieve each assigned mission was not possible. A better approach is for the commander responsible for achieving an objective to be given both his mission and control of required forces. Obtaining the objective becomes the responsibility of the commander with the mission and the forces. If circumstances do not allow the accomplishment of the mission in some agreed way, the commander is expected to find another.

There are three exceptions to the concept of centralized command as it is commonly understood. The first pertains to those airpower systems with the speed, range, or flexibility to meet the needs of more than one theater. Examples include space reconnaissance assets and certain long-range systems that can operate across theaters. With these, centralization of control should be at a higher level. In the former Soviet Union, such systems were controlled by the supreme high command.

The second exception applies to systems that lack the speed, range, and flexibility to operate throughout the theater or over large portions of it, such as light observation helicopters and corps-level reconnaissance assets.

The third exception is for naval air assets, which, due to the unique features of naval air operations, should be controlled by the battle group or fleet commander. Naval air assets at sea have unique operational requirements that demand specific attention from the designated naval commander. One such requirement is the need to defend against a submarine threat. Another is the management of tightly scheduled deck cycles to ensure fuel reserves during launch and recovery. With regard to such naval air operations, when land-based air is operating with naval air and unique naval air requirements predominate, land-based air should be subordinated to the naval air commander, unless the land-based air provides the predominant portion of the fighting force or there are other extenuating circumstances. Conversely, when maritime superiority, to include air superiority, is obtained and operations are routine, naval air activities should be under the general direction of the air component commander when naval air assets are part of the overall operation. Often this subordination is implemented by making those sorties that are excess to internal requirements available to the other commander for tasking.

Organization for Airpower

The method of organizing for airpower, which generally means organizing air forces, has been contentious since World War I. The importance of the issue turns on the development of national doctrine and on the allocation of budgets. Airpower systems are extremely expensive and can distort budgets even for the richest nations. For some countries, the procurement of new aircraft can mean no new major equipment for land and naval forces for that period. For a nation to develop even limited airpower, it must ensure that an airpower establishment is part of its bureaucratic structure so that there will be an effective voice for airpower in defense councils and in the budget allocation process.

The establishment of independent air forces did not come automatically, but rather derived from the work of airpower advocates who claimed to be acting on the lessons of past wars. By World War II, a number of nations had independent air forces, including Great Britain, France, Germany, and Italy. This national independence was not necessarily accompanied by independence of thought or by equipment that would allow independent action. The ability of major participants in World War II to apply airpower was limited not only by national bureaucratic considerations but also by doctrine, the development of the relationship of the air arm with other services, technical capabilities, and the financial resources to produce the required air force.

Subsequent to World War II, the development of airpower has moved in two directions. Some nations have followed the Western approach of an independent air force while others have seen airpower as a component, albeit vital, of land and naval power. In fact, few nations have a path that is totally committed to one of these organizational patterns. Furthermore, lessons learned from the control of civil aviation have influenced the organization and employment of airpower. A final factor complicating the issue of organization has been the technical advances that have led to the development of missiles and remotely piloted vehicles. Strong arguments have been made that surface-to-surface and surface-to-air missiles are correctly land and naval systems. As a result of the lack of consensus concerning the control of these new systems, unmanned aerial vehicles are to be found in all the services in many nations.

In the postwar years, the way nations organized their civil and military airpower activities depended upon their national war-fighting style, prewar preferences, wartime experiences, entrenched bureaucracies, and budgets. For the United States, the development of a separate air force evolved with the concept of a centralized Department of Defense. In a compromise, the air capabilities of naval forces remained separate. Within a decade of this new arrangement, the military was becoming more dependent on space, but in 1958, the president elected to orient the new national space organization along civilian lines. Thus, direction of airpower is somewhat diffuse in the United States.

In the former Soviet Union, the strength of the Red Army was felt throughout the military bureaucracy. Independence for airpower evolved through the splitting off of separate services that specialized in airpower functions. These included the air force, the air defense troops, and the strategic rocket forces. Other nations have followed paths dictated by their own circumstances.

Nuclear Weapons

The advent of nuclear weapons added a new dimension to the issue of air superiority. With their promise of facilitating a crippling first blow, nuclear weapons make the defeat of an opposing air force much more likely. During the 1950s and 1960s, the world's most powerful nations spent enormous sums on systems designed to defeat enemy nuclear-armed bombers. Soviet defensive forces constituted a tremendous portion of their armed forces. The advent of the ballistic missile caused both the Soviet Union and the West to abandon efforts at a virtually leakproof strategic, or homeland, defense. The concept of a crippling first blow gave way to the concept of retaliation and a secure nuclear reserve force. Thus, the offense remained dominant, being countered only by an equally devastating offense in the hands of the other side.

The dominance of the strategic offense came under question in the 1980s by those who believed that the strategic defense can, through the use of advanced computers and beam weapons, again gain the upper hand. For strategic defense to move into a position of dominance it will have to demonstrate that it can reduce the civilian losses in an enemy nuclear attack to an acceptable level.

Civilian Contributions to Airpower

An often overlooked aspect of airpower is the contribution of the civilian sector. One of the most important points is the need to develop an air-minded population from such things as exposure to a nation's air and space programs. From this air-mindedness comes support for airpower. Further, the existence of a civilian aircraft industry provides a reserve of pilots and mechanics and of aircraft production facilities. Also, civil airlines provide a reserve of strategic lift capability.

For the United States, this airlift reserve is formalized in the Civil Reserve Air Fleet. Under this program, the U.S. government pays airline companies to modify designated aircraft to meet wartime airlift requirements. The government offsets increases in operating costs due to the modifications. In addition, the program includes the flight and maintenance crews needed to operate the aircraft. Similarly, the former Soviet Union maintained a close relationship between its air force and its national airline, Aeroflot.

Other actions in the civil sector that foster airpower are programs such as the Civil Air Patrol in the United States. This organization serves three functions: it provides peacetime domestic search and rescue on a volunteer basis, conducts aerospace education for its members and the public at large, and operates a cadet program for the training and educating of young adults with regard to airpower.

Future Developments

The future of airpower is tied to the advance of technology. Advances in space-related technologies, including potential space-based offensive and defensive capabilities, offer new possibilities and suggest that it may become necessary to replace the concept of airpower with the broader concept of aerospace power. Exploitation of these possibilities depends upon the decisions of nations regarding investments and treaty limitations. The cost of space systems excludes all but a small number of nations from participating in space activities. Even among those that have moved into space, only the United States and the Soviet Union have developed major capabilities. The European nations, working together, have developed a significant launch capability, but cost continues to hold back many desired projects.

Closer to the surface of the earth, advances in low-observable technologies could well tilt the offense-defense balance in the direction of the offense for the next twenty years or more. Such advances, coupled with the significantly increased accuracy of unmanned systems, offer the potential to realize, without resort to weapons of mass destruction, the concepts of early airpower thinkers such as Gen. Giulio Douhet. The costs will strongly affect what directions these advances take. It is becoming increasingly difficult to offer tailored systems to meet the needs of all who could benefit from airpower. Thus, in the twenty-first century, it is likely that some classic airpower missions and modalities will be abandoned so that others may be better exploited. Given the unsettled international situation, it is unlikely that there will be an end to technological advances and thus in the continuing development of air or aerospace power.

CLIFFORD R. KRIEGER

SEE ALSO: Airpower, History of; Airpower, Strategic; Airpower, Tactical; Airspace Control, Military; Chaff; Douhet, Giulio; Electronic Warfare, Air; Flexible Response; Organization, Air Force; Radar; Radar Technology Applications; Technology and Warfare.

Bibliography

Armitage, M. J., and R. A. Mason. 1983. *Air power in the nuclear age.* Urbana, Ill.: Univ. of Illinois Press.
Bacon, H. R., et al. 1983. *Aerospace: The challenge.* Maxwell Air Force Base, Ala.: Civil Air Patrol.
Higham, R. 1972. *Air power: A concise history.* New York: St. Martin's Press.
Mason, R. A. 1986. *War in the third dimension.* London: Brassey's.
———. 1987. *Air power: An overview of roles.* London: Brassey's.
Momyer, W. W. 1978. *Air power in three wars.* Washington, D.C.: Government Printing Office.
Murphy, P. J. 1984. *The Soviet air forces.* London: McFarland.
Proektor, D. M. 1973. World War Two. In *Great Soviet encyclopedia.* Vol. 5. New York: Macmillan.
Radziyevskiy, A. I., ed. 1965. *Dictionary of basic military terms, a Soviet view.* Washington, D.C.: Government Printing Office.
Singh, J. 1985. *Air power in modern warfare.* New Delhi: Lancer International.
Tedder, A. W. 1966. *With prejudice: The war memoirs of Marshal of the Royal Air Force, Lord Tedder.* London: Cassell.
———. [1948] 1975. *Air power in war.* Westport, Conn.: Greenwood Press.
Vershinin, K. A. 1973. Air force. In *Great Soviet encyclopedia.* Vol. 5. New York: Macmillan.

AIRPOWER, HISTORY OF

Airpower is the use of the air to further defensive or aggressive national objectives. The means by which they are pursued will be an air force, of whatever composition is appropriate to achieve the objectives. But airpower also implies the use of less direct resources such as industry, logistics (including, for example, communications and the supply of fuel), and many other facets of the potential of a nation as a whole for warlike operations. Airpower has developed since the earliest days of aviation and has had failures and successes.

Earliest Steps

The use of the air in war swiftly followed the inventions which enabled man to fly. Unmanned balloons were used in an attempt to bombard Venice with shrapnel as early as 1849 during the Austrian siege of that city; the United States used balloons for surveillance during its Civil War in the 1860s, and the British army used observation balloons in the Boer War. The Wright brothers, while still perfecting their flying machine in 1903, twice offered their invention to the U.S. Army. Military employment has never been far from the minds of aerial inventors. In fact, throughout the history of airpower, the military potential of the use of the air has been a principal stimulus to progress in the field of aviation technology.

The activities of the Wright brothers stirred U.S. military interest in the possibilities of aviation, and on 1 August 1907 the first U.S. military aviation unit was formed, the aeronautics section of the U.S. Army Signal Corps. One year later a nonrigid airship built by Thomas Scott Baldwin, and carrying Glenn Curtiss as flight engineer, was purchased by the corps after a demonstration at Fort Myer, near Washington, D.C.

In 1909, also at Fort Myer, Orville Wright completed the trials of his *Flyer* for the U.S. Army and demonstrated an endurance of 72 minutes and an average speed of 68 kilometers (42 mi.) per hour (Fig. 1). The U.S. Army thus became the owner of the first and only military aircraft in the world at that time.

In the years that followed, small aircraft construction companies sprang up in most industrial countries. During the last three years of peace (1911–14) before World War I, all the major powers were purchasing the new machines for military purposes and training their pilots. Meanwhile in a modest foretaste of what was to follow, the Italian army used aircraft to drop 2-kilogram grenades on enemy targets during its Libyan Campaign of 1911.

Figure 1. Orville Wright preparing for a flight at Fort Myer, Virginia, 1909. (SOURCE: U.S. Library of Congress)

First World War

But it was during the First World War that use of the air developed from a popular curiosity into an effective means of prosecuting war. When the war began in August 1914 military aviation was limited to a few hundred elementary machines integrated into existing military structures. These aircraft were expected to perform reconnaissance over land and sea, artillery spotting, and courier work. Aircraft were viewed as a supplement to fleets and armies during what was expected to be a short war. Initially, there were no bombs, bombsights, integral weapons, or other equipment for combat in these early machines.

Military aircraft, however, soon took on more robust characteristics as technology was harnessed to the demands of intensive warfare. Three developments were particularly noteworthy. First, more powerful engines and more sturdy machines were produced. Second, the introduction of lightweight machineguns, synchronized to fire through the propeller arc of single-engine aircraft, transformed the early fighters into effective weapon platforms. Third, long production runs meant standardized machines, which in turn made possible formation tactics.

Air-to-Air Combat

The demands of air-to-air fighting that emerged began to use resources that might otherwise have been used to meet the growing requirements of land and naval forces for air support. The result was an even more urgent demand for more aircraft, men, and supporting services. Operational pressures for higher performance, so that aircraft could outmaneuver their opponents, led by 1916 to speeds of up to 150 kilometers (93 mi.) per hour in the British DH2 and to ceilings up to 4,600 meters (15,000 ft.) for the French Nieuport II. Endurances of two hours also became common, and although these improvements over the machines of 1914 were not dramatic, they were accompanied by new levels of reliability and maneuverability.

Bombers

Long-range bombing, that is, bombing beyond the immediate battle areas, was also introduced. Lighter-than-air airships first undertook this role. Antwerp and Warsaw were attacked in this way by German zeppelins in the early months of the war in raids intended to undermine the morale of the inhabitants rather than to cause any serious physical destruction. These attacks were followed in January 1915 by zeppelin raids on British east coast towns, and by others on London during the spring of 1915, the first strategic bombing offensive in history.

Airships continued to make these sorties, particularly against London and Paris, sporadically throughout 1915 and 1916. Although the raids caused only modest damage and casualties in Britain (556 killed and 1,357 injured; small numbers compared to the slaughter at the war fronts), they alarmed the urban populations and caused grave concern at government level. Defensive measures were put into place in the form of antiaircraft artillery and interceptor aircraft, eventually equipped with deadly tracer and incendiary ammunition.

Rather more serious were the raids made against Britain by Gotha bombers starting in May 1917. On 13 June the first such raid against London killed 162 and injured 432. This and following raids led to a reorganization of the defenses created to counter the zeppelin attacks. Extra searchlights were deployed, as well as barrage balloons that supported curtains of steel cables in the air up to altitudes of 2,400 meters (8,000 ft.). Above that height, intercepters flew patrols.

At the same time as the Gothas were being developed, the British and the French were producing similar machines so that by 1917 all the principal powers had long-range bombers in their inventories. One significant organizational consequence of the Gotha raids was that partly in response to the public outcry about the bombings, the decision was made to amalgamate the air elements of the British army and the Royal Navy—the Royal Flying Corps (RFC) and the Royal Navy Air Service (RNAS)—to form the first independent air arm, the Royal Air Force. This took place in April 1918.

Throughout the war aircraft were also used extensively for support of ground and naval forces. Efforts at coordinated air support for ground forces were made from March 1915 onward, so that at the Battle of the Somme in July 1916, 360 French and British aircraft were engaged. By 1918 air operations had become so extensive that, for example in July of that year, the Allied air forces lost over 500 aircraft in a single month during a counteroffensive that was launched between Soissons and Château-Thierry. Air warfare on other fronts tended to follow the tactics developed in the west, although far fewer numbers were engaged. In Italy, Macedonia, Palestine, East Africa, Gallipoli, and Mesopotamia, aircraft played some part in the operations on land.

Naval and Other Missions

Once convoys were instituted in 1917, naval aircraft and airships had an important role in escorting merchant ships. As to main fleet activities, seaplane carriers were able to launch fighters designed to operate from airfields, but the ships were not fast enough to keep up with the fleet. After unsuccessful experiments with a cruiser modified to take an aircraft hangar and a flying-off deck, the Royal Navy in October 1918 introduced the first real aircraft carrier, HMS *Argus*, armed with torpedo bombers, but it joined the fleet too late to enter combat.

By the end of the First World War, aviation had made enormous progress. Some aircraft produced during the conflict, such as the Avro 504N, were still in use as trainers as late as the mid-1930s. At the technical level, the war had produced far more powerful, maneuverable, and reliable aircraft. Special air weapons such as synchronized fixed machine guns, as well as innovations like bombsights, airborne radios, survey cameras, and a host of lesser technologies had all been developed and produced during the war. The war had brought an awareness of the potential of military aviation, and because of the huge numbers of people involved in flying, in support of flying, or in the aviation industry during the conflict, this awareness was widespread throughout the fighting nations. The war had seen the birth of effective airpower.

Interwar Years

During the First World War, the air forces of all the major powers had grown to enormous fleets of machines. Britain, for example, began the war with 110 aircraft. During the war it produced 55,093 machines, and by the 11 November 1918 Armistice over 20,000 were in the inventory, including trainers. After the war, however, the great air fleets of the belligerents were dismantled almost to the point of abolition. As one example, the wartime U.S. Army Air Service grew to about 200,000 men, but by July 1920 only 10,000 remained.

In terms of organization, the air arms of the army and navy in the United States remained apart during and after the war, and bitter bureaucratic argument marked the efforts of Maj. Gen. William L. ("Billy") Mitchell and others in the interwar years to create an independent air force and to gain recognition of Mitchell's claim that the airplane was "the arbiter of our nation's destiny." The two services thus went their own ways, but they did so with some success. In the early 1920s, the U.S. Navy converted a collier into its first aircraft carrier, and two battle cruiser hulls were modified to produce the carriers USS *Saratoga* and USS *Lexington* in 1928. The new carrier USS *Ranger* was launched in 1934, followed by the USS *Enterprise* and the USS *Yorktown* in 1936.

In the case of the U.S. Army Air Corps, the role of coastal defense was stressed. Meanwhile the Air Corps Tactical School at Maxwell Field, Alabama, was exerting a formative influence on the development of airpower thinking, including the importance of the offensive role. On the technical side, aircraft such as the Boeing 299 and the XB-15 of 1935, which contributed to the design of the B-17 and the B-29, were emerging from the advancing technologies of aeronautics.

In Britain, modest resources were spread over the various roles of the Royal Air Force, including that of policing overseas possessions, such as Iraq and the northwest frontier of India, where relatively inexpensive air elements substituted for costly field forces.

Interwar Doctrine

In terms of doctrine during the interwar years, Douhet's theories of 1921 offered a sweeping vision of how the decisive impact of strategic airpower could replace the attrition of the First World War. His assumptions about the destructive power of the heavy bomber, its ability to prevail in spite of modern air defenses and the likely effect of bombing on industrialized societies were based on slender evidence, but he offered a very persuasive argument for independent air forces. At the same time, most of the same major powers to whom strategic airpower might have been expected to appeal, had a more immediate preoccupation with security on their frontiers. This concern emphasized the priority of tactical air and of short-range aviation, rather than the expenditure of scarce resources on the long-range heavy bomber. The paradoxical consequences of all this was the emergence of independent air forces in Italy (1923), Sweden (1926), and France and Germany (both in 1933), but very little progress toward a strategic bomber force in any nation.

Spanish Civil War

The emphasis on tactical air seemed to be endorsed by the events of the Spanish Civil War of 1936–39. Certainly the experience of the German Condor Legion in that war had a formative influence on the German concept of war fought by a combination of infantry and armor, with airpower acting in direct support and in the interdiction role. Largely because no accurate bombsight was available, bombing from medium levels was found by the Luftwaffe to be less effective than dive bombing, and the use of Panzer divisions, first formed in 1936, together with dive-bombing Stukas was thus to become familiar in the opening stages of the German campaigns in the Second World War.

Preparations for War

Meanwhile, in Britain different conclusions were being drawn, this time from the experience of German bombing attacks during the First World War. In analyzing the air threat that Germany was expected to pose to Britain, the Air Ministry fell back on the evidence of the Second German air offensive against Britain in 1917. This purported to show that each ton of high explosive would cause 50 casualties. Later revised upward, then extrapolated to the size of the Luftwaffe, this estimate was used to project the casualties that would be produced by the knock-out blow the Germans were expected to deliver at the very start of the war. The official forecast of air casualties for the first day of the war became 1,700 killed and 3,300 injured, with 850 killed and 1,650 injured in each subsequent 24-hour period.

In fact, air-raid casualties in Britain during the whole first year of the war were only 257 killed and 441 hospitalized. But the widely inaccurate forecast led to two developments. One was a massive investment in passive defense measures such as air-raid shelters, fire-fighting equipment, and so on that were to prove invaluable during the later and prolonged German air attacks. The other was a sharp and, as it turned out, decisive acceleration in the air defense program of the Royal Air Force leading to a state of high preparedness by the time of the Battle of Britain.

The Second World War: Early Campaigns

The disparity between expectations and reality was one of the most striking features of the early days of World War II. In fact, the first stages of the war were dominated by tactical, rather than strategic airpower. This was most strikingly the case with German air efforts. Although before the war many Luftwaffe leaders had seen strategic bombardment as the principal mission of the air arm, German rearmament had by 1939 been able to produce only twin-engined bombers. In any case, at the strategic level the German intention was not merely to wage blitzkrieg campaigns, but to wage a blitzkrieg war, in other words, a war that would be swift in execution and short in duration. Strategic bombing might not be necessary.

This certainly proved to be the case in Poland, Norway, France, and the Low Countries. In Poland during the single month of September 1939, both the army and the air force of that country were destroyed. In Norway, the Luftwaffe made a decisive contribution to successful operations by the German army and navy. Against France and the Low Countries, the German offensive began with priority given to air superiority, and although the Allied air forces fought well, those on the Continent were virtually eliminated in the first few days. Thereafter, German aircraft were able to contribute to the assault on the Allied ground forces, which were defeated within a very short time. Notably, however, the evacuation from Dunkirk would not have been possible without air cover provided by the RAF fighter command from bases in Britain.

Battle of Britain

Despite considerable losses during the campaign in France, by July the Luftwaffe was able to launch a major air offensive against the British Isles as the precursor to a full invasion. The initial air objective was defeat of the RAF and its supporting echelons, and the destruction of the British aircraft industry. The limited size of the German fighter escort force, and the restricted range of the bomber and fighter aircraft, however, confined almost all the attacks to the south of Britain, thus providing immunity to the considerable aircraft industry located in the north, and affording sanctuary areas for the training and recuperation of the defending fighter forces.

During August 1940 the air battles of the Battle of Britain developed into costly confrontations as the Luftwaffe pressed home its campaign. For example, between "Eagle Day," 13 August, the day originally planned for the invasion, and 19 August, the Germans lost 284 aircraft, approximately 10 percent of their available force in the west. But just when a collapse of the defenses was within reach, the Luftwaffe switched its efforts to London in a massive daylight attack on 9 September against the docks. The results were highly destructive, and huge fires raged out of control. The damage was then compounded by day and night attacks over the following week. Another massive and destructive daylight attack was made on 15 September, but this raid proved to be the climax of the campaign, and the Luftwaffe scaled down its later efforts. The offensive had been defeated by a skillful defense, greatly assisted by radar and ground control, against German aircraft that were well matched by the defending fighters. But it is doubtful if the defeat would have occurred had the Luftwaffe single-mindedly pursued its attacks against the Royal Air Force's fighter command.

The serious losses suffered by the Luftwaffe in the daylight raids of this period had three consequences. The German invasion plan was cancelled; the Luftwaffe switched to night bombing raids; and the RAF was afforded a respite in which to rebuild some of its badly depleted strength.

Meanwhile, the German High Command turned its attention to the east. This left the British (and later the Americans and their allies) free to build up massive airpower resources in the United Kingdom, although German bombing of the United Kingdom continued sporadically throughout the rest of the war, reinforced by V-1 pilotless aircraft attacks and bombardment by V-2 ballistic missiles in 1944.

In the East

In the campaign against Russia, the Luftwaffe again concentrated its initial efforts against the opposing air force, this time in a devastating blow starting in the early hours of the day of the invasion, 22 June 1941. No fewer than 3,275 German aircraft—1,945 of them frontline combat aircraft—had been deployed for the campaign, and the initial air assault was made on 31 Soviet airfields. By the next day 1,811 Soviet aircraft had been destroyed, 1,489 of them on the ground, with a loss of only 35 Luftwaffe aircraft. By the end of June, 4,614 Soviet aircraft had been destroyed, with a loss of only 330 German aircraft. This was an overwhelming air victory, and one that gave German forces the virtual total air superiority. In the months that followed, the Luftwaffe was able not only to give valuable direct support to land operations, but also to operate almost unhindered over the Soviet rear areas.

As the war progressed, and particularly as the Allied air offensive over Germany from late 1943 onwards drew in more and more of the resources of the Luftwaffe, the Russian air force gradually recovered until it was able in its turn to wrest air superiority from the Luftwaffe in the east.

The Luftwaffe had no answer to this steady and massive buildup. Its aircraft production program was inadequate, and the aircrew training program could not replace the losses of valuable men. But the main failure was a long-term one; the early and easy Luftwaffe victories had caused a misappreciation of the attrition rates likely to be experienced in the prolonged war that became inevitable once the German offensive failed at the gates of Moscow. The result was that by the time the Red army launched its greatest offensive against the German Army Group Center on 22 June 1944, the Luftwaffe was outnumbered in the East by about 6 to 1.

Strategic Bombing Offensives: Europe

The early RAF daylight raids on the Continent proved to be expensive failures, and most of the available effort was switched to night bombing. But this, too, was largely ineffective, as well as wildly inaccurate, so in November 1941, bombing by the Royal Air Force was virtually suspended altogether to allow for the re-equipment and expansion of the Bomber Command. It was not until mid-February 1942 that the long strategic bombing campaign could begin in earnest. The first major raid was made by 1,000 aircraft on Cologne on 30 May 1942, and heavy raids against Essen and Bremen followed. On 17 August of the same year, the U.S. Army Air Forces (USAAF) flew their first strategic bombing mission, and from then on a pattern of complementary daylight raids by the USAAF and night attacks by the RAF developed.

The U.S. Army's Eighth Air Force of the USAAF, based in Britain, applied its efforts to specific targets such as oil refineries, shipyards, factories, and other objectives that directly supported the German war effort. Large formations of B-17s and B-24s, escorted from July 1943 onwards by early models of long-range fighters, battled their way to the targets and back, sometimes with heavy losses. One of the worst setbacks was the raid on Schweinfurt in October 1943, a target beyond the range of escorting P-47s. Of 291 bombers engaged in the raid, 28 were lost en route to Schweinfurt, and 32 on the return flight. Only 92 suffered no damage at all.

Partly because of the technical difficulties of accurate night bombing, and partly because of a conviction that the will and ability of the enemy to continue the war could be broken by area bombing, the Royal Air Force generally attacked large area targets. Pathfinder techniques were developed by specialist squadrons that made possible concentrated and devastating attacks on major German cities. The bombers flew under the cover of night, relying on the modest protection afforded by on-board machineguns, and on the concentration of the bomber force in time and space to overwhelm the German night-fighter defenses. On many raids the loss rate to the bombers was very low, while on others it was intolerably high. The worst RAF losses were sustained during an unsuccessful raid on Nuremberg on 30–31 March 1944 when 95 out of 795 aircraft were lost, a loss rate of 11.9 percent.

The results of this long campaign of strategic bombing by day and by night were manifold. First, although it did not prevent an overall increase in German arms production, it did set a ceiling on that production at a time when the Germans were desperately short of weapons and equipment on the eastern front. Second, German defensive efforts against the air campaign and the need to repair the vast damage caused, absorbed a huge proportion of the total German war potential. Massive resources in manpower, materiel, guns, and aircraft were all drawn into the battle. German fighter losses during these raids were particularly serious, and led to virtual Allied air superiority over Germany from March 1944. In effect, and as Albert Speer admitted, a second front had been opened above Germany long before the Allied invasion of Normandy, and this led to a diversion and attrition of Luftwaffe forces that might otherwise have been available to the German High Command, for example, over the Normandy beachhead. Third, the inability of the Luftwaffe to defeat the attacks led to a loss of confidence in the German air force, and encouraged Hitler to devote more of the available limited air resources to tactical support in the East.

Japan

Strategic bombing against Japan during the war in the Pacific took a different form. After initial successes in the early months of the war, the fortunes of the Japanese were swiftly reversed. From February 1943, the Japanese were on the defensive, and by the time Saipan and other island bases in the Pacific were recaptured or seized from the Japanese, some 500 B-29 bombers were available for the strategic bombardment of the Japanese home islands. The main air offensive against the Japanese home islands was launched in November 1944, at a stage of the war when Japanese industry was already in decline and the economy hard pressed, due to shortages in raw materials caused by the destruction of Japanese shipping.

Faced with operational conditions that raised questions about the efficacy of precision bombing relative to area attacks, a policy of area targets that would lead to victory through blockade and bombing alone was decided upon. Attacks using firebombing techniques against the densely built and highly vulnerable Japanese cities were begun in March 1945. Although Japanese industry was very concentrated geographically, and the ground-based defenses could thus be densely deployed, the attacking USAAF XXI Bomber Command suffered only modest losses in these raids. For the Japanese, however, the result was the virtual destruction of 58 cities between May and August 1945. This so undermined morale and the effective functioning of civil and military machinery that surrender became inevitable.

The surrender was hastened by the use of atomic bombs on Hiroshima and Nagasaki in August 1945. These two attacks were a fulfillment of the kind of prophecy that Douhet had made two decades before, yet were on a scale that even he had not envisaged.

The strategic air bombardment of Japan was more effective than that against Germany for several reasons. First, the lessons learned in Europe were incorporated into the plans for the offensive against Japan. Second, the Japanese air defenses were no match for the American air effort. Third, the Japanese economy was already in decline as the result of the American sea blockade. And last, the construction of Japanese cities, which made extensive use of flammable materials, made them far more vulnerable to air attack than those of Europe. Together these factors produced an air campaign of overwhelming success.

Highpoint of Tactical Air

As Germany was gradually forced onto the defensive, Allied tactical airpower was increasingly brought to bear in North Africa, Italy, and finally in western Europe. It took two main forms. One was the direct support of land forces; and starting in North Africa, techniques of close control of tactical air in the battle area were perfected. Those techniques were then used with great effect in northwest Europe by the new Allied tactical air forces. On D-Day no fewer than 12,837 aircraft including 5,400 fighters were engaged, many of the latter in the close support of armies.

The second form of air support for land operations was that of interdiction. This entailed the destruction in rear areas of enemy resources such as reinforcements before they could reach the battle area and severing and disrupting the routes along which those resources were to travel. Again, the techniques were perfected in the Mediterranean during the campaign in Italy, and applied with devastating effect in preparation for the Allied invasion of Normandy, as well as in operations such as that at the Falaise Gap in 1944 during that same campaign. Interdiction was a highly effective application of airpower; its successes in these instances were enhanced by the massive air superiority that had meanwhile been achieved by the Allied air forces.

At Sea

At sea, airpower played a key role throughout the Second World War. In the Atlantic and the Mediterranean, both land-based and carrier-borne aircraft helped sustain the vital lines of communication by defeating the German submarine threat. Nearly 60 percent of all U-boats lost in the war were sunk by aircraft. Airpower was also significantly engaged in attacks on German and Italian main fleet units, notably at Taranto in November 1940 and in the sinking of the German battleship *Tirpitz* in 1944.

In the Pacific, it was airpower that opened Japan's war against the United States with the surprise attack on Pearl Harbor by Japanese carrier-borne aircraft on 7 December 1941. In an attack lasting less than two hours, 167 Japanese torpedo and dive bombers sank four U.S. battleships, damaged another four, and destroyed or damaged many smaller vessels and shore facilities. At the same time, 105 other bombers together with 78 fighters destroyed or put out of action 310 of the 400 U.S. Army, Navy, and Marine aircraft, mostly on the ground, on Oahu Island. Meanwhile, other Japanese formations attacked U.S. bases in the Philippines and British forces in Malaya. The Japanese lost only 29 aircraft at Pearl Harbor, but in one critical aspect the raid failed; both of the U.S. aircraft carriers based at Pearl Harbor were at sea, and thus survived to fight in later, decisive battles.

During the next twelve months, the Japanese advance in the Far East was gradually halted, and in the Pacific a series of maritime engagements (including carrier battles at the Coral Sea, Midway, and the Eastern Solomons) took place. During these and other engagements, all fifteen of the Japanese aircraft carriers that had joined the fleet after 1941 were sunk or put out of action, while of the 27 carriers added to the U.S. fleet, only one was lost. This huge imbalance was decisive in a campaign that was essentially maritime in all its characteristics.

In the entire Far East campaign, because of the vast distances involved, air supply was a crucial feature of Allied operations. Fleets of transport aircraft increasingly supported land and maritime operations, whether in the India-China air link, in Burma, or across the vast reaches of the Pacific Ocean.

World War II in Retrospect

By the end of the Second World War, airpower was widely acknowledged as the dominant arm in warfare. In quantity and quality, the development of the air weapon over a period of six years had been phenomenal. Over 300 different types of aircraft saw service during the war, and the principal belligerents produced some three-quarters of a million airframes. The United States alone produced 272,000, and supplied over 45,000 to allies.

In terms of quality, the conflict saw the development not only of the decisive airborne weapon, the atomic bomb, but also of electronic warfare, particularly radar, but including many other devices. It also saw the emergence of the first effective guided weapons in the form of remotely controlled bombs; and finally it greatly accelerated developments in aircraft engines, including jet engines, leading to entirely new levels of aerodynamic performance. If the First World War had seen the birth of airpower, then the Second World War had seen it grow to full maturity.

Postwar Air Power: The Strategic Role

By the end of the Second World War, the United States was overwhelmingly the leading proponent of airpower, and within the United States, military aviation had become the largest industry. Meanwhile, and well before the end of the conflict, the leaders of the U.S. Army Air Forces were planning a continuation of this national emphasis on the air arm. They had two objectives: (1) to form an independent U.S. Air Force to give airpower both the voice and the share of national resources that they believed it deserved, and (2) to equip that air force with a minimum of 70 active combat groups.

Within that figure of 70 groups, the emphasis was to be on strategic bombardment. But continuing demobilization, budgetary cuts, and the many problems inherent in separating the new U.S. Air Force (USAF) from the U.S. Army Air Forces meant that the new service was hard-pressed to maintain any strategic force at all after its formation in 1947. Some impetus to the emergence of a separate air force was given by growing Soviet hostility in 1946, and in particular by the U.S.-British Berlin Airlift from June 1948 to September 1949, during a blockade of the city which also served to demonstrate the unique qualities of a logistic air bridge.

Although the Strategic Air Command (SAC) and the strategic mission were given first priority by the USAF in 1948, it was not until the outbreak of the Korean War in June 1950 that the resources to turn intentions into capabilities began to be available. Progress in rebuilding U.S. airpower was then rapid. For example, at the end of 1949, SAC had fourteen bomb groups with 610 strategic bombers, two fighter groups, and six air-to-air refueling squadrons. By 1953, this force had expanded to 37 bomb groups with more than 1,000 aircraft (mainly B-36s and B-47s), as well as six fighter wings and 28 air-to-air refueling squadrons. Between 1951 and 1963, almost 3,000 strategic bombers entered service with the USAF.

This was a high point in postwar U.S. airpower, but two events were to change the strategic situation again toward the end of the Korean conflict. First, Dwight D. Eisenhower became president with a mandate not only to end that war, but to reduce U.S. defense spending. And second, the U.S. exploded the first thermonuclear device in October 1952, followed by the Soviet Union ten months later. The qualitative change that the thermonuclear bomb represented is sometimes overlooked; yet it meant a weapon that was over 500 times more powerful than the atomic bombs that had destroyed Hiroshima and Nagasaki. It also soon became clear that the new weapons could be made smaller in size and in weight than had at first been supposed.

This fact led to profound changes in USAF procurement policies. At the end of the Second World War, air force planners had believed that the manned bomber would remain the principal strategic weapon for many years, and that it would eventually be replaced by cruise missiles. But the development of the lightweight thermonuclear weapon now led the USAF in March 1954 to accelerate the modest Atlas Intercontinental Ballistic Missile (ICBM) program and later to add Titan, Minuteman, and Thor to the USAF missile procurement list. By 1957 it had become clear that Atlas would overtake the most promising cruise missile that had been under development, the Navajo, and the belief that there would be a steady progression from manned aircraft through cruise missiles to ICBMs was abandoned. Progress toward ICBMs became very rapid as technology solved many of the problems that had seemed to argue against ballistic missiles, and by 1963 ICBMs had become the principal U.S. strategic weapon.

This marked the end of an era. Total dependence on conventional aircraft for strategic bombardment was now replaced by a combination of: (1) ICBMs with instantaneous reaction, short flight time, high accuracy, and ability to penetrate all defenses; and (2) an aging, but operationally flexible, force of B-52s supported by tankers.

In the only other Western nuclear power at that time, the United Kingdom, the development of atomic weapons owed much to the wartime cooperation with the United States, and the Royal Air Force was able to deploy a sizable force of nuclear-armed medium bombers from the early 1950s until 1969, when Polaris submarines took over the deterrent role. In the United Kingdom the air-atomic strategy had lasted a little longer than it did in the United States.

Korean Conflict

The invasion of South Korea by the forces of North Korea on 25 June 1950 was thought to be only the first move in a wider Soviet plan of communist expansion. The attack therefore stimulated a rapid and comprehensive Western rearmament program including expanded air forces, but the campaign itself was limited both geographically and in terms of the forces engaged.

From the start, the United Nations (UN) air forces (composed overwhelmingly of U.S. Air Force and U.S. Navy and Marine Corps aviation), held air superiority over all but the northern extremities of the Korean peninsula. The early stages of the campaign were marked by an emphasis on close air support as UN land forces were driven back to the Pusan perimeter. One interesting circumstance was that Second World War piston-engined P-51 Mustangs (redesignated F-51 in 1947) were found to be more effective than the available F-80 Shooting Stars because the jets could not be forward-based from Japan onto the poor airfields of South Korea.

As UN reinforcements arrived in preparation for their counteroffensive, the application of airpower was widened to include attacks by B-29 bombers, not without loss, against strategic targets in North Korea, and growing air efforts against the communists' lines of communications. These and later bombing attacks were indecisive because the real sources of enemy military power lay not in North Korea, but in China and in the Soviet Union. In some respects the attacks were counterproductive, since the Communists were able to make propaganda play out of what they claimed were indiscriminate attacks.

The early interdiction attacks were only the first in a series of eight interdiction campaigns during the three-year war. None was decisive, and all disappointed the air planners. Whether aimed at road, rail, or both networks, these interdiction efforts all failed for the same reasons. First, the logistic needs of Asian-style armies was consistently overestimated. For example, a North Korean division could fight on as little as 50 tons of resupply per day; Western logisticians were more accustomed to thinking in terms of 650 tons per division per day. Second, the staff skills, the ingenuity, and the field engineering capabilities of coolie-styled armies had been seriously underestimated. Cuts in roads and railways were quickly repaired, and damaged bridges were rebuilt or replaced with remarkable speed. Third, the Communists learned to disperse their supply columns by day and to move forward under cover of darkness. Fourth, and most telling, the Communists learned to adjust the intensity of their military effort to match the logistic effort that was escaping the interdiction.

In air combat over the extreme north of Korea, the UN forces were more successful. Because Soviet-supplied MiG-15 jet fighters based in Manchuria were unable to dominate airspace over North Korea, the airfields sited there could be kept out of action by UN air bombardment. Thus, the Communists were never able to extend their air effort over the ground battles farther south.

In spite of the application of airpower, the war turned into a stalemate. As a result, it led to considerable rethinking about the future role of airpower. Before Korea, airpower, with its ability to strike the sources of enemy war-making potential, had come to be the apotheosis of total war. In Korea, not only was it important to prevent the conflict from becoming a total, global war, but the sources of enemy power were in what amounted to sanctuaries. Korea was the first demonstration of limited conventional war in the nuclear era, but it was not to be the last.

Suez Campaign, 1956

Two years after Korea, airpower was again engaged in conventional operations, this time in a struggle for control of the Suez Canal. This brief Anglo-French campaign against the Egyptians was conducted on a considerable scale. Five division equivalents were assigned to the Anglo-French commander, as well as a combined fleet that included five aircraft carriers. Available combat air strength was 125 bombers, 118 fighter/ground attack and reconnaissance aircraft, 159 carrier-borne aircraft, and 24 helicopters; a total of 426 machines, not including the Israeli Defense Force/Air Force or three squadrons of French aircraft based in Israel. The Egyptian air force was composed of about 200 combat aircraft, including 80 MiG-15s.

The air plan for the brief campaign comprised three stages: the destruction of the Egyptian air force; interdiction against military and other installations in what was called an aero-psychological campaign; and direct air support for the amphibious and parachute landings. Although the offensive counter-air effort destroyed about 60 Egyptian aircraft on the ground, the Egyptians succeeded in dispersing the rest of their air force. The limited success of the British and French air forces against airfields was due largely to the fact that the modest force available could not cover all targets adequately. Additionally, the attacks that were made were often too inaccurate to put the airfields out of action. The remaining Egyptian air force was too weak to offer serious opposition to the Anglo-French offensive, however.

With only weak opposition from the Egyptians, the direct air support portion of the campaign was more successful. However, the results of the aero-psychological attacks totally failed to meet expectations. In the first phase of these particular attacks, raids were made against a Cairo radio station, two barracks, and a large railway marshaling yard. The attacks produced an international outcry that caused further attacks to be cancelled. The Suez campaign itself was brought to an end by political pressure on the governments of France and Britain after only six days.

Thus at Suez as in Korea, the exercise of airpower was shown to be no longer a question of the uninhibited selection and destruction of targets. Airpower, which in 1943–45 had been able successfully to extend warfare beyond the boundaries of conventional land and sea operations, now found itself restricted by other considerations, including those of international opinion.

Vietnam

A decade later, the United States became involved in another war, this time in Vietnam. Air activity during the Vietnam war from 1965–73 is best viewed in components: strategic and tactical air transport; support to ground forces; air superiority; interdiction; and the use of airpower against strategic targets.

Strategic air transport made an indispensable contribution to logistics, while within Vietnam itself a network of airstrips able to take twin-engine transports had been built across the country as early as 1965 in one of the first U.S. contributions to the defense of South Vietnam. As the conflict developed, some highly adaptive uses of basic transport aircraft were seen, notably when they were employed as flare-ships, as gunships, and in operations to defoliate the forests that covered Vietcong logistic routes.

Considerable air effort was applied in direct support of U.S. and South Vietnamese ground forces throughout the war. On a typical day, between 750 and 800 sorties were flown, either in preplanned missions or in unscheduled support missions. These latter could normally be executed within 35 or 40 minutes by forces in a ground-alert posture. In crisis operations such as that during the Tet offensive of 1968, surge operations could be flown that raised the direct air support effort by about 50 percent.

Against an elusive enemy able to concentrate and scatter with ease, this ability to bring mobile and responsive firepower to bear, particularly since artillery was often not available, was a vital element in the U.S. campaign. A further important ground support contribution was made by B-52 bombers used in the tactical role. Their ability to carry the equivalent warload of about five fighter-bombers each meant that they could lay down massive carpets of firepower on areas known to harbor Vietcong concentrations.

A different kind of support was provided in Vietnam by a very considerable force of U.S. helicopters. But all efforts to employ helicopters and tactical transport aircraft in major air-landing operations demanded massive logistic support, and served to confirm again the essential prerequisite of air superiority, the need to suppress all ground antiaircraft fire. In smaller operations, however, and particularly in a locally benign air environment, the use of helicopters became an essential and ubiquitous feature of U.S. activity throughout the war.

Air superiority was essential to virtually all other operations in the U.S. air effort, and the Vietcong and North Vietnamese devoted considerable efforts to challenge U.S. domination of the airspace. At the lowest level of effectiveness this included Vietcong small-arms fire in South Vietnam. More telling were the scattered antiaircraft guns used before 1967 along the Ho Chi Minh trail, which was actually a comprehensive system of well-developed roads and tracks. After 1967 the deployment of surface-to-air missiles (SAMs) and more effective AA weapons along the trail made it necessary to cover attacking aircraft with defense suppression missions. North Vietnam deployed highly effective ground-based antiaircraft systems. Those around Hanoi were particularly well sited and efficiently served. Most of the communist surface-to-air missiles (SAMs) in the North were deployed in a 65-kilometer (40-mi.) circle around the capital in some 20–30 battalions that operated a total of perhaps 2,000 launchers.

The effectiveness of the Soviet-supplied SAMs required a considerable U.S. effort to counter them, and by the end of the war the ratio of support to attack aircraft in U.S. attack packages had risen to 4 to 1. These packages were, however, very successful. In 1967 there had been one aircraft lost to each 55 missiles fired; this later fell to one per 100, and by 1972 had fallen to one per 150. Later, during the Linebacker II offensive of December 1972, the Hanoi SAM system was overwhelmed by the density and persistence of U.S. air attacks.

Comprehensive U.S. use of electronic countermeasures (ECM) from 1967 onward made it possible to penetrate North Vietnamese airspace at medium altitude with some assurance of invulnerability from SAMs, and yet be above the range of most of the antiaircraft gunfire. As to enemy fighter defenses, by 1967 there were some 100 MiG-17s and MiG-21s deployed on airfields in North Vietnam. The air-to-air engagements provoked by these fighters were never on the scale of those seen over the Yalu River fifteen years before, and although the communist fighter threat could not be ignored, the MiGs were never a serious inhibition to U.S. air activities.

Efforts to cut the supply routes from the Chinese border and from the port of Haiphong absorbed a great deal of the U.S. air effort in Vietnam. Many of the difficulties encountered during the interdiction campaign in Korea now reappeared. The U.S. air effort still had to deal with a coolie-maintained logistic system and with the proven ingenuity and skill of communist engineers. This made very difficult all attempts to interdict the diffuse and highly resilient network of roads and paths that formed the Ho Chi Minh Trail. Farther north, where limited road and rail communications were being used by the Communists to move their supplies to the combat areas, the American effort was hampered by serious political restrictions that were applied to the air campaign in deference to world opinion and to keep from provoking North Vietnam's Chinese and Soviet allies. In neither the interdiction campaign of 1965 to 1968 nor in that of 1972 could Hanoi or the key harbor of Haiphong be attacked. Furthermore, a 200-kilometer (125-mi.) buffer zone along the Chinese border prevented attacks in that region, while key bridges along the route such as the 1,686-meter (5,532 ft.) long Paul Doumer bridge were off limits until August 1967. The predictable result of these restrictions was that the North Vietnamese instituted a shuttle system between the numerous sanctuary areas, storing military supplies in them by day and moving them forward at night. Thus was interdiction prevented from exercising its full potential, and, as in Korea, the Communists learned to adjust the intensity of their activities to match the supplies evading the U.S. interdiction efforts.

Finally in the Vietnam War, strategic air bombardment was employed by the U.S. air forces. In retrospect, however, one of the principal flaws in the U.S. conduct of the war was the use of air bombardment to send political signals to the North and its supporters, instead of applying the massive military-economic pressure of which U.S. airpower was undoubtedly capable.

Only in the last stages of the war was airpower able to have a decisive impact. There had been various bombing pauses before early 1972 in the hope of persuading the North to come to terms, and pressure was increased again by the mining of Haiphong harbor and by reducing the sanctuary zones around that city and around the capital, Hanoi. This appeared to produce a softening of the communist line at the Paris peace talks and from October all bombing above the 20th parallel was halted. But when it became clear that the Communists were once again procrastinating, the decision was at last made to attack targets in Hanoi and Haiphong with maximum effort.

This was the Linebacker II campaign. It lasted for

eleven days beginning on 18 December 1972, and consisted of heavy, coordinated, and escorted B-52 raids. After three nights of bombardment, the efforts by the SAM defenses decreased, and on 26 December a climax was reached when 120 attack and 100 escort aircraft in seven waves struck their targets. All told, 389 sorties were flown by B-52s in these raids, and sixteen of the aircraft were lost. A total of 13,395 tons of bombs was dropped during Linebacker II, and a wide range of targets was hit including railway yards, airfields, petroleum installations, munition depots, docks, and power plants.

It was an expensive war for the United States, and for the U.S. air forces involved. In flying 1,248,105 fixed-wing combat sorties, 1,324 aircraft had been lost to enemy action; and for well over 37 million helicopter sorties, 2,112 machines had been lost in combat and 2,475 to other causes. One reason for the length of the war and for these and other losses was that the slow escalation of the air effort during the whole conflict not only gave the enemy the opportunity to mobilize his population militarily and psychologically against future attacks, but also allowed him to invoke worldwide protest at the same time. The war had seen a serious misuse of airpower, and only when airpower was properly applied during Linebacker II were the desired results forthcoming. The North Vietnamese signed the peace agreement on 15 January 1972, within weeks of Linebacker II.

Falklands/Malvinas Conflict

In another brief campaign in the Falkland Islands/Islas Malvinas in 1982, airpower—both potential and applied—had a considerable impact on both protagonists, although the number of aircraft engaged was small.

On the Argentinian side, the most powerful weapons were five Exocet-armed Super Etendard aircraft, of which only four were serviceable. Yet they not only sank two major British warships, they also obliged the Royal Naval carrier group to operate at the extreme range of its Harrier aircraft. This determined much of the character of the campaign. The British conducted very long-range attacks by bombers that had to be refueled in flight so they could operate from their base on Ascension Island some 6,400 kilometers (4,000 mi.) to the north. These attacks compelled the Argentinians to deploy their most important squadrons of fighters away to the north in defense of Buenos Aires, thus almost certainly tipping the overall balance of power in favor of the British.

Middle East Wars

Three short but intense conflicts took place in the Middle East in 1967, 1973, and 1982, each with its own characteristics from the standpoint of airpower.

Six-Day War

In the first of these wars, the Israeli Defense Force/Air Force (IDF/AF) on 5 June 1967 launched a pre-emptive attack against nineteen Egyptian airfields in the Sinai and in Egypt proper. These carefully planned attacks achieved complete tactical surprise, and within a few hours, some 75 percent of Egyptian combat air strength had been destroyed. Equally destructive attacks followed on the small Jordanian air force and on that of the Syrians. By the end of the day more than 500 Arab aircraft had been destroyed with a loss of only 20 Israeli machines.

This overwhelming blow enabled the Israeli army to inflict defeats on the Arab land forces, while the Israeli air force followed up its initial success by inflicting heavy losses on large enemy ground forces, particularly in the Mitla Pass in the Sinai Desert. One important and wider consequence of the Israeli destruction of so much enemy airpower on the ground was the construction by the Warsaw Pact of hardened aircraft shelters, starting in 1968, while the North Atlantic Treaty Organization (NATO) followed with a long overdue program in 1974.

War of Attrition

The 1967 defeat of the Arabs was followed in the succeeding years by a long Egyptian-inspired campaign of attrition, consisting of constant minor harassing attacks against Israeli positions. The Israeli response took the form of a progressive destruction of most of the Egyptian SA-2 missile batteries. The Egyptians gradually replaced these batteries so that by the end of 1969 a Soviet-supplied, comprehensive air defense system of missiles and guns was in place along Egypt's entire eastern frontier.

October 1973 War

With their air defenses now secure, the Egyptians planned a surprise assault across the Suez Canal. The Israelis meanwhile had calculated that since they had a superiority in tanks and in operational aircraft, it was extremely unlikely that the Egyptians would risk an attack. In fact the Egyptians had drawn quite different conclusions from the same assessment of comparative strengths. Instead of pitting armor against armor, they employed infantry-fired missiles against tanks and used surface-to-air missiles to dominate the airspace above their army formation when they attacked across the Suez Canal on 6 October 1973. Simultaneously the Syrians attacked the Golan Heights, and both in the north and in the south, the forward Israeli positions were overrun.

The Israeli ground forces were soon so hard pressed that there was no opportunity for the IDF/AF to achieve air superiority. In contrast to the 1967 war, no Arab airfield could be closed by air attack for more than a few hours, and only 22 Arab aircraft were claimed to have been destroyed on the ground. Instead, the IDF/AF, with its 340 or so combat aircraft, was obliged to devote virtually all its efforts to the direct or indirect support of the ground forces.

This meant flying in airspace dominated by SAMs, particularly the SA-6, and by ZSU-23 guns. The Israelis lost about 40 aircraft in the first 48 hours of the conflict. This represented 14 percent of the combat strength of the IDF/AF, and a loss rate of some 3 percent of combat sorties flown. Although the Egyptians contented themselves with a limited advance into the Sinai (and thus retained the dense nature of their ground-based antiaircraft defenses), on the Golan front the pressure became critical, and only the remorseless efforts of the IDF/AF prevented a Syrian breakthrough into the open plains of Israel. Overall, the intensity of the conflict led to a critical shortage of war materiel on both sides; on 9 October the United States, and on 10 October the Soviet Union, began flying in replacement stocks of arms. The resulting airlifts were a convincing demonstration of the ability of airpower to transfer massive military resources very rapidly over intercontinental distances.

On 15 October, the Israelis were able to launch a counterattack across the Suez Canal, which succeeded in overrunning four of the Egyptian SAM sites. This opened a gap in the air defenses which the IDF/AF was then able to exploit by giving air support to the Israeli ground forces. Ground forces thus contributed to the air superiority necessary to their own continuing operations.

A cease-fire came on 22 October after the Soviets had made preparations to fly in airborne forces and the United States had declared a state of alert. There was much to be learned from the war, particularly about intelligence failures. But as far as airpower was concerned, the Israeli ability to switch effort between the north and the south to meet crises on the Syrian and on the Egyptian front had been crucial. The mobility of air at the operational level was paramount. At the tactical level, the protection afforded to ground forces by a careful combination of SAMs and antiaircraft guns was highly effective, although the static nature of the complex deployment carried clear limitations; in highly mobile operations the density of cover would have been less lethal. In any case the lethality was diluted when the United States supplied early warning equipment to counter the new Soviet antiaircraft systems.

Technical surprise had again played an important part in the air facet of a war, this time in the deployment of the Soviet SA-6 and the ZSU-23 and their high effectiveness. This had been crucial when the Egyptians attacked across the canal. On the other hand, their reliance on this ground-based air defense system, together with the fact that most of their air strength was also used in forward areas, meant that Israeli mobilization and reinforcement efforts could proceed virtually unhindered behind the battle zone. The Egyptian offensive lacked the depth that effective airpower might have given it.

The third Middle East conflict took place in June 1982 over the Bekaa Valley in Syria. Employing careful intelligence, excellent training, and superb timing, the Israeli Defense Force/Air Force drew the Syrian air force into an air-to-air battle in which some 86 Syrian aircraft were destroyed and only one Israeli machine was lost. It was a remarkable illustration of the effectiveness of a carefully coordinated air campaign, taking advantage of all the enemy's known weaknesses in the air and in the deployment of SAMs, to achieve a devastating victory.

The Bekaa engagement was also a striking example of an emerging trend in the application of airpower—the rapid execution of independent and accurate air strikes that are carried out with or without a declaration of war. Recent years have seen three other operations of this kind. First was the Israeli air raid on the Iraqi nuclear plant at Tuwaitta near Baghdad in June 1981, carried out with devastating precision by fourteen attack aircraft flying a 2,260-kilometer (1,400 mi.) round-trip mission. Second was the Israeli raid on the Palestine Liberation Organization (PLO) headquarters in Tunis, probably carried out by only six or eight combat aircraft making a round-trip flight of almost 4,840 kilometers (3,000 mi.). Third was the U.S. attack on Libya in April 1986, when aircraft attacked carefully selected targets in Tripoli and Benghazi. For the U.S. Air Force F-111 aircraft, the raid involved a round-trip flight from the United Kingdom of some 8,870 kilometers (5,500 mi.).

1991 Gulf War

The unprecedented air campaign in the 1991 Persian Gulf War was perhaps the most dramatic use of airpower in history. Analysts will study and seek lessons from the following major departures from the past that occurred in the 1991 Gulf War:

- use of large numbers of stealth and other high-technology aircraft.
- extensive use of high-technology and precision-guided munitions including sea- and air-launched cruise missiles; and of satellites and airborne systems to provide: intelligence; attack warning; control of air defense, strategic and tactical navigation, target selection, and attack.
- development and execution of an integrated air campaign that centralized the targeting and scheduling of aircraft and helicopters of allied air force, army, and navy forces.
- use of army forces at the outset deep within enemy territory against enemy air defenses.
- execution of the campaign as planned with little interference from higher level authorities.
- virtual destruction and demoralization of a large, well-equipped enemy air force and a massive, seasoned, well-equipped army prior to ground combat.
- denial to Iraq of virtually all strategic and tactical intelligence because of the allied airpower threat.
- limitation of allied aircraft losses to far below expectations.
- the demonstration that airpower could achieve all the above if based upon reliable and sophisticated equip-

ment, highly qualified and trained personnel, excellent leadership, and allied cooperation.

Analysts will also study what airpower did not achieve: finding and destroying the leader of Iraq; being able to destroy all mobile Scud missiles; locating and attacking all sites where weapons of mass destruction were made or stored; and successfully enforcing the embargo of materials. Finally, analysts will try to fathom how future wars will be affected by live worldwide television coverage of aerial attacks and suffering in the opposition's homeland.

One thing is certain. The history and the future of airpower were forever altered in this short war.

MICHAEL ARMITAGE

SEE ALSO: Airpower; Airpower, Strategic; Airpower, Tactical; Arab-Israeli Wars; Bombardment, Strategic; Close Air Support; Douhet, Giulio; Electronic Warfare Technology Applications; Korean War; Radar; Vietnam and Indochina Wars; World War I; World War II.

Bibliography

Armitage, M. J., and A. R. Mason. 1985. *Air power in the nuclear age.* London: Macmillan.

Beaufre, A. 1969. *The Suez expedition.* London: Faber and Faber.

Boog, H. 1983. *Die Luftwaffe. Das Deutsche Reiche und zer Weltkrieg.* Freiburg: Militärgeschichtliches Forschungsamt.

Collier, B. 1957. *The defence of the United Kingdom.* London: Her Majesty's Stationery Office.

Craven, W. H., and J. L. Cate, eds. 1949. *The army air forces in World War II.* Chicago: Univ. of Chicago Press.

Douhet, G. 1942. *Command of the air.* Trans. D. Ferrari. New York: Coward McCann.

Emme, E. M., ed. 1959. *The impact of air power.* New York: Van Nostrand.

Ethel, J., and A. Price. 1983. *Air war South Atlantic.* London: Sidgwick and Jackson.

Futrell, R. F. 1984. *Ideas, concepts, and doctrine.* 2 vols. Salem, N.H.: Ayer.

Futrell, R. E. 1983. *The United States Air Force in Korea.* New York: Duell, Sloan, and Pearce.

Goldberg, A. 1957. *A history of the U.S. Air Force 1907–57.* New York: Van Nostrand.

Momyer, W. W. 1978. *Air power in three wars.* Salem, N.H.: Ayer.

Slessor, J. 1956. *The central blue.* London: Cassell.

Speer, A. 1970. *Inside the Third Reich: Memoirs.* Trans. R. Winston and C. Winston. New York: Macmillan.

Terraine, J. 1985. *The right of the line.* London: Hodder and Stoughton.

AIRPOWER, STRATEGIC

The airpower theorists of the 1930s were the first to develop the concept of strategic airpower. They envisioned large air forces built around bomber fleets that could carry warfare to the industrial heartland of the enemy. As the sophistication and expense of bomber aircraft increased, however, most nations had little choice but to procure tactical fighters. These states came to the erroneous belief that strategic airpower was beyond their grasp.

In reality, strategic airpower is tied only indirectly to the type of aircraft employed. Airpower is strategic when it is targeted against resources whose destruction results in desired political objectives. Therefore any nation that possesses a tactical air force has the inherent capability to employ it strategically.

Although strategic airpower's impact on warfare has been revolutionary, its development has been evolutionary and bears further examination to appreciate fully its unrealized potential.

Evolution of Strategic Airpower

By the time of Alexander the Great (356–323 B.C.) reliance on strategic military operations to achieve political goals had reached a level of sophistication on a par with that of the modern era. In antiquity man first witnessed the development of great land powers and wide-ranging seafaring peoples. In practice, nations developed one capability in preference to and at the expense of the other.

The operational limits imposed by the combined effects of ship design and logistics worked to promote the primacy of land armies. Indeed the commonly held—but in fact myopic—belief that a nation needs a conquering land army to win a war can be traced to this period. Generalized conclusions drawn from the inability of the Persian fleet to prevent the rise of Macedonia may have held true in the distant past, but they do not hold today.

As he began his drive eastward, Alexander faced a serious problem of securing his lines of communication because of the constant threat of being cut off by the Persian fleet. Had Alfred Thayer Mahan (nineteenth-century naval strategist) been there, he undoubtedly would have advocated development of a strategic plan for acquiring, training, and then employing a Hellene navy. Such a course certainly would have been in keeping with prevailing wisdom.

Whether based on his strategic genius or on an unchallenged mastery of land campaigns, Alexander developed an alternative strategy that obviated the need for building a navy. His strategy capitalized upon the absolute reliance of the Persian fleet upon its existing ports. In a brilliant littoral campaign Alexander pushed southward, capturing each port in turn. Deprived of sanctuary and vital land support, the fleet had no choice but to surrender. Assured at last of secure communications Alexander was able to drive eastward in an unprecedented and subsequently unparalleled series of successful campaigns. For centuries these campaigns have served as the standards for strategic application of land power. However, it is for an entirely separate reason that Alexander warrants mention in an essay on strategic airpower. It is because of his Sogdiana Campaign, wherein he achieved victory through a strategic deception while at the same time disproving two pervasive doctrinal myths, that he is relevant today.

Alexander's opponent, Oxyartes, had taken refuge on the Rock of Sogdiana. This natural fortress was well provisioned and thought to be impregnable. Alexander's first reaction was a political one, similar to that of the Byzantine general Belisarius or, more recently, U.S. general Westmoreland's Chieu Hoi program. Alexander offered clemency to the king and his people if they would ally themselves with him. From the safety of their fortress they cast insults in response to this offer. They told Alexander to find soldiers with wings to fight his battle, for no other force could prevail.

Again, he displayed the ingenuity that was perhaps his greatest gift. He waited for the cover of darkness, then offered incentives to soldiers who would attempt to climb the rock face. A small contingent of volunteers reached the summit and hid themselves among the rocks. The next morning Alexander again addressed the defenders. This time he called for their surrender because he had gained the strategic advantage—he had found the winged soldiers. He gestured toward the summit and, as previously arranged, his men stepped into view.

In the eyes of the defenders there was only one explanation: winged Macedonians had landed upon the summit and were now in position to attack from above. Overwhelmed by this perception, they immediately surrendered.

There were no winged soldiers and certainly there were no aircraft, but the essential elements that characterize airpower were present in the minds of the defenders. They believed they were subject to a military force unfettered by physical constraints. This perception resulted in the surrender of an otherwise impregnable fortress. Alexander achieved a strategic victory over an enemy who possessed a formidable army and the capability to employ it. Their army had not been defeated, but their will to resist had been destroyed. With it had gone their sense of invulnerability. Today airpower can similarly achieve strategic victory without engaging, much less destroying, the opposing land army. The chief difference is that technology, not deception, is the key determinant of airpower's worth. Today's strategic air force is effective across the entire spectrum of conflict when it places the enemy's most valued assets at risk.

The more traditional view of airpower begins much later, with the use of lighter-than-air balloons. Their introduction into the American Civil War was championed by visionaries of the time as being a great technological breakthrough. In reality, they were of no strategic importance because of their use in a tactical role. In most cases they simply served as higher trees for artillery spotters. Even in this role they were ill-used because of prevailing military bias. Officers schooled in the traditional methods of warfare were unwilling to accept the introduction of something so far beyond their experience. (The airplane was to suffer a similar fate 50 years later, just as remotely piloted vehicles are misunderstood today.) But the critical shortcoming that doomed the balloons' existence was technological.

To be useful, balloons had to be within visual range of the front. Lacking powered flight, they could either be loosed and allowed to drift with prevailing winds or be tethered to a vulnerable ground position. To see, they must be seen; thus they became essentially defenseless targets in full view of the enemy. There were also problems associated with the prototype equipment and with communicating data to the ground. With all these shortcomings it is understandable that they made no meaningful strategic contributions to either side.

World War I saw the first large-scale use of airplanes. Initially they served the same artillery-spotting role as the balloon. However, the nature of warfare encourages modification, change, and innovation as advantages gained are countered and negated. As with every previous addition to the battlefield, airpower expanded in usefulness as it underwent this rapid adaptation and change.

To challenge the presence of enemy observation aircraft, crudely fashioned "fighters" began to appear. These underwent rapid technological improvement and achieved a degree of sophistication. During this period the first specialized bombers ushered in the concept of strategic airpower. Strategic operations were planned and undertaken. Indeed, every type of mission currently ascribed to aircraft was successfully demonstrated or at least attempted during that war.

At that point in history, when the old was reluctantly giving way to the new, airpower captured popular imagination and reintroduced gallantry. People were fascinated by aerial combat, and a "knights of the air" syndrome developed. Attention focused on personal one-on-one combat. The fledgling strategic applications of airpower, plagued as they were by accuracy and ordnance problems, took second place. Only during the final two campaigns of the war were centralized air efforts mounted.

Following the war, visionaries began publishing works that called for revolutionary changes in warfare. Chief among these was Giulio Douhet, whose *Command of the Air* argued for the immediate formation of an independent and institutionally predominant air force. In his analysis, wars had always involved attrition of the enemy until a decisive action was possible. Rivers, mountain ranges, deserts, oceans, and forests had since the dawn of time dictated the battlefields and campaign strategies. Victory was totally elusive as long as an army or fleet stood between you and the enemy's heartland. This form of warfare favored the defense, but airpower with its unlimited axes of attack could concentrate on the offensive. Thus, Douhet identified the strategic value of airpower.

To him the guiding principle was simple: inflict the

greatest damage in the shortest possible time. As with land and sea warfare, wanton damage is not an end unto itself. Rather, it is the carefully directed damage or destruction of the vital elements of the enemy's forces, society, or resources that results in political concessions.

Traditionally, land armies could serve as moving buffers to prevent the enemy from reaching vital areas and at the same time counter with maneuver to gain advantage. Navies could perform similar functions on a global scale. Their advantage lay in the ability to project their power across vaster distances. With this greater mobility they had more control over the timing and location of engagements, but their advantage ended at the shoreline. Under such constraints, oceans provided the best defense against invasion. Douhet accurately predicted the revolutionary impact airpower would have on the world.

Airpower provided the capability to direct campaigns over and around fielded forces and natural defenses. The dictates of terrain that had made the defense of any particular country a known constant were irrelevant to airpower. For centuries Italy had the Alps as a natural ally while Poland had only its armies; now each was equally vulnerable to airpower. Similarly, the Channel and a strong navy had protected England's population from the ravages of war; neither could prevent an airborne attack.

Douhet was writing about a future world. He had witnessed the effects of aerial bombing during World War I and knew that air forces as they existed could not achieve more. His vision required extensive preparations and independent air forces. Nations would have to address three issues in order to develop strategically important air forces. The first concern was equipment. An independent air force must have acquisition priority over both the army and navy. Only investment in research and development could produce aircraft capable of executing his strategy. Procurement of these aircraft would have to be on a scale geometrically expanded beyond existing standards. The second factor was ordnance. To Douhet, strategic power was synonymous with destructive power. He envisioned mass attacks with explosives, incendiaries, and gas. These attacks would require tremendous quantities of weapons. The final and essential quality that his air force must possess during operations was command of the air.

This third factor must be addressed separately due to its enduring importance and the general misinterpretation of Douhet's belief that the bomber offensive would always get through. For Douhet, command of the air resulted from mass. Large bomber formations would be accompanied by large numbers of well-armed escorts. The role of these escorts would be to sweep away any fighters that might be encountered. The bomber formation would always get through because: (1) air force primacy would assure the proper aircraft quality and quantity to overcome the opposition; and (2) the large number of potential targets accessible from unlimited axes of attack would make it impossible to have enough defensive aircraft to cover all possibilities. His was a pre-radar world.

Douhet believed that all countries would invest in bomber-oriented air forces. In this attack-centered warfare the winner would be the country that could endure attacks while successfully mounting unbearable attacks against the opponent. His prediction was not borne out during World War II for two reasons: air forces never received primacy, and fighter escort technology and techniques had lagged behind bomber development.

Douhet's theories influenced the theories of airpower advocates around the world. In the United States a group of U.S. Army officers at the Air Corps Tactical School made a major contribution to strategic thought when they modified and expanded on Douhet and others during the 1930s. At that school the multiple theories and concepts of airpower coalesced into a mainstream bombardment viewpoint that became the basis of the U.S. position on strategic airpower.

The Air Estimate of the Situation for
Strategic Air Warfare
(Air Corps Tactical School)

1. Define clearly the purpose, the goal that you want to accomplish.
2. Consider the obstacles and opportunities in the broad situation.
3. List the actions (tasks) which, if successfully accomplished, will attain the purpose, in order of desired priority.
4. Consider the forces needed to accomplish each task.
5. Consider the capacity of your own forces and determine which of the tasks come within your capability.
6. Consider the risks and losses for each task.
7. Select the tasks which will accomplish most effectively your purpose without unacceptable risk and loss, and which come within your capability.
8. Prepare a plan to carry out the tasks.

The concept of strategic airpower had matured. This view broke it into three basic questions: What do you want to accomplish? What does it take? How will you do it? It forced clear definition of the purpose or desired outcome, unlike Douhet's rather generalized goal of winning. Further, it pointed out the need to define target sets and to estimate their ability to withstand air attack. Finally it called for developing a plan that embraced all known factors to accomplish the goal set in the beginning.

This process, developed in the 1930s, has value even today as a guide for planning strategic air operations. Operations should have clearly articulated goals, focus on target sets that put the enemy's survival at risk, and follow realistically developed plans.

The airpower advocates who developed this process became the Air Staff planning team who created AWPD-1 (Air War Plans Division 1). It was AWPD-1 that served as the guide for U.S. air operations in Europe during World War II. Conceptually, "strategic airpower" had gone from infancy to adolescence.

It was an awkward adolescence. Strategic airpower did not achieve its predicted goals because of three interactive reasons. First, no country fully subscribed to its primacy; second, the targeting process failed to properly assess the absolutely critical nature of petroleum; most important, there were technologically based and often operationally ignored discrepancies between task and capability.

All major participants in World War II used airpower extensively, but strategic air operations were valued primarily by the Allies. Japan's attack on Pearl Harbor lacked the depth of planning required to be considered strategic. Had the Japanese more clearly defined their desires and more fully assessed the level of military force required to achieve them, they would have expanded the attack beyond a single strike or abandoned it completely. Although airpower was crucial to the German successes early in the war, they, too, failed to exploit strategic airpower. Soviet doctrine and recent Israeli operations had their roots in the German blitzkrieg, but both expanded the role of airpower to strategic proportions by targeting their air forces against objectives aimed at ultimate victory rather than at direct, day-to-day support of the army.

The Allies undertook multiple strategic air operations, but generally gave priority to land and sea campaigns. In the European theater air campaigns were aborted, changed, and directed in response to a strategy focused on invasion. In the Pacific theater the strategic use of airpower became more pronounced, culminating in the use of the atomic bomb. At no point during the war did the equipping, manning, and employment of the air forces achieve a one-to-one correlation to what the prewar advocates had called for.

The most telling deleterious effect on strategic airpower resulted from consistent failure to reconcile technological capabilities with attempted operations. The goal was Axis surrender; the selection of the strategic target sets that would achieve this goal and their ability to withstand air attack was faulty. Bombing accuracy in Europe resulted in approximately 20 percent of the weapons hitting within 300 meters (1,000 ft.) of the target (Fig. 1). This had not been anticipated or properly incorporated into the air operations. Expectations generally exceeded results.

Tactically oriented historians, who focus on battles rather than on war, have suggested that this amounts to the failure of strategic airpower. The U.S. Strategic Bombing Survey, begun during the final months of the war, cites airpower as a decisive factor in the war's outcome. This polarity of opinion persists.

Figure 1. Würzburg, Germany, after heavy Allied bombing, 1945. (SOURCE: U.S. Library of Congress)

Strategic Airpower Today and Tomorrow

Current explanations of strategic airpower can take one of three directions, depending upon which characteristics are stressed and what is expected of the capability.

1. Strategic airpower is most commonly considered to be the aerial delivery of nuclear weapons, primarily large bombs against the enemy homeland. Smaller weapons used against advancing forces constitute theater nuclear operations. This view gained acceptance when the British, American, and Soviet air forces fielded nuclear bombers.

2. Others describe strategic airpower as long-range aviation. Advocates of this school tend to consider strategic operations those that can launch from the homeland and conduct intercontinental missions. Airlift is the best example, being separated into strategic (intertheater) and tactical (intratheater) components. The linking of long-range to nuclear as in the TU-95 and B-52 bombers has tended to cause this definition and the one above to overlap.

3. A third school believes strategic airpower strikes at and destroys the enemy's will and capability to resist. The claims of airpower advocates before and during the Second World War centered on this definition.

Although each of the definitions above has some credibility as well as staunch advocates, official definitions tend to focus on the elements of the third. The two closely related examples that follow serve to illustrate this point.

> *strategic air warfare:* air combat and supporting operations designed to effect, through a systematic application of force to a selected series of vital targets, the progressive destruction and disintegration of the enemy's war-making capacity to a point where the enemy no longer retains the ability or will to wage war.
>
> —Inter-American Defense Board

strategic air warfare: air operations designed to effect the progressive destruction and disintegration of the enemy's war-making capacity.
—North Atlantic Treaty Organization

The NATO definition is wholly contained within that of the IADB and seems to be little more than a compact rendering of the latter. In fact, it is a greatly generalized definition in that it makes no provision for a systematic selection of vital targets nor does it seek to affect the enemy's will. As such, the NATO countries acknowledge the existence of strategic airpower without addressing the issue of its capability to affect an enemy's will to wage war. This capability is not repudiated; rather, it is ignored.

Strategic airpower goes well beyond both definitions, but can be stated in simple terms if one accepts an underlying premise that *all* strategic power relies upon threat analysis, capability assessment, and operational planning. These three elements are always essential to strategic operations. Constructs for their application will be discussed in the section on The Strategic Air Campaign.

strategic airpower: air operations or the perceived capability to conduct those operations which achieve political objectives.

This definition varies considerably from those that precede it, in that:

1. It recognizes the peacetime use of strategic airpower.
2. It allows for exploitation of perceived capabilities.
3. It shifts the focus from chiefly military targets to political outcomes.
4. It provides for the use of reconnaissance and other support missions.

The primary purpose of strategic airpower is to achieve political outcomes. It is a recognized fact that every country attempts to direct, alter, or negate international relationships to secure its own national objectives. When nations use airpower to achieve these outcomes, they use strategic airpower. It is this political intent rather than the use of a particular class of weapons that differentiates strategic operations from tactical encounters.

The Strategic Air Campaign

John A. Warden III, in his 1989 book *The Air Campaign*, has proposed a useful model for developing a strategic air campaign. He postulates that for a modern state to conduct modern war it must have a command structure; possess or have access to industry suited for war production; have a distribution, transportation, and communication infrastructure; have a population capable of supplying workers and soldiers with agricultural needs; and have a fielded military force.

These five areas can be envisioned as concentric rings with increasing strategic importance as one goes from fielded forces to the political-military command structure. There is target overlap between rings, but basically five levels of modern society serve as the foundation for strategic planning.

Strategic Rings

Outer:	fielded military forces
Fourth:	population
Third:	infrastructure
Second:	critical war industry
Inner:	political-military command structure

This apparently inverted order reflects the importance of political influences in the execution of modern war. Clausewitz rightly determined that all wars are political, but his was a time of transition. Technology had moved the battlefield away from the ruler's castle to a more distant location, but had not yet provided the communication capability to permit near real-time political direction. With few exceptions (such as the Roman Empire), warfare before gunpowder allowed for on-scene political control since state leaders led armies. As this changed, military and political considerations began to take on distinctive characteristics.

The generals in the field operated under political direction that was anywhere from a few hours to several days old. It was an understood reality that they would face unexpected circumstances and situations. Their responsibility to provide victories demanded a military prowess that was both an impetus to and a result of doctrinal refinement. By the nineteenth century, one could envision and engage in warfare without on-the-scene political constraint. Clausewitz viewed an end result, but saw clearly the essential oneness of politics and war that many had forgotten.

Today, communications technology once again permits the natural applications of political constraints to individual battles and combatants. This is not a new phenomenon that confronts the strategist, but it does force changes in the application of the military doctrine that is designed to optimize unrestrained military might.

The model given above reflects these military priorities and will necessarily be subject to political constraints like those imposed during the Korean, Falkland/Malvinas, and Middle East conflicts. However, it is inherently useful as the basis for a strategic air campaign. We do not suggest that military planning be prematurely constrained by models overly imbued with political considerations.

Used as overlays, Warden's strategic rings allow for and demand that each country's political-military-social essence be examined for strengths and weaknesses. Each of these must in turn be examined for its vulnerability to airpower. This process provides a plan that accurately pits a nation's airpower capabilities against vital enemy targets. This military exploitation of national vulnerabilities lies at the heart of strategic airpower.

Two Israeli uses of strategic airpower serve to illustrate the point. In 1967 a pre-emptive air strike against Arab airfields proved to be the determining factor in the ensuing conflict. Again in 1981 airpower provided the basis for Israel's successful attack on an Iraqi reactor. In neither instance could land or seapower offer an alternative course of action. The first case was a clear example of operating against fielded forces (outer ring); in the second instance the Israelis addressed a power plant (third ring) that eventually could have become a source for nuclear weapons (second ring). But in both cases the political outcome was identified, the actions required to effect this outcome were determined, and airpower was strategically applied.

The peacetime uses of strategic airpower can be equally effective in achieving political goals. The Berlin airlift of 1948 was responsible for ensuring the survival of West Berlin; the Soviets' exaggerated claims of missile superiority (a subset of airpower) in the 1950s served to enhance their "world power" status; while the peaceful removal of missiles from Cuba in 1962 was to a significant degree aided by the timely presentation of reconnaissance photographs at the United Nations.

In each of the aforementioned instances, air operations or the perceived capability to conduct those operations achieved political goals. Success was determined by the application of airpower against crucial targets within particular strategic rings or within combinations of those rings. It is critically important to identify and subsequently attack the vital target sets in each ring. Furthermore, to qualify as strategic, it is imperative that airpower be capable of exacting a required level of damage, destruction, or disruption of those nodes targeted.

Capabilities Versus Tasks

The Air Estimate of the Situation for Strategic Air Warfare first highlighted the importance of matching tasks to capacity. Beginning with World War II, there have been several notable abandonments of the principle.

It was only during the latter stages of the war that the targeting of Germany's petroleum industry effectively matched Allied capabilities to a strategic target set. During neither the Korean War nor the French experience in Indochina was airpower employed strategically. Again in Vietnam, airpower was not employed with strategic effectiveness until the Linebacker II Campaign in December 1972.

Stated in the most basic terms, airpower cannot achieve strategic effect unless its capabilities are targeted against strategic targets that are vulnerable. The results of airpower must be crippling, causing damage, destruction, or diversion that cannot be tolerated. The capability to inflict such damage must be equal to or greater than the enemy's capability to withstand that damage.

There are two general ways to misdirect airpower that prevent strategic outcomes. First, airpower can be directed against target sets that have no strategic importance to the enemy. Second, it can be directed against strategic targets that it cannot adequately affect. This would include targets too numerous, dispersed, protected, or hardened to be handled by the existing airpower capability. The following discussion outlines these concerns.

In each strategic ring there will be any number of target sets. For example, a country may have the following assets in the second ring, critical war industry: tank factories, artillery factories, small arms factories, aircraft plants, shipyards, missile factories, fuel refineries, truck factories, munitions factories, repair depots, training centers, and so forth.

The order of importance of such assets varies with the country, nature of the conflict, and time. Consequently, the importance of quality ongoing analysis cannot be overstated in regard to the preparation and maintenance of such lists. A direct relationship between list accuracy, capability assessment, and strategic success will always exist.

To illustrate that relationship, let us examine a hypothetical example (the numbers in parentheses represent the number of individual target sites in each target set). The strategically most important target sets from the list given above are: munitions factories (100), aircraft plants (17), fuel refineries (15), repair depots (50), and small arms factories (13). Nonstrategic target sets from the same list are: artillery factories (2), truck factories (3), and training centers (4).

It is conceivable that items in the first list could represent equally critical nodes. That is: sufficient damage, destruction, or disruption of any one of the five separate categories would produce the political outcome desired by the opposing country. The bottom three could represent nodes that would not achieve the desired political outcome even if totally eliminated.

The strategic importance of a particular target category is determined by the degree to which a nation is dependent upon or values it. For example, an island nation's survival may be dependent on shipping, whereas it could survive the elimination of its steel industry but values it sufficiently to make major political concessions to protect it. Both would therefore possess strategic importance. Within given categories the value of individual targets is determined by factors such as excess production, reserves, and replacement/substitution capability.

Whatever strategic airpower capability the opposing nation has is situationally finite. When it is expended in a given manner, a given level of damage will occur. This level is dependent on the nature, quality, and quantity of ordnance available and the hardness of the targets attacked. With this in mind, the most basic requirement for the successful employment of strategic airpower is *that capabilities be equal to or greater than the force required to sufficiently damage, destroy, or disrupt a strategic target set.* To illustrate this relationship we shall assume a situation where:

- Airpower has the capability to totally negate ten sites in any category (in reality, capability is never the same value across all target sets).
- Excess production and existing reserves result in surplus capabilities in every target set.
- Each target within an individual set is equal.

	Existing Sites	Strategic Requirement
Munitions factories	100	50
Aircraft plants	17	7
Fuel refineries	15	8
Repair depots	50	20
Small arms factories	13	1
Artillery factories	2	0
Truck factories	3	0
Training centers	4	0

The capability to eliminate ten targets is strategically sufficient in only one category—fuel refineries. It is strategically irrelevant that the opposing power could eliminate all the artillery and truck factories along with the training centers. Tremendous destruction would result, but it would not effect the desired political outcome. It would be equally futile to destroy nearly 77 percent of the small arms factories, since the opponent requires only one factory to successfully conclude hostilities. The single obvious conclusion one must draw is that airpower cannot be strategically effective unless it is targeted strategically.

All strategic power draws its utility from its ability or the perception of its ability to meaningfully damage, destroy, or disrupt something an opponent sufficiently values or requires. Strategic airpower gives each nation the capability of directing its military power to these ends in the most timely and effective manner yet discovered.

Summary

Strategic airpower exists when air operations or the perceived capability to conduct those operations achieve political goals. This capability is only indirectly tied to the size or wealth of a country. Although it is generally exercised through combat, it can be successfully employed in peacetime or during war through support airlift or reconnaissance.

An air force that is planned, procured, and employed based on a model such as Warden's Strategic Rings and is targeted against vulnerable strategic nodes is a strategic air force. An abdication of any element of this stratagem eliminates the possibility of strategic airpower and relegates airpower to a secondary role.

Addendum

Since this article was originally submitted for publication, the 1991 Gulf War has incontrovertibly proved the efficacy of strategic airpower. That strategic air campaign was firmly based in the principles described above and benefited tremendously from the technological advances of stealth and precision. The intense initial countrywide attack overwhelmed Iraqi defenses and generated a strategic paralysis. The devastating effectiveness of the 43-day air war is unparalleled and led a former U.S. Air Force Chief of Staff to describe the new capability as "hyperwar."

Thomas M. Kearney

See Also: Airpower; Airpower, History of; Arab-Israeli Wars; Bombardment, Strategic; Cuban Missile Crisis; Douhet, Giulio; Gulf War, 1991; Strategy; Vietnam and Indochina Wars; World War I; World War II.

Bibliography

Douhet, G. 1983. *Command of the air.* Washington, D.C.: Government Printing Office.

Emme, E. M. 1959. *The impact of air power.* Princeton, N.J.: Van Nostrand.

Kennet, L. B. 1982. *A history of strategic bombardment.* New York: Scribner's.

Warden, J. A., III. 1989. *The air campaign: Planning for combat.* Washington, D.C.: Pergamon-Brassey's.

AIRPOWER, TACTICAL

Tactical airpower appeared almost simultaneously with the development of aircraft. The military quickly found use for air units in supportive or tactical functions: carrying messages, supplies, and men; observing the battlefield and enemy movements; attacking enemy forces with various munitions; and defending friendly airspace from hostile enemy air forces.

As early as World War I, some air forces won an independent role, forming strike or strategic bomber forces with the ultimate objective of forcing surrender of an enemy nation without the necessity of destroying armies or occupying land. By World War II some air forces, challenging further the original subordination of airpower to control by ground army commanders, won greater centralized command over tactical air resources as well. Throughout, there has been a dichotomy in the aims of airpower, and a competition for funding between tactical airpower dedicated to the support of ground armies, and independent bombardment airpower. Each of these two manifestations of military aviation limited and defined the role of the other.

Over time, large nations organized air forces as elements of the existing military services (land and naval) and many divided their air forces into separate, functionally designed, organizations such as strategic, defense, and tactical air commands. Some nations went further, allocating tactical resources and distinct support responsibilities to each of the services, as the United States did with its air force, army, navy, and marines air resources. Beginning in the 1950s, large nations established combat-ready tactical air forces, and sponsored generous tactical research and development programs. Advancing technology continues to improve propeller, jet, and helicopter aircraft to include armor, electronics, weapons, and armament.

Smaller nations, too, are interested in tactical airpower, not only for transport, supply, and air attacks, but also for reconnaissance of enemy territory and support of ground forces. Although smaller nations tend to have less sophisticated aircraft—often trainers or obsolescent models from the airpower nations—a few have raised enough funds to compete with major nations in tactical airpower.

From Observation to Air Combat

In the first two decades of the twentieth century, pioneer aircraft designers and military leaders in all major nations were quick to see a use for the new heavier-than-air flying vehicles. When models were developed that had endurance, range, and carrying capacity, airplanes replaced the balloons and airships that performed tactical observation and reconnaissance.

Some nations experimented with offensive airpower. In 1910 American air pioneer Glenn Curtiss practiced bombing a battleship-shaped target. In 1912 Lt. Riley Scott, an American Army officer, developed a bombsight that won a bombing contest held in Rheims, France. Both England and Italy experimented with air-launched torpedoes. The first actual air attack occurred in 1911, when a small Italian air unit, accompanying ground forces to Turkish-held Tripoli, dropped small bombs on enemy troop concentrations.

World War I

Warring nations in World War I had purchased large numbers of aircraft prior to the outbreak of war, and employed them in the very first operations. As German armies performed their great wheel through northeast France, in a modified version of the so-called Schlieffen Plan, they were accompanied and preceded by aircraft reconnoitering the enemy. From the beginning, British, French, and German ground commanders relied on air observer reports for flank protection and the tracking of the opponent's movements.

The several high commands soon identified problems with this new air warfare. Under mobile conditions, air units failed to keep up with the ground forces without extensive administrative and service organizations. Observation proved ineffective when enemy troops maneuvered under cover of darkness or in bad weather. Expense and operational limits notwithstanding, the generals demanded more air resources, including pilots, observers, mechanics, and more high-quality, competitive aircraft.

The technology of tactical airpower evolved quickly in a competitive environment. Advances came in aircraft, aircraft systems, and maintenance and repair as airmen demanded, among other things, higher-altitude performance to avoid fire from guns on the ground, photographic gear to aid reconnaissance, and wireless radios to facilitate air-to-ground communication. By the spring of 1915, both sides armed aircraft with machineguns and bombs to attack targets beyond the range of artillery. Soon, observation aircraft required fast, well-armed, escort fighters to run interference against defending pursuit planes. Competition encouraged a rapidly evolving technology of high-speed, well-armed, maneuverable fighters, and the ensuing air-to-air war quickly captured public attention.

By the summer of 1916, Gen. Hugh M. Trenchard, commander of the British Royal Flying Corps in France, articulated the first standard doctrinal concepts still associated with tactical air operations. He maintained that an air force was more effective in offensive attacks against enemy air and ground than flying defensive missions over friendly forces. He felt that defensive air patrols should be avoided for two reasons: (1) because they debilitated aircraft and pilots without a guarantee of profitable action; and (2) defensive air cover was false security as it could be defeated any time the enemy mounted a large air attack.

Trenchard inspired two practices that have been held inviolable by airmen ever since: (1) centralized command of all aircraft in a ground theater to facilitate concentration of air resources for carefully chosen, significant missions; and (2) dominance in the air as a prerequisite for victory on the ground.

Germany developed similar practices, but also initiated the concept of assigning air liaison officers to ground commanders to facilitate joint operations. Germany was the first to develop an armored tactical aircraft, the Junkers J.4, for close air support.

Airmen on both sides found that the rising demand for various tactical support tasks—along with a demand for air defense and strategic bombing air units—spread thin the available air resources. In the great British Somme Offensive, July–November 1916, for example, Trenchard failed to collect sufficient aircraft to accomplish successfully any of his tactical tasks: observation for the Fourth Army, reconnaissance for headquarters, air superiority, and interdiction bombing of enemy communication centers. Air superiority seesawed back and forth then and throughout the war. Only in 1918, when Germany was nearing military collapse, did the Allied air forces gain superiority in the air.

Interwar Years: The 1920s

Through the 1920s, colonial powers applied tactical airpower in their territories. British, French, and Italian air units assisted civil authorities and ground-based military guards maintaining order in the undeveloped lands. The harsh tactical lessons of World War I were ignored in warfare against weaker peoples, nor did airpower experiences against developing countries translate well in succeeding European war conditions. Military leaders may well have developed misleading impressions about airpower because the absence of effective antiaircraft defense permitted generous low-level air operations. Meanwhile, military aircraft development took a back seat to technological work for the private sector. First-line aircraft were not needed to intimidate colonials, transport arms and men, or bomb undefended villages.

Interwar Years: The 1930s

Three events and conditions in particular affected tactical airpower in the 1930s. First, a surge in aviation technology produced larger and much faster aircraft, and that factor, along with the development of new antiaircraft artillery, made close support of ground forces or attack on heavily defended army positions exceedingly difficult and dangerous. Second, as the European nations began to rearm, Britain and France expended great energy developing fighters for air defense. The need for air defense was also recognized by the navies of the seapower nations, and they began to develop carriers and naval tactical airpower to include observation, air superiority, and surface-attack missions as with land airpower.

The third event that affected tactical aviation was the development of strategic bombardment. The British Royal Air Force became enamored with bombardment to the point that tactical aviation was significantly neglected. Germany, Italy, and the United States, also attracted to the idea of strategic warfare, invested funds and effort in bomber development. Germany constructed hundreds of long-range bombers by 1940; however, with no plan for strategic warfare, it continued to view aircraft as part of the combined weapons team in ground operations.

The Spanish Civil War, as a dress rehearsal for World War II, gave greater impetus to tactical air warfare. Operations in that war put a new light on mobility in ground operations, especially in a combination of tanks and supporting aircraft. German forces fighting for Gen. Francisco Franco showed that airpower could be substituted for artillery. Germany then organized some of its air forces into close-air-support units, which coordinated their efforts with the ground forces by radio links.

World War II: Modern Tactical Aviation

Germany started the war with a massive tactical air effort, as the Luftwaffe attacked Poland's air forces in the air and on the ground. Thereupon, the Luftwaffe employed the whole range of tactical roles, including interdiction of ground force concentrations, supply lines, and communications; close support of the ground forces; airlift for an independently operating armored force, and continuing air reconnaissance and liaison.

The blitzkrieg, an extensive, coordinated, employment of the Luftwaffe and armor through Belgium and France in May–June 1940, provided a model for ground and air forces everywhere. The ground forces kept in radio contact with the armored columns, while the Luftwaffe, guaranteeing air supremacy, attacked important chokepoints until German artillery units could be moved into place. Air support was under unified control, air and ground corps commanders sharing headquarters and relying on liaison officers, control centers, and an effective radio net to link intelligence and command between air and ground. The Allies could neither raise sufficient tactical forces to win the air superiority battle, coordinate forces for an effective interdiction battle, nor even provide effective air reconnaissance. The ineffectiveness of the Allied aviation hastened the French collapse and British withdrawal.

This fast-moving warfare suggested again, as in World War I, a need for expansive tactical aviation forces. Both Britain and the United States fostered progress in tactical as well as strategic aviation. With limited time and technological ability, the Soviet Union decided to concentrate its energy on building ground-support aircraft. Meanwhile, because Germany controlled the continent during 1940–41, there were no ground engagements, and attention was given to other forms of aviation. Britain allocated resources both to air defense (until after the Battle of Britain in late 1940) and to strategic bombing as the most effective way to hit back at Germany. Along with the considerable efforts of long-range bombers to destroy German military and, eventually, civilian facilities, Britain sent out fighters and light bombers to engage enemy air forces and destroy air facilities to gain some control in the air, to soften the enemy for the eventual invasion, and to take some pressure off Russia, after that country was invaded by Germany in June 1941.

Mediterranean: Seedbed of Tactical Doctrine

The United States joined the war against Germany in late 1941. But for several reasons, the Allies delayed the invasion of northwest Europe. Allied tactical aviation was tested and reformulated in the Mediterranean and other war theaters. The German air support system worked efficiently at first as contenders faced each other in Greece, Crete, and North Africa. When Germany sent great numbers of air units to the Russian front, the stretched-out Luftwaffe lost air superiority in the Mediterranean. By the autumn of 1942, British forces in the western desert gained superiority in aircraft, tanks, and trucks, as well as service facilities and manpower.

After a short learning experience, American, French, and additional British tactical air forces operating in northwest Africa helped corral German and Italian forces in Tunisia. Eventually developing consistency in its support of infantry and armor, Allied tactical aviation offered a wide variety of support functions: bombardment of ports, troop concentrations, and control centers; interdiction of shipping; attack of airfields; bomber escort; area defense; occasional close support of friendly forces; and air transport. Even with many incidents of friendly fire, from both air and ground, air support became increasingly important to the success of the ground campaigns.

The West learned new lessons and relearned a few old ones: (1) ground commanders could not rely on air support as they could on a tank or artillery unit; (2) weather at the air base and over the target affected air support reliability; (3) enemy antiaircraft defenses and recognition problems by friendly troops made close air support expensive and inefficient; (4) likewise, high speeds and flying altitudes limited target recognition by aircrews; (5) air units needed air bases built quickly as the battlefield advanced or retreated; (6) aircraft needed prodigious amounts of maintenance, replacement parts, bulky fuel, and munitions; (7) air warfare required sophisticated communications systems, powerful enough for wide coverage and security from jamming; (8) bombers, used occasionally for close air support, were often inaccurate; and (9) air leaders demanded greater influence over extensive air operations. Feelings were permanently sensitized on this last point. British airmen, followed by the Americans, declared that they would give tertiary priority to close-air-support missions; the first priority for tactical aircraft would be to gain control of the air, and secondarily to hit enemy lines of ground communications behind the battle fronts.

Northwest Europe

This, in fact, was the way the air war was prosecuted in northwest Europe. The Allies organized enormous tactical air forces to attack enemy aircraft in the air, at their bases, and at manufacturing locations. German air forces were so reduced in numbers and effectiveness that they rarely conducted attacks the rest of the war. Having gained general air superiority by D-Day, Allied air units turned to interdiction and close support tasks.

Tactical aviation for the Allies was very successful in 1944 and 1945. Tactical air units paved the way for Eisenhower's ground troops and provided almost complete protection from the constrained enemy. On occasion, the Allies employed heavy bombers in both the interdiction and close support roles. An air-ground team composed of fast-moving tank columns protected by continual air cover for observation and flank protection, brought good feelings between air and ground forces, and facilitated deep advances against German defenses.

Many airmen maintained that their tactical success (with some exceptions such as the accidental bombing of friendly troops in a carpet bombing attack or the interdiction program destroying bridges that subsequently slowed the offensive) owed much to the centralized command of air units by airmen.

Eastern Front

As in the West, the Luftwaffe served almost universally in support of the ground battle, especially beginning in 1942 when the German offensive stalled. Proper tactical use of aircraft became more difficult as the Luftwaffe, along with other German forces, tried desperately to avoid a Napoleonic defeat.

The Russians employed vast numbers of aircraft, including American lend-lease P-39s and their own popular IL-2s and IL-10 Stormoviks, and overwhelmed the Germans in the air. Ignoring doctrinal axioms professed by the West, the Russians assigned air units permanently to armies and army groups. Air activities were decided more by circumstances and expediency than by deliberate planning. Fighter operations were mostly defensive; ground attacks were generally inefficient due to a lack of flying skill and poor intelligence about German targets. Nonetheless, by the end of 1942, the Russians could concentrate more of their qualitatively inferior—numerically superior—fighters and ground attack aircraft than the Germans, and they slowly gained air superiority.

Far East

Japan employed support aviation in all its battles in Asia and the Pacific, also considering destruction of enemy air forces the top priority for its air forces. In this theater, too, Allied air forces came under a central command structure. The weaker Japanese air forces permitted a wider, less selective, employment of Allied air forces for bombardment, transportation, and reconnaissance support for the amphibious assaults and for the island-hopping ground operations unique to war in the Pacific. The retreat of the Japanese Empire occurred when Allied air resources became numerically and qualitatively superior. The U.S. Marines, with dedicated air support, developed a reputation for unselfish close air support to the frontline troops.

Postwar Decline of Tactical Aviation

The atomic bombs dropped on Japan in August 1945, signaled not only the end of World War II, but the primacy of atomic deterrent forces and the temporary eclipse of tactical aviation. At least for the United States, the emphasis was on high-altitude bombers, swift interceptors, and air superiority fighters rather than aircraft suited specifically for and dedicated to operations with the ground forces.

Korea

Tactical airpower was revived during the Korean War. The UN forces employed World War II fighters and tactical bombers before introducing jet aircraft. Eventually American F-84s and F-86s competed against Chinese or Russian MiG-17s and MiG-19s. American and Soviet fighters, confirming the tradition that fighters be multipurpose aircraft, also carried bombs and cannons for operations in support of the ground forces. Close-in observation, administrative liaison, reconnaissance, and tactical transport tasks (now employing helicopters) followed the pattern of previous wars. Unlike World War II, however, big bombers played a less prominent role and were employed mostly in tactical missions.

Cold War

Most nations continued to modernize their tactical air forces: Britain with its de Havilland Venom and Hawker Hunter; France its Sud-Ouest Vautour and Dassault Super Mystère; and Sweden, its Saab 32. In the 1960s the Soviet Union expanded its support for insurgencies in the developing nations, employing Sukhoi Su-7, Su-11, and other dedicated ground support aircraft and rethinking its own doctrine for conventional warfare. As jet fighters gained the capability to carry nuclear weapons and extended their range with aerial refueling, the United States joined the Europeans in developing modern air superiority fighters for tactical missions. Americans equipped the F-100, F-104, and F-101 (all fast, high-altitude performers) with bomb racks, cannons, and missiles for ground roles.

Some nations developed multipurpose aircraft to carry tactical weapon systems. The French Mirage series and Sweden's Draken are examples. Others saw a market for smaller, less expensive, tactical fighters. Italy's popular Fiat G91, built to NATO specifications, served Italy and Germany for many years. The U.S. Navy followed a similar course with the Douglas A-4 lightweight attack fighter, employed in air forces worldwide.

Southeast Asia and Middle East

War in Southeast Asia and the Middle East magnified and accelerated the technological advances in tactical aviation hardware, especially because of new developments in surface-to-air missiles and other electronic ground defense systems. Tactical aircraft predominated as Americans employed their most capable operational aircraft, those made for speed and range, to fight North Vietnamese MiG-17s and MiG-21s in air combat. The Americans also modified many fighters to fill interdiction and close-air-support tasks. Tactical bombing missions called for a complex organization of air resources. A fighter-bomber mission over North Vietnam might consist of sixteen F-105s, escorted by twelve F-4s for fighter protection, with four additional F-105s to suppress enemy flak and surface-to-air missiles, supported by EB-66 radar-jamming aircraft, and EC-121 radar aircraft to keep track of all aircraft, enemy and friendly.

Helicopters acquired the firepower of light airplanes and were employed in the ground battle, new elements in the pantheon of offensive tactical airpower. The American Bell Huey series and the Westland/Aerospatiale Lynx in European armies, were the first to signify rotor aircraft success, giving the ground commanders potential for very close transport and fire support. Desire for extensive air reconnaissance continued as primary tasks for tactical air forces as war involvement expanded.

Contemporary and Future Tactical Airpower

Many tactical air issues have not changed since World War I. Doctrine for joint operations is not substantively different, especially in organization and command relationships, even if methodology is different in scale and technique. Command and control centers are large, sophisticated collectors of intelligence, necessary as major battlefield operations are conceptualized as large complex problems. The battlefield is differentiated into areas close in and farther from the battle line, and may or may not be less linear and more fast-moving and fluid than in World War I. Tactical aircraft, encountering improved surface-to-air missiles, antiaircraft fire, and hand-held missiles, will have increasingly protective countermeasures and sophisticated delivery systems.

Current tactical aviation continues to find air combat and air superiority harsh taskmasters. All nations have approached the problem with a range of fighters. The big jets, however, such as American F-15s and Soviet Su-27 Flankers—with greater speed, powerful radar and electronics for all-weather operations, and maneuverability—are the premier air combat aircraft.

For the critical close-air-support tasks, multipurpose fighters, carrying modern air-to-air missiles, guided bombs, radar, and digital computer and inertial navigation systems for accurate targeting, continue to improve and are employed by nations of all sizes. Moderately sized attack aircraft, such as the multination NATO Panavia Tornado and Sepecat Jaguar, Swedish Viggen, American F-16, and French Mirage F1, have less air combat ability but are also less expensive and still effective in ground attack. As production costs increase, these aircraft appear to be the tactical models of the future. Many can carry tactical nuclear weapons. The British-built Harrier, with the ability to land vertically or on small isolated strips near the battlefield, serves with several air forces.

American and Soviet air forces acquired specialized, armored, air-support aircraft, the A-10 Thunderbolt, and Su-25 Frogfoot. These have good loiter time and fly relatively slowly for better targeting—but are vulnerable in modern air-land warfare. Both the Soviets and Americans have heavy, multirole, fighter-bombers such as the American F-111 and Russian Su-19 for long-range ground attack missions. The future promises night vision systems, voice-actualized computers, fire-and-forget weapons, and helmet-mounted displays for all sizes of aircraft as funding is available.

Ground commanders in Vietnam discovered the usefulness of the helicopter for tactical air support, and thousands were acquired for observation, transportation, and eventually for fire support. Being quite vulnerable to ground fire, however, thousands of helicopters were destroyed in battle. Still, many nations have modified helicopters with weapons and even designed fast new models with computer management systems dedicated for the potential of modern armored warfare. The American AH-1 Cobra and AH-64 Apache, Soviet MiG-24 Hind, French Aerospatiale Panther, Italian Mangusta, and British Lynx lead the current trend. The Apache can carry as much munitions (such as antitank missiles, rockets, and cannons) as a fighter-bomber and still have room for antiradar detectors, laser designators, advanced navigational devices, and other modern electronics so much a part of tactical aviation. Nonetheless, low-flying aircraft, winged or rotor, remain vulnerable to ground fire.

With the proliferation of surface-to-surface missiles, the question has been asked since the 1970s whether these missiles will replace close air support by aircraft. At the same time, other aspects of tactical aviation such as transport and reconnaissance requirements are becoming increasingly important. Tactical airlift continues to attract development in terms of size and rough-field capability whether a battle on the German plains or in developing countries. New twists have been added for special airlift operations. Transports carry extensive electronic suppression equipment or powerful guns to add firepower to ground battles, and the American tilt-rotor Osprey, a cross between a helicopter and a winged aircraft, offers new challenges for rapid troop deployment.

Technology continues to offer potential for changes in tactical airpower. With stealth technology, for example, aircraft may avoid radar-directed antiaircraft weapons, allowing more security for air operations. Another significant technology for future airland battle is the development of autonomous systems such as pilotless or remotely piloted vehicles for reconnaissance and even for offensive attack. Israel's successful employment of remotely piloted aircraft helped gain acceptance for these agile, stealthy vehicles. Their smaller airframes, easy to build in large numbers, may fill part of the requirement for close support attack, reconnaissance, interdiction, and destruction of enemy air bases, communication nodes, and weapon sites located beyond the battlefield.

Nevertheless, ground commanders of all nations continue to insist on an air-ground attack capability, integrated smoothly into ground activities. They want it quickly and want it to be accurate against precisely defined targets, day, night, and in all-weather conditions. Air commanders want centralized management of tactical resources to ensure that they have the ability to respond flexibly and with mass. In the Gulf War of 1991, the air forces of the coalition of nations that engaged Iraq in combat operated under a single air commander. The results were very impressive.

Smaller nations have not neglected tactical air resources. Their inventory is as varied as are the aircraft developed over the last 30 years. American Northrop F-5s and Cessna A-37s, British Hawks, multination European Alpha Jets, Soviet Union MiG-17s, Su 20s, and other second-string aircraft will continue to be employed as tactical aircraft in smaller air forces throughout the world.

DANIEL MORTENSEN

SEE ALSO: Air Interdiction; Air-land Battle; Airpower; Airpower, History of; Blitzkrieg; Close Air Support; Helicopter.

Bibliography

Baumbach, W. 1960. *The life and death of the Luftwaffe*. New York: Coward-McCann.

Bilstein, R. E. 1984. *Flight in America, 1900–1983: From the Wrights to the astronauts*. Baltimore, Md.: Johns Hopkins Press.

Collier, B. 1974. *A history of air power*. New York: Macmillan.

English, J. A., J. Addicott, and P. J. Kramers, eds. 1985. *The mechanized battlefield: A tactical analysis*. Washington, D.C.: Pergamon-Brassey's.

Gibbs-Smith, C. H. 1985. *Aviation: An historical survey from its origins to the end of World War II*. London: Her Majesty's Stationery Office.

Hardesty, V. 1982. *Red Phoenix: The rise of Soviet air power, 1941–45*. Washington, D.C.: Smithsonian Press.

Higham, R., and J. W. Kipp. 1978. *Soviet aviation and air power: A historical view*. London: Brassey's.

Jackson, R. 1987. *NATO air power*. London: Airlife.

Lissarague, C., and P. Lissarague. 1986. *A history of French military aviation*. Washington, D.C.: Smithsonian Press.

Mason, R. A. 1987. *Air power: An overview of roles*. Washington, D.C.: Pergamon-Brassey's.

Murray, W. 1986. *Luftwaffe*. Baltimore: Nautical and Aviation.

Smith, P. M. 1987–88. Air battle 2000 in the NATO alliance. *Air Power Journal* 1:4–15.

Ulanoff, S. M., and D. Eshel. 1985. *The fighting Israeli air force*. New York: Arco.

AIRSPACE CONTROL, MILITARY

Airspace control is the attempt by military commanders to discriminate their forces from the enemies' and to define, separate, and support the movements of their own, and allied, aircraft and space vehicles. When airspace control is successfully planned and implemented, it results in the maximum attrition of enemy air and space vehicles while at the same time ensuring that friendly vehicles are not mistakenly engaged and attacked by friendly air defense units.

History

During World War I it became apparent that aviators needed to ensure that their aircraft could be easily distinguished from the enemy's. During that war, when concepts of employment of airpower were being rapidly developed and implemented, it was not unusual for a pilot to have survived an air-to-air encounter with one or more enemy aircraft only to be shot at or shot down by his own squadron mate. In addition, there were casualties of friendly airmen as a result of fire from friendly ground forces. The men in the trenches were not averse to the "shoot-first-and-ask-questions-later" approach. The unlucky aviator who nursed his wounded bi-wing or tri-wing aircraft back over the front lines in an attempt to make a landing in friendly territory often had a rude shock when he received deadly fire from the soldiers he was trying to support. Fresh in the minds of the infantrymen, of course, was the pounding they had received shortly before from other aircraft that they had allowed to get too close. Although losses from ground fire were not particularly high, due to the limited range and accuracy of the soldiers' weapons, steps were taken to make the aircraft more visible and more readily identifiable. Insignia were painted in letters large enough to be seen and read from the ground before the aircraft was within firing range. This primitive form of airspace control set the stage for the developments that occurred in the interwar period (1918–39).

Airspace control at the end of World War I consisted of little more than well-marked aircraft and aircraft identification training programs to help ground troops and aviators recognize friendly and enemy aircraft silhouettes. Airspace control was based on visual cues and identification. Only when an aircraft came within visual range of fighters or ground troops was it subject to attack. This concentration on visual identification changed dramatically with the introduction of radar just prior to World War II.

World War II

Both the Axis and Allied powers used radar to guide fighters toward (and to alert antiaircraft artillery crews to) incoming enemy aircraft. Commanders were quick to grasp the significance of this advancement in technology and to use it to concentrate their fighter resources where they could do the most good. By the summer of 1940, the interface between radar and interceptor aircraft became absolutely crucial. The Battle of Britain is a brilliant example of the marriage of technology, airmanship, and airspace control. Outnumbered, exhausted, and reduced to very few resources, Fighter Command of the British Royal Air Force took to the air upon the warning provided by the primitive fixed radar sites and met the determined waves of the German *Luftwaffe*. The summer and early autumn of 1940 was unusually hot and dry and most of the engagements took place in clear weather when visibility was excellent.

There were many problems for the Royal Air Force besides the persistent attacks by the Germans. The radars provided enough warning time to ensure that the British aviators took off at the right time and in the right direction to intercept the incoming waves of enemy aircraft, but these same radars sometimes caused British antiaircraft sites to shoot down returning Allied fighters based on misidentified radar plots at the radar control centers in southeastern England. All sides quickly recognized the need to develop and produce a system of identification that would work in all weather conditions and in the "beyond visual range" environment of modern air warfare. The predominance of the eyeball had to give way to electronics if airspace control was to work.

Electronics

Identification Friend or Foe (IFF) and Selective Identification Feature (SIF), which consist of a transponder and interrogator system installed on the aircraft and at selected ground sites, paved the way for modern airspace control systems and procedures. With such a system, aircraft could be tracked and identified as they moved through various air defense sectors. Even if they appeared unannounced on the radar screen, they could be challenged electronically and classified as friendly or unknown long before they came within the range of orbiting fighters or gun emplacements on the ground.

Gradually, sophisticated airspace control procedures evolved around this electronic identification capability. Because battle commanders recognized that these new systems were susceptible to enemy jamming or even "spoofing" (i.e., copying the friendly signal to make an enemy aircraft appear to be a friendly one), elaborate procedures involving special flight paths and altitude authentication procedures were developed.

Many groups of specialized air force and army personnel were dedicated to producing and disseminating "airspace control orders." Command centers that previously used wooden sticks to represent formations of incoming aircraft now pulsed with electronic systems that displayed radar plots of aircraft. These plots were the result of interrogation and the correct routes and altitude for the friendly aircraft. Large sums and countless man-hours were spent getting ever-changing airspace control orders to pilots who would have to fly in that environment. The entire system required great discipline on the part of every participant. Aviators had to be sure to turn on and off their IFF/SIF at the correct times and places; they also had to fly the proper routes and altitudes over friendly territory. Radar controllers and plotters in the radar sites and command centers had to be careful in their identification and plotting of all aircraft. The antiaircraft gunners had to withhold fire against friendly aircraft and fire aggressively and accurately at enemy aircraft. The interceptor pilots had to observe a great deal of self-discipline not only to comply with all the procedures but also to constrain their aggressive nature when friendly aircraft were in the vicinity.

An Airspace Control Plan

Today, a workable airspace control plan must meet a number of very tough requirements. It must satisfy many constituencies: the ground commander, the air commander, the aircraft attack communities from the various services and allied nations, the short-range surface-to-air missile community, the antiaircraft artillery community, the high performance long-range surface-to-air missile community, the various radar communities (early warning, tactical mobile), the interceptor community, and the infantry, artillery, and armor communities on the battlefield. In addition, it should be a plan that can be exercised on occasion to give confidence to all the users and to iron out difficulties in the application of the plan.

The plan also must have built-in flexibility so that in wartime, procedures that are not working can be changed quickly and easily. If, for instance, an airspace control plan should have low-level corridors over the battlefield area for friendly aircraft to fly to and from enemy territory, these corridors must be changed often and in an unpredictable way so that the enemy cannot take advantage of these corridors for safe transit over the battlefield. In addition, if the plan is to have transit routes for airlift and other support aircraft to ensure that they have safe passage into theater bases (for instance, for aircraft coming from great distances to resupply bases that are launching and recovering combat aircraft), these routes also may have to be changed periodically to ensure the enemy does not take advantage of them.

In the immediate battlefield area, the ground commander must have authority to establish special zones where his antiaircraft artillery and surface-to-air missile commander can fire without worrying about positive identification of aircraft. When the ground commander establishes these zones, however, he pays a certain price, because friendly aircraft will not be able to operate within these zones except at great peril to the pilots and other aircrew members. Hence, the ground commander cannot expect to get close air support, reconnaissance, battlefield air interdiction, or helicopter support flights during the time that these zones are in operation.

With more and more interceptor aircraft having a "beyond visual range" air-to-air missile capability, airspace control plans should be designed to maximize this capability. This is a very delicate issue between the interceptor community and the attack-aircraft community. An attack pilot who has just returned from an extremely hazardous mission over enemy territory does not like the thought of aggressive interceptor pilots hoping to become aces (by shooting down five or more aircraft) having the authority to fire before positively identifying his aircraft. Unfortunately, aircraft that are approaching at a 900-knot closure speed (e.g., if both aircraft are flying toward each other at 450 knots) are very difficult to identify visually until both are in close proximity. If the interceptor can positively identify the aircraft as an enemy (electronically, visually, using photonics, or any other way), then the interceptor pilot will want to shoot at the approaching aircraft at a range of at least 16 kilometers (10 mi.). But what if the identification cannot be made positively (i.e., the aircraft is probably an enemy but it just *might* be a friendly aircraft)? Then the interceptor pilot must hold fire until he makes a positive visual identifcation; by that time the approaching aircraft may be inside the minimum range of the interceptor's missile. At the time of positive identification, if the aircraft is an enemy, then the interceptor must make a rapid "high-G" turn and try to shoot the enemy aircraft from the rear. This is a very hazardous maneuver for the interceptor because, if the enemy aircraft is being followed by an enemy escort fighter, the friendly interceptor may have turned just in front of this trailing enemy aircraft, making his demise quite likely. Of course, the interceptor flying over friendly territory must on occasion turn back toward friendly territory, but he would prefer to make this turn at a time and place of his own choosing.

To give an example, an F-15 pilot operating out of Bitburg, Germany, has a very tough mission. Armed with eight missiles and 20mm ammunition for his rapid-fire Gatling gun, his job is to defend vital targets from enemy air attack. He would prefer to attack the ingressing enemy aircraft frontally and to launch his missiles as soon as feasible to have a good possibility of a kill on the first shot. He wants to shoot before the enemy aircraft shoots and to shoot well before the two opposing aircraft "merge," or cross paths.

Another example of the problems that make the development of a comprehensive airspace control plan so difficult is the dilemma of the ground soldier. A soldier on the battlefield, who sees an aircraft begin its roll in for an air-to-ground attack, may want to shoot at it even if the aircraft may be friendly and may be attacking a nearby enemy ground position. When in doubt and when feeling threatened, it is natural for a soldier to react by defending himself using all available means. The ground observer has a very hard time predicting the geometry of an attacking aircraft. The soldier wants complete freedom to fire on any aircraft that appears to be rolling in on him. The friendly pilot wants the soldier to fire only when he has positive identification that the aircraft is an enemy.

The result of these different perspectives is a plan that is a multidimensional compromise. The temptation is strong to duck the issue and try to live with no plan at all. This is not a prudent course of action because, in the transition from peace to war, it is vital that the rules for airspace control be well established, practiced, and understood.

The Present

The valiant open-cockpit aviator of World War I would scarcely recognize today's combat environment. He flew with relative freedom and impunity in his brightly marked aircraft over friendly territory; the modern pilot is afforded no such freedom. Airspace control procedures dictate that he follow preplanned routing and correct transponder settings or risk engagement by friendly fighters, antiaircraft artillery, and surface-to-air missile sites. His aircraft is prodded and poked by unseen electronic fingers, demanding coded responses that prove time and time again that he is friendly. It is ironic that these evolutionary airspace control procedures, born out of a need to identify and protect against friendly fire, should be at the heart of a major new command and control controversy—Is it more important to identify friendly aircraft or enemy aircraft? Where should the emphasis and money be put?

A growing number of military professionals believe that airspace control should concentrate on identifying enemy, rather than friendly, aircraft. They argue that in today's highly volatile combat environment, with its limited number of surface-to-air missiles and interceptor aircraft, it is more important and effective to detect and quickly neutralize the enemy than to spend time trying to interrogate and correlate every airborne object to determine if it meets "friendly" criteria.

They advocate the development and use of "passive" systems that "hear" and "see" the incoming enemy aircraft and missiles rather than "active" systems like radar. Such developments, if successful, could free the pilot from the constraints imposed on him by current control procedures.

The Future

Airspace control, which has become so complex and expensive, will face many challenges and opportunities in the decades ahead. A number of technical developments will have impact. Stealth technology will mean that many "invisible" or, more correctly, low-observable platforms, both manned and unmanned, will be flying around the modern battlefield area. Developments in the area of antiradiation missiles (ground-to-air, air-to-ground, and air-to-air) will make it more and more hazardous for anyone to turn on a radar set. Hence, the role of radar in combat is quite likely to diminish in the next century. Photonics and other nonradiating systems will play an ever-increasing role in air warfare.

Some feel that airspace control, which has been a combination of geographically derived missile and fighter engagement zones, published flight procedures, radio challenges, and radar interrogations, will give way to more assured and direct means of detection and tracking. New sensors may be able to detect aircraft and space systems from launch to recovery and be able to track them throughout their entire flight. If positive identification of all airborne objects becomes a reality, there may be less need for complicated route restrictions and other limiting aspects of airspace control. If this comes to pass, aircraft will be able to take the most direct and effective routes to their destinations without fear of engagement from friendly systems. In any case, it will be vital for military professionals in all the military services and nations of the world to track developments carefully. The fog of war will never completely disappear. The wise commander of the future will outsmart the enemy and operate within the enemy commander's "decision cycles." By using air and space vehicles in a way that not only outsmarts the enemy but reduces losses due to friendly fire to a minimum, the enlightened commanders of the future will succeed.

PERRY M. SMITH

SEE ALSO: Command, Control, Communications and Intelligence; Fog of War; Identification Friend or Foe; Radar; Radar Technology Applications.

Bibliography

Cimbala, S. J. 1987. *Soviet C^3*. Washington, D.C.: AFCEA International Press.

Hwang, J. 1982. *Selected analytical concepts in command and control*. New York: Gordon and Breach.

Rotchford, F. C. 1988. Hawk and patriot, the mix that wins. *Air Defense Artillery*, October, pp. 22–27.

Van Creveld, M. 1985. *Command in war*. Cambridge, Mass.: Harvard Univ. Press.

Walburton, K. E. 1988. AWACS and FAAD. *Air Defense Artillery*, February, pp. 28–30.

ALEXANDER, HAROLD RUPERT LEOFRIC GEORGE [1891–1969]

Field Marshal Earl Alexander of Tunis was one of the outstanding British military commanders of the twentieth century (Fig. 1). Optimistic and self-confident, "Alex" played a significant role in virtually every theater where British troops were involved during World War II.

Early Life and Career

Harold Rupert Leofric George Alexander was born on 10 December 1891, the third son of the fourth Earl of Caledon. He inherited a tradition of public service and a good life marked by dignity, orderliness, and discipline. Alexander attended Harrow, and after graduating from Sandhurst in 1911 he joined the Irish Guards.

Figure 1. Harold Rupert Leofric George Alexander. (SOURCE: U.S. Library of Congress)

When World War I broke out, Alexander's battalion formed a part of the original British Expeditionary Force (BEF), in which he was a 22-year-old lieutenant and platoon commander. Alexander was a chivalric, cheerful, and charismatic leader; during the war he became the youngest lieutenant colonel in the British army, and when the Great War ended he was in temporary command of a brigade. During four years of fighting on the western front he was wounded twice; he won the Military Cross at Loos and the Distinguished Service Order at the Somme. Rudyard Kipling noted, "It is undeniable that Colonel Alexander had the gift of handling the men on the lines to which they most readily responded . . . his subordinates loved him, even when he fell upon them blisteringly for their shortcomings; and his men were all his own."

Alexander emerged from the crucible of the Great War a solid professional soldier. In 1919–20 he commanded a Landwehr Brigade of German and expatriate soldiers that fought under appalling weather and political conditions to prevent Latvia from succumbing to Bolshevik domination. Successful in this mission, Alexander returned to England with an enhanced reputation for imperturbability, and in time to become a battalion commander in Turkey during the 1922 Chanak crisis. Other interwar assignments included service at Gibraltar and in England, attendance at the Staff College (1926), a short stint in the War Office, then assignment as General Staff Officer 1 (GSO1) in Northern Command at York.

In 1934 Alexander took command of the Nowshera Brigade on the North-West Frontier, an appointment considered exceptional for an officer who had had no connection with the Indian Army. He commanded the brigade for three years in two frontier campaigns: the Loe Agra, as Force Commander, in early 1935; and the Mohmand campaign later that year. Once again Alexander demonstrated his tactical mastery and astute organizational and leadership abilities.

In the wake of Secretary of State for War Hore-Belisha's program to rejuvenate the army, in January 1938 Alexander returned to England as a major general to command the 1st Division, a division designated as part of the British Expeditionary Force in the event British forces were again committed to the continent of Europe.

World War II

At 47 years of age Alexander was indeed fortunate in being at the peak of his intellectual and physical powers when World War II began in 1939. His division, one of the original four of this second BEF, deployed to France and saw little action during the "phony war" of the winter of 1939–40. After the German onslaught in May 1940, the 1st Division was never intensively engaged, but at Dunkirk Alexander was given a task that brought him national renown. He was designated to command the rearguard of the BEF and adroitly conducted the evacuation of the last British soldiers from Dunkirk.

Alexander had earned the trust of Prime Minister Winston Churchill and General (later Field Marshal Viscount) Sir Alan Brooke, the future Chief of the Imperial General Staff (CIGS). Shortly after his return to England, he was promoted to lieutenant general and given command of the I Corps. His mission was to prepare his corps to resist an anticipated German invasion of England.

In December 1940 Alexander was selected to become General Officer Commanding Southern Command, and was later designated to command the first major expeditionary force in a counteroffensive against Europe. The Japanese attack in December 1941 in the Pacific altered these plans, and Alexander was appointed Commander in Chief, Burma, serving under General (later Field Marshal Earl) Sir Archibald P. Wavell, Commander in Chief, India. It was impossible to save Burma and Rangoon, and only by conducting a difficult retreat was Alexander able to save his force.

The defeats of Dunkirk and Burma would have ruined the career of an ordinary general, but shortly after Alexander returned to England in July 1942 he became Commander in Chief, Middle East. He has been criticized for his handling of his difficult subordinate, Lieutenant General (later Field Marshal Viscount) Bernard Montgomery (who later said: "First-class general, Alex—did everything I told him to do."), but North Africa was cleared of Axis forces by May 1943. Alexander reported to Churchill that, "We are masters of the North African shores."

Alexander commanded the 15th Army Group during the invasion of Sicily, then became commander in chief of the polyglot Allied armies in Italy during the difficult advance up the well-defended peninsula. The apex of Alexander's military career was the capture of Rome on 4 June 1944, for which he received his field marshal's baton.

On 12 December 1944 he was appointed Supreme Commander, Mediterranean, and after the success of his Po offensive and the capture of a million German prisoners, Alexander on 29 April 1945 accepted the first unconditional surrender signed by the Germans. Of Alexander's generalship, Harold Macmillan observed: "If Montgomery was the Wellington, Alexander was certainly the Marlborough of this war."

Aftermath

Alexander was selected to succeed Brooke as CIGS, but was requested by Canada to serve as its governor-general. He skillfully and happily served in that position from 1946 to 1952, when he returned to England and served as Churchill's Minister of Defense from 1952 to 1954. Alexander spent the last fifteen years of his life in semiretirement, serving as director of a number of companies and performing many honorary appointments, including Constable of the Tower of London from 1960 to 1965. He was persuaded to allow his *Memoirs* to be ghost-written in 1960, but they are considered a great disappointment and unworthy of his actual accomplishments. Alexander died of a perforated aorta on 16 June 1969.

Field Marshal Earl Alexander of Tunis, K.G., P.C., O.M., G.C.B., G.C.M.G., C.S.I., D.S.O., M.C., was undoubtedly one of the most skillful, courageous, and charismatic British generals of this century. "Alex's" reputation will rest on his signal achievements as a professional soldier whose life was dedicated to his sovereign and country.

HAROLD E. RAUGH, JR.

SEE ALSO: Civil War, Russian; Montgomery, Bernard Law; Wavell, Archibald Percival; World War I; World War II.

Bibliography

Barnett, C. 1960. *The desert generals.* London: Kimber.
Blaxland, G. 1979. *Alexander's generals.* London: Kimber.
Clark, M. 1950. *Calculated risk.* New York: Harper.
Hillson, N. 1952. *Alexander of Tunis.* London: Allen.
Jackson, W. G. F. 1967. *The battle for Italy.* London: Batsford.
———. 1972. *Alexander of Tunis as military commander.* New York: Dodd, Mead.
Linklater, E. 1977. *The campaign in Italy.* London: Her Majesty's Stationery Office.
Nicolson, N. 1973. *Alex.* London: Weidenfeld and Nicolson.
North, J., ed. 1962. *The Alexander memoirs, 1940–1945.* London: Cassell.
Shepperd, G. A. 1968. *The Italian campaign, 1943–45.* New York: Praeger.

ALEXANDER THE GREAT (Alexander III) [356–323 B.C.]

Alexander III, King of Macedonia from 336 to 323 B.C., was, quite literally, a legend in his own time. His accomplishments were so unusual and so far removed from those of ordinary men that within his lifetime he achieved a sort of superhuman status, and the process continued after his death. He was a very complex individual, and there is sufficient evidence to see a man who was at one and the same time a visionary, a dreamer, a shrewd politician, and a brilliant military commander. His profound impact on human history is undeniable; he changed the world.

Early Life

Alexander was born in the summer of 356 B.C. to King Philip II of Macedonia and his queen, Olympias. The marriage of Philip and Olympias seems to have been a love match as well as a political arrangement, but the passion died soon after Alexander's birth. Olympias was the second of Philip's seven wives, and a deep hatred developed between them and lasted for as long as they both lived. Nevertheless, Alexander seems to have been genuinely devoted to both of his parents. There are many charming anecdotes told about Alexander's childhood, most of them of questionable validity, but they all seem to indicate an extremely precocious child who learned quickly and was not anxious to remain a child any longer than necessary. When Alexander was about 13, his father decided that he needed nothing less than the famed philosopher Aristotle as his tutor. When he was 16, Alexander was sufficiently skilled and trusted by his father to be given his own army command. Two years later, in 338 B.C., he commanded the victorious right wing of the Macedonian army at the fateful battle of Chaeronea, which confirmed Philip's total mastery of Greece. When Philip was assassinated in 336 B.C. (by one of his bodyguards with a private grudge), Alexander, now 20, was hailed as king without opposition. Nevertheless, as a precaution, he brought about the deaths—by execution or murder—of all possible pretenders.

Preparations for the Invasion of Persia

Philip had been planning the invasion of Persia for several years. Indeed, if he had not been overshadowed historically by his more famous son, his own accomplishments might have entitled him to be called Philip the Great.

Early in his reign, Philip had reformed the Macedonian army into a highly disciplined fighting force equipped with 4.1-meter-long (14-foot-long) pikes (called sarissas [they may have been even longer than this]), which easily overwhelmed the traditional armies of the Greek city-states; yet he was also an able diplomat who rarely had to use his army. After the battle of Chaeronea, Philip forcibly united the Greek city-states into an unequal alliance, called by historians the League of Corinth after the city where the arrangements were made. Philip was the leader of the league with full military command and power to demand troop commitments from each member.

Soon after Philip's assassination, Alexander marched south into Greece with his army and demanded to be installed in his father's place. The demand was not refused. Alexander was tested early in his kingship. Semicivilized Thracian tribes that had been subdued by Philip fought to reassert their independence, believing that with the powerful king of Macedonia dead, they could easily overwhelm a mere boy of 20. Alexander surprised them with the rapidity of his movement and quickly subdued them. Many of the Greek city-states also sought to reassert their independence, and the result was that Alexander destroyed the city of Thebes. These events delayed his carrying out Philip's plan to invade the Persian Empire. He finally crossed into Asia in the spring of 334 B.C. An advance party had been sent over two years earlier and controlled the crossing of the Hellespont (Dardanelles).

REASONS FOR THE INVASION

Alexander, carrying out the plans his father had already formed, made such alterations or adaptations as he thought necessary. The intentions of Philip, and later Alexander, are the subject of much speculation by historians. Philip's invasion of the Persian Empire may have had limited goals—the conquest of Asia Minor, the coast of which was inhabited by Greek-speaking people—or they may have been more extensive. Alexander probably planned much more than the conquest of Asia Minor from the beginning, although whether he planned as much as he actually accomplished is debatable.

An invasion of Persia had been a subject much talked about among Greeks for two generations. Greece was overcrowded and underemployed, and Persia was the traditional enemy since the Persian invasions in the early part of the fifth century. It was also obvious to the Greeks, including Philip, that the Persian Empire was in a state of advanced decay with serious internal problems. Indeed, Darius III, the Persian king at the time of Alexander's crossing, was a usurper who had acquired the throne only three years earlier. The opportunity was simply there.

Resources, Organization, and Planning

Alexander's conquest of the Persian Empire was a carefully planned operation. In addition to the fearsome Macedonian phalanx of heavily armed infantry with their sarissas, well drilled and very maneuverable, his cavalry was equally well trained and always deployed to cover the vulnerable flanks of the phalanx. His army included competent engineers for siege warfare, which he used to great effect. His logistics and intelligence operations, although not glamorous, were crucial to his success, and he seems to have appreciated the importance of this kind of support. He had no fleet worthy of the name, but overcame Persian seapower by defeating the Persian fleet on land: he simply overran all of its Mediterranean naval bases. For this early part of the campaign, the presence of the Athenian fleet was useful, but perhaps more as a hostage for the good behavior of Athens than for any operational necessity. Alexander was always outnumbered, yet he never lost a battle because of his combination of good intelligence, astute deployments, skillful maneuvers, and more than a little daring. He was willing to try what was not expected of him.

Conquest of Persia and Egypt

The Battle at the Granicus River in northern Asia Minor was Alexander's first encounter with Persian military forces (see Fig. 1). The Persian plan was apparently to expend all possible effort to kill Alexander himself and thus behead the opposing army. That was not successful, and the Persians were unable to withstand the sudden assault of the Macedonian forces in a bold and skillful river crossing.

For the rest of the year, Alexander continued his march down the coast of Asia Minor, in many cases accepting the submission of the cities along the coast; in some cases it was necessary to lay siege to the cities—always successfully. During the winter months, he campaigned in the interior of Asia Minor and brought under his control some isolated tribes that had not even acknowledged the suzerainty of the Persian king.

The next major encounter with the Persians was the Battle of Issus in Cilicia, where Darius III was himself present. The king's presence did not make his troops fight any better against Alexander, and he fled the scene.

Alexander continued down the coast and was delayed by the siege of Tyre for most of the year 332 B.C. (Tyre was an extremely well-fortified island city and Persia's

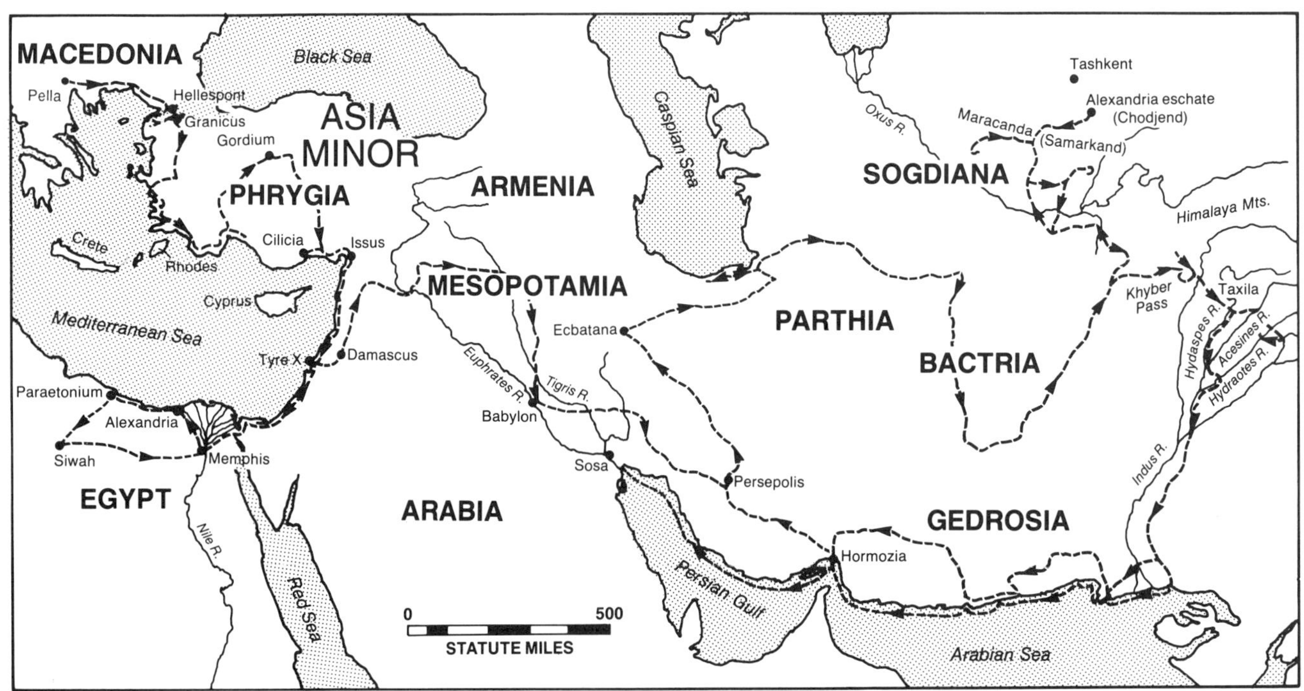

Figure 1. Route of Alexander's army (334–323 B.C.).

principal naval base.) The city refused to submit. Alexander's conduct of the siege of Tyre was indicative of his unorthodox character, and it shows his frequent recourse to engineering skills. Alexander determined that the siege of Tyre would be more likely to succeed if Tyre were not an island; therefore, he put his troops and other manpower to work building a causeway from the mainland to the island. It was a time-consuming process, but when he was finished Tyre was connected to the mainland, and it remains so today. It took seven months, but the city finally fell in July of 332 B.C. amid much slaughter by exhausted Macedonian soldiers.

Alexander continued on to begin his conquest of Egypt, where he was happily received by the Egyptians, who were willing to trade a Persian master for a Greek. While in Egypt, he made arrangements for the building of a city, to be called Alexandria, that would be located at the westernmost outlet of the Nile River. This city, begun in 331 B.C., soon became the greatest city of the ancient world.

Pursuit of King Darius

Technically, Persia was still ruled by Darius III. The empire had not fallen and would not until Darius had been captured or killed. Having captured all Persian dominions in the Mediterranean, Alexander left Egypt to pursue Darius into Mesopotamia.

The Battle of Gaugamela took place on 1 October 331 B.C. (the date is secured by a lunar eclipse). This was the largest battle Alexander fought and it proved decisive for the campaign. With only about 47,000 men, Alexander was heavily outnumbered. Darius had assembled an army of more than 200,000 men and had every possible resource at his disposal, including scythed chariots. However, the discipline and training of the Macedonian army, applied in Alexander's brilliant battle plan, prevailed, and Darius fled the field of battle.

Alexander proceeded at leisure to the Persian capitals of Babylon and Persepolis, and whether by accident or design, the royal palace at Persepolis was burned to the ground.

After consolidating control of central Persia, Alexander resumed the pursuit of Darius, who had fled north to Sogdiana and Bactria. As Alexander and his cavalry escort were closing in on Darius, the Persian king was murdered by one of his noblemen, Bessus. Alexander soon caught up with Bessus and had him tortured and executed. There was now no rival claimant for the throne of the Persian Empire. Alexander, king of Macedonia, leader of the Greek league, was now also king of Persia. He would have several other titles before he died.

Campaigns in Afghanistan and Central Asia

Alexander now marched into the Persian provinces of Sogdiana and Bactria (modern Afghanistan, Turkmenistan, and Uzbekistan). The local tribes were more difficult than any people he had encountered on his journey. In one encounter, the inhabitants took refuge at a place called the Sogdian Rock. It was surrounded by sheer cliffs and the leader, Oxyartes, challenged Alexander to reach him at the top of the rock. Alexander called for volunteers to scale the rock, and after that demonstration, Oxyartes and his people surrendered to Alexander. The endeavor had been sufficiently difficult that Alexander thought it prudent to cement the new friendship with the Sogdians by marrying the daughter of the chief, a girl named Roxane, who would bear him a son (born a few months after Alexander's death).

Alexander marched north into Central Asia, crossing both the Oxus and the Jaxartes rivers, decisively defeating and subduing the wild Scythian tribes in that region.

Returning south to Sogdiana, Alexander marched east into what was called India (modern Pakistan, the Punjab area); again he relied on his engineers to defeat the stubborn hill people. A large group had taken refuge in the Rock of Aornos, which was a sheer rock separated from a neighboring hill by a ravine. Alexander simply ordered earth to be moved until the ravine was filled and he could erect a ramp to the top of the rock, at which point the inhabitants surrendered.

War Elephants

Alexander apparently crossed the Khyber Pass and then crossed the Indus River. At the Hydaspes River (a tributary of the Indus) he encountered an Indian force led by their king, Porus, a majestic figure who was reputedly seven feet tall. More impressive than Porus, however, was his use of elephants in warfare. This was the first time the Macedonians had encountered elephants in battle, but by sheer discipline and bravery, as well as excellent tactical moves by Alexander, they won that battle as well. Alexander learned the usefulness of elephants in this encounter, and so did his staff officers, many of whom would later become kings in their own right. Use of the elephant in warfare would become common in the next century.

Mutiny at the Hyphasis River

Alexander then continued his march eastward. But at a small river called the Hyphasis, another Indus tributary, Alexander's troops mutinied. Many of them were veterans who had been with him for fully eight years now, and they had gone as far as they wanted to go. They had conquered the Persian Empire and more, and they saw little need to go on. With great disappointment, Alexander relented and agreed to lead them back home—but he took them home the hard way. They marched and sailed south along the Indus to near modern Karachi. There he built a fleet that he sent westward along the coast of Baluchistan to the Persian Gulf, where it was to rejoin the army near Susa. Meanwhile, Alexander led his army overland through the desert, no doubt planning to secure provisions for the fleet when it reached the shore. The army and the fleet soon lost contact, however, and there was great loss of life on the march through the desert.

Alexander and the remnants of his army finally returned to Susa in 324 B.C. There he took a second wife, Barsine, the daughter of the late King Darius, to cement his position as king of Persia. At the same ceremony, 80 of his officers took Persian wives, and 10,000 of his troops married local women. This was a symbolic attempt to establish the unity of his empire, an empire composed of Macedonians, Greeks, Persians, and many other peoples. The marriages, in general, did not long outlive Alexander.

Death of Alexander

Alexander returned to Babylon early in 323 B.C. and busied himself with administrative details and plans for future expeditions. He became ill in the spring and slowly worsened. He died on 11 June 323 B.C., probably of pernicious malaria. The legend that he died after a roisterous drinking bout is almost certainly inaccurate.

Problems in the Empire

Alexander was not yet 33 years old when he died. It is natural to wonder what more he might have accomplished had he lived, and there were many problems with which he would have had to deal. Many of the governors and other officials he had appointed had become corrupt and disloyal. Although his officers and troops remained fiercely loyal to him to the end, there were grumblings. The occasional conspiracies that arose against Alexander were dealt with rather harshly. On one occasion, not long before his death, he ordered the execution of his boyhood friend on a charge of treason, and also ordered the execution of the man's father Parmenio—who had been an important staff officer—just to be safe. Many of the Macedonians were displeased with Alexander's growing tendencies to adopt Persian practices and even Persian dress. Yet most of them grudgingly obeyed when instructed to prostrate themselves before their king, something no Macedonian had ever done. The Greek city-states were quite restive because Alexander had insisted that each city take back all of its political exiles, which caused no small amount of political turmoil. He also asked that he be deified and worshiped as a god, something that met with derisive compliance. It remains open to speculation whether a great military commander and an inspired leader could have solved such problems.

Assessment

Alexander changed the world—of that there is no doubt. He changed the political situation, military practices, and the economy. When he was born, the civilized world consisted of the mighty Persian Empire and the independent but very small Greek city-states, with the inconsequential small kingdom of Macedonia on its fringe. Shortly after his death, the political arrangement of the civilized world consisted of three major kingdoms, a few minor independent kingdoms, inconsequential Greek city-states that were under the sovereignty of one of the successor kingdoms, and, significantly, some people called Romans beginning to make their mark in the west. When Alexander was born, strategy was almost unknown and tactics were crude. It was rare for any military encounter to involve more than ten thousand armed men on each side; siege warfare was primitive, and naval activity had not changed for several centuries. After Alexander's death, his successors frequently waged war with 50,000 or more armed soldiers on each side, often mercenaries. Siege warfare under Alexander reached a sophistication not equaled in the West until modern times. He even began a ship design and building program that would result in the large supergalleys of the Hellenistic age. His conquest of the Persian Empire opened up economic opportunities for industrious Greeks, and his dispersal of the hoarded Persian treasure spread wealth unevenly throughout the civilized world and caused considerable inflation. Greek became the common language throughout the civilized world and remained so for over a thousand years in many places. Thus, the Romans learned the Greek language and culture when they eventually conquered most of what had been Alexander's empire.

JANICE J. GABBERT

SEE ALSO: History, Ancient Military; Persian Empire; Siege; Strategy.

Bibliography

Some contemporary accounts are preserved in the *Anabasis of Alexander* by Flavius Arrianus, written in the second century A.D., and Arrian is probably the best source for Alexander. Quintus Curtius Rufus also wrote a useful history of Alexander in the first century A.D. Also useful for personal anecdotes is Plutarch's *Life of Alexander*. Modern literature on Alexander is extensive; a complete overview can be found in the *Cambridge Ancient History*, vol. 6 (Cambridge, 1927).

Adcock, R. E. 1957. *The Greek and Macedonian art of war*. Berkeley, Calif.: Univ. of California Press.

Bosworth, A. B. 1980. *A historical commentary on Arrian's history of Alexander*. London: Oxford Univ. Press.

Engels, D. 1978. *Alexander the great and the logistics of the Macedonian army*. Berkeley, Calif.: Univ. of California Press.

Fox, R. L. 1980. *The search for Alexander*. Boston: Little, Brown.

Fuller, J. F. C. 1960. *The generalship of Alexander the great*. New Brunswick, N.J.: Rutgers Univ. Press.

Hammond, N. G. L. 1981. *Alexander the great: King, commander, and statesman*. Park Ridge, N.J.: Noyes Press.

Holt, F. L. 1988. *Alexander the great and Bactria: The formation of a Greek frontier in central Asia*. Leiden: E. J. Brill.

Tarn, W. W. 1948. *Alexander the great*. Boston: Beacon Press.

Warry, J. 1980. *Warfare in the classical world*. New York: St. Martin's Press.

Wilcken, U. 1967. *Alexander the great*. Trans. G. C. Richards. New York: W. W. Norton.

ALGERIA, POPULAR AND DEMOCRATIC REPUBLIC OF

The Algerian armed forces have their origin in the struggle for independence from France in the 1950s and early 1960s. The major role played in that struggle by insurgent armed forces has in turn led to a major political role for the armed forces in independent Algeria. Algeria has not been involved in any long-term major military conflicts since independence in 1962. Algeria's main rival for power and influence in the region is Morocco, and these two nations have had border disputes in the past.

Power Potential Statistics

Area: 2,381,740 square kilometers (919,590 sq. mi.)
Population: 26,288,200
Total Active Armed Forces: 125,500 (0.477% of pop.)
Gross Domestic Product: US$54 billion (1990 est.)
Annual Defense Expenditure: US$857 million (1.8% of GDP, 1991 est.)
Iron and Steel Production:
Crude steel: 1.710 million metric tons (1988)
Pig iron: 1.1 million metric tons (1986)
Fuel Production:
Coal: 0.008 million metric tons (1985)
Crude oil: 52 million metric tons (1989)
Natural gas: 50,000 million cubic meters (1985)
Electrical Power Output: 14,900 million kwh (1990)
Merchant Marine: 75 vessels; 903,179 gross registered tons
Civil Air Fleet: 42 major transport aircraft; 134 usable airfields (53 with permanent-surface runways); 3 with runways over 3,659 meters (12,000 ft.); 30 with runways 2,440–3,659 meters (8,000–12,000 ft.); 66 with runways 1,220–2,440 meters (4,000–8,000 ft.).

For the most recent information, the reader may refer to the following annual publications:
The Military Balance. International Institute for Strategic Studies. London: Brassey's (UK).
The Statesman's Year-Book. New York: St. Martin's Press.
The World Factbook. Central Intelligence Agency. Washington, D.C.: Brassey's (US).

History

At the time of the conquest of Algeria by the French between 1830 and 1842 there was no real sense of nationhood. Algerian troops, serving in formations with French officers, served in the French army and won particular distinction in World War I; during World War II, two of four divisions in Gen. Alphonse Juin's Free French expeditionary force in Italy were Algerian. In the years after World War II, Algerians began to develop a national identity, and open warfare between the French and the Algerian FLN (*Front de Libération Nationale*) began in 1954. The Algerian War for Independence eventually involved half the French army, and cost 10,000 French soldiers and 70,000 Algerians dead. The conflict was complicated by the presence in Algeria of nearly 1,000,000 *pied-noires,* French settlers of modest means, many of whom had lived in Algeria for generations. In the long run, despite the adamant and violent resistance of some elements in the French army, *pied-noire* interests were sacrificed for the sake of a permanent tenable settlement, and the French gave Algeria independence on 3 July 1962.

Algeria's history since independence has been generally peaceful, but the armed forces have seen some action. A major Berber revolt in the Kabylia Mountains (between Algiers and Constantine) in October 1963 provided the spark for a major but short-lived border war with Morocco between 13 and 30 October 1963. Morocco has remained Algeria's principal rival in the area, and partly for that reason Algerian governments have generally favored the Soviets while Morocco has sided with the United States and Western Europe. Algeria, as a member of the Arab League, sent a small expeditionary force to Egypt on 29 May 1967 just prior to the outbreak of the Six Day War (1–6 June). Over the last two decades, Algeria has lent considerable support, notably sanctuaries and supplies, to the Polisario guerrillas fighting against the Moroccans in Western Sahara, thereby harassing the Moroccans at little cost to themselves.

The worldwide decline in oil prices in the late 1980s has brought hard times to Algeria. Partly as a response to its inability to maintain high levels of social spending, the government has introduced economic and political reforms, and conducted open parliamentary elections but the economic situation remains poor.

The success of the fundamentalist Islamic parties in elections in January 1992 led to a coup d'état by the armed forces to forestall an Islamic regime, which would have undone much of the FLN's social reforms. The Islamic parties remain restive and are a powerful political force.

Politico-Military Background and Policy

Algeria's policy historically has been one of aggressive support of revolutionary movements tempered by realistic caution. Algeria has supported several wars of liberation against regimes it views as reactionary, racist, or imperialist, and has given considerable backing to the cause of the Palestine Liberation Organization (PLO). The Algerians have also played a growing role in the Arab League. Although the Algerian armed forces were originally volunteer forces, the manpower demands of Algerian security compelled the government to decree two years of compulsory military service for all 19-year-old males beginning in April 1968.

Strategic Problems

During most of the years since independence, Algeria has not gotten along well with neighboring Tunisia and Morocco. In recent years, however, the Algerians and their neighbors have begun to see possibilities for cooperation, and recent relations between the three states of the Maghreb have been relatively good. The domestic unrest in

Algeria (September–October 1988) occasioned by necessary, but highly unpopular, austerity measures after years of economic mismanagement, has weakened the government's authority.

Defense Industry

Algeria produces virtually no weapons of its own, although it does apparently manufacture small-arms ammunition. The bulk of its materiel has been imported from the former Soviet bloc countries.

Alliances

Algeria is a member of the Arab League, the Organization of Arab Petroleum-Exporting Countries (OAPEC), the Organization of African Unity (OAU), and the Organization of Petroleum-Exporting Countries (OPEC). It has no clear military alliances with any other nations at this time, although the former Soviet navy had been given access to Algerian ports, perhaps in return for past weapons shipments.

Defense Structure

The supreme commander of Algeria's armed forces is the president of the republic. He is assisted in this role by the Higher Council of Defense, which includes the cabinet ministers for defense, interior, and foreign affairs as well as a parliamentary representative and two other officials named by the president. Because the current president, Col. Chadli Bendjedid, is at the same time the leader of the only functioning political party (the FLN), in actual practice the president deals directly with the heads of the armed services and with the general staff.

(For an explanation of the abbreviations and symbols used in the following section of military statistics, see the list of Abbreviations and Acronyms in each volume.)

Total Armed Forces

Active: 125,500 (70,000 conscripts). Terms of service: Army only 18 months (6 months basic, 1 year civil projects).
Reserves: Army: some 150,000, to age 50.

ARMY: 107,000 (70,000 conscripts).
6 Military Regions.
3 armd bde (3 tk, 1 mech, 1 arty, 1 engr bn, recce coy, ATK, log bn).
8 mech bde (3 mech, 1 tk, 1 arty, 1 engr bn, 1 recce, ATK, log bn).
9 mot inf bde (3 inf, 1 tk, 1 arty, 1 engr bn).
1 AB/SF bde.
31 indep inf, 4 para bn.
7 indep arty, 5 AD bn.
4 engr bn.
12 coy desert troops.
Equipment:
MBT: some 960: 330 T-54/-55, 330 T-62, 300 T-72.
Recce: 120 BRDM-2.
AIFV: 915: 690 BMP-1, 225 BMP-2.
APC: 460 BTR-50/-60.
Towed arty: 415: 122mm: 15 D-74, 100 M-1931/37, 40 M-30, 190 D-30; 130mm: 10 M-46; 152mm: 60 M-1937.
SP arty: 200: 122mm: 150 2S1; 152mm: 25 ISU-152, 25 2S3.
MRL: 128: 122mm: 48 BM-21; 140mm: 50 BM-14-16; 240mm: 30 BM-24.
Mortars: 120mm: 120 M-43, 60 M-160, 150 M-1937.
ATGW: 40 AT-3 Sagger (some SP/BRDM-2), Milan.
RCL: 178: 82mm: 120 B-10; 107mm: 58 B-11.
ATK guns: 296: 57mm: 156 ZIS-2; 85mm: 80 D-44; 100mm: 10 T-12, 50 SU-100 SP.
AD guns: 880: 14.5mm: 65 ZPU-2/-4; 20mm: 100; 23mm: 100 ZU-23 towed, 210 ZSU-23-4 SP; 37mm: 150 M-1939; 57mm: 75 S-60; 85mm: 20 KS-12; 100mm: 150 KS-19; 130mm: 10 KS-30.
SAM: SA-7/-8/-9.

NAVY: 6,500. Bases: Mers el Kebir, Algiers, Annaba, Jijel.
Submarines: 2: 2 Sov Kilo with 533mm TT; (plus 2 Sov Romeo† that may be used for trg).
Frigates: 3 Mourad Reis (Sov Koni) with 2 × 12 ASW RL.
Patrol and Coastal Combatants: 20:
Corvettes: 3 Rais Hamidou (Sov Nanuchka II) with 4 × SS-N-2C Styx SSM.
Missile Craft: 11 Osa with 4 × SS-N-2 SSM.
Patrol: 6.
Coastal: 2 local-built C-58 PFC.
Inshore: about 3 El Yadekh PCI, 1 ⟨.
Mine Warfare: 1 Sov T-43 MSC.
Amphibious: 3: 2 Kalaat beni Hammad LST, capacity 240 tps, 10 tk, 1 hel; 1 Polnocny LSM, capacity 100 tps, 5 tk.

Coast Guard (under naval control): 500; about 6 El Yadekh PCI, 16 PFI ⟨.

AIR FORCE: 12,000; 241 cbt ac, 58 armed hel.
FGA: 3 sqn: 1 with 30 MiG-17; 1 with 17 MiG-23BN/MF; 1 with est. 6 Su-24.
Fighter: 10 sqn: 6 with 95 MiG-21MF/bis; 1 with 14 MiG-25; 3 with 40 MiG-23B/E.
Recce: 1 sqn with 3 MiG-25R.
MR: 1 sqn with 2 Super King Air B-200T.
Transport: 2 sqn with 6 An-12, 10 C-130H, 4 C-130H-30, 3 SE-210, 1 Aero Commander 680 (survey); *VIP:* 1 Il-18, 2 Falcon 20, 3 Gulfstream III, 2 Super King Air 200, 4 Il-76, 3 F-27.
Helicopters: 7 sqn: *Attack:* 4 sqn with 38 Mi-24, 1 with 20 Mi-8/-17. *Transport:* (hy): 1 sqn with 1 Mi-4, 1 Mi-6, 8 Mi-8/-17; (med): 1 sqn with 4 Mi-6, 1 Mi-8/-17.
Training: 3 MiG-15, 25* MiG-17, 3* MiG-21U, 5* MiG-23U, 3* MiG-25U, 6 T-34C, 19 Yak-11, 24 L-39, plus 24 ZLIN-142 in store.
AAM: AA-2.
AD guns: 3 bde+: 85mm, 100mm, 130mm.
SAM: 3 regt: 1 with 30 SA-2, 2 with SA-6, 21 SA-3.

FORCES ABROAD
UN and Peacekeeping:
Angola (UNAVEM II): observers.

PARAMILITARY
Gendarmerie: (Ministry of Interior): 23,000; 44 Panhard AML-60/M-3 APC, 28 Mi-2 hel.

Future

Algeria appears to have reached a crossroads since the early 1980s, marked by a rapprochement with Morocco and by a more pragmatic economic and foreign policy. The nation will certainly continue to champion the cause of Arab nationalism, and is unlikely suddenly to become openly friendly with the West, but waning regional tension will reduce foreign support for domestic dissident groups. As a result, the armed forces will probably retain their close ties to the former Soviet bloc, but the likelihood of conflict in the Maghreb will decrease as the states of that region realize that the ties that bind them are stronger than the issues that divide them.

David L. Bongard
Trevor N. Dupuy

See Also: Arab Conquests; Arab League; France; Morocco; North Africa; Tunisia.

Bibliography

American University. 1979. *Algeria: A country study.* Washington, D.C.: Government Printing Office.
Horne, A. 1977. *A savage war of peace.* New York: Viking Penguin.
Hunter, B., ed. 1991. *The statesman's year-book, 1991–92.* New York: St. Martin's Press.
International Institute for Strategic Studies. 1991. *The military balance, 1991–1992.* London: Brassey's.

ALLENBY, EDMUND HENRY HYNMAN (1861–1936)

At the close of World War I, Gen. Edmund Henry Hynman Allenby (Fig. 1) was the most accomplished and respected British general. His 1918 Palestine campaign is considered one of the most brilliantly conceived and executed successes of the war. The final British offensive in the campaign, initiated by the Battle of Megiddo, was a flawless operation that included the last great horse cavalry battle. It is with justification that Allenby, the architect of the victory, is considered the last great horse cavalry commander. Known for his violent temper and equally violent verbal reprimands, he was respected, if not liked, by those who served under him.

Background and Early Career

Allenby was born 23 April 1861 in East Anglia, of relatively affluent parents. He decided on a military career after failing to pass the Indian Civil Service exam. In February 1881 he entered the Royal Military College at Sandhurst, and upon completing his studies in December 1881 he received a commission in the Sixth Inniskilling Dragoons, stationed in South Africa at the time. He saw considerable service between 1883 and 1888 in South Africa and at-

Figure 1. Edmund Henry Hynman Allenby. (Source: U.S. Library of Congress)

tended the Staff College at Camberley during 1896–97. At the outset of the Boer War in 1899, Allenby returned to South Africa, where he gained valuable experience in the mobile, hard-hitting style of warfare employed in the conflict. At the end of the war he returned to Britain, where he was promoted to colonel and placed in command of the Fifth Lancers. His competence and proven ability as a cavalry leader were largely responsible for his rise to the rank of major general by the spring of 1910 and his appointment as Inspector-General of Cavalry, a position he held until the outbreak of World War I.

Early World War I Service

Allenby took command of the Cavalry Division of the British Expeditionary Force in France during the battles of August and September 1914. Between 29 October and 11 November Allenby's Cavalry Corps (another division had arrived in the meantime from Britain) was heavily engaged south of Ypres by German forces attempting to take the channel ports. Allenby then assumed command of Seventh Corps from Gen. Sir Hubert Plumer in May 1915, at the height of the Second Battle of Ypres. Eight months later he took command of the Third Army from Gen. Sir Charles Monro, who was assigned to the Dardanelles Front. The

Third Army was relatively inactive during the Somme offensive of 1916, but in April 1917 it took part in the Arras offensive, making the largest one-day gain on the western front since 1914. But the army quickly lost momentum, and the offensive gradually ground to a halt.

Palestine Campaign of 1917–18

In June 1917 Allenby was sent to Palestine to replace Gen. Sir Archibald Murray as commander of the Egyptian Expeditionary Force (EEF), which to that point had been unsuccessful. Once in command, he used his exceptional leadership and organizational talents to boost morale and prepare the EEF for an offensive against the Turkish Seventh and Eighth Armies in Palestine as soon as cooler temperatures set in. The heavy casualties and poor results on the western front made it vital for morale at home that British troops in Palestine achieve a victory. The British Prime Minister David Lloyd George therefore expected Allenby and his EEF to achieve victory and asked that Jerusalem be taken by Christmas 1917.

The Turks held a heavily fortified position extending from Gaza, on the Mediterranean coast, to Beersheba, approximately 55 kilometers (34 mi.) inland. On 27 October, as a diversion, Allenby opened the offensive with an intense land and sea bombardment of Gaza, while massing the bulk of his force secretly in the vicinity of Beersheba for the main assault. The attack on Beersheba began on 31 October with good results: the city was occupied within 24 hours. The assault on Gaza began on the night of 1–2 November, and Gaza was occupied by the British on the 7th. The retreating Turks occupied a new defensive position at Junction Station, which was taken on 15 November after a two-day fight. The Turks continued their retreat, eventually evacuating Jerusalem, which was occupied by the British on 9 December.

In early 1918 much of Allenby's force was sent to France to help contain the German spring offensives, leaving the EEF depleted of many of its veteran troops. Reinforcements coming from India and Mesopotamia had to be trained and organized throughout the summer. By mid-September Allenby was ready to launch a carefully planned offensive that would drive Turkey from the war.

A series of feints and deception plans carried out by the British caused the Turks to believe the main blow would come on their left flank, north of Jerusalem, and to prepare accordingly. Reversing the procedure of the Gaza battle, the actual attack was launched against the Turkish right on 19 September, achieving complete surprise. A breach in the line was made by the British infantry, and the waiting cavalry pushed through, making deep penetrations, while the Royal Flying Corps harassed the retreating Turkish columns. By 20 September British cavalry spearheads had entered the Plain of Esdraelon, near Megiddo, and shifted east, cutting off retreating elements of the Turkish Seventh and Eighth Armies. Allenby continued the pressure on the Turks as British troops entered Damascus on 1 October. In late October, realizing that any further resistance was impossible, Turkey began to make peace overtures, and on 30 October an armistice was signed.

Postwar Service and Later Life

In March 1919 Allenby was appointed Special High Commissioner for Egypt and was instrumental in Egypt's move from protectorate to sovereignty. Allenby's final days in Egypt were clouded by the murder of the sirdar, Sir Lee Stack, and a confrontation with Foreign Secretary Austen Chamberlain, over which he ultimately resigned. He left Egypt in June 1925 and returned to England to spend the rest of his life in retirement. He died in London on 14 May 1936, leaving no heirs (his only son, Michael, had been killed in France in 1917). For his accomplishments in the war, he had been promoted to field marshal and raised to the peerage as Viscount Allenby of Megiddo and Felixstowe (the ancient city of Megiddo, the Armageddon of the Bible, was chosen as the name of the climactic battle of the Palestine campaign).

ARNOLD C. DUPUY

SEE ALSO: Cavalry; World War I.

Bibliography

Dupuy, R. E., and T. N. Dupuy. 1970. *Encyclopedia of military history.* New York: Harper and Row.

Gardner, B. 1965. *Allenby of Arabia.* New York: Coward-McCann.

Mansfield, P. 1971. *The British in Egypt.* New York: Holt, Rinehart and Winston.

Savage, R. 1926. *Allenby of Armageddon.* Indianapolis: Bobbs-Merrill.

Wavell, A. P. 1940. *Allenby: A study in greatness.* London: George G. Harrap.

ALLIANCE, MILITARY AND POLITICAL

An alliance is a long-term politico-military relationship between two or more nations designed to improve their security through the aggregation of state power. In its pure form it may be considered a classic "if . . . then" proposition through which the parties agree to take certain actions—ranging from vague promises of military assistance to specific pledges to declare war or send troops, if a given event takes place—such as an armed attack, subversion, or threat of some kind (the *casus foederis* or *casus belli*).

Traditionally this promise is formalized in a treaty (public or secret) between the parties. Paul Schroeder (1976) defines an alliance as "a treaty binding two or more independent states to come to each other's aid with armed force under circumstances specified in the *casus foederis* article of the treaty." Modern alliances are also often characterized by ongoing political and defense cooperation designed both to improve military capabilities and reinforce the pact's deterrent effect. This cooperation may include foreign military and economic aid or arms sales, the construction of military facilities by one ally in the other's country, joint planning and military maneuvers, high-level contact between their political and military leaders, and the establishment of ongoing combined military commands and organizations with a full range of political organs and military infrastructure.

Typologies and Varieties of Alliance

The extraordinary variety of alliances and their rapidly evolving character in recent times makes a precise definition difficult. Alliance typologies abound in the literature, but no standard categorization is generally accepted. Alliances may be bilateral or multilateral, permanent or temporary, mutual or one-sided, broad or limited, equal or unequal, offensive or defensive, formal or informal, specific or vague. They can be grouped according to the kinds of interest that underlie them (identical, complementary, or ideological), their degree of formality and specificity (de jure, de facto, or apparent), the number and kind of states they encompass, their duration and effectiveness, their decision-making processes, the kind of obligations assumed by the parties, and on many other grounds.

As Roger Dingman (1979) points out, there is no standard definition of the term among statesmen or historians; even distinguishing alliances from similar arrangements is problematical:

1. Alignments, the most general analog, are less intentional and explicit than alliances, and may be merely a simple "coming into line" of states' political postures without any purposeful or explicit relationship between them.

2. Coalitions are more temporary than alliances, and are undertaken for a specific and limited purpose. This term is often applied to relationships formed expressly for prosecution of a war that has already begun. States in coalitions (like parties in coalition governments) may thus have opposing interests in many areas.

3. Ententes, historically often a prelude to alliances, are soft or weak understandings based on unwritten conventions or declarations for an unspecified period of time. They are likely to be of a more general nature than an alliance, although some writers argue that they go deeper than alliances to include a broad sharing of goals and perceptions (Kimball 1978); the Triple Entente of World War I was an alliance in all but name.

4. On the multilateral side, it is clear that groupings like the North Atlantic Treaty Organization (NATO) and the former Warsaw Pact, properly considered examples of collective defense, are different from collective security arrangements like the League of Nations and the United Nations. The latter consist of mutually agreed upon provisions for dealing with conflict among their members, while the former (like bilateral alliances) are aimed at attack from outside and usually have an external enemy in mind. There are also multilateral security groupings which include collective security and defense characteristics but are not alliances (e.g., the Organization of American States [OAS] and the Arab League), and regional agreements which give a guarantee to outside parties (like the agreements guarding the straits to the Black Sea, or the Southeast Asia Treaty Organization's protection of South Vietnam as a protocolary state).

Alliances and interstate security relationships have taken on a different character in the postcolonial era of superpower nuclear parity than they possessed even in the immediate postwar years. A practice that goes back at least to ancient China and the city-states of classical Greece, alliances became a key policy instrument in the bipolar cold war confrontation—used for containment by NATO and for socialist solidarity by the Soviet bloc. Increasingly, however, the superpowers seem to view their alliances as artifacts of "imperial overstretch" or "adventurism" which provide little security against the missile-driven intercontinental nuclear threat, while the majority of developing nations fear that alliances may compromise recently won national sovereignty, expose them to nuclear risk, and offer domestic opponents political ammunition.

Although it is possible that the use of alliances may decline, "wherever in recorded history a system of multiple sovereignty has existed, some of the sovereign units when involved in conflicts with others have entered into alliances" (Wolfers 1968). Thus, a satisfactory definition must take into account the enormous diversity of the kinds and purposes of alliances, the tools and techniques used for their creation, maintenance, and dissolution, and their characteristics and effects on the international system.

Purposes of Alliance

The fundamental purpose of all alliances is to aggregate state power. Nearly all postwar American realist writers from Hans Morgenthau to Inis Claude view alliances as "a necessary function of the balance of power operating within a multiple state system" (Morgenthau 1968):

> The balance of power system is aptly characterized as an *alliance* system. States struggling for what they regard as appropriate places in the distribution of power discover readily enough that they can enhance their power not only by the "natural" method of building up their own resources, but also by an "artificial" method of linking themselves to the strength of other states. Indeed this is the only method available to the bulk of states in the actual circumstances of modern history. Small states obviously cannot hope individually to balance . . . their great power neighbors; the only active course open to them in the quest for security within a balance of

power system is to seek a position in a grouping of states. . . . (Claude 1962)

As Friedman (1970) puts it, an "alliance combines the capabilities of nation-states . . . essentially to preserve, magnify, or create positions of strength for diplomacy or war." But within this broad purpose of power aggregation, writers and statesmen adduce at least four more specific goals:

War

Although the term *coalition* is used more frequently to denote an alliance formed explicitly to prosecute a war (as in the four engineered by Britain against Napoleon I), alliances, too, have been used for this purpose. That was the case with the first alliance undertaken by the United States, with France in 1778, which after two years of French-assisted war against England, brought France into the war (and the war into Europe) within six months of its signing. It was also the case with the nations which fought World War II, and with the Berlin-Rome Axis and Tripartite Pact preceding that war.

Fighting a war may be offensive or defensive in nature, and alliances similarly may be formed for offensive or defensive purposes. The treaty language of alliances is almost always defensive in character, however, and military preparations differ little whether the intent is to defend against an anticipated attack or initiate one. Hence, analysts can only subdivide war-fighting alliances into defensive or aggressive via the general foreign policy aims and behavior of the states, not from the attributes of their alliance.

Protection Against Attack

Whether or not the Triple Alliance and Triple Entente helped precipitate World War I (see below), there is little question that at least some of the statesmen who formed them were trying to prevent war by presenting an image of combined strength sufficient to deter aggression. This was certainly one of the purposes behind the alliances formed by Pres. Harry S. Truman in the late 1940s (NATO, ANZUS, and the bilateral treaty with Japan), and especially so regarding the military aspects of NATO, which were put in place after the 1950 invasion of South Korea made the threat of armed attack on Europe plausible.

Entirely deterrent alliances often spend most of their effort improving military capabilities, an activity which may appear warlike but which is essential to the credibility of deterrence and even more important if it fails. Moreover, part of the agenda for deterrent alliances is to provide a sense of confidence to weaker allies so that they are less vulnerable to peacetime politico-military-economic pressures from potential adversaries, a job difficult to do from afar without major local defense improvements. Confidence-building, in addition to deterrence, was a major reason for NATO in its 1949 form, as well as for the later Eisenhower-Dulles alliances in the developing nations (SEATO, CENTO, and the Mutual Security Treaties with South Korea and the Republic of China).

Management or Control of the International System

No superpower in the nuclear age wants its allies to be too confident, however, especially if they are located near the other superpower or its allies. As Schroeder (1976) argued, alliances have often been used by great powers as tools for managing the international system in order to reduce the potential for violence. They may wish to restrain reckless junior partners who might provoke larger conflicts, or even to group and conciliate an opponent within an alliance rather than isolating and intimidating him by keeping him outside. For example, the American alliance with Taiwan in 1954 was made at least as much to restrain Chiang Kai-shek from setting off an American war with China by invading the People's Republic as to protect Formosa and the Pescadores from Beijing's assaults. Those limitations were made as explicit as diplomatic language would allow when the U.S. Senate consented to the treaty.

More generally, a great power may simply use alliances based on vague treaty promises as vehicles for regularizing its relationships with a variety of countries and ensuring itself access to their decision-making processes and elites, a purpose served to some extent at least by all of the United States postwar compacts. Control, of course, can work both ways, and smaller states may equally wish to regularize their international relationships. Thomas Schelling (1966) is one of many observers who have noted the paradox of weak allies' control over their stronger partners. Junior allies exercise their influence by threatening to reverse alliances and side with their allies' opponents, by capturing the senior ally's prestige in their cause, by leveraging its decision-making processes and elites, and by providing services the great power would find it difficult to do without.

Force Projection

A powerful motive for many alliances in the post colonial world has been acquisition of access to facilities and bases that a power needs if it is to project military forces to defend its own interests and protect other allies. This contains an Orwellian suggestion that some allies are more equal than others, with these "secondary" or "instrumental" allies being reluctantly taken on so that "primary" allies, those of intrinsic strategic importance, can be defended. Many of the nontreaty security partners acquired by the United States during the Carter and Reagan administrations in the Persian Gulf, Africa, and elsewhere are of this variety, and it is difficult not to connect Soviet support of Vietnam and the PDRY with its use of facilities at Cam Rahn Bay and Aden, respectively.

For the smaller power, this kind of relationship has a different purpose, that of deterrence/attack protection noted above. This illustrates a broader point about alliance purposes: they may differ among parties in the same compact. That may not make much difference, as long as they are complementary and the states' overall foreign policy actions are not too contradictory.

A word should also be said about purposes for which states, contrary to popular wisdom, generally do not ally. Steve Walt (1985) points out that a common ideology does not predispose states to alliance, that strong ideologies are more frequently a cause of divisions, as illustrated by the Sino-Soviet, Sino-Vietnamese, Russo-Albanian, and other communist rifts. Walt also argues that states do not generally ally with, rather than against, a stronger nearby power in the hope of dissuading aggressive intent on its part. Such "bandwagoning" is resorted to only by those who have no other choice, and the geographic distribution of powerful, threatening states across the world allows most governments the opportunity to use alliances for the kind of deterrent "balancing" noted above.

Commitment and Alliance Management

Regardless of its specific purpose or form, the bedrock of any alliance is the commitment of one state to come to the aid of another. If this commitment is to have meaning, it must also restrict the freedom of action of the committed state at least to some degree.

This does not mean that alliances reduce the state's *overall* freedom of action: as noted above, alliances are usually intended to increase a state's capabilities for various diplomatic or military purposes. Even in relations between two allied states directly governed by an alliance, the response to a *casus* does not happen automatically (e.g., the currency-equilibrating effects of the nineteenth-century gold standard) in a crisis. There will always be a decision by the government as to the interpretation of its pledge and the precise nature of its response. Thus, an alliance commitment is not an either/or thing, but a matter of degree.

However, if an alliance is to have meaning, it must predispose the decision makers to some response if the *casus* occurs. The first thing to look for in evaluating an alliance, then, is how that binding force, that restriction on the allied state's freedom of action, may be generated.

The most obvious place to look is the legal obligations springing directly from the language of the written compact. If states are bound by international law, the legal force of the alliance will obviously depend greatly on the breadth of the *casus belli* and the specificity with which the response is defined. The *casus* may be described narrowly, as an armed attack in a particular geographic area (as in most U.S. alliances), perhaps by a specified party; or broadly, as subversion, infiltration, or some other threat. Similarly, the response can be very specific—going to war or delivering a certain number of troops within a certain time period, as in some nineteenth-century European alliances—or very general, as in American promises to respond as it deems necessary (NATO) or in accordance with its constitutional processes (for U.S. Pacific alliances). The more broad and definite the *casus* and the more specific the response, the stronger the legal force of the alliance.

There is ongoing debate about how binding international treaty law really is in an anarchical state system with no enforcement mechanism and extremely weak judicial organs. If the promise is public and recent, whether or not in treaty form, political factors will come into play to reinforce legal ones. As Henry Kissinger wrote regarding his sense of U.S. obligations to Pakistan during the 1971 Indo-Pakistan war:

> The decisions of a great power will be shaped by the requirements of the national interest as perceived at the moment of decision, not only by abstract legal obligations whether vague or precise. . . . But equally a nation that systematically ignores its pledges assumes a heavy burden; its diplomacy will lose the flexibility that comes from a reputation for reliability; it can no longer satisfy immediate pleas from allies by promises of future action. . . . The image of a great nation conducting itself like a shyster looking for legalistic loopholes was not likely to inspire other allies who had signed treaties with us or relied on our expressions in the belief that the words meant approximately what they said. . . . A reputation for unreliability was not something we could afford. (*White House Years*, p. 895)

A nation's words thus have a binding effect quite apart from treaty language, although in a constitutional system it is important to know who has the power in internal law to bind the state. Pledges may be given publicly (or privately) by heads of government or their representatives, either orally (e.g., during state receptions) or in writing (like the Shanghai communique or President Nixon's secret letter to President Thieu of South Vietnam), by parliaments in the law-making process (e.g., the U.S. Taiwan Relations Act of 1979), or through executive agreements—none of which follows the treaty-making requirements and each of which has different legal and political impacts on a commitment.

Other means of commitment, however, may be far more powerful than words. A nation can become physically committed by stationing troops in "tripwire" positions on allied territory so that they will be automatically involved if an attack comes, as have several NATO nations in West Germany and the United States in South Korea. Commitments can be engendered by participation in combined defense organizations and planning (e.g., by the presence of an American general as SACEUR), particularly if they lead to military divisions of labor by which one country becomes physically dependent on its ally for certain aspects of its defense. Economic ties can also have a committing effect if a country must rely on a key commodity supplied by its ally or on sales to allied markets, and to a lesser extent if its citizens or government hold allied debt instruments or own a sizable amount of plant and equipment in the ally's economy. Even a major presence of a state's civilian nationals there may predispose their government to come to the ally's rescue in order to protect them.

Other, less quantifiable factors may also push a government to come to an ally's defense. Many examples show that decision makers become committed by their own behavior; that is, by acting as an ally, particularly if they have responded to past threats or attacks, they come to see themselves as being an ally. One country's past and current support of another through military and economic aid tends to commit the donor, if only because officials are loath to see such investments wasted. Governments in a democratic society may also be pressured to respond by public opinion, particularly if sizable numbers of voters have ethnic, religious, or other ties to an ally (the case of Israel in American policy is illustrative).

That each of these factors has an impact on the strength of alliance commitments underlines the complexity of relationships that in simpler times might have seemed to depend only on the language of a treaty. This complexity in turn makes it extremely difficult for a nation, its allies, and its adversaries to know exactly to whom and to what degree it is committed. It is a sobering conclusion that there is no necessary correspondence among those three views of a given commitment, and thus no clear relationship between commitment, allied confidence, and adversary deterrence. Another point is the extreme difficulty of alliance management, a task in which all of these aspects of allied relationships (except the original treaty) play a part. For although commitments are never involuntary in a strict sense, the various forces which bind states to each other often seem beyond a government's ability fully to understand and regulate.

Characteristics and Effects of Alliances

Alliances have been a frequent subject for scholarly inquiry, not only because of their long and important history in the modern state system, but also because their characteristics are intriguing and their effects open to considerable dispute. Alliances are, after all, first-order foreign policy decisions. Like fundamental or constitutional law, which sets the parameters under which all other laws are made, alliances shape the real and psychological structure of foreign relations around which other policy decisions flow. Although they are a means to an end of greater security, alliances often become ends in themselves. For large states, the permanence of alliances is reinforced by their psychological interconnectedness: a great power's credibility is at stake externally (and its national honor internally) if it abandons its allies. For smaller states, alliances can often involve issues of national identity, especially if (like South Korea or Taiwan) the alliance was a critical part of the country's birth as a nation-state.

This is not to say that alliances never change. Indeed, one of the problematical aspects of depending on alliances for security is whether they can be expected to be there when needed, to last for decades (as has NATO and the American alliance with Japan), or to disintegrate (like SEATO or CENTO). Historians have noted a life cycle in most alliances, a tendency for growth or decay depending on a variety of factors. Certainly the coincidence of the states' interests over time is important, as is their sense of a common threat to those interests. But many writers argue that the underlying complementarity of the societies involved is equally important: common ties of culture, language, economic organization or stage of industrialization, and form of government. Though alliances have on occasion been precursors of permanent international bodies or even confederal nation-states, the more usual pattern is disintegration as the parties' interests and purposes change. What seems clear is that alliances more reflect than preserve the underlying relationship; governments must be ready to alter the terms and conditions of membership as conditions change if the association is to endure.

Statesmen approach alliance policy with respect and ambiguity because the permanence and importance of security commitments is matched by the difficulty of controlling and calculating their effects. At the heart of all alliances there is a paradox: that security is a primary requirement of sovereignty, yet linking one state's fate to that of another as a means of security is a derogation of sovereignty and always involves additional risk. On the one hand, both great and small powers fear that their commitments will involve them against their will in conflicts they might otherwise avoid. On the other hand, the track record of alliances provides little confidence that allies will come to a state's aid when they are needed. Caught by these conflicting pressures, governments often seem uncertain whether they are more fearful of being entrapped by their allies or abandoned by them.

Even if allies can be counted on to respond, there is the further issue of whether the likelihood of their response will be credible enough to enhance deterrence and their aid sufficient to ensure defense. In fact, many analysts have argued a contrary case: that alliances tend to move the world toward war even when their purpose is to move states away from it. Certainly the lesson of 1914 seemed to be that a world divided along the lines of alliance is a dangerous world, one where tensions can build between opposing groups of states and war plans become so interlinked that small conflicts inevitably spread into major conflagrations. That the world since 1945 has avoided hegemonic war in spite of rigid alliance divisions may be attributed either to the special circumstances of 1914 or the sobering impact of nuclear weapons.

The question remains: Do alliances really make states more secure? Given the above considerations, the answer is problematical. If the alliance lasts until it is needed, if the ally does not involve the state in additional conflicts and can be counted on to respond when needed, if the likelihood of that response is credible enough to enhance deterrence, if the divisions in world politics ratified by alliance ties do not cause more wars than they deter—in short, if the costs do not outweigh the benefits—then an affirmative answer may be given. For a great power measuring commitments against resources, the yardstick of cost/benefit analysis may ultimately be determined by the statesman's sense of political leverage, of the degree to which commitments can safely exceed power. Leverage is a psychological phenomenon, impossible to calculate; and so the tendency to be careful is reinforced.

In the modern world all these factors have gone far to end the practice of precise, treaty-based alliances. Today, except for alliances from the postwar years, interstate security relationships tend to fall short of formal alliances as statesmen attempt to fashion ties that combine enough commitment to enhance deterrence with sufficient freedom of action to avoid dangerous involvement. The distinction between alignments, coalitions, and alliances is becoming increasingly blurred by relationships that are cemented by little more than arms sales, facilities construction, and informal promises of support. Whether states can remain committed while retaining their freedom of action is open to question, but such are the alliances of the future.

TERRY L. DEIBEL

SEE ALSO: Arms Trade and Military Assistance; Coalition Warfare; Combined Operations; Deterrence; Strategy, National Security.

Bibliography

Claude, I. L., Jr. 1962 *Power and international relations.* New York: Random House.

Deibel, T. L. 1980. *Commitment in American foreign policy.* Washington, D.C.: National Defense Univ. Press.

———. 1987. Hidden commitments. *Foreign Policy* 67:46–63.

Dingman, R. V. 1979. Theories of, and approaches to, alliance politics. In *Diplomacy: New approaches in history, theory, and policy*, ed. P. G. Lauren, pp. 245–66. New York: Free Press and Macmillan.

Fay, S. B. 1935. Alliance. In *Encyclopaedia of the social sciences*, vol. 2, pp. 3–4. New York: Macmillan.

Friedman, J. L. 1970. *Alliance in international politics.* Boston: Allyn and Bacon.

Holsti, O. R., P. T. Hopmann, and J. D. Sullivan. 1973. *Unity and disintegration in international alliances.* New York: Wiley-Interscience.

Kimball, W. F. 1978. Alliances, coalitions, and ententes. In *Encyclopedia of American foreign policy*, ed. A. DeConde, vol. 1, pp. 1–15. New York: Scribner's.

Morgenthau, H. J. 1968. Alliances. In *The restoration of American politics*, pp. 176–97. Chicago: Univ. of Chicago Press.

Osgood, R. E. 1968. *Alliances and foreign policy.* Baltimore, Md.: Johns Hopkins Univ. Press.

Liska, G. 1962. *Nations in alliance: The limits of interdependence.* Baltimore, Md.: Johns Hopkins Univ. Press.

———. 1968. *Alliances and the Third World.* Baltimore, Md.: Johns Hopkins Univ. Press.

Sabrosky, A. N., ed. 1988. *Alliances in U.S. foreign policy.* Boulder, Colo.: Westview Press.

Schelling, T. C. 1966. *Arms and influence.* New Haven, Conn.: Yale Univ. Press.

Schroeder, P. W. 1976. Alliances, 1815–1945. Weapons of power and tools of management. In *Historical dimensions of national security problems*, ed. K. Knorr, pp. 227–62. Lawrence, Kans.: Univ. Press of Kansas.

U.S. Senate. 1969–70. *United States security agreements and commitments abroad.* 2 vols. Hearings before the Symington Subcommittee of the Committee on Foreign Relations, 91st Congress. Washington, D.C.: Government Printing Office.

Walt, S. M. 1985. Alliance formation and the balance of world power. *International Security* 9:3–43.

Wolfers, A. 1968. Alliances. In *International encyclopedia of the social sciences*, vol. 1, pp. 268–71. New York: Collier-Macmillan.

AMERICAN REVOLUTIONARY WAR

After a decade of controversy concerning the place of the colonies of British North America within the empire and in relation to the home country, hostilities erupted near Boston in April 1775. They continued until September 1783 when the Peace of Paris, resulting in an independent United States of America, was signed. During the revolutionary war, the British sought to subdue American insurgents (who composed only a minority of the population) in the thirteen colonies and who were dispersed over several thousand square miles of largely wooded terrain, more than 4,800 kilometers (3,000 mi.) from the British Isles. Because British policy toward the rebels vacillated between conciliation and subjugation, no consistent strategy was pursued. In 1778 France declared war against Great Britain in support of the Americans. Spain, allied with France but not with the United States, entered the war in 1779; and in 1780 Britain declared war on Holland. Thus, the revolutionary war, originally a rebellion, or civil war, became an international conflict.

Balance Sheet

It appeared that Great Britain, a world power by any criterion, had a decisive advantage over the colonists because of its larger population, and material and military superiority. By contrast, the Americans had no proven continental government, no treasury or credit, no regular army or navy, no military tradition beyond the short service of militia and volunteers, and little experience in continental cooperation of any kind.

INTERNAL DIVISIONS

The American people were fragmented into three groups of roughly equal proportions: the indifferent, the Tories, and the patriots. Class and sectional antagonisms, manifest in disagreements as to wartime objectives, also proved divisive. Only after adoption of the Declaration of Independence (4 July 1776) did a determination to persevere characterize the patriot cause. There were also serious disagreements within the British body politic. The Friends of America (men such as Isaac Barré, Edmund Burke, Charles James Fox, and William Pitt) believed that the rebels were merely protecting their historic rights as Englishmen against the tyranny of King George III. Some of Britain's ablest generals and admirals declined service against the Americans.

The Armies

While the British army was composed of professional regulars trained and disciplined on the European model, the Americans had only their militia tradition and the limited experience gained in the colonial wars on which to build. To confront forces, which grew to about 42,000 British regulars and nearly 30,000 German mercenaries, the Americans organized two sets of forces: the Continental, or national, Army and the various state militias. The Continental Army ranged in size from roughly 5,000 to 20,000, depending on its fortunes. The largest single American field army numbered about 17,000 and was composed of Continentals and militia. By 1778 the Continental Army was reliable and, considering its brief history, surprisingly well trained, but the militia was unpredictable throughout the war. There were notable exceptions, such as at Bunker Hill and Cowpens, where militiamen performed well. South Carolina irregulars under Francis Marion, Andrew Pickens, and Thomas Sumter were especially effective in harassing British outposts, field armies in motion, and lines of supply and communications.

The generalship of both British and American commanders was undistinguished. Service in North America tarnished the reputation of every major British general who fought there: Thomas Gage, William Howe, John Burgoyne, Henry Clinton, and Charles Cornwallis. There were no geniuses among the American generals, but Henry Knox, Daniel Morgan, Nathanael Greene, and George Washington were competent. An enigma, Benedict Arnold showed great promise in the Quebec campaign at Valcour Island and in the Saratoga campaign, but his name became synonymous with treason when he defected to the British. Commander in chief George Washington's leadership was crucial to American military success. Although he sometimes took dangerous risks, Washington kept his army intact and demonstrated in all circumstances a determination to endure until independence was achieved (Fig. 1). He became the embodiment of the patriot cause.

The Navies

The greatest disparity between Britain and the United States was in naval forces. The Americans had no navy when hostilities began, while the British had 131 ships of the line and 139 ships of other classes. From the first Washington feared British naval supremacy, and as early as September 1775 he sought to arm New England merchantmen so that they might interrupt the flow of British supplies to Boston. "Washington's Navy," a flotilla of six schooners and a brigantine, took 35 prizes valued at more than US$600,000 before it was disbanded in 1777.

Figure 1. On the night of 25 December 1776, Washington's army crossed the Delaware River and attacked a Hessian garrison at Trenton, New Jersey. Of 1,400 Hessians, more than half were captured by Washington's forces. (Source: U.S. Library of Congress)

Meanwhile, the Continental Congress created an American navy composed initially of eight ships. These ships, mounting only 110 guns among them, were ordered to clear American waters of 78 British ships armed with 2,000 guns. While the Continental and state navies eventually commissioned nearly 100 ships, the British fleet was increased from 270 to 468 ships between 1775 and 1783.

Clearly overmatched, the American navies prudently engaged in actions against isolated warships and unarmed merchantmen. Some 2,000 privateers were authorized to prey on British commerce, but they had little effect in offsetting the supremacy of the Royal Navy in American waters. Capt. John Paul Jones, whose exploits became legend, emerged as America's greatest naval hero, but he did little more than harass British ships around Britain's home islands. Fortunately for the Americans, at the outset of the war the British fleet was in deplorable condition and was poorly directed by Lord Sandwich.

Because of unchallenged British naval predominance before the French entry into the war, British armies were easily transported from one military objective to another. Not until 1780, with the British fleet divided among American, West Indian, and European waters, did the United States and its allies overcome Britain's naval superiority. Reorganized after 1763, and in a high state of morale and efficiency, the French navy was essential to the American victory at Yorktown.

The War

At some time between 1775 and 1781 the British occupied every major American city—Boston, New York, Philadelphia, Charleston, and Savannah—but were never able to destroy Washington's army or the American will to resist.

Strategy

The British appear to have envisioned several strategic initiatives, including the following:

1. to occupy major American seaports and to pacify the surrounding countryside;
2. to isolate New England by controlling Lake Champlain, Lake George, and the Hudson River;
3. to divide the southern states along the line of the Santee River from a base at Charleston;
4. to use naval superiority to blockade the American coast, to transport army units as necessary, and to provide logistical support; and
5. to enlist the support of American Loyalists wherever and whenever possible.

None of these strategies was pursued with vigor, imagination, or consistency. After 1778 British priorities shifted to protection of the empire as the long struggle with France resumed.

Washington clearly recognized that the British had naval superiority, Canada as a base of operations, and larger, more professional armies; but he also knew that the British were faced with the problem of controlling a vast geographic area and subduing a widely dispersed populace. He understood that patriot hopes depended on the survival of the Continental Army. It was essential that he avoid decisive defeat and keep the army in the field.

Campaigns and Battles

Except for the abortive American invasion of Canada (1775–76), the successes of Brig. Gen. George Rogers Clark in the West (1778–79), and George Washington's joint Franco-American action against Cornwallis at Yorktown, the military initiative in the revolutionary war lay with the British. After it became apparent that occupation of American cities would not result in general submission, the British undertook two major campaigns, one prior to European intervention and one after.

The Saratoga Campaign

Perhaps the best prospect for British success lay in the 1777 campaign proposed by Lt. Gen. John Burgoyne for a three-pronged advance on Albany, New York. Burgoyne was to invade New York from Canada via the Richelieu River–Lake Champlain route so as to reach the upper Hudson River Valley; a smaller force of British regulars and Indians, under Brig. Gen. Barry St. Leger, was to reach Lake Ontario via the St. Lawrence, land at Oswego, and advance down the Mohawk to Albany; and Maj. Gen. George Clinton, with a portion of Howe's army, then ensconced in New York City, was to proceed up the Hudson. The combined forces of Burgoyne, St. Leger, and Clinton would isolate New England from the other rebellious colonies, and American resistance would then be broken. Lord George Germain, British secretary of state for the American colonies, and principal architect of British strategy, approved Burgoyne's plan; but he also approved a contradictory plan whereby Howe would occupy Philadelphia. Because of the consequent division of effort, and Washington's recognition of its implications, the Saratoga campaign, a British disaster, ensued. St. Leger was forced to turn back, and Clinton never started up the Hudson. Moving overland from Canada, Burgoyne, burdened by excess baggage and troubled by poor supply, moved slowly through dense New York forests. Near Saratoga he met an American army under Horatio Gates, reinforced by major contingents sent from Washington's army. Isolated there without hope of relief from St. Leger or Clinton, Burgoyne gave battle at Freeman's Farm (19 September) and Bemis Heights (7 October) before surrendering his army of 5,000 to the Americans on 17 October 1777. Burgoyne's defeat was symptomatic of other British failures during the revolutionary war. The campaign plan was too complex, given the poor transportation and communications prospects; poor planning and coordination in Britain and America also contributed to the defeat. News of the American victory at Saratoga was partly responsible for France's decision to enter the war against Britain.

The Southern Campaign

Subsequently, although British strategists considered North America a less important theater of war than the West Indies, Europe, and India, another major campaign to crush the American rebellion was mounted. The British had long believed that, because of the large number of Loyalists in Georgia and the Carolinas, victory in the South was attainable. As early as 1776 a joint army-navy expedition to capitalize on Loyalist sentiment among Southerners was undertaken, but the British arrived in North Carolina waters after Loyalists had been defeated in the Battle of Moore's Creek Bridge (27 February 1776) and were thereafter unable to capture Charleston.

The British concentrated their efforts elsewhere until late 1778. Then the British, at the urging of George III, who still believed that thousands of Loyalists were awaiting an opportunity to serve their king, took Savannah easily. From that base, the Georgia backcountry was pacified and royal government was restored. After a bitter siege, Charleston fell to the British on 12 May 1780, and Maj. Gen. Benjamin Lincoln surrendered 5,500 American defenders, the largest army captured by either side to date. Events in the South had taken an ominous turn for the Americans. Against Washington's advice, the Continental Congress sent Horatio Gates, the victor of Saratoga, to command its Southern Army with instructions to hold the Carolinas. From Charleston the British moved inland, and Cornwallis surprised and routed Gates at Camden,

South Carolina, on 16 August 1780. Gates was replaced by Nathanael Greene who found the army battered and demoralized. Moreover, thousands of Tories were entering the king's service. Intensive fighting characterized the conflict between patriots and Tories in the Carolinas. At the Battle of King's Mountain (7 October 1780) about 1,700 patriots from the mountains and beyond attacked about 900 Tories holding high ground in a bloody fight. The Tory commander, Maj. Patrick Ferguson, the only Briton in the fray, was slain and his entire force either killed or captured. Thereafter it was more difficult to recruit Tories.

A series of small engagements in 1780 and 1781 were interspersed with two battles of major importance. Greene split his army, and Brig. Gen. Daniel Morgan moved westward in hopes of menacing the British flank and rear. He was pursued and forced to give battle by Lt. Col. Banastre Tarleton at Cowpens in northwestern South Carolina. There, on 17 January 1781, Tarleton with some 1,100 men (slightly more than Morgan had) attacked the Americans, who had the swollen Broad River at their backs. Mistaking a readjustment of Morgan's lines as a panicky retreat, Tarleton ordered his men to attack. Morgan dealt a stunning defeat to the British, utilizing green militiamen to good advantage. The main armies of Cornwallis and Greene met at Guilford Courthouse on 15 March 1781, where the British gained a Pyrrhic victory in a bloody engagement. Consequently, Cornwallis decided to link up with the British navy, first at Wilmington, North Carolina, and then at Yorktown, Virginia. Hopelessly trapped at Yorktown by the French fleet under Admiral De Grasse and a combined Franco-American army of superior numbers, Cornwallis surrendered his army of about 8,000 men to Washington and French Gen. Jean Baptiste, Comte de Rochambeau on 19 October 1781. The victory at Yorktown virtually ended the war and made possible the final separation of the thirteen colonies from the British Empire.

Assessment of the Revolutionary War

The Whig historians George Otto Trevelyan, Sir Lewis Namier, Richard Pares, and others have contended that the Americans were defending their rights as Englishmen against royal tyranny and that the government of George III was shamefully inept in prosecuting an unpopular war. Eric Robson believed that the scales were weighed against the British from the outset because of distance, difficult terrain, poor communications, and the British commitment to European strategy and tactics. Many scholars have emphasized European intervention as critical; Samuel Flagg Bemis has stated flatly that the outcome was determined by France. More recently Richard B. Morris has postulated that the American patriots would have won the War for Independence in any event.

Perhaps, as Robert Middlekauff has argued, American morale and commitment to the "Glorious Cause" of liberty and self-government were of paramount significance in determining the outcome. Based on the experience of the American Revolutionary War, it would appear that an insurrectionary movement, upheld by a determined, highly motivated minority willing to sacrifice life and fortune for its cause, might well prove impossible to quell. The Napoleonic French in Spain, the British in South Africa, the Americans in Vietnam, and the Russians in Afghanistan might have studied the American Revolution to advantage.

MAX R. WILLIAMS

SEE ALSO: Alliance, Military and Political; Coalition Warfare; Combined Operations; Joint Operations; Seapower; Suffren de St. Tropez, Pierre André; Washington, George.

Bibliography

Alden, J. R. 1962. *The American Revolution, 1775–1783.* New York: Harper.

Bonwick, C. 1977. *English radicals and the American Revolution.* Chapel Hill, N.C.: Univ. of North Carolina Press.

Flexner, J. T. 1968. *George Washington in the American Revolution, 1775–1783.* Boston: Little Brown.

Gruber, I.D. 1972. *The Howe brothers and the American Revolution.* Chapel Hill, N.C.: Univ. of North Carolina Press.

Higginbotham, D. 1971. *The war of American Independence: Military attitudes, policies, and practice, 1783–1789.* New York: Macmillan.

Mackesy, P. 1964. *The war for America, 1775–1783.* Oxford: Oxford Univ. Press.

Middlekauff, R. 1982. *The glorious cause: The American Revolution, 1763–1789.* New York: Oxford.

Miller, J. C. 1948. *Triumph of freedom, 1775–1783.* Boston: Little, Brown.

Robson, E. 1966. *The American Revolution in its political and military aspects 1763–1783.* New York: Norton.

Shy, J. W. 1976. *A people numerous and armed: Reflections on the military struggle for American independence.* New York: Oxford.

Ward, C. 1952. *The war of the revolution.* 2 vols. New York: Macmillan.

AMMUNITION

Ammunition is "a device charged with explosives, propellants, pyrotechnics, initiating composition, or nuclear, biological, or chemical material for use in connection with defense or offense. Certain ammunition can be used for training, ceremonial, or nonoperational purposes" (U.S. Department of Defense 1987). Generally, ammunition for firearms may be divided into two categories: small caliber—usually less than 20mm to 40mm—and large caliber—usually greater than 20mm to 40mm. The categories overlap in the 20mm to 40mm range.

Small-Caliber Ammunition

There is a wide variety of small-caliber ammunition, virtually all of which is fixed—that is, the cartridge case is permanently attached to the projectile. Each round of small-caliber ammunition is an assembly of all components—the cartridge case, primer, propellant, and bullet (projectile) or shot—required to fire a weapon one time. A typical small-caliber cartridge with its components is shown in Figure 1.

The cartridge case, which holds the primer, the propellant, and the projectile that is fired from the weapon, conforms to the shape of the specific weapon's chamber, and is usually made of brass but may also be steel or some other material. The case also seals the weapon's barrel, so it must be sufficiently flexible first to expand and then to return to its approximate original size, permitting the extraction of the case and the insertion of a fresh round of ammunition. It must also be strong enough to withstand the great pressures generated by firing. Experimental weapons using caseless rounds have been developed, but none has yet seen widespread use. Heckler and Koch has developed a rifle, the G-11, that uses 4.7mm caseless ammunition. This rifle is scheduled to enter service with the German armed forces in 1992.

The primer of a round of ammunition is the assembly that fits in the center of the cartridge base and ignites the propellant when struck by the weapon's firing pin. Some cartridges, usually 20mm or larger, may use electric priming to speed ignition and improve reliability; this type is almost always used in aircraft. Rimfire priming is also used in some low-power ammunition; today, this is limited to .22-caliber bulleted breech (BB) caps; conical breech (CB) caps; and short, long, and long-rifle ammunition. All other mechanical primers consist of a primer cap, primer composition, and anvil. Most modern center-fire cartridges use Boxer priming, in which the anvil is integral to the primer assembly. Cartridges that are Berdan-primed have the primer anvil machined into the center of the primer pocket with two small flash holes on either side of the anvil. Ironically, Boxer priming, traditionally used in the United States, was invented by a British officer, Edward Boxer, while Berdan priming, more common in Europe, was invented by an American, Col. Hiram Berdan. Most primers today are made of noncorrosive materials so that the residue of the burned primer will not cause corrosion

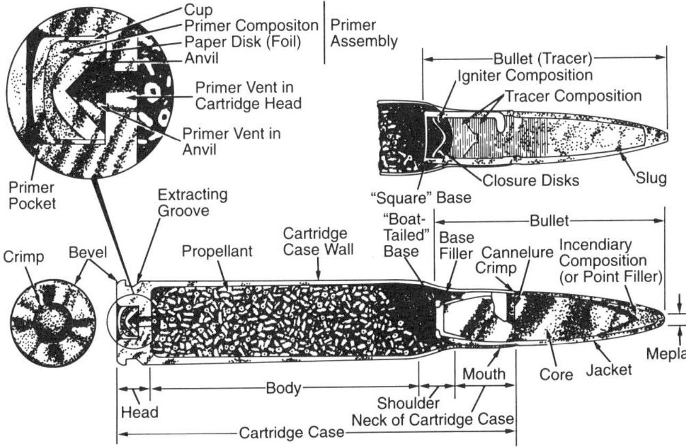

Figure 1. Cartridge terminology. (SOURCE: U.S. Army)

in the barrel of the weapon, a common problem prior to the 1950s. A primer is a mixture of ingredients extremely sensitive to shock; the most important characteristics are sensitivity, impulse, gas volume, and duration of flash.

The propellant is a low-explosive fine-grained substance that burns at a controlled rate and produces gases that expand with sufficient energy to propel a bullet out of the weapon's barrel. From the time firearms were invented until the late nineteenth century, black powder was used as the propellant. Black powder had several disadvantages: (1) it was very susceptible to moisture, which drastically changes its burning characteristics; (2) because it was a mixture of charcoal, sulphur, and saltpeter by volume, its explosive value was very dependent on the care with which it was mixed; (3) the manufacturing process of black powder required extreme care because the ingredients could explode during mixing; (4) when fired, black powder generates huge volumes of smoke, which obscured the battlefield and enabled the enemy to pinpoint the location of the shooter; and (5) black powder leaves a dense gummy residue when burned, requiring weapons to be cleaned frequently in order to remain operational. Black powder is still used in some artillery igniters, fuzes, and in other specialized ammunition applications.

Modern ammunition uses smokeless powder, which not only overcomes the problems associated with black powder but also makes possible the use of small-caliber, high-velocity ammunition. Although it is called smokeless powder, the propellant that pushes the bullet down the bore of modern weapons is neither smokeless nor is it truly a powder. The grains of modern powder are made by an extrusion process into a variety of forms—flakes, rectangles, cylinders, crosses, or any other desired shape. The shape of the powder grain is critical because it determines the burn rate and thus the amount of pressure in the weapon's barrel, and therefore the velocity of the projectile. Velocities may be as low as 45 meters (150 ft.) per second for mortar projectiles or as high as 1,200 meters (about 4,000 ft.) per second for some tank ammunition. The velocity of most military rifle ammunition is between 750 and 900 meters (2,500 and 3,000 ft.) per second. The burn rate of the propellant must be carefully designed to take advantage of the characteristics of the weapons in which the ammunition will be used. If all propellants were to be burned before the bullet moved very far down the barrel, undesirably high pressures would be generated. Thus, most propellants are designed to burn at a given rate so that the powder is not completely consumed until the bullet has traveled along approximately two-thirds of the barrel. This results in a larger volume for the expanding gases with a concomitant decrease in pressure.

Smokeless powders may be either single-based or double-based. Single-based powders are composed primarily of nitrocellulose and are manufactured by the "nitration of cotton" method. Double-based powders have nitroglycerin added to the nitrocellulose, to form a gel or plastic-like substance, and small quantities of stabilizers.

The bullet is the component of the cartridge that is fired from the weapon. It may be a single projectile or, in rare instances, more than one projectile. Shotgun cartridges usually fire a mass of round shot that may be of varying sizes, depending on the purpose of the cartridge. Bullets are made of various materials. At one time almost all bullets were made of a lead/tin alloy, but the introduction of smokeless powder engendered several problems with lead bullets. First, lead-alloy bullets fired at high velocities do not readily engage the rifling of a weapon's barrel and may in fact override the lands and grooves of the bore, which leads to erratic accuracy. This phenomenon is called *swaging*. Another problem associated with lead-alloy bullets fired in high-velocity military weapons is *leading*. As the bullet is swaged down the bore without engaging the rifling, it overrides the lands and grooves of the rifling, leaving a deposit of lead in the barrel. This deposit, if not removed, may cause inaccuracy and higher-than-desired pressures. Also, lead bullets tend to be easily deformed prior to firing, causing malfunctions in feeding. Finally, lead bullets have a relatively low penetrating capability. These problems led to the introduction of what is termed *ball ammunition*. Such bullets have a lead-alloy core and a gilding metal jacket, such as copper, that positively engages the rifling in the weapon bore and can be fired without swaging. The most common military small-caliber ammunition fires an armor-piercing (AP) bullet. This type of bullet consists of a gilding metal jacket surrounding a tungsten or molybdenum steel core, with a point filler of lead alloy or incendiary mixture. The lead-alloy point filler initially stresses the point of impact and supports the steel core so that the latter has a good chance of penetrating without breaking up. About one-third of the way forward from the bullet base is the cannelure, a machined groove around the circumference of the bullet that is used to crimp the case to the bullet. Bullet bases are of two shapes, boat tail or square. The boat-tail design is better at velocities under 900 meters (3000 ft.) per second. At higher velocities, either design delivers adequate performance. Other common types of small-caliber bullets include incendiary, armor-piercing incendiary, and tracer bullets. All incendiary bullets function on impact; they are ignited by the heat generated when they strike their target. Incendiary bullets are derived from ball-bullet design; they are filled with an incendiary mixture ahead of the lead-alloy core. Armor-piercing incendiary (API) bullets have the incendiary mixture in front of their steel core. Tracer bullets are ignited by the cartridge propellant and allow the gunner to observe the path of the bullet. Tracers, however, do not burn for the full range of the bullet. Most 7.62mm bullets are limited to a trace length of approximately 1,500 meters (4,950 ft.). Tracers are usually used in machine-gun ammunition loaded in belts in which every fifth round is a tracer, the other four rounds being AP or API.

Multiple bullets have been in existence since the early 1900s and consist of two or more bullets in one cartridge. Typical was the U.S. design of the late 1950s. These multiple bullets consisted of two 7.62mm rounds in one standard North Atlantic Treaty Organization (NATO) cartridge. The intent was to increase the odds of hitting a target with one shot. The first bullet had a conventional shape and a flat base; the second bullet's nose nested in the face of the first with the base of the second slightly slanted. The trajectories of both bullets were thus somewhat offset because the gases leaking past the offset base of the second bullet as it emerged from the muzzle of the rifle caused it to be slightly canted. The cant was carefully engineered so that the strike of both bullets was predictable over given ranges. The multiple bullet, however, was not particularly successful in service and was withdrawn by the late 1960s.

Cartridge cases are, with the exception of shotgun cartridges, usually made of brass, although steel is occasionally substituted. The cartridge case is drawn from flat brass stock in such a way that the thickness of the case tapers from base to mouth. Cases may be rimmed, semirimmed, or rimless. Most military cartridges have rimless cases. Rimless and semirimmed cases have an extraction groove around the circumference of the case head. In rimless cartridges, this is often mistakenly referred to as the cartridge rim, but rimless cartridges do not have a rim, only an extraction groove. Belted cases, rare in military cartridges, have a belt forward of the extracting groove to reinforce the case head against extremely high pressures. This type of case is usually associated with cartridges of very high power, such as the .300 Winchester Magnum or the .375 H&H Magnum. During the Vietnam conflict, some U.S. sniper teams used rifles of .300 Winchester Magnum caliber.

Complete rounds of small-caliber ammunition are classified according to purpose. The most common classifications are: AP, API, API tracer (API-T), ball, grenade launching, incendiary, tracer, blank, dummy, high-pressure test (HPT), match, practice, and shotgun. Ammunition is also color-coded to facilitate recognition. Representative NATO standard color codes for small-caliber ammunition are as follows:

AP	Black
API	Silver
API-T	Silver/Red
Ball	None

The principal types of small-caliber ammunition are listed below.

Ball. At one time the most common type of small-arms ammunition, ball ammunition has been largely supplanted by AP ammunition for combat use. Ball ammunition has a bullet of lead with a gliding metal jacket and is now used primarily for marksmanship training.

Armor piercing. AP ammunition has a hardened steel or tungsten carbide core behind a lead-point filler inside a gilding metal jacket. It is used against personnel and in larger calibers, such as 12.7mm and 20mm, against lightly armored vehicles. A variant of AP ammunition being developed in the United States is called "saboted light armor piercing" (SLAP) ammunition. It is being developed in 7.62mm and 12.7mm calibers and consists of a subcaliber penetrating projectile in a discarding sabot of light plastic—that is, the outer shell of plastic peels off the steel projectile after it leaves the muzzle of the weapon, allowing the projectile to continue. The light weight of these rounds gives them very high velocities and improved armor penetration over normal AP rounds.

Tracer. Tracer (T) ammunition is similar to ball ammunition, but the bullet has its rear portion replaced by a composition of magnesium powder and barium nitrate with metallic compounds added to provide colors. This is usually strontium nitrate, which produces a red color when the compound burns. It was developed originally for use by aircraft machine gunners, and eventually came to be used in all machine guns.

Incendiary. Incendiary (I) ammunition is designed specifically to start a fire in a target. Like tracer ammunition, incendiary ammunition was originally designed for use in aircraft to set fire to enemy planes. Its use has gradually declined, as small-caliber weapons are rare in modern high-performance aircraft, which are often capable of flying faster than bullets of this type.

Armor-Piercing Incendiary and Armor-Piercing Incendiary Tracer. Both API and API-T ammunition combine the features their names imply. Like incendiary ammunition, both were designed for use against enemy aircraft, and again, both are becoming less common due to less frequent use of small-caliber weapons in aircraft.

Blank. Blank ammunition consists of a powder charge in a cartridge case with no bullet, and is used for training, for simulating weapons fire, and in ceremonies.

Dummy. Dummy ammunition, also known as drill ammunition, is completely inert but looks like an actual round of ammunition. It is used for training, has no propellant or primer, and can usually be identified by holes or longitudinal grooves in the cartridge case. In Great Britain, dummy ammunition is used by weapons inspectors for testing the mechanical functions of weapons and is made of tool steel to precise tolerances.

High Pressure Test. HPT is similar to ball ammunition except that it has a heavier bullet and an excess propelling charge for proof-testing weapons. Firing of proof loads is performed with the weapon under a hood and the trigger pulled mechanically.

Rifle Grenade. This ammunition is similar in appearance to blank ammunition but has distinguishing features to set it apart. It has no bullet but does have a large propellant charge designed to fire a grenade from the end of the rifle barrel. Rifle grenade cartridges are no longer widely used due to the development of rifle grenades that may be launched using standard AP ammunition.

Shotgun. This ammunition consists of a propelling charge; a load of shot, a projectile, or flechettes; and primer in a case of paper, plastic, or brass. The head of the cartridge, usually brass, contains the primer and encloses the propellant. On top of the propellant are several wads of paper or plastic, followed by the shot or other projectiles. The case may be closed by either placing a closing wad over the shot and rolling the case down tightly to seal it, or, more commonly, crimping the case mouth over the shot. Military shotguns are usually loaded with 00 buckshot (.34 inch) or flechettes. A typical 12-gauge shotgun round will contain nine balls of 00 buckshot or twenty flechettes. Shotguns may also fire a solid ball or a rifled slug. Shotguns are especially useful in jungle warfare, where ranges of engagement seldom exceed 50 meters (165 ft.). Indeed, they were widely used by U.S. forces in Vietnam. Shotgun gauges are determined by the number of lead balls of the diameter of the bore required to weigh one pound. The exceptions to this rule are the .410 and 9mm shotguns, which have a bore diameter of .41 inch and 9mm, respectively. Shotgun gauges and bore diameters follow.

Shotgun Gauge/Bore Diameter

Gauge	Bore Diameter
4 Gauge	.935 inch
8 Gauge	.835 inch
10 Gauge	.775 inch
12 Gauge	.729 inch
16 Gauge	.662 inch
20 Gauge	.615 inch
28 Gauge	.550 inch

Large-Caliber Ammunition

Large-caliber ammunition starts at 20mm to 40mm. At the lower end of the scale, from 20mm to approximately 75mm, large-caliber ammunition is usually fixed—that is, the projectile and case are permanently attached until the time of firing, similar to small-caliber ammunition. Larger-caliber ammunition may be semifixed or separate-loading. In the former case, the projectile and case are separate but are put together prior to firing. In the latter, there is no case; instead, powder bags are used as the propellant. Separate-loading ammunition is employed only in the largest calibers of cannon either because of a need to vary the charge of propellant or because of handling requirements.

The basic types of large-caliber ammunition are high explosive, which has a filler of TNT or some other explosive; AP, which may be of either kinetic energy or chemical energy varieties; chemical, which also includes smoke and white phosphorus (WP) ammunition; canister, which has balls, flechettes, or other type of fragments in a matrix; and illuminating, which contains a magnesium flare and a parachute for lighting a battlefield at night. Within these categories are many varieties of ammunition. For the purposes of this discussion, large-caliber ammunition is divided into ammunition for guns and howitzers, ammunition for mortars, and ammunition for recoilless rifles.

Guns and Howitzers

High Explosive (Fig. 2). The high-explosive (HE) artillery shell is by far the most common in most military establishments; there are several types. Typically, an HE projectile is cylindrical, tapering to a point at the nose. The tapered portion is called the *ogive,* and the fuze is tapered to closely match the contour of the ogive. The *bourrelet* is a smooth, machined surface of the projectile just to the rear of the ogive; it rides the bore lands of the gun tube, supporting the projectile as long as it is in the tube. The rotating band is slightly larger than the bore of the gun and performs a number of functions, one of which is to impart spin to the projectile by engaging the lands and grooves of the bore. Another function is that it provides obturation, or sealing, thus preventing the propellant gases from blowing by the projectile as it travels down the bore. Some projectiles have a separate obturator. Finally, the rotating band provides a rear bearing surface for the projectile while it is in the bore of the gun.

Some projectiles also have a base cover or plug. The base cover is sheet steel and prevents hot gases from bleeding through the projectile body, which may be porous. Such an occurrence would ignite the projectile filler while it was still in the bore of the weapon, a highly undesirable event. Base plugs are employed in HE-improved conventional munitions projectiles that are base ejecting and in other projectiles, such as smoke, illuminating, and leaflet rounds.

Conventional HE shells are used to obtain demolition effects against materiel and fragmentation effects against both materiel and personnel. Fragmentation is a serious design consideration of the projectile engineer and is the result of the careful selection of explosive filler and metallic composition of the projectile body. An explosive of overly high brisance—the ability of an explosive to shatter a surrounding medium—will cause the projectile to shatter into fragments that are small and ineffective, as will a projectile body that is too brittle. An explosive that is of low brisance will result in fragments that are large and of low velocity and thereby of limited range. Projectile designers strive for a balance between explosive brisance and projectile metallurgy to deliver fragments of optimum size for the intended purpose. This is generally considered to be in the range of 150–750 grains for effects on both materiel and personnel. Most HE shells of conventional design, however, deliver no more than 60 to 75 percent of fragments in this range. This limitation led to the development of controlled-fragmentation projectiles in the late 1960s, in which fragmentation and explosive effects are optimized to achieve greater effectiveness than conventionally designed HE rounds.

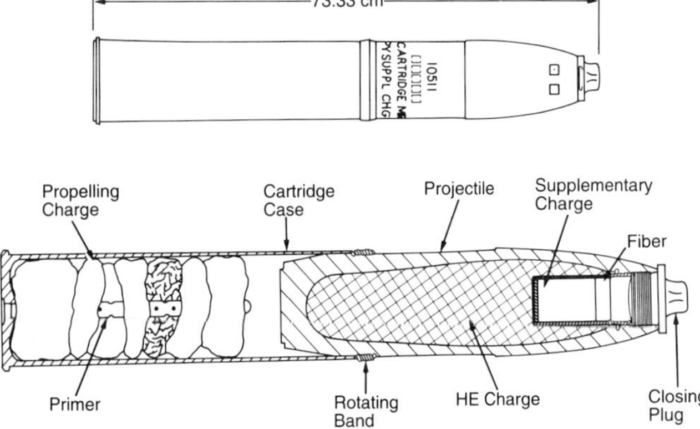

Figure 2. High-explosive round (semifixed). (Source: U.S. Army)

Another type of HE projectile is the improved conventional munition (ICM). ICMs carry a number of submunitions—for example, grenades or mines—that are ejected from the base of the shell over the intended target or in an area in which targets might occur. Developments in this type of munition have resulted in a dual-purpose, improved conventional munition (DPICM) that is effective against both light armored vehicles and personnel. Developmental ICMs carry submunitions that, when ejected over the target, will seek out and destroy armored vehicles using millimeter-wave radar and infrared seekers. This type of munition is characteristic of the U.S. Army seek-and-destroy armor (SADARM) program, which utilizes either 155mm or 203mm projectiles to carry the SADARM submunitions.

Armor Piercing. There are two basic types of AP ammunition: kinetic energy and chemical energy. The former defeats the armor by a combination of pressing, spiking, or punching its way through. Pressing fractures the armor by overstraining it; spiking defeats the armor by forcing the armor material aside as it strikes at a very high velocity; punching defeats the armor by punching its way through, actually pushing a plug the size of the projectile diameter out of the armor plate. A typical kinetic-energy AP round is a fin-stabilized, discarding-sabot tracer round (APFSDS-T). In this type, the weapon bore is unrifled, although APFSDS-T rounds are used in rifled guns. Smoothbore guns are capable of higher velocities because the problem of swaging is eliminated. The capability of a kinetic-energy projectile to defeat armor is a function of its weight and velocity; higher velocity generally results in greater penetration. When fired, the light metal sabot surrounding the arrow-shaped penetrator falls away, leaving the penetrator to fly to the target. Penetrators were originally made of tungsten alloy steel, but they are now constructed of depleted uranium, a very heavy alloy of uranium that has little radioactivity but is very hard and heavy in comparison to its overall size. Most smoothbore cannons are employed in tanks. The first was fitted to the Soviet T-62 in the 1960s, and such cannons have been adopted by the Bundeswehr in the Leopard II. The same 120mm gun used by the Germans is fitted to the U.S. M1A1 tank.

Chemical-energy ammunition is usually associated with

shaped-charge (also known as hollow-charge) ammunition. The principle of the shaped charge lies in the fact that an explosive, usually cylindrical, with a cavity at one end will inflict more damage than an equivalent charge without the cavity. Most shaped-charge cavities are lined with a material such as copper. To achieve maximum effect, they are detonated some distance from their targets.

The shaped charge is detonated at its base. Detonation waves pass over the liner, causing it to collapse upon itself. When the collapsing liner reaches the axis of the detonating warhead, it forms two parts. A small portion forms a high-velocity jet while the bulk of the charge forms a slower moving but more massive slug. The jet is responsible for the deep penetration of the shaped charge. The jet itself varies in velocity along its length, the tip moving at about 7,500 meters (25,000 ft.) per second while the base moves at approximately 1,500 meters (5,000 ft.) per second. This is caused by the mass of the liner increasing as it collapses while the amount of explosive remaining to move it decreases. Thus, the elements of the liner reach the axis of the charge at progressively lower velocities, which causes the formation of a jet with various velocities along its length.

When the jet strikes armor, or any material, it generates tremendously high pressures, typically 4^{10} pounds per square inch (psi), which causes both the target and the jet to deform hydrodynamically. The jet and material displaced from the target merge together and flow radially until the jet is used up or its velocity falls below a critical point and penetration ceases. The depth of penetration into a given material is directly proportional to the length of the jet and the square root of its density, which is considered to be the same as the original liner material. Depth of penetration is also dependent on the strength of the target material.

The more time a jet has to form the better, as it will have more time to lengthen and increase penetration. This is true, however, only up to a point, because once a certain jet length is reached, the jet separates into discrete particles that no longer stretch and the jet length becomes constant. Once this point is reached, penetration falls off because of an inherent asymmetry in shaped charges called "jet waver." In this phenomenon, the separate particles tend to follow different paths and thus do not contribute to the penetration already attained. This condition sets in very shortly after optimum standoff; this is why spaced armor and stand-off devices are very effective against normal shaped charges. Reactive armor, which explodes on impact of a shaped-charge jet, is also effective because the jet is displaced and separated into particles. Several shaped-charge countermeasures against both spaced and reactive armor have been developed. One is a tandem-shaped-charge warhead in which a small charge makes the initial penetration and a larger charge follows to defeat the main armor.

The design of shaped charges compensates for the characteristics of the warhead or projectile into which they are fitted. For example, a shaped charge designed for a spinning projectile will have flutes on its surface to induce tangential velocity on detonation, which counteracts the spin of the projectile and increases penetration.

The pizeoelectric element in the tip of the stand-off spike generates an electrical charge on impact. This charge flows back through the wire lead to the point-initiating base-detonating (PIBD) fuze and detonates the charge. This round is designated a high-explosive antitank tracer (HEAT-T).

A third type of antiarmor ammunition is the high-explosive squash head (HESH) projectile, also known as high-explosive plastic (HEP). This type of ammunition was originally developed for attacking concrete fortifications, but it later came to be used against armored fighting vehicles. Rather than actually penetrating the armor, the HESH round explodes against the armor, causing a huge amount of spalling on the opposite side of the armor plate. The fragments resulting from this spalling ricochet throughout the inside of the vehicle, wrecking the interior and killing or injuring the crew. It is still in use by many armies, and is particularly favored by the British, but it is less effective against composite armors than are other types of antiarmor ammunition.

The newest development in antiarmor cannon ammunition is the guided artillery round exemplified by the U.S. M712 Copperhead. In this type of projectile, a laser designator–equipped forward observer calls for a fire mission from a remote artillery unit. The projectile's code detector is keyed by the gun crew to match that of the observer. When the projectile is fired, fins are deployed by centrifugal force and after a time delay, the main batteries activate and the projectile wings deploy. The projectile then receives and decodes the laser energy that is reflected from the target by the forward observer. It steers itself into a gliding intercept path to the target while the fuze electrically arms the warhead. When it hits the target, the Copperhead projectile functions as a conventional HEAT round.

Chemical ammunition is filled with a chemical agent such as mustard, a nerve agent, or some other type of chemical. It is usually associated with poison gas of some sort but may also include smoke ammunition such as white phosphorus. In most international treaty definitions chemical ammunition encompasses those munitions that deliver a substance intended for use in military operations to kill, seriously injure, or incapacitate personnel through physiological effects. Primary types of chemical ammunition in use today are nerve agents, either persistent (V-agent) or nonpersistent (G-agent); mustard (blister) agents; and tear gas. Binary nerve agent projectiles have also been developed. In these rounds, two chemicals, which by themselves are not poisonous, are contained in the same projectile. Once fired, the chemicals are mixed and transformed into a highly toxic nerve agent. Chemical ammunition has not been used on a wide scale by a major power since World War I. The United States, however, used tear gas in Vietnam, and there have been scattered reports of a chemical agent having been used by the Soviet Union in Afghanistan. Because chemical ammunition is relatively cheap, it has been used in several Third World conflicts, notably by Iraq in the recent Persian Gulf War against Iran.

Some countries also classify smoke ammunition as chemical munitions; for the sake of convenience they will be covered here, but they are not properly chemical ammunition. Smoke ammunition includes WP and a variety of screening smokes, such as hexachloroethane-zinc (HC). In addition to creating smoke, white phosphorus causes casualties and is effective as a high explosive. It burns on contact with air and can be extinguished only by immersion in water or by otherwise cutting off its air supply. Smoke shells are used for a variety of purposes, including spotting charges for artillery, but they are most commonly used to screen troops from enemy observation. Advances in smoke technology have given smoke shells new life as countermeasures against thermal imagers. These are referred to as multispectral smokes, because they cover more than one wavelength of the electromagnetic spectrum, including not only visible light but also infrared, ultraviolet, radio, and radar waves. Smoke projectiles may be of either the bursting or base-ejecting type; screening smokes are usually white while signaling smokes are various colors.

Traditionally, canister ammunition had no explosive charge and consisted of a projectile filled with a large number of slugs, balls, pellets, or flechettes enclosed in a light metal casing. It has been used for many years by artillery for close defense and in tank cannons against personnel. Conventional canister ammunition functions in a manner similar to that of a huge shotgun. The latest canister rounds may be filled with balls or flechettes. When fired, they eject forward from the projectile in a conical pattern propelled by a base charge. When loaded with flechettes, such modern canister rounds are often referred to as "beehive ammunition."

In one significant respect, the modern "beehive" and similar canister ammunition is really a version of a now-obsolete form of artillery ammunition called shrapnel. It was so named after its early-nineteenth-century inventor, British general Sir Henry Shrapnel. The principal differences between shrapnel and the traditional canister are (1) an explosive charge in the shrapnel projectile shell permitted it to be a long-range version of canister; and (2) a time fuze set so as to detonate the internal explosive charge as the shrapnel projectile's trajectory approached the ground. In this way, the shrapnel projectile sprayed the contents of its shell against targets on the ground just before the projectile would otherwise strike the surface. The contents were usually steel or lead balls, often about 12 centimeters (almost 5 in.) in diameter. Shrapnel was the principal antipersonnel artillery ammunition of World War I. Toward the end of that war, however, shrapnel began to be displaced by an HE shell with a time fuze also set to detonate as the projectile approached the ground. It became evident that the jagged fragments from an HE shell were substantially more lethal—and thus more effective—than were the pellets of the shrapnel shell. Further, it was more cost-effective to use an HE shell for both antipersonnel and antimateriel targets. Except to use up old stocks of ammunition, shrapnel was little used in World War II, and it is not believed that (except for the "beehive version") shrapnel ammunition has been produced since about 1940.

The term *shrapnel* has been widely misused by non-artillerymen since the closing months of World War I. The origin of this misuse seems to have been reports by British surgeons on their treatment of wounds. Apparently aware that shrapnel had been the principal artillery ammunition against personnel, the surgeons began to refer to shell fragments as "shrapnel." This misuse of the word *shrapnel* was quickly adopted by journalists. And so it has become common practice to refer to shell fragments (quite incorrectly) as shrapnel, and to wounds inflicted by such fragments as shrapnel wounds.

Another even-more-obsolete version of canister was grapeshot. These were large pellets, iron or lead, often about 2.5 centimeters (1 in.) in diameter, that were held together by a wire net or some adhesive compound rather than being enclosed in a container, as was canister. Grapeshot was a short-range antipersonnel ammunition, like canister, and was widely used in the eighteenth and early nineteenth centuries. It was certainly in use as late as the Mexican War (1846–48), and some grapeshot may have been used as late as the American Civil War.

Illuminating ammunition is used to light an area at night in order to detect targets. Illuminating projectiles are base ejecting and consist of an open-ended projectile filled with a magnesium compound attached to a parachute. The illuminant is packed in the forward position of the projectile with the parachute and its shroud lines toward the rear. A small ejecting charge of black powder is fired by a mechanical time fuze that expels the illuminating flare from the projectile while simultaneously igniting the flare's first-fire composition. As the flare is ejected from the projectile, the parachute deploys, allowing the flare to slowly descend. Typically, the luminosity of illuminating projectiles ranges from 450,000 to 1,000,000 candlepower lasting from 60 to 120 seconds depending on the size of the projectile and the composition of the flare.

Rocket-assisted and base-bleed artillery ammunition are described separately because of their unique characteristics. Both represent efforts to achieve greater range than possible with conventional projectiles, although each is a different approach to the problem. Rocket-assisted projectiles have a rocket motor to boost their range. The first efforts at rocket-assisted ammunition for artillery were undertaken by the Germans during World War II. They were able to achieve experimental ranges of up to 200 kilometers (120 mi.), although accuracy was poor. The latter has always been a problem for the rocket-assisted projectile (RAP) designer because the gradual consumption of the rocket's fuel during the flight of the projectile upsets the balance of the projectile, which results in pitching and yawing. The Germans solved this problem by placing the rocket motor in the center of the shell and venting it through side nozzles or through a long center tube. The yaw problem persists, however, because any deviation from trajectory at the time of rocket firing results in inaccuracy. RAP ammunition is a compromise.

Base-bleed projectiles represent another approach to extending the range of artillery projectiles. Base-bleed projectiles have a small chamber filled with propellant in the base of the projectile. This propellant ignites and "bleeds out" the base of the projectile, filling the low pressure area created by the passage of the round through the air and thereby reducing drag. The effect of base bleeding has been to extend by as much as 20 percent the range of 155mm artillery projectiles.

Ammunition for Mortars

In the West, mortars are defined as muzzle-loaded, indirect-fire weapons that may have either a smooth or rifled bore, although the former is more common (Fig. 3). Mortars have shorter ranges than howitzers and employ a higher angle of fire. A mortar tube (barrel) is usually 10 to 20 calibers in length. A few large-caliber mortars, such as the Soviet 240mm mortar, are breech-loaded. Most mortar projectiles are different from artillery ammunition in that they are "tear drop" shaped and fin-stabilized. Because of this shape, mortar projectiles are often referred to as "bombs" even though they are not true bombs. The fin assembly is screwed into the base of the projectile. Mortar projectiles are also lighter in construction than artillery projectiles because chamber pressures and setback forces are far lower than in cannons and howitzers. Since most mortars are smoothbore, they have no rotating band and usually contact the bore of the weapon at two places. One is on the forward portion of the mortar projectile, where older mortar rounds had a series of machined bands called the gas check. More modern mortar projectiles have an obturator rather than a gas check. The other bearing surface is the outside portion of the fins. A few mortars, such as the U.S. 4.2-inch (107mm) rifled mortar, use projectiles similar in appearance to artillery projectiles. This type of mortar projectile is spin-stabilized rather than fin stabilized, but otherwise it has characteristics similar to "tear drop" mortar projectiles. Early versions of this type of projectile had rotating disks instead of bands, but the latest 107mm mortar projectiles have rotating bands and are very similar in appearance to artillery projectiles, except for the projectile base spike to retain the propellant increments. Mortars have been traditionally used as area weapons inasmuch as they lack the accuracy of guns and howitzers. Developments in munitions technology have resulted in mortar ammunition with a homing capability for use against armor. Mortar ammunition in this category includes the Bussard projectile manufactured by Diehl of West Germany; the Stryx munition by Saab-Scania of Sweden; and the Merlin terminally guided projectile produced by British Aerospace.

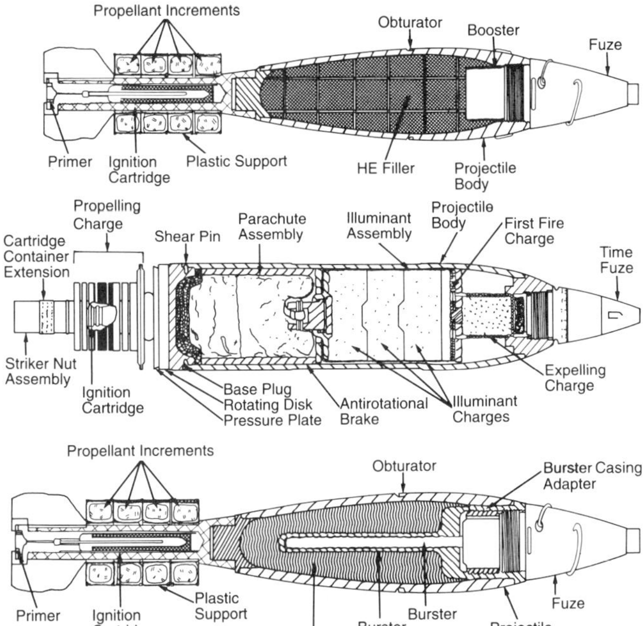

Figure 3. Typical mortar projectiles. (Source: U.S. Army)

In their role as "the infantryman's artillery," mortars use a variety of ammunition similar to that used in artillery guns and howitzers. A panoply of munitions is available, from conventional HE to "smart munitions." Only direct-fire antitank ammunition is not available for mortars. With the widening use of the 120mm mortar as standard in most armies, it will be only a matter of time until ICMs and DPICMs find their way into mortar use.

The HE mortar in Figure 3 illustrates the construction of a typical mortar projectile. The mortar fuze is similar to that utilized in an artillery round. It may be of any one of a number of types. Like the artillery projectile, the mortar round has a steel body that carries the filler of explosives or other material. Unlike artillery projectiles, most mortar rounds have a fin assembly (includes the tail boom and fins). Inside the tail boom are a primer and an ignition cartridge that set off the propellant increments to launch the projectile out of the mortar tube. Like the separate bags of propellant and charges used in artillery ammunition, mortar increments are used to achieve variations in range. Virtually all mortar rounds, whether spin or fin stabilized, consist of a fuze, body, and tail boom. Those rounds that are spin stabilized lack fins.

The functioning of mortar rounds is different from artillery, or even small arms, in that the majority of mortars remain the only modern weapon that is muzzle loaded.

Those few mortars that are breech loaded are very large caliber and are in service primarily with forces of the former Soviet Union and its allies. Having selected the appropriate charge for firing, the mortarman removes increments to adjust the range. The fuze is set, in the case of mechanical time or proximity fuzes, and the mortar round is dropped down the tube of the weapon, which contains a fixed firing pin in the base cap of the tube. When the projectile strikes the firing pin, the primer fires, igniting the ignition charge, which in turn ignites the propellant increments, firing the round.

Other than the firing procedure and the design of the projectile itself, the differences between mortar rounds and artillery projectiles is one of degree. The functioning of mortar and artillery projectiles after firing is similar and the range of munitions available for both is likewise congruent. As can be seen from the accompanying illustrations, the general designs of mortar rounds of HE, chemical, smoke, and illuminating types differ little from their artillery cousins.

The newest developments in mortar ammunition are the antiarmor "smart munitions." Instead of being like the "area weapons" of the past, these mortar rounds are highly accurate projectiles that seek their targets through millimeter wave radar, infrared seeker, or semiactive laser sensors. In the case of the millimeter wave radar and infrared seekers, the round is fired toward an area where a target is known to be located. No further action on the part of the crew is necessary. Once over the target area, the seeker "looks down" onto the battlefield. When it acquires a target, the seeker "locks on" and guides the projectile to it using either wings or canards that are folded until after launch. These mortar rounds carry a shaped-charge warhead capable of defeating the top armor on almost any known tank. The functioning of this type of warhead is the same as that in HEAT ammunition.

Ammunition for Recoilless Rifles

A final type of artillery ammunition is that for recoilless rifles. The projectiles for such weapons are similar to those fired from traditional guns and howitzers, but the functioning of the recoilless gun is quite different from any other, and as such it deserves mention.

A recoilless gun consists of a light artillery tube and a lightweight mount. Recoilless guns are typically employed by infantry as antitank artillery, although most fire a variety of ammunition. The tube is open at both ends. The recoil of fired rounds is counterbalanced by the thrust of gases generated by the burning of the propellant. The thrust of the burning gases acts as if it were a "rocket motor" to offset the recoil of the gun. Recoilless guns can be constructed in a far lighter configuration than other weapons of similar caliber. The lack of recoil and the light weight of the recoilless gun is offset somewhat by the backblast inherent in such weapons. In larger calibers, the backblast can be lethal to personnel who are caught in it.

While recoilless guns fire HE, HEAT, and other munitions, their propellant cases are different, characterized by many perforations to allow propellant gases to escape when the weapon is fired. Some recoilless gun ammunition uses a "blowout disk" instead of case perforations, but the effect is the same: release of propellant gases from the vent of the weapon.

Grenades

A grenade is a small explosive or chemical missile originally designed to be thrown by hand but currently capable of being fired from a variety of launchers that may be fitted to the end of a rifle or carbine barrel or attached underneath. In the latter instance, the grenade is a small cartridge of fixed ammunition in the 30mm to 40mm range. The projectile warhead contains an explosive, smoke, illuminating, or shot grenade. This type of weapon was originally developed in the 1960s for use with the U.S. M-79 grenade launcher, a single-shot weapon that resembles a single-barreled, break-open shotgun. Grenades launched from the end of a rifle barrel either are specifically designed as rifle grenades or are hand grenades adapted for the purpose. Traditionally, rifle grenades required the use of special cartridges, but developments have led to the introduction of "bullet trap" rifle grenades. While this concept is not new, previous efforts at firing rifle grenades using standard ammunition have not been especially successful. Generally, grenades are classified as either hand or rifle, but there are several variations of both types.

Hand grenades are among the oldest firearms, having been in use almost since the recorded advent of gunpowder. Early hand grenades were simply earthenware pots filled with black powder and a fuze, which were dropped or thrown at the enemy. Such grenades were used to defend fortifications. By the seventeenth century, specialized grenadier units were formed to carry and throw grenades. Many such units later became elite elements within their national military establishment. All hand grenades consist of a body, a filler, and a fuze. Modern hand grenades are classified as to purpose and type. They may be offensive or defensive and may be classed as fragmentation, incendiary, smoke, or antitank (the last category is rare). Most grenades have a fixed delay fuze that is activated by a pull ring. There is a safety lever, or "spoon," on the fuze and it prevents fuze actuation until after the grenade leaves the thrower's hand. Once the safety lever flies off, most grenades explode in three to five seconds.

The idea of a "rifle" grenade is also old. The first concept for launching a grenade from a musket dates to the seventeenth century. The rifle grenade did not develop until the early years of the twentieth century when grenade cups were introduced to allow firing grenades from service rifles. Such a grenade cup, the British 6.5cm grenade launcher, was officially in service from 1917 to 1962.

During World War II, rifle grenades were developed by the Germans and Americans. These were fitted to a "spigot" attached to the muzzle of the rifle. The grenade had a hollow tail assembly with fins and appeared very similar to a small mortar projectile. In use, the hollow-tail assembly was placed over the launcher "spigot" and a special cartridge was used to launch it. Rifle grenades have been developed that allow the use of standard ammunition to fire them. Most modern Western rifles have standardized integral grenade adapters on their muzzles that have eliminated the need for a separate grenade adapter, as "bullet trap" rifle grenades have begun the elimination of grenade cartridges.

Offensive grenades contain a high explosive charge in a thin container and do most of their damage by demolition or lethal shock rather than by fragmentation, although some offensive grenades have a fragmentation effect. In this case, the fragments are designed to be of a range that is less than the distance the grenade can be hand thrown to allow an advancing soldier to throw his grenade without having to take cover from its fragments. "Stun grenades," developed for use in antiterrorist operations, are a form of offensive grenade with a loud report and vivid flash. These temporarily disorient victims in the vicinity of the explosion. They do not produce fragmentation or lethal blast effects.

Defensive grenades contain a high explosive charge in a metallic body and achieve their effects primarily through fragments. The grenadier must take cover when he throws this type of grenade to prevent wounding himself because the range of the fragments is greater than the distance the grenade can be thrown.

Smoke grenades, like artillery and mortar smoke rounds, are used for screening and signaling. White smoke grenades are almost universally of the HC or WP types. Colored smoke grenades come in a variety of colors for use in signaling, especially for air-ground operations. The most common colors are red, green, yellow, and violet. The chemical compounds used in smoke grenades are identical to those used in artillery and mortar ammunition.

Incendiary grenades are used for starting fires. They are filled with thermite, a compound of iron oxide and aluminum powder that burns at a temperature of approximately 2,000 degrees Celsius. Incendiary grenades are widely used to destroy artillery and mortars when their capture is imminent; all that is necessary is to drop them down the weapon's barrel. Otherwise, WP is better suited to general incendiary effect under battlefield conditions because of its more widespread effects and the fact that few materials found on the battlefield require 2,000 degrees Celsius to ignite them.

Antitank grenades are used against armored vehicles, but they are rare in modern armies. All consist of a shaped charge and a stabilizing mechanism. In the case of the Soviet RGK-3 antitank grenade, for example, a small drogue parachute keeps the warhead of the grenade oriented after it is thrown. Such hand-thrown antitank grenades have little effect against all but the most lightly armored vehicles. Antitank rifle grenades are in widespread use by many armies, but their effectiveness against modern tanks in other than flank or rear shots is marginal.

Rockets

A rocket is a self-propelled vehicle whose trajectory cannot be controlled while it is in flight. It is propelled by hot gases ejected to the rear by a motor or a burning charge. Rockets are among the oldest weapons, having been used in Asia since the fourteenth century and in Europe since the eighteenth century, in essentially the same form as today. Rockets are used in a variety of roles by modern military forces on air, sea, and land. Rockets are launched from aircraft against ground and sea targets; at one time they were also used against other aircraft, but guided missiles supplanted them in that role. Rockets are extensively used by ground forces in multiple-launch rocket systems (MLRSs). These systems launch from 12 to 40 individual rockets ranging in caliber from 122mm to 240mm. Their primary advantage over conventional artillery lies in their ability to saturate a target area with a large number of warheads in a very short period of time. One battery of Soviet BM-27 or U.S. MLRS rockets can fire 64 or 48 rockets, respectively, almost simultaneously, while a cannon battery can fire only 6 or 8 rounds at one time. The accuracy of modern rocket artillery has improved since World War II. As of the early 1990s, rockets are being equipped with a variety of warheads in addition to traditional HE. Some rocket launching systems include not only HE but also ICM, DPICM, chemical, and terminal homing warheads for use against armored vehicles. These warheads function as do those employed in cannon artillery projectiles.

Rockets are also used as antitank weapons, mostly as last-ditch defenses by infantry. Such weapons were employed beginning in World War II and have continued in use to the present time. Almost all antitank rockets employ HEAT warheads and are disposable—that is, the rocket and launcher are issued as a complete round of ammunition and the launcher is thrown away after firing. A notable exception is the Soviet RPG-7 system, which not only launches a HEAT rocket but can also fire a number of other rocket-propelled projectiles. A few other countries manufacture systems similar to the RPG-7, but all work much like the original and many are outright copies of this venerable and effective system. These rockets, of marginal effectiveness against modern tanks utilizing composite armors, are of great utility in urban combat and against snipers and weapons emplacements.

CHARLES Q. CUTSHAW

SEE ALSO: Artillery, Rocket and Missile; Artillery, Tube; Fuze; Grenade; Gun, Antitank; Machine Gun; Missile, Antitank Guided; Missile, Guided; Mortar; Munitions and Explosives: Engineering and Handling; Munitions and Explosives Technology Applications; Small Arms.

Bibliography

Campbell, C., ed. 1987. *Understanding military technology.* New York: Gallery Books.

Courtney-Green, P. R. 1991. *Ammunition for the land battle.* Vol. 6 of *Land warfare: Brassey's new battlefield weapons systems and technology series.* London: Brassey's.

Germershausen, R., et al. 1982. *Rheinmetall handbook on weaponry.* English ed. Frankfurt am Main: Broenners Druckeri Breidenstein GmbH.

Hogg, I. 1985. *The illustrated encyclopedia of ammunition.* Secaucus, N.J.: Chartwell Books.

———. 1988. *The illustrated encyclopedia of artillery.* Secaucus, N.J.: Chartwell Books.

Miller, D., and C. Foss. 1987. *Modern land combat.* New York: Portland House.

Ohart, T. 1947. *Elements of ammunition.* New York: Wiley.

Quick, J. 1973. *Dictionary of weapons and military terms.* New York: McGraw-Hill.

U.S. Department of Defense, Joint Chiefs of Staff. 1987. *Department of Defense dictionary of military and associated terms.* Washington, D.C.: Government Printing Office.

AMPHIBIOUS FORCES

Some 37 nations of the world maintain military forces that possess the capability to conduct one or more types of amphibious operations. Most of those forces are comparatively small in number and limited in capability. The U.S. Marine Corps represents the largest amphibious force in the world by a large margin. Forces of other countries are modest and, in general, do not have the ambitious tasks that are assigned to the U.S. force.

Types of Amphibious Operations

Amphibious operations range in complexity from small-unit raids to expeditionary-force amphibious assaults. The most common amphibious operations are: (1) strategic deception—to force an opponent to disperse his defenses along all vulnerable littorals; (2) raids—to destroy selected installations, units, or individuals that may have significant bearing on the course of the campaign; (3) forcible entry—to establish beachheads or airheads from which to introduce large-scale military forces; (4) extractions—to evacuate expeditionary forces or noncombatant civilians from a threatened area; (5) strategic reserve—to exploit opportunities and counter threats that develop during the course of a campaign; (6) reinforcement—to assist in conducting a land campaign as a part of a joint or combined command; (7) naval campaign—to control the landward flank of a naval command.

U.S. Amphibious Forces

Since World War II, the U.S. Marine Corps has set the standard by which all other national amphibious forces are measured. It is by far the world's largest naval infantry force, numbering about 195,000 personnel.

The U.S. Marine Corps is a separate military service within the Department of the Navy. It maintains two major operational commands organized, trained, and equipped primarily for the amphibious assault role, the Fleet Marine Forces (FMF) Atlantic and FMF Pacific. These FMFs are integrated components of the U.S. Atlantic and Pacific fleets, respectively. The corps is not only the largest naval infantry force in the world, but also the only combined-arms naval infantry force, possessing organic armor, artillery, and air forces.

The corps maintains three divisions and three aircraft wings in the active force structure, one division and one aircraft wing in the reserves, and an integrated force service support structure to maintain these major units. In addition, the corps supports the president of the United States with security and helicopter transportation and the U.S. Department of State through the maintenance of security guard detachments at U.S. embassies around the world.

The operational organization of the Marine Corps is the Marine Air/Ground Task Force (MAGTF). This structure draws forces from the FMFs to build combined-arms forces called Marine Expeditionary Units (MEUs), Marine Expeditionary Brigades (MEBs), and Marine Expeditionary Forces (MEFs). Two MEUs are continuously embarked in U.S. Navy amphibious ships and deployed with the Pacific and Atlantic fleets. The MEUs are built around a battalion landing team; the larger MEB is built around a marine regiment, and the MEF around one to three marine divisions.

The Marine Corps is equipped with a variety of modern individual and crew-served weapons. These include tanks, armored infantry fighting vehicles, armored personnel carriers, self-propelled artillery, towed artillery, mortars, TOW and Dragon antitank guided missiles, and both Redeye and Stinger air defense systems.

Marine Corps Aviation includes aircraft and systems that provide virtually every combat function of aviation: fighter (F/A-18), ground attack (A-6E, or AV-8B), reconnaissance (RF-4B), electronic warfare (EA-6B), airborne FAC (OV-10B), tankers (KC-130), transport (CH-46 and CH-53), armed escort (AH-1), and three battalions each of improved Hawk and Stinger air defense systems.

Soviet Amphibious Forces

The naval infantry of the Soviet navy corresponded in many respects to the U.S. Marines and the British Royal Marines. The Soviet naval infantry (SNI), however, did not appear to have the mission of conducting long-range, large-scale amphibious operations. The total strength of the naval infantry was about 18,000, reflecting a slow but steady growth in the USSR's last years. Each of the four Soviet naval fleets had a naval infantry component. The Northern, Baltic, and Black Sea fleets each were assigned a brigade, while the Pacific fleet had an SNI division. In addition, the Soviets maintained four fleet special forces (*Spetsnaz*) brigades.

SNI units were trained to carry out assaults against hostile shores from amphibious ships. They were equipped with amphibious tanks and armored personnel carriers, self-propelled artillery, rocket launchers, mortars, and numerous air defense missile systems, and employed both helicopters and air-cushioned vehicles (ACVs) to move troops. The Soviets invested significant research into amphibious specialized weapons and lift platforms. The most impressive of their recent efforts was the ORLAN wing-in-ground effect (WIG) aircraft.

SNI were deployed afloat with fleet units on a regular basis beginning in the mid-1960s. The Soviets conducted periodic amphibious landing exercises in the various fleet areas. They also made larger landings during Soviet worldwide fleet exercises, culminating in a practice amphibious assault during exercise Zapad 81 near the Polish border.

Other Nations Possessing Amphibious Forces

NATO Amphibious Forces

France. The French marine corps (*Fusiliers-Marins*) numbers some 2,600. Of these, 600 are organized into commando units: four assault groups, one attack swimmer unit, and one headquarters section. The remaining 2,000 are used to provide naval base protection for the French fleet.

Italy. The Italian navy includes the San Marco Brigade, a special forces unit similar to a marine corps. The brigade consists of approximately 750 personnel organized into one raiding group, one underwater operations group, one special operations group, one marine battalion, and two training groups. The brigade is equipped with armored personnel carriers, and it employs recoilless rifles and mortars as well as antitank missiles.

The Netherlands. The Royal Netherlands Marine Corps has a total active manpower of 2,800. It is organized into two amphibious commando groups, one mountain/arctic warfare company, and one reserve amphibious commando group. These units are equipped primarily with individual infantry weapons and rely upon the Netherlands army and navy for heavy artillery support. The marines maintain a highly specialized company, the Close Combat Unit, whose mission is to respond to terrorist incidents. The unit is authorized about 115 men and has trained with similar units in the Royal Marines, the U.S. Marines, and the German army.

Portugal. Portugal maintains a force of 2,800 marines, half of whom are conscripts. They are organized into two separate regiments, one designated the Continental Marine Force and the other Marine Corps Schools. The continental force is composed of one headquarters battalion and three infantry battalions, together with necessary supporting units. The schools include one training battalion and one service battalion. The principal weapons systems used by the Portuguese marines are armored personnel carriers, grenade launchers, and mortars.

Spain. The Spanish marine corps is one of the three components of the Spanish navy; it musters about 8,500 marines. The corps is organized into a single regiment of five marine garrison regiments. The regiment is composed of two infantry battalions, one support battalion, and three artillery batteries. The garrison units include specialized landing operations (TEAR) groups. These TEAR units are expected to support the tri-service Rapid Action Force being formed for operations in noncontinental Spanish territories. The marines are equipped with tanks, armored reconnaissance vehicles, and amphibious assault vehicles. They employ recoilless rifles, howitzers, and self-propelled howitzers. They are armed also with TOW and Dragon antitank weapons.

Turkey. Turkish marines number 4,000. They are administratively subordinated to the army and operationally controlled by the navy. The marines are organized into a single brigade consisting of a headquarters command, three infantry battalions, and one artillery battalion.

United Kingdom. There are about 7,700 Royal Marines, organized into one commando brigade and necessary support structure. The brigade contains three commando infantry regiments, one commando artillery regiment, one battery of artillery, two commando engineering squadrons, one logistics regiment, and one helicopter squadron. The Royal Marines also maintain one mountain and arctic warfare cadre, the Special Boat Service, and one assault squadron. They are equipped with antitank guided missiles, both Javelin and Blowpipe SAMs, and Lynx helicopters.

Other European Amphibious Forces

Poland. The Seventh Naval Assault Brigade or "Blue Berets" are the Polish marines and, next to the former Soviets, were the largest naval infantry unit in the Warsaw Pact. The brigade numbers 4,500 men. It is organized into three naval assault regiments, one tank battalion, one artillery battalion, one signals battalion, one engineer battalion, one multiple rocket launcher company, and one chemical defense company. The brigade is equipped with amphibious armored personnel carriers, T-55 and PT-76 tanks, and scout vehicles. It also maintains Frog missile launchers and antiair weapons.

Yugoslavia. There are two Yugoslavian marine brigades comprising two regiments with two battalions each.

MIDDLE EAST/AFRICA AMPHIBIOUS FORCES

Egypt. The Egyptian navy has one special operations brigade.

Iran. Iran maintains three battalions of naval infantry.

Israel. Israel has a naval commando unit of 300.

Kuwait. Kuwait has two battalions of commandos.

Morocco. Morocco maintains one naval infantry battalion of 1,500 men.

Saudi Arabia. Twelve hundred Saudi marines are organized into one infantry regiment with 140 armored fighting vehicles.

South Africa. There are 900 South African marines organized into one brigade headquarters, nine harbor/base defense units, and one amphibious company.

Zaire. Zaire has a naval infantry of 600.

SOUTHEAST ASIA/PACIFIC AMPHIBIOUS FORCES

Burma. Burma's naval infantry numbers 800. They are organized in one battalion.

China. China maintains a naval infantry force of 6,000, organized into one brigade special plus reconnaissance units. The Chinese keep a large naval infantry reserve. On mobilization, the naval infantry gains eight divisions (24 infantry, 8 tank, 8 artillery regiments), and two independent tank regiments. In addition, the Chinese army identifies three divisions specifically for the amphibious role. Chinese marines are equipped with main battle tanks, light tanks, amphibious personnel carriers, multiple rocket launchers, and howitzers.

India. The Indian marines number some 1,000 in one active regiment with an additional regiment forming.

Indonesia. The Indonesian marine corps is administratively supported by the navy but operationally controlled by the chief of the armed forces. The corps numbers over 12,000 marines (organized into 2 infantry brigades of 6 battalions each), one administrative regiment, one combat support regiment, and one training regiment. The corps is equipped with tanks, armored fighting vehicles, armored personnel carriers, towed howitzers, multiple rocket launchers, and air defense guns.

Peoples' Republic of Korea (PRK). The PRK maintains three amphibious light infantry brigades (ALIBs) within a larger special-purpose force. The brigades are specifically trained in amphibious assault, special operations, and unconventional warfare. The amphibious brigades are operationally controlled by the VIII Special Purpose Corps. The brigades include ten battalions and number some 5,000 soldiers. Each brigade contains a headquarters element, signal company, up to five infantry battalions, and a service support element. The ALIBs do not have organic heavy weapons but are equipped with Soviet standard infantry weapons including AK-47s, recoilless rifles, mortars, antitank weapons, and the SA-7 GRAIL air defense missile.

Republic of Korea (ROK). The ROK marine corps is an independent command under the ROK chief of naval operations. The corps is 25,000 strong organized into two divisions, one brigade, and support units. It is equipped with tanks, armored personnel carriers, towed artillery, and land-based Harpoon antiship missiles.

The Philippines. The Philippine marine corps is a 10,000-man force, organized into three brigades of three infantry battalions each and one brigade of combat support/combat service support assets. The corps also includes a 700-man rapid reaction force. The commandant of the marine corps is responsible to the commander of the navy for both operational and administrative control. The marine corps is equipped with howitzers and mortars, and it employs some U.S.-variant armored personnel carriers.

Taiwan. The Taiwanese maintain 30,000 marines in two divisions plus supporting elements. The marines are equipped with armored personnel carriers, towed artillery, and recoilless rifles.

Thailand. The Royal Thai Marine Corps is the largest element of the navy, yet comes under direct operational control of the army during war. The corps is some 20,000 strong with two infantry regiments, one artillery regiment, one security regiment, and one service support regiment. In addition, there are separate amphibious assault, reconnaissance, communications, engineer, and military police battalions. The corps is equipped with armored personnel carriers, towed howitzers, and both TOW and Dragon antitank guided weapons.

Vietnam. Vietnam has 27,000 naval infantry, both amphibious and commando.

LATIN AMERICAN AMPHIBIOUS FORCES

Argentina. The Argentine marine corps is headed by the chief of naval infantry who is a member of the navy general staff. The corps is organized into two major commands: the fleet force, which supports both of the regional fleets, and the amphibious support command, which provides logistic, training, and land-based support to the marine corps. Total active manpower is 5,000.

The fleet force is divided into two separate commands each comprising two infantry battalions, one field artillery battalion, one amphibious reconnaissance group, one heavy mortar company, one antitank company, and one engineer company. The amphibious support command includes one antiaircraft regiment, one signals battalion, one logistics battalion, one independent infantry battalion, and six independent infantry companies. The marine corps is equipped with combat vehicles and three different types of personnel carriers. It also maintains a variety of artillery pieces including towed howitzers, air defense guns, and recoilless rifles.

Bolivia. Marines maintain one battalion with a company in each district. There is a separate naval infantry with one battalion plus five independent companies.

Brazil. The Brazilian marine corps (*Corpo de Fuzileiros Navais*, or CFN) is the largest and best-equipped amphibious force in Latin America. It is commanded by the commandant of the marine corps who reports directly to the minister of the navy. The corps numbers some 16,500 and is organized into two major commands: the fleet marine force and the support command. The fleet force includes the amphibious division and the reinforcement troop. The division is further divided into one command, three infantry, one special operations, one artillery, and one service battalion. The reinforcement troop is made up of five separate battalions: one engineer, one transportation, one special operations, one maintenance, and one command battalion. In addition, there is an amphibious reconnaissance company and eight marine barracks detachments for internal security located in the naval districts. Brazilian marines are equipped with reconnaissance vehicles and armored personnel carriers, towed howitzers, a variety of rocket launchers, and towed air defense guns.

Chile. The Chilean marine corps (*Cuerpo de Infantería de Marina*) is an integral part of the navy, directly under the control of the navy commander. The commandant of naval infantry is responsible for 5,200 marines organized into four battalion-sized detachments, one of which is specifically identified as amphibious. Each detachment includes one commando company, one field artillery battery, and one air defense artillery battery. Chilean marines are equipped with armored personnel carrier variants and operate Roland ATMs, towed howitzers, mortars, and the Blowpipe SAM.

Colombia. The Colombian marine corps numbers 6,000, organized into five infantry battalions and two naval police battalions. The corps employs personal infantry weapons but no heavy equipment.

Cuba. Cuba has 550 troops organized into one amphibious assault battalion.

Ecuador. The corps of the naval infantry (*Cuerpo de Infantería de Marina*, or CIM) is headed by the commander of the marine corps under the operational control of the chief of naval operations. The CIM is organized into an operations group, a security force, and the support force. The operations group includes a commando and a special warfare group; the security force includes three security companies at major naval bases, and the support force includes instruction, training, administration, and military police units. The CIM has about 1,700 personnel but employs no heavy weapons or vehicles.

Honduras. The Honduran marine corps (*Infantería de Marina*, or IMH) includes some 700 personnel whose primary mission is to provide security for naval assets. The commander of the marine corps is the intelligence officer of the naval general staff. The IMH is organized into two companies and equipped with personal infantry weapons only.

Mexico. The Mexican marine corps is a force of some 9,000 marines, organized into 36 companies assigned to 17 naval zones. It does not have an overall operational commander, but is administered instead by the director of the marine corps subordinate to the Mexican naval staff. Marine units are under the direct control of the naval zone commanders. The marines also include one brigade with two battalions, and one presidential guard battalion.

Paraguay. Paraguay's marines number 500 organized in one marine battalion and one commando battalion.

Peru. The Peruvian marine corps (*Fuerza de Infantería de Marina*, or FIM) is an integral part of the navy, and its commander is directly subordinate to the Peruvian chief of naval operations. The corps numbers some 5,000 personnel, organized into one marine brigade of two battalions, one reconnaissance company, and one commando company. It is equipped with armored personnel carriers, and employs a variety of individual weapons together with rocket launchers, mortars, howitzers, and antitank guns.

Uruguay. Uruguay has 500 marines organized into one battalion.

Venezuela. The Venezuelan marine corps numbers some 4,500 personnel organized into four infantry battalions, one artillery battalion, one amphibious vehicle battalion, one river patrol, one engineer unit, and two commando units. The corps is equipped with armored personnel carriers, towed howitzers, and air defense guns.

The Future of Amphibious Forces

Amphibious operations by their very nature require expensive, specialized equipment and naval infantry with a high degree of combat readiness. There are only a handful of nations willing to maintain these prerequisites. A few more keep some form of amphibious raid or commando capability. In the years ahead the single most influential determinant for the maintenance of these forces will be economic.

For those nations that persist, their future amphibious force will face more formidable defensive capabilities around the world. The profusion of modern technology—which includes long-range surveillance systems, precision-guided munitions, sophisticated land-based airpower, and high-technology naval mining capability—

will offer major advantages to defenders. The fact that these technologies are available to developing nations makes even small amphibious operations in their areas a difficult undertaking.

Those same technologies, however, have been modifying the attacker's capabilities as much as those of the defense. While surrendering the *strategic* surprise of earlier years to improved surveillance, amphibious forces will find it easier to gain *operational* and *tactical* surprise, such as landing where the enemy is not ready. Air-cushioned vehicles, tilt-rotor transports, and VSTOL fighter-bombers will make over-the-horizon landing operations the norm. Assaults will take place with unprecedented speed, from greater distances, and using both air and sea transport. The enemy might well find both his front and rear attacked at the same time. In the final analysis, geography will still play a central role. Today, there is not a single nation with the military capability to defend all of its coastline from amphibious assault. As long as nations seek solutions to their problems through conventional combat, the seas will offer one alternative that combatants must consider to achieve their directives—in some instances, the only way.

THOMAS L. WILKERSON

SEE ALSO: Amphibious Ships and Craft; Amphibious Warfare; Combined Operations; Joint Operations; Marine; Special Operations Forces.

Bibliography

Bermudez, M. 1987. North Korean marines. *Marine Corps Gazette*, January, pp. 32–35.
Eshel, D. 1984. *Elite fighting units*. New York: Arco.
International Institute for Strategic Studies. 1990. *The military balance, 1989–1990*. London: Brassey's.
International Media Corporation. 1989. *Defense and foreign affairs handbook*. Alexandria, Va.: International Media Corporation.
Polmar, N. 1988. *Amphibious warfare: An illustrated history*. London: Blandford.
U.S. Marine Corps. 1991. *FMFM 2: The Marine air/ground task force*. Quantico, Va.: U.S. Marine Corps. Draft.
United States Naval Institute. *Military data base*. Annapolis, Md.: United Communications Group.
Walmer, M. 1986. *An illustrated guide to modern elite forces*. Englewood Cliffs, N.J.: Prentice-Hall.
Zaloga, S. 1987. The Blue Berets: Poland's marines. *Amphibious Warfare Review*, vol. 5, no. 2.

AMPHIBIOUS SHIPS AND CRAFT

A perusal of the world's naval inventories yields an interesting fact: more than 50 nations include amphibious ships and craft in their naval forces. The use of amphibious ships and craft is generally divided into two categories. The majority of nations use these naval assets primarily for logistics support to nearby islands or to resupply military or civilian outposts that are difficult to reach by overland routes. The military purpose of amphibious ships and craft—to project power—is less widely used. By far the largest fleets of amphibious ships belong to the United States and to the former Union of Soviet Socialist Republics. From different directions, each of these nations is proceeding toward the goal of power projection, maintaining the capability to seize the territory of another state and to preserve the option to hold that territory by reinforcing the troops put on that foreign shore.

The Ships

Because amphibious warfare is a unique military art, a few words of description are required for the major types of amphibious ships in the world's navies.

MULTIPURPOSE AMPHIBIOUS ASSAULT SHIP (LHD)

The LHD, the newest type amphibious ship in the world, is peculiar to the U.S. Navy. It is a follow-on design from the American general-purpose amphibious assault ship (LHA). The LHD is similar in appearance to a small aircraft carrier; in fact, the LHD has a secondary mission as a sea control ship, operating vertical and short takeoff and landing aircraft (V/STOL). Its length is 272 meters (844 ft.) overall, only 17 meters (53 ft.) shorter than the Soviet Kiev-class aircraft carrier. The LHD's island is displaced to starboard, and the flight deck is straight instead of angled, as in U.S. attack aircraft carriers. The LHD carries 42 (CH-46 equivalent) helicopters or a mixture of helicopters and the AV-8B Super Harrier. It also carries three air-cushioned landing craft (LCAC) and more than 1,800 troops. The LHD is equipped with a 600-bed emergency medical facility. Its full load displacement is more than 40,000 tons, and its maximum speed is over 20 knots.

GENERAL-PURPOSE AMPHIBIOUS ASSAULT SHIP (LHA)

The LHA is the forerunner of the American LHD. It combines the capabilities of the helicopter assault ship (LPH) and the dock landing ship (LSD). It has a large, open well-deck for transport of landing craft, including four utility landing craft (LCU) and six medium landing craft (LCM). It can also carry one LCAC. Its length is 264.5 meters (822 ft.) overall. In addition to the surface landing craft, it can also transport 38 helicopters and more than 1,700 troops. The LHA and LHD are very similar in appearance. The LHA may be distinguished by its much larger island.

AMPHIBIOUS ASSAULT SHIP (LPH)

This older American helicopter carrier is being replaced by the newer LHDs. Its overall length is 195 meters (602 ft.), and its full load displacement is 18,000 tons. The LPH carries 27 helicopters and more than 1,700 troops. It has no well-deck and thus carries no surface landing craft. Although the U.S. Navy is the only force with designated amphibious helicopter carriers, several nations have small aircraft carriers that can provide a similar capability if assigned an amphibious warfare mission.

AMPHIBIOUS CARGO SHIP (LKA)

The LKA is basically a break-bulk cargo ship built to U.S. Navy specifications. It can carry 226 troops and has four organic medium landing craft. The Charleston-class LKAs were built on the same hull design as the Iwo Jima–class LPHs. They are capable of operating helicopters, but they are primarily off-loaded over the side by booms.

AMPHIBIOUS TRANSPORT DOCK (LPD)

The LPDs have been in service since the early 1960s by the U.S. Navy and the British Royal Navy, since the late 1970s by the former Soviet Navy, and most recently by the Italian Navy. The LPD can carry landing craft in a floodable well-deck similar to but not as large as that in the LSD. They also have permanent flight decks for helicopter debarkation of troops and equipment. They carry tanks, vehicles, heavy equipment, and more than 500 troops. The Russian Ivan Rogov class has a beaching capability. The American Raleigh and Austin classes do not, nor does the British Fearless class or the Italian San Giorgio class. Full load displacement of LPDs varies from 12,000 to 17,000 tons. The Italian LPD resembles a small LHA with an overall flight deck and island displaced to starboard.

DOCK LANDING SHIP (LSD)

Built for the U.S. and French navies, some older American LSDs have been transferred to other nations. Similar in appearance to American LPDs, LSDs feature a much longer floodable well-deck with a correspondingly greater capacity to carry landing craft. They carry less cargo and fewer troops (around 300). The LSDs can operate helicopters on a much smaller, usually removable, flight deck than found on the LPDs.

TANK LANDING SHIP (LST)

The LSTs comprise the amphibious forces for most navies with amphibious capability. They have been built primarily by the United States, the former USSR, and Poland. They feature a covered tank deck for tanks and vehicles and generally have the capability to land them directly on a beach. Except for the U.S. Newport class, LSTs are identifiable by the bow doors through which cargo vehicles are discharged. Newports have a dual ramp system that delivers vehicles up and over the bow and distinctive derrick arms to support the ramp. The Newport LSTs can operate helicopters for vertical off-loading of troops and cargo.

The Craft

Amphibious landing craft vary widely by mode of propulsion and capacity. They are usually transported in mother ships but may operate at short ranges independently from bases.

AIR-CUSHIONED VEHICLES

AIST (USSR) — Displacement of 250 tons, a range of 350 nautical miles at 80 knots, and a capacity of four light tanks.

LEBED (USSR) — Displacement of 87 tons, a range of 150 nautical miles at 70 knots, and a capacity of two light tanks.

GUS (USSR) — Displacement of 27 tons, a range of 230 nautical miles at 60 knots, and troop-carrying capacity.

LCAC (U.S.) — Displacement of 150 tons, a range of 300 nautical miles at 50 knots, and a capacity of one 60-ton tank.

HOVERCRAFT

BH-7 (U.K.) — Displacement of 55 tons, a range of 400 nautical miles at 58 knots, and troop-carrying capacity.

VCA-36 (SP) — Displacement of 36 tons, a range of 145 nautical miles at 60 knots; can carry troops and light vehicles.

HULLBORNE

LCU, LCM, LCVP, LCT, LCP, LCA, RPL — These are all designations for hullborne landing craft, normally carried aboard or within amphibious ships or designed for short-distance assault support or logistics lighterage.

The U.S. Program

The United States has been the leader in the design of amphibious ships and craft. The American experience in World War II taught the value of amphibious warfare in the Pacific campaign. That experience drove home the importance of a mixture of ship types and pointed out the desirability of including vertical assault in the amphibious war-fighting equation.

The helicopter subsequently revolutionized amphibious warfare and has led to the development of the present LHD and LHA amphibious assault ships. Since the early 1960s, helicopter carriers (LPHs) were incorporated into the American amphibious forces to make assault possible on shores impregnable to surface assault and to enable the landing force to land behind initial enemy defensive positions.

The numerous types of American amphibious ships reflect the synergism required for modern amphibious warfare. Heliborne and surface assault capabilities are melded into ships' design to facilitate the rapid buildup of personnel, equipment, and supplies ashore. Highly specialized individually, the American ships selected for an amphibious operation complement each other to support that mission. The present building program for amphibious ships and craft represents an enhancement of this capability, as well as replacement for aging ships, and will result in a more highly capable and versatile force.

Amphibious lift capacity is defined in terms of the shipping required to deliver amphibious assault echelons. The assault echelon is that portion of an assault force that must be put ashore within the first three to five days of the beginning of the assault, the "teeth" of the assault force. The figures for this force, in terms of personnel, vehicle capacity, and cargo stowage, are fixed by agreement between the navy and the marines. The assault follow-on echelon is composed of everything else the Marine Corps needs to keep its assault force fighting (the "tail") and includes supplies for up to 60 days. This latter echelon is planned to be carried in "black bottoms," merchant ships provided by the Military Sealift Command.

Former American amphibious ships constitute the majority of the amphibious ships in the navies of the rest of the world. Hundreds of tank landing ships (LSTs) that beached at Saipan and Guadalcanal and later at Inchon during the Korean War were sold to friendly nations throughout the world during the 1950s and 1960s. The last World War II–vintage amphibious ships, the amphibious personnel carriers (LPAs), were stricken from the American navy in the 1970s and sold to Spain.

Balanced between the U.S. Atlantic and Pacific Fleets, highly capable and, in some cases, revolutionary amphibious ships provide a fast force (all capable of speeds over 20 knots) that can sail long distances and land more than a battalion's worth of marines from each fleet.

The air-cushioned landing craft (LCAC) caused a virtual revolution in amphibious shipbuilding. Although the 1960s generation of amphibious ships could transit large expanses of ocean quickly and stealthily and the concept of vertical envelopment had evolved to the point where a large percentage of the personnel, light weapons, and vehicles of the assaulting force could be landed via helicopter, an American amphibious assault remained tied to the 7 percent of the world's ocean littorals accessible to traditional hullborne landing craft. This was because all tanks and heavy equipment carried in the assault echelon as well as virtually all of the assault follow-on echelon, had to be off-loaded in conventional surface landing craft. The U.S. amphibious force, composed of the 1960s-vintage ships, would also be so close to these beaches as to make the defender's task relatively easy.

The LCAC significantly alters the equation. Capable of speeds over 50 knots and ranges of nearly 400 nautical miles, LCAC brings the threat of assault to as much as 70 percent of the world's shores. It also enables the mother ships to stand off the beach beyond coastal battery and shore-based reconnaissance range and makes surprise a true ally in the assault. Air-cushion vehicle technology, in use commercially throughout the world, has led the U.S. Navy into an amphibious assault capability that will make it an effective and viable power projection tool into the twenty-first century.

Ninety LCACs are programmed as the minimum number required to land the assault element of the landing force in two waves. Twenty-eight meters (88 ft.) long, with a 15-meter (47-ft.) beam, LCAC is capable of carrying 60 tons of vehicles or cargo, equivalent to one main battle tank. The LCAC requirement was central to the design of the Whidbey Island–class (LSD-41) dock-landing ships and to the transition from the LHAs to the newest U.S. amphibious ships, the Wasp–class (LHD-1) multipurpose amphibious assault ships.

The U.S. Navy shipbuilding plan calls for delivery of eleven Wasp-class LHDs by the turn of the century. Wasps will replace the LPHs as well as add to the capacity of the U.S. amphibious forces in the longer term. Besides being the most versatile and capable amphibious ship in the world today, LHDs could also supplement the U.S. aircraft carrier force in time of emergency by carrying V/STOL strike, fighter, and antisubmarine aircraft. The LHDs could serve as the carrier component of battle groups in low-threat areas or as the primary escort vessels for high-priority resupply convoys.

The eight Whidbey Island–class LSDs were designed specifically to carry four LCACs each. The older Austin LPDs and Anchorage LSDs have been modified to carry LCACs.

The addition of the MV-22A/Osprey tilt-wing aircraft to the American amphibious forces would make them a true over-the-horizon force. The aging CH-46 helicopter force, which forms the backbone of the medium-lift air assault force, requires replacement in the 1990s. The range, lift capacity, and flight characteristics of Osprey make it an ideal choice to complement LCAC and the future ship mix. Osprey would permit vertical envelopment operations from beyond 300 nautical miles at sea and significantly enlarge the battlefield area. Its speed would enable it to fly around heavily defended areas and further complicate defensive problems.

The Soviet Program

Since the early 1960s, the USSR has built an impressive amphibious power projection capability. Early Soviet amphibious ships were primarily coastal in nature, the Polnocny-class medium landing ships. The more capable Alligator tank landing ships built in the mid-1960s greatly enhanced the available amphibious lift and provided a contingency response capability throughout the world. Alligator LSTs have been deployed for long periods in distant areas, including the east and west coasts of Africa. They were usually deployed with Soviet naval infantry troops (the Soviet counterpart of the U.S. Marine Corps) embarked.

In the late 1970s, the introduction of the Polish-built Ropucha LSTs and the Ivan Rogov large landing ships gave the Soviet Navy a credible distant power projection capability. The Kiev-class aircraft carrier, which was introduced at about the same time, is an excellent helicopter platform that could function as a vertical envelopment platform in an amphibious assault, as could the Moskva and Leningrad helicopter-carrying cruisers.

Numerous auxiliary amphibious ships subordinated to the Russian Navy offer the heavy lift required for amphibious power projection without modification. Many of these commercial types of ships have sophisticated fast discharge capabilities. Roll on/lift off (RO/LO), roll on/float off (RO-FLOW), and roll on/roll off (RO/RO) equipped ships, as well as numerous barge carriers, are excellent for carrying heavy cargo and tanks and for independent organic off-loading. These auxiliary amphibious ships give the Russian Navy the greatest capability in the world for carrying what was described in the "U.S. Program" section above as the assault follow-on echelon of the amphibious landing force. They cannot be used for assault operations against armed resistance, however.

The extensive interest shown by the former Soviet Navy in air-cushioned vehicles (ACV) has resulted in a significant rapid assault capability within the immediate range of bases and staging areas, including against the northern and eastern North Atlantic Treaty Organization (NATO) flanks and in the Far East. A force of ACV landing craft could stage amphibious landings near these Russian-controlled areas independent of amphibious ships because they could use nearly any Russian combatant ship for command and control purposes.

The wing-in-ground-effect machines (WIG), under development since the mid-1960s and reportedly now under construction in two versions, offer the possibility of a very high speed amphibious assault, landing up to 900 troops each from these revolutionary craft (Fig. 1). Capable of speeds of 300 knots, these unusual craft could skim across water and low terrain and discharge their cargo before any reaction could occur.

Seen in total context, Russia has an excellent amphibious assault capability across open oceans and against lightly defended territory. It has a much greater capability near its home territory. Once established ashore, the resupply capability of amphibious forces inherent in its large merchant fleet provides Russia with the ability to sustain forces in place for a long time.

Figure 1. An artist's concept of a Soviet wing-in-ground-effect vehicle. (Source: U.S. Department of Defense)

Other Programs

Few nations other than the United States and the former USSR have ongoing amphibious shipbuilding programs. The British are building a replacement Fearless LPD for the one lost in the Falklands/Malvinas conflict. Italy is building the San Giorgio LPD, which will have an important function as a vertical assault platform.

Most other nations' amphibious forces are made up of U.S.- or Soviet Polish-built LSTs that they have purchased. Some American-built LSDs and assault personnel carriers (LPAs) have been sold to other nations after service with the U.S. Navy.

These smaller amphibious forces are used either as logistics lighterage for remote area resupply or for power projection on a limited, regional scale. The reduction in scale does not make the amphibious forces less effective in their intended area of operation. These forces still provide the ability to reach out and take the territory of an opposing belligerent or to put an occupying force ashore on a disputed island. In other words, they offer power projection. Amphibious ships and craft are inexpensive relative to aircraft carriers or guided missile cruisers and submarines, and no other naval force is capable of putting one nation's troops onto the territory of another nation.

Future Developments

Amphibious ships and craft are highly versatile assets to national naval forces. During the cold war, the United States and the former Soviet Union had building programs to augment and expand their power projection capabilities; however, as of mid-1992, the United States, Russia, and Ukraine were reducing the size of these programs. The United Kingdom and Italy are building amphibious ships to maintain a complementary amphibious capability as part of the NATO alliance. Many other nations have amphibious ships and craft for power projection on a regional scale, and others use them for logistics purposes. Amphibious ships and craft are generally easy to operate and relatively inexpensive to build or purchase.

William L. Eldred

See Also: Amphibious Forces; Amphibious Vehicle; Amphibious Warfare; Coast Defense; Helicopter, Naval; Tooth-to-Tail: Ground Forces.

Bibliography

Couhat, J. L., and B. Prezelin, eds. *Combat fleets of the world.* Annual. Annapolis, Md.: U.S. Naval Institute Press.
Gregory, B. 1987. *Amphibious operations.* Poolc: Blandford.
Jane's fighting ships. Annual. London: Jane's.

Polmar, N. 1988. *Amphibious warfare: An illustrated history.* London: Blandford.

U.S. Congressional Budget Office. 1989. *Moving the Marine Corps by sea in the 1990s.* Washington, D.C.: Congressional Budget Office.

AMPHIBIOUS VEHICLE

Amphibious vehicles are those vehicles that possess the capability of moving both on land and in the water. For military applications they are primarily designed with a high interior volume-to-weight ratio so that they are able to float without preparation in fresh or salt water. Tightness of seals and protection against salt water are important considerations. Such vehicles move on land exactly as do other wheeled or tracked vehicles, and with the same performance in terms of agility and mobility.

Military amphibious vehicles are used in army and marine operations. They are employed in crossing waterways during deep reconnaissance or a tactical approach to engagement, and to land on the shore from the sea in the course of special landing operations. In army operations, amphibious vehicles normally approximate in size such armored vehicles as the armored personnel carrier or the infantry fighting vehicle. The number of crewmen is determined by the mission and normally ranges between three and thirteen. Marine operations employ both vehicles similar to those used by army forces and a larger size; the latter may or may not be armored, and can accommodate as many as thirty troops. Amphibious vehicles of such size can disembark from maritime vessels and move to the shore.

Hovercraft

Hovercraft are also amphibious vehicles, but of a specialized type that operate without any part of the drive train being in contact with the terrain being traversed, whether on land or over water. Hovercraft achieve this by riding on an air cushion, free of all contact with the underlying surface. This technique was introduced in modern form by British engineer Sir Christopher Cockerell in 1955, when he demonstrated the first prototype hovercraft. A first experimental passenger service was operated in 1962.

Features and Function of Amphibious Vehicles

Although most amphibious tracked and wheeled vehicles have the same technological basis as armored vehicles, they also have some distinctive features in their design and construction that help them perform their specialized mission effectively. Thus they require the following features:

A streamlined hull section that provides minimal resistance and higher speed in the water. This can be achieved more easily in wheeled amphibious vehicles than in armored ones.

High ground clearance for axles and hull, and large angles of approach and departure to ensure quick and easy entry to and exit from bodies of water with steep banks.

High volume-to-weight ratio, useful in making the vehicle float, and a reasonably high roof that projects above the waterline, taking into account the effect of waves.

Balanced distribution of weight in both longitudinal and transverse planes, and a low center of gravity.

Low ground pressure to facilitate crossing muddy, slippery, and soft terrain and steep banks safely and quickly, since the amphibious vehicle is very vulnerable in water and especially while climbing banks during exit from the water. The recommended ground pressure may be as low as 55 KN/m (0.55 bar). This is the normal ground pressure for tracked vehicles. Wheeled vehicles can achieve it by using low-pressure, wide-tread, large-diameter tires with air pressure regulation that can reduce ground pressure to 0.65 bar.

High power-to-weight ratio to ensure enough tractive power to push the amphibious vehicle out of the water and up steep banks by means of the driving wheels or tracks already in contact with the soil and the propellers still in the water, using both simultaneously.

Low fuel consumption to enhance cruising range, especially important for vehicles performing deep reconnaissance missions in uncharted terrain. Such vehicles should also be provided with large fuel tanks, as they may be employed in coastal and shore patrol operations.

Design

Achieving a streamlined hull section presents no problem in the design of wheeled amphibious vehicles, which can even have a rhomboidal hull that provides an adequate safety margin against waves and water spray and also a reasonable degree of protection against land mines. For tracked amphibious vehicles the necessary installation of the suspension system torsion bars, trailing arms, and road wheels in the bottom of the hull does not allow for such a streamlined hull design.

The required volume-to-weight ratio (the total outer volume of the vehicle as compared with the volume of displaced water) may reach 1.15. That ratio will ensure the vehicle of adequate buoyancy, draft (submerged depth), and height above the waterline. In wheeled vehicles the pneumatic tires, especially those with large diameter and wide tread, also help to provide flotation.

The greater the width of the vehicle, the more stable it will be in water. Tightness should not present difficulties, since most amphibious vehicles are airtight by virtue of their installed NBC (nuclear, biological, chemical) protection systems. But the possibility of accidental leakage through upper hatches due to high waves, splashing, and spray make it advisable to mount one or more bilge pumps that can be electrically operated as soon as the vehicle enters the water. A hand pump may also be provided as an emergency backup.

The only preparations the driver of an amphibious vehicle must take before entering the water are to erect the trim vane at the front of the hull and switch on the electric bilge pumps. The trim vane, which is carried folded back onto the glacis plate when not in use, may have a transparent panel in its center to provide the driver a clear view to the front. The trim vane functions as a wave barrier.

PROPULSION

Motion in water is achieved by two main means: positively by the use of propellers, as in motorboats, or of hydrojets; or passively by use of the same running train that moves the vehicle on land—its wheels or tracks. Positive propulsion produces greater speed and better steerability and maneuverability in water, but providing it is complicated and expensive.

Passive propulsion of amphibious vehicles, whether wheeled or tracked, produces a limited speed in the water (e.g., about 6 km/hr in still water). Tracks can be provided with buckets or inverted water grousers to help push the vehicle through the water; such means can increase the speed to some degree. Tire tread configuration can also help to provide motive power. Such considerations should not be allowed to conflict with dictates of the original land mobility requirements for either wheeled or tracked vehicles. For many missions, in fact, the time spent in the water is minor.

The most positive method for propulsion of amphibious vehicles in water is the use of driving propellers, using a single propeller centered in the rear part of the hull or twin propellers positioned one on either side. This solution is more suitable for use with wheeled vehicles than with tracks. Propellers should be positioned under the floor or elsewhere at that same level so that they remain in the water at considerable depth, thus enabling them to provide their full thrust to the vehicle. Either two- or four-bladed propellers are used. Steerable propellers are also employed, including some that can be traversed through 360 degrees. Such swivelling propellers give amphibious vehicles outstanding maneuverability in water and are more active in steering than a rudder, which is rarely used on amphibious vehicles except with fixed propellers.

The speed in water of amphibious wheeled vehicles with propellers can be as high as 12 kilometers per hour (7.4 mph). Propellers are driven by a power takeoff from the transmission of the vehicle, usually mounted on the main gearbox and driven by its lay-shaft. The driver engages the propellers immediately prior to entering the water, in the same manner as he engages the front wheel drive. Consequently the wheels will drive the vehicle in the water after descending the bank, while as soon as the propellers are at a suitable depth they begin to deliver their thrust to push the vehicle forward. The driver can then disengage the wheels until it is time to exit the water (See Fig. 1).

The exiting maneuver is the more critical. Entering the water requires descending a bank, during which the vehicle uses its own weight and gravity; getting back out requires ascending or climbing a possibly steep and slippery bank against the vehicle's weight. The driver must engage all wheels early in the maneuver so that the vehicle can begin climbing the bank as soon as its wheels touch, while the propellers are still deep in the water and can add their thrust. In this way the propellers and the front and rear wheels can all work together to help push the vehicle out of the water. (Exit from the water may be further complicated if an enemy places obstructions for the vehicles.)

In some designs of amphibious vehicles, the axles can be retracted hydraulically to reduce drag during movement in water. The usefulness of this arrangement does not seem to warrant the complications in construction required to implement it.

For tracked vehicles, propulsion in water may be achieved through the use of water jets, sometimes called

Figure 1. U.S. DUKW-type amphibious vehicle hits moderate surf after high-speed run off high beach, 1953. (SOURCE: U.S. Army)

hydrojets, which are induced by water pumps driven off the vehicle's transmission. These suck in water and then discharge it to the rear of the vehicle through one or two jets that thus push the vehicle forward. Steering in water can be accomplished by use of a rudder in the middle part of the water jet outlet, although more positive steering can be derived from a double water jet. Covers over the jets are manipulated to turn the vehicle in the desired direction; to go left, for example, the left water jet would be covered. To make a more pronounced turn, the left water jet can be made to suck in water while the right jet pushes it out. Speed in the water using such an arrangement averages 10 to 12 kilometers per hour (6.2 to 7.4 mph). When exiting the water, tracked vehicles should employ the same technique as wheeled vehicles, using tracks and water jets simultaneously to propel the vehicle up the bank.

In both types of vehicles, the torque transmitted should be sufficient to drive the land running train (tracks or wheels) and the water propulsion element simultaneously. This is a function of the amphibious vehicle's location on the power-to-weight ratio maps of both wheeled and tracked vehicles, where it will be found to have one of the highest ratios.

Amphibious landing vehicles, both wheeled and tracked (but especially tracked), may come in many different versions—including recovery, engineer, fighting, mine clearing, and similar applications—that can act in conjunction with the landing forces.

Fording

Military vehicles can ford in water of different depths, according to their construction. Fording depth can be increased by certain preparations. A few vehicles can ford water as deep as their full height or more by using a special snorkel that rises above the water surface and supplies air to the vehicle's engine. Such vehicles are not considered amphibious, since they do not float but rather move over the bottom of a waterway of limited and known depth.

Typically military vehicles can ford at depths of up to 1.3 meters (4 ft.) without special preparation, and with a fording kit to 2.2 meters (7 ft.). A snorkel can increase fording capability to more than 5 meters (16 ft.). Some logistical vehicles can be equipped with either folding or fixed outboard motors or with large inflatable side cushions (called borthons) that can make them temporarily amphibious for certain missions.

Upgrading and retrofitting existing amphibious tracked vehicles (e.g., the provision of add-on armor) offered designers an opportunity to simultaneously improve their vehicles' buoyancy and stability in water by favorable distribution of the foam used to counterbalance the additional weight, thus producing higher cruising speed in water.

Examples of Amphibious Vehicles

The German Spähpanzer Luchs armored amphibious reconnaissance vehicle was developed in West Germany as part of a new generation of military vehicles for the 1970s. The quiet-running Luchs has excellent cross-country mobility, achieved by its eight-wheel configuration powered by a Daimler-Benz multifuel engine. Fully amphibious, the Luchs has a hydraulic trim vane on the front, and can achieve speeds up to 9 kilometers per hour (5.6 mph) in water from its steerable twin propellers mounted on each side at the rear of the hull. It is capable of entering water obstacles at an angle of 66 degrees and exiting water at 53 degrees. Armed with a 20mm cannon and a 7.62mm machine gun, the Luchs provides its four-man crew battlefield with flexibility and mobility, which, with its quiet engine, are essential to reconnaissance activities.

The Hungarian FUG (Felderítö Usó Gépkosci) is an example of an amphibious scout car that is powered in water by twin water jets at the rear of the hull. Fulfilling a role similar to the Soviet BRDM-1 amphibious scout car, the FUG entered service in Hungary in 1964 and in Poland and Czechoslovakia in 1966. Powered by a diesel engine that develops 100 horsepower at 2,300 rpm, it can achieve speeds up to 9 kilometers per hour (5.6 mph) in water (with the trim vane lowered) and 87 kilometers per hour (54 mph) on roads. Additional cross-country mobility is provided by a set of four belly wheels that can be lowered to augment four primary wheels. A two-man crew operates the vehicle, which can carry four additional soldiers. The main armament is a 7.62mm machine gun, although the Czech version (the OT-65) has been fitted with an external 82mm recoilless gun.

The American LVTP7 (landing vehicle, tracked, personnel) armored amphibious assault vehicle, fielded by the United States Marine Corps in the early 1970s, is a fully amphibious tracked vehicle that requires no trim vane in front and is propelled in the water by two water jets at the rear of the hull. Its tracks, which provide excellent cross-country mobility, can also be used to move the vehicle in water. The LVTP7 has a vehicle commander and crew of three and can carry 25 fully equipped marines. Designed to support marine amphibious operations, the LVTP7 can be launched at sea or used over water obstacles on land. Its diesel engine develops 400 horsepower at 2,800 rpm, and it achieves forward water speeds up to 13.5 kilometers per hour (8.4 mph) and rearward speeds to 7.2 kilometers per hour (4.5 mph). Its speed on land is about 74 kilometers per hour (45.9 mph). The LVTP7's main armament is a 0.50-caliber machine gun, but it can mount other weapon systems as well. It is in wide service around the globe in Argentina, Italy, South Korea, Spain, and Venezuela.

Conclusion

One of the more significant problems amphibious operations must deal with today is the increased use of underwater mines. New techniques and technologies for detecting and negating underwater mines will involve amphibious vehicles and considerations for their landing characteristics. Thus, while there is no question that amphibious vehicles will continue to play an important military role, their future is linked to this particular challenge.

Regardless, with three-fourths of the globe covered with water and countless waterways coursing across its land mass, the need for amphibious vehicles in warfare will continue as long as there are militaries to use them. Continuing research in composite materials will enable future amphibious vehicles to be lighter and more mobile. New, more powerful engines and streamlined hull shapes will improve water speeds and range.

Whether or not amphibious operations are conducted depends on the physical environment of the battlefield and the desires of military commanders. Nonetheless, amphibious capabilities will be maintained by armed forces even if, as was the case with the U.S. Marines in Operation Desert Storm, they are not used.

MOUSTAFA ALY MORSY ALY

SEE ALSO: Amphibious Forces; Amphibious Ships and Craft; Amphibious Warfare; Combined Operations.

Bibliography

Hasso, E. 1987. New multi-purpose amphibious armored vehicles for EWK. *International Defense Review* 8:54–58.
Jane's Armor and Artillery. 1983, passim.
Leibston, M. 1985. The U.S. Marine Corps and amphibious warfare. *Military Technology* 8:22–38.
———. 1987. The USMC: Key issues. *Military Technology* 8:37.
Miller, S. 1986. U.S. Marine Corps amphibious operations and technology. *Military Technology* 8:54–81.
Ogorkiewicz, R. 1981. LVTP 7A1: The latest tracked landing vehicle. *International Defense Review* 4:104–106.
Trainer, B. 1985. We are ready and will remain ready. *Military Technology* 9/8:34–41.

AMPHIBIOUS WARFARE

Amphibious warfare is that dimension of naval warfare in which an attack is launched from the sea by naval and landing forces, embarked in specialized ships and craft, against a hostile shore. It integrates all elements of military force (air, land, naval, logistics, command, and control) and is useful in the entire spectrum of political conflict. Amphibious warfare is also risky and complex, hence requiring an extraordinary degree of coordination.

Amphibious warfare is distinguished from other forms of warfare by the three primary requirements that shape its distinctive organizational and doctrinal priorities. First is the requirement for rapid buildup of combat power in the amphibious objective area (AOA) from zero capability to full striking strength. Second is the requirement to maintain unity of command between naval and landing force commanders throughout the transition of the assault from sea to land. Third is the requirement to minimize the inherent vulnerability of the landing force to natural obstacles and hostile fire during the ship-to-shore movement.

To succeed, the amphibious task force should therefore be assured of at least temporary naval superiority against enemy surface and submarine forces, preponderant control of the air, and a substantial superiority over enemy forces ashore. Because these conditions are uncommon, amphibious forces seek to maximize tactical surprise and reduce vulnerability by means of mobility, deception, and decisiveness. It is not surprising that amphibious warfare—the forcible assault from the sea against a hostile shore—has been described as the most difficult of all military operations.

Historical Perspective

Amphibious warfare has been practiced for as long as people have taken to the open seas in armed conflict. King Darius, for example, landed his Persian army on the Plains of Marathon by means of an amphibious operation in 490 B.C. The Roman Empire brought the war to Carthage in 254 B.C. with an amphibious landing at Panormus. Julius Caesar landed 22,000 legionnaries and cavalrymen on the beaches near Dover in 55 B.C. to commence the Roman conquest of Britain. William the Conqueror's victory over the Saxon King Harold at Hastings in 1066 was also a product of a massive amphibious landing. During the Napoleonic Wars, amphibious assaults by Abernathy at Aboukir in 1801, Baird at Capetown and Stuart at Calabria in 1806, and Wellington at Bayonne in 1814 served to project British seapower ashore to thwart, distract, and ultimately help defeat the French. Likewise, the American landing at Vera Cruz in 1847 led eventually to the capture of Mexico City and the termination of the war with Mexico.

Employment of the amphibious option in naval warfare sustained a major setback in World War I with the catastrophic failure of allied attempts to seize the Dardanelles by landing at Gallipoli in 1915. So conspicuous and costly was this failure that many military analysts concluded that modern weaponry had rendered obsolete such large-scale, opposed amphibious landings. Others—including U.S. Navy and Marine Corps planners and certain Imperial Japanese Navy strategists—recognized the continued utility of this form of warfare to any maritime nation and applied the lessons learned from Gallipoli to improve doctrine. This farsightedness led to widespread and effective use of amphibious warfare in World War II by the Japanese initially and then by the Allies in both the Pacific and

European theaters. The pivotal amphibious landings at Guadalcanal, North Africa, Iwo Jima, Anzio, Okinawa, and Normandy represented the refinement of this operational technique to perhaps its highest degree. Indeed, the forcible seizure of the Normandy beaches in 1944 enabled the Allies to assault "Fortress Europe" with 2,086,000 troops and 3,446,000 tons of supplies in the first 90 days after D-Day.

Advent of the nuclear age seemed to render amphibious warfare obsolete yet again. Although the vulnerability of any large concentration of forces to nuclear weapons is undeniable, amphibious forces have been successfully employed throughout the nuclear era. General MacArthur's brilliant surprise landing of allied forces at Inchon in 1950 significantly altered the war in Korea. The British in the 1982 Falklands/Malvinas War and the Americans in their 1983 landing in Grenada provide more recent examples.

Enduring Principles

A survey of amphibious warfare history produces several enduring characteristics or features that have emerged over the centuries. The first of these is the need for command of the sea. Amphibious warfare's dependence on temporary command of the sea has been amply demonstrated in history. When the Royal Navy had command of the sea during the British expedition against Quebec in 1759, they won a subcontinent. When they were unable to establish command of the sea off Yorktown in 1781, Cornwallis had to surrender, and the success of the American Revolution was ensured. Likewise, Napoleon's assembly of landing craft and a large invasion force in the Low Countries for an assault of the British Isles was in vain when the French navy was unable to attain even temporary command of the English Channel during 1803–05.

A second historic characteristic is the requirement for unity of command. The amphibious task force commander (typically a naval officer) and the landing force commander (typically an army, marine, or navy infantry officer) must maintain thoroughly coordinated relations. Only one of the two officers can be in command at any given time, and the command must be painstakingly phased from naval to land commander as the operation progresses through prearranged milestones. Violation of this principle throughout the Gallipoli campaign was a major contributor to that spectacular failure. Similarly, lack of unity of command led to the failures of the British amphibious operation against Camaret Bay, France, in 1696; the allied amphibious landings in the Crimea in 1854; and the first attempt by the Federal forces in the American Civil War to invest Fort Fisher, North Carolina, in 1864. Maintaining unity of command has usually paid valuable dividends: the British at Aboukir in 1801, the reorganized Federal forces at Fort Fisher in 1865, the Japanese at Timor in 1942, the Americans at Iwo Jima in 1945.

A third historic feature is the requirement to pay special heed to weather and hydrographic conditions in the landing area. Here again, the extraordinary vulnerability of the ship-to-shore assault becomes a factor. All ships are vulnerable to these conditions, but troop ships and landing craft have historically been the most vulnerable. The huge storms that thwarted Kublai Khan's invasion of Japan in 1274 and the Spanish Armada in the English Channel in 1588 are examples. The failure of American landing boats to traverse the fringing reef at Tarawa in 1943 nearly caused that bloody operation to be aborted. Then again, a wise strategist can sometimes turn adverse conditions to advantage, as did MacArthur in the tidal flats of Inchon in 1950 and Eisenhower at Normandy in 1944.

Another consideration is that amphibious operations rarely win wars by themselves, despite the exceptions of the Norman invasion of Britain in 1066 and perhaps the Allies' defeat of Japan in World War II. In most historic cases, amphibious warfare has been best employed as a supporting operation to open a new front, relieve a defensive position, divert enemy attention and resources, or seize the initiative. Gallipoli was an attempt to accomplish all of these. The Normandy and Inchon landings best exemplify this principle: massive, risky, surprise landings that successfully altered the fighting but did not on their own directly terminate either conflict.

A fifth characteristic of amphibious warfare is its adherence to the ancient Chinese theoretician Sun Tzu's axiom of initiating a strategic offensive to assume a tactical defensive position. Most amphibious operations follow this pattern as a matter of course. A forcible landing is made to seize a beachhead and the nearby key terrain and transportation features—ports, bridgeheads, road junctions, and airfields. The landing force then consolidates its position to repel the inevitable counterattacks or counterlandings until sufficient combat power is delivered ashore to permit a sustained offensive. Amphibious warfare and airborne operations are similar in this regard.

A sixth feature of amphibious warfare is the value of specialized landing craft. Negotiating open seas, plunging surf, rocks or reefs, and possibly a seawall while under fire in an open boat is exceptionally difficult. Those who survive typically wind up drenched, disorganized, and decimated on the beach. They have lost offensive momentum, created a backlog to successive landing waves, and provided the enemy with lucrative targets. The historic requirement has been for special landing craft, compatible with the ships of the amphibious task force, that can convey assault troops and their weapons with reasonable protection to the beach and preferably beyond to inland objectives. Julius Caesar's *Fabricatores* built ships for the invasion of Britain with a very shallow draft forward and folding landing ramps; Caesar used such a ramp himself in landing his three-horse war chariot on the beach in the first wave. Roman and, 1,000 years later, Byzantine success with these craft was undeniable, but the art seems to have been lost during the next millennium. Both Japanese and American forces, reading the lessons of Gallipoli during the 1930s and 1940s, developed specialized landing craft that were widely used throughout World War II. Several innovations of that period, such as the landing ship tank (LST) and the landing vehicle tracked (LVT) or assault amphibious vehicle (AAV), continue to be employed by amphibious forces throughout the world.

The single greatest breakthrough in special landing craft was the application of transport helicopters to the ship-to-shore assault in the 1950s and 1960s. Although helicopters have limitations of their own in terms of payload, designated loading spots on helicopter-capable amphibious ships, landing zones ashore, and vulnerability to enemy fire, they have added a new dimension to amphibious warfare. Indeed, the most combat-effective means of executing an opposed amphibious assault now appears to be a combination of helicopter-borne and waterborne landing forces.

A seventh and frequently overlooked feature of amphibious warfare is its utility for extracting embattled forces under fire. Sir Charles Munro's evacuation of the remaining 35,000 allied troops from the bloody Gallipoli beaches without the loss of a single man in January 1916 has been described as a masterpiece of deception; it provided the one allied success in that catastrophic campaign. Other examples abound: Sir John Moore at Corunna in 1809, Ulysses S. Grant at Belmont in 1861, and the spectacular evacuation of Dunkirk in 1940.

Current Doctrine

Currently, amphibious forces are expected to be employed throughout the spectrum of conflict, particularly in the seizure of advanced bases or airfields in support of a naval campaign. Emphasis is placed on teamwork between naval and landing forces in both training and operations, and also on combat readiness, forward deployment of amphibious forces, and combined training with allied nations. This emphasis reflects the naval roots of amphibious warfare, an overall appreciation for the general utility of amphibious forces, and the value of sharing what in effect are global amphibious responsibilities with similar forces of friendly nations. Current doctrine also reflects respect for the growing counterlanding defensive weaponry of nearly all potential adversaries vis-à-vis the historic vulnerability of amphibious task forces. In this regard, a significant focus within the United States and the North Atlantic Treaty Organization (NATO) throughout the 1980s has been the "over-the-horizon" concept of amphibious warfare. This concept seeks to maximize the relative speed and sustainability of the amphibious task force to enable it to maneuver, converge, or loiter off an enemy's coastline, well beyond the range of conventional weapons, and then execute the ship-to-shore assault from extended ranges of 50 to 75 kilometers (31–47 mi.) with helicopters and air-cushioned landing craft. Military planners generally concede that strategic surprise in amphibious operations against a capable adversary may never again be attained in the age of reconnaissance satellites. Nevertheless, intelligent application of the over-the-horizon concept still lends the advantage of tactical surprise to the amphibious task force commander.

Other combat operations involving waterborne movement such as river crossings, shore-to-shore ferrying, and administrative landings without opposition are not part of amphibious warfare. The key ingredients remain an assault launched from the sea by naval and landing forces embarked in ships or craft against a hostile shore.

Phases of Amphibious Operations

Amphibious doctrine in the U.S. military (used as an example here as the United States maintains the world's foremost amphibious warfare capability by a very large margin) defines five cyclical phases of amphibious operations: planning, embarkation, rehearsal, movement to the objective area, and assault.

Planning phase. Although planning continues throughout the operation, it is dominant during the first phase. Planning begins with the initiating directive from the commander exercising overall responsibility for the operation. The initiating directive establishes the amphibious task force, assigns the mission and forces, designates both the amphibious task force commander and the landing force commander, sets target dates, and defines the amphibious objective area (AOA) in terms of sea, land, and airspace surrounding the objective. The amphibious task force commander and the landing force commander are on equal levels of command, but the former coordinates the joint planning process.

Command and staff actions during this critical phase are characterized by concurrent, parallel, detailed planning. Basic decisions include determination of amphibious task force and landing force objectives in support of the assigned mission and designation of landing sites and beachheads that will permit the continual landing of troops and equipment and provide sufficient maneuver space for projected operations ashore. The landing force commander and staff then develop their concept of operations ashore, which includes selection of specific landing beaches and helicopter landing zones. Because the naval forces must be able to execute the ship-to-shore assault plan and support the proposed scheme of maneuver ashore, the amphibious task force commander, in consultation with the landing force commander, then selects the tentative date and hour of landing. Other concurrent and parallel planning addresses intelligence, supporting arms coordination, communications, and logistics issues.

Once the basic decisions have been rendered, the planning phase ends and the operational phases commence. At this point, the commander of the amphibious task force assumes full responsibility for the entire force and operation and is vested with commensurate command authority to ensure successful execution of the plan until the operation is terminated.

Embarkation phase. The embarkation phase involves the orderly assembly of troops, supplies, and equipment and their subsequent loading aboard assigned shipping in the proper sequence to support the requirements of the landing force concept of operations ashore. Embarkation for an opposed amphibious assault differs markedly from administrative loading of ships. Embarkation of the landing force must be organized in such a way as to make it compatible with the ship-to-shore movement plan, which in turn supports the proposed scheme of maneuver ashore. Tactical integrity of troop units must be maintained as much as possible. Ships should nonetheless be loaded to minimize the possibility of a catastrophic loss—all of the landing force's artillery, for example—should a single ship be sunk. Combat loading is done on the basis of the phased requirement for specific troops, weapons, and supplies in accordance with the landing plan, as opposed to economical use of shipboard spaces. The last units and equipment to be embarked will probably be those first needed in the assault waves. Additionally, both horizontal and vertical stowage practices are used, the former permitting lateral distribution of supplies and equipment for simultaneous unloading from multiple cargo holds on several ships and the latter permitting storage in depth of specific items that then become continually available for unloading. Embarkation planning is obviously a science in its own right, whereas the execution of those plans remains very much the art of the possible.

Rehearsal phase. The individual components of the amphibious task force should have attained a satisfactory level of training prior to embarkation. Training should include rehearsal of the landing plan under conditions approximating those expected in the AOA to test the adequacy of plans, timing of execution, communications capabilities, and overall readiness for combat operations. In a general war, however, a full-scale rehearsal may become an unaffordable luxury. The necessity for wide dispersal of most elements of the amphibious task force and the imperative requirement to strive for tactical surprise both seem to rule out taking the time and risk involved in assembling the force, conducting and evaluating the plan, making the necessary adjustments, and retesting the revisions. Yet good rehearsals generally lead to effective amphibious operations, and their omission adds to the risk. As alternatives, modified rehearsals can be conducted with subcomponents of the force; landings can be effected across imaginary lines established in the open ocean; or the critical command, control, and communications elements of the plan can be rehearsed without troops.

Movement to the objective area. During this phase, the amphibious task force sorties from embarkation and rehearsal sites, forms into movement groups escorted by naval and air forces, executes its collective passage by sea, and approaches assigned positions within the objective area. Advance force operations are conducted as necessary. Emphasis is placed on collective security, deceptive measures, electronic emission control, intelligence updating, continual planning, and limited physical training and briefings for embarked troops.

The amphibious task force commander, in consultation with the landing force commander, must decide to what extent, if any, to engage in preassault operations with an advance force. If attaining tactical surprise is paramount, then advance force operations would be severely curtailed or canceled altogether. If tactical surprise is less important than ensuring effective delivery of most of the assault forces against enemy opposition, then the commander might opt for extensive use of a designated advance force. The mission and objectives, plus a reading of enemy capabilities and intentions, determine the decision.

Advance force operations serve the purposes of isolating the objective area, gathering intelligence on enemy dispositions, and facilitating the main assault. Such preassault operations typically include reconnaissance, minesweeping, naval gunfire, air strikes, underwater demolition, and destruction of beach obstacles. In certain cases, clandestine forces may be inserted to provide terminal guidance at designated helicopter landing zones or as advance beachmasters at critical landing points. In other cases, small combat forces may be landed surreptitiously to seize and defend critical terrain features surrounding the immediate landing area, such as mountaintops or offshore islands. All such operations remain the responsibility of the amphibious task force commander.

The assault. The assault phase commences when the assault elements of the main body arrive in designated positions within the objective area and terminates with the accomplishment of amphibious task force missions. The assault phase includes: preparatory air strikes and naval gunfire; ship-to-shore movement of the assault elements of the landing force by helicopters, amphibious vehicles, landing craft, and landing ships; subsequent operations ashore to seize designated objectives and effect linkups between waterborne and helicopter-borne units or with allied or special forces operating nearby; continual provision of logistic, air, and naval gunfire support; and off-loading of remaining landing force troops and equipment to support the assault forces.

The amphibious task force commander is responsible for control of the ship-to-shore movement of both waterborne and helicopter-borne assault forces. Maximum coordination and flexibility are demanded of both commanders at this critical point. Alternate plans may need to be executed or new ones improvised on the spot, depending on the unanticipated effects of enemy action, weather, or terrain conditions.

Tactical integrity of troop units must be maintained to facilitate control ashore by the landing force. Essentially, the waterborne elements of the landing force are organized into scheduled waves (predetermined time and place of landing), on-call waves (early requirement anticipated), "floating dumps" of emergency supplies (preloaded and launched early to loiter on call near the line of departure), landing force supplies (landed selectively as requested by the landing force), and nonscheduled units (generally combat support and combat service support units whose need ashore and sequence of landing have been estimated but held in abeyance until called for). Similarly, helicopter-borne forces are divided into scheduled, on-call, and nonscheduled movements. To facilitate and help to coordinate the massive flow of troops and units ashore, a tactical-logistical group (TACLOG) is established afloat to monitor tactical and logistic radio nets and maintain information on current landing force requirements.

Employment of supporting arms during the assault phase emphasizes close support of the landing force by coordinated air, artillery, and naval gunfire. Initially, the amphibious task force commander maintains complete control of airspace throughout the AOA and coordinates air support operations through the tactical air operations center afloat. As the assault gains momentum ashore, control of close-air-support and certain other air operations is passed to the landing force commander, once the latter's tactical air command center is fully established and as the tactical situation dictates. Similarly, control of other supporting arms is phased ashore once certain prearranged conditions have been met. From the beginning of the assault until shortly after the first waves land, coordination of all fire support is typically achieved by execution of a planned schedule. Once the first control teams of the landing force reach shore, however, fire support becomes responsive to requests from troop units directly engaged in the fight for the initial objectives.

When the progress of the assault and the tactical situation ashore permit discontinuance of the tightly controlled movement of selected units and supplies, the amphibious task force commander can, on the recommendation of the landing force commander, commence general unloading. Emphasis is then switched to rapid administrative unloading of the supplies and equipment remaining aboard. In larger amphibious operations, an assault follow-on echelon arrives a few days after "D-Day" to provide long-term sustainability and replacements.

Termination of any amphibious operation is predicated on the accomplishment of the missions specified in the initiating directive. The usual precondition for completing the mission involves the firm establishment of the landing force ashore. Attainment of this condition reflects the opinion of the landing force commander, not just the naval counterpart, and reflects a conviction that the beachhead has been secured; sufficient tactical and supporting forces have been established ashore to permit continual landing of additional troops and equipment as required; command, communications, and supporting arms coordination facilities have been established ashore; and the landing force commander is ready to assume full responsibilities for subsequent operations. When both commanders agree that the conditions of the initiating directive have been met, the amphibious task force commander reports these facts to their common superior. That higher commander then terminates the operation, dissolves the amphibious task force, and issues instructions for subsequent operations, as necessary.

A significant factor in the success of any amphibious operation is the degree to which the amphibious task force commander and the landing force commander coordinate with each other. Good professional and personal relations between the two commanders is important throughout the operation; it is vital during the assault phase.

The Future of Amphibious Warfare

Opponents of amphibious warfare usually contend that it is obsolete, suicidal, or both. Others argue that it constitutes a tangential operation at best and an expensive waste of scarce assets better used in a more continental approach to campaign planning. All the positions have merit. Amphibious warfare remains an option—possibly a very useful one—to policymakers and war planners. In any protracted conflict in which one or more of the antagonists is a maritime power, the opportunity invariably arises for affecting the outcome by forcible entry against hostile shores. The capability to exploit that opportunity remains an attractive option for many maritime nations.

Nevertheless, amphibious capability requires significant capital investment. Most nations have difficulty maintaining modern, trained forces in peacetime. Rarely are enough ships available for immediate execution of general war plans, should the need suddenly arise. Some nations have attempted to lessen the shipping shortfall by selective pre-positioning of supplies and equipment near likely theaters of engagement. During the 1980s, the United States invested significantly in pre-positioning combat materiel both ashore (Norway and Germany) and afloat in three squadrons of commercial cargo ships permanently at sea in the Pacific, Indian, and Atlantic oceans. These programs are not substitutes for amphibious capability. For the most part, they represent strategic mobility enhancement initiatives. In times of heightening tension, troops would be flown to a nonhostile site for an administrative joining with their pre-positioned equipment and subsequent deployment to the theater of conflict. A natural amphibious scenario would be the seizure and protection of a suitable port and airfield complex to enable maritime pre-positioned forces to execute their linkup and then reinforce or relieve the amphibious forces. Pre-positioned forces have no immediate forcible entry capability until "reconstituted."

Vulnerability of amphibious forces will continue to be a concern to nations planning to use such a capability. Wide dispersion, rapid convergence, and conduct of operations in low visibility and under adverse weather conditions will always help mitigate the threat. However, all components of the amphibious task force must have similar speed, range, and control features to minimize vulnerability and maximize concentration of forces to attain tactical surprise. The Achilles' heel of amphibious warfare continues to be the vulnerability of the waterborne ship-to-shore assault. Over-the-horizon capability does the commander little good if some ships have to be sent close ashore to launch landing craft and amphibious vehicles. Air-cushioned landing craft may ultimately solve that long-standing weakness. For years, Soviet amphibious forces employed such craft, and the U.S. Navy has recently begun to acquire its own. The vulnerability factor is still present, but the vastly increased speed and range of air-cushioned landing craft are a quantum improvement.

Military research and development activities seem on the verge of fielding several other new items that could improve amphibious capabilities. Foremost among these is the tilt-rotor aircraft, which combines the range and some of the speed of conventional aircraft with the vertical takeoff and landing capabilities of the helicopter. Acquisition of the global positioning system (a constellation of U.S. space satellites used for navigation) should enable amphibious task forces to improve their navigation capabilities by an order of magnitude and thereby enhance high-speed dispersed operations at night. Significant developments in the detection and neutralization of mines in the surf zone and along landing beaches appear to be forthcoming as well. With these technical advances, amphibious operations will be improved, but still risky. The enduring principles will remain as they have throughout the history of maritime warfare.

JOSEPH H. ALEXANDER

SEE ALSO: Amphibious Forces; Amphibious Ships and Craft; Maritime Strategy; Naval Warfare.

Bibliography

Bartlett, M. L. 1983. *Assault from the sea: Essays on the history of amphibious warfare*. Annapolis, Md.: U.S. Naval Institute Press.

Dupuy, R. E., and T. N. Dupuy. 1970. *The encyclopedia of military history from 3500 B.C. to the present*. Rev. ed. New York: Harper and Row.

Heinl, R. D., Jr. 1979. *Victory at high tide: The Inchon-Seoul campaign*. Annapolis, Md.: Nautical and Aviation.

Iseley, J. A., and P. A. Crowl. 1951. *The U.S. Marines and amphibious war*. Princeton, N.J.: Princeton Univ. Press.

Thucydides. 1954. *The Peloponnesian war*. Trans. R. Warner. Harmondsworth, Middlesex, U.K.: Penguin Books.

ANGOLA, PEOPLE'S REPUBLIC OF

Angola, located on the southwest coast of Africa between Namibia and Zaire, is a former Portuguese colony that gained its independence in 1975. Angola includes the oil-rich Cabinda enclave, separated from the rest of the country by part of Zaire. Angola draws its name from the title of the rulers of the Kongo kingdom, who were called *ngola*.

Power Potential Statistics

Area: 1,246,700 square kilometers (481,354 sq. mi.)
Population: 10,323,600
Total Active Armed Forces: 96,000 est. (0.930% of pop.)
Gross Domestic Product: US$7.9 billion (1990 est.)
Annual Defense Expenditure: not available
Iron and Steel Production:
  Crude steel: 0.01 million metric tons (1985)
Fuel Production:
  Crude oil: 24 million metric tons (1989)
  Natural gas: 154 million cubic meters (1986)
Electrical Power Output: 770 million kwh (1989)
Merchant Marine: 12 vessels; 66,348 gross registered tons
Civil Air Fleet: 27 major transport aircraft; 183 usable airfields (28 with permanent-surface runways); 1 with runways over 3,659 meters (12,000 ft.); 13 with runways 2,440–3,659 meters (8,000–12,000 ft.); 58 with runways 1,220–2,440 meters (4,000–8,000 ft.).

For the most recent information, the reader may refer to the following annual publications:
The Military Balance. International Institute for Strategic Studies. London: Brassey's (UK).
The Statesman's Year-Book. New York: St. Martin's Press.
The World Factbook. Central Intelligence Agency. Washington, D.C.: Brassey's (US.)

History

Much of the history of Angola before the arrival of the Portuguese in the late fifteenth century is not well known, obscured by the lack of written records. The Bantu-speaking peoples who now inhabit the country arrived over a period of centuries following A.D. 1000, displacing the earlier Bushmen and Khoikhoin (Hottentot) settlers. The Portuguese arrived on Angola's coast in 1483, and established close relations with the greatest native power in the area, the Kongo kingdom, a highly centralized state on the lower Congo River.

Conflict with the Kongo resulted in several wars, after which the Portuguese took control of Kongo in the late seventeenth century. Portugal had meanwhile founded the fortified settlement of Luanda in 1575, but over the next two centuries founded only a handful of other settlements on the northern coast and in the lower Cuanza River valley, with a total population of perhaps 5,000 Europeans. The slow Portuguese expansion was interrupted by Dutch occupation of Luanda and Benguela from 1640 to 1648. The Portuguese drew considerable wealth from the slave trade, exporting 5,000 to 10,000 slaves annually in the early seventeenth century. The Portuguese expanded their control inland in the late nineteenth century, bringing most of modern Angola under their control between 1850 and 1900.

Angola's borders were not established until 1884–85, and the southern frontier was not defined until a dispute with South Africa was resolved in 1926. Sporadic armed resistance to Portuguese rule continued until 1930. By the late 1950s, Western-educated natives and people of mixed European and African ancestry had begun to agitate for independence, even though Angola had become an overseas province of Portugal in 1951. Following an extensive unsuccessful rural uprising in the old Kongo areas of the north in February–March 1961, several guerrilla groups began operating in the countryside. There were three such groups: the Marxist-oriented *Movimento Popular de Libertaçao de Angola,* or MPLA (Popular Movement for the Liberation of Angola), led by Dr. Agostino Neto and drawing its support from the Mbundu people; the Western-oriented *Frente Nacional de Libertaçao de Angola,* or FNLA (National Front for the Liberation of Angola), led by Holden Roberto and based among the Kongo of the north; and the neutralist *Uniao Nacional para la Independencia Total de Angola* or UNITA (National Union for the Total Independence of Angola), led by former FNLA member Jonas Savimbi and based among the Ovimbundu and Chokwe of central Angola.

By the early 1970s the government had over 50,000 troops, mostly African, engaged against perhaps 5,000 to 7,000 guerrillas of all factions. However, there were at least 30,000 more guerrillas in bases in Zambia and Zaire. The leftist army coup in Portugal (24 April 1974) installed a regime that promised rapid independence for Portugal's African colonies, but also further confused the already complex politico-military situation in Angola. Civil war between the MPLA on one side and UNITA and the FNLA on the other began in earnest in mid-summer 1975 even before independence was formally granted on 11 November 1975. Lack of cooperation between UNITA and the FNLA, coupled with extensive Soviet and Cuban support for the MPLA, including the commitment of Cuban ground troops, enabled the MPLA to gain the upper hand. By March 1976 the FNLA was virtually powerless, and UNITA's forces had adopted guerrilla tactics out of desperation, limited to their strongholds in the rural southeast.

Since 1976 the MPLA has worked to consolidate its rule in Angola, but Savimbi's UNITA forces have disputed this, and effectively rule the southeastern third of the country. As part of the multinational agreement granting full independence to Namibia, Cuba agreed to withdraw its 50,000 troops from Angola by mid-1991. This settlement helped pave the way for UNITA's entry into the government and an end to the civil war.

This process began with a preliminary settlement concluded on 14 December 1990, following extensive negotiations. Further talks followed in Lisbon in January 1991, leading to a formal peace accord signed in Lisbon on 31 May 1991.

Politico-Military Background and Policy

The MPLA, or MPLA-*Partido de Trabalho* (MPLA-Labor Party) as it has been known since the first party congress in December 1977, exercises complete control over Angolan government and armed forces. MPLA-controlled Angola suffered several incursions by South African armed forces from 1979 to 1989. These were in part occasioned by MPLA support for SWAPO (South West African People's Organization), the principal organization opposed to South African rule in Namibia. The MPLA government maintained close association with the former Soviet Union and Cuba.

Strategic Problems

Angola faces two major sets of strategic problems. First are severe difficulties related to economic development. Most of the people are farmers, and many of Angola's exports are agricultural. Limited education and poor health care contribute further to a low standard of living.

Second, the UNITA insurgency made any development efforts doubly difficult. The presence of large numbers of Cuban troops in the country, and South Africa's hostile reaction to the Cuban presence, caused further problems. Despite its guerrilla origins, the MPLA had little success combating UNITA, due in part to UNITA's foreign backing and to its secure base of popular support.

Military Assistance

Angola received extensive military assistance from the former Soviet Union, Cuba, and until recently from several countries in Eastern Europe. The MPLA received aid from these sources since the early 1960s. This assistance included tanks and armored vehicles, artillery, combat aircraft and helicopters, trucks, and naval vessels. This aid was decisive during the civil war of August 1975–March 1976. It amounted to some US$3 billion between 1983 and 1987. Further, the MPLA inherited some equipment from the Portuguese colonial establishment just after independence.

Defense Industry

Angola's limited industrial capacity ensures that most materiel must be imported. Angolan factories do supply some small arms ammunition, and domestic refineries supply the fuel and lubricants needed for operations.

Alliances

Angola is a member of the Organization of African Unity (OAU) and the United Nations. Angola also retains some ties with Portugal and has a close security arrangement with Cuba, as it did with the former Soviet Union. A twenty-year treaty of friendship and cooperation was signed with the former Soviet Union on 8 October 1976; two aid agreements with Cuba date from July 1976.

Defense Structure

Under the 1977 Constitution, the president of the republic is commander in chief of the *Forcas Armadas Populares de Libertaçao de Angola* (FAPLA, or Popular Armed Forces for the Liberation of Angola) as the Angolan armed forces are officially known. Control of the FAPLA is entrusted to the Ministry of Defense, which is directly responsible to the president, unlike other ministries, which report to the prime minister through one of three deputy prime ministers. As in other Communist-dominated countries, policy decisions are controlled by the party (MPLA-Labor Party) apparatus.

(For an explanation of the abbreviations and symbols used in the following section of military statistics, see the list of Abbreviations and Acronyms in each volume.)

Total Armed Forces

Following the end of a fifteen-year civil war, the Angolan government and its opponent UNITA have agreed to merge their armed forces to form a new 50,000 strong National Army. Details outlined below reflect the position prior to merger, which was scheduled to commence on 15 July 1991.

Active: est. 96,000 (incl some 10,000 recalled ODP militia, 24,000 conscripts). Terms of service: conscription, 2 years.
Reserves: Militia (ODP): 50,000.

ARMY: est. 91,500 (est. 24,000 conscripts, 10,000 ODP).
15 Military Zones (some may be fd HQ).
73+ bde (each with inf, tk, APC, arty and AA units as required. Bde = est. 1,000 men).
Equipment:†
MBT: 500+: 100 T-34†, 300 T-54/-55, 100+ T-62.
Light tanks: some 25 PT-76.
AIFV: 100+ BMP.
Recce: some 100+ BRDM-2.
APC: 300 BTR-60/-152.
Towed arty: 500: incl 76mm: M-1942 (ZIS-3); 85mm: D-44; 122mm: D-30; 130mm: M-46.
Assault guns: SU-100.
MRL: 122mm: 75 BM-21, some BM-24.
Mortars: 82mm: 100; 120mm: 40+ M-43.
ATGW: AT-3 Sagger.
RCL: 500: 82mm: B-10; 107mm: B-11.
AD guns: 300+: 14.5mm: ZPU-4; 23mm: ZU-23-2, 20 ZSU-23-4 SP; 37mm: M-1939; 57mm: S-60 towed, 40 ZSU-57-2 SP.
SAM: SA-7/-14.
Reserves: People's Defense Organization (ODP): 35,000; 11+ 'bde'. 10,000 serving with the Regular Army at any one time.

NAVY:† est. 1,500. Bases: Luanda (HQ), Lobito, Namibe.
Patrol and Coastal Combatants: 17:
Missile Craft: 6 Sov Osa-II with 4 × SS-N-2 Styx SSM.
Torpedo Craft: 4 Shershen with 4 × 533mm HWT.
Patrol, Inshore 7: 4 Port Argos†, 2 Sov Poluchat, 1 (.
Mine Warfare: 2 Sov Yevgenya MHI.
Amphibious: 3 Sov Polnocny LSM, capacity 100 tps. 6 tk. Plus craft; 1 LCT, about 8 LCM.
Coastal Defense: SS-C-1 Sepal at Luanda.

AIR FORCE/AIR DEFENSE: Est. 3,000; 160 cbt ac, 40 armed hel.†
FGA: 25 MiG-17, 51 MiG-23, 15 Su-22, 10 Su-25.
Fighter: 35 MiG-21 MF/bis.
COIN/Recce: 16 PC-7.
MR: 2 EMB-111, 1 F-27MPA.
Attack helicopters: 28 Mi-25/35, 6 SA-365M (guns), 6 SA-342 (HOT).
Transport: 2 sqn with 12 An-12, 20 An-26, 6 BN-2, 3 C-47, 6 C-212, 2 L-100-20, 4 PC-6B.
Helicopters: 2 sqn with 30 IAR-316, 10 SA-316, 25 Mi-8, 13 Mi-17, 1 SA-315, 10 SA-365.
Liaison: 10 An-2, 5 Do-27.
Training: 3 Cessna 172, 3 MiG-15UTI, 6 MiG-21U, 5* Su-22, 6 Yak-11.
AD: 5 SAM bn. 10 bty; with 40 SA-2, 12 SA-3, 75 SA-6, 15 SA-8, 20 SA-9, SA-13.
Missiles:
ASM: HOT.
AAM: AA-2 Atoll.

FORCES ABROAD
São Tomé: some 500; 1 bn.

PARAMILITARY
Border Guard (TGFA): 7,000.

OPPOSITION
UNITA (*Union for the Total Independence of Angola*): some 28,000 'regulars' (1–2 years service), 37,000 'militia' (spt and log); to merge with government forces.
Equipment: captured T-34/-85, 70 T-55 MBT reported, misc APC (not in service); BM-21 122mm MRL; 75mm, 76mm, 122mm fd guns; 81mm, 82mm, 120mm mor; 85mm RPG-7 RL; 75mm RCL; 12.7mm hy machine guns; 14.5mm, 20mm and ZU-23-2 23mm AA guns; Stinger, SAM-7;
FNLA (*National Front for the Liberation of Angola*): (Bakongo tribesmen) claims up to 5,000, actual strength est. 250; small arms only.
FLEC (*Front for the Liberation of the Cabinda Enclave*): (200–300); small arms only.

FOREIGN FORCES
USSR: 1,000 advisers and technicians (numbers reducing)
ANC: African National Congress, up to 250.
United Nations: (UNAVEM II) 350 military observers and 90 police observers from Algeria, Argentina, Brazil, Canada, Congo, Czechoslovakia, Egypt, Guinea-Bissau, Hungary, India, Ireland, Jordan, Malaysia, Morocco, Netherlands, New Zealand, Nigeria, Norway, Senegal, Singapore, Spain, Sweden, Yugoslavia, Zimbabwe.

Future

The implementation of the United Nations Angola/Namibia settlement provides the first real opportunity for peace in those two countries in fifteen years. Despite the UN arrangements and the potential for an internal settlement with UNITA, Angola and its government still face severe problems relating to public health, education, and economic development.

DAVID L. BONGARD
TREVOR N. DUPUY

SEE ALSO: Organization of African Unity; South Africa; Sub-Saharan Africa.

Bibliography

American University. 1979. *Angola, A country study.* Washington, D.C.: Government Printing Office.
Bridgland, F. 1986. *Jonas Savimbi, A key to Africa.* New York: Paragon House.
1990 Britannica Book of the Year. 1990. Chicago, Ill.: Encyclopedia Britannica.
Hunter, B., ed. 1991. *The statesman's year-book, 1991–92.* New York: St. Martin's Press.
International Institute for Strategic Studies. 1991. *The military balance, 1991–1992.* London: Brassey's.

ANTISUBMARINE WARFARE

Antisubmarine warfare (ASW) is fought mainly at sea and is aimed at defeating the war-fighting purposes of the submarine. ASW is practiced at three levels of planning: strategic, operational, and tactical. There are three types of strategic planning: (1) destruction of the opponent's submarines, (2) containment of enemy submarines, and (3) limitation of the war-fighting efficiency of the hostile submarine fleet. The operational level of ASW planning is concerned with where and how to destroy, contain, or limit the efficiency of hostile submarines. The operational choice is whether to defeat the submarine (1) at its sources (i.e., operating bases and construction yards), (2) in the transit areas that the submarine must pass through to and from its sources, or (3) in the patrol areas. ASW tactics are concerned with the local coordination of platforms, weapons, and sensors in the area of encounter. The tactical ASW encounter consists of four phases: (1) surveillance and reconnaissance, (2) detection, (3) tracking, and (4) attack.

Knowledge about wartime ASW is drawn almost exclusively from the experience from World War I and World War II, for there have been very few examples since those conflicts.

ASW Strategies of Destruction

The preferred ASW strategy is one that results in the physical destruction of the submarine; the outcome is permanent and, with the underwater opponent eliminated, resources can be released for other wartime duties. Strategies of destruction have also proven to be the most difficult and risky. Depending on the quality and quantity of the opposing submarine force, its complete elimination may take more time and tie up more resources than can be afforded. A different kind of risk is associated with ASW operations against strategic missile submarines. The destruction (or even the threat of destruction) of this particular type may undermine the stability of mutual strategic deterrence and force a decision to "use them instead of lose them."

DESTRUCTION AT THE SOURCE

The preferred operational strategy of destruction is aimed at the sources of the submarine menace (i.e., operating bases, construction, repair and maintenance yards, and industries that manufacture critical components). The most important advantage of this approach is that it circumvents ASW's most difficult problem: finding the opponent. Unfortunately, enemy submarine bases and building yards also tend to be heavily defended and can usually be attacked only at great risk to one's own forces.

Destruction at the source can be accomplished in four ways: (1) physical seizure and occupation of bases and yards, (2) fleet bombardment, (3) aerial bombardment, and (4) mining. The first method is the most decisive, but seizure and occupation of enemy submarine bases and yards is likely to be attempted and successful only if it is part of a general campaign of territorial conquest. The Anglo-American and Soviet occupations, in 1944–45, of the French and Baltic coastal areas, respectively, deprived the German U-boat fleet of key operating and construction sources. This outcome was not the result of ASW strategy, but instead a "bonus" of the Allies' general advance.

But for sporadic shelling by the Royal Navy of Germany's U-boat bases on the Belgian coast in World War I, the strategic choice to destroy submarines at their source by bombardment has been stymied by the fear of disproportionate losses. Consequently, the destructive record of mining and aerial bombardment of submarine bases and yards is mixed. During World War I, only one U-boat was destroyed by the more than 44,000 mines that were scattered in the Heligoland Bight. In World War II, however, fourteen U-boats were destroyed in their Baltic Sea training grounds. The most productive result of the Baltic mining offensive was the interference with crew training and new construction work (i.e., with the U-boat's efficiency). The official British history of *The Strategic Air Offensive Against Germany 1939–1945* suggests that the campaign may have prevented 20 Type XXI U-boats from becoming operational.

The results of the World War II air offensives against the operational and industrial sources of the U-boat were especially disappointing. Principal operational targets were the concrete submarine shelters on the French and Norwegian coasts. Even the heaviest bomb of the war, the 12,500-pound "Tallboy," failed to penetrate shelter roofs, which were up to 8 meters thick. Postwar tests by the Americans indicated that a future air assault against hardened submarine pens would probably require nuclear weapons.

The British Bombing Survey Unit's (BBSU) report on *The Effects of Strategic Bombing on the Production of German U-Boats* concluded that the bombings directly and indirectly contributed to a production loss of 111 U-boats. It reported that another 42 operational units were destroyed in port. The report acknowledged, however, that the estimated production loss of 30 Type XXI submarines due to the "indirect" effect of the bombings was merely an "educated guess." Furthermore, most of the U-boat production losses caused by the "direct" effect of bombing occurred in 1945, when no time remained for the boats to become operational.

The reasons for the low profitability of the antisource bombing campaign were: (1) the inadequacy (mainly in accuracy) of contemporary bomb-laying techniques, (2) the enemy's better-than-expected recovery capabilities, (3) the efficient German air defense system, and (4) the sporadic pattern of the direct offensive against U-boat pens, yards, and other facilities.

Destruction in Transit and Patrol Areas

With the difficulties involved in destroying the submarine at the source, the ASW practitioner must find ways to defeat it at sea in the transit and operational patrol areas.

A key factor for a successful strategy of destruction in transit areas is local geography (i.e., the length, width, and depth of the "chokepoint" through which the submarine must pass). For example, if the submarine must pass through a long, narrow, and shallow area, there will be: (1) a high predictability of the submarine's comings and goings, (2) multiple opportunities for attack, and (3) minimum submarine escape volume.

The opposite conditions exist if the submarine is in a patrol area on the high seas. An ASW strategy aimed at finding and destroying the opponent in the open ocean is highly dependent on strategic intelligence about the submarine's general location, strength, and direction of movement. A hunt-and-kill (HUK) strategy without the benefit of strategic intelligence has proved to be a cost-ineffective search for a "needle in the haystack."

Strategies of destruction in transit areas have generally relied on minefields, sometimes supported by mobile surface and air patrols linked to detection devices. A successful ASW barrier system will destroy few enemy sub-marines because after the first few losses the submarines will be diverted to another, less dangerous route. If another route does not exist, they are effectively blockaded. This was the fate of the submarines of the Soviet Baltic Fleet during World War II. From the spring of 1943 until the capitulation of Finland in September 1944, the German-Finnish barrier of steel nets, mines, and mobile patrols across the Gulf of Finland prevented the Soviet submarines from entering the Baltic Sea.

ASW destruction strategies in the patrol areas have been practiced in two basic forms. These are HUK and armed escort of the targets of the submarine (i.e., the convoy system). Between these two lies the system of protected lanes, or defense of the so-called focal points of friendly shipping. This last strategy combines intensive HUK and close escort operations in the approaches to ports and harbors, where seagoing traffic is funneled, and where enemy submarines may be expected to concentrate.

Today, as in the past, a HUK strategy is vitally dependent on strategic intelligence. The success of the Allied hunting groups during World War II was a result of two sources of strategic intelligence: (1) the interception and location of U-boat radio traffic through high-frequency direction-finding (HF/DF), and (2) the decryption of the U-boat fleet's cipher. Contemporary strategic intelligence about enemy submarine movements still relies, in part, on the interception of communications. In addition, much time and money are being invested in extremely long-range acoustic and nonacoustic ocean-floor-mounted and satellite-carried ASW early warning systems.

Today the convoy system is frequently labeled a "defensive" ASW strategy and, by connotation, inferior to "offensive" HUK. However, during the two world wars convoys were the single most successful means for defeating the purpose of the U-boats (i.e., to sever the Allies' economic and military arteries); and the ships and aircraft on convoy escort duty destroyed more submarines than did their counterparts that engaged in HUK operations. Table 1 summarizes submarine losses in the two world wars. Not shown are submarine losses due to scuttling, collisions, and other marine accidents, capture, or own forces.

ASW Strategies of Containment

The objective of the ASW strategist is to defeat the war-fighting purposes of his opponent; destruction of the enemy's submarines is a bonus. Containment strategies have historically depended on physical obstruction of the submarine's movements, including the use of minefields, nets, and "blocking ships." The creation of the strategic missile submarine has added the idea of psychological containment (i.e., the threat of retaliation by similar forces).

The advantage of an ASW strategy of containment is twofold: (1) it minimizes the risk of casualties, which is central to destruction strategies, and (2) it reduces the need for current intelligence about the enemy submarines' plans and movements. The disadvantage of containment is also twofold: (1) it is quite difficult to create a leakproof barrier, and (2) containment schemes are likely to require forces that are badly needed elsewhere.

TABLE 1. *Submarine Losses Due to Enemy Action in the Two World Wars*

	Surface ships[a]	Aircraft[b]	Surface ships & aircraft	Submarines	Mines[c]	Other	Unknown	Total
WORLD WAR I								
Germany	73	1	0	18	48	0	19	159
Great Britain[d]	7	1	0	5	10	0	8	31
WORLD WAR II								
Germany	246	349	50	21	26	7	29	728
Great Britain	25	5	1	4	27	0	7	69
United States	18	5	6	1	5	0	9	44
Japan	65	13	7	21	2	0	16	124
Italy	32	23	4	19	2	1	4	85
Soviet Union	20	5	0	5	41	1	43	115

[a] Includes naval and nonnaval surface ships, using ramming, gunfire, explosive sweeps, and depth charges.
[b] Includes submarines destroyed in port.
[c] Includes losses "probably" due to mines.
[d] Includes 3 Canadian and 2 Australian submarines.

CONTAINMENT AT THE SOURCE

Most close-in ASW containment schemes have relied on minefields, and most have been ineffective for the same reason that direct action against the sources of the submarine has been ineffective. Success in mine warfare ultimately depends upon the relative stamina of the two sides (i.e., the relative persistence of the minelayer and the minesweeper). The Allied minelaying campaigns of the two world wars failed to contain the U-boats inside their bases because Allied navies were unable or unwilling to patrol the fields within easy reach of enemy counterattack, and thus prevent the Germans from clearing a safe passage through the cordon. British efforts in World War I to contain the U-boats inside their bases by sinking blockships failed, in part, for the same reason.

CONTAINMENT IN THE TRANSIT AND PATROL AREAS

"Static" containment strategies without the presence of mobile reactive forces have proven equally unproductive in the submarine's transit and patrol areas. The reason is that a determined submarine opponent is likely eventually to find a crack. The most famous (if not most successful) antitransit barriers of the two world wars were the Dover and Northern barrages. The first involved a combination of minefields and tripwires laid across the English Channel; the second depended on tens of thousands of mines planted in the Greenland–Iceland–United Kingdom (GIUK) "gap." The World War I version of the Dover barrage failed because the British did not maintain reactive patrols after daylight hours or during the winter months from December through April. The World War II Dover barrage was circumvented by the German occupation of France. The northern barrage of World War I stretched across the 400 kilometers of water between the Orkney Islands and Norway. Established in the spring of 1918 (when the convoy system had already proven its effectiveness), the system proved more dangerous to the Triple Entente minelaying force than to the U-boats. Of greater importance, the patrol ships of the Triple Entente sent to harass the intruders and force them into the minefields were withdrawn for other duties. Only four to six U-boats were lost on the barrier. In World War II, one U-boat might have fallen victim to the Northern barrage, but more Allied ships were lost to mines broken loose from their moorings.

Contemporary barrage schemes combine containment and destruction tactics, using mines, mobile or stationary acoustic fences, and long-range patrol aircraft. One technique is to encircle completely the submarine's suspected patrol area with air-dropped acoustic buoys, and methodically shrink the fenced area by placing one buoy row inside another until the enemy has been pinpointed for final prosecution.

Strategies for Limiting the Submarine's War-Fighting Efficiency

If the enemy submarine cannot be destroyed or contained, yet can be denied the use of its destructive capabilities, the ASW strategist has succeeded. The choice of efficiency-limiting strategies is dependent on the war-fighting purpose of the enemy submarine fleet. For example, if the purpose is economic strangulation, the ASW defender may counter by reducing dependence on seaborne commerce (e.g., food rationing, boosting domestic sources of supplies). If the threat is a strategic missile attack, various passive and active damage limitation measures are possible.

LIMITING EFFICIENCY AT THE SOURCE

One way to reduce the submarine's operational efficiency is to mine the training areas. Production efficiency may be reduced by aerial "harassment raids" aimed at forcing yard workers to stop work and seek shelter. One of the hoped-for effects of the Allied city bombings was to lower the morale and hence the fighting efficiency of U-boat crews.

LIMITING EFFICIENCY IN THE TRANSIT AND PATROL AREAS

The purpose of efficiency-limiting strategies in the transit or patrol areas is to minimize the submarine's operational patrol time. As already noted, the measure of success of a barrier system is not necessarily the number of submarines destroyed, but may be instead the extent to which it forces the enemy to seek an alternate and more time-consuming route. For example, the success of the improved Dover barrage of 1917–18 lay in the rerouting of

U-boats via the more distant waters between Norway and Scotland.

Another successful method to reduce the submarine's productivity has been broad area search and surveillance by patrol aircraft. The tendency of the submarine to avoid an opponent who can look over the horizon was discovered by the use of kite balloons (ship-towed balloons with a human observer) in the Mediterranean theater in World War I. During World War II, the fear of airborne discovery forced U-boats in transit through the Bay of Biscay to spend increasingly more time at slower underwater speeds. Similarly, an unquantifiable measure of effectiveness of the World War II convoy air escorts was how frequently their presence forced U-boats to break tactical contact and look for easier prey elsewhere.

The submarine's productive period is determined, in part, by the amount of fuel and weapons it carries. The first consideration is irrelevant for a nuclear submarine, but the second is still valid today. Thus, a submarine, nuclear or otherwise, can be denied its full potential by interfering with its logistics infrastructure. The best-known illustration of this particular strategy is the systematic Allied campaign of World War II to destroy the "Milch Cows"—the U-boats' fuel replenishment submarines.

The Foreseeable Future

The choice of ASW strategy is determined by two factors: (a) the prevailing balance between submarine and antisubmarine technologies, and (b) the particular war-fighting purposes of the submarine. The foreseeable technological balance will hinge on both the submarine's stealth versus ASW detection capabilities, and the ability of the ASW defender to attack the submarine quickly and accurately at long range. The submarine no doubt will continue to evolve and assume tasks that have traditionally been performed by surface fleets—for example, air defense of the aircraft carrier. Accordingly, new submarine roles will prompt new ASW strategies.

JAN S. BREEMER

SEE ALSO: Convoy and Protection of Shipping; Maritime Strategy; Naval Warfare; Sea Control and Denial; Submarine Warfare; Surveillance, Ocean; Underwater Management.

Bibliography

Blair, C., Jr. 1975. *Silent victory: The U.S. submarine war against Japan.* New York: Lippincott.
Daniel, D. 1986. *Anti-submarine warfare and superpower stability.* Urbana and Chicago, Ill: Univ. of Illinois Press.
Doenitz, K. 1981. *10 jahre und 20 tage.* Münich: Bernard & Graefe Verlag.
Grant, R. M. 1964. *U-boats destroyed: The effect of anti-submarine warfare 1914–1918.* London: Putnam.
Hackmann, W. 1984. *Seek & strike: Sonar, anti-submarine warfare and the Royal Navy 1914–54.* London: HMSO.
Hill, J. R. 1984. *Anti-submarine warfare.* Shepperton, England: Ian Allan.
Jellicoe, Viscount of Scapa. 1920. *The crisis of the naval war.* New York: George H. Doran.
Marder, A. J. 1961–70. *From the Dreadnought to Scapa Flow: The Royal Navy in the Fisher era, 1904–1919.* 5 vols. London: Oxford Univ. Press.
Meigs, M. C. 1990. *Slide rules and submarines: American scientists and subsurface warfare in World War II.* Washington, D.C.: National Defense Univ. Press.
Middlebrook, M. 1976. *Convoy.* New York: William Morrow.
Ministry of Defence (Navy). 1990. *The U-boat war in the Atlantic 1939–1945.* London: HMSO.
Price, A. 1973. *Aircraft versus submarine.* London: Kimberg.
Roskill, S. W. 1957. *The war at sea.* 3 vols. London: HMSO.
Terraine, J. 1989. *The U-boat wars 1916–1945.* New York: Henry Holt.
United States Strategic Bombing Survey (1945 and 1947). *German submarine industry report.* Washington, D.C.
Watts, A. J. 1976. *The U-boat hunters.* London: Macdonald and Jane's.
Y'Blood, W. T. 1983. *Hunter-killer: U.S. escort carriers in the Battle of the Atlantic.* Annapolis: U.S. Naval Institute Press.

ANTITACTICAL BALLISTIC MISSILE (ATBM) POLICY

The idea of missile defenses is not new. It can be traced back at least to 1944 when London came under attack by German V-2 missiles. The British found themselves almost defenseless against these new, supersonic means of attack. The fact that hundreds of missiles launched against the Greater London area inflicted only limited damage on the capital was, considering the limited defensive countermeasures, exclusively due to the poor accuracy and the deficient warhead of the missiles.

Since then, active defense against ballistic missiles has been an ambition of military planners in East and West. Active defenses against V-2–type ballistic missiles (i.e., the precursors of today's tactical ballistic missile [TBM]) were under investigation before the emergence of the intercontinental ballistic missile (ICBM).

In 1951, the U.S. Army initiated the "Plato" guided antimissile project, but it was terminated in 1958 for lack of well-defined characteristics and inadequate funding. Successor projects were the Field Army Ballistic Missile Defense System (FABMDS) in 1960–62, and SAM-D between the years 1962 and 1976 (Davis 1986). When the SAM-D was redesignated "Patriot" in 1976, its ATBM capabilities had already been deleted. It was not until 1982–83 that the U.S. Army took a fresh look at the issue of antitactical missile defense and started a Patriot conventional ATBM program. This program was accelerated in the ensuing years and promises to yield a robust self-defense and a limited area-defense capability for the Patriot system.

It is worth noting that the U.S. Nike-Hercules surface-to-air missile (SAM) possessed ATBM capabilities from 1967 on and was explicitly labeled an air defense and

ATBM system. Successful intercepts by the Corporal and other short-range ballistic missiles date back to 1960. The Nike-Hercules had one major disadvantage: its inaccurate guidance system required nuclear warheads for effective ATBM missions.

Resurgence of ATBM in the 1980s

Aside from the fact that technological progress had rendered conventional ATBM a distinct possibility, two developments in particular led to renewed interest in antitactical missile defense in the West:

1. *Initiation of the U.S. Strategic Defense Initiative (SDI) program in 1983–84.* Many U.S. analysts viewed ATBM merely as an offshoot of SDI or as an "intermediate option" on the way toward a comprehensive ballistic missile defense (BMD) of the continental United States (CONUS), as recommended by the so-called Hoffman panel in the fall of 1983 (Hoffman 1983).

Soon after the launching of the SDI, however, it became apparent that the U.S. efforts were geared primarily toward protection from intercontinental-range ballistic missiles (ICBMs/SLBMs) and longer-range intermediate-range nuclear forces (INF) of the SS-20 type. This led European political leaders to call for a European Defense Initiative (EDI) to complement SDI, a proposal motivated not only by defense but also by technological and economic considerations. The common denominator of all EDI supporters was that their proposals (regardless of what they emphasized independently—research policy, economic aspects, or security policy) were invariably justified by the existence of the SDI program. This SDI fixation prevented any analysis of the antimissile defense option within the context of military-strategic parameters and developments both in the West and the East. In particular, SDI-independent considerations by the North Atlantic Treaty Organization (NATO) were widely, if not totally, ignored.

2. *The fact that NATO gave consideration to the question of an active defense against ballistic missiles before President Reagan's SDI speech in March 1983.* In the late 1970s, when drafting an air defense program for the period 1980–94 as part of NATO's Long-Term Defense Program (LTDP), military experts concluded that the Warsaw Pact air threat of the 1990s and beyond would bear little resemblance to the threat situation of the 1970s. Most notably, besides operating thousands of deep-penetration attack aircraft, the Warsaw Pact would also be able to field a formidable number of relatively small-sized, high-speed, and highly accurate tactical missiles. It was recognized that NATO's integrated air defense in Europe had virtually no means to actively defend against this emerging threat. This led to various study efforts (e.g., a report by NATO's "Advisory Group for Aerospace Research and Development" [AGARD] entitled "Defence against Missiles," released in March 1980).

The actual and anticipated fielding of a new generation of Soviet TBMs—the SS-21, with a range of 120 kilometers (75 mi.); SS-23 with a range of 500 kilometers (310 mi.); and SS-12/22 with a range of 900 kilometers (558 mi.)—was especially worrisome. The reason for concern was not modernization per se, but the prospect of effective, highly accurate conventional employment options for these missiles some time in the future, especially in light of the remarkable shift of Soviet strategy toward conventional nonnuclear weapons.

Active defense against tactical ballistic (and nonballistic) missiles was also considered during NATO's "Counterair" discussions in 1982–83. The U.S. "Counterair '90" study laid down the requirement for ATBM defense as one element within the overall Counterair framework. And in 1983 the Military Committee assigned AGARD to investigate "Anti-Tactical Ballistic Missile Concepts." The resulting AAS-20 study (Enders 1986) had important political repercussions since it provided decision makers with the first, albeit tentative, guidance as to which ATBM approach should be pursued.

"Extended Air Defense"—NATO's Integrative ATBM Approach

NATO's studies probably would have had only minor political impact if high-ranking European politicians had not boosted the idea of missile defense. Most notably, German Defense Minister Wörner, in the fall of 1985, began arguing for an "Extended Air Defense" system in NATO-Europe. According to the minister, NATO had to develop a response to the increase in the Soviet Union's conventional offensive capability, especially in the TBM field, in order to preclude the Soviets acquiring a conventional-only attack option. Wörner pointed out that the Western Alliance was bound to consider how a strictly nonnuclear defensive system against conventional TBMs, cruise missiles, and aircraft equipped with standoff missiles, could be developed and set up for the European NATO nations. Furthermore, the goal would be a point defense of militarily important NATO assets and not an area defense or large-scale protection of populations.

Perhaps the most important difference between SDI/EDI concepts and the Extended Air Defense approach is that the latter does not alter the military strategy of the Western Alliance. Building upon NATO's well-proven, fully integrated air defense structure, it merely aims at keeping NATO's Flexible Response operable in the foreseeable future. Also, whereas SDI addresses the "old" (i.e., nuclear Soviet attack option), the Extended Air Defense concept is much more concerned about the emerging "new" conventional-only option.

Wörner's initiative had already been endorsed by NATO Secretary General Lord Carrington, Supreme Allied Commander Europe (SACEUR) General Rogers, U.S. Secretary of Defense Weinberger, and Dutch Defense Minister de Ruiter when the Western Alliance's defense ministers, during their Defense Planning Committee (DPC) meeting in May 1986, added political impetus to the initiative. For the first time, the concept of antitactical missile defense was included in a ministerial communique, and the NATO Air Defense Committee (NADC) was assigned the task of leading further studies. Various possibilities of enhancing NATO's integrated air defense to enable it to deal with the full spectrum of the Warsaw Pact air threat (most prominently: TBMs) were to be investigated. Ministers were particularly interested in a comprehensive threat assessment as a basis for further discussions and decisions. Simultaneously, the U.S. Army Strategic Defense Command (USASDC) awarded multiple contracts for "Theater Missile Defense" architecture studies to American and European defense industry firms.

The TBM Threat in Perspective: Recent History

The reader should keep in mind that the former Soviet military has recently undergone a dramatic transformation. It will take years before the new independent states of the former USSR define their new militaries and design their own force structures, organizations, and doctrines of use. Nevertheless, this recent history of the interaction between NATO and the former USSR/Warsaw Pact remains important because the Soviets exported to the developing countries TBM technology, training, and doctrine.

Current trends in the development of air attack assets in East and West are: increased range and increased standoff capabilities, higher accuracies, higher attack velocities, reduced radar signatures, use of all altitudes, application of an increasing variety of ever more effective conventional munitions and submunitions, and increased utilization of electronic warfare devices. Most of these trends apply to nonballistic as well as ballistic tactical missiles, although the latter have very high close-in (terminal) speed, extremely short flight times, and altitude regime utlilization.

Proper threat analysis requires at least two important analytical steps: making fair assumptions about the opponent's capabilities, and, most important, putting these capabilities in the right strategic and operational context. Only then can appropriate countermeasures be devised.

With respect to TBMs this translates into considering that these missiles were organic to Soviet fronts, armies, and divisions, and did not belong to the Strategic Rocket Forces. Failing to take this fact into account (i.e., proceeding on the assumption of a quasi-autonomous TBM force) can lead to very divergent conclusions: one can exaggerate the threat by overestimating the number of available missiles for attack on Western Europe (counting every missile between the Baltic Sea and the Pacific), perhaps even assuming an independent conventional TBM first-strike option; or one can underestimate the threat by neglecting the combined-arms approach of Russian offensive air operations (aircraft plus missiles). These errors were common in early analyses of the subject.

Two interdependent factors form the background against which the TBM threat facing NATO was viewed. *First*, for Soviet military planners "conventional-only" wars on a strategic level were not merely a probable, but a definitely preferred, conflict scenario. The architects of Soviet military strategy seemed to be confident that the USSR, having achieved escalation dominance—at least in the European theater—could succeed in suppressing NATO's nuclear options.

Second, acceptance of the possibility to wage major conventional wars forced Soviet military planners to find a surrogate for the initial mass nuclear strike. Offensive air operations with conventional means were the obvious solution. This requirement resulted in a radical restructuring of Soviet air forces. From 1965 to 1977 the offensive load capacity of Soviet frontal aviation in Eastern Europe grew by some 90 percent. As of 1989, some 3,000 offensive Soviet aircraft were facing NATO-Europe, many of them ultramodern variable-geometry third-generation planes that can execute deep-strike operations. One can assume that at least 1,000–1,500 aircraft would have been available for the first mass strike in the Western theater of military operations (TVD).

Offensive air operations comprising the employment of various delivery platforms with different flight and weapon characteristics is the context in which Soviet planners viewed the utility of conventional TBMs. They were not treated as an autonomous means of attack but would have been assigned certain supportive functions depending on their specific capabilities. Velocity and assured penetrability are TBM features that were most appealing to the Soviet planner. A major disadvantage of short-range ballistic missiles, however, is their limited payload capacity compared with that of aircraft. This underscored the need to employ TBMs in conjunction with aircraft operations rather than independently.

Suppressing Western air defenses and disrupting NATO's major air bases at the outset of a conventional war in Europe were tasks crucially important for the success of the Soviet air operation. A Rand study concluded that the first generation of conventionally armed TBMs in the 1990s would probably only threaten fixed, soft, and highly time-critical targets (i.e., air bases) (Rubenson and Bonomo 1987). TBM effectiveness against air bases is still a matter of intense debate among Western experts. The main reason for profound disagreement is that different experts base their calculations on different attack scenarios. For instance, if one assumes that the objective was to close air bases permanently with TBM attacks only, this leads to extraordinarily high missile requirements. But the Soviet approach to offensive air operations seemed to bear little resemblance to such a scenario. According to Western sources, Soviet military specialists concentrated on examining ways for missiles to disrupt air base operations for short intervals (minutes) before fighter-bombers arrive (Gormley 1988). Such precursory TBM raids would maximize the effects of follow-up aircraft attacks.

Outside NATO, Israeli interest in ATBMs grew throughout the 1980s due to the progressive proliferation of ballistic missiles in Israel's immediate neighborhood. Especially worrisome from the Israeli perspective was the former Soviet Union's transfer of 120-kilometer (75-mi.) range SS-21s to Syria and Syria's request for longer-range ballistic missiles. The INF Treaty prohibits Russia from supplying ground-based missiles with a range of 500 kilometers (310 mi.) or more to Syria or any other state. Despite this, the number of potential missile suppliers worldwide is increasing. Chinese sales to Saudi Arabia, Argentinian efforts to enter cooperative ventures with Arab countries, and Indian and Pakistani test and development programs highlight this development.

In addition, the Gulf War between Iraq and Iran (1980–88) heightened Israeli apprehensions. The extensive use of rockets by both sides and the employment of chemical weapons by Iraq led Israel to examine possible defenses against TBMs armed with chemical warheads. In contrast, NATO countries focus their ATBM efforts almost entirely on meeting the conventional threat. In 1988, the Israeli Ministry of Defense conducted "an ATBM architecture study to examine the near- and far-term TBM threat and potential countermeasures" (Payne and Berkowitz 1988). Israeli research and development of ATBM systems was ostensibly advancing rapidly. In late 1987, the United States and Israel signed an agreement for a joint technology demonstration of Israel's Arrow antimissile system. At the same time, Israel showed great interest in additional partners from NATO-Europe.

NATO's Search for Countermeasures

In NATO, the initial enthusiasm among ATBM supporters faded when thorough analyses indicated that active defense could only be part of the solution to the TBM problem and was extremely costly. Budgetary and other constraints, as well as allegations that active defenses against short-range missiles might violate the 1972 Soviet-American ABM Treaty (Daalder and Boutwell 1988), compelled planners to abandon ambitious ATBM concepts. The leading question became: What can be done with present and prospective air defense systems? Since the AAS-20 study had already concluded that any ATBM defense in Europe would have to rely on SAM systems for at least the next two decades, NATO's major SAM assets were scrutinized for their ATBM capabilities.

The Patriot turned out to be the most potent ATBM candidate. The development of the Patriot low-to-high altitude SAM system (max. range: about 80 km, 50 mi.) started as early as the 1960s (at that time its designation was SAM-D). The new system was expected to be effective not only against aircraft, but also (under the original plan) against nuclear TBMs. The ATBM requirement was cancelled at an early stage, however, for funding, technological, and NATO policy reasons. As a result, the mobile Patriot, as originally fielded in the mid-1980s, was not ATBM capable. It could only engage aircraft and cruise missiles with relatively large radar cross-sections. But since the system possesses a considerable growth-potential, Patriot ATBM Capability programs (PAC) were begun as early as 1986.

In a first step (PAC-1) the Patriot software was upgraded to provide the system with an ATBM self-defense capability via "mission kill" (i.e., diversion of an incoming missile warhead from its preplanned trajectory, resulting in the failure of the attack mission) and a capability against larger TAMs. The Patriot's software was further improved under a program known as PAC-2, which also involved modifications to the missile itself. U.S. and Israeli operators launched 158 PAC-2 missiles against 47 Iraqi missiles during the 1991 Persian Gulf War, intercepting 45 of them. With 53 Patriot batteries (a total of 1,696 launch tubes) already fielded, the U.S. Army is seeking funds for a total of 6,000 Patriot missiles. One-third of these would be PAC-2 versions and designated ATBMs; the other two-thirds, PAC-1s, would be designated for defense against aircraft.

The U.S. Army and the German and Netherlands air forces planned to procure 84 Patriot units by the early or mid-1990s. Each battery is to be equipped with eight launcher vehicles with four guided missiles each (in the case of the Netherlands, 5 × 4) and each launcher carries four spare SAMs. This adds up to a total of more than 5,300 missiles in NATO's Central Region. The basic concept for employment of these missiles is the protection of German forward airspace. The United States, however, also uses the Patriot system for the protection of essential rear area installations and air bases in the Federal Republic of Germany. Hence, NATO in the 1990s will presumably field some ATBM defense, although this defense will not be leak-proof. Technology is clearly pushing in the direction of utilizing "traditional" SAM systems for ATBM missions. NATO is not likely to succeed in completing such a vigorous and coordinated ATBM program because the INF Treaty should eliminate all INF from the Atlantic to the Ural Mountains in the former USSR. Limited ATBM options are bound to accrue to the Western Alliance as a result of ongoing air defense modernization. European NATO nations already plan to replace the aging Hawk, a medium SAM (MSAM), which went into service in the early 1960s, with a new MSAM with limited ATBM (and comprehensive ATAM) capabilities.

Active defensive measures are, of course, only part of the answer to the tactical missile challenge facing NATO.

Passive measures taken to minimize the effectiveness of air attacks (e.g., hardening, mobility, target proliferation, dispersal, camouflage-improved deployment, alert and mobilization patterns, more redundant C^3-structures) are an important complement. The NATO Air Defence Committee (NADC) concluded that passive measures offer good prospects for near- to mid-term application. It is important to note their general significance because they contribute to protection against the full spectrum of the air threat. NADC proposals for passive defense in the near- to mid-term include: mobility improvements for SAM fire units, decoys and electronic deception, splinter protection of the Kevlar-type, improved emission-control for SAM radars, barracks hardening, aircraft dispersal over all air bases (including civilian airfields and airports), procurement of rapid-runway-repair facilities, and an expanded shelter program.

To cope with a Warsaw Pact air threat, NATO had always relied heavily on Offensive Counter-Air (OCA). If a Warsaw Pact attack had been initiated and SACEUR had given Border Crossing Authority (BCA), NATO air forces would immediately have attacked the opponent's air assets (i.e., aircraft and missiles). Successful forward defense depended on NATO air superiority. Counterair '90 gave rise to the notion of striking Soviet TBM batteries and related command, control, and communications systems with Western conventional TBMs. Because NATO is a defensive alliance, however, the OCA component of the overall Counterair posture cannot be overemphasized. Furthermore, OCA could not prevent an initial mass air strike at the outset of a war in Europe. NATO would have to ride out the first blow by employing active and passive defense measures. All of these plans have become merely historical documents since the disintegration of the USSR and the Warsaw Pact.

The Soviet Union's ATBM Potential

The former Soviet Union traditionally showed great interest in providing an effective air defense for the homeland. This was reflected in the extensive SAM network the USSR fielded on Soviet and non-Soviet territory in Eastern Europe. Contrary to NATO deployment patterns, Warsaw Pact SAM systems were deployed on an area-coverage basis. The density of coverage was such that Western fighter-bombers had a good chance of penetrating it only at night and at low altitude. Within the first 480 kilometers (300 mi.) beyond the intra-German border, some 4,300 radar-guided and more than 11,000 optical- and infrared-guided SAM systems were deployed, not counting the Warsaw Pact mobile SAM systems.

However, not only could Western manned systems be effectively engaged by the Warsaw Pact's air defense posture, but also cruise missiles and TBMs. The SA-10, which reached operational capability in 1980, represented the Soviet's first credible capability against targets with a small radar cross section. The SA-10 can be employed not only against low-flying aircraft but also against cruise missiles. A limited ABM capability, primarily against sea-based ballistic missiles (SLBMs), is also attributed to this system. It was believed that the former Soviet Union had at least 1,400 SA-10 launchers.

The newest and most advanced Russian SAM system is the SA-12. This highly mobile, all-altitude system exists in two different configurations: the currently deployed "Gladiator" is intended for traditional air defense while the SA-X-12B/"Giant," which will become operational in the 1990s, is likely to be used for ATBM missions (U.S. Department of Defense 1988).

After the INF Treaty: What Happened to the TBM Threat?

It is doubtful whether the renewed interest in ATBM, which arose in 1984–85, would have been so significant if the INF Treaty had already been in place. Pondering the impact of the treaty on ATBM, a British analyst in 1988 posed the rhetorical question: "Without a credible large-scale conventional TBM threat, what remains of the rationale for pursuing ATBMs?" (Cuthbertson 1988). Many ATBM critics have praised the "second zero" of the INF Treaty (banning all TBMs with a range of 500–1,000 km, [310–620 mi.]) as the crucial achievement since it would render all Western ATBM planning obsolete. However, experts have never suggested that the TBM threat already exists but rather have pointed to it as an emerging threat. So the correct question to ask is: Has the conventional TBM threat ceased to emerge in the wake of the INF Treaty?

Although the "second zero" of the INF Treaty provides for the elimination of the SS-12/22 and of the SS-23 (the only missile system assumed to have been the most plausible candidate for a strategically significant conventional TBM option of the former Warsaw Pact), TBMs below the 500-kilometer (310-mi.) threshold remain unconstrained. Furthermore, the INF Treaty does not require the destruction of guidance and warhead sections of missiles. Even more important, further technological development in this field is not restricted since such restrictions are not verifiable.

Some experts assume that additional Russian follow-on TBMs with ranges of just under 500 kilometers (310 mi.) are already "in the pipeline" (Payne and Berkowitz 1988). This is, against the backdrop of previous Soviet armament patterns, a legitimate assumption. It does not, however, suffice to make a compelling case for a vigorous ATBM program in a time of sweeping arms control agreements and shrinking defense budgets.

Even if Russia had a SS-23 missile with a shorter range "in the pipeline," it should have good reasons to exercise self-restraint. Aiming at the gradual denuclearization of Europe, Russia will probably avoid providing NATO with a reason for short-range TBM modernization (Lance follow-on). This appears to be one lesson the Soviet Union learned from the SS-20 controversy of the late 1970s and early 1980s when NATO argued that Pershing II and cruise missile deployment was necessary to offset the new Soviet INF weapon. It is therefore unlikely that Russia will field a new TBM to close the "range gap" between the Scud and the SS-23.

The Scud, upgraded by Iraq from its 300-kilometer (188-mi.) range to a range of 500 kilometers (310 mi.), demonstrated its poor accuracy, but showed its value as a "terror weapon," in the 1991 Gulf War. Furthermore, much like NATO's Lance, the Scud is rapidly approaching operational obsolescence. An interesting question is: Can the guidance and warhead technology of the SS-23 or any future technology be retrofitted into the Scud in order to make this missile system an effective (i.e., highly accurate with advanced munitions) conventional TBM and can its lifetime be extended throughout the 1990s? The differences between the Scud and the SS-23 lead to the conclusion that the inherent improvement capability of the old Scud using SS-23 technology is very limited. However, the Iraqis demonstrated that not only could they increase its range, but also that they could design a chemical warhead for the Scud.

In sum, the INF Treaty has certainly not increased the conventional TBM threat to NATO, as is sometimes suggested. The immediate effect of the treaty was to curtail the Soviet TBM arsenal. As stated above, the new states of the former Soviet Union have good reasons not to take the lead in fielding a new TBM (i.e., a decreased-range follow-on to the SS-23).

Whatever the possibilities and probabilities pertaining to future TBM developments, the INF Treaty will certainly fuel efforts in the air-to-surface missile (ASM)/TAM field. From NATO's perspective, and especially under the Pentagon's "Competitive Strategies" approach, this might be a positive "channeling" effect of the treaty. If it was right to point out that the TBM problem must be assessed against the whole Warsaw Pact air threat to NATO before the conclusion of the INF agreement, it is even more important today. The conventional TBM threat is (and is likely to stay so in the next ten to twenty years) only a small portion of the overall air threat confronting the NATO Alliance. "NATO's TBM problem in the 1990s may be largely a problem of airbase defense" (Rubenson and Bonomo 1987). Therefore, the main effort of NATO's Extended Air Defense planning will have to be directed against a dramatically reduced nonballistic air threat. In Israel and other countries outside Europe, however, the situation might be entirely different.

Finally, even if one were absolutely certain that no TBM threat existed or could ever emerge, future air defense would have to have some intrinsic ATBM capability. Otherwise, an opponent would feel tempted to devise nonballistic missiles with TBM-like terminal attack angles. Furthermore, provided that all TBMs were to be eliminated in Europe and that even if a production ban could be verified, it would certainly not stop the accelerating TBM proliferation outside the East-West context. Developing nations could use such missiles against NATO or former Warsaw Pact forces outside Europe, or against their allies. Also, clandestine reintroduction of such missiles into Europe cannot be excluded. Therefore, in the not too distant future, ATBM capabilities will be an integral part of all major ground-based air defense systems.

The Changing Context For Tactical Defense

Until 1987, ATBM systems had been of interest primarily in the context of a war between NATO and the Soviet Union. The relaxation of tensions between NATO and the former Soviet Union, the implementation of the INF treaty, and the 1991 Persian Gulf War has, however, cast ATBM into a different light.

The sight of U.S. Patriot air defense missiles arcing up to intercept Iraqi ballistic missiles in the night sky over Israel and the Gulf states has reinvigorated the debate in the United States over the future of ballistic missile defense. Shortly after the war, the Bush administration announced that it was redirecting the SDI away from research on defenses to counter an intentional Soviet nuclear attack on the United States, in favor of protection against accidental or unauthorized missile launches or attacks from developing countries. This new concept, called "global protection against limited strikes" (GPALS), confronts policymakers with important new questions. How effective would such defense be? Would it be prudent to amend or to withdraw from the ABM treaty?

While investment in ATBMs for the defense of NATO seemed to make sense in the 1980s, similar costs or new programs may be more difficult to justify in a regional context. In comparison with the former Soviet Union, new nuclear states in the developing world are likely to have relatively few missiles and nuclear warheads for the foreseeable future; thus their ability to use these weapons against ATBM defenses before attacking their primary targets is limited. Their relatively small and perhaps more vulnerable and less tightly controlled nuclear arsenals may, however, increase the probability that they would be involved in a nuclear war with a neighbor.

Critics question whether expensive advanced ATBMs are a cost-effective response to the relatively inexpensive threat posed by older missile technology currently in the developing world. ATBM supporters point out that political factors can be as important or more important than military considerations, as demonstrated by the moderating effect the presence of Patriot missiles may have had on Israeli decision making during the 1991 Persian Gulf War. Concerns about TBMs and ATBMs can be expected to be very much a part of the world's future.

THOMAS ENDERS

SEE ALSO: Arms Control and Disarmament; Ballistic Missile Defense; Ground Defense of Air Bases; Missile, Ballistic; Missile, Cruise; Space, Military Aspects of; Space Weapons; Strategic Defense Initiative; Strategic Defense Initiative: Policy Implications; Technology and Arms Control.

Bibliography

Cuthbertson, I. M. 1988. *The anti-tactical ballistic missile issue and European security*. New York: Institute for East-West Security Studies.

Daalder, I. H., and J. Boutwell. 1988. TBMs and ATBMs: Arms control considerations. In *ATBMs and western security: Missile defenses for Europe*, ed. D. L. Hafner and J. Roper, pp. 179–208. Cambridge, Mass.: Ballinger.

Davis, W. A., Jr. 1986. *Regional security and anti-tactical ballistic missiles*. Washington, D.C.: Pergamon.

Enders, T. 1986. *Missile defense as part of an extended NATO air defense*. Bonn, St. Augustin: Konrad-Adenauer-Stifting.

Gormley, D. M. 1988. The Soviet threat. In *ATBMs and western security: Missile defenses for Europe*, ed. D. L. Hafner and J. Roper, pp. 75–79. Cambridge, Mass.: Ballinger.

Hafner, D. L., and J. Roper, eds. 1988. *ATBMs and western security: Missile defenses for Europe*. Cambridge, Mass.: Ballinger.

Hoffman, F. S. 1983. *Ballistic missile defenses and U.S. national security*. Washington, D.C.: Institute for Defense Analyses.

Nerlich, U. 1985. Missile defenses: Strategic and tactical. *Survival*, May–June, pp. 119–127.

Payne, K. B., and M. J. Berkowitz. 1988. Anti-tactical missile defense, allied security and the INF treaty. *Strategic Review* 16(1):24–34

Rubenson, D., and J. Bonomo. 1987. *NATO's anti-tactical ballistic missile requirements and their relationship to the strategic defense initiative*. R-3533-AF. Santa Monica, Calif.: Rand Corp.

U.S. Department of Defense. 1988. *Soviet military power*. Washington, D.C.: Government Printing Office.

ARAB CONQUESTS [A.D. 632–732]

The Arab conquests dramatically altered the political and religious status quo in the Mediterranean basin. United into one nation by the Prophet Muhammad and motivated by the tenets of Islam, the Arabs destroyed the Persian Empire and from the Byzantine Empire won Palestine, Syria, Egypt, eastern Anatolia, and the north coast of Africa. In the space of 100 years, the Arabs conquered an empire extending from the Pamirs in the east to the Atlantic coast of Morocco in the west, and northward into southern France.

The Arab Military

An Arab field army consisted of four elements: vanguard, center, wings, and rearguard. The troops in each element were recruited from the same tribe.

The cavalry, drawn from the nomadic Bedouin tribes, were either lancers, armed with swords and lances, or horse archers, armed with swords and bows and arrows. Some cavalrymen also carried javelins. During their early campaigns, the horse archers did not use stirrups, and as a result, their effectiveness was limited. The Arab cavalry, therefore, relied primarily on the lance and the sword.

Initially, the cavalryman was lightly armored, his personal armor consisting, usually, of a helmet and mail shirt. After contact with the Byzantine and Persian heavy cavalry, the Arabs adopted the armor of their opponents.

The infantry, drawn from the town-dwelling Arabs (al-Hadhar), consisted mainly of foot archers who, along with their bows and arrows, carried swords. Occasionally, other weapons—including javelins, slings, and spears—were used. Infantry armor consisted of a helmet and mail shirt. In Arabia and the conquered territories, Arab townsmen formed militias for both garrison duty and field operations.

TACTICS

The cavalry deployed either in extended order (line) or in a compact mass (column). When present, the infantry formed the center and the cavalry the wings. Tactics were centered around the cavalry charge with supporting fire supplied by the horse archers and the infantry, the latter serving as both a tactical pivot and a fire-support base. The objective of the charge was to break the enemy's formation. Once the enemy forces were in disarray, the Arabs attacked and defeated each unit separately.

Arab tactics were based upon the *razzia*, the traditional Bedouin raid. In fact, most campaigns were just a series of raids. The traditions of the *razzia* also explain a major weakness of Arab tactics. After the cavalry had driven home the charge, each warrior engaged in single combat with an enemy soldier—just as if he were on an intertribal raid in Arabia. All unit cohesion disappeared.

REASONS FOR ARAB VICTORIES

Despite the glaring weaknesses of their tactical system, the Arabs won victory after victory over the Byzantines and Persians, the dominant military powers of the day. The superior mobility of the Arabs, their high morale, the weakness of both the Byzantine and Persian empires following the conclusion of their 25-year war, and the support of native populations all contributed to Arab victories. Another contributing factor was Arab generalship. The victories of Khalid ibn al-Walid, Amr ibn al-As, and Saad ibn Abu Waqqas were won against superior enemy forces. The ability of the Arab commanders to exploit the advantages of terrain, especially the desert, and to draw the enemy into fighting on ground favorable to the Arabs, accounts in large part for the string of Arab victories.

The Conquests: First Phase (632–56)

Initial Operations in Iraq

Abu Bakr, the successor (caliph) of the Prophet Muhammad, chose Iraq and Palestine as the initial targets for Arab expansionism. In 634, Khalid ibn al-Walid led a force of 4,000 cavalry into southwestern Iraq. He was joined there by Muthanna ibn Haritha, chief of the Beni-Bakr, and his warriors. With his reinforced army, Khalid took al-Hira and transformed it into his operational base. Located 320 kilometers (200 mi.) northwest of Basra (up the Euphrates River), al-Hira was strategically situated. Its strong walls also made it a highly defendable refuge in case of trouble. From al-Hira, Khalid raided the Persians at will, penetrating as far as Ctesiphon, the Persian capital (located approximately 80 kilometers [50 mi.] south of modern Baghdad, on the Tigris River). Advancing northwestward up the Euphrates, Khalid defeated a Persian army at Firad (480 kilometers [300 mi.] upriver from al-Hira). In recognition of his success, Abu Bakr named Khalid governor of Iraq.

Operations in Palestine and Syria. While Khalid was advancing along the Euphrates, Abu Obeida, with a force of 24,000, commenced operations in Palestine. His army was divided into four columns. The first column, commanded by Amr ibn al-As, was to advance from Akaba to Gaza, then to Jerusalem. The second column, commanded by Yazid ibn Abu Sufyad, had Damascus as its objective. The third and fourth columns formed the reserve.

Amr occupied Akaba, then crossed the Negev Desert and captured Gaza. Initial Byzantine resistance was light, but as Amr neared Jerusalem, resistance stiffened. Both the first and second columns were stopped.

His advance stalled, Abu Obeida faced a new threat: rebellion behind his lines. Fearing that Abu Obeida's forces would be cut off and destroyed, Abu Bakr ordered Khalid from Iraq to Palestine. In July 634, Khalid led a force of 9,000 cavalry across the Great Syrian Desert, entered Palestine, and overwhelmed the rebels. Joining forces with Amr, Khalid defeated the Byzantines at Ajnadayo. The advance northward resumed, bypassing Jerusalem. Khalid and Abu Obeida laid siege to Damascus in March 635; the city surrendered, on lenient terms, in September. Homs and Aleppo surrendered shortly thereafter.

Persian counterattack in Iraq. While Khalid was conducting operations in Palestine and Syria, the Persians counterattacked in Iraq. At the Battle of the Bridge, the Persians defeated Muthanna ibn Haritha. Arab losses totaled 4,000. In October 634, Muthanna stopped the Persian offensive at the Battle of Buwaib. During the battle, Muthanna was mortally wounded.

Byzantine counterattack in Syria. In 636, the Byzantine emperor Heraclius led a force of 200,000 men to Antioch. He sent most of these, under his brother Theodorus, toward Damascus. As the Byzantines approached, Khalid abandoned Damascus and withdrew southward. The Byzantines pursued. Khalid continued to fall back until he reached the confluence of the Yarmuk and Jordan rivers (near the modern towns of Baqura and Ashdot Ya'aqov). Under cover of a sandstorm, Khalid launched his army of 40,000 against Theodorus's 150,000. The Battle of Yarmuk lasted three days. Khalid maneuvered his forces so that eventually the Byzantines were caught in a narrow passage between two converging Arab columns. Theodorus was slain and his army annihilated. So decisive was the Battle of Yarmuk that Heraclius withdrew from Antioch and returned to Constantinople. Khalid, at the head of his victorious army, reentered Damascus only to be deprived of his command and recalled by the new caliph, Omar, who had appointed Abu Obeida governor of Syria. In January 637, Amr ibn al-As occupied Jerusalem. With the exception of Caesarea and Antioch, all of Palestine and Syria—two of the richest provinces of the Byzantine Empire—were in Arab hands.

Conquest of Iraq. Omar appointed Saad ibn Abu Waqqas governor of Iraq in 636. Saad, with 30,000 men, defeated a Persian army 100,000 strong at Qadisiya. Advancing up the Tigris River, Saad occupied Ctesiphon. At Jalula (80 kilometers [50 mi.] north of Baghdad), Saad again defeated the Persians. Saad wished to pursue the Persians into Iran, but Omar, the caliph, forbade it. The victories of Saad ibn Abu Waqqas gave the Arabs control of all of Iraq except for the Mosul region.

Conquest of Egypt

The conquest of Egypt was entrusted to Amr ibn al-As, the conquerer of Jerusalem. With a force of 4,000—later increased to 10,000—Amr crossed the Sinai isthmus into Egypt in December 639. Pelusium and Heliopolis quickly fell to the Arabs. In April 640, Amr besieged Babylon, a mighty Byzantine fortress on the site of modern Cairo. Babylon surrendered in March 641 on condition that the garrison be allowed to withdraw to Alexandria. Three months later, Amr laid siege to Alexandria, capital of the province of Egypt and headquarters of the Byzantine fleet in the Levant. In November 641, Cyrus, the Byzantine viceroy, surrendered the city to Amr. Once again, Amr granted the Byzantines lenient terms and allowed the defenders of Alexandria to withdraw from Egypt. All of Egypt was secured by 643, and Amr was appointed governor of the province. In 645, Alexandria revolted, spurred on by the appearance of the Byzantine fleet offshore. Amr, however, quickly quelled the rebellion, and the Byzantines withdrew.

Abdullah ibn Saad replaced Amr as governor of Egypt in 646. To counter the threat posed by the Byzantine navy, Abdullah created an Arab navy, and in 649, it captured Cyprus. At the Battle of the Masts (Dhat al-sawaib) in 655, the Arabs soundly beat the Byzantine navy, thereby wresting control of the eastern Mediterranean from the Byzantine empire.

Conquest of Persia

Saad ibn Abu Waqqas recommenced operations in northern Iraq in 641, securing Mosul. Then, in 642, he crossed into Persia (Iran) and, at Nehawend, decisively defeated the Persian emperor Yazdagird, who fled eastward leaving 60,000 Persian dead on the battlefield. After Nehawend, the Arabs gradually extended their control over all of Persia. In 649, Saad ibn al-As, governor of Kufah, commenced operations along the Hamadan-Ray-Jurjan-Khurasan axis, while Abdullah ibn Amir, governor of Basra, advanced along the Fars-Kerman-Tabas-Nishapur-Marv axis. Although the Arabs encountered sporadic, and sometimes stiff, resistance, their advance was aided by the conversion of many Persian aristocrats to Islam. The once mighty Persian Empire was finally secured by 652.

End of the First Phase

The first phase of the Arab conquests was ended by the outbreak of the First Arab Civil War. Fought between the Alids, followers of Ali—the son-in-law of the Prophet Muhammad—and the followers of the Omayyads, the war revealed deep religious and tribal divisions within the Arab nation.

The Conquests: Second Phase (661–80)

The victory of the Omayyads in 661 restored stability to the Arab Empire—at least temporarily. Unity restored, Arab expansion continued, with Arab forces becoming active in North Africa and Central Asia.

The conquest of North Africa was assigned to Oqbah ibn Nafi, nephew of Amr ibn al-As. By 670, Oqbah had reached Tunisia, where he founded Kairouan (Qairawan).

Ziyad ibn Abihi campaigned in Afghanistan and occupied Kabul in 664, after which he proceeded northward into Transoxiana, reducing Samarkand in 676.

The outbreak of the Second Arab Civil War ended the second phase. Hussein, son of Ali, revolted against the Omayyads in 680. The war ended quickly, Hussein was slain in the Battle of Kerbala, and his followers were ruthlessly suppressed.

The Conquests: Third Phase (680–732)

The defeat of the Alid rebels paved the way for the resumption of operations in North Africa and Central Asia.

Oqbah ibn Nafi resumed his westward march in 683. Tangier fell and all of the Moroccan coast as far as modern Agadir (on the Atlantic coast) came under Arab control. Oqbah's conquests, however, were short-lived. On the journey back to his base at Kairouan, Oqbah divided his army into a number of columns—it was a fatal blunder. At Bishra, Berbers ambushed and annihilated Oqbah's column.

Twenty-two years passed between the death of Oqbah and the resumption of operations in North Africa. The capture of Carthage from the Byzantines was the only Arab success of note. In 704, however, Musa ibn Nosair was named governor of North Africa. Through a combination of military action and diplomacy, Musa persuaded the Berbers to make peace with the Arabs and to accept Islam. With the conquest of Mauritania in 705, all of the Atlantic coast of North Africa was added to the domain of the caliph.

Central Asia

While Musa ibn Nosair was pushing the western frontiers of Islam to the Atlantic, Qutaba ibn Muslim began operations to reconquer Transoxiana where, during the Second Arab Civil War, the Turks had reasserted their independence. This proved a formidable task. The Arabs met stiff resistance from the Turkic horse archers, whose skill with horse and bow far surpassed that of their Arab counterparts. Bokhara was taken in 709; Samarkand not until 712. By 714, Qutaba had pushed the eastern frontiers of Islam as far as Farghana, though tradition claims he reached Kasghar in Chinese Turkestan.

Between 710 and 715, Arab forces commanded by Mohammed ibn Kasim reconquered Afghanistan and extended Arab rule over the Punjab and Sind, thus adding the Indus River valley to the empire of the Omayyads.

Iberian Peninsula

Tariq ibn Ziyad, the governor of Tangier and a subordinate of Musa ibn Nosair, crossed the straits of Gibraltar (Tariq's Rock) with 7,000 men in 711. Taking advantage of Visigothic disunity, Tariq rapidly occupied Algeciras, Cadiz, Malaga, and Cordoba. On 19 July 711, Tariq annihilated the army of the Visigoth king, Roderick, at the Battle of Wadi Bekka (Salado River). With the death of King Roderick, all organized resistance ended. Granada and Toledo, the Visigoth capital, surrendered.

Musa ibn Nosair, upon learning of Tariq's adventure, crossed over to Spain with 10,000 men. By the end of 713, all of Iberia except for the northern provinces of Asturias and Navarre had been secured.

Southern France

From their base in Spain, successive Arab governors launched operations against southern France. In 717, al-Hurr ibn Abd al-Rahman al-Thakafi conducted the first of these raids. Al-Samh ibn Malik al-Khaulani occupied Septimania in 720 and established a forward base at Narbonne. In 721, al-Samh laid siege to Toulouse. It was during this siege that al-Samh was slain and the Arabs withdrew to Narbonne. In 732, Abd al-Rahman ibn Abdullah al-Ghafiqi advanced northwestward along the Garonne River with about 50,000 men and occupied Bordeaux. Advancing northward from Bordeaux, the Arabs penetrated central France, reaching the Loire River near Tours. Charles Martel, de facto ruler of the Merovingian Frankish borders, led an army of more than 50,000 to meet the Arabs, who retreated to protect their train of booty. Somewhere between Tours and Poitiers, near the confluence of the Clain and Vienne rivers, the Franks caught up with the Arabs, and decisively defeated them. This Battle of Tours (October 732) marked the farthest Arab penetration of Europe. Although the Battle of Tours blunted Arab expansionism, it did not end Arab military activity in France. In 734, Arab raiders seized Avignon. In 743, they raided Lyon. The Arabs remained a military threat until the loss of their base at Narbonne in 759.

End of the Conquests

The Arab conquests lost momentum after 732 for a number of reasons. After withstanding four Arab attacks on Constantinople, and repeated attempts to occupy Asia Minor, the resurgent Byzantine Empire took the offensive, reoccupied the Syrian coast, and threatened Arab possession of Palestine.

In the east, Arab expansion into Chinese Turkestan was blocked by the Uigher Turks. And behind the Uighers stood the Chinese Empire. In the west, the growing power of the Franks under the son and grandson (Charlemagne) of Charles Martel, proved a barrier to further Arab expansion into western Europe.

Arab disunity also contributed to the end of the Arab conquests. The simmering hatred between the Omayyads and the Alids, reflected in the continuing Sunni-Shiite split, undermined both the stability and unity of the Arab nation. The overthrow of the Omayyads in 750 by the Abbasids—a Persian family of Arab origin—further undermined Arab unity. The banner of Islam passed from the Arabs to the Seljuk and Ottoman Turks.

Lawrence D. Higgins

See Also: Byzantine Empire; Charlemagne; History, Medieval Military; Khalid ibn-al-Walid.

Bibliography

Brice, W. C., ed. 1981. *A historical atlas of Islam.* Leiden: E. J. Brill.

Butler, A. J. 1902. *The Arab conquest of Egypt.* London: Oxford Univ. Press.

Gibb, H. A. R. 1923. *The Arab conquests in central Asia.* London: Royal Asiatic Society.

Glubb, Sir John. 1963. *The great Arab conquests.* London: Hodder and Stoughton.

Hitti, P. K. 1956. *History of the Arabs.* 6th ed. New York: Macmillan.

Levy, R. 1957. *The social structure of Islam.* Cambridge: Cambridge Univ. Press.

Lewis, B. 1958. *The Arabs in history.* 4th ed. London: Hutchinson.

Nutting, A. 1964. *The Arabs: A narrative history from Mohammed to the present.* New York: New American Library/Mentor Books.

Pipes, D. 1981. *Slave soldiers and Islam: The genesis of a military system.* New Haven: Yale Univ. Press.

Spuler, B. 1960. *The age of the caliphs.* Leiden: E. J. Brill.

ARAB-ISRAELI WARS [1947–82]

The long struggle between Israel and various coalitions of surrounding Arab nations began with the Israeli War of Independence (First Arab-Israeli War) in 1948–49 and has since included four more wars, plus almost continual conflict with various levels of violence, ranging from military interventions to terrorism. The last three wars have served Western and Soviet military planners as paradigms for a hypothetical clash in Central Europe.

The basic issue concerns territorial rights in the former Ottoman-Turkish administrative district of Palestine, which is located in the heart of what the Arabs of the Middle East regard as an exclusively Islamic domain. Britain and France had, since 1918, administered (under League of Nations mandates) the lands in the Fertile Crescent liberated from Germany's Turkish ally in World War I. This arrangement was intended to midwife the native nationalist movements to independent nationhood. British wartime diplomacy, however, resulted in separate and conflicting promises of self-rule in Palestine to both the native Arab populace and the Jewish Zionist nationalist movement. It was subsequently impossible to satisfy the claims of either the Zionists or the Palestinian Arabs, and spiraling violence from both parties, directed primarily at the British occupation apparatus but also at each other, ultimately brought the matter to the attention of the United Nations (UN) in 1946. That body voted to partition the mandate into separate Jewish and Arab areas, with Jerusalem a neutral international zone. The Zionists accepted this (as half a loaf), but the Arab League nations vowed to nullify the decision by force. Israeli success in 1948 resulted in the flight of most of the original Arab inhabitants ("Palestinians"). Confined to tent cities in countries of refuge, the plight of the stateless Palestinians was the impetus (some say pretext) for their patrons' revanchist efforts to undo the Zionist fait accompli. Since then, brief bursts of intensive all-out warfare punctuated extended truces during which the conflict continued in economic and guerrilla-terroristic modes.

Arab-Israeli War of 1948–49

The first round officially lasted one and a half years. It was a stop-start series of clashes, the longest of which lasted four weeks, with combat operations totaling about ten weeks. Long truces divided the war into distinct phases.

Phase I was the period of "civil war" between the Palestinian irregular armed bands—remnants of a 1936–39 uprising—and the Jewish self-defense force. The waning yet vigilant British presence prevented the Arab League states from invading Palestine, but they could not prevent village-based Arab bands from waging a guerrilla war. There were two irregular "fighting organizations" loyal to the exiled Grand Mufti of Jerusalem, each numbering about 1,500 men, which had on call some 35,000 armed villagers, an informal local militia available for short-term and rather static actions. Car-bombing and random sniping in the towns was expected to wear down Jewish morale while the Battle of the Roads would choke isolated Jewish settlements. The patchwork pattern of Jewish settlement meant that the Arab villages sat astride vital communications links. Thus the Palestinians were able to mount roadblocks and ambushes on an ad hoc basis. Haganah, the underground Jewish army, had to rely upon armed convoys for resupply and reinforcement at this early stage. This method was only sporadically successful and exacted a high toll in lives and vehicles.

A small "Arab Liberation Army" composed of Palestinians and volunteers from other Arab countries was operating against Zionist settlements by January 1948. By the end of March 1948, in anticipation of invasion by neighboring Arab countries on expiration of the British League of Nations mandate, Haganah had mobilized and integrated various contingents: a core of 3,000 idealists in the elite Palmach striking force, with another 1,000 in reserve; a mobile field force, HISH, about 10,000 strong with a pool of 35,000 World War II veterans on tap; and a home guard–style static settlement defense force, HIM, numbering 20,000. There were nine brigade-sized units activated, enough to implement Plan D, an offensive designed to seize and hold the Arab wedges separating Jewish sectors. There were also two politically dissident independent terrorist groups, Irgun and Stern, totaling about 1,500. By 15 May, the Jewish consolidation effort was girded for the all-out Arab invasion on the heels of the departed British.

On 15 May—the day following British abandonment of the League of Nations mandate—Egypt, Transjordan, Syria, Iraq, and Lebanon sent forces into Palestine against the Israelis, thereby initiating Phase II of the war. Of all of these, only the Transjordan contingent—the Arab Legion—was a truly effective fighting force. Forces allocated to the task by each of the mutually suspicious Arab allies were quite small relative to strength left at home to check dissident domestic rivals. Each sent brigade-sized expeditions (Egypt allocated two brigades) reinforced by tanks, ground attack planes, artillery, and armored cars. Much has been made of the imbalance of these assets, but the Arab forces could not coordinate the various arms and had to employ them piecemeal, in rigid field-manual fashion.

Most serious was the lack of a unified war plan, which left the various armies to run independent operations without provision for mutual support. All were stunned by tenacious and aggressive reaction of the Jewish border settlements and considerably altered their initial "Anaconda" program (a plan to cut off incoming resources by closing Israel's borders) to settle for a few threatening bridgeheads on the periphery of the Jewish state. Egyptian columns stalled far short of their objectives—Tel Aviv and Jerusalem—unable to eliminate the chain of Negev settlements from whence wasp stings paralyzed overextended communications. The Arab Legion, however, had secured most of the Old City of Jerusalem. Had the invasion forces made a concerted, coordinated attack instead of accepting an 11 June 1948 truce, it is likely that there would be no Israel today.

Phase III operations were all Israeli initiatives using enlarged and up-gunned mobile brigades. The Israeli Defense Force (IDF) succeeded in blunting the Arab Legion east of Tel Aviv, in containing the Iraqi probe at the narrow "waist," and in decisively thrashing the volunteer army in central Galilee. The Legion still menaced the main corridor between Tel Aviv and West Jerusalem at Latrun, but an improvised bypass rendered Latrun less relevant.

In October 1948, the Israelis began Phase IV with maneuvers that achieved a new sophistication, primarily directed at the Egyptian picket line across the main roads to the Negev. The offensive shattered the Egyptian front, leaving a defiant Egyptian pocket at Faluja and a main threat at Gaza-El Arish, which was dealt with in Phase V (December 1948–January 1949).

This phase began with a wide envelopment presaging the freewheeling maneuvers in Sinai of 1956 and 1967, including the coordinated use of armor, artillery preparations, and air support. A series of armistices (no treaties or recognition was in sight) and a last-minute grab for the Negev's deep "V" corridor to the Gulf of Aqaba left the Jews in control of a considerably larger Israel than the UN had contemplated, but with a crazy-quilt border that was particularly vulnerable opposite the Transjordanian (later Jordanian) salient, now known as the West Bank since it is west of the Jordan River.

Sinai Campaign, 1956 (Operation Kadesh)

Israel had been frustrated by the failure of its reprisal raids to deter border incursions and sabotage by Palestinian exile terrorist/commando groups during the early 1950s. The escalating pattern of reprisals only seemed to intensify these fedayeen attacks, which in 1954 were openly sponsored by Egypt's Gamal Abdel Nasser. In early 1956, Israel decided to stop these terrorist incursions.

In his bid for leadership of the Arab world, Nasser sought to head the confrontation with Israel, stepping up the pressure by sealing Israel's Red Sea outlet with artillery that commanded the narrow Tiran Straits and declaring a military alliance with Syria directed against Israel.

Most worrisome for the IDF was Egypt's massive purchase of Czech and Soviet arms in summer 1955, which would provide Egypt with a decisive edge in one to two years. Thus, the Israeli decision to take military action to halt terrorist attacks was probably to some extent influenced by a determination to prevent the Egyptian forces from integrating their new and sophisticated equipment into effective field units. This then was to some extent a "preventive war," but firm evidence of Egyptian war plans is lacking.

Shortly before the planned Israeli attack on Egypt, France "invited" Israel to coordinate its own campaign with an imminent Anglo-French operation, Musketeer, to seize the Suez Canal. Nasser had recently nationalized the canal in retaliation for withdrawal of Western capital from his Aswan High Dam project. Israel's opening gambit would be to pose a credible "threat" to the canal zone, bringing Egyptian units into the area, in turn triggering Musketeer, ostensibly to buffer the two converging forces in order to keep the canal open. The "distraction" of the Anglo-French maneuvers would draw off sufficient Egyptian strength to allow Israel to accomplish its objectives of wiping out the Gaza fedayeen bases and removing the Egyptian forces covering the Tiran Straits, neither of which entailed incursions near the canal.

To avoid alerting Egypt's armored forces held west of the canal as well as its worrisome air strength, the first phase of "Kadesh"—an airborne incursion east of the Mitla Pass—was to appear to be merely a deep-strike counter fedayeen raid. If the Egyptian High Command were deceived by this and thought they were dealing only with another Israeli retaliation, they would hold back their air support and not alert the strong, well-dug-in defenses holding the northeast Sinai "triangle": El Arish–Rafah–Abu Ageila. The second phase would be the opening of an alternate supply corridor to the first phase units deep in Sinai by breaching the formidable Egyptian defense "hedgehog" at Abu Ageila. The final operations would involve the annihilation of the pocketed raider bases in the Gaza Strip while mobile units overran the Egyptian artillery bases at Sharm el Sheikh.

Phase I went according to plan, although some unauthorized probes into the Mitla Pass created a perilous situation for a few hours. The Egyptian air and armored reserves were not drawn off from the canal—largely because of the diversion created in Nasser's rear by the concentration of the Anglo-French task force on Crete. The Israeli airborne brigade near Mitla turned south to Sharm el Sheikh, while an infantry brigade from Eliat began an arduous trek along the converging axis through terrain barely passable for wheeled vehicles; civilian transport borrowed for the job often broke down.

Two Israeli mechanized infantry brigades opposite the Um-Katef/Um Shehan hedgehog in the center were held at bay by accurate preranged fire from dug-in Egyptian armor and artillery. Impatient with delay, the IDF's sole all-tank brigade, supposedly in reserve, probed along the southern fringes of the defensive complex and found an unguarded pass through which to circle to the rear of Abu Ageila. Contrary to the plan, and without informing headquarters, one tank battalion filtered through and began pounding the Egyptian self-propelled guns from the rear, while the other battalion raced southwest to assist the mechanized brigade beginning its thrust to Sharm el-Sheikh.

The northern Israeli task force then began its combined-arms reduction of the second major Egyptian fortified zone between Rafah and Gaza, one unit racing westward flanking the sector along "impassable" terrain and disrupting its rearward communications, while the other assaulted from the front, exploiting the rather rigid Egyptian defense plans. Finally, the mopping up of the Gaza Strip's Palestinian and Egyptian raiding forces occurred while the two columns descending toward Sharm el Sheikh besieged the garrison there. By this time, the Egyptian high command had ordered all forces in Sinai to pull back to reinforce the main effort against the Anglo-French landings at Suez; this facilitated Israeli operations under way in the two main fortified belts in northeast Sinai. The IAF had dealt decisively with two Egyptian armored columns that had attempted to relieve the hard-pressed units at Abu Ageila and Rafa, proving the value of air superiority over the battlefield, especially in herding retreating vehicles into killing zones at bottlenecks. The inability of Israeli mechanized infantry to penetrate the Um Katef defenses, combined with the success of the armored spearheads, led the Israelis to decide that the tank was the decisive weapon, and that infantry should be used to exploit *after* the armor had punched through or bypassed the main enemy concentrations.

Although Israel won a clear-cut military victory, the war was a political disaster for her Anglo-French allies, who were compelled by pressure from the UN, and especially from the United States and the Soviet Union, to withdraw from Suez. This in turn compelled the Israelis to withdraw from Sinai, although the Straits of Tiran were opened and the postwar UN force in the Sinai limited terrorist attacks on Israel from Egyptian bases. The war left Nasser in a much stronger political position, as he had successfully weathered a crisis and frustrated Anglo-French goals.

Six-Day War, June 1967

After his 1956 military defeat, and political triumph, Nasser rebuilt his forces with Soviet equipment and deployed much of his revitalized army in the forward positions that had caused the entire Sinai command structure to unravel when these linchpins were cracked in 1956. His claim to military leadership of the confrontation with Israel was questioned by Syria in May 1967 when Nasser failed to honor his military commitment (another alliance was patched together in 1966) after an Israeli retaliatory air patrol shot down six Syrian MiGs. Reacting both to the goad and to a supposed threat of an imminent Israeli invasion of Syria (contrived by Soviet incitement), Nasser reimposed the blockade against shipping from Eilat, demanded the evacuation of the UN buffer force from the border areas in Sinai, stirred up the Egyptian masses with martial rhetoric defying Israel, and signed a pact with Jordan and Iraq, placing the alliance forces under Egyptian command. Thus, all the previously announced Israeli tripwires to war had been broken. Yet apparently Nasser did not really expect Israel to attack.

Preliminary Air Strike, 6 June 1967

Israel adopted a low-key posture while secretly mobilizing reserves, updating war plans, and apparently demonstrating a concentration toward Jordan. The Arab air threat was seen as the most crucial factor, both in terms of equipment and numbers. So the Israelis opened their unambiguously preventive war with a meticulously executed, simultaneous air strike on eighteen Egyptian air bases, exploiting the predictability of the Egyptian morning stand-down pattern, underflying Egyptian radar, and dodging SAM-2 missile shields by flying out to sea and circling back from the west. An incredible turnaround time one-third that of the United States Air Force standard, effectively trebled the Israeli Defense Force/Air Force (IDF/AF) order of battle and convinced Nasser that the United States was participating in collusion. Later that day, Jordan and then Syria, crediting Egyptian propaganda that the Israeli attackers had been blown from the sky, launched limited, futile fighter-bomber attacks on Israeli bases and depots. This spurred the IDF/AF to mount additional strikes against their air bases, including an Iraqi base in Jordan, catching planes on the ground as they returned from their initial missions. In all, over two-thirds of total Arab airpower was eliminated in eight hours, thereby giving the IDF/AF a free hand to neutralize the Arab superiority on the ground in armor, artillery, and manpower.

Sinai Front

Taking advantage of intelligence that Nasser's war "coalition" was a self-deluding myth, the IDF resolved, as it had in 1948, to exploit its central position to deal separately with each threat, trusting the unmolested partners to sit on their hands. The first priority was the most dangerous adversary, Egypt, to be dealt with by three divisional task forces (*ugdahs*), each designed and structured for a unique tactical situation along its designated line of march. Southern front commander Gavish employed his 700 tanks and 50,000 troops to punch through the two northernmost Egyptian blocking positions and race to the passes along the Sinai's western ridge line. There he trapped and destroyed the withdrawing Egyptian forces as they channeled through the gorges, utilizing unopposed air support to suppress dug-in firepower and block counterattacks.

Meanwhile, a deceptive feint, where a brigade masqueraded as a division using dummy tanks and illusory reinforcements, opposed the one offensively oriented Egyptian division (Division Shazli) poised along the southern Negev gateway to Tel Aviv and ensured that it would stay there, safely away from the main thrusts.

Ugdah Israel Tal slashed through Egyptian fortifications along the north coast while isolating and reducing Palestinian infantry units entrenched in Gaza. Ugdah Yoffe exploited a soft, heretofore "impassable," seam between two major hedgehogs to join with Tal's southern detachment in racing to the Khatmia Pass and trapping an Egyptian counterattack force at Bir Gifgafa. Yoffe was also able to send part of his force southwest toward an Egyptian deployment at Jebel Libni. Ugdah Ariel Sharon, farther east, mounted a complex, set piece concentric night attack on the greatly expanded (since 1956) Um Katef–Abu Ageila defensive complex. Then, moving cross-country southwest to Nakhl, Sharon cut off Egyptian forces lining the southern axis. Although dangerously overextended and depleted, Yoffe's force captured garrisons at Bir Hasneh and Bir Thamada before sealing the Mitla and Giddi passes. Sharon's force was able to ambush an Egyptian column near Thamad and hold it for the IDF/AF to finish off.

Central Front

The campaign on the central front was to some extent improvised, since the Israelis had expected Jordan to abstain from the fight. Under pressure from Nasser to show solidarity, King Hussein seems to have hoped that perfunctory long-range shelling of Israeli air bases, Jewish Jerusalem, and Tel Aviv with 155mm "Long Toms" would satisfy Nasser yet at the same time demonstrate enough restraint to stay Israel's hand. However, the long-range artillery threat to the runways at the important Ramot David air base set Gen. Uzi Narkiss's central front forces in motion. This readiness demonstrated that the contingency was not entirely unexpected.

The Israelis immediately attacked in Jerusalem to contain a Jordanian battalion in its defensive position, while other elements of the Jerusalem Brigade advanced south toward Hebron. Reinforcements released from Southern Command reserve allowed Narkiss to send three brigades into the Battle of Jerusalem, the main task falling to Col. Mordechai Gur's paratroop brigade. A reinforced Jordanian brigade commanded by Brig. Ata Ali garrisoned the old walled city, Gur's assigned objective. The night assault stalled in the face of obstinate resistance, but elements of Gur's brigade were more successful in driving out two Jordanian infantry brigades holding commanding positions northwest and east of Jerusalem. This action enabled the main effort force to capture intervening posts along the northern ridge line, making contact with a beleaguered Jewish outpost on Mount Scopus.

Meanwhile, early on 6 June, elements of Ben Ari's armored brigade took up positions astride key terrain north of Jerusalem and worked cross-country through territory considered impassable to tanks to gain control of Ramallah by dawn on the seventh. A reserve infantry brigade, striking toward Ramallah in a wide arc through Jordanian positions at Latrun, consolidated Israeli control of the heights dominating the Jerusalem area while the infantry brigade holding the southern approaches closed the ring.

The Jordanian 60th Armored Brigade, held in reserve around Jericho, mounted an effort to relieve the Jerusalem garrison. The relief column, consisting of a battalion each of tanks and infantry, was caught by the IDF/AF and Israeli ground forces. It was wiped out on the night of 5–6 June. Another relief attempt mounted by the Qadisiyeh infantry brigade on 6–7 June also failed.

Concurrently with operations around Jerusalem, Northern Command and elements of Central Command mounted a series of concentric pincer thrusts into Samaria. Jordanian antitank defenses at Jenin stalled one armored brigade, but a mechanized brigade hooked around from the southeast to surprise the Jenin garrison. A particularly effective Jordanian armored counterattack was halted at Kabbatya junction.

An Israeli feint down the Jordan Valley distracted other Jordanian units, as did the advance from the coastal strip by a Central Command infantry brigade, threatening Jordanian armor at Jenin from the rear. The infantry brigade had to fight its way through determined Jordanian armored counterattacks and move cross-country to encircle Nablus from the southwest, while the mechanized brigade could only extricate itself from desperate fighting in Jenin with the help of air support, allowing it to approach Nablus from the northwest, completing the conquest of that town and, with it, the West Bank.

Northern Front

True to expectations, the Syrians, stripped of their air force, largely confined their activities to artillery bombardment of Israeli targets from their formidable fortified complex atop the more than 600-meter (2,000-ft.) Golan escarpment. Shuffling forces from the Jordanian front, the Israeli attack went in on the fourth day of the war. Facing six Syrian brigades on line, with six more in reserve east of Kuneitra, Northern Command concentrated its available forces along the northern anchor of the Syrian line at the Dan-Banyas area, flanking the foothills of Mount Hermon, for an initial advance onto the Golan Plateau. Israeli attack planes concentrated on silencing Syrian gun positions. The key to the Syrian defenses was the fort of Tel Fakhr. There was no scope for maneuver; tank-backed APCs took the hedgehogs straight-on, assisted by armored bulldozers moving ahead to clear boulders littering the steep gradient. Infantry dismounted for the final lunge for the trench lines. Fresh troops passed through depleted units, picking up the remnants. The next day, other Israeli units forced their way up the ridge north of the Sea of Galilee and units fresh from the heavy fighting in the Jenin-Nablus action crossed into Syria along the sea's southern shore. Heliborne troops, leapfrogging with an armored column, menaced Kuneitra from the south.

Meanwhile, the breakthrough units to the north pushed through the crumbling Syrian Golan defenses and pressed on across the plateau to converge on Kuneitra from the north and west, joining the units redeployed from the Jordanian front coming up through the Yarmuk Valley to surround Kuneitra, as an armored unit entered and held the key Syrian assembly point. The imminent Israeli threat to Damascus was warded off by a bluntly worded Soviet ultimatum. The previously announced UN cease-fire took hold on 10 June, with Israeli forces controlling the entire Sinai Peninsula, the West Bank salient, and the Golan Heights—all three declared by Israel as nonnegotiable, essential strategic buffer zones.

War of Attrition

Victory in the Six-Day War netted Israel a strategic warning belt against Egypt in the Sinai. However, the security demands of policing thousands of restive Arabs in the captured territories left Israel with a new internal security problem, tying down troops that were thereby unavailable to guard the distant Suez defense line, which in itself posed logistical and deployment problems in the event of war.

The Egyptians were reequipped massively by the Soviets with modern tanks and field guns. They determined to make life along the canal untenable for the Israeli garrison force and, in September-October 1968, fired intermittent intense artillery barrages from 150 positions along the canal, initially inflicting heavy casualties on the unprepared Israelis. Nasser, anticipating heavy Israeli retaliation, also evacuated civilians from the canal zone. Saboteurs and small raiding parties infiltrated through unguarded sectors, but these were almost always intercepted and this tactic was abandoned. Israeli artillery could not match the Egyptian barrages, and Israel came to rely instead on deep air strikes on industrial sites and arms depots in the Egyptian hinterland as well as spectacular commando forays into ostensibly impenetrable Egyptian military installations.

The air strikes prompted Nasser's Soviet patron to set up an integrated air defense net of antiaircraft guns overlapped by SA-2 ground-to-air missiles. When this system failed to deter the IDF/AF, Soviet pilots began to fly air cover in the Egyptian interior. The United States engineered a cease-fire after several Soviet pilots were shot down in dogfights and the situation threatened to create a superpower showdown. Egypt defied the cease-fire terms by secretly installing an interlocking line of SAM emplacements along the canal's west bank. For their part, the Israelis constructed fortified observation bunkers with a linking command and communications network on their side of the canal. This so-called Bar-Lev line was designed to be a line of observation posts and a delaying tripwire rather than a rigid rampart against an Egyptian attack.

October 1973 Mideast War

Underlying the failure of Israeli intelligence to accurately read the incipient two-front attack of 6 October 1973 was their conviction that the Arabs would not attempt to move forward without absolute air supremacy and their belief that the IDF/AF had developed effective tactics to foil the SAMs in 1970. Nor did the IDF contemplate Arab willingness to settle for a *limited* objective under the protection of a static, tightly integrated, multilayered air defense shield. Nor could the Israelis imagine the precision of the Egyptian attack plan, a well-rehearsed, precisely orchestrated, shallow mass assault. Inconceivable as well, based on the lessons of 1967, was the very idea of Arab initiative and multifront coordination between allies. Egyptian ingenuity and the adaptation of Soviet doctrine and technology combined with a successful deception plan contributed to the successful cross-canal assault. This began with a massive artillery preparation, which covered the opening stages of the assault. Once across, teams of sappers ingeniously cut pathways through the Israeli sand rampart and blew holes for bridging units while 70,000 infantrymen fanned out laterally from the crossing points to set recoilless rifle and antitank missile ambushes. The IDF/AF's scramble to wipe out the widening bridgeheads was foiled by the deadly SAM umbrella underpinned by radar-guided AA batteries and hand-held infrared SAMs. Reserve armor was sent forward as it mobilized—piecemeal—and was badly mauled on D + 2 as it entered the infantry antitank killing grounds.

The Egyptians crossed two corps-sized armies that consolidated shallow bridgeheads along an 80-kilometer (50-mi.) front. On the second day, the bulk of the IDF/AF was redirected to the northern front to try to stem the Syrian advance, also begun on 6 October.

Syria had committed about 75 percent of its total armor (800 tanks) to the attack, which sent four columns westward north of the Sea of Galilee. Preceded by heavy artillery fire, three mechanized infantry divisions (in 2,800 APCs) preceded two armored divisions, ultimately 1,400 tanks, against less than 200 Israeli tanks that redeployed to specially prepared chokepoint ambushes with interlocking fields of fire. By this method, the Israeli armor was able to make the Syrians pay dearly for their initial breakthrough. An assault by heliborne infantry seized the fortified Israeli observation post on the commanding heights of Mount Hermon.

The IDF turned its major attention to this front as posing the most immediate threat to Israeli territory. By the second day, Israeli reserves were arriving in sufficient numbers (an entire division) to put their highly accurate long-range tank gunnery to good use. The IDF/AF at first flew into the missile umbrellas regardless of cost, but soon developed evasive tactics and was able to hit a fresh column of armor along the southernmost axis by coming in at treetop level over Jordanian territory, stopping it after an advance of almost 29 kilometers (18 mi.)—the Syrians' deepest penetration. The Syrians soon outran their lines of communication and then changed their formation to line abreast, whereupon Israeli air chewed them up. In this way, the Israelis bought 36 vital hours. Without a follow-on echelon to extend its incursion, and lacking the improvisational capacity to regroup and explore alternate lines of advance, the Syrians were driven back with hammer blows, making a stubborn fighting withdrawal toward Damascus and Sasa, clear off the Golan Heights to their start line by the 10th. On 11 October, advancing Israeli tanks were able to turn to deal decisively with Iraqi and Jordanian armored attacks on their southwest flank.

On the 14th, the Egyptians responded to desperate Syrian appeals by launching a major assault out of their secure defensive laagers. Backed by unmolested air cover, the Israelis were able to neutralize the infantry antitank teams with artillery fire, while long-range precise tank fire picked off advancing Egyptian T-62s before they could bring their turret guns to bear, disabling over 250 tanks.

The next day, exploiting a seam discovered between the two Egyptian bridgeheads during the early containment probes, the IDF activated a contingency plan to bridge the canal into Egypt proper. Using improvised bridging equipment, the Israelis advanced to the canal through the gap between the two Egyptian army sectors. The Egyptian Second Army, on the northern flank of the crossing, belatedly recognized the threat and mounted a concerted effort to seal the corridor (Battle of the Chinese Farm). This effort was repulsed by Gen. Abraham (Bren) Adan's division, which then crossed the canal into the bridgehead held by General Sharon's division. As Adan passed through to the southwest, Sharon attempted to seize Ismailia but was stopped. Adan's southward push toward Suez City began the Israeli main effort. The Egyptian Third Army—astride the canal—was encircled. By this time international pressure brought about a cease-fire, just as Adan was repulsed from Suez City. Israel had managed to turn near disaster into a muted victory, losing 3,000 men in the effort. The losses were commensurate with the intensity of the fighting but unacceptable by Israeli standards. The grand strategical winner appears to have been Egypt, which secured eventual return of the Sinai and a "cold peace" with Israel.

1982 War in Lebanon

In 1976 civil war flared in Lebanon, partly due to the activities of the Palestine Liberation Organization (PLO), which was able to establish a base for terrorist operations against Israel in southern Lebanon, and partly a result of long-standing hostilities between Lebanese Muslims and Christians. In March 1978, the Israelis made a limited incursion to crush the PLO presence in southern Lebanon. This had led to the establishment of a UN Emergency Force in Lebanon, but this proved to be unable to halt PLO rocket attacks on settlements in northern Galilee. In early 1982, Israel decided that it must eliminate the PLO bases.

The attempted assassination of Israel's ambassador to England by Arab terrorists on 4 June was the starting gun for Israel to initiate the long-planned sequel to the truncated 1978 effort. The problem was that there were actually two war plans. The first, known as Operation Peace for Galilee, had been agreed to by the full Israeli cabinet and known to the Israeli staff and field command. It involved the removal of PLO bases from a security belt running 40 kilometers (25 mi.) north from the Israeli border, designed to place PLO gunners beyond range of Israel. The second, the so-called Big Plan, a secret apparently shared between defense minister Ariel Sharon and the IDF chief of staff, was concealed from the cabinet and IDF commanders. It involved scouring the entire country up to Beirut to eliminate the entire PLO presence in Lebanon and install a Phalangist Christian government in full consonance with Israel's security goals.

Massive air strikes on 5 June on PLO installations throughout Lebanon drew the expected heavy PLO artillery and rocket retaliation along the entire northern frontier. The next day—6 June—the IDF pushed north on three main axes. Believed ultimately to be comprised of seven *ugdahs* (divisional task forces), the easternmost combined three *ugdahs* into a corps-sized task group of 35,000 men and 800 tanks. The westernmost column, proceeding along the coastal plain, was allocated 22,000 men and 220 tanks. The central column, about 20,000 men and 200 tanks, was to link its operations with those of the two main efforts on the flank. Total Israeli manpower mobilized for the operation amounted to 76,000 troops, with 1,250 tanks and 1,500 APCs. The PLO regular fighting forces were organized in brigades of 1,000 to 1,500 men each, totaling about 9,000, with another 12,000 militia in the refugee camps. They had arsenals of heavy weapons, including tanks, APCs, field guns, rocket launchers, and mobile antiaircraft and antitank weapons sufficient to equip two division equivalents, though much of this was either in storage or parceled out haphazardly among the various units.

The Syrians had two tank divisions and other units in Lebanon, totaling about 50,000 men and 600 tanks. In the central Bekaa Valley area, PLO concentrations were shielded by Syrian forward elements.

On the coast, major PLO camps near Tyre were enveloped by a small Israeli amphibious landing and units moving up from Galilee on 6 June. That evening, a larger amphibious force landed at Sidon and began the isolation of trapped PLO formations, sending detachments north to Damour on the coast and inland to push PLO defenders into the mountains, while fresh units coming up the coastal highway bypassed PLO camps that were left to mop-up crews. The latter had to stalk PLO fighters in street fighting in the camps, attempting to avoid hitting civilians interspersed with and often indistinguishable from the PLO militia. The militia generally gave a good account of themselves, though fighters in the uniformed "regular" units often fled after their officers shed their uniforms and melted away.

A central column entered the "pivot" at the bend of the Litani River, heights that commanded roads north and west, a vital crossroads from which the coast could be reinforced through Nabatiye and other units sent north along the key Arsouf-Jezzine axis. A small force took Beaufort Castle, a PLO mountaintop observation post that overlooked northern Galilee. The Syrian outposts in the southern Bekaa Valley were quiet, being under constraint not to engage the Israelis unless directly threatened, the PLO plight notwithstanding. For its part, the IDF sought initially to avoid a fight with the Syrians. On the third day, with the western and central columns advancing toward Beirut and the Beirut-Damascus highway, the Israelis decided to move against the Syrians. The IDF/AF moved decisively to take out seventeen of the nineteen SAM batteries in the northern Bekaa, applying advanced electronic countermeasures devised for the task. Dogfights with Syrian MiG-21s and -23s on that day destroyed 29 of the Soviet-built aircraft with no Israeli losses. Another 60 Syrian planes were shot down over the next few days.

At the same time, the Bekaa Valley Group advanced to engage the Syrian 1st Armored Division, facing T-72s for the first time, defeating it in a major tank battle east of Lake Kairouan. The arrival of Syrian reinforcements slowed the Israeli advance. An Israeli-Syrian cease-fire on 11 June left the Syrians bleeding, the PLO inert, and the Israelis within long artillery range of Damascus and closing on Beirut.

The cease-fire applied only to the Bekaa sector, and IDF units in the west continued the encirclement of Beirut through the Shouf hills on the southeast perimeter in the teeth of tenacious PLO-Syrian resistance. Fierce resistance of the PLO in the Ein Hilweh camp near Sidon was bypassed by Israeli armored columns. Other Israeli forces advanced up through the Beirut airport on the south. After a sharp fight near the southeastern quadrant of Beirut, the Israelis linked with Phalangists and closed the ring around Beirut on 12 June.

In renewed fighting south of the Beirut-Damascus road on 22–26 June, the Israelis succeeded in controlling the highway for ten miles east of Beirut. A second cease-fire, this one on 26 June, ended offensive combat operations. Sharon, however, continued to press for his grand strategic solution through siege operations. While American mediator Phillip Habib negotiated the terms of disengagement in Beirut, the IDF and Phalangists surrounding the city sent artillery shells and bombs into the Muslim western half after dropping leaflets urging all noncombatants to evacuate southward via the Israeli-controlled coastal highway. Periodic barrages, air strikes and utilities stoppages continued for two months amid growing international condemnation of the Israeli siege, unprecedented protest demonstrations in Jerusalem and Tel Aviv, and dissension among the IDF commanders themselves.

The PLO withdrawal and dispersal among several reluctant Arab states was finally arranged at the end of August and was completed by 2 September, when the siege was lifted and an international truce supervisory force entered. The assassination of the newly elected Christian Phalangist president in mid-September prompted the Israelis to cross into Muslim West Beirut on the pretext of protecting Palestinian civilians from the wrath of rioting Christian mobs. The northern front commander was ordered by General Eitan, the chief of staff, to allow Phalangist militia to enter the Sabra and Shatila Palestinian camps in Beirut to root out any PLO combatant remnants. Predictably, the Phalangists indiscriminately slaughtered hundreds of unarmed residents. A chastened and internationally scorned IDF immediately pulled out and was replaced by the international force. A commission of inquiry several months later placed indirect blame for the massacre upon war minister Sharon, Chief of Staff Eitan, and Prime Minister Menachem Begin, all of whom either resigned or were relieved of their positions.

The Israeli army left an occupation force in the area of Southern Lebanon controlled by the allied Christian Southern Lebanese Army. Its presence, as well as the overreach of the 1982 invasion, drew the wrath of Muslim and Druze fighting factions that had at first applauded Israeli actions against their unwelcome PLO neighbors. These former friends began their own resistance struggle against the Israelis and their Phalangist surrogates. The financial and human cost of continued occupation forced the Israelis to withdraw from all save a strip of southern Lebanon within the year, leaving a fractious and evermore hostile neighbor to their north and the Syrians in firmer control than before. Though operationally impressive, the deceit that the defense minister and chief of staff exercised toward both the cabinet and their field commanders obscures the "lessons." On balance, the 1982 war marks a low point for vaunted Israeli purity of arms.

JAMES J. BLOOM

SEE ALSO: Arab League; Egypt; History, Modern Military; Iraq; Israel; Jordan; Lebanon; Middle East; Syria.

Bibliography

Adan, A. 1980. *On the banks of the Suez.* Novato, Calif.: Presidio Press.

Barker, A. J. 1980. *Arab-Israeli wars.* New York: Hippocrene Books.

Bloom, J. J. 1982. From the Litani to Beirut: A brief strategic assessment of Israel's operations in Lebanon, 1978–1982. *Middle East Insight*, November/December.

———. 1983. Six days plus ten weeks war. *Middle East Insight*, January/February.

Cordesman, A. H., and A. R. Wagner. 1990. *The lessons of modern war.* Volume I: *The Arab-Israeli conflicts, 1973–1989.* Boulder, Colo.: Westview Press.

Dayan, M. 1966. *Diary of the Sinai campaign.* New York: Harper and Row.

Dupuy, T. N. 1984. *Elusive victory: The Arab-Israeli wars, 1947–1974.* Fairfax, Va.: HERO Books.

Dupuy, T. N., and P. Martell. 1985. *Flawed victory: The Arab-Israeli conflict and the 1982 war in Lebanon.* Vienna, Va.: HERO Books.

Eshel, D. 1989. *Chariots of the desert: The story of the Israeli armored corps.* London: Brassey's.

Gawrych, G. 1990. *Key to the Sinai: The battles for Abu Ageila in the 1956 and 1967 Arab–Israeli wars.* Fort Leavenworth, Kans.: U.S. Army Command and General Staff College.

Herzog, C. 1984. *The Arab-Israeli wars.* Rev. ed. New York: Vintage Books.

Lorch, N. 1961. *The edge of the sword: Israel's war for independence.* New York: Putnam.

———. 1976. *One long war.* Jerusalem: Keter.

Marshall, S. L. A. 1958. *Sinai victory.* New York: William Morrow.

Safran, N. 1969. *From war to war.* New York: Pegasus.

———. 1981. *Israel: The embattled ally.* Cambridge: Harvard Univ. Press.

Schiff, Z. 1985. *A history of the Israeli army: 1874 to the present.* New York: Macmillan.

Young, P. 1968. *The Israeli campaign 1967.* London: Kimber.

ARAB LEAGUE

Officially the League of Arab States, the Arab League is an association of Arabic-speaking nations created to foster common goals and to provide a united front for the community of Arabic nations.

Origins

The Arab League was formed in 1945, inspired by the awakening of pan-Arab nationalism from the middle of the nineteenth century. Arab desires for a national state after World War I had foundered both on Arab factionalism and on British and French colonial designs in the Middle East; only after World War II were most Arab-speaking lands at last independent. At a meeting in Alexandria, Egypt, in the summer of 1944, seven Arabic nations signed the "Alexandria Protocol," which outlined the character of the Arab League. The League, comprising Egypt, Iraq, Jordan, Lebanon, Saudi Arabia, Syria, and Yemen, was neither a union nor a federation, only an alliance of sovereign states.

History

The League's first major undertaking was its intervention in Palestine at the end of the British mandate, in an effort to prevent partition and the creation of the state of Israel.

Egypt, Iraq, Jordan, Lebanon, and Syria invaded Palestine after the British departed, but the Arab armies were poorly coordinated and often worked at cross-purposes. The infant Jewish state of Israel therefore survived and prevailed, and the Arab failure left the League with the problem of Palestinian refugees and their desire for a state of their own.

The League survived this crisis, and during the 1950s several conferences resulted in a collective security treaty (17 June 1950) and a system of economic ties (1957); an Arab oil office was also set up in 1957. Differences in political goals, to say nothing of the different characters of the member states, prevented these measures from producing significant tangible results. A major meeting in Baghdad (January–February 1961) was for the first time attended by all members (twelve at the time) and saw the start of several economic initiatives. In June 1961, however, the League faced another serious crisis over Iraq's desire to annex Kuwait; this was forestalled only by Kuwait's admission to the League and the installation of a League peacekeeping force.

During the 1960s, the League's members took steps to foster their collective economic development. The cornerstone of this effort was the creation of the Arab Common Market, which began operation on 1 January 1965. Although open to all League states, it has so far been joined only by Iraq, Jordan, Syria, and Egypt. It provides for the gradual abolition of import duties on agricultural goods and natural resources and for the gradual elimination of all import duties among the signatories. There are also provisions for joint development, capital and labor movement among members, and the imposition of common external tariffs. The original ten-year timetable has not been met, and many provisions are in limbo, but the machinery and framework remain intact.

The Arab League was involved in several later efforts against Israel, ranging from military alliances to economic measures and efforts to isolate Israel diplomatically. Many League members sent troops to aid Syria and Egypt during the October 1973 war; similar efforts at assistance had not been effective during the Six-Day War in 1967 because the conflict was so brief.

The next major activities of the League were in connection with Lebanese civil war. On 10 June 1976 the League set up a peacekeeping force in Lebanon to restore internal order. This move was followed by a grant of full League membership to the Palestine Liberation Organization (PLO) on 6 September, and with the creation of the Arab League Deterrent Force for Lebanon on 17 October. As with the earlier peacekeeping force, the Deterrent Force was dominated by the Syrians, although there was limited participation by North Yemen, Saudi Arabia, Sudan, and the UAE. Those non-Syrian forces subsequently withdrew their contingents in June 1979, and the League decided not to renew the Deterrent Force mandate on 17 July 1982.

In the meantime Egypt's peace treaty with Israel, signed on 26 March 1979 and brought about in part through U.S. diplomatic initiatives, had provoked a storm of protest in the Arab world. The League imposed sanctions on Egypt on 31 March, culminating in Egyptian expulsion from the League. The headquarters of the League was moved from Cairo to Tunis, but returned to Cairo after Egypt's readmission in 1989. The League has since played a significant role in mobilizing Arab support for Iraq in its war with Iran (1980–88), helping to provide loans and economic assistance as well as military aid.

Current Membership

There are currently 21 members of the Arab League: Algeria, Bahrain, Djibouti, Egypt, Iraq, Jordan, Kuwait, Lebanon, Libya, Mauritania, Morocco, Oman, Palestine Liberation Organization, Qatar, Saudi Arabia, Somalia, Sudan, Syria, Tunisia, United Arab Emirates, and Yemen.

Organization and Purposes

The League of Arab States is organized with a Council, a Permanent Secretariat, and a number of Special Committees. Each member state of the League has one vote on the Council, which may meet in the capital of any member state. One of the Council's principal roles is the mediation of disputes between two League members, or between a League state and any nonmember state. The Council also has a Political Committee, composed of the foreign ministers of each member state.

The Permanent Secretariat is run by the secretary-general, but the seat of the secretary-general is currently (1991) vacant. The secretary-general and his senior associates have full diplomatic status; further, the secretary-general is a permanent observer at the United Nations. Besides its special committees, the League also contains 22 special agencies, which deal with a variety of cultural and economic issues.

For the most recent information on this organization the reader may refer to the following annual publications:

The Military Balance. International Institute for Strategic Studies. London: Brassey's (UK).

The Statesman's Year-Book. New York: St. Martin's Press.

The World Factbook. Central Intelligence Agency. Washington, D.C.: Brassey's (US).

DAVID L. BONGARD

SEE ALSO: Arab Conquests; Arab-Israeli Wars; Colonial Empires, European; Ottoman Empire; Peacekeeping; United Nations.

Bibliography

Gomaa, A. M. 1977. *The foundation of the League of Arab States: Wartime diplomacy and inter-Arab politics, 1941 to 1945*. London: Longman.

Hunter, B., ed. 1991. *The statesman's year-book 1991–92.* New York: St. Martin's Press.

ARCHIVES, MILITARY

Archives, from the Greek word *archeion* (office building), is defined by the *Oxford English Dictionary* as "a place in which public records or historic documents are kept; a historical record or document so preserved." To be considered archives, the materials present must have been created or accumulated for a purpose, whether governmental or private in nature. The materials also must have been preserved for reasons other than those for which they were originally created. This latter point is best understood with regard to government documents. The files of documents created or acquired by a government department in the course of its conduct of official business are considered working records as long as they remain in current use by that department. Once they have been turned over to an archival repository or have been designated for one, however, they become archival records or archives.

Military archives, then, are organized bodies of records pertaining to military subjects, including matters such as the establishment and maintenance of armies, navies, and air forces; the role of armed services within societies in time of peace or war; and the conduct of warfare. Military archives consist not only of papers but also of books, reports, maps, sound recordings, and other documentary records—in short, of the wide variety of material that is most often present in the various individual collections of records that have been brought together for purposes of preservation and research.

Military archives are to be found in almost every country today. Public access to such archives, however, most of which remain under control of the central governments in each country, varies widely. Similarly, many countries that allow private individuals to conduct research in their military archives have records closure rules that preclude looking at documents written less than 30 or 50 years ago. Even when blocks of military records have been opened to the general public, security restrictions on some remaining portions of the records exempt them from being examined by researchers who do not have special clearance to see them.

Following are descriptions of particular military archives in selected countries. The archives discussed represent only a few of those present in these countries.

Federal Republic of Germany

The principal military archive in Germany is the *Bundesarchiv-Militaerarchiv* located in Freiburg im Breisgau. Originally created in 1954 as a division of the *Bundesarchiv* in Koblenz, the military archive was moved to Freiburg in 1967. The *Bundesarchiv-Militaerarchiv* houses the military record collections that were originally captured by the Western Allies during and after World War II and that were returned to the Federal Republic beginning in 1959. Additional material there has been collected in Germany.

The archival material is classified according to several headings: PH (Prussian army to 1919), RH (German army 1920–45), RM (German navy 1871–1945), RL (German air force), and RS (Waffen-SS). The actual amount of material available for studying any particular aspect of the pre-1946 German military varies significantly because large portions of Germany's military records were destroyed in the course of World War II, either by enemy bombs or intentional German destruction.

Of the five categories of material mentioned, the collection relating to the Prussian army shows the greatest evidence of the war's damage. In April 1945, bombing destroyed almost all of the *Heeresarchiv* in Potsdam. The records that remain on the origins and development of Germany's army prior to 1919 are insubstantial. Luckily, however, the personal papers of several of Germany's most important generals, including Scharnhorst, Gneisenau, and Moltke the Elder, were saved from the flames. The material at Freiburg on the German army from 1920 to 1945 shows a similar, although not so dire, fate. Of particular concern to a historian of the early wartime period is the absence of records of the German army's campaigns in Poland, France, and Norway, records that were destroyed by a fire in 1942.

Historians interested in the German navy are in a far better situation, thanks to a series of fortunate circumstances at the close of the war. The German Naval Archive (now at Freiburg) had been transferred to Schloss Tambach in Bavaria in 1944 to escape the bombings of Berlin, although it had been slated for destruction by the German staff overseeing it prior to its capture by the Western Allies. Only the unexpected absence of the admiral in charge of the archive, a shortage of fuel for burning the records, and the fast-moving advance of the American army in the final days of the war kept the German navy's records from oblivion.

The collection of material relating to the German Air Force (Luftwaffe) is very small. Although some air force files were moved to Karlsbad in Czechoslovakia late in the war, they suffered almost complete destruction at German hands, and the vast bulk of Luftwaffe material that remained in Berlin was intentionally destroyed before the Russians captured the city. Of the papers remaining, those of Field Marshal Erhard Milch, which he had originally donated to the British Imperial War Museum, are among the most important. Similarly, the collection of material on the Waffen-SS is very limited. The records that do exist, however, include documents on the armored divisions, the mountain units, and the SS units staffed by foreign personnel.

Large portions of the German records were microfilmed by Great Britain and the United States prior to their return to West Germany. These microfilms are available to researchers in the United States at the National Archives. However, some 400 personal papers collections available at Freiburg—including the papers of officers such as Schlieffen, Mackensen, Moltke the Elder, Seeckt, Keitel, Model, Beck, Hipper, Tirpitz, and Pohl—have not been copied and must be consulted at the *Bundesarchiv-Militaerarchiv.*

France

The primary repository for French military records is the vast complex of the Château de Vincennes, located on the eastern extremity of Paris. Housed in the Pavilion of the King, records relating to the French army are administered by the Army Historical Service (*Service historique de l'Armée*). The records of the revolutionary and Napoleonic periods have long been used at Vincennes by scholars, but documentary collections for the later nineteenth (post-1870) and the early twentieth centuries have been available to researchers only since the late 1960s because of the French archival practice of making documents available (with some exceptions) only after 50 years.

Of the twentieth-century collections now available, that dealing with World War I (the N series) is by far the most rewarding. It is a mass of documents in more than 20,000 cartons. The papers of the General Staff of the Army (*Etat-major de l'Armée*) are especially valuable for materials dealing with the high command's view of the war. Documents of interest for people researching French perceptions of the administration and performance of the American Expeditionary Force in France can be found in some profusion in subscrics ss13N (Franco-American military affairs) and ss17N (French military missions).

The major portion of the archives of the French navy has also been housed at the Chateau de Vincennes since 1974. Administered by the Naval Historical Service (*Service historique de la Marine*), the naval archives are housed in the Pavilion of the Queen, located across from the building in which the army archives are kept. Archival material relating to particular maritime regions, both contemporary and older records, is kept at the French ports of Cherbourg, Brest, Lorient, Rochefort, and Toulon. During the Second World War, however, significant portions of the older material at Brest, Lorient, and Cherbourg were destroyed in the fighting.

In all, the archives consist of approximately 40,000 linear meters (43,747 yd.) of material, including documents useful for studying French political, diplomatic, and administrative history, in addition to purely naval subjects. Toulon, for example, holds material relating to French interests in the Levant, and Rochefort has the documents concerned with emigration to the New World. The archival material available in Paris represents some 14,000 linear meters (15,311 yd.) of documents; most are at Vincennes, but 4,000 meters (4,375 yd.) of the oldest (primarily prerevolutionary) material is deposited at the French National Archives. The collections in Paris are composed primarily of documents dealing with the central administration of the navy (naval headquarters, personnel, naval weapons, and the like) and with the navy's participation in France's wars.

Italy

For researchers interested in twentieth-century Italian military history, Rome is the location of the most important archives. Navy and Air Force ministry files can be consulted at the *Archivio Centrale dello Stato.* The material on prewar military preparations is particularly rewarding. Unfortunately, the *Archivio Centrale* has no similar army collection. This lack must be made up as best one can by reference to personal papers, such as the Graziani collection.

Also in Rome are the service historical offices, each with significant amounts of archival material. However, the reception given to researchers is dependent upon suitable recommendations and the other demands that are being made upon the staff's time during one's visit. The Army Historical Office's archives (*Archivio dell'Ufficio Storico dell'Esercito*) has manuscript material dating to the 1860–70 period, as well as outstanding collections of photographs. The navy archives (*Archivio dell'Ufficio Storico della Marina Militare*), which allow researchers to see material only on a case-by-case and file-by-file basis, and the air force archives (*Archivio dell'Ufficio Storico dell' Aviazione*) are also worth visiting. The navy archives, for example, hold a vast amount of material dealing with Italy's naval participation in the First World War.

For those looking for archival material dealing with earlier periods of Italy's military history, the provincial state archives are the appropriate places to visit. Material on the Crimean War and on the Sardinia-Piedmont disputes during risorgimento are in the State Archives (*Archivio di Stato*) of Turin. Similarly, documents on the Napoleonic Kingdom of Italy can be found in the State Archives at Milan, and military records relating to the Kingdom of the Two Sicilies can be found in the Bourbon collection of the State Archives in Naples.

Great Britain

The most important repository of military documents in Great Britain is the Public Record Office, Kew (London). Indeed, its holdings are so vast that utilizing its documentary resources to attempt to research many twentieth-century topics can seem an overwhelming task.

The records at the Public Record Office are divided into series, with the most important for military historians being the Cabinet Office (CAB) Series, the Admiralty (ADM) Series, the Air Ministry (AIR) Series, the War Office (WO) Series, the Ministry of Defense (DEFE) Series, and the Prime Minister's Office (PREM) Series. Within each series are many numbered subseries.

In the Cabinet Office Series, some of the more important subseries include

CAB 2—Committee of Imperial Defense: Meetings;
CAB 4—Committee of Imperial Defense: Memoranda;
CAB 23—Cabinet Minutes to September 1939;
CAB 53—Committee of Imperial Defense: Chiefs of Staff Committee to September 1939, Meetings and Memoranda;
CAB 54—Committee of Imperial Defense: Deputy Chiefs of Staff Sub-Committee to September 1939, Meetings and Memoranda;
CAB 65—War Cabinet: Minutes;
CAB 79—War Cabinet: Chiefs of Staff Committee Meetings;
CAB 80—Chiefs of Staff Committee Memoranda;
CAB 82—War Cabinet: Deputy Chiefs of Staff Committee, Meetings and Memoranda;
CAB 84—War Cabinet: Joint Planning Committee, Meetings and Memoranda;
CAB 86—War Cabinet: Committee on Anti-U-Boat Warfare, Meetings and Memoranda;
CAB 106—Historical Section: Files;
CAB 122—British Joint Staff Mission Washington File

These files provide detailed accounts of the day-to-day thinking and activities in the Cabinet and its subordinate committees and subcommittees.

Important admiralty files for the researcher are

ADM 1—Admiralty and Secretariat Papers, which contain the registered files of the admiralty that were selected for preservation;
ADM 116—Admiralty and Secretariat Cases (files that were detached from the registered files and put into cases because of their size);
ADM 137—Admiralty Historical Section, 1914–1918 War Histories, which includes various operational papers that passed into the hands of the Historical Section;
ADM 199—War History Cases and Papers;
ADM 205—First Sea Lord's Papers;
ADM 223—Naval Intelligence Papers (including Admiralty Ultra Signals)

Similarly, valuable War Office record series include (for the Second World War period)

WO 106—Directorate of Military Operations and Intelligence;
WO 169—War of 1939–1945: War Diaries, Middle East Forces;
WO 171—War of 1939–1945: War Diaries, North-west Europe;
WO 175—War of 1939–1945: War Diaries, British North Africa Forces;
WO 205—War of 1939–1945: Military HQ Papers, 21st Army Group;
WO 208—Directorate of Intelligence;
WO 219—War Diaries: SHAEF

War Office documents on the First World War are also voluminous, although some materials are missing because of intentional destruction of certain war records.

Valuable Air Ministry files are to be found in

AIR 2—Registered Correspondence Files;
AIR 5—Air Historical Branch Records, Series II;
AIR 8—Chief of Air Staff's Papers;
AIR 9—Director of Plans Papers;
AIR 23—Overseas Commands;
AIR 40—Directorate of Intelligence and Other Intelligence Papers;
AIR 41—RAF Monographs and Narratives.

For the Second World War period, the Ministry of Defence Series that is of utmost importance is DEFE 3, which covers intelligence from enemy radio communications. Finally, the Prime Minister's Office (PREM) Series, which has been used so effectively for the wartime period by Winston Churchill's biographer, Martin Gilbert, is important but is incomplete for certain periods, including the late 1930s.

Personal papers collections in Great Britain are more difficult to consult because many are scattered throughout the country, and significant numbers of them remain in private hands. However, repositories with important personal papers collections include the British Library, formerly the British Museum (the Balfour and Jellicoe papers); the Imperial War Museum (the Montgomery and De Guingand papers); the Liddell Hart Centre for Military Archives, King's College, London (the Liddell Hart, Chester Wilmot, and Alanbrooke papers); and Churchill College, Cambridge University (the Hankey and Keyes papers).

United States

The United States boasts an impressive number of military archives, the most important of which are administered by the federal government. The National Archives in Washington, D.C., the largest, has among its numerous federal records collections many directly related to military subjects. Army collections of greatest interest include

RG (Record Group) 107—Records of the Office of the Secretary of War;
RG 335—Records of the Secretary of the Army;
RG 165—Records of the War Department General and Special Staffs;
RG 319—Records of the Army Staff.

Record Group 165 is particularly useful for students of twentieth-century U.S. military history because it includes the records of the chiefs of staff from 1903 to 1947 and the records of the War Plans Division from 1917 to 1942. Also of particular importance for the World War Two period are the records of the Office of the Assistant

Chief of Staff, G-2, Intelligence, and the Office of the Assistant Chief of Staff, G-3, Operations, both found in RG 319.

Navy material at the National Archives of particular interest comprises the following record groups:

RG 80—General Records of the Department of the Navy, which includes the office files of Navy Secretaries Frank Knox and James Forrestal;

RG 45—Naval Records Collection of the Office of Naval Records and Library;

RG 38—Records of the Office of the Chief of Naval Operations, most of the material pre-1946;

RG 127—Records of the United States Marine Corps.

Air force collections of great value at the National Archives include

RG 18—Records of the Army Air Forces (material dating from 1914 to 1952);

RG 340—Records of the Office of the Secretary of the Air Force;

RG 341—Records of Headquarters United States Air Force, which encompass a number of documentary groupings such as the Records of the Office of the Deputy Chief of Staff, Operations;

RG 342—Records of the United States Air Force Commands, Activities, and Organizations.

Additional record groups at the National Archives that are of particular value are RG 218, Records of the United States Joint Chiefs of Staff, and RG 330, Records of the Office of the Secretary of Defense. Record Group 218 is especially useful for those researchers interested in the Western Allies' military strategy and strategic planning in World War II or U.S. military planning in the early postwar period.

Three other important military archives in the Washington, D.C., area are the navy's Operational Archives, located at the Washington Navy Yard, which houses U.S. Navy strategic planning, operations, and Office of the Chief of Naval Operations documents, primarily from 1941 to the present; the Office of Air Force History, located at Bolling Air Force Base, which holds microfilm copies of much of the massive compilation of archival material that is housed at the Air Force Historical Research Center at Maxwell Air Force Base, Alabama; and the Manuscript Division of the Library of Congress, whose collection houses the personal papers of numerous senior U.S. military officers, including Sims, Benson, Pershing, Harbord, Leahy, King, Halsey, Arnold, Spaatz, Eaker, and LeMay. Many of the Manuscript Division's collections of naval papers are there on deposit from the Naval Historical Foundation.

A final U.S. military archive that should be mentioned is the United States Army Military History Institute, Carlisle Barracks, Pennsylvania. This repository, founded about 1970, now holds an important collection of personal papers, including those of Generals Bradley, Ridgway, Gay, and Bull. In addition, it holds significant material relating to subjects such as the Philippine Insurrection and the Boxer Rebellion.

JEFFREY G. BARLOW

SEE ALSO: History, Military.

Bibliography

Burdick, C. 1972. The Tambach archive: A research note. *Military Affairs* 36:124–26.

Chatelle, R. A. D. M. 1986. Historical service of the French navy. *Military Affairs* 50:143.

Guide to the National Archives of the United States. 1974. Washington, D.C.: National Archives and Records Service.

Herwig, H. H. 1972. An introduction to military archives in West Germany. *Military Affairs* 36:121–24.

Higham, R., ed. 1977. *A guide to the sources of British military history.* Berkeley: Univ. of California Press.

Hodson, J. H. 1972. *The administration of archives.* Oxford: Pergamon.

Kennett, L. 1973. World War I materials in the French military archives. *Military Affairs* 37:60–61.

Koenig, D. 1971. Archival research in Italy. *Military Affairs* 35:11–12.

Nelson, A. K. 1978. Government historical offices and public records. *The American Archivist* 41:405–12.

Schellenberg, T. R. 1956. *Modern archives: Principles and techniques.* Chicago: Univ. of Chicago Press.

Wolfe, R., ed. 1974. *Captured German and related records: A national archives conference.* Athens, Ohio: Ohio Univ. Press.

ARCTIC WARFARE

The arctic and antarctic regions make up roughly one-twentieth of the surface of the globe and consist primarily of ice-covered barren rock (Antarctica) or water dominated by ice floes (Arctic Ocean). The Arctic Circle, at 66°30′N, and the Antarctic Circle, an equivalent distance south of the equator, delineate the so-called frigid zones of the planet. The harsh climate of these regions, including the subarctic and subantarctic areas, has proscribed warfare there, and armed forces that have been assigned there have found that weather and terrain pose a far greater challenge than enemies. However, these regions—especially the arctic region during the Cold War—have played a strategic role in past confrontations, conflicts, and wars and are likely to retain some significance in the future. Because of this, arctic warfare has been a much-studied and -practiced subject, particularly by the militaries of the former Soviet Union, the United States, and Scandinavian countries.

History

The arctic has been the scene of ground and sea combat several times in the twentieth century; Antarctica, by contrast, has been the subject of international disputes, but not war.

The Bolshevik assumption of power in Leningrad in November 1917 presaged the withdrawal of Russia from World War I and signaled the beginning of the Russian Civil War. After the defeat of Germany a year later, the Western Allies sought to assert their power in Eastern Europe; in the Russian north, multinational forces pushed south from the ports of Murmansk and Archangel. Leon Trotsky's newly formed Red Army eventually threw back the Western and White Russian forces, dispersing them by the spring of 1920. Despite this southward movement, arctic warfare characterized the northernmost campaigns of the war; harsh lessons would be remembered by some, forgotten by others.

Bitter winter fighting describes the short Russo-Finnish War (30 November 1939–1 March 1940). The Finns, well prepared and equipped for arctic warfare, initially surprised superior Soviet forces, achieving a series of tactical and operational victories. However, Soviet forces, improved in training, preparations, and equipment, eventually prevailed; Finnish territory along the Arctic Circle and farther south along the Gulf of Finland were ceded to the Soviet Union.

Part of the German invasion of Russia (Operation Barbarossa, 22 June 1941) was an offensive in the north to seize Murmansk. After initial gains, German forces bogged down in the arctic tundra, and failed to reach Murmansk. But the success of the German invasion elsewhere led to a massive commitment of aid to Russia from Britain and the United States. The Battle of the Atlantic extended to arctic waters as convoys of supply transports struggled against German U-boats to deliver equipment and stores to northern Soviet ports.

Also during World War II, the subarctic region of the Aleutian Islands saw warfare under arctic conditions between Japanese and American air, land, and sea forces. Arctic weather predominated along the Aleutian Chain, and proved the greater foe for both sides. The bloody, costly Battle of Attu, which eliminated Japanese presence on American soil, featured the rugged, inhospitable conditions of arctic warfare.

By contrast, the antarctic region has not specifically been visited by war (though an argument may be made for subantarctic warfare as a feature of the Falklands/Malvinas War between Britain and Argentina in 1982). However, Antarctica is the subject of international disputes regarding claims to its territory. The Antarctic Treaty, which went into force in 1961, provided a 30-year period of peaceful use and suspension of claims.

While Antarctica may have played an important role in control of sea lanes around Cape Horn in Africa and around the southern tip of the South American continent, the emerging geopolitical realities of the 1990s portend a much more dominant strategic role for the arctic region.

Economic Aspects

The arctic is an area of immense natural resources. In addition to rich fishing grounds, it contains as much as 50 percent of the world's known oil reserves, as well as abundant natural gas, coal, and strategic minerals. The costs of exploitation are high, however, and must consider the expense of environmental protection along with those of extraction, processing, and transportation to southern markets. According to Canadian arctic specialist Nils Ørvik (1983), the core of the northern debate is not whether natural resources will be developed, but when and by whom.

The same probably applies to Antarctica, though very little is known about the region's resources. It is believed that the continent once existed in close juxtaposition with Australia, South Africa, South America, and India, forming the supercontinent known as Gondwanaland. Since the latter areas are well endowed with minerals, it is assumed that Antarctica must be as well.

Strategic Considerations

Modern technology has changed the arctic's geostrategic role dramatically. Whereas the Japanese in World War II sought strategic control of the northern flank of the Pacific Theater by establishing bases in Alaska, today, the shortest air routes between vital strategic areas of the United States and the Commonwealth of Independent States cut across the arctic. Distant early warning systems of both militaries encircle this region. Further, modern nuclear ballistic missile submarines—and their hunters—have a vast area of operation in arctic oceans, especially under the cover and concealment of the polar ice cap. Those on station in the region play an important role in the strategic nuclear balance.

Over most of the arctic, ground operations in relation to sea and air operations will play a subordinate role due to the extreme hostility of the environment and the limited strategic objectives (with the exception of Norway and Iceland). While many installations would probably be the targets of cruise missiles or long-range bombers, operations involving special and orthodox forces can not be ignored.

Arctic Environments

Arctic warfare is strongly influenced by the environment—terrain, climate, and especially weather, which may have severe effects on personnel, equipment, and operations. Though ice and snow are features typically associated with the northern and southern frigid zones—2 percent of Antarctica is exposed barren rock, the rest is covered by ice to a mean depth of between 2 and 4 kilometers (between 1.25 and 2.5 mi.)—the arctic region comprises substantial land areas that support nomadic herding, have a variety of terrain, and demonstrate a surprising range of temperatures. Temperatures in the arctic interior of Alaska, for example, can reach over 38°C in July, compared with wintertime lows of −62°C or colder.

Another aspect common to arctic and antarctic climates is a lack of precipitation, which averages less than 10 inches annually. In this respect, these regions fit the criteria of deserts; Antarctica, the second smallest of the continents, is also the largest desert. Precipitation in Antarctica almost always falls in the form of snow, while in the arctic the warmer part of the year will bring some rain.

Terrain

The polar ice cap dominates the arctic environment; doubling in size during winter, it revolves clockwise about the North Pole, completing a revolution every two to four years. The thickness of the ice varies from 1 to 20 meters (about 3 to 65 ft.), and its surface is covered with jagged ice ridges and fissures. Elsewhere, the arctic littoral features a variety of terrains: mountains with barren peaks, glaciers, coniferous forests, rolling hills, extensive bogs ("muskeg"), and tundra.

Established transportation networks are either sparse or nonexistent in arctic regions; frozen or navigable waterways and aircraft provide alternatives. While extremely rare, heavy snows to depths of several feet are sufficient to prevent movement of heavy mechanized vehicles. Lightweight, specially designed vehicles and alternative modes of transportation such as dog sleds must be considered in winter operations.

Climate and Weather

For military operations in the arctic, the use of terrain must always be considered in the context of annual climatic changes and weather variations. Climatic change has a pronounced effect on arctic terrain, particularly tundra and watercourses, and can be decisive to military operational outcomes. Perhaps the most fragile of ecosystems, tundra is a thin layer of low vegetation beneath which is a substrate of frozen earth—permafrost—which can extend to a depth of a mile. In winter, the tundra offers no obstacle to cross-country movement. In the warmer months, however, permafrost recedes somewhat, leaving a water-saturated subsurface. During this time, movement across tundra is all but impossible for vehicles without extremely low specific pressures.

Rivers and lakes that aid ground movement when frozen become obstacles with spring thaws; ice jams and rapid melting cause extensive flooding. In the summer and fall months, however, many arctic waterways support movement by boat and raft.

Weather varies seasonally; its primary feature is that of extremes in temperature, but high winds and storms, thermal inversions, ice fog, and bright sun reflecting from snow and ice can all impair military operations. Operations over water can be particularly hazardous. A downed aviator's survival in icy, below-freezing winter seas is measured in hours, or less if proper precautions are not taken. In the Aleutians during World War II, storms and fog caused more aircraft to crash at sea or into rugged mountains than opposing air forces or air defenses.

Even in summer, weather and terrain can severely affect military operations. American amphibious landings on Attu on 11 May 1943 were characterized by dense fog (visibility was little more than the length of a landing craft), rocky shoals, unmelted snow that extended to the water's edge in places, and a thick bog just inland from the beaches that mired vehicles and artillery pieces. So challenging was the terrain that for every infantry battalion initially committed to battle, another was dedicated to carrying supplies to forward positions—resupply vehicles simply could not function.

Visibility

In addition to the problems of thick fog and windblown snow and grit, visibility in the arctic is also affected by glare—bright sunlight reflecting from nearly pure-white snow in the winter months. Snow blindness is a common occurrence for unprepared soldiers, and special goggles are worn to prevent damage to eyes.

Daylight conditions also affect visibility. At the winter solstice, latitudes north of the arctic circle will have one or more days where the sun does not rise above the horizon; midday features conditions of twilight, and the remaining twenty or more hours will be in darkness. Visibility in the winter nights is improved somewhat by the ambient light from stars and the moon, especially when it is reflected by snow. At other times in winter, long shadows are cast at sunrise and sunset from relatively small folds in the terrain, making distance and object determinations difficult. Arctic summers have the opposite daylight conditions, and 24-hour days are witnessed.

Intense Cold

Extended periods of extreme low temperatures can slow arctic military activity dramatically. This is especially true of inland areas, where temperature inversions can trap cold air in localized pockets for days and weeks. Metal becomes brittle and is easily fractured under nominal stress; the same is true of rubber tires, which have been known to shatter at the kick of a soldier's boot. Special care must be taken to warm lubricating oils, as they tend to become viscous or solid at low temperatures.

Cold weather also poses risks to personnel; for example, exposed or poorly protected skin can quickly become frostbitten, and extended exposure when inadequately protected can mean the loss of extremities. Care must be taken to avoid touching bare metal to skin, and heavy work can cause perspiration that can later freeze, or inhalation of cold air that can damage lungs.

Habitation

Human populations in the arctic are sparse. Indigenous peoples depend upon cooperative efforts for survival, and isolated individual dwellings are rare. Small villages and clusters of installations, widely separated, are the rule, and are more hospitably located in coastal areas or along rivers.

Nomadic herding is a feature of the arctic, as are fishing, hunting, and trapping. Increasing commercial interest and exploitation of natural resources have brought a corresponding increase in trade and commerce to native peoples.

The northern frigid zone provides natural habitat to reindeer, caribou, and musk-ox, and also to polar bears, seals, and walrus. Different species of whales and salmon provide rich sea and river harvests. In the summer months, swarms of biting insects—mosquitoes, gnats, and flies—can make life miserable for the unwary visitor, and challenge the resourcefulness of local inhabitants. Small rodents provide sustenance for different birds of prey. Vegetation varies from the meager lichen and moss of rocky plateaus and tundra to rare stands of coniferous timber.

Fighting in the Arctic

The harshness and variability of arctic conditions affect friend and foe alike. Successful operations will be conducted by those leaders who have best prepared and conditioned their force, and who are both patient and resourceful.

Personnel

For arctic fighting, physical conditioning of troops must be of the highest order, but more important is the mental toughness necessary simply to survive the elements, let alone deal with a determined enemy. The psychological effects of extended adverse weather and cold conditions, and of isolation, have been shown to take a severe toll on a soldier's morale and physical ability. These effects are compounded by periods of winter darkness.

Protection from winter cold is essential, and frequent warming in addition to insulated clothing is an important consideration. In the summertime, protection against insects is necessary. Since arctic environments can vary greatly, careful leaders will ensure that adequate study and preparations involve all soldiers at all levels.

Equipment

The arctic environment poses a challenge to all military equipment, from personal gear and clothing to weapons and mobility platforms. The effects of wind, fog, cold, temperature variations, terrain, light and dark, static electricity, vast distances, and snow must be considered.

The development of new, lightweight synthetic cloth has helped considerably in reducing the loads soldiers must carry along with the bulk of clothing they wear. Previously, warmth in cold weather equated to the number of layers of clothing. This is no longer true, and a few layers of the proper material can keep a person warm, or at least from freezing, at low temperature extremes. Other items of personal equipment include chemical hand- and foot-warmers, means of heating packaged rations and water, and goggles for protection against arctic glare.

The weapons soldiers carry need constant attention and inspection. Expansion and contraction of metal-on-metal parts require extra application of special lubricants, and the knowledge that the ballistic trajectory of rounds fired will change as a weapon warms with repeated use.

Weapons' effects also vary in the arctic; artillery rounds, for example, have less effect in snow and bogs than on firm countryside. Ranging and sighting can be problematic without the benefit of range-finding instruments and accurate position-location systems. Extended arctic winter nights make night vision devices critical.

Light, tracked vehicles, because of their low specific pressure, are generally better suited to cross-country arctic environments than wheeled vehicles. The construction of ice roads can support heavier track and wheel traffic in winter, as can log (corduroy) roads in summer, especially across bogs. Where road nets do not exist, or road construction material is unavailable, air transport, particularly helicopters, provides a viable alternative.

Vehicle refueling operations, especially for aircraft, must allow for the presence of static electricity. Vehicle operation also depends on maintaining a variety of lubricants, particularly lightweight oils for cold weather, and antifreeze/coolant for radiator-based engines. Proper engine warming before starting is necessary, and de-icing procedures for aircraft are essential in winter. Moreover, the weight of any vehicle parked on ice or hard-frozen ground will tend to melt the ice beneath its wheels or treads. When the melted ice refreezes, the vehicle can become stuck, and often is difficult to extricate.

Arctic environments are hard on all vehicles, and preventive maintenance concerns should be heightened. The fact that operations under such harsh conditions are maintenance- and logistics-intensive should signal to commanders and staffs the need for close attention to all pertinent details.

Military Operations

The unforgiving nature of the arctic requires that the military force consider carefully the doctrinal concepts of command and control, intelligence, maneuver, fire support, mobility/countermobility, air defense, survivability, and combat service support. Of these, combat service support requires the most effort in personnel and materiel, and most of this effort will be directed toward survival in an inhospitable countryside. Ensuring friendly mobility is perhaps of next importance, for without the ability to move in the arctic, adequate maneuver, fire support, and intelligence collection are hampered, with the result of handing the initiative to the opposition. The provision of reliable mobility assets again depends largely on preventive maintenance and combat service support.

The variance in weather and terrain will determine the

nature of intelligence generation, maneuver, and fire support. Open, frozen tundra tends to support mobile warfare practices, but with little in the way of key terrain, the destruction of enemy forces, either directly or by cutting their lines of supply and communications, becomes the primary mission intent. Defensive operations (if proper cover and concealment can be arranged) also can have a devastating effect on an exposed attacker.

Command and control infrastructures in arctic warfare must place additional emphasis on operational plans and communications. Clearly prepared, unambiguous plans and orders coupled with rugged, redundant communications systems complement ground maneuver and fire support elements, and ensure proper coordination with air and sea forces. Mission execution must be swift; extended operational distances do not favor lengthy engagements.

Long-range reconnaissance and surveillance are particularly essential to arctic warfare. These, combined with target acquisition and electronic warfare systems, will enable a commander to shape battles and engagements before they are joined on the ground. The importance of the interaction of these systems is illustrated by the mixed success of U.S. forces when the Japanese opened their invasion of the Aleutians with an air attack against Dutch Harbor on 3 June 1942.

Japanese intentions were known as early as 15 May, when coded radio transmissions had been intercepted and the code broken. But because of exceptionally bad weather, constant air and sea patrols failed to detect the invasion fleet, and the Japanese launched a carrier-based air strike against Dutch Harbor early on 3 June. Shipboard radar detected the incoming bombers and relayed the information to Dutch Harbor defenders. An ineffective communications link with American fighters at nearby Umnak failed, and Japanese warplanes bombed Dutch Harbor unmolested from the air.

Because ground-attack aircraft can have a devastating effect on a ground force in open, arctic terrain, good air defense is necessary. Better still is to maintain air superiority over an opponent. For joint, combined arms operations in the far north, the battle for air supremacy will dominate the initial stages of a war.

Outlook

Nobody has yet mastered the arctic or antarctic. Technological developments and applications will, however, improve the chances for people to live and work in this inhospitable environment, and arctic warfare will constantly be influenced by such advances.

The probable scale of ground operations must be considered when planning possible future force deployments, and clearly technology has been the key factor in developing the utility of a military force for arctic warfare. The military potential of the arctic probably will continue to grow in the future, even though the relative importance of land operations may not always be as significant as that of sea or air.

GERHARD SCHEPE

SEE ALSO: Desert Warfare; Jungle Warfare; Land Warfare; Mountain Warfare.

Bibliography

Eyre, K. 1981. Canada's far distant flanks. *NATO's Fifteen Nations* 2:46–48.

Garfield, B. 1969. *The thousand-mile war.* Garden City, N.Y.: Doubleday.

Hulbert, J. H., III, and M. R. Lloyd. 1987. Cold weather CSS. *Marine Corps Gazette* 2:52–58.

Natkiel, R., and J. Pimlott. 1988. *Atlas of warfare.* New York: W. H. Smith.

Ollivant, S. 1985. The strategic and economic importance of the arctic. *Conflict Studies,* 172.

Ørvik, N. 1983. Northern development: Northern security. *Northern Studies Series 1–83.* Kingston, Ontario: Queen's Univ., Centre for International Relations.

Skagestad, G. 1975. The frozen frontier: Models for international cooperation. *Cooperation and Conflict* 3:167–87.

ARDANT DU PICQ, CHARLES JEAN JACQUES JOSEPH [1821–70]

Charles J. J. J. Ardant du Picq was a French soldier and military theorist of the mid-nineteenth century whose writings, as they were later interpreted by other theorists, had a great effect on French military theory and doctrine.

Life and Career

Ardant du Picq was born at Périgueux in the Dordogne on 19 October 1821. On 1 October 1844, upon graduation from the Ecole de St. Cyr, he was commissioned a sublieutenant in the 67th Regiment of Line Infantry. As a captain, he saw action in the French expedition to Varna (April–June 1853) during the Crimean War, but he fell ill and was shipped home. Upon recovery, he rejoined his regiment in front of Sevastopol (September). Transferred to the 9th Chasseurs à Pied battalion (December 1854), he was captured during the storming of the central bastion of Sevastopol in September 1855. He was released in December 1855 and returned to active duty. As a major with the 16th Chasseur battalion, Ardant du Picq served in Syria from August 1860 to June 1861 during the French intervention to restore order during Maronite-Druse sectarian violence. Like virtually all his peers, he also saw extensive service in Algeria (1864–66), and in February 1869 was appointed colonel of the 10th Regiment of Line Infantry. He was in France at the outbreak of war with Prussia on 15 July 1870 and took command of his regiment. He was killed leading his troops at the Battle of Borny, near Metz, on 15 August 1870.

Military Theorist and Author

Ardant du Picq's fame rests more with his writings than with his martial exploits. By the time of his death, he had already published *Combat antique* (Ancient Battle), which was later expanded from his manuscripts into the classic *Etudes sur les combat: Combat antique et moderne*, often referred to by its common English title as *Battle Studies*. This work was published in part in 1880; the complete text did not appear until 1902.

Although comparatively little is known of his life, his small corpus of writings has earned him a place in the ranks of the great military analysts. His principal interest was in the moral and psychological aspects of battle; as he himself wrote of the battlefields of his day: "The soldier is unknown often to his closest companions. He loses them in the disorienting smoke and confusion of a battle which he is fighting, so to speak, on his own. Cohesion is no longer ensured by mutual observation." Nor did Ardant du Picq neglect the decisive importance of modern firepower, noting that it was necessary for the attacker to "employ fire up till the last possible moment; otherwise, given modern rates of fire, no attack will reach its objective." Despite these words, much of his work was later used to help justify the unfortunate doctrine of the *offensive à l'outrance*, put forward principally by Colonel Grandmaison.

Assessment

In sum, Ardant du Picq was a talented analyst and, had he lived, would have gained a fine reputation as a military historian. His analyses stressed the vital importance, especially in contemporary warfare, of discipline and unit cohesion. With Karl von Clausewitz, he was one of the first military analysts to pay particular attention to psychological and behavioral factors in combat.

DAVID L. BONGARD

SEE ALSO: Clausewitz, Karl von; Combat Stress; History, Modern Military; Morale; Psychology, Military; Social Science Research and Development, Military; Unit Cohesion.

Bibliography

Ardant du Picq, C. J. J. J. 1942. *Etudes sur les combat: Combat antique et moderne*. Paris: N.p.

———. 1921. *Battle studies: Ancient and modern battle*. Trans. J. M. Greely and R. C. Cotton. Harrisburg, Pa.: Military Service.

Porch, D. 1981. *The march to the Marne*. Cambridge: Cambridge Univ. Press.

Possony, S. T., and E. Mantoux. 1943. Du Picq and Foch: The French school. In *Makers of modern strategy*, ed. E. M. Earle, et al. Princeton, N.J.: Princeton Univ. Press.

Snyder, J. 1984. *The cult of the offensive in European war planning, 1870–1914*. Ithaca, N.Y.: Cornell Univ. Press.

ARGENTINA (Argentine Republic)

Argentina occupies approximately three-quarters of southern South America. Its topography ranges from semiarid patagonia to fertile but virtually treeless pampa, to subtropical and tropical northern plains and the Andes mountain chain in the west. It borders on Bolivia, Brazil, Chile, Paraguay, and Uruguay, and faces the Atlantic and the Antarctic oceans. Its population is composed of immigrants from Spain, Italy, the United Kingdom, France, Germany, and other European countries. Argentina's national language is Spanish and Catholicism is the official religion.

Power Potential Statistics

Area: 2,766,890 square kilometers (1,068,296 sq. mi.)
Population: 33,082,400
Total Active Armed Forces: 83,000 (0.251% of pop.)
Gross National Product: US$82.7 billion (1990 est.)
Annual Defense Expenditure: US$700 million (1% of GNP, 1990 est.)
Iron and Steel Production:
  Crude steel: 2.85 million metric tons (1986)
Fuel Production:
  Coal: 0.505 million metric tons (1988)
  Crude oil: 23 million metric tons (1989)
  Natural gas: 13,500,000 million cubic meters (1983)
Electrical Power Output: 45,580 million kwh (1990)
Merchant Marine: 129 vessels; 1,663,884 gross registered tons
Civil Air Fleet: 54 major transport aircraft; 1,575 usable airfields (135 with permanent-surface runways); 1 with runways over 3,659 meters (12,000 ft.); 31 with runways 2,440–3,659 meters (8,000–12,000 ft.); 336 with runways 1,220–2,440 meters (4,000–8,000 ft.).

For the most recent information, the reader may refer to the following annual publications:

The Military Balance. International Institute for Strategic Studies. London: Brassey's (UK).
The Statesman's Year-Book. New York: St. Martin's Press.
The World Factbook. Central Intelligence Agency. Washington, D.C.: Brassey's (US).

History

At the time of its discovery by Europeans, Argentina was inhabited by small bands of nomadic plains indians. The first of several Spanish expeditions to Argentina was led by Juan Díaz de Solis in 1516. Magellan stopped in Argentina in 1520, and Sebastian Cabot conducted the first serious explorations in 1526. Other explorers followed. Buenos Aires was permanently founded by Juan de Garay in 1580. Argentina was part of the Viceroyalty of Peru until the establishment in 1776 of the Viceroyalty of the River Plate. The British attempted to take over the viceroyalty during the Napoleonic occupation of Spain. But local forces, led by Santiago de Liniers and Juan Martin de Pueyrredon, defeated them in 1806 and again in 1807. Local government was established on May 25, 1810, to rule in the name of the king of Spain.

On July 9, 1816, the congress at Tucuman formally declared independence from Spain without a fight. Gen. José de San Martín began training an army after independence and, together with the defeated Chilean army that had taken refuge in Argentina, crossed the Andes to liberate Chile and Peru. San Martín's efforts to join forces with Bolívar were rebuffed. He resigned, returned to Argentina, and, because of political rifts that had developed while he was away, voluntarily went into exile. Rivalries that had originated in the colonial period between Buenos Aires and the provinces over strong central government based in Buenos Aires (Unitarians) versus a decentralized, loose federation (Federalists) continued after Independence. Strained relations with Brazil over the status of Uruguay between 1817 and 1825 led Brazil to declare war on Argentina in 1825. With no effective army in Argentina after independence, conscription was instituted, levying forces from the provinces in proportion to their population. Peace was negotiated in 1828 and Uruguay gained its independence.

In 1835, Gen. Juan Manuel de Rosas, an advocate of strong central government, became president. In his second term, he became a dictator and ruled in a bloody reign of terror until defeated in 1852 by Gen. Justo José de Urquiza. In 1853, Juan Bautista Alberdi drafted a constitution using that of the United States as a model; it was approved with minor changes and remained in effect until 1949, and was then readopted in 1983 with minor modifications. Between 1853 and 1862, Buenos Aires fought the provinces for control. Under Bartolome Mitre, Buenos Aires won control of the government in 1861.

Between 1862 and 1930, Argentina expanded economically and in population due to large European immigrations. Technological innovations and capital investments made Argentina one of the fastest-developing countries in the world. During this period the army, under Gen. Julio A. Roca, conquered the Pampa Indians and their territories south of Buenos Aires. Border disputes with Chile were peacefully resolved around the turn of the century. Political and electoral reforms, especially the introduction of the secret ballot, ended conservative rule and brought the Radical party to power in 1916; it remained in power until ousted in a Conservative coup in 1930. Political instability dominated the period between 1930 and 1943. Pro-fascist elements in the armed forces overthrew the government in 1943 and banned political parties, dissolved congress, and instituted censorship. The army took over a splinter faction of the General Confederation of Labor and appointed Col. Juan Domingo Perón to head an opposition labor union. There he began to build the power base that in the 1946 elections propelled Perón and his Justicialista (Peronist) party into the presidency. Perón's wife, Eva Duarte de Perón, exerted tremendous influence over workers. Between the two of them, they purged the labor leadership. In 1949 a new constitution was adopted insuring Peronist control of all segments of government. Foreign enterprises were nationalized. Generally, the fiscal, economic, and political policies instituted during this period continue to plague Argentina to this day. During World War II, Argentina remained officially neutral. During the war years, Argentina's relations with the United States, the United Kingdom, and other Allies were strained. However, in 1945, Argentina declared war on the Axis.

Perón was overthrown in September 1955 by elements of all three armed services, and the Peronist party was declared illegal. Gen. Pedro Aramburu emerged in control and his administration served as a transition to democracy. Arturo Frondizi was elected and inaugurated president in 1958. He instituted economic reforms with varying degress of success as he tried to attract other political parties into his sphere of influence. However, Peronist elements won several governorships and a sizable block of seats in the Congress in the 1962 elections after the party had been legalized. As a result, the armed forces overthrew Frondizi. In 1963 Arturo Illia was elected president, but was forced out unceremoniously in June 1966. Gen. Juan Carlos Ongania became president, followed by Gen. Roberto Levingston in 1970, and he in turn by Gen. Alejandro Lanusse in 1971. With the assassination of Gen. Pedro Aramburu in 1968, political unrest and violence escalated, further undermining Argentina's stability. By 1971, leftist elements and neo-Peronist guerrillas were active and disruptive. In 1972, Perón returned from exile, but after a brief stay he returned to Spain. Elections held in 1973 were won by the Peronist Hector Campora, who invited Perón to return and run for president in his own right. Perón won and was inaugurated with his wife Isabel as vice-president in September 1973. In less than a year Perón died, and his wife succeeded to the presidency.

General unrest and dissatisfaction with the economic and political situation led to Isabel Perón's ouster by the military in March 1976. The intervening period until 1982 was marked by turmoil, terrorism, political repression, human rights violations, and changes in military junta presidents. In December 1981, Gen. Leopoldo Galtieri became president. Public protests mounted until April 1982. General Galtieri took advantage of the stalled negotiations with the British over the Falkland/Malvinas islands and the South Georgias to invade the islands. The British mounted a counteroffensive and retook the islands on 14 June 1982. With the election of Dr. Raul Alfonsín in 1983, Argentina returned to constitutional government. President Alfonsín served his term, and Carlos Menem was elected in 1989, marking the first time in decades that the presidency had been constitutionally transferred. After some initial economic successes under Alfonsín, economic instability returned, actually forcing Alfonsín to advance Menem's inauguration by several months.

Politico-Military Background and Policy

The origins of the Argentine army date from the middle of the eighteenth century. The colonial militia defeated two British attempts to take Buenos Aires in 1806 and 1807. Their success fostered an independence movement that eventually led to the peaceful revolution in May 1810. New units were formed in unsuccessful attempts to assert control over Bolivia, Paraguay, and Uruguay. These efforts ended with Argentina's formal declaration of independence from Spain in 1816. Gen. José de San Martín's forces defeated the Spanish, and Chile and Peru declared their independence. Following independence, political instability led to the disintegration of both the army and navy. In May 1825, with the threat of war with Brazil over Uruguay, a national army was formed with each province providing a contingent proportionate to its population, while a naval force was organized to confront the Brazilians. After initial failures, Argentina defeated Brazil in 1828. Uruguay became an independent buffer state. Again the army and naval forces disintegrated and political instability ensued.

Juan Manuel de Rosas was appointed governor by the Buenos Aires legislature in 1829 for a three-year term. He was reappointed in 1835. Rosas trained an army, made national unification his objective, and created a paramilitary police organization that terrorized all opposition. Rosas was ousted by Gen. Justo José de Urquiza in 1852. With the Constitution of 1853, the Army of the Confederation was created. Bartolome Mitre commanded the Army of Buenos Aires. Both forces coexisted until 1861 when Urquiza's forces were defeated by Mitre's. Mitre became the first president of a united Argentina in 1862. He opened the army to troops that had fought with Urquiza and created a national Argentine army. Argentina was drawn into the War of the Triple Alliance (1865–70) with Brazil and Uruguay against Paraguay. Neglected, the Argentine army again was forced to call on volunteers from the provinces.

After the war, Argentina began the modernization and professionalization of its armed forces. In 1868, under president Domingo Faustino Sarmiento, the military and naval academies were established. During the 1890s the general staff was modernized with the help of former Prussian military advisers. Border disputes with Chile in the 1890s led to expansion of the fleet. The need for trained personnel in the enlisted ranks led to the creation in 1897 of the Naval Mechanics School. During the two presidential terms of Julio A. Roca, 1880–86 and 1898–1904, the armed forces were modernized and consolidated. He also attempted to limit the political involvement of the armed forces in national politics. Roca, himself a military man, established civilian control over the military. He established a permanent general staff and created separate ministries of war and navy. With German military advisers, Roca established the Superior War College and the national obligatory military service system. By 1907, the Argentine army had adopted the German army's organizational structure and training manuals. German military doctrine was firmly established prior to World War I. After Germany's defeat, relations were resumed and continued until the outbreak of World War II.

Argentina's democratic system and rapid economic development between 1880 and 1930 were ended by the September 1930 military coup that ousted President Hipolito Yrigoyen. Argentina's military entered the national political arena and remained there in one form or another until 1983.

During this time, two factions emerged in the army officer corps: (1) those who supported democratically elected governments; and (2) the corporatists and authoritarians who favored military involvement in and control of national politics. In 1943, corporatist army officers had formed a secret military lodge, Grupo de Oficiales Unidos (GOU), and engineered a military coup that brought Col. Juan Domingo Perón to prominence and, ultimately, to the presidency in 1946. During the 1930s, in spite of the economic depression, the Argentine armed forces had doubled in size; their organizational structure changed to keep pace with its expanded size. The air force, established in 1912 under the command of the army, was made an independent service in 1945. In 1941, the Dirección General de Fabricaciones Militares (DGFM) was established to coordinate, under military control, the manufacture of military equipment. Through the years, the DGFM's increased sophistication placed Argentina second to Brazil in Latin America in the export of military hardware, and the DGFM was one of the largest enterprises in Latin America. The armed forces were downsized and the army reorganized after Perón's ouster in 1955. During the 1960s, factionalism in the armed forces grew as a result of increased involvement in politics. The hardline faction, which favored indefinite military control of the government, was most powerful. However, all factions in the armed forces were united in opposition to the Peronists.

After the 1966 coup that brought General Ongania to the presidency, the armed forces developed the National Security Doctrine, which linked national security to economic development. Under Ongania in 1966, the Act of the Argentine Revolution reorganized Argentina's armed forces command structure in accordance with the National Security Doctrine. Two councils were created: the Consejo Nacional de Seguridad (CONASE) and the Consejo Nacional de Desarrollo (CONADE); they were responsible for coordinating all government policies and strategies with regard to development and national security. Under this concept the military became involved in civic action programs and other national development programs.

By 1968, opposition to the armed forces began to emerge. In 1976, with the increase of political violence and left-wing subversion, the National Reorganization Process was implemented by the government of Gen. Jorge Rafael Videla to justify the steps taken by the military against segments of the population that opposed military rule. This period has been called the "Dirty War" and the "War Against Subversion," among others. The armed forces were granted extraordinary powers by statute. Under the National Reorganization Process, the governing junta, composed of the army, navy, and air force chiefs of staff, became the supreme body of the nation with powers previously attributed to the three branches of government. The process remained in force until just before President Alfonsín's inauguration in December 1983, when it was repealed and the constitution of 1853 restored.

The restoration of a democratically elected government is directly traced back to the defeat of the Argentine armed forces by the British. The military's performance led to a series of studies on the entire military. The best known of these was prepared by the Rattenbach Commission. Its findings, after being submitted in September 1983, led to the decision to prosecute the members of the junta that was in power during the Falklands/Malvinas (South Atlantic) War. The charges against the military junta and leadership stated in the commission's findings were those of gross negligence in planning, preparedness, military intelligence, diplomacy, timing, and, ultimately, judgment. Formal charges were presented by the military prosecutor to the Supreme Council of the Armed Forces in August 1985. All were found guilty and sentenced to dismissal from the armed forces and varying prison sentences.

With the inauguration of Dr. Raul Alfonsín in December 1983, the president of the republic once again became the commander in chief of the armed forces. One of the first acts of the Alfonsín government was to order a study to plan the reorganization of the armed forces. A plan was submitted to the Congress in April 1985 and approved after debate. The reorganization law approved by the Congress superseded the 1966 National Security Doctrine. The law provided for the creation of a number of new bodies responsible for defense matters. The National Defense Cabinet was to advise the president on appropriate strategies and coordinated plans of action for the resolution of conflicts. The Military Committee was to advise the president on military affairs and the conduct of military operations. Under the administration of President Carlos Saúl Menem, civilian control over the military continued.

Strategic Problems

Argentina's greatest strategic problem is its limited natural resources. While self-sufficient in petroleum, it is dependent on the importation of most of the basic materials needed by an industrialized nation. Its primary source of foreign currency is from its agricultural sector. Another problem for Argentina is its distance from the world's most lucrative markets and the cost of transporting its exports to these markets. Militarily, while Argentine armed forces have had a long tradition of strategic planning and political involvement, they lack combat experience against a trained military force. In the Falklands/Malvinas War, this inexperience produced deficiencies in supply, logistics, communications, and intelligence which limited the nation's ability to project military forces. Most of Argentina's strategic problems are internal and related to its economic and political stability. Its external strategic problem remains its claims to the Falklands/Malvinas and the South Georgia Islands. These claims are at the negotiating table. The Argentine dispute with Chile over the Beagle Channel and Picton Island was resolved through negotiation.

Military Assistance

Argentina does not now receive military assistance nor does it give military assistance.

Defense Industry

The Dirección General de Fabricaciones Militares has been the entity responsible for the manufacture and acquisition of military equipment for the armed forces. Fabricaciones Militares rapidly expanded when it was cut off from its traditional suppliers during World War II. Its capabilities include everything from small weapons to artillery and armor to small naval patrol craft and submarines to counterinsurgency aircraft. Other equipment is produced under foreign license. Argentina is second to Brazil in Latin America in the exportation of military equipment. In 1985, a coordinating committee was created to review requests to export military equipment produced in Argentina. Argentina has created a solid research and development capability, including space and nuclear programs. Its nuclear development is considered one of the best in Latin America, and it is believed that Argentina has had, for sometime, the capability to produce and detonate a nuclear device. Its first nuclear research program was established in 1950. It was the first country in Latin America to build a research reactor (1957), and later built the first commercial power reactor (1974) and the first reprocessing and uranium enrichment plant. With its own source of uranium, Argentina controls its nuclear fuel cycle. Argentina assists other countries with nuclear development programs subject to international safeguards, and the government stresses that its research is for peaceful uses of atomic energy.

Alliances

Argentina is one of the original members of the Organization of American States (OAS), the successor of the Pan American Union. It is also an original member of the

United Nations. Argentina has no formal alliances with other countries. Argentina signed the Act of Chapultepec in 1945. Argentina is also a member of the Inter-American Defense Board, which was created during World War II and extended by a resolution calling for the creation of a permanent body responsible for addressing problems threatening hemispheric defense. In 1947, Argentina signed the Inter-American Treaty of Reciprocal Assistance (Rio Treaty). Argentina became a member of the International Atomic Energy Agency in 1956 and has signed, but not ratified, the Treaty for the Prohibition of Nuclear Weapons in Latin America (Treaty of Tialtelolco). During the 1991 Gulf War, Argentina joined the coalition forces and dispatched two naval warships to the Persian Gulf. These ships participated with other coalition naval forces in guaranteeing the UN embargo against Iraq.

Defense Structure

The president of the republic is the commander in chief of the armed forces. As such as he has the right to determine the organization and distribution of the armed forces as required. Officers holding the rank of colonel, or its equivalent, are appointed by the president with the consent of the Senate. The constitution provides that the president may declare war, pending congressional authorization and approval. The president is also empowered to negotiate and to sign peace treaties, alliances, and border treaties and to declare neutrality. The president may declare a state of siege, as dictated by internal security, but only when Congress is in recess; otherwise he needs the consent of the Senate. Congress is empowered to authorize the president to declare war or make peace. The Congress is empowered to declare a state of siege, as dictated by internal security, while it is in session. The Congress can confirm or suspend a state of siege declared by the president while it was not in session. The Congress establishes the size of the armed forces, authorizes the use of the armed forces outside of Argentina, and authorizes the entry of foreign forces. The Congress has exclusive jurisdiction throughout the country over military facilities.

(For an explanation of the abbreviations and symbols used in the following section of military statistics, see the list of Abbreviations and Acronyms in each volume.)

Total Armed Forces

Active: 83,000 (est. 16,000 conscripts). Terms of service: all services up to 14 months; some conscripts may serve less.
Reserves: 377,000: Army 250,000 (National Guard 200,000; Territorial Guard 50,000); Navy 77,000; Air 50,000.

ARMY: 45,000 (est. 10,000 conscripts). Many units cadre status only.
3 corps HQ (to reorganize on div basis).
2 armd bde (each 3 tk regt, 1 SP arty bn, 1 armd recce sqn, 1 engr coy).
2 mech inf bde (each 2 inf regt of 1 bn, 1 tk regt, 1 arty bn, 1 armd recce sqn, 1 engr coy).
2 mtn inf bde (each 3 inf, 1 arty bn, 1 SF, 1 engr coy).
2 inf bde (1 with 3 inf regt each 1 bn, 1 arty bn, 1 armd recce sqn, 1 engr coy, 1 with 1 inf, 1 jungle, 1 mtn regt, 1 arty bn, 1 armd recce sqn, 1 engr coy).
1 jungle bde (4 lt inf, 2 arty (how) bn, 1 armd recce sqn, 2 engr coy).
1 AB bde (3 AB regt of 1 bn, 1 arty bn, 1 engr coy).
Army tps:
Army HQ Escort Regt: 1 mot inf regt of 1 bn (ceremonial).
Presidential Escort: 1 mot cav regt (ceremonial).
1 indep mech inf bde (3 inf regt of 1 bn, 1 arty bn, 1 armd recce sqn, 1 engr coy).
2 AD arty, 2 engr, 1 avn bn.
1 SF coy.
Corps tps: each corps 1 armd cav regt (recce), 1 arty, 1 AD arty, 2 engr bn.
Equipment:
MBT: 250: 100 M-4 Sherman, 150 TAM.
Light tanks: 60 AMX-13.
Recce: 50 AML-90.
AIFV: 45 AMX-VCI, some 175 TAM VCTP.
APC: 100 M-3 half-track, 240 M-113, 70 MOWAG Grenadier (mod Roland).
Towed arty: 326: 105mm: 200 incl M-101 and M-56; 155mm: 126 CITEFA Models 77/-81.
SP arty: 125: 155mm: Mk F3, L33.
MRL: 105mm: SLAM Pampero; 127mm: SLAM SAPBA-1.
Mortars: 81mm: 1,000; 120mm: 130 (some SP in VCTM AIFV).
ATGW: 600 SS-11/-12, Cobra (Mamba), 2,000 Mathogo.
RCL: 75mm: 75; 90mm: 100; 105mm.
ATK guns: 105mm: 106 SK-105 Kuerassier SP.
AD guns: 20mm: 130; 30mm: 40; 35mm: 15; 40mm: 80 L/60, 15 L/70; 90mm: 20.
SAM: Tigercat, Blowpipe, Roland, SAM-7.
Aviation:
Aircraft: 5 Cessna-207, 3-500, 5 Commander 690, 2 DHC-6, 3 G-222, 1 Merlin IIIA, 4-IV, 3 Queen Air, 1 Sabreliner, 5 T-41.
Helicopters: 6 A-109, 3 AS-332B, 5 Bell 205, 4 FH-1100, 4 SA-315, 3 SA-330, 10 UH-1H, 8 UH-12.

NAVY: 25,000 incl naval air force and marines (incl 3,000 conscripts). 3 Naval Areas: Centre: from River Plate to 42° 45′ S; South: from 42° 45′ to Cape Horn; and Antarctica. Bases: Buenos Aires, Puerto Belgrano (HQ Center), Mar del Plata (submarine base), Ushuaia (HQ South), Puerto Deseado.
Submarines: 4: 2 Santa Cruz (Ge Tr-1700) with 533mm TT (SST-4 HWT); 2 Salta (Ge T-209/1200) with 533mm TT (SST-4 HWT) (both in major refit).
Principal Surface Combatants: 14:
Carrier: 1 Veinticinco de Mayo CVS (UK Colossus): (in major refit, currently proceeding very slowly) capacity 18 ac and hel, complement: ac: 4 Super Etendard, 3 S-2; hel: 4 S-61D.
Destroyers: 6:
2 Hercules (UK Type 42) with 1 × 2 Sea Dart SAM; plus 1 SA-319 hel (ASW), 2×3 ASTT, 4 × MM-38 Exocet SSM, 1 × 114mm gun.
4 Almirante Brown (Ge MEKO-360) ASW with 2 × SA-316 hel, 2 × 3 ASTT; plus 8 × MM-40 Exocet SSM, 1 × 127mm gun.
Frigates: 7: 4 Espora (Ge MEKO-140) with 2 × 3 ASTT, hel deck; plus 8 × MM-40 Exocet; 3 Drummond (Fr A-69) with 2 × 3 ASTT; plus 4 × MM-38 Exocet, 1 × 100mm gun.
Patrol and Coastal Combatants: 13:

Torpedo craft: 2 Intrepida (Ge Lürssen-45) PFT with 2 × 533mm TT (SSt-4 HWT)
Patrol Craft, Offshore: 7:
1 Teniente Olivieri (ex-US oilfield tug).
2 Irigoyen (US Cherokee AT).
2 King (trg) with 3 × 105mm guns.
2 Somellera (US Sotoyomo AT).
Patrol Craft, Inshore: 4 PCI ⟨.
Mine Warfare: 6: 4 Neuquen (UK 'Ton') MSC; 2 Chaco (UK 'Ton') MHC.
Amphibious: 1 Cabo San Antonio LST (hel deck), capacity 600 tps, 18 tk. Plus 19 craft; 4 LCM, 16 LCVP.
Support and Miscellaneous: 9: 1 AGOR, 3 tpt, 1 ocean tug, 1 icebreaker, 2 trg, 1 research.

Naval Air Force: (2,000); 41 cbt ac, 10 armed hel.
Attack: 1 sqn with 11 Super Etendard.
MR/ASW: 1 sqn with 3 L-188, 6 S-2E.
EW: 1 L-188E.
Helicopters: 2 sqn: 1 ASW/TPT with 4 ASH-3H (ASW) and 4 AS-61D (tpt); 1 spt with 6 SA-316/-319 (with SS-11).
Transport: 1 sqn with 1 BAe-125, 3 F-28-3000, 3 L-188, 4 Queen Air 80, 7 Super King Air, 4 US-2A.
Survey: 4 PC-6B (Antarctic flt).
Training: 2 sqn: 7*EMB-326, 9*MB-326, 5*MB-339A, 10 T-34C.
Missiles:
ASM: AGM-12 Bullpup, AM-39 Exocet, AS-12, Martín Pescador.
AAM: AIM-9 Sidewinder, R-550 Magic.

Marines: (5,000).
Fleet Forces: 2: each 2 bn, 1 amph recce coy, 1 fd arty bn, 1 ATK, 1 engr coy.
Amph spt force: 1 marine inf bn.
1 AD arty regt (bn).
2 indep inf bn.
Equipment:
Recce: 12 ERC-90 Lynx.
APC: 19 LVTP-7, 15 LARC-5, 6 MOWAG Grenadier, 24 Panhard.
Towed arty: 105mm: 15 M-101/M-56; 155mm: 6 M-114.
Mortars: 81mm: 20.
RL: 89mm: 60 3.5-in M-20.
ATGW: 50 Bantam, Cobra (Mamba).
RCL: 105mm: 30 M-1968.
AD guns: 30 mm: 10.
SAM: Tigercat.

AIR FORCE: 13,000 (3,000 conscripts); 176 cbt ac, 14 armed hel, 9 air bde, 10 AD arty bty, SF (AB) coy.
Air Operations Command (9 bde):
Bombers: 1 sqn with 4 Canberra B-62, 2 T-64.
FGA/Fighter: 4 sqn: 2 (1 OCU) with 20 Mirage IIIC (17-CJ, 1 -BE, 2 -BJ), 15 Mirage IIIEA; 2 with 8 Mirage 5P, 23 Dagger (Nesher; 20 -A, 3 -B).
FGA: 2 sqn with 16 A-4P.
COIN: 3 sqn: 2 ac with 36 IA-58A, 18 IA-63, 24 MS-760; 1 armed hel with 11 Hughes MD500, 3 UH-1H.
MR: 1 Boeing 707.
Survey: 3 Learjet 35A, 4 1A-50.
Tanker: 2 Boeing 707, 2 KC-130H.
SAR: 4 SA-315 hel.
Transport: 5 sqn with:
Aircraft: 3 Boeing 707, 6 C-47, 2 C-130E, 3 -H, 1 L-100-30, 6 DHC-6, 12 F-27, 6 F-28, 15 IA-50, 2 Merlin IVA. Antarctic spt unit with 1 DHC-6, 1 LC-47.
Helicopters: 7 Bell 212, 1 CH-47C, 1 S-61R.
Calibration: 1 sqn with 2 Boeing 707, 3 IA-50, 2 Learjet 35, 1 PA-31.
Liaison: 1 sqn with 12 Cessna 182, 1 -320, 7 Commander, 1 Sabreliner.
Air Training Command: 28 EMB-312, 10* MS-760, 40 T-34B ac; 4 Hughes 500D hel.
Missiles:
ASM: ASM-2 Martín Pescador.
AAM: AIM-9B Sidewinder, R-530, R-550, Shafrir.

FORCES ABROAD
UN and Peacekeeping:
Angola (UNAVEM II): 6 observers.
Central America (ONUCA): 30; 4 patrol craft.
Middle East (UNTSO): 4 observers.
Iraq/Kuwait (UNIKOM): 7 observers.

PARAMILITARY
Gendarmerie (Ministry of Defence): 15,000; 5 Regional Comd.
Equipment: Shorland recce, 40 UR-416; 81mm mor; ac: 3 Piper, 5 PC-6; hel: 5 SA-315.
Prefectura Naval (Coast Guard): (13,000); 7 comd. Equipment: 5 Mantilla, 1 Delfin PCO, 4 PCI, 19 ⟨; 5 C-212, 4 Short Skyvan ac; 3 SA-330, 6 MD-500 hel.

Future

Argentina has been beset with economic problems since 1930. From then to the present, there have been military governments and constitutionally elected ones. Argentina has fallen from being one of the richest nations in the world to one of the most financially troubled, with one of the largest external debts among the developing countries. Its early economic success and growth were based on a rich agricultural base. Since 1930, attempts to industrialize have drained its economic resources. Argentina does not have the population, internal market, or natural resources to support a cost-effective industrial base. The Alfonsín administration elected in 1983 attempted unsuccessfully to reverse Argentina's economic downtrend. The Menem administration implemented various economic measures, including privatization of state industries, but with no visible success. Argentina has the potential to reverse its current economic dilemma, but for the foreseeable future it will continue to struggle with austerity budgets and hope that current economic measures will pay off. Continued political stability will be essential, as well as disciplined economic efforts, to attract foreign investment and capital to Argentina to return the country to economic growth and expansion.

DONALD STEWART

SEE ALSO: Latin American Wars of Independence; Organization of American States; South America; Spanish Empire.

Bibliography

American University. 1985. *Argentina: A country study.* Washington, D.C.: Government Printing Office.
Dupuy, T. N., ed. 1972. *The almanac of world military power.* San Rafael, Calif.: Presidio Press.

English, A. J. 1984. *Armed forces of Latin America: Their histories, development, present strength and military potential.* London: Jane's.
Fitzgibbon, R. H., comp. 1974. *Argentina, a chronology and fact book, 1516–1973.* Dobbs Ferry, N.Y.: Oceana.
Looney, R. E. 1986. *The political economy of Latin American defense expenditures: Case studies of Venezuela and Argentina.* Lexington, Mass.: Lexington Press.
Lynch, J. 1981. *Argentine dictator: Juan Manuel de Rosas, 1829–1852.* Oxford: Oxford Univ. Press.
Moreno, S. L. 1937. *La Argentina, futura gran potencia mundial.* Buenos Aires.
Poneman, D. 1987. *Argentina, democracy on trial.* New York: Paragon House.
Potash, R. A. 1969. The army and politics in Argentina. Stanford, Calif.: Stanford Univ. Press.
Rock, D. 1985. *Argentina, 1516–1982: From Spanish colonization to the Falklands War.* Berkeley: Univ. of California Press.
Stewart, N. K. 1991. *Mates & Muchachos.* Washington, D.C.: Brassey's.
Di Tella, G. 1983. *Argentina under Peron, 1973–76: The nation's experience with a labor-based government.* New York: St. Martin's Press.
Weil, T. E. 1974. *Area handbook for Argentina.* Washington, D.C.: Government Printing Office.
Whitaker, A. P. 1964. *Argentina.* Englewood Cliffs, N.J.: Prentice-Hall.
Wynia, G. W. 1986. *Argentina: Illusions and realities.* New York: Holmes and Meier.

ARMED FORCES AND SOCIETY

The term *armed forces and society* summarizes the complex relationship that exists between military organizations and social systems, while the term *armed forces* relates to just the organized groups that are involved in the managed application of violence. Since the former term refers to regular and irregular military organizations and standing armies as well as voluntary or auxiliary formations, it is wider in its coverage than the term *armed services*, which applies specifically and exclusively to those institutions and organizations that are part of the state. The concept of "society" is also more extensive in scope than the notion of the "state," for while armed forces are, as a rule, national instruments, they are also an international type of social institution, the characteristics, structure, and functions of which transcend political boundaries.

General Characteristics

Although the study of armed forces over the centuries has created an extensive literature of military science and history, specific interest in the analysis of the relationship between those forces and the parent society is of more recent origin. Two contributions that were prepared in the 1930s provide a multidisciplinary approach to the study of the field. The first of these major works was Karl Demeter's pioneer study, *Das Deutsche Heer und Seine Offiziere*. This constituted the first extensive and major historico-sociological research on a specific group of military personnel. It drew heavily on both historical and sociological methodology even though its sociological stance was more implicit than explicitly formulated. Nevertheless, the sociological theory that is used is an important contribution to study in this field, for it is a development of Max Weber's brilliant and penetrating analysis of military institutions. In the same way that this theory has had a continuing impact on the social scientific community, the work of Demeter is also a valuable commentary on Alfred Vagt's *The History of Militarism*, which appeared in 1937 and which offered a clear and noteworthy distinction between "militarism" and the "military way."

In his classic study of the German officer corps, Demeter meticulously laid down the framework of much subsequent research into the social origins, education, and career development of an elite group. This later research owed a very considerable debt to the earlier work. It is no exaggeration to conclude that Demeter's study was the prototype for a whole generation of more elaborate and more explicitly sociological analysis of military professionals, professionalism, and professionalization. At the same time, Demeter recognized that the military professional is also an armed bureaucrat who works in a highly structured organization. The emphasis that is increasingly placed on the more systematic application of organizational theory to this field reflects the evolution of this analysis of the military profession and the military organization as one of the most developed aspects of the study of armed forces and society.

In the second area—that of civil-military relations—the genesis of much subsequent study was the publication in 1941 of Harold D. Lasswell's classic essay, "The Garrison State." Drawing on his earlier conceptual statements, Lasswell refined the analysis of the dangers of militarism in an advanced industrialized society that was subject to a sustained threat of war. His basic hypothesis completely rejected earlier notions of military dictatorship, for he argued that militarization and militarism in these advanced societies could not be—and would not be—characterized by direct rule by military elites. Rather, it would be identified by expansion of the military into those political roles that are traditionally held by civilian elites. The trend of the time, he argued, was away from the dominance of the specialist on bargaining—the businessman—toward the supremacy of the soldier as the specialist in the application of violence.

This general study of society and social systems expanded rapidly in the 1940s and early 1950s, particularly in the United States. During World War II and immediately afterward, social scientists began a critical examination of the military system. In *The American Soldier*, S. A. Stouffer and his colleagues produced a classic study of combat behavior, morale, and buddy relationships under stress. This complemented other work that looked at the contribution of the primary group to the maintenance of military cohesion. This type of research paralleled the interest shown by social scientists, on the basis of their experience, on the concept of the military as an ideal-type bureaucratic organization. One important study, S. Andreski's *Military Organization and Society*, was a major contribution to the analysis from a general perspective of the relationship between armed forces and society. This introduced the concept of the military participation ratio (MPR)—that is, the ratio of military-utilized individuals to the total population—as an indicator of postulated changes in the structure of the parent society. Even so, specific interest in the further analysis of the relationship between armed forces and that society did not truly develop until the late 1950s.

The most significant development was the publication of two major studies, one by Samuel Huntington and one by Morris Janowitz. These studies share a common overall perspective, for they both stress the concept that the military career-officer is a member of a profession that possesses certain characteristics which contribute to effectiveness and responsibilities. However, it is the difference between these two theorists that highlights the conceptual and problematic questions associated with the study of armed forces and society.

In *The Soldier and the State*, Huntington argues that military officership is a fully developed profession because it manifests, to a significant degree, three principal characteristics of the ideal type of professional model: expertise, corporateness, and responsibility. The military, however, carries out its purpose within a political environment without regard to political, moral, or other nonmilitary considerations, so its professionalism can be summarized as its expertise over lethal violence, a corporate self-identity, and ultimate responsibility to the larger polity.

According to Huntington, only officers involved in and dedicated to the central expertise of the management of violence are members of the military profession. This implies that neither commissioned specialists such as lawyers and doctors nor enlisted personnel can be typed as military professionals. Furthermore, the characteristics of the latter are derived from and are shaped by the content and function of the military task. Thus, the professional officer is, above all, obedient and loyal to the authority of the state, competent in military expertise, dedicated to using his skill to provide for the security of the state, and politically and morally neutral. His sense of professional commitment is shaped by a military ethic that reflects a carefully inculcated set of values and attitudes. These are seen to constitute a unique professional outlook or military mind that may be characterized as pessimistic, collectivist, historically inclined, power-oriented, nationalistic, militaristic, pacifist, and instrumentalist—in short, realistic and conservative. Huntington approaches the analysis of the relationship between armed forces and society from the perspective of interest group politics. Civil-military relations constitute a subsystem of a pluralistic political system; the nub of most problems of civil-military relations, accordingly, is the issue of the relative power of the armed forces and other groups within society. Huntington suggests that the more professionalized the officer corps, the more likely it is to be an efficient and politically neutral instrument of state policy. The dominant political beliefs affect the nature of this relationship. Huntington argues that a conservative ideology (rather than a liberal, fascist, or Marxist one) is most compatible with the military ethic and professionalism.

This widely read and influential text was complemented in 1960 by the publication of Morris Janowitz's seminal work, *The Professional Soldier*. In common with Huntington, Janowitz was concerned with the critical issue of the subordination of the military to the duly-elected government. He, however, treated the military as a social system in which the professional characteristics of the officer corps change over time. They are variable in that they encompass norms and skills, including, but also going beyond, the direct management of violence. While he specifies the characteristics that make officership a profession—expertise, lengthy education, group identity, ethics, standards of performance—he identifies the profession not as a static model but as a dynamic bureaucratic organization that changes over time in response to changing conditions. This recognizes the extent to which the form of existing military organizations and professionalized officer corps has been shaped since the turn of the century by the impact of broad social transformations. This implies that armed forces are experiencing a long-term transformation toward convergence with civilian structures and norms. It can be hypothesized that as a result of broad social changes, the basis of authority and discipline in the armed forces has shifted to manipulation and consensus; military skills have become more socially representative; membership of the elite has become more open and the ideology of the profession has become more political. As a result of this, the traditional heroic warrior role has given way to an ascendant managerial-technical role. In short, the military profession as a whole has become similar to large, bureaucratic, nonmilitary institutions. It has, in effect, become "civilianized."

The Military Community

A common feature in this research is the emphasis placed on the significance of the military community. Armed forces are something more than a bureaucratic organization. They are not simply "General Motors in Uniform." Their characteristics as a profession resemble those of other occupational groups claiming this status, but they also uniquely reflect the nature of the military task. Armed forces form a community that unites the work and life of its members much more completely than do most other social organizations. Within this milieu, two distinctive lifestyles can be identified. That of officers is characterized by a ceremonialism that is a heritage of the long historical traditions of officership. Seen by its critics to be anachronistic, this military style of life is expected to enhance group cohesion, encourage professional loyalty, and maintain martial spirit. Political indoctrination is effective in this milieu because of the relatively closed community environment in which military officers continue to work and live.

The community life of enlisted men is very different. The distinction between officers and men is visibly reflected in differences in uniforms and insignia. It is seen in differences in remuneration and types of accommodation. Socially, greater privileges and status are attached to officership. Although gradations in the lifestyle of enlisted personnel can be made between noncommissioned officers (NCOs) and privates, the separation of officers and enlisted personnel is most marked. This is particularly noticeable with reference to recruitment, socialization, rights, and privileges (Moskos and Wood 1988). Although the increased recruitment of women into national armed forces has modified traditional customs and mores, the characteristics of the exclusively male combat unit constitute the archetypal image of this military community. With its distinctive subculture, characterized by a distinctive language and a strongly developed informal organization, socialization and life in this tightly knit occupational community produce a self-image that reflects its self-sufficiency.

The Military Bureaucracy

Armed forces constitute a purposive organization. The formal structure of the military closely resembles the classic model of bureaucracy described by Weber. Since the primary function of armed forces is the effective management and application of violence, an organizational form is required that is designed to do this effectively and the defining characteristics of bureaucracy—hierarchy of command, impersonality, precision, routine, and regulations—are seen to ensure this. This is particularly so when these qualities can be linked to an emphasis on the importance of patterns of traditional authority. The creation of a bureaucratic structure with a formal, highly detailed and often monolithic body of rules and regulations also recognizes the presence within armed forces of a specialized division of labor. From a very early point in the historical development of armed forces, the training of the military man as a multiskilled generalist was paralleled by the evolution of the military specialist. This encourages the development of armed forces as bureaucracies, many features of which are also to be found in civilian organizations. Theories of military organization are, therefore, closely related to general theories of sociology. For all the romance, ritual, and history associated with the regiment, ship, or air squadron, the military is a rational-legal institution in which the structure of power and authority closely resembles that of other large-scale organizations. As in any other bureaucracy, the principle of hierarchy prevails. The office guarantees that the individual will enjoy all the authority associated with his rank. The military, however, now faces the major problem of bringing this traditional authority into line with technological developments that have materially affected ways of waging war.

In the past, the authority structure widely associated with the military was that of a rigid hierarchy of command. The model was simple. The principle of hierarchy rested on a broad base of basically unskilled enlisted men under the command of an officer who was aided by a few trusted noncommissioned officers who put his orders into practice. At each successive echelon or rank grade, there was an officer of higher rank who directed several more or less functionally similar units. This created the traditional hierarchical pyramid that is a defining characteristic of all bureaucracies.

The introduction of new weaponry and increasingly sophisticated technology materially affected this structure. Many enlisted men—and women—possess vital skills not easily replaced. This can give rise to major questions about their reluctance to accept orders solely on the basis of the authority of rank of the person from whom such orders emanate. This is very noticeable if such orders should be seen to go contrary to their own technical judgment. The diverse components that nowadays come under the direction of even a unit commander often exceed the technical competence of the officer in command. To direct them effectively he is therefore forced to rely on the knowledge of others, either from within his own unit or from a technical expert attached to a higher staff. Dependence on highly technical knowledge at ever lower echelons gives the technical staff officers a set of informal roles in which they enjoy considerable de facto authority, resolving problems outside the regular command channels and frequently without the knowledge of the commanding officer. Such deviation from "correct" procedures may be widely condoned. Thus, many relatively junior officers exercise authority to which they are entitled neither by their rank nor by their formal position in the hierarchy. This implies that too precise an adherence to hierarchical channels will discourage this type of informal communication among officers sharing responsibility for a mission.

The issues that are implicit in this debate can be seen more clearly in the wider discussion of the difficulties of introducing innovation into military organizations. Armed forces are traditionally held to distinguish between *structural* innovation and *operational* innovation. The former may be more readily accepted because it supports the quest for certainty about the internal and external environment. By contrast, dismantlement of one weapon system in favor of a new one always has a destabilizing effect on military organization, and the remote and uncertain advantages promised by their adoption in peacetime must always be balanced against the costs and disruptions of change of any sort. Hence, in the past, armies have almost invariably gone into battle with strategic concepts and weapons whose only improvement over those used in the previous war consisted of the elimination of obvious deficiencies. Such generalized resistance to new weapons is shown by the unwillingness to motorize the cavalry, to switch from battleship to carrier, and to give up the bomber in favor of missiles.

In view of the current emphasis both armed forces and the parent society place on weapons development, the problem of introducing major innovations into the military is of critical importance. There are some indications that despite their comparative willingness to accept structural changes and notwithstanding their innate organizational advantages, armed forces lag behind comparable civilian organizations in their ability to innovate. And it can be argued that, despite a heavy commitment to research and development, change in the military cannot be readily effected other than in peripheral matters. If, therefore, military organizations continue to insist on some outmoded structural forms, there must be some reason.

To begin with, investing structural means with a special sanctity is a feature of military organizations. Individuals everywhere who hold authority and responsibility fear being bypassed by subordinates. In addition, however, there are some specific factors within the military that encourage adherence to some routines, even after their utility has been questioned. Clear channels and routinized procedures are thus thought to help reduce uncertainty. They are considered to create a sense of confidence that during a crisis officers and soldiers at all levels of the organization will respond in accordance with their training. The second factor that inhibits the introduction of innovation is the tendency of every military institution to build its routines on the normal and its expectations on the expected. This being so, there can be no adequate test of the appropriateness of many military practices short of actual war.

The Military Professional

Traditionally, the term *military professional* referred to those soldiers whose lifetime career in the armed forces contrasted markedly with the lesser commitment of the citizen soldier, reservist, or auxiliary volunteer. Today, it also means that a member of the armed forces has characteristics in common with others who identify themselves with the professional self-image: doctors, lawyers, priests, accountants, and so on. It is, however, very evident that the military self-image predates the evolution in the nineteenth century of other occupational groups claiming professional status. Accordingly, while many of the characteristics of that early military self-image were adopted without change by those groups, others remain uniquely military. The degree of collegiality that is implicit, for example, in the notion of officership is not replicated in other occupations. The traditions of the officers' mess, the willing acceptance of a code of ethics, the retention of a sense of honor, and so on, emphasize the uniqueness of this form of professionalism. Not unexpectedly, therefore, the concept of the profession of arms is traditionally associated with officers and not enlisted personnel. This can be readily rationalized. The particular set of values and attitudes that makes up the professional ethos is seen to be most prevalent among commissioned officers, is rarely to be found among noncommissioned officers, and is thought not to exist among enlisted men.

Increasingly, however, this traditional image of the military profession is under critical review. There are two particular developments. First, armed forces are a unique example of the total fusion of profession and organization. Since the military professional can only be employed within the structure of the total institution, many of the characteristics of the ideal type are modified. As the organization becomes increasingly bureaucratized, these characteristics begin to change very markedly. Expertise becomes skill; the commitment of the professional to the client is recast as the subordination of the soldier to the government of the day; professional responsibility is confused with organizational loyalty; collegiality conflicts with the rigid hierarchy of formal rank. For many members of the military, this change to the traditional military image is the source of considerable personal stress and occupational strain. This is particularly marked among those whose perception of the armed forces recognizes that the military is more than just an organization.

A second development encourages a shift away from the traditional professional model of the military toward an occupational model. The concept of the professional soldier has never been static. Over time, a number of significant changes have transformed the officer corps from a group of part-time employed, neo-feudal soldiers to a well-educated, technologically competent, and managerially trained group of experts recruited on the basis of their achievement and skill. As part of this transformation, there has been a shift away from the concept of the soldier as the professional working within an institutional format to one that resembles more and more an occupational ideal type.

In the institutional model, the military profession is legitimized in terms of its values and norms. Self-interest is subservient to a presumed higher good. Membership in the armed forces is seen to be a vocation in which a paternalistic remuneration system based on rank and seniority may not be comparable with marketplace trends. The high status enjoyed by the military is, however, some compensation for employment conditions and the dangers inherent in combat. In the occupational model, the military career is defined in terms of the marketplace. The cash-work nexus implies a priority of self-interest that contrasts markedly with the traditional preference for community interest. The military professional is now seen to be no different from any other worker in terms of the attitudes and values that are projected.

An alternative approach sheds doubt on the efficacy of this model as an indicator of the dimensions of change within the military organization. This argues that institution and occupation are not opposite poles in a comparable dimension but are really two relatively autonomous positions, the developmental trends of which may well be in the same direction. This does not reflect a zero-sum situation; rather, it draws attention to the utility of the concept of pragmatic professionalism as a measure of institutional and occupational concerns. The central feature of this interpretation of military professionalism is the conclusion that the military is essentially a bureaucratic profession. Here, the fusion of profession and organization is most evident. The introduction of unions into the military is a case in point. Traditionally, the absence of trade unions within armed forces, other than for civilian employees, seemingly confirmed the validity of the institutional model. Linked to the innate conservatism of armed forces and their tendency to promote a traditional self-image that was heavily dependent on established norms and values, this rejection of unionization implied an extreme stance. Yet the gradual introduction of military unions into the organization did not lead to the loss or replacement of the unique features of the military organization. Many military unions resemble professional associations rather than civilian trade unions. Although there has been a change in the basis of authority and discipline in the military establishment by virtue of a shift from authoritarian domination to greater reliance on manipulation, persuasion, and group consensus, it has not gone as far as it has in civilian organizations. The armed services in industrialized and many developing nations remain a highly professionalized and distinctive social organization. In some instances, however, armed forces do not attain this status. Guerrilla units, for example, are noticeably distinctive social organizations with well-developed cohesion and ideology, but they do not fall into the category of highly professionalized organizations.

Originally, the issue of recruitment was of significance solely in terms of the numbers inducted into the military. Subsequently, it was important because of the level of professionalism associated with entry into the armed forces. The types of people who were recruited provide valuable information on changes in social composition and in the motivation of personnel. The issue was also important since, as the officer corps became more socially representative and more heterogeneous, it became difficult to maintain organizational effectiveness. In addition, the recruitment process was of fundamental significance because it provided the means to continue the organization's existence.

For many years, a major issue in industrialized countries was the debate about the legitimacy and potential effectiveness of a system of universal conscription or national service as a means of recruitment, as opposed to a selective service system in which lotteries, appeals to local draft boards, and the like meant that only a fraction of those potentially liable to conscription were actually inducted. Extensive sociological studies were complemented by perceptive analyses of the economic advantages and disadvantages of conscription. In the United States, however, the end of the war in Vietnam and the concomitant cessation of the draft meant that the major issue became that of the problematic nature of recruitment into an all-volunteer force (AVF). This led very naturally to an evaluation of the probable social composition of an all-volunteer force in the United States. Two conflicting schools of thought could be identified. One viewpoint, influential at top American policy-making levels, argued that with proper monetary inducements an all-volunteer force could be recruited that would in general terms be representative of the larger society. The opposite view held that an all-volunteer force, especially in the ground combat arms, would grossly overrepresent less well educated and minority groups.

Outside the United States, much of this debate reflected a specific rather than universal management problem. Few issues could be readily identified as methodological and conceptual questions that were of more than local interest. One of these, however, is the vigor and emotive issue of the role of women in armed forces. This has a wider importance than the basic question of the general problems of recruitment into the contemporary military organization. Three questions of critical import can be identified. First, there is the major issue of the identification and evaluation of the role of women in the military organization. Second, there is an increasing awareness of the effect upon organizational issues of enhanced recruitment of female personnel: relative costs, problems of socialization, morale and attrition rates, and fundamental questions of operational effectiveness. The third issue, in common with much research into the complex area of race relations and ethnicity in armed forces, is more concerned with the societal implications of changing established and traditional manpower policies. In this context the issue is not simply the technical competence of women soldiers. Nor is it solely a question of the impact that the recruitment of women has had on the organizational effectiveness of the military. Rather, the critical area of interest is part of a more general concern with the implications for society of contemporary manpower changes within the military organization.

To a very great extent, the crux of these manpower issues is the fundamental problem of recruiting an adequate number of suitably qualified personnel. This is linked not only to immediate questions of cost but also to more fundamental issues of social policy. Maintaining the armed forces is a classic example of choice under uncertainty. It involves politicians in choices about the desirable size and composition of various budgets. This in turn encourages a welfare-warfare controversy in which the competing claims of the military and civil sectors of society have to be judged. For some countries, the choice is between guns and butter. Since the military is a heavy user of material and human resources, the creation of large and expensive armed forces prevents the development of other parts of the social system. This trend may be justified if the military makes a qualitative and quantitative contribution to the creation and perpetuation of innovation. This modernizing role is rationalized on the grounds that the military is the most modern institution in a country, that its leaders are the most effective managers, that military socialization most readily transmits culture, and that it serves as the symbol of nationhood. Such justification is less rational in those industrialized countries where the choice is more dichotomized as welfare or warfare.

The problem is particularly acute when the scarce resource is that of manpower. When faced with this problem, governments have traditionally adopted one of five options. First, some relied heavily on conscription as a means of bringing into the military organization an adequate number of recruits. Alternatively, in adopting an all-volunteer force structure, governments depended on a whole variety of motivating factors, ranging from market forces to appeals to patriotism, as a means of meeting manpower targets. Third, smaller and, it can be argued, less vulnerable states in the West created military structures based on the notion of the "citizen-soldier," which is the assumption that a small cadre of professional soldiers could be readily supplemented in time of emergency by civilian reservists. A fourth option, in contrast, depended for its effectiveness not on the mass availability of manpower but on substitution policies that replaced men with machines. Finally, governments continually used their preferences for compromise solutions to devise mixed strategies that combined one or more of these options.

Military Effectiveness

Initially, the effectiveness of a military organization is linked to the suitability of its organizational structure. The simple system of organization, which is adequate for peacetime operations, is transformed in time of conflict into a complex form capable of responding to the exigencies of wartime. Effective combat performance is thought to result from the effective operation of the formal military organization. This includes positive military leadership, discipline, and the esprit de corps of the military formation. Military effectiveness is also defined in terms of combat effectiveness. Many studies of the latter originated during the course of World War II. These stressed that a key explanation of such effectiveness was the solidarity and social cohesion of military personnel at the small-group level. In the abnormal situation of combat, men from different socioeconomic backgrounds, of different ethnic origins and lifestyles are expected to unify as a single fighting unit. Individual and group performance in terms of courage, discipline, enthusiasm, and willingness to endure is initially very dependent on the solidarity of the small group with whom the individual identifies. Cohesion can be identified with the peer relationships that occur within the primary group. Participant observation in Korea suggested that while the basic unit of cohesion in World War II followed squad or platoon boundaries, this had changed to the two-man or "buddy" relationship. Subsequent operations indicated that the "brick" or four-man patrol was the smallest effective subdivision. In all instances, this horizontal cohesion or peer bonding is associated with a common sense of mission within a specific technical proficiency, a deep appreciation of the importance of teamwork, and a reliance on mutual trust, respect, and friendship.

It is complemented by other forms of bonding. Vertical cohesion involves the relationship within the organization of enlisted personnel, noncommissioned officers, and officers. This comprises not only formal military authority but also more subtle features of leadership such as concern, example, trust, and sharing of risks, which transcend the officially laid down bureaucratic hierarchy. Organizational cohesion, in contrast, stresses the importance of normative concepts of tradition, patriotism, valor, heroism, nationhood, and ideology; these bond the individual soldier or officer to the subunit within the broader context of the military system. These explanations of combat motivation, originating in the social science studies of World War II, tend to deemphasize ideological considerations. The attention they give to the role of face-to-face or primary groups in formulating the motivation of the individual stresses that this motivation is a function of his solidarity and social intimacy with fellow soldiers at small-group levels. An alternative explanation, however, finds combat motivation resting on the presumed national character of the general populace. The varying effectiveness of different national armies has often been popularly ascribed to the putative martial spirit of their respective citizenries. The use of national-character explanations of military effectiveness, however, is not unique to popular folklore. In recent American history, certain prominent spokesmen invoked such broad cultural determinants to explain the allegedly poor performance of American prisoners of war in the Korean War. All of this can be seen, in part, as cultural cohesion—that is, the relationship of the military and the individual to society at large. An increasingly important aspect of this is the willingness of a society to support the military system it has established. Some of this support will be reflected in the size of the national defense budget; some will be linked to the expressed preference for a conscript or all-volunteer military force. All will reflect the extent to which armed forces are recognized by society as a reflection of the norms, values, mores, and cultural ethos of that society.

Civil-Military Relations

The term *civil-military relations* summarizes the complex network of political interests that exists between the various branches of the military and the various sectors of civilian society. Traditionally, the doctrine of civil-military relations presumes a series of checks and balances. Armed forces are identified as the managers of violence; civil power on the other hand exercises political control over the military. This democratic model of civil-military relations ensures that the civilian and military elites are sharply differentiated, for the civilian political elites exercise control over the military through a formal set of rules that ensures the objective control of the armed forces. This model is seen not as a reflection of historical reality but rather as an objective of governmental policy. It contrasts markedly with an aristocratic model where the civilian and military elites are socially and functionally integrated. The narrow base of recruitment for both elites and the presence of a relatively monolithic power structure combine to provide for the comprehensive subjective control of the military. It is also different from a totalitarian model in which political regimes manipulate a whole series of control mechanisms to ensure the politicization of military personnel. It can also be distinguished from the garrison state model, which identifies the rise to power of the military elite under conditions of prolonged international tension.

The contemporary preference for the ideology of the democratic model is most marked. Even so, the dangers inherent in the perception of civil-military relations are not ignored. The danger of praetorianism is very real. Praetorianism characterizes a situation in which the military elite within a society exercise independent political power by virtue of an actual or theoretical use of force. In terms of organization and coherence, armed forces possess many advantages over comparable civilian organizations. Centralization, a hierarchy of authority, discipline, a communications network and a commonly accepted ethos, indicate that the military is more highly organized than civilian bodies. A concern with order, which stems from the function of armed forces as crisis organizations, encourages the development of hyperbureaucratization. This ensures that armed forces are not only the most highly organized association but are also a continuing corporation with an intense sentiment of solidarity.

This power makes it possible for armed forces to intervene in the domain of the civil authority and, under certain conditions, to supplant that authority. Whether the military will have the motive or, indeed, the opportunity to so intervene will depend on a number of complex factors. In some countries, the tendency of armed forces to intervene, the motive to intervene, and the opportunity to intervene are such that the military coup d'état is an almost endemic feature of political life. This is not a new phenomenon. In the nineteenth century, many European and Latin American countries were plagued by coups. In the present day, military intervention frequently occurs in the states that have won their freedom from colonial domination. This is especially noticeable where the civilian government cannot assert its legitimacy, or where such a government is ineffective. In the latter case, the military represents a relatively efficient and stable instrument of power.

Once power has been seized, the ability of the armed forces to continue in office and to govern efficiently invites critical evaluation. Notwithstanding their structural and organizational advantages, armed forces have little technical ability to administer the complex modern state. The demands of a sophisticated economy, the promotion of schemes of social welfare, the need for a highly developed division of labor, and the wish to ensure the effective management of innovation favor the employment of civilian technicians and bureaucrats. Tasks such as resource allocation, the provision of specialized skills, and the need to respond to "civilian" problems create cross-pressures for armed forces. It may be possible for a military organization to respond to these pressures through enhanced internal differentiation. Alternatively, a valid response may result in the creation of specialized units, either on an ad hoc basis or as part of a more regular plan of activity. A third solution, however, is for the military to cooperate more and more with civilian agencies.

A more major and persistent critical issue is the legitimization of the military's claim to remain in power. Following a military coup, the questions that ultimately arise are: How is the intervention in politics to be legitimized? And to whom can the military look in search of legitimacy? In rare instances, the legitimacy of armed forces is unquestioned. The military is uniquely identified with the national interest. Armed forces are seen to be the origin of the independent nation-state and the last bastion of nationhood. Armies are not merely part of the administrative bureaucracy. Their claim to a monopoly of arms gives them a special status that enables them to symbolize, as well as make effective, the distinctive identity of the state. From this point of view, no other national institution so symbolizes independence, sovereignty, or equality with other peoples as a country's armed forces. Armed forces are the synthesis of the nation and the purest image of the state. Their power is legitimate, because it is based on an authority exercised in the establishment and maintenance of goals that are defined in terms of the basic needs of the state.

In most cases, the claim of the military to effective and general legitimacy is less easily established. True legitimacy can only be ensured by the transfer from direct military rule to various types of civilian rule. There are two major modes of transfer: abdication and civilianization. In the former, armed forces willingly or unwillingly hand back the reins of power to the civilian elite; in the latter, the military elite itself becomes civilianized. In both instances the pattern of civil-military relations recognizes that true legitimacy exists only when the respective political roles of the military and civil elite can be sharply differentiated. Even the special relationships between the military and industry that are implicit in the controversial term *military-industrial complex* do not weaken this preference for the distinctiveness of those political roles.

Future Developments

The traditional interpretation of the concept of armed forces and society draws heavily on historical models. These were very well established in Western society. The pattern of relationships that evolved from the seventeenth century onward was not only accepted in Western Europe, it was exported overseas and retained by new nations as they gained independence. The basis of the relationship was the role and function of the military in two distinct but related areas. First, armed forces were seen to have the major objectives of protecting the state from an external aggressor and the promotion of its political interests through the coercion of other states. Second, the legitimate role of the military was identified with the protection of the state from internal threats. This objective included maintaining the duly-elected government. Both distinctive external and internal functions represented the formal purpose of the military organization.

Over time, this formal structure has been considerably amended. The domestic function of the military has been extended to include the responsibilities of armed forces as agents of modernization. In many developing countries, the social and political significance of these armed forces as agents of economic development are most marked. A wider analysis of the role of the military in national modernization questions the changes that the intervention of armed forces brings about. Structural and attitudinal changes contrast with the effects of sociodemographic change. The potential for sustained natural growth invites an examination of the quality and quantity of military-sponsored change in terms of economic differentiation, communication, urbanization, and political development. In the latter area, the military's effectiveness invites a particularly critical examination. This reflects the awareness of the major role of armed forces in such areas of political growth as natural integration and the institutionalization of political organization.

An alternative feature of this future development is the changing role of armed forces in an era of nuclear stalemate and the effect of this change upon traditional interpretations of the relationship between armed forces and society. The use of force as an instrument of foreign policy has been so changed that the future role of the military can be identified with the constabulary concept. While this provides a continuity with the past experience of armed forces, it reflects a radical interpretation of future military purpose. The military establishment is seen to become a constabulary force where it is always prepared to act and committed to the minimum use of force. Its goal is the attainment of satisfactory international relations rather than victory, and it incorporates a protective military position (Janowitz 1960). When the trend toward the internationalization of these constabulary forces is added to this adoption of a pragmatic doctrine, the traditional perception of the relationship between a military organization and the parent society is much altered. Nevertheless, for the moment, the complex relationship between armed forces and the parent society persists. Change in the internal dynamic of the military organization will be inevitable; society will reflect, in its attitudes toward the military, the impact of altered norms and values. Armed forces and society, however, will continue to be an important example of a necessary and realistic public discussion about the control of an all-powerful purposive organization.

GWYN HARRIES-JENKINS

SEE ALSO: Civil-Military Relations; Combat Effectiveness; Manpower, Military; Militarism; Morale; Organization, Military; Professionalism, Military; Social Science Research and Development; Sociology, Military; Unit Cohesion; Women in the Armed Forces.

Bibliography

Andreski, S. 1954. *Military organization and society.* London: Routledge and Kegan Paul.

Demeter, K. 1935. *Das Deutsche Heer und Seine Offiziere.* Berhn: Verlag von Reimar Hobbing.

Edmonds, M. 1988. *Armed services and society.* Leicester: Leicester Univ. Press.

Harries-Jenkins, G. 1977. *The army in Victorian society.* London: Routledge and Kegan Paul.

———, and C. C. Moskos. 1981. Armed forces and society. *Current Sociology* 29:1–170.

Huntington, S. P. 1957. *The soldier and the state: The theory and politics of civil-military relations.* Cambridge, Mass.: Harvard Univ. Press.

Janowitz, M. 1960. *The professional soldier.* New York: Free Press.

———. 1977. *Military institutions and coercion in the developing nations.* Chicago: Univ. of Chicago Press.

Lasswell, H. D. 1941. The garrison state. *American Journal of Sociology* 46:455–68.

Moskos, C. C., Jr., and Frank R. Wood, eds. 1988. *The military—More than just a job?* McLean, Va.: Pergamon-Brassey's.

Stouffer, S. A., et al. 1949. *The American soldier.* Princeton, N.J.: Princeton Univ. Press.

Van Doorn, J. 1975. *The soldier and social change.* Beverly Hills, Calif.: Sage.

ARMENIA

Armenia, one of the fifteen former republics in the Union of Soviet Socialist Republics (USSR), joined ten other Soviet republics in dissolving the Union on 21 December 1991 when they agreed to form the new Commonwealth of Independent States. This dramatic end to the Soviet and Communist state followed several years of dynamic and unprecedented change. For several more years, relations between members of the new Commonwealth and with the rest of the world are likely to continue to change. Over time, new structures and patterns will emerge in economics, trade and commerce, politics and government, finance, manufacturing, religion, and virtually all aspects of human life. New arrangements must be devised for dealing separately as sovereign states and as a Commonwealth with the world outside the boundaries of the former Soviet state. If the history of the Soviet Union since 1985 is any guide, we can expect dramatic surprises and dynamic change.

An important question for the world is how the new states and the Commonwealth will organize and provide for their security. The Soviet Union's armed forces, formerly the largest in the world, are likely to be withdrawn from foreign territory, reduced in size, and divided up between the former republics. Also of great concern is the disposition of the largest arsenal of nuclear weapons, the security of these weapons, the command and control of their potential use, and compliance with arms control agreements entered into by the former Soviet government. The world can only hope these issues are settled amicably.

It will be years before all of these issues are resolved for Armenia and some time before events settle down into more routine and measurable patterns. No accurate description of this new country's policies, defense structure, and military forces was available to be included in this encyclopedia. Only time will reveal the future of Armenia as a separate sovereign state. The reader is thus referred to the historic information contained in the article "Soviet Union," and to the latest annual editions of the *Military Balance*, published by Brassey's (UK) for the International Institute of Strategic Studies; the *Statesman's Year-Book* published by the Macmillan Press Ltd and St. Martin's Press; and the *World Factbook*, developed by the U.S. Central Intelligence Agency and published commercially by Brassey's (US).

F. D. MARGIOTTA
Executive Editor

ARMOR

Armor serves to protect men and vehicles on land, at sea, and in the air by means of protective covering and specialized equipment. The term *armor* is used here as a collective term for all armored combat vehicles.

Historical Development

By the early Bronze Age (ca. 3500 B.C.) primitive fighting among groups of Paleolithic men had evolved to include concepts of organized warfare. Protection against rocks, clubs, and arrows was provided by hand-held shields, often of leather stretched and hardened over wooden frames, but all-wood and wicker shields were also used. Protection covering was also developed for the head, torso, and legs.

The dagger and the sword were the first new weapons of the metallic era, and bronze-reinforced shields, helmets, breast plates, and greaves evolved to become entirely made of bronze and later of iron. Early armor extended to horses and chariots, small armored carts drawn by one or more armor-clad horses. Prior to about 700 B.C. chariots constituted the elite force of ancient armies. The great Kurusch (Cyrus) of Persia is supposed to have built chariots for twenty warriors, who dismounted to continue fighting. This early version of the armored personnel carrier shows that the concept of delivering men swiftly, and protected, into fighting is not new.

Although the designed use of protective armor in warfare is limited only by the imagination, in practical application it is limited by the physical or mechanical ability to transport it about the battlefield. Before the industrial revolution made mechanization possible, the weight of armor used in combat was no more than could be borne by man or animal. Interesting applications appeared: Germanic warriors in the time of Ceasar used barricades of wagons, maneuvering these in close formation to engage Roman forces; in Italy in 1335 Guido Da Vigerano, and in 1482 Leonardo Da Vinci, designed armored combat vehicles, but they were too heavy to be of practical use; the use of protective wagons was revived and used by the Hussites in the fifteenth century; in Korea (ca. 1592–99), an ironclad ship in the shape of a tortoise helped defeat a Japanese fleet.

By the end of the Middle Ages (ca. 1400–1500), refinements in metalworking had advanced to the point where further improvements to armor would be only marginal, or would reduce mobility. Mounted knights, heavily clad in protective chain mail, armor plate, and helmets, their horses similarly encased, represented the elite shock troops of the day (Fig. 1). The evolution of weapons had generally surpassed the ability of armor to keep pace. The famous English longbow (of Welsh origin) had good penetrating power even at long ranges; crossbows were lethal at close range; determined Swiss pikemen could unseat a heavy cavalry charge. Most importantly, however, technology enabled the fielding of a new class of weapons—gunpowder cannon and small arms.

Gunpowder was known in China as early as the eleventh century, and made its way to Europe via East-West trade routes in the thirteenth century. The first gunpowder cannon in Europe were used in the early 1300s; small arms made their appearance in the latter half of the century.

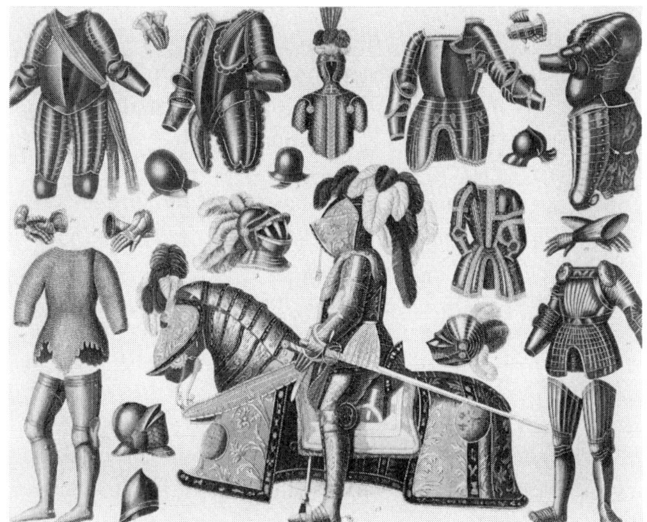

Figure 1. Examples of European armor in the Middle Ages. (SOURCE: U.S. Library of Congress)

The use of gunpowder began a new era of warfare. The armor of knights could not withstand projectiles propelled by gunpowder. With cannons, muskets, mortars, and later rifles and modern artillery, it became possible to fight an enemy from increasingly greater distances. As technology progressed, the rate of fire, range, and penetration power increased and handling became easier. Body armor for man and beast, already heavily leveraged by its weight, could not keep pace. Thereafter, efforts to improve protection and maintain mobility focused on a revival of the chariot. Various experiments included: a Scottish war chariot from the year 1456; a war chariot by Vaturio in 1472; a war chariot by Holzschuher in 1558; an armored steam tractor by Applegarth in 1886; and an armored wagon by Batter in 1888.

The object of these developmental efforts was to direct fire on the enemy and to make renewed use of mobility, which had brought the knight success. The power to move these vehicles, however, was insufficient. Muscle power was inadequate, and steam power was too cumbersome. The internal combustion engine would eventually improve to the point where it could provide a solution, but not until World War I.

With the introduction of the machine gun, in addition to the repeating rifle, the fire cadence of the individual soldier became equivalent to that of a whole company previously, and cover, or protection, from enemy fire increased dramatically in importance. The soldier dug his foxhole, and trench warfare began.

Otto's internal combustion engine led to Daimler's motor vehicle and soon to the idea of armoring the latter, thus making it a mobile means of combat. In the dynamics of modern combat, mobility had once again become significant. One of the first armored vehicles of modern times was built by Austro-Daimler in 1904. The prototype was remarkable for its revolving turret with built-in machine gun and all-wheel drive. It earned no recognition, however, and was never produced.

Ten years later, the Belgium army became the first to use vehicle-mounted machine guns in combat against attacking German troops. The Minerva armored fighting vehicle saw action in the autumn of 1914, and the British and French soon followed this example. The German supreme command did not decide to use this means of combat until 1916.

Because they lacked cross-country mobility, these armored vehicles were forced to stay on hard-surface roads, and street fighting did not provide opportunities to prove the value of these armored vehicles. These limitations were recognized before the war, and motivated Austrian First Lieutenant Burstyn to develop a combat vehicle that was inspired by the idea of sliding bands, or caterpillars. These endless bands of wire-netting mounted over two wheels offered armored vehicles a cross-country capability.

Burstyn's idea for a small, fast armored vehicle with catapillar treads, however, was rejected by the same institutions that had rejected Daimler's fighting vehicle. Germany acknowledged the need for a chain-driven combat vehicle only after the British, under the code name "Tank," developed and fielded a treaded armored vehicle in World War I in 1916.

Development of the Tank

The British First Lord of the Admiralty, Winston Churchill, had the mobility of sea warfare in mind when he called for the development of "land ships" in 1915 to break the deadlocked trench warfare on the Western Front. William Foster and E. D. Swinton conceived the first heavy battle tank. It weighed 27 tons, was adapted to the speed of marching soldiers, and was intended to accompany them when overcoming enemy field fortifications. Although their first use, at Flers-Courcelette on 15 September 1916, involved heavy losses because the crews were inexperienced, some tanks succeeded in making a deep penetration that reached their objectives and overpowered all resistance. This success led the army command to give orders for further production.

World War I Operational Doctrine and Technical Limitations

The introduction of tanks implied a return to mobile warfare. For the first time since the days of knights in armor, there was a sufficiently compact source of energy (the internal combustion engine) to make effective armored vehicles possible. The tank afforded protection against fire and made possible the penetration of the trench systems. This had the same effect on warfare as catapults of the early Middle Ages: fortifications were breached and provided the foot soldier with access to the defenders.

The first tanks had limited mobility, and thus were confined to overcoming field fortifications, while simultaneously holding down enemy infantry fire and affording covering fire to their own accompanying infantry. Although technology had broken the deadlock on the Western front, the infantry escort tank was developed on a narrow technical base: the motorized vehicle was not yet twenty years old, gear technology for heavy vehicles was very rudimentary, and the track and suspension configuration was based on that of U.S. Caterpillar farm tractors.

Interwar Period

After the end of the war, opinions on the operational potential of the tank diverged. Although the idea of tank warfare originated in Great Britain, no logical consequences followed their experience in combat. The British expert Liddell Hart described modern operational possibilities for the tank, but prior to World War II all Western countries, with the exception of Germany, had forgone the opportunities inherent in the tank.

By contrast, the German Wehrmacht paid attention to the lessons of the war and the German general staff listened to the suggestions, proposals, and reflections of Liddell Hart. After Hitler's rearmament, a modern tank force was organized. General Guderian created independent tank divisions equipped with new combat tanks that were fast and well-armored. The objectives of mobility, firepower, and protection had been achieved, and German tanks, operating on roads or across country and formed into independent divisions, became tools for Hitler's lightning war (blitzkrieg).

In addition to combat tanks, the Wehrmacht produced combat vehicles, known as assault guns, to support the infantry. These assault guns emphasized firepower, were more lightly armored than combat tanks, and took over the task of accompanying the infantry during an attack. The idea was to use these guns, mounted in a mobile casemate, primarily against machine gun emplacements to open a breach for the infantry.

World War II

At the beginning of the war, antiarmor weapons and munitions technology had not kept pace with tank armor. As the penetrating power of shells fired from antitank guns improved, however, armor plating on tanks was also thickened and improved. This increase in armor led to an increase in weight, and some tanks at the end of the war weighed more than 70 tons. Because engine power did not keep up with increases in weight, tank mobility began to suffer. The development of the hollow-cone, or shaped-charge ammunition provided the capability to defeat even the most heavily armored tank by the end of the war.

On the Eastern front, the strengthening of the Russian adversary brought an end to the success of the blitzkrieg, and the war degenerated into defensive combat against advancing tanks, first on the Russian and then on the German side. The combat tank turned into an antitank means of combat. The criticism of Liddell Hart was: "The wastage of such an effective force as the tank corps, by using it to combat enemy tank forces, is as foolish as the chess-player who opens his game by disposing of the queens."

Both sides followed this criticism and developed vehicles on the basis of tanks, but without a turret and with a high-velocity gun mounted in a casemate. These weapons, well armored at the front, usually had better cannon than an equivalent battle tank, but the mounting restricted movement in traverse and they were not suited to unaided defense. These tank destroyers were known as the "best tank killers."

The fighting doctrine was not to engage in battles of long duration, but to conduct short operations of limited length and proportions. The basic principle was the formation of points of main effort (i.e., concentration of greatest fighting capacity at decisive points).

Post-World War II

During the war the effect of the tank corps had been considerable, but the concluding event—the dropping of two atomic bombs on Japan by the United States—brought a momentous turn to world history. For a time, the tank seemed to have lost significance; atomic weapons had made all others obsolete. The Soviet development of atomic weapons and intercontinental ballistic missiles to deliver them seemed to result in a nuclear standoff between East and West, but this view proved illusory. Tanks again became important: in a conventional war without nuclear weapons, tanks would be a critical feature; in a war with nuclear weapons, the tank offered the best protection against blast, heat, and radiation of nuclear bursts.

Tank designers re-evaluated the parameter of mobility. Hit probability by ballistic missiles and rockets is largely dependent on the maneuverability and acceleration of the tank, and on its dimensions or outline. The operating range of tanks was extended, and lower fuel consumption was emphasized even as engines became more powerful. Maintenance features received attention; high reliability and thus high availability were deemed necessary for defenders who might be outnumbered.

The parameter of firepower was also studied in terms of system stability during firing, and fire control. Accuracy at ranges beyond 2,000 meters (6,600 ft.) was improved, and sighting systems aided fast target acquisition. Emphasis was placed on improved munitions in terms of an increase in caliber and in the penetration and detonation characteristics of the warhead.

When the Bundeswehr recommended tank development, it emphasized protection through mobility, an example that was followed by other countries. New armor protection developed in the late 1960s (armored bulkhead plating, compound plating) was further strengthened by the use of reactive armor. With these technical advances in protective materials, aided by improved engines, the parameter values of mobility and of protection became equivalent for the first time. This, combined with improved firepower through better ammunition and electronic fire control systems, gives the present-day tank an almost inconceivable fighting value in the dynamic course of any future conflict.

The Tank and Combined Arms Concepts

The original combat tanks were successful from a tactical point of view, but they were unable to hold their own for any length of time in captured territory without the coordinated support of other combat arms. The assistance in combat of infantry, artillery, engineers, scouts, and air support is vital to ensure the operational success of tank warfare.

Infantry

The British acquired the following basic knowledge from the first tank operations in World War I:

- The speed of the tank assault is determined by the accompanying infantry. A slow attack pace gave the defender time to take countermeasures in the depths of the battlefield.
- If the tank broke through without infantry, it became an easy target for the defender, especially if he could keep his nerve and had tank destroyer weapons at hand.

Successful attempts that breached defenses, therefore, were only successful if the infantry was brought up rapidly with the tanks, and with necessary protection from small arms and shell bursts. The British experimentally developed the first armored personnel carrier (APC), the Mark IX. After World War I, the French were the first to construct a combat vehicle for transporting infantrymen on the basis of a 15-ton lorry. The armored plating contained apertures for firing during mounted combat.

Some early theories expounded noncooperative "all-tank" themes. In 1919 J. F. C. Fuller, then chief of staff of the British tank corps command, presented "Plan 1919," in which he defined the question of collaboration between tanks and infantry: "Up till now the prevailing theory for the tactical use of tanks revolved around the reconciliation of their strength with existing combat methods, i.e., with the infantry and artillery tactics. Indeed, the tank idea, which revolutionized warfare methods, was applied to a system it was destined to destroy." He concluded, "the infantry as equipped at present, will become first an auxiliary weapon and later an impracticable weapon on any territory which can be driven through by tanks." The crux of the statement was that the equipment of the infantry was unsatisfactory.

The German Wehrmacht did not accept this view, and focused on turning infantrymen into motorized infantry. Using lightly armored semi-tracked vehicles, they were able to keep pace with tanks moving cross country. The modern armored personnel carrier concept was born and gave the armored infantry the possibility for tank assault "instantly followed in quick succession by exploitation and supplementation" (Guderian). The combination and cooperation of the battle tank with the APC in the German Wehrmacht created the basis for the blitzkrieg successes.

After World War II, the Bundeswehr retained this concept. It was consistent with the experience of military organizers and with the ideas of the Anglo-American expeditionary corps, evolving from their experiences. Initially, the Bundeswehr used American equipment and vehicles, but soon began development of its own fully-tracked armored personnel carrier, and later, the development of a German main battle tank.

By the 1970s, the concept of combining mechanized infantry in APCs with tank forces was well developed. The German Marder (the original Western armored personnel carrier) pioneered the concept with the Leopard I tank. The former Soviet Union's version of the APC, the multi-wheeled BTR-70, was used in a similar role. The U.S. M-113 was replaced in the 1980s by the M-2 and M-3 Bradley Infantry Fighting Vehicle (IFV) and Cavalry Fighting Vehicle (CFV), and emphasis continued on cooperation between the two combat arms.

One drawback of mechanized and motorized infantry forces is the relatively light armor plating of APCs and IFVs. Increasing the armor protection is impractical for several reasons: cost; battlefield mobility; and vehicle size, or payload.

Armored personnel carriers are designed to carry an infantry squad of 8 to 12 soldiers. In the attack, it is important that the infantry be delivered into the breach made by tanks as quickly as possible. Armored and mechanized tactics have adapted so that the APCs follow the tanks instead of being commingled with them, where they would become initial targets for antiarmor systems. The U.S. Bradley has somewhat offset this, but it is still a far more vulnerable vehicle than a main battle tank.

Some critics have suggested that the proliferation of effective antitank weapons, especially antitank guided missiles (ATGM), will lead to the end of the mobile tank warfare. The 1973 October War led to intensive analysis of the value of the combat tank in light of the numerous successes of antitank missiles. The French military historian Mischke implied that the tank had reached its limit of development and cost effectiveness. He cited that in the first 10 days of the October War 2,700 of 6,000 tanks involved had been destroyed.

Counterarguments that focused on tactical countermeasures for antitank defenses prevailed, however, and the Israelis succeeded in breaking through Arab antitank systems, and restored the full mobility of their tanks. The prerequisite for the restoration of offensive mobility was the optimal collaboration of all arms, the infantry in particular. At the beginning of the war the cooperation of Israeli armor and infantry was minimal, and lacked a strong collaborative structure. When this was changed and an effective structure implemented as a battlefield tactic, the war turned in favor of the Israelis.

Artillery

Indirect fire support units form the essential third leg of the combat triad of armor, infantry, and artillery. As a consequence of increasingly effective methods of counter-battery artillery fire, improvements in artillery protection resulted in lightly armored, self-propelled artillery howitzers.

Improvements in artillery-delivered munitions, such as scatterable mines and smart munitions, have been a cause of concern for tanks and APCs. Concepts for employment have varied, and depend on the situation. To achieve surprise, German attacks in World War II often held the use of artillery until the last moment, or it was not used at all. Blitzkreig emphasized dive bombers in providing fire support for attacking tanks, and surprise was often achieved because there was no extensive artillery preparation to give away the plan.

In contrast, extensive use of artillery fire in support of attacking armor and mechanized formations was used in Operation Desert Storm (February 1991). Artillery rockets were used in a counterbattery role and to scatter mines to deny Iraqi forces maneuverability. Howitzer fire suppressed Iraqi formations, pinning them so that tank-gun fire and infantry antitank guided missile fire could have maximum effect.

Armored, self-propelled mortars are also a feature of indirect fire support weapons. At firing ranges of 6 to 8 kilometers (approx. 4–5 mi.) self-propelled mortars come into their own, with a firing efficiency greater than that of longer-range artillery pieces. Originally mounted in caterpillar-tracked chassis, they have evolved with all-around protection against shell splinters, small-arms fire, and possible nuclear-biological-chemical (NBC) attack.

Engineers

Antitank mines were one of the early devices used to stop or slow tanks and deny them use of terrain. Mines can be effective in destroying a tank, but often they take them out of action by damaging a tread, thus eliminating their mobility. Other methods of hindering tank advances involve tank ditches and traps, and uncrossable blocks of concrete (dragon teeth).

To counter these obstacles, the support of combat engineers is necessary. Engineer tanks, equipped with dozer blades, mine-clearing flails or wheels, excavator shovels, and jib cranes, help to fill trenches, clear paths through mine fields, and breach obstacles. In defensive operations, engineer tanks can help prepare defilade fighting positions for tanks and APCs.

An interesting feature of combat engineer vehicles is the armored vehicle launched bridge (AVLB). The AVLB is a bridge-laying tank with the turret removed and replaced by a bridge with powered hydraulics to extend the frame in scissors or cantilever fashion. AVLBs have protection against small arms and shell fragments, and can accommodate spans from 15 to 20 meters (50–66 ft.) over rivers and ditches.

Armored Scouts

Despite electronic, optronic, and optical reconnaissance by aircraft, drones, and satellites, the tank corps still cannot dispense with the human scout: the reconnaissance soldier. In mechanized fighting, the scout is equipped with an armored reconnaissance vehicle, a lightly armored combat vehicle that emphasizes silent operation, obstacle negotiations capabilities (e.g., fording, flotation, and water navigation), maneuverability, and a low profile.

The use of optical, optronic, and electronic sensors, combined with a long-range method of communication and precise navigation instruments, enable a scout patrol leader to carry out comprehensive missions and transmit findings quickly to appropriate command levels. Because reconnaissance vehicles are only lightly protected by armor plate, a good scout will avoid becoming involved in combat as far as possible.

The armament on reconnaissance vehicles varies from light machine guns to antitank missiles in accordance with different concepts for their use. The U.S. M-3 Bradley is used as a scouting vehicle with armored and mechanized forces and is designed to withstand more punishment than lighter scout vehicles such as the versatile French Panhard VBL. The M-3 also mounts TOW ATGMs, which can kill tanks at ranges exceeding 3,500 meters (approx. 2.5 mi.).

Close Air Support

Armored and mechanized forces derive a great benefit from the fire-support capability of attack helicopters and mission-specific aircraft such as the U.S. A-10 Warthog. By necessity, these flying machines cannot be too heavily armored, yet some armor plating around sensitive areas is incorporated into their design. More important is the contribution they make to the ground fighting forces by overcoming opposing armor and APCs with ATGMs, rockets, and rapid-firing mini-guns.

The value of attack helicopters is their high mobility and capability to deliver fire support quickly to different parts of the battlefield. Some modern concepts view the mobility advantage as permitting the tank to be replaced by the attack helicopter. In certain situations—surprise attack, or where terrain is difficult—this may be partly true, but the attack helicopter is not intended to be an airborne replacement for the tank. Rather, the cooperation of this air arm with the ground arms remains as originally conceived.

Other Armored Support Vehicles

With the possible exception of airborne and light infantry forces, armored protection of some sort has become ubiquitous in modern warfare. Armor plating has evolved from frontal shields on antitank guns of World War II to enclosures of the entire gun casemate mounted on a mobile platform today. Other armored fighting vehicles consist of self-propelled antitank missile launchers such as the combination BMP-1 with a Sagger ATGM mounted on top of its 73mm gun (Hungary), and self-propelled air defense tanks that use a search radar to acquire airborne targets and guide munitions to distances of 6 to 8 kilometers (approx. 4–5 mi.). In addition, there are armored recovery vehicles used to pull damaged tanks and APCs from the battlefield under fire, and armored transport vehicles to deliver combat supplies to the fighting troops.

Combined Arms Performance

The combat tank of today requires the support of other combat vehicles to guarantee an effective performance. In order to achieve optimal collaboration, the latter should have comparable mobility and protection. The combined armored forces should represent the synthesis of firepower, mobility, and protection. If one of the component arms lacks a particular characteristic, the combined force may be unable to fulfill its mission.

The main battle tank and the combat vehicles that support it can be the most potent tool in the hands of an aggressive commander. Operational possibilities of the combined armored force symbolize a potential for implementing aggressive policy; equally, they symbolize the ability to deter, or to defeat, such action.

Future Tank Development

Since their first use at Flers-Courcelette on 15 September 1916, tactics and technology have influenced, complemented, and made demands on the primary tank features of firepower, mobility, and protection. Early ammunition has moved from high-explosive to shaped-charge to high-velocity, kinetic energy rounds with pinpoint accuracy at increasing ranges. Electro-optic technology has vastly improved target acquisition, firing speed, and accuracy. Mobility has improved with advances in automotive technology that has continually increased the power-to-weight ratio of internal combustion engines. Protection has improved in terms of armor thickness (initially), improved steel plating techniques, and design of sloping front and sides. Although perhaps at an optimal position vis-à-vis trade-offs between the key parameters, there seems still to be room for improvement.

Future improvements in firepower will come from several sources: improved auto-loading mechanisms; larger-caliber warheads; so-called "smart" munitions with target recognition microelectronic guidance systems; higher-speed kinetic energy penetrators powered by new propulsion mechanisms; and advances in intelligence collection, filtering, fusion, and distribution systems.

Of these, auto-loaders are of particular interest because they can lead to a reduction in crew size, and thus to a different tank configuration. The possibility of automating, or of semi-automating, other crew functions is also being researched. Also of interest are developments in electromagnetic, or rail, guns that have demonstrated the ability to hurl rounds at hypervelocity speeds approaching 10 kilometers (6.2 mi.) per second. Power requirements at present prohibit the development and fielding of a practical weapon, but should one become possible, it is difficult to imagine armor that might provide protection from such a weapon.

Advances in mobility will come from either a reduction in the overall weight of the armored vehicle, or an increase in engine power for the same weight of engine; gears and power train components will have to keep pace. Developments in lighter-weight engines with ceramic materials and lighter metal alloys have shown promise, particularly for aircraft engines. These advances could extend to engines for ground mobility platforms. Reductions in the weight of armor while maintaining the same protective capability can also contribute to improved mobility.

New classes of composite materials are being researched and developed for use in many applications. Light-weight plastic composites are used in some armor plating; other types of composite materials have already been used for body armor, and extensions of this existing technology may find applications in armored vehicles. Improvements in reactive armor plating may also be developed, and can be a defense against both kinetic-energy rounds and shaped-charge rounds.

One possible future for armored vehicles is the combination into one system of the tank and the armored personnel carrier. If the power-to-weight ratio of engines can be increased and composite armor can afford the same protection for less weight, and if crew size can be reduced, it will be possible to combine tank and APC in one vehicle. This concept would be a further development of the Israeli combat tank Merkava (Chariot). The Merkava, with its engine and drive train forward, features a tank turret and space in its rear for 6 to 8 infantrymen. Improvement on this idea is possible and would not mean a reduction in fighting value. In sum, it would be cheaper than fielding a tank and an infantry APC team, and could perform the same cooperative mission.

Paul-Werner Krapke

See Also: Arab-Israeli Wars; Armored Ground Vehicle; Blitzkrieg; Guderian, Heinz; Gun, Antitank; Helicopter, Battlefield; Manstein, Erich von; Mechanized Warfare; Patton, George Smith, Jr.; Rommel, Erwin; Tank; Tukhachevsky, Mikhail Nikolaevich; World War II; Zhukov, Georgii Konstantinovich.

Bibliography

Albrecht, W. 1973. *Gunther Burstyn (1879–1945) und die Entwicklung der Panzerwaffe.* Osnabrück: Biblio-Verlag.

Chamberlain, P., and Ellis, C. 1972. *Britische und amerikanische Panzer des Zweiten Weltkrieges.* München: Verlag Lehmann.

Dupuy, R. E., and T. N. Dupuy. 1986. *The encyclopedia of military history.* 2d rev. ed. New York: Harper and Row.

Eimannsberger, L., Ritter von. 1934. *Der Kampfwagen.* München: I. F. Lehmann Verlag.

Foss, C. F. 1971. *Armoured vehicles of the world.* London: Allan.

Frentag, Taktische und oerative Verwendung moderner Tanks in der Roten Armee. 1932. *Militär-Wochenblatt,* no. 3.

Fuller, I. F. 1937. *Erinnerungen eines freimütigen Soldaten.* Stuttgart: Rowolt Verlag.

Gaulle, C. de. 1935. *Frankreichs Stossarmee.* Potsdam: Voggenreiter.

Guderian, H. 1937. *Die Panzertruppe und ihr Zusammenwirken mit den anderen Waffen.* Berlin: Union Verlag.

———. 1952. *Erinnerungen eines Soldaten.* London: Michael Joseph.

———. 1957. *Panzer-Marsch.* München: Schild Verlag.

Heigl's Taschenbuch der Tanks. 1971. Teil III: *Der Panzerkampf.* München: Verlag Lehmann.

Hillgruber, A. 1940–41. *Hitler's Strategie Politik und Kriegführung.* Koblenz: Bernard und Graefe.

Hubatsch, W. 1958. *Hitler's Weisungen für die Kriegführung.* Frankfurt/Main: Verlag für Wehrwesen.

Justrow, K. 1938. *Der technische Krieg.* Berlin: Claasen-Verlag.

Krapke, P. W. 1986. *Leopard 2, sein Werden und seine Leistungen.* Herford: Mittler und Sohn.

Liddell Hart, B. H. 1940. *Das Buch vom Heer.* Potsdam: Voggenreiter.

Miksche, F. O. 1941. *Blitzkrieg.* London: Faber and Faber.

Mostowenko, W. D. 1940. *Panzer gestern und heute.* Berlin: Deutscher Militärverlag.

Nehring, W. K. 1974. *Die Geschichte der Panzerwaffe von 1916–1945.* Stuttgart: Propyläen Verlag.

Ogorkiewicz, R. R. 1960. *Armour.* London: Stevens and Sons.

Spannenkrebs, W. 1939. *Angriff mit Panzerkampfwagen.* Oldenburg: Gerhard Stolling.

ARMOR TECHNOLOGY

Armor ranges from personal armor designed to protect individuals from shell fragments and small-arms projectiles to battleship armor intended to resist penetration by naval shells and large missile warheads. If stationary armored fortifications are included, the range of possibilities is further enlarged. The threats against which armor provides protection range from milligram-sized fragments to warheads weighing hundreds of kilograms, and in velocity from a few hundred meters per second to more than 10,000 meters per second. Furthermore, although the chief purpose of armor is to prevent penetration by projectiles, it may also be called upon to provide structural support, resistance to blast, reduction of damage by penetrating hits, and protection against radiation—both nuclear and that from focused-energy weapons.

Given the variety of levels of protection required, and the diversity of the threats, it is understandable that armor has evolved in a complex manner and that it exploits a wide variety of technologies. The limitations on the protection that armor can afford are usually imposed by competing requirements for mobility, safety of accompanying vehicles or troops, or economics.

This article addresses only the use of armor for protection against ballistic threats. The requirements for radiation protection are very different and they compete for weight and cost allowances in overall survivability design.

Threat-Damage Mechanisms

The kinds of ammunition against which armor is used to provide protection may be divided into two general categories: kinetic energy ammunition (Fig. 1) and explosive warheads (Fig 2).

Kinetic Energy Ammunition

Antipersonnel bullets. These are small arms projectiles designed specifically for use against personnel rather than for armor penetration. The masses of such projectiles are in the range of 10 to 100 grams; velocities are usually in the range of 200 to 1,000 meters per second (m/s).

Armor-piercing (AP) shot. These full-caliber projectiles are designed specifically for penetration of armor. They range from small arms bullets with a mass less than 10 grams to battleship-fired projectiles of more than 1,000 kilograms. The most important class of AP shot, historically, has been antitank rounds ranging in caliber from 75mm to 120mm and weighing as much as 20 kg. They have universally been made of very hard steel; the ratio of length to diameter (L/D) is usually about 2:1. The length is limited by the conditions required for flight stability.

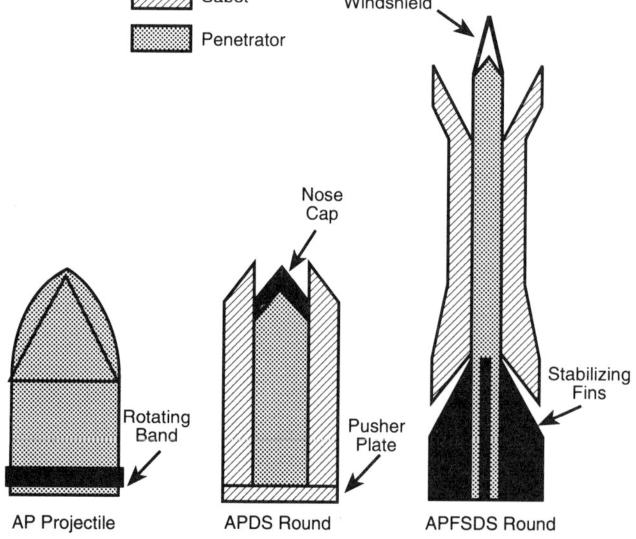

Figure 1. Kinetic energy projectiles. NOTE: *Schematic only; scale approximate, same for all.*

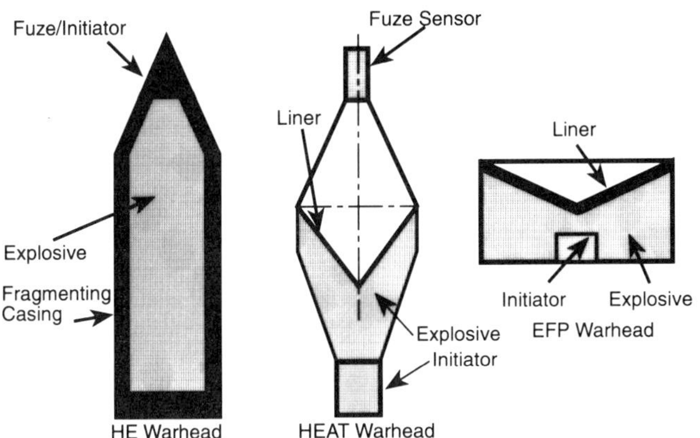

Figure 2. High-explosive warheads. NOTE: *Schematic only; to approximate relative scale*

Velocities range from 700 to 1,000 m/s. Such rounds are capable of penetrating about a 1-caliber thickness of conventional, rolled homogeneous (steel) armor plate (RHA; hardness about 350 Brinell).

Armor-piercing, discarding sabot (APDS) shot. These subcaliber penetrators, usually of high-density material such as tungsten carbide or sintered tungsten composition, are encased in a metal or plastic sabot that is discarded very soon after emergence from the muzzle of the gun. Penetrator diameters are typically less than half the caliber of the gun, the L/D ratios are less than 4:1, and such rounds are fired at velocities between 850 and 1,000 m/s. These penetrators are capable of penetrating as much as a 2-caliber thickness of RHA (i.e., about one penetrator length). Penetration is largely of the purely mechanical deformation type, the penetrator being almost undeformed during the process (except for shattering upon perforation). Moderate cavitation occurs, the hole in homogeneous armor being slightly larger than the penetrator.

Armor-piercing, fin-stabilized, discarding sabot (APFSDS) shot. These are long, fin-stabilized, rod-shaped penetrators; each is enclosed in a sabot that is discarded very early in flight. Originally made of hardened steel, they are now universally made of sintered tungsten compositions or depleted uranium (DU). L/D ranges from 6:1 to 20:1, and increases as technology improves. Diameters of rods range from 17mm to 30mm for major caliber guns. Velocity ranges from 1,200 to 1,750 m/s and also increases with improving technology. Penetration into RHA can exceed the length of the penetrator and in some cases approaches 1 meter. Cavitation of the crater is considerable, the crater diameter being as much as 50 percent greater than that of the penetrator. The penetrator erodes by a quasi-hydrodynamic process, so that its length is continually decreasing during the process. The penetration is described with reasonable accuracy by a Bernoulli form of equation (Eichelberger 1956; Tate 1967):

$$(1/2)a(v - u)^2 + s = (1/2)bu^2 + t \qquad (1)$$

where
a = density of penetrator material
b = density of armor material
s = strength of penetrator material
t = strength of armor material
v = velocity of penetrator
u = velocity of contact surface between penetrator and armor

The integral of u over the time required for the penetration to be completed is the penetration depth. If the deceleration of the rod and continuing cavitation after complete erosion of the rod are neglected, this is given, approximately, by:

$$p = L(y/z) \qquad (2)$$

where $y = -av + [a^2v^2 - 2(a - b)(av^2/2 - t + s)]^{1/2}$

$$z = bv - [a^2v^2 - 2(a - b)(av^2/2 - t + s)]^{1/2}$$

and L is the length of the rod.

EXPLOSIVE WARHEADS

Blast-fragmentation (HE) rounds. High explosive (HE) ammunition, including grenades, mortar and artillery shells, and missile warheads, produces a combination of air shock wave and fragments, the latter from the warhead casing. The air pressure wave is of consequence only for light structures, logistical vehicles, and personnel; even in those cases, it is usually of less importance than the accompanying fragments. Exceptions include buried land mines, in which case the air blast is augmented by earth propelled by the explosion; and underwater mines and torpedo warheads, which produce much higher pressures because of the confining effects of the water.

The fragments produced by conventional HE warheads range in mass from milligrams to hundreds of grams and are almost always steel; velocities are in the range of 500 to 2,000 m/s, with occasional designs yielding somewhat higher velocities. Some specialized warheads contain preformed fragments of high density metals—such as tungsten or depleted uranium (DU)—with velocities and masses in the same range as for conventional shells.

High explosive antitank (HEAT) warheads. Sometimes fired as full caliber, fin- or spin-stabilized projectiles from guns, these are more often used as rocket-propelled missile warheads. They use the shaped charge principle (Birkhoff et al. 1948; Eichelberger 1955) to form a jet with velocities as high as 10,000 m/s, so that flight velocity of the missile is of only secondary importance in contributing to penetrating power. Jets are small in diameter—less than 0.1 times the diameter of the warhead—and are usually of copper, with high density metals becoming more desirable as armor technology and metallurgical technology advance. L/D ratios are of less meaning, varying during flight, but are on the order of 50:1 to 200:1. Penetrating capability ranges from five to ten times the diameter of the warhead. Cavitation is significant, the crater usually being tapered because of the velocity gradient in the jet and ranging from four to two times the diameter of the jet. Penetration follows equation (1) more closely than do rod penetrators, and strength terms are much less important because of the higher pressures produced by the jets. Current and future technology emphasize multiple HEAT warheads in tandem to counter advances in armor. For jets, the pressures produced at the point of contact with the target are so much larger than the strength of materials that equation (1) can be simplified by omitting the two strength terms, and the depth of penetration is given, to a good approximation, by

$$P = L(a \div b)^{1/2} \quad (3)$$

where L is the length of the jet (or the sum of the lengths of the particles, if the jet has become particulated). The velocity gradient in normal jets makes the length dependent upon the distance the jet travels before reaching the target, and thus makes straightforward integration of equation (1) very complicated.

Explosive-formed penetrator (EFP) warheads. These are similar to HEAT except that the jet-forming mechanism is not exploited. They produce a more massive but slower and shorter penetrator. Diameters are typically 0.1 to 0.2 times the charge diameter; L/D ratios range from 1:1 to 6:1. Velocities range from 1,000 to 2,000 m/s. Relatively soft, ductile metals are used: copper, iron, tungsten, and DU. Penetrating capability in RHA is close to the length of the penetrator, or between 0.5 and two times the diameter of the warhead. Cavitation is usually considerable, lying between that caused by APFSDS and HEAT penetrators. Penetration also follows equation (1), with strength terms more important than for jets.

High explosive plastic (HEP) warheads. These superficially resemble HE rounds, but are made with a thin, ductile steel casing, plastic explosive, and delayed action fuzes. Sometimes called HESH (high-explosive squash head), they are designed to crush against the surface of armor and spread over as large an area as possible before detonating. The resultant pressure wave produced in the armor causes spallation of the inner surface without necessarily perforating, the spall being the medium for causing damage to the target.

Defeat Mechanisms

The mechanisms devised to defeat various threats are as varied as the threats themselves. The main ones are described below.

Elastic Resistance

Fabrics woven of high-strength, very elastic fibers can absorb the energy and redistribute the impulse of fragments and conventional antipersonnel bullets by stretching under the force of impact, without perforation. This mechanism is most commonly used for personnel armor; it is also used in liners for armored vehicles and fortifications to reduce internal damage from penetrating hits.

Plastic Deformation

Homogeneous, metallic armors (usually steel or aluminum) absorb energy and momentum by plastic deformation (see schematic diagrams in Fig. 3). Especially at the low-impact velocities of AP rounds, there is little deformation other than a projectile-diameter hole formed in the armor. Friction and heating due to the deformation constitute small, second-order energy sinks. The higher the strength of the armor, the greater the energy absorption and the higher the resistance to perforation. Hard metals are also brittle, however, and fail with less energy absorption than more ductile materials; this failure is significant because strikes that cannot perforate the armor may nonetheless cause spallation from the inner surface. Brittle failure in the form of spallation also contributes to the damage and lethality of perforating hits, so it is avoided to the extent compatible with efforts to prevent perforation.

At higher impact velocities, cavitation of the armor occurs, the crater being greater in diameter than the projectile. This absorbs greater energy from the penetrator, but does little to affect the depth of penetration attainable. Cavitation is, however, accompanied by greater stresses in the armor and a greater tendency to cause spallation.

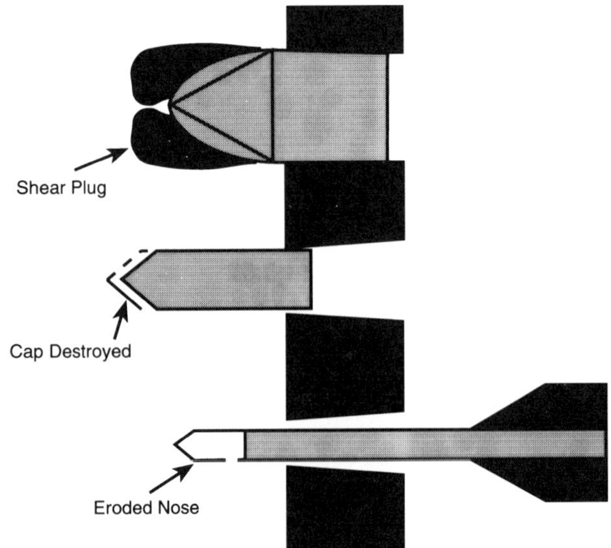

Figure 3. Penetration by kinetic energy projectiles. NOTE: *Homogeneous armor at 0 deg. obliquity; schematic only.*

Shock Absorption

Spallation caused by a shock wave initiated at the exterior surface, as by a HEP shell, is readily prevented by use of either space or low-shock impedance materials layered in the armor to cause reflection and attenuation of the shock. Ceramics also perform well against such damage mechanisms by absorbing the shock energy in cracking and comminution. Since almost all modern armors include spaces, low impedance materials, or ceramics, HEP shells have become obsolete—at least for the time being.

Deflection, Bending, Fracture

By placing homogeneous armor at large angles of obliquity to the direction of attack, AP and APDS penetrators can be made to ricochet or, in extreme cases, to fracture. Even under less favorable conditions, the path of the projectile through thick armor can be altered. Care must be taken in exploiting this mechanism, however, because the path is often changed so as to reduce the path length through oblique plates. The use of multiple, spaced plates does not enhance the deflection, but adds the useful probability that the hard, brittle projectiles will shatter upon release of the compressive stress created by the penetration process upon emergence from the rear of the first plate. The fragments will be distributed over a larger area than the projectile's cross-section; the area increases with the square of the distance between plates, making the stoppage of the scattered, smaller fragments relatively easy for a second plate. The plates must be sufficiently rigid, or reinforced, to maintain the integrity of the array under repeated impact or the blast from large HE rounds.

APFSDS penetrators impact at too high a velocity to be easily deflected, but can be subjected to sufficient stress to reduce their effectiveness. The shattering effect of stress relief after emergence from a plate affects long-rod penetrators, but much less than AP or APDS; a length of only about one diameter of the rod is lost as a result of each layer traversed. Bending of the relatively weak rods due to bending stresses induced by obliquity is a more important factor, if several plates are used with substantial spacing; the remaining, bent portions of the rod are much less effective penetrators than the same length of material in a straight configuration.

Deflection and bending have essentially no effect on the jets from HEAT or the slugs from EFP warheads. Each will lose some length to shattering by stress relief at each rear surface perforated, in addition to that used in hydrodynamic erosion, but will not be deflected or bent.

Inert "Reactive" Materials

There is a class of materials, composed of glasses, ceramics, cermets, and composites reinforced with glass or ceramic fibers, that reacts violently to high-pressure, impulsive loading. The precise mechanism is a matter of argument, but is variously called a dilatation, rebound, or dust-storm effect. It is of little consequence for AP, APDS, or APFSDS rounds. It is also of only marginal importance to EFP slugs. For shaped-charge jets, however, because of the extraordinarily high pressures they produce during penetration (several hundred kilobars), the reaction is particularly violent. (See schematic illustration of the effects in Fig. 4.) Jets are also much less substantial than any of the other penetrators and thus more vulnerable to lateral displacement forces. The result is that a moderate thickness of the more "reactive" of these materials can deflect substantial portions of a jet from its trajectory and scatter it over a large area; only a thin plate of metal is required to stop the residual material. The materials of the classes named vary greatly in the violence of their reaction to impulsive loading; the best of them can drastically reduce the effectiveness of HEAT warheads with much less weight of protection than is needed for homogeneous armor.

The violent reaction of these armor materials (inert as well as explosive) creates engineering problems. If rigidly confined in an armor shell, they tend to disrupt the structure of the vehicle as well as disrupt the actions of an attacking warhead. Design of a vehicle using this mechanism must take this characteristic into account.

Explosives have also been used in this manner with a high degree of effectiveness. The violence of the reaction, however, has prevented the fielding of such armor. This use of explosives in armor should be distinguished from reactive armor, discussed in the next section.

Crossing Velocity

Reactive armor consisting of thin layers of metal with a thin layer of explosive sandwiched between them has become well known because of its prolific use by the Israeli army as an applique armor for its tanks. Reactive armor operates on the principle of creating a crossing velocity in elements of the armor with respect to the trajectory of the penetrator. (See Fig. 5 for a schematic illustration.) Ideally, the entire penetrator could be absorbed by hydrodynamic erosion in a single thin plate if the crossing velocity were great enough. Practically, because of the

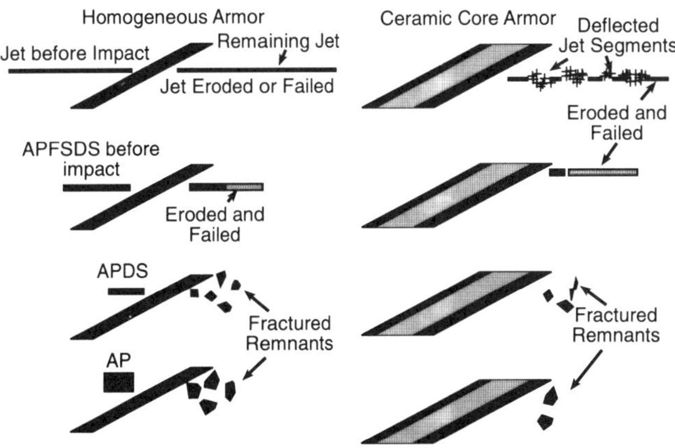

Figure 4. Effects of passive armor on penetrators.

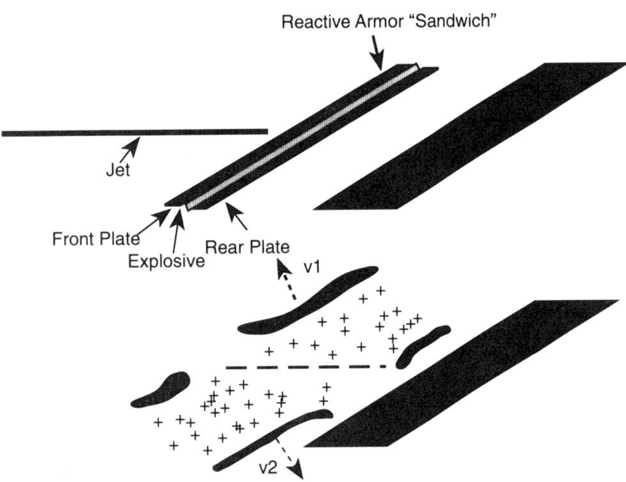

Figure 5. Explosive reactive armor defeating jet.

size of the crater produced by high velocity penetrators and the large amounts of explosive required to achieve the ideal condition, something less is usually attained.

Since the effectiveness of reactive armor depends explicitly on the crossing velocity, the plates must be given a substantial velocity component transverse to the trajectory of the threat. That is usually provided by using the armor at a high angle of obliquity to the expected path of attacking warheads. The obliquity can be built into the armor package, so that the exterior appearance is that of a vertical array, but obliquity must be provided. It is impractical to impart a large component of velocity parallel to a plate surface, so reactive armor plates have velocity vectors nearly normal to their surfaces. Attack at any angle less than 45 degrees to the normal to the actual plate surface will effectively defeat reactive armors.

Reactive armor is commonly used in applique boxes that often contain two "sandwiches," each consisting of two thin steel plates and a layer of explosive.

Reactive armor was initially conceived for use against, and is by far most effective against, HEAT warheads. While jets are seldom completely stopped by the moving plates, they are so severely disrupted by the combination of plates that only light armor backing is required to absorb the residue.

Against the short, relatively slow AP and APDS rounds, reactive armor as currently applied has essentially no effect. It could conceivably cause fracture, but the great disparity of weight and momentum between the projectiles and the armor plates makes such a result unlikely. Rod (APFSDS) penetrators and EFP slugs are somewhat more affected, but reactive armor as it is currently used is only a minor contributor to their defeat.

Interception/Destruction

"Active armor" functions by intercepting an approaching projectile and destroying it before it impacts the defended vehicle. It requires two basic components: (1) an electronic/optical system to detect and make measurements on an attacking warhead and provide controls for the intercepting device; and (2) a projection system to propel one or more projectiles to intercept and damage the attacking warhead.

Active armor falls into two general categories. Some is designed to detect an approaching threat at considerable distance, make the necessary trajectory measurements and predictions, signal through a computer to an aimable "gun" to aim at the appropriate point in space to intercept the threat, and fire a "shotgun" pattern of fragments at the threat. The second type is designed to detect at a moderate distance, track for a sufficient time to permit gathering precise trajectory data, and trigger the appropriate components of a system of explosive devices to project jets or slugs to intercept and destroy the threat.

The former class is most effective against explosive warheads, such as HEAT or EFP, which have large frontal areas and sensitive guidance and control components at the front, and the vulnerable explosive body behind light protection (the windshield, guidance and control components, and the warhead liner). This class is not very effective against APFSDS rounds, and even less so against AP or APDS.

The second class is designed mainly for protection against APFSDS rounds, but has a high potential effectiveness against HEAT and EFP as well. It could not provide protection against AP or APDS rounds without using an excessive amount of explosive in the protective devices.

Armor for Classes of Targets

The following paragraphs describe seven types of "systems" that require armor to provide ballistic protection.

Personnel

The chief threats specific to personnel are blast, fragments, and small arms bullets. Armor is irrelevant for protection of personnel against blast. For protection against fragments and "ball" ammunition fired by small arms, vests made of fabric are favored for their low heat retention and their flexibility. (Ball ammunition is the type designed specifically for antipersonnel use; it has little armor-penetrating capability.) For crews of aircraft or ground vehicles, vests made of metal (often titanium) or ceramic tiles contained in pockets of the vest may be used, despite their bulk and weight, for the greater protection they afford against small caliber AP ammunition.

Aircraft

Aircraft are threatened mainly by blast and fragmentation warheads delivered either by antiaircraft cannon or by missiles and small- and medium-caliber AP projectiles. Protection against blast is a structural problem rather than one to be solved by armor. Weight constraints make it impossible to protect all parts of an aircraft from penetration by fragments and projectiles. Hence, armor for aircraft is usually designed to protect only specific, critical components, including the crew. Light metals such as aluminum and titanium are sometimes used in thicknesses sufficient to prevent perforation by AP shot of 30mm or lesser caliber. Ceramics, particularly boron carbide, are most commonly used in seat bottoms and backs for crew protection. Redundancy of vital parts and protection of "soft" components by more robust and/or less critical ones are more effective ways to provide survivability where weight is of dominant importance.

Light Armored Vehicles

Armor for light armored vehicles is usually designed to protect against penetration by medium-caliber (up to 40mm) automatic cannon fire, AP and APFSDS, and infantry-portable missile warheads, as well as fragments from artillery HE shells.

Because of the need for rigidity of the hull for travel over rough terrain, a substantial amount of the weight assigned for armor must consist of double-purpose hull structure. Consequently, aluminum is the most common base material for armor for armored personnel carriers (APCs) and similar vehicles. The material added exclusively as armor may be spaced metal plates—often perforated to reduce the weight, as in the Israeli P900 armor—or ceramic tiles mounted on brackets to provide some space between them and the basic hull armor. Neither of these methods provides significant protection against HEAT warheads.

On a light vehicle, reactive armor appliques offer the only real promise for defense against HEAT; these are in use on a tentative, experimental basis by several armies. Active armor offers even greater hope of protection against HEAT missiles but is still in the exploratory stages of development.

Because of the severe problems of maintaining mobility, especially flotation for water travel, the armor for light vehicles cannot offer complete protection using present technology. Therefore, great emphasis is placed upon mitigation of the damage caused by perforating hits. Crew, passengers, and critical components are provided with protection against spall fragments caused by perforation of the armor. This protection often is in the form of a plastic or composite lining of the compartments, or fabric curtains surrounding the personnel compartments. The spall protection is usually designed to provide some protection against nuclear radiation as well.

Tanks

Tanks require the highest level of protection in mobile, land-based combat units. Armor is needed to prevent penetration of a large part of the area of a tank by major caliber (100 to >150mm) ammunition designed specifically to defeat armor, and by explosive warheads of missiles mounted on ground and air craft.

As in the case of light armored vehicles, hull rigidity requirements for tanks dictate that a thick basic layer of steel be a component of the armor. It is no longer feasible, however, to make a solid steel hull or turret sufficiently thick to provide protection without additional material. For protection against APFSDS rounds, a great variety of configurations of spaced metal plates and ceramics has been developed. (See Fig. 6 for illustrations of typical configurations.) Reactive armor is used as an applique to provide additional protection against large HEAT warheads; it is designed to be applied when protection is needed against large HEAT warheads, and to be a replaceable rather than a permanent part of the structure.

Internal protection of crew and components (especially ammunition) from fragments produced by perforating hits can also afford considerable enhancement of survivability. This protection is usually a thick layer of plastic lining the crew compartment. The liner also provides significant protection against nuclear radiation; it can be boron-impregnated in order to increase radiation protection. At present, only the Soviet army has consistently used such liners.

Sea-Craft, Surface

Surface ships cover such a great range of designs and purposes that many levels of protection are required. Ships are subject to attack by AP shot of caliber up to 800mm, missiles of almost unlimited size, mines, and torpedoes. The wide range of weapons and the variety of modes of attack make the complete protection of even capital ships essentially impossible. Active armor in its most sophisticated form (e.g., the U.S. Phalanx/Aegis system) constitutes the main line of defense against missiles. Decks and hulls are made of sufficient thickness of steel armor to provide the needed rigidity, with a modicum of additional armor as protection against AP shot. In particularly critical locations, layered construction is used, providing a kind of spaced armor. Major emphasis is placed upon protection of critical components and stores by in-

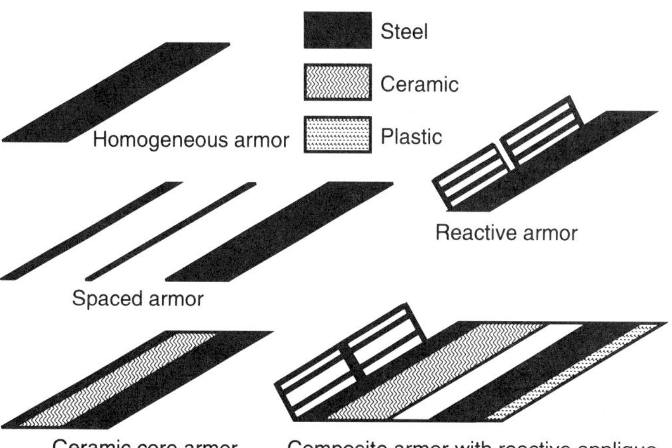

Figure 6. Armor classes.

ternal armoring. Materials used include light metals, composites, and spaced arrays.

Submarines

Submarines are threatened mainly by sophisticated torpedoes carrying large (to >800mm) blast, shaped-charge, or EFP warheads, and by depth charges. Protection from blast is a structural design problem rather than one to be addressed by armor. Protection from HEAT and EFP warheads is accomplished mainly by use of widely spaced hull components, often with water in the space between layers. Reactive armor, using either explosive or inert materials, is of little use because of the probability of damage to the hull by the action of the armor.

Stationary Facilities

Bunkers and other stationary facilities are subject to threat from the full range of gun-fired and missile warheads carried by artillery and armored vehicles, and occasionally by navy vessels. Although blast has been the historically important damage mechanism, penetrating warheads are now and for the future the main concern. Sophisticated armor has little role in the design of such facilities, however; neither weight nor volume of protection needs to be limited (as they do in a vehicle), so facilities are usually constructed of concrete, earth, and wood thick enough to provide the desired level of protection. In response to the increased penetrating ability of large HEAT warheads and of possible large-caliber APFSDS rounds, attention has been given to interior lining to limit damage from perforating hits. Wooden barriers can be used for this purpose, or plastic or fabric liners similar to those used in armored vehicles.

Table 1 presents a simple evaluation of the relative importance of the various classes of armor for protection against the several kinds of threat. No distinction is made concerning the kind of system being protected. The numbers in the cells of the table indicate the relative importance of each class of armor against each kind of threat, 1 being the highest level and 7 the lowest. Foreseeable future prospects are taken into account, as well as current technology.

Prospects for the Future

Passive Armor

Future advances in passive armor are likely to be limited. The exploration of new materials has been nearly exhausted. The greatest advances in passive armor will be in engineering design to permit more efficient use of materials whose capability is already known; this can be achieved particularly by designing vehicles with the use of modern armor materials as a priority design feature from the initial concepts. Improvements in design of armor arrays using combinations of materials and mechanisms can be anticipated, but they will not provide more than evolutionary, incremental improvements.

Reactive Armor

Reactive armors, using both inert and explosive materials as drivers, can be expected to improve rapidly in the near future. Their integration into the basic armor of heavy armored vehicles is one direction in which improvements can be expected, eliminating the need for appliques except for added, emergency applications and for light armor. Improvements in the armor itself are likely to result in increased effectiveness against APFSDS penetrators and EFP warheads, greatly increasing its importance as a protective mechanism.

Active Armor

Active armor holds the real promise for the future. The competition between the two basic types of active armor will be resolved, perhaps by using a combination, since one is most effective against HEAT and EFP warheads, the other against APFSDS penetrators. There is a great deal of engineering design to be done to make active armor practical and reliable, and innovations are needed to increase its versatility and effectiveness.

One possible direction for long-range evolution of antimissile active armor would be to use high-energy lasers or particle beams rather than fragments or projectiles as interceptors. This would apply only to the long-range interception systems, and would require very high energy beams to produce more than a "soft" kill (i.e., more than

TABLE 1. *Relative Effectiveness of Armor Technologies Versus Various Threats*

	Threat							
Armor	*Fragments*		AP	APDS	APFSDS	HEAT	EFP	HEP
	P	*V*						
Fabric	1	4	7*	7*	7*	7*	7*	N/a
Solid	N/a	5	2	5	6	6	6	6
Spaced	N/a	2	1	2	5	5	4	2
Composite	2	3	4	3	4	4	5	3
Ceramic	3	1	3	1	3	3	1	4
Reactive	N/a	6	5	4	2	1	2	5
Active	N/a	(7)	(6)	(6)	(1)	(2)	(3)	(1)

P = Personnel armor. *Used as spall inhibitor. N/a not applicable. V = Vehicular armor. ( ) = Future capability.

destruction of guidance and control components). A "hard" kill, achieved by detonating the explosive of the warhead, is a much more desirable result. In no case would this direction provide defense against kinetic energy (AP, APDS, or APFSDS) penetrators.

Possible Consequences

Assuming that the projected advances in armor design occur, certain collateral consequences can be expected.

1. By taking full advantage of either reactive or active armor, armored vehicles will become much lighter in weight, at least for an interim period.
2. To counter the effectiveness of reactive and active armor, weapon designers may revive the currently obsolete AP and APDS ammunition in refined forms. Neither is likely to be defeated by any practicable reactive or active armor.
3. The armor designer will then be confronted by a broader range of threats and will be forced, once again, to develop heavy vehicles to provide protection against all of the threats. In this competition, the weapon designer has the advantage; guns, missiles, ammunition, and warheads can be altered more quickly and with less expense than can the vehicles that carry them.

The competition between armor and antiarmor weapons will continue indefinitely and will engender more innovations on both sides, most of which cannot be foreseen.

Robert J. Eichelberger

See Also: Ammunition; Armor; Armored Ground Vehicle; Armored Land Vehicle Technology Applications; Fortification; Gun, Antitank; Mechanized Warfare; Missile, Antitank Guided; Tank.

Bibliography

Birkhoff, et al. 1948. Explosives with lined cavitics. *Journal of Applied Physics* 19:563.

Courtney-Green, P. R. 1990. *Ammunition.* London: Brassey's.

Eichelberger, R. J. 1955. Reexamination of the nonsteady theory of jet formation by lined cavity charges. *Journal of Applied Physics.* 26:398.

———. 1956. Experimental test of the theory of penetration by metallic jets. *Journal of Applied Physics* 27:63.

Hilmes, R. 1987. *Main battle tanks: Developments in design since 1945.* Trans. R. Simpkin. London: Brassey's.

Nürnberger, W. 1981. Technical trends and possibilities for the armoured vehicles of the future. *Defense Today* 33/34:56ff.

Tate, A. 1967. A theory for the deceleration of long rods after impact. *Journal of the Mechanics Physics of Solids* 15:387.

ARMORED GROUND VEHICLE

Armored ground vehicles include tanks, infantry fighting vehicles, many self-propelled artillery weapons, armored cars, personnel carriers, cargo carriers, recovery vehicles, and fire direction centers. Usually, the design, equipment, and production of specialized vehicles are adapted from the basic design of the armored personnel carrier (APC) (Fig. 1).

An important example of this flexibility of design is the armored infantry fighting vehicle (AIFV), which can be adapted to serve for close air defense; as an antitank missile carrier; as a command post carrying communications systems; as an ambulance for medical first aid and evacuation; as a mine layer; as a mortar carrier; as an artillery forward observation platform; as a field workshop and a recovery vehicle; and for internal security.

Specialized Vehicles

The following descriptions of five important categories of armored ground vehicles will serve to illustrate the broad range of highly specialized roles for which these vehicles can be adapted.

Reconnaissance Vehicle

Reconnaissance vehicles are wheeled or tracked armored vehicles designed primarily for scouting and reconnaissance, either by visual observation or through the use of other detection methods. The key characteristics of these vehicles are a high degree of mobility, capability for long-distance deployment, and the ability to maneuver over rough ground even under hostile fire. These requirements mandate a certain degree of survivability linked to protection, but design compromises are required because adding armor sufficient to protect against heavy fire could increase vehicle weight to such a level that cross-country mobility would be impaired.

At present, no ideal design for a universal reconnaissance vehicle exists, and compromises tend to consider mission requirements as determined by military doctrine. Generally, wheeled, rather than tracked, armored vehicles have come to be used for a variety of low-intensity missions such as scouting, liaison, communications, and

Figure 1. A Soviet BTR-50 amphibious-tracked APC used in training exercises with U.S. Army units. (Source: Robert F. Dorr Archives; U.S. Army)

surveillance. This is because of their greater speed and mobility when used along established road networks and trafficable terrain, and their more economical production and operation. More heavily armored tracked reconnaissance vehicles tend to be used when doctrine stipulates a more active role in fighting and where terrain is more difficult.

Amphibious capabilities are of paramount importance for reconnaissance vehicles, which should be able to navigate water obstacles and "move" at high speed in water rather than merely "swim" as other wheeled and tracked vehicles do. Hence positive propulsion by propellers or waterjets is required. In some versions, the vehicle has a second driving position aft, which enables another member of the crew to drive the vehicle backward for a short distance should it become necessary to immediately disengage from contact with heavily armed enemy units. Reduced width of such vehicles is an important consideration, given that they are often required to move through wooded or built-up areas.

These 3- to 5-ton vehicles can typically transport up to six men, including the driver. The provision of large windows of bulletproof glass helps drivers to drive comfortably. An automatic weapon can be fired from within the vehicle over a frontal arc, or from a small turret at the expense of a limited increase in weight. This modification can be adapted so as to be employed in counterreconnaissance.

Armored Infantry Fighting Vehicle

Armored infantry fighting vehicles (AIFV) give the infantryman a level of mobility comparable to that of the main battle tank (MBT), and a substantial degree of protection from enemy fire. The AIFV may be equipped with light, medium, or heavy turrets, and a variety of armaments, depending on its role.

Turrets may be either one-man or two-man. The first type is smaller and lighter, and thus suited to light vehicles. In this configuration, only the gunner can occupy the turret, while the commander remains in the hull with a limited field of vision. In a two-man turret, the commander can override the gunner for all combat functions, besides making use of the installed optics and command devices. Achieving this advantage entails greater dimensions, however, especially in width.

Turrets should have the same level of protection as the overall vehicle, or even higher, due to the inclination and thickness of the armor. They feature all-around vision blocks or periscopes for observation of the surrounding field. They can rotate 360 degrees continuously, which is accomplished manually, hydraulically, or electrically, depending on the weight of the turret.

AIFVs may be either wheeled or tracked. They are excellent platforms for different weapons, which can range from 100mm guns to 30-caliber coaxially mounted machine guns. Other popular armaments include antitank guided missiles, 25mm chain guns, and externally mounted grenade launchers. Some vehicles feature firing ports for individual weapons of the occupants.

The primary weapon on an AIFV is mounted and balanced about its trunion on the front part of the turret. Weapon elevation is controlled through a gearbox (pinion and toothed arc), and traverse depends on the turret itself. Subsystems, such as magnification sights, thermal and infrared sights, and searchlights, are used to improve weapon effectiveness.

Consideration must be given to the weight and placement of the main armaments. Larger-caliber weapons require greater structural support and thus add to the weight of the AIFV, which in turn affects the weight of the vehicle's engine, transmission, and suspension systems. For example, high-pressure guns need about a 1.6-meter turret ring, which is best adapted only to heavy AIFVs (about 12 tons), while a 1.4-meter turret ring is suitable for lower-pressure guns and can be mounted in AIFVs of about 7 tons. Asymmetrical designs (e.g., offset mounting of the main gun) can impair amphibious operations through listing caused by uncorrected torque along the axis of movement of the vehicle.

Grenade launchers provide AIFVs, as well as tanks, armored personnel carriers, and other armored ground vehicles, with a unique and variable defensive capability. The launchers may fire smoke, phosphorus, tear gas, or illumination rounds in addition to antipersonnel grenades. They may also fire infrared and radar-jamming munitions. These are fired from inside the vehicle individually or in salvo, and can form a considerable screen to conceal the vehicle as it safely changes position. Some armored vehicles are provided with smoke generators that can rapidly provide a dense smoke screen produced by fuel being sprayed onto the exhaust outlet.

Many AIFVs are equipped to maintain a slight overpressure inside the vehicle. While this feature may complicate the design of the turret, it serves to prevent exposure of the crew and occupants to the conditions of nuclear, biological, and chemical (NBC) warfare.

Some sophisticated AIFVs are equipped similarly to the latest generation of main battle tanks, and even two-axis stabilization is being adapted to AIFVs. This system compensates for the vehicle's movement in roll, pitch, suspension travel, and tire behavior. Once so equipped, an AIFV turret lacks only adequate firepower to become an MBT turret.

Internal Security Vehicle

Internal security vehicles are designed for missions involving territorial security, antiguerrilla combat, restoration of order, and repression of riots in urban areas. Their high maneuverability, wide range of vision, and special ancillary equipment gives such vehicles outstanding performance characteristics. They feature large and comfortable interior space, which enables crews to remain on alert for several hours in the vehicle. These vehicles may be equipped with turrets fitted with a medium 12.7mm machine gun or a light 7.62mm machine gun. They are found in a 4 × 4 or 6 × 6 configuration, but tracked vehicles are absolutely unsuitable. The latter also have political disadvantages in that they are often confused with tanks. An amphibious capability is necessary only for coast or border patrol missions. Vehicles of this type can typically accommodate about ten men in the crew compartment.

To minimize the "dead zone" in front of the vehicle, the depression capability of the mounted machine gun may be as low as −12 degrees. These vehicles are usually also equipped with smoke and CS (tear gas) grenade launchers, searchlights, a magnifying telescope mounted coaxially with the weapon, all-around observation glass vision blocks, and episcopes or periscopes.

Vehicles intended for antiriot duty should be provided with protection of the engine air intake against flammable liquids, protection of the exhaust port, fuel tank locking, suppression of outside handles on doors and hatches, vision blocks with swivelling tight firing ports permitting protected firing from inside the vehicle, and CS protection. For repression of riots in urban areas such vehicles may be equipped with a hydraulic cleaning blade, windscreen shutter, tear gas dispenser, siren, outside public address system, rotating light, turret, video camera, and water cannon.

Armored Workshop Vehicle

The armored workshop vehicle transports mechanics and necessary spare parts and tools to the combat zone, where maintenance operations and first- and second-level repair can be performed under the full protection of an armored hull. The workshop is equipped with the necessary tools and equipment, such as a welding set, bench, tool boxes for mechanical and electrical repairs, and lifting gear. Also included are a vise, portable drilling machine, disc grinder, electric generator, and battery charger. Lightly damaged vehicles can thus be repaired and put back into operation without being towed to the rear. The workshop has both an external radio set and internal communications. It is also usually armed with a small-caliber machine gun. Mechanics can work in a standing position through two large roof hatches with about a 90-degree opening while being protected by the sides of the vehicle's hull. The same workshop can be fitted to a wheeled or a tracked vehicle.

Recovery Vehicle

Armored recovery vehicles are used to evacuate partially disabled military vehicles suffering battle damage and those experiencing severe technical failures that cannot be repaired in place. Such inoperable equipment is extracted and towed to the rear, where a higher-level repair facility can deal with the problem.

Recovery vehicles have a hydraulically driven crane that can rotate within a minimum arc of 180 degrees to the rear, and often a full 360 degrees. Two or four jacks, manually or hydraulically operated, provide additional stability for lifting, and heavier recovery vehicles may feature outriggers to widen the range of stable operations.

Ground clearance, fording ability, and a short turning radius are other important attributes of recovery vehicles. There are usually two driver's work stations, one on the vehicle for road travel, the other on the crane mechanism for movement about work sites and over rough terrain at low speed. These vehicles also mount various pulleys, wire, and tools to be used to facilitate recovery operations.

Mobility Characteristics

Regardless of the type of armored ground vehicle or its mission, its main purpose is to provide mobility to a military force. Since speed is one mainstay of mobility, military vehicles are designed to attain high speed both on hard-surface roads and on different kinds of cross-country terrain.

Another key element of mobility is traction. When roads and cross-country terrain are slippery—from ice, snow, sand, or mud—friction is often insufficient and the driving wheels or tracks spin in place instead of pushing the vehicle forward. This may combine with the reduced resistance to shear of certain soils to result in the sinking of the vehicle's tracks or tires and a mired, immobile vehicle.

Tracks are more effective than driving wheels in achieving traction. More driving wheels, however, will enhance a vehicle's mobility. The specific pressure of tracked vehicles on soil may be as low as 0.5 bar, but the lowest value using normal low-pressure tires is not less than 0.9 bar, and even deflating tires can only reduce the pressure to 0.7 bar.

Generally a vehicle's mobility can be improved by the following: (1) low specific soil pressure, so that the friction in the contact area plus the resistance to shear are enough to withstand the tractive force and thus sufficient to push the vehicle; (2) firm contact of the rolling driving element (track or wheel) with the terrain by transferring the weight of the vehicle via the elastic element of the suspension system (springs or torsion bars) so as to maintain this contact at all times; and (3) absence of the probability of spinning due to lack of adhesion in the contact areas. This can be achieved by positive connection of different components of the drive line through locking the interwheel and interaxle differentials during movement on slippery roads. Tracked vehicles have a distinct advantage in terms of these factors. The specific soil pressure is limited by the length of track contact and its width, and the contact with the ground is secured by the tracked vehicle's suspension system (road wheels and torsion bars).

Thus the track throughout its length can adapt its configuration to that of the terrain being traversed, something that cannot be achieved by wheeled vehicles. Multiaxle wheeled vehicle designers try to approach this configuration by increasing the number, width, and diameter of the wheels, by decreasing their inflation pressure, and by improving their tread pattern and applying independent suspension. By these means the design of 8×8 vehicles has realized a satisfying mobility despite its complexity; this seems to be the optimum possible solution.

The Map of Armored Vehicles

According to their function, armored vehicles differ widely in their characteristics, especially in weight and power. Weight depends mainly on the available interior room and the amount of armor protection, while the power depends on the resulting weight and the required dynamic performance. Even vehicles having similar functions have variations in these parameters, mainly combat weight and specific power (the power-to-weight ratio).

Infantry fighting vehicles, having taken over essential battlefield tasks formerly performed on foot, are capable of moving more rapidly when tanks cannot or need not be employed. They are able to keep up with tanks tactically, defend themselves, and even be used offensively against a light enemy. They are designed to discharge their embarked infantry from the rear of the vehicle for dismounted combat. They are armed with heavy small arms (a 20–30mm cannon) and antitank guided missiles, but arming these vehicles with powerful weapons has also left them with less room for carrying infantrymen and their equipment; thus fewer soldiers are available for dismounted action.

Tracked armored vehicles enable the infantry to follow the tanks, but unfortunately most of them as currently designed prevent the crew from firing their weapons without exposing themselves. Some versions have a one- or two-man turret, or vision blocks and firing slots in the sides and rear of the vehicle; these permit infantry to fire their weapons from within the vehicle, and also reduce the risk of their becoming claustrophobic or disoriented.

Clearly, the roles of infantry carriers and fighting vehicles are quite different. Infantry carriers must deliver infantry to their objective by a series of tactical bounds, while fighting vehicles must deliver them to suitable firing positions. The various factors deriving from the disparate missions have affected the design of the vehicles for performing them. For infantry carriers, the priority is to transport eight or ten soldiers rapidly and under maximum protection, then dismount them to go into action on foot. Such vehicles have suffered heavy losses when they tried to function as fighting vehicles.

Well-designed wheeled vehicles with independent suspension have the advantage of a lower silhouette than tracked vehicles, while their running gear enables them to operate effectively off the road as well as on it. They also provide the base vehicle for an entire family of variations.

In order to identify the main tendencies in combat weight and in power-to-weight ratio of existing armored vehicles, a survey was conducted of about 70 military armored vehicles fielded by the American, European, and Soviet armed forces. A specific power (power-to-weight ratio) versus weight diagram was then plotted for both armored wheeled vehicles and armored tracked vehicles. A number of considerations go into the design of the various systems considered, constituting a series of tradeoffs, in effect a calculus of vehicle design.

Ultra-light and light reconnaissance wheeled vehicles, for example, with their extremely light combat weight and small crew designed for conducting deep reconnaissance missions in the forward battlefield, lack the capability to conduct major engagements and must avoid such confrontations. They must have instead outstanding agility, mobility, and maneuverability. Conversely, medium and heavy reconnaissance and heavy reconnaissance/armored personnel carriers, although heavier in weight, may not need such high power.

On the other hand, infantry fighting vehicles have more offensive missions that necessitate an increased level of protection of the hull and turret, larger-caliber weaponry, more powerful observation and aiming devices, more ammunition stowage, and accurate tactical and navigation systems. All these in the aggregate result in an enormous increase in weight, and thus require a corresponding increase in power to ensure adequate levels of mobility and maneuverability to perform their offensive tasks. These considerations are, to some extent, similar to those affecting main battle tanks.

Ultra-light and light reconnaissance vehicles weighing up to five tons have high specific power to suit their missions of scouting, liaison, transportation of commanders, and surveillance patrols, all of which require high mobility and rapid maneuverability. This can be provided by 4×4 light vehicles of 3.0 to 5.5 tons with a power-to-weight ratio of about 20 to 34 horsepower per ton. Heavy reconnaissance vehicles sacrifice high dispensible dynamic performance to gain more room. Thus their weights range from 7.5 to 20 tons for 4×4 up to 8×8 configurations, with lower power-to-weight ratios of about 13 to 27 horsepower per ton.

Armored personnel carriers have a similar character and similar power-to-weight ratios, as their main operating theater is often in the rear. Their configuration varies from 4×4 up to 8×8 with weights of 4 to 18 tons and power-to-weight ratios of 15 to 30 horsepower per ton. Since an infantry fighting vehicle's weight increases with the increase in its gun caliber and the addition of missiles, its power-to-weight ratio must increase correspondingly to maintain high mobility and maneuverability. These vehicles may be as heavy as 15 to 26 tons and have power-to-weight ratios of 10 to 22 horsepower per ton.

Tracked vehicles having the same function as comparable wheeled vehicles show the same tendencies. Increase in weight is accompanied by a decrease in power-to-weight ratio as the vehicle version shifts from reconnaissance to reconnaissance/armored personnel carrier to pure armored personnel carrier.

Monocoque Version of Armored Wheeled Vehicles

In the monocoque version of armored wheeled vehicles, the hull represents the infrastructure on which all the main drive line aggregates and components of the vehicle are mounted. These include the engine, transmission, axles, steering, and suspension. When all, or at least most, of the vital aggregates and components are installed within the hull armor, it is called an "all-in" design.

In this form the hull completely replaces the frame. As a result of eliminating the frame, the dead weight of the vehicle is considerably reduced; the saving can be added to the useful payload. At the same time, the design is not restricted by the classic frame. Consequently, road clearance can be increased, height reduced, the center of gravity lowered considerably, and the angles of approach and departure increased during the design process. The bottom of the hull of this version has a v-shape to provide additional protection against mines and a lower level that enables the crew to embark and disembark more easily and quickly. The v-shape also helps to reduce water resistance in the amphibious version, which can be equipped with propellers or water-jet pumps for propulsion in water.

In the monocoque version most suitable for armored military vehicles, the designer can make use of "leftover" places and pockets to arrange crew seating and their accommodations. The suspension can easily be adapted as independent and, since the axles and final drives are related to the sprung mass in this type of suspension, the comfort and riding quality of these vehicles are noticeably improved.

The hull may be covered by an armored roof to protect the crew. It may also be provided with hatches for observation by the commander and crew and for use as emergency exits. The sides of the hull may have as many vision blocks and firing ports as the number of crewmen. The windshield in front of the commander and driver, along with the crew vision blocks, are made of armored glass that provides the same degree of protection as the hull. All crew members, and especially the commander and driver, are afforded wide fields of vision with a minimum dead zone.

The level of protection afforded by the front part of such vehicles is usually higher than that on the sides, and can withstand 7.62mm fire at a range of 30 meters.

NBC Protection

Ground forces are especially threatened by nuclear, biological and chemical (NBC) warfare. Main battle tanks and most military armored vehicles, especially those subject to operation in the forward battle area, are provided with a sealed, airtight, and pressurized compartment that excludes the entry of radioactive dust, harmful chemicals, and microorganisms. Filtered fresh air is ducted to the crew compartment; crew members can thus maintain maximum efficiency since they can work freely without the need to wear respirators or breathing aids.

Air Conditioning

NATO countries have been slow to adopt any form of air conditioning on military vehicles, preferring to rely on forced air ventilation. Equipment intended for export to tropical areas, especially those characterized by high humidity, may have better marketability if it is air conditioned to maintain a more comfortable crew environment. This is particularly important in tightly closed vehicles designed to include NBC protective systems. These types of vehicles are subject to operation in a "closed down" mode for long periods in a contaminated environment. Under such conditions a satisfactory atmosphere for the crew cannot be achieved without air conditioning. Ambient temperatures in certain tropical climates may reach 50–60 degrees centigrade in summer with accompanying humidity up to 90 percent. No human body can withstand such conditions for more than several minutes, much less work and fight effectively under them.

Various approaches have been devised to solve this problem, each a function of the characteristics and operating requirements of the vehicle being conditioned. The simplest solution is a direct descendent of the automobile air-conditioning system. That is, to drive the compressor off the vehicle engine and to locate the discrete components of the system in suitable places within and on the outside of the vehicle. If this approach is not taken, retrofitting installation costs for existing vehicles are certain to be high, and probably nonstandard components will have to be designed to fit into the "leftover" spaces. The main drawback of this design is that it can only operate when the vehicle engine is running. Also, if the system is designed and sized for operation at low engine speed, then it will have surplus capacity at higher engine speeds. Ambulance vehicles, in particular, should be fitted with air-conditioning systems. This provides a cooling capability that permits personnel survival in ambient or tropical humidity and desert solar loading. Compactness can be attained primarily by use of a high-efficiency heat exchanger.

An internal and completely independent power pack that is entirely protected within the armored hull may also be used, although such a system takes up considerable interior space. Usually it comprises a small 2- or 3-cylinder diesel engine using the same fuel as the vehicle engine but equipped with a separate fuel tank, its own battery starter, and a powerful alternator to drive the system's fans. The condenser of the system is cooled, together with its engine radiator, by the same fan through the same armored grill. An adjustable thermostat is provided for switching the system on and off automatically within a temperature range preset by the crew. The main feature of this independent version is that it can air-condition the vehicle even when the main engine is not running. This is important for ambulance, command post, internal security, and patrol vehicles. In both systems heating can be provided only when the vehicle engine is running.

Wheels versus Track

Practical experience has shown that ground pressure of a two-axle wheeled vehicle may amount to twice that of a tracked vehicle of the same weight. Therefore, and in order not to lose the other advantages of wheeled vehicles, the solution has been to provide more axles so as to maintain ground pressure within a range that could compete with tracked vehicles.

The mean maximum pressure is sometimes used as the unit of measure, rather than nominal ground pressure; the former is more critical, especially since the difference between the two figures is considerable for tracked vehicles with a small number of road wheels. Due to the provision of large tires and a tire inflation pressure control system, this approach is deemed acceptable.

On roads, the rolling resistance of tracked vehicles is double that of wheeled vehicles (0.04 times the tracked vehicle weight versus 0.02 times that of wheeled vehicles fitted with cross-country tires). Wheeled vehicles can cover longer distances on roads before they require refueling, especially if they are driven by diesel engines. They can also cover longer distances faster and with less fatigue for their occupants, since the vibrations generated by tires are negligible in comparison with those produced by tracks.

The suspension of tracked vehicles is simpler, lighter, and more compact than that of wheeled vehicles. Tracked vehicles are sprung by transverse torsion bars, which are lighter than springs. Tracked-vehicle wheel travel due to torsion bar suspension may be as much as 230 to 280 millimeters, and even up to 380 millimeters in the case of hydropneumatic suspension.

Steering in tracked vehicles may depend on a clutch-and-brake system, formerly the standard. A controlled differential is now considered more effective, but it provides only one radius of steering.

It is generally accepted that the main battle tanks should be tracked rather than wheeled, but the same conclusion does not necessarily follow for light armored vehicles. The relative cross-country performance depends on vehicle weight. Within the weight range of the main battle tank, tracks are required, but the light weights of other armored vehicles may or may not favor wheels. Wheeled vehicles with up to eight driving wheels are, despite the accompanying steering and transmission difficulties, currently being produced. The low ground pressure that favored the track has also been achieved in wheeled vehicles by using large-diameter tires with a high loading capacity and central tire-pressure control that permits adjustment of tire pressure in accordance with the terrain being traversed. This system is both more convenient and easier than making adjustments in track tension. Also, if run-flat tires are used, then puncture of one or more tires will not immobilize the vehicle, whereas any track link damage does halt a tracked vehicle.

Other advantages of the wheeled armored vehicle include fuel economy and longer range, especially with diesel engines; high road speeds; simplicity; relative quietness; long service life as compared with track life, which rarely exceeds 4,000 kilometers (2,480 mi.); better riding quality, without the vibration associated with tracks; ability to be towed or recovered more easily; lower procurement and in-service costs; easier driver training; and higher mobility on semi-soft terrain and hard surfaces. While 4 × 4 wheeled vehicles are inferior to tracks in their ability to cross wide trenches, 6 × 6 and 8 × 8 versions have approximately the same capability as tracked vehicles in this respect.

Wheeled vehicles have lighter armor protection than tracked vehicles. To be able to withstand 12.7mm, 14.5mm, and 20mm armor-piercing shells, wheeled armored vehicles would have to be brought up to combat weights that would result in unacceptably high ground pressure. Thus they are not a substitute for tracked armored vehicles. Rather, wheeled and tracked vehicles should be viewed as complementary, not competitive, and tailored according to the geographical characteristics of the theater of operations.

Semitracked vehicles, sometimes known as half-tracks, were first produced in large numbers in Germany by 1940. During the next five years the Americans quickly followed suit, producing some 40,000 half-tracks for themselves and their allies. None of these vehicles proved completely satisfactory, as they proved to be difficult to maintain, awkward to drive, of poor reliability, inadequate in cross-country mobility, and too expensive. It was reported, for example, that their cost per unit of weight was higher than a tank's. By 1944 the Allies had turned toward fully tracked and armored solutions based on the tank chassis.

Semitracked vehicles should probably be excluded from consideration for modern use, since they lack the respective advantages of wheeled and tracked vehicles while at the same time having many of the disadvantages of both.

Military Tires

Since the greater part of the distances covered by wheeled armored vehicles is on hard or dirt surfaces, their tires must have good resistance to abrasion and good adhesion even on wet roads.

Military tires cannot operate as close to their maximum

load-carrying capacity as commercial tires because of "up sizing" to provide an extra margin of safety against possible structural failure, higher ground clearance, and extra flotation on yielding surfaces. Military applications also emphasize the importance of tire-ground contact area more than commercial uses. Military vehicle designers seek to improve mobility and agility by achieving the largest possible area of tire contact with the ground at the lowest possible inflation pressure, minimizing soil pressure while also limiting tire dimensions. Thus a single, wide, variable-pressure tire is often used on heavy military vehicles where an equivalent commercial vehicle would utilize a double tire.

Tire rubber will always remain vulnerable to penetration due to enemy action, ground litter, and debris. To counter this difficulty and become competitive with, and possibly to displace, metal tracked systems or solid rubber tires, pneumatic tires must provide good flotation and tractive characteristics and must have an acceptable degree of continued mobility in terms of distance and speed even after being punctured. This translates into a quick-escape capability of 30 to 50 kilometers (18.6 to 31 mi.) of travel at 40 to 50 kilometers per hour (25 to 31 mph) for heavy vehicles and 50 to 100 kilometers (31 to 62 mi.) at 50 to 70 kilometers per hour (31 to 43.4 mph) for light vehicles.

For medium and heavy vehicles (1,100 kg/tire or more), flat tires generate high internal heat that causes rapid breakdown and disintegration of the tire structure. One solution is to provide thick-wall, self-supporting tires that can bear the load without totally collapsing on the rim. Such tires use low-hysteresis, high-structure compounds that limit bending of tire walls as they go into compression with the basic casing reinforcement in tension. The base of the tire is held in the correct relationship with the rim by insertion of a reinforced rubber spacer. There is a penalty in terms of reduced shock absorption and flotation, especially in the deflated mode. An alternate solution involves filling the torroidal void within a tire with a rubber core that incorporates nitrogen-filled cavities within its structure.

The dominant advantage of radial tires is the extension of tread life that results from stabilization of the ground contact area, along with decreased rolling resistance and consequently reduced fuel consumption. In terms of run-flat capability, radial tires provide better performance, although this is not essential if a limited post-deflation performance is acceptable. When running on partially or fully deflated tires, serious failures of the inner tube can occur; the valve can be torn from the tube by the increased rotational forces imposed and the increase in circumferential strain. Such failures are not present, of course, in tubeless tires.

Military requirements for tire performance have tended to concentrate on optimizing off-road capabilities and operation in soft soils, sand, mud, loose rock, and the like, often to the detriment of performance on hard surfaces. Uni-directional patterns of tire design are generally not favored, so as to avoid extra complications in tire fitting. Certain other designs have been found highly advantageous. A full run-flat design with an efficient bead-locking system, for example, has been evaluated as doubling tractive capability in snow when fully deflated. For optimum performance in loose sand (which has very poor shear strength), a high-flotation, low-pressure tire is required. A rounded-profile tire edge helps to avoid excessive sinkage due to milling into the sand when a spin occurs. But there are always tradeoffs; such tires provide rather hard road performance in terms of abrasion resistance. Sectional height-to-width ratios for military vehicle tires vary from 0.3 to 0.7.

The provision of run-flat tires, together with a pressure-control system for them, on armored fighting vehicles and armored personnel carriers is indispensable on the modern battlefield, where these vehicles are continually subject to enemy action, and the need often arises for continued use of the tires even after they have been punctured; indeed for the vehicle to be able to cover a considerable distance at relatively high speed after punctures have occurred. The construction of run-flat tires does not adversely affect maneuverability of the vehicle. Only tubeless tires, however, can incorporate the run-flat emergency running ring, a solid rubber ring made from two different special types of rubber. Its base is reinforced with steel wire, which provides a good interference fit so that the ring remains in place on the rim even at high speed. The outer section of the running ring contains rubber tubes filled with a lubricating paste. In case of an emergency breakdown involving complete loss of air pressure inside the tire, the tire lowers down to the emergency running ring; under this pressure, the sections of the ring open. The lubricating tubes come free and are broken between the tire and the running ring. The "freed" lubrication reduces friction between the parts. Such rings are easy to fit, have a homogeneous structure without imbalance, incorporate safe-to-use lubricating tubes, and are extremely light.

Another type of run-flat tire uses a circular bead lock of molded rubber to keep the bead against the sides of the rim, regardless of low or zero tire pressure. It thus avoids tire separation and the entry of sand or other foreign matter into the tire casing. The contact surface is increased when tire pressure is reduced. The bead lock can be installed in either tubeless or tubed tire types; standard air valves are used.

A third type of run-flat tire uses an inner tube of cellular core manufactured with a specially processed elastomer. Each cell is independent and is inflated with some type of inert gas during manufacture. This system also includes a lubricant to prevent overheating while running flat.

Run-flat tires eliminate the need for a spare wheel, thus saving space and payload for military vehicles. Besides military utilization, such tires are useful for police vans and commercial armored cars.

Conclusion

Different types of armored ground vehicles, their characteristics, attributes, and performance comparisons have been described above. While the primary role of these vehicles varies greatly—direct combat assault, reconnaissance, communications, repair and recovery, medical aid—the common denominator is mobility: their ability to operate effectively over various road surfaces and different terrain.

In terms of mobility, these vehicles are divided into wheeled and tracked classes, each with its own particular advantages and disadvantages. Effective employment of armored ground vehicles in combat and combat support operations depends on using them in a complementary manner, rather than arguing the relative value of one over the other. In the final analysis, use of these vehicles by military forces will "depend on the situation," and the astute commander will organize all mobility assets accordingly.

MOUSTAFA ALY MORSY ALY

SEE ALSO: Amphibious Ships and Craft; Amphibious Vehicle; Armored Land Vehicle Technology Applications; Engine Technology, Ground Vehicle; Mechanized Warfare; Mobility; Tank.

Bibliography

Bekker, M. 1980. Tracked vehicles: Terrain damage and economy. International Off-Highway Meeting and Exhibition, Milwaukee, Wis., September. SAE Technical Paper Series 800953.

Enrico, P. 1985. Scout and reconnaissance combat vehicles. *Military Technology* 9 (12):68–78.

Flume, W. 1987. Towards a new generation of wheeled vehicles. *Military Technology* 11 (11):115–17.

French, T. 1985. Tyres for the military. *Military Technology* 9 (4):36–41.

Howarth, M., and R. Ogorkiewicz. 1986. Tracked and wheeled light armoured vehicles. *International Defense Review*, editorial supplement 8:37, 40–47, 52–62.

Meckenheim, H. 1978. New multi-purpose amphibious armoured vehicles from EWK. *International Defense Review* 8:54–58.

Ogorkiewicz, R. 1986. Tracked and wheeled light armoured vehicles. *International Defense Review*, editorial supplement 8:19–23, 25–30, 31–34.

Vial, D. 1984. Armoured vehicles from Cardoen. *International Defense Review* 2:179–81.

ARMORED LAND VEHICLE TECHNOLOGY APPLICATIONS

The armored land vehicle traditionally leads the assault and affords breakthrough opportunities to the ground forces. The assault itself is a coordinated effort between air, land, and sometimes sea forces. The armored land vehicle as typified, for example, by the main battle tank and the armored infantry fighting vehicle is exposed to a large and increasing number and level of threats. The technology of the threats themselves is becoming increasingly diverse and lethal. The threats include: tank cannon; antitank guided missiles; free-flight rockets and guns; aircraft and artillery cannon; bombs and bomblets; high-energy lasers; electromagnetic radiation; nuclear, bacteriological, and chemical agents; and mines.

The application of new technologies to the armored land vehicle has as its purpose the provision of capabilities to overcome these threats and to improve the three principal functions that determine the effectiveness of the fighting vehicle: lethal firepower, crew and vehicle survivability, and mobility.

The mix and degree of lethality, survivability, and mobility in an armored vehicle varies according to the combat mission it is intended to perform—assault leader, fire support, reconnaissance, transport and logistics—and the likely type of opposing weapons. Accordingly, vehicle design is tailored to provide the desired balance of these attributes for optimal mission effectiveness. As Table 1 shows, there is a wide range and mix of these attributes from tracked main battle tanks to wheeled armored personnel carriers.

Technology Applications

The application of technology requires an assessment of the technologies either presently or potentially available for the various components or subsystems that comprise the entire armored vehicle. (The subsystems include structure, armor, propulsion system, suspension, auxiliary automotive systems, armament, vetronics, fire

TABLE 1. *Armored Vehicle Characteristics*

	WGT. (TONS)	ENG. HP	MAX. ROAD SPEED (MPH)	MAIN GUN CALIBER	CREW
U.S. M1A1 main battle tank	63	1,500	44	120 mm	4
USSR 2S3 self-propelled howitzer	30	520	38	152 mm	5
FRG Marder infantry fighting vehicle	32	600	46	20 mm	9
USSR BTR-70 armored personnel carrier	12.6	240	50	14.5 mm	2+9
UK Fox scout vehicle	6.7	190	65	30 mm	3

control, command, control and communications, and nonballistic survivability.) These subsystems are then assessed for specific technologies that have application to future vehicles.

Structure

The hull (and the turret for turreted vehicles) provides the structure to accommodate the crew and the armament, ammunition, and automotive system, and the integral armor that has traditionally provided protection against penetration. In many vehicles a cast-steel structure was used; but increasingly the trend is toward fabrications of welded rolled plates, with space allocated for the inclusion of armor, and more recently provision for the addition of modular armor. The latter design approach is expected to predominate in the future because of the capability to modify or replace the armor as the threat changes, or to accommodate to specific threats. In effect, the approach provides for a vehicle structure that serves as a carrier for the functioning components, but with replaceable or modifiable protection levels.

Heavy armored vehicles are fabricated principally of ballistic steel, with aluminum used in certain applications. Plastics, such as polymer composites, are increasingly being investigated, initially for weight reduction applications but also as principal components of the structure or armor. Various candidate configurations for vehicle structures include those listed below.

- Steel monocoque (welded)
- Aluminum monocoque (welded)
- Composite monocoque
- Steel casting
- Aluminum casting
- Steel rib-stiffened
- Aluminum rib-stiffened
- Composite integral rib
- Composite cored
- Steel frame + aluminum skin
- Aluminum frame + steel skin
- Steel frame + composite skin
- Aluminum frame + composite skin

Heavyweight vehicles are expected to continue to utilize structures principally of monocoque steel and aluminum, with selected application of steel castings; medium-weight vehicles, either rib-stiffened aluminum or rib-stiffened steel; and lighter vehicles a combination of aluminum and composite materials. The trends will be influenced by progress in manufacturing technology, principally in the techniques of fabrication and fastening.

A significant past trend in armored land vehicles has been the steady growth in weight for virtually all types of vehicles as both the lethality and protection levels have been increased. This trend is expected to be reversed as new weight-saving technologies emerge, but also as some tradeoffs in survivability are made in favor of lighter vehicles, particularly for airborne and rapid-response forces.

Armor

Reliable protection is required against a diversity of weapons, including armor-piercing kinetic energy projectiles and shaped-charge ammunition. Each has a different effect on the armor and requires different protection mechanisms. Figure 1 is an armor technology tree delineating the threats to the armored vehicle and the analyses made in determining the final armor design. The armor is tailored for the range of threats included in the design requirements. The candidate armors and combinations of armors include passive solid or spaced-composite, various laminates, and reactive. Recognizing the constant technological battle between improved threats and improved armor, vehicle designers are reluctant to rely solely on integral armor, which requires a major vehicle rebuild to improve the armor protection. Future applications increasingly will utilize replaceable armor packages, either contained within cavities in the basic structure or attached to the structure. This approach is advantageous for several reasons:

- ease of incorporating improved armor technologies as they evolve;
- ease of design upgrade for future threat changes;
- the flexibility of changing vehicle armor protection levels to meet the battlefield threat environment;
- the ability to minimize vehicle weight (operational efficiency) and maximize vehicle safety by removal of all armor (or only reactive armor) for certain operations such as training.

It is recognized that there is a limit to the amount of armor that can be applied for protection. As the lethal threat increases, the required weight of protective armor can become excessive.

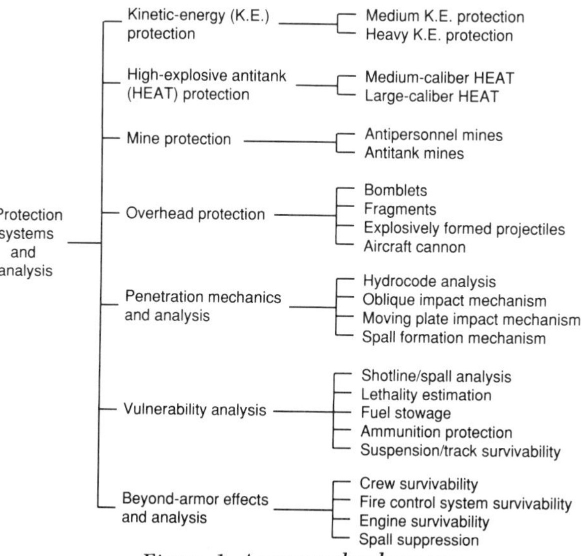

Figure 1. Armor technology tree.

Nontraditional methods of survivability and protection include techniques for signature reduction to avoid being detected and countermeasures to defeat threat sensors, as described further in the section entitled "Nonballistic Survivability."

Propulsion System

The propulsion system includes the entire powerpack and drive train, from the primary power source at the engine to the final drives for the track sprockets. Included are the engine, transmission including provision for steering and braking, final drives, cooling for engine and transmission, air filter, inlet and exhaust ducting, ancillary power generation, batteries, fuel tanks, and other auxiliary equipment. The engine and the transmission represent the bulk of the propulsion system in terms of both volume and cost and are key factors in establishing the design of the vehicle. One of the principal requirements is a high power-to-weight ratio to minimize the space requirement.

Propulsion system technologies can be categorized into three major areas:

1. Primary power source, which includes combustion energy engines, electrical energy, and fuel cells;
2. Power transmission device to provide speed and torque control, steering and inhibitors, drive trains to transfer power from transmissions to the vehicle sprocket/wheel; and
3. Auxiliary systems, which include air induction system, exhaust system, cooling system, fuel system diagnostic systems, and other ancillary equipment.

While a large variety of engine-transmission combinations have been developed and used in armored land vehicles, the preferred engine has been a four-stroke cycle diesel engine, with more recent applications of gas turbines. The latter are compact and reliable, and start up easily under cold conditions, but have a higher fuel consumption than the diesel. Future trends indicate continued activity in improving the power-to-weight ratio. As shown in Figure 2 for main battle tanks, a steady growth has been experienced. The trend is expected to be applied to all components of the propulsion system with the objective of reducing the armored volume requirement. Current systems under development have the objective of a 40 percent reduction in volume and a 50 percent reduction in fuel consumption for equivalent power.

One negative effect of the increased power in land combat vehicles has been the dramatic increase in operational fuel requirements. Vigorous efforts to reduce fuel consumption will be a challenge for future technology. A combination of efforts is required—weight reduction, improved fuel efficiency, and operational choices in the mix and utilization of various types of combat vehicles. It is expected that the drive for increased power and weight will have to be modified to fit logistical and operational realities.

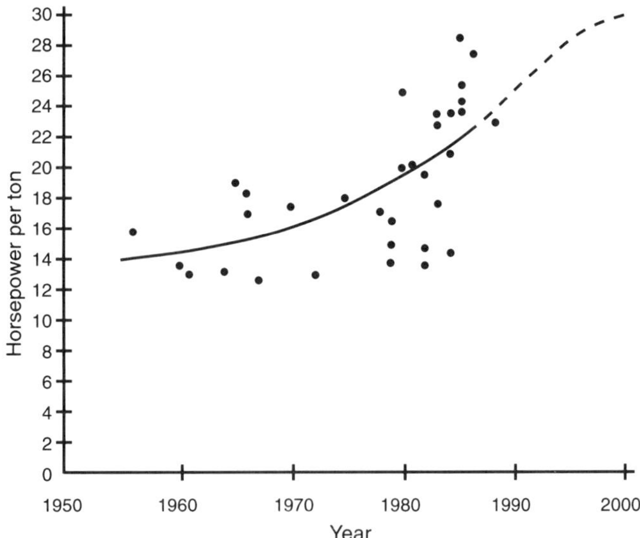

Figure 2. Power-to-weight ratios for main battle tanks.

One of the most promising technologies for future propulsion systems is the application of electrical drive, particularly as electrical weaponry is developed and a significant electrical power generation capability is developed that can serve both the propulsion and the weapon system.

Many configurations for the electrical drive are possible. Perhaps the simplest version has individual motors at each sprocket, but a number of experimental and operational vehicles have been built and tested. Electrical drive trains offer greater flexibility in design due to the modularization of electrical components and the lack of a rigid mechanical drive train. Critical component technologies that have shown marked progress are in the areas of power semiconductors, permanent magnet materials, and brushes for high current collection. Power storage devices have improved, and the entire field has profited from high-energy laser and space power programs. In particular, the promise of superconductivity at moderate to high temperatures, as that technology develops, will open the doors to electrical propulsion systems.

Suspension System

The suspension system, coupled with the track or wheel drive of the armored vehicle, is the critical element in effective transfer of power from the propulsion system to the tractive effort required for vehicle movement. The suspension consists of the springing and damping subsystems linking the hull with the wheel axles. The performance of the suspension system determines the stability of the vehicle platform, which in turn affects the degree of crew fatigue, vehicle speed over various terrains, accuracy of fire on the move and, by absorbing impact energy, the service life of the vehicle components and mechanisms.

The majority of modern tracked armored vehicles utilize a passive suspension system designed for a specific loading condition, frequently with some provisions for minor adjustment to the system for other operating conditions. For example, a tank may have torsion bars for springing and rotary hydraulic shock absorbers for damping. Each side of the vehicle incorporates a compensating idler with an adjustable track tension link, road arm stations with road arm, axle, and road wheel, and support rollers for top support and alignment of the track.

Some modern tanks incorporate external coil springs instead of torsion bars for the springing action in order to eliminate the weight and space occupied within the vehicle by a torsion bar system. A more recent advance is the use of pneumatic or hydropneumatic units external to the vehicle as the springing device. A further advantage is that the system can be made adaptive by modifying or adjusting the springing and damping with changes in the gas or hydraulic fluid, and by relief pressure adjustment. The technology has made steady progress and it is anticipated that the next generation of armored vehicles will incorporate adaptive suspension systems. But the added cost and complexity will be a consideration in finalizing the vehicle design, and for some armored vehicles the passive system will continue to be adequate, particularly for locales where the traversing of difficult terrain is not a major requirement.

The highest level of suspension control technology is the incorporation of an active suspension with controlled changes in the springing and damping rates during dynamic vehicle operation based on sensor data from the terrain, suspension rates, and vehicle speed, all processed and controlled by an on-board computer.

The electromagnetic suspension system is an infant technology holding promise as progress is made in magnetic materials and in electric power generation and conditioning. With continued developmental effort on electrical drive and electrical weaponry, the prospects are excellent for this technology application to the suspension system as well.

The tracks consist most frequently of metallic track shoes connected by pins, usually in rubber bushings, with rubber pads on the shoes to reduce road damage. Tracks are high-mortality service items with relatively poor durability requiring frequent servicing, maintenance, and replacement. Tracks are by far the highest-operational-cost item for suspension systems and will gain the most from innovative design and from technological advances in rubber development.

The preceding discussion has emphasized the suspension system for the tracked combat vehicle, which is decidedly superior to the wheeled armored vehicle in terms of adverse terrain mobility and in combat survivability of the drive system. But for many combat-related roles, the wheeled vehicle has been and will continue to be employed. Wheeled vehicles are more economical to acquire and operate; have higher reliability, with component life four to five times that of the tracked vehicle; are less costly to maintain and repair; and can rely on national truck and automotive production bases. Both the armor and the armament can be equivalent to that of a tracked vehicle of similar weight, limited generally to 20–25 tons. Wheeled vehicles that operate at higher speeds on road marches are quieter and less fatiguing for the crew and consume less fuel than tracked vehicles. All of the suspension technologies for tracked vehicles are applicable to wheeled vehicles.

Auxiliary Automotive Systems

In armored vehicles, the auxiliary systems most amenable to technology application are the fire detection and suppression system and the fire control system, which includes the gun and turret drive systems.

Automatic fire detection and suppression systems with provision for manual actuation are widely used in modern armored vehicles. Detectors sensitive to ultraviolet or infrared radiation rapidly sense the radiation emitted by flames, with a response time of two to three milliseconds. An electronic control unit processes the sensor signal data, interprets the data for such factors as false alarms, and activates the installed fire extinguishing system. In the past, carbon dioxide has been the principal suppressant for military vehicles, but modern vehicles use halogenated compounds that are two to three times more effective on a unit weight basis. Once the fire suppressant is released, it is effective in protecting the crew and the engine compartment. In terms of the application of new technology, principal effort will be in improving the detectors with regard to response time, false alarms, sensitivity to lens obscuration, and reliability.

Hydraulic pressure has traditionally been used for gun and turret drive at pressures most commonly in the 1,500- to 2,000-psi range. Other types of vehicles, such as modern construction equipment, operate at 3,000–6,000 psi, and some aircraft applications are being designed for 7,000–8,000 psi. In an armored vehicle, increased hydraulic pressure constitutes a hazard to personnel due to fire potential endangering the crew from an equipment leak or a ballistic hit. Hydraulic systems constitute an ever-present danger in the vehicle, exacerbated as the pressures are increased to provide additional functions such as robotic hardware for ammunition autoloaders. Technology application efforts are being directed at the development of nonflammable hydraulic fluids and the development of suitable materials and fabrication techniques for hydraulic hardware that is subjected to elevated pressures.

One approach being effected in some armored vehicles is to avoid the problem by totally eliminating hydraulic fluids, replacing hydraulic actuators and motors with electrical drives. Electrical gun turret drives have been designed and are operational, a trend which is expected to continue.

Armament

A wide range of armaments is carried by various land combat vehicles, including main tank guns, automatic cannon, cupola-mounted self-defense weapons, scatterable mine dispersers, field artillery armament, antitank missiles and guided munitions, air defense missiles, and mortars. One prevailing characteristic has been the growth increase in gun caliber over time and the continuing effort to increase muzzle velocity and the penetration capability of the projectile warhead. The effect on the vehicle has been weight growth due to the heavier guns and ammunition, and to the increased armor required to afford self-protection against equivalent-threat weapons. At the same time, the requirements for improved fire control and gun stabilization systems have resulted in increased complexity of electronics and display systems. The overall lethality of the armored vehicle, therefore, is affected not only by the gun and ammunition but by the effectiveness of the gun control mechanisms.

New technologies applicable to main armament include principally liquid propellant and electrical weapons.

From a vehicle viewpoint, liquid-propellant guns are advantageous because the liquid can be stowed in tanks in a more efficient manner than can individual solid propellants. On the other hand, the added valves, pumps, and piping increase vulnerability and complexity. Handling of projectiles is easier with elimination of the solid propellant. From the viewpoint of application of liquid gun technology, the effect on the overall vehicle system is expected to be positive. With proper design, the liquid propellant can be stored and compartmented for protection purposes, and the requirement for ammunition handling would be limited to the projectile, easing the handling and storage requirement. The promise would be even better if progress were made in the bipropellant liquid approach, with one of the propellants being engine fuel, thereby easing somewhat the liquid handling problem. From an armored vehicle viewpoint, the development and incorporation of a liquid-propellant gun could be accommodated.

The application of the electrical gun, either electrothermal (ET) or electromagnetic (EM, either the rail or coil type) would have a much greater impact on the vehicle. The electrothermal gun uses a conventional gun tube with modified breech, which is easier to accommodate than the more radical reconfiguration required for the electromagnetic gun. The elimination of the chemical-propellant charge improves the survivability of the crew and vehicle, as well as reducing the logistics of ammunition supply, since only projectiles are required. Fuel logistics would be increased because more fuel would be required for the prime power source to provide the electrical energy for the gun.

From a technology application viewpoint, the development of electrical weaponry will provide the most significant change in future armored vehicles. The lethality of the system will increase. Radical changes will be possible in other subsystems, including the potential for electrical drive, electromagnetic suspension, even the possibility of electromagnetic protection. All of this potential is highly dependent on technological progress in efficient power generation and conditioning techniques. The drive toward electrical weapons, therefore, has an ancillary benefit—the parallel effort for technological progress in power generation and power conditioning techniques. Once those are in hand, additional electrically powered weaponry like lasers and microwave devices will be possible.

Vetronics

Vetronics (*ve*hicle elec*tronics*) is the major new technology to be applied to future armored land vehicles—the techniques of using modern computer systems to achieve precise control through electrical and electronic integration. These subsystems are becoming more complex and more costly than the automotive and armament subsystems in the current vehicles. Vetronics, initiated by the U.S. Army Tank Automotive Command in 1981 to develop a standard electronic and electrical architecture for all land combat vehicles, is a total systems integration approach to the electronic and electrical subsystems on a land vehicle, similar to avionics systems in aircraft. In the past, armored land vehicles, even those of more modern design, focused on the development of individual electronic subsystems without much thought to how vehicle integration would be accomplished. The result has been extensive use of hard wiring, manual actuation devices, and little capability for upgrading without a major retrofit of the vehicle. Vetronics utilizes a distributed architecture design and modular building blocks that allow efficient integration and the flexibility to accommodate change. Management of computer assets and automation of vehicle tasks is facilitated, as well as on-board fault diagnosis and prognosis.

One possible vetronics architecture showing functional allocation to subsystems is given in Figure 3. Variations of this generic architecture will be made for different vehicle types and to meet the degree of sophistication demanded by the mission. In this generic example, the data control and distribution subsystem manages the information flow between the crew stations and the subsystems, as well as between subsystems. The power generation and management subsystem distributes electrical power from the generator or batteries. The computer resources subsystem provides the automated data collection, manipulation, and control. The crew stations consist of controls and displays that allow the crew members to access and control all of the vehicle subsystems.

Figure 4 depicts the vetronic system's integrating elements: controls and displays, computers, and busses for digital communication. These basic elements provide the design flexibility needed to integrate easily mission-

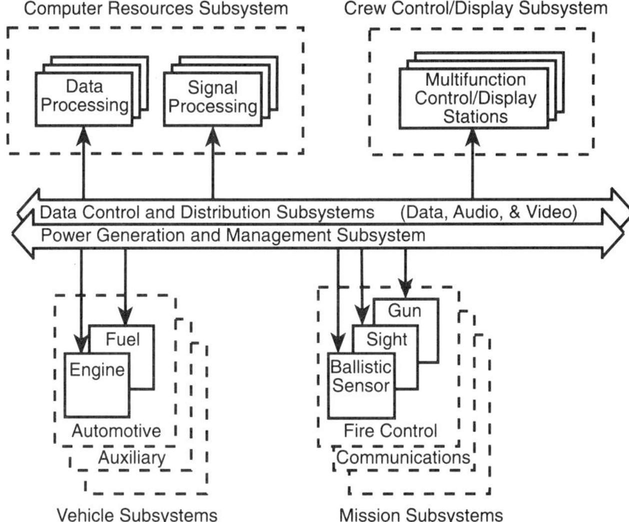

Figure 3. Vetronics generic systems architecture.

specific subsystems such as navigation, electro-optical, radar, etc. The advantage of this system is that the integrating elements can be replaced by improved units without altering the wiring systems, and additional units and displays can be installed as required for particular vehicles, for example engine controls, additional threat sensors, communication equipment, command and control devices—whatever the design requires. The individual modules of the integrating elements will be designed so as to have application to a number of vehicle types, with the vehicle architecture software tailored for the specific application.

Fire Control

The lethality of a gun-firing armored vehicle requires an effective method of detecting the target by means of an on-board observation and sensing device, and accurate laying of the gun with aiming devices. To increase gun-firing accuracy, corrections need also to be made for relative motion between the vehicle and the target, the environmental conditions, the condition of the gun, and ammunition type. All of these data are fed into an on-

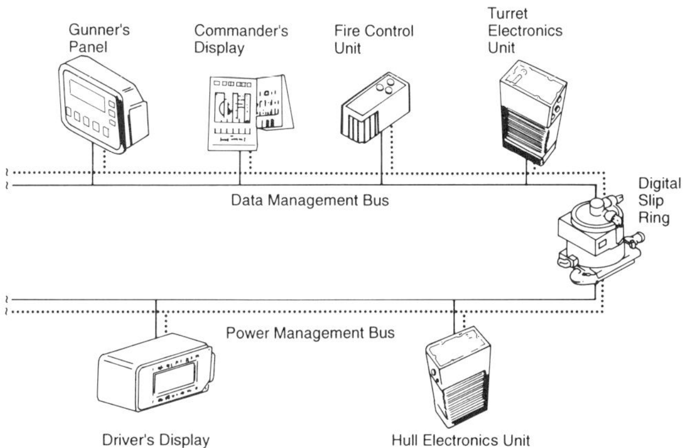

Figure 4. Some data and power management connections.

board digital computer that accurately controls gun pointing for putting a round on target. As technology has progressed, each generation of armored gun vehicle has increasingly utilized automatic inputs from sensors to the computer rather than mechanical inputs from the gunner.

A wide field of view is needed for surveillance of the battlefield, with capability for high magnification for target identification and enhanced target detection. Optical sights continue to be the preferred sighting device; however, other sensors such as infrared devices are the primary device in the case of night fighting. Active infrared searchlights have been employed, but are readily detectable. Passive night-vision devices based on image intensification are in use, but do not perform well on dark nights or in other poor-visibility conditions. Increasingly, armored vehicles are being equipped with thermal imaging devices in the 8 to 14 micrometer range to detect the radiation given off by target objects. The initial high cost of these sensors gradually has been reduced. As the technology improves, techniques for the integration of thermal with optical sights will be enhanced, as well as the wider application of the sighting devices to additional crew members, to remotely positioned sensors, and for robotic devices. Other types of sensors under development, and candidates for future technology application, include low-light-level television and millimeter-wave radar sensors. The latter are superior to infrared devices in battlefield operation with obscurants and smokes.

Once a target has been detected, the range to it must be ascertained and included in the ballistic computation. In early armored land vehicles, determination of range by eye under good conditions resulted in an error of about fifteen percent of the range. The use of sight scales within the optics improved the acuracy to an eight percent error. Further improved optical rangefinders utilizing the coincidence principle are in wide use, but more recently laser rangefinders with an error of about ± 10 meters (32 ft.) have dramatically improved accuracy and reduced the first-round engagement time. Development of laser rangefinders will continue, probably moving from the current Neodymium-Yag laser to the CO laser for better smoke penetration.

Initially, ballistic computers were mechanical devices into which the gunner fed data such as ballistic firing conditions (charge conditions, gun tube wear, vehicle cant, angle of sight), meteorological conditions (wind direction and velocity, air temperature, atmospheric pressure), and speed and direction of target movement. Subsequently, automated electromechanical ballistic computers were developed, and today the fully digital ballistic computer has been placed in service on several vehicles. Coupled with the signal and data processing capabilities previously described with the development of the vetronics architecture, and the potential application of electrical drive for the gun and turret stabilization systems, the time required for first-round engagement will continue to be reduced.

Additional technology applications to the fire control system will include automated target acquisition and identification, improved techniques for target handoff from commander to gunner or from vehicle to vehicle, and automatic target tracking. The latter already is being developed based on thermal sensors and will be the next principal addition to the fire control suite. With vision devices, automatic target acquisition is a processing function that automatically finds targets by searching an image to find localized areas that are most likely to be targets. Automatic target recognition is a software function based on a pattern recognition system to discriminate between targets. The technology will be applied as algorithms are developed and as computer processing capability increases. Laboratory devices already have been demonstrated and the on-board architecture system design will be able to accommodate the software functions.

Command, Control and Communications

As rapid technological progress is made in all subsystems of the armored land vehicle, including increased mobility, higher weapon lethality with reduced times for engagement, improved first-round hit probability, and better protection mechanisms, the environment for the commander is changing to a high-paced battlefield with an overriding need for improved tactical and troop-leading procedures. The same technological progress being made in mechanical and electronic subsystems and in systems integration is required for the acquisition, processing, transmittal, and utilization of battlefield information. Four areas of technology development are anticipated: navigation, digital map display, enhanced communications, and tactical data processing.

Navigation systems are important to the control of armored land vehicles in battle and on the march. With good visibility and with adequate time, the use of maps and local topography features is adequate, but with poor visibility or in difficult terrain, automatic navigation systems are becoming a basic requirement. Navigation information is needed in combat situations to determine the route and disposition of troops and for the plotting of vehicle and troop movements. With advances in lethality, the use of purely visual devices and crew observation is becoming too hazardous; automatic techniques are required.

Navigation and position-reference systems of the self-contained passive gyroscopic type will be developed initially, with eventual coupling to satellite-based position-locator systems to provide increasingly accurate position information.

For topographical maps, the paper maps traditionally used will continue for certain applications. However, with the extensive electronic display and computer capabilities of future armored vehicles, maps can be generated using integrated computer graphics generators embedded into the vehicle host computer. It is anticipated that map generation and display technology will be included in the next-generation commander's display functions for armored land vehicles.

Communications equipment is the most critical component in the command function and in the control of armored combat vehicle forces. It also is the most vulnerable in view of threat jamming efforts and the volume of message traffic. Technology applications include improved data link security by encryption techniques and the use of data compression to provide for increased traffic and a reduction in the time of transmission.

Just as on-board data is processed and managed by the vetronics architecture design, a corresponding procedure will be developed for the handling and display of tactical data. Protocols for the handling of data at various levels of battle management (including and beyond the armored land vehicle level), such as formatting of messages and automatic transmittal and acknowledgment procedures tailored for specific mission roles, will be applied as the development of specifications, software, and hardware continues.

It is anticipated that tactical data processing will become a major effort because armored vehicles are increasingly being utilized as team members in combined operations. The lack of adequate command and control mechanisms otherwise would negate the progress made in individual vehicle capability and performance.

Nonballistic Survivability

In addition to the improvement of the armored land vehicle itself and of its components, a major effort is developing in the technology of avoiding detection and increasing vehicle and crew survivability by means other than the use of antiballistic armor. As the range of threats to the armored vehicle has expanded, the range of protective mechanisms under investigation and development similarly has been expanded, covering a diversity of techniques and technologies. The field is too broad for a detailed discussion, but a brief summary follows.

Active protection requires the detection of a threat and activation of a defeat mechanism. For example, an incoming missile can be detected and defeated by a countering blast warhead missile fired from the armored vehicle. Various techniques of passive protection are afforded by utilizing smoke or chaff generators to evade attack. The vehicle can be equipped with warning receivers to alert the crew to a threat, triggering either an automatic or a manually actuated response. With the variety of sensors and response mechanisms available, integration of the countermeasures is required and sensor fusion techniques will be applied. To avoid detection, a variety of signature-reduction methods can be employed, with initial emphasis on the infrared signature because of the large number of infrared threat sensors. NBC (nuclear, biological, chemical) protection is required for the crew. Several modern armored vehicles carry both collective and individual crew protection devices against chemical and bacteriological attack. Nuclear survivability techniques include gamma ray absorption devices and, in most instances, armored vehicles are designed to resist electromagnetic pulses (EMP). Lasers and microwaves have as a first target the optical systems; various protective schemes are in development. As power levels increase, additional attention will be placed on protection for other components of the vehicle.

One of the greatest threats to the armored vehicle, and one of the most difficult to counter, is the mine, either self- or command-actuated. The technology for mine defeat is perhaps the least advanced technologically. Traditional methods continue to be used for mine clearing or for mine lane marking. A great advance in nonballistic survivability would be the development of methods for neutralizing mines. Armored vehicles continue to be vulnerable to this threat.

Conclusion

The current trends in armored land vehicles will continue, with expanded technology applications in sensors, electronics, and computers, benefitting greatly from developments in more sophisticated weapons. Correspondingly, the sophistication and cost of the systems will increase, although major progress is expected in the ability to operate the vehicle with the inherent complexity transparent to the crew.

- Welded monocoque steel and aluminum structures will predominate, with increased application of polymer plastic composites. Armor packages will be replaceable to permit upgrade of a vehicle's protective capabilities without requiring a complete vehicle rebuild. Emphasis will continue on reducing vehicle size and weight.
- The vehicle propulsion system will increasingly move to more compact designs with higher power-to-weight ratios to conserve armored volume. The growing overall fuel consumption due to weight and power growth in the vehicles will become a more significant factor in future design considerations, with greater emphasis on reversing the trend.
- The vehicle running gear, consisting of the suspension system and tracks or wheels, will continue to use mechanical springing with damping for many applications, but the technology of adaptive suspensions and active suspensions with external hydropneumatic devices will be applied to selected high-performance vehicles.
- In terms of armament, higher-caliber main guns will appear in the next generation of fighting vehicles, but the promise of electrical weaponry in increasing lethality and reducing the ammunition logistics burden is such that major effort is expected to continue and expand. Electrical power generation and conditioning are the key technologies; once they are achieved, it is expected that electrical drive for vehicle propulsion, electromagnetic suspensions, and electromagnetic protection systems will move to the demonstration phase.
- The continuing technological battle between improved lethality and improved protection has contributed to the growth in weight, complexity, and cost; all of these likely will continue, but with more attention devoted to alternate solutions. A range of techniques to improve survivability by other than ballistic armor protection—for example, by such methods as reducing detectability, countermeasures, and active protection—are expected to receive greater emphasis.
- Major technology application in future vehicles will feature the expanded use of electronic devices and software architecture utilizing displays, automated controls, and a variety of aids to relieve the crew tasks and improve the decision-making process. Data will be selectively distributed within the vehicle and between vehicles.

In summary, the technologies directly associated with the components and subsystems of the armored land vehicle, coupled with the wealth of technologies from other weapons developments, as well as the general progress in commercial fields, provide a host of opportunities for application to land combat vehicles. All are expected to continue to be candidates for consideration, requiring a selective process of determining the optimum combination of performance and cost suitable for each particular design.

E. N. PETRICK

SEE ALSO: Armor; Armored Ground Vehicle; Armor Technology; Engine Technology, Ground Vehicle; Mechanized Warfare; Mobility; Tank.

Bibliography

Hilmes, R. 1987. *Main battle tanks: Developments in design since 1945*. Trans. R. Simpkin. London: Brassey's.
Nürnberger, W. 1981. Technical trends and possibilities for the armoured vehicles of the future. *Defence Today* 33/34:56ff.
Senger und Etterlin, F. M. von. 1983. *Tanks of the world*. London: Arms and Armour Press.
Zaloga, S., and J. Loop. 1982. *Modern American armour*. London: Arms and Armour Press.

ARMS CONTROL AND DISARMAMENT

Many nations have pursued a policy of arms control and disarmament, in treaties as well as in their political declarations. The two nuclear superpowers and the European states have been foremost for many years in seeking to limit their armaments potential through multilateral and bilateral negotiations.

Despite this fact, in the period since the Second World

War the arsenals of most states have proliferated. Most international arms control agreements limit the military and strategic options of the parties involved only marginally, if at all. Only after the confrontation between East and West ended did arms control negotiations begin to herald structural changes. It is questionable whether these concepts could have been implemented successfully without the fundamental changes in the East-West conflict, and uncertain to what extent they can be applied to the conflicts of the future.

To comprehend and judge the significance of arms control with regard to the foreign and security policies of the second half of the twentieth century, one must clearly understand the concepts of arms control, particularly the objectives envisaged and the instruments developed for these purposes. Arms control policy itself is not a static act; it should be regarded as a dynamic process operating under specific conditions that evolve in certain historic situations. This article assumes the following definition of arms control: "The essence of arms control is some kind of mutual restraint, collaborative action for exchange of facilities between potential enemies in the interest of reducing the likelihood of war, the scope of war if it occurs or its consequences" (Schelling and Halperin 1988).

History

Arms control in its various manifestations has always been an element in the theory and practice of international politics. It was only in the age of nuclear deterrence, however, that it developed beyond disarmament policy into a sophisticated instrument for regulating and managing the military strategy and political aspects of the relationships between antagonistic states.

Traditional Disarmament Policy

Arms control until the time of the Versailles treaties manifested itself mainly in the form of disarmament terms that victors in war imposed on vanquished powers. As early as the period between the two world wars, some powers attempted to conclude mutual voluntary agreements on reducing their military potential. A milestone of arms control in that period was the Washington Naval Agreement of 1922. In the late 1920s the Soviet Union presented a plan for comprehensive and complete disarmament to the Disarmament Conference of the League of Nations; negotiations began in 1932 but soon failed.

After World War II, plans for general disarmament were discussed again, this time under the auspices of the United Nations. Four initiatives deserve mention. The first, the Baruch Plan, aimed to abolish all nuclear weapons by subjecting the development and utilization of nuclear energy to the control of an international agency. When the first Soviet nuclear bomb exploded in 1949, this plan quickly lost currency. In the 1950s the Western powers began to focus on the limitation of conventional armaments. The five-power negotiations of London in 1957 dealt with almost the entire spectrum of modern arms control questions, ranging from reduction of conventional forces to nuclear test bans and questions of inspection. A third major attempt at comprehensive disarmament was initiated by the McCloy-Sorin Agreement, in which the United States and the USSR agreed on the fundamentals of a disarmament policy aimed at total abolition of nuclear and conventional weapons. This agreement formed the basis for the negotiations of the eighteen-nation Disarmament Committee in Geneva between 1962 and 1964. When these negotiations failed, all comprehensive disarmament plans were shelved until, in the late 1970s, the First Special Session of the United Nations on Disarmament brought them back into focus. Even in recent times, repeated initiatives have aimed at general disarmament.

All these ideas reflect a somewhat idealistic approach to arms control and one that has a fairly low chance of implementation. All focus on disarmament, with the reduction or abolition of certain categories of weapons and/or armed forces regarded as an objective in itself. It is a peculiarity of this approach that it concentrates on military hardware, completely neglecting the political and strategic context. It ignores the political causes of the dynamism of armaments, and it makes only perfunctory allowance for the interrelationship between disarmament and arms control on the one hand and strategic and military interests on the other.

A number of multilateral arms control agreements (such as the Antarctic Agreement and the Space Treaty) are fully within the traditions of this idealistic approach to arms control. The negotiations of the Geneva Disarmament Conference seeking a global ban on chemical weapons, which have been "nearing completion" for years but have so far been fruitless, belong in that same category. On the other hand, these very negotiations prove that such an approach can succeed only in realms where military and strategic interests are not seriously involved. Whenever the focus is on controlling the dynamism of armaments or the arms race as a form of military competition under antagonistic political conditions, in an attempt to obviate situational instability or escalation into open conflict, traditional disarmament policy always proves unsuitable.

Modern Arms Control

Political and technological developments in nuclear strategy made it appear probable that a nuclear confrontation might erupt involuntarily and uncontrollably. As a result, new theories and concepts developed in the early 1960s in the United States that laid the foundations of modern arms control. Their essential innovations vis-à-vis traditional thought can be summed up as follows: The supreme goal of arms control is the prevention of war. Notwithstanding military and political antagonism between nations, there must be a way of defining areas where strategic interests coincide so that the risk of war can be reduced. To prevent war by arms control primarily implies creating and safeguarding strategic stability, with the abolition or reduction of certain weapons categories being of secondary importance. Modern arms control also implies exchanging information on military potential, its technical specifications, and the doctrines and procedures that govern its application. Modern arms control is not limited to the issue of reducing or banning certain weapons systems or armed forces but embraces the entire regime that controls their deployment. Arms control starts with the readiness of antagonistic states to subject these processes to cooperative control, be it through negotiations or through other forms of communication.

U.S.-Soviet agreements. Modern arms control theory quickly became an element of American security policy. Thus, its practical manifestation bears the stamp of the nuclear strategy relations between the United States and the Soviet Union. Among the milestones of this new policy in the 1960s and 1970s is a series of agreements concerning the strategic nuclear regime. The 1963 Nuclear Test Ban Treaty, to which 160 nations have now acceded, is of political significance because it marks the start of the new era. In 1968 the Nuclear Nonproliferation Treaty came into force, designed to limit the number of states disposing of nuclear weapons. In 1972 the United States and the Soviet Union signed two agreements on stabilizing their strategic situation; these became the cornerstone of further dialogue on the limitation and reduction of strategic armament. The Anti–Ballistic Missile Treaty (ABM Treaty), in which both sides to all intents and purposes renounce the deployment and development of anti–ballistic missile systems (each side was permitted two sites at first, later only one each), codified the agreement of the two nations on the fundamental principles of the deterrence strategy of mutual assured destruction. The SALT I Agreement (Strategic Arms Limitation Talks) for the first time defined limits of growth for offensive strategic systems (intercontinental ballistic missiles; sea-launched ballistic missiles). In addition, a number of flanking measures were designed to stabilize the bilateral nuclear regime (e.g., accidents measures agreements, AMA). Issues regarding the limitation of conventional arms in Europe, long blocked because of links to a change in the political status quo, remained outside the scope of modern arms control. Multilateral negotiations on mutually balanced forces reduction in Europe (MBFR) that began in 1972, soon degenerated into a forum for propaganda or, at best, a laboratory for testing new ideas in arms control policy.

In the late 1970s, modern arms control came under severe attack. Critics asked whether the Soviet Union was indeed in agreement with the premises of American arms control policy, especially whether it shared the American concept of stability or was instead attempting to turn processes of arms control into instruments to attain its own foreign policy goals. In final consequence, such questioning led to the conclusion that arms control was feasible only between states that stood in no need of it.

As the East-West relationship began to deteriorate across the board, the continued criticism led to a temporary collapse of arms control policy. Only after decisive changes occurred in the parameters of the East-West conflict did it become possible to initiate new arms control agreements in the field of nuclear strategy and, for the first time, in conventional strategy as well.

Recent trends. Within the framework of the Conference on Security and Cooperation in Europe (CSCE), a comprehensive agreement on confidence- and security-building measures (CSBM) was concluded in 1985, by which the military structures and procedural patterns of NATO and the Warsaw Pact were partially revealed, and which laid down the principle of on-site verification for the first time. In 1988 an American-Soviet agreement on the limitation of land-based short- and medium-range (500–5,500-km, or 310–3,410-mi.) nuclear missiles came into force (INF Treaty). In this by-no-means undisputed agreement, two states for the first time in history agreed to destroy an entire category of weapons. The last weapons of this type in American and Soviet possession were scrapped in the summer of 1991.

In 1990 the member states of both the Warsaw Pact and NATO signed an agreement on conventional stability in Europe (CSE) that remains significant even after the revolutionary developments in Eastern Europe and the dissolution of the Eastern military alliance. It codified new structures of security from the Atlantic Ocean to the Ural Mountains. The arsenals of weapons systems that constitute the core of conventional offensive capability were limited or reduced considerably, and the options available for dislocating them within the area covered by the agreement were circumscribed. In July 1991, after nine years of negotiation, the Soviet Union and the United States signed an Agreement on the Reduction of Strategic Armaments (START); it provided, for the first time, for the effective reduction of strategic nuclear weapons (launching systems and warheads); contained bans on modernizing the strategic arsenal; and introduced a long-term process of restructuring the military potential of both sides with a view toward more stability. Tables 1 and 2 list significant bilateral (U.S.–USSR) and multilateral arms control agreements.

Goals of Arms Control

In practice, arms control and/or disarmament are subservient to goals and expectations of varying priority. The theory and practice of modern arms control suggest three major goals: (1) to prevent war; (2) to contain the damage in the event of a conflict; and (3) to reduce defense expenditure. These goals by no means form a monolithic

TABLE 1. *U.S.–USSR Bilateral Arms Control Agreements*

"Accidents Measures" Agreement (AMA)—Signed 30 September 1971; entered into force 30 September 1971; unlimited duration

Anti-Ballistic Missile (ABM) Treaty—Negotiated 1969–72; signed 26 May 1972, entered into force 3 October 1972; duration unlimited; review called every 5 years

Strategic Arms Limitation Talks (SALT I)—Interim agreement; negotiated 1969–72; signed 26 May 1972, entered into force 3 October 1972; 5 year duration

Threshold Test Ban Treaty (TTBT)—Signed 3 July 1974; renegotiated 1986–87, 1987–90; treaty entered into force 11 December 1990

Strategic Arms Limitation Talks (SALT II)—Negotiated 1972–79; signed 18 June 1979; has not entered into force

Nuclear Risk Reduction Center—Negotiated 1985–87; signed 15 September 1987; U.S. Nuclear Risk Reduction Center opened 23 March 1988

Intermediate-Range Nuclear Forces (INF) Treaty—Negotiated 1980–87; signed 7 December 1987; entered into force 1 June 1988; duration unlimited

Strategic Arms Reduction Talks (START)—Negotiated 1982–91; signed 30 July 1991; to be ratified; indefinite duration

system. While they are not fundamentally irreconcilable, they contain partial contradictions.

Conflicting Goals

The range of objectives associated with the prevention of war is at the center of modern arms control, damage containment being rather a side effect. The same applies to the reduction of expenditure—although political debates have shown that this argument is sometimes foremost in the motivation of arms control policy.

At first glance, the goal of damage containment logically contradicts the main goal of preventing war; its relevance begins with the failure of the latter. However, it is highly significant with regard to specific weapons systems and categories that are used only when a conflict has escalated to a certain level. What comes particularly to mind in this context is the role of chemical or biological weapons, or other instruments of violent conflict such as climatic manipulation (environmental weapons).

Under the nuclear-strategy aspect of arms control, the significance of damage containment was secondary. Nuclear overkill capacities were reduced hardly at all. To be sure, the comprehensive nuclear test ban certainly had a protective effect on the environment. On the other hand, such measures may to some extent counteract the goal of containing collateral damage, insofar as they diminish our understanding of the controllability of nuclear forces.

The goal of cutting defense expenditure conflicts with the other two goals as well. The psychological effect of the cost argument is certainly significant with regard to more than one aspect of the arms control process. For instance, tight national budgets, especially in the Western democracies, increased political pressure to resume arms control negotiations. Another fact is that arms control helps save opportunity cost, especially in the conventional field.

However, any arms control policy that is founded mainly on cost cuts is apt to lead in the wrong direction. Strategic arsenals account for only a small proportion of the defense budgets of the superpowers; most of the money is spent on research and development. Research is beyond the scope of arms control, but from the point of view of stability it may be vital—for example, in developing weapons systems and their mechanisms of control.

Stability and the Prevention of War

In the context of a policy founded not on a vision of collective security but on a balance-of-power approach, security cannot be enhanced by the reduction of weapons per se. (Conversely, such reduction might even increase the risk of war.) This being so, modern arms control focuses on stability in the strategic and military relations between states. Theoretically, this stability is present "whenever the military sector does not generate any specific or intrinsic elements of risk, and whenever it is impossible for one side to make political use of military instruments to the detriment of the other" (Forndran 1988).

The major challenges in formulating such a policy of arms control are to translate the goal of stability into operative terms, or to define it in terms adequate to the situation; to analyze politically correctly what developments might endanger stability; and, following this, to identify adequate measures in arms control policy.

The founders of modern arms control defined stability in terms of safeguarding the nuclear deterrent, especially

TABLE 2. *Major Multilateral Arms Control Agreements*

Antarctic Treaty—Signed 1 December 1959; entered into force 23 June 1961; duration unlimited after 1991 review

Limited Test Ban Treaty (LTBT)—Signed 5 August 1963; entered into force 10 October 1963; duration unlimited

Outer Space Treaty (OST)—Signed 27 January 1967; entered into force 10 October 1967; unlimited duration

Tlatelolco Treaty—Treaty for the Prohibition of Nuclear Weapons in Latin America—Negotiated 1962–66; signed 14 February 1967; entered into force 25 April 1968; permanent duration

Non-Proliferation Treaty (NPT)—Negotiated 1957–68; signed 1 July 1969; entered into force 5 March 1970; duration until 1995 with option of continuation

Seabed Arms Control Treaty (SACT)—Signed 11 February 1971; entered into force 18 May 1972; review conferences

Biological Weapons Convention (BWC)—Signed 10 April 1972; entered into force 26 March 1975; duration unlimited

Moon Treaty—Signed 18 December 1979; entered into force 11 July 1984; duration unlimited

Confidence and Security-Building Measures (CSBM; part of the CSCE)—Measures negotiated at "Stockholm Conference" from 17 January 1984 to 22 September 1986; Vienna CSBM negotation from 15 January 1989 to 17 November 1990 (Vienna Document); ongoing

Treaty on Conventional Armed Forces in Europe (CFE; part of CSCE)—Negotiated 1989–90; signed 19 November 1990; not yet in force; duration unlimited in terms of preventing surprise attacks and instability in crises. In their opinion, the most critical dangers were the dynamism of armament and the arms race that enhanced the risk of accidental war and the probability of surprise attack. Last, but not least, were the dangers associated with nuclear proliferation.

The initial development of strategic arms control in the 1960s reflected these definitions of the problem. The relatively swift agreement to install a "hot line" to ensure instant contact between Moscow and Washington in the event of a crisis or some other unintentional development, and the cooperation between the American and Soviet sides with regard to the Nonproliferation Treaty, seemed to corroborate the premise that the two antagonistic superpowers indeed could define areas where their interests coincided. Negotiations on bilateral strategic arms control (in the narrower definition of the term) began as the Soviets were developing an antimissile system that put American retaliation capability at risk in addition to bringing Soviet offensive nuclear potential up to par.

That both the ABM Treaty and the SALT I Treaty were concluded successfully seemed to indicate that the Soviet Union had accepted the U.S. doctrine of nuclear retaliation and the definition of stability on which it was founded. However, the policy of arms expansion pursued by the USSR in subsequent years, as well as Moscow's behavior in the area of strategic and conventional arms control, increasingly imperiled the premises of Western policy.

Differing definitions. The traditional interpretation of stability came under the cross fire of fundamentalist critics, who said that the narrow focus on strategic stability was neglecting the political dynamism of Soviet arms control policy. They claimed that under the cloak of arms control the Soviet Union was striving not merely for parity with the United States but for nuclear supremacy—aiming to create a first-strike capability by modernizing its nuclear arsenal partially in defiance of the agreement, particularly by developing heavy intercontinental missiles. Similarly, they held that the Soviet Union was attempting to exploit the negotiations on conventional arms control in Europe: attempting to codify military imbalances that were in its favor, at the same time ratifying the political status quo (i.e., its hegemony over Eastern Europe) and undermining the U.S. presence in Western Europe. Moreover, the definition of stability derived from the theory of games was criticized for its artificial distinction between global and regional equilibrium. This argument was corroborated by the Soviet deployment of medium-range missiles in the 1970s that threatened Western Europe alone, but because of their reach did not come within the scope of strategic arms control (grey-area problem).

In fact, the Soviet Union agreed to only a limited extent with the American model of stability and with American strategic thought in general. The USSR had developed its own strategic culture, which had imposed itself on the country's security policy and, consequently, on its interests in arms control policy. Moreover, Soviet comprehension of stability was different; at times, the USSR defined stability as a "correlation of forces." However, with the conclusion of the START Agreement and the CSE Treaty—which include provisions for containing particularly destabilizing systems as well as measures to reduce the risk of surprise attacks—it appeared that a rapprochement between these differing definitions was under way.

The scope of stability. In defining the goal of stability, arms control policy must go beyond mere numeric relationships; it must encompass differences in the security doctrines that govern the leadership and deployment of troops, the structure of the armed forces, the general style of leadership, hierarchic and historic preferences, and military thinking in general. Moreover, certain key indicators of strategic stability, such as targeting precision, system reliability, or the structure of leadership and command (C^3), are difficult to measure in quantitative terms; they may even be completely beyond the compass of arms control. Finally, when analyzing the causes of instability, arms control policy must allow for the fact that the dynamism of armament is not simply a matter of action and reaction, as the term *arms race* suggests. Rather, armaments competition should be regarded as a specific form of military interaction, an instrument of mutual influence.

Instruments of Arms Control

Today, the spectrum of the instruments of arms control ranges from straightforward bans with quantitative and qualitative limitation of military potential to confidence-building measures and general declarations in international law. This breadth reflects the complexity of the goals of arms control with their plethora of operative aspects as well as the multitude of objects that may come within range. The measures involved can be subdivided into those aimed primarily at limiting or reducing the scope of military potential (vertical arms control) and those aimed at limiting the proliferation of certain weapons (horizontal arms control).

Bans on Weapons and Weapons Systems

Theoretically, the simplest instrument of arms control is a global ban on a specific weapon or weapon category. Such a ban may call for the abolition or annihilation of existing weapons systems or may be designed to prevent the introduction of new systems. When we define the dynamism of armament in terms of an arms race fuelled by a process of action and reaction in technological development, the call for a ban on the qualitative innovation of existing systems and the development of new systems becomes especially important.

In practice, this instrument has proven difficult to wield. In the entire postwar period, the INF Treaty was the only one that agreed upon the abolition and destruction of a weapon capable of operative deployment; and this treaty is binding upon only the two signatory powers. Worldwide, the number of states possessing medium-range missile systems has increased, with no agreement on a global ban in sight. The military strategic consequences of the INF Treaty were long under dispute, which suggests that in the future states will agree to renounce the use of certain weapons only when they have become obsolete in terms of military usefulness (e.g., nuclear artillery in Europe).

Qualitative arms control, to prevent the birth of new weapons systems, is theoretically attractive; in practice, it is problematical in several respects. The two superpowers were reluctant to agree on modernization bans. In the ABM Treaty they renounced the development, testing, and deployment of new sea-, air-, and space-launched as well as mobile land-launched anti–ballistic missile systems. However, in the dispute on the Strategic Defense Initiative (SDI), the U.S. administration held the view that this regulation did not cover antimissile systems based on new physical principles.

The SALT II and START Agreements on strategic arms control also contained bans on the introduction (of, e.g., heavy intercontinental ballistic missiles, ICBMs) and development (of, e.g., heavy sea-launched ballistic missiles, SLBMs; mobile launchers) of precisely defined weapon systems as well as on testing of specific devices (such as fast-reloading heavy ICBM launchers). In principle, modernization is still permitted. Interference with research in this field is beyond the scope of serious negotiation.

One item on the agenda of the United Nations Disarmament Committee is a ban on new weapons of mass annihilation that, with the exception of so-called radiology weapons, are not identifiable in concrete terms. Such a convention would need to cover virtually all technological breakthroughs that could be applied in any military sense whatsoever; in consequence, research institutes would have to be included in the inspection and control procedures.

Any ban on modernization would require precise technical definitions, especially demarcations between innovation and replacement, and would call for highly sophisticated verification procedures.

Quantitative and Qualitative Limitation

The achievement of numeric parity, the definition of an adequate quantitative balance between armaments and armed forces, or at least the mutual agreement to freeze certain arsenals are still at the core of all political arms control concepts. Originally, the central objective was not to reduce armaments but to create stability, containing the dynamism of armaments by introducing ceilings. From the point of view of safeguarding or creating stability, mere numeric limits are inadequate unless they contain qualitative elements. This qualitative aspect relates not to the containment of technological innovation but to the creation of specific structures that govern the disposition of the armed forces. This implies that the codification of quantitative arms control must meet highly complex requirements.

Problems begin with the need to define a common database. Negotiations on establishing a balance of conventional armaments (MBFR) failed not least because the military capability figures quoted by the Warsaw Pact nations deviated considerably from the information gathered by NATO. Thus, it was impossible to arrive at a mutually agreeable foundation on which to base verifiable and balanced reductions.

The second hurdle is to identify and define comparable objects for limitation. For instance the United States and the Soviet Union agreed relatively quickly on which missiles should be defined as strategic simply by referring to their range (above 5,500 km, or 3,410 mi.). However, the question of whether and how other weapons systems with a nuclear deterrent capability should be included in considerations of relative strategic strength—and, consequently, in the agenda—repeatedly disturbed both SALT and START negotiations. In later years, a need arose to find criteria by which heavy and light missiles could be differentiated. During the CSE negotiations there was much dispute on what should fall under heavy personnel carrier or assault helicopter categories. There need to be precise definitions of which service a specific part of the armed forces belongs to. The geographic regions to which agreed limits should refer also need to be defined.

The complexity of modern weapons systems calls for ever-more-differentiated categories of counting. The SALT I Agreement merely set limits for carrier systems (ICBMs and SLBMs). More refined, the SALT II Agreement specified upper limits for their equipment with single or multiple warheads. The treatment of strategic bombers and cruise missiles could be handled only in a protocol. To include these systems in the strategic equation, START provides some complex rules of counting; for instance, the number of cruise missiles allocated to each bomber is less than its actual carrying capacity. Furthermore, the counting procedures agreed upon were complicated by the need for verification, spawning a complex system of accounting for bombers and their bomb or nuclear cruise missile payloads.

The arms control agreements signed in the 1990s show that numeric upper and lower limits are indeed suitable instruments for inducing structural modifications that are equivalent to qualitative change. The first task is to ascertain the stabilizing or destabilizing character of a weapon system. Thus, the START Agreement set various subceilings for carrier systems and their equipment with single or multiple warheads, to reduce the risk of a pre-emptive strike. By pointing the way toward a theoretical reconfiguration of the strategic triad, allowing more room for slower bombers and cruise missiles, it increases early-warning timespans. The CSE Treaty not only did away with conventional disparities in favor of the Warsaw Pact;

it also imposed limits on weapons systems (tanks, armored vehicles, artillery, assault helicopters, and fighter planes) that are designed for offensive military action and are capable of surprise attacks.

Nonproliferation

The core proper of horizontal arms control is nonproliferation, a special form of arms export control policy. Nonproliferation is an undertaking by states that possess certain technologies or materials not to pass these on to other states and to deny access to such materials and technologies to other states that are interested in them.

The best-known case in point is the Nuclear Nonproliferation Treaty of 1968 (NPT), to which more than 140 states have acceded; these states include, however, neither the entire group of nuclear-weapons powers (France, China) nor all so-called "threshold" countries. Those signatory states that possess nuclear arms undertook not to transmit fissionable material and fission technology; the remaining states renounced the production, acquisition, and deployment of nuclear weapons. The access of the non–nuclear-weapons states (NNWS) to materials or technologies that permit the manufacture of nuclear explosive devices is controlled by an international safeguard system administered and supervised by the International Atomic Energy Commission. This regime is also designed to promote the peaceful application of nuclear energy.

Recently, the concept of nonproliferation is being applied to chemical weapons and certain missile technologies, especially medium-range missiles. In 1987 the states belonging to the Group of Seven (G7) agreed on a missile technology control regime (MTCR) that obligates them to pursue a restrictive policy of export, following jointly agreed guidelines for specific technologies. The list of restricted goods concerns ballistic (but not cruise) missiles with a range of 300 kilometers (186 mi.) and above, a payload of more than 500 kilograms (1,100 lbs.), and relevant technologies. Most Western industrialized nations have joined this regime; some manufacturers still hold out.

The weaknesses of the nonproliferation concept are becoming increasingly clear: States interested in possessing controlled weapons are little inclined to agree to such a regime. In the NPT agreement, the nuclear-weapons powers offered material aid and support in the peaceful use of nuclear energy to the states without nuclear weapons while at the same time undertaking to defend these states against nuclear attack and to reduce their own potentials drastically. The two last-named obligations have been met in only a sketchy manner. If a state regards the possession of nuclear weapons as an outward sign of its own sovereignty, relatively little will induce it to renounce these putative insignia of power. Any nonproliferation regime automatically discriminates against one group of states, the have-nots. Moreover, the transfer of nuclear technology has enabled some states in the course of time to create their own research and development capabilities that conceivably might be put to military use as well. In nonnuclear areas, it is even more difficult to identify and define relevant technologies that might lend themselves to abuse or even encourage it (dual-use problem) and therefore need to be controlled. Fraud is impossible to preclude. While the International Atomic Energy Commission is one of the most effective systems of controlling and verifying infringements of the Nonproliferation Agreement, experiences in Iraq and other countries have verified its suspected defects.

Furthermore, the practice of nonproliferation is made or marred by the producer's individual interests. The less specific the technology, the higher is the probability that an oligopoly can be broken. Thus, certain countries have not hesitated to supply supposedly controlled material and technology to less-developed states for economic or political reasons.

Geographic Limitations of Military Use

In the past, certain geographically limited regions have successfully been kept free of military use. The Antarctic Treaty of 1968, the Seabed Treaty of 1972, the Space Treaty of 1976, and the Moon Treaty of 1984 basically forbid the construction of military installations as well as the dislocation and testing of nuclear weapons and other instruments of mass annihilation. They do not specify exclusively peaceful utilization in any generally accepted way. The Seabed and Space treaties permit military activities of other kinds; the Space Treaty expressly permits using satellites for espionage and verification.

Another variant of this horizontal arms control instrument is found in the concept of peace or nuclear-free zones that was popular especially in the 1970s and 1980s. Pacifists, opponents of nuclear weapons, and socialist governments proposed the establishment of so-called zones of peace in the Mediterranean region, the Indian Ocean, and the Southern Atlantic, with the objective of barring all military activity there. None of these proposals ever was the subject of serious negotiation; they were confined to general declarations, mostly within the UN framework. None ever clearly specified to what area the proposal would apply, what powers would be involved, and what their obligations would be. Fundamentally, these proposals were ideologically motivated instruments to combat the global presence of the superpowers, especially the United States. They are unsuitable as instruments of true arms control.

The same appraisal applies to the proposals for nuclear-free zones made in the context of the East-West conflict, especially for Europe. Establishing such zones does nothing to enhance security if the area concerned is within the range of a launching system of a third country and might so become a target for a nuclear strike. Nuclear-free zones may even degrade security, insofar as they undermine the material premises of a strategy that relies on the interaction of conventional and nuclear elements. As an instrument to keep regions free of nuclear powers, such as the Tlatelolco Treaty for Latin America, the concept has gained new currency whose usefulness still has to be proven.

Confidence- and Security-Building Measures (CSBM)

Since the middle 1950s, confidence- and security-building measures have had their place in arms control negotiations; they began to move back into prominence in the 1980s. The term refers to agreements designed to improve information on military activities. The benefit to arms control policy is that such an agreement limits the role of military factors in international relations and helps to clarify misunderstandings and misinformation concerning activities of the other side. Its purpose is to reduce and, if possible, eliminate the risk of a military conflict arising from misunderstanding, communication failure, technology breakdown, and to clear away the motives and chances of surprise attacks.

The range of confidence-building measures includes the establishment of direct information links between governments as well as aerial inspection, the creation of ground observation posts, and even the exchange of military missions. To codify the inspection and observation procedures involved requires the regulation of an immense amount of technical detail.

In the field of strategic arms control, the United States and the Soviet Union have agreed on a number of technical confidence- and security-building measures. These include the setup of the "hot line" in 1963, the Accidents Measures Agreement (AMA) of 1971 (similar agreements exist between France, Great Britain, and the Soviet Union), and the Agreement for the Prevention of Incidents on the High Seas. In 1987 Moscow and Washington agreed to establish a permanently staffed Nuclear Risk Reduction Center to handle implementation of these agreements.

The confidence- and security-building measures agreed upon within the framework of the CSCE conferences—as laid down in the Helsinki Communiqué of 1975, the Stockholm Agreement of 1985, and the Vienna Agreement of 1989—were a major breakthrough. The participating nations agreed to exchange information on the structure and strength of their armed forces, to give advance notice of planned military maneuvers, to exchange observers in such exercises, and to permit the inspection of military activities outside of military facilities. So far, these agreements cover only ground forces; efforts are being made to extend their scope to air and naval forces. Another dimension is opened by the Open Skies proposal: that unarmed reconnaissance planes be entitled to traverse the air spaces of all European countries.

Conventions under International Law

Wherever the above-mentioned instruments of arms control have no effect, the only recourse is to international conventions that expressly forbid the use of specific weapons systems. Such global measures are relatively weak instruments. For example, the Geneva Protocol of 1925 forbade the use of biological and chemical weapons except in retaliation or for use against a nonsignatory state. A 1983 Convention on Inhuman Weapons was designed to preclude the use of brutal weapons (such as shrapnel) and of systems (such as land and antipersonnel mines) that cannot distinguish between legitimate and illegitimate targets. The signatory states of the Weather Modification Convention of 1978 undertake not to manipulate natural processes (e.g., the biosphere or the atmosphere) for military purposes.

Arms Control as a Process

Arms control should be viewed as a complex process that is influenced by many factors in foreign and domestic policy as well as technology. Generally, the process comprises two distinct but equally important features: the negotiations to reach an agreement and the management and implementation of agreements once they are concluded.

Factors of International Arms Control Negotiations

The very initiation of arms control negotiations presumes some measure of mutual trust; a qualitative change in the relations between the parties is implicit. To this extent, arms control is inextricably interrelated to developments in foreign and security policy and strategy. Any hope to isolate arms control from such influences by permanently institutionalizing arms control bodies within the framework of the United Nations is illusory. Even in instances where arms control policy as exercised in United Nations bodies has not degenerated into ideological ritual, it has been characterized by national interests, by the international distribution of power, or by the confrontation between East and West, especially the antagonism between America and the Soviet Union.

Readiness to institute arms control negotiations depends mainly on four factors: The assessment of strategic stability and/or the perception of any threat to that stability; the rise of new weapons technologies; the extent to which agreements can be verified; and, finally, the political climate in general.

It is important to remember that the last-named factor is inextricably related to arms control itself. Arms control negotiations are distinguished from diplomatic negotiations in other fields mainly by the extent to which relevant military information must be disclosed and by the wealth of technical detail and definition that requires clarification and regulation. Today, an arms control agreement is an instrument comprising hundreds of pages of text, protocols, definitions, explanatory statements, and so forth. Technical questions may attain paramount significance in certain phases of the negotiations themselves or for the support they enjoy in domestic policy, sometimes delaying or even endangering the conclusion of an agreement.

The domestic politics dimension of arms control negotiations should not be underrated. The negotiations bear the stamp of bureaucratic conflicts of interest between defense and foreign ministries or among the armed services. Depending on the characteristics of the political system, governments need to conduct more or less intense public debates with the legislature, the parliamentary opposition, as well as interested sections of the public, the media, research institutions, and pressure groups. In the United States especially, political disputes have repeatedly arisen between Congress and the president, delaying agreements or barring the ratification of an agreement already signed.

This kind of democratization may severely affect the process of arms control. It is more difficult in an open society to conduct negotiations coherently and consistently. Negative side effects may also occur if a government feels it must make promises regarding the procurement of new weapons systems, not covered by the agreement under negotiations, in order to ensure the support to conclude a specific arms control agreement (buying-off theory). Conversely, governments have met political resistance to the development or manufacture of new weapons systems by arguing that these were necessary as bargaining chips at the negotiating table.

All these factors contribute to the fact that arms control negotiations usually last for years. There is always a risk of initial mandates being rendered obsolete by technological developments or political events. Critics of confining the arms control process to negotiations suggest alternative informal arms control procedures, involving individual but parallel policies or a gradualist approach, which means unilateral decisions that elicit similar responses by the adversary. Some feel that this procedure is better adapted to the problems involved and opens up more political options. For example, to better control the situation after the Soviet Union crumbled, the U.S. government took unilateral steps to destroy or remove land- and sea-based tactical nuclear warheads that were reciprocated in kind.

The differences between the two approaches should not be overemphasized. Informal procedures always have been part and parcel of arms control policy, although unilateral U.S. actions were seldom honored by the Soviets, as in the U.S. decision to stop the manufacture of chemical weapons in the 1960s.

Both types of procedures will certainly be used in the future. In view of the complex interdependence between strategy, military arsenals, and the instruments of arms control policy, it will likely be increasingly difficult to formulate consistent mandates for negotiations. On the other hand, the mere fact that governments are sitting at the negotiating table may build confidence. It is more difficult to withdraw from negotiations than from informal arms control measures. Moreover, negotiated agreements ensure more predictability and especially better verification.

Management of Treaties and the Role of Verification

The management of agreements involves enforcing and verifying the implementation of the provisions of an agreement and instituting sanctions in the event of infringements.

The implementation of an agreement presents problems that are political and technical (the definition of destruction procedures, for instance), as well as financial and social problems, such as those related to the closure of military installations and to questions of conversion (i.e., of refitting the armaments industry for other production purposes). The political aspects of implementation involve not only exploiting the positive effects of the agreement but also taking steps to ensure that its provisions are interpreted in conformance with the spirit of the agreement, and are updated and adapted to political and technological developments. For these reasons, most arms control agreements set either expiration or renewal dates or provide for periodic review conferences or, alternatively, for the institution of standing consultative commissions (SCCs).

An arms control agreement can be effected only if the signatories abide by and observe its terms. Thus the inclusion of an adequate system of verification is an element of extraordinary importance. The efficiency of any regime of verification depends, first, on how clearly an agreement has been worded and, second, on the methods of verification to be employed. Traditionally, three instruments are available: (1) classical espionage, or reconnaissance with the aid of cognitive instruments (desk control); (2) so-called national technical means (satellite reconnaissance, electronic or seismic surveillance); and (3) on-site inspection.

With the exception of the Nonproliferation Treaty, multilateral arms control agreements provide rather weak regimes of verification comprising mainly consultation mechanisms. In bilateral agreements, parties have tended to rely on national technological means. It was only in the mid-1980s (Stockholm CSBM Agreement; INF Treaty) that the Soviet Union and the other members of the former Warsaw Pact agreed to accept on-site inspection. There are many variants to the practical implementation of this verification procedure. What is politically important is to distinguish between routine inspections scheduled beforehand and the option of mounting an inspection on grounds of suspicion within a certain term and on a specific site (challenge inspections).

The acceptance of verification procedures implies great

willingness to cooperate and share military secrets. For instance, weapons systems need to be marked specifically to facilitate verification, and test procedures must be designed to be comprehensible to the other side. Certain forms of verification, such as the inspection of industrial facilities to verify a chemical weapons ban, are regarded by some states as unwarranted interference in their internal affairs. Other states fear that such measures might affect their economic competitiveness.

Verification goes beyond merely detecting infringements; it is at the same time an instrument of deterrence. Furthermore, it serves to contain damage by keeping the consequences of infringements below the threshold of creating military or political conflict. Consequently, the use of the instrument of verification is affected by the perception of the military risk posed by infringements identified too late or not at all.

The dearth of powerful sanction mechanisms must be viewed with this as background. In keeping with the general progress of international law, multilateral agreements rarely name anything more severe than referring infringements to some UN institution (e.g., the Secretary General, the Security Council, or the International Court of Justice). The community of nations has no effective means beyond international public censure and diplomatic pressure. In addition to some disputes on violations of the spirit of an agreement, there have been two well-publicized cases of infringement by the Soviet Union: the coding of telemetric data (radio signals indispensable for the monitoring of missile tests) and the construction of the Krasnoyarsk radar installations, which ultimately the Soviet side conceded as an infringement of the ABM Treaty. The United States responded to these incidents with public pressure. However, a solution—Soviet readiness to dismantle Krasnoyarsk—was only found in the context of further negotiations.

Past Performance and Perspectives of Arms Control

Both in theory and practice, arms control policy after World War II bore the stamp of the East-West conflict. But there is no way to predict which of today's approaches and experiences will remain valid in the changing international framework. The performance of modern arms control must be regarded as positive. It culminated in the conclusion of the START and CSE treaties that both promised to provide for a certain increase in international security and can be built on even under changed circumstances. In addition, arms control aided the end of the East-West conflict, however difficult it is to measure its impact.

Contextual Arms Control

In the past there was much dispute whether arms control is or should be an instrument to reach detente or other foreign policy goals or whether detente should precede arms control. Some people feared that the Soviets might reap far-reaching political benefits in return for marginal military concessions. Utilizing the political spillover of arms control—not to be confused with explicit linkage strategy in negotiations—is, however, both legitimate and reasonable. For example, a major political side effect of the negotiations on confidence-building measures was the restriction it imposed on the USSR with regard to exerting its military power on its satellite states. On the other hand, the strategy of contextual arms control is risky.

To the extent that the process of arms control promotes detente, cooperation, and mutual restraint, it may support and even induce political change. If it is viewed as a comprehensive concept to keep external threats in check, contextual arms control may contribute materially toward harmonizing changes in military structures and political evolution. In this sense, it should gain currency not only in post–Cold War Europe but also in other regions of the world, especially the Middle East.

Arms Control in the 1990s

With the radical recent changes in East-West relations, the classical function of arms control—creation of stability—will face new challenges but has lost none of its importance.

Since the propagation of the Strategic Defense Initiative (SDI), the United States has proposed to overcome by arms control the strategy of nuclear deterrence and to establish instead a nuclear strategic regime characterized by defensive structures. While the former Soviet Union's attitude toward these ideas was reserved if not antagonistic, the new Russia has expressed interest in joining the United States in establishing a nonnuclear global protecting system against limited strikes, while at the same time reducing their strategic offensive capabilities way below the START limits. This will affect all other nuclear powers. Moscow also had urged a system of minimum deterrence to be negotiated by "all five" nuclear powers within the framework of the United Nations. This assumes that Great Britain, France, and the People's Republic of China are prepared to subject their nuclear arsenals to international arms control, a step toward which they have been little inclined so far. In any case, a new model of stability will have to be developed. Its structure will become more complex the less the community of nations manages to contain the group of nuclear powers.

Nonproliferation issues will have top priority. It is already evident that the axis of confrontation is shifting from antagonism between the United States and the former Soviet Union to animosity between the industrialized nuclear states and the nuclear have-nots. With the collapse of the former Soviet Union, its nuclear arsenals are no longer under central control of one sovereign state; the spread of relevant knowledge must also be contained. Measures to control the proliferation of modern missile technology are of outstanding urgency, since these systems can be utilized by less-developed nations to carry nuclear as well as chemical or biological weapons to medium-range targets (1991 Paris Conference of the five standing members of the Security Council). Negotiations on the reduction of substrategic and/or tactical nuclear weapons in Europe, high on the agenda in the recent past, have been rendered obsolete by events.

The continuation of the Vienna CSBM and the CSE Ia negotiations and the agreement to renegotiate mandates after the CSCE Summit of Helsinki in 1992 have set the stage for further conventional arms control in Europe. What concrete steps will be taken is still a matter of dispute. Two schools of thought are emerging. One group of states under the leadership of Germany aims to use the momentum generated by the existing agreements to reduce armament potential and especially personnel; others prefer to concentrate for the time being on confidence-building questions. After the dissolution of the military blocs and the Soviet Union and Yugoslavia, it is likely that the structure of stability among the 50 or so states of the CSCE process will be more complex. The effects of the European balance of power on the international distribution of power will have to be taken into account as well.

The negotiations of Vienna might also open access to another dimension of arms control; there is increasing pressure to begin negotiating on the limitation of naval capacities, starting with confidence-building measures. Such a step would lead to unknown territory in arms control policy. A number of agreements already in existence provide for the restriction of naval activities in the field of nuclear strategy and elsewhere. However, because of the differences in the geographical situation and maritime role of the powers involved, the establishment of nondiscriminatory arms control regimes will be difficult.

Outside Europe, the only conventional arms control agreements of any significance to date have been mere approaches (the demilitarized zone in Korea; the Arias Plan in Central America). The perspectives of the future are no better, although the developing countries are among the most vociferous supporters of disarmament resolutions. Their policy, with frequent reference to a causal relationship between the arms race among the industrialized nations on the one hand and underdevelopment on the other, plays to the gallery and is an attack on the rich nations. Most of these young nations regard military power as an expression of national eminence, and power rivalries are important. Awareness of a need for arms control, as it developed in the East-West conflict under the nuclear threat, is underdeveloped. The conflicts in these regions, which are often civil or guerrilla wars, call for special arms control concepts. Moreover, the dynamism of armament in these countries is influenced by the strategic and economic interests of extra-regional powers. One important approach is to restrict politically the export of armaments, and there are increasingly frequent attempts by donor countries and development aid organizations to link development aid to conditions imposed on the arms policy of the receiving countries.

On a worldwide scale, the Geneva Disarmament Conference will need to step up its efforts to establish a global ban on the development, production, and stockpiling of chemical weapons, analogous with the Biological Weapons Convention of 1975. By binding themselves to the almost complete annihilation of their stockpiles of chemical weapons, the United States and the Soviet Union had attempted to impart a new impetus to these negotiations. However, in view of the verification problems, the prospects of reaching agreement on a convention or arriving at a nonproliferation approach are poor.

The change in East-West relations and the emergence of a still hazily defined international order have altered the traditional frame of reference for international arms control policy. Future arms control will be challenged by new issues, the redefinition of operative targets (especially the development of stability concepts), the modification and refinement of the instruments of arms control policy, and the restructuring of the arms control process, which is sure to evolve through formal negotiations.

PETER R. WEILEMANN

SEE ALSO: Arms Control and Disarmament: Mathematical Models; Arms Trade and Military Assistance; Cold War; Deterrence; Nuclear Nonproliferation; Nuclear Theory and Policy; Strategic Stability; Technology and Arms Control.

Bibliography

Adelmann, K. L. 1984. Arms control with and without agreements. *Foreign Affairs* 2:240–63.

Berkowitz, B. D. 1987. *Calculated risks: A century of arms control, why it has failed, and how it can be made to work.* New York: Simon and Schuster.

Blacker, C. D., G. Duffy, eds. 1984. *International arms control, issues and agreements.* 2d ed. By the Stanford Arms Control Group. Stanford, Calif.: Stanford Univ. Press.

Brennan, D. G. 1961. *Arms control, disarmaments and national security.* New York: CRASL McGill Univ.

Brodie, B. 1959. *Strategy in the missile age.* Princeton, N.Y.: Princeton Univ. Press.

Bull, H. 1965. *The control of the arms race: Disarmament and arms control in the missile age.* 2d ed. New York-Washington: Praeger.

Carnesale, A., and R. N. Haas, eds. 1987. *Superpower arms control. Setting the record straight.* Cambridge, Mass.: Ballinger.

Forndran, E. 1988. Stabilität als Problem der Strategie und der internationalen Rüstungskontrollverhandlungen. In G. Schwan, Hrsg., *Bedingungen und Probleme politischer Stabilität*, pp. 179–206. Baden-Baden: Nomos Verlag.

Gray, C. S. 1976. *The Soviet-American arms race.* Farnborough, U.K.: Heath.

International Institute for Strategic Studies (IISS). 1986. Power and policy: *Doctrine, the alliance and arms control.* Parts 1–3, Adelphi Papers nos. 205–207. IISS Annual Conference Papers. Letchworth, N.Y.: Garden City Press.

Krass, A. S. 1985. *Verification: How much is enough?* Lexington, Mass.: Heath.

Mahncke, D. 1987. *Vertrauensbildende Maßnahmen als Instrument der Sicherheitspolitik.* Ursprung-Entwicklung-Perspektiven, Forschungsbericht d. Konrad-Adenauer-Stiftung Nr. 59, Melle, Germany: Knoth Verlag.

Navias, M. 1990. *Ballistic missile proliferation in the Third World.* Adelphi Papers no. 252. Oxford: Nuffield Press.

Nerlich, U., and J. A. Thomson, eds. 1983. *Soviet power and Western negotiation policies.* Vol. 2, *The Western panacea, Constraining Soviet power through negotiation.* Cambridge, Mass.: Ballinger.

Potter, W. C. 1982. *Nuclear power and nonproliferation: An interdisciplinary perspective.* Cambridge, Mass.: Oelschlager, Gunn and Hain.

Rudolf, P. 1991. *Non-Proliferation und internationale Exportkontrollpolitik.* Ebenhausen, Germany: Stiftung Wissenschaft und Politik.

Schelling, T. C., and M. H. Halperin. 1988. *Strategy and arms control.* 2d ed. Twentieth Century Fund. Washington, D.C.: Pergamon-Brassey's.

Talbott, S. 1979. *Endgame.* New York: Harper and Row.

de Jonge Oudraat Ch. and P. G. Alves. 1990. *UNIDIR Repertory of Disarmament Research 1990.* New York: United Nations.

Additional Sources: *Arms control and disarmament agreements,* texts and histories of negotiations, irreg. since 1972, publ. U.S. Arms Control and Disarmament Agency (ACDA); Stockholm International Peace Research Institute (SIPRI), annual since 1970, *World armaments and disarmament,* SIPRI Yearbook, London; *Strategic survey,* annual report since 1967, publ. International Institute for Strategic Studies (IISS), London; *The arms control reporter,* monthly since 1982, a chronicle of treaties, negotiations, proposals, weapons, and policy, publ. Institute for Defense and Disarmament Studies, Brookline, Mass.

ARMS CONTROL AND DISARMAMENT: MATHEMATICAL MODELS

Whether arms control and disarmament will ever display a set of acceptable rules and procedures for its universal implementation within national and international political affairs will depend upon, among other things, how well the fundamental issues are understood. To this end, models have been created that permit us to study, in a highly structured and detached manner, the properties and dynamics of the complex processes and systems underlying arms control and disarmament. Such models are necessarily abstract in nature and they describe the subject of study in terms of logical relations and mathematical equations. Some regard this as a weakness, others as a strength.

There seems to be general agreement that the basic issues of arms control and disarmament revolve around four questions (Avenhaus, Huber, and Kettelle 1986):

1. Why do nations arm?
2. What are stable military regimes that arms control and disarmament should aim for?
3. Whether and how agreements can be verified?
4. How should negotiations be structured to maximize their chance of success?

Modeling Approaches and Issues

All of these questions have been studied to some degree by means of mathematical models. Among the earliest modeling attempts was Richardson's 1939 mathematical description of an arms race. The stability question first became of major interest in the 1960s in the context of the strategic nuclear balance between the superpowers (Kaysen 1986). Interest was renewed during the debate on the strategic defense initiative (SDI) (Avenhaus et al. 1986, pp. 183–206) and it has become a key topic for conventional arms control as well (Huber 1988). In regard to verification, the safeguard systems of the International Atomic Energy Agency (IAEA) for monitoring adherence to the Non-Proliferation Treaty have been developed by means of mathematical models of the materials balance concept (Avenhaus 1977). There are also mathematical models for bargaining situations and negotiations that are relevant to arms control (Avenhaus et al. 1986, pp. 295–306; Raiffa 1982).

Arms Race Modeling

In a general sense, an arms race may be defined in terms of an action-reaction mechanism between two parties X and Y, whose military power is represented by x and y, respectively. A real or perceived change Δx_i in the military power x at time step i causes the other party to implement a countervailing change Δy_i in its military power y. This in turn leads to a further reaction Δx_{i+1} by party X at the next time step $(i+1)$ followed by a reaction Δy_{i+1} by party Y, and so on (Fig. 1).

Richardson's model describes this mechanism as a continuous process in terms of a system of coupled linear differential equations:

$$dx/dt = ky - ax + g$$
$$dy/dt = k'x - a'y + g'$$

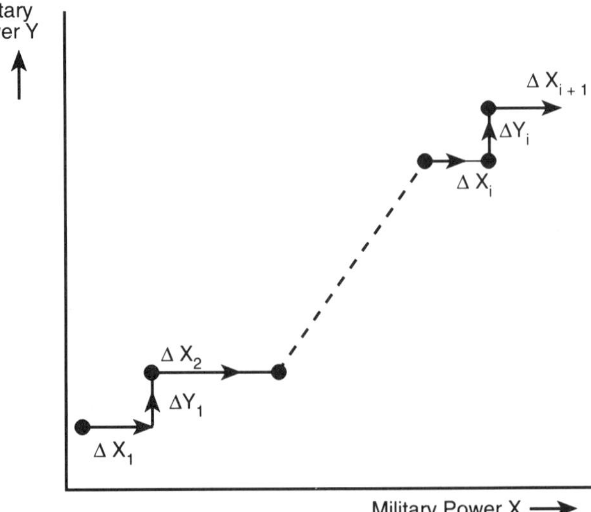

Figure 1. The arms race mechanism.

in which k and k' are defense coefficients, a and a' are fatigue coefficients, and g and g' are grievance terms of the parties X and Y, respectively. These equations imply that (1) the stronger the adversary the more a party will arm; (2) due to the costs associated with the existing arms inventories, the increase in the arms level of a party will be less the higher the level of arms of that party; and (3) a party dissatisfied with its situation will arm regardless of existing arms levels in order to achieve its objectives, by war or by intimidation.

Rapoport's (1957) review of Richardson's model triggered a veritable avalanche of theoretical and empirical research on arms races. A well-documented bibliography of the literature was compiled in 1979 by Cioffi-Revilla. Rattinger provided a summary review of the many efforts to empirically validate the model as well as the problems and difficulties encountered. He concluded that, while the analysis of the formal properties of arms race models may be less relevant for empirical research, it still provides valuable insights for understanding why and how particular forces drive processes in the real world (Rattinger 1984, p. 198). The results published by Pastijn and Struys (Avenhaus et al. 1986, pp. 239–256) on their attempt to validate the Richardson model—by analyzing the mutual defense expenditures of NATO and the Warsaw Pact over a period of twenty years as a measure of their respective military power—leads one to conclude that the Warsaw Pact's motives for the arms competition with NATO may have been driven less by threat perceptions than by the internal dynamics of the Soviet military-industrial bureaucracy. Contrary to Richardson's first assumption, their data suggest that, during the same time period, the rate of increase of the Warsaw Pact's defense expenditures increased with the strength of the military-industrial bureaucracy, and that it decreased when NATO increased its expenditures.

In addition to the Richardson-type arms race dynamics models, several researchers proposed to formulate the arms race as a *game* between two parties. The simplest such game-theoretical model is the two-person non-zero-sum game of Prisoner's Dilemma in which each player has two strategies, namely to arm or to disarm, with well-defined pay-offs (Rapoport and Chammah 1965; Brams 1976). Despite its drastic oversimplification of reality, this game provides a plausible explanation of the fundamental intractability of arms races. In 1979, Brams, Davis, and Straffin extended the Prisoner's Dilemma model to investigate a possible solution to the arms race by considering the game as a sequence of moves by the two parties. Each side is able to detect what the other side is doing with a specified probability and pursues a tit-for-tat policy of conditional cooperation (i.e., disarm when signs of disarmament are detected on the part of the other side, otherwise no cooperation).

In the context of their research on conventional stability, Avenhaus, Güth, and Huber (1988) analyzed a series of noncooperative non-zero-sum games between two antagonists who may be either status quo or revisionistic powers and have the option of choosing between offensive and defensive force postures. It is shown that under certain circumstances reciprocal cooperation between a status quo and a revisionistic power may be brought about by an initial noncooperative move of the status quo power.

Force Balance and Stability

The fundamental aim of arms control and disarmament is to bring about conditions that preclude the use of military force in the solution of international disputes and, should war occur, to limit its consequences. There seems to be widespread agreement that, short of complete disarmament, a balanced military situation between two antagonistic parties or camps is a necessary condition for the resolution of their disputes without military force. A balance alone, however, is not sufficient to provide for strategic stability in the sense of removing the military incentives for arms competition (arms race stability) and preemptive attacks (crisis stability). In addition to a balanced situation, stability requires that the opponents perceive their mutual military force postures as being defensive in nature. Otherwise, there is no escape from the so-called security dilemma, which implies that an increase in one side's security decreases the security of the other (Jervis 1973). This dilemma is the fundamental force behind arms races between status quo powers. However, there is neither a military nor an economic incentive to adopt defensive force postures, which could never be perceived as offensive by the opponent, unless the defense efficiency hypothesis (DEH) holds. The defense efficiency hypothesis implies that defensive force postures may exploit the intrinsic defense advantage more efficiently than offensive postures (Huber 1988).

There are two primary analytical approaches to force balance assessments: static analysis and dynamic analysis. Static analysis compares "inputs" such as defense expenditures and manpower under arms, combat equipment, mobilization potential, and so on; dynamic analysis measures the balance in terms of likely war outcomes if deterrence fails. The stability of a balance can only be assessed by dynamic analyses, which permit one to measure the rate of change in the balance as the conflict progresses (Davis 1988; Huber 1988; Avenhaus et al. 1986, pp. 151–69).

Thus, dynamic analysis requires models that can simulate, in a sufficiently realistic manner, a military conflict between two parties. (For a brief discussion of the various dynamic modeling techniques, the reader is referred to the article entitled "Defense Decision Making, Analysis and Models for." It should be noted that the highly aggregated analytical models are primarily suited for the communication of specific concepts and fundamental prerequisites for stability (Boulding 1975; Huber 1988). They are not useful, however, for numerical assessments, as shown by the debates about Kaufmann's use of the Lanchester equations for regional force balance assessments and about the "Adaptive Model of War" proposed by Epstein as "the" alternative (Kaufmann 1983; Epstein 1985; Leppingwell 1987; Mearsheimer 1989). First of all, Lanchester formulated his equations as a model of mutual attrition in *local* battles in which all participants on both sides are within weapon range of their opponents (Lanchester 1914). Thus, its use as a dynamic model for *regional* force balance assessments implies, among other things, that war between the two camps consists of a large number of battles fought in parallel and simultaneously by all of the forces deployed uniformly along an uninterrupted front line by both sides. Epstein's model pictures war in exactly the same manner, as a front-wide steamroller operation, with the additional option that the defender may control his attrition by universal withdrawal. Furthermore, he considers airpower as merely another source of firepower, uniformly available to the ground forces in form of close air support (Davis 1988, p. 29), which is unrealistic.

In order to account for factors such as mutual operational strategies and tactics, command and control, surprise or short warning, sustainability, and many others, the models need to be designed to simulate, to a sufficient degree of detail, the dynamic interactions of forces and terrain on the theater level. To keep the model's complexity manageable, hierarchical model designs are preferable to so-called "nested" models (Huber 1988, p. 97). Also, the models must be able to cope with the large number of parametric variations that need to be processed in view of the uncertainties associated with the scenario parameters. In addition, they must be able to take into account important random processes that cause considerable variance in the course and outcome of battles. Tactical and operational variance, caused by stochastic elements in command and control, is still largely ignored in most models even though its exploitation, by systematically taking advantage of the opponent's vulnerabilities as they arise, is the essence of operational and tactical art.

Thus, for force balance assessments, two versions of the same simulation model should be available: one for testing the sensitivity of large numbers of scenario parameter constellations by means of parametric variations, a fast-running *deterministic* or *expected-value* version, which "averages out" random effects; and another for the subsequent investigation of "sensitive" scenarios, a *stochastic* version (using Monte Carlo sampling techniques to determine the outcome of random events) that permits one to perform a sufficient number of replications for the determination of probability distributions on battle and war outcomes rather than merely some "average" outcomes, which never occur in reality.

The significance of outcome distributions is illustrated in Figure 2, which shows that for two alternative arms

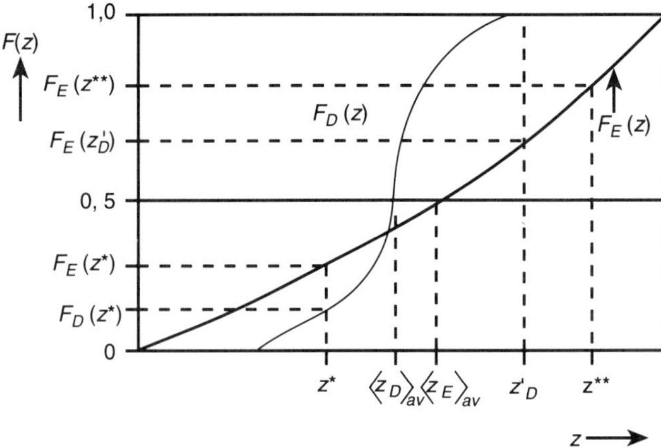

Figure 2: Probability functions F(z) *of conflict outcomes measured in terms of the parameter* Z *(e.g., force ratio between the antagonists).*

control proposals D and E, the distribution functions $F(z)$ of conflict outcomes measured in terms of the parameter z, which might, for example, represent the force ratio between parties X and Y at conflict termination. Clearly, based on the average results z_{av}, party X would prefer the proposal E because $(z_E)_{av} > (z_D)_{av}$. For alternative E, however, the probability $F_E(z^*)$ for ending up with a force ratio of less than z^* (which might imply unconditional surrender for party X) is almost three times higher than $F_D(z^*)$ for alternative D. On the other hand, alternative E provides some probability of ending up with a force ratio above z^{**}, which might imply unconditional surrender for the opponent Y. Thus, the choice between the two alternatives depends on the risk attitude of the political leadership of X. A cautious leadership would certainly prefer D and consider E only if $1-F_E(z_{D'}) >> F_E(z^*)$ (i.e., the probability of obtaining values above $z_{D'}$ [the maximum value for D] were significantly higher than the probability of ending up with outcomes below z^*).

Together with the variance resulting from parametric scenario variations, this type of information is indispensable for assessing the robustness of arms control proposals and the stability of force balances. The availability of commonly accepted simulation models and data bases to generate such information on comparatively short notice will very likely become a decisive issue for successful negotiations on the complex arms control proposals related to conventional and theater nuclear forces (Kokoshin 1987).

Verification

With regard to the means and procedures of verification, Cleminson and Gilman (1984) identified three categories for analysis:

1. *Verification Regimes* (level of confidence required): The major determining factor would be the application of political judgment influenced by deployment practices, developed and agreed cooperative measures, and security perceptions.

2. *Verification Methods* (concepts of inspection and detection methodology): The major determining factors would be the technological level of monitoring systems and the capability of existing and projected analytical techniques.
3. *Verification Systems* (existing and projected national and international systems available): Systems would include the physical hardware developed nationally and internationally to accomplish the monitoring, synthesis, analytical, and dissemination tasks.

Mathematical modeling support is relevant for all of these categories. With regard to the verification regimes, it is their importance for stability that is of primary interest. Therefore, the relevant modeling tools are those discussed in the previous section for dynamic force balance analysis. For the verification systems, models are required for (1) the performance assessment of sensors (including human inspection teams), (2) the analysis and fusion of sensor information, and (3) the estimation of the associated probabilities of detecting violations given certain acceptable thresholds for false alarms. For the assessment of verification methods, mathematical abstractions of the inspection process permit simulation of that process so that the effectiveness of alternative concepts can be tested in a possibly deceptive environment (Avenhaus, Huber, and Kettelle 1986).

Negotiations

How negotiations should be structured to maximize their chance of success involves the analysis of four primary issues, to each of which modeling may contribute (Avenhaus et al. 1986, pp. 279–93):

1. *Linkage:* Any treaties on negotiation theory quickly establish the advantage of widening the issues that are to be put on the negotiating table. In fact, that is the grist for the "yes-yes" results that third-party negotiators relish modifications that benefit both sides (Raiffa 1982). Theoretically, the cooperative forces associated with the search for agreements that both parties consider efficient are enhanced by increasing the scope of negotiations. However, complication of negotiations is the price for linking issues.
2. *Information Management:* A particular difficulty with arms control negotiations (as opposed, for example, to trade negotiations) is the background of sensitive military secrets that presumably underlies the logic each side must apply to the assessment of potential agreements. Just as centrally, *any* negotiation typically suffers if the adversary knows one's bargaining position: the values put on the various components of a possible deal, and the limits to which one is prepared to go. The search for efficient treaties is thus complicated by the nonavailability of information about the desires of *both* sides.
3. *Sequential Unilateral Moves:* A remarkable part of the arms control negotiations process has not been in the form of explicit treaties or agreements, but rather a sequence of unilateral moves or nonmoves (Avenhaus et al. 1986, pp. 51–98). What can be said about this form of de facto negotiation? Recent work in game theory has addressed what seems to be a similar problem, namely repeated plays of the Prisoner's Dilemma game. The result seems to be a consensus that the best strategy (or at least a robust and effective one) is "tit-for-tat."
4. *Multilateral Aspects:* A treaty considered as efficient by the principal negotiating parties may have very inefficient implications for their allies or for third parties. With regard to interalliance arms control, a natural procedure would be first to get agreement among component members of one side, and then negotiate with the opposing side. An essential complication of this procedure, at least for an alliance of nations with open societies, is secrecy—not just military secrets, but negotiating policy secrets such as reserve prices and trade-off values.

Summary

The present state of modeling for arms control is limited. Except for the arms race models, most existing models considered relevant to arms control originate in issues related to national defense planning. A comprehensive analysis of arms control problems and its modeling requirements has not yet been attempted, even on a conceptual level. This is in contrast to the public attention that arms control gets, at least in the open societies of the Western countries. Historical evidence indicates that arms control is a poorly understood process of great complexity, one that is embedded in an international environment of wide socio-economic, technological, and cultural diversity; and, until very recently, an East-West competition characterized by largely incompatible value systems. Indeed, the oversimplified, if not faulty, conceptual models frequently seem to be responsible for counterproductive arms control proposals and agreements. Thus, an interdisciplinary research effort aimed at the development of adequate conceptual and mathematical models of the dynamics of international security systems is considered to be of the utmost importance.

Reiner K. Huber

See Also: Arms Control and Disarmament; Crisis Management; Defense Decision Making: Analysis and Models; Lanchester Equations; NATO Policy and Strategy; Policy, Defense; Strategic Stability.

Bibliography

Avenhaus, R. 1977. *Material accountability—Theory, verification, applications.* International Institute for Applied Systems Analysis. New York: Wiley.

Avenhaus, R., W. Güth, and R. K. Huber. 1988. Implications of the defense efficiency hypothesis for the choice of military force postures. Federal Republic of Germany: Universität Bielefeld, Zentrum für Interdisziplinäre Forschung.

Avenhaus, R., R. K. Huber, and J. D. Kettelle, eds. 1986. Systems analysis and mathematical modelling in arms control. *Operations Research Spektrum*, Band 8, Heft 3, pp. 129–41.

Boulding, K. E. 1975. *International systems: Peace, conflict resolution, and politics.* Collected Papers Vol. 5. Boulder, Colo.: Associated Univ. Press.

Brams, S. J. 1976. *Paradoxes in politics: An introduction to the nonobvious in political science.* New York: Macmillan.

Brams, S. J., M. D. Davis, and P. D. Straffin, Jr. 1979. The geometry of the arms race. *International Studies Quarterly* 23(4):567–88.

Cioffi-Revilla, A. 1979. *Mathematical models in international relations: A bibliography.* IRSS Technical Paper No. 4. Chapel Hill, N.C.: Institute for Research in Social Science.

Cleminson, F. R., and E. Gilman. 1984. Proposals and technology for arms control verification—A survey. In *Quantitative assessment in arms control*, ed. R. Avenhaus and R. K. Huber, p. 359. New York: Plenum Press.

Davis, P. K. 1988. *The role of uncertainty in assessing the NATO-Pact central region balance.* Rand report P-7427. Santa Monica, Calif.: Rand Corp.

Epstein, J. M. 1985. The calculus of conventional war: Dynamic analysis without Lanchester theory. Washington, D.C.: Brookings.

Huber, R. K. 1985. On current issues in defense systems analysis and combat modelling. *Omega* 13 (2):95–106.

———. 1988. On structural prerequisites to strategic stability in Europe without nuclear weapons: Conclusions from the analysis of a model of conventional conflict. *Systems Research* 5(3):211–23.

Jervis, R. 1973. Cooperation under the security dilemma. *World Politics* 30:167–214.

Kaufmann, W. W. 1983. The arithmetic of force planning. In *Alliance security: NATO and the no-first-use question*, ed. J. D. Steinbrunner and L. V. Sigal. Washington, D.C.: Brookings.

Kaysen, C. 1986. Keeping the strategic balance. *Foreign Affairs* 46(4):672.

Kokoshin, A. 1987. Militärpolitische Aspekte der Sicherheit in den Ost-West-Beziehungen. *Politik und Zeitgeschichte*, 7 November, pp. 45–53.

Lanchester, F.W. 1914. Aircraft in warfare: The dawn of the fourth arm—no. 5, The principle of concentration. *Engineering* 98:422–3.

Leppingwell, J. W. R. 1987. The laws of combat? Lanchester reexamined. *International Security* 12(1):89–134.

Mearsheimer, J. 1989. How to measure the conventional balance: The 3:1 rule and its critics. *International Security* 13(4):54–89.

Raiffa, H. 1982. *The art and science of negotiation.* Cambridge, Mass.: Harvard Univ. Press.

Rapoport, A. 1957. Lewis F. Richardson's mathematical theory of war. *Journal of Conflict Resolution* 1:249.

Rapoport, A., and A. M. Chammah. 1965. *Prisoner's dilemma: A study in conflict and cooperation.* Ann Arbor, Mich.: Univ. of Michigan Press.

Rattinger, H. 1984. Empirical validation of Richardson models of arms races. In *Quantitative assessment in arms control*, ed. R. Avenhaus and R. K. Huber, pp. 179–203. New York: Plenum Press.

Richardson, L. F. 1939. Generalized foreign politics. Monograph Supplement No. 23. *British Journal of Psychology.*

ARMS TRADE AND MILITARY ASSISTANCE

Since the end of World War II, the transfer of conventional arms has become an important part of the world's international trade system and a major foreign policy tool for the participating countries. Some states seek to extend their area of influence with the sale or procurement of weapons. Others hope to deter aggression with them. Because states view arms as vital to their national interests, attempts to control their spread have met with little success. In recent years, as new states have entered the international community, the size of the arms market has grown and its character has altered.

Trends in the Arms Trade (1964–84)

Although the international arms market changed in many ways between 1963 and 1984, two trends stand out: the increasing amount of money involved and the participation of developing countries. Exports of military hardware and services more than doubled. In 1964, before the war in Vietnam escalated, world exports of defense items amounted to US$13 billion in contrast to the US$57 billion spent in 1984, an increase of about 340 percent. (All dollar values are constant US$1985 unless otherwise noted.) See Table 1.

Furthermore, the number of states importing arms rose—from 94 countries (69% of the world's states) in 1964 to 118 (81%) by 1984. Those in the Middle East were the largest customers. Between 1979 and 1984 the four biggest importers of arms worldwide were, in descending order, Iraq, Libya, Syria, and Saudi Arabia.

The number of exporting countries also grew, from 29 in 1964 to 48 in 1984. The rise in arms exports by developing countries was more striking. In 1964, five developing countries exported US$41 million worth of arms, less than 0.3 percent of the world's total. By 1984, 21 developing countries delivered more than US$5 billion, or 9 percent of the total. The People's Republic of China (PRC) was a key actor here. In 1984, China delivered more than two billion dollars worth of defense equipment, or more than 40 percent of all arms exports by developing countries.

Trade between developing countries expanded as well, altering the traditional flow of arms from the industrialized North to the less-industrialized South. In 1964, South-South trade was a mere US$101 million worth, or 4.5 percent of total major weapon exports to developing countries; by 1984 it had risen to US$2.4 billion—more than 10 percent of the total.

Just as the number of buyers and sellers grew, so too did the number of weapons producers among the developing countries—from six states in the early 1950s to 27 in 1984. The number of major weapon systems they made more than trebled during the same time period. By the

TABLE 1. *World Exports of Military Goods and Services by Value of Deliveries*: A Comparison of 1964, 1974, 1984, and 1987 (constant US$1985 millions)*

	1964 $VALUE	%WORLD TOTAL	1974 $VALUE	%WORLD TOTAL	1984 $VALUE	%WORLD TOTAL	1987 $VALUE	%WORLD TOTAL	%CHANGE 1964–1987
NATO Europe [a]	1,969.59	14.69	3,728.60	13.85	10,938.60	19.30	6,627.36	14.32	236.48
Other Europe [b]	64.41	0.48	339.90	1.26	2,698.60	4.76	575.47	1.24	793.45
United States	6,418.29	47.86	12,096.28	44.94	13,888.81	24.51	13,483.84	29.14	110.08
Canada	223.74	1.67	247.20	0.92	195.70	0.35	113.21	0.24	−49.40
Japan	44.07	0.33	41.20	0.15	288.40	0.51	75.47	0.16	71.25
Soviet Union	3,722.22	27.75	8,446.00	31.38	19,982.00	35.26	20,000.00	43.22	437.31
Other WTO [c]	894.96	6.67	1,442.00	5.36	3,563.80	6.29	2,712.26	5.86	203.06
Oceania [d]	33.90	0.25	61.80	0.23	72.10	0.13	28.30	0.06	−16.51
Developing countries [e]	40.68	0.30	515.00	1.91	5,041.85	8.90	2,660.38	5.75	6,439.77
Total	13,411.86		26,917.98		56,669.86		46,276.29		
%Change									245.04

* *Source:* U.S. Arms Control and Disarmament Agency (ACDA), World Military Expenditures and Arms Transfers, 1963–73, 1985, & 1987 for all countries except the United States. The dollar value of U.S. exports was derived from the Department of Defense Security Assistance Agency (DSAA), Fiscal Year Series (as of September 30, 1987), which includes deliveries of construction, training, and other services. The ACDA data includes these services in the dollar value of exports for all countries other than the United States. The DSAA figures for the United States were used rather than ACDA's in order to make U.S. and non-U.S. export figures comparable.

[a] NATO Europe = Belgium, Denmark, France, Federal Republic of Germany (FRG), Greece, Iceland, Italy, Luxembourg, Netherlands, Norway, Portugal, Turkey, United Kingdom
[b] Other Europe = Albania, Austria, Finland, Ireland, Malta, Spain, Sweden, Switzerland, Yugoslavia
[c] Other WTO = Bulgaria, Czechoslovakia, German Democratic Republic (GDR), Hungary, Poland, Romania
[d] Oceania = Australia, Fiji, New Zealand, Papua New Guinea
[e] Developing countries = Africa, Asia (without Japan), Latin America, Middle East

mid-1980s, eight countries (Argentina, Brazil, China, Egypt, India, Israel, South Africa, Taiwan) had the ability to produce all four types of major weapon systems: aircraft, ships, armor, and missiles.

This worldwide growth in arms manufacture was facilitated, in part, by offset agreements—forms of industrial and commercial compensation designed to reduce the foreign exchange needed to buy a military item or to create revenue to help pay for it. In a direct offset, the compensation is related to the item purchased. For example, the seller might offer coproduction, licensed production, joint ventures, or technology agreements to lower the foreign currency cost to the buyer. In an indirect offset, the seller offers to invest in nonmilitary sectors, to market unrelated goods and services, or to engage in barter agreements. Sometimes the two forms are combined (Neuman 1985, pp. 183–213). For example, the Turkish government's 1988 purchase of US$1.07 billion worth of armored fighting vehicles from the Ford Motor Company provided for US$405 million direct offsets and US$300 million in indirect offsets. These arrangements generally are made between developed countries or between them and developing countries; but some producers among the developing countries are now transferring manufacturing know-how to other countries as well. The result is that direct offsets, when they involve transfers of technology, help ever more countries enter the defense production business.

Because of these developments, both the United States and the Soviet Union lost part of their arms markets. The United States, as the largest supplier, lost the most. From 1963 through 1968, U.S. transfers accounted for more than 50 percent of the world's military exports; from 1979 to 1984, about 27 percent. The Soviet Union, with only a 29 percent share of the world market during the 1960s, saw its exports peak at 46 percent in 1979, then decline to 38 percent for 1979–84.

Many observers feared that the escalating transfers fostered greater, more violent conflicts and had created a less stable world order. Such concerns were expressed most frequently during the late 1970s, when it appeared that the military expenditures of states would continue to rise indefinitely and the size of the arms trade increase exponentially. U.S. president Jimmy Carter tried unsuccessfully to institute an arms restraint program. A subsequent multilateral initiative, the Conventional Arms Transfer (CAT) talks, also failed by the end of the 1970s.

A Contracted Market (1984 to the Present)

The growth of the weapons trade ended in the mid-1980s as a by-product, not of arms restraint programs, but of worldwide economic and political developments. For two decades, beginning in 1964, arms transfers grew at an average rate of 8 percent a year. But during the mid-1980s arms deliveries stopped growing and then reversed, contracting by an average of 11 percent per year. In 1987, this trend again reversed. Arms exports grew about 6 percent over the previous year but remained well below the peak dollar values set in the early 1980s. Even with this increase, the period 1984–87 averaged a negative growth of 6 percent in arms deliveries.

World military expenditures followed a similar, if less dramatic, downward pattern. They increased steadily, from an average 2.6 percent growth rate between 1963 and 1973 to 3.3 percent between 1973 and 1983; by 1983–1987 they had dropped to 1 percent. Since then the downward trend has continued. World military spending totaled about US$950 billion in 1989, 2 percent less than in 1988. The number of major weapon systems transferred, particularly to developing countries, dipped as well. Between 1978 and 1987, some categories of arms exports to developing countries (such as tanks) declined by as much as 33 percent. Antiair artillery declined by 52 percent (Table 2).

Five economic and political developments are associated with the unanticipated slowdown of the arms trade: dwindling funds, rising costs and technological improvements, reduced assistance, the lessons of war, and fewer conflicts.

Dwindling Funds

The same factor principally responsible for inflating the 1970s arms market caused its deflation in the 1980s—the ups and downs in the oil market. The rise in oil prices after 1970 made possible the massive influx of arms into the Middle East. The governments of Iran, Iraq, Saudi Arabia, and the other oil-rich states increased their military purchases and sometimes subsidized the procurements of other Muslim countries (principally Egypt, Jordan, and Syria). Between 1973 and 1982, Middle Eastern defense-related purchases amounted to more than one-third of the world total. In the peak years of 1983 and 1984, the region's purchases rose to 43 percent of that total, largely due to the Gulf War between Iran and Iraq.

Nevertheless, even the oil-rich states began feeling the pinch of falling oil prices in the mid-1980s, and were forced to slow their arms purchases commensurately. Even before the August 1988 cease-fire in the Persian Gulf, arms sales to the Middle East began to level off, declining from a high of US$22 billion in 1984 to US$15 billion in 1985 and US$13 billion in 1986 (less than one-third of the world total). Although they rose again in 1987 to US$17 billion as a function of the continuing Iran-Iraq war, since the 1988 cease-fire the downward trend has continued.

Table 2. *Number of Weapons Delivered to Developing Countries, Cumulative 1978–82 and 1983–87*

	1978–82	1983–87
Tanks	12,335	8,325
Antiair artillery	6,890	3,309
Major surface combatants	125	103
Combat aircraft supersonic	3,505	2,058

Source: ACDA, World Military Expenditures and Arms Transfers, 1972–82 and 1988.

Note: "Antiair artillery" includes weapons over 23mm.
"Major surface combatants" includes aircraft carriers, cruisers, destroyers, destroyer escorts, and frigates.

The 1988 Saudi budget, for example, was notable for its US$10 billion deficit, its first foreign borrowing in 25 years (US$8 billion), and its imposition of taxes for the first time since 1975. Like many others in the region, the Saudis responded by slowing their arms purchases. Between 1985 and 1988, their defense spending declined an average 16 percent annually. By the end of 1989 it was reported that the Saudi government was having difficulty keeping up with payments of the "Al-Yamamah" arms package, which included among other items Tornado fighter aircraft and Westland helicopters, purchased from Britain.

Oil prices will continue to be an important factor in Middle East procurements. Although analysts disagree about the future, indications are that during the 1990s oil prices will stay below the levels reached in the 1980s, thus moderating arms purchases as well (Kanovsky 1990).

The oil boom and its aftermath had consequences for other developing countries, too. Higher oil prices during the 1970s drained their foreign exchange reserves, and the petrodollars that had been lent to them with abandon had to be repaid. From about 1980 on, this created a debt crisis in much of the Third World, especially in Latin America and Africa. The growing indebtedness of these states, combined with high interest rates and the reluctance of lending institutions to extend more credit to them, sharply curtailed their buying power. By the mid-1980s, the International Monetary Fund required many developing states to apply stringent budget cuts if they were to qualify for debt rescheduling and new loans. The result was a further reduction in defense allocations in many of the non–oil-rich nations.

Even governments that previously had given military expenditures a high priority now cut back. In 1980, for example, Israel was spending almost 30 percent of its gross national product on its military. But later in the decade the government faced interest payments amounting to over US$700 million a year, a foreign debt estimated to be 65 percent of Israel's GNP, and a GNP growth rate that dropped from 6.3 percent in 1980 to 2.6 percent in 1986 and 1987. By 1988 Israel's GNP was growing less than 1 percent annually. Under these circumstances, Israel's military spending declined an average of 11 percent each year between 1984 and 1988, in contrast to an average 4 percent annual increase between 1981 and 1984. Brazil also reduced its military expenditures, which showed a drop of 65 percent between 1987 and 1988. Likewise, the PRC's estimated military expenditures decreased between 1985 and 1988 (an average decline of about 1% each year). In general, between 1984 and 1988, defense expenditures dropped an average of 7 percent each year in developing countries.

RISING COSTS AND TECHNOLOGICAL IMPROVEMENTS

The price of Western military technology has escalated rapidly, further reducing the number of weapons states can afford to buy. For example, in the early 1960s an American Phantom combat aircraft reportedly cost about US$10 million. By the 1970s, US$15 million was needed to replace it with an F-15; and by the mid-1990s, it is estimated, US$50 million will be the price of the Advanced Tactical Fighter. Similarly, France's Rafale, which will not be ready for service until the mid- to late 1990s, is projected to cost 44 percent more than its predecessor, the Mirage 2000. In addition, warplanes last longer than before and therefore need to be replaced less frequently. Across the board, modern major weapon systems have experienced price increases and technological improvements, further depressing the number purchased worldwide.

REDUCED FOREIGN AND MILITARY ASSISTANCE

The oil-rich states. Poorer states have depended upon foreign financial help to buy weapons and services. The decline in the oil-rich states' funds has meant they are less able to assist others with military procurement. Arab aid to Jordan, for example, fell from US$1 billion per year in 1979 to US$357 million in 1987 and 1988. The Saudis no longer give aid to Pakistan, and reduced oil revenue caused Libya to cut back its support, estimated at some US$400 million annually, for Brazilian missiles in 1988. Since then, Avibras-Aerospaciale, the Brazilian rocket and missile company, has filed for bankruptcy.

Other suppliers. In the current economic climate, few governments have the resources and inclination to provide large-scale, long-term concessional military aid. Other wealthy countries such as Japan and Germany prefer to provide economic assistance. Other European states cannot afford to give grants or long-term concessions because of their need for foreign exchange to sustain their own defense industries and procurements.

As economic conditions have deteriorated and sources of financial assistance have diminished, the ability to provide military assistance has become the prime consideration in choice of supplier for most economically strapped states. Germany, for example, has had difficulty finding customers for its tank and armored fighting vehicle upgrade/conversion kits. The problem, one German official explained, is not mechanical or technical: "Customers are usually dependent on some kind of out-of-country financial aid to buy equipment of this kind. This they don't get from Germany" (*Defense News* 25 January 1988:19). Egypt, unhappy with the many U.S. restrictions imposed upon the coproduction of the M-1 tank, nevertheless chose the M-1 over British, French, and Brazilian alternatives. An American official observed: "The bottom line was that they could use our grants to buy in. It's not going to cost them a thing" (*Wall Street Journal* 23 February 1988:26).

The United States and the Soviet Union. Even the military assistance programs of the United States and the former Soviet Union have been negatively affected by recent trends, and neither is likely to offer major financial help to others except when important foreign-policy considerations are involved. In the case of the United States, congressional reluctance to expand military assistance has been the principal constraint. Although Congress in recent years increased the grant-aid component of the U.S. military assistance program, aggregate funding levels have fallen 26 percent since 1984. For FY 1989, Congress reduced funding for military aid by US$10 million, and in 1990, Senator Dole recommended a 5 percent cut in U.S. aid for all earmarked countries—Egypt, Greece, Israel, Pakistan, and Turkey—in order to provide economic assistance to Eastern Europe. As a result Washington has made only exceptional additions to its concessionary military programs.

The Soviet Union, with its economic problems, also was less forthcoming with grant-aid during the late 1980s. A 1986 Communist Party program reformulating Soviet policy toward the developing countries contained an explicit disavowal of continuing Soviet support, declaring that the USSR would offer assistance only to the extent of its ability. In line with this approach, the Soviets began reassessing their military-aid commitments. They asked the Syrian government (to which they sent about US$10 billion worth of military equipment between 1983 and 1987) to repay its US$15 billion debt to the Warsaw Pact, and they demanded prompt payment in hard currency for new weapons transfers. Moscow also warned Syria to abandon its drive for strategic parity with Israel.

The Peruvians, unable to repay their debt of about US$1 billion in hard currency (mainly for military equipment supplied in the 1970s), were obliged to provide the Soviet Union with naval vessels. The Vietnamese export crude oil to help repay the US$2.5 billion they reportedly received annually from Moscow, and the Soviet government warned them of dwindling Soviet foreign assistance resources. In Ethiopia, the Soviet Union reportedly terminated its military aid program, which amounted to some US$10 billion between 1979 and 1989. Nicaragua, too, experienced cuts; Soviet military aid declined 20 percent between 1988 and 1989 and halted in 1990. By 1991 the disintegrating Soviet Union had announced its intention to phase out its arms sales to Cuba and was negotiating with the United States to stop all arms transfers to combatants in Afghanistan; its shipments reportedly were already declining. Assistance to North Korea was also being withdrawn (*New York Times*, 12 September 1991; 14 September 1991; 15 October 1991).

Many producers have arms to sell, but most potential customers cannot pay for them. As long as current economic and political conditions persist, the procurement of military technology will continue to be restrained.

Lessons of War

The recent experiences of combatants fighting conventional wars and insurgencies indicate that more modern weapons do not necessarily translate into enhanced fighting capabilities or short-term military power. Instead, countries such as Iran and Syria found themselves overburdened with unrealistic requirements for infrastructure and technical skills.

Argentina found its logistic infrastructure inadequate to the task of modern war in the Falklands/Malvinas. For example, fewer than one-half the Argentine bombs that hit British ships actually exploded. (The most likely reason was that the Argentines were trying to sink ships with bombs intended for destroying land targets.) Furthermore, without an air-refueling capability, Argentina's aircraft were operating at the extreme end of their combat radii at a distance of 400 miles. Pilots often had only one opportunity to pass over the target and drop bombs before being forced to turn back. Other logistic problems, such as inadequate spares and inexperienced mechanics, particularly for the newer French- and Israeli-built aircraft, also plagued the Argentine air force.

Military leaders in many developing nations, such as Saudi Arabia, Argentina, and the PRC, have concluded that military forces are effective only if they have sufficient support. Investing in infrastructure, training, logistics, command and control, communications, and intelligence systems takes precedence over the acquisition of major new armaments. This means upgrading human skills along with weapons already in inventory, and hoping that skill and quality compensate for declining quantity. Given the rising costs of military technologies, this is probably the direction that developing countries, as well as developed countries, will follow. In the future, not only will the number of major weapons purchased continue to decline, but the type of military transfers will probably change as well.

Fewer Conflicts

Peace initiatives since 1988 also have supported the trend toward a diminished arms trade. As war ebbs so will the flow of arms to such countries as Afghanistan, Angola, Vietnam, and Nicaragua. During the Iran-Iraq war, oil revenues made Iran and Iraq the world's largest market for arms, and, with the exception of Saudi Arabia, the only solvent customers with a large demand. From 1982 through 1986, they jointly absorbed 17 percent of worldwide arms deliveries, 18 percent of the Soviet Union's total military exports, 23 percent of France's, and 70 percent of the PRC's (see Table 3). For some smaller suppliers the proportion was still higher. During 1980–83 alone, some 40 countries supplied Iran or Iraq with weapons or other services (SIPRI 1984, p. 198). If peace prevails, the sharp reduction in demand will mean hard times for suppliers around the world. French sales, for example, were adversely affected by the slack in Iraqi orders beginning in 1987; this was reported as an important factor in the first layoffs in history at the French Avions Marcel Dassault. Similarly, Brazil's Engesa, a manufacturer of armored vehicles and tanks which were used heavily by Iraq in its war with Iran, is in economic difficulty now. In the future, Iran is expected to buy fewer major systems and to concentrate its spending on upgrading and updating its arsenal with sophisticated components and support systems, such as air- and sea-launched missiles, and command and control radar. Iraq, after its defeat in the 1991 Persian Gulf War, will in all likelihood be subject to restrictions on its military procurements for some time to come.

TABLE 3. *Arms Exports to Iran and Iraq as a Percent of Total Exports, 1982–1986 (1987 US$ millions)*

Supplier*	Total exports US$ value	US$ Value exports to Iran & Iraq	% Total exports
Soviet Union	87,100	15,540	17.84
United States	69,561	10**	00.01
France	20,500	4,540	22.51
United Kingdom	6,925	150	2.17
West Germany	6,685	625	9.35
China (P.R.C.)	6,475	4,500	69.50
Poland	5,125	545	10.63
Czechoslovakia	4,775	440	9.21
Others	34,530	13,795	39.95
World total	241,676	40,145	16.60

Source: U.S. Arms Control and Disarmament Agency (ACDA), World Military Expenditures and Arms Transfers, 1987. The dollar value of total U.S. exports was derived from the Department of Defense Security Assistance Agency (DSAA), Fiscal Year Series (as of September 1987) (author's calculations).

* The suppliers included here are not necessarily the major suppliers to Iran and Iraq. Rather they are the only suppliers for which ACDA provides export figures to specific recipients.

** Value of exports to Iraq. Values of U.S. covert deliveries to Iran in 1985–86 are not included.

A combination of factors, then, has deflated a formerly expanding arms market. The increasing number of producers notwithstanding, demand for major weapons has stopped growing, especially in the developing countries. Major activity in the arms market, other than services, components, upgrades, improved electronics, and the transfer of older equipment, is not expected during the 1990s.

The Future Shape of the Arms Trade

Some analysts predict that a new multipolar international environment is evolving, in which there will be no hegemonic power. The arms trade, however, shows little sign of change in this direction. The shrinking of the arms market has had little effect on its overall structure. On the contrary, contraction has exposed the relative weaknesses of some supplier states—often concealed in a rapidly expanding buyer's market—and emphasized the commercial and productive power of its strongest members. Although the volume of trade has decreased, the hierarchy of suppliers (their relative position in the arms market) has not changed substantially. While the pie may be smaller and the size of the slices may vary dramatically, to date the United States and the former Soviet Union continue to dominate the arms trade.

UNITED STATES

Technology, Research, and Development. In spite of its reduced market share, the United States retains its competitive advantage over other suppliers. In part, this is because the market seeks what the United States has to sell: manufacturing know-how, sophisticated components, and advanced technologies. The fastest growth rates in the U.S. aerospace industry are not in the airframe and engine sectors but among the avionics and space/satellite equipment suppliers. Overall, the demand for American electronics and space technologies is expanding.

The United States has the largest military research and development (R&D) budget in the world—on average US$39 billion annually, accounting for three-quarters of total U.S. federal government spending for research—about 42 percent of the world's total in 1983 (SIPRI 1984, pp. 165–67). According to the Senate Armed Services Committee, 48.5 percent of U.S. R&D allocations are earmarked for conventional weapons research and development. Such a large R&D budget enables the U.S. to dominate the production and sale of advanced technologies, such as gallium arsenide components, carbon fibers, ceramics, high-speed integrated circuitry, stealth technology, and terminal missile defense.

In today's fast-changing technological environment, the gap between the U.S. and its competitors is widening. New systems such as sensor and communications technologies, advanced data processing capabilities mated with new delivery systems, low observable aircraft and missiles, and long-range surveillance systems are placing ever more exacting demands on the R&D and production capabilities of producers. During the next 20 years as other technologies enter development (such as directed energy weapons, autonomous smart weapons, new families of explosives, earth-penetrating sensors and weapons, "brilliant" information processing, and advanced robotics), they will further strain the manufacturing capabilities of the world's arms producers and the absorptive capabilities of the world's militaries. These state-of-the-art systems as well as other high-technology manufacturing systems (such as advanced tooling equipment, computer-driven industrial mills, and high-temperature ceramic superconductors) are expected to be in demand in the future arms trade (Future Security Environment Working Group 1988, pp. 9–11).

Impact on the future battlefield. These and other projected systems are expected to have a revolutionary impact on the future battlefield. They can provide real-time, all-weather reconnaissance and surveillance capabilities and increased warning time, and allow for unprecedented weapon lethality, real-time target acquisition, and high-kill probability per ammunition round. In this new military environment, some observers predict, "the advantages once associated with large standing forces eventually will fade along with those of [strategic] surprise" (Pilat and White 1990, pp. 82–83). The strategy and tactics of war will change, as well as force structures, placing a premium on unmanned weapons and long-range stand-off weapons.

Some analysts claim that the power and accuracy of modern armaments have blurred the distinction between conventional and strategic weapons—indeed that "if a full scale conventional war broke out in Europe, the battlefield two weeks later . . . would be, in visual terms, little different from an attack by Hiroshima class nuclear weapons" (Hoag 1987, p. 79). Whether the lethality and accuracy of new conventional weapon systems will provide the same deterrent effect that nuclear weapons have since the end of World War II remains to be seen. But as the implements of war change, so will demand, affording a competitive advantage to the country capable of designing and producing the new technologies. To date, in part due to its R&D resources, that advantage attends to the United States.

Military and commercial markets. The weight of the United States in the international arms trade derives partly from its physical and economic size, especially the size of its defense sector. With an annual procurement budget of about US$80 billion (Carlucci 1989, p. 219; Cheney 1990, p. 64), the United States, even after budget cutting, is the largest military market in the world. The Pentagon claims that, in the area of new weapons, it outspent its nearest rival, the USSR, by about 32 percent in 1987, before the disintegration of the Soviet army (*Soviet Military Power* 1988, p. 140). As a result, the United States is an attractive market for other arms producers.

Furthermore, the size of its commercial market augments the competitive advantage and influence of the United States in the arms trade. The US$5.2 trillion U.S. economy is the largest in the world, making it an attractive market for other nations' products. The Swiss decision to buy American F/A-18s, rather than replace its French Mirage 3s with Mirage 2000s, reportedly was due not just to technical and operational considerations but also to Swiss expectations of offset offers that included additional large sales of Swiss industrial and electronic equipment to the American market. Similarly, Japan's Honda Motor Company Ltd. yielded to U.S. pressure to stop selling military-related items to Vietnam, Cambodia, and Laos because it feared compromising its automobile-manufacturing position in the United States.

Lack of dependence on arms exports. The United States is not dependent upon exports to support its military-industrial sector. Only 5 to 15 percent of total U.S. defense production is exported, which insulates U.S. military industries from some of the consequences of a contracted world market. Dependence on foreign sales does vary from industry to industry. Some U.S. firms are more sensitive to recent defense budget cuts than others; for them, foreign markets provide important supplementary earnings. Sikorsky's international sales, for example, grew from 5 to 25 percent of its total revenues in the late 1980s and early 1990s, and the company hopes to increase that percentage significantly. Overall, however, because of the size of its military market, the United States remains less dependent on exports than other arms producers.

All of these factors sustain U.S. influence in the arms trade. Arms-producing countries with relatively small domestic markets face the challenges of rapid technological change and declining demand. They need to achieve economies of scale to maintain their defense industries. These countries now look to the United States as a source of technological innovation and as a customer for their military and civilian wares.

Former Soviet Union

In the past, little was known about Soviet R&D expenditure. It was thought to be somewhat less than that of the United States. The USSR's many efforts to acquire U.S. technology attested to its technological deficiencies. According to the Pentagon, the Soviet Union lagged behind the United States in many areas of technology with military importance such as composite materials, semiconductors, and software productivity. This situation continues today in the Russian Republic, which inherited the bulk (80%) of the former Soviet Union's defense industrial infrastructure (*Jane's Defense Weekly*, 23 November 1991, p. 995).

Economic problems. Economic difficulties, as well as technological lags even before the disintegration of the Soviet Union, raised questions about the USSR's ability to maintain its standing in the international arms trade. Bad weather combined with disruptions in the Soviet industrial sector in 1987 led to a slowdown in industrial growth and a decline in agricultural output. As a result, Soviet GNP grew less than 1 percent in 1987, the lowest rate since the 1970s (CIA and DIA 1987, pp. 2–3, 23). In addition, the Soviet state budget deficit increased from 11 billion rubles in 1984 (1.4% of Soviet GNP) to 64 billion rubles in 1987 (7.4% of GNP). Relative to GNP, the Soviet deficit was roughly twice the size of the peak U.S. deficit in 1986. In 1989, President Mikhail Gorbachev announced that the Soviet Union intended to reduce its defense expenditures by one-seventh and its arms production by one-fifth. Estimated to have declined about 6 percent in 1989 and 1990, Soviet defense spending reductions resulted in cutbacks in military production as well as in research.

A declining market. Partly in response to these developments, major Soviet clients such as India increasingly began to shop for their expensive high-technology systems in the West. Even Eastern Europe now looks to the United States for computer innovation, and many developing countries, perceiving Soviet-built equipment as inferior, are increasingly unwilling to buy it (SIPRI 1988, p. 180).

A comparison of arms imports during two periods, 1978–82 and 1983–87, shows that India, Iraq, Peru, and the Warsaw Pact states were importing an increasing share of their arms from non-Soviet suppliers (USACDA 1984, pp. 95–98; 1988, pp. 111–14). Even Syria appears to be opening more to the West, which it sees as a potential source of economic assistance and advanced technology. In the future, this trend may be more pronounced as arms production cutbacks reduce the number of the former Soviet Union's most modern weapons, making them less available for export.

Although the dollar value of Soviet military exports remained high in 1986 and 1987, more than 40 percent of these transfers were outright grants to impoverished clients. In addition, many were paid for with low-interest loans, soft currency, or commodities, earning little in hard currency for the hard-pressed Soviet economy (Carlucci 1989, p. 66). Afghanistan, Angola, Iraq, Nicaragua, and Vietnam, belligerents in conflicts that are now winding down or in remission will, in all likelihood, require less Soviet equipment in the future. The market share of the Soviet Republics—both in volume and in monies earned—is therefore likely to decline further in the 1990s and beyond. This trend has already begun; Soviet weapon sales (deliveries) to developing countries fell 13 percent between 1988 and 1989 and 28 percent between 1989 and 1990 (Grimmett 1991, Table 2A, p. 59). Further declines are expected for the new republics in 1991. Unless the former Soviet Union is able to resolve its internal problems, establish some form of military unity, and maintain a sophisticated R&D and industrial infrastructure over the long term, its dominance in the world's arms production and transfer system is likely to diminish.

Eastern Europe

Most major weapon systems procured by former non-Soviet Warsaw Pact (NSWP) states have been of Soviet manufacture or Soviet design. This has impeded the indigenous R&D and military production capabilities of these countries. NSWP states were dependent on imports from the USSR, particularly fighter aircraft, sophisticated missiles, and warships larger than frigates. Only Czechoslovakia and Poland were permitted to manufacture older Soviet tanks. As a result, the export capabilities of NSWP countries were constrained both by their own military production limitations and by Soviet third-party transfer restrictions. Given the new political climate, it is difficult to predict how the military-industrial sector in Eastern

Europe will develop. Some political leaders have declared an end to military exports. Others talk of new arms production and sales ventures. But whatever the outcome of these policies, given their limited production capabilities, military transfers from Eastern Europe are unlikely to figure prominently in the arms trade of the 1990s.

Western Europe

R&D expenditures and procurement. The United States spends an estimated three to four times more than all of Western Europe on conventional military R&D. In spite of their considerable production capabilities, individual European countries must rely on the United States for many of their most advanced weapons and components. Their unfavorable military sector trade balance with the United States, averaging roughly 7 to 1 between 1978 and 1988, reflects this dependence (ACDA 1988).

In today's political and economic climate, most European states are cutting their defense expenditures, particularly procurement budgets. (British defense spending, for example, is expected to fall by 3% in 1990–91.) In addition, military exports upon which most European states depend to support their defense industries and foreign procurements are dropping. Export orders for French defense equipment, for example, fell by more than 40 percent in 1989, the industry's lowest figure in ten years; Italian military sales dropped from a high of US$1.5 billion in 1981 to US$390 million in 1988; and Swiss arms exports in 1989 declined more than 22 percent from 1988 levels. Many governments are being forced to cut back defense production.

The European Community. Europe's ability to remain competitive in the world's military industrial sector depends, in large part, upon the degree of real economic and military cohesion it develops in 1992 and on the level of technological independence it achieves. The Treaty of Rome, which governs the European Community (EC), specifically excludes defense affairs from the community's jurisdiction; Article 223 of the treaty exempts defense equipment from import duties. The EC plans eventually to impose duties on foreign military systems, in its drive to create a single European market by 1992. The EC has not yet embraced major defense items, however, and many observers doubt that it will. In some technologies Western Europe is hard-pressed to provide any fully viable supplier (Curtis 1990, p. 10). Therefore, it continues to see the United States as a critical source of advanced technology. As the military market has contracted, many European defense firms have begun to restructure. While some have divested themselves of their defense units, others have opted to become as big and wide-ranging as possible, seeking acquisitions and consolidation within and across borders. (For example, Daimler-Benz AG has taken over Messerschmitt-Boelkow-Blohm GmbH, and combined it with MTU and Dornier to establish a large German aerospace and defense company; the United Kingdom's General Electric Company PLC in conjunction with Germany's Siemens AG has taken over the Plessey Company of Britain.) There has also been a move toward more joint projects as companies build cross-border alliances in order to save R&D costs, achieve economies of scale, and lower unit costs.

In spite of the ongoing rationalization and consolidation of Europe's defense industries, it remains uncertain whether the Europeans will achieve integration of their defense sectors or the desired economies of scale. Past efforts at military-industrial cooperation have not been encouraging; current disagreements over military requirements, work-share arrangements, cost, and the need for political compromise have placed a number of joint projects in doubt.

Furthermore, experience to date has been that collaborative projects are inefficient and costly. With the huge gap in R&D expenditure, it would appear that even with cooperative efforts, unless Europe decides to invest significantly more resources in military R&D, it will not be competitive enough to either produce what it needs independently or to increase its exports substantially.

Japan

Japan constitutes another unknown factor in the future arms trade. It is clear that Japan has the industrial capability to produce and export a variety of advanced weapons systems. To date, however, political considerations—deriving from a legislated arms-export ban, public antiwar sentiment, and the sensitivity of their neighbors to signs of increasing Japanese military capabilities—have limited the nation's defense production and exports. Few analysts foresee a wholesale dismantling of the country's restrictions on rearming and weapons sales abroad. Consequently, Japan remains dependent on American defense equipment, sustaining a four-to-one military trade imbalance with the United States in 1987.

Other Producers

Already the rising expense of military R&D and production has caused many smaller defense producers to curtail their more sophisticated manufacturing programs. In today's market it can cost up to US$5 billion to develop modern commercial aircraft and another US$1.5 billion to design and build a new engine. The cost to develop modern military aircraft is even higher, and few countries can afford that much risk capital.

Moreover, as the technological complexity of modern major weapons has risen, so have the challenges to the industrial capabilities of the developing countries. Because of inadequate industrial infrastructure and scarce skilled personnel, moving the process from design and development into production often has entailed major technical setbacks and excessive time delays. In many instances, by the time a weapon is delivered it is virtually obsolete.

The Indian Ministry of Defense, for example, has conservatively estimated that sophisticated weapons take more than twenty years from the point of design and development to production and delivery. When the weapon is finally delivered, after years of delay and budgetary overruns, the quality is lower and the cost higher than an equivalent off-the-shelf imported weapon (Thomas 1989, p. 192). The modest aspirations of the South Koreans underscores the difficulty. They hope their new fighter program will achieve 25 percent of the capabilities of developed aerospace industries in the manufacturing and management fields by 1995 and 75 percent by the year 2000.

Retrenchment in the manufacture of major systems is already occurring in the developing countries. The Israeli decision not to produce the Lavi advanced fighter bomber and the bankruptcy of the Brazilian rocket manufacturer Avibras-Aerospaciale are only two examples. For other potential producers, financial constraints will serve as an effective barrier to market entry. As it is, the number of major arms producers has remained fairly static since the beginning of the 1980s.

In the current environment, the less-industrialized countries and smaller producers will have to depend upon others for technological innovation in the military sector. In 1987 Australia, Egypt, Israel, Pakistan, South Korea, and Switzerland, all sustained significant military trade imbalances with the United States.

There is little to suggest that this will change in the future. To stretch their shrinking defense dollars, many of these countries are now searching for innovative cost-cutting ways to acquire new and used weapon systems and are looking to the United States to assist them. Brazil, for instance, instead of buying new ships, is renting four aging Garcia-class frigates and a landing ship dock that were to be retired from the U.S. Navy. Israel is obtaining the Raytheon MIM-104 Patriot missile from the United States under a special leasing agreement. Other states hope to acquire surplus equipment from U.S. conventional forces reduction in Europe. Egypt, for example, is scheduled to receive up to 700 M60A1 surplus tanks; talks have been held with India, Morocco, Oman, Pakistan, Thailand, and Tunisia about 300 remaining excess tanks. Egypt will also receive U.S. assistance to upgrade four submarines originally supplied by China, 86 percent of which (US$97.3 million) will be paid for with foreign military sales (FMS) credits.

Changing Realities: A More Complex Arms Trade System

The U.S. Role

The picture for the United States in future arms trade is ambiguous. A number of factors point to a position of dominance, but foreign policy considerations and changing economic realities may intervene to diminish the American share of the arms market and obscure its central role in the arms trade.

Increased imports. To date, the U.S. market has been supplied essentially by domestic manufacturers. In 1988 it was reported that more than 94 percent of the Pentagon's prime contracts were awarded to U.S. firms. But the U.S. government is under increasing pressure to buy more military items from its friends and allies and to adopt a more liberal trade policy. In response to these demands, Washington has agreed to enter more international cooperative defense ventures, buy more foreign military products, relax controls over the transfer of some sensitive technologies, and permit the sale to third parties of more U.S. systems—often embedded in foreign-produced weapons. These measures have encouraged U.S. friends to expect more generous transfers of technology and to look to the U.S. market for future sales. More foreign firms are now bidding to sell equipment directly to the U.S. military, and are also joining in a variety of cooperative and investment ventures with U.S. firms in order to gain access to the U.S. market and its technology.

Tacit offsets. Pressures are also building for the United States to share its foreign customers with its friends and allies who need military sales to support their own industries. As weapon systems grow more sophisticated and expensive, and defense budgets contract, small- and medium-size producer countries depend more upon foreign sales to maintain their own defense industries. (For example, Israel Aircraft Industries depends on exports of 70% of its production to achieve economies of scale.) Meanwhile, most developing countries cannot afford U.S.–built first-line weapon systems. Together these facts suggest that Washington will forgo some of its market as a tacit offset to help friends and allies, earn needed foreign exchange, achieve economies of scale, and enable them to procure sophisticated U.S. technologies necessary to maintain their own defense industries and military readiness. (A similar dilemma faced the Soviet Union which, during the past decade, bought weapons from NSWP countries as a means of helping them pay for their Soviet manufactured military equipment.)

This type of U.S. offset is not without precedent either. In the 1960s, for example, the British sold Lightning aircraft, missiles, a radar system, and training services to Saudi Arabia in spite of the Saudis' declared preference for U.S. equipment. This was done with the direct encouragement of the Kennedy Administration, since Britain would use the profits to buy fighter aircraft from the United States.

When it has been politically expedient, Washington has even permitted U.S. security assistance to be used to pay for military equipment sold by its friends to third parties. After the Iranian revolution, for instance, Egypt purchased from Italy helicopters ordered by the shah, and it paid for them, in part, with U.S. security assistance funds. Special arrangements also allowed Israel to use foreign-military-sales funds to pay a West German shipyard for two Dolphin submarines.

Given the current economic climate, indirect aid of this sort may be a more prominent feature of U.S. security assistance in the future. If so, it could serve to moderate U.S. arms sales to developing countries, expand the export earnings of U.S. allies and friends, and increase the dollar value of Washington's military imports. The latter will occur if the United States, in fact, buys more foreign military products as an offset to its friends and customers. This would represent a significant change in U.S. practice, since U.S. foreign military purchases amounted to only one percent of the world's total during the 1980s.

Increasing International Cooperation

The arms trade clearly is in a state of transition, becoming vastly more complex and variegated than in the past. The risk of doing business has increased due to tight defense budgets, the ever more complicated weapons, the costs of R&D, and the declining number of weapon systems being produced. These factors are moving military industries everywhere, including those in the United States, toward greater international cooperation and out-of-country manufacturing. For example, some U.S. defense manufacturers are looking to Europe for industrial alliances as 1992 approaches and the prospect of an enlarged, truly common market promises increased sales opportunities. Others are transplanting production to Asia in an effort to cut costs and satisfy the offset requirements of the host country.

East-West collaboration. East-West industrial collaboration will expand as the products and peoples of these formerly alienated regions flow through increasingly porous political boundaries. Bonn and Moscow have discussed possible collaboration in aerospace, and in 1988 a West German delegation was allowed to visit Soviet aircraft and aero-engine factories previously closed to Westerners. Soviet aerospace firms also sought joint ventures with U.S. manufacturers. Yugoslavia reportedly has sought British help with engine, transmission, suspension, and electro-optical systems for a new tank, and France's Dassault is cooperating on the design of Yugoslavia's Novi Avion light-combat aircraft.

Combined-design weapons. As joint or consortium R&D projects, coproduction, licensing, and foreign investment in defense industries become more commonplace, military technologies will increasingly represent a conglomeration of design and manufacture. Indeed, this type of collaboration is rapidly becoming the norm worldwide. The British have teamed with the Brazilians in a joint venture to produce night vision equipment. China has led in this sort of enterprise, entering cooperative agreements with Pakistan to develop an advanced trainer; with France and Singapore for the design, development, and production of a new light helicopter; and with companies in the United States and Britain for the design of a new low-cost tank intended for sale to developing countries and possibly the Chinese Army. Although the 1989 Tiananmen Square uprising has rendered the status of these projects unclear in China, the worldwide trend continues.

Cross-national services and upgrades. In the years ahead, buying a system from one country will not necessarily be accompanied by upgrades or technical training from that country. An example of the growing size and complexity of the international service market is McDonnell Douglas Training Systems, Inc., which is using former U.S. Air Force pilots to train Kuwaiti pilots using Brazilian (Tucano) airplanes built in Britain. Upgrades of military items produced in one country by technicians from another have also become more common. Despite expected downturns in military spending, the demand for and sales of this type of service is expected to rise.

Integration of Civilian and Military Industries

In the future, the divide between civilian and military industries will become less defined. Companies worried about profits in a time of declining defense budgets already are looking to the civilian sector for business opportunities. Political leaders, too, are beginning to understand the interdependence of their civil and military industrial sectors, and are attempting to integrate them in support of larger economic goals.

Conversion. In some countries, slack military-industrial capacity is being diverted to the production of civilian products or dual-use items. Germany's Krauss-Maffei, which for more than two decades has produced the Leopard battle tanks, is now dealing with falling military orders by widening the company's civilian business in transportation, environmental technology, and machines for making plastic compact discs. Civil sales now claim a larger portion of France's aerospace industry relative to military sales. In 1989, more than 60 percent of French aerospace orders were for civil products. Of the military orders, only 23 percent came from foreign customers.

Indonesia's leaders are now demanding that up to 30 percent of capacity in defense plants be employed for production of nonmilitary goods. Chile's Cardoen arms group, which was one of the chief weapons suppliers to Iraq during its long conflict with Iran, is diversifying to nonmilitary products and engineering services. In the PRC, two-thirds of all military factories now also make consumer goods. To compensate for cuts in the defense budget, the PRC's military hopes the share of China's consumer goods made in China's military factories will rise by one-half by the year 2000, providing more money for the needs of the armed forces. In India, even state-owned ordnance factories are contemplating diversification due to a shortfall in orders. Israeli defense manufacturers have been forced to shift their marketing focus to civilian projects. Elta Electronic Industries, for example, hopes to increase its overall share of civilian products to half of its product line, and civil items already account for more than 20 percent of Israel Aircraft Industries sales compared with 10 percent a decade ago.

Similar efforts were underway in the United States and in the USSR before 1991. The Soviet Union's economic reforms required defense industries to integrate with civilian industries. At least one-third of Soviet shipbuilding, aircraft, and electronic production reportedly was to go to the civilian sector. The share of civilian goods produced by Soviet defense industries was expected to increase from 40 percent in 1989 to some 60 percent by 1995. In addition, Soviet defense industries were to be self-financing. The practice of *khozraschot* (self financing) already widespread in the civilian economy was to be extended to many Soviet defense plants, notably major tank and armored vehicle factories and naval shipyards. This meant they were no longer eligible for state subsidies and had to operate on a commercial footing, working to achieve a profit. This policy is expected to be continued in the Russian Rebublic's defense sector. American companies are also looking to the civilian sector to compensate for declining defense contracts. The Boeing company, as one example, is depending upon demand for commercial aircraft to keep it going until the military market improves.

Some governments encourage technological transfers from the military to the commercial sector to stimulate growth there. Others, because of the overwhelming expense and technical demands involved in producing modern weapons, are looking to the civilian sector for help with R&D. Even the Pentagon is arguing for broad U.S. industrial policies to benefit civilian high-technology industries, in the hope that the rewards will benefit military R&D as well.

Dual-use technologies. Economic considerations are also fostering the production of more "dual-use" items—technologies that satisfy both civilian and military requirements. Civilian satellites capable of producing photographs of military interest; inexpensive commercial receivers that can be used to guide or deliver a nuclear, chemical, or other warhead; microelectronics, superconductors, computers, and composite materials are only some examples of products produced in the civilian sector that have military applications (Welch 1990). In the new global industrial environment, it is becoming ever less possible to distinguish between civilian and military products.

Accounting Problems

It is also increasingly difficult to determine the relative market share of the world's arms exporters. As weapon systems incorporate more foreign and civilian intellectual properties, components, subcomponents, and materials, tracing their origins and disaggregating their dollar value will become a futile task. The "world tank" will soon follow the "world car." According to the U.S. General Accounting Office, the Department of Defense has "virtually no idea what percent of subcontractor parts and components come from foreign sources (USGAO 1988), nor are there accurate records on the number of U.S. components and parts embedded in foreign systems.

Current accounting procedures are simply inadequate for the task. Royalties, fees, and repatriated profits are not reflected in trade statistics; given the growing complexities involved, they may not be calculable. A related problem will be that of tracking and analyzing arms export data that fall into the gray area of intellectual property, dual-use application, and covert third-party military sales. Clearly, it is becoming more difficult to ascertain the actual weight of individual producers and suppliers and, therefore, the real structure of the arms trade system. In the future, arms transfer statistics may mask more than they clarify. Changes in the type of technology transferred will make it more difficult to determine exactly what is and is not a military transfer.

Despite these many uncertainties, factors are at work that will limit the number of weapons most countries can buy or make, and that will foster their dependence on the economic and technological strengths of the system's largest, most industrially advanced members. Recent developments suggest that the United States will be in a position of dominance during the 1990s and beyond, as other states struggle to adjust to changes in the arms trade. Whether arms transfer statistics reflect the primary U.S. role in the arms trade or not, directly or indirectly the United States is likely to be the central actor. The extent to which other states will be able to match American industrial and export strength in the long run remains unclear.

Stephanie G. Neuman

See Also: Arms Control and Disarmament; Arms Control and Disarmament: Mathematical Models; Assistance, Military; Economics, Defense; Procurement, Military; Research and Development Establishments and Policies; Technology and Arms Control; Technology and Warfare.

Bibliography

Carlucci, F. C. 1989. *Report of the Secretary of Defense Frank C. Carlucci to the Congress on the FY1990/FY1991 biennial budget and FY 1990–94 defense programs,* 17 January, p. 66, 219. Washington, D.C.: Government Printing Office.

Central Intelligence Agency (CIA) and Defense Intelligence Agency (DIA). 1988. *Gorbachev's economic program: Problems emerge.* Paper prepared for the Subcommittee on National Security Economics of the Joint Economic Committee, Congress of the United States (DDB-1900-187-88), April, pp. 2–3, 23.

Cheney, D. 1990. *Report of the Secretary of Defense Dick Cheney to the President and the Congress,* January, p. 69.

Curtis, I. 1990. Europe's defense industry faces turbulent times.

Defense and Foreign Affairs, January/February, pp. 7–14.
Future Security Environment Working Group. 1988. *Sources of change in the future security environment*. Paper submitted to the Commission on Integrated Long Term Strategy, April, pp. 9–11. Washington, D.C.: Government Printing Office.
Grimmett, R.F. 1991. *Trends in conventional arms transfers to the third world by major supplier, 1983–1990* [series]. Washington, D.C.: Congressional Research Service. 2 August.
Heisbourg, F. 1988. Public policy and the creation of a European arms market. In *European armaments market and procurement cooperation*, ed. P. Creasey and S. May, pp. 60–88. London: Macmillan.
Hoag, P. W. 1987. Hi-tech armaments, space militarisation and the third world. In *The sociology of war and peace*, ed. C. Creighton and M. Shaw, p. 79. London: Macmillan.
Kanovsky, E. 1990. An oil shock in the 1990s: Another case of crying wolf? Paper presented at a forum of the Washington Institute for Near East Policy, 22 March.
Neuman, S. G. 1985. Coproduction, barter and countertrade: Offsets in the international arms market. *Orbis*, Spring, pp. 183–213.
Pilat, J. F., and P. C. White. 1990. Technology and strategy in a changing world. *Washington Quarterly*, Spring, pp. 82–3.
Sampson, A. 1977. *The arms bazaar: From Lebanon to Lockheed*. New York: Viking Press.
Soviet military power: An assessment of threat [series]. 1988. Washington, D.C.: Government Printing Office.
Stockholm International Peace Research Institute (SIPRI). 1984, 1988. *SIPRI Yearbook: World armaments and disarmaments* [annual]. New York: Oxford Univ. Press.
Thomas, R. 1989. Strategies of recipient autonomy: The case of India. In *The dilemma of third world defense industries: Supplier control or recipient autonomy?* Ed. K. Baek, R. D. McLaurin, and C. Moon. Boulder, Colo.: Westview Press.
U.S. Arms Control and Disarmament Agency. 1972–1982, 1985, 1987, 1988. *World military expenditures and arms transfers* [annual]. Washington, D.C.: Government Printing Office.
U.S. General Accounting Office. 1988. *Industrial base, defense-critical industries*. Washington, D.C.: Government Printing Office. August.
Welch, T. J. 1990. Technology change and security. *Washington Quarterly*, Spring, p. 113.

ARMY

See Land Warfare; Organization, Army.

ARMY AVIATION

Army aviation is a term applied to air mobile forces that belong to the ground forces as a branch of service in the armies of various countries.

The growing need of ground forces for operational, tactical, and logistic mobility necessitated the exploitation of the air dimension. The army aviation forces are equipped primarily with helicopters, also with some fixed-wing aircraft.

The spectrum of air mobile operations extends from liaison flights over friendly territory to the independent operation of an airmobile division with assault, antitank, escort, transport, C^3 (command, control, and communications), and electronic warfare helicopters up to 300 kilometers (186 mi.) from a friendly base.

Historical Development

The origins of all air forces lie in the exploitation of "lighter than air" means, that is, balloons, which were anchored to the ground and were used to observe the battlefield. The first use of a tethered balloon for aerial reconnaissance occurred at Maubeuge, France, on 2 June 1794, when a French balloon was used to observe Austrian troops. Subsequently, balloons were used in many conflicts, including the U.S. Civil War (1861–65). Prior to World War I, individual army officers in various countries investigated the suitability of early aircraft for military purposes.

From the very start, aircraft were instruments for observation, reconnaissance, and the direction of artillery fire. Between World Wars I and II the already-existing air forces, which had developed their own profile with pursuit and bomber aircraft, sought new fields of operation.

At the beginning of World War II, the German army (Wehrmacht) used the air force for tactical close support of army operations on the ground. In 1942, in the endeavor to accelerate target acquisition and adjustment of artillery fire, army aviation was founded in the United States and the army air corps in Great Britain. In the same year the Soviet Union combined its army and front air forces, which had been separate, into one air force.

In the period after World War II, several countries' armed forces began the use of helicopters. Although they were limited in performance, it soon became apparent that rotary-wing aircraft were ideal for supporting armies. This encouraged the formation of army aviation units in many countries. France supported its ground forces in the Indochinese and Algerian wars with her *Aviation Légère de l'Armée de Terre*. The United States made use of helicopters for the first time in the Korean War.

The extensive use of army aviation units came to the fore in the Vietnam War. With the deployment of the 1st Cavalry Division, for the first time a major airmobile unit was committed in a war. The massive use of helicopters for transport, logistics, reconnaissance, fire control, command, rescue, salvage, repeater stations, and messenger services increased their vulnerability to grounded antiaircraft defense and infantry fire.

Roles and Functions

Organization

The organizational form of army aviation forces varies from nation to nation and is influenced by the number of missions of the ground forces requiring support, by the dimensions of threat, by the geographical features of the operational area, and by financial aspects of force structure.

With the introduction of antitank and assault helicopters equipped with efficient weapons, as well as observation and fire control systems with improved survival capacity, a radical change in the organization of larger armies took place, attributable to the increased significance of airmobile operations.

The outline of army aviation structures in four countries is described below. The current structure of U.S. army aviation focuses on the combat aviation brigade (CAB).

Each U.S. Army corps contains a CAB with two attack regiments, each with three battalions and a combat aviation regiment. The regimental attack helicopter battalions of the corps CAB are the corps commander's most mobile maneuver force, each with approximately 120 assault helicopters. Battalions of the combat aviation regiment perform combat, combat support, and combat service support tasks.

Depending on the type of division, the CAB comprises one or two attack helicopter battalions and assault helicopter companies and the divisional cavalry, with 97 or 131 helicopters respectively.

The U.S. 101st Airborne (Air Assault) Division's battlefield mobility depends on the aviation brigade. The brigade in this division consists of four attack helicopter battalions, two assault helicopter battalions, and a command aviation battalion, with altogether approximately 350 helicopters.

In the Soviet Union, helicopters were originally subordinate to the transport and more particularly to the first-line air forces. As assault helicopters became an important element in the ground combat battle, and in close air support, an assault helicopter regiment with about 75 helicopters was provided at the army level. Similar regiments (with 20 helicopters each) were provided to divisions. Similar formations exist in other East European countries.

Of the Western countries, France undertook a radical alteration of its army aviation organization in 1985; the *Force d'Action Rapide* (FAR) was built up and the army light aviation (*Aviation Légère de l'Armée de Terre*—ALAT) was considerably reduced. Each French corps has a combat helicopter regiment with five squadrons and a light helicopter group with two squadrons. One of the five divisions of the FAR is the 4th Airmobile Division, which concentrates on the employment of 90 Gazelle helicopters, equipped with the antitank guided missile HOT. The three combat helicopter regiments have a total of 60 helicopters; in the command and support regiment there are 60 more, mainly PUMA helicopters.

At approximately the same time that the army of the Federal Republic of Germany was reorganized, service introduction of the PAH-1 antitank helicopter weapon system made it necessary to reorganize army aviation as well. It is currently structured as follows: An army aviation command is assigned to each corps, with one helicopter regiment of 56 PAH-1, two transport helicopter regiments with 32 CH-53 and 48 UH-1D, and one army aviation squadron with 15 liaison and observation helicopters (LOH). Each division has one army aviation squadron with 10 LOH.

Capabilities and Limitations

The following list of functions illustrates the possibilities of army aviation: battlefield reconnaissance, aerial patrols, aerial observation and adjustment of indirect fire, command and control actions, aerial fire support for ground forces, day and night air assault operations, destruction of tanks and other combat vehicles, rear area combat operations, offensive and defensive air-to-air operations, deep attacks, electronic warfare, laying of minefields, radiological surveys and chemical reconnaissance operations, aerial radio relay, aerial resupply, aeromedical evacuation, and dispersion of riot control agents and smoke.

Army aviation is subject to several important restrictions: limited NBC protection and decontamination capabilities; vulnerability to air defense, aircraft, and artillery; personnel and maintenance requirements, which may preclude sustained 24-hour-a-day operations; and adverse weather, extreme heat and cold, driving snow and sand, which may hinder operations.

Employment

The tactical use of aviation systems and forces differs little from classical ground fighting techniques. For example, army aviation forces seldom will fight alone; they will be employed alongside other combat and combat support arms.

Although employment on a tactical level was the rule over a long period of time, nowadays the larger-scope operational significance is rapidly taking over where numbers and equipment permit. No other branch of the services in the army is in a position to concentrate forces and firepower over long distances, at critical points, so fast—and consequently with surprise effect—as is aviation.

Certain principles can be formulated for army aviation operations that apply in varying degrees depending on the situation. The requirement to fight as an integral part of the combined arms team on the battlefield is always applicable.

Employment as support for the armored or mechanized infantry forces is planned in advance in most combat situations. Possible conflicts with the artillery fire plan, air defense, and close air support should not only be avoided, but on the contrary should be turned to advantage. The capabilities of as many as possible of the troops fighting in the combined arms team should be optimized to maximum reciprocal advantage. For example, the helicopter flight course should not result in a reduction in the use of arms by the air defense system.

Army aviation is in a position not only to employ its own firepower but also for the manipulation and support of other firepower. The aerial transport of artillery guns, antitank and air defense commandos, engineer blocking forces, ammunition supplies, and maintenance teams are only a few examples. Irrespective of ground features, obstacles, and blockades, surprise, and consequently success, can be achieved even where the local situation favors the opponent.

Armed Helicopters

Armed helicopters are divided into categories according to the nature of the armament and the operational mission.

1. Relatively simple antitank helicopters (ATH), originally conceived as liaison and observation helicopters on which an air-to-ground, antitank guided missile system has been fitted; ATH are generally used defensively and not usually armored (e.g., Bo 105 P, SA-342 Gazelle). They are used by many NATO countries.
2. Attack helicopters (AH), which have a more offensive range of operation depending on the weapons with which they are equipped (e.g., Mi-24, AH-64). This type of helicopter is found predominantly in the former Warsaw Pact countries but also is becoming increasingly popular in NATO countries.
3. Multirole helicopters that, depending on the situation, can conduct attack or transport functions (e.g., Mi-8, Lynx).

Helicopter Armament

Although U.S. Army and Marine Corps test groups began experimenting with various weapons on helicopters in the early 1950s, it was the French experience in Algeria, and shortly thereafter the American experience in Vietnam, that created the first specific needs.

At the beginning of the Algerian War, the vulnerability of the unarmed helicopters rapidly became apparent, particularly when hovering while engaged in enemy territory. CH-21 helicopters were subsequently armed with two containers for 18 68mm missiles, with two mobile 7.62mm machine guns mounted under the fuselage and with a 20mm gun in the cabin door.

With the large-scale introduction of American forces in Vietnam, it soon became evident that their utility helicopters required armament for self-defense. In 1967 the first attack helicopter, the AH-1G Huey Cobra, was used in Vietnam, equipped with a six-barreled 7.62mm machine gun or 40mm automatic grenade launcher. Up to 76 2.75-inch free-flight rockets can be carried under the body. A 20mm gun can also be used in a special turret.

Antitank Missiles

Following the introduction of antitank missiles, their utilization by helicopters was investigated.

France tested the antitank missile SS-11 on its Alouette II as early as 1958, and the Soviet Union integrated the AT-3 missile (Sagger) into the Mi-1, Mi-2, and Mi-8 helicopters.

These missiles belong to the first generation, are wire-guided, and require optical pursuit from the helicopter, which is not easy (manual command to line of sight—MACLOS principle).

The second generation of missiles used the semiautomatic target cover procedure SACLOS (semiautomatic command to line of sight), for which the control gunner follows the target with his sighting mechanism. The missile is tracked automatically, in the course of which an infrared sensor measures the divergence of the missile from the line of vision to the target and brings the missile on target by means of guiding signals through the wire.

The most common antitank missiles today are the TOW (tube-launched, optically tracked, wire-guided), manufactured by Hughes, and HOT (*haut subsonique, optiquement téléguidé, tiré d'un tube*), manufactured by Euromissile. Both work on the SACLOS principle.

The radio-controlled Soviet AT-6 and the Hellfire laser homing missile manufactured by Rockwell constitute further developments of second-generation missiles. Ranges vary between 3,750 meters (2.3 mi.) and 6,000 meters (3.7 mi.), with a penetration capacity of up to 700 millimeters (27 in.).

Antitank missiles of the third generation are currently being developed. These operate on a "fire-and-forget" principle.

Other Munitions

Bombs. The dropping of bombs from helicopters has occurred only sporadically in recent conflicts.

Rockets. The customary helicopter armament since the Vietnam War is with rockets, usually with HE, HEAT, antiradar, and fragmentation warheads. However, 70mm FFAR (free flight aerial rocket) are also in use. These are able to carry hollow-charge subammunition over a distance of 6,000 meters.

Cannon. Aircraft cannon are the usual armament for assault helicopters, and views differ on their suitability for combating aerial targets. Commonly, 7.62mm ammunition is used, but Soviet helicopters use, in the main, 12.7mm, and other armies use 20mm; with single-, double-, or triple-barreled guns. In Soviet helicopters, mobile machine guns built into the nose predominate, but fixed arrangements are more common elsewhere.

The engagement of helicopter against helicopter in air-to-air combat is being taken with increasing seriousness. Tests with high-cadency automatic cannon (up to 4,000 shots/min.) and rockets (Stinger, Blowpipe, etc.) have been underway for some time. The antitank missiles available are unsuitable from the point of view of construction. In the long run, only a fire-and-forget rocket with a range of 6,000 meters (3.7 mi.) or at least an autonomous end-phase guidance system, comes into consideration.

Mines. Mine-laying from helicopters has been applied by the Soviet army for a long time. The U.S. Army also has a scatterable mining system in use, and a considerably more efficient version is being tested as assembly for the ESSS (external stores support system) for the UH-60A Blackhawk. This could lay a minefield 1,000 meters by 30 meters (3,280 × 98 ft.) in 30 seconds.

Aids for Weapon Employment

As a general principle, arms are dependent on auxiliary aids, including equipment for identification, for obtaining target data for fire control, for the selection of weapons and their activation, and above all for directing or guiding. Assault helicopters are frequently equipped with radar warning systems. Laser warning systems will have to follow.

Sighting mechanisms are increasingly being installed as mast-mounted sight (MMS). This allows the helicopter to remain below the horizon and yet observe and even attack on the far side without giving away its position. The MMS is mounted above the rotor disc and the images it sees are transferred electronically to the observer in the helicopter.

Very few helicopters at present have sighting mechanisms suitable for night and bad-weather flight. This presumably will not change soon in many countries for economic reasons. The introduction of night-vision glasses and instruments with forward looking infrared (FLIR) or low light level television (LLLTV) has begun. The advanced attack helicopter AH-64 Apache possesses the most efficient target acquisition and designation system available to date, TADS (target acquisition and designation system), which can be used at night and to a certain extent under unfavorable weather conditions. TADS provides the gunner with a search, detection, and recognition capability with direct-view optics, television, or forward-looking infrared sighting systems. Once acquired, targets can be tracked manually or automatically for an autonomous attack with 30mm guns, rockets, or Hellfire missiles.

The pilot night-vision sensor (PNVS) is used by the pilot for night navigation and consists of an FLIR sensor system packaged in a rotating turret. The PNVS is slaved to the pilot's helmet display line-of-sight and provides imagery that allows the helicopter to be flown in a NOE (nap-of-the-earth) fashion.

Combat Operations

Antitank Helicopter (ATH) and Attack Helicopter (AH) Operations

Operational procedures for ATH and AH are almost identical with regard to combat against armored weapon systems. However, in the 1990s there will be a considerable number of nonarmored AH in use in the NATO countries, although their operational capability against ATH will be restricted.

Both ATH and AH operate with ground combat forces, which they reinforce and support for a specific length of time. Depending on the situation, various ways of employing ATH or AH can be selected: maximum destruction, continuous attack, or phased employment. The maximum destruction technique employs all assets forward to provide massed firepower over a relatively wide area. This technique severely limits the capability to maintain continuous fire.

The advantage of the continuous attack technique is that one-half of the ATH or AH available will be fighting while the other half is being serviced. Thus an enemy can be engaged for a longer period of time without need to break contact.

The third technique, phased employment, is a modified form of the continuous attack. After engagement of one company or echelon, a second is brought in. A third replaces the first unit requiring relief.

Companies or echelons usually consist of five to seven ATH and additional scout helicopters for reconnaissance and coordination, depending on the equipment of army aviation units.

Operations may take the following sequence:

1. flight from an assembly area to a holding area;
2. coordination with the forces requiring support or scout helicopters;
3. approach in NOE flight in battle positions, maintaining radio contact with the troops in position; and
4. ATH/AH conduct of fire action at the greatest possible fighting distance. Because of dissimilar observation capabilities, specific target designation procedures will be used only in exceptional cases.

Soviet army aviation units equipped with Mi-24 and Mi-8 AH concentrate largely on close air support (CAS) and pursuit operations. Thanks to their high disposable load of weapons, these helicopters are particularly suitable for CAS. Soviet attack helicopters are therefore in a position to release aircraft for other missions. As the Mi-24 is also able to transport eight soldiers, it can combine fire action with transport.

Important targets are tanks, armored infantry fighting vehicles, vehicles in general, emplacements, antitank weapons, and command positions. Further targets include assembly areas for combat and combat support forces and nuclear delivery means, as well as assaults on fortified positions with the aid of dropped troops.

Helicopters and aircraft engaged in CAS collaborate in the accomplishment of these tasks. Harmonization and collaboration with friendly CAS aircraft, artillery, missile troops, and maneuver units are essential for the effective identification, allocation, and combating of targets. These CAS tactics also require neutralization of the enemy's short-range air defense, aerial disposition, signals coordination, and identification systems.

Three types of fire support are open to helicopters: (1) preparation (firing prior to attack); (2) close support (firing during attack), and (3) escort (helicopters escort the attacking unit and combat any resulting targets). Friendly ground forces mark their positions with smoke to facilitate helicopter operations. Artillery observers illuminate targets for the helicopters using lasers.

Assault helicopter operations usually take place with flights composed of two sections, although other formations are possible. A flight can be stationed on an airfield 30 or more kilometers (19 mi.) away from the FLOT (forward line own troops). On being requested for support, the helicopters fly from the airfield to just before the combat area at a height of 100 to 150 meters (330 to 490 ft.) above ground. At this point they reduce their altitude to 5 to 10 meters (16 to 33 ft.). On target acquisition, the altitude is increased to a maximum of 100 meters in order to fire on the target. Targets are approached preferably at a gradient; this restricts the enemy's chances of air defense firing to a minimum. Combat begins at the greatest possible distance from the target. (Swatter can be launched from 3,500 meters [2.2 mi.], Spiral from 4,000 meters [2.5 mi.]). When engaged in combat against area targets, missiles can be fired at a maximum of 1,500 meters (0.9 mi.) and fire opened with 12.7mm machine guns at 1,000 meters (0.6 mi.). Disengagement occurs by veering sharply at very low altitude.

The most important operation for army aviation units equipped with the Soviet Mi-24 is presumably low-flying combined combat in conjunction with the mechanized infantry and CAS.

Deep-line Operations

Helicopters operating in depth in enemy occupied territory are included in the doctrine of countries such as the United States and the USSR. Within the framework of the AirLand Battle doctrine, even rear area forces may be attacked, and their commitment either decelerated or prevented.

Target fighting in depth requires adequate helicopter strength (e.g., the combat aviation brigade reinforced by the air force, artillery, and electronic countermeasures). Targets need not be confined to enemy fighting forces. "Soft" targets such as command and control or logistics elements are struck by attack helicopters. Airmobile reconnaissance and operations by dwindling daylight give the attacking forces a greater measure of safety. Depending on the depth and duration of a deep attack, it may be necessary to hold airmobile supply points with fuel and ammunition at the ready in the depths.

Deep-attack operations have high priority for Soviet assault helicopters. These operations comprise at least five combat missions: capture of bridgeheads near water; capture of important terrain; destruction of enemy nuclear delivery means; disruption of the enemy's reserves, command and communications networks, and logistics systems; and exploitation of nuclear and chemical impacts.

Soviet attack helicopters fulfill these missions by supporting the operational maneuver groups (OMG), by raiding parties and by helicopter *desant* (landings).

A Soviet OMG generally consists of a reinforced unit of division strength or larger, with extensive helicopter and aircraft support. Its task is to penetrate the enemy's defense on a narrow front and to destroy the defense system by attacking vulnerable targets in the enemy's rear. OMGs are threatened by enemy air attacks, multiple missile launcher and artillery systems, and counterattacks from ground forces. Attack and multipurpose helicopters are required for flexible fire support, reconnaissance of enemy troops, surveillance of open flanks, evacuation of casualties, material supplies, and for dropping airmobile assault landing forces to capture key terrain or crossing points prior to arrival of the ground forces.

On completion of a certain mission, the helicopters can land on a base within the OMG forces, be prepared for further operations, carry out supporting missions and finally return to bases behind the lines, which are some distance from the main forces of the OMG.

A helicopter *desant* takes place either as part of an OMG operation or as an independent undertaking initiated by an army to capture an obstacle or key terrain. The depth of thrust is determined by the expected speed of the ground forces detached to receive the airhead. A helicopter *desant* carried out as part of an OMG-operation may comprise *desant* forces with the strength of a rifle regiment. Armies usually carry out *desant* in battalion strength, whereas divisions carry out *desant* in company strength. In accordance with the principles of operation, relief of the *desant* forces should take place within two to three hours (5 to 30 km), but in Afghanistan assault landings with helicopters occurred up to 50 kilometers (31 mi.) ahead of the front lines. A Soviet helicopter *desant* begins by neutralizing the enemy's air defense with air force and artillery. A strike group of attack helicopters flies ahead, above the assault landing forces transporting the *desant* troops. A forward air controller in the strike group coordinates the air attack by the helicopters and ground fighting aircraft in the target area. The fire support from the ground attack fighters is stopped when the *desant* forces are about three minutes from the target area, although the assault helicopters continue to attack the target until the final phase of the assault landing.

Air Transport Operations

This is the classical form of helicopter employment by army aviation. Air movement operations serve to support the combat, combat support, and logistics forces at points of main effort and are clearly distinct from air assault and airmobile operations. The task involved is the transport of troops, casualties, equipment, ammunition, fuel, and other supplies.

The volume of these operations can vary considerably. Depending on the situation, such transports may require protection by assault helicopters or aircraft.

Special Operations

Special operations are overt, clandestine, or covert military operations conducted during periods of peace or war. They are conducted in direct support of national and strategic objectives. They are outside the typical spectrum of the army aviation units, which provide flying equipment, mainly helicopters, and practice and carry out operational procedures with special forces. Air force assets, with their higher capacity, are also employed for these special operations. Operations can include unconventional warfare, intelligence and electronic warfare, strike, psychological warfare, and civil affairs.

Air-to-air Combat

The increasing number of helicopters, in particular assault helicopters, has led many nations to consider how these can be combated in the air by other aircraft.

Helicopters have a flight profile that makes it hard for ground radar to detect them and fire antiaircraft weapons to engage them in good time. Enemy helicopters and fixed-wing aircraft constitute the greatest danger for friendly helicopters at present. At close range, stabilized automatic cannon are wholly suitable for utilization against helicopters, and mounted machine guns are useful to a certain extent. Accuracy of fire and penetration capacity give satisfactory results only within a range of 3,000 meters (1.9 mi.). Unguided missiles are effective only against concentrations of helicopters. Antitank guided missiles are unsuitable due to their restricted lateral and vertical target tracking ability and long flight time. At best they can be employed only against helicopters that are maneuvering slowly.

Air-to-air missiles are regarded as the most effective means of combating helicopters. For this, the use of helicopters rather than fixed-wing aircraft with limited look-down/shoot-down potential has definite advantages.

For helicopter-against-helicopter combat, several maneuvers have evolved that are applied depending on the type of armament, the type of helicopter, and the operational area. Unlike fixed-wing aircraft, the helicopter conducts its maneuvers in the horizontal plane; even the slightest alteration in flight altitude can be decisive and can foil an attack or win a tactical advantage. Yoyo, horizontal scissors, and wing-over are maneuvers that are generally combined for use in attack and defense.

Joint Air Attack Team (JAAT) Operations

JAAT, used by the U.S. Army, provides for the combination of army aviation and air force aircraft to conduct independent operations or actions integrated into combined arms operations.

The advantage lies in the high mobility of A-10 aircraft and AH-64 helicopters, which are able to conduct night combat and have specialized equipment for antitank defense (Fig. 1).

Operations are directed against enemy penetrations, against sensitive fòrces in the depths, and against enemy air assaults or air-landed insertions in friendly territory toward the rear.

Airspace Management

Airspace management is necessary if a variety of participants will be using the airspace; an additional complication is that the airspace will also be monitored on the ground by air defense forces. It is an objective of airspace management to impose as few restrictions as possible on the utilizers, who may have partially conflicting interests.

Airspace management must contribute to the overall operational plan; a rigid system would be unable to accommodate changing situations. Certain altitudes, corridors, and zones are laid down in a plan and are binding on the different users. Army aviation, air defense, artillery, and air force units participate in this plan.

Generally speaking, helicopters fly below the monitored airspace on the battlefield. They avoid entering zones especially protected by air defense and zones of planned artillery fire or CAS. However, the identification of aircraft remains a problem until a friend/foe identification system (IFF) is introduced.

Future Development of Army Aviation

Development in the years ahead will depend primarily on the future assessment of land warfare and consequently on the supporting role of army aviation.

Improved intelligence systems already render it almost impossible to conceal military movements whether by day or night or under bad weather conditions. Combat tanks

Figure 1. U.S. AH-64 Apache attack helicopter. (Source: Robert F. Dorr Archives)

will continue to exist in large numbers in most armies into the next century and will threaten their enemies with firepower and mobility. Their armament and armor will be improved; but the vulnerability of the drive mechanisms, tracks, and track rollers will remain. However, decisive improvements will be made in barrier systems and intelligent long-range ammunition, both costly items. Consequently, land warfare in the future will increasingly risk stagnation, subject to the availability of finances.

Use of the third dimension is also subject to these restrictions, although to a lesser extent. It may therefore be able to maintain and considerably improve its place in combined-arms combat as a highly mobile form of warfare that is independent of terrain and, increasingly, of visibility.

Equipment

It is generally agreed that present-day helicopters will not measure up to requirements beyond the year 2000 with respect to efficiency, survivability, and flight and combat effectiveness.

For armed helicopters, whose main task will be to intercept and repel tank attacks, future models need to be improved in the following ways:

- Ability to fly NOE missions at night and in bad weather;
- Accurate all-weather navigation, target acquisition, and communication and identification systems;
- Maneuverability and sustainability of flight performance;
- Endurance in the 2.5- to 3-hour range;
- Light-weight weapon systems capable of engaging and defeating armor, ground defenses, and airborne targets; and
- Up-to-date equipment enabling one-man operation.

In the 1990s the United States plans to introduce a new helicopter generation now known as the light helicopter experimental (LHX), which will come up to these and further requirements.

The U.S. Army will replace the helicopters UH-1M, OH-58C, OH-6A, AH-1G, and AH-1S with the LHX-SCAT (Scout/Attack). In addition to a multibarreled, turret-mounted Gatling automatic cannon, the SCAT version will also carry guided antitank missiles of type AGM-114 Hellfire, Stinger aerial target rockets, and nonguided missiles.

The LHX is to replace the OH-58A and UH-1H and will transport up to six fully equipped soldiers and/or payload. Its main task will be to transport fighter, antitank and/or defense detachments as well as logistics transports in the battle area.

The Soviet Union soon will introduce the Mi-28 as replacement for the Mi-24. It can be assumed that this helicopter is at least equivalent to the American AH-64 and consequently possesses fire-and-forget systems for tank and aerial target combat.

For the countries of Western Europe it is highly unlikely that they will be able to equip armed helicopters to a similar extent in the foreseeable future, due to financial constraints. However, the helicopters being developed, such as the Franco-German joint production of antitank and escort/support helicopters (PAH-2/HAC) and the Italo-British production of a multirole combat helicopter (TONAL), constitute a considerable step forward toward a helicopter fleet that is independent of the United States.

The Boeing Vertol Company is working on a replacement for the CH-47 Chinook, a medium-weight assault transport helicopter. The design, known as army cargo rotorcraft (ACR), should be able to transport a load of approximately 14 tons over a distance of 500 kilometers (310 mi.) and take a maximum load of 40 tons.

Work is also being carried out in the United States on an advanced tilt-rotor aircraft, which is to fulfill multiple duties. This aircraft, named V-22, will position the two wing-tip-mounted engines vertically for a helicopter-style takeoff and then progressively tilt the rotors forward for transition to forward flight. The tilt-rotor concept combines the low-speed flight of a helicopter with the speed and range of an airplane.

The role of such aircraft will be in intertheatre and intratheatre movement of troops with their vehicles, guns, and stores, flying over long distances at speed, direct to their operational locations.

Doctrine

The increasing number of armed and armored helicopters in many countries can be taken as an indication that helicopters will assume a more active role in combat than they have in the past.

The United States, the USSR, and France already have strong army aviation units that are able to conduct air assault and airmobile operations. Discussions are still in progress in some NATO countries as to the size and role of airborne mechanized units. However all acknowledge the great significance of such forces, in situations where insufficient armored operative reserves are available, if they are brought into play decisively, rapidly, and effectively.

Arno Möhl

See Also: Airborne Land Forces; Airlift; Airpower, Tactical; Helicopter; Helicopter, Battlefield; Helicopter, Naval; Logistic Movement; Low-intensity Conflict: The Military Dimension; Rapid Reaction Force; Rotary-Wing Aircraft Technology; Special Operations Forces.

Bibliography

Gunston, B. 1986. *Modern fighting helicopters*. London: Salamander Books.

Harrison, P. 1985. *Military helicopters*. London: Brassey's.

Jane's all the world's aircraft, 1987–88. 1987. London: Jane's.

ARNOLD, H. H. ("HAP") [1886–1950]

"Hap" Arnold played a vital role in the history of United States military airpower (Fig. 1). As chief of the U.S. Army Air Forces during World War II, he established the doctrinal patterns and organizational structures that influenced the U.S. Air Force for many years subsequently.

The Emergence of Airpower

Arnold was born at Gladwyne, Pennsylvania, on 25 June 1886. He entered West Point in 1903 and in 1907, after graduation, he received an infantry assignment. His first post was in the Philippines, where the Army Signal Corps was forming an Aeronautical Division. The new flying machine's obvious potential for observation suggested its assignment to the Signal Corps. Arnold decided to become an aviator.

In 1911, Arnold was assigned to aeronautical duty with the Signal Corps at the Wright Aircraft flying school, Dayton, Ohio. After flight training, he became the 29th pilot licensed in the United States. With a small cadre of airmen, Arnold brought two Wright planes to the College Park, Maryland, airfield. The group trained pilots and mechanics and established a nomenclature for airplane parts. They also experimented with bomb sights and mounting guns on planes and practiced air-to-ground communications.

Figure 1. Henry Harley ("Hap") Arnold. (SOURCE: U.S. Library of Congress)

In 1911, Arnold became the first pilot to deliver U.S. mail by air. In 1912, he gained national publicity by flying to an unprecedented altitude of 6,540 feet, and an aerial reconnaissance won him the first Mackay Trophy for "the most meritorious flight of the year." A near-fatal accident that same year grounded him for a short time, but he soon tired of desk jobs and reapplied to the infantry. There he participated in the Batanga, Philippines, maneuvers under the command of Lt. George C. Marshall. The two developed a mutual respect that played an important part in their future military careers.

In 1916, Arnold returned to the Aviation Section of the Signal Corps. When the United States entered World War I the next year, he was assigned to Washington with the temporary rank of full colonel—at 31, the youngest in the Army at the time. Arnold was appointed executive officer of the Signal Corps Air Division. In May 1918, the Aviation Section separated from the Signal Corps and became the Air Service of the Army of the United States. Arnold became assistant director of military aeronautics, the number–two man in the Air Service.

The Armistice ended World War I before Arnold got to Europe. Disappointed because he had not been in combat, he considered resigning. However, his broad experience in aviation was much respected, and he became an articulate spokesman for a concept of national airpower. Military operations were only a part of Arnold's vision of airpower. He advocated mass production of aircraft by companies dedicated primarily to making planes (rather than automobile manufacturers). He also promoted civilian air transportation and, in 1925, was involved in the beginnings of Pan American Airways.

Arnold was promoted to temporary brigadier general in 1935 and became commander of the First Wing of the newly created General Headquarters Air Force. Now in a position to influence military doctrine and policies directly and officially, he saw distinct objectives and operations in air warfare, and struggled for an independent air arm. He supported the basic tenet of airpower advocates that long-range bombers were the nation's primary defensive need. Seeking to develop a long-range, high-altitude strike force, Arnold promoted the development of the B-17 bomber (the "Flying Fortress") and sought appropriations to develop pressurized cabins in such aircraft.

In 1939, Arnold became chief of the Air Corps. With the support of his old friend General Marshall, Arnold developed an air plan that allowed the Air Corps to sustain Britain's air forces when the United States entered the European War, but did not compromise the buildup of the U.S. Army Air Corps. Arnold faced an enormous and complex task. He obtained funds, directed development of improved aircraft designs, prodded companies to work faster, built air bases, recruited and trained air crews, and selected leaders. A major problem was whether primary emphasis should be placed on developing bomber or fighter planes. Arnold favored bombers and struggled to acquire long-range aircraft capabilities. General Marshall's support of Arnold in initiating development of the B-29 "Superfortress" was taken as an official recognition of the independent, strategic mission of the Air Corps. When Marshall appointed him deputy chief of staff for air, Arnold became the first airman to serve on the General Staff.

World War II: Airpower Comes of Age

After the attack on Pearl Harbor, Arnold's challenge was to train and organize effectively the massive resources of men and materiel being mobilized for the new Air Corps. Fortunately, he knew many outstanding airmen, like Doolittle, Spaatz, Eaker, and others, whom he appointed to critical command and logistical support positions.

Early in the war, the United States established the Joint Chiefs of Staff (JCS) to work with the British Chiefs of Staff Committee. Arnold's participation in the JCS rendered him equal to General Marshall and Admiral King, chiefs of the Army and Navy services, and to Admiral Leahy, chief of staff to the President. He also became a member of the seven-man Combined Chiefs of Staff (CCS), which included three members of the British Chiefs of Staff Committee. The CCS, under the direction of President Roosevelt and Prime Minister Churchill, was responsible for the strategic direction of the Allied global war effort.

In addition to the strategic responsibility he carried as a member of the JCS and CCS, Arnold faced many difficult airpower issues. His major concern was to make strategic bombing work in the fashion he and others had envisioned. Allied air commanders learned many exacting lessons. The daylight raids over Germany were more costly than most had estimated. Long-range escort fighters were needed to protect the bombers, and target selection was often ineffective, as postwar analyses were to point out. But over all, U.S. airpower prevailed with quality air crews, innovative technology, and sheer numbers—elements of U.S. airpower for which Arnold was fundamentally responsible.

The U.S. air effort was sustained by an exceptional new logistical system. Arnold understood airpower's reliance on emerging aeronautical technology and airmanship skills, much of which depended upon civilian institutions. He gave the fullest attention to training and efficient support activities, and pushed the military airlift to its fullest potential. In operational matters, Arnold also resorted to special civilian support. In 1942, he authorized a Committee of Operations Analysis, mostly civilians, to assess selection of bombing targets and to study penetration tactics.

After the success of the D-Day landings in Normandy (6 June 1944), Arnold knew that the war was won and that the air war in Western Europe had entered its final phase. He turned his attention more fully to the Far East. His hope that airpower could reduce further Allied casualties in ending the Pacific war depended mainly on the use of new long-range bombers in sufficient numbers. In 1944, the 20th Air Force, composed of B-29s, was established. Arnold followed the bomber's progress with keen interest, for he believed strongly in its evolutionary potential. The pace of wartime production presented many difficulties in the aircraft's development. The initial attempts to bomb the Japanese mainland from bases in China were not successful. In November 1944, B-29s flying from Saipan began a devastating campaign against Japan. In 1945, the B-29 was matched with the atomic bomb; the consequences of that match demonstrated once and for all the utility of the long-range bomber.

After Arnold suffered four heart attacks during the last two years of the war, General Spaatz became his deputy and assumed many of his responsibilities. Following the Japanese surrender, Arnold retired with five-star rank—the only U.S. Air Force officer to hold that rank. Marshall and Arnold were the only members of the American-British CCS to serve in the same post from the first day of the war to the last.

Arnold died 15 January 1950 at his home in Sonoma, California. He had lived to see the independent U.S. Air Force he always sought. He left the Air Force with an abiding model for long-range planning. Well aware of the revolutionary impact the atomic bomb and jet propulsion were having an airpower, he knew that military planning would have to deal more effectively with the increasingly rapid development of technology. One of his last acts was to engage Dr. Theodore von Karman to conduct an extensive study of a science-oriented military future. Many findings of the study influenced U.S. Air Force developments, and civilian scientists have continued to contribute to long-range U.S. military planning.

ALBERT D. MCJOYNT

SEE ALSO: Airpower; Airpower, Strategic; Bombardment, Strategic; Marshall, George Catlett, Jr.; Spaatz, Carl A.; World War II.

Bibliography

Arnold, H. H. 1949. *Global mission.* New York: Harper.
Coffey, T. M. 1982. *"Hap."* New York: Viking Press.
Copp, D. S. 1980. *A few great captains: The men and events that shaped the development of U.S. air power.* New York: Doubleday.
Kuter, L. S. 1973. How Hap Arnold built the AAF. *Air Force Magazine* 56(9):88–93.
Mason, H. M. 1976. *The United States Air Force: A turbulent history, 1907–1975.* New York: Mason/Charter.
Mauer, M. 1987. *Aviation in the U.S. Army, 1919–1939.* Washington, D.C.: Office of Air Force History, U.S. Air Force.
Sherry, M. S. 1987. *The rise of American air power.* New Haven: Yale University Press.

ART OF WAR

The art of war refers to the skill or ability of individuals or groups to wage war. While the term *art* can be applied to either utilitarian or nonutilitarian purposes—that is, aesthetic purposes—the art of war encompasses only the basic utilitarian abilities pertinent to the prosecution of war.

Ancient War

Primitive war refers to war that occurred before written histories were recorded and generally involved fighting between tribes with the object of vindicating offended mores. Battles were nearly always fought on foot, and the common weapons were the club, spear, and knife. Until the advent of herding and agricultural tribes, war was seldom fought for conquest or economic advantage.

The first recorded images of war date to about 4000 B.C. Babylonian carvings from that period depict men wearing helmets, armed with spears, carrying shields, and arranged in close order. One of the significant innovations in warfare in the ancient period was the introduction of the horse as a participant in battle, first as the motive power of a chariot, later as the mount of a horseman. Early horsemen had neither saddles nor stirrups to control their beasts, but their size and strength alone altered the balance in a battle.

In the 500 years before the birth of Christ, the Greek city-states were in frequent conflict. The chief protagonists in these wars were Athens and Sparta, and their chief fighting formation was the phalanx. Battles were generally won by brute force, but notable exceptions occurred at the Battle of Marathon (490 B.C.) and at Leuctra (371 B.C.). At Marathon, the Greeks defeated the invading Persians by presenting a weak center and then, with the strength of both flanks, routing the whole of the Persian force. At Leuctra, a Theban force of 6,000 under Epaminondas defeated a Spartan force of 11,000 by weighting the left flank and thereby defeating the strong right of the Spartans, a maneuver since referred to as the oblique order, using the techniques of the refused flank.

Further significant developments in the art of war of the ancients occurred during the reign of Alexander the Great of Macedonia (336–323 B.C.). Two years after ascending the throne, Alexander began a campaign against Persia that lasted eleven years and ended with his death. Although only 23 years old at the start of the campaign, Alexander combined the skill and discipline of his foot soldiers with the mobility of his cavalry and consistently defeated more numerous forces.

The conquest of the Mediterranean basin by the Romans, and Rome's subsequent decline, marked both the zenith and the end of the ancient period of war. The first major wars for control of the Mediterranean, known as the Punic Wars, occurred between Rome and Carthage. Hannibal commanded the Carthagenian forces in the second Punic War, and although successful in his invasion of the Italian peninsula, particularly at the Battle of Cannae (216 B.C.) where he annihilated a larger Roman army in a classic double envelopment reminiscent of Marathon, Hannibal was ultimately forced to return to Carthage after the Roman senate adopted a successful strategy of sending forces to attack Carthage. The most notable achievement in the rise of Rome was the defeat of Hannibal and Carthage by Publius Correlius Scipio at the Battle of Zama (202 B.C.).

Julius Caesar's contribution to the art of war was initiated by his conquest of semi-civilized Gaul, today made up of France, Switzerland, Belgium, the Netherlands, and the Rhineland of Germany. His conquest was marked by significant engineering achievements, notably his bridging of the Rhine, the construction of an extensive system of military roads, and the successful conduct of siege warfare. From this beginning he demonstrated his genius by consistently defeating the best (next to him) Roman generals in the Great Civil War.

Warfare in the ancient period was characterized by close formations, a tradition of citizen-soldiers, and a predominance of thrusting and throwing weapons. The Romans replaced the thrusting spears of the Greeks with throwing spears, such as the pilum or javelin. Some machines of war—such as the catapult, onager, and trebuchet—were widely used, particularly in siege warfare. Toward the end of the empire, the citizen-soldiers were replaced by barbarian mercenaries, an act typical of the social and political decline of Rome.

Navies consisted of oared vessels that sought to defeat their enemies by ramming or by boarding an enemy's ship and gaining control through hand-to-hand combat.

Medieval War

The Middle Ages span the 1,000 years from the fall of Rome (ca. A.D. 500) to the emergence of gunpowder as a significant force in the art of war (ca. 1500). Cavalry was in its prime, and religion increasingly dominated the affairs of citizens and states. Threats to the remnants of the western portion of the Roman Empire came from Scandinavian pirates known as Vikings and from Magyar horsemen. Threats to the Eastern Empire came first from Persian and later from Muslim invaders. Heavy cavalry dominated the fighting forces, and the bow and arrow was the arm of distant engagement.

Technology was largely responsible for the growing importance of both cavalry and archers. The introduction of the saddle and stirrup (ca. A.D. 300–800) gave the rider a stable seat to support the traditional mounted weapons of war: the sword, the spear, and the lance. The crossbow, a bow set crosswise on a stock, which had dominated warfare in China since the second century B.C., appeared in Europe in the eleventh century. Although it was slow to arm, its arrow, or bolt, could pierce light armor. Bows were commonly used by Eastern horsemen, and in the thirteenth century the longbow, a 2.7-meter (6-ft.) bow made of yew or ash, became a favorite weapon of English foot soldiers. It could shoot farther and much more rapidly than the best crossbow and was equally good at penetrating armor.

In the west, the fragmentation of the Roman Empire meant that local leaders had to organize defensive forces to protect against barbaric invaders, and the resulting social system was known as feudalism. Local autonomy prevailed except when strong leaders were able to impose organization and discipline over vast geographic areas. Charlemagne was such a leader. Although semiliterate, his edicts established a military standard that brought unity and strength to what is today France, the Low Countries, Switzerland, most of Germany, and large parts of Austria, Italy, and Spain. Charlemagne strengthened the cavalry by forbidding the export of armor; he levied subordinate leaders for troops and equipment. His greatest contribution to the art of war was really the revival of an old Roman practice: the building of fortifications that were permanently manned in order to maintain control of a region after the army had passed through. These sites—at Bremen, Magdeburg, and Paderborn, for example—became important political and economic centers.

Charlemagne's empire passed intact to his son, Louis the Pious, but Louis's three sons fought bitterly and hastened the empire's decline. Feudalism thrived, partly in response to the military necessity resulting from Viking invasions. Feudalism achieved its most thorough development in the ninth and tenth centuries.

During this period, the power of the Christian church was expanding. The church restricted the use of the crossbow, calling it a barbaric and highly destructive weapon that allowed the lowly archer to best the chivalrous and noble knight. And the church attempted to excommunicate anyone who fought between Thursday night and Monday morning. The church was also responsible, as a result of an appeal from Pope Urban II in 1095, for the Crusades, military expeditions to the Holy Land that spanned a period of over 150 years.

The purpose of the Crusades was to recover the holy sites of Christendom from Muslim occupiers, to avenge mistreatment of Christian pilgrims, and to protect both the sites and the pilgrims from Seljuk Turks and other Muslim warriors. The logistical effort necessary to support the Crusades was enormous, and the dominance of the mounted horseman was challenged by both mounted and dismounted bowmen. But neither the logistics system devised nor the effectiveness of the Eastern bowmen had a profound effect on the prevailing state of the art of war in western Europe. The horseman remained the dominant force on the continent of Europe, but the longbows and the crossbow were increasingly used with good effect. The lasting military impact of the Crusades was the bringing to Europe of new ideas regarding fortifications and the opening of commerce between East and West.

Warships remained oared during the Middle Ages, and ramming and boarding continued as the principal options available to naval commanders.

Having successfully defended its institutions from the Vikings, from the Moors in Spain and southern France, from pagans of Prussia and Lithuania, and from periodic Muslim threats to the Byzantine Empire, the feudal system began to weaken. The church, a central feature of feudalism, was threatened by greed and corruption. The feudal lords were increasingly in conflict with their neighbors and their vassals. And the dominance of the mounted warrior was threatened by the longbows of England, the discipline and pikes of the Swiss infantry, and the introduction of gunpowder in the middle of the fourteenth century. Primitive hand cannon were used during the Hundred Years' War (1337–1453), but the potential of the destructive power of gunpowder was not fully evident until the walls of Constantinople fell to the artillery of the Turks in 1453. By the dawn of the sixteenth century, significant new conditions influenced the art of war.

Discovery, Renaissance, and Reason

Columbus's discovery of the New World half a millennium ago corresponded with the rebirth of knowledge in European cities. The accumulation of wealth and the consequent growth of banking further spurred the growth and magnified the importance of cities. The protection of cities also increased in importance as feudal arrangements were supplanted by the power of hereditary kings. Through war, inheritance, and marriage, new centers of power arose around the Tudors in England and the Valois in France, around Ferdinand of Aragón and Isabella of Castile in Spain, and around the institution of the Holy Roman Empire in German-speaking lands. The feudal arrangement of exchanging military service for land gave way to a system of exchanging military service for money or gold, and mercenary armies were hired and rigorously trained to protect and defend the new monarchs.

As sovereigns attempted to protect and extend their temporal powers, they needed larger and better-equipped armies. New methods of recruitment were introduced, and new, highly disciplined formations were created. No longer was the soldier a peasant who took up arms from time to time to fulfill a feudal obligation; he became instead a full-time professional who was trained, equipped, and paid to serve the monarch's wishes.

The first writer to explore the new forces operating in renaissance society was Niccolo Machiavelli (1469–1527). Disgusted with the *condottieri*, mercenary fighters of the Italian city-states, Machiavelli proposed that a trained militia be established. He argued that a militia would be more effective than mercenaries because motivation by identification with institutions would lead to a more effective soldier than would motivation by money only. He also believed that peace was maintained by power, and that war was a natural condition between states. Though marked by wisdom and a timeless quality, Machiavelli's ideas had little general effect on the art of war in the renaissance era.

The impact of technology and organizations on the art of war, however, was profound. The Swiss had shown that the mounted horseman could be defeated by mass, phalanxlike formations armed with the pike and halberd. The Spanish used similar mass formations but with large numbers of gunpowder weapons in the hands of the infantry. Late in the fifteenth century, Gonzalo de Córdoba combined harquebuses and pikes in a formation that became known as the Spanish *tercio*. The harquebus was the first of the shoulder-fired weapons to come into general use. It consisted of a metal tube mounted on a stock. The tube was loaded with a measure of gunpowder, followed by a metal ball or round stone. A touchhole in the tube allowed a glowing match to ignite the powder and fire the ball or stone in the general direction in which the tube was pointed. Inaccurate and unreliable, particularly in wet or damp weather, the harquebus was nonetheless effective when used in mass. Tercios commonly numbered between 1,500 and 3,000 men.

The tercio was still in use during the Thirty Years' War (1618–48), but the harquebuses had been replaced by muskets, which used a lock, or trigger mechanism, to ignite the powder in the breech of the weapon. The Thirty Years' War had its roots in religious conflict, but as the war grew more general, it directly or indirectly involved all the major powers of Europe.

The destruction and horror of the war were extreme. The town of Magdeburg, for example, was destroyed in 1630, and its 30,000 inhabitants slaughtered. Some historians have claimed that three-quarters of the German-speaking people of the world were killed in that war or died of disease, particularly of plague, which was carried from town to town by the itinerant armies.

The art of war seemed hardly an art form in the midst of such wanton destruction, yet it was greatly advanced during the Thirty Years' War through the efforts and genius of Gustavus Adolphus, King of Sweden. He instituted a national military service obligation to replace the mercenary system that Machiavelli and others had complained of. He instituted a training system that ensured that soldiers were well drilled in battle evolutions. He reduced the weight of weapons by replacing the heavy wooden rest used to support the early muskets with a light iron pole. He further lightened the infantryman's load by discarding armor, which had little protective value against musket fire. He introduced the paper cartridge, which combined ball and powder in a single package and greatly simplified the loading of the musket. He changed the basic fighting formation from one ten ranks deep to one only six ranks deep, and occasionally utilized formations in which the musketeers were formed three ranks deep. The increase in mobility and firepower was significant. He standardized the sizes of artillery pieces and lightened the weight of artillery gun tubes. He established a system of depots to supply his army on campaign. He returned shock action to the cavalry by restoring the charge with sword rather than the standoff that often resulted from the use of fire tactics with ineffective pistols. The Gustavian reforms proved their worth at Brietenfield in 1631, when the unwieldy tercios of the Imperial armies were routed by the Swedish force. Gustavus's genius covered the gamut of the art of war. He established a solid base, had a superb system of supply, moved his army quickly, struck decisively, and employed all the tools of war in a masterful way.

In England during the civil wars (1642–49), the lessons of the Swedish reform were generally adopted, although it is not clear that it was simply a case of emulating success. Oliver Cromwell, like Gustavus, recognized that discipline, training, and a professional force were necessary components of victory. Through discipline and leadership, Cromwell bested the king's forces and became the first to conquer and rule over all the British Isles.

In the late seventeenth century, France became the leading military power in the Western world, and like the Macedonians, the Romans, the Swiss, the Spanish, the Swedes, and every other group that had set the pace regarding the development of the art of war, France took the lead as a result of innovation and reform. The key to French reform was wealth and the desire for greater wealth. Gold from the New World had filled the coffers of the Spanish during the Thirty Years' War, and now France sought to be a leading power in Europe and a major colonial power. The sinews of war are said to be gold, and Louis XIV's finance minister, Jean Baptiste Colbert, put the finances of France on a firm footing through taxation and a mercantile policy. Military reform, led by Louis's secretary of state for war Michel le Tellier and his son, the Marquis de Louvois, who succeeded him, was greatly facilitated by the wealth of the state. Uniforms were adopted for general use throughout the army. Arsenals, hospitals, and retirement centers were built. And an efficient quartermaster department was established to correct the abuses in the supply system that had earlier prevailed. Civil servants ran the army, and the modern system of bureaucracy imposed itself on the art of war.

By the early eighteenth century, all the armies of Europe recognized the value of fixed magazines and depots for the successful prosecution of war. To protect these depots and the frontiers of the modern states, fortifications were built to block the advance of any invading army. Thus, fortifications became the key to a nation's defense, and fortification design and construction became important aspects of the art of war. Chief among the military engineers of this and every other era was Louis XIV's military engineer, Sébastien Le Prestre de Vauban.

Vauban developed three systems of complex defensive works, each designed to stop the progress of an invading army by exhausting it in time-consuming sieges. To counter his virtually impregnable defensive works, Vauban devised a system of offense against defensive works that was known as the system of parallels. By digging approach trenches, parallel trenches, and establishing artillery batteries at critical points, Vauban was able to again turn to geometry and mathematics to solve the practical problems facing commanders in the field.

Although the armies of Louis XIV were well trained, well disciplined, well financed, and well supplied, they were sometimes defeated by superior generalship and powerful coalitions. The generals who served France so skillfully in the seventeenth and eighteenth centuries, chief among them Henri Turenne; Louis, Prince de Condé; and Hermann Maurice, Comte de Saxe, were sometimes defeated when faced by forces commanded by such luminaries as Raimondo Montecuccoli; John Churchill, Duke of Marlborough; Eugene, Prince of Savoy; and finally, Frederick the Great of Prussia. By the time of the Seven Years' War (1756–63) France's military hegemony was eclipsed by Britain at sea and Prussia on land.

The limited warfare that generally prevailed in Europe after the Thirty Years' War continued during Frederick the Great's reign (1740–86), but the limitations did not affect Frederick's willingness to take risks, to commit to battle, or to the skill and discipline that he demanded of his soldiers and their leaders. The key to Frederick's success lay in his own energy and determination. His army was well equipped, particularly with regard to the iron ramrod and artillery—the former being far superior to the wooden version still used by other European armies. Frederick's artillery was light in comparison with that of other European powers, but it was highly mobile. Furthermore, one-third of Frederick's artillery consisted of very effective howitzers. The discipline instilled in the army paid dividends when Frederick was compelled to fight a major battle against the French at Rossbach (7 November 1757), then march 270 kilometers (170 mi.) to defeat the Austrians at Leuthen just one month later.

Much discussion about Frederick as a general concerns his use of the oblique order, which had been used with success by Epaminondas at Leuctra over 2,000 years earlier. It worked for Frederick on two of four occasions (at Leuthen and Torgau—it failed at Zorndorf and Kunersdorf), but he gave greater credit for his success to his use of artillery. Significantly, Frederick won only half his battles, but he established Prussian military institutions as the preeminent in the Western world. He mastered the use of the army as an instrument of policy and raised the art of war in the age of limited war to unprecedented heights.

Like war on land, war at sea was greatly affected by the introduction of gunpowder. The ship was an ideal platform for the heavy siege cannon of the period, but the weight of the cannon made ships too heavy to be propelled by oars. The great age of sail began in the sixteenth century and extended well into the nineteenth. Cannon facing outward along the sides of ships meant that a line of ships maneuvered to place its broadsides toward its enemy so that maximum firepower could be brought to bear. A strong navy was essential to any state that sought to be a colonial power, and the French victory off the Chesapeake capes, which led to the surrender of Cornwallis at Yorktown (1781), demonstrated the dominant role that seapower would play in a world joined by oceans but contested on land.

The Napoleonic Age

No military commander has dominated the events of the age in which he lived to the extent Napoleon did. Yet he is surrounded by controversy. He was a hero to some, a villain to others; an innovator and superb strategist who was lucky when successful and foolish when defeated; a military genius and a brazen exploiter of the ideas of others.

Without question, the events following the overthrow of the Bourbon regime in 1789 had extraordinary impact on the art of war. Of greatest significance was the institutionalization of the *levée en masse*, the concept that the entire population of the state had obligations in time of war. The *levée* meant large armies—not since the time of Attila the Hun had such large armies been placed under arms. It also meant that the rigorous training that had typified the professional, mercenary armies of Frederick the Great and Louis XIV would be impractical. Instead of the common soldier's being a valued commodity in the system of war, he could be quickly and readily replaced. The generals who commanded the French forces in the early years after the *levée* recognized the difference, but Napoleon saw in the *levée* an opportunity to change the fundamental nature of war. With greater resources, Napoleon expended his resources more readily and sought not just victory but the annihilation of his foes. Thus the *levée* gave Napoleon the opportunity to command a nation in arms, not just an army.

The larger armies also made command, training, and logistics far more complex. But Napoleon was equal to the task. He established a corps system in which his corps commanders were given considerable autonomy. He used his cavalry extensively as a reconnaissance force, and he was demanding in the face of adversity. The strict linear formations employed during the period of Frederick the Great were put aside, and columns were more widely used in the attack. The column required far less training and gave depth and staying power to the attack, and it mattered little if it was inefficient. Manpower in the Napoleonic Age was an expendable resource. A further change in the formations for battle involved the use of skirmishers, men sent in advance of a main formation as a reconnaissance and early reaction force. Their role was simply to find the enemy and disrupt his formations before the arrival of the main body of troops.

To supply his army, Napoleon relied on the system of depots and magazines established by his predecessors, but the larger armies also meant that foraging as a means of supply had to be used extensively. Far more factories were needed to generate the materiel of war, and the beginnings of industrialization helped by meeting the voluminous demands of the army and by making weapons with interchangeable parts. The system worked effectively until 1812 when distances, the Russian army, Russia's deliberate destruction of abandoned crops and supplies, and the Russian winter combined to bring the first major defeat on land to Napoleon's French Empire.

Technologically, there was little innovation in the arsenal of weapons employed by Napoleonic armies. The smoothbore muzzleloading musket was still the dominant firearm of infantry, and even though Gribeauval had standardized French artillery late in the reign of Louis XVI, Napoleon had little or no technological advantage in artillery. He introduced heavier armor for some of his cavalry and experimented with a mechanical telegraph system, but generally he relied on the weapons of war that had been available to his predecessors.

As a planner, Napoleon was unrivaled. He was a man of infinite detail, and his knowledge and constant updating of the disposition of his forces was essential to his ability to concentrate superior force against his enemies at the decisive moment. He constantly looked for opportunities to divide his enemies and defeat them in detail or to maneuver his force in a way that blocked his enemy from their base of supply. His example became the school for leaders and generals in the post-Napoleonic world.

American Civil War to World War I

The wars of Napoleon were characterized by little technological innovation and superb generalship; the American Civil War was characterized by significant technological innovation and generally poor generalship. Both the Industrial Revolution and the benefits of commerce contributed to the significant changes that occurred in the manufacture and design of the weapons of war between the defeat of Napoleon at Waterloo and the close of the American Civil War. The developments that had the greatest impact were the rifling of muskets and the introduction of railroads.

The basic shoulder arm of the infantry had changed little in the 100 years before the introduction of the rifled musket. Effective rifles had been used by hunters and some elite soldiers since the sixteenth century, but, with few exceptions, they were muzzleloaders and very slow to load since the bullet had to be forced down the grooves of the rifling as it was inserted into the barrel. For some models, a mallet was needed to tamp the bullet into the barrel. The key to the development of a militarily effective muzzleloading rifle was the creation of an undersized bullet called a "Minie ball." Named after its inventor, Claude Minié, the elongated bullet had a hollow base into which an iron thimble was placed. When the weapon was fired, the thimble was driven into the bullet, the walls at the base of the Minie bullet expanded into the grooves of the rifling, and the bullet was given spin as it traveled down the barrel. The spin gave increased velocity, accuracy, and range to the bullet. The new rifle-muskets of the U.S. Army also employed a percussion cap system. Instead of relying on a flint to provide the spark necessary to ignite the powder in the chamber, a small cap containing fulminate of mercury was placed over a nipple that took the spark to the chamber. This percussion cap gave much greater reliability to the weapon, since the ignition system was now essentially watertight. Some breechloaders and a few repeating rifles were introduced during the Civil War, but the net effect of the rifle-muskets and other rifles was to increase the lethality of the most common of the weapons of the battlefield and to force soldiers to dig trenches for protection even from small arms.

The development of a system of railroads affected the strategy and logistics of war. Troops could now be moved rapidly from one theater of war to another, and the delivery of mass supplies was greatly facilitated.

Communications on the battlefield was aided by experimental telegraph systems, and balloons were again used to facilitate reconnaissance. Improvements in iron allowed cast-iron artillery to be mass produced, and Robert P. Parrott developed a method of reinforcing the breech of rifled cannon by heat-shrinking a heavy wrought-iron band around the breech. Like the rifled musket, the Parrott guns used an elongated projectile, similar in design to the Minie ball. Artillery was also improved by the adoption of the friction primer, which consisted of a tube of primer that was placed in the touchhole and a roughened, twisted wire that was perpendicularly inserted in the tube. When the wire was yanked from the tube by the lanyard, a sulphurous substance on the wire ignited the primer, and the tube carried the flame to the main powder charge in the breech.

Innovation came to naval vessels, too. The first ironclads opposed each other in the American Civil War, and the invention of the screw propeller in 1836 meant that steam engines could be used on ocean-going ships armed with cannon and guns. Steam gave predictability to the navy because movement at sea was no longer dependent on the winds.

Despite the many innovations in technology, the Civil War saw few, if any, consistently bold strokes of leadership. Stonewall Jackson was brilliant in the Shenandoah Valley campaign in 1862, but tardy when needed near Richmond. Robert E. Lee was brilliant at Chancellorsville in May 1863, but reverted to bloody, unrewarding frontal assaults at Gettysburg less than two months later. Ulysses S. Grant was effective in the western theater, but ordered repeated, costly assaults in the Virginia campaign of 1864. Ambrose Burnside was ineffective; George McClellan was slow. Positive contributions to the development of the art of war seemed confined to the world of logistics and technology.

The attention savants gave to the Civil War was short-lived, for the wars of German unification quickly turned military interest to the world of the Prussian military machine. Quick victories over Denmark (1864) and Austria (1866) were followed by an equally impressive victory over the French in 1870–71. The Prussians employed the Dreyse needle gun in their victories; it was the first breech-loader to be standardized for use on the battlefield. Still, far more than technology influenced the Prussian victories. Perhaps the greatest innovation regarding the art of war to be demonstrated in the Prussian victories was the staff work accomplished by the great general staff. Efficiency was the byword, and success was the result.

The World Wars

Continued improvements in the weapons of war and wholly new dimensions of war marked the most significant changes that occurred in the art of war during the two great wars of this century. Among the notable technological advances was the invention of smokeless gunpowder, which was not literally smokeless but burned white rather than black and caused far less fouling of small arms and artillery. It made rapid-fire weapons effective, and rapid-fire weapons made life between heavily manned, entrenched lines impossible.

New ideas and new weapons were used in attempts to breach the enemy's trenches. Gas warfare was attempted. Mass attacks were attempted. Radios facilitated communications. Tanks were tried. New tactics, among them the Hutier tactics of the Germans, were tried. And airplanes were used, but without any decisive result. Submarines prowled the seas and wrecked havoc on commercial shipping, but the stalemate in the trenches continued. The arrival of Gen. Jack Pershing and the American Expeditionary Force (AEF) had only a minor impact on the outcome of the war; ultimately, the Germans sued for peace because in a bloody war of exhaustion, they were the first to be exhausted.

In the years following World War I, diplomatic initiatives sought to outlaw the use of chemical weapons, to limit the size of navies, and to eliminate war as an instrument of policy among nations. Meanwhile, the tank was further developed as an effective ground fighting vehicle. The airplane became an effective weapons platform, and advocates of airpower argued that an independent air force would be the decisive arm in future conflicts. The French believed that the defensive would dominate future wars and invested in an elaborate series of fortifications, known as the Maginot Line, that extended in depth all along France's border with Germany. While the Western powers focused on hopes of peace, the Germans, Italians, and Japanese focused on plans for retribution and conquest.

In stark contrast to the stalemate of the defensiveness of World War I, World War II was a war of vast and rapid movement. Tanks and airplanes dominated the land and air, and at sea, battleships, aircraft carriers, and submarines engaged in costly battles throughout the oceans of the world. Sophistication marked further weapon developments. Radar provided eyes to see distant attacks developing in and from the air. The Norden bombsight improved the accuracy of high-level bombers. Guidance instruments allowed planes to navigate effectively at night and in marginal weather. Machine guns were improved. Huge railroad guns were developed. Antiaircraft weapons were perfected, and pilotless bombs, the dreaded Vergeltungswaffen rockets, were unleashed. The ultimate weapon of war, the nuclear bomb, was developed and used with devastating effect on Hiroshima and Nagasaki to bring an end to the destruction in the Pacific.

Open formations were used by all ground forces, and the combined arms team of infantry, tanks, and artillery was employed wherever possible. Aircraft were used in close support roles, but the bulk of air resources were used in strategic bombing offensives against the enemy homeland and industrial base.

Examples of good and bad generalship occurred on all sides, and major problems in war leadership involved the resolution of differences between civilian heads of government and the generals in the field. Hitler's megalomania, Mussolini's obsequiousness, Stalin's lack of resources, Churchill's dogged determination, and Roosevelt's poor health all affected the conduct of the war.

Man remained the ultimate determinant of the outcome of war, but as technology made some tasks easier, it made moral choices much harder.

Cold War to the Present

Notable changes have affected the art of war since the conclusion of World War II. Nuclear weapon arsenals have increased dramatically—to the point where it is possible to destroy the world many times over. Attempts to limit the number of nations possessing nuclear arms have been moderately successful, and attempts to reduce the size of the great power arsenals have met with limited success. Improved delivery systems, from sophisticated stealth bombers to midget intercontinental ballistic missiles, continue to demand high production and deployment costs. Nations have agreed to the peaceful uses of space, but spy satellites, communications satellites, and a continually manned Soviet space station ply the heavens.

Closer to the firmament, new weapons of war are still in abundance. Jet aircraft continue to improve in speed, maneuverability, carrying power, and staying power. Their electronic navigation and target acquisition systems are complex, yet reliable—and made possible in large part by computers and electronic miniaturization. Supersonic transports routinely fly from continent to continent, and helicopters perform myriad functions in support of the soldier on the ground. Computers are pervasive, and their role in future wars will be extensive.

Tactics have changed from the preponderance of frontal attacks that marked World Wars I and II and the Korean War to a preference for guerrilla methods where stealth and surprise can overcome the sophisticated and lethal weapons of one's enemies, particularly if a developing nation is in conflict with a major power. A logical extension of guerrilla war is the terrorist war, and Western nations have invested costly resources in special operations commands to deter and counter acts of terrorism. While nations meet to place further bans on the use of chemical, biological, and nuclear weapons, evidence of chemical use is abundant.

This review illustrates some of the dominant factors—among them economic, social, and political institutions—that have affected the art of war. Other factors are generalship, the state of military thought and doctrine, the state of logistics and administration, strategy, and tactics. Clearly, technology has been, and will continue to be, a major factor. The constant in the art of war is man, his avarice and greed, his sacrifice and his courage. The future of war is a great unknown, but the obligation of civilized nations to be prepared for war when it comes is absolute. Skill in the practice of war and study of the art of war are essential features of man's existence.

JOHN I. ALGER

SEE ALSO: Alexander the Great; Charlemagne; Civil War, American; Crusades; Feudalism; Fortification; Frederick the Great; Gonzalo de Córdoba; Graeco-Persian Wars; Gustavus Adolphus; History, Ancient Military; History, Early Modern Military; History, Medieval Military; History, Military; History, Modern Military; Napoleon I; Professionalism, Military; Punic Wars; Roman Empire; Science of War; Seapower; Thirty Years' War; Vauban, Sébastien Le Prestre de; Vikings; World War I; World War II.

Bibliography

Adcock, F. 1957. *The Greek and Macedonian art of war.* Berkeley, Calif.: Univ. of Calif. Press.
Amstutz, J. B. 1986. *Afghanistan: The first five years of Soviet occupation.* Washington, D.C.: National Defense Univ. Press.
Chandler, D. G. 1966. *The campaigns of Napoleon.* New York: Macmillan.
Delbruck, H. 1975. *History of the art of war.* Trans. W. J. Renfroe, Jr. Westport, Conn.: Greenwood Press.
Esposito, V. J., ed. 1959. *West Point atlas of American wars.* New York: Praeger.
Griess, T. E., ed. 1985. *The West Point military history series.* Wayne, N.J.: Avery.
Hastings, M., and S. Jenkins. 1983. *The battle for the Falklands.* New York: Norton.
Howard, M. 1979. *The Franco-Prussian war.* London: Granada.
Liddell Hart, B. H. 1931. *The real war, 1914–1918.* Boston: Little, Brown.
Montross, L. 1944. *War through the ages.* New York: Harper.
Oman, C. W. 1885. *The art of war in the Middle Ages.* Oxford: Oxford Univ. Press.
Parker, G., ed. 1988. *The Thirty Years' War.* London: Routledge, Chapman & Hall.
Preston, R. A., and S. F. Wise. 1970. *Men in arms.* New York: Praeger.
Rees, D. 1964. *Korea: The limited war.* New York: St. Martin's Press.
Ritter, G. 1954. *Frederick the Great.* Heidelberg: Quelle and Meyer.
Ropp, T. 1959. *War in the modern world.* Durham, N.C.: Duke Univ. Press.
Spaulding, O. L., H. Nickerson, and J. W. Wright. 1925. *Warfare: A study of military methods from the earliest times.* New York: Harcourt, Brace.
Thucydides. 1954. *The Peloponnesian war.* Trans. R. Warner. Middlesex, Eng.: Penguin.
Williams, T. H. 1952. *Lincoln and his generals.* New York: Knopf.
Wright, G. 1968. *The ordeal of total war, 1939–1945.* New York: Harper.
Wright, Q. 1942. *A study of war.* Chicago: Univ. of Chicago Press.

ARTILLERY

Modern artillery weapons play a dominant role in land combat. The effects of massed fire of these weapons combined with the shock action of armor and the ground-gaining ability of infantry is often decisive; artillery is the greatest killer on the battlefield.

The use of the word *artillery* predates the use of gunpowder and the development of guns and cannon. Many scholars consider the word to be a combination of *arcus*, bow, and *telum*, projectile. Others attribute the word to the Latin *ars tolendi*, or *ars* and *tirare*, meaning the art of catapulting or shooting, or *ars telorum*, the art of long-range weapons.

French fortress-builder Vauban (1633–1707) traces the word *artillery* to the old French *artillier*, to fortify or arm. German philologist Diez assumes an association with the Provençal word *artilha*, for fortification, and usage of the word was adopted into the German language by 1500.

Regardless of its derivation, the present-day definitions of *artillery* include the following: a general term, usually referring collectively to large-caliber gunpowder weapons (such as howitzers, cannons, and rockets), too large to be hand-carried, and served by a crew (although all large, pregunpowder devices for firing missiles may be considered artillery); the branch of an army that is equipped with such weapons; and, in the Russian sense, the science of construction as well as the peculiarities and methods of implementation in combat of artillery weapons.

History

Early Development to the First Gunpowder Weapons

Pregunpowder throwing machines were known to the Assyrians (ca. 700 B.C.) and were employed by them against fortifications. It was several hundred years later, however, before the principles of engineering and mathematics were applied to advance the state of early catapults and ballistae—weapons using tension and/or torsion to propel various projectiles through a range of trajectories. Dionysius of Syracuse is considered by most historians to be the father of these early progenitors of modern artillery (399 B.C.).

The origins of the first firearms—weapons using the power of expanding gases from exploding gunpowder to shoot projectiles—are obscure. Gunpowder was introduced in China in the eleventh century and may have made its way to Europe via east-west trade routes in the mid-thirteenth century, although an Englishman, Roger Bacon, and a German monk, Berthold Schwarz, have been credited with its discovery. The Chinese used gunpowder in pyrotechnic weapons (rockets) and developed crude, cannon-like projectors, but it was the Europeans who invented the first gunpowder-operated cannon.

This development, in the early fourteenth century, became possible when advances in metalworking technology produced bronze and iron tubes strong enough to withstand the tremendous pressures generated by exploding gunpowder and rapidly expanding gases. The first cannon were bulbous, vase-shaped devices with a touchhole at the rear used to ignite the powder charge and a muzzle opening for loading and expelling a missile. Early projectiles varied from iron bolts and arrows, usually with some wadding at the base of the shaft to permit a closer fit in the tube, to round stones and later to iron and lead balls.

The first use of cannon in warfare may have been as early as 1326, when such weapons were described in a Florentine document. Austrians made their first use of cannon in an attack against Cividale in 1331, and the English used the weapon against the French in the Battle of Crécy in 1346. Other scholars point to the first use of guns at Metz in 1324 and agree to their later use at Algeciras in 1342. During this period, cannon became features in the English and French forces in the Hundred Years' War, and became known throughout Europe.

Evolving Doctrine, Tactics, and Technology

As militaries became increasingly aware of the impact that cannon had on waging war, they began adapting the structure of their forces to accommodate the new weapons. Concurrently, tactics evolved to better suit the new capabilities, and arms makers sought to design and construct guns of varying size and arrangement.

In the early 1500s the collective term *gun*, which until then had applied to all equipment used for shooting (bow, crossbow, fire tubes, etc.), was restricted to heavy weapons. Later the name was used for each individual gun, often with a second name descriptive of the type of fire or tactical use. In the fourteenth and fifteenth centuries the crewmen of a gun became known as bombardiers, the word deriving from the Latin *bombus*, meaning a muffled sound. By contrast, cannon are managed by cannoneers or master gunners. The term *cannonier* was used in France as of 1411 and spread from there to the artillery of other countries.

During this period the art and craft of designing, manufacturing, and employing artillery were handed down exclusively from gunsmith to apprentice. Thus the circle of the initiated was intentionally kept small and knowledge was transferred by word of mouth and hands-on practice. The first books concerning artillery appeared toward the end of the sixteenth century.

In the 1400s the Dukes of Burgundy, Philip the Good and his son Charles the Bold, who appointed noblemen as *maîtres d'artillerie*, were the first to include artillery in an army structure. They no longer used artillery guns individually in field battles but assembled them into batteries to increase the effects of their fire.

As technology and gun designs improved, cannon were transformed from simple iron tubes sealed at one end (muzzleloaders) on wooden frames (trestles) into early breechloading cannon (although muzzleloaders remained a common feature of guns until the mid-nineteenth century). These were followed in the fifteenth century by gun barrels cast from copper or bronze, with trunnions to allow pivoting. These were mounted on wheeled gun carriages; thus the artillery gained mobility.

In addition to the destruction of fortifications, artillery could be employed in other tasks in the course of battle, such as shattering close formations of foot soldiers and horsemen. Stone, iron, and lead shot continued in use as ammunition; these were effective against walls and entrenchments, but against living targets they had effect only in the event of a direct hit. Therefore, antipersonnel ammunition (grape or canister) was developed, which resembled large shotgun rounds. The range of this ammunition was less than that of a solid projectile, but had a broader spread and was more effective against personnel targets.

As the weight-to-caliber ratio of guns decreased, mobility improved, resulting in the separation of field artillery from siege artillery. The field artillery, positioned in front of closed infantry formations at the commencement of battle, attempted to disrupt enemy formations. However, reinforcement of infantry weapons alone did not contitute a sufficient task for field artillery; greater scope was sought for these firearms.

Maurice of Orange (1567–1625) assigned some light guns to the infantry regiments in certain battles. Typically employed on the flanks, they reinforced musket fire and advanced as best they could with the musketeers.

Gustavus Adolphus (1594–1632) of Sweden, however, is considered the father of modern field artillery and of massed, mobile artillery fire. He devoted much time and effort to solving artillery mobility problems: gun weight was reduced by shortening the barrel and reducing the thickness of the tube; improved, standardized gunpowder permitted greater accuracy despite the shortened barrel; calibers were standardized for heavy (24-pound), medium (12-pound), and light (3-pound) regimental guns. Equally important, Gustavus abandoned the practice of hiring civilian contract gunners and replaced them with his own soldiers, responsive to his discipline and training; thus he ensured far better command and control in battle.

A Frenchman, Vauban (1633–1707), dominated developments in both siegecraft and fortification. At a time when sieges were the most common activity of warfare, Vauban provided a systematic approach for attackers and their heavy siege artillery to blow a breach in walled fortifications and exploit the breach with an infantry assault. Likewise, he devoted much effort to designing fortifications that could withstand such attacks.

Toward the end of the eighteenth century, technological developments brought new artillery advances. Improvements in powder and more resistant metal alloys resulted in an increased range up to 600 meters (1,970 ft.) and a rate of fire of two shots per minute. Aiming and sighting devices were developed in France, and an era of more accurate artillery fire began.

Napoleon Bonaparte (1769–1821), who began his career as an artillery officer, owed his success in battle largely to his intensive use of artillery as the backbone of the post-revolutionary mass armies. An infantry attack was preceded by concentrations of artillery fire that were greater than ever before. The artillery of Napoleon's Imperial Guard, which he held in reserve at the beginning of a battle, wore down enemy infantry forces at the point of intended penetration: "My Artillery Guard decides the majority of battles. As I always have them at the ready, I can deploy them anywhere they are needed."

In this way artillery reserves, alongside infantry reserves, became a means in the hands of the commander to force an issue during the course of combat. The effectiveness of artillery was enhanced not only by ambitious tactics, but also by improved powder, which increased the effective range to 1,000 meters (3,280 ft.). To a greater extent fire was now delivered over the heads of friendly troops—artillery had become the dominant, and most lethal, combat arm.

Napoleon's influence on warfare extended to the middle of the nineteenth century, at which time the organization, doctrine, tactics, and weapons of militaries had come together in a congruent and optimal way. The arms of artillery, cavalry, and infantry combined on the battlefield in a consistent and effective manner; their weapons had achieved something nearing their technological potential. It was the end of one era and the beginning of another.

Age of Technological Innovation

The congruence of Napoleonic warfare was shattered in the mid-nineteenth century by the introduction of the conoidal bullet (Minié ball) in battle during the Crimean War of 1853–56. Combined with technological developments in percussion ignition, breech loading, rifled barrels, and cartridge cases, the conoidal bullet initially provided a new firepower and lethality for the infantry. It was to have a profound effect on warfare. Military strategists such as the Prussian chief of staff Helmuth von Moltke (1800–1891), recognizing its destructive power, began adapting tactical and strategic concepts.

The technological innovations applied equally to artillery. In autumn 1857 the Prussian army began to replace smoothbore guns with rifled barrels. The new steel gun, manufactured by the Krupp concern, used a crucible casting process and was breechloaded. The barrel had grooves and lands, enabling the projectile to be spin-stabilized. The use of cast steel resulted not only in increased resistance of the material, but also in decreased wall thickness and therefore a reduction of the barrel's weight.

In 1877 the development of explosive gelatin and of smokeless powder made possible the manufacture of high-explosive charges for the shell and of guns that would not obscure battlefields with smoke. The rifled gun barrel and elongated shells with ranges up to 4,250 meters (14,000 ft.) resulted in greater accuracy of fire. Easy loading from the rear increased the rate of fire, and aiming devices continued to improve.

In the late nineteenth century the introduction of the field telephone permitted indirect fire. Artillery was now able to fire into the depth of the battlefield from defiladed positions, to transfer fire, and to have drastic effect on the course of combat. Massed targets, which had originally encouraged the introduction of artillery, gradually diminished as a result of all these developments, but artillery tactics and techniques had become so versatile and reliable that the enemy could be struck even in loose formation. The old cast-steel shells were gradually replaced by modern shrapnel and high-explosive (HE) ammunition.

Simplified loading, recoil mechanisms, and aiming devices increased the rate of fire to 8–10 shots per minute; the range was now up to 8,000 meters (26,000 ft.). Along with the development of guns came innovations in artillery ammunition. In 1897 the laminated shell produced an effect five times that previously achieved. Shrapnel ammunition with time fuzes was developed further. The time fuze caused the shell, filled with lead pellets, to explode while still in the air, projecting the pellets in the direction of the target. This effect was increased by fitting a booster charge and a pusher plate into the base of the shell casing. Shrapnel soon became the main shell for field guns.

Artillery in World War I

By the beginning of World War I, artillery development had spawned a wide assortment of weapons in the world's militaries. Artillery was divided into light field artillery (drawn by horses or tractors), heavy field artillery, and heavy artillery/siege artillery (emplaced semipermanently). Corps and divisions had light field artillery and (where appropriate) mountain artillery; guns were of 65–77mm and howitzers were in the 105–122mm range. Howitzers of 120–155mm were available at corps and army level; the heavy artillery with guns, howitzers, and mortars above caliber 155mm was subordinate to the supreme command. Antiaircraft artillery and trench mortars existed only as experimental models or in very restricted numbers at the beginning of 1915.

In principle the main artillery function was to support infantry combat. Artillery fire was largely dependent on visual observation, and adjustment fire was followed by fire for effect. During the course of the war the artillery developed into the main firepower of the ground forces.

In support of infantry troops the most important task of the artillery was to suppress enemy firepower throughout the depth of the defense, to destroy defense installations, and thus to provide the infantry attack with a chance of success. To facilitate breakthrough operations, artillery was employed in large concentrations in the most important sectors. For example, the Germans used 1,051 guns (722 light, 329 heavy and very heavy) for the attack near Verdun on 12 February 1916, along a 25-kilometer (15.5-mi.) front—42 guns per kilometer of front, three times the artillery concentration of the defender. The German armies attacking at Chemin des Dames on 27 May 1918 used 5,263 guns along a 55-kilometer (34-mi.) front (95 guns per kilometer of front, and a ratio of 3.7:1 against the defender). British troops attacking at Wytschaete on 7 June 1917 along a front width of 16 kilometers (9.9 mi.) had an artillery density of 140 guns per kilometer of front.

In trench warfare, artillery firepower afforded the defender high resistance; at the same time, it constituted the strongest and most reliable means of destroying the defense. As a result artillery duels and lengthy artillery preparations characterized the war. The German artillery preparations at Verdun in February 1916 lasted nine hours; the French fired on the Somme in July 1916 for seven days and in Flanders in July 1917 for sixteen days.

The heavily fortified nature of trench warfare, and the emergence of artillery as the dominant firepower weapon, challenged employment of these pieces. Both the railway as means of transport for deploying and the tactical march with mainly horse-drawn transport could be easily observed, triggering countermeasures by the other side. The resulting battles of attrition and subsequent stalemates affected artillery organization and tactics. The numbers of howitzers and heavy artillery rose five- to tenfold. Flat-trajectory fire was unable to reach defiladed targets effectively, so new howitzers were introduced that fired at high angles of elevation (45 degrees or greater), thus enabling the destruction of protected enemy infantry.

Artillery observers on hills or tall buildings were often far from the infantry struggle and could not see operational details. For that reason, as well as to enable prompt compliance with infantry requests for fire support, artillery liaison units and forward observers were detached to the infantry. In this way collaboration between the two branches of the service became closer than before. Another need was for artillery to accompany the infantry. This requirement was met principally with 37mm guns and trench mortars. These weapons were intended to close the artillery's fire gap and constitute a sort of "pocket artillery" for the infantry.

In an attempt to regain tactical mobility on the battlefield, the Germans reorganized their field forces in the spring of 1917. The reform was based on the close relationship between fire and movement, but the fronts were already so firmly established by trenches that only limited movements were achieved on the battlefield.

Under such conditions, the objective of the artillery could not be the destruction of the enemy army, but merely the acquisition of territory. Even the introduction of tanks made little difference, particularly as no new guidelines were elaborated for their employment; they were spread wide apart rather like mobile machine-gun nests, in successive waves, with the object of supporting the infantry in the sporadic conquest of sectors. The introduction of armored vehicles led to the creation of antitank artillery.

Artillery observation facilities were improved by the use of tethered balloons and aircraft. Observers in the sky above the battlefield could see a larger area and direct artillery fire more effectively. The rapid development of aviation in general resulted in the creation of antiaircraft artillery. In 1918 the armies in action had approximately 4,200 guns for air defense. Special field guns on carriages were similarly used to combat aircraft.

New developments in artillery ammunition continued throughout the war. Shrapnel was replaced by a fragmenting or splinter-producing shell as the principal antipersonnel round. Special projectiles were developed: incendiary shells, smoke shells, and shells filled with chemical agents.

New methods and procedures for commanding and controlling artillery were developed. Forces were centralized at the outset of an operation and decentralized as combat progressed. This necessitated uniform fire control and good signals communications. Firing commands required precise calculations, as adjustment fire was abandoned in order to achieve surprise. Internal and external ballistic influences were increasingly taken into better account in such calculations. The groundwork for this was provided by newly created artillery meteorological services, which permitted calculation of the effects of wind currents on projectiles at different levels of ballistic trajectory. As a result, indirect fire could be placed on target areas with reasonable accuracy and effectiveness.

Despite various techniques for employing artillery fire, such as rolling barrages that moved ahead of attacking infantry formations, artillery firepower in World War I was unable to overcome the static, entrenched positions of the opponent. On the contrary, increasing consolidation of artillery contributed to the "freezing" of the fronts, and to stronger underground positions and greater defensive depth. The element of movement was missing. The potential of the tank used with artillery fire support was never recognized.

Between the World Wars

Technological innovation of artillery weapons and procedural development of their uses continued after World War I, albeit with varied emphasis and focus in different countries. In the 1920s and 1930s artillery weapons were modernized and developed further in the countries of Western Europe, the United States, Japan, and the Soviet Union. Range, rate of fire, mobility, and firepower all increased, the result of new types of powder, semiautomatic and automatic breech mechanisms, motorization, and the introduction of self-propelled artillery. The heaviest and longest-range artillery was loaded onto specially designed artillery carriages.

The artillery branches of the armies of France, Italy, and Great Britain were to some extent neglected due to the fascination with emerging possibilities for employment of tanks and airplanes in battle. Germany, by contrast, increased its artillery from negligible quantities in the early 1930s to approximately 50,000 guns and mortars of varying caliber by the end of the decade. Soviet artillery consisted of about 67,000 guns and mortars.

Although the United States had only a small number of artillery weapons in 1939, this was to some extent made up for by an intensive production effort beginning in 1940. Even more important, however, was a new and revolutionary method of fire control developed at the U.S. Field Artillery School during the 1920s and 1930s. Using this new method, built around battalion fire direction centers, U.S. artillery proved to be more effective than that of any other belligerent in World War II.

Basic artillery employment concepts evolved, such as the concentration of artillery fire in prioritized areas, close collaboration between infantry and tanks, use of artillery to combat tanks, and emphasis on achieving surprise. Surprise was to be achieved by dispensing with adjustment fire, and placing accurate, effective fire on known target locations; simultaneous opening of fire from all batteries; using brief artillery preparations, even if this meant the enemy's positions were not completely destroyed; and by great artillery density and high rate of fire.

Artillery in World War II

Although all major belligerents in World War II employed artillery, the German and Soviet experiences provide an excellent illustration of the use of artillery at that time.

The motorization and mechanization of armies, the development of tactical air forces, and progress in communication systems were all prerequisites for reestablishing mobility in combat, which had been frozen in World War I. These elements fathered the German "blitzkrieg"; the technical method called for the concentrated employment of the mechanized forces in collaboration with the air force while the remaining components, including the artillery, played a subordinate role in combat.

In Poland in 1939, and in the west in 1940, German tank units broke through the front and the motorized divisions that followed widened the breakthrough with artillery support. Dive-bombers joined in ground combat and destroyed enemy artillery firing positions, thus to a certain extent sparing the attacker the need to establish heavy artillery concentrations. Offensives were made with no prior artillery preparation, only with air support. It was typical of the blitzkrieg to select weak points where an issue could be decided with concentrated superiority, enabling rapid penetration into the depths of the defender's position. This led to tremendous dynamics between opposing forces in battle and to the creation of a much deeper battlefield. The artillery was unable to keep pace with this development, particularly the heavy artillery, which in most armies was still horse-drawn. Movement, considered more important than fire, was the movement of motor-driven, mechanized units. The artillery of the German army played a minor role in the lightning campaigns in 1939 against Poland and Norway, in 1940 against Western Europe, and in the 1941 Balkan campaign.

This situation was altered with the German attack on the Soviet Union that began in June 1941. After a series of successful battles of encirclement similar to the blitzkrieg, the mobility of the motorized units was drastically curtailed in early October due to the weather. The offensive drowned in mud, and then the Russian winter set in.

The greatest artillery concentration of World War II was accumulated on the German side in 1942 for the third attack on Sebastopol (93 batteries of heavy artillery, 88 batteries of light artillery, 24 mortar batteries, three detachments of self-propelled assault guns, including howitzer and mortar batteries with 305mm, 350mm, and 420mm weapons, two 600mm mortars, and the 800mm gun known as Dora). Approximately 12,500 shells of the heaviest caliber were fired.

In the summer of 1943 the density of the German artillery was 70 to 80 guns per kilometer of front, this in preparation for a renewed assault operation in the Kursk offensive. The artillery, despite its concentration, was unable to shatter the double-echelonned Russian defense, and the main effort of attacking tanks and infantry was repulsed.

In the extensive Soviet operations that ensued as a strategic counterattack between 1943 and 1945, the Soviet artillery was employed en masse. Depending on the situation it supported attacking operations with successive concentrated fire, with the creeping barrage, and, in numerous cases, with the double creeping barrage. Soviet artillery density in the breakthrough sectors often amounted to 200–300 guns and mortars per kilometer of front. In spring of 1945, approximately 45,000 Soviet guns, mortars, and missile launchers participated in the battle for Berlin.

The Soviet Supreme Command placed heavy emphasis on the production of artillery, and by the end of the war the Red Army had nearly 50 percent of all artillery in the world. The Soviets used artillery to accomplish operational objectives. By the end of 1942 artillery brigades and divisions began to appear; in 1943 a special artillery breakthrough corps was established. The artillery was increasingly centralized, which made rapid deployments more difficult but permitted numerical concentrations of weapons beyond what was possible in other armies.

A significant German contribution to artillery was the development of jet propulsion systems. On 3 October 1942 the first A-4 rocket was launched from the Peenemünde, Germany, test area. Its flight lasted 296 seconds, covered 192 kilometers (119 mi.), and it fell with a lateral deviation of 18 kilometers (11.2 mi.) from its target. Although even the long-range V-1 and V-2 weapons (V stands for *Vergeltungswaffe*, which means retaliatory weapon) were not able to alter the outcome of World War II, the creation of the jet propulsion system began a development that has decisively influenced artillery right up to the present.

Altogether World War II encouraged the allround development of artillery, particularly antiaircraft artillery, antitank artillery, self-propelled artillery, and missile artillery.

Artillery Today

Roles, Missions, and Concepts

The role of artillery has changed since World War II. In that war artillery was characteristically used for direct-fire support of combat troops and containment of first-echelon enemy forces, including accompanying artillery units. Today, with better reconnaissance, greater range, and more effective ammunition, artillery is also in a position to contain and destroy the following echelons (reserves) of the major units and operational alliances.

This has served to broaden the operational focus of artillery support. In addition to providing direct-fire support for maneuver forces, artillery also focuses on neutralization of enemy artillery and other important targets throughout the depth of the battlefield. These latter missions are assigned to general-support artillery units. Overall, combat operations are influenced by the commander to the extent that he effectively neutralizes enemy troops (in echelon), heavy weapons, logistics installations, battle headquarters, and facilities so that the threat to friendly major units is diminished or crushed and the way opened for accomplishment of his own mission.

For the artillery, this complex role requires rapid and accurate target acquisition; conversion of reconnaissance information into firing data with minimum action and reaction time between location of and effective fire on the target; engagement of static and moving targets of various size and hardness with effective ammunition; and safeguarding one's own survival against attacks of any kind, including enemy artillery fire.

Of contemporary interest is that the Russians also consider artillery a science that comprises all knowledge of structure and organization, deployment and employment, development and manufacture, and military technology, as well as combat characteristics, firing procedures, and use in action. The spectrum corresponds to the components of the artillery training in Western armies, but with somewhat different emphases.

Organization

Artillery is found as a branch of the service in different countries in artillery formations and units of various sizes (division, brigade, detachment, regiment, battalion, battery). The size of the artillery force relative to the overall size of the armed forces varies from country to country. These differences reflect differences in military doctrine, operational concepts, tasks of the armed forces in general and of the artillery in particular, and the strategies of alliances and nations.

Historical experiences frequently affect operational thought. Changes in technology increasingly determine the internal organization and structure of artillery units, as well as the task assignment for the combined forces' effort within the general concept of the armed forces.

Western organizational concepts. The artillery of the Western armed forces is composed of artillery divisions, brigades, regiments, battalions, and batteries of firing and reconnaissance (target acquisition) artillery. For example, German artillery consists of detachments (corps level), regiments (division level), and battalions (brigade level). Western artillery formations are defined as corps, division, or brigade artillery, depending on their organizational assignment to major units. They support combat troops with conventional and atomic fire and by reconnaissance.

The use of reconnaissance artillery by Western armies provides basic data for firing during combat and contributes to the commander's estimate of developing situations. It covers terrain with technical reconnaissance means that include optical control means, flash-ranging apparatus, radar apparatus, sound-ranging systems, and reconnaissance aircraft (drones). Regardless of time of day or weather, it locates targets in the area of interest of the senior commander, with the aim of conducting combat and as a basis for the operational activity of the firing artillery. In addition, it has apparatus for ascertaining meterological data.

The firing artillery consists of tube and rocket artillery. Tube artillery includes barrel weapons of all kinds, able to fire bomblet, high-explosive, and smoke ammunition. Weapon types include field howitzers and field guns of various range and caliber (field artillery), as well as armored and nonarmored self-propelled howitzers and guns. Field artillery includes towed guns, mounted guns, and self-propelled guns.

Warsaw Pact organizational concepts. The structure of artillery in the armies of the nations of Eastern Europe was dictated by the requirements and agreements set by the Warsaw Pact. Accordingly, all of these nations still have a similar organization, which is described here. They may evolve in varying forms over the coming decade.

The structure of artillery in these armies comprises the troop artillery and the reserve artillery of the supreme command. At army level the troop artillery consists of an artillery brigade with howitzers and a brigade with self-propelled guns, as well as a battalion for artillery reconnaissance.

Each motorized infantry division has an artillery regiment with armored howitzers and multiple rocket launchers and a battery of reconnaissance artillery. The armored divisions have fewer armored howitzers, but are otherwise similarly equipped. Motorized infantry and tank regiments each have a battalion of armored howitzers.

The reserve artillery of the supreme command in each nation's forces consists of artillery and rocket launchers that are easily attached to support the general tactical and operational units. The front artillery division has four regiments consisting of field guns, howitzers, armored howitzers, and multiple rocket launchers, as well as three artillery reconnaissance battalions.

This artillery is employed for the qualitative and quantitative reinforcement of the troop artillery in the sector of main effort. This range of weapons is considered necessary for any extensive operational artillery maneuver and to allow for a high artillery density in the breakthrough sectors. According to doctrine, an attack is inconceivable without integrating the necessary support weapons into the attacking command. The air force, combat helicopters, and heavy artillery elements all constitute important means of support.

Since 1973 the artillery of these armies has been reinforced and modernized. The tube artillery has been reequipped with 122mm and 154mm armored howitzers, which have automatic fire-control and data-transfer systems. This has increased the survivability and effectiveness of the artillery.

Command regulations have aimed at an artillery support ratio of 10:1 in the main effort sector. This is obtained by the concentrated use of the troop artillery of the divisions attacking in echelons and the army artillery brigade, and with the help of artillery forces detached from the artillery front division (reserve artillery of the supreme command).

Concept Variations among Armies

In some armies, artillery includes mortars, recoilless guns, and launching installations for antitank weapons as well as air-force/air-defense guns and rocket launchers. Some nations subdivide their artillery into light, medium, and heavy artillery, depending on the caliber or weight of the weapons. Light artillery is intended primarily for direct support of infantry and armor and includes cannon with calibers up to 105mm; the largest (and only) light artillery piece currently in the U.S. Army is the 105mm howitzer (see Fig. 1). Medium artillery includes weapons that range in size from 105mm to 155mm howitzers. Heavy artillery includes guns of at least 155mm and howitzers of larger calibers.

Rocket artillery is equipped with multiple rocket launchers and rocket launchers that fire guided or nonguided missiles. Multiple rocket launchers use bomblet, mine, splinter, and smoke rockets. The rocket artillery is able to obstruct sectors of terrain, especially against attacking enemy tanks.

The artillery in national armed forces is either allocated decentrally to the various formations or centrally organized. An example of decentralized organization is the German Bundeswehr. Tube artillery battalions are assigned to the brigades, regiments with a field artillery

Figure 1. A U.S. Army 105mm gun shielded by a camouflage net during the Korean War. (Source: U.S. Library of Congress)

battalion to the divisions, and a battalion with multiple rocket launchers to the reconnaissance battalions.

Other armies may have armored artillery battalions in the brigades and artillery regiments with tube weapons of various caliber on division level. In addition, the corps often has available comprehensive artillery forces that provide heavy artillery support and air defense for the divisions. This is the case in the British corps artillery division.

A similar situation exists in the corps of the U.S. forces stationed in Germany. In addition to the artillery of the armored and infantry divisions, the corps also has strong artillery forces available in brigade strength. This artillery organization, which is primarily for the central command, enables the commander to form points of main artillery effort at his own discretion.

Tube Artillery or Rocket Artillery?

At present, a burning question concerning armament revolves around the relative values of rocket and tube artillery.

The advantages of rocket artillery include consistent action where area targets are involved; an increase in range with minimal technical expenditure; low gas pressures in the barrel of the rocket launcher, and therefore a thinner, lighter covering on the warhead. The interior of the barrel is larger, although the caliber is the same, which allows more space for ammunition than in the shell. Rocket artillery has lower personnel requirements (operating crew) and lower cost.

The disadvantages of the rocket are several. The dispersion of rounds on the target is greater than that of guns, firing positions are restricted, and they are farther from the target. No uninterrupted fire support is possible because usually it is best to have only one fire mission per firing position with preselected ammunition. Since rockets are easy to observe, the launch position is very vulnerable to enemy artillery, and there is usually no armored protection available for the crew.

The advantages of tube artillery include greater hit accuracy, faster firing sequence, faster target acquisition, and faster change in type of ammunition. Consequently, tube weapons are more suited for use against smaller area targets and moving targets.

With the current state of engineering, the two weapon systems complement each other. The decision to choose rocket launcher or gun must depend in the last instance on the future development of ammunition for use against hard targets. In the meantime, several armies in the Western alliance have also recognized the possibilities of multiple rocket launcher systems.

A significant step toward increasing conventional firepower was made with the introduction of the multiple launch rocket system (MLRS). This system, which was inspired by weapons used by both Germany and the USSR in World War II and developed in the United States, has several advantages: its three-man crew can continue to fire even under nuclear-biological-chemical conditions; the launcher can be adapted to fire rockets with different calibers or ranges and is therefore effective against targets of any hardness; it has a short reload time (up to three refills per launcher per hour); and its range of up to 40 kilometers (24.8 mi.) enables echelonment in depth, which means that not all firing units are compelled to change position, even if the enemy penetrates. The MLRS was used successfully by coalition forces during Operation Desert Storm (February 1991) against area targets and also as a counterbattery weapon.

Antiarmor Artillery

Antitank, or antiarmor, artillery is that which combats armored vehicles by direct fire. This branch is equipped with antitank guns (towed) or with armored and nonarmored self-propelled guns, as well as recoilless guns and weapon carriers with antitank guided missiles. The most modern electronics are used in connection with these antitank guided missiles, which have ranges up to 4,000 meters (13,000 ft.). In modern armies, antitank helicopters are also equipped with these missiles.

Tanks and armored infantry fighting vehicles pose a constantly increasing threat due to their special armor, greater mobility, better firepower, improved ammunition, electronic fire-control equipment, and longer ranges. This threat is steadily being countered by the increased effectiveness of antitank artillery. Special antitank fighting vehicles and antitank missile systems with longer range, as well as hand-carried "fire-and-forget" weapons, are under development. In some countries antitank artillery does not belong to the artillery branch but to the supported troops (armored corps, antitank corps, mechanized infantry).

Air Defense Artillery

Air defense artillery is that part of the artillery used on the battlefield to combat enemy helicopters and aircraft with tube or rocket antiaircraft weapons. It is equipped with cannon that are towed or are carried on armored or nonarmored self-propelled carriages, as well as with towed or self-propelled rocket launchers. In modern armies the air defense weapon systems are autonomous with regard to target identification and tracking. In some armies this type of artillery is a separate branch of service, as an army air defense corps. In some nations air defense is a separate service, on a level with army, navy, and air force. It conducts battle against aircraft at low to medium altitude and protects ground combat forces and artillery as well as important installations against enemy reconnaissance and air attacks.

Coast Defense Artillery

In a few nations rockets have been put to use for coastal defense and controlling sea straits. It is conceivable that the compulsion to minimize costs in national defense budgets will result in expansion of such use. The guided missiles of today are already able to safeguard and defend coast and sea routes effectively using available technology.

Tasks of Artillery within Different Forms of Combat

Within the combined arms effort the artillery supports other troops with indirect fire and reconnaissance. The principal task attributed to the artillery on a world-wide scale is the direct support of the combat forces (tanks, mechanized infantry). Consequently, the artillery is largely responsible for nonatomic firepower on the battlefield. It may also make use of atomic warheads, depending on what options are open to the commander. Thus this branch of the services is a decisive means for the operational command of the land forces to combat enemy forces in the depths of the battlefield or directly ahead of combat troops, with fire of any quality and density.

The range of the various weapon and reconnaissance systems and the ability to open or shift fire quickly and precisely on the battlefield can decide a battle. Defense is, in the first instance, a battle with fire. An army whose main form of combat is defense therefore requires strong firepower. The perspectives for successful defense are increased if long-range fire can prevent follow-up units from being moved up and causing heavy losses, and if the effect of support weapons can be diminished.

The classical sphere of artillery action therefore lies in the area beyond that of the direct-fire weapons of frontline combat troops, and out to the maximum range of the reconnaissance means, guns, and rockets. The artillery has technical reconnaissance means and weapon systems available that enable it to react quickly and fire effectively within this area at any time.

The early crushing of enemy forces as far as possible ahead of friendly front troops obviously results in fewer casualties for supported forces than if penetrations must be suppressed during the course of combat. It is therefore imperative that artillery be integrated in adequate strength with other ground and air forces for modern combat.

Russian theory. According to Russian theories, the attacking artillery has the following tasks in combat: crush the adversary's defensive fire capability, making way for motorized infantry and tank elements; shatter the enemy by breaking through its defense sectors; beat off enemy counterattacks (counterblows) together with other forces and means; engage the enemy while introducing the second echelon; support friendly forces in pursuit of the enemy and when confronted with water obstacles; combat the enemy by supporting tactical air landings.

For an attack with penetration of the defense sectors, the artillery's actions take place in three related periods: (1) artillery preparation of the assault; (2) artillery support of the assault; and (3) artillery accompaniment of the troops exploiting a successful assault into the rear areas of the enemy's defense.

The main tasks of defensive artillery include the following: engagement of the enemy during its attack preparations as well as during the assembly and deployment of its troops; repulsion of enemy assaults in front of the foremost line of defense; attrition of enemy groups that have penetrated the defense, so that they cannot push forward into the depths and flanks; protection of boundaries, flanks, and sectors between defensive areas; attrition of enemy airborne troops and advancing reserves, and the disorganization of the enemy's military command; and support of friendly troops conducting counterattacks. Artillery counterpreparations and fire against enemy tanks are important parts of artillery defense action.

Western theory. According to Western doctrine, defense artillery should harrass enemy movement at an early stage and destroy or damage enemy elements as much as possible while they are preparing for attack. Later, it should block tank attacks and crush lightly armored and nonarmored enemy forces with fire. The enemy is to be struck with concentrated fire at penetration points, and open flanks should be controlled. In particular, enemy artillery that has engaged friendly antitank weapons or reserves should be neutralized or crushed.

Attacking artillery should provide constant support for friendly troops without restricting their movements. Concentrated firing is required where enemy forces most strongly hinder friendly assault operations. Fire protection before an attack is normal; artillery firing action may also commence simultaneously with the attack, particularly if surprise is desired.

When delaying tactics are applied, the artillery engages enemy forces with concentrated fire in the depths of the battlefield, decelerating the hostile advance by using heavy fire and supporting the combat troops in delaying positions. This should compel the enemy to deploy his forces, thus contributing to the delay.

Artillery of the Future

The entire spectrum of artillery tasks will benefit from anticipated technological developments. Since artillery is responsible for indirect fire in the combined arms effort, it will bear more responsibility than previously. Future artillery capabilities will counteract other achievements of modern technology, such as an eventual increase in the fighting power of the armored elements of the armed forces, an increase in their speed due to reduction of their specific weight, and reinforced hardness. The spheres of reconnaissance and fire coordination will be of particular importance.

Artillery reconnaissance, command, and fire control should be optimized in a combined system that includes coordination of close air support. This could be achieved by an artillery system with the following elements:

reconnaissance/target acquisition; command/fire-control; weapon system/surveying; and ammunition. The scope and responsibilities of each element are suggested below. Reconnaissance and target acquisition:

- Regular reconnaissance of the battlefield in sufficient depth, day and night and in any weather
- Identification of targets as to type and activity, as well as location, with adequate accuracy
- Passing on and evalution of information without loss of time; situation and target information on the spot
- Provision of information in degree of detail adequate for the requirements of the respective level of command
- Combined use of infrared, laser, heat image, dwarf wave (millimeter wave), and radar techniques

Command and fire control:

- Connection of the reconnaissance and acquisition systems with artillery command positions, fire-control points, and weapon systems
- Integration of the elements of reconnaissance, evaluation, tactical and technical fire control, weapons, and ammunition
- Guarantee of short artillery reaction and response times

Weapon systems and surveying:

- Use of a variable mixture of artillery weapons, consisting of autonomous armored artillery guns and rocket launchers
- Optimization of the range, rate of fire, and accuracy of artillery weapons and protection of the operating crew
- Integration of artillery weapons into computer-assisted operational systems
- Use of combat drones to continually seek, find, and directly engage targets

Ammunition:

- Development of ammunition to achieve maximum effect on armored targets
- Use of bomblet ammunition and hollow-charge ammunition
- Construction of fully guided missiles, ejected as subammunition, that approach and destroy individual targets
- Construction of homing ammunition that probes the target area and fires a projectile as soon as a target appears

Realization of these objectives depends on the degree of threat involved, on the operational and tactical concepts, and on the finances available in the defense budget.

The efficiency of the combined artillery effort can be increased in collaboration with modern technology to such an extent that this branch of the services can cope with all conceivable threats in the future. All in all, a new quality of artillery will result from the existence of three conditions: (1) the battlefield is totally under surveillance; (2) fire can be opened on any target that appears, without adjustment fire and without time delay; and (3) soft, semihard, and hard targets—in front of friendly troops, in the depths of the enemy, and across the whole breadth of the scene of action—can be effectively engaged with optimal and economic use of ammunition. Thus the commander possesses new possibilities for the use of artillery.

The role of artillery in the postnuclear age, with radiating weapons such as laser or electromagnetic weapons, has yet to be determined. In view of its technical knowhow, the artillery will continue to bear heavy responsibility.

MANFRED KÜHR

SEE ALSO: Ammunition; Artillery, Antiaircraft; Artillery, Rocket and Missile; Artillery, Tube; Blitzkrieg; Combat Support; Combined Arms; Fire and Movement; Firepower; Gun, Antitank; Gun Technology Applications; Indirect Fire; Land Warfare; Mechanized Warfare; Mobility; Rocket, Antiarmor; Tank; World War I; World War II.

Bibliography

Cocino, A. 1971. Artillerie-Entwicklungen beim italienischen Heer. *Internationale Wehrrevue*, Jg. 4, Nr. 2:139–41.

Die Artillerie. 1986. *Entscheidende Waffe im Konventionellen Kampf in Allgemeine Schweizerische Militärzeitschrift*, Beih. Jg. 152, Nr. 7/8:3–22.

Dodd, N. 1973. Die Royal artillery des britischen Heeres. *Wehrkunde*, Jg. 22, lt. 5, 253–59.

Dupuy, R. E., and T. N. Dupuy. 1986. *The Encyclopedia of military history.* 2d rev. ed. New York: Harper and Row.

Graf, K. 1987. Artillerie 2000. *Allgemeine Schweizerische Militärzeitschrift* Jg. 153, Nr. 4:229–32, und Nr. 6:377–8o.

Hahn, F. 1986. *Waffen und Geheimwaffen des deutschen Heeres* 1933–1945. Koblenz: Bernhard und Graefe Verlag.

International Institute for Strategic Studies. *The military balance.* Annual. London: Brassey's (U.K.).

Krug, H. 1982. *25 jahre Artillerie der Bundeswehr.* Friedberg: Podzun-Pallas-Verlag.

Manuel du gradé d' artillerie T. 1-3. 1952. Paris: Charles-Lavanzelle.

Mausbart, F. 1969. Die Entwicklung der Artillerie in den letzten 3o jahren. *Österreichische Militärische Zeitschrift* Jg. 7:22–32.

Ministère de la Défense Nationale. 1955. *Artillerie au combat.* Paris: Charles-Lavanzelle.

Neuzeitliche Artilleriesysteme. 1983. Forum der Deutschen Gesellschaft für Wehrtechnik an der Artillerieschule in Idar-Oberstein, 6–7 Oktober. Koblenz: Bernhard und Graefe Verlag.

Reid, W. 1976. *Arms through the ages.* New York: Harper and Row.

Ryan, J. W. 1982. *Guns, mortars and rockets.* Vol. 2 of *Brassey's battlefield weapon systems and technology series.* Oxford: Brassey's.

Speisebecher, W. 1977. *Taschenbuch für Artilleristen.* Koblenz: Wehr und Wissen Verlagsgesellschaft.

ARTILLERY, ANTIAIRCRAFT

Antiaircraft artillery (AA) is a means of providing direct protection from air attack to troops during combat, as well as for protection of various objectives against enemy low-

and medium-altitude air strikes. In some cases, AA can also be brought to bear against enemy tanks and airborne and seaborne forces. AA may be employed independently or combined with surface-to-air missile (SAM) units. It is intended to destroy enemy aircraft on close approaches to and over the protected objective.

National air defense artillery is employed to protect individual rear-area objectives and vital military installations such as airfields, naval bases, and SAM launching sites.

According to caliber, AA is classified into the following categories:

- antiaircraft machine guns
- light antiaircraft artillery (20mm–60mm)
- medium antiaircraft artillery (60mm–100mm)
- heavy antiaircraft artillery (over 100mm)

NATO designates altitude bands for antiaircraft artillery: very low level, below 150 meters (500 ft.); low level, 150–600 meters (500–2,000 ft.); medium level, 600–7,500 meters (2,000–24,500 ft.); and high level, 7,500–15,000 meters (24,500–50,000 ft.).

The performance of AA guns used for low-level air defense is continually being improved by advances in propellants, explosives, projectile design, fuzing, and control. The high destructive power of gun ammunition is gained from its high impact velocity, large explosive content, naturally shaped fragments, and considerable blast and incendiary effect. The proximity fuze, which is based on the Doppler principle, initiates the shell at a distance of several meters from the target. The prefragmented shell produces a large quantity of fragments that have great penetrating ability and high effect even at a distance.

History

During World War I (1914–18), antiaircraft machine guns were employed to engage low-flying and slow aircraft and to prevent accurate bombing by forcing the attacking aircraft to fly at higher altitudes. Forcing the aircraft to a higher altitude also provided a better opportunity for medium-caliber guns to engage such aircraft.

The .303 Lewis light machine gun was the first to be introduced, entering service with the British Army in 1915. It was used as an antiaircraft defense weapon, both ashore and afloat, against low-flying and dive-bombing aircraft. The Lewis gun was air-cooled, gas-operated, and magazine-fed by means of a circular rotating steel drum. Aiming and controlling fire were by observation of tracers. The weapon was fixed on an antiaircraft mount, either a folding tripod or vertical pillar. By the end of the war, existing antiaircraft artillery included the .303 Lewis and Bren light machine gun, Hotchkiss guns, and mobile three-inch (76mm) guns.

During World War II (1939–45) a wide range of antiaircraft weapons of different calibers, along with radars and mechanical computers, were introduced to meet the increased threat of air attacks. Following World War II, aircraft development continued with the manufacture of jet engines, increasing aircraft speeds to supersonic levels and providing the capability for high-altitude operation. These developments greatly complicated the problem for antiaircraft guns because of the long flight time of the projectile en route to the target and the distance covered by the enemy aircraft during that time. In addition, although the speed of the projectile decreased after firing, there was no way to make corrections to compensate for aiming errors arising from this deceleration.

The improved performance of tactical support aircraft (in terms of range, speed, ability to operate at low and very low altitudes, and the effectiveness of on-board weapon systems), and particularly the appearance of armed helicopters, has greatly increased the danger to combat units on the battlefield, both those in contact with the enemy and others dispersed over the full depth of the combat zone. Defense against this growing threat requires short-range, highly mobile weapon systems with immediate reaction capability that can counter low- and very low-level strikes by enemy aircraft that are exploiting the terrain to escape long-range detection.

Main Combat Properties of AA

Capability to repel enemy air strikes at very low, low, and medium altitudes

Capability to repulse enemy air attacks under any conditions of weather, day or night, by weapons equipped with radar

High maneuverability to permit combined operations with maneuver elements and rapid concentration of large forces of AA in desired areas

Rapid reaction capability to permit engagement of attacking aircraft from fixed firing positions or while on the move

Capability to rapidly maneuver the fire of several AA batteries so as to concentrate fire on a single target; such fire must be possible during short halts or while on the move

Capability to destroy ground targets such as tanks and armored personnel carriers, and—in coastal areas—ships and landing craft

Antiaircraft Machine Guns (AAMGs)

AAMGs are used for self-defense against very low-flying enemy aircraft to provide direct protection of troops, SAM positions, AA units, and radar subunits. They are also used in naval craft, where they are mounted in pairs or in multiple units, to engage enemy dive aircraft that attack ships in convoy. Table 1 shows types of AAMGs and their technical data.

All types of antiaircraft machine guns are mounted so that they can be traversed and elevated rapidly. They

TABLE 1. *Technical Characteristics of Antiaircraft Machine Guns*

Characteristic	14.5 Quad	14.5 Dual	14.5 Single	12.7 Quad	12.7 Single	0.5 -inch Dual
Caliber (mm)	14.5	14.5	14.5	12.7	12.7	0.5-inch
Effective range* (meters)	up to 3,000	2,000	1,500	1,500	500–1,500	1,500–2,200
Muzzle velocity* (meters/second)	990–1,000	990–1,000	820–850	830–850	760–1,035	n/a
Theoretical rate of fire (rpm)	2,200–2,400	1,100–1,200	550–600	2,160–2,400	540–600	450–550
Practical rate of fire (rpm)	800–1,200	400–600	200–300	800–1,200	200–300	200
Traverse (degrees)	360	360	360	360	360	360
Elevation (degrees)	+85–−10	+90–−7	+90–−7	+90–−7	+90–−7	+85–−10
Weight of projectile (grams)	61–63.6	61–63.6	61–63.6	45.5–49.5	45.5–49.5	n/a
Weight of charge (grams)	20	20	20	18–19	18–19	n/a
Short burst (rounds)	4–8	4–8	n/a	n/a	5–7	n/a
Long burst (rounds)	12–16	12–16	n/a	n/a	10–15	n/a
Sustained burst (rounds)	24–50	24–50	n/a	n/a	26–50	n/a
Sight means	auto	semi-auto	cir	cir	cir	n/a
Can engage target with airspeed of*	300 m/sec	900 km/hr	1,000 km/hr	1,000 km/hr	500 km/hr	n/a

*Note: 1,000 meters = 3,280 feet; 1 kilometer = 0.62 miles. n/a = not available.

have a short range; a flat trajectory and short flighttime; a high rate of fire; are air cooled (which means that barrels must be able to be changed if engagement is continuous); and have projectiles involving solid bullets and propulsion fitted with a tracer element.

Fire direction and control for AAMGs are performed by the "fire hose" method of continuous fire, aided by the observation of tracers. Observing the stream of tracers at or near the target permits correcting fire onto the target until hits are obtained. To ensure maximum effect against aircraft, fire is withheld until the most favorable moment for fire effect, which depends on the path of the target and where it comes into closest range.

The U.S. 0.5-inch (12.7mm) Browning heavy machine gun is the standard weapon in many armies. It was designed as a mobile support weapon with a high rate of fire that could be used by combat units against air and ground targets. The U.S. M16 has quadruple .50-caliber machine guns mounted on a half-track. The combined rate of fire is 1,600–2,000 rounds per minute (rpm), enabling the weapon to destroy point targets. The half-track carriage of the M16 gives it a fair amount of battlefield mobility, and the bed of the half-track provides protection against shell fragments and small-arms fire.

Light Antiaircraft Artillery

Light antiaircraft artillery (LAA) is used mainly for the immediate cover of troops and command posts during combat actions, and for the protection of small objectives such as airfields and SAM sites, against low-altitude enemy air attack. It is designed for point and area defense and is also used to cover missile dead zones. A primary advantage of such systems is that guns and the ammunition they expend are far cheaper than missiles.

LAA systems require high maneuverability based on high mobility. They must be rapidly deployable, which means that the gun and fire control equipment must be integrated. High muzzle velocity, automation, and short reaction time are essential, as are a high rate of fire, short time of projectile flight, air transportability, the ability to conduct fire while on the move or during short halts, and a fire control system providing high kill probability against aircraft flying at low levels. The kill probability is a factor of the destructive power of the ammunition used and the overall efficiency of the system.

Day/night and all-weather operation are required. Firepower may be increased by using multiple barrels on a single mount. Target effect may be a function of an accurate aiming system or the use of proximity-fuzed ammunition. The system must offer considerable resistance to an increasingly intense electronic countermeasures (ECM) environment and must be able to continue to fire when radars have been blinded and infrared seekers have been decoyed. This means that high ECM resistance must be obtained by means of ECCM features and increased use of passive optronic devices. Finally, the system must be effective when defending point targets against approaching aircraft at short ranges.

The mounting system must provide for 360-degree traverse, and an arc of elevation from lowest to highest angles that will permit following a fast-moving target at close range. Projectiles must be fitted with direct-action or proximity fuzes.

LAA weapons are mounted on wheeled or tracked vehicles to ensure that mobile infantry units and armored columns can be adequately protected. The guns can be either towed or self-propelled.

The kill probability of LAA is dependent on hit probability and range, both primarily a function of the rate of fire, muzzle velocity, caliber, and accuracy.

The effect of the rate of fire on kill probability depends on range to the target, size of the target, and accuracy of the gun. Rate of fire can be increased by increasing the number of barrels and breechblocks, but rates of fire must be very high to meet current requirements.

An increase in muzzle velocity, which reduces the projectile flight time, can have a significant effect on the kill probability. For targets accelerating across the line of fire, the hit probability under simplified conditions is proportional to the fourth power of the muzzle velocity. Thus increases in muzzle velocity pay very high dividends in enhanced kill probability. Within a given caliber, increases in muzzle velocity can be obtained in basically three different ways: reduction of projectile mass, increase in propellant charge, or increase in specific energy of the propellant.

The caliber influences the kill probability through the destructive effects of the projectile and its tactical range. The kill probability of a cannon plotted against the caliber of the projectile, produces an optimum between 30 and 40 caliber.

Regarding accuracy, it has been established that ballistic errors of guns and ammunition must be adjusted to compensate for the aiming errors of the fire control system.

Fire Control and Sighting Systems

Fire control equipment for LAA, such as that for the Bofors 40mm, consists of optical sights with a light amplifier for nighttime combat, a laser range finder, and a computer. For target detection, the system can be linked to a search radar and an optical target indicator. Against a low-altitude threat an autonomous pulse-Doppler search radar can be used, in combination with LAA batteries in the 20–30mm range, for point defense.

Gun King sighting system. Based on the latest technology, the Gun King sighting system enables both air and ground targets to be engaged with great success using autonomous gun operation. In this system, precise fire control data are automatically determined and updated by a modern high-speed computer coupled with laser range finding. During engagement the computer controls the combat sequence of the entire gun system.

There is a common optical path in the periscope for the laser beam and the aiming line of sight. These beams are deflected with high accuracy by a gimbaled mirror. The periscope has an extremely high light transmittance and is fitted with a multispectral optical system. For night operation, the normal eyepiece is replaced by one with an integrated residual-light amplifier. Spectral beam splitting is effected by a system of lenses and prisms specially coated to ensure operator safety. Range finding is accomplished by means of a multi-divergency Neodyme laser.

An accessory television camera may be mounted on the periscope casing for direct observation of the operator's view over the identical optical path. This enables operator performance to be monitored, recorded, and evaluated for training purposes.

The modular Gun King design ensures unlimited adaptation to various gun systems. The modules can be grouped as necessary to fit different guns. When AA guns are fitted with their own drives, the Gun King system controls the guns servo systems.

Gun King includes a periscope with eight-power magnification and an eight-degree field of view, a laser range finder, and a microcomputer that processes all sensor data such as target range, muzzle velocity, and meteorological information, thus generating lead-angle data for the gun control system when the weapon is being operated autonomously.

Gun King is a tactically optimized laser/computer-controlled sighting system that significantly improves the combat efficiency of an AA gun by providing the following capabilities: accurate tracking of aircraft flying at very high speed; precise calculation of the intercept point, thereby allowing a high kill probability against air and ground targets; servo control of the gun by direct current motors; and one-man operation.

Self-propelled AA Guns (SP AA Guns)

Self-propelled AA gun vehicles are armed with guns and provided with sensors for target tracking. The operational criteria for such a vehicle includes high mobility, at least equal to that of the tanks and other combat vehicles it must accompany; great reliability; simple operation; total autonomy on the battlefield; and the shortest possible reaction time. Such a system comprises electrohydraulic control systems; optical systems for AA and ground firing; loading systems; and vehicular radio equipment.

30mm AMX-30 gun system. This French system is most effective against armed aircraft, although the firepower of its guns also enables it to effectively engage armored combat vehicles and troop concentrations in the open. The system's TG 230 A turret is armed with two Hispano-Suiza 30mm HSS 831A cannon. The turret can be operated from the vehicle commander's station or the gunner's station. The commander is provided with a panoramic viewer and radar control panel, a direct view device for AA fire, a control lever with fire control buttons, a periscope for firing against ground targets, and a panel that provides firing data when firing manually. The gunner is equipped with a control lever incorporating switches for surveillance, tracking and fire control, and a six-power magnifying viewer for AA fire.

To improve performance of the cannon, a dual belt-loading system provides the capability of firing single rounds, short bursts of five to fifteen rounds, and sustained bursts. A pulse-Doppler radar provides excellent performance; it features rapid reaction time, elimination of fixed echoes, excellent separation of moving-target sub-clutter, and good short-range detection with immediate intervention. The radar electronic equipment is housed inside the turret or in an external armored housing.

AA armored truck. This system is a six-wheeled armored vehicle with a hull that resembles that of an armored personnel carrier. It carries a turret mounting two 30mm Mauser cannon, each with a rate of fire of 800 rpm. Fire control is performed by a combination of search radar, a TV-tracker/laser combined sight unit, a digital computer, and an optical periscope. The search radar permits continuous air surveillance over an 18-kilometer (11-mi.) radius even when the vehicle is moving, and is resistant to ECM interference.

Once a target has been selected on the radar screen, the periscope is automatically directed to the correct azimuth and elevation for optical search and acquisition. The TV tracker locks on and tracks the target, while the laser unit keeps continuous track of range. A digital computer calculates the requisite lead angle and takes into account meteorological and ballistic factors and the vehicle's cant and muzzle velocity variations.

Twin 35mm SP system. The high performance of the 35mm weapon is clearly based on the fire control system, the weapon itself, and the ammunition. All components of the weapon system are housed in or on the turret, mounted on a Leopold battle tank chassis. The system essentially consists of a search radar, a tracking radar, a fire control system with computer, and the 35mm twin-gun mounting.

Autonomy of this weapon system is achieved by the search radar, which carries out continuous and reliable surveillance of the surrounding airspace whether the vehicle is stopped or moving. The system ensures target acquisition and tracking even under severe ground clutter conditions.

The commander and gunner are each provided with their own periscopes, which are used for optical target acquisition and tracking zone observation and for laying the gun on ground targets. A miniaturized and transistorized analog computer calculates the lead angle for the weapon, taking into account the meteorological data, the continuously measured muzzle velocity, and the tilt angle of the vehicle. This precise and rapid electronic computation results in high hit probability. The computer also simultaneously calculates the duration of fire in relation to the programmed range, thus minimizing ammunition expenditure.

For engagement of aerial targets, the 35mm AA tank utilizes two types of ammunition: an armor-piercing high explosive (APHE) that contains the maximum quantity of explosives, and a high explosive antitank (HEAT) round that is fitted with a base fuze.

The weapon system consists of two automatic 35mm Oerlikon cannon with belt feed and a rate of fire of 550 rounds per minute (rpm). They can fire continuously or single shot, with the length of burst programmed by the fire control computer as a function of range. Combat range with adequate hit probability is about 4,000 meters (2.5 mi.). The laying limits of the weapons are +85°/−5° in elevation and full 360-degree traverse. The ammunition supply consists of 660 AA rounds in internal magazines, plus 40 rounds of ground combat ammunition in an external armored magazine. Armor protection against infantry automatic weapons and artillery shell fragments is provided.

Both the search radar and the pulse-Doppler tracking radar have a maximum range of 15 kilometers (9 mi.). The search radar includes an integrated IFF unit.

Falcon AA gun system. Falcon is used to provide a cost-effective mobile defense for troops and armored vehicles against attacks by low-flying aircraft and armed helicopters and to provide the additional capability of engaging lightly armored ground targets.

The weapon system is mounted in a turret equipped with two Hispano-Suiza Type HSS 831 L 30mm guns on the well-proven Abbot armored chassis. The guns have an estimated effective range of 2,000 meters (approx. 6,500 ft.) against aircraft flying at up to 250 meters (820 ft.) per second.

The turret is armored against shell fragments and small-arms fire, and contains the commander's and gunner's positions, arranged side by side. The crew compartment is sealed from the gun and ammunition compartment, thus reducing exposure to fumes and noise when operating the guns. The system is fitted with VHF radio equipment and internal communications facilities.

The guns provide a combined rate of fire of 1,300 rounds per minute at a muzzle velocity of 1,080 meters (3,540 ft.) per second. Single-shot or automatic fire can be selected for either or both guns, which are cocked and fired electrically. Ammunition is fed to the guns from two 310-round boxes located in the base of the turret, through chutes into belt-feed mechanisms operated by gun recoil. Empty cartridge cases and belt links are ejected sideways through the elevation trunnion bearings. Reloading is quick and simple.

An electric power-control system drives the turret in traverse and the stabilized twin guns in elevation. The gunner tracks the target by operating a two-motion joystick that is energized by depressing a foot pedal. The commander has a similar control, which can override the gunner's. The weapons can be traversed 360 degrees and elevated through the +85°/−10° range.

For fire control the gunner uses a periscopic gunsight with a dual optical system—one for antiaircraft use and the other with appropriate graticules for accurate laying on ground targets. Superimposed on the gunner's antiaircraft line of sight is a moving circle on a cathode ray tube, which makes it possible to calculate the lead-angle from the tracking speed of the guns and range to the target. The commander has a similar periscope gunsight, but without the moving lead-angle display. Both sights have fixed graticules for emergency use. The driver also has a periscope; head-out vision and infrared night driving equipment can be supplied.

TA-20 mobile antiaircraft system. The M3 VDA antiaircraft vehicle (France) is fitted with twin 20mm guns, and its turret houses a computerized sight, which the gunner keeps aligned on the target. The Doppler-type radar, which can be folded down during travel, has a range of 8–10 kilometers (5–6 mi.) against low- and very low-flying targets. The control panel is positioned at the commander's station.

Continuous surveillance is maintained during target tracking. Using the target information provided by the radar, the computer (already programmed with ballistic table data) calculates the predicted angle and controls the lead of the weapon relative to the sights.

The TA-20 turret and its derivatives can be fitted with a suitable IFF, a TV tracking system (possibly a low-light-level TV), and a laser range-finder system. The rate of fire is 900–1,000 rounds per minute per gun. Both single-shot and single-barrel fire are possible.

Vulcan M-163 system. This system (U.S.) comprises the Vulcan gun, a linked ammunition feed subsystem, and a fire control subsystem, all mounted in an electrically powered turret.

The 20mm gun used in the system is a modified version of the air-cooled six-barrel M61 Vulcan gun, mounted on a modified M113A1 armored personnel carrier chassis, the M741. It has two rates of fire, 1,000 or 3,000 rounds per minute, and the gunner can select bursts of 10, 30, 60, or 100 rounds. The use of six barrels results in longer weapon life because it reduces the problems of barrel erosion and heat generation, since each barrel fires only once each six shots. This method of operation also eliminates the excessive recoil forces normally associated with multiple-gun installations.

The effective range of the Vulcan gun is 1,600 meters (5,250 ft.). It can traverse 360 degrees and move in elevation through the +85°/−5° range. The turret has full power traverse and elevation.

The fire control subsystem consists of a gyro lead-computing gunsight, a ranging radar, and a sight current generator. The gunner visually acquires and tracks the target with his gyro gunsight. The antenna axis of the radar is served onto the optical line of sight. The radar supplies target range and range rate data to the sight current generator. These data are then converted to the correct current for use in the sight. With range, range rate, and angular tracking of the optical line of sight measured by a freely gimbaled gyro, the sight automatically computes the future target position and adds the super-elevation needed to hit the target.

The ranging radar is a coherent Doppler moving-target indicator type that can acquire targets at 5,000 meters (16,410 ft.). When the radar has acquired a target at a range within the capability of the turret system, a green light appears in the sight optics. The gunner need only acquire the target in the sight reticule, track it, and fire after the green light appears. The turret can also be operated using manual fire control if necessary, in which case the gunner must estimate target range and speed and set these estimates on indicator dials on the control panel. The gyro lead-computing sight then computes the lead angle based on the estimates.

The linkless ammunition feed system used in the Vulcan turret incorporates stowage for 1,100 rounds in a feed drum mounted beneath the turret body. A variety of ammunition can be used, including armor piercing (AP), AP incendiary, and high-explosive incendiary. The Vulcan cannon can also be used in the ground role to support infantry.

Gepard SP AA gun system. The Gepard system (Germany/Switzerland), which replaced the M42 twin 40mm AA system, ensures AA defense of German armored and mechanized units (see Fig. 1). It consists essentially of an Oerlikon twin turret 35mm mounted on the modified hull of the Leopard I main battle tank. A new version, designated 5 PEZ-B, is aimed at incorporating advances in electronic technology and would provide greater target acquisition capacity and superior tracking capability at very low altitudes. The main characteristics of this system are a rate of fire of 550 rpm per gun, muzzle velocity of 1,175 meters per second, range of 3,000 meters (10,000 ft.), elevation in the +85°/−5° range, and a hydraulically operated belt ammunition-feed system. Ammunition stockage includes 640 rounds of AA-type high explosive (HE) and 40 rounds of AP for use against ground targets.

Italian SIDAM 25 SP system. This system is mounted on a modified M-113 chassis, which accommodates a one-man turret equipped with four Oerlikon KBA-B 25mm automatic cannon providing a combined rate of fire of as much as 2,280 rounds per minute. SIDAM 25 is equipped with a day/clear-weather optical sight, a laser low-light-level TV camera, a laser range finder, and an automatic day/night optronic tracker system. This combination results in a short-range, rapid reaction and a high rate of fire against low-flying aircraft, thereby fully exploiting the few seconds for which they remain under aim.

Figure 1. West German Gepard twin 35mm SP AA gun with surveillance radar. (SOURCE: U.S. Army)

Soviet ZSU-23 4AA SP gun "Shilka." This system is designed primarily for protection of land-force elements against low-altitude aerial attacks. It may also serve to protect individual vital objectives, as well as SAM launch sites and airfields, in cooperation with other air defense means.

Shilka is intended to destroy enemy aircraft at very low altitudes in any weather, day or night. Its accuracy, achieved by installing its radar on the same mount as the gun, and the great volume of fire it can deliver also make it effective against diving targets. The Shilka system is mounted on a hull derived from the PT-76 amphibious tank. A low, wide turret mounted on the hull houses the four 23mm cannon and the fire control radar. The guns are all on the same mounting and are synchronized so that they all fire together, thus providing a high volume of fire. The guns are gas-operated and use a vertical sliding breechblock.

Both HE and AP incendiary rounds make the ZSU-23-4 a threat to APCs and IVCs as well as to aircraft. The Shilka carries 500 rounds per gun and is accompanied by support vehicles that carry another 3,000 rounds per gun, thus permitting the high rate of fire to be maintained for relatively long periods.

The four guns are controlled by B-76 radar (called "Gun Dish" by NATO) whose circular antenna is folded behind the turret when the vehicle is on the move. This radar has a range of twenty kilometers (12.4 mi.), acquires and tracks the target, functioning as a fire control radar with a secondary search function. The information gathered by the radar is processed by a digital computer and translated into fire control data.

The main characteristics of the ZSU-23-4 are a maximum road speed of about 44 kilometers per hour (27 mph) on-road and 30 kilometers per hour (19 mph) off; a theoretical rate of fire of 1,000 rpm per gun, and a practical rate of fire of 200 rounds per minute per gun; muzzle velocity of 970 meters (3,180 ft.) per second; and a range of 2,000 meters (6,560 ft.) against ground targets and about 1,800 meters (5,900 ft.) against aerial targets.

Soviet ZSU-57-2 SP AA gun. This 57mm twin-barreled SP is used mainly to provide immediate cover to armored and mechanized troops during combat actions, protecting them against low-level enemy air attack. The system has a maximum effective range of 5,500 meters (18,000 ft.) in ground use and 4,800 meters (15,750 ft.) against aerial targets. The muzzle velocity is 1,000 meters (3,280 ft.) per second, and the practical rate of fire is 120 rounds per minute. It takes one minute to go into action and half a minute to resume the march. A crew of four operates the system.

Towed Light Antiaircraft Artillery Guns

U.S. M167A1 towed version. This is a modified version of the air-cooled six-barrel Vulcan cannon, mounted on a two-wheeled carriage that is normally towed by an M715 or M37 truck. It uses linked ammunition and has 500 rounds in ready-use stowage. The weapon's main characteristics are similar to those of the M163 SP AA gun.

Oerlikon 35mm twin field AA gun. (Switzerland) This system, also called the Type GDF-002, is converted from traveling to firing mode electrohydraulically. In the process the lateral outriggers are slewed out and locked, the spindles are extended, and the wheels are swiveled clear of the ground. Then the entire system is lowered and automatically leveled.

The guns are remotely controlled by the fire control unit. In the event of a fire control unit failure each gun can engage autonomously, using a Ferranti auxiliary sight. The optical alignment system is permanently installed on the gun to ensure high precision.

Ammunition for this gun is characterized by high muzzle velocity and aerodynamic shape, producing a flat trajectory and short time of flight. The high destructive power of the ammunition is the result of high impact velocity, large explosive content, naturally shaped fragments, and considerable blast and incendiary effect. The system has 112 rounds maintained in ready-for-firing stowage and another 126 rounds in a reserve container.

The other main characteristics of this system are an 1,100-rpm rate of fire, muzzle velocity of 1,175 meters (3,850 ft.) per second, high aiming speed and acceleration, joystick control in the local operation mode, and a maximum tactical effective range of 4,000 meters (13,120 ft.).

Soviet ZU-23 towed twin AA gun. This system is mounted on a wheeled carriage. It is a fully automatic weapon with a high rate of fire but lacks any provision for radar control. It is therefore used only during clear weather conditions.

Ammunition is fed from two large box-type magazines located outboard of the trunnions, each containing 50 rounds of ammunition in a belt. The guns have a muzzle velocity of 970 meters (3,180 ft.) per second, maximum effective horizontal range of 2,000 meters (6,560 ft.), maximum altitude of 1,500 meters (4,920 ft.), and a practical rate of fire of 500–600 rounds per minute. Ammunition includes HE and AP rounds, the latter providing an antitank capability. It takes half a minute to put the system into or take it out of action.

BOFI towed 40mm AA gun. Bofors has introduced a third generation of its well-known 40mm L70 AA gun, the BOFI (Bofors optronic fire control instrument) 40mm system. It consists of a sight, a laser, and a computer, all completely integrated with the gun.

The sight can be used under all light conditions by adaptation of light-intensification equipment; the laser is used for range finding. The computer processes the data about the lead to be taken on the target (by establishing the future position of the target and giving the actual line of aim necessary to effect the meeting of projectile and target) and also produces guidance signals for the aiming system, using a completely new principle known as continuous-lead correction. The barrel and the line of aim remain continuously parallel; when the firing pedal is pressed, the barrel automatically follows the actual line of aim and continues to do so while firing on the basis of data continuously provided by the computer.

The gun has been modified in a number of ways, the most important of which is provision of a generator to power the system. The BOFI may be used with existing guns, giving these main advantages: great speed in coming into action; high resistance to ECM because the only active component is the laser, which is difficult to deceive; night and day operating capability; and a high degree of effectiveness, especially when proximity fuzes are employed. BOFI employs an on-mounted multi-sensor tracking system comprising KU-band radar, laser range finder, image intensifier, and daylight telescope.

Soviet 57mm towed AA gun C-60. This system is used to provide direct protection to troops during combat operations, as well as protection of various objectives against air strikes. In some cases it can also fight against enemy tanks, and airborne and seaborne forces.

The gun has a muzzle velocity of 1,000 meters (3,280 ft.) per second; a theoretical rate of fire of 100–120 rounds per minute and a practical rate of 60 rpm; a 360-degree traverse; water cooling; elevation in the +87°/−4° range; and highway speed of up to 60 kilometers per hour (37 mph) and 10 kilometers per hour (6.2 mph) cross country. The maximum effective horizontal range is 6,000 meters (20,000 ft.); maximum altitude of effective fire is 5,000 meters (16,400 ft.). The gun fires HE and AP shells and takes one minute to go into firing position from the march.

RH 202 light field mounting AA gun. This system, deployed by West Germany, meets the need for increased firepower for infantry support and AA defense, particularly of mountain warfare units. It can be operated by one man and can be dismantled into manpack loads without tools. The gun is equipped with a gas-operated three-way belt feed, permitting various types of ammunition to be fired as desired. Two 25-round capacity magazines are located to the left and right of the breech. A flat magazine is also available for top feed. In ground combat operations, with barrel elevation limits of +20°/−5°, the gunner uses a precision laying mechanism and a ground combat sight.

Medium and Heavy Antiaircraft Guns

These guns were designed for protection of individual objectives against low- and medium-altitude attacks. They are employed mainly to protect vital objectives, large groups of troops, SAM installations, and fighter aviation.

The employed systems of medium-caliber AA guns are the U.S. Skysweeper 75mm; the 76mm gun; U.S. 90mm; British 3.7-inch gun; German 88mm gun; and Soviet 100mm gun. In the heavy category are the British 4.5-inch, the 120mm, and the 130mm.

In the early 1950s, air defense missiles began to challenge the supremacy of antiaircraft artillery. Because of the ballistic constraints of gun ammunition, projectiles are relatively slow and lack range in comparison with missiles, which are powered for the majority of their effective time of flight. For these reasons medium- and heavy-caliber antiaircraft guns have been retired by most countries and replaced by missile systems.

Mixed Gun-Missile Air Defense Systems

Effectiveness against helicopters has become a major battlefield problem. The increasing ranges from which stand-off helicopters can fire at their prime targets, tanks, have correspondingly reduced the kill probabilities of AA guns. The demise in August 1985 of the U.S. DIVAD (division air defense) system, also known as Sgt. York, resulted from its inability to counter the known Soviet air threat of the armed helicopter. The U.S. Army then formed a forward area air defense working group; its task was to develop a way to counter both existing and anticipated Soviet threats, including those presented by helicopters, fixed-wing aircraft, and remotely piloted vehicles across the entire battlefield spectrum.

Research concentrated on an air defense system that combined guns and missiles and could be mounted on either tracked or wheeled vehicles. There are many options for such a system, including 25mm or 30mm AA guns and short-range AA missiles such as Stinger or Blowpipe/Javelin. The guns would have an effective range of two to three kilometers (1.2–1.9 mi.), while the missiles would have an engagement range of six to ten kilometers (3.7–6.2 mi.) (depending on the missile selected). This system is equipped with a search/acquisition radar, a laser range finder, and forward-looking infrared tracking.

Another system combines the Vulcan cannon with Stinger missiles. Yet another example of the integrated gun and missile defense system is Skyguard, which performs as the fire control system for the Skyguard-Sparrow launchers, as well as for two Oerlikon 35mm twin AA guns, forming a fully integrated gun/missile air defense system.

In light of the stand-off engagement threat posed by armed helicopters, AA guns are still needed and a gun/missile mix is required. The correct composition of that mix is best determined by utilizing different types of weapons that can complement each other.

Current and Future Development Trends

Current development activity is concentrated on ammunition, which in turn influences the technical design of cannon. The following are areas of focus:

- external drive systems, with the aim of simplifying the cannon to increase its availability rate
- low-weight construction technology that can increase cost effectiveness
- ammunition developments—such as caseless ammunition, fluid propellant charges, and telescopic ammunition—to increase muzzle velocity and rate of fire
- proximity-fuzed ammunition and guided projectiles that will increase the hit probability of a burst.

The main trend in gun design appears to be movement toward the use of higher calibers such as 25mm, 30mm, and 35mm; this results partly from the wide variety of highly effective ammunition types available in the larger sizes.

The cannon design principles of the future will consider balance between such performance parameters as rate of fire and the crucial issue of reliability. The hit probability of automatic cannon will be increased by greater muzzle velocity, which in turn will require new materials technology in the construction of cannon and development of guided projectiles.

All development efforts may be most attractive when they can show some positive relationship to kill probability, availability, or cost reduction. Combinations of guns and missiles may produce a mixed defense capable of overcoming the air threat. There is also a trend toward combining a new and highly accurate gun—one that has an on-mount fire control system and fires a new multipurpose round—with a programmable proximity fuze.

A number of weapon systems are under development that promise improved antiaircraft capabilities. The trend toward dual role capability also continues; the prospect is that such developments will provide defense capability for units facing both ground and aerial threats.

KHEIDR K. EL DAHRAWY

SEE ALSO: Ammunition; Firepower; Fleet Air Defense; Gun Technology Applications; Missile, Surface-to-air.

Bibliography

Chant, C. 1989. *Air defense systems and weapons.* London: Brassey's.

Friedman, R., et al. 1985. *Advanced technology warfare.* London: Salamander Books.

Jane's Weapons Systems 1987–1988. 1987. London: Jane's.

Lee, R. G. 1985. *Introduction to battlefield weapons systems and technology.* 2d ed. Vol. 12 of *Brassey's battlefield weapons systems and technology series.* London: Brassey's.

ARTILLERY, ROCKET AND MISSILE

Free flight rockets (FFRs) provide a means for delivering massive firepower in a short time, at long range, and from comparatively light equipment. Furthermore, they are ideally suited to the new range of improved submunitions being developed. Despite their logistical penalties and the ease with which they can be detected, there will probably be more FFR systems employed by Western armies in place of heavy guns.

FFRs characteristically receive all their guidance instructions prior to launch. A rocket may be conveniently broken down into two parts: the forward part, which contains the warhead; and the rear part, which contains the motor, the fuel propellant, and the combustion chamber. The gas produced by the burning propellant escapes out the rear of the rocket, imparting a forward thrust to the rocket itself. Because the mass of the escaping gases is less than the mass of the rocket, however, the rocket moves at a lower velocity than the gases. The fuel can be either liquid or solid. Liquid fuels have a higher energy content than solid fuels, but solid fuels are easier to produce and safer to handle. FFRs are generally less accurate than guns due to the effects of wind, thrust misalignment, and the variability of velocity after all the fuel has been burned (which will affect the range of the rocket). There are three ways to overcome the problems of stabilization: fin stabilization, spin stabilization, and a combination of the two.

ROCKET MOTOR (CASING)

A rocket motor for an FFR is simply a casing that provides a combustion chamber in which the propellant can burn. The rocket's forward end is closed and attached to the warhead. It contains an igniter and, at the rear end, a nozzle. The motor casing must be strong enough to withstand the high temperature and pressure reached during combustion. If the casing is susceptible to bending when the motor is fired, or if it is not geometrically precise, there can be problems in dispersion at the target. Cold-worked flow-forming manufacturing techniques have been used for rocket motor casings and have produced good results in terms of material strength and of precision in producing the required dimensions. Other manufacturing techniques include the use of glass fiber.

RANGE COVERAGE

The accuracy of free flight rocket systems has improved greatly since World War II, with system accuracies of one percent of range or better now attainable. Nevertheless these systems still cannot compete with conventional gun systems for many tasks, particularly close support, because of their inferior range coverage and reloading times. "Spoilers," or air brakes, can be used to increase the drag on a rocket in flight, modifying its trajectory and range at a given quadrant elevation. The French RAFALE 145mm rocket system, for example, has air brakes positioned between the tail fins. When necessary, these can be actuated at the launcher before firing so that they deploy at the same time as the folding fins as the rocket leaves the launcher. Their effect is to reduce the minimum range of the rocket from 18 kilometers to 10 kilometers (from 11 mi. to 6 mi.).

It is possible to design a rocket with sets of air brakes that present different surface areas so as to vary the range. However, the use of air brakes can be regarded as primarily a means of reducing minimum range rather than a method of achieving range coverage similar to that of a conventional multi-charge gun or howitzer. Mechanical loading systems have slashed FFR reloading times. The Italian FIROS-25 122mm rocket system, for example, is said to be able to reload 40 rockets in five minutes. Regardless of such advantages, it is highly unlikely that FFR systems will ever be able to match conventional gun systems or mortars at sustained fire rates.

Warheads

Free flight rockets and missiles (Fig. 1) can be adapted to carry a wide variety of warheads: nuclear (at calibers of 150mm and above), high explosive, chemical, preformed fragments, and submunitions (including terminally guided). They also have a greater degree of inherent flexibility than guns. A general feature of fin-stabilized rocket ammunition is that different types, weights, and sizes of warheads can be fitted to the same motor. Spin-stabilized rockets are more limited, because any alteration in warhead shape and weight may upset the stability of the rocket. Both fin-stabilized rockets and those stabilized by fin and spin combined also have warhead limitations, but the limits within which the same launcher and motor can be used are much greater. Moreover, with some FFRs the fins are larger than required for stability purposes, permitting changes in warhead with little or no difference in stability. Some launcher tubes with helical guide rails have been designed so that the warhead protrudes from the tube; in such cases the diameter of the tube does not limit the size of the warhead. Currently the trend is toward larger-caliber rockets firing to long ranges, with warhead flexibility being more a function of the rocket's ability to carry either a full-caliber warhead or submunitions.

Launchers

A rocket launcher serves to support and aim the rocket. A launcher in its simplest form may be expendable. Most modern launchers, however, are designed for reloading. Rocket launchers may be built to carry a single rocket or a number of rockets. Since a rocket moves forward by ejecting gases backward, there is no significant recoil on the mounting, apart from a small amount of friction between the rocket and its guide rails. To prevent recoil, the escaping gases must be allowed to pass unimpeded to the rear of the launcher. In practice, this is difficult to achieve because the escaping gases, in expanding, impinge on parts of the launcher, even though the net effect is small. Unlike a gun, there is no trunnion pull to consider; therefore an increase in maximum range does not necessarily mean an increase in the weight of the launcher, as is often the case with a gun.

With no great recoil forces to be withstood, the mounting for a rocket system need be only as heavy and as strong as required to support—and in some cases to transport—the desired size, weight, and number of rockets. It is possible for an armored self-propelled rocket launcher such as MLRS (multiple launch rocket system) to transport and fire twelve rockets, each weighing more than 270 kilograms.

There are two main types of launcher: positive length or "rail launchers," and "zero length launchers." A zero length launcher is one in which the first motion of the rocket removes it from the restraint of the launcher. The purpose of a zero length launcher is simply to hold and point the rocket in the required direction; it does not influence the subsequent trajectory of the rocket. Although zero length launchers can be lighter and smaller than rail launchers, they are generally unsuited for FFR system applications because their use results in high ini-

Figure 1. U.S. Improved Lance missile. (Source: Robert F. Dorr Archives)

tial dispersion. They are, however, normally employed for guided weapon systems.

In contrast, a positive length rail launcher is long enough to influence the flight of the rocket after it has begun to accelerate. The term *rail launcher* is used to describe a wide variety of launchers, including tubes and ramps as well as rails. Tubes seem to be favored in modern FFR system design because the tube can be used to provide protection for the rocket from shell fragments and small arms fire. In addition, tubes can provide good support for the rocket as it accelerates on the launcher and can be readily adapted to impart spin.

In the following sections, a variety of rocket and missile artillery systems are described.

Rocket and Missile Artillery Systems

Soviet 132mm BM-13-16 (16-Round) Multiple Rocket System (MRS)

The 132mm BM-13-16 MRS was standardized in August 1941 in a configuration mounted on a Soviet ZIS-6 or an American 6×6 truck chassis. After World War II the launcher was mounted on the ZIL-15 6×6 truck chassis, the only model seen today. The system is no longer in front-line service in Eastern Europe, but it is used for training. Each Chinese artillery division has one rocket launcher regiment with 32 BM-13-16 (16-round) or 32 updated BM-14-16 (16-round) systems, or 32 Chinese BM-21 variants, or 32 of the more recently developed Chinese 130mm MRS. The 132mm BM-13-16 can easily be distinguished from other Soviet MRSs, as the launcher uses rails rather than the frames or tubes common to all other Soviet postwar launchers. The launcher consists of eight shaped launcher rails with eight fin-stabilized rockets on the top and another eight underneath. Before launching, two stabilizer jacks are deployed at the rear of the vehicle. A full load of sixteen rockets can be launched in seven to ten seconds.

The weapon system requires a crew of six and has a reload time of five to ten minutes. Its maximum range is 9,000 meters (5.6 mi.).

240mm BM-24 (12-Round) Multiple Rocket System

The 240 BM-24 MRS was introduced into the Soviet army in the early 1950s as the replacement for the World War II 300mm BM-31-12, which by then had been found to have insufficient range. When originally introduced, the system was mounted on the rear of a ZIL-151 6×6 truck chassis. This was later replaced by the ZIL-157 6×6 chassis, distinguishable from the earlier model by its single rather than dual wheels and its central tire-pressure regulation system. Soviet tank divisions normally had the tracked 240mm (12-round) BM-24, whereas the Soviet motorized rifle division had the 122mm (40-round) BM-21 MRS. The lighter weapon has a barrel rather than frame launcher and is mounted on the rear of an AT-S medium tracked artillery launcher.

The BM-24's accuracy at two-thirds maximum range for projectile error is 61 meters (200 ft.) in range, 46 meters (150 ft.) in deflection, and 93 meters (305 ft.) CEP (circular error probable). At maximum range the corresponding figures are 40 meters (131 ft.), 95 meters (312 ft.), and 118 meters (387 ft.), respectively. The system has twelve launcher frames and a maximum range of 10,300 meters (6.4 mi.). Reload time is three to four minutes.

130mm M51 (32-Round) Multiple Rocket System

The Czechoslovakian 130mm V51 MRS was developed in the 1950s and is a standard Praga V3S 6×6 truck chassis with the rocket launcher mounted in the rear. No armor protection is provided for the cab, so the launcher is traversed left or right before the rockets are launched. Spare rockets are carried in stowage boxes on either side of the hull under the launcher. The rockets are spin stabilized, and it is believed that a rocket with an increased range has been introduced in recent years. Austria uses the M51 launcher mounted on the rear of a Steyr 680 M3 6×6 truck (q.v.) and Romania uses it on the rear of a Soviet ZIL-151 or 157 truck. The 130mm M51 (32-round) is sometimes called the RM-180 and is issued on the basis of one battalion of eighteen launchers to each motorized rifle division and tank division. The system includes 32 barrels. It has a maximum range of 8,200 meters (5.1 mi.) and a reload time of two minutes. The crew consists of six men.

250mm BM-25 (6-Round) Multiple Rocket System

The 250mm BM-25 entered service with the Soviet army in the 1950s and is the largest caliber MRS to have been deployed since World War II by any member of the former Warsaw Pact. It is no longer in front-line service, but numbers are probably held in reserve. The system was used in combat by South Yemen against North Yemen.

The rocket is believed to use a storable liquid propellant and to have a range of around 55,900 meters (34.7 mi.). The launcher is mounted on the rear of a KRAZ-214 6×6 truck chassis. Before launching the rockets, two stabilizers are lowered at the rear of the vehicle and armored shutters are lowered over the windshield. The launcher has six launcher frames. It requires a crew of eight to twelve.

122mm RM-70 (40-Round) Multiple Rocket System

The Czechoslovakian 122mm RM-70 MRS, which also carries the Western designation M1972, was first seen in public during a parade in Czechoslovakia following the SHIELD-72 maneuvers. It was since identified with East German and Libyan units. The system is essentially an armored version of the Czech Tattra 813 8×8 truck fitted with the same launcher as the Soviet BM-12 MRS at the rear of the hull, with an additional hull for preparing firing positions and clearing obstacles. It is probable that the M1972 is fitted with a winch with a 20,000-kilogram capacity.

The M1972 is issued on the basis of one battalion of eighteen in each of the motorized rifle divisions and tank divisions. Two basic types of fin-stabilized rocket can be fired by the M1972: the BM-21, a short rocket with a range of 11,000 meters (6.8 mi.), and a long rocket with a 20,380-meter (12.6-mi.) range. In addition, there is a combination of the short rocket with an additional rocket motor, producing a range of about 17,000 meters (10.5 mi.).

128mm YMRL 32 OGANJ (32-Round) Multiple Rocket System

The YMRL 32 (its Western designation, for Yugoslav multiple rocket launcher, 32-barrel) was developed in the early 1970s to meet the requirements of the Yugoslav army. It is normally found in batteries of six launchers. The system performs a role similar to that of the Czech 122mm M1972 (40-round) MRS, but has neither the armored cab nor the excellent cross-country performance of the Czech system. The YMRL 32 consists basically of an FAP 2220 BDS 6×4 forward control truck with a 32-barrel 128mm rocket launcher mounted at the rear of the hull. An additional pack of 32 rockets is located at the rear of the cab to provide the capability of rapid reloading. The system fires a twenty-kilogram warhead, containing some 5,000 fragments that are lethal in a radius of more than 30 meters (98 ft.), to a range of 20,000 meters (12.4 mi.). A fuze with preselected superquick, inertia, and delay options is standard. The rockets may be launched singly or in a ripple salvo; the latter takes a total of eighteen seconds. Launching can be accomplished by manual, semiautomatic, or fully automatic means. Once the rockets have been launched, the launcher is traversed to the rear and depressed to the horizontal, permitting the reserve pack of 32 rockets to be mechanically loaded. This operation can be completed in two minutes. The system can be emplaced and commence firing in twenty seconds; in a total of only four or five minutes it can occupy a position, fire both loads, and be on the move again.

220mm BM-27 (16-Round) Multiple Rocket System

The BM-27 was introduced into service with the Soviet army in 1977 and is thus sometimes referred to in the West as the M1977. The system was found in a multiple rocket launcher battalion consisting of a headquarters, one support battery, and three firing batteries (each with six BM-27s). These units were attached to the combined arms army-level artillery brigades. In a tank army the artillery brigade was replaced by a regiment of three battalions of BM-27s. The system provides chemical, high-explosive, and submunitions (including fragmentation bomblet, incendiary bomblet, and minelet) support fire to maneuver units. The rocket weighs some 360 kilograms and has a range of 5–40 kilometers (3–25 mi.). The launcher is configured with one layer of four tubes and two layers of six tubes and is mounted on the ZIL-135 8×8 truck chassis. Four stabilizing jacks are used during firing. A rapid reload capability is provided by another ZIL-135 carrying sixteen rockets and a single-round capacity reloading arm on its rear platform. Reloading time is an estimated fifteen to twenty minutes.

122mm Type 81 (40-Round) Multiple Rocket System

The Chinese are known to have in service a locally built modified version of the Soviet BM-21 122mm system. The 40-tube launcher is carried on a CQ261 Hongyan (a locally built variant of the French Berliet GB4) 6×6 truck chassis. The launcher tube is 3 meters (9.8 ft.) long; each 122mm round weighs 66.8 kilograms. The rocket has a maximum range of 20,580 meters (12.8 mi.).

The launcher can also be mounted on a 4×4 truck with an enlarged cab to accommodate the crew of four and twelve reload rounds. During firing the vehicle suspension system is locked. If necessary, the entire launching system can be removed from the vehicle and placed on a towing carriage. The launcher can be fired from within the cab or from a remote position. This vehicle-mounted version is designated the Type 81.

A pack model developed for use by airborne and mountain units weighs 281 kilograms in firing position and can be dismantled into manpack loads. A lighter version of the Type 63, recently developed, has been designated in the West the Type 63-1. It is some 136 kilograms lighter than the basic model and is distinguishable from it by its smaller spoked roadwheels and four banks of three rockets. Both high-explosive and incendiary rockets are used. China is also known to use the Soviet 132mm BM-13-16 and the 140mm BM-14-16, each of which is mounted on the rear of a ZIL-151 6×6 truck chassis. Each Chinese artillery division has one rocket launcher regiment with 32 MRS.

Egyptian Multiple Rocket Systems

The Egyptian army uses a number of rocket systems provided by Czechoslovakia and the Soviet Union, including the 122mm (40-round) BM-21, 130mm (32-round) M51, 132mm (16-round) BM-13-16, 140mm (16-round) BM-14-16 and 240mm (12-round) BM-24. A straight copy of the BM-21 system has also been produced by the SAKR factory. This system can be mounted as a 40-round launcher on a ZIL 6×6 truck chassis or as a 30-round launcher on a Soviet ZIL-131 or a Japanese Isuzu truck chassis.

The Egyptian army has also deployed locally made rocket launchers on tanks (two quadruple box-like launchers on either side of a T-62 turret) and on wheeled armored personnel carriers (a rectangular system of three superimposed quadruple rail launchers in the rear of a Walid 4×4 APC). The purpose of these systems is to lay smokescreens.

In May 1981 Egypt successfully tested in firing trials the SAKR-30, which is an indigenously developed 122mm multiple rocket launcher system with interfaces that allow it to be fired from the Soviet BM-21 launcher vehicle. The rockets that can be fired include one with an HE-fragmentation warhead, an antitank submunition round containing five mines, and a submunition round containing either 28 antitank or 35 antipersonnel bomblets. An increase in range to 30 kilometers (18.6 mi.) has been achieved through use of an improved lightweight rocket motor and case and a composite bonded star-grain propellant.

Another system of the same caliber, designated the SAKR-18, has also been developed. It has a range of eighteen kilometers (11 mi.) and fires a rocket that can be fitted with either of two warhead types—one carrying 28 antipersonnel bomblets, each with a lethal radius of 15 meters (49 ft.); the other including 21 antitank bomblets, each of which can pierce up to 80 millimeters (3.2 in.) of steel armor. The number of launcher tubes can be varied between 21 and 40.

Egypt has also developed the 12-round 80mm VAP light vehicle-mounted multiple rocket launcher system. The rocket has a range of 8 kilometers (5 mi.) and can be fitted with illumination or HE-fragmentation warheads. Fire is by remote control from an off-vehicle system.

U.S. Multiple Rocket Systems

From World War II to the 1980s, the United States employed only two multiple rocket systems: the M21 (24-round), which was phased out of service some years ago; and the M91 (45-round), which has been declared obsolete.

Early in 1976 the U.S. Army Missile Command initiated feasibility studies and concept formulation for a general support rocket system (GSRS) that would have a high rate of fire and would use a low-cost rocket that could be handled like a round of conventional ammunition. This system was designed for use against troops and light-equipment air-defense systems, and command centers. Later directives reoriented the GSRS toward a standard NATO weapon to be developed and produced in both the United States and Europe. France, Italy, West Germany, and the United Kingdom signed a memorandum of understanding with the United States for joint development and production of the GSRS.

Following completion of a test firing competition in February 1980, the U.S. Army planned for procurement of 491 self-propelled launcher loaders, more than 362,000 tactical rockets, and supporting systems by 1990. Each system, now redesignated the Multiple Launch Rocket System (MLRS), has two pods, each containing six rockets, that can quickly be replaced once the rockets have been fired.

The warhead-carrying rocket, with a range of about 45 kilometers (28 mi.; a German variant has a range of about 40 km, or 25 mi.), supports several different munitions. Among these are a German-developed mine-laying warhead, the AT2, which carries seven mine distribution canisters; and the M77 warhead, which delivers 644 explosive submunitions. The MLRS is mounted on a light armored vehicle based on the U.S. M2 infantry fighting vehicle (IFV), which has a crew of three. In extreme emergencies, one man can operate the entire system.

The MLRS had its baptism by fire in Operation Desert Storm in February 1991 and proved highly effective in counterfire against Iraqi artillery. According to Iraqi prisoners the MLRS's submunitions were called "steel rain" and were the most terrifying threat they faced.

Germany, Italy, and the United Kingdom collaborated on an FFR project for development of a weapon called RS80. The system was to have a range of 40–60 kilometers (25–37 mi.), depending on the warhead used, and was designed to complement conventional 155mm weapon systems. After the RS80 project was discontinued, the United Kingdom and Germany adopted the U.S. Army's MLRS, while the Italian firm SNIA Viscosa produced two other systems, the 51mm FIROS-6 and the 122mm FIROS-25. Although these three systems are by no means the only ones produced in the Western world, they are good examples of the state of the art at opposite ends of the performance spectrum. The FIROS-25 and other modern rocket systems are described below.

FIROS-25

The Italian FIROS-25 field rocket system is an area saturation weapon system based on the 122mm SNIA BPD unguided rocket. The launcher consists of two removable modules with twenty launch tubes each. The escort unit can carry four launch modules. Loading operations are carried out by removing the empty module with a jib crane fitted on the support vehicle, then installing a filled module ready to fire.

Rockets are available in two models with different maximum ranges. They can carry a variety of warheads, from the conventional types (HE, PFF, WP) to the submunition types dispensing antitank or antipersonnel mines and bomblets. The rocket has a single solid-propellant motor with a burn time of just under one second. The system is suitable for massed use or individual missions, and can cover large-area targets in the 8- to 33-kilometer (5- to 20.5-mi.) zone.

A typical battery would consist of a command post equipped with a fire direction system, six firing units, and six escort units. The firing unit is a modular rocket launcher installed on a heavy 6×6 truck. The system comes in two versions: a standard version with a motorized manual movement system that is simple to operate; and an automatic version equipped with an inertial navigator, a servo control system, and a ballistic computer. This firing unit configuration enables the crew to perform topographic and ballistic calculations and aiming procedures by means of an automatic control unit installed in the vehicle cab.

110mm Light Artillery Rocket System

The 110mm LARS was developed in the 1960s and accepted for service with the West German army in 1969. First production systems were delivered the following year. The prime contractor for the launcher was Wegmann and Company of Kassel, with GUF responsible for the rockets. The system has 36 launcher tubes and a range of 14,000 meters (8.7 mi.). It is called the Artillery Raketenwerken 110 SF by the German army and issued on the basis of one battery of eight launchers per division; each battery has two Fieldguard fire control systems (mounted on a 4×4 truck chassis) and a resupply vehicle carrying 144 rockets. There are 209 LARS in service with the German army.

The system has been upgraded from LARS-1 to LARS-2 over the past few years. The program has included a new fire control system, more rocket types, and mobility improvement achieved by fitting the launcher to a new MAN 6×6 truck chassis. An air-transportable, towed, two-wheel, 15-round launcher was also developed by Dynamit Nobel, but it was not adopted by the German army.

140mm Teruel (40-Round) Multiple Rocket Launcher System

The 140mm Teruel-2 MRS, which has a maximum range of 18,000 meters (11.2 mi.), was developed to replace an older MRS in service with the Spanish army. The launcher has two 2-round packs arranged in five rows of four launcher tubes each. Mounted on the rear hull of an IASA-Pegaso 6×6 truck chassis, the vehicle is fitted with an armored crew cab that can mount a light machine gun for local defense and antiaircraft purposes. The launcher is deployed in a battalion of three batteries, each with six firing units.

A Teruel-3 system with new longer-range rockets, effective to 28,000 meters (17.4 mi.), has also been developed. The new rocket is fitted with a double-grain solid-fuel motor that, when equipped with aerodynamic air brakes, allows three distinct trajectories to be flown while using the same firing elevation. The rockets also have pop-out fins for stabilization in flight. The warhead can be either high explosive or, in the case of the Teruel-3, a submunition-carrying warhead in five versions: 42 antipersonnel grenades filled with steel pellets; 28 hollow-charge grenades with contact fuzes that are capable of penetrating 110 millimeters (4.4 in.) of armor; six pressure-activated antitank mines including antidisturbance features; 21 smoke grenades that can each provide four minutes of smoke; or a number of antipersonnel mines. The rockets can be equipped with contact, proximity, or time fuzes. All six versions of the rocket can be mixed on the launcher, which has 40 barrels, and selected according to the target to be engaged. The minimum range for both Teruel-2 and Teruel-3 is 6,000 meters (3.7 mi.).

A resupply vehicle with four blocks of twenty Teruel-3 reload rounds or six blocks of Teruel-2 reload rounds is assigned to each system. Reloading is manual and takes five minutes. The time required to emplace a launcher is two minutes; to fire, 45 seconds; and to displace, another two minutes. The system has a crew of five or six men.

MAR 290mm Multiple Rocket System

This Israeli 290mm artillery rocket has a 25,000-meter (15.5-mi.) range. In the mid-1960s it entered Israeli Defense Force (IDF) service mounted in frame racks, holding four rockets, mounted on Sherman tank chassis. The basic 290mm rocket weighs 600 kilograms at launch and carries a warhead weighing 320 kilograms. The tube launcher can fire four rockets in ten seconds. The MAR-290 system is still in IDF use, but it is now mounted on a new launching system using Centurion tank hulls as the platform and consisting of four launching tubes. On the turretless Centurion chassis, the four tubes are carried in a horizontal layer on a new superstructure positioned on the original turret ring. These tubes can be traversed through a full 360 degrees and through elevations ranging from 0 to +60 degrees. Each launching tube has a diameter of 700 millimeters (27.5 in.) to accommodate the rocket's tail span of 570 millimeters (22.5 in.).

160mm LAR Multiple Rocket Launcher System

Following the 1973 Yom Kippur War, the Israeli Ground Defense Force generated a requirement for an unguided rocket artillery system that could be rapidly deployed to engage large mechanized units supported by artillery and protected by sophisticated air defenses. The result was Israeli Military Industries' Light Artillery Rocket System 160, which anticipated combat in the 1982 Lebanon campaign.

This system consists of a tracked or wheeled all-terrain vehicle on which is mounted a multiple rocket launcher with expendable launch-pod containers that contain sealed-in fuzed 160mm rockets. The pods can be rapidly replaced from resupply vehicles after firing. The number of aluminum/fiberglass tubes per launch-pod container varies according to the size and type of platform vehicle used.

The 110-kilogram LAR 160 rocket is of the solid-propellant, wraparound fin-stabilized type. It carries a 50-kilogram warhead that can be changed to suit the mission. The types available include a cluster munition with 187 M42 bomblets, the FASCAM scatterable mine, chemical or biological agents, the Skeet "smart" antitank submunition, battlefield illumination, and adaptation of any

155mm howitzer shell payload if required. All the rounds use an M445 electronic time fuze that can be remotely set. The minimum and maximum firing ranges are 12 and 30 kilometers (7.4 and 18.6 mi.). The maximum number of tubes per pod is 25 for the system mounted on an M47 MBT chassis, although the more usual number is 13. In Israeli army service the LAR 160 is mounted on a modified M548 chassis and is deployed with the 240/290mm MRS already in service.

Conclusion

Artillery rockets and missiles, particularly in multiple launch configurations as discussed here, will continue to play a significant role on future battlefields. For example, senior officials, recognizing the value of rocket artillery used by the UN coalition forces in Operation Desert Storm, have recommended increasing the range as well as the use of MLRS.

Improved technology and international cooperation will enable this to occur, just as the same combination has helped solve the problem of accuracy. This will also contribute to an increased variety of warheads and submunitions employed by FFR, especially the new generation of "smart" munitions. The future of artillery rockets and missiles as part of combined arms forces seems assured.

ALAA EL DIN ABDEL MEGUID DARWISH

SEE ALSO: Artillery; Artillery, Tube; Explosives Technology, Conventional; Firepower; Missile Propulsion Technology.

Bibliography

Farrar, C. L., and D. W. Leeming. 1983. *Military ballistics: A basic manual.* Vol. 10 of *Battlefield weapons systems and technology.* London: Brassey's.

Jane's armour and artillery, 1987–1988. 1987. London: Jane's.

Pearson, P. F., and G. K. Otis. 1991. *Desert Storm fire support: Classic airland battle operations.* No. 91-2. Association of the United States Army Essay Series. Washington, D.C.: Brassey's (US).

Ryan, J. W. 1981. *Guns, mortars and rockets.* London: Brassey's.

ADDITIONAL SOURCES: *Military Technology: NATO's Sixteen Nations.*

ARTILLERY, TUBE

Some of the earliest devices for hurling projectiles at an enemy were catapults, trebuchets, and ballistas. They were simply mechanical implements for the sudden release of energy to propel projectiles. Modern artillery, in contrast, relies on the ability to harness the energy released by burning propellant to push the projectile to the required range.

The earliest cannon probably had wrought-iron barrels fashioned by lashing iron bars or staves around a white-hot metal core, then arranging equally hot wrought-iron hoops, which contracted when they cooled, over the staves. Some of the earliest cannon were breech-loaded because this method of loading and obturation was favored by the manufacturing technique.

The standard of obturation in early versions proved unsatisfactory, however, and the breech-loading approach was dropped. The purpose of the barrel in those early guns was simply to provide a vessel for the burning propellant, which at that time was black powder, and to enable the projectile to be held and pointed in the right direction. In this regard they were truly forerunners of modern guns. But it was the use of black powder propellant that was perhaps the most significant innovation, for without it the cannon would not have been introduced.

During the fifteenth century, cannon with trunnions began to appear. These were short-stub axles fitted at the barrel's point of balance and about which the elevation and depression of the piece were effected. Obviously gunners were becoming interested in being able to vary, quickly and easily, the range achieved by their weapons.

Benjamin Robins (1707–51), an English mathematician and engineer, invented a device called the ballistic pendulum for use in determining muzzle velocity. Unfortunately, the manufacturing techniques available during Robins's lifetime were unable to cope with the production of rifled cannon so as to prove his theories. Nevertheless, the application of ballistics had begun; well before this time, also, new concepts for the tactical employment of artillery weapons were being put into practice.

Before the time of Gustavus Adolphus (1594–1632), artillery was comparatively immobile, with its most common task being to demolish fortifications or to fire from prepared positions at an advancing enemy. Gustavus Adolphus introduced a new dimension to artillery with the use of light and mobile 4- and 9-pounder demiculverins to support his troops. Frederick the Great of Prussia (1711–86) followed this lead with his employment of artillery during the Seven Years' War, extending the concept to include horse artillery.

The eighteenth century saw the arrival of one of the most significant artillerists in history, Jean Baptiste de Gribeauval (1715–89). His reforms as the French Inspector General of Artillery were the basis of the artillery triumphs of the Napoleonic era. Among other initiatives, he grouped artillery resources into coastal/garrison, siege, and field elements. The United States Army adopted his system in 1809 and retained it until the 1840s. The improvement in techniques for the tactical employment of artillery was not at this time, however, accompanied by many significant developments in the design of guns.

The early nineteenth-century artillery pieces still lacked many of the refinements apparent in modern weapons. A typical gun was muzzle-loaded, smooth bored, and lacking any efficient mechanism to stop it from careering backward upon firing. In the second half of the century, however, developments in gun design began to move swiftly. Before that time, guns had been able to fire from exposed positions on advancing infantry with relative security beyond ranges of about 400 meters (1,308 ft.), and beyond such ranges guns could be used to some advantage.

The invention of rifled small arms made gunners vulnerable at much greater ranges. At the same time, the logical extension of the innovation of rifling to artillery became apparent. The French and the Prussians had rifles in quantity before 1850; rifled field artillery was first employed in 1856.

After many earlier attempts to produce an efficient recoil mechanism, the French came up with their now famous M1897 75mm field gun. The French 75 design included a hydropneumatic recoil mechanism capable of performing two important functions. It absorbed the recoil forces acting on the gun during firing and, unlike other methods under examination at the time, also returned the barrel to its original position. The design of the French 75mm recoil mechanism incorporated a hydraulic brake, which absorbed recoil by the action of forcing oil through a small orifice. The weapon had a high muzzle velocity, thus producing a flat trajectory that was thought to be desirable because it produced a wide spread of shrapnel at the target.

Modern artillery claims the distinction of being the "greatest killer on the battlefield," causing more injuries and personnel casualties to the enemy than other combat arms. That distinction has resulted partly from the continued improvements to artillery pieces to increase range, enhance the lethality of projectiles, and improve mobility, durability, and rates of fire. Selected examples of modern artillery weapons, both towed and self-propelled, are discussed on the following pages (see Fig. 1).

Figure 1. The M-198 155mm howitzer is a typical example of the modern towed artillery weapon. (SOURCE: U.S. Department of Defense)

Towed Artillery

25-POUNDER FIELD GUN (UNITED KINGDOM)

The 25-pounder field gun (Mk 1) was developed and produced in the late 1930s. Initially, many were mounted on 18-pounder field carriages and these were commonly known as 18/25-pounders. The first production 25-pounders with a humped box trail for towing (Mk 2) were completed in 1940. In 1942 the ordnance was fitted with a two-port Solothurn muzzle brake to enable it to fire an armor-piercing projectile with a higher muzzle velocity. This was designated the Mk 3, and is the only version likely to be encountered today.

The 25-pounder is an 87.6mm weapon with a vertical sliding breech mechanism. Served by a crew of six, it can elevate and depress in the range of +40°/−5° and traverse 8 degrees. Its rate of fire is 5 rounds per minute to a maximum range of 12,250 meters (7.6 mi.).

76MM MOUNTAIN GUN M48 (YUGOSLAVIA)

This weapon, often called the "Tito Gun," was developed in the post–World War II period specifically to meet the requirements of Yugoslav mountain units, although it can also be used as a field gun. Its low weight has attracted the attention of other countries, especially in the developing world, where weight, rather than range, is often the overriding consideration.

There are at least four variants of the M48, all of which have split trails, with each trail hinged in the center so that it can be folded forward 180 degrees for towing. The M48 (B-1) has pneumatic tires and a maximum towing speed of 60 kilometers per hour (37 mph). It can also be towed by animals in tandem, or be broken down into eight pack loads. The M48 (B-1A2) has light alloy wheels with solid rubber tires and a modified suspension, but a maximum towing speed of only 30 kilometers per hour (18 mph). Featuring a multi-baffle muzzle brake and hydraulic recoil system, the M48 has a rate of fire of 25 rounds per minute to a maximum range of 8,750 meters (5.5 mi.).

Ammunition for these guns is of the semifixed type with four charges. It is based on that used by the obsolete Soviet 76mm regimental gun M1927, which fired fixed ammunition. The high-explosive (HE) M55 projectile weighs 6.2 kilograms (13.7 lb.) and has a muzzle velocity of 222–398 meters per second (728–1,305 fps). The high-explosive antitank (HEAT) projectile, weighing 5.1 kilograms (11.2 lb.), will penetrate 100 millimeters (4 in.) of armor at a range of 450 meters (1,475 ft.). There is also WP M60 smoke shell that weighs 6.2 kilograms.

85MM FIELD GUN TYPE 56 (CHINA)

The Soviet 85mm divisional gun D-44 was first supplied to China during the Korean War. China began production during the early 1960s under the designation Type 56. Some slight changes were made in the D-44 design to suit Chinese production methods, one being the location of a push rod firing device in the center of the elevating handwheel. The Type 56 does not appear to use the Soviet infrared searchlight and sight system.

Ammunition currently available for the Type 56 includes HE, HEAT-FS (fin stabilized) and high-explosive squash head (HESH). The only current projectile for which definite information is available is the HEAT-FS. Its direct-fire maximum range is 970 meters (3,180 ft.), at which range it will penetrate 100 millimeters (4 in.) of armor set at an angle of 65 degrees.

The Chinese army assigns twelve Type 56 guns to an artillery regiment. The weapon uses a double-baffle muzzle brake and has a hydraulic recoil system. The breech mechanism features a semi-automatic vertical sliding block. Maximum range is 15,650 meters (9.7 mi.). A crew of from six to eight serves the piece, which can elevate and depress in the range +35°/−7° and traverse through 54 degrees. The rate of fire is 15 to 20 rounds per minute. The gun can be towed at a maximum on-road speed of 60 kilometers per hour (37 mph).

100mm Field Gun (China)

This gun, a copy of the 100mm Soviet BS-3 (M1944), is basically the same gun found on the SU-100 and T-54 tanks. It is being introduced to replace the 85mm Type 56 in border area artillery regiments. The gun is effective as a counterbattery artillery piece. The Soviet UBR-412 AP-T round is used in the antitank role, while the HE-FRAG UOF-412 round (with a point-detonating fuze Type 429) is also produced in China.

The gun has a double-baffle muzzle brake; an easily identified massive square-shaped breech system; a cradle-enclosed recoil system; and a vertical sliding-wedge breechblock operating semiautomatically. The breech ring apparently doubles for the long gun tube. The gun is simple and rugged. Eighteen such weapons are assigned to an artillery regiment, although they may be found mixed with the 85mm Type 56 at army level.

The elevation and depression range is +45°/−5° and the gun can traverse about 50 degrees on its carriage. Its maximum range is 20,000 meters (12.4 mi.). Rate of fire is 7 rounds per minute.

GIAT 105mm LG1 Light Gun (France)

During the mid-to-late 1960s, GIAT (Groupement Industriel des Armements Terrestres) developed the prototype of a 105mm light gun known as the Canon 105 LTR. The prototype was not further developed, but the formation of the French Rapid Action Force created a need to replace the French army's existing 105mm M101 and 105mm Model 56 pack howitzers. The Canon 105 LTR was thus revived during the mid-1980s and has now been replaced by an updated model known as the LG1.

The 105mm LG1 light gun is the result of a private venture developed by GIAT's Etablissement d'Etudes et de Fabrications d'Armement de Bourges. By early 1987 three prototypes had been produced. The LG1 follows the same general lines as the earlier LTR, using a split trail carriage, a small shield, a barrel approximately 30 calibers long, and generally light construction. A circular firing jack is provided, and the barrel has a double-baffle muzzle brake and a vertical sliding-wedge breech mechanism. The time required to go into or out of action is 30 seconds.

The LG1 fires the standard HE M1 OE 105 projectile to a maximum range of 11,680 meters (7.2 mi.). Using an HE hollow-base OE 105 DTC projectile, it has a range of 15,000 meters (9.3 mi.); with the HE base bleed OE D105 DTC the range is 17,500 meters (10.8 mi.). In the direct-fire role the weapon can fire the HEAT OCC 105 projectile to an effective range of 1,000 meters (.62 mi.).

The LG1 can be towed by a jeep-type light vehicle. The crew is specified as seven, although the gun can be operated by a reduced crew of five. The gun can elevate and depress in the range +70°/−5° and traverse 40 degrees; its rate of fire is 12 rounds per minute.

105mm Howitzer M102 (United States)

The requirement for a light towed 105mm howitzer to replace the 105mm M101 was established in 1960. The howitzer, first used in combat in South Vietnam, subsequently underwent major successful modifications to solve design problems. Today the M102 is the standard 105mm howitzer of airborne and airmobile divisions and other selected units. Each M102 battalion consists of three batteries of six howitzers each. In 1985 the U.S. Army had a total of 526 M102 howitzers in its inventory.

The weapon has no muzzle brake or gun shield. It uses a hydropneumatic recoil system and a vertical sliding-wedge breech system. It weighs 1,496 kilograms (3,300 lb.). Light and flexible, it can elevate and depress in the range of +75°/−5° and traverse a full 360 degrees. Its rate of fire is 10 rounds per minute. Maximum range is 15,100 meters (9.4 mi.) with HERA M548 or 11,500 meters (7.1 ml.) with HE M1. A crew of eight serves the piece.

105mm Light Field Gun Mark 2 (India)

This Indian Ordnance Factories weapon resembles the British 105mm Royal Ordnance light gun; both were derived from the same 105mm L13 gun used on the FV433 Abbot self-propelled gun. The first 105mm barrel developed in India from the British original was used on the 105mm Field Gun Mark 1. The Mark 2 uses tubular bow trails similar to those of the British 105mm light gun.

The Mark 2 was developed for use in various types of terrain, ranging from mountains to the desert. To reduce its weight, the system is constructed using light, high-strength alloy steels. The resultant weapon in action weighs 2,275 kilograms (5,005 lb.).

Normal towing position is with the barrel folded back across the trails. A 360-degree traversing platform is provided. The gun can be parachute dropped or transported by helicopter. It fires separate ammunition using an eight-charge system. Projectiles include HE, smoke, base ejection star, and HESH.

The Mark 2 has a double-baffle muzzle brake and a vertical sliding-breech system. It can elevate and depress in the range of +73°/−5° and traverse 10 degrees on its carriage (or 360° on the platform). Its normal rate of fire is 4 rounds per minute; maximum range is 17,425 meters (10.8 mi.).

105mm KH178 Light Howitzer (South Korea)

In the preliminary design stages of a new 105mm light howitzer for the South Korean army, the Kia Machine Tool Company procured examples of the British Royal Ordnance 105mm light gun and the West German Rheinmetall conversion of the American 105mm M101 howitzer. Aspects of both have been incorporated in the KH178 105mm light howitzer, production of which began in 1984. The weapon is now in service with the South Korean army.

The KH178 comprises the CN78 cannon, the RM78 recoil mechanism, the GG78 carriage, and a new fire control system. The barrel is 34 calibers long and fitted with a double-baffle muzzle brake. A horizontal sliding breechblock is used with a percussion firing mechanism.

The weapon can elevate and depress through the range +65°/−5° and traverse 45.5 degrees. It has a maximum rate of fire of 15 rounds per minute and a sustained rate of 5 rounds per minute. Its maximum range using HE is 14,700 meters (9.1 mi.); with RAP it can reach 18,000 meters (11.2 mi.).

122mm Howitzer M1938 (M-30) (Soviet Union)

This weapon entered service with the Soviet army in 1939. Until introduction of the D-30 in the 1960s, it was the standard division howitzer of Warsaw Pact armies, issued on the basis of 36 per motorized rifle division (organized into 2 battalions of 3 batteries, each with 6 howitzers) and 54 per tank division (in three battalions).

The weapon's carriage is of the same riveted box-section split trail type used for the 152mm howitzer M1943 (D-1), but the latter can easily be distinguished from the 122mm weapon by its longer and fatter barrel with a double-baffle muzzle brake. The top half of the M1938's gunshield slopes to the rear; in the center is a section that slides upward so the weapon can be elevated. The gun has a hydraulic buffer recoil system and a hinged screw breech mechanism. A crew of eight serves the piece, which can be towed by a variety of tractors and 6x6 trucks. The weapon has a rate of fire of 5 to 6 rounds a minute; can be elevated and depressed through a range of +63.5°/−3° and traversed 49 degrees; and has a maximum range of 11,800 meters (7.3 mi.).

The M1938 fires a variety of case-type, variable charge, separate loading ammunition including FRAG-HE and HEAT. With the HEAT round it can penetrate 200 millimeters (8 in.) of armor at zero degrees obliquity.

The M1938 has also been manufactured in China as the Type 54 and Type 54-1. There it is issued on the basis of twelve per infantry and armored division.

122mm Howitzer D-30 (Soviet Union)

This weapon was introduced into service with the Soviet army in the early 1960s as the replacement for the 122mm howitzer M1938 (M-30). Its main improvements over the earlier system are increased range and the ability to traverse quickly through 360 degrees.

The D-30 is towed muzzle first. Upon arrival at the battery position, the crew must first unlock the barrel traveling lock. A firing jack under the carriage is lowered, raising the wheels clear of the ground. Three trail ends are then staked down, and firing can commence. An unusual feature of the D-30 is that the recoil system is mounted over the barrel.

Some projectiles fired by the D-30 are interchangeable with those fired by the M-30, but the D-30 also fires a HEAT projectile of the nonrotating fin-stabilized type, which can penetrate 460 millimeters (18 in.) of armor at zero degrees obliquity and any range. There are also at least two chemical projectiles for the D-30, one containing Sarin, the other viscous Lewisite. In both cases the chemical agent is dispersed by a TNT bursting charge.

The D-30, with a crew of seven, uses a multibaffle muzzle brake and a semiautomatic vertical sliding breechblock mechanism. It can be elevated and depressed through the range +70°/−7° and has a rate of fire of 7 to 8 rounds per minute. Maximum range is 15,400 meters (9.5 mi.) or, with RAP, 21,900 meters (13.6 mi.).

In the Soviet Army the D-30 is issued on the basis of 36 per tank division (2 battalions of 18 howitzers each) and 72 per motorized rifle division. The D-30 is also produced in China.

130mm Field Gun M-46 (Soviet Union)

This weapon, developed in the early 1950s, was first seen in public during the 1954 May Day parade. It replaced the 122mm M1931/37 (A-19) Field Gun and is ballistically similar to the 130mm guns used by the Soviet navy. The weapon uses a pepperpot muzzle brake and a hydraulic buffer and hydropneumatic recuperator recoil system. The breech mechanism is of the horizontal wedge sliding type. The weapon can be elevated and depressed through the range +45°/−2.5° and traversed 50 degrees. It has a crew of nine, can sustain a rate of fire of 5 to 6 rounds a minute, and has a maximum range of 27,150 meters (16.8 mi.). The weapon can be towed by a variety of artillery tractors or tracked armored vehicles.

During travel the gun's barrel is withdrawn from the gun by a mechanism on the right trail, reducing the overall length. The carriage is a split trail arrangement provided with a two-wheeled limber. The M-46 has direct fire sights, including an active/passive night sight. Modified M-46s with a longer barrel, recuperator, and cradle appeared in Soviet army service in the mid-1970s. India has deployed a self-propelled model called the Catapult, based on the Vijavanta MBT chassis. The first 130mm field gun produced by China was the Type 59, a direct copy of the Soviet M-46.

The M-46 fires FRAG-HE and APC-T rounds. With the latter it can penetrate 230 millimeters (9.2 in.) of armor at a thousand meters. It also uses illuminating and smoke rounds, and at least two chemical rounds filled with Sarin and VX. An RAP is also known to be in service; it was used by Syria during the 1973 Middle East war. The SRC Group of companies, based in Belgium, has produced a conversion package to allow existing M-46 guns to accommodate a new 155mm barrel capable of firing ERFB ammunition.

In the Soviet army the M-46 is issued on the basis of 72 per artillery division (two brigades of 36 each). It is also found in Soviet army artillery brigades.

Factory 100 Artillery Systems (Egypt)

Abu Zaabal Engineering Industries, also known as Factory 100, has reverse engineered the Soviet 122mm D-30 towed howitzer and the Chinese 130mm Field Gun Type 59. The first D-30 was completed in Egypt early in 1984, with Royal Ordnance Nottingham providing some machined-part components that were completed in Egypt. The 122mm based on the D-30 is called the D-30-M by the Egyptians; the copy of the 130mm Type 59 is designated the M59-1M.

Factory 100 is also closely involved with Royal Ordnance Nottingham in upgunning the Soviet-supplied T-55 main battle tank with the 105mm L7A3 rifled gun and will also be involved in whichever of the two competing 122mm D-30 self-propelled howitzers is eventually selected for production or coproduction in Egypt.

152mm Howitzer M1943 (D-1) (Soviet Union)

This weapon was introduced into the Soviet army in 1943 as the replacement for the earlier 152mm Howitzer M1938 (M-10). The D-1 is basically a strengthened carriage and recoil system of the 122mm Howitzer M1938 (M-30) fitted with the ordnance of the 152mm Howitzer M1938 (M-10), but with the addition of a large double-baffle muzzle brake.

The D-1 has a hydraulic buffer and hydropneumatic recoil system and a hinged screw breech mechanism. It features a split trail carriage and has a gunshield. The range of elevation and depression is +63.5°/−3°, the range of traverse 35 degrees. Rate of fire is 4 rounds per minute and maximum range is 12,400 meters (7.7 mi.). The system requires a crew of seven.

The D-1 fires variable charge, case-type, separate loading ammunition, including FRAG-HE and CP rounds. There are also chemical, illuminating, smoke, semi-AP (which will penetrate 82 mm of armor at 1,000 m) and HEAT (which will penetrate 300 mm of armor at zero degrees obliquity and 1,000 m) rounds available.

In the Soviet army the D-1 is being replaced by the 152mm self-propelled gun/howitzer 2S3.

Soltam 155mm M-71 Gun/Howitzer (Israel)

The Soltam M-71 is a further development of the Soltam 155mm M-68 Gun/Howitzer and uses the same recoil system, breech, and carriage. The main differences are that the M-71 has a longer barrel and is fitted with a rammer driven by compressed air. This permits rapid loading at all angles of elevation.

The system has a single-baffle muzzle brake, a hydropneumatic recoil system, a horizontal wedge breechblock, and a split trail carriage. Total traverse is 84 degrees, while elevation and depression can be carried out in the +52°/−3° range. The sustained rate of fire is 2 rounds per minute, and can be doubled for short periods of time. Maximum range is 23,500 meters (14.6 mi.). The weapon has a crew of eight.

155mm Field Howitzer 70 (FH-70) (Multi-national)

In the early 1960s West Germany, the United Kingdom, and Italy agreed on a requirement for a new 155mm field howitzer that would be able to sustain a high rate of fire with a burst fire capability, have high mobility and be deployable with minimum effort, and achieve increased range and lethality by means of a new family of ammunition.

The United Kingdom became project leader for the FH-70. Trilateral responsibilities were assigned for production of various components and accessories.

The system has a double-baffle muzzle brake, a semiautomatic wedge breech mechanism, and a split trail carriage. There is no gunshield. Elevation and depression can be carried out in the +70°/−5° range and the weapon can traverse through 56 degrees. Normal rate of fire is 6 rounds per minute. With the standard projectile, maximum range is 24,700 meters (15.3 mi.). A crew of seven or eight is required.

The FH-70 can be towed using a variety of trucks and is air transportable in a Lockheed C-130 aircraft or slung beneath a CH-47D helicopter. A new family of 155mm ammunition significantly increases the range and lethality of both direct and indirect fire against armored targets. The FH-70 can also fire NATO standard ammunition, including the American Copperhead CLGP. The new family includes HE, smoke, and illuminating rounds. The ERP (extended range projectile) being actively considered for tri-national use is the American M549A1, which would increase the range of the FH-70 to more than 30,000 meters (18.6 mi.).

The Japanese Self-Defense Force has selected the FH-70 to replace its 155mm M114 towed howitzers. Production is being undertaken under license in Japan.

Rheinmetall has produced a 46-caliber length barrel that replaces the standard 39-caliber barrel and enables standard HE projectiles using charge 9 propellant to reach a range of 30,000 meters (18.6 mi.) and base bleed projectiles to a range of 36,000 meters (22.3 mi.). Existing FH-70 howitzers can be modified to this longer barrel FH-70R configuration without being sent back to the factory. Development trials of the modified version began in mid-1984. The FH-70R was shown at the 1986 British Army Equipment Exhibition.

155mm Towed Gun TR (France)

This weapon (Le Cannon de 155mm Tracte), developed to meet the requirements of French motorized infantry divisions, has now started to replace the older 155mm Model 50 towed howitzers. The weapon was shown for the first time at the 1979 Satory Exhibition of Military Equipment. First production 155mm guns were completed in 1984, with the first 79 units to be delivered to the French army by 1988. A special version for possible NATO customers is now in the design stage. It will have a modified chamber configuration and the maximum elevation will be increased to 70 degrees.

A crew of eight is required to man this weapon's tractor and gun. In the self-propelled mode, the gunner doubles as driver. The gun has a double-baffle muzzle brake, a hydropneumatic recoil mechanism, a horizontal wedge breechblock and a split trail carriage. There is no gunshield. The gun can be elevated and depressed through a +66°/−7° range and traversed 65 degrees. Sustained rate of fire is 2 rounds per minute. Maximum range is 24,000 meters (14.9 mi.) using a hollow base projectile and 33,000 meters (20.5 mi.) with a rocket-assisted projectile.

5.5-Inch Medium Gun (United Kingdom)

This weapon was developed by the Armament Research and Development Establishment in the late 1930s to meet a requirement for a 5-inch gun that could fire a projectile weighing 41 kilograms (90 lb.) to a maximum range of 14,600 meters (9.1 mi.). The gun entered production in 1941 and was first used in action in the Middle East the following year. It remained in British army service in diminishing numbers until 1978–80, when it was finally phased out and replaced by the 155mm FH-70.

In 1982 and 1983 four 5.5-inch medium guns were reintroduced into service with the British army at the Royal School of Artillery. The 5.5-inch gun has a hydropneumatic recoil system, an interrupted screw thread breech mechanism, and a split trail carriage. There is no muzzle brake or gunshield. Elevation and depression can be carried out in the +45°/−5° range and the weapon can traverse 60 degrees. Rate of fire is 2 rounds per minute; maximum range is 16,460 meters (10.2 mi.). The weapon requires a crew of ten.

180mm Gun S-23 (Soviet Union)

This gun was developed in the early 1950s from a naval weapon. It was first seen in public in the 1955 May Day parade in Moscow. During travel the barrel is withdrawn out of the gun to the rear and linked to the trails to reduce overall length. In action the S-23 is supported on a base that is retracted under the carriage during travel.

The weapon uses a pepperpot muzzle brake, a screw-type breech mechanism, and a split trail carriage. It is towed by a heavy artillery tractor and requires a crew of sixteen. Elevation and depression range from +50° to −2°, while the weapon can traverse 44 degrees total.

The S-23 fires using a bag-type variable charge and several different types of separate loading ammunition including FRAG-HE, HE/RAP, a concrete-piercing projectile, and a 0.2 KT tactical nuclear shell. Its maximum range is 30,400 meters (18.8 mi.), increased to 43,800 meters (27.2 mi.) with the use of RAP. The weapon can sustain fire at one round per minute for short periods, but the sustained rate is one round every two minutes.

In the Soviet army the S-23 is issued on the basis of twelve weapons in the heavy artillery brigade of the artillery division.

8-Inch Howitzer M115 (United States)

Following World War I, the United States developed two 8-inch (203mm) howitzers, the M1920 and the M1920M1, that could traverse 360 degrees, elevate from 0 to +65 degrees, and had a common carriage that could also be used for a 155mm gun. It was not until 1940, however, that modifications of these designs resulted in a standardized 8-inch howitzer (the M1) for U.S. forces. After World War II, the M1 was redesignated the Howitzer, Heavy, Towed: 8-inch: M115.

Capable of hurling a 90.72-kilogram (200-lb.) projectile to a range of 16,800 meters (10.4 mi.), the M115 can fire as fast as a round per minute, with a sustained rate of fire of one round every two minutes. The howitzer fires several different projectiles including HE, antipersonnel mine-dispersing, chemical (agent GB or VX), and nuclear (5- to 10-kiloton range).

The M115 has a hydropneumatic recoil system with interrupted screw-stepped thread breech mechanism and a split trail with limber carriage. It is designed to be served by a crew of 14 and is towed by a tractor or 6x6 truck. A self-propelled version was developed during World War II, but is no longer in service.

The 8-inch howitzer saw service in Vietnam by U.S. forces in the 1960s and early 1970s, where it gained a reputation for uncanny accuracy. Today, it remains prominent as heavy artillery and can be found in corps artillery groups.

Self-Propelled Artillery

122mm Self-Propelled Howitzer M-1974 (2S1) (Soviet Union)

This weapon is commonly known as the Gvozdika (Carnation), although NATO usually calls it the M-1974, referring to the year it was first seen in public. It entered service with the Soviet and Polish armies in 1971 and was first seen by Western observers at a parade in Poland in July 1974. In appearance it is similar to the American M109 self-propelled howitzer, which entered service in 1962.

The M-1974 is issued on the basis of 36 per artillery division, 36 per motorized rifle division, and 72 per tank division. It can be distinguished from the heavier 152mm self-propelled gun/howitzer M-1973, which has six road wheels and four return rollers, by its seven road wheels and the absence of return rollers.

The M-1974's main armament is a modified version of the 122mm D-30 towed howitzer. It has a semi-automatic vertical sliding wedge breechblock and a firing pin that can be recocked in the event of a misfire. A power rammer and extractor provide a higher rate of fire and permit loading at any angle of elevation. The maximum sustained rate of fire is 5 rounds per minute. The basic load of 40 rounds carried aboard is normally divided into 32 HE, six smoke, and two HEAT-FS. The HE projectile has a maximum range of 15,300 meters (9.5 mi), with HE/RAP, that can be extended to 21,900 meters (13.6 mi.). AP-HE, flechette, leaflet, and chemical projectiles are also available. The system requires a crew of four. It is amphibious and has a maximum road range of 500 kilometers (310 mi.). The turret has both electrical and manual controls and full 360-degree traverse. The range of elevation and depression is +70°/−3°.

152mm Self-Propelled Gun (2S5) (Soviet Union)

Since 1978 the Soviet Union has deployed two new 152mm guns, one self-propelled and one towed. The SP version is believed to have reached full operational capability with the Soviet army in 1980. So far it has not been identified in service outside the Soviet army.

The self-propelled gun is based on the chassis of the GMZ minelayer or the 152mm M1973, with the weapon well to the rear in an unprotected mounting. The ordnance is fitted with a muzzle brake, but does not have a fume extractor. A large spade is lowered at the hull before firing commences.

This weapon has a nuclear capability. Maximum range with a conventional HE round is 17,000 meters (10.5 mi.), increased to 37,000 meters (22.9 mi.) with a rocket-assisted projectile. In addition to high explosive and tactical nuclear projectiles, the 2S5 can also fire chemical, concrete-piercing, and improved conventional munitions.

203mm Self-Propelled Gun M-1975 (2S7) (Soviet Union)

Soviet ground forces began receiving the M-1975 during 1975; reportedly some 400 have now been deployed, although fewer than half are aligned against NATO forces. This gun equips heavy artillery units at front level and is capable of firing nuclear projectiles. It is believed that an artillery regiment equipped with the M-1975 has 24 weapons organized in three batteries of eight weapons each.

The M-1975 is based on a large chassis that is probably the biggest armored vehicle currently in the Soviet inventory. An armored cab at the front can carry two to four crewmen. Immediately behind the cab is the engine compartment. The transmission is forward-mounted below the cab so as to power the forward track drive sprockets. The suspension is of a new type and features seven road wheels. Storage bins are located midway of the hull; the gun is mounted at the rear in the conventional manner. The gun is equipped with a form of power-assisted loading, with its operator seated in a crow's nest position at the left rear of the vehicle. At the extreme rear is a large hydraulically operated recoil spade. The M-1975 has no cover for the gun crew when in action. It is possible that a second tracked vehicle carries the ammunition and the bulk of the gun crew.

A maximum range of 30,000 meters (18.6 mi.) has been quoted for this gun. It is understood to have a maximum rate of fire of two rounds a minute and a sustained rate of one round every two minutes. Types of ammunition fired include high explosive and tactical nuclear.

240mm Self-Propelled Mortar M-1975 (2S4) (Soviet Union)

This Soviet army system is known in the West as the M-1975. It is normally retained at front or high command levels of control for special-purpose use, since it can fire a nuclear projectile. The system reached full operational capability in 1975, but has yet to appear in public. It is believed that each 240mm mortar regiment has from 36 to 54 systems.

The M-1975 consists of a much-modified GMZ tracked minelaying vehicle on the hull rear. The mortar is carried complete with a baseplate and is hydraulically lowered from its traveling position around a pivot on the rear of the hull. The baseplate is hinged to the hull rear; when emplaced, the mortar barrel faces away from the hull. Probably some rounds are carried inside the vehicle hull and some form of assisted loading is provided. Rate of fire is estimated at one round a minute.

The 240mm mortar has a minimum range of 800 meters (0.5 mi.) and a maximum range of 9,700 meters (6 mi.); it is possible that the mortar barrel used on the M-1975 has an enhanced range of 12,700 meters (7.9 mi.). In addition to nuclear projectiles the mortar fires a high-explosive round weighing 130 kilograms (287 lb.) and a chemical projectile. A concrete-piercing round for use against urban targets has also been reported.

M109A1 (United States)

The M109A1 is basically the M109 fitted with a new and much longer barrel, an improved elevation and traversing system, and a strengthened suspension system. It fires an HE projectile to a range of 18,100 meters (11.2 mi.), compared with 14,600 meters (9.1 mi.) for the M109; an RAP extends that range to 24,000 meters (14.9 mi.). The weapon can also fire other projectiles including one filled with agent H/HD, an HE round, a grenade-filled round, an antitank mine round, and an antipersonnel mine round.

M109A2 (United States)

This system entered production in 1978 with the first deliveries made early the following year. The major changes from the M109A1 include a redesigned rammer and improved recoil mechanism, engine operation warning devices, redesigned hatch and door latches, an improved hydraulic system, and a bustle designed to carry an additional 22 rounds of ammunition. The weapon can be elevated to +75° and depressed to −3°, while the turret can traverse 360 degrees. Turret control is both hydraulic and manual. In addition to the main armament there is a 12.7mm or 7.62mm machine gun for antiaircraft defense.

Manned by a crew of six and powered by a Detroit Diesel turbo-charged engine developing 405 brake horsepower, the system has a maximum road speed of more than 90 kilometers (56 mi.) per hour and a maximum road range of some 354 kilometers (220 mi.). It can ford more than a meter of water, climb a 60 percent gradient, and span a trench 1.83 meters (6 ft.) wide. The cross-drive transmission has four forward and two reverse gears. Independent torsion bar suspension is provided.

155mm GCT Self-Propelled Gun (France)

The GCT (Grande Cadence de Tir) was developed beginning in 1969 to meet a French army requirement for a self-propelled gun to replace the 105mm and 155mm self-propelled weapons then in service. First production GCTs were delivered in 1978—to Saudi Arabia. The weapon was officially selected by the French army in July 1979 and is now being deployed in five-gun batteries, with each regiment consisting of three batteries. The French army has an overall requirement for 190 GCTs.

The GCT basically consists of a modified AMX-30 main battle tank chassis fitted with a new turret and armed with a 155mm gun and an automatic loading system. The vehicle has a crew of four: the commander, gunner, loader, and driver.

The hull is almost identical to that of the AMX-30, with modifications that lighten the hull by 2,000 kilograms (4,400 lb.). The 105mm ammunition racks in the hull have been removed, and a 5KVA 28-volt generator and a ventilator system to supply the turret with cold air have been installed.

The system, powered by a Hispano-Suiza 12-cylinder water-cooled and supercharged multi-fuel engine developing 720 horsepower, has a maximum road speed of 60 kilometers (37 mi.) per hour. Maximum road range is 450 kilometers (279 mi.). The vehicle has five forward and five reverse gears and torsion bar suspension; it can ford more than two meters and climb a 60-percent gradient. Turret control is both hydraulic and manual; the turret can traverse 360 degrees. Gun elevation and depression are in the +66°/−4° range. Equipment includes a 7.62mm or 12.7mm machine gun for antiaircraft defense and two smoke dischargers.

OTO Melara Palmaria 155mm Self-Propelled Howitzer (Italy, for export)

The Palmaria was developed beginning in 1977 by OTO Melara specifically for export. The first production vehicles were ready in 1982. The first customer, Libya, placed an order for 210 systems. Nigeria placed an early order for 25, while Argentina ordered 25 Palmaria turrets to be fitted on the TAM medium tank chassis. All were completed by late 1986.

The system's chassis is similar to the OF-40 main battle tank's, apart from the engine. The driver is seated at the front of the hull. The other four crew members (commander, gunner, charge handler, and magazine operator) are seated in the aluminum turret in the center of the hull. The commander, in the right forward part of the turret, has eight periscopes for all-around observation and a single-piece hatch cover that opens to the rear. Additional large rectangular hatches are on either side of the turret. A 7.62mm or 12.7mm antiaircraft machine gun can be mounted on the roof, and four smoke dischargers are mounted on either side of the turret.

The system has a maximum road speed of 60 kilometers (37 mi.) per hour and a maximum cruising range of 500 kilometers (310 mi.). The power shifting transmission provides four forward and two reverse gears. Torsion bar suspension is used. The main gun can elevate and depress +70°/−4° and traverse 360 degrees.

M107 175mm Self-Propelled Gun (United States)

The U.S. M107 has a crew of five, can attain a maximum road speed of 56 kilometers (35 mi.) per hour, and has a maximum road range of 725 kilometers (450 mi.). The cross-drive transmission provides four forward and two reverse gears. Torsion bar suspension is utilized. Turret control is both hydraulic and manual, with an elevation and depression range of +65°/−2° and gun traverse of 30 degrees in each direction.

In the U.S. Army, M107s were deployed in battalions of twelve guns and were held at corps level. All M107s in U.S. corps were, by 1981, converted to M110A2s (see below). It is expected that other countries deploying the

M107 will follow suit; Italy and the Netherlands have already effected such conversions.

M110A1 AND M110A2 (UNITED STATES)

In 1969 the United States Army Armament Command began development of a new version of the M110, one that would have longer range and fire a new family of improved ammunition. The result was standardized as the M110A1 and entered service in January 1977. It replaced both the M110 and the M107, which were phased out of service with the U.S. Army in Europe by 1980.

The M110A1 203mm howitzer has a new and much longer barrel, a direct-fire elbow telescope, and a chassis identical to the M110's. The M110A2, which was standardized in 1978, is the M110A1 fitted with a double-baffle muzzle brake. It can thus fire charge 9 of the M118A1 propelling charge, whereas the M110A1 can fire only up to charge 8.

The M110A1 and M110A2 have a crew of five. Their maximum road speed is 56 kilometers (35 mi.) per hour, using a Detroit Diesel 8-cylinder turbocharged engine, and maximum road range is 725 kilometers (450 mi.). The transmission provides four forward and two reverse gears. Torsion bar suspension is used. Turret control is both hydraulic and manual. The gun can be elevated and depressed through a +65°/−2° range and traversed 30 degrees to each side.

Conclusion

The U.S. Army envisages that a new artillery system will be required to follow the present M109 howitzer improvement program (HIP). It currently anticipates that a new weapons system will be required from the late 1990s onwards; that requirement is now generally known as the advanced field artillery system (AFAS). Although AFAS is still in its early stages, two guiding principles have been established: to reduce personnel-to-weapon system ratios and to enhance survivability. Other requirements include increased range, a higher rate of fire, and a smaller crew, all related to existing systems; mobility equal to other anticipated AFVs; a nuclear-hardened capability; and the ability to be carried in a C-141 transport aircraft. AFAS will also have to be "soldier friendly."

Technologies under investigation for possible inclusion in AFAS are robotics, artificial intelligence, a single-charge propellant system, liquid propellants, electromagnetic propulsion, and a chassis common with the projected future combat systems.

Electromagnetic (EM) and electrothermal (ET) propulsion systems hold particular promise for the future of guns, especially in direct-fire roles. Conventional guns cannot push projectiles any faster than the 2-kilometer-per-second (1.25 mps) expansion speed of solid propellant. Recent experiments have used electric power to achieve projectile (1.1-kg; 2.5-lb.) speeds in excess of 3 kilometers (1.86 mi.) per second. While substantial challenges remain, a conceptual design for an electric 120mm gun with twice the kinetic energy of conventional guns has been developed. Where the future leads is tied to continuing research and development efforts.

ALAA EL-DIN ABDEL MEGUID DARWISH

SEE ALSO: Artillery; Artillery, Antiaircraft; Artillery, Rocket and Missile.

Bibliography

Jane's armour and artillery, 1988–1989. 1988. London: Jane's.

Metzgar, T. L. 1991. Electric guns. *National Defense*. Arlington, Va.: The American Defense Preparedness Association.

U.S. Dept. of Defense. 1988. *Soviet military power: An assessment of the threat*. Washington, D.C.: Dept. of Defense.

ADDITIONAL SOURCES: *Military Technology; NATO's Sixteen Nations*.

ASSISTANCE, MILITARY

Military assistance covers two types of activity: the provision of military aid by one nation to another and the rendering of assistance to the civil community.

Military Aid to Another Nation

In this context, military assistance covers all the functions and activities by which one nation furnishes military aid to another, but excludes fighting alongside it in war. This is an important distinction. A formal defense treaty commits the signatories to armed alliance against another nation or a perceived threat. Military assistance agreements are usually a part of normal diplomatic treaties of friendship between nations.

Military assistance is not normally pre-planned. Requests for aid are forwarded from one nation to another, to be met or not as the diplomatic situation dictates. However, these requests fall into various categories and can be described in an ascending order of magnitude.

The first stage is often the sale of a weapon system or equipment from one country to another, accompanied by training courses in its use and maintenance.

The second stage occurs when a nation agrees to assist another by giving it quantities of equipment and weaponry, together with personnel to instruct in its use.

The third stage is the commitment to provide training for the armed forces of another nation. This is done by sending military training teams and advisers, as instructors in military colleges or as training officers in units.

The fourth stage is very close to a formal military alliance and has occurred often in recent years. A government, faced with severe internal disorder or insurrection, seeks help from another nation. The assistance requested in this case can be for fully equipped army, air, or naval units to assist in suppressing the disorder or insurrection. Examples are the Russian involvement in Afghanistan and the Cuban units in Angola.

The categories of assistance described above are not comprehensive, but indicate the scale and type of aid that can be given.

Military Assistance to the Civil Community

Military assistance to the civil community is normally considered under two heads: peace and war. The principle is the same in both cases—that the armed forces, because of their organization, training, and equipment, are able to carry out certain tasks beyond the scope or capabilities of the civil community.

Military Assistance in Peacetime

The civil community will look to the military forces for assistance in such matters as the disposal of explosives, emergency medical transport, and rescue operations (shipwrecks, mine disasters, etc.). Their aid will also be needed in natural disasters such as earthquakes, floods, and forest fires.

Military Assistance in Wartime

The role of the military in the civil community in wartime is sometimes overlooked, but it forms an important element in the national war effort. Sea convoys and civil air movement will come under military control and military liaison officers will be appointed to ports, airfields, and main railheads. Military teams will also be required for bomb disposal, monitoring of nuclear and chemical fallout, and for such tasks as the urgent restoration of damaged bridges, roads, and public utilities along the lines of communications.

N. T. P. Murphy

See Also: Arms Trade and Military Assistance; Assistance, Mutual; Cross-servicing.

Bibliography

Congressional Quarterly. 1969. *Global defense: US military commitments abroad.* Washington, D.C.: Congressional Quarterly Service.

Dunn, M., and J. Ackerman. 1986. Life history of a foreign military sale. *Defense and Foreign Affairs* 14:7–13.

Gosztony, P. I. 1977. The Spanish civil war and Soviet aid. *Military Review* 57:26–33.

Gruhn, I. 1972. *British arms sales to South Africa: The limits of African diplomacy.* Denver, Colo.: Univ. of Denver Press.

Heymont, I. 1968. US Military assistance programs. *Military Review* 48:89–95.

Lyons, G. M. 1961. *Military policy and economic aid: The Korean case, 1950–1953.* Columbus, Ohio: Ohio State Univ. Press.

Stevens, J. C., and W. W. Sedlacek. 1986. Security assistance. *Army Logistician* 18:36–37.

ASSISTANCE, MUTUAL

Mutual assistance is a generic term covering two concepts: mutual aid and mutual support. Because of the wide area covered by these two terms, specific definitions are necessary for each and those adopted by the North Atlantic Treaty Organization (NATO) are in general use.

Mutual aid covers those arrangements made at government level between one nation and one or more other nations to assist each other.

Mutual support is the support that military units render each other against an enemy on the battlefield because of their assigned tasks, their position relative to each other and to the enemy, and their inherent capabilities.

Mutual Aid

Mutual aid agreements between governments are made in both peace and war, and cover the complete field of government activities.

These agreements, often called mutual aid programs, are not confined to purely military aid. They may commit one nation to provide technological assistance, engineering expertise, or heavy industrial equipment to another in exchange for preferential trade tariffs or free use of ports and airfields. This type of agreement can be considered as diplomatic or economic mutual aid.

Regarding defense, mutual aid agreements may be part of a formal defense treaty or may stand on their own, to provide lesser defense needs. A simple example is an agreement whereby one nation allows the military forces of another to transit through its territory or make use of refueling and maintenance facilities for aircraft and naval vessels. Host nation support or military assistance often forms the basis of such agreements.

The detail of such agreements normally specifies the type of aid to be given and the limitations and conditions under which it will be implemented. These conditions normally include methods of payment for services or use of utilities and may impose a time limit on the agreement.

Mutual aid can cover all or any aspect of cooperation between nations. The important factor is that it is formally agreed upon at national government level.

Mutual Support

Mutual support embodies the same concept of assistance, but specifically covers cooperation among armed forces in combat. It can be agreed upon at any level and includes tactical, administrative, medical, and logistic support. It may take place between units of the same service or nation or among different national contingents.

The simplest example is that of neighboring infantry companies agreeing to cover each other's front with a joint fire plan. This basic cooperation should be exercised at every military level as a matter of routine.

Although mutual support is common within national formations, special arrangements are necessary if the force comprises contingents from different nations. Mutual support, in this instance, requires much preparatory work and consultation between the force commander and the planning staffs of the nations concerned.

This consultation takes into account any differences in nations' military organizations or practices. Particular attention must be paid to the detailed planning and exercising of cross-servicing and logistic cooperation among the different contingents.

N. T. P. MURPHY

SEE ALSO: Alliance, Military and Political; Assistance, Military; Cross-servicing; Host Nation Support.

Bibliography

U.S. Department of the Army. Headquarters. 1977. *Field Manual 100-5: Operations*. Washington, D.C.: Government Printing Office.

ASSOCIATION OF SOUTHEAST ASIAN NATIONS (ASEAN)

A regional organization of global significance, ASEAN is an example of successful self-organization by developing nations to deal cooperatively with political and economic matters. It includes six nations: Brunei, Indonesia, Malaysia, the Philippines, Singapore, and Thailand, which represent more than 3 million square kilometers (1 million sq. mi.) in area and more than 300 million people.

Expressly intended *not* to become involved in military activity, ASEAN nevertheless has been intimately concerned with such matters as the Vietnamese intrusion into and occupation of Cambodia (State of Kampuchea) and the former USSR's growing military presence in Southeast Asian waters. Dynamics of the demand for and transportation of oil and other energy resources are major concerns, together with the realities of controlling choke points for global ocean transport in Southeast Asia. The increasingly complex economic and political (and military) implications of national zones of control provided for by Law of the Sea agreements are further issues.

Most recently, ASEAN has been concerned with the changing nature of the global economy, serious economic matters that will require major cooperative efforts in ASEAN, together with related issues of succession to national leadership and power.

Forerunners of ASEAN

The Association of Southeast Asia (ASA) was formed in 1961 by Malaysia, the Philippines, and Thailand but was replaced by ASEAN in 1967. ASA dealt with only a small geographic and political part of Southeast Asia and its problems. In 1963 the president of the Philippines initiated Maphilindo, named for member nations *Ma*laysia, the *Phil*ippines, and *Indo*nesia, an effort that was soon aborted. The Asia and Pacific Council (ASPAC), a cooperative group founded in 1966, was composed of Australia, Japan, Malaysia, New Zealand, the Philippines, South Korea, South Vietnam, Thailand, and Taiwan. It dissolved in 1975.

The Southeast Asian Treaty Organization (SEATO), while not a lineal ancestor of ASEAN, nevertheless was important at one time to the current members of ASEAN. Although criticized continually and seriously from both external and internal sources, SEATO had considerable impact on the region, both prior to and following its collapse after the Vietnam War ended. SEATO's diverse membership included Australia, France, New Zealand, Pakistan, the Philippines, Thailand, the United Kingdom, and the United States. It was organized under the Southeast Asia Collective Defense Treaty of Manila in 1954, which came into force on 19 February 1955, to resist aggression against the Asian parties and other regional territories the parties might designate.

SEATO was a response to communist expansion, presumably stimulated further by the defeat of France in Vietnam. The Indo-Chinese countries were not invited to participate; other Southeast Asian countries did not wish to. It had no standing forces, although it was used as a basis for significant military activities (and interference with such activities) by member nations. The Secretariat had a large headquarters building in Bangkok. Support for wide sociocultural research resulted in extensive publications. An Asian Institute of Technology and a SEATO Graduate School in Engineering, along with a Military Technical Training Institute, were fruits of the alliance. Increasingly SEATO shifted from military to civil functions, as its structure was reduced. Pakistan withdrew in 1973; France maintained inactive status after withdrawing financial support in 1974. In 1975 the prime minister of Thailand and the president of the Philippines publicly called for dissolution of the organization. Although the permanent mechanism was disbanded in 1975, SEATO held its last military exercise on 20 February 1976. It officially went out of existence on 30 June 1977, but the U.S. Department of State nevertheless maintains that "obligations under the treaty remain in force."

Founding and Development of ASEAN

At Bangkok on 8 August 1967, Indonesia, Malaysia, the Philippines, Singapore, and Thailand formed ASEAN to help accelerate economic, social, and cultural progress and to ensure the stability of Southeast Asian noncommunist states through consultation and cooperation. In part this initiative resulted from the devastating near state of war between Indonesia and the Philippines on the one side, and U.K.-supported Malaysia on the other (Jackson et al. 1986).

Initially ASEAN was an anticommunist organization, but in 1972, following the reconciliation of the United States and Japan with the People's Republic of China, ASEAN members also changed their attitudes. Indeed, ASEAN seems to have had more success in political matters than in economic negotiations, although the latter are not insignificant. To the surprise of some, ASEAN has stood firmly against post–Vietnam War expansion by Vietnam and has realistically influenced politico-military affairs without the use or threat of military force. ASEAN member-nations' production of some of the world's significant raw materials, their strategic location, and their potential for effective control of critical passageways between the Indian and Pacific oceans have enabled it to do so.

ASEAN states were bothered by increasing intrusion of the former Soviet fleet into the Pacific, particularly Soviet use of Vietnam's Cam Ranh Bay and Danang military and naval facilities, and construction of facilities in Cambodia's port of Kampong Som. Those Soviet moves reflected an overarching strategic threat to China, the ASEAN countries, and the United States Pacific Command. ASEAN attempted to neutralize potential superpower rivalry in the area by backing a proposed "zone of peace, freedom, and neutrality (ZOPFAN)" in the region. More significant were ASEAN's efforts at the international level to terminate Vietnam's occupation of Kampuchea.

Membership and Structure. Upon achieving independence from the United Kingdom in 1984, Brunei Darussalam joined the original five members to make up the present ASEAN. The organization incorporates a Ministerial Conference of member states' foreign ministers, together with a steering committee that meets monthly. There are also a Council of Economic Ministers and permanent committees on communication, shipping, food production, aviation, commerce and industry, science and technology, transport, and telecommunication. These are supported by a small Secretariat. ASEAN committees of the members' diplomatic mission chiefs make representations of common interest in key foreign capitals and in Geneva.

Of particular interest are bilateral and joint discussions that take place after the annual ministerial conferences with the secretary of state of the United States and other principal political and diplomatic participants from the European Community, Australia, Canada, Japan, and New Zealand.

Current Issues and Activities

After more than a decade of exemplary and rapid annual economic growth (up to 10% in some countries) the ASEAN states are in serious trouble. The collapse of prices for most Southeast Asian commodity exports (copra, sugar, rubber, tin, copper) and a disastrous fall in the international price of oil were accompanied by political turmoil in the Philippines. The many serious economic problems that affect the superpowers and the more developed nations of the world have now reached Southeast Asian nations, even such "Little Tigers" as Singapore. In addition to current international problems, such as too-rapid urbanization and attempts to gain access to Chinese and Japanese markets, ASEAN states are also affected by prior investments in uneconomical "prestige" projects and "official" corruption, despite their real potential for rapid economic growth, social progress, and political stability. In addition there are serious issues of political succession to aging but still powerful leaders. The timing of transitions from cheap labor to high-tech industry has been adversely influenced by world market shifts and international declines in oil and gas consumption, as well as stock market crashes and entrepreneurial manipulation. The very success of efforts to produce larger rice harvests, through their effect on markets, has also made for difficulties.

Future

The original needs of ASEAN have multiplied, and there are many more reasons for the existence of this now-experienced organization. Despite the seriousness of the issues it faces, there are hopeful indicators: China wants to develop its relations with ASEAN members "energetically" under its policy of the "four requirements": peaceful coexistence; opposition to hegemony; equality and the mutual benefit and attainment of common prosperity in economic relations; and independence and mutual restraint, with close cooperation and mutual support in international affairs. In addition, Thailand, for one, seems to have settled into less fragile political dynamics and greater government stability—a situation yet to be achieved in the Philippines.

ASEAN recognizes that its economic and political (and de facto military-political) problems and their solutions are globally based, not just regional. Its members are also aware of the international power they wield by the practical control of passageways for global traffic between the Pacific and Indian oceans.

For the most recent information on this organization, the reader may refer to the following annual publications:

The Military Balance. International Institute for Strategic Studies. London: Brassey's (UK).

The Stateman's Year-Book. New York: St. Martin's Press.

The World Factbook. Central Intelligence Agency. Washington, D.C.: Brassey's (US).

DONALD S. MARSHALL

SEE ALSO: Alliance, Military and Political.

Bibliography

ASEAN Secretariat. 1987. *ASEAN: The first twenty years.* Singapore: Federal Publications.

Jackson, K. D., S. Paribatra, and J. S. Djiwandono, eds. 1986. *ASEAN in regional and global context*. Berkeley, Calif.: Institute of East Asian Studies.

Martin, L. J. 1987. *The ASEAN success story: Social, economic, and political dimensions*. Honolulu: East West Center, Univ. of Hawaii Press.

Miller, R. J. 1968. Is SEATO obsolete? In *U.S. Naval Institute Proceedings*, November.

Palmer, R. D., and T. J. Reckford, with a Foreword by J. H. Holdridge. 1987. *Building ASEAN: 20 years of Southeast Asian cooperation*. The Washington Papers/127. New York: Praeger. Published for the Center for Strategic and International Studies, Washington, D.C.

Sopiee, N., Chow Lay See, and Lim Siang Jiu, eds. 1988. *ASEAN at the crossroads: Obstacles, options, and opportunities in economic cooperation*. Malaysia: Institute of Strategic and International Studies (ISIS).

Tangsubkul, P. 1982. *ASEAN and the law of the sea*. Singapore: Institute of Southeast Asia Studies.

ASSYRIA, MILITARY HISTORY OF

Assyria began as a small northern Mesopotamian city-state called Assur. Under a succession of aggressive, warlike kings, Assyria created a highly professional army and, with it, an empire that, at its height, included the entire Fertile Crescent as well as much of Asia Minor. Although Assyria's rise to supremacy was a slow process, its fall was swift and complete.

Militarization of Assyria

Located at the junction of important caravan routes in northern Mesopotamia, Assyria was open to attack from all directions. During the second millennium B.C., it suffered greatly from the chariot forces of Indo-European invaders.

Threats to Assyrian Security

By 1550 B.C., Assyria was, in effect, encircled and threatened by potential and actual enemies. To the southeast, Babylonia, under the Indo-European Kassites, constituted a perennial threat. To the east, it was prey to frequent raids by various mountain tribes. To the north, the Kingdom of Mitanni, and later the Kingdom of Urartu, seriously threatened both the commerce and survival of Assyria. The most formidable threat, however, lay to the northwest. The Hittites, with their chariots and iron weapons, were an aggressive, expansive power. Under Mursilis I (1550–1530 B.C.), the Hittites not only conquered Syria but also sacked Babylon.

Assyrian Army

Assyria answered the threats confronting her by creating a professional, standing army. Assuruballit I (1366–1331 B.C.) reorganized the army according to weapon type: chariots, infantry, and engineers—including sappers and siege artillery. While his opponents emphasized the chariot, Assuruballit made the heavy infantry the core of his army. Following the Hittite example, he armed his soldiers with iron weapons and provided them with light body armor.

Assuruballit marshaled his troops in formations according to branch. The smallest unit consisted of ten men. Building on the basic unit of ten, formations of 100 (company), 1,000 (regiment), and field armies of 120,000 or more were mobilized.

Information on Assyrian military tactics is fragmentary. On the strategic level, the Assyrians proved themselves masters at exploiting terrain to the best advantage. In Mesopotamia, for example, the Assyrians used the rivers and canals not only for logistical purposes but also to screen movements, to provide flank protection, and to channel enemy movements. The Assyrians also developed riverine and amphibious warfare capabilities, as demonstrated by the campaigns of Sennacherib (705–682 B.C.) against the Elamites.

Assyrian Expansion

Assyrian expansion occurred in two distinct phases: the Middle Assyrian Empire and the New Assyrian Empire.

Middle Assyrian Empire, 1356–1209 B.C.

Enlilnirari I (1330–1321 B.C.), son of Assuruballit, established the unalterable, central principle of Assyrian policy in Mesopotamia: control of Babylonia. Although Enlilnirari succeeded in reducing Babylonia to vassalage, his successors were frequently required to remind the Babylonians of their duty to Assyria.

Under Adadnirari I (1308–1276 B.C.) the Assyrians first clashed with the Hittites. The Assyrian conquest of Mitanni, a Hittite vassal, provoked numerous border skirmishes. Although the bulk of the Hittite forces were engaged in the ongoing struggle with Ramses II of Egypt over control of Syria and Palestine, the Hittites were too strong to be challenged directly.

Blocked by the Hittites to the northwest, Shalmaneser I (1275–1246 B.C.) attempted to expand northward at the expense of the Urartu, a tribal confederacy. His operations met with only limited success. Tukultininurita I (1245–1209 B.C.), angered by Babylonian collusion with the Hittites, crushed the Kassites, thereby ending their 450-year rule over southern Mesopotamia. Babylonia was incorporated into Assyria as a province and Tukultininurita took for himself the ancient title of the kings of Babylon, "King of Sumer and Akkad."

The disintegration of the Hittite Empire around 1200 B.C. offered Assyria an opportunity to expand westward to the Mediterranean Sea. Assyria, however, came under attack from Aramean and Chaldean tribesmen moving eastward from Syria. From 1200 to 1117 B.C., Assyria fought to survive against these new invaders as well as a reinvigorated Babylon.

NEW ASSYRIAN EMPIRE, 1115–612 B.C.

The first great king of the New Assyrian Empire was Tiglathpileser I (1115–1077 B.C.), who accomplished what his predecessors had been unable to do: conquer Syria to the Mediterranean coast. He also reimposed Assyrian suzerainty over the troublesome Babylonians.

Tiglathpileser was the ruler to initiate the terror tactics that have become synonymous with the name Assyria: the mass deportation of conquered people, or their mass execution by immurement, flaying alive, or impalement. Faced with barbarian invaders and rebellious vassals, the Assyrians employed barbarous means of coercion.

Tukultininurita II (890–884 B.C.) continued the policies of his ancestors. His great innovation was the introduction of cavalry, which was done in response to the depradations caused by a new wave of invading Indo-European cavalrymen, ancestors of the later Medes and Persians.

Tiglathpileser III (745–728 B.C.) extended Assyrian power over most of Asia Minor and Palestine to the Egyptian border.

Shalmaneser V (726–722 B.C.) suppressed a rebellion by the Arameans of Damascus and their ally, the Kingdom of Israel. Israel was destroyed and its people deported to northern Mesopotamia. Sargon II (722–705 B.C.) defeated the Elamites and brought the Babylonians to heel once again.

Sennacherib (705–682 B.C.) added no new territory to the empire. He did reassert Assyrian suzerainty over the Kingdom of Judah (Judea) and devastated Elam in the 690s B.C. Against Babylon, Sennacherib took drastic measures. In 689 B.C., he ordered the ancient city destroyed and forbade its rebuilding for 80 years.

Esarhaddon (681–670 B.C.) lifted his father's ban on Babylon in 679 B.C. and rebuilt the city on a grand scale. He also imposed Assyrian suzerainty over the Phoenician city of Sidon. Esarhaddon's most significant achievement was the conquest of northern (Lower) Egypt, completed in 671 B.C. with the occupation of Memphis. Esarhaddon, however, never completed his conquest of Egypt. He died in 670 B.C. while leading a new expedition against the Egyptians, and with him died the last period of Assyrian expansion.

Decline and Fall of Assyria

With the exception of Assurbanipal III (668–625 B.C.), under whom Mesopotamian civilization experienced its penultimate flowering, the last Assyrian kings were weak nonentities. In the summer of 612 B.C., Nineveh, the Assyrian capital, fell to the Medes and Babylonians. Although a junior member of the royal family attempted to revive Assyria, by 609 B.C. mighty Assyria was no more.

Cyaxares, king of the Medes, imposed his rule over the former Assyrian provinces of northern Mesopotamia and the vassal states of Asia Minor and Urartu.

Nabopolasser, founder of the Neo-Babylonian Empire, accepted the homage of the states of Syria and Palestine. His son, Nebuchadnezzar II (605–561 B.C.), destroyed the rebellious Kingdom of Judah in 586 B.C. and deported the Judeans to Babylon, where they remained until freed by Cyrus the Great.

LAWRENCE D. HIGGINS

SEE ALSO: History, Ancient Military; Persian Empire.

Bibliography

Olmstead A. T. E. 1908. *Western Asia in the days of Sargon of Assyria*. Ithaca: Cornell Univ. Press.
———. 1923. *History of Assyria*. New York: Scribner's.
Rigg, H. A. 1942. Sargon's "eighth military campaign." *Journal of the American Oriental Society* 62:130–38.
Saggs, H. W. F. 1962. *The greatness that was Babylon*. New York: New American Library (Mentor Books).
Smith, S. 1928. *Early history of Assyria to 1000 B.C.* London: Chatto and Windus.
Tadmor, H. 1958. The campaigns of Sargon II of Assur: A chronological-historical study. *Journal of Cuneiform Studies* 12:22–40; 77–100.
Wright, E. M. 1943. The eighth campaign of Sargon II of Assyria. *Journal of Near Eastern Studies* 2:173–86.

ATLANTIC-MEDITERRANEAN AREA

The Atlantic-Mediterranean region is one of the two great world regions (the other being the Pacific-Indian Ocean Region). It embraces the Western Hemisphere, the Atlantic Ocean, Europe, and Africa. Since this article treats this region in a geostrategic and military context, it is focused on the Atlantic and Mediterranean littoral nations within that area. However, because European nations have been the primary actors in most of the major wars in history, and because certain nonlittoral nations have been involved in many of these wars and have had Atlantic security interests, this article also includes Eastern European nations and the European area of the former USSR.

The Western Hemisphere consists of three subregions: North America, Central America, and South America. Europe consists of six subregions: Scandinavia and Great Britain, Western Europe, Central Europe, Eastern Europe, Southern Europe, and the European area of the former USSR. For topographic and ethnic reasons, Africa is customarily divided into North Africa and Sub-Saharan Africa.

The Atlantic Ocean is divided into the North Atlantic and the South Atlantic. The military significance of Africa pertains chiefly to the Mediterranean littoral, the Atlantic coast of Morocco, and South Africa.

Politico-Military Background

The Primacy of Conflict in Europe, and Its Expansion into the Atlantic

Europe has throughout history been the scene of major conflicts and wars. This is the result of several factors: the concentration in large numbers of different ethnic groups within a relatively small region; the early emergence of energetic, dynamic, and aggressively acquisitive peoples; the successive migrations and conflict-provoking contacts among very diverse ethnic groups; the early and persistent development of military technologies; and the failure to develop or to make permanent very large political units. In respect to the latter, the Roman Empire, the Holy Roman Empire, the French Empire under Napoleon, the Austro-Hungarian Empire, and the Union of Soviet Socialist Republics all collapsed in the face of the enormous diversity of ideas, religions, and cultural perspectives, and the remarkably dynamic, change-oriented vigor of the peoples of the area.

In place of empires, the peoples of modern Europe developed separate, often multiethnic nation-states, each organized under strong leaders, their authority usually sanctioned by divine right. Each took care that its rivals did not gain superior power. This often meant choosing war over compromise.

Beginning in the fifteenth century, Portugal discovered a sea route to India and the East Indies, while Spain opened the Atlantic route to the New World and the Pacific. In the following centuries, the Netherlands, England, and France followed. European wars took on an extra-European meaning as nations contended for colonies and trade: Spain against England, France, and Holland; Portugal against Spain; and France against England. The independence of the United States, in part a consequence of these rivalries, and British dominance of the seas after Napoleon's fall, ensured that Central and South American countries acquired independence from Spain and Portugal.

European Politics and the Balance of Power

Meanwhile, the rulers of the European powers, unimpeded by popular emotion, had learned to restrain the most powerful of them by the judicious forming of alliances. With the fall of Napoleon, the European nations restored and refined this balance of power system to ensure that no one country would dominate Europe. Each power shifted its alliances to ensure a balance of power, and thus preserve the peace. This resulted in European peace from 1815 until 1914, with the exception of the wars attending the unification of Germany (the Schleswig-Holstein Wars, 1848 and 1864; the Austro-Prussian War, 1866; the Franco-Prussian War, 1870–71).

The system broke down because of the fragile balance of power, leaders' errors in assessing the relative power of states with precision, and fundamentally incompatible national aims. Additionally, Germany reached nationhood much later than the other major states, thus missing an "equitable" opportunity to acquire colonial territories and overseas trade. The dynamic, aggressive rise of German power, a period of strong nationalism, ethnic unrest in the Austro-Hungarian Empire, intense competition for colonies, and the resultant hardening of the opposing alliances (the Triple Alliance and the Triple Entente)—all were major contributing causes. Finally, the close proximity of dynamic nations placed a high premium on the capacity of all to mobilize and strike fast in the event of perceived danger. All these conditions led to World War I.

After World War I, the formation of new (and resurrection of old) smaller states with ethnic minorities, together with the formation of a communist Russia, so different in ideology from its neighbors, sowed the seeds for further conflict. The causes of World War II include perceived economic inequities, ethnic irredentism, ideological polarization, and the failure of leaders to act decisively to preserve the balance of power when it threatened to break down.

After World War II, the Western European nations, unable to deter or balance the enormous military power of the Eastern bloc, turned to the United States as the "balancer." A bipolar strategic balance was created, relying on the awesome deterrence value of nuclear weapons. The United States and the Western European nations formed the North Atlantic Treaty Organization (NATO) and established a multinational defensive posture in Central Europe. Under the leadership of the USSR, the Warsaw Pact, comprising most of the nations of Eastern Europe, was formed to face the NATO forces. This uneasy confrontation endured for over 40 years. Only after the rise to power of Mikhail Gorbachev in the USSR, and the breakup of the USSR, has a significant change begun to occur in the size and structure of these opposing forces.

This unprecedented peacetime system of forward deployments, backed by strategic and tactical nuclear deterrence systems, maintained peace between these blocs. In the light of the enormous changes underway in Eastern Europe, the future suggests the real possibility that this bipolar confrontation will gradually be supplanted by a more diversely structured Eastern and Western Europe, with many of its countries less ideologically polarized, perhaps within a broadened form of European Economic Community. The relation of the now independent parts of the former Soviet Empire to this Europe will continue to evolve for some time. The precise lines of this development are still obscure, depending on internal Soviet change as much as on such imponderables as the future of the united Germanies.

The progress of the European Economic Community toward a single market, and even possibly political confederation, will be fundamentally affected by the changes in Eastern Europe that began in 1989. Whether strengthening of the European Economic Community with its present membership accelerates because of these events, or a broader, less integrated European Community will emerge, can strongly affect both European stability and the military mission, size, and force structure of the one-time alliances.

In the Western hemisphere, most conflict has been more localized. However, five major wars occurred after the wars of independence in the nineteenth century: the United States–Mexican War (1846–48); Peru's war with Spain (1864–66); the War of the Pacific between Peru and Bolivia against Chile (1879); the War of the Triple Alliance (1865–70), Paraguay against Argentina, Uruguay, and Brazil; and the Spanish-American War (1898).

The first of these resulted from a period of American nationalism and belief in its destiny to become a great power—this in a period of political weakness, corrupt leadership, and stagnant development in Mexico. In the peace settlement of the U.S.–Mexican war, Mexico lost more than one-third of its territory to the United States; the result was a century of distrust and hostility. Only since the administration of Pres. Franklin D. Roosevelt did Mexico renew friendly relations with the United States, and American intervention elsewhere in Latin America has permanently complicated its relations with that area. The Alliance for Progress under Pres. John F. Kennedy greatly facilitated a new acceptance of American purposes and cooperation among the nations of the area. The Organization of American States (OAS) has opened a new era in efforts to bring peace to the subregion.

In the War of the Pacific, Peru lost its southern provinces and Bolivia lost its Pacific coastline to Chile. In the War of the Triple Alliance, Paraguay lost over half its population in a remarkable struggle against overwhelming odds, and took decades to recover. (In 1935 Paraguay also fought and won another exhausting war—the Chaco War—against Bolivia.)

The Spanish-American War began as a Cuban war of independence. The United States sided with the Cuban rebels in a domestic atmosphere of patriotic fervor. Spain lost the Philippine Islands and Puerto Rico to the United States, and Cuba gained its independence. The Philippines remained an American dependency until granted independence in 1946. In 1903, the United States acted to ensure that Panama gain its independence from Colombia, then built the Panama Canal through its territory, connecting the Atlantic and Pacific Oceans. In 1979 the United States ratified a treaty with Panama, neutralizing the Panama Canal and agreeing to yield sovereignty over it to Panama on 31 December 1999.

Since World War I, Latin America has played a significant economic role, and a lesser military role, throughout the Atlantic area. Brazil deployed a division to Europe in World War II and provided major airbases for the United States. Argentinian and Chilean naval forces also supported the Western Allied effort.

In 1982, Argentina invaded the Falklands/Malvinas, which it had claimed ever since Britain occupied them early in the nineteenth century. Britain defeated and expelled the Argentine forces in an amphibious operation conducted over an enormous distance. The United States, after futilely seeking a compromise, finally secretly supported Britain diplomatically and with munitions and communications assistance.

The North Atlantic and Mediterranean Areas: Politico-military Role in the Twentieth Century

Since the beginning of this century, Atlantic and Mediterranean waters have played a major role both in the economic development of nations and in the nature, locus and scope of politico-military conflict. Beginning with the Algeciras Conference in Spain (1906–1907), French, German, and Spanish rivalry resulted in the French and Spanish partition and annexation of Morocco and German occupation of Cameroon, while Britain consolidated its domination of Egypt. During World War I, Britain landed forces in Turkey and with its Middle East campaign supplanted Turkey as the dominant force among the Arab states of that area. Italy, in the same period, annexed Libya, and in 1935 conquered Ethiopia. Both countries regained their independence with the defeat of Italy in World War II.

The North Atlantic was of critical importance to the outcome of both world wars. In World War I it was the route by which the United States and Canada deployed their forces to Europe and augmented the supplies of France and Britain. In World War II the American supply lines saved Britain from defeat. The American and Canadian forces convoyed to Europe played a critical part in the defeat of Germany and Italy. They and the British were supported by French, Polish, and Dutch forces, which were equipped mainly with American and some British arms and materiel. Both Britain and the United States sent vast quantities of war materiel to the Soviet Union via Murmansk and Arkangel. The German submarine assault on these numerous convoys made the North Atlantic a critical area of warfare in both world wars.

Military Geography

The Atlantic Ocean Area

In time of conflict, the Atlantic Ocean area, because of the enormous space and distances involved, requires the operation of very large naval, sea, and air forces which can remain at sea over periods of months. They must incorporate accompanying seaborne logistic support means, as well as a strong support system in their home ports. Atlantic navies must maintain equivalent home-based forces or force components which can rotate to ensure a continuously sustained ready posture. Western Ally and U.S. commands (see "Regional Alliances and Collective Security Arrangements" below) currently control such forces. They also must be complemented by large merchant fleets, largely privately owned, which in wartime are put to the single-minded mission of sustaining the war effort.

The American, Canadian, and Latin American naval forces deployed in the Atlantic rely upon exceptionally numerous and highly developed ports. The Atlantic coast of the Western Hemisphere is blessed with innumerable rivers, bays, gulfs, and harbors superbly suited to these purposes: in Canada, Montreal, Quebec, and Halifax; in the United States, Boston, New York, Philadelphia, Baltimore, Norfolk, Wilmington, Charleston, Jacksonville, Miami, and New Orleans; in Brazil, Bahia, Rio de Janeiro, and Santos; and in Argentina, the La Plata estuary (Buenos Aires). Chile, though a Pacific nation, regularly operates naval forces in the Atlantic. Among its major ports are Valparaiso, Concepción, and Punta Arenas.

On the European Atlantic littoral the major ports are: Belfast, Edinburgh, Glasgow, Bristol, Portsmouth, Dartmouth, Southampton, and London in Britain; Bremerhaven and Wilhelmshaven in West Germany; Rotterdam in the Netherlands; Antwerp in Belgium; Le Havre and Bordeaux in France; and La Coruña and Cadiz in Spain. The main African Atlantic ports are Casablanca, Morocco; the Gambia, Senegal; Freetown, Sierra Leone; Port Harcourt and Accra, Nigeria; Brazzaville, the Congo; and Cape Town in the Union of South Africa. Except for Cape Town and Casablanca, the importance of the African ports in a major war is chiefly for access to critical raw materials, and as refueling stations.

The Mediterranean area has innumerable important bases and ports: Marseilles, France; Algeciras, Ceuta, Málaga, and Barcelona in Spain; Genoa, Livorno, Naples, Catania, Palermo, Messina, Reggio Calabria, and Venice in Italy; Trieste and Split in Yugoslavia; Piraeus (Athens) and Salonika in Greece; Istanbul and Izmir in Turkey; Latakia, Syria; Beirut, Lebanon; Nicosia, Cyprus; Herakion, Crete; Haifa, Israel; Port Said and Alexandria in Egypt; Benghazi, Libya; Tunis, Tunisia; Algiers and Oran, Algeria; and Tangier, Morocco.

European Military Geography

European military geography can best be treated by subregions. There are vital chokepoints controlling access to the European landmass. In the north the Arctic and White sea approaches to Murmansk and Arkangel, as well as the Atlantic approaches to the Orkneys and Shetland Island areas, are critical to the operation of Russian, Western European, American, and Canadian surface and submarine forces and shipping. The English Channel, North Sea, and Skaggerak-Kattegat Straits are critical to the West and Central European and Scandinavian countries. Opposing forces must in wartime seek to control these waters.

On the continent, the major military geographic features are: the very advanced highway and rail systems; the Rhine River as an avenue for communications and transport, as well as an obstacle in land warfare; the estuary, swamp, and river-dominated lowlands of the Netherlands and Belgium; the relatively open, rolling tank-friendly terrain of northern and southwestern France and northern Germany; the heavily forested, hilly, rugged terrain of central and southern Germany and Czechoslovakia, which is nonetheless suitable for large-scale mobile land warfare; and the flat plains and enormous distances from the eastern half of Germany through Poland and European Russia and the Ukraine. In the latter, the Volga River is a dominant feature, both as an obstacle and as a transportation route. The road network in the former USSR is extensive but primitive when compared with that in central and western Europe. The rail network is extensive, and far more important than trucking as compared with the rest of Europe. Western defense in Europe is hampered by the short distances to the seas.

A continuous chain of high mountains separates southern and southeastern Europe from the rest of the continent. This, combined with the northern indentations of the Mediterranean Sea, dictates the need to fight on separate fronts in a major war, and consequently the fundamental importance of the Mediterranean as an access route. In the north, the unique position of Britain, protected as well as isolated from the continent by water, allows it to serve as a relatively secure base and logistics zone in wartime. The English Channel tunnel, due to open in 1993, will be an important supplementary supply route, but only if its French terminus is in friendly hands and the entrances and approaches are well protected against hostile air action.

The Mediterranean subregion is of critical military importance. Its main significance has long been as a supply route and avenue for deploying forces on the European continent. Its military geography has taken on new importance as the Arab nations, since the founding of Israel, have assumed important roles on the international scene. The North African coastal zone is important for its ports, now useable not simply as entrepots, but for the operation of small, swift naval craft. The northern rim of the Sahara Desert, from Algeria to the Suez Canal, remains a military route for gaining control of the ports, airbase sites, and access to the Middle East.

Strategic Significance

The Region

The Atlantic-Mediterranean Region is strategically the primary world region because of the high industrial production, economic development, and military strength of countries within the region, as well as the extent of international trade. This would be particularly important in the event of a major war.

The Atlantic shipping lanes are by far the busiest of any ocean. Moreover, the exposed position of West European countries and their industry require reliance on the United States and Canada to serve as arsenals and protectors of these routes of commerce. This region contains a preponderance of raw materials critical to warmaking. Most uranium, used in nuclear weapons, is mined in Africa and in the former USSR. The primary source of petroleum is the Middle East, and most of this is transported via pipeline and the Suez Canal through the Mediterranean to the Atlantic Ocean. Other important petroleum sources are Russia, North Africa, Nigeria, and Mexico. Most iron sources are located in the United States, Brazil, and the former USSR. Most steel is fabricated in the United States, the former USSR, and the two Germanies.

The Atlantic Ocean

The narrow accesses to the Atlantic Ocean—from the Mediterranean through the straits of Gibraltar, and from the Pacific Ocean through the Panama Canal—would be risky to use in wartime. For example, for a hostile power to use the Panama Canal in wartime would require a major military operation; but a hostile power could easily deny use of the canal to a friendly power by air action or blockade. The only "easy" (i.e., that could not be readily closed) sea access to the Atlantic Ocean from the Indian Ocean is south and east around the Cape of Good Hope and the tip of South Africa; from the Pacific Ocean to the south and west around Cape Horn and through the Drake Passage off the tip of South America. Within the Atlantic, the North Atlantic is the primary subregion, though important food products and some manufacturing, including significant amounts of military equipment, are transported from Latin America. Winter weather severely hampers ocean traffic. Icebergs south of Greenland and northeast Canada severely inhibit shipping operations in winter.

There are relatively few islands in the North Atlantic (the Caribbean Islands, really part of the Western Hemisphere, are an exception), especially beyond the continental shelves. Aside from Iceland, in the extreme north, only Bermuda and the Azores are plausible bases, or obstacles which must be controlled or neutralized to protect the advance of military forces. The great distance across the North Atlantic, averaging 4,300 kilometers (2,700 mi.), requires that all but strategic air forces be based in the Eastern Hemisphere for a conflict in Europe. Similarly, only strategic (long-range) Europe-based aircraft can reach the Western Hemisphere. Because of the lack of mid-ocean islands, the United States relies upon a friendly Brazil for bases. The distance from northeastern Brazil to western Africa (Senegal) is about 2,560 kilometers (about 1,600 mi.).

Continental Europe

Europe is the strategic heart of the region. The maritime powers (chiefly the West European powers) must preserve their territorial integrity to ensure the industrial and trading bases of their strength. In wartime, they exploit their character as seapowers to control trade and to deploy their forces to capitalize upon their naval mobility. The essentially landlocked nations of central and eastern Europe, as well as those of the former USSR, are compelled by geography to break through to the seas and the ocean by means of land warfare (supported, of course, by airpower). The inherent advantage of maritime nations in a long war compels the landlocked nations (if not allied with maritime powers) to strike fast and seek early victory in war. This unchanging geostrategic fact goes far to explain the successes of Germany in the early stages of both world wars, and its eventual defeat when it was unable to win the war early.

The Mediterranean Subregion

The Mediterranean Sea is the world's largest inland sea. Its maximum dimensions are about 3,840 kilometers (about 2,400 mi.) long by about 1,600 kilometers (1,000 mi.) wide, but the width at most points is much less. It includes numerous bays and seas, and many rivers empty into it. Among the many nations that border it, hostility is common. The Mediterranean is of critical importance in a major war, as a supply route and as a route for forces entering continental Europe. For this reason, and because it controls access to and from the Black Sea and the Asian waters beyond the Suez Canal, an early struggle in wartime to control its waters and the airspace above it is basic to success. In peace as well as in war, rival nations seek access to, if not control of, its waters. Currently, the United States, Britain, France, and Italy maintain major maritime forces there, while Russia and the Ukaine keep a smaller naval force in the Mediterranean, and Turkey and Greece also have small but competent navies.

For ready forward deployment of airpower, carrier forces must be deployed in the Mediterranean in peacetime. It demands active submarine and antisubmarine operations. As in any confined waters, disastrous naval actions can readily occur. A complicating factor is that because of the constant threat and actuality of small wars, all Mediterranean nations maintain significant naval and air forces. These forces are configured for such wars. Uncertainty about their posture and military alignments in wartime complicates strategic calculations for the major powers, who must rely heavily upon diplomacy and threats to neutralize this possible source of strategic uncertainty.

The chokepoints of the Turkish Straits (Dardanelles, Sea of Marmora, and Bosporus), the Suez Canal, and the Strait of Gibraltar are in peacetime open to the naval forces of all nations (the first has special rules of notification). In wartime their control and denial are basic to competing strategies.

Regional Alliances and Collective Security Arrangements

The three regional security arrangements discussed below are paralleled and supplemented by an extensive and complex set of bilateral security treaties.

The North Atlantic Treaty Organization (NATO)

This treaty was formalized under Article 51 of the United Nations Charter, in April 1949, by Belgium, Canada, Denmark, France, Britain, Iceland, Italy, Luxembourg, the Netherlands, Norway, Portugal, and the United States. Greece and Turkey joined in 1952, the Federal Republic of Germany in 1955, and Spain in 1980 (France partially withdrew in 1966). The treaty provided for a common defense, primarily because of the threat created by the USSR in occupying and influencing the governments of some of the East European countries, as well as establishing formidable military forces on their territories. Under the North Atlantic Treaty Organization (NATO), a multinational forward-based European land and tactical air force was soon established, under the command of an American (Supreme Allied Commander, Europe, or SACEUR). It includes a naval counterpart, the Atlantic Command, also under an American commander (Supreme Allied Commander, Atlantic, or SACLANT). The NATO forces are backed up by a strategic nuclear force of American and British aircraft and missiles, which is complemented by an equivalent, independent French force.

The European Command extends from Norway's North Cape to the Mediterranean Sea, and from the Atlantic Ocean to the eastern border of Turkey. The Atlantic Command extends from the North Pole to the Tropic of Cancer, and from the Atlantic coast of North America to the coasts of Europe and Africa.

The Warsaw Treaty Organization

The Warsaw Treaty Organization was formally created at Warsaw, Poland, in 1955, under Soviet leadership and pressure. The immediate stimulus was the remilitarization of West Germany under the Paris Pacts of 1954, and its incorporation into NATO in 1955. The signatories of the Warsaw Treaty were Albania, Bulgaria, Czechoslovakia, East Germany, Hungary, Poland, Romania, and the Soviet Union (Albania withdrew in 1968 in protest against the invasion of Czechoslovakia). The treaty provided a formalized legal framework for the already-existing presence of military forces, principally Soviet forces, in Eastern Europe. It provided the basis for a multinational force under unified Soviet command. The Warsaw Treaty Organization was disbanded 1 April 1991.

The Organization of American States

The Organization of American States (OAS), formed in 1948, and now including all nations of the Western Hemisphere, has no military component or counterpart. It serves chiefly as an institutional umbrella for the use of diplomacy and public pressure to resolve disputes among its members, to forestall conflicts, or to bring wars to an end. It has repeatedly opposed the unilateral use of force, but has characteristically been cautious about the adoption of sanctions.

Recent Conflicts

Central Europe

The following uses of force involved the suppression of resistance related to Soviet occupation of Eastern Europe or to oppression by Soviet-installed regimes.

In 1948–49, the Soviet Union, using East German forces, blockaded the land approaches to West Berlin in an attempt to force an end to Western Allied control of the city. The U.S. Air Force (assisted by the British Royal Air Force) airlift into West Berlin of some 8,000 tons per day over fifteen months induced the Soviet Union to lift the blockade.

In East Berlin in 1953, a general strike and popular riots were suppressed by Soviet armored forces.

In October 1956, an uprising in Hungary against communist and Soviet domination occurred when a reform government declared Hungary neutral and sought to withdraw from the Warsaw Pact. This was suppressed by Soviet armored forces, "invited" to invade by a Soviet-installed puppet government. The reform premier, Imre Nagy, was arrested, tried, and executed by the puppet Kadar regime.

After popular demonstrations in Prague, Czechoslovakia (1968), a reform communist regime took power and introduced elements of democracy. As a result, Soviet, Polish, and Hungarian forces invaded Czechoslovakia, overthrew the regime, and suppressed popular resistance. The reformist premier, Alexander Dubček, was arrested and removed from the party.

The Mediterranean Area

The most important and frequent recent conflicts in this area have involved Israel and various Arab states over the issue of a homeland for the Palestinians, and the related civil war. Since its creation as a state in 1948, Israel has been engaged in four wars (1948–49, 1956, 1967, and 1973) over the status of Palestine as well as in intermittent guerrilla warfare in border regions. Since 1987, Israel has been faced with a low-key but persistent Palestinian uprising in the West Bank and Gaza areas.

The origins of the Lebanese Civil War lie, first, in centuries-old hostilities among the diverse religious sects of the region; second, in the Christian majority control of the government and armed forces in a period when the Muslim population outnumbers the Christians; and, third, the arrival in Lebanon of major elements of the Palestine Liberation Organization forces, after their expulsion from Jordan in 1971. In 1973 there was widespread fighting between the Lebanese army and the Palestinians. In 1975, civil war ensued, leading eventually to the virtual paralysis of governmental authority. Among many factions engaged in fighting are the Christian militia of north central Lebanon, the Amal (Druze) forces, the Iran-sponsored Hezbollah Shiite zealots, the Syrian military, the Lebanese military, and an Israeli-armed puppet Lebanese force in southern Lebanon. The Israeli invasion of 1982, in response to repeated local incursions of Palestinian guerrillas into northern Israel, resulted in the Israeli capture of Beirut and the expulsion of the Palestine Liberation Organization forces from Lebanon. For a variety of complex reasons, however, the Israeli invasion failed to achieve stability, and Israeli forces withdrew from all except southern Lebanon.

Another war in the Mediterranean was fought between Greece and Turkey (1963–74). In response to a strong movement in Cyprus (encouraged by the military regime in Greece) for union with Greece, Turkey mobilized to protect the large Turkish minority in Cyprus. Greece also mobilized, but its military regime soon fell, leaving Greek Cypriot forces without military support. The Turkish army landed in Cyprus and soon controlled the northern half of the island. The resulting peace settlement allowed Turkish forces to remain in the area they occupied.

Future

Any analysis of history and recent happenings suggests that conflict will continue in the Atlantic-Mediterranean region. The likelihood of major superpower conflict and confrontation seems much diminished, but the world can expect continued strife in the Middle East, in Central and Eastern Europe, and perhaps on the northern coast of Africa. The conflicts are likely to be smaller, but there will be continuing terrorism. This region will continue to contain unresolved sources of conflict: boundary disputes; Arab-Israeli hostilities; ethnic and national independence movements; rivalry for predominance in a region; and resentment of migrants crossing borders to flee violence, prejudice, or poor economic conditions. All these sources of tension may be made more critical by the spread of nuclear, chemical, and biological weapons. Thus, although the threat of a major world war has diminished, that will be of little consolation to those caught in the crossfire of smaller conflicts in this region.

For the most recent information, on this region, the reader may refer to the following annual publications:

The Military Balance. International Institute for Strategic Studies. London: Brassey's (UK).

The Stateman's Year-Book. New York: St. Martin's Press.

The World Factbook. Central Intelligence Agency. Washington, D.C.: Brassey's (US).

PAUL C. DAVIS

Bibliography

Chaliand, G., and J. P. Rageau. 1985. *Strategic atlas: A comparative geopolitics of the world's powers.* New York: Harper and Row.

De Porte, A. W. 1986. *Europe between the superpowers: The enduring balance.* New Haven, Conn.: Yale Univ. Press.

Keegan, J., and A. Wheatcroft. 1986. *Zones of conflict: An atlas of future wars.* New York: Simon and Schuster.

Nitze, P., and L. Sullivan. 1978. *Securing the seas: Soviet naval challenge and Western Alliance options.* Washington, D.C.: Atlantic Council of the United States.

Rouse, F. C., ed. 1977. *To use the sea: Readings in seapower and maritime affairs.* Annapolis, Md.: U.S. Naval Institute Press.

Snyder, J. C. 1987. *Defending the fringe: NATO, the Mediterranean and the Persian Gulf.* Baltimore, Md.: School of Advanced International Affairs, Johns Hopkins Univ. Press.

Snyder, L. L. 1960. *The war: A concise history, 1939–1945.* New York: Julian Messner.

Stokesbury, J. L. 1981. *A short history of World War I.* New York: Morrow.

ATTACHE, MILITARY

A military attache is an officer sent abroad as a member of an embassy or legation staff. Although he advises the ambassador and represents his country's armed forces at official functions, his primary duty is to observe, evaluate, and report on military activities in the country in which he is stationed. The attache studies developments in military technology, organization, theory, and doctrine by using information from open sources. His reports are important components of military intelligence and affect national defense planning.

History

Although the word *attache* is of modern derivation, and the assignment of officers with that title is a relatively recent historical development, the functions of attaches have been carried out in various guises for centuries. The need for military information is as old as armies. In one of the earliest recorded examples, Moses sent twelve spies, one for each of Israel's tribes, into Canaan. These men were to evaluate the military potential of the inhabitants and report on the topography and resources of the country. Attaches are not spies but seek essentially the same type of information.

More immediate precursors of the military attache were the specialized military observers who appeared in Europe during the wars of coalition in the seventeenth and eighteenth centuries. Subsidies were an important feature of coalition war, and the nations providing financial support to their allies began to send officers to allied armies to ensure that the money was spent for the purpose for which it was intended.

The first true military attache was appointed by Napoleon. In 1806, Bonaparte sent a captain to the French embassy in Vienna to serve as the second secretary. The captain was ordered to keep accurate and detailed information on the location of Austrian regiments. He did so with an index card file, and his findings were reported every month to the French general staff. This officer was the precursor of the modern military attache because he was the first soldier assigned to engage in constant and systematic observation of a potential enemy. Other nations soon recognized the value of this activity, and a Prussian military attache appeared in that country's embassy in Paris in 1830. The United States did not follow suit until 1889, when American officers were sent to Berlin, Paris, London, Rome, and Vienna.

Initially the European powers sent military representatives to one another, but soon smaller and even militarily insignificant states received accredited attaches. Small states sent officers to large states because the latter were military innovators, but large states often sent attaches to the former to emphasize the former's client status. The Russian attache in Serbia, for example, did not realistically hope to learn anything of value from the Serbian army but was there as a demonstration to the other powers of Russian influence and interest in that Balkan country.

Sending attaches abroad does not ensure that the intelligence they procure will be acted on or even believed. Prussian attaches sent detailed and accurate reports to their government before the Austro-Prussian War of 1866 and the Franco-Prussian War of 1870. The intelligence in these reports was the cornerstone of each Prussian victory. Before the Franco-Prussian War, conversely, the French ignored the reports of their attache in Berlin, with predictable consequences. One explanation of the poor performance of British arms in the early stages of the Boer War is that the high command ignored attache reports that warned of Boer military preparations and decried the lack of British strength in South Africa.

By the outbreak of World War I in 1914, 305 service attaches were on duty around the world. Of these, 214 were military attaches and 85 were naval attaches. Most were accredited to Berlin, which is an indication of the regard with which the world held the German military. The size of individual countries' attache corps varied. The United States, for example, had one of the most active attache corps and sent 23 military attaches to other countries. No other country had more, although several had as many (Vagts 1967).

The end of World War I and the subsequent disillusionment with the military temporarily focused public attention on attaches. Socialists and pacifists had long urged the abolition of the post because they equated attaches with militarism. The victors in World War I agreed with this equation as it applied to the Central Powers, not to themselves. They did not eliminate their own attaches, but in Article 179 of the Treaty of Versailles forced the Germans to agree not "to send to any foreign country any military, naval, or air mission, nor to allow any such mission to leave [German] territory."

Despite the temporary decline in military attaches following World War I, technical advances in warfare during and after the war, such as the development of airpower and increased mechanization, led many nations to expand and specialize their attache corps.

The number of attaches and their average rank crept upward in the 1930s. In the nineteenth century, the attache was usually a lieutenant or captain. After World War I, attaches were often colonels, major generals, or even lieutenant generals. Higher rank went with the perceived prestige of a post. Great powers sent high-ranking officers to one another, whereas a second- or third-rate military power could expect to receive a relatively low-ranking officer from a militarily preeminent state.

The slow but deliberate inflation of rank reflected two important trends. First, the importance of military affairs in formulating national policy was bcoming more widely appreciated in the capitals of the world. Second, attaches are members of their country's embassy staff. Diplomatic protocol is based on rank, not competence, so a high rank is always given precedence over a low rank. High rank ensures that a military representative is treated with the respect he and his country deserve.

The tendency for nations to send large numbers of attaches abroad continued in the cold war. One reason was the misperception that more attaches meant more information. Information itself took on a heightened importance with the advent of atomic weapons and the formation of permanent alliances like the North Atlantic Treaty Organization (NATO) and the Warsaw Pact. Accurate prediction of a potential enemy's intentions seemed more likely if more attaches were trying to deduce those intentions.

Contemporary military attaches are members of the diplomatic community and are so recognized under international law. The Vienna Convention on Diplomatic Relations of April 1961 codifies the practice of centuries. Diplomats enjoy certain privileges and immunities in their work. Attaches, as members of the diplomatic staff, have the same protection. They are immune from the criminal and civil processes of the host government, which means that they cannot be arrested, tried, or otherwise subjected to local jurisdiction. They have the right to travel freely, except where laws and regulations prohibit their entry into militarily sensitive areas (Article 26). Attaches enjoy freedom of communication under the convention. Official correspondence is privileged, and the diplomatic bag in which it is sent cannot, except under exceptional and carefully defined circumstances, be opened or detained (Article 27).

A country is not forced to accept the officers another country wishes to send as attaches. The convention recognizes the right of the receiving state to require the names of prospective attaches and to approve them before they are posted (Article 7).

Should an attache engage in improprieties, the host country cannot take direct action against him. Nonetheless, a state is not powerless to deal with foreign officers who spy or commit crimes while members of a foreign embassy staff. The convention provides that in the event an attache becomes undesirable, for whatever reason, the host country can declare him a persona non grata and demand and secure his recall (Article 9). Consequently, the attache has wide legal protection but also has a great responsibility to ensure that his activities—both on and off duty—are beyond reproach. Being declared a persona non grata and recalled is the end of an attache's career and may be the beginning of a diplomatic incident.

Functions

Attaches are not posted randomly, but the countries to which they are sent are chosen for different reasons. One country may be a potential enemy. Information on that state's current military capability, probable future capability, and intentions is critical to the national planning and defense structure of the state sending the attache.

Another country may be a military innovator. Information from an innovator is used to improve the attache's own armed forces and not necessarily to neutralize the armed forces of the host state. The purpose of intelligence collection in these circumstances is cooperation, not confrontation.

A third country may be sent an attache to improve diplomatic and military relations by establishing a close liaison between the countries' services. In this capacity the attache acts as a "military diplomat" by making contacts and encouraging cooperation between two armies.

Regardless of the reason he is posted, the attache's primary function is to collect intelligence. Secondarily, he advises the ambassador on military matters and represents his service to the corresponding service of the host country.

Despite a reputation to the contrary, attaches are not spies and are expected to collect information by overt means through open sources. Open sources include but are not limited to material distributed by official government agencies, including the armed forces, maneuvers and parades, lectures, newspapers, journal articles, travel within the host country, and informal conversations with national officers. Foreign colleagues in the attache corps are also valuable resources because they may have learned something different and would find an exchange of information beneficial.

Attaches gather information on two aspects of their host country's military forces. The first is current or actual military power, which comprises tangible and intangible elements. Tangibles are the things usually quantifiable and include the number of personnel under arms, quantity of equipment, and nature of fixed defenses and military installations. Intangibles are nonquantifiable and encompass methods and standards of recruitment and training, combat experience, quality of officers, quality of staff work, and existing military traditions (Kent 1949). The indications of potential military power include the state of military technology, nature of the economy and its capacity for growth, and birth rate.

A surprising amount of information is available for the asking, and reciprocity is the mechanism that enables attaches to work openly. A country provides the equivalent of information that it receives. As a general rule, all attaches posted overseas are regularly informed of the types of questions that their counterparts ask. With this list as a guide, an attache can justifiably argue that he should be given the same quality of information that his counterpart receives. The 1939 edition of the U.S. Army's *Standing Instructions for Military Attaches* provided that "An exact equivalent of information furnished is not necessarily required, but it is the practice to withhold information and to make desired visits when it is apparent that the government concerned is not inclined to grant our reasonable request."

The attache must work through the host country's military bureaucracy to obtain information directly from official sources. When the foreign officer arrives at his post, he is usually assigned a host officer who serves as his contact. This officer's job is to ensure that the attache's requests for material are met insofar as possible.

The arrangement has many advantages for both sides. The attache knows someone to whom he can address his questions, and the host country has a means of keeping records of the types of information each attache seeks. These records are useful when disputes arise, as they sometimes do, whether one country is supplying either more material or more sensitive material than another.

Attaches in a particular country need not be treated equally. The amount and quality of intelligence an attache secures is largely a function of the state of political relations between the two countries. As an illustration, before World War II Germany divided the foreign attaches in Berlin into four groups. Class I attaches were those with the best opportunity to gather useful information; class IV attaches had to rely on their counterparts in the attache corps for scraps. In March 1937, the Bulgarian, American, Hungarian, Italian, Japanese, Swedish, and Spanish attaches were in class I; class II comprised the British, Dutch, and Polish military representatives; class III members included the French and Czechoslovakian observers; and, as one might expect, the Soviet attache was in class IV. Favored attaches—those whose countries maintained "correct" relations with the Reich—were allowed to visit almost all combat formations after proper clearance. Those disfavored, like the Soviet attache, saw almost nothing.

The military attache can and does exchange information with other members of the attache corps. When he represents a neutral country with military representatives in two or more belligerents, he must guard against the appearance of impropriety. The attache's function is to collect information for his country, not act as a conduit for intelligence to the other side. Belligerent states often suspect neutral attaches of passing reports to the other side and thus restrict or eliminate access to sources. To ensure that their neutral military observers retain the trust so carefully established, many nations follow the practice of the United States, which, as a neutral in 1940, did not let the American attaches in belligerent capitals know what their colleagues were doing.

Attaches are recalled from prospective belligerents when hostilities are imminent. Recall does not mean that the attache corps in warring countries disappear. Neutrals maintain their presence and continue as before. Belligerents keep their attaches in neutral countries, and these nations often become "listening posts." War does not mean a lessening of attache activity; the work load increases, but the location changes. This circumstance was a common feature of both world wars.

As a Source of Military Information

Attendance at maneuvers is a valuable source of intelligence, and attaches seek invitations to these exercises whenever possible. Not only do they have an opportunity to see how units operate under near combatlike conditions but also they get an idea of an army's tactical doctrine.

Conclusions cannot be drawn indiscriminately. Maneuvers—or more accurately, the maneuvers to which attaches are invited—may be deceptive because they may involve second-line units or units equipped with obsolete equipment. If the attache is not able to tell the difference, he may draw the conclusion that the host country's troops are not sufficiently trained or are poorly armed. In addition to the participants and their equipment, the location and size of the maneuvers sometimes indicate their value. A maneuver that includes a small armored force in hilly terrain may not be as important as a maneuver with large armored forces over flat terrain.

Attaches also collect technological specifications of weapons and equipment. Frequently these details can be obtained from open sources, but exact technical specifications may not be available on prototype or recently introduced equipment. An educated guess is possible by viewing the hardware occasionally displayed in public. This method is most useful in totalitarian states where military parades are part of national celebrations. Foreign attaches in Berlin were able to deduce a surprising amount of technological data otherwise unavailable simply by watching the Wehrmacht's parades on Hitler's birthday or at Nazi party rallies.

Depending upon the country in which they serve, attaches may have a relatively unrestricted right of travel. Travel can be an important source of new information or confirmation of old. An observer can acquire a significant amount of knowledge just by noting the presence and type of local construction, general economic activity, presence and type of military units, and general condition of roads and bridges.

Military attaches receive many invitations to social functions and are expected to participate fully in the social life of the embassy or legation to which they are posted. Entertaining is not just a way to practice social graces; it is a way to establish and strengthen informal relationships with other officers. The attache does not expect to uncover state secrets at these gatherings, but he can and often does have an opportunity to determine whether personal opinions deviate from official positions and whether official positions are flexible.

The extent to which an attache can entertain is a function of the financial support he receives from his government. Until recently, such support was inconsistent. The officers whose governments did not give them lavish expense accounts had to rely on their own financial means, which, if their means were not limitless, resulted in a great disparity. Under the Third Reich, for example, the German government assumed the cost of the social obligations their attaches incurred. In contrast, in 1935 the U.S. government gave its military attache in Berlin US$500 for entertaining for the entire year. He split the money with the assistant military attaches because they also had to return social obligations (Hessen 1984).

One of the most important duties an attache can perform during war is observing battle. He cannot, of course, observe the army of a country with which his country is at war, but he may watch the efforts of his allies or of belligerents if his country is neutral. Frequently a belligerent will arrange tours of the front or areas close to the front for members of the attache corps. A trained observer can spot many details and make accurate inferences from them even though his tour is guided and may include only those things his hosts wish him to see.

Once an attache has accumulated facts, he must convey them to his intelligence bureaucracy. He does so by submitting reports to intelligence specialists for analysis, evaluation, and interpretation. The value of these documents is a function of how well they are prepared. The contemporary attache, unlike his predecessor, receives extensive training in how to write a succinct report. Training emphasizes accuracy and the attache's conclusions based on original thinking. Compilations of news clippings or copies of journal articles alone are insufficient. The attache is the officer on the scene, and his intelligence organization wants to know his ideas, concentrating on combat capability and intentions.

As Adviser to the Ambassador

The military attache advises his ambassador on military affairs. The value of this advice depends upon the relationship between the ambassador and the attache. Cooperation benefits both. If friction exists, the ambassador is free to disregard advice the attache gives him and indeed may not even feel the need to consult him at all. William Dodd, the American ambassador in Berlin before World War II, did not trust his military aides. He believed their training deficient, their grasp of social and political problems inadequate, and their ability to resist the appeal of Nazi military power nonexistent. Truman Smith, one of Dodd's military attaches, recalled that not once in two years did Dodd ask him for an evaluation of the pace and scope of German rearmament (Hessen 1984).

The official relationship between the attache and ambassador is not always sharply defined. The officer reports on military matters and is a member of the embassy staff and is subordinate to the civilian ambassador. The attache's ultimate loyalty is sometimes in question. Some ambassadors want to approve the attache's reports, especially those dealing with nonmilitary matters. Attaches and ambassadors may disagree on the significance of a particular event because they have different perspectives. Most often these problems are avoided or resolved with the attache routinely providing the ambassador with copies of reports that contain political or economic matters. Differences of opinion may be noted, but the attache must, in order to remain effective, send his own impressions and interpretations to his military intelligence analysts.

If the line between the attache and diplomat is occasionally blurred, so too is the distinction between a military and political report. Diplomats submit their own reports on political developments, and attaches do not duplicate these efforts. Sometimes, however, attaches must comment on political affairs because they are so closely related to military developments. Many countries today are under military rule, and reporting on the military is synonymous with reporting on local politics. Such "duplication" is not wasted effort because the attache's perspective differs from the diplomat's. The same fact is almost always interpreted and used differently by civilian political leaders and military intelligence specialists. The diplomat needs information to guide relations between his country and his host country; the attache needs it to protect the national security of his state.

Contemporary attaches enjoy greater autonomy within the embassy than their predecessors. One reason is the growing importance of security and military affairs in international relations. Just as increasing technological sophistication in warfare created the need for military attaches, the dominance of military considerations in post–World War II diplomacy encourages deference to defense specialists. Specialization promotes and fosters autonomy.

Other Functions

Besides gathering information for their governments, attaches have acted as impartial observers in the resolution of international disputes. In the most outstanding example, the British, French, and Italian attaches in Belgrade were invaluable in helping settle the Greco-Bulgarian border dispute of October 1925. The League of Nations appointed a commission to investigate the shooting of a Greek border guard and subsequent exchange of gunfire between Bulgarian and Greek troops, and the commission asked for help from the neutral attaches in Belgrade.

The officers went to the disputed area and interviewed participants on both sides in an effort to understand what had happened. They also supervised the temporary withdrawal of Greek and Bulgarian troops from the scene. The attaches contributed to settling the dispute because they were able to evaluate the military posture on both sides and recommend ways to prevent violence from recurring. Because this work was not that for which they were originally intended, the attaches asked for and received an allowance from the league to cover their expenses.

Just as the attache provides a valuable service in war by viewing battle, in peace he may be called upon to aid the cause of arms limitation. International disarmament conferences usually have current or former attaches attending as members of their country's delegation. One of the Russian representatives at the First Hague Peace Conference in 1899, Colonel Gilinsky, had been an attache with the Spanish army in Cuba during the Spanish-American War. Gilinsky proposed, on behalf of the czarist government, that the attending nations prohibit the manufacture of new guns for a period of years and that existing guns not be modified into automatic weapons.

Selection and Training

The ideal attache is able to determine the significance of what he sees and can spot subtle changes. He is imaginative in his search for sources of information and does not merely consult the most obvious. He can evaluate critically the information he obtains and distinguishes the credible from the noncredible. Finally, he has the patience and objectivity of a competent scholarly researcher (Kent 1949).

The ideal is rarely present in reality. Most officers serving as attaches have only a few or none of the ideal qualities. Part of the problem in attracting qualified officers has been the perception of the job. Attache duty was not regarded as important and in many armies was to be avoided as a career-damaging detour. In a few services attache duty was welcome not for the challenge, but because it promised "freedom, prestige, and fun with an undemanding job" (Kahn 1978). Because much of the attache's work is social and few governments gave their attaches the necessary financial support, only those officers with sufficient incomes outside their regular pay could accept the assignment. Some officers worked hard, but the perception that the military attache was nothing but a polo-playing aristocrat was widespread and too frequently based on fact.

Few officers had the broad military, political, and economic knowledge necessary to be an effective attache. Different criteria had to be found. The German army selected attaches on the basis of overall character, social skills of both the officer and his wife, pleasing physical appearance, military experience, and expertise in a military specialty. The ability to dance was desirable, as was a knowledge of art. In short, the prospective German attache had to be a "gentleman" (Halder et al. 1951).

At the same time, the U.S. Army was designating attaches similarly. In general, the best officer available was the one chosen, with consideration given to suitability and availability. Availability meant that he had no mandatory duty impending that would interfere with his ability to be overseas for three years. Curiously, knowledge of the host country's language was not a prerequisite. One school of thought held that such knowledge was invaluable, whereas another school maintained that attaches should not go too far in learning the customs of the host country. The danger of excessive familiarity was the tendency for the attache to evaluate facts from the perspective of the host country and not from his own. The American standards specifically included the need for an income independent of military pay because the U.S. government did not give its attaches an adequate expense account to cover the necessary social obligations.

Once the prospective attache was selected, he had to prepare for his post. Before World War II, little if any formal training was available. At best, a new attache may have been given some rudimentary instruction in how to code his messages and in basic office practices. This lack of preparation and training was not considered serious. General Franz Halder was satisfied with the performance of German attaches before World War II even though they had almost no training before they were sent abroad. Halder explained the apparent paradox by observing that the attaches "made up for their lack of systematic training by their own tireless efforts in the foreign country" (Halder et al. 1951).

The military attache today is a highly trained professional whose preparation and qualifications are impressive. He is no longer selected on superficial qualities such as appearance, and independent wealth is not a determining factor. Officers volunteering and selected for attache duty take courses in the administration of an attache office, diplomatic duties, security, and observation and reporting techniques. They also become familiar with the defense requirements and national security policies of their own country so that the attache knows the significance of what he sees and can estimate its importance in light of his country's defense objectives.

Training in observation and reporting emphasizes the overt nature of intelligence collection and stresses the attache's rights and obligations under the 1961 Vienna Convention. Preparation is not, however, narrowly focused on technical matters. The attache represents his service and his country and must live and work in a culture that may be strange. His effectiveness depends upon his ability to work with local people and feel at ease with their customs. The prospective attache learns about the history, geography, politics, culture, and armed forces of his new post. In this way, he is prepared to perform his duties efficiently on the first day of his assignment.

Future

The attache was formerly the only contact between his service and a foreign service. The contemporary proliferation of military assistance missions has made this aspect of the attache's work less important than it once was. These missions allow broader and more numerous contacts than one attache, or even an attache and several assistants, is likely to have.

To say that a major aspect of the attache's job has changed does not mean that he is no longer useful. Given the near indistinguishability of political and military matters, the attache may evolve into a politico-military expert rather than a collector of military information. Most officers are not currently prepared by education or training to assume this responsibility, so extensive education in political, economic, and social subjects would be required before the transition would be complete.

Despite this probable evolution, that attaches may eventually abandon their traditional intelligence-gathering duties seems unlikely, at least for the foreseeable future. The complexity of modern warfare requires information in unprecedented quantities. Attache reports are devoted to increasingly technologically sophisticated topics, and as a result attaches will become more specialized and their expertise more in demand. This trend will increase rather than diminish the importance of attaches, not only as liaisons between armed services but also as advisers to their ambassadors. Ambassadors, given their diplomatic duties, cannot hope to keep current on the quantum changes in military technology and their effects on the contemporary international system. The disappearance of the attache, therefore, is not likely. As long as nations believe that they need an armed force to survive in international politics, the attache's place is certain.

SCOTT A. KOCH

SEE ALSO: Intelligence Collection; Intelligence, General.

Bibliography

Bidwell, B. D. 1986. *History of the military intelligence division, department of the army general staff: 1775–1941.* Frederick, Md.: University Publications of America.

Geyr von Schweppenburg, L. 1952. *The critical years.* London: Allan Wingate.

Halder, F., E. von Rintelen, E. Koestring, and L. Buerkner. 1951. *Selection and training of German officers for military attache duty.* Washington, D.C.: U.S. Army Historical Division Foreign Military Studies No. P-097. U.S. National Archives, RG 338.

Hessen, R. 1984. *Berlin alert: The memoirs and reports of Truman Smith.* Stanford, Calif.: Hoover Institute Press.

Hittle, J. D. 1961. *The military staff: Its history and development.* Harrisburg, Pa.: Stackpole Books.

Huntington, S. P. 1957. *The soldier and the state: The theory and politics of civil-military relations.* Cambridge, Mass.: Belknap Press of Harvard Univ. Press.

Kahn, D. 1978. *Hitler's spies: German military intelligence in World War II.* New York: Macmillan.

Kent, S. 1949. *Strategic intelligence for American world policy.* Princeton, N.J.: Princeton Univ. Press.

Leutze, J. 1971. *The London journal of General Raymond E. Lee 1940–1941.* Boston: Little, Brown.
May, E. R., ed. 1984. *Knowing one's enemies: Intelligence assessment before the two world wars.* Princeton, N.J.: Princeton Univ. Press.
Mott, T. B. 1937. *Twenty years as a military attache.* New York: Oxford Univ. Press.
Vagts, A. 1956. *Defense and diplomacy: The soldier and the conduct of foreign relations.* New York: Columbia Univ. Press.
———. 1967. *The military attache.* Princeton, N.J.: Princeton Univ. Press.

ATTACK

Attack is an aggressive action in which one side uses force to impose its will on the other side. One of the four fundamental operations of military force (the others are defense, reinforcement, and withdrawal), attack intends to destroy the effectiveness of enemy forces and, generally, to decide an issue. The main elements involved are fire and movement.

Historical Development

During the Thirty Years' War, battle was characterized by relatively deep quadrangular formations composed of several thousand men armed with pikes and matchlock muskets forcing the issue by sheer mass and impact (Regling 1979, p. 31f.). The Swedish forces under Gustavus Adolphus, however, began a transition to linear tactics.

Linear Tactics

As a result of the initiative of Gustavus Adolphus, tactics changed in the latter part of the seventeenth century. Battle drill was introduced, and armies became more professional. The quadrangular formation commonly used up to this time was replaced by shallow linear formations in which attacking armies took on echelon formations several ranks deep. The long, muzzle-loading muskets demanded a complicated loading procedure; consequently, firing took place rank by rank. This meant that three ranks knelt while the fourth rank stood and fired over them. Then the third rank stood and the fourth rank reloaded, and so on.

Training now had to concentrate on increasing the rate of fire. With the introduction of flintlocks for muskets and the improvement of weapon drill, the rate of fire rose from one shot in three minutes to five shots in two minutes.

Fire effect was greatly enhanced also, and this benefited the momentum of attack. This was complemented by the invention of the socket bayonet, which made it possible for an infantryman to load his musket with fixed bayonet, thus rendering the pike superfluous. The Prussian king, Frederick II (the Great) considered the bayonet a more suitable offensive weapon than fire. So between 1753 and 1757, priority was given in the Prussian army to practice in bayonet fighting.

At the turn of the eighteenth century, the infantry was largely re-equipped with new muskets. This and the endeavor to fire all muskets simultaneously meant that troop formations thinned out and became broader, leaving a single linearly formed line of attack two ranks deep. The Battle of Leuthen (1757, Prussia against Austria) is an example of successfully applied linear tactics.

A prerequisite for success was that troop movements on the battlefield should proceed in accordance with drill, with the cavalry commonly operating on the flanks. In the Battle of Leuthen, however, transversal battle array was successfully used. Although the Prussians were inferior in strength, this was compensated for by successful flank attacks and commitment of cavalry at a propitious moment.

Rifle Columns

Linear tactics gradually lost significance late in the eighteenth century, largely due to the battles in the American Revolutionary War (1776–83) and the Napoleonic Wars in the first decade of the nineteenth century. Battles were fought not only in closed formation in North America, but also in partisan-style dispersed form. This partisan-style warfare, which was partly due to poor drill training and lack of discipline of the infantry, caused the English considerable losses.

In Europe, a lesson was learned from these tactics, particularly by the German armies. Light infantry units were formed to which swarms of riflemen were allotted. The latter were equipped with rifles (as opposed to smoothbore muskets) that increased the accuracy of an aimed shot.

Usually, riflemen were sent in advance of the deployed units, which could no longer proceed in a closed front because they had to shoot their muskets past preceding riflemen. This resulted in greater dispersal. Firing tactics developed definitively during the French Revolution, because the masses could not be adequately drilled for linear tactics. The French also sent swarms of riflemen ahead of their line, and they bore the brunt of battle: "There were no valid regulations and therefore no instructions [on] what to do if an attack failed" (Regling 1979, p. 203). Attack, therefore, was dependent on improvisation.

Assault Column

Linear tactics retained their form until 1805, when the French attempted to coordinate the linear formation with the deployment of swarms of riflemen. Column tactics were the result, and they were adopted by all European armies with the exception of the British.

A battalion was drawn up as a combat or assault column in four lines (three men deep) that stood at intervals behind each other, making the column, therefore, twelve men deep. Intervals between the lines and the distance between the sections divided the column, from front to back, into two halves, thereby allowing a measure of elasticity when approaching the enemy in the attack (Regling 1979, p. 205).

ARTILLERY

Owing to its low mobility and short range, artillery played an insignificant part in attack up to the middle of the eighteenth century. As the firing range of rifles and cannons lengthened, greater importance was lent to artillery. Moreover, it was realized that effective support of the infantry (creeping barrage) could only be achieved by mobile batteries with a longer range. Frederick the Great was particularly instrumental in the development of rapidly moving horse-drawn artillery.

CAVALRY

As of the mid-nineteenth century, due to the use of the rifle-musket and, later, machine guns, horse cavalry was no longer used as an assault force. After 1916, it became insignificant in that attack role.

INFANTRY

In World War I, increased fire effect compelled the infantry to thin out its originally closed and continuous-firing line and make greater use of terrain. Firing lines in the attack were spaced out to approximately three meters (3.3 yd.), with an interval of 30–50 meters (33–55 yd.) between lines. The infantry's firing strength was greatly reinforced by the increased allocation of trench mortars as well as heavy and light machine guns.

The decisive tactical innovation of attack in World War I was the creeping barrage, first devised by the French and brought about because of positional, trench warfare. Shock troop actions, with machine guns and flamethrowers, assisted by engineers, often dictated the shape of battle.

TANKS

Tanks were used in World War I to support attacking infantry. Then, between the two world wars, they were designated attacking weapons. The difference in the concepts of operations was whether tanks should continue to be assigned to support infantry assaults or whether they should attack as independent units. The mobility of a mechanized unit, adequately equipped for reconnaissance and battle, meant that an attack could be made at the enemy's weakest point, either deep in the flanks or from the rear. Other arms in the vicinity of the tank assault could then be deployed accordingly. This included support from pursuit and attack aircraft.

The great mobility of tank units, consequently, was conducive to the element of surprise, which was particularly effective in attacks.

Deployment of self-contained tank units led to concentrations not only of a tactical nature but also of an operational and strategic nature. These are emphasized by the massing of additional troops, reserves, and fire effect. Concentration goes a long way toward the success of an attack; often it is a prerequisite.

Attack in the Late 1980s

THE WEST

In the Western world, attack in the military sense implies an offensive operation, taking the initiative with armed forces to capture or regain a certain area and/or to destroy the enemy.

By prior or simultaneous defense, enemy forces can be repelled and one's own territorial integrity restored (Lutz 1980).

Attack is a type of combat in its own right, alongside defense, delaying action, and reinforcement. An attack can be made within other types of combat, but it is the only type that can decide an issue.

THE USSR

From the Soviet point of view (and, consequently, for the other countries of the former Warsaw Pact), attack was the main type of combat. The aim of a Soviet attack was to destroy enemy forces, disarm those forces, and capture enemy territory.

An attack or offensive is implemented by means of combat, battles, and operations. On land, an attack can be made on an enemy in the defensive, on an enemy who is himself intending to attack, or on a retreating enemy.

A variant of an offensive is the counteroffensive. Depending on the objectives, scale, and number of the forces and means deployed, the attack can be of strategic, operational, or tactical importance.

"Modern military encounters generally take the form of attack, although defense operations may also occur in the course of attack" (GDR 1984, pp. 13f.). Defense only serves as a repellent against superior enemy numbers, as a means of maintaining positions, or for creating conditions favorable to a sustained attack.

General

Attacks can be made on strategic, operational, and tactical levels with the aim of deciding an issue, and require the deployment of strong fighting power at the crucial point. For an attack to be successful, the size of the attacking force should be greater than the enemy's. "The successful attack is the result of superiority with regard to both physical and moral strength" (Clausewitz 1952, p. 777).

To be effective, an attack must consist of concentrated fire and rapid systematic movements, preventing the enemy from taking successful countermeasures. The attacker has the advantage of freedom of action because he can determine target, direction, and timing. In addition, the attacking troops often have a feeling of superiority.

Types of Attack

Attacks can take various forms: frontal, flank, envelopment, preliminary, and counterattack.

Frontal Attack

The advantage of frontal attack is that it offers the shortest route to the objective and facilitates the coordination of fire and movement. The disadvantage is that the attacker is confronted with the greatest enemy strength, and therefore requires considerable firing superiority and striking power.

Flank Attack

The advantage of the flank attack is that one is generally confronted with a weaker enemy and therefore can be successful even with fewer troops. The disadvantages are often that a greater distance needs to be covered, the coordination of firing and striking is more complicated, and one's own flanks are exposed and vulnerable.

Envelopment Attack

The advantage of an envelopment attack is that the attacker is confronted with a weaker enemy whose communication lines are disrupted and whose logistics are cut off. The disadvantages are again that a greater distance needs to be covered, there is a danger of being encircled by the enemy, and the coordination of firing and striking are more complicated, particularly when encircling comes from both sides.

Preliminary Attack

The preliminary, or "spoiling," attack (Fig. 1) is made on a nearby objective with only part of the attacking force in order to facilitate the main attack or to create a situation whereby the main attack force can form bridgeheads or overcome obstacles.

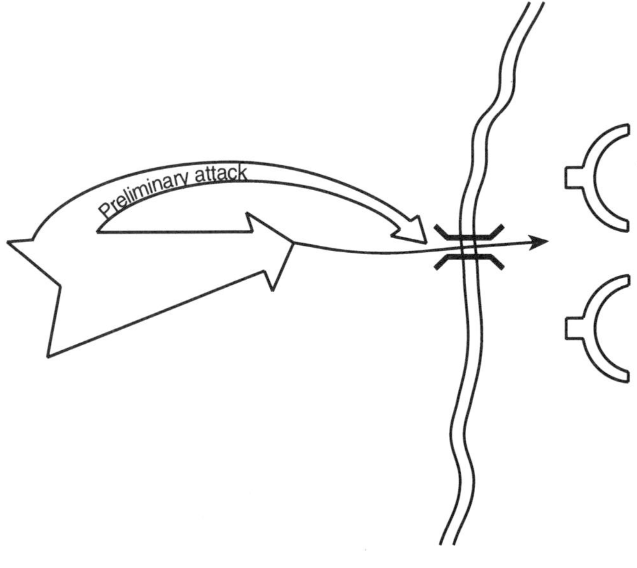

design: Axel von Netzer

Figure 1. Preliminary attack. (Source: Axel von Netzer)

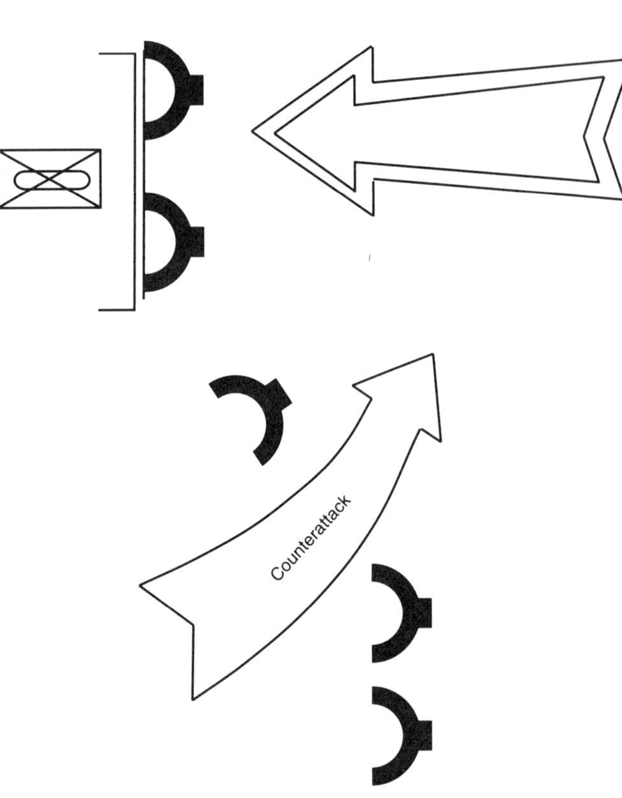

design: Axel von Netzer

Figure 2. Counterattack. (Source: Axel von Netzer)

Counterattack

The counterattack (Fig. 2), made with prepared reserves, is used according to a preconceived plan to destroy advancing or intruding enemy forces, to recover lost territory, or to capitalize on a favorable situation with readily available troops. Counterattacks should, if possible, be unexpected and against enemy flanks; in this way, the attacks can be successful with fewer troops than those of the enemy.

Preparations for Attack

Attacks are generally made after careful preparation. Apart from an assessment of the situation, preparations comprise the timely establishment of combat readiness and the coordination of the combined participating forces—for example, fire support, engineer support, and logistics.

Either broad or deep formations can be used when attacking. The advantage of a broad formation is that attacking troops can deliver more fire on the enemy at one time, splitting up enemy fire and establishing the enemy's weak spots and breaches at an early stage. The disadvantage is that the attacker has to determine when to put the main point of his advance effort; this is difficult to change if circumstances change. In addition, the flanks and rear are then at greater risk and reserve strength is purely nominal.

The advantage of a deep formation attack is that the direction and point of main effort can be easily changed, threatened flanks can be better protected, and adequate reserves can remain in the rear. The disadvantage is that, in the first instance, only a part of the fire can have any effect on the enemy, and the enemy can concentrate his return fire.

For any attack, troops require freedom of movement so they can circumvent local obstacles or persistent enemy resistance and select a favorable line of attack.

Course of Attack

An attack is composed of two basic steps: the phased approach and the breach (Fig. 3). In an attack on a deeply staggered enemy, approach and breach may be repeated. A breakthrough is decisive insofar as the attacker succeeds in penetrating the enemy lines to a point where the latter can no longer maintain continual resistance.

AXEL VON NETZER

SEE ALSO: Echelon; Envelopment; Fire and Movement; Firepower; Maneuver; Mobility; Schwerpunkt.

Bibliography

Bauer, E. 1955. *Der Panzerkrieg.* Books 1 and 2. Bonn: Verlag Offene Worte.

Clausewitz, C. von. 1952. *Vom Kriege.* 16th ed. Bonn: Ferd. Dümmlers Verlag.

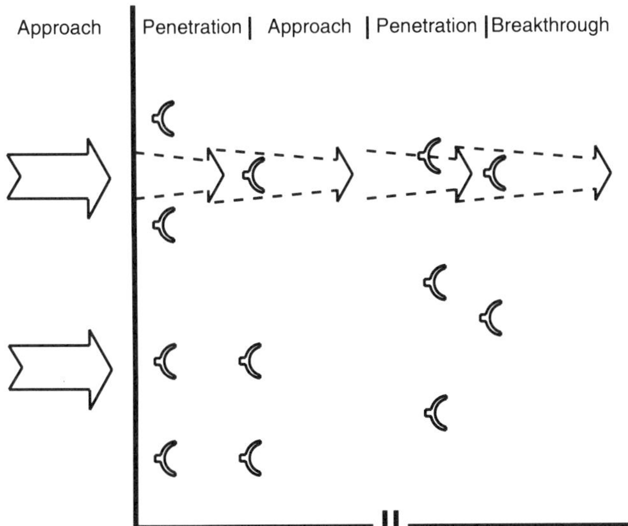

Figure 3. Course of attack. (SOURCE: Axel von Netzer)

Dinter, E. 1985. *Nie wieder Verdun.* Herford: Verlag Mittler und Sohn.

Fuchs, T. 1977. *Geschichte des europäischen Kriegswesens.* Part 3. München: Bernhard und Graefe Verlag.

German Democratic Republic (GDR). 1984. *Junior lexicon for military affairs.* East Berlin: Military Publishers.

Heilbrunn, O. 1967. *Konventionelle Kriegführung im Nuklearen Zeitalter.* Frankfurt am Main: Verlag E. S. Mittler und Sohn.

Herzog, C. 1975. *Entscheidung in der Wüste.* Berlin: Verlag Ullstein.

Lutz, E. 1980. *Lexikon zur Sicherheitspolitik.* München: C. H. Beck.

Regling, V. 1979. *Handbuch zur Deutschen Militärgeschichte.* Section 9. München: Bernhard und Graefe Verlag.

Sowjetische Militärenzyklopädie. 1978. Militärverlag der Deutschen Demokratischen Republik, no. 14.

Wallach, J. 1967. *Das Dogma der Vernichtungsschlacht.* München: Bernhard und Graefe Verlag.

ATTILA THE HUN

The Huns, a people of Turanian stock, began to appear as a political and military power during the second century B.C. They emerged from the pastoral peoples living on the northern steppes of Europe and Asia and reached the height of their power in the West between A.D. 350 and A.D. 470. From their earliest appearance in Europe (fourth century A.D.) they gained a reputation as fierce warriors.

The Eastern Huns (chronicled by the Chinese as *hsiung-nu*) attained their greatest power under King Mao Tun in the early first century A.D. In central Asia, some nineteen tribes, known as the Southern Huns, consolidated their power during the first and second centuries A.D. They gained control of the Altai region and modern Kazakhstan, expanding into northern India, Pakistan, and Afghanistan.

The Huns, or hsiung-nu, became known to the Romans after the defeat of Crassus's legions by the Parthians at the Battle of Carrhae in 54 B.C. The captured legionaries were resettled on the Parthian's eastern frontiers where they became mercenaries in the service of Chih-chih, hsiung-nu shan-yu, the king of the Southern Huns. The term *hsiung-nu* (archaic Chinese) derives from the ancient Iranian word for ruling king and was used by the Huns when referring to themselves.

Recent excavations of early Hun sites have provided evidence that the Huns had both agrarian knowledge and weapons-fashioning skills. Agricultural tools and large storage areas for cereal grains were found along with weapons made from iron and bronze. The Hun ruling class (Logades), as best as can be determined, spoke an ancient Eastern dialect similar to Saka-Iranian.

There is little reason to believe that there was a concerted sociopolitical life within the Hun empire that would have united the Eastern, Southern, and Western Huns.

Instead, each evolved separately, modifying their languages and sociopolitical and military organizations as they formed alliances, subjugated other peoples, and developed political, economic, and military spheres of influence.

Also, it is evident, from the brief period of Western Hun supremacy (A.D. 350–470) and its rapid decline after the death of Attila (A.D. 453) that it was Attila's political and military skills, as opposed to consolidated Hun political and military power, that held his part of the empire together. This is further strengthened by the fact that the Western Huns were far outnumbered by the people they ruled, the majority of whom were Germanic.

The Western Huns' peak military power occurred sometime after Attila's birth (ca. A.D. 406) with the unification of the Western Hun tribes under one all-powerful king, Karaton (A.D. 412). Prior to this, Balamer (ca. A.D. 320–390), Karaton's father, appeared to be "first among equals" in his relationship with the loosely federated tribal chieftains.

Organization and Equipment

The Hun military organization was based on the tribe. Each tribe numbered 50,000–60,000 individuals, of whom about 10,000 were military-age males. This 10,000-man unit of mounted archers, which represented the tribe's war-making capability, was called a *tumen.* The basic building block of the tumen was ten light horsemen, who were combined into elements of 100 and then 1,000. The highest title among the Huns, next to that of king, was "commander of the Ten Thousand Horsemen," also known as the khan among many Turanian peoples.

The Hun tumen were the epitome of fast, light cavalry. The horse was essential to their way of life and mode of fighting. The Hun horses were small and hairy with long manes and long, bushy tails. They had large, long heads and short legs with broad hooves. Their eyes were large, and they were apparently faithful companions to their masters. These hardy horses survived quite well on grass and sparse vegetation, could tolerate extreme cold or heat without noticeable fatigue, and were rarely sick.

These horses responded equally well to bridle commands, the rider's verbal commands, and the unit commander's signals, thus leaving the rider's hands free to handle the war bow and other weapons. When the enemy's defensive line was penetrated, the Hun horses would bite and kick the enemy's troops, wreaking great havoc and consternation.

The saddle consisted of a wooden frame covered with leather and stuffed with horse hair or other materials. The stirrups were wood covered with leather. The leaders rode horses whose saddles and bridles were richly decorated with silver and gold.

The Hun's principal weapon was the reflex composite bow, which measured 140–160 centimeters (55–63 in.) in length, and which when unstrung curved outwards. In fact, the entire Hun system of warfare and tactics evolved around this bow, which was still used by the Hungarians as late as the early fifteenth century. The bow was not symmetrical, the bottom extending a shorter distance from the grip than the top. It was made of seven different materials—including wood, bone, and sinew—by expert bow makers. The quiver consisted of a wooden frame covered with leather and highly ornamented. It hung from either the saddle or the rider's belt.

The effective combat range of the Hun bow was 70–100 meters (230–330 ft.). The maximum range for "arrow showers" was 175 meters (575 ft.). The war bow was commonly referred to as the Scythian bow, and its origin and design were most likely Iranian.

The Huns complemented their use of the bow with the lasso, which was used to thin an enemy line by roping enemies out of the ranks and dragging them away. Other weapons included short, curved Iranian-type swords, daggers, maces, and pickaxes. Thrusting and jabbing lances, while known to have been used, were rare. A small shield of wood covered with leather completed the Hun warrior's equipment. Depending on the owner's rank and wealth, the weapons were decorated with silver, gold, and precious stones.

Clothing and combat attire were equally rich and again were used to display rank and wealth. The warrior wore a leather-covered conical helmet (made on a metal frame), with a peak that pointed forward. Chain mail covered the neck and shoulders, and sometimes the upper body, but body armor was usually made of hard leather, which was greased with animal fat for waterproofing. The leather armor was skin tight and bone plaques were sewn to the outer part for additional protection. Up to four layers of this armor were worn over a shirt or blouse. The warriors also wore baggy pants of goat skin, and soft boots. The boots were only good for riding as they were too fragile for dismounted use. Over this clothing, the warrior wore a knee-length split-felt or fur coat, often richly embroidered.

The Hun warrior rarely cut his hair or beard. His hair was combed and parted on top of his head. Sometimes his beard was also parted, and both the beard and hair might be plaited with colorful ribbons. During cold and rainy seasons, animal fat was thickly smeared over the warrior's face and hair for protection against the elements.

Tactics and Strategy

The Hun system of warfare was characterized by rapid movement during tactical marches toward an objective, as well as during combat itself. The Huns had no infantry or siege equipment and, therefore, depended upon rapid movement to catch their enemies off guard with city garrisons ill-prepared for defense. Movement over great distances occurred so quickly that no one, regardless how distant from the great Hungarian plains, felt secure. This mobility was provided by the horse, with each warrior having at least one remount. Some sources indicate that the Huns had as many as seven remounts. When a mount was killed in combat, the warrior changed to another. The mounts were saddled and equipped with a spare quiver and standard rations, which made each horse an individual logistical package, enabling units of 1,000 and more to travel hundreds, even thousands, of miles from home without the need for an operational support base.

In addition to individual horses, the Huns used light, two-wheeled, chariot-like carts drawn by two to three horses.

It must be noted that the armies of Balamer, Mundzuk, and Attila became progressively less Hun-like as they absorbed Gothic elements, which were mainly infantry. The Goths, Gepids, and Quadi fought dismounted, as infantry, preferring hand-to-hand combat. The Huns rarely dismounted and preferred to use their bows from a distance. Close combat was used only for finishing off the enemy in the final assault.

The Huns and other Turanians preferred to avoid hand-to-hand combat for several reasons: first, while their armor was quite effective against arrows, it offered almost no protection against the heavy cut-and-thrust weapons used by the Roman legions or Germanic tribes. Second, the Hun horses were vulnerable to the spear and lance at close combat range. Third, a limited population base and the ever-present need to protect the tribe made the heavy losses sustained in close combat unacceptable.

If the tumen of 10,000 warriors incurred heavy casualties, the tribe was endangered, since it could no longer protect itself and its livestock from marauders. Therefore, the tribal tumen was usually split. Half the warriors would remain behind to protect the tribe, while half would go on military expeditions and raids. Thus, even if the tribe's entire offensive capability was lost in war, it remained formidable defensively.

The Huns placed great value on long-range reconnaissance, deception, and concealment. The full force was never within view of their enemy. Any part of the main body might be hidden in forests, ravines, or riverbeds. In battle, units would be arrayed over wide fronts.

Skirmishes, aimed at thinning the enemy ranks, would always precede an assault. Groups would dash out from the line, fire a few well-placed arrows, wheel right, fire several more arrows, and return to their position in the line. This maneuver was repeated until the enemy ranks had been thinned sufficiently to permit the decisive tactical maneuvers to be initiated.

Units of 1,000 would then approach within bow range (70–100 m, 230–328 ft.). The front ranks would then fire direct, well-aimed shots, while the rear ranks would fire arrow showers overhead. These arrow showers would force the enemy troops to lift their shields to protect their heads and shoulders, thereby exposing their bodies to the direct fire from the Hun front ranks.

The attacking tumens would move forward quickly, then turn back and move forward again. Some elements would ride around to the enemy's rear and flanks and engage his cavalry and rear guard. Through these seemingly random forward and rearward movements the attacking Huns would attempt to lure the enemy's main body into pursuit, which was always attended by some disorganization. Another ruse was the simulation, on signal, of the flight of the entire Hun force. If the enemy pursued into the trap, units that had been kept out of sight attacked from all sides and destroyed him. If the enemy did not fall for the feint and kept his formation, a frontal assault was executed in wedge formation by units of 1,000 or by massed tumen, depending on the total size of the army.

Rivers were never an obstacle to the Hun warriors. They all carried inflatable skins. In addition rafts would be built to carry heavy equipment and carts. Individual warriors normally would ride their horses into the water and swim across. The major river-crossing sites were well guarded.

The Attila Period

Attila was brought to kingship as co-ruler by his brother Bleda (Buda, A.D. 434–445), who was the ruling king. This dual kingship was common among the pastoral peoples of the East. The elder partner was responsible for general administration and political and spiritual leadership, while the younger partner led the military forces.

Attila was by nature cautious and preferred above all to gain his political and military objectives through cunning political maneuvers rather than bloodshed as the Roman chronicler Ammianus Marcellinus noted. If he had to fight, he used his confederates and allies as much as possible rather than risking Hun forces. Although he was called a savage and a barbarian by his enemies, this assessment may not be entirely fair, particularly when considering his abilities as a military commander. Attila often led armies of 60,000 to 100,000 troops from what is now central Hungary into Gaul, Italy, Illyria, Greece, and Spain. There, he conducted siege operations and fought pitched battles. What is even more impressive is the fact that his armies were multilingual, making command and control difficult.

Attila's main adversaries were the Roman legions, at that time the best trained, disciplined, equipped, and supplied military formations in the world. They were ably led by professional noncommissioned officers and officers. Attila's ability to effectively meet and defeat the Roman legions places his military and intellectual powers on a par with the great commanders of his time.

After the death of Attila's uncle, Ruga, in A.D. 434, good relations with the Roman Empire ceased. Bleda and Attila engaged in almost constant warfare with the Eastern Roman Empire until Bleda's death in A.D. 445. When Attila assumed sole rule, he ruthlessly made war against the Western and Eastern empires, enjoying great success.

It appears from historical accounts that no amount of monetary tribute from the Roman Empire satisfied Attila, who was bent on conquering Rome. At that time Roman military strength was heavily committed to Asia Minor, Africa, and Gaul. This left Rome the option of paying off the Huns to keep peace.

Attila made peace in the East to free his southern flank for an attack on the Western Roman Empire. He used, as justification for this attack, the refusal of Valentinianus III to accede to his demand for the hand of his sister, Honoria, in marriage. Attila appeared, unexpectedly, at the gates of Metz on Easter Sunday, 7 April 451. His army killed and looted as far south as the Loire River. At Orléans, he reached the frontier of the kingdom of the Visigoths, having burned everything in his path. When the Roman army, under Aetius, arrived, Attila and his allies were still besieging Orléans. Attila immediately raised the siege to look for a battlefield where he intended to fight a pitched battle. This decision to stand and fight was uncharacteristic of the Huns, who avoided close combat, especially when conditions were not totally in their favor.

Attila found a suitable field on the plains of Châlons (Catalaunian Plains). Here, near the city of Troyes, close to a small village called Mauriacum, he prepared for battle. Because he was superstitious and believed he would lose, he placed his Huns in the center around himself. The Ostrogoths with Walamir were placed on the left, facing the Visigoths, and Ardaric and the Gepids were on the right facing the Romans. Aetius, who was concerned about the loyalty of his Alans, placed his Romans on the left flank, the Alans in the center, and Theodoric and his Visigoths on the right.

The battle, which began around 3:00 P.M., ended late in the evening. Although Theodoric was killed, Attila clearly lost control toward evening, and the battle then turned in Aetius's favor. At dark, the Huns withdrew into the wagon fort that was their camp. When morning came, the Romans and Visigoths had withdrawn from the field. Aetius, for political expediency, had left Attila free to depart. Attila, however, turned south, invading Venetia and Aquileia (452), devastating northern Italy, and taking Milan and Apuleia. In desperation, Pope Leo I came out of Rome to meet Attila and dissuade him from sacking Rome. It is said that the pope succeeded in persuading Attila to relent and spare Rome, but it is more likely that the invasion of his home territory (modern-day Hungary) by the armies of the East Roman Emperor Marcianus cut short his Italian expedition.

Attila died a year after returning home (453) of a sudden nosebleed on the evening of his marriage to Ildiko. None of his sons was strong enough to keep Attila's allies subjugated and his empire intact. The Hun empire, within twenty years of Attila's death, disintegrated from bloody internal power struggles and fighting with the Romans. The main Hun tribes, under the leadership of Attila's two Hun sons, Irnik and Dengizik, returned to the areas between the Dniester and Don rivers. Some Hun tribes remained in the Carpathian Basin, but these either posed no threat to Rome or they entered Roman military service. Irnik also entered Roman service at some later date. Dengizik tried stubbornly to reestablish his father's empire, but was killed in combat against East Roman forces.

SZABOLCS M. DE GYÜRKY
CHERYL DE GYÜRKY

SEE ALSO: Cavalry; History, Ancient Military; Hungary; Roman Empire.

Bibliography

Eckhardt, S., et al. 1986. *Attila es Hunjai* (Attila and his Huns). Ed. G. Nemeth. Budapest: Hungarian Academy Press.
Fuller, J. F. C. 1954. *A military history of the Western world*. Vol. 1. New York: Funk and Wagnalls.
Maenchen, O. J. 1973. *The world of the Huns*. Berkeley, Calif.: Univ. of California Press.
Padanyi, V. 1956. *Dentu Magyaria*. Buenos Aires: Transylvania.
Phillips, E. D. 1969. *The Mongols*. London: Thames and Hudson.
Zajti, F. 1939. *Magyar Evezredek* (Hungarian millennia). Budapest: Arpad Fodor Press.

ATTRITION: PERSONNEL CASUALTIES

Attrition is a reduction in the number of personnel, weapons, and/or equipment in a military unit, organization, or force. There are two basic kinds of attrition: personnel and materiel. Personnel attrition, which is treated here, results from the killing, wounding, capture, injury, or illness of military personnel or civilian employees.

Significance and Causes of Attrition

Other things being equal, victory in battle is a function of the numbers of troops and weapons on each side. While leadership, morale, tactics, and chance do influence the outcome of a battle, so do the number of troops and the number and type of weapons. Thus, a commander wants as large a force as possible.

The primary factor in attrition is losses. The number of losses caused by enemy action can be only partially influenced by a commander, who can minimize his losses by good leadership, strategy, and clever tactics.

Attrition has three major causes: enemy action, accidents, and illness or wearout. Enemy action causes the most attrition in modern wars; people and equipment are hit with bullets or fragments (both large and small) from artillery or mortar shells, aerial bombs, or missiles. In addition, both people and equipment can be wounded or damaged by fire, toxic chemicals, or germs. It will be possible in the future to damage people and equipment with laser beams and particle beams.

Accidents are usually caused by carelessness and violations of good health or safety practices. They occur in armed forces in peacetime because people are using dangerous weapons and equipment. During wartime there are more accidents because the operating tempo is increased, matters must be accomplished urgently, people are tense, and safety rules are relaxed.

Illness has always been a significant element of personnel attrition. Disease was the single most important cause of attrition until the end of the nineteenth century. It can still be an important cause of personnel attrition, particularly in environments that are inherently hostile to humans.

Personnel Loss Categories

There are two basic categories of personnel losses: (1) battle casualties and (2) nonbattle injuries.

Battle casualties. Battle casualties are caused primarily by enemy action. Commanders can influence to some degree the rate, number, and kinds of battle casualties by the way in which they lead their units. There are three kinds of battle casualties: killed in action (KIA), wounded in action (WIA), and captured-missing in action (CMIA).

Personnel killed in action are killed or die of wounds on the battlefield before receiving any medical treatment. Most fighting forces place great importance on the proper and respectful treatment of their dead. Thus a significant effort is made to recover, identify, record, and provide a proper burial for the deceased.

Personnel wounded in action who enter the medical system while still alive are classified as WIA even if they later die of wounds. All armed forces place great stress on the prompt and effective treatment of wounds for two reasons. First, early and effective treatment provides a greater number of returns to duty. Second, the timely treatment of wounds helps morale and increases the willingness of troops to enter combat.

Personnel who become separated from their units during combat are listed as CMIA. Some may have been captured by the enemy and become prisoners of war (POW), at least temporarily (some POWs escape and return to duty). Some of the CMIA are lost or stragglers, and thus under friendly control, although they are not with their unit; these MIA personnel often are returned to duty. Some CMIA are neither captured nor separated from their unit but have, in fact, died or been killed or wounded under circumstances unknown to other surviving members of their units. Sometimes wounded CMIA personnel are recovered and placed in the medical treatment system.

Nonbattle casualties. Nonbattle casualties in the U.S. armed forces are called Disease and Non-Battle Injuries (DNBI). The three major categories are disease, mental illness, and injuries.

Disease is illness caused by bacteria, viruses, parasites, or other organisms. Patients can be mildly debilitated, severely debilitated, or killed by disease. In the past, disease has been a major factor in maintenance of the strength and health of armies, but (due to modern medicine) disease has become a relatively minor factor for modern armies.

Mental illness is a form of disease caused by emotional or psychological traumas; for example, the reaction of soldiers to the stresses of combat. It was called *shellshock* in World War I, *battle fatigue* in World War II, and *post-combat stress disorder* in Vietnam, but the causes and effects remain largely the same. Psychological stress affects the mental processes of an individual in such a way that he cannot effectively perform his duties. Mental illness is seldom fatal, but it can lead to the long-term inability of the victim to perform effectively in a combat unit or in the theater of operations.

Injuries are caused by accidents. In general, these have the same physical effects as WIA and are treated much the same. Some people die of their injuries; others are treated and either returned to duty in the theater or returned to the Zone of the Interior for further treatment, where they will return to duty there or be discharged from the service.

Personnel Attrition Process

A generalized, schematic diagram of the attrition process for personnel is shown in Figure 1. The three areas of interest are the Combat Zone (CZ), the Theater Support Zone (TSZ), and the Zone of the Interior (ZI). (For the United States, the ZI is the Continental United States, or CONUS.) A theater of operations may be divided into several geographical areas or commands depending on the circumstances, but only one TSZ is shown in this diagram. The CZ is generally considered to be forward of the corps rear boundary. These three basic zones exist in all wartime situations, but there can be as many variations as there are wars.

The three basic categories of casualties are processed differently. Personnel who are killed—whatever the cause—are collected at graves registration points for identification and subsequent burial in a temporary or permanent cemetery.

Personnel formerly in the CMIA category are gathered at designated collection points for processing. Depending on their condition, they are placed in the medical treatment system or returned to duty in the replacement system.

The most complicated process involves personnel who require medical treatment. These are the WIA, injured, and sick (all are indicated in the diagram as WIA). Initial treatment is likely to be at a battalion or brigade aid station. A decision is made at each treatment facility either to treat the patient and return him to duty or evacuate him to another, more capable, medical facility. The diagram shows only one forward medical unit in the CZ, but in

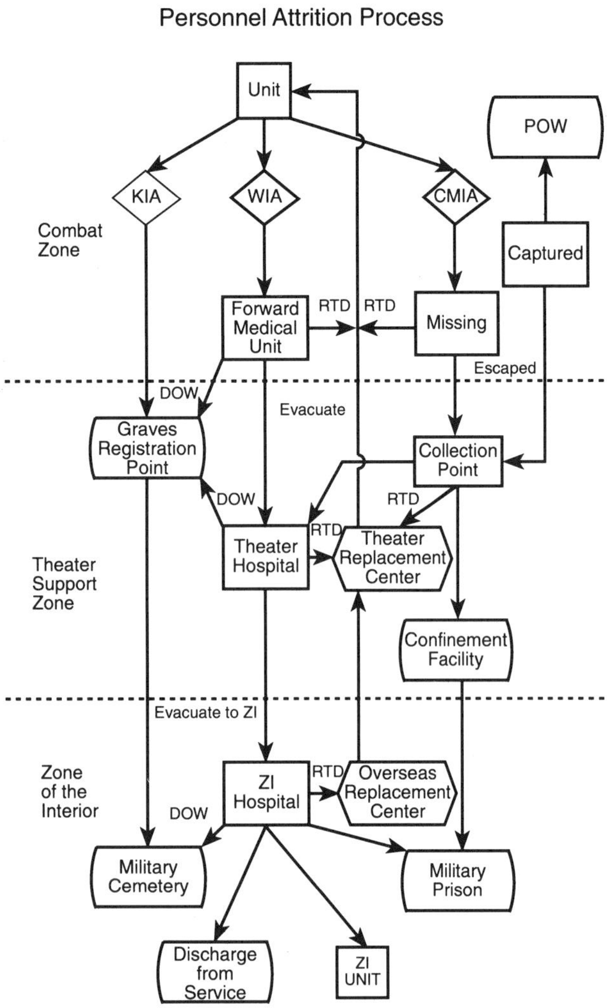

Personnel Attrition Process

Unit
POW
KIA
WIA
CMIA
Combat Zone
Captured
Forward Medical Unit
RTD
RTD
Missing
Escaped
DOW
Evacuate
Graves Registration Point
Collection Point
DOW
RTD
Theater Hospital
RTD
Theater Replacement Center
Theater Support Zone
Confinement Facility
Evacuate to ZI
Zone of the Interior
ZI Hospital
RTD
Overseas Replacement Center
DOW
Military Cemetery
Military Prison
Discharge from Service
ZI UNIT

Figure 1. Schematic of personnel attrition process.

reality there would be several: battalion or brigade aid stations, a division medical battalion, an evacuation hospital, a forward surgical hospital, and a field hospital. Personnel treated at medical facilities in the CZ generally return directly to their original unit when declared fit for duty.

Once the patient is moved to a theater-level hospital or to a ZI hospital, he is unlikely to be returned directly to his original unit. Patients released from these hospitals are usually reassigned to the theater or ZI personnel replacement system for reassignment to units needing certain skills and grades.

Lethality versus Casualties

In military units exposed to hostile firepower, the percentage of those hit per day of combat has declined steadily, albeit unevenly, over four centuries, despite tremendous increases in the lethality of weapons.

All weapons have at least one common characteristic: lethality. This is the ability to injure and, if possible, to kill people. Lethality is comparative. Nothing is more lethal than a sword, in the hands of someone who can wield it, to kill a single opponent within reach of the sword. But the sword's lethality is limited by the factors of time, range, and the physical limitations of the man using it. By assigning values to these and other factors it is feasible to compare the lethality of the sword with the lethality of the hydrogen bomb, or the tank, or any other actual or hypothetical weapon. Weapons that kill more people in shorter periods of time have greater lethality.

Figure 2 is a semilogarithmic plot of trends in weapon lethality over history. It is not surprising that through the period called the "Age of Muscle," the increase in lethality is quite flat. Since the introduction of gunpowder weapons, however, and particularly since the mid-nineteenth century, the lethality of weapons has increased steadily and sharply. Because of this great and steady increase in the lethality of weapons over the past 400 years—particularly as the trend has become pronounced in the past century-and-a-half—it would be logical to assume that the damage inflicted by these weapons, in terms of killed and wounded in battle, would have increased commensurately. But such an assumption would be wrong.

Despite the increase in the lethality of weapons, the battlefield has become steadily less deadly over these same four centuries. Figure 3 shows average daily battle casualty rates for winners and losers in combat from 1600 to 1973.

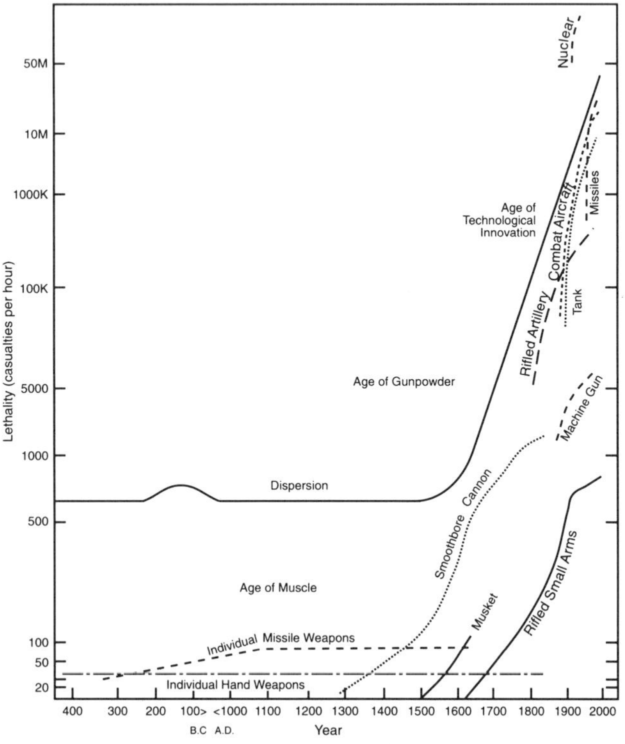

Figure 2. Increase of weapon lethality and dispersion over history.

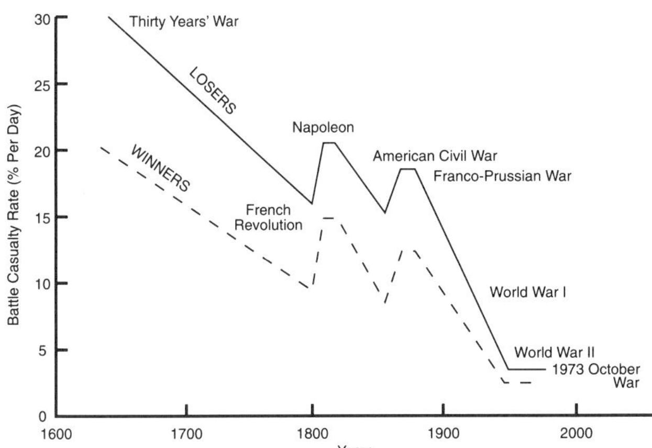

Figure 3. Average daily battle casualty rates, 1600–1973.

Casualty Rates

Effect of Dispersion on Casualty Rates

The principal reason for a decrease in casualties despite an increase in weapons lethality has been greater dispersion of combat troops on the battlefield. This greater dispersion has occurred primarily in response to the increase in lethality of new weapons. As weapons lethality increased, tactics were adopted that minimized the effectiveness of the enemy's weapons by increased dispersion of the combat forces. The way this has occurred is shown in Table 1, which compares the area occupied over history by a typical army or army corps with a strength of about 100,000 men.

In antiquity an army of 100,000 men occupied an area of about 1.0 square kilometer, with each soldier's share being about 10 square meters on the average. It was not often that armies as large as 100,000 men were assembled in antiquity, but it did occur. For instance, the army of Xerxes that crossed the Hellespont in the year 480 B.C. was certainly larger than 100,000 men, as was the army that Darius III brought to the field of Arbela against Alexander the Great. Roman armies on several occasions faced more than 100,000 men in their wars against Mithridates and such barbarian hosts as those of the Teutones and Cimbri.

By the time of the Napoleonic Wars, an army of 100,000 men occupied an area of about 20 square kilometers, with the average space per soldier being 200 square meters. The troops were not distributed uniformly at this density, being grouped in more compact unit formations with relatively large spaces between units, both laterally and in depth.

In the twentieth century the average space occupied by each soldier increased steadily as weapon lethality increased. The dispersion increased dramatically in World War I and even more so in World War II.

By the time of the 1973 October War the area occupied by an army of 100,000 men (that of the Egyptians, for instance) was about 3,500 square kilometers, with an average density of 29 men per square kilometer, or 35,000 square meters per man.

The increase in troop dispersion is represented graphically in Figure 2 by a dispersion line superimposed over the lethality curves.

The interaction of increased dispersion with increased weapons lethality is demonstrated in Table 2. In this table the lethality of all of the weapons in a typical army of 100,000 men has been estimated for several important historical periods. The relationship between dispersion and lethality varies, but both lethality and dispersion have increased over two centuries. Compared with antiquity, the lethality of a modern army of 100,000 has increased 2,000-fold, while dispersion has increased 5,000-fold. Thus, the average lethality density of a modern army is less than half that of an army of antiquity. It is notable that the average lethality densities of World War II were half as great as for World War I, due primarily to the availability of motor vehicles to move reserves in World War II. This permitted greater dispersion without fear of breakthrough because there had not been a significant increase in weapons lethality. This in turn resulted in substantially lower casualty rates in World War II than in World War I.

There were two periods shown in Figure 3 in which the general downward trend of the casualty rates since 1600 was temporarily reversed. The first was a period of about ten years during the Napoleonic Wars; the second was a period of similar duration encompassing the American Civil War, the Austro-Prussian War, and the Franco-Prussian War.

The first of these countertrends reflects the higher casualty rates in Napoleon's imperial battles, beginning with Eylau early in 1807. There appear to be two principal

TABLE 1. *Historical Army Dispersion Patterns (Army or Corps of 100,000 Troops)*

	Antiquity	Napoleonic Wars	American Civil War	World War I	World War II	1973 October War
Area Occupied by Deployed Force of 100,000 (sq km)	1.00	20.12	25.75	248	2,750	3,500
Front (km)	5.00	8.05	8.58	14	48	54
Depth (km)	0.20	2.50	3.00	17	57	65
Men Per sq km	100,000	4,970	3,883	404	36	29
Square Meters Per Man	10.00	200	257.5	2,475	27,500	35,000
Football Fields/Per Man	1/500	1/25	1/20	1/2	5+	7

TABLE 2. *Trends in Lethality of Ground Armies (Typical Armies of 100,000 Men)*

	ANTIQUITY	NAPOLEONIC WARS	AMERICAN CIVIL WAR	WORLD WAR I (1914–18)	WORLD WAR II (1939–45)	OCTOBER WAR 1973	EUROPE (1985–90)
Area (sq km)	1	20	26	250	2,750	3,500	5,000
Lethality (TLI units, millions)	2	5.5	14.3	233	1,281	1,650	4,098
Lethality (normalized)	1	2.80	7.20	117	641	825	2,049
Lethality (sq. m)	2.0	0.28	0.55	0.94	0.47	0.47	0.82

reasons for this. One was that Napoleon's enemies had begun to learn his method of warfare, which led to an increase in the efficiency of battlefield performance by both sides, with an inevitable rise in casualty rates on both sides. The other reason was a general overall decline in the quality of forces Napoleon led to battle, forcing him to rely more on the effect of mass attacks and less on skillful maneuver, again with an inevitable rise in casualty rates.

EFFECT OF THE CONOIDAL BULLET ON CASUALTY RATES

The second perturbation in the downward casualty trend shown in Figure 3 for the period between 1861 and 1871 was caused by a very different phenomenon. This was the introduction, during the American Civil War, of the conoidal bullet—the so-called Minié "ball"—and its substitution for the old spherical ball in rifle muskets. This caused a remarkable improvement in the range, accuracy, and power of the infantryman's weapon. Effective ranges were increased from less than 200 meters (218 yd.) to over 1,000 meters (1,094 yd.). Even at that extended range, the conoidal bullet could penetrate 10.16 centimeters (4 in.) of solid pine.

Prior to 1850, as shown in Table 3, artillery had caused about one-half of the battle casualties, infantry small arms about one-third, and the saber and bayonet the rest. A short time later, during the three major wars between 1861 and 1871, these proportions had changed dramatically. The saber and bayonet became only incidental causes of casualties. The major change was the reversal of relative lethality between infantry weapons and artillery, with the rifle-musket firing the conoidal bullet accounting for 85 to 90 percent of the casualties, and artillery for only 10 percent.

For all practical purposes, the infantryman's rifle had achieved the same effective range as the artilleryman's cannon—as far as the next ridgeline. Riflemen could fire effectively at hostile artillery cannoneers on that ridge, and the cannoneers were much more exposed to such fire than the generally prone riflemen nearby. Artillery effectiveness declined as infantry lethality soared, and all casualty rates doubled. Infantry bayonet charges and cavalry saber charges became suicidal against hostile riflemen and were rarely used.

TABLE 3. *Nineteenth-century Causes of Battlefield Casualties*

WEAPON TYPE	% OF CASUALTIES BEFORE 1850	% OF CASUALTIES AFTER 1860
Artillery	40–50	8–10
Infantry Small Arms	30–40	85–90
Saber and Bayonet	15–20	4–6

In terms of immediate effects upon doctrine, tactics, and casualty rates, the introduction of the conoidal bullet to the battlefield was the most significant change in weapon lethality in all of military history. Not even the machine gun, the tank, or the fighter-bomber has had such a dramatic impact on casualty rates.

Subsequently, however, artillery gradually regained its predominance as the principal cause of casualties on the battlefield. Improvements in recoil mechanisms, in the accuracy of rifled cannon, and in the destructiveness of high-explosive projectiles played important but secondary roles in this evolutionary process.

The principal reason for the return of artillery as the cause of more than 50 percent of the casualties in World Wars I and II was the simple field telephone, an implement with no inherent lethality. The field telephone permitted the artillery to leave exposed positions on ridges and take position behind the cover and concealment of terrain and man-made masks, and to place fire on targets by indirect fire techniques. Only the observer needed to expose himself to observe the target and direct the fire of the concealed and protected artillery weapons upon it.

IMPACT OF SUSTAINED COMBAT ON CASUALTIES

Simply because casualty rates have been declining fairly steadily over the past 400 years (Fig. 3) does not mean that war has become less dangerous. The daily battle casualty rate is a measure of the percentage of a force that incurs casualties during exposure to hostile fire for 24 hours. Prior to the twentieth century battles usually lasted one day or less, and there were periods of days, weeks, and months between battles. In the twentieth century, particularly during World War I, troops were exposed to hostile fire in battles that continued day after day. The fact that daily battle casualty rates have been lower during the past century has been offset by the fact that these lower daily losses have been sustained day after day on a continual basis.

The effect of sustained daily losses upon total attrition is shown in Table 4. This shows clearly the importance of

TABLE 4. *Casualty Rates of U.S. Armies, 1846–1971*[a]

WAR	AVERAGE ANNUAL CASUALTY RATE (%)	AVERAGE DAILY CASUALTY RATE (%)	AVERAGE DAILY DIVISION ENGAGEMENT CASUALTY RATE (%)
Mexican War (1846–48)	9.90	0.03	8.0
Civil War (1861–65)	24.26	0.07	13.0
Spanish-American War (1898)	5.62	0.02	b
Philippine Insurrection (1899–1903)	2.64	0.01	b
World War I (1918)	52.86	0.14	4.0
World War II (1942–45)	17.79	0.05	1.2
Korean War (1950–53)	14.72	0.04	0.9
Vietnam War (1966–71)	14.17	0.04	b

[a] Rates for ground combat troops in the combat theaters.
[b] No comparable division casualty rates are available or applicable.

specifying the exact casualty rate. The daily engagement rates, which tend to measure casualties during actual combat, are much higher than the daily rates for the army as a whole.

The most deadly war in U.S. history was World War I when, for a six-month period in 1918, U.S. Army casualties were 26.4 percent of combat strength in France. This is the equivalent of an annual casualty rate of 52.8 percent of the average strength of forces in the combat theater. Although the average daily engagement casualty rate (for a division) was less than one-third of the average daily casualty rate (for a force of about 50,000 men) in the Civil War, the accumulated casualty rate per year was more than twice as great. This apparent paradox is due to the fact that there were lulls of days and weeks between relatively brief battles in the Civil War, whereas in World Wars I and II battles often continued day after day for weeks or months.

Equally interesting is the comparison of annual casualty rates for the principal armies in World Wars I and II (Table 5). Two phenomena should be noted. First is the marked decline in the daily engagement casualty rates of all participants in World War II, which is consistent with the trend shown in Figure 3. Second, this decline in engagement casualty rates is reflected in both average annual and average daily casualty rates for all participants except Germany and the Soviet Union. For Germany, these average rates were about the same (slightly lower) for World War II as for World War I. For the USSR the average rates were greater for World War II. This is an indication of the ferocity of the Russo-German War of 1941–45. Note, in particular, the average annual loss rate of the USSR in World War II. With the possible exception of Paraguay in the Lopez War (1864–70), this is probably the highest national annual casualty rate of history.

Table 6 indicates that the daily engagement casualty rates in the Arab-Israeli wars of 1967 and 1973 were close to those for World War II. The average daily rates, of course, were much higher because of the brevity of those wars.

RELATIONSHIP OF CASUALTY RATES TO FORCE SIZE

Small-force casualty rates are invariably higher than those of larger forces under the same circumstances. The first person to notice this phenomenon, apparently, was The-

TABLE 5. *Casualty Rates in World Wars I and II*[a]

WAR	AVERAGE ANNUAL CASUALTY RATE (%)	AVERAGE DAILY CASUALTY RATE (%)	ESTIMATED DAILY ENGAGEMENT CASUALTY RATE (%)
World War I			
United States	52.9	0.14	4.0
British Empire	42.8	0.12	4.0
France	46.9	0.13	4.0
Russia	63.3	0.17	6.0
Germany	47.2	0.13	3.0
Italy	46.6	0.13	b
World War II			
United States	17.8	0.05	1.1
United Kingdom	17.5	0.05	1.2
France	16.3	0.04	1.2
USSR	88.2	0.24	3.5
Germany	44.9	0.12	2.0
Italy	19.8	0.05	b
Japan	25.1	0.07	b
China	12.2	0.03	b

[a] Rates for ground combat troops in the combat theaters.
[b] Not estimated.

TABLE 6. *Casualty Rates for Arab-Israeli Wars*

WAR	DURATION (DAYS)	AVERAGE DAILY CASUALTY RATE (%)	AVERAGE DAILY ENGAGEMENT CASUALTY RATE (%)
1967 War			
Israel	6	0.37	2.5
Egypt	3	2.07	3.0
Jordan	3	1.90	3.5
Syria	2	1.50	3.0
1973 War			
Israel	19	0.21	1.5
Egypt	19	0.42	1.9
Syria	17	0.41	2.5

odore Ayrault Dodge, an American historian in the late nineteenth and early twentieth centuries. There are two principal reasons for this phenomenon. The first is that small combat forces, at least through company size, have very few individuals not directly related to combat. Battalions, regiments, and brigades, however, have increasing numbers and proportions of staff and support personnel and units, who are involved only rarely in direct combat.

This phenomenon of higher casualties for smaller forces is essentially a manifestation of Clausewitz's concept of "friction in war." The larger a force, the greater the number of human interactions among individuals and groups, imparting an inherent inefficiency to combat activities, which can be kept to a minimum, but not eliminated, by efficiency in organization, training, communications, and control procedures. Thus, as forces become larger, there are increasing delays in the performance of missions and compliance with orders on both sides of interactions between opposing forces. Troops are exposed to hostile fire less promptly, and there is comparable diminution in the promptness and efficiency with which response is made to that hostile fire.

There is an apparent anomaly created by this strength-size attrition phenomenon. The daily casualty rates of a corps will always be less than the rates of the engaged divisions of the corps for the same day; the casualty rate of a division will be less than the rates of its component brigades that are engaged on that same day, and so on down the line. This is only to a small extent the result of the large staffs and support units in the larger formations. It occurs primarily because small units will be engaged more intensively, but for briefer periods, than will the larger formations to which they belong.

Relationship of Killed to Wounded in Battle

One of the most consistent relationships in battle statistics over history has been that between the number killed and the number wounded in battle. In his books on ancient warfare, Dodge (1890–1904) noted that the standard relationship in ancient battles was between 2.2 and 2.1 men wounded for every man killed—for the winners. For the losers he simply states: "Usual massacre." In the casualty statistics for Napoleon's wars the relationship is similar to that in antiquity; but Dodge notes that the relationship of wounded to killed in the German armies in the Franco-Prussian War was 2.6 to 1.0.

Dodge did not distinguish between KIA and died of wounds (DOW) as is done in compilations of modern casualty statistics in most countries. This would not have made much difference in antiquity; wounded men who survived the battle generally recovered, although some were maimed. About one in three of those hit on the winning side did not survive; two in three did. It is doubtful if the records available to Dodge would have permitted him to be more discriminating. The average relationship between wounded and killed in a number of wars between 1704 and 1871 is about 4.4 (Longmore 1872). Official U.S. Army records for the Mexican and Civil Wars show that the relationship of wounded to killed was 3.72 and 4.55, respectively, in those wars, while the relationship of surviving wounded to KIA and DOW was 2.18 and 2.38, respectively.

Table 7 shows the ratios of the numbers wounded to the numbers killed in American wars of the nineteenth and twentieth centuries, and the ratio of the surviving wounded to total battle deaths, which includes those who were killed outright and those who died later because of wounds in battle. (The raw statistical data is not entirely reliable.) There is reason to believe that the KIA figures for the Union Army in the Civil War may be low, perhaps by a factor of 10 percent to 20 percent. Official sources are both contradictory and unreliable for the Spanish-American War. There are two sets of numbers for WIA in the Vietnam War. One set includes all who were recorded at the aid stations. The other set (which is used here, and which is 30% smaller) includes only those who were evacuated from the aid stations for treatment. Since consistent medical records for the U.S. Army do not exist before 1819, the first war on this list is the Mexican War, 1846–48.

These ratios do not reveal any significant trends in the relationship between wounded and killed in battles, until possibly the beginning of World War II. Otherwise, the relationship appears to have been fairly steady over the course of history, and certainly for most of the past two centuries.

Lethal weapons have killed one man in battle for about every four men wounded. Of those who are hit in battle by lethal weapons, approximately three men survive for every one who dies, when those who subsequently die of wounds are considered. The proportion of survivors has increased in recent wars due to modern evacuation and medical techniques.

Two sets of data are shown in Table 7 for the U.S. experiences in both World War I and World War II. This

Table 7. *Ratios of Wounded to Killed in U.S. Wars*

War	Ratio of wounded to killed	Ratio of surviving wounded to battle deaths
Mexican War	3.72	2.18
Civil War	4.55	2.38
Spanish-American War	5.88	3.94
Philippine Insurrection	3.81	2.72
World War I	5.96	4.10
World War I w/o Gas	4.20	2.88
World War II	3.57	2.41
World War II w/o USAAF	4.25	2.77
Korean War	4.02	3.56
Vietnam War	4.45	4.16

is because there were special circumstances relating to the statistics, which need to be noted.

The raw data for World War I show a ratio of wounded to killed of 5.96, significantly higher than in most of the other wars. This is because 72,773 casualties, slightly more than one-third of the total casualties, were caused by poison gas. However, less than 2 percent of the total gas casualties were killed in action, and less than 2 percent of the survivors of gas injuries died of their gas-related injuries. If all of the gas-related casualties are deducted from the World War I statistics, the killed and wounded ratios for those hit by bullets or shell fragments come quite close to those of other modern combat.

In World War II, the overall U.S. Army figures show a low ratio of wounded to killed, mainly because a substantial portion of the casualty figures are for the U.S. Army Air Forces (USAAF). Only a small proportion of aircraft crews survived after being shot down. Thus, the USAAF had a much lower ratio of wounded to killed than was the case for the rest of the U.S. Army. When the USAAF figures are not used, the U.S. Army ground casualties for World War II are very close to the normal ground combat pattern.

Complicating Vietnam War data was the large number of personnel MIA, for whom data is confusing and still not complete as of 1990. Those known to have died while in MIA status and those still listed as missing are shown as having been wounded and then died of wounds. This assumption tends to degrade the effects of modern evacuation and treatment with respect to DOWs.

These are U.S. Army figures. Marine Corps casualty rates for twentieth century wars are similar. Air Force figures would be less consistent for the same reason that the USAAF figures were. Figures for other nations are similar to those for the United States.

Impact of Improved Medical Care

Survivability on the battlefield has increased significantly as a result of the tremendous improvements in medicine in the past century. Table 8 shows, for American wars, the percentage of survivors of hits, the ratio of nonbattle deaths to battle deaths (KIA and DOW), and the ratio of deaths from disease to deaths from injuries.

All three of the ratios shown in Table 8 indicate that improvements in military medicine have caused a dramatic increase in survivability on the battlefield. The percentage of personnel who get hit and survive has increased since the Mexican War, and the significance of this increase is explained below. It is also evident that the proportion of total casualties caused by disease has decreased significantly.

While the trend to increased survivability is clear, the figures shown in the first column of Table 8 might be interpreted to mean that the effect of improvements in medicine and battlefield evacuation is relatively insignificant. The chances of surviving a hit in the Mexican War and Civil War were 69 percent and 70 percent, and the chances of surviving a hit in the Korean and Vietnam wars were 78 percent and 76 percent, only a modest improvement. This comparison fails to consider, however, two fundamental attrition facts.

TABLE 8. *U.S. Casualty Ratios Influenced by Medical Progress*

War	Survivors as % of hits	Ratio of nonbattle to battle deaths	Ratio of deaths from disease to deaths from injuries
Mexican War	69	7.30	27.80
Civil War	70	2.27	21.29
Spanish-American War[a] [b]	80	13.34	16.65
Philippine Insurrection[a]	73	3.15	4.59
World War I[c] (w/o gas casualties)	74	1.43	11.64
World War II (ground forces only)[a]	73	0.36	0.28
Korean War	78	0.13	0.23
Vietnam War	76	0.24	0.24

[a] Ratios influenced by tropical climate.
[b] Malaria epidemic.
[c] Influenza epidemic.

First, almost exactly one casualty in five (19% to 21%) has been killed outright in all of the U.S. wars. (The slightly lower percent shown for the Civil War is because official statistics have probably omitted approximately 10,000 soldiers KIA.)

Second, approximately 65 percent of all of those hit on the battlefield suffer relatively minor wounds and will almost certainly survive even without medical attention.

This means that approximately 15 percent of those who are hit on the battlefield are seriously wounded and are likely to die without medical care. Table 9 shows how these seriously wounded men have fared in U.S. wars. When the survival rate for the seriously wounded group is considered separately, the trend to greater survivability is indeed significant. In the Mexican War only 27 percent of the seriously wounded survived. In the Korean War 87 percent of the seriously wounded survived.

The figures for Vietnam, like those for World War II, are slightly depressed by the higher incidence of infection in tropical climates. Otherwise the trend is a dramatic testimonial to the improvements in modern medicine and battlefield evacuation.

The effects of improvements in modern medicine are also clear from the decrease in the ratios of nonbattle to battle deaths and disease deaths to injury deaths from the Mexican War through the Vietnam War, also shown in Table 8. With the exception of the Spanish-American War and the Philippine Insurrection, these ratios decrease steadily until the Vietnam War. The Spanish-American War anomaly is explained by the malaria epidemic which nearly destroyed the U.S. Army expeditionary force in Cuba. The Philippine Insurrection figure may also be an indication of a higher incidence of disease and infection in the tropics than in temperate climates. This explanation may also account for the very slight increase in the ratio of nonbattle to battle dead between the Korean and Vietnam War.

Disease and Nonbattle Injuries

Four factors affect the disease rates of a military force: (1) the season of the year in temperate climates; (2) a tropical climate; (3) the quality of medical care; and (4) the incidence of battle casualties.

In northern and northwestern Europe and the northern United States, the hospital admission rate for disease is approximately twice as high in early winter (about 0.30% per day in December and January) as in summer (about 0.15% per day in June, July, and August). This seasonal variation almost disappears in subtropical and tropical regions.

In tropical climates, however, the disease rate throughout the year is approximately 1.35 times greater than the average rate for temperate climates. In other words, if the average disease admission rate per day in a temperate climate is about 0.22 percent, the average rate in a tropical climate will be about 0.30 percent per day.

The effect of high-quality, sophisticated medical care upon disease death rates is shown in Table 8. While admissions to hospitals are not greatly affected by the quality of medical care (with the exception of the effect of malarial suppressants such as quinine and Atabrine upon malaria admissions in the tropics), the length of hospital stay and the number of deaths from illness are reduced sharply when quality medical care is applied.

Regardless of the other effects upon disease rates discussed above, there is a clear and consistent correlation between disease rates and battle casualty rates in the combat zone. The following quotation from Beebe and DeBakey (1952) is relevant:

> It is of the nature of man to react with his entire being to strong stimuli. If men are placed in a combat situation their attrition is not well estimated by adding a casualty rate to their previous rates of non-battle causes. Life under combat conditions will interfere with preventive measures otherwise considered routine and effective, will transform anxiety into somatic symptoms, particularly those referable to the gastro-intestinal and cardiovascular systems, and may bring new risks of disease and non-battle injury.
>
> That non-battle attrition depends upon combat is well established but the numerical relationship is not one which can be specified for all places and for all times. Environmental circumstances and the previous experience of the troops shape the relationship in myriad ways. The most uniform and strongest of these relationships is the correlation between wounding and psychiatric breakdown in combat troops. . . .

This explains why there is usually a noticeable rise in nonbattle injuries (as opposed to disease) when a unit is suffering battle casualties. Otherwise, there is no apparent relationship between nonbattle injuries and either disease or battle casualties. In the American wars of the nineteenth and twentieth centuries, the hospital admission rate for nonbattle injuries has been quite constant, about 0.03 percent per day, with deaths about 0.001 percent per day.

Causes of Casualties

There have been major changes in the causes of casualties over the last 150 years. Prior to the middle of the nineteenth century, as noted earlier, nearly half of all casualties were caused by artillery. Then, for the three major wars of the mid-nineteenth century (American Civil War, Austro-Prussian War, and Franco-Prussian War) artillery caused barely 10 percent of the casualties, while infantry small arms (almost entirely the conoidal bullet of the rifled musket) inflicted nearly 90 percent of the losses.

By the early twentieth century, however, the relationship of the lethality of small arms and artillery in terms of casualties caused had more than returned to the pre–Civil War situation. In fact, as shown in Tables 9 and 10, artillery and mortar shell fragments caused nearly seven out of ten WIA and DOW in World War I. The increased effectiveness of artillery was the result of indirect fire techniques (i.e., the ability of the artillery to fire effectively while out of range and observation of hostile infantrymen).

If we assume that the proportions of those killed in action by different causative agents (for which data is not available) were approximately the same as for those dying of wounds, then the percentages of those hit by artillery or mortar shell fragments were approximately as shown in

TABLE 9. *Causes of Wounded in Action for Twentieth-century Wars (U.S. only)*

	Percent of WIA caused by				
War	*Small arms*	*Shell fragments*	*Mines & booby traps*	*Toxic gas*	*Other*
World War I	19	46	*	32	3
World War I w/o gas	28	68	-	-	4
World War II	32	53	3	-	12
Korean War	33	59	4	-	4
Vietnam War	51	36	11	-	2

* = n.a.

TABLE 10. *Causes of Died of Wounds in Twentieth-century Wars (United States only)*

War	Percent of DOW caused by				
	Small arms	*Shell fragments*	*Mines & booby traps*	*Toxic gas*	*Other*
World War I	18	71	*	9	2
World War I w/o gas	20	78	-	-	2
World War II	20	62	4	-	14
Korean War	27	61	4	-	8
Vietnam War	16	65	15	-	4

* = n.a.

Table 11 for the four major U.S. wars of the twentieth century.

The proportion of artillery casualties was so much higher for World War I because the combatants relied so heavily upon artillery in dealing with the trench warfare stalemate of that conflict. The inability of either side to achieve major breakthroughs until near the end of the war greatly inhibited maneuver and the employment of weapons other than artillery. Since most of the toxic gas used in the war was projected by artillery shells, it could be considered that the proportion of all casualties caused by artillery in World War I was actually between 75 percent and 79 percent.

There was a much lower proportion of casualties caused by artillery in the Vietnam War. World Wars I and II and the Korean War were conventional wars, fought between traditional armed forces with the most sophisticated weapons available and in accordance with doctrines keyed to those weapons. The Vietnam War was very different. The guerrilla nature of the actual combat engagements unquestionably has been overemphasized, since much of the fighting was between the conventional U.S. and South Vietnamese armies on one side and the conventional North Vietnamese Army on the other. Unlike other wars, however, there was no front line, and the manner in which the conventional forces were employed was such that there were no large formation battles involving divisions and larger organizations. Most combat engagements were between companies and platoons. Seldom were full battalions and brigades (or regiments) employed conventionally against each other. The engagements were relatively brief and without the lengthy artillery preparations typical of other twentieth-century conventional conflicts that involved linear tactics. The Americans and South Vietnamese were supported by a substantial amount of artillery. The North Vietnamese had a much lower proportion of artillery, although their mortar support was ample. It is surprising that under these conditions as much as 40 percent of the casualties inflicted upon the American troops came from hostile artillery and mortars. The proportion of North Vietnamese casualties caused by U.S. artillery was undoubtedly much higher.

TABLE 11. *Proportion of Battle Casualties Caused by Artillery or Mortar Shell Fragments*

War	Percent (%)
World War I	50
World War II	55
Korean War	59
Vietnam War	40

Casualties by Branch of Service

Table 12 shows the distribution of casualties among the combat arms and the noncombat services in the major U.S. wars of the twentieth century (except for the Vietnam War; the battle casualties of the Vietnam War have not yet been analyzed at those levels). The infantry has suffered the highest proportion of casualties by far.

The relatively low proportion of armor casualties in these wars may be misleading. In World War I, tank warfare was just beginning, and only a small proportion of the American Expeditionary Force was in the tank corps. In World War II the proportion of armor troops, and of casualties, was considerably higher in the European theater in the closing months of the war than this average suggests. Armor branch personnel made up only 1.4 percent of the average strength deployed overseas in World War II. However, particularly in the European theater, armored units included a large proportion of troops of other basic branches, particularly infantry and artillery. There was relatively little use of armor in operations against the Japanese in the Pacific and Asiatic theaters. The small proportion of deployed armor forces in the Korean and Vietnam wars is also reflected in the casualty statistics for those wars.

TABLE 12. *Hypothetical Force and Casualty Relations by Branch (1980s and 1990s)*

	% Theater strength	% Branch casualties	% Casualties
Infantry	15	26.0	55.0
Armor	10	18.0	27.0
Artillery	8	5.0	6.5
Engineer	10	2.0	3.5
Air Defense	12	1.0	2.0
Medical Dept.	10	2.5	3.5
Other	35	0.5	2.5

Conclusions: Attrition Verities

Based upon observed patterns of attrition in modern combat as discussed above, hypotheses about personnel and materiel attrition have been formulated, which have been called "attrition verities" (Dupuy 1987). The first two of these verities do not deal with attrition directly but have great significance for understanding attrition. The following attrition verities include those that relate to materiel attrition as well as to attrition casualties (see Dupuy 1987 for details).

1. *In the average modern battle, the attacker's numerical strength is about double the defender's.*
2. *In the average modern battle, the attacker is more often successful than the defender.*
3. *Attrition rates of winners are lower than those of losers.*
4. *Small-force casualty rates are higher than those of large forces.*
5. *More effective forces inflict casualties at a higher rate than less effective opponents.*
6. *There is no direct relationship between force ratios and attrition rates.*
7. *In the average modern battle, the numerical losses of attacker and defender are often similar.*
8. *Loss rates for defenders vary inversely with the strength of fortifications.*
9. *Loss rates of a surprising force are lower than those of a surprised force.*
10. *In the average modern battle, attacker loss rates are somewhat lower than defender loss rates.*
11. *In bad weather, casualty rates for both sides decline markedly.*
12. *In difficult terrain, casualty rates for both sides decline markedly.*
13. *The casualty-inflicting capability of a force declines after each successive day in combat.*
14. *Casualty rates are lower at night than in daytime.*
15. *Casualty rates are higher in summer than in winter.*
16. *The faster the front line moves, the lower the casualty rates for both sides.*
17. *Casualty rates seem to decline during river crossings.*
18. *An "all-out" effort by one side raises loss rates for both sides.*
19. *A force with greater overall combat power inflicts casualties at a greater rate than the opponent.*
20. *The distribution of killed and wounded casualties in twentieth-century warfare is consistent.*
21. *Materiel loss rates are related to personnel casualty rates.*
22. *Tank loss rates are five to seven times higher than personnel casualty rates.*
23. *Attacker tank loss rates are generally higher than defender tank loss rates.*
24. *Artillery materiel loss rates are generally about one-tenth to one-third personnel casualty rates.*
25. *Self-propelled artillery loss rates are about three times greater than for towed guns.*
26. *Average World War II division engagement casualty rates were 1 percent to 3 percent per day.*
27. *Attrition rates in the 1973 October War were comparable to World War II.*
28. *Casualty rates in minor hostilities after 1945 are about half those experienced in World War II.*

TREVOR N. DUPUY

SEE ALSO: Casualties: Evacuation and Treatment; Chemical Warfare; Combat Stress; Indirect Fire; Medical Research and Technology; Medicine, Military; Replacements: Personnel and Materiel; War of Attrition.

Bibliography

Beebe, G. W., and M. E. DeBakey. 1952. *Battle casualties: Incidence, mortality, and logistic considerations.* Springfield, Ill.: Thomas.

Clausewitz, C. von. 1976. *On war.* Ed. and trans. M. Howard and P. Paret. Princeton, N.J.: Princeton Univ. Press.

Dodge, T. A. 1890–1904. *Great captains.* Vols. 1–4. Boston: Houghton Mifflin.

Dupuy, T. N. 1985. *Numbers, predictions, and war.* Rev. ed. Fairfax, Va.: HERO Books.

———. 1987. *Understanding war.* New York: Paragon House.

———. 1990. *Attrition: Forecasting battle casualties and equipment losses in modern wars.* McLean, Va.: HERO Books.

Livermore, T. L. 1957. *Numbers and losses in the Civil War in America, 1861–1865.* Reprint. Bloomington, Ind.: Indiana Univ. Press.

Love, A. G. 1931. *War casualties.* Carlisle Barracks, Pa.: Medical Field Service School.

Longmore, T. 1872. *A treatise on gunshot wounds.* Philadelphia, Pa.: J. B. Lippincott.

Neel, S. 1973. *Medical support of the U.S. Army in Vietnam, 1965–1970.* Washington, D.C.: Department of the Army.

Reister, F. A. 1973. *Battle casualties and medical statistics: U.S. Army experience in the Korean War.* Washington, D.C.: Surgeon General.

Stanton, S. 1981. *Vietnam order of battle.* Washington, D.C.: News Books.

Thayer, T. C. 1985. *The U.S. in Vietnam: War without fronts.* Boulder, Colo.: Westview Press.

U.S. Army. Armed Forces Information School. 1950. *The Army almanac.* Washington, D.C.: Government Printing Office.

Note on sources: For wars before World War II, data is based almost entirely upon Beebe and DeBakey and Love. In the light of the reliability of these authors, their careful research in the medical archives, and their sometimes deliberate deviations from the official figures, it is assumed that their figures are accurate. The World War II figures are based upon the official records, as reflected in the *Army Almanac*, and the *World Almanac* with some minor modifications based upon Beebe and DeBakey. The Korean War figures are based upon official data as presented in Reister; the Vietnam War data comes from Neel, Stanton, and, particularly, Thayer.

AUFTRAGSTAKTIK

Auftragstaktik is a German term referring to a method of issuing orders so that subordinate commanders are allowed maximum freedom of action to accomplish assigned missions. The U.S. Army, while not formally embracing this term to describe its recently developed "mission-type orders," has in effect accepted what many regard as the methodological essence of the German military system. Some have argued for the official adoption of Auftragstaktik to formalize what they regard as a practical *fait accompli.* U.S. Army literature frequently uses the term to describe what some officers regard as the best way to master the problems of command and control on a fluid battlefield. A perusal of the U.S. Army's journals *Military Review* and *Parameters* indicates the depth to which what are believed to be German methods have been infused into current military thought. Other writers—in particular the late British Brig. Richard Simpkin—have also stressed Auftragstaktik as the key to understanding the German system and as a possible model for other modern Western armies (Simpkin 1985). A number of self-styled military reformers in the United States have also praised the concept as one of the key elements in the German Army's tactical performance in World War II. Hughes's word of caution (1986) about potential difficulties in copying this and other German methods was disputed by van Creveld (1987). Clearly, the issue of Auftragstaktik is not merely an academic quest for understanding of past events and theories; it goes to the very heart of current Western command and control systems, and to one of the central issues in what has come to be known loosely as "maneuver warfare."

Traditional German Usage

Auftrag by itself conveys little of the essence of the Prusso-German method of command. As Simpkin (1985) and Hughes (1986) have pointed out, the term *Auftrag* cannot be properly translated to the British or American concept of "mission." Moreover, linking the term with *tactics* and translating the result as "mission-type orders" obscures the essence of the Prussian method and reduces a comprehensive approach to warfare to a slogan.

Although the central ideas in the German system of command and control date at least to the elder Moltke, the first comprehensive statements are found in the military literature published after his death. Official regulations written after World War I contain the clearest statements of how the basic concepts fit together. None of these sources used the term *Auftragstaktik*. Indeed, *Auftrag* itself is but one part of the concept, which had as its objective independent and rapid action by subordinate commanders.

German theory used three key concepts to define how a commander must prepare himself to act independently on the basis of the local situation and yet remain within the larger framework of his superiors. These three concepts were simple in essence but difficult in execution. They were *Absicht* (the intention of the higher commander), *Lage* (situation), and *Entschluss* (resolution, or decision). The key to the entire concept was *Absicht*, the higher commander's concept of executing his plans for a battle. The subordinate commander received an *Auftrag* from his superior in the form of an order, which also outlined the overall concept of the operation or battle. He then considered the broad, local, and geographical complexities of the situation (*Lage*). Together, the higher commander's intent, the task he assigned, and the situation produced what the Germans called a "problem," an approach used both in peacetime training and in battlefield situations. After considering these three factors, the subordinate commander reached his *Entschluss*, or resolution of the problem.

Commander's Intent

The key to the entire process was the intention of the higher commander, rather than the specific task (*Auftrag*) he had assigned to any particular subordinate. The commander's intention gave unity to the entire undertaking and was the fundamental precondition of successful cooperation in war (Moltke 1916; Blume 1896).

Local circumstances changed, as did the broader conditions that had given rise to the task. In some cases, such altered circumstances warranted changes either to the subordinate's resolution or to the task assigned by the higher commander. In the absence of further orders from his superiors, the subordinate commander thus had to decide if he should change his plan or abandon his task, or both. German theory, with its emphasis on speed in adjusting to new circumstances and in maintaining the initiative, allowed such alterations to original plans, although they were not to be undertaken without good reason. German officers were fond of quoting Frederick the Great's statement that it would be better to make a mistake in a resolution than to delay and reach no resolution (Boetticher 1930). By 1921, official regulations had acknowledged what leading theorists had been saying for many years: delay in reacting to changed situations was worse than making a mistake. The semiofficial literature, even before World War I, emphasized that immediate action, even if flawed, was always preferable to lengthy searches for the perfect resolution. As the unofficial handbook on command stated, "Only inactivity is always wrong" (*Truppenführung* 1914, privately published, not to be confused with the later official manual of the same name).

Altering Plans

The willingness to alter plans according to changed circumstances extended to a subordinate commander and the task he had received from his superior. In his instructions for high commanders of 1869, Moltke authorized junior commanders to subordinate tasks to their own considerations of the situation, especially when a battle was in progress (Moltke 1916). Gen. Wilhelm Blume, a leading military writer before World War I, also pointed out that it was the duty of the subordinate to act upon his own initiative when his orders had become irrelevant due to changed circumstances. The subordinate should act according to his understanding of the higher commander's intention when the original task was established, even if this meant acting in direct opposition to the orders. The first post-1918 regulation, *Führung und Gefecht* (1921), gave official authorization to abandoning the task when necessary as long as the commander acted within the larger framework. The *Truppenführung* regulation of 1933 also recognized the occasional need to abandon an outdated task within the overall framework (*im Rahmen des Ganzen*).

Improvisation

Implementing a system of command based on intent was no easy task. The Prussian and German armies lacked a rigid structure or format for orders because it might not allow sufficient flexibility for local situations. The result was that commanders frequently failed to convey their intent in a clear manner. This remained a problem on the eve of World War II, despite the emphasis placed on such clarity for at least 75 years. Volkmann's short handbook on techniques for orders (1936) emphasized that *Absicht* was the key to a good order but warned that too many commanders framed it poorly or not at all. "Whoever does not force himself to the sharpest self-education on this point remains a tactical bungler" (Volkmann 1936).

"It is easier to shepherd sheep than lions, but with the latter one has more effect on the enemy, even if the sheep wear wolf's fur." These words of Gen. Walter Reinhardt, used in reference to the need for a sense of independence and responsibility in high military commanders, captures the goals of the Prusso-German approach to command (Reinhardt 1932). The object was to develop subordinate commanders who would act on their own initiative regardless of the risks and who would willingly accept the responsibility of independent decisions. The German Army's theorists and historians consistently attributed the past successes of Prussian armies to the initiative of commanders at all levels. The reverse of this was the frequent discussion of lost opportunities, which in retrospect seemed to have been more harmful in the long run than defeats. German theorists believed that the difference between an ordinary victory and a decisive battle of annihilation was either timidity in exploiting fleeting opportunities provided by local success or the unwillingness of local commanders to act without orders. Improvisation was the basis of the entire Prusso-German approach to warfare. In the case of unit command, an important issue related to the Auftragstaktik principle was the question of how to develop commanders who would take the initiative, exercise independent judgment, and act on the basis of local circumstances.

Officer Preparation

The Prusso-German approach to officer education and development used several methods to develop the kind of battlefield leaders who could act in the expected manner. The Prussian system of professional education stressed the "applicatory" method of studying strategy and tactics, with military history and current theory receiving nearly equal emphasis. Of more relevance was officer training through field maneuvers and map exercises. During field maneuvers, command of Prussian units frequently passed to lower commanders. Lieutenants commanded companies in such training, while captains and majors commanded battalions. Officers who read the Prussian literature on the Franco-Prussian war were well aware of cases such as that of the Sixth Grenadier Regiment at Sedan—where in 1870, Napoleon III capitulated. A major commanded the regiment, while three first lieutenants commanded battalions. At lower levels, six lieutenants commanded companies, as did four noncommissioned officers. It thus made good sense to allow officers to gain command experience at levels higher than their normal assignment.

A second aspect of officer training was the practice of placing officers in situations, either in field or map exercises, where they would be forced to act either without orders or in direct disobedience to orders from their superiors. The 1908 *Field Service Regulation* (paragraph 12) established that practical exercises should have as one of their purposes the development of independent decisions and actions. Some German theorists found support for this in Clausewitz, who concluded his discussion of the dangers of disobedience that might endanger the superior's plans with the observation that undue timidity was a thousand times worse than undue audacity (Freytag-Loringhoven 1935; Blaschke 1934). Numerous writers were quick to attribute part of the German successes in 1870 to the willingness of subordinates to disobey their orders when the local situation demanded it (Blume 1896; Kutschka 1903). After World War I, Gen. Wilhelm Groener went so far as to argue that Gen. von Kluck should have disobeyed Lieutenant Colonel Hentsch's directive to break off the battle along the Ourcq (part of the battle of the Marne) (Groener 1931). Thus, by the end of the nineteenth century, the Prussian army had established a long tradition of encouraging independent action and initiative in its commanders at all levels.

The Twentieth Century

Reliance on individual judgment of local circumstances within one's understanding of the overall framework of the higher commander's concept for battles or operations was a staple of the military literature before and after World War I. The theoretical basis lay in Clausewitz, in a variety of regulations, and in the writings of leading officers from Moltke onward. The Prussian Army's interpretation of the events of 1870 offered further justification for this view, which had become something of a cliche by 1914—despite Count Alfred von Schlieffen's mixed opinion. Both von Schlieffen's methods and the events of 1914–18 provided reasons for reopening what by 1914 had been considered a firmly decided issue.

Schlieffen's Position

Count Alfred von Schlieffen, who headed the Prussian General Staff from 1891 through 1905, was of the opinion that Moltke had erred when he tried to lead entire armies with general directives (Mette 1938). However, historians disagree on whether Schlieffen encouraged or discouraged continuing the principle of independent action by subordinates. Helmut Otto, a leading East German scholar of Prussian theory under Schlieffen, argued that Schlieffen was not in the tradition of Moltke on this point (Otto 1966). Guenther Rothenberg (1986) has argued to the contrary, pointing to Schlieffen's support of the infantry regulations of 1888 and his efforts to encourage initiative among his general staff officers. On the other hand, Rothenberg quite rightly cites the arguments of a number of Schlieffen's contemporary critics who felt that his view of war was mechanistic and actually tended to stifle initiative in subordinates. The German general and historian Baron Friedrich von Cochenhausen (1933), writing after World War I, pointed out Schlieffen's reverence for the strict methods of control used by Frederick the Great. Regardless of the details of these widely divergent interpretations, the East German historian Gerhard Förster (1967) was probably correct in his argument that the German methods of World War II marked a move away from Schlieffen's tendency toward schematism in conducting battles.

Experience of World War I

The experience of position warfare between 1914 and 1918 produced decisive, although temporary, changes in German command methods. As the encounter battles of August and September 1914 turned into the bloody stalemate of static trench warfare, and as its prewar officer corps fell victim to Western firepower, the German army gradually adopted the rigid command methods typical of other armies of the period. Orders became longer and reached into details that would have been unthinkable in the old Prussian army. The greatly expanded use of sketches and improved communications provided further opportunities for nervous commanders to dictate details to their subordinates and to interfere in tactical minutiae. This doubtless served to stifle initiative at lower levels (Geyer 1925). On more practical grounds, the need for close coordination between artillery barrages, poison gas, engineer support, and so forth tended to produce setpiece battles entirely at odds with the tradition of Clausewitz and Moltke. The much-heralded "storm troop" tactics of the German offensives of 1918 were essentially an effort to find tactics capable of restoring mobility to the battlefield, but the attempt to restore the initiative of local commanders was an even more important development in the long run. As the best and most influential study of breakthrough efforts in World War I pointed out (Krafft von Dellmensingen 1937), the experiences of both failed and successful attacks illustrated the dangers of excessively detailed command and showed that clever improvisation by subordinate commanders was the foundation of all battle leadership. Indeed, the strong emphasis on subordinate initiative in the postwar regulations was doubtless in response to the view of World War I as an aberration in this area as well as in that of tactics at large.

Modern Communications

The steady improvements in modern communications methods raised new challenges to the principle of independent local commanders during and after World War I. Even before 1914, Gen. Wilhelm von Blume had warned that the telegraph was a threat to local initiative. In 1928, retired General Feeser warned that improved wire and wireless communications narrowed the range of local initiative, a process which he regarded as having been a problem in World War I (Feeser 1928). Five years later, William Justrow's important *Feldherr und Kriegstechnik* (1933), which was harshly critical of the old army, repeated this warning. In 1939, Col. Hermann Foertsch, then in the General Staff, predicted that improved communications would allow more strict control and that specific orders would replace general directives as the basis for command (Foertsch 1939).

The actual command and control methods of German units in World War II have been the subject of much speculation by Western army officers seeking to learn the secrets of the early German successes. Nevertheless, little serious research exists on the topic. Generalizations are particularly difficult because of the wide range of units and the drastic internal changes within units as the war progressed, as well as the great variety of circumstances dominant on the various fronts.

Hitler's Orders

Hitler's interference in the conduct of operations and battles, and in particular his "stand fast" order after the repulse at Moscow, marked a new departure in the struggle between strict command from above and the exercise of local initiative below. The German army's wartime literature reflected this tension and the difficulties of maintaining local initiative in the changed circumstances after 1942. Erich Weniger's article in *Wehrwissenschaftliche Rundschau* (1944) was a massive attack on the army's entire tradition of local initiative. Weniger argued that for decades German officers had distorted military history to justify their enthusiasm for independent subordinate commanders. Drawing upon examples from 1870–71, Weniger argued that by 1914 *Auftragsverfahren* (action based on task) had gone too far. He stressed the limits placed on subordinates by both Schlieffen and Hindenburg and even represented Seeckt as one of those who disliked independent subordinates.

The Broader Perspective

Finally, one must consider the so-called Auftragstaktik principles within the broader framework of the Prusso-German approach to warfare. Individual factors in this approach, including command and control methods, were effective only to the extent that they harmonized with other important aspects. The Prussian system and principles of officer selection, promotion, education, and assignment were just as important as the Auftrag principle. In fact, they were integral to the effective functioning of the command and control system. Lengthy command tours, to cite only one example, allowed officers to develop their abilities and restricted command positions to the capable few. German military literature, both official and semiofficial, provided no formulas for simplifying complex situations nor recipes to guide those who could not think for themselves.

A Lifestyle, Not Merely a Command Method

As one distinguished German officer has recently pointed out, Auftragstaktik was more than merely a system of command; it was part of a particular lifestyle typical of Prussian officers for more than a century (Uhle-Wettler 1984). From the days of Moltke through the early years of World War II, aristocratic German officers regarded themselves as independent individuals with special rights and responsibilities. The officer corps' code and courts of honor and its internal grievance system reflected its unique social and political position, which continued until the entire structure (as well as much of its ethical base) collapsed under the pressures of the rapid expansion after 1934 and the subsequent large-scale surrender to Nazi ideology. The paucity of centralized training and educational facilities for most officers reflected the extreme German reliance upon individuals to develop their own skills and upon commanders to prepare their subordinates.

Problems of Modern Application

Wrenching the *Auftrag* principle from its broader context in the Prussian-German approach to war might well be an undertaking of questionable validity. For purposes of clarity, this article has used the term *system* to describe the German approach to command and other matters. In a larger comparative sense, however, the Prusso-German armies had no system in the modern military meaning of that word. The systematic approach to warfare, which shaped most Western armies as well as those of the Soviet Union and its former allies, may well be contradictory to and incompatible with old German practices. Two questions emerge from the broad issues, of which Auftragstaktik is but the most visible sign: (1) can modern Western armies imitate this approach? (2) should they?

In answering these questions, one immediately leaves the sphere of history and enters the uncertain future. One can infer from the current literature of the American army that it has adopted the concept of Auftragstaktik, if one equates that with mission-type orders. Yet the results of the National Training Center and the original "lessons learned" concepts from the Joint Readiness Training Center (for light forces) suggest that the most successful units continue to use detailed orders. The commander of the National Training Center, in a letter circulated throughout the U.S. Army in 1986, recommended detailed planning and orders, even at the level of brigade and battalion task force, despite the fact that such were contrary to the army's current doctrinal emphasis. Implementation of the Auftragstaktik principle in realistic peacetime maneuvers or in wartime would be very difficult for armies whose daily style of command emphasizes strict reliance upon detailed regulations of all types. An army cannot raise its junior officers for 20 years in a system that issues the death penalty to careers for a single mistake and then expect them to become the bold risk takers of the future. As long as Western armies regard Auftragstaktik simply as a policy of short or general orders, rather than as a fundamental principle governing all matters requiring decisions and judgment, their officers will not even understand what the principle entails, let alone implement it on the battlefield.

One thinks of Lord Carver's (1986) repeated observations of the consistent failure of British units in North Africa to take action, because they had no orders, even while other units were destroyed before their very eyes. Regardless of what its regulations might have said in theory, such an officer corps could never have adopted the Auftragstaktik principle in wartime when its entire peacetime tradition was quite the contrary. The question remains whether the equally bureaucratic Western armies of today can do so.

Daniel J. Hughes

See Also: Clausewitz, Karl von; Command; Command, Control, Communications, and Intelligence; Education, Military; Initiative in War; Leadership; Moltke the Elder; Prussia and Germany, Rise of; Schlieffen, Alfred, Count von.

Bibliography

Balck, W. 1908. *Taktik*. 6 vols. Berlin: R. Eisenschmidt.
Blaschke, R. 1934. *Karl von Clausewitz*. Berlin: Juncker und Dünnhaupt.
Blume, W. von. 1896. Selbstätigkeit der Führer im Kriege. *Beiheft zum Militärwochenblatt*, pp. 479–534.
Boetticher, F. von. 1930. Gehorchen und Führen. Gedanken über militärische Persönlichkeiterziehung. *Wissen und Wehr*, pp. 513–535.
Carver, F. M., Lord. 1986. *Dilemmas of the desert war*. Bloomington, Ind.: Indiana Univ. Press.
Cochenhausen, F. von. 1933. Kampf gegen übermacht. In *Wehr-*

gedanken. Eine Sammlung wehrpolitischer Aufsätze. Hamburg: Hanseatische Verlagsanstalt.
Feeser, Lt. 1928. Winke für das selbständige Studium der Kriegschichte. *Wissen und Wehr,* pp. 275–93.
Förster, G. 1967. *Totaler Krieg und Blitzkrieg.* East Berlin: Deutscher Militärverlag.
Foertsch, H. 1939. *Kriegskunst Heute und Morgen.* Berlin: Zeitgeschichte Verlag Wilhelm Andermann.
Freytag-Loringhoven, H. 1935. *The power of personality in war.* Harrisburg, Pa.: Military Service Publishing.
German War Ministry. 1921. *Führung und Gefecht der verbunden en Waffen.* Berlin: E. S. Mittler.
Germany, Chef der Heeresleitung. 1933. *Truppenführung.* Berlin: E. S. Mittler.
Geyer, Maj. 1925. Lehren für den Kampf um Festungen aus den Ereignissen des Weltkrieges auf dem Westlichen Kriegsschauplatz. *Wissen und Wehr,* pp. 441–456, 499–512.
Groener, W. 1931. *Der Feldherr wider Willen. Operative Studien über den Weltkrieg.* Berlin: E. S. Mittler.
Hughes, D. 1986. Abuses of German military history. *Military Review* 66(12):66–76.
Justrow, W. 1933. *Feldherr und Kriegstechnik.* Oldenburg: Gerhard Stalling.
Krafft von Dellmensingen, K. 1937. *Der Durchbruch. Studien an Hand der Vorgänge des Weltkrieges 1914–1918.* Hamburg: Hanseatische Verlagsanstalt.
Kutschka, Capt. 1903. Das Begegnungsgefecht. *Militärwochenblatt,* pp. 3494–3500.
Mette, S. 1938. *Vom Geist deutscher Feldherren. Genie und Technik 1800–1918.* Zurich: Scientia.
Moltke, H. von. 1916. War lessons, part 1. *Moltke's military works,* vol. 4. Fort Leavenworth, Kans.: Army Service Schools.
Otto, H. 1966. *Schlieffen und der Generalstab.* East Berlin: Deutscher Militärverlag.
Paret, P. 1986. Clausewitz. In *Makers of modern strategy: From Machiavelli to the nuclear age,* ed. P. Paret and G. A. Craig. Princeton N.J.: Princeton Univ. Press.
Rothenberg, G. 1986. Moltke, Schlieffen, and the doctrine of strategic envelopment. In *Makers of modern strategy: From Machiavelli to the nuclear age,* ed. P. Paret and G. A. Craig. Princeton, N.J.: Princeton Univ. Press.
Simpkin, R. 1985. *Race to the swift: Thoughts on twenty-first century warfare.* London: Brassey's.
Die Truppenführung. 1914. Berlin: R. Eisenschmidt.
Uhle-Wettler, F. 1984. *Höhe- und Wendepunkte deutscher Militärgeschichte.* Mainz: Hase and Koehler.
van Creveld, M. 1987. On learning from the Wehrmacht and other things. *Military Review* 68(1):62–71.
Vigor, P. 1983. *Soviet blitzkrieg theory.* New York: St. Martin's Press.
Volkmann, H. 1936. *Befehlstechnik. Winke und Anregungen für ihre Anwendung im Rahmen der Division und des verstärkten Regiments.* Berlin: E. S. Mittler.
Weniger, E. 1944. Die Selbstätigkeit der Unterführer und ihre Grenzen. *Wehrwissenschaftliche Rundschau* 9:100–15.

AUSTRALIA, COMMONWEALTH OF

The Commonwealth of Australia is the only nation which occupies an entire continent. Although Australia has a history unmarred by domestic warfare, it contributed manpower and resources to the Allied war effort in both World Wars. More recently during the Korean War, the Malayan insurgency, and the Vietnam War, Australia has given substantial assistance to United Nations (UN), British, and U.S. forces engaged in conventional and antiguerrilla operations in Asia.

Power Potential Statistics

Area: 7,686,850 square kilometers (3,146,240 sq. mi.)
Population: 16,906,000
Total Active Armed Forces: 68,300 (0.404% of pop.)
Gross Domestic Product: US$254.4 billion (1990 est.)
Annual Defense Expenditure: US$6.6 billion (2.2% of GDP, 1990 est.)
Iron and Steel Production:
  Crude steel: 6.65 million metric tons (1988–89)
  Pig iron: 5.88 million metric tons (1988–89)
Fuel Production:
  Coal: 183.86 million metric tons (1988–89)
  Coke: 0.003 million metric tons (1986)
  Crude oil: 31,264 million metric tons (1987–88)
  Natural gas: 15,249 million cubic meters (1987–88)
Electrical Power Output: 150,000 million kwh (1990)
Merchant Marine: 77 vessels; 2,249,926 gross registered tons
Civil Air Fleet: 150 major transport aircraft; 524 usable airfields (270 with permanent-surface runways); 1 with runways over 3,659 meters (12,000 ft.); 17 with runways 2,440–3,659 meters (8,000–12,000 ft.); 401 with runways 1,220–2,440 meters (4,000–8,000 ft.)

For the most recent information, the reader may refer to the following annual publications:
The Military Balance. International Institute for Strategic Studies. London: Brassey's (UK).
The Statesman's Year-Book. New York: St. Martin's Press.
The World Factbook. Central Intelligence Agency. Washington, D.C.: Brassey's (US).

History

Australia's settlement by Europeans brought little conflict with the native peoples, unlike the bitter Maori Wars in neighboring New Zealand. The bulk of Australia's military experience has come from its involvement in overseas wars, beginning with the Boer War of 1899–1902. Australian forces played a major role in World War I, particularly at Gallipoli and in the Palestine campaign; an Australian corps also fought on the western front in 1917–18. Australian forces were also heavily involved in World War II, not only in the nearby Pacific theater but also in North Africa and Italy. The cooperation between Australian and U.S. forces during World War II established a close alliance which has endured since that time, strengthened by the gradual British withdrawal from its Asian defense commitments after 1945.

That reliance led to Australian commitment of several thousand combat and noncombat troops in South Vietnam in the late 1960s and early 1970s. The recent coolness between the United States and New Zealand over the presumed presence of nuclear weapons on U.S. ships visiting New Zealand has placed Australia in an awkward position between her two allies. It is unlikely that any change in Australia's government would see a major shift in military policy, although the last decade has seen an orientation away from overseas commitments and toward a regional defense.

Politico-Military Background and Policy

Traditionally, Australia, as a British colony and then as a dominion, had very limited standing armed forces backed by a large militia system, an arrangement similar to that which existed in Canada and New Zealand. Their experience in World War II and the postwar situation has convinced successive governments that this is no longer adequate, and Australia now maintains (in terms of the nation's historical practice) a moderately large peace-time army. Extensive ties with neighboring nations, notably New Zealand, Papua-New Guinea, Indonesia, and the new Melanesian and Polynesian states, show a sincere concern for regional security and stability. Australia is the only nation in the region that can undertake such a leadership role.

Strategic Problems

At the end of World War II, a consensus emerged in Australia not to send large expeditionary forces overseas in a future war, and that conviction has strengthened since the late 1940s. Australians, as citizens of a large and rich but sparsely settled nation, view densely populated Southeast Asia with unease. Australia enjoys friendly relations with nearly all its neighbors, but the most populous of them, Indonesia, is regarded a serious potential threat because the region of Australia closest to Indonesia is among the country's least-settled and least-developed. The Australians are also suspicious of Indonesian territorial ambitions toward Papua-New Guinea. Although Australia and Indonesia have generally enjoyed good relations, especially since the early 1970s, Indonesia's absorption of West Irian (Western New Guinea) in 1963 and of Portuguese Timor in November 1975 provides a basis for Australian concerns. Much of current Australian military planning is therefore oriented toward ensuring the security of the northern and western coasts against potential infiltration and commando-type raids. Since Australia does not possess sufficient manpower to garrison these areas effectively, armed forces planners are relying on mobility, especially that provided by helicopters, to maintain a strong military capability in the unsettled northwest of Australia.

Military Assistance

As part of its role as a regional power, Australia renders considerable military assistance to its neighbors. Although in the past Australia provided cash assistance to both Singapore and Malaysia, currently it is not providing cash or material assistance to any neighboring nation (although it continues to contribute other forms of aid). Australia's largest overseas military commitment is in the form of an infantry company and a P-3C Orion patrol aircraft detachment at Singapore. There is a 100-man unit of advisers, engineers, and trainers in Papua-New Guinea, as well as advisers in Indonesia, Malaysia, Thailand, Singapore, the Solomon Islands, Vanuatu, Tonga, Western Samoa, and Kiribati. In addition, many Indonesian military officers gain some or all of their professional education in Australia.

On a wholly cooperative basis, Australia exchanges students at military schools with the United Kingdom, New Zealand, Canada, and the United States. Australia also exchanges information with these nations within the framework of existing alliances, but otherwise receives no military assistance of any kind.

Defense Industry

Australia's domestic arms industry is limited by the nation's relatively small industrial base, and made less essential by secure sources of sophisticated modern weapons in Great Britain and the United States. Australia constructs a large proportion of its own naval vessels, including River-class FFGs, Fremantle-class coastal patrol ships, and several smaller ship types. The Australians also produce most of their own ammunition (missiles excepted) and small arms, and often conduct extensive modifications on the equipment purchased abroad.

Alliances

Australia is a member of the United Nations and the Commonwealth. Its principal and most important alliance is the Australia–New Zealand–United States (ANZUS) Pact, dating from 1952. This alliance is further strengthened by separate bilateral agreements with both New Zealand and the United States, but has suffered some strain since the United States broke with New Zealand in 1985 over that nation's refusal to allow U.S. ships (some of which might be carrying nuclear weapons) to visit New Zealand ports. In addition to the ANZUS Pact and its linked agreements, Australia has been a member of the Southeast Asian Treaty Organization (SEATO) since its inception in 1955, and maintains close ties with several other Commonwealth nations, notably Great Britain and Canada.

Defense Structure

The nominal commander in chief of Australia's armed forces is the governor-general, an appointee of the monarch. (The monarch of the United Kingdom—currently Queen Elizabeth II—is also the monarch of Australia.) Actual executive power is vested in the Prime Minister and his cabinet, who are responsible to Parliament. Within the Cabinet, responsibility for defense matters rests with the Minister of Defence, who exercises control through the individual service ministers, who are not members of the Cabinet. The three services (army, navy, and air force) are each administered by a board, consisting of the service minister, the service's chief of staff, and four or five senior civilian officials and military officers. Joint operations fall under the control of unified commands, and overall defense planning is in the hands of a joint staff, but in other respects the three services remain separate.

(For an explanation of the abbreviations and symbols used in the following section of military statistics, see the list of Abbreviations and Acronyms in each volume.)

Total Armed Forces

Active: 68,300 (incl 8,500 women).
Reserves: 29,200. Army: 26,000; Navy: 1,600; Air: 1,600.

ARMY: 30,300 (inclu. 3,100 women).
Land Comd: 6 military districts, 1 northern comd.
Comd tps: 1 AD regt +, 1 engr regt (construction), 1 avn regt.
1 SF reg (3 sqn)
1 inf div
1 mech bde (1 armd, 1 mech, 1 para inf bn)
2 inf bde (each 2 inf bn)
1 recce regt +
1 APC regt
3 arty regt (1 med, 2 fd)
1 engr regt +
1 avn regt (3 hel, 1 ac sqn).
(2 reserve inf bde see below)
Reserves:
1 div HQ, 7 bde HQ, 2 recce regt, 1 APC regt plus 2 APC sqn, 15 inf bn, 1 cdo, 5 arty (1 med, 4 fd) regt, 1 fd arty bty, 4 engr (2 fd, 2 construction) regt, 3 regional surveillance units.
Equipment:
MBT: 103 Leopard 1A3.
AIFV: 53 M-113 with 76mm gun.
APC: 725 M-113 (incl variants, 205 in store), 15 LAV.
Towed arty: 105mm: 142 M2A2/L5, 63 Hamel; 155mm: 34 M-198.
Mortars: 81mm: 294.
ATGW: 10 Milan.
RCL: 84mm: 597 Carl Gustav; 106mm: 68 M-40A1.
SAM: 20 Rapier, 19 RBS-70.
Aircraft: 13 GAF N-22B Missionmaster, 14 PC-6.
Helicopters: 35 S-70 (Army/Air Force crews), 44 OH-58 Kalkadoon, 6 UH-1H (armed).
Marine: 16 LCM, 85 LARC-5 amph craft.

NAVY: 15,700 (incl 900 Fleet Air Arm, 1,900 women). Maritime Command, Support Command, 6 Naval Area cmd. Bases: *Sydney*, NSW (Maritime Command HQ), base for: 4 SS, 3 DDG, 6 FF, 1 patrol, 1 LST, 1 AOR, 1 AGT, 2 LCT. *Cockburn Sound*, WA, base for: 2 SS, 3 FF, 3 patrol, 1 survey, 1 AOR. *Cairns*, Qld., 5 patrol, 1 survey, 2 LCT. *Darwin*, NT., 6 patrol, 1 LCT.
Submarines: 6 Oxley (mod UK Oberon) with Mk 48 HWT and Harpoon SSM.
Principal Surface Combatants: 10.
Destroyers: 3 Perth (US Adams) DDG with 1 SM-1 MR SAM/ Harpoon SSM launcher; plus 2 × 3 AST T (Mk 46 LWT), 2 × 127mm guns.
Frigates: 7: 4 Adelaide (US Perry) FFG, with S-70B-2 Seahawk, 2 × 3 ASTT; plus 1 × SM-1 MR SAM/Harpoon SSM launcher. 2 Swan, 1 Paramatta FF with 2 × 3 ASTT; plus 2 × 114mm guns.
Patrol and Coastal Combatants: 18: Inshore: 18: 15 Fremantle PFI, 3 Attack PCI (Reserve trg). (plus 2 PCC in store).
Mine Warfare: 6: 2 Rushcutter MHI. 2 Bandicoot and 2 Brolga auxiliary MSI.
Amphibious: 1 Tobruk LST, capacity 14 tk, 350 tps, hel deck. Plus craft; 5 LCT, capacity 3 tk (1 more in store).
Support and Miscellaneous: 10: 1 Success (mod Fr Durance) AOR, 1 Westralia AO, 1 Protector sub trials and safety, 1 trg/log spt (ex-ferry), 2 AGHS, 4 small AGHS, (1 AGOR in store).
Fleet Air Arm: (900); no cbt ac, 15 armed hel.
ASW: 1 hel sqn with 7 Sea King Mk 50/50A (ASW), 8 S-70B-2 (ASW/trg).
Utility/SAR: 1 sqn with 6 AS-350B, 3 Bell 206B; 1 with 2 BAe-748 (EW trg).

AIR FORCE: 22,300 (incl 3,500 women); 158 cbt ac, no armed hel.
FGA/Recce: 2 sqn with 18 F-111C, 4 RF-111C.
Fighter/FGA: 3 sqn with 53 F-18 (50 -A, 3 -B).
Training: 2 sqn with 46* MB-326H.
MR: 2 sqn with 19 P-3C.
OCU: 1 with 18* F-18B.
FAC: 1 flt with 4 CA-25 Winjeel.
Tanker: 4 Boeing 707.
Transport: 7 sqn: 2 with 24 C-130 (12 -E, 12 -H); 1 with 6 Boeing 707 (4 fitted for air-to-air refueling); 2 with 21 DHC-4; 1 VIP with 5 Falcon-900; 1 with 10 HS-748 (8 for navigation trg, 2 for VIP tpt).
Training: 42 PC-9 (increasing to 64 by Jan 1992), 45 CT-4/4A.
Support: 4 Dakota, 2 Nomad, 2 DHC4.
Missiles:
ASM: AGM-84A.
AAM: AIM-7 Sparrow, AIM-9L/M Sidewinder.
AD: Jindalee OTH radar: 1 experimental, 3 planned. 3 control and reporting units (1 mobile).

FORCES ABROAD
Malaysia: Army: 1 inf coy (on 3-month rotational tours). Air Force: det with P-3C ac.
Papua New Guinea: 100; trg unit, 1 engr unit, 85 advisers.
Advisers in Indonesia, Solomon Is., Vanuatu, Tonga, W. Samoa and Kiribati.
UN and Peacekeeping: Middle East (UNTSO): 13 observers.

PARAMILITARY
Bureau of Customs: 10 GAF N-22B Searchmaster MR ac; 6 boats.

FOREIGN FORCES
U.S.: Air Force: 270; Navy: 450, joint facilities at NW Cape, Pine Gap and Nurrungar.
New Zealand: Air Force: 6 A-4K/TA-4K (providing trg for Australian Navy).

Future

A recent reassessment of Australia's defense needs judged that the most likely threat would be a low-intensity campaign directed against isolated settlements, outlying island possessions, or overseas trade routes. To secure against such an eventuality, the Australians have begun radar surveillance systems at three sites along the nation's northern coast, set up a naval squadron in Western Australia to provide a presence in the Indian Ocean, and undertaken a ten-year naval building program to add six new submarines and four to five major surface combatants to the navy. The army will receive additional lift helicopters, and a larger portion of its strength will be deployed to the north. Although Australia will keep its infantry company in Singapore, it will not deploy any of its planned fleet of 75 F/A-18s there, but will keep them in Australia. Notwithstanding the low-intensity threat, the Australian armed forces very sensibly maintain as wide a spectrum of capabilities as possible for the foreseeable future.

DAVID L. BONGARD
TREVOR N. DUPUY

SEE ALSO: Commonwealth of Nations; Indo-Pacific Area; New Zealand; South and Southwest Pacific.

Bibliography

Albinski, H. 1982. *The Australian-American security relationship*. St. Lucia: Univ. of Queensland Press.
American University. 1974. *Area handbook for Australia*. Washington, D.C.: Government Printing Office.
Crowny, F., ed. 1974. *A new history of Australia*. Melbourne: Wm. Heinemann Australia Pty.
Hughes, R. 1987. *The fatal shore*. New York: Knopf.
Hunter, B., ed. 1991. *The statesman's year-book, 1991–92*. New York: St. Martin's Press.
International Institute for Strategic Studies. 1991. *The military balance, 1991–1992*. London: Brassey's.

AUSTRIA, REPUBLIC OF

Austria is a small and mountainous country that occupies a strategic position in central Europe. Its neutrality is enshrined in the Austrian State Treaty of 1955, whereby the country regained full sovereignty from Allied occupation after World War II.

Power Potential Statistics

Area: 83,850 square kilometers (32,364 sq. mi.)
Population: 7,546,200
Total Active Armed Forces: 44,000 (0.583% of pop.)
Gross Domestic Product: US$111.0 billion (1990 est.)
Annual Defense Expenditure: US$1.4 billion (1% of GDP, 1990 est.)
Iron and Steel Production:
  Crude steel: 4.718 million metric tons (1989)
  Pig iron: 3.823 million metric tons (1989)
Fuel Production:
  Coal: 2.066 million metric tons (1989)
  Coke: 1.744 million metric tons (1986)
  Crude oil: 1.323 million metric tons (1989)
  Natural gas: 1.265 million cubic meters (1988)
Electrical Power Output: 49,290 million kwh (1989)
Merchant Marine: 32 vessels; 150,735 gross registered tons
Civil Air Fleet: 25 major transport aircraft; 54 usable airfields (20 with permanent-surface runways); none with runways over 3,659 meters (12,000 ft.); 5 with runways 2,440–3,659 meters (8,000–12,000 ft.); 4 with runways 1,220–2,440 meters (4,000–8,000 ft.).

For the most recent information, the reader may refer to the following annual publications:
The Military Balance. International Institute for Strategic Studies. London: Brassey's (UK).
The Statesman's Year-Book. New York: St. Martin's Press.
The World Factbook. Central Intelligence Agency. Washington, D.C.: Brassey's (US).

History

Although Austria in its current form has existed only since 1918, the country has a long and colorful history. It formed part of the Roman provinces of Noricum and Pannonia, and was incorporated in Charlemagne's empire after he defeated the Avars. Austria's greatest claim to fame is its status as the homeland of the Hapsburgs, who ruled from 1275 to 1918. Austria in general, and Vienna in particular, became the center of the Hapsburgs' Germanic empire, which at its greatest extent included most of modern Czechoslovakia and Hungary, as well as Austria and portions of Germany, Poland, and Yugoslavia. Although Austria lost the struggle for leadership of Germany when it was defeated by Prussia in 1866, its reorganization the following year as the dual Austro-Hungarian monarchy gave the state another half century. Defeat in World War I, however, led to the dissolution of the empire, and the creation of the modern states of Eastern Europe.

Between 1918 and 1938, Austria was faced with several difficulties. It had to adapt a multinational imperial administration to the government of a small national state, a situation complicated by the hyperinflation of the early 1920s and the general economic depression of the early 1930s. The fragile political consensus, which permitted republican government, collapsed under these pressures. In 1933 Chancellor Engelbert Dolfuss became virtual dictator and effectively suspended the constitution. The Social Democrat revolt of 12 February 1934, and the attempted Nazi coup of 25 July 1934 (which resulted in Dolfuss's murder) further destabilized the country.

Dolfuss's successor, Kurt von Schuschnigg, was a milder man, and Austria drifted for the next few years without clear direction. A second attempted Nazi coup, uncovered by the police in January 1938, provoked the final crisis. Schuschnigg called for a plebiscite to decide on unification with Germany (*Anschluss*), slated for 13 March, but Hitler, knowing how a plebiscite could be rigged, invaded Austria on 12 March. A rescheduled plebiscite on 10 April 1938 gave Hitler and the *Anschluss* support from 99 percent of the voters. (Hitler did indeed know how to rig plebiscites.) For the next seven years, Austria was an integral part of the Third Reich.

Austria, like Germany, was occupied by Soviet, American, British, and French forces in 1945, but unlike Germany avoided the fate of partition. Although limited self-government was restored with elections in November 1945, full sovereignty was not regained until 1955. On 15 May that year, the four occupying powers and Austria signed the Austrian State Treaty in Vienna; it formally established the Austrian republic on its pre-1938 frontiers, and provided for an end to occupation and for monetary compensation to the Soviets (later reduced slightly) for "occupation costs."

Since 1955, Austria has pursued a policy of general neutrality, although it has close economic ties to Western Europe. Austria has often served as a meeting ground for Soviet and Western interests, and Austria conducts considerable trade with neighboring East bloc nations. Postwar internal politics have been dominated by the conservative, Catholic-oriented People's Party and by the moderate Socialist Party, which have often formed governing coalitions.

Politico-Military Background and Policy

Under the Austrian State Treaty, Austria may not possess nuclear weapons, and the declaration of permanent neutrality, which was voted into law in October 1955, prohibits Austria from entering any military alliances. The armed forces are maintained through conscription of all able-bodied males reaching age 19 for six months' initial training. After that initial service, men enter the reserve, where they are liable for call-up for periodic refresher training and have a service obligation through age 51 (for enlisted men) or 65 (for officers, NCOs, and specialists).

Strategic Problems

Austria's small size and its strategically important location in central Europe astride the Danube Valley corridor, coupled with self-imposed constitutional limits on defense policy, dictate a purely defensive military stance. The geography of the northern and eastern frontier areas (open country well-suited for mechanized warfare) would make it difficult for Austria to resist a full-scale attack from those directions. The rugged southwest half of the country would be difficult to either invade or subdue, and helps to limit Austrian vulnerability.

Military Assistance

Between 1955 and 1977, Austria received nearly US$100 million in military assistance from the United States, including the training of 429 personnel. During the same period, Austria received some limited assistance from Great Britain, but since the late 1970s has borne its entire defense effort on its own resources.

Defense Industry

Most of Austria's armaments are produced domestically by state-owned industrial concerns, with the exception of aircraft and main battle tanks, both of which are purchased abroad. The Saurer 4K4 APC and the Steyr Kuerassier light tank or tank destroyer have proved highly successful, and have been exported to African, Latin American, and Middle Eastern countries. Austria also produces most of its own artillery, mortars, and light weapons, and the SAF aircraft concern sells light utility and liaison aircraft abroad.

Alliances

Although prohibited by law from joining any military alliances, Austria is a member of the United Nations and the European Free Trade Association (EFTA). As part of its UN obligations, Austria has a 410-man infantry battalion in Cyprus (UNFICYP), a second battalion of 530 men in Syria (UNDOF), seventeen men with the United Nations Truce Supervisory Organization (UNTSO) in the Middle East, and seven observers in Iraq/Kuwait.

Defense Structure

The president of the republic (currently Kurt Waldheim, former secretary-general of the United Nations) is the nominal commander in chief of the armed forces. Administrative and operational authority is in the hands of the secretary of defense, under the prime minister.

(For an explanation of the abbreviations and symbols used in the following section of military statistics, see the list of Abbreviations and Acronyms in each volume.)

Total Armed Forces

(Air service forms part of the army):

Active: 44,000 (22,400 conscripts; some 68,000 reservists a year undergo refresher training, a proportion at a time). Terms of service: 6 months recruit trg, 60 days reservist refresher trg during 15 years (or 8 months trg, no refresher); 30–90 days additional for officers, NCO and specialists.

Reserves: 242,000 ready (72 hrs) reserves; 1,342,000 with reserve trg but no commitment (men to age 51; specialists, NCO, officers to 65).

ARMY: 38,000 (est. 20,000 conscripts).
Army HQ.
Standing Alert Force: (some 15,000):
- 1 mech div of 3 mech bde (each 1 tk, 1 mech inf, 1 SP arty; 2 with 1 SP ATK bn); 1 recce bn (cadre), 1 AA, 1 engr bn.
- 1 air-mobile, 1 mtn bn.

Field Units:
- Army: 1 HQ, 1 arty (cadre), 1 guard, 1 SF bn.
- Corps: 2 HQ, 2 arty (cadre), 1 SP ATK, 2 AA (cadre), 2 engr bn (cadre), 2 log regt (cadre).
- 9 Provincial Commands: Peacetime: trg and maint; on mob: equates to div HQ (with 1 inf bde, 1 or more territorial defense regt and indep units).
- 30 Landwehrstammregimenter (trg regt, no war role).

Reserves:
8 inf bde HQ: with 24 inf, 8 arty.
Territorial tps: (82,000): 25 inf regt, 90 inf coy, 42 guard coy; 16 hy, 15 lt inf, 11 inf/ATK bn, 5 hy arty bty (static), 13 engr, 6 ATK coy.

Equipment:
MBT: 159 M-60A3.
APC: 460 Saurer 4K4E/F.
Towed arty: 105mm: 108 IFH (M-2A1); 155mm: 24 M-114.
SP arty: 155mm: 54 M-109A2.
Fortress arty: 155mm: 24 SFK M-2.
MRL: 128mm: 18 M-51.
Mortars: 81mm: 551; 107mm: 80 M-2; 120mm: 200 M-43.
ATGW: 38 RBS-56 Bill.
RL: 400 LAW.
RCL: 74mm: Miniman; 84mm: Carl Gustav; 106mm: 446 M-40A1.
ATK guns:
SP: 105mm: 225 Kuerassier JPz SK.
Towed: 85mm: 240 M-52/-55;
Static: 90mm: some 60 M-47 tk turrets; 105mm: some 200 L7A2 (Centurion tk);
AD guns: 20mm: 560; 35mm: 74 GDF-002 twin towed; 40mm: 38 M-42 twin SP.
Marine wing: (under School of Military Engineering): 2 river patrol craft (; 16 boats.

AIR FORCE: 6,000 (2,400 conscripts); 54 cbt ac, no armed hel.
1 air div HQ; 3 air regt; 1 AD regt.
FGA: 1 regt with 30 SAAB 105.
Fighter: 1 regt with 24 J-350e.
Helicopters:
Recce: 12 OH-58B, 12 AB-206A.
Transport: (med): 23 AB-212; (lt): 8 AB-204 (9 in store).
SAR: 24 A-316 B Alouette.
Liaison: 1 sqn with 2 Skyvan 3M, 15 O-1 (10 -A, 5 -E), 11 PC-6B.
Training: 16 PC-7, 8 SAAB 105, 14 SAAB 91D.
AD: 3 bn with 36 20mm, 18 M-65 twin 35mm AA guns; Super-Bat and Skyguard AD, Goldhaube, Selenia MR(S-403) 3-D radar systems.

FORCES ABROAD
UN and Peacekeeping:
Cyprus (UNFICYP): 1 inf bn (410).
Iraq/Kuwait (UNIKOM): 7 observers.
Middle East (UNTSO): 17.
Syria (UNDOF): 1 inf bn (530).

Future

With the easing of East-West tensions in the late 1980s, and Mikhail Gorbachev's conventional disarmament initiatives of late 1988, Austria's main strategic problem in the 1990s will be its response to increasing integration in the European Community. Also, the political situation in the former Yugoslav Federal Republic could pose some problems, especially in regard to Austria's Slovenian minority. Austria's economy is sound, but declining numbers of young people (a common development in the industrialized world) may compel a reorganization of armed forces service and an expansion of the term of service to maintain the army's strength.

DAVID L. BONGARD
TREVOR N. DUPUY

SEE ALSO: Eugene, Prince of Savoy-Carignan; Prussia-Germany, Rise of; Western Europe; World War I.

Bibliography

American University. 1976. *Area handbook for Austria.* Washington, D.C.: Government Printing Office.
Crankshaw, E. 1963. *The fall of the house of Hapsburg.* London: Longmans.
Dupuy, T. N., et al. 1980. *The almanac of world military power.* San Rafael, Calif.: Presidio Press.
Hunter, B., ed. 1991. *The statesman's year-book, 1991–92.* New York: St. Martin's Press.
International Institute for Strategic Studies. 1991. *The military balance, 1991–1992.* London: Brassey's.
Society for the Promotion of Science and Scholarship. 1981. *Modern Austria.* Palo Alto, Calif.: Society for the Promotion of Science and Scholarship.

AUTOMATIC WEAPON

The need to provide individual soldiers with a weapon that enables them to engage numerous enemy targets for short periods led to the development of multiple-firing, rapid-firing, and automatic-firing weapons. True automatic fire is associated only with gunpowder weapons and depends upon either the energy generated by the expanding gases of the fired cartridge or recoil energy. The first fully automatic firearm was developed by Hiram Maxim—the father of the machine gun—in the late nineteenth century and gave soldiers the firepower they sought.

Britain's colonial forces first used Maxim guns in the Matabele War of 1893–94. In one engagement, 50 police of the Rhodesian Charter Company with only four machine guns fought off 5,000 Matabele warriors. Today, automatic weapons comprise rifles, submachine guns, machine guns, assault rifles, and various other weapons.

Operation of Automatic Weapons

Automatic firing is the process of feeding a cartridge, firing a round, and ejecting the casing, carried out by the mechanism of a weapon after a primary manual, electrical, or pneumatic cocking, and continuing as long as the trigger is held to the rear and there is still ammunition in the belt, feed-strip, or magazine. The same process describes semiautomatic fire from self-loading weapons, except that the trigger is pulled once per shot and must be released between shots.

This sequence of operations, which leads from the firing of one round to the firing of the next, comprises a basic cycle that is common to almost all automatic weapons, and a series of associated operations that vary with the weapon type. The energy required can come from only two sources: recoil energy or the energy that would otherwise be wasted as muzzle blast. These two sources of energy lead to one or another of the three methods used today in all automatic weapons: blowback, recoil, or gas operation.

BLOWBACK OPERATION

In this method of operation the energy required to carry out the cycle of operation is supplied to the bolt by the backward movement of the cartridge case caused by gas pressure. There are four systems of blowback operation: simple blowback, advanced primer ignition, delayed blowback, and blowback with a locked breech.

Simple blowback. This system in its simplest form allows for a totally unlocked breech and relies merely on the mass of the breechblock and the strength of the return spring to prevent the cartridge case from coming back too quickly after firing. This form of operation is suitable only where the cartridge is of low power relative to the weight of the breechblock. Simple blowback operations are effectively restricted to pistols and submachine guns.

Advanced primer ignition. More sophisticated blowback designs have been incorporated into large-caliber machine guns. These take advantage of the fact that a cartridge fired before being fully chambered allows half the available firing impulse to force the block back again. This in effect allows the breechblock to be made lighter. In such weapons the fixed firing pin of the simple blowback design is replaced by a controlled pin that strikes the cap at the desired point in the forward travel of the cartridge being chambered.

Delayed blowback. This method is also known as retarded blowback or hesitation blowback. Here, as in the previous blowback systems, the breechblock is not locked, but some mechanical delay is incorporated to ensure that the breechblock cannot move back so rapidly as to allow the unsupported cartridge case to emerge from the chamber while the pressure is still high. The delay may be achieved by means of a lever, or by a system of rollers that must be forced out of engagement with the barrel extension before the breechblock can move backward.

Blowback with a locked breech. In this system the breechblock is physically locked to the receiver of the weapon during the time the pressure is high, then unlocked in time to allow the residual pressure to blow the breechblock to the rear. This allows for use of the lightest possible breechblock with a high-powered cartridge, but the timing of breech opening is critical and the system tends to be expensive. It is also sensitive to variations in ammunition.

Advantages and disadvantages of blowback operation. The blowback method is cheap, simple, and reliable, and it allows for a configuration that makes for ease of changing barrels. Its disadvantages are that it allows no adjustment for power, fouling is left in the breech, and it is not suitable for vehicular use.

Recoil Operation

In this method of operation the energy required to carry out the cycle of operations is supplied to the bolt by the rearward movement of the bolt and barrel, locked together, caused by gas pressure. The system differs from the blowback in having a fully locked breech and in having the barrel move back with the breechblock. There are two types of recoil operation: long recoil and short recoil.

Long recoil. In the long recoil system both the bolt and barrel recoil a distance that is greater than the length of the unfired round. This method produces a very slow rate of fire, but is advantageous in those cases where it is important to minimize the forces exerted on the mounting. Except where that special requirement exists, this approach is rarely used.

Short recoil. Here the breechblock remains locked to the barrel only while the pressure is high. In practice, as with a round of rifle caliber, this involves a barrel travel of only a centimeter or so. This approach reduces the weight of the breechblock compared with that required in a blowback system. In smaller-caliber weapons, however, there is less recoil energy and the system will not function unless steps are taken to maximize the available energy and use it to best advantage.

Advantages and disadvantages. Machine guns based on recoil operation are particularly well suited for use in armored vehicles. They are generally sturdy, can have their rate of fire slowed down when desirable, and allow for easy change of barrels from the rear. A disadvantage is that there is no way of adjusting the power under adverse conditions.

Gas Operation

In this system of operation, the required energy is obtained from the pressure of gas tapped off from the barrel. The amount of gas required to operate a machine gun is not very great, and the effect on the pressure in the barrel—and hence on the velocity of the projectile—is correspondingly small.

The required gas can be tapped off anywhere between the breech and the muzzle, and examples can be found of every conceivable gas position. Different effects are obtained at different positions. At the muzzle the gas is at a relatively low pressure and is much cooler. As a result, more gas must be led off to obtain the same working force. Here too the carbon is desublimated, which results in a lot of fouling. The working parts can be light, but since they are so far from the breech they tend to be thin and spidery.

At the other extreme, a gun has been produced that has a hole in the chamber wall through which a small section of the brass cartridge is blown to release the gas to drive back a very short tappet. In general a compromise is made, with a tap-off point somewhere about 20 to 30 centimeters from the muzzle, depending on caliber and barrel length. The gas pressure obtained can be used in one of three ways to operate the gun: long- or short-stroke piston, or direct gas operation.

Long-stroke piston operation. In this system the piston is connected directly to the breechblock and controls the position of the block at all times. This type of arrangement is found in by far the greatest number of modern machine guns. The piston tends to be long and heavy, and the resultant recoiling mass is considerable.

Short-stroke piston operation. Here the piston moves back a distance that can be as short as a millimeter or two, but it imparts its energy to an operating rod that forces the breechblock to the rear. This arrangement is found on the great majority of gas-operated rifles; because the operating rod and the bolt can be quite light, this system avoids large changes in the center of mass of the weapon during firing, and thus tends to have less effect on the firer's aim than a long-stroke system.

Direct gas action. No piston at all is used in this method. The gas is tapped off from the barrel and ducted back along a tube, where it imparts energy to the bolt carrier. The direct gas action system produces the lightest possible moving mass, but it can also result in heavy fouling, because the gases cool in the duct and bolt carrier, depositing solid residue in a critically inaccessible area where the accumulation of carbon can lead to difficult and prolonged stoppages.

Advantages and disadvantages. Gas operation is the only system that can genuinely regulate the power available and control it according to the needs of the moment by means of a simple regulator. A disadvantage is that special modifications are needed to alter the gas system when it is used in an armored vehicle because of fouling and the emission of toxic fumes. Also, because of the mating of barrel and gas cylinder, barrel changes must be made in a forward direction, which is a disadvantage in an armored vehicle.

Conclusion

Automatic weapons vary in caliber, size, weight, and mission, and are ubiquitous to militaries throughout the world. They are neither likely to disappear nor to change in the fundamental way in which they function. The rates at which they fire will remain the same (anywhere from a low of about 100 rounds per minute to as fast as many thousand rounds per minute), although some new developments in caseless ammunition promise to greatly increase firing rates for submachine guns and assault rifles. Other advances in light-weight, composite material technology and advances in munitions will contribute to the flexibility and lethality of automatic weapons.

Samir H. Shalaby

See Also: Machine Gun; Small Arms.

Bibliography

Jane's infantry weapons 1984–1985. 1984. London: Jane's.

Reid, W. 1976. *Arms through the ages.* New York: Harper and Row.

AVIATION, MILITARY

On 17 December 1903 the *Wright Flyer* traveled 3 meters (10 ft.) per second. Today, aircraft consistently operate up to 2.5 times the speed of sound. With improved technology has come a proliferation of aerospace forces and roles, including reconnaissance, military airlift, training, bombardment, air-to-air combat, and even deterrence. However, that these basic roles survive illustrates an uncomfortable truth for airmen—the impact of technology and the actions of operators have had a far greater influence on the development of aerospace forces than modern military or strategic theory.

Lighter-than-Air Ships and Nonpowered Flight

An Italian priest, Francesco de Lanza Terzi (1631–87), first suggested the use of military aircraft in modern times. In his writings, Terzi visualized airships hurling balls and bombs against ships, houses, and other ground targets. However, with the development of hot-air and hydrogen balloons in the eighteenth century, military aviation first played a reconnaissance role.

The French Montgolfier brothers pointed the way by launching barnyard animals in a pear-shaped balloon as early as 1783. Two years later, and much to the dismay of the British, Jean-Pierre Blanchard crossed the English Channel in two hours. Such feats soon convinced the French of the military utility of balloons. As early as 9 June 1794, Revolutionary France used its tethered aerostatic corps for reconnaissance against the Austrians at Maubeuge and later at the Battle of Fleurus. Napoleon I used reconnaissance balloons during the siege of Mantua in 1797, and he considered using troop-carrying balloons in his planned invasion of Britain. However, it was Napoleon's ultimate antipathy toward balloons that provoked their demise in 1798–99. Yet, while they operated over the "fog and friction" of French battlefields, balloons provided valuable information on troop movements and challenged Karl von Clausewitz's later belief that the "fog of war" compromised all intelligence.

In 1849 the Austrians developed a new application for balloons. In their campaign against the Venetians, they unleashed 100 unmanned balloons that carried explosives triggered by time fuses (ironically, capricious winds forced the Austrian balloons back over their own lines). The Japanese attempted the same thing during World War II. They released thousands of explosives-laden Fugo balloons, some of which rode the jet stream to North America and caused negligible damage and casualties.

In due time, reconnaissance balloons experienced new popularity in the United States. Aerial observation occurred during campaigns against the Seminole Indians of Florida and at Veracruz during the Mexican War. In October 1861, Federal forces used John La Mountain's reconnaissance balloon at Cloud's Mill, Virginia. Its presence forced the Confederate General Beauregard to camouflage his artillery, since his dummy pieces were now identifiable from the air.

Competing for influence with La Mountain was Thaddeus Lowe, the first man to direct artillery fire from a balloon by using a telegraph, and the first to devise flag signals to communicate enemy positions to gunners. Lowe also designed a field hydrogen generator, using a sulfuric acid and iron mixture, that could fill a balloon in several hours. He and his nine "aeronauts" used seven balloons to supply the Union Army of the Potomac with accurate and timely reports on Confederate movements during the Virginia and Peninsular campaigns. Yet, since most Union generals thought balloons were vulnerable to artillery, they forced the retirement of the balloon corps after the Chancellorsville campaign of May 1863. Lacking formal recognition, the corps would not reappear in the U.S. Army until the 1890s, although countries like Italy, Spain, Russia, Britain, Germany, and France all had military balloon corps by 1884.

In Europe, 66 French balloons were employed during the siege of Paris during a four-month period of the Franco-Prussian War. They carried 167 people out of the city and delivered over 3 million pieces of mail over German lines. The siege also instigated the first reported aerial combat, when Felix Nadar traded rifle fire with a German balloonist sent aloft to prevent his return to Paris.

Subsequent to the wars spanning from 1860 to 1871, interest in balloons survived, but at a modest level. The U.S. Army, for example, purchased only eight balloons from the end of the Civil War until 1907. The transfer and control of these airships remained a problem, soldiers still questioned their utility, they remained comparatively expensive, and dirigibles were gaining in popularity.

Henri Giffard performed the first flight in a powered airship in Paris on 24 September 1852. A three-horsepower steam engine propelled Giffard's 43.8-meter (144-ft.) ship, tapered to two sharp points, over 24.3 kilometers (17 mi.). Subsequently, dirigible development stalled as builders sought faster and more dependable means of propulsion. Yet, technology did improve the dirigibles. The mass production of aluminum, beginning in 1886, enabled builders to construct rigid tubular frames that held gas bags in compartments. Gas and diesel engines became increasingly dependable (nonrigid German airships traveled up to 40 knots during the first decade of the twentieth century). Because of improving technology, different countries began to use dirigibles for military purposes.

The British abandoned their experiments with man-lifting kites and introduced their first army dirigible in 1907. By World War I, British airships traveled at speeds up to 50 knots and performed reconnaissance patrols lasting up to 24 hours. They searched for U-boats in the English Channel and later acted as scouts for Atlantic convoys.

In 1912 the Italians operated dirigibles over Tripolitania during the Italo-Turkish War. The airships performed artillery and tactical reconnaissance and some bombing. During World War I, Italian airships served as submarine hunters in the Mediterranean and provided fleet support.

However, no one rivaled the Germans and Count Ferdinand von Zeppelin (1838–1917) in airship development. The Germans had 72 metal-framed Zeppelins in commission during the First World War, ten of which were military airships built before 1914. The Zeppelins performed hundreds of effective naval reconnaissance sorties around Heligoland and the Baltic Sea. They also conducted a notorious night bombing campaign against Britain.

Beginning with their first attack on 19 January 1915, the Germans conducted 285 sorties against reputedly military targets. In fact, German airships indiscriminately used bombs and incendiaries to kill 557 people and wound 1,358. The raids caused over £1.5 million in damage and seriously affected public morale. They also forced the British to use twelve aero squadrons (110 airplanes) and over 14,000 people for British home defense. Yet, the bombing campaign was short-lived. The destruction of Zeppelin LZ-33 introduced a note of caution in German airship activity. The LZ-33 cost US$1.75 million to build, and the Germans could ill afford the loss of such expensive ships. As a result, the combined tonnage of bombs dropped by dirigibles and heavier-than-air aircraft on Britain during the war was 249,433 kilograms (275 tons), while the British, in contrast, dropped 4,535,147 kilograms (5,000 tons) of bombs on Germany in 1918 alone.

After World War I, the military utility of balloons and dirigibles declined because of their vulnerability. All belligerents effectively used tethered reconnaissance balloons during the war. Even the Americans, who did not enter the war until 1917, made 1,642 ascensions at the front. In World War II, however, balloons saw only limited action. The British used them to funnel enemy aircraft into narrow fire zones where ground defenses could concentrate their antiaircraft fire. The British also used balloons for passive defense over strategic targets—of the 3,957 V-1 flying bombs destroyed over England, 232 became entangled in mooring cables and failed to strike their targets. The Americans, in turn, used approximately 160 blimps as submarine spotters along their coastlines and with naval convoys. In the latter case, the U.S. Navy subsequently claimed no merchant vessel in a blimp-escorted convoy was ever sunk by a submarine. The Americans continued airship patrols after the war and suspended them only in 1961.

A final type of airship that saw service, particularly during World War II, was the glider. The Soviet Union pioneered its use, and by 1934 the Soviets had ten glider schools, 57,000 trained pilots, and the GN-4 Groshev, the world's first military glider transport. The Germans, in contrast, first used the glider as a modern Trojan Horse. On 10 May 1940, ten German gliders carrying 78 men assaulted the Belgian fort Eben Emael, causing the surprised defenders to capitulate the next day.

The German example sparked universal interest in the military utility of gliders—they bestowed mobility to ground units, introduced the possibility of airborne warfare, and provided the element of surprise. Following the German lead, the United States spent over US$500 million to build approximately 16,000 assault, transport, and training gliders. Over 14,000 of them were Waco CG-4As, a high-wing monoplane with a hinged nose. Built at US$18,000 each, the CG-4A was large enough to carry one jeep or a 75mm howitzer. The British built 412 Hamilcar Gs. The aircraft could carry 8,163 kg (nine tons) and supported operations at Normandy and Arnhem. The Germans, in contrast, also had the ME 321 Gigant. The Germans built 200 ME 321s and expected them to carry tanks, 88mm guns, and troops (200 fully equipped men per aircraft) in a cross-channel invasion of Britain. When the invasion failed to materialize, the Germans used the Gigants as transports on the Russian front. Argentina, Australia, China, India, and Italy also had glider programs during World War II. However, because gliders damaged easily and were operationally limited, their large-scale use did not survive after 1945.

The Airplane through World War I

The Americans Wilbur and Orville Wright ushered in the era of powered and controlled flight on 17 December 1903. The *Wright Flyer* traveled 36.56 meters (120 ft.) in the air for 12 seconds. Warping the wings with wires and using rudders allowed for controlled flight. Yet the Americans did not sustain their early momentum in aviation. Between 1909 and 1917, the U.S. Army acquired only 224 aircraft, all of which were second-rate by European standards. Poor funding was partly to blame—between 1909 and 1916, the army received only US$630,000 for aeronautics. In contrast, Belgium spent approximately US$2 million on military aviation from 1908 to 1913. The United States thus relinquished an early technological lead it would not regain until the B-17 appeared in the mid-1930s.

In Europe, others soon matched the success of the Wright brothers. Alberto Santos Dumont accomplished the first controlled flight in France when his *14 bis* flew 50 meters (164 ft.) on 23 October 1906. Two years later, J. H. C. Ellehammer, a Danish citizen, was the first to fly from German soil, while the American Samuel Franklin Cody performed the first officially recognized flight in Britain. Igor Sikorsky first flew in his native Russia in 1910.

Still the public saw the airplane as an oddity. It was the Prussian general staff that first believed airplanes were superior to dirigibles. A shift in opinion also occurred because of technological progress, the growth of aircraft companies and flying clubs (to include the German Air Fleet League and All Russian Aero Club), and the growing support of the European nobility. By 1911, most of the world's major powers were training pilots and buying military aircraft.

The Italians were the first to use the airplane as a military weapon. On 23 October 1911, Captain Piazza flew a Blériot aircraft on a reconnaissance mission over Turkish lines at Azizia, Libya, during the Italo-Turkish War. Subsequent sorties involved dropping hand grenades and propaganda leaflets on Turkish positions. Yet, it took the First World War to convert sporadic activity to systematic application.

The French began the war with 150 to 200 pilots and 24 aero squadrons. At war's end, they had 260 squadrons on the western front alone and around 4,500 front-line aircraft. The Italians had 150 aircraft in 1914 and ended with 1,700, while even industrially backwards Russia built about 4,700 airplanes by the end of the war. The Germans built approximately 44,000 airframes and 48,000 engines. The Americans, in turn, built over 3,400 de Havilland D.H. 4s and 15,000 Liberty engines, the first mass-produced airplane engine with interchangeable parts. Such productivity was necessary to compensate for airplane losses on the front lines—the French aircraft replacement rate was 50 percent during the last two years of the war, while in the German offensive of 1918, the British alone lost over 80 percent of their front-line aircraft in just two months. Clearly, by war's end, the belligerents had traded handicraft production for the standardized assembly line. Synchronized machine guns, internally braced cantilever wings, and early rockets fired by electrical impulses were just a few of the technological innovations introduced during the war.

World War I also formalized different combat roles for aircraft. The Germans were the first to use airplanes for bombardment. On 13 August 1914, Lt. Hermann Dressler dropped small bombs by hand on Paris. The British, in contrast, conducted their first successful strategic raid two months later. A single-seat Sopwith Tabloid carrying 9-kilogram (12-lb.) Hale bombs struck the Cologne railway station, while another attacked the Zeppelin shacks at Düsseldorf and destroyed the Z-9 airship.

In striking the British, the Germans followed the increasingly ineffectual dirigible attacks of 1915–16 with daylight airplane raids in the summer of 1917 and night attacks beginning late in the same year. There were a total of 52 attacks that killed 857 people, injured 2,058, and caused over £1.4 million in damage. The primary instrument of destruction was the Gotha bomber, a two-engine "pusher" biplane. With a wing span of 23.7 meters (77 ft. 9.25 in.) and a length of 12.2 meters (40 ft.), it was a huge aircraft. Its 260-horsepower engines propelled the Gotha up to 140 kilometers per hour (87.5 mph) and lifted it to 6,500 meters (21,325 ft.). It carried up to 500 kilograms (1,102 lb.) of bombs and protected itself with two to three machine guns. On 13 June 1917, a single Gotha raid against London killed 162 people and injured 432 others.

The origins of the heavy bomber may be traced to the family of Italian Caproni multiengine aircraft developed as early as 1913, and from similar Russian developments. Igor Sikorsky's Il'ya Mourmetz, for example, was a four-engine bomber whose E version had a wingspan of 38 meters (124 ft. 8 in.). Despite its carrying 2,721 kilograms (6,000 lb.) of protective armor, the E version flew up to 137 kilometers per hour (87 mph) and had an operational ceiling of 4,000 meters (13,120 ft.). The plane had mechanical navigation aids, a bombsight, and bomb-release gear. Despite the approximately 400 raids the 75 Sikorsky bombers made before the Russian Revolution, the fleet was even more valuable in a reconnaissance role (7,000 photographs helped Russian intelligence efforts).

The British contributions to the early development of bombardment included the Handley Page 0/400, a heavily armed plane with five 7.7mm (.30 caliber) machine guns, which appeared in 1917. The British built 550 of these airplanes and used them in 1918 to strike German industrial centers. The 0/400 carried up to 813 kilograms (1,800 lb.) of bombs, including "block-busters" weighing up to 792.5 kilograms (1,650 lb.) each.

Another British workhorse was the single-engine de Havilland D.H. 4. Appearing in 1917, the plane was soon characterized as the best daylight bomber in the war. Its comparatively small size gave the D.H. 4 exceptional speed and climbing ability. It could travel up to 230 kilometers per hour (143 mph) and soar to 7,163 meters (23,500 ft.). As a result, the D.H. 4 could often outrun enemy fighter attacks. Additionally, its complement of two to four machine guns meant it could often fend off an attacker it could not outrun.

Clearly, bombardment aviation progressed during the war. Although few countries had multiengine military aircraft at the beginning of hostilities, roughly four years later (9 October 1918) the Allies mustered 200 bombers to drop 58,050 kilograms (69 tons) of bombs on German positions in one day. The basic technology that would ensure the future importance of bombardment was now in place.

In the case of air-to-air combat, the Germans relied on standardized aircraft designs to establish air superiority until May 1916. The Fokker E.III was the instrument of German success. It was the first aircraft to use a machine gun synchronized with its propeller, although the British accomplished the same effect in 1913 with the Vickers Destroyer. This was an experimental aircraft with a "pusher" engine placed behind the crew and a belt-fed machine gun placed in its nose. German success with the E.III provoked a reaction from the Allies that resulted in the last year of the war with equally capable aircraft. Mere qualitative equality was not enough for the Germans, since the Allied air forces had a 4:1 numerical advantage in 1918.

The Germans followed the Fokker E series with a highly maneuverable triplane, the DR-1. The aircraft's internally braced cantilever wings accounted for its mobility, as demonstrated in 1917 by Lt. Werner Voss's downing of 22 Allied planes in 21 days. But the best fighter in World War I was the Fokker DVII, which was introduced in May 1918. This biplane could travel up to 200 kilometers per hour (124 mph) and climb to 6,000 meters (19,685 feet). It had an immediate impact, as its 217 victories during the first month of operations illustrated.

The British entered the war with the Sopwith Tabloid and Avro 504, both inadequate for aerial combat. True progress began only in late 1916 with the introduction of new Sopwith and Royal Aircraft Factory designs. The Sopwith Camel, with a wingspan of 8.53 meters (28 ft.) and length of 5.72 meters (18 ft. 9 in.), served as a ground support fighter, reconnaissance aircraft, and deadly air superiority fighter (the Camel claimed 1,294 victories in one year alone). The RAF S.E.5 and the Bristol F.2B also enhanced the performance of the Royal Flying Corps. The S.E.5, along with the French Spad S.XIII, was the fastest fighter in World War I (222 km/h, 138 mph). The F.2B, in turn, could go up to 198 kilometers per hour (132 mph) and climb to 6,553 meters (21,500 ft.). Although it was a two-seat aircraft, it could outmaneuver almost any single-seater.

French contributions centered on the Nieuport and Spad series of aircraft. The small and agile Nieuport Bébé was the scourge of German troops at the battle of Verdun. The Nieuport 17 was a versatile biplane used by six Allied countries as early as 1916. The Spad S.VII introduced a sturdy Hispano-Suiza V-8 engine that presaged the demise of less durable rotary engines. And the speedy Spad S.XIII, of which the French built 8,472, gave the Allies temporary air superiority in late 1917.

By war's end, advances in aircraft technology had benefited every belligerent. In contrast to the slow and stable reconnaissance aircraft of 1914, the typical fighter of 1918 was a biplane powered by a 200-horsepower engine. It could travel 190 to 210 kilometers per hour (120–130 mph), climb to 6,000 meters (20,000 ft.), and fire synchronized machine guns at enemy targets. In many respects, this prototypical fighter would remain the standard for the world's air forces until the early 1930s.

The Interwar Years

During the interwar years, technology continued to revolutionize military aviation, but postwar demobilization, politics, and economic instability slowed the process. The British RAF, for example, disbanded over 80 percent of its front-line flying squadrons, while the draconian Treaty of Versailles assured the confiscation of 20,000 German aircraft and 27,000 engines. French aviation spending lagged until 1938, when it comprised only 19 percent of the country's defense budget. Given the postwar surplus of military aircraft (57,000 in France, Britain, and Germany alone), the French government's unwillingness to spend money on aviation was typical.

Throughout the 1920s, the preference was for inexpensive, general-purpose aircraft that could, in the case of those nations with colonial responsibilities, act as a police force. On the organizational level, several countries established independent air forces or air ministries (Italy in 1923, Japan in 1925, Sweden in 1926, France in 1928, and Germany in 1933). In the realm of technology, commercial aviation inspired research that eventually had military applications. The Germans, for example, incorporated technology developed for their national air carrier, Lufthansa, into military aircraft like the Junkers Ju 52 and the Heinkel He 111. Competitive events, represented by the Pulitzer races and contests for the Collier and Schneider trophies, also nurtured improvements in airframes, engines, and armaments.

By the 1930s, wood and fabric biplanes, with their externally braced wings, yielded to faster and lighter all-metal monoplanes. The typical monoplane featured wing flaps, an enclosed cockpit, and a retractable landing gear. It also had a variable-pitch propeller, an innovation the Messerschmitt company introduced in its Me 109 fighter during the Spanish Civil War (the idea was to shift the angle of the propeller during takeoffs and at cruising altitude, and thus improve aircraft performance). Furthermore, major engine manufacturers like Fiat, Rolls Royce, Hispano-Suiza, and Curtiss built superchargers to enhance engine output at high altitudes. At the same time, cowled and air-cooled radial piston engines increasingly replaced rotary and liquid-cooled varieties. With improved engine capability, and the introduction of a rudimentary oxygen system, the common operational ceiling for aircraft increased to 6,100 meters (20,000 ft.). Finally, with improved design and performance came better armament. Armor plating in the rear of the cockpit and bulletproof glass protected the pilot while he fired large-caliber machine guns and even cannon (the Me 109 introduced the latter innovation as well). British bomber crews, in contrast, could rely on turret-mounted machine guns as early as the Boulton Paul Overstrand bomber of 1934.

In addition to basic revolutions in airframe construction, engine design, and armament, the interwar years saw other important developments. Deicing equipment, improved bombsights, and relatively reliable radios appeared. Aerial refueling was demonstrated in January 1929 by American airmen who flew a trimotor Fokker monoplane for 150 consecutive hours. This feat involved 43 midair hookups with a transport plane that used a fire hose to transfer fuel. In the same year, James Doolittle was the first to fly blind by relying solely on cockpit instruments. Finally, by the autumn of 1939, the British deployed a chain of new radar stations. The twenty stations, working with an IFF (Identification Friend or Foe) capability, dotted the southeast coast of England and directed British fighters with stunning success during the Battle of Britain, the first battle in history fought exclusively in the air. These additional innovations proved increasingly important as the major powers accelerated aircraft production in the 1930s.

As World War II approached, the British began to emphasize the development of fighter aircraft. One aircraft that benefited from this decision was the Hawker Hurricane, the first British fighter to exceed 483 kilometers per hour (300 mph). Equipped with eight 7.7mm (.303-in.) Browning machine guns, the Hurricane became operational at the end of 1937. The legendary Spitfire, developed by R. J. Mitchell from his previous Supermarine design, followed in 1938. It had a 1,030 horsepower Rolls Royce Merlin II engine that powered the aircraft up to 10,360 meters (34,000 ft.) at 571 kilometers per hour (355 mph). In a four-month period (July–September 1940), Hurricanes and Spitfires shot down 1,733 German aircraft, most of which had inadequate defensive armament, and saved Britain from a cross-channel invasion. This timely emphasis on fighter development was in direct contrast to the French, who invested 69 percent of their 1939 defense budget in a mad dash to upgrade their air force before the war began.

In the United States, 90 percent of the aircraft industry had disappeared in the early 1920s. Eventually, the industry recovered and began to produce the first truly modern bombers. The first of these, the Boeing B-9, was introduced in 1931. An all-metal monoplane with a cantilever wing structure and semiretractable landing gear, it could travel nearly twice as fast as the Keystone B-4A bombers then in service and incorporated advanced engineering features like variable-pitch propellers that later appeared in the classic Boeing B-17. Yet another improvement was the Martin B-10, which became operational in 1935. The B-10B, with enclosed cockpits and fully cowled engines, was capable of speeds up to 343 kilometers per hour (213 mph), and thus was faster than contemporary fighters. It also featured an internal bomb bay capable of carrying 1,025 kilograms (2,260 lb.) of bombs.

The development of the B-9 and B-10 showed that airplane manufacturers could increase aerodynamic efficiency with size. The success of these aircraft encouraged further experimentation, and on 28 July 1935, the first prototype of the B-17 flew. Built in seven major variations, the four-engined B-17 came to symbolize the high-altitude, precision daylight bombardment that was carried out against key German industries during World War II. The E model could travel up to 510 kilometers per hour (317 mph), climb to 11,150 meters (36,000 ft.), range over 4,800 kilometers (3,000 mi.), drop 7,985 kilograms (17,600 lb.) of bombs, and defend itself with ten to thirteen machine guns. The B-17 incorporated the most advanced technology available at the time, but it would ultimately require fighter escorts in order to survive Luftwaffe attacks.

As in the United States, the aircraft industry of the Soviet Union also experienced a decade of neglect after the First World War. Through 1928, the Soviet aviation industry was short of raw materials, machine tools, and skilled laborers. Four years later, however, the labor force alone had grown by 750 percent. In 1929, the Soviet Air Force was a motley collection of 1,000 outdated aircraft. A decade later, it had 2,500 planes, most of which were made in the 1930s. The most common aircraft were the Polikarpov I-15 and I-16 fighters, and the Tupolev TB-3 and SB-2 bombers. However, Soviet military aviation suffered a setback during the Stalin purges that claimed 75 percent of the senior Soviet air force commanders by 1939. The result was a severe shortage of leaders for an aviation establishment that now included 28 aircraft, 14 engine, and 32 component factories, as well as 100,000 Russians who had received rudimentary flight training through the Society of Defense, Aviation, and Chemical Warfare. One consequence of the purges was the poor Russian showing in its 1939–40 war with Finland. Although the Soviet Air Force began the conflict with a 15:1 numerical advantage, the Finns achieved a kill ratio of over 10:1. In the case of Operation Barbarossa (the June 1941 German invasion of Russia), the Luftwaffe destroyed 1,200 aircraft (800 on the ground) during the first nine hours of the assault. The Soviets would not recover from this disaster until mid-1942.

The most technologically developed air forces prior to the Second World War belonged to the Germans and Japanese. The Germans circumvented military restrictions imposed by the Treaty of Versailles by signing the Treaty of Rapallo with the Soviet Union in 1922. In exchange for *de jure* recognition of the Bolshevik state, the Germans were allowed to set up secret arms factories, test centers, and flight training bases in Russia. Through 1933, they trained 120 German pilots and 100 observers far from the prying eyes of other European nations.

The German aviation industry produced three major new aircraft that played important roles in the European air war that started in 1939. From 1935 to 1940, the Messerschmitt Me 109 was the best fighter in the world. It first appeared in combat with the German Condor Legion in the Spanish Civil War. Fighting for the Nationalists, the Condor Legion soon dominated the Republican Air Force, 90 percent of which was made up of Russian aircraft. The Germans built 35,000 Me 109s in nine years and entered World War II with the sturdy E model. The Me 109E-1 had a 1,050-horsepower Daimler-Benz engine that gave the aircraft a speed of up to 550 kilometers per hour (342 mph) and a service ceiling of 10,500 meters (34,450 ft.).

Similar in character was the Focke Wulf Fw190, which appeared in 1939. The Germans made both a fighter and a fighter-bomber version of this plane, producing a total of 13,367 of the fighter's ten different models and 6,634 of the fighter-bomber variant.

The third major new aircraft was the Junkers Ju 87 Stuka dive bomber. The Luftwaffe received over 5,700 Ju 87s in ten versions through 1944 and used them on all fronts (the Germans borrowed the concept of dive bombing from the U.S. Navy, which introduced its widespread use in 1926).

In Japan, aircraft companies like Mitsubishi, Nakajima, and Kawasaki spurred the growth of military aviation in the 1930s. The Japanese increased their yearly production from 445 aircraft in 1930 to 4,768 in 1940. On 7 December 1941, they had a total of 7,500 planes, of which 2,900 were combat ready. The premier aircraft was the Mitsubishi A6M Reisen (known as the Type 0 or Zero, and nicknamed Zeke by the Western Allies), which first became operational in July 1940. The Japanese navy used over 10,000 Zeros during the war, and they became the mainstay of Japan's carrier-based aviation. The A6M2 Zero was more than the equal of the Curtiss P-40 Warhawk, the most versatile land-based American fighter from 1941 to 1943. The Zero could travel 534 kilometers per hour (332 mph), climb to 10,000 meters (32,810 ft.), and range over 3,105 kilometers (1,930 mi.). In addition to having two machine guns and a 20mm cannon, the Zero also could carry 120 kilograms (264 lb.) of bombs.

The Zero was a formidable weapon in the hands of early Japanese pilots, half of whom had combat experience in Japan's undeclared war against China or in the 1939 Khalkhin-Gol Incident with Russia. Further, Japanese pilots received excellent initial training. In 1941, for example, Japanese trainees received 300 hours of flight training, while their American counterparts were given only 200 hours. Like the Germans, prewar Japan was in the vanguard of military aviation.

World War II

During World War II, the production capabilities of the competing alliances proved crucial once blitzkrieg warfare gave way to a war of attrition. Where aircraft production was concerned, the Axis was no match for the Allied powers. From 1939 to 1944, the Germans built approximately 111,800 aircraft, while the Japanese constructed 74,656 from 1940 to 1945. The total figure (186,456) was only 35 percent of the combined number of airplanes produced by Britain, Russia, and the United States. The Americans alone built 297,199 aircraft from 1941 to 1945, including 99,742 fighters and 97,592 bombers. The balance between single and multiengine airplanes in American production figures contrasts sharply with those of the Japanese, who increasingly shifted to fighter production as their defensive needs rose toward the end of the war. For example, in 1944, the Japanese built 13,811 fighters, but only 4,189 bombers. The mismatch in production just described was one major reason why the Allied powers ultimately won.

Allied air forces also benefited from timely modernization cycles. Here, the Soviet Union is a good example. Prior to the German invasion, the majority of Soviet military aircraft were obsolete. When the Germans destroyed 4,000 of these airplanes during the first week of Operation

Barbarossa, the losses simply underscored the need for modernization. The Russians consequently moved their industrial plants, along with the skilled laborers that worked in them, east of the Volga. Russian aircraft production dropped only during the relocation (June 1941–March 1942). New aircraft like the Pe-2, Il-4, and Il-2 bombers soon appeared, as did the MiG-3 (the equal of the Me 109 above 4,877 meters or 16,000 ft.), the La-5, and the Yak series of fighters. By 1942–43, the Soviets were introducing massive numbers of new airplanes.

In contrast, the Luftwaffe standardized its aircraft production too early. The technological innovations the Germans introduced in the 1930s, along with their combat experiences in the Spanish Civil War, caused the Luftwaffe's modernization cycle to peak in 1939. When Hitler subsequently restricted research and development to those programs that promised results within one year, he essentially forced the Luftwaffe to replace battlefield losses with existing aircraft models. This temporary hiatus meant that significant improvements over the airplanes first designed in the 1930s would not appear until very late in the war.

The Japanese suffered the same fate as the Germans, although for different reasons. Japan's industrial capacity was too limited to produce first-line aircraft like the Zero and Nakajima Ki-43 Hayabusa and also develop a new generation of improved airplanes. Second, Japanese industry could not make good the devastating air losses their navy suffered at Midway, the Coral Sea, and the Marianas Islands. At the 1942 Battle of Midway, for example, the Japanese lost four carriers, 275 aircraft, and 30 percent of their carrier pilots.

Like that of the Russians, the American modernization cycle peaked in 1942–43. The United States produced more of the Consolidated B-24 Liberators, which played a key role in the daylight strategic bombing of the Axis powers in Europe, than any other type of aircraft. A total of 18,888 B-24s rolled off the assembly line. The B-24J, with four Pratt-Whitney turbo-supercharged engines, could carry 4,000 kilograms (8,800 lb.) of bombs over 3,380 kilometers (2,100 mi.) at 480 kilometers per hour (300 mph). In the Pacific theater, the Liberator dropped 575,963,710 kilograms (635,000 tons) of bombs and shot down 4,189 enemy aircraft in just three years.

The heavy armament of B-24s and B-17s was designed to enable these bombers to overcome fighter defenses and reach their targets with acceptable losses. However, American attempts to bomb German targets without fighter escort resulted in catastrophic losses. During the third quarter of 1943, for example, 42 percent of the American strategic bomber force incurred battle damage on every mission. On 14 October 1943, better known as "Black Thursday," 291 B-17s attacked the ball-bearing plants at Schweinfurt. The German defenders destroyed or damaged 198 of the bombers. By the end of October, the American Eighth Air Force lost almost 30 percent of the B-17s and B-24s in its inventory.

The turnabout came with the introduction of the North American P-51 Mustang and jettisonable external fuel tanks. The key to the Mustang's success was the installation of the 12-cylinder Rolls Royce Merlin engine. The P-51B could now travel at 708 kilometers per hour (440 mph) and climb to 12,800 meters (42,000 ft.). With its six machine guns, it became a deadly fighter—it could outperform and outmaneuver German aircraft at all altitudes. With the subsequent addition of expendable drop tanks, the P-51B nearly doubled its range to 1,300 kilometers (810 mi.). When strategic bombing resumed in February 1944, P-51s and P-47 Thunderbolts joined the attacks on Germany and helped to establish Allied command of the air in Europe.

In the Pacific theater, the P-40 and F4F Wildcat yielded in 1943–44 to the P-47 and carrier-based aircraft like the Vought F4U Corsair and the Grumman F6F Hellcat, fighters that were superior to the Zero. The performance characteristics of both aircraft were slightly less than the P-51, although their range extended up to 1,670 kilometers (1,040 mi.). As in Europe, the Americans acquired command of the air through attrition. At the mid-1944 "Marianas Turkey Shoot," for example, navy pilots downed 315 aircraft in one day (an almost 14:1 kill ratio). Japanese air defenses subsequently became so weak that the Americans lost only 52 aircraft over the home islands from December 1944 to early March 1945.

Lost aircraft often meant lost pilots, and this translated into a Japanese air force composed of less experienced, less capable pilots. Not only were hundreds of veteran Japanese pilots killed (the loss rate was 50% in 1944), but the training hours for replacements decreased from 300 to 100 hours. In the case of *kamikaze* suicide missions, the volunteers received only the most basic training.

The weakening of the Japanese air force was well along by the spring of 1944 when the U.S began to deploy the Boeing B-29 Superfortress in the Pacific. This behemoth had a wingspan of 43.05 meters (141 ft., 3 in.) and a length of 30.18 meters (99 ft.). It could travel 6,000 kilometers (4,100 mi.) and carry 9,090 kilograms (10 tons) of bombs. Unarmed B-29s were used to make nightly low-level incendiary attacks on paper and wood Japanese cities with devastating results. The 9–10 March 1945 area bombing of Tokyo, for example, obliterated 27 square kilometers (16.8 sq. mi.) of the city, killed 84,000 people (half of whom suffocated because of street-level fire storms), and eliminated 18 percent of Japanese industry. The Americans lost only 14 of 334 attacking B-29s. As in Europe, the combination of mass production and new technology proved unbeatable in the Pacific theater.

Overall, the necessities of war provided a strong stimulus to technological innovation. As mentioned earlier, the turbo-supercharging of engines allowed bomber aircraft to regularly operate above 9,100 meters (30,000 ft.).

Self-sealing fuel tanks prevented the spread of fire in the event of a rupture. The bomb-carrying capacity of aircraft increased, as did the size of individual bombs. The British Bristol Blenheim Mk.IV, for example, appeared in 1939 and could carry 600 kilograms (1,320 lb.) of bombs into the heart of Germany. Three years later, the Lancaster Mk.I could carry a 9,980 kilogram (11-ton) payload, to include individual bombs weighing 1,859 kilograms (4,000 lb.). In time, Allied aircraft carried single bombs weighing as much as 9,980 kilograms (22,000 lb.).

Yet large munitions loads meant nothing if they could not be placed accurately on targets. A major reason the British abandoned their early experiment with precision daylight bombing and adopted night area bombing was that only three bombs in every 100 landed within eight kilometers (5 mi.) of the target. In the case of the Americans, the top secret Norden bombsight soon provided some improvement in accuracy, but overcast skies restricted its effectiveness. Still, the Americans kept the bombsight classified until 1955 and did not share it with the British, who made a number of important advances that improved bombing operations. For one thing, they dramatically improved radio navigation technology in 1942. Two devices, code-named Gee and Oboe, enabled the British to attack cities under all-weather conditions. The British also pioneered the development of airborne radar which they called H_2S. Unlike the Americans, the British quickly shared these developments with their ally.

World War II also saw the introduction of several types of missiles. The most revolutionary was the German V-2, a large surface-to-surface ballistic missile. It was almost 14 meters (47 ft.) long, traveled 320 kilometers (200 mi.), and carried a 907-kilogram (1-ton) conventional warhead. The Germans launched approximately 4,000 V-2s during the war, but they did not have a decisive impact due to their inaccuracy. In the case of air-to-surface missiles, Germany, the Soviet Union, Japan, Great Britain, and the United States all developed this type of weapon for use against transportation and supply targets. The Soviet Ilyushin Il-2, better known as the "flying tank," was the first close air support aircraft to use rockets in large numbers. Tube, straight-rail, or zero-length launchers held them under the aircraft's wings. Lastly, the Germans introduced unguided air-to-air missiles that proved effective against aircraft traveling less than 740 kilometers per hour (440 mph). The German Me 262, the world's first operational jet fighter, for example, carried 48 missiles and at times used them to good effect. On 7 April 1945, sixteen rocket-armed Me 262s downed 25 B-17s over Westphalia, Germany. However, missile technology was still in its infancy when the war ended.

Other wartime innovations that pointed to the future were airborne assaults, military airlift, and jet aircraft. The German Heinkel He 178 was the first jet to fly (27 August 1939), although an Englishman, Frank Whittle, was the first to operate a jet engine (12 April 1937). The Messerschmitt Me 262A-1a entered service in mid-1944. It could travel 869 kilometers per hour (540 mph) and range over 1,050 kilometers (652 mi.). The Germans built 1,430 Me 262s, but less than a quarter of them became operational (primarily because of an aviation fuel shortage). Also, German leaders marred its effectiveness by trying to assign it multiple roles, rather than using it solely as an interceptor.

Complementing the Me 262 was the Me 163B-1a Komet, a rocket-powered aircraft popularly known as the "flying coffin." After catapulting from a take-off trolley, it would sustain 2.5 minutes of powered flight and reach speeds up to 959 kilometers per hour (596 mph). The Komet would then land on a skid, sometimes exploding when the propellants unexpectedly mixed (the Japanese Mitsubishi J8M Shusui, appearing in 1945, was a direct copy of the Me 163 and was equally maladroit).

Great Britain was the only other country to introduce a jet-powered aircraft during the war. The Gloster Meteor Mk I saw limited service during the war, starting in August 1944 when it was used in an attempt to intercept V-1 flying bombs. The 200 Mk IIs that followed depended on two Rolls Royce engines to range over 2,156 kilometers (1,340 mi.) at speeds up to 793 kilometers per hour (493 mph). However, these aircraft did not appear until late 1944, and massive production by the Allies, coupled with timely new weapon cycles, already had the Axis powers facing defeat.

The Postwar Era

Subsequent to the war, the development of supersonic aircraft began in earnest. While countries like Sweden and Israel developed sophisticated aerospace programs, the dominant innovators proved to be the Soviet Union, Great Britain, the United States, and France. In three successive stages these countries developed multirole, semiautomatic combat aircraft; "smart" weapons; and increasingly computerized avionics (a word coined in the 1950s and referring to the application of electronics to aeronautics).

The first generation of supersonic jet aircraft appeared soon after the American Charles Yeager broke the sound barrier in a rocket-propelled aircraft on 14 October 1947. Between 1947 and 1949, the United States introduced three front-line fighter aircraft. The Lockheed F-80, actually designed and built in six months toward the end of World War II, participated in the first all-jet air battle in history during the Korean War. The Republic F-84, the second of the three, went through five straight-wing versions before the F model introduced a 45-degree swept-wing design intended to minimize shockwave effects at high speeds—3,723 F-84s saw service as one of the North Atlantic Treaty Organization's (NATO) earliest fighters. Lastly, the swept-wing F-86 Sabre saw twenty years of front-line, all-weather service in numerous allied countries.

The Soviets built the MiG-15 and -17. Appearing in late 1948, the MiG-15 was an impressive aircraft with swept wings, but it had poor aerodynamics in transonic flight. The MiG-17 was more effective, having an all-weather capability, an afterburner for quick bursts of speed, and air-to-air missiles. The latter aircraft saw wide use in Warsaw Pact air forces and in developing countries.

The second generation of jet aircraft first appeared in the 1950s and continued to evolve into the 1970s. France's Marcel Dassault, father of the distinguished Mirage fighter series, introduced the Ouragan, Etendard, and Mystère (the last a fighter-bomber). The United States developed the Century-series fighters. The F-102 was the first delta-wing aircraft to have all-missile armament, while the F-104 pushed speeds up to Mach 2. The F-105 Thunderchief had the twin capacity to carry 6,350 kilograms (14,000 lb.) of bombs and yet travel up to 2,237 kilometers per hour (1,390 mph). Such characteristics made it a mainstay of the U.S. Air Force in the Vietnam War, where F-105s carried out 75 percent of the air assault missions from 1965 to 1968. Complementing these fighters was the F-4 Phantom, a sturdy fighter-bomber that operated from land and from aircraft carriers.

The most impressive bomber of the era was the legendary B-52 Stratofortress. This plane could travel 13,680 kilometers (8,500 mi.) and carry a 30,000-kilogram (33-ton) bomb load. With the introduction of tankers such as the KC-135, used for aerial refueling, the range of the B-52 and other combat aircraft was extended, as was the time they could stay aloft for airborne alert. Crew fatigue now became the most significant factor in limiting aircraft operations.

Soviet aircraft evolved in parallel with those of the United States. The MiG-21 fighter appeared in 1956 and saw service in India, China, and over twenty other countries. The F model could travel 2,000 kilometers per hour (1,243 mph) and climb to 20,000 meters (65,610 ft.). Its armament included one 30mm cannon and two K-13 air-to-air missiles, a combination of unguided rockets and a heavy caliber gun that quickly became universal. The MiG-25 and -27 soon followed, with the MiG-25 setting a speed record for fighters of 3,529.56 kilometers per hour (2,193 mph) in September 1978 (30 years earlier, the record stood at a modest 710.9 km/h, or 441 mph). The Tupelov Tu-26 bomber appeared as an air-to-ground missile carrier.

Finally, Britain and Sweden developed second-generation jet aircraft suited to their particular needs. The British began a full conversion to jets in 1950. The Hunter and Javelin fighters soon followed, as did the Vulcan and Victor bombers. In recognition of the growing need to operate from short, unprepared airstrips, the British in 1969 also introduced vertical short takeoff and landing (VSTOL) aircraft. The single-seat British Aerospace Harrier accomplishes vertical take-off through the use of a vectored-thrust engine, with rotating exhaust nozzles. In normal level flight, it can travel at 1,186 kilometers per hour (737 mph) and carry 2,270 kilograms (5,000 lb.) of bombs. The neutral Swedes developed a series of first-rate Saab self-defense fighters. The multirole AJ37 Viggen, for example, travels at Mach 2, carries 6,000 kilograms (13,200 lb.) of bombs, and ranges up to 1,000 kilometers (620 mi.).

The third generation of postwar multirole aircraft began to appear in the mid-1970s. Panavia, a consortium of German, British, and Italian interests, produced the Tornado, an aircraft that is well suited for all-weather air-to-ground NATO operations. The Tornado can travel at 2,335 kilometers per hour (1,450 mph) and yet carry 8,810 kilograms (18,000 lb.) of assorted weapons. Other members of this third generation of fighters include the American F-16 Falcon and the French Dassault Mirage 2000, both of which have performance characteristics broadly similar to those of the Tornado. The American F-15 Eagle has singularly impressive capabilities—the A model can travel up to 2,701 kilometers per hour (1,678 mph), climb to 30,500 meters (100,000 ft.), and carry 7,620 kilograms (16,800 lb.) of bombs. Overall, these specifications exceed those of the Soviet MiG-29 Fulcrum (Fig. 1), which first appeared in 1985, and the Sukhoi Su-27 Flanker. Both of these new-generation Soviet aircraft, however, can operate at Mach 2 and carry effective radar-homing air-to-air missiles.

Third-generation combat airplanes may have unique capabilities, but they also share similar operating procedures and technology. AWACS (airborne warning and control system) aircraft like the American E-3A Sentry or the Soviet Ilyushin Il-76 Mainstay, both of which have a large rotating "saucer" radome mounted on the plane's fuselage, can identify low-flying combatants or cruise missiles and guide interceptors to them. Complementing the AWACS radar is pulse Doppler look-down/shoot-down radar on the interceptors themselves. The interceptor's radar search range can extend to 306 kilometers (190 mi.), as in the case of the radar aboard the MiG-31 Foxhound. Once the radar has "interrogated" a target, it can "lock

Figure 1. Soviet MiG-29 Fulcrum. (SOURCE: U.S. Department of Defense)

on" self-homing guided weapons with long-range capability (the Soviet AA-9 Amos, a standard air-to-air missile on the MiG-31 and an alternate weapon for the MiG-29, has a range of 40–45 kilometers [25–28 mi.] at high altitude). Radar, infrared sensors, or optical sensors in the missile then work with the aircraft's computerized fire-control system to guide it to the target. The pilot, rather than risk looking down at a display panel for information, scans a head-up display that visually projects data up to his helmet visor or windscreen. These systems have the capacity to engage multiple targets at the same time.

While an attacker is closing in on his target, the opponent is relying on electronic countermeasures like radar homing-and-warning receivers to identify what type of hostile radar is tracking him, establish the location of the attacker, and warn him when "lock on" occurs. In the case of multiple threats, this system accounts for all of them and assigns a priority number to each threat. Evasion of radar and infrared guided weapons is accomplished through jamming the threatening radar, dispensing chaff and flare decoys that create false signals, or using countermeasure pods on the aircraft to generate false return signals to the attacker. Once joined, air-to-air combat remains basically the same, but the combatants now try to fix or disengage from each other by electronic means, rather than by visual means.

In the air-to-ground arena, very accurate guided free-fall bombs and missiles are now common. Television and laser-guided free-fall bombs such as the American Maverick and the British-French Martel TV-guided rockets are widely used. The Soviets, however, rely on infrared imaging to guide their AS-7 and AS-9 missiles. Another new munition is the West German BD-1 cluster bomb, which saturates an area 181 × 1,212 meters (604 ft. × 4,044 ft.) with small bomblets. Finally, France, the former Soviet Union, Israel, Great Britain, and the United States have introduced antirunway bombs that, in the case of the French Durandal, use a booster rocket to drive the explosive charge deep into the concrete.

In addition to the above developments, strategic bombardment has been revitalized by the introduction of cruise missiles. The Soviet Blackjack bomber, which is capable of Mach 2 speeds, carries the AS-15 Kent air-launched cruise missile, while the U.S. B-52 and B-1 bombers carry the American equivalent of the Kent. Penetration of hostile air space to perform bombing missions is no longer necessary.

In the future, technology will continue to have a major impact on air forces. One scenario may include operational aircraft that travel to and from space and regularly fly at speeds over Mach 5. Airframes will evolve from heat-resistant alloys and exotic metals to composite, radar-absorbing materials that minimize an aircraft's electronic image and provide it with the ability to escape radar detection. While in flight, adaptable-variable camber wings will change shape to improve aerodynamic efficiency. Such "smart skins" that can transmit and receive signals may replace bulging pods and domes. There will likely be advances in optical aircraft computers that will be immune to electromagnetic interference and capable of processing 50 million bits of information per second. Pilots may control these fiber-optics systems by voice or eye movements.

Further, today's "smart" armaments will evolve into "brilliant" weapons. "Shoot-and-forget" technology will allow aircraft missiles to truly guide themselves to targets far over the horizon. Laser and directed energy weapons will also appear. Their extremely high "muzzle velocity" will be invaluable, given that sustained supersonic flight without afterburners will be common. Aircraft sensors will be able to "see" over great distances. The aircraft will be able to fight for long periods of time under virtually any conditions and will possess improved automatic terrain-following equipment such as is now found in the American FB-111. If a particular environment appears too dangerous to fly in, remotely piloted vehicles or aircraft flown by sophisticated computers will operate in the area. With such advancements, many of which are currently in the research and development stage, aerospace forces will continue to have a decisive impact on warfare in the twenty-first century.

PETER R. FABER

SEE ALSO: Aircraft, Military; Aircraft, Unmanned; Airpower, Strategic; Airpower, Tactical; Air Reconnaissance; Bombardment, Strategic; Chaff; Close Air Support; Electronic Warfare, Air; Engine Technology, Aircraft; Radar; Reconnaissance and Surveillance; Technology and Warfare; World War I; World War II.

Bibliography

Angelucci, E. 1981. *The Rand McNally encyclopedia of military aircraft.* New York: Military Press.

Armitage, M. J., and R. A. Mason. 1983. *Air power in the nuclear age.* Urbana and Chicago, Ill.: Univ. of Illinois Press.

Boog, H. 1978. Higher command and leadership in the German Luftwaffe, 1935–1945. In *Air power and warfare*, ed. R. C. Ehrhart and A. F. Hurley, pp. 128–58. Washington, D.C.: Government Printing Office.

Coox, A. D. 1978. The rise and fall of the Imperial Japanese air forces. In *Air power and warfare*, ed. R. C. Ehrhart and A. F. Hurley, pp. 84–97. Washington, D.C.: Government Printing Office.

Emme, E. M. 1959. *The impact of air power.* Princeton, N.J.: Van Nostrand.

Gunston, B. 1982. *The encyclopedia of world air power.* New York: Crescent Books.

Higham, R. 1972. *Air power a concise history.* New York: St. Martin's Press.

MacIsaac, D. 1986. Voices from the central blue: The air power theorists. In *Makers of modern strategy*, ed. P. Paret, pp. 624–48. Princeton, N.J.: Princeton Univ. Press.

Nordeen, L. O. 1985. *Air warfare in the missile age.* Washington, D.C.: Smithsonian Institution Press.

AZERBAIJAN

Azerbaijan, one of the fifteen former republics in the Union of Soviet Socialist Republics (USSR), joined ten other Soviet republics in dissolving the Union on 21 December 1991 when they agreed to form the new Commonwealth of Independent States. This dramatic end to the Soviet and Communist state followed several years of dynamic and unprecedented change. For several more years, relations between members of the new Commonwealth and with the rest of the world are likely to continue to change. Over time, new structures and patterns will emerge in economics, trade and commerce, politics and government, finance, manufacturing, religion, and virtually all aspects of human life. New arrangements must be devised for dealing separately as sovereign states and as a Commonwealth with the world outside the boundaries of the former Soviet state. If the history of the Soviet Union since 1985 is any guide, we can expect dramatic surprises and dynamic change.

An important question for the world is how the new states and the Commonwealth will organize and provide for their security. The Soviet Union's armed forces, formerly the largest in the world, are likely to be withdrawn from foreign territory, reduced in size, and divided up between the former republics. Also of great concern is the disposition of the largest arsenal of nuclear weapons, the security of these weapons, the command and control of their potential use, and compliance with arms control agreements entered into by the former Soviet government. The world can only hope these issues are settled amicably.

It will be years before all of these issues are resolved for Azerbaijan and some time before events settle down into more routine and measurable patterns. No accurate description of this new country's policies, defense structure, and military forces was available to be included in this encyclopedia. Only time will reveal the future of Azerbaijan as a separate sovereign state. The reader is thus referred to the historic information contained in the article "Soviet Union," and to the latest annual editions of the *Military Balance*, published by Brassey's (UK) for the International Institute of Strategic Studies; the *Statesman's Year-Book*, published by the Macmillan Press Ltd and St. Martin's Press; and the *World Factbook*, developed by the U.S. Central Intelligence Agency and published commercially by Brassey's (US).

F. D. MARGIOTTA,
Executive Editor

B

BALKAN WARS

First Balkan War, 1912–13

In 1912 Bulgaria, Serbia, and Greece—each seeking to eliminate Turkish power in its region of the Balkans, and each seeking to increase its own territorial area—entered into a military alliance to take advantage of Turkey's involvement in a war with Italy. Tiny Montenegro was informally associated with the allies. The pretext for war was Turkish misrule in Macedonia.

Turkey had about 140,000 troops in Macedonia, Albania, and Epirus, and another 100,000 in Thrace. The allies were rightly confident that Greek command of the Aegean would prevent rapid and direct transfer of other Turkish forces to the Balkans. Bulgarian active military strength was approximately 180,000, Serb 80,000, and Greek 50,000, and each had about an equal number of trained, readily mobilizable reserves. Montenegrin militia strength, capable only of guerrilla operations, was about 30,000. Courage and stamina of the opposing forces were equal, but the tactical leadership of the allies was superior to that of the Turks, despite recent German assistance in reorganization of the Ottoman army.

Allied Invasions

Almost simultaneously, the allies moved into Turkey's European provinces on 17 October 1912. Three Bulgarian armies under Gen. Radko Dimitriev invaded Thrace, moving generally on Adrianople. In Macedonia, Gen. Radomir Putnik's three Serbian armies from the north, and Crown Prince Constantine's Greek army from the south, converged on the Vardar Valley with the intention of compressing hastily grouping Turkish elements between them.

Operations in Macedonia. While a small Greek force invaded Epirus in the west, Constantine's main army pressed on to the lower Vardar Valley. He defeated the Turks at Elasson on 23 October. Most of the Turkish force withdrew toward Monastir, but Constantine did not pursue since, contrary to prior agreements, a Bulgarian division (ostensibly aiding the Serbian invasion) was advancing toward Salonika, which was coveted by both Bulgaria and Greece. Constantine headed eastward to try to forestall the Bulgarians. Turkish resistance in unexpected strength at Venije Vardar on 2 November at first held up the Greek advance. At the same time, other Turkish units defeated Constantine's flank detachments at Kastoria and Yiannitsá. Despite these setbacks, on 5 November Constantine finally overwhelmed the Turks at Venije and pressed on to Salonika (Thessaloniki). The isolated Turks to his northwest withdrew to Yannina (Ioánnina).

Meanwhile, the Serbs met and defeated a Turkish covering force at Kumanovo on 24 October. Turkish resistance stiffened in the Babuna Pass, near Prilep, and checked the Serbs until a threatened double envelopment in the hills forced the Turks to evacuate Skoplje and retreat to Monastir. There, reinforced to a strength of 40,000, they again gave battle.

At Monastir, on 5 November, a Serb division impetuously stormed commanding ground to threaten an envelopment of the Turkish left. An Ottoman counterattack, with reinforcements drawn from the center of their line, retook the height, almost annihilating the Serb division. But the Turk center was so weakened that a Serbian frontal attack broke through. Faced with a threatened Greek advance from the south, Turkish resistance collapsed. Nearly 20,000 Turks were killed or captured. The remainder, scattering to the west and south, finally reached the fortress of Yannina, where they were besieged by the Greeks.

In the face of Greek preparations for an all-out assault on Monastir, the Turkish garrison of 20,000 surrendered on 9 November. Constantine occupied the city one day before the frustrated Bulgarian division arrived. This incident, and the subsequent dispute over possession of Salonika, worsened relations between the Bulgarians and the Greeks.

By the end of the year, the only Turkish forces still holding out west of the Vardar were the garrisons of Yannina (besieged by the Greeks) and Scutari (Shkoder, besieged by the Montenegrins).

Operations in Thrace. In Thrace, a Turkish army group commanded by Abdalla Pasha met Dimitriev's Bulgarians in a series of fiercely contested engagements (22–25 October) and was driven back to a line between Lülé Burgas and Bunar Hisar, where it regrouped. The Bulgarian Second Army, on the right, invested Adrianople, while the other two Bulgarian armies wheeled to the east against the position of the Turkish field armies. The Battle of Lülé Burgas ensued.

The Bulgarian battle plan envisioned a strong frontal attack against the Turkish position followed by an envelopment of the Turkish left (southern) flank, intended to drive the Turks off their line of communications to the south and Istanbul. The Bulgarian attack, however, when it developed on 28 October, was poorly coordinated. On the first day only the Bulgarian left engaged the Turks. On the second day the fighting became general, but the Bulgarian units again failed to coordinate their efforts, and the attacks were delivered piecemeal. Nonetheless, the Bulgarian right was successful in turning the Turkish left, and the Turks were forced to withdraw in some confusion. The Bulgarians did not pursue. The Turks subsequently reorganized behind the permanent fortifications of the Chatalja Line, between the Black Sea and the Sea of Marmara, protecting Constantinople.

The Bulgarians, launching a premature assault, were driven back with heavy losses (17–18 November). A stalemate continued along the Chatalja Line until, on 3 December, an armistice between Bulgarians and Serbs on one side, and Turks on the other, temporarily ended hostilities. Adrianople remained in Turkish possession. Greece and Montenegro ignored the armistice.

Abortive Peace Negotiations

Beginning on 27 December, representatives of the combatants and of the European Great Powers met in London, where they vainly tried to settle their conflicting aims with respect to the Balkans and the crumbling Turkish Empire. The conference collapsed.

On 23 January 1913 the Turkish government was overthrown by the Young Turk nationalistic group, led by Enver Bey. The Young Turks denounced the armistice and, on 3 February, hostilities resumed.

Resumption of Hostilities

On 3 March the Turkish garrison of 30,000 surrendered Yannina to Crown Prince Constantine. This was followed on 26 March at Adrianople by a combined Bulgarian-Serb assault against the eastern face of the fortress, breaching the Turk lines despite an allied loss of 9,500 men. Shukri Pasha surrendered Adrianople with his garrison of 60,000.

Meanwhile, in mid-March, a Serb force had come to the assistance of the irregular Montenegrin besiegers at Scutari, but they left on 16 April after a month of continuing disagreements. The Turks then surrendered to the Montenegrins.

Treaty of London

On 30 May the Great Powers finally imposed an uneasy peace, the Treaty of London, on the combatants. Turkey lost all of her European possessions save the tiny Chatalja and Gallipoli peninsulas. Bitter squabbles broke out between Bulgaria, on the one hand, and the Greeks and Serbs, on the other, over the division of conquered Macedonia. Montenegro was forced to abandon Scutari to the newly established state of Albania.

Second Balkan War, 1913

At the end of the war, Bulgaria's five armies were arranged as follows: the First faced the Serbs between Vidin and Brokovitsa, with the Fifth on its left; the Third lay above Kustendil; the Fourth about Koccani and Radaviste (Radovic); the Second faced the Greeks between Strumitsa (Strumica) and Serres (Serrai).

The Serb Second Army was on the old Serb-Bulgarian frontier; the First, in the center, at Kumanovo and Kriva Palanka; the Third, on the right of the First, was concentrated along the Bregalnica.

The Greeks were assembled between the lower Vardar and the mouth of the Struma.

Bulgarian Offensive

On 30 May the Bulgarians attacked Serbia and Greece without a declaration of war. The Fourth and Third armies, moving to the Vardar, attacked the Serbs. The Second Army drove in Greek advance elements. Both Serbs and Greeks were disposed in depth, however, and the Bulgarian attack soon lost its momentum.

Serbia's General Putnik, responsible for the success of the Serbian defensive, seized the initiative on 2 July. While the Third Serbian Army checked the Bulgarians on the upper Bregalnica, the First Army broke through, driving on Kyustendil and pushing the Bulgarians back in a northeasterly direction. On 3 July the Greeks attacked the Bulgarian Second Army, forcing it back. On 7 July the Greeks outflanked the Bulgarian left and drove them north up the Struma Valley. A counteroffensive by Bulgaria's Third and Fourth armies against the Serbian Third, toward the upper Bregalnica, was checked on 10 July.

Intervention of Romania

Romania declared war on Bulgaria on 15 July, and Romanian troops advanced into Bulgaria toward Sofia practically unopposed. At the same time, the Turks issued from the Chatalja Line and from Bulair (Bolayr) to reoccupy Adrianople. A Bulgarian attempt to regroup and attack the Greeks in the Struma Valley was unsuccessful. On 13 July Bulgaria sued for peace and hostilities were formally ended by the Treaty of Bucharest (10 August).

Bulgaria's brilliant successes in the First Balkan War caused her to underestimate her former allies' military capacity. The end result of the Second Balkan War was to deprive the Bulgarians of all gains made in the previous conflict.

Trevor N. Dupuy

See Also: Bulgaria; Greece; Ottoman Empire; Turkey; Yugoslavia.

Bibliography

Ashmead-Bartlett, E. 1913. *With the Turks in Thrace*. London: W. Heinemann.

Barby, H. 1913. *La guerre des Balkans*. Paris: B. Grasset.

Dupuy, R. E., and T. N. Dupuy. 1986. *The encyclopedia of military history*. New York: Harper and Row.

Ford, C. S. 1915. *The Balkan wars*. Fort Leavenworth, Kans.: Press of the Army Service Schools.

Howell, P. 1913. *The campaign in Thrace, 1912*. London: H. Rees.

Kiraly, B. K., and D. Djordjevic, eds. 1987. *East central European society and the Balkan wars*. Boulder, Colo.: Social Science Monographs.

Schurman, J. G. 1914. *The Balkan wars, 1912–1913*. Princeton, N.J.: Princeton Univ. Press.

Wagner, H. 1913. *With the victorious Bulgarians*. Boston: Houghton Mifflin.

BALLISTIC MISSILE DEFENSE

Ballistic missile defense (BMD) is active defense against ballistic missiles, a mode of defense that destroys or negates ballistic missiles in one or more phases of their flight path from lift-off to arrival at their target. The term *BMD* is synonymous with antiballistic missile (ABM), a name that was popular during the SALT I negotiations in the late 1960s and early 1970s and the one that is affixed to the U.S.–Soviet treaty limiting deployment of such defenses, the ABM Treaty (signed on 26 May 1972).

The characterization of BMD as "active defense" differentiates it from passive defense, a class of defensive measures to protect against ballistic missiles that includes hardening, mobility, and deception. Passive measures have been varied for protection of military targets, such as hardened Minuteman silos, the MX multiple protective shelters (MPS) concept, and the mobile Midgetman concept. For protection of cities against ballistic missiles and other strategic nuclear weapons, Civil Defense shelters have been the primary approach. In a number of studies, a combination of active and passive defenses has been analyzed.

Strategic defense is the term popularly used today for BMD, as in the Strategic Defense Initiative (SDI). Strictly speaking, strategic defense connotes a broader class of defense, including defense against manned bombers; but common usage has narrowed the term *strategic defense*, and SDI, to mean defense against ballistic missiles. The term *air defense* is applied to defense against manned aircraft. The Air Defense Initiative (ADI) is a national U.S. program, comparable to SDI in mission but of smaller scale, to develop defenses against strategic manned bombers and cruise missiles. The term *space defense* is commonly used to mean defense against satellites, as with antisatellite (ASAT) defense weapons.

In the ensuing discussion, the acronym BMD will be used with reference to early history, when ABM was the term of choice, and recent U.S. developments, when strategic defense and SDI have become more commonly used terms.

Early History

The spark that ignited U.S. interest in defending against ballistic missiles was the German V-2 ballistic missile, used against the Allies in World War II. Although this was a primitive ballistic missile by today's standards, it marked the first use of a supersonic missile at long ranges against a wartime adversary. The historical importance of the V-2 lies in the fact that there was no defense against this class of weapon. It could be used with impunity against area targets, such as cities and military bases, subject only to the limitations imposed by air raids against the launch sites. Capable of delivering a high-explosive warhead of nearly one ton to a range of 290 kilometers (180 mi.) in a time-of-flight of about 5 minutes, the V-2 presaged the evolution of strategic nuclear missiles and an offense-dominant era in military history.

In 1944, the U.S. Army initiated a program called Project Thumper to investigate the feasibility of a high-altitude air defense missile and the potential of creating a defense against the V-2. A second air defense program was launched by the army in 1945: Project Nike, a program destined to have far greater visibility and longevity than the earlier program. Project Nike led to the deployment of the Nike Ajax and Nike Hercules air defense systems in the 1950s. Early BMD developments in the United States were an outgrowth of these air defense systems. With the realization in the 1953–55 period that the Soviet Union was making progress in the development of long-range ballistic missiles, the impetus for U.S. investigation of BMD systems was intensified.

In March 1955, the U.S. Army contracted with Bell Telephone Laboratories (BTL) of the Western Electric Corporation to conduct an 18-month study of defense of the continental United States agasint both the air-breathing threat and ballistic missiles. At this time, the daunting objective of intercepting ballistic missiles was likened to "hitting a bullet with a bullet." Nevertheless, this ground-breaking study concluded that such a defense was feasible, using radar command guidance and a nuclear-tipped interceptor (active radar homing guidance was proposed for the air-breathing threat). In February 1957, the army contracted with BTL/Western Electric to develop a defense system for countering strategic ballistic missiles (the requirement to defend against manned aircraft as well was dropped). This was the origin of the Nike-Zeus system, which was under development from 1957 to 1963. The Nike-Zeus system achieved the first successful intercept of an intercontinental ballistic missile (ICBM) at Kwajalein Missile Range in December 1962.

A competitive approach to BMD in the mid-1950s was

the U.S. Air Force Wizard concept. The Wizard concept never progressed beyond the study stage, and the army was assigned the BMD system development mission in January 1958. At the same time, the decision was made (by Secretary of Defense McElroy) to assign the mission of ballistic missile early warning to the air force, and BMD advanced concepts and technology were centered in the newly created Advanced Research Projects Agency (ARPA).

In 1963 the Nike-Zeus system was succeeded by the Nike-X system, a more capable system employing phased-array radar and a high-acceleration interceptor. Nike-X overcame many of the technical deficiencies of Nike-Zeus, notably the problem of handling high traffic threats with dish antenna radars and the inability to discriminate between decoys and reentry vehicles (RVs). With a high acceleration interceptor, Sprint, the Nike-X system could wait for the threat cloud to reenter the atmosphere before launching an interceptor, and the resultant slowdown of the threat objects provided a physical basis for discrimination.

The first U.S. national BMD deployment decision was made in September 1967, the decision to deploy the Sentinel system for population defense against a first-generation Chinese ICBM threat. Sentinel was based on Nike-X technology. In early 1969, the Sentinel system was changed to the Safeguard system, a system with the same components and technology but reoriented to emphasize defense against a Soviet attack on Minuteman silos rather than protection of U.S. cities.

A single Safeguard site was deployed at Grand Forks, North Dakota, in 1975 and the site was closed, by direction of the Congress, in 1976. By this time, the ABM Treaty had been signed, allowing both the United States and the Soviet Union to deploy one site with 100 interceptors, but the U.S. Congress directed closure of the Safeguard site, primarily for economic reasons.

The Soviet Union embarked on deployment of the Galosh BMD system around Moscow in the early 1960s, later to be called the Moscow system. This system, upgraded with improved radars and two different types of interceptors, is still operational today.

U.S. BMD developments after Safeguard included prototype development of the Site Defense system (1971–78) and concept formulation and early development of the LoAD/Sentry system (1977–84). These generations of BMD systems employed progressively smaller components than Safeguard, while retaining the basic features of radar command guidance and nuclear interceptors. In parallel with the U.S. system development programs, advanced technology programs were carried out to investigate BMD phenomena and to demonstrate improved capabilities. In 1984 the homing overlay experiment (HOE) was conducted at Kwajalein Missile Range, demonstrating the capability to destroy an RV with a nonnuclear intercept.

The SDI Program

In March 1983, President Reagan announced the SDI Program. This program was described as an approach to make nuclear weapons "impotent and obsolete," and to "save lives rather than to avenge them." It marked not only a large escalation in U.S. investment in BMD research and development, but also a policy shift away from mutual assured destruction (MAD) in the direction of damage limitation. For all of the early history of U.S. BMD development, MAD was the principal policy to assure nuclear deterrence, a policy of threatened retaliation against any aggressor that employed nuclear weapons. With the introduction of the SDI program, President Reagan signaled an intent to develop defenses against nuclear missiles that would lessen U.S. dependence on MAD as a guarantor of deterrence.

For the first four years of the SDI program, the keynote of the program was research on highly advanced weapons to defend against massive ballistic missile attacks. Directed energy weapons (DEW), based in space, became both a high-priority research objective and a popular image of the program ("Star Wars"). In 1987 the Phase I SDI architecture was announced by the SDI program office, embodying a mix of ground-based and space-based interceptors and sensors and a relatively modest defense objective of negating about 40 percent of a 5,000-reentry-vehicle attack. Both the ground-based and space-based weapons (interceptors) in the Phase I architecture were kinetic energy weapons (KEW), rather than DEW, in deference to the immaturity of DEW technology.

In 1990 the SDI program office announced a refocused program that centered on a concept called global protection against limited strikes (GPALS). GPALS is comprised of three primary parts: national missile defense (NMD), theater missile defense (TMD), and global missile defense (GMD). An early part of NMD is a limited defense system element, ABM-Treaty compliant, which was advocated by the U.S. Congress in FY1992. It appears that a limited defense system will be deployed at Grand Forks, North Dakota, the same location as the Safeguard site, in the period 1996–98.

GPALS is a broadened defense concept, including defense of allied and friendly nations as well as the United States, against accidental, unauthorized, and developing nations' ballistic missile threats. While it envisions defense against quantitatively smaller threats than Phase I, it has as an objective the achievement of lower system leakage (the fraction of RVs that penetrate the defense). Ultimately, GPALS is seen as a global, space-based umbrella to protect against ballistic missiles launched "from anywhere to anywhere." A key feature of GPALS is the use of single, space-based interceptors, with autonomous acquisition sensors and battle management capability (Brilliant Pebbles), as opposed to the Phase I space weapons designed for multiple kill vehicles per platform and dependence on external sensors and control.

The success of the Patriot system in the Persian Gulf War significantly bolstered U.S. public and congressional awareness of BMD and the level of support for the SDI program. Patriot is an air defense system that has been upgraded to defend against short-range ballistic missiles, and its success against the Iraqi SCUD missiles marked the first time in history that hostile ballistic missiles have been shot down by a defense system. While Patriot was not developed under the SDI program, the TMD part of SDI is devoted to the development of more capable follow-on TMD systems. Beyond this direct relevance of Patriot to the SDI program, the Persian Gulf experience lifted confidence that the complex and challenging goals of SDI are achievable.

BMD Phases and Elements

Figure 1 shows the phases of a strategic ballistic missile trajectory and typical defense elements that are designed to operate in the various phases. It illustrates a multiple, independently targetable RV (MIRV) strategic missile; some strategic missiles have only one RV and all current tactical missiles have only one warhead. Tactical ballistic missiles, also called theater ballistic missiles, have shorter ranges and they frequently carry a nonseparating warhead. The defense elements shown in the figure are representative of those currently under development in the SDI program. This figure will be used to describe the BMD functions that are performed and to characterize BMD system performance.

At the left side of Figure 1, the boost phase of a ballistic missile is illustrated, the phase in which the main engines of the missile are burning and the missile is accelerating to the velocity required to cover the desired range. Boost phase typically has a duration of 5 minutes. The Satellite Early Warning System (SEWS), shown at the top left of the figure, detects the bright infrared signal of the main engine plumes and performs the function of early warning. The Brilliant Pebble (BP) interceptors shown heading toward the missile in both the boost phase and post-boost phase are launched from space; they achieve leverage by killing more than one RV per intercept. BP interceptors home on the infrared signal of the booster and post-boost vehicle (PBV).

The post-boost phase lasts for about 4 minutes. During this phase, multiple RVs are released from the bus. If penetration aids are included in the payload, they are also released from the bus during the post-boost phase. The small engines used on the missle bus emit

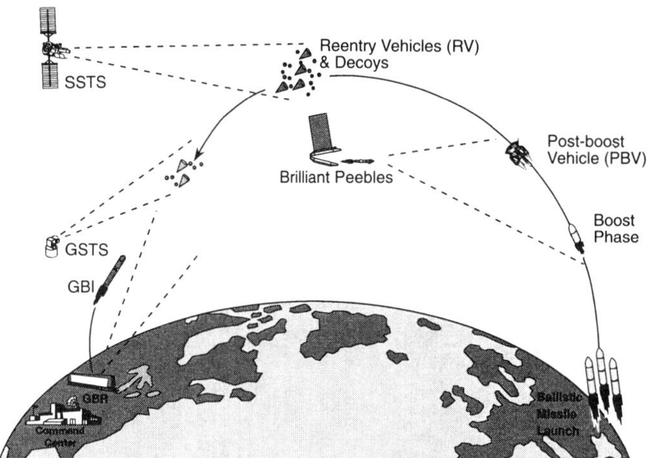

Figure 1. BMD phases and elements.

relatively weak infrared signals that are difficult to detect at long ranges, but they can be used by BPs to achieve bus kill.

The midcourse phase, during which the missile payload coasts in space, is the longest-duration phase, lasting about 20 minutes. In this phase, the booster and bus stages have dropped off and only RVs and penetration aids (if present) comprise the threat complex. The active "signatures" of the objects are weaker than in the boost and post-boost phase because there are no emissions from rocket engines.

The natural black body radiation from the objects in the midcourse phase can be detected by sensitive long-wave infrared (LWIR) sensors at long ranges. It is this radiation that is sensed by the Ground Surveillance and Tracking System (GSTS) and the Space Surveillance and Tracking System/Brilliant Eyes (SSTS/BE) sensors. Upon early warning, GSTS is launched by a rocket motor from ground basing up to exoatmospheric altitudes, while SSTS/BE operates in space orbits. A third sensor, the ground-based radar (GBR), can also sense targets in midcourse using active microwave radiation. The GBR can also be used in the terminal phase.

In the terminal phase, the ballistic missile payload reenters the earth's atmosphere and lightweight objects, such as light midcourse penetration aids, are stripped away by the resultant heating. The duration of this phase is on the order of 1 minute, requiring quick reaction by terminal defense elements.

Two ground-based KEW interceptors are depicted in Figure 1: the exoatmospheric ground-based interceptor (GBI) and the exoatmospheric and endoatmospheric interceptor (E^2I). GBI is generically related to the HOE experiment previously mentioned, and it engages the threat in the midcourse phase. E^2I is a more versatile interceptor than its predecessor, the high endoatmospheric defense interceptor (HEDI), in that it can be used in both the midcourse and terminal phases. These two ground-based interceptors, as well as BP, are nonnuclear interceptors that employ homing guidance to achieve small miss distances or "hit-to-kill" performance.

A fundamental advantage of a BMD architecture that operates in all phases of a ballistic missile trajectory, constituting a multi-tiered defense, is that very low defense leakage can be achieved. As an example, a defense architecture that has 50 percent leakage in the boost/post-boost phases, 20 percent leakage in the midcourse phase, and 10 percent leakage in the terminal phase has an overall defense leakage of only 1 percent ($0.5 \times 0.2 \times 0.1 = 0.01$). This means that such an architecture, defending against a threat composed of 1,000 RVs, would allow only 10 RVs to penetrate. Lower leakages than this example are feasible against smaller attack sizes, and advanced SDI concepts envision lower leakages even against massive attacks.

This brief discussion of BMD phases and elements has emphasized KEW interceptors and optical and microwave sensors that are under development to perform BMD functions in all phases of a ballistic missile trajectory. Two important additional elements are directed energy weapons, a follow-on element; and battle management/communication, command, and control (BM/C^3). DEW devices, including lasers and particle beams, were prominent in the early years of the SDI program. They offer the promise of providing highly lethal, zero-time-of-flight weapons that may ultimately replace KEW interceptors. The rate of maturation of DEW is a subject of some controversy in the scientific community, but it is clear that they will ultimately have a revolutionary influence on the effectiveness of BMD systems.

BM/C^3 is the element that ties together all of the other elements of BMD; it contains the computer hardware and software necessary to execute the incredibly large number of calculations, in a short span of time, to make the system work against a large-scale threat. It is considered by many defense specialists to be the most complex part of a BMD system and the most difficult element to develop. Compounding the challenge imposed by the size of BM/C^3 systems that have been defined is the difficulty of confidently testing the systems. Critics have argued that it will never be known whether the system will work until it is used against a real attack; defense analysts respond that modern software techniques and simulation tools will provide the necessary degree of confidence.

Future BMD Trends

As previously noted, the SDI program has evolved through several phases, responding to changing world conditions and the constraints imposed by the U.S. Congress. The Congress has cut the SDI budget request every year since the program started, and it has consistently opposed plans for early deployment of space-based weapons. With the dissolution of the Soviet Union, the demise of the Warsaw Pact, and the signing of the U.S.–Soviet START agreement, the magnitude of the perceived Soviet ballistic missile threat has diminished, and congressional support for SDI plans to defend against that threat has dissipated. The GPALS concept, with its near-term priority on Soviet accidental and unauthorized launches and the threat of missile attacks from developing countries, has been responsive to changes in the missile threat; however, the continued long-term emphasis on global, space-based defenses remains controversial.

The break-up of the Soviet Union raises questions about the disposition and control of the large Soviet inventory of strategic ballistic missiles. If these forces are dispersed in a number of Soviet republics, the paradigms of U.S.–Soviet strategic stability will be invalidated, and new security policies will have to be formulated. Added to the problem of proliferation, underscored by the estimate that twenty nations will possess ballistic missiles by the year 2000, the potential fragmentation of Soviet strategic missile forces creates a scenario that is potentially more dangerous than that of the cold war period. Depending on the future directions of Soviet government reforms and the pace of proliferation, the ballistic missile threat to the U.S. and other nations could become of increasing concern and lead to greater emphasis on BMD.

It appears doubtful that the original vision of the SDI program, involving massive defense deployment against large-scale Soviet attacks, will return to the prominence it enjoyed in the first few years of the program. A gradual, evolutionary approach to BMD deployment is more likely to occur. Beginning with the Limited Defense System, compliant with the ABM Treaty, the concept of national missile defense (NMD) could proceed to the deployment of four to six ground-based sites in the continental United States, and Alaska and Hawaii. This growth path would necessarily be accompanied by negotiations with Russia and other former Soviet republics on expansion of the ABM Treaty and agreement on deployment levels by all these nations. Beyond negotiations, other nations will probably develop or buy theater missile defense systems to protect against regional threats and to insulate against coercion and intimidation.

William A. Davis, Jr.

See Also: Ballistic Missile Defense; Strategic Defense Initiative; Strategic Defense Initiative: Policy Implications.

Bibliography

Bell Laboratories/Western Electric Corp. 1975. *ABM Research and Development at Bell Laboratories, Project History.* Whippany, N.J.: Bell Laboratories.

Carter, A. B., and D. N. Schwartz. 1984. *Ballistic missile defense.* Washington, D.C.: Brookings.

U.S. Congress, Office of Technology Assessment. 1985. *Ballistic missile defense technologies,* OTA-ISC-254. Washington, D.C.: Government Printing Office.

BALLISTICS

Ballistics deals not only with the motion of projectiles, but also is linked closely with a variety of technologies. Essentially there are four fundamental phases of ballistics. Interior ballistics involves the initial propulsion, or what happens in the gun or launcher; intermediate ballistics studies and analyzes the complex events related to the initial projectile flight just out of the gun or launcher; exterior ballistics describes the flight motions and performance characteristics of the projectile; and terminal ballistics determines the effect of the projectile on the target.

Currently, ballistics is in transition: both traditional and newer technology projectiles are in the field. Basic stockpiles of ammunition for a large number of weapon systems still consist essentially of "dumb" projectiles. That means that these projectiles, both kinetic energy (KE) and high explosive (HE), do not incorporate means to alter their trajectories once they are launched, nor can they sense the target or recognize the type of target. The newer generation of projectiles, however, is being designed to include guidance and sensing.

Thus one can generally differentiate between projectile types by broadly designating them as dumb (or conventional), "competent," "smart," or "brilliant." These designations require brief explanations. Conventional is usually a traditional ballistic projectile (spin-stabilized or fin-stabilized), whether KE or HE. The projectile (other than perhaps its fuzing) does not include any electronic sensing or subsidiary propulsion and guidance.

A competent munition consists of a conventional projectile that has been somewhat upgraded by the addition of one or more smart devices so that the projectile has gained a multiple increase in utilization and effectiveness over its basic form.

A smart munition is designed to be based on guidance and/or sensors to allow it to have in-flight (trajectory) flexibility unattainable by a conventional ballistic projectile.

Brilliant munitions are technology extensions beyond smart. They integrate guidance, control, and various sensors in conjunction with algorithms and high-speed microprocessing to represent the most advanced form of the state of the art.

As technology relentlessly advances in scope and complexity, smaller and more cost-effective devices will drive the application and design of future projectiles. Ballistics will no longer be based on a series of firing tables involving muzzle velocity, elevation angles, and range. Automatic fire-control systems will dominate and offer the user a variety of options.

The computer, with its ability to become increasingly miniaturized while providing high-speed data processing, will underlie a new style of ballistics. These will be a blending of the technologies between gun-launched projectiles and guided missiles. Of fundamental importance is the currently accepted methodology of using high-speed computing to analyze warhead designs and potential terminal (target) effectiveness with amazing accuracy. Warhead design is then integrated with appropriate sensor and fuze technologies. Concurrently, new materials are evaluated and selected for application (for example, sabots) and mating with the propulsion elements.

Wind tunnels and instrumented ballistic ranges are a traditional, proven, and continuous means for deriving the aerodynamic coefficients required for input into realistic six degrees of freedom (6 DOF) equations that, in turn, can be used to simulate external and mass effects upon flight stability and potential performance. These analyses are critical to achieving a successful ballistic item. The new field of computational fluid dynamics (CFD) is making strides and will provide an efficient method for design evaluation and performance prediction.

The increased use of high-speed, high-capacity computers is rapidly altering the overall traditional methodology of design, preliminary analysis, fabrication, testing, and performance analysis. What is strongly indicated is that much of the warhead design, flight performance, and terminal effects potential can be sufficiently well predicted from computer-based mathematical models so as to move more rapidly and confidently into building and testing the actual hardware. Nonetheless, gun-launched testing is still required, as is overall testing to verify system performance.

An anomaly continues to exist in ballistic testing, namely that small-scale ballistic systems (e.g., small arms and medium-caliber weapons) require testing of many thousands of rounds. By contrast, since the large-caliber and smart systems are individually expensive, relatively fewer numbers are actually tested. Thus, it is necessary to have highly instrumented test ranges and the supporting database to undertake the complete system analyses and associated acceptance decisions.

Interior Ballistics

Potentially, one of the ballistics areas for the next stage of significant improvement will be the efficiency of gun propulsion. This area divides into two diverse technologies. The first is in advanced propellant technology, specifically retaining the conventional gun design and obtaining substantial performance increments through use of different propellants. Examples are liquid, gelled, and a form of compacted conventional propellant referred to as "very high burn rate" (VHBR). These new propellants could add approximately 10 percent to 20 percent to the present muzzle velocities without completely changing the current gun systems.

The second technology trend relating to propulsion started about a decade ago with official support for a major research program based on electromagnetic propulsion. While this is still a long-term technology area, several new variations offer promise of intermediate performance improvement in a shorter time frame. These hybrids include electrothermal (ET), which combines electrical and chemical energy to launch conventional shapes at velocities significantly above the current standard, and combustion augmented plasma (CAP).

Light gas guns are a major ballistics research tool for conducting hypervelocity-impact and penetration-design studies leading to future armor/antiarmor systems. Two-stage light gas guns are capable of launch velocities up to 7,620 meters per second (25,000 ft./sec.). These fundamental research tools provide the means for obtaining the database upon which major changes and resultant advances in ballistic technology are dependent. Research is trying to determine whether these laboratory fixtures can become actual military weapons by means of unique redesigns and by applying the latest in materials and other advanced components. This work will require some unusual design and engineering to reduce size, weight, and complexity to a point where the proposed system has attractive military potential.

Intermediate Ballistics

In intermediate ballistics studies, KE investigations involve the launch dynamics of saboted projectiles. Emphasis is on achieving uniform sabot discard, thereby minimizing the dispersion error due to launch asymmetries. This is a form of fine-tuning the round to achieve reduced dispersion at ever-increasing ranges, since improved propellants are resulting in increased muzzle velocity with shorter time of flight to greater ranges. This results in the need to reduce those contributions to the total dispersion.

Projectile Configurations

In addition to modifying current projectile shapes, such as adding on rocket boost to long-rod penetrators, extensive research is being undertaken to increase significantly the length-to-diameter (l/d) ratio of rod penetrators. However, practical limits to the l/d will have to be considered because of the dimensions of munitions storage compartments within various fighting vehicles.

Currently, consideration is being given to including a multipurpose projectile in the small family of tank ammunition. This projectile would serve in a variety of roles, from antihelicopter, using a proximity fuze, to bunker-busting, antiarmor, and antipersonnel.

Future projectile designs will be required as launch velocities are increased and there is need to extend the effective range of these projectiles. Designs to be evaluated could be tubular, ramjet, or low-drag conical nose shapes, as well as wave-rider configurations. Each of these designs offers specific advantages and will have to be applied accordingly. For example, tubular projectiles, while generally having low mass, also have very low drag and can be used for both combat and training missions. On the other hand, ramjet projectiles can provide increased kinetic energy and extended range.

Another approach will be the weight reduction of sabots, so that additional energy can be imparted to the projectile and not lost through sabot discard. Rocket-assisted projectiles will be utilized to gain more downrange kinetic energy.

With so many tanks equipped with the 105mm cannon system, it would be economically feasible to use increased energy propellants and/or a rocket boost—initiated just out of the gun muzzle—to reduce time of flight to target while adding significantly to the downrange kinetic energy. If this approach proves to be relatively successful, simple, terminal correction means will be added. Later, in view of the longer range performance potential, more intricate guidance will be incorporated, particularly against maneuvering targets. These systems become complex when integrated, however, and require very detailed engineering design analyses, as well as experimental verification.

One of the key challenges will be integrating multisensors and fuzing without affecting the necessary, or required, warhead volume. Considering the continuing miniaturization of sensors and electronic fuzing, this design and packaging efficiency should be attainable within the next two generations of smart munitions.

Partial Ballistic Flight Modes

Free-flight, unguided projectiles and munitions are becoming converted to several terminal trajectory modes. Examples of these are guided mortars, where the first portion of the trajectory is ballistic, followed by terminal guidance. Artillery shells are being developed to deliver sensor-fuzed munitions. The shell's free-flight trajectory places it in a desired target area , and then the submunitions are base ejected to disperse, search, and fire on the target from above. In a similar manner, medium artillery rocket systems launch carrier rockets in a ballistic mode to reach a target area and then eject terminally guided submunitions that can detect and fly to the target. This combination of ballistic ammunition and electronic technologies is also applicable for future aircraft-delivered stand-off weapon dispensers.

Aircraft-Delivered Munitions

One specialty generally overlooked in ballistics is air-delivered munitions, particularly submunitions or bomblets carried by aircraft to the target area and then released. Currently, the aircraft has to launch the dispenser in a free-flight ballistic trajectory.

The present dispensers are capable of spinning, then opening and releasing the bomblets above the target area. The effective area coverage is determined by the centrifugal force generated by the spinning dispenser. What is of concern is the vulnerability of the aircraft, in that it must approach and fly near (if not over) the target zone to achieve the required ballistic trajectory release. Future dispenser versions in research will have a long stand-off range capability. They will contain on-board thrust generators and guidance, so that the delivery aircraft will be able to launch the dispenser farther from the target and thus be able to "launch and leave" while the powered dispenser seeks and homes in on the target area, much like an advanced cruise missile. However, until the "smarts" become smaller and very affordable, the bomblets will tend to be ballistic. Eventually, technology is expected to transition dumb munitions into competent munitions by applying basic sensors and through maneuvering or guidance means. At this point, self-dispersing bomblets or submunitions will no longer be a direct function of their former ballistic characteristics. Additionally, air-launched munition dispensers will share some of the flight and performance characteristics of cruise missiles.

Small Arms

The current technology trend is on improving the hit probability at ranges beyond 250 meters (820 ft.). Ballistic effort is focusing on multiple rounds launched per trigger pull to increase the dispersion in a relatively controlled area or target zone, thus increasing the probability of a hit. Both conventional projectiles and flechettes are being tested for this improved hit probability.

Caseless ammunition is continuing to be developed by a small segment of the small-arms community. Concurrent with a trend toward smaller, lightweight projectiles launched at higher muzzle velocities is a trend toward larger capacity magazines as a means of supporting the higher rate of fire, or expenditure of ammunition.

A new trend in the ballistics of infantry weapons that is in its earliest stage is the concept of a small-arms shoulder-fired weapon that can launch an exploding projectile, or bursting munition, to ranges in excess of 500 meters (1,640 ft.). Since the impulse required for achieving this range is beyond the human factors limit for that of normal rifle or grenade-launched munitions, this calls for a rocket-propelled grenade or an aeroballistic projectile whose shape can produce sufficient lift in flight, in conjunction with low drag, to result in a relatively flat trajectory and extended range. This technology trend also calls for a compact fire-control system that computes range and time of flight and communicates to the fuzing to achieve either an airburst near the ground or a direct impact, whichever may be required by combat conditions.

The focal point of this technology trend is to reduce significantly the major deficiency in small-arms infantry weapons, the large number of bullets that must be fired to achieve an incapacitating hit. By developing a shoulder-launched explosive fragmentation projectile that has both a relatively flat trajectory and extended range, two key results accrue. Area coverage rather than point target accuracy is required, and a suppressive effect is achieved at a range well beyond that of current shoulder-fired infantry weapons. This unique requirement has emerged from the U.S. Army Infantry School study, *Small Arms Strategy—2000.*

Medium-Caliber Ballistics

Progress in medium-caliber ballistics is gradual, as this tends to be an area for continuing the conventional rather than for undertaking radical change.

A major effort is under way to apply finned-rod penetrators to the entire range of medium-caliber ammunition. The rods are scaled down from the kinetic-energy tank-penetrator designs. In the medium calibers the accuracy of the rods becomes very sensitive to the tolerances of the projectiles' components and to the uniformity of sabot discard. To achieve higher muzzle velocities for the rods to increase penetration at longer ranges, newer propellant formulations are being applied.

Another area of slow, but continuing, progress in medium-caliber ballistics is telescoped ammunition. The projectile is completely enclosed within a cylindrical case containing compacted (or consolidated) propellant. The key is to launch each projectile into the barrel at, or very close to, the same initial velocity so as to achieve near-uniform muzzle velocity from shot to shot. Current studies have shown that launch velocities of 1,525 meters per second (5,000 ft./sec.) and higher can be obtained. This performance, combined with the more efficient case geometry, results in a larger number of stowed rounds per given volume, making this area of ballistic technology attractive for future application for both aircraft and ground systems.

Larger Caliber—Tank Cannon

As discussed previously, one of the key goals in obtaining increased muzzle velocities is to be able to launch kinetic-energy rod-type projectiles having higher length-to-diameter (l/d) ratios. This area of ballistics includes the development of new sabots of lighter weight materials, mainly of stronger composites.

Further, in view of the increased emphasis on tank protection, and through new material combinations and the addition of reactive armor, it will not be surprising to see larger caliber tank cannon come into use. Alternatively, new hypervelocity gun designs may also be introduced, and this could signal a new family of projectiles combining the best features of both the kinetic-energy and high-explosive types. Additional emphasis is currently being placed on projectile designs having a form of dual warheads to overcome the protective use of reactive armor and to be able to penetrate the main target. Again, ballistics is being challenged by the measure/countermeasure aspect from continuing advancements in technology.

Larger Caliber—Artillery

The trend in long-range artillery delivering submunitions that can independently seek, acquire, and destroy armor will continue. The keys to further advancements in this area are cost effectiveness of the electronics and sensor sensitivity countermeasures.

Fire control will play a major role in the ballistics of artillery systems, particularly for self-propelled units. With the use of land navigational systems and autoloaders it will be possible to increase significantly firepower effects.

As more sensor-electronic systems become part of projectile design, various control systems will be used in ballistics. For example, in tank weapons, command and control from the tank could correct and guide the projectile toward the target. In artillery, studies have shown that to achieve accuracy at long range, application of a form of the Global Positioning System (GPS), combined with an on-board correction system, could play a key role in future artillery tactics.

Advances in ballistics must be integrated with concurrent advances in guidance and control, target acquisition, and fire control.

Training Systems

During peacetime, additional emphasis is placed on low-cost training systems. Tank cannon training systems are starting to utilize subcaliber ammunition whose ballistics are designed to match the combat rounds to a reasonable range and then rapidly decelerate so as to not overfly the maximum range or safety limits.

In artillery, new training rounds are being developed that allow for an airburst and that have an acoustic signature similar to combat antipersonnel rounds. This will allow for appropriate troop training.

A current mortar training system uses scaled trajectories and simulates full-scale ammunition handling.

Materials

Various near and future weapon systems will use more high-strength lightweight materials. For example, there are programs under way to develop medium-caliber gun barrels of composite materials in combination with special ceramics.

Some calibers of cased ammunition will have thinner, stronger walls of new high-strength steel. Also, the development of high-strength plastic cartridge cases will significantly reduce weight.

Lightweight composite materials are being used to fabricate sabots. The reduction in weight will allow the payload (projectile) to be heavier or to be launched at a higher muzzle velocity.

As new gun designs, such as the electromagnetic gun or its variants, produce increased muzzle velocities, there will be a need for heat-resistant materials for the projectile nose and the leading edges of the fins. This will be necessary to eliminate or minimize the configurational asymmetries due to ablation from atmospheric heating and the resultant effect on dispersion.

All told, new materials and their applications will be a vital factor in future ballistic systems.

Miscellaneous

Naval Systems

In the area of naval defense, while the 20mm Gatling gun (Phalanx system) is an accepted ballistic weapon, the trend is toward an increased caliber system so that a larger projectile can be launched at higher muzzle velocity, have shorter time of flight to the target, and arrive with more kinetic energy to hit and damage the target.

Larger caliber naval guns will make use of improved fuzes, explosives, and materials. New projectile designs are under development, from submunition carriers to extended range configurations.

An extension of the long-range large gun role will be in the form of ship-launched cruise missiles. Potential payloads will include submunitions.

Caseless Ammunition

There is a near-term trend to caseless or consumable ammunition. Accepted and in use for the large-caliber 120mm NATO tank ammunition, a similar methodology is being intensively developed by the Germans for small arms (for example, the German G11 rifle in 4.92mm). Other infantry weapons using caseless ammunition also are being studied.

Lasers

Research continues on laser weapons. Although feasibility studies have determined the lethality of laser weapons, it remains to be seen how rapidly the power supply and associated components can be packaged into a reasonably sized and militarily rugged mobile weapon platform.

Summary

The trends show continuing competition between gun systems and missile systems, with a gradual merging or combination of these technologies. Emphasis in the gun area will be on developing new interior ballistic systems such as electromagnetic and electrothermal. These systems are capable of launching projectiles at hypersonic velocities, but they need to reach practical size and weight limits to become useful weapon systems. In turn, the hypervelocities will result in new projectile shapes using heat-resistant materials and other components developed for the space program. Although the higher launch velocities will result in shorter times of flight, the use of command or terminal guidance may be necessary to ensure higher hit probabilities.

Concurrently the large investment in conventional ballistic systems represents a basis for product improvement in a variety of technical areas associated with ballistics. These range from more energetic propellants to the materials composing the projectiles, (e.g., high-strength metals and lightweight composites for saboted kinetic-energy penetrators and the use of new materials in explosive warheads).

Much of the supporting research and development in ballistics is being done through the use of complex mathematical modeling programmed on some of the world's fastest and largest capacity computers. These high-speed computers enable designers to evaluate and predict the complete ballistic performance of advanced weapon systems, ranging from interior ballistics through flight and then terminal ballistic effectiveness. What was once done very slowly and in a separate or compartmented manner is now being approached in a more unified way. Nonetheless, despite emphasis on the in-laboratory aspects, verification of ballistic systems performance must still be undertaken on highly instrumented and specialized test ranges.

It appears that competent, smart, and brilliant munitions will dominate in the coming era, leaving small arms and some of the medium-caliber areas as the remaining fields for high technology to enter. Fundamental operations studies might show whether it is cost-effective to fully apply high technology to these lower calibers.

Again, weight, size, and muzzle velocities will be key factors in future launch systems, while what flies through the atmosphere will depend in great part upon advances in electronics, miniaturization, and on-board propulsion and guidance systems.

The guns-versus-missiles debate may gradually diminish as the best elements of a variety of technologies are integrated into future weapon systems. Ballistics will produce a powerful combination of free-flight and guided dynamics.

ABRAHAM FLATAU

SEE ALSO: Ammunition; Artillery; Artillery, Rocket and Missile; Artillery, Tube; Fuze; Gun Technology Applications; Missile, Ballistic; Missile Technology Applications; Mortar; Munitions and Explosives: Engineering and Handling; Munitions and Explosives Technology Applications; Sensor Technology; Small Arms.

Bibliography

Defense Technical Information Center. 1974–. Proceedings of Hypervelocity Impact Symposiums, nos. 1–7.

Deitchman, S. J. 1987. Exploiting the revolution in conventional weapons. *Aerospace America* (June).

DeMeis, R. 1987. Looking ahead to tactical missiles. *Aerospace America* (June).

Farrar, C. L., et al. 1982. *Military ballistics*. London: Brassey's.

Flatau, A. 1982. Non-spinning projectile, U.S. Patent No. 4,337,911.

Goad, K. J., et al. 1982. *Ammunition*. London: Brassey's.

Hooten, T. 1986. More punch for the infantry: The intelligent mortar round. *Miltech* (4).

Lenaerts, J. 1987. Automatic grenade launchers and their role. *Miltech* (10).

Ryan, J. W. 1982. *Guns, mortars & rockets*. London: Brassey's.

Swift, H., et al. 1979. Feasibility of hypervelocity ordnance. *U.S. Army ARDC*. AD-E400 338. July.

U.S. Army Infantry School. 1986. *Small arms strategy—2000*. Fort Benning, Ga.: U.S. Army Infantry School.

Zukas, J. A. 1982. *Impact dynamics*. New York: Wiley.

BANGLADESH, PEOPLE'S REPUBLIC OF

Bangladesh occupies the eastern, Muslim half of the old Indian region of Bengal. It is the most densely populated agricultural nation on earth, and is also one of the poorest.

Power Potential Statistics

Area: 144,000 square kilometers (55,126 sq. mi.)
Population: 115,880,800
Total Active Armed Forces: 106,500 (0.092% of pop.)
Gross Domestic Product: US$20.4 billion (1990 est.)
Annual Defense Expenditure: US$319 million (1.5% of GDP, 1991 est.)
Iron and Steel Production:
  Crude steel: 0.0955 million metric tons (1986)
Fuel Production:
  Petroleum products processed: 1.31 million metric tons (1986)
  Natural gas: 4,175 million cubic meters (1987–88)
Electrical Power Output: 5,700 million kwh (1990)
Merchant Marine: 47 vessels; 339,081 gross registered tons
Civil Air Fleet: 15 major transport aircraft; 12 usable airfields (12 with permanent-surface runways); none with runways over 3,659 meters (12,000 ft.); 4 with runways 2,440–3,659 meters (8,000–12,000 ft.); 6 with runways 1,220–2,440 meters (4,000–8,000 ft.)

For the most recent information, the reader may refer to the following annual publications:

The Military Balance. International Institute for Strategic Studies. London: Brassey's (UK).

The Statesman's Year-Book. New York: St. Martin's Press.

The World Factbook. Central Intelligence Agency. Washington, D.C.: Brassey's (US.)

History

Bangladesh has a rich historical past and cultural heritage, the result of the repeated influx of various peoples, most recently the Persian- and Turkish-influenced Moguls in the mid-sixteenth century, and the British in the mid-eighteenth century. Bangladesh and the neighboring Indian state of Bengal (to the west) formed the British province of Bengal, the first large area of India directly governed by the British. By the 1930s and 1940s, as movement toward independence from British rule gained impetus, the Muslim League gained influence and support among the Muslims of eastern Bengal. When independence came in 1947, the Muslim areas of Bengal were joined with other Muslim-majority areas along the Indus valley as the new nation of Pakistan, eastern Bengal becoming known as East Pakistan.

This arrangement, and the domination of the Pakistani government by West Pakistan, did not please the citizens of Muslim Bengal. By the mid-1960s an independence party, the Awami League, had gained considerable support; the party won 70 percent of the popular vote and 167 of 169 seats allotted to East Pakistan in the elections of 1970–71 for the 313-seat National Assembly planned by Gen. Yahya Khan's government. Dismayed by such unexpectedly strong support for the Awami League and independence, Yahya Khan postponed the pending National Assembly session on 1 March 1971.

The infuriated supporters of the Awami League organized a provisional government in India on 26 March, where many Awami leaders had fled to escape arrest. Open warfare erupted between the Pakistani army and the Bengali *Mukti Bahini* (freedom fighters), and refugees fled to India by the thousands to escape the fighting. India lent considerable support to the rebels, and in retaliation the Pakistanis launched a major strike against Indian air bases on 3 December 1971. The Indians had expected an attack (and so suffered little damage), and immediately launched an invasion of East Pakistan with nearly 300,000 men. Within two weeks, Indian troops had overwhelmed the 90,000-man Pakistan army force in East Pakistan and captured Dhaka (16 December). The independence of Bangladesh became official on 17 December.

Independence did not solve Bangladeshi political problems, and the assassination of Pres. Sheikh Mujibur Rahman by mid-level army officers in August 1975 resulted in a new government. Successive military coups on 3 and 7 November 1975 led to the emergence of Gen. Zia ur Rahman (no relation) as strongman. General Zia dissolved the parliament, but held new elections in June 1978 in which he won a 5-year term as president and his broad-based center-left coalition won 207 of 300 elected parliamentary seats. General Zia was assassinated in Chittagong in May 1981 as part of an unsuccessful coup. Former vice president Abdus Sattar's administration was ineffective, and he was replaced by Gen. Hussain Mohammed Ershad in a bloodless coup on 23 March 1982.

General Ershad was elected president in December 1983 and was re-elected in October 1986. He ended martial law in November 1986, and restored the constitution after confirming the legality of his acts under martial law. After declaring a state of emergency in November 1990, however, he was forced to resign in December. An interim president, Shahabuddin Ahmed, was then appointed by the caretaker government.

Politico-Military Background and Policy

As its history shows, the armed forces have played a pivotal role in the development of Bangladeshi politics. A rift with India, which began in 1974–75 during the later stages of President Mujibur's regime, has led to good relations with Pakistan, China, and the United States. Dissident members of the Awami League still pose some threat to internal stability and are not fully reconciled to the current government. The armed forces are manned entirely by volunteers.

Strategic Problems

Bangladesh's greatest strategic problem stems from the density of its population, coupled with its largely agricultural economy and its lack of natural resources. Most Bangladeshi foreign credit is earned from the export of jute (1.158 million metric tons in 1985; 70% of world output), and any depression of the market has severe repercussions.

Bangladesh is also afflicted with an indigenous guerrilla movement. The *Shanti Bahini* (Peace Force) is based in Comilla Province (east-central Bangladesh), and fields perhaps 8,000 active fighters. At present it does not pose a serious threat to the regime, but it might gain support if the economic situation worsens.

Military Assistance

Bangladesh receives some grant-aid assistance from the United States for training of officers and enlisted men, but most military assistance comes from China.

Defense Industry

Bangladesh has no domestic arms industry, and relies on imported equipment, most of which comes from China. China has provided tanks, artillery, and naval vessels. Three British-made frigates are also in service.

Alliances

Bangladesh is a member of the United Nations (UN), the Commonwealth, and several other international organizations. Bangladesh has close relations with the United States (from which it has received considerable economic aid) and with China.

Defense Structure

The president is commander in chief of the armed forces, and exercises administrative and operational control through the service chiefs of staff.

(For an explanation of the abbreviations and symbols used in the following section of military statistics, see the list of Abbreviations and Acronyms in each volume.)

Total Armed Forces

Active: 106,500

ARMY: 93,000.
6 inf div HQ.

14 inf bde (some 26 bn).
1 armd bde (2 armd regt).
6 arty regt.
6 engr bn.
Equipment:†
MBT: 20 Ch Type-59, 30 T-54/-55.
Light tanks: some 40 Ch Type-62.
Towed arty: 105mm: 30 Model 56 pack, 50 M-101; 122mm: 20 Ch Type-54.
Mortars: 81mm; 82mm: Ch Type-53; 120mm: 50 Ch Type-53.
RCL: 106mm: 30 M-40A1.
ATK guns: 57mm: 18 6-pdr; 76mm: 50 Ch Type-54.
AD guns: 37mm; 57mm.

NAVY: † (following April 1991 cyclone) 7,500. Bases: Chittagong (HQ), Dhaka, Khulna, Kaptai.
Frigates: 4: 1 Osman (Ch Jianghu II) with 2 × 5 ASW mor, plus 2 × 2 CSS-N-2 Hai Ying-2 (HY-2) SSM, 2 × 2 100mm guns. 1 Umar Farooq (UK Salisbury) with 1 × 3 Squid ASW mor, 1 × 2 114mm guns. 2 Abu Bakr (UK Leopard) with 2 × 2 114mm guns.
Patrol and Coastal Combatants: 35:
Missile Craft: 8: 4 Durdarsha (Ch Huangfeng) with 4 × HY-2 SSM. 4 Durbar (Ch Hegu) PFM with 2 × HY-2 SSM.
Torpedo Craft: 4 Ch Huchuan PFT (with 2 × 533mm TT.
Patrol, Coastal: 5: 2 Durjoy (Ch Hainan) with 4 × 5 ASW RL. 2 Meghna fishery protection. 1 Shahjalal.
Patrol, Inshore: 13: 8 Shahead Daulat (Ch Shanghai II) PFI 2 Karnaphuli, 2 Padma, 1 Bishkali PCI.
Riverine: 5 Pabna (.
Amphibious: 1 Shahamanat LCU; plus craft: 4 LCT, 3 LCVP.
Support and Miscellaneous: 3: 1 coastal tanker, 1 repair, 1 ocean tug.

AIR FORCE: † 6,000; 85 cbt ac, no armed hel. (A number of ac and hel were destroyed and many others were damaged during the cyclone in April 1991. The figures only indicate reported losses.)
FGA: 3 sqn with 18 J-6/JJ-6, 16 Q-5, 12 Su-7BM (ex-Iraqi ac).
Fighter: 2 sqn with 17 J-7M, 16 MiG-21 MF, 2 MiG-21U.
Transport: 1 sqn with 1 An-24, 4 An-26, 1 DHC-3.
Helicopters: 3 sqn with 2 Bell 206L, 10 -212, 6 Mi-8, 3 UH-1N.
Training: 20 Ch CJ-6, 8 CM-170, 4* JJ-7, 4 MiG-15UTI, 3 Su-7U.

FORCES ABROAD
UN and Peacekeeping:
Iraq/Kuwait (UNIKOM): 7 observers.

PARAMILITARY
Bangladesh Rifles: 30,000 (border guard); 37 bn.
Armed Police: 5,000.
ANSARS (Security Guards): 20,000.

OPPOSITION
Shanti Bahini (Peace Force), Chakma tribe Chittagong Hills, est. 5,000.

Future

Bangladesh faces no serious external threats. Geographically, India poses the greatest potential threat, but despite a cooling relationship does not show any interest in invading. A collapse of central authority in Burma might generate a refugee problem, but would likely lead only to small-scale conflict. The greatest Bangladeshi challenges, therefore, are internal: to achieve real, steady economic growth and development while at the same time maintaining a stable legal and representative government.

DAVID L. BONGARD
TREVOR N. DUPUY

SEE ALSO: India; Indo-Pacific Area; Pakistan; South and Southeast Asia.

Bibliography

Baxter, C. 1986. *Bangladesh: A new nation in an old setting.* Boulder, Colo.: Westview Press.
Hunter, B., ed. 1991. *The statesman's year-book, 1991–92.* New York: St. Martin's Press.
International Institute for Strategic Studies. 1991. *The military balance, 1991–1992.* London: Brassey's.
O'Donnell, C. 1986. *Bangladesh: Biography of a muslim nation.* Boulder, Colo.: Westview Press.

BATTLESHIP

For most of the first half of the twentieth century, the battleship was considered the primary type of warship in the world's navies. It carried the largest guns and heaviest armor and, until supplanted in World War II by the aircraft carrier, was considered the principal embodiment of a nation's naval might. Also considered a capital ship, and closely related, was the battle cruiser, which also carried large guns but was generally faster and less heavily armored than the battleship. Fleet tactics and naval strategy were built around the concept of using a nation's battleships to defeat those of an enemy on the high seas. In practice, such encounters seldom took place, with the result that the battleship's strength was for the most part potential rather than actual. Two battleships, both in the U.S. Navy, are now in active service.

Predecessors

The battleship derived its name and general function from the heavily gunned wooden ship of the line of the eighteenth and nineteenth centuries. Naval tactics in the age of sail called for enemy fleets to maneuver in line formations as they opposed each other. The name *battleship* resulted from the contraction of the term *line-of-battle ship*. The first seagoing ironclad, a forerunner of the modern battleship, was the French *Gloire*, essentially an armored frigate of 5,600 tons, completed in 1860. The British ironclad *Warrior*, completed in 1861, was bigger and faster than the *Gloire* and is generally considered the prototype of the eventual battleship.

Battleship Components

In their physical makeup and fighting abilities, battleships have a number of elements in common.

Armament

The primary component that distinguishes battleships (and battle cruisers) from other types of warships is the number and size of their guns. The battleship carries the biggest guns of any ship in the fleet. In 1862, the USS *Monitor* carried a pair of 11-inch guns in a rotating armored turret on its main deck. Both 9- and 10-inch guns were popular in nineteenth-century battleship designs, and a few ships mounted guns as large as 16¼ inches in diameter. The USS *Indiana*, completed in 1895 as the first true U.S. battleship, mounted four 13-inch guns. Contemporary European battleships had comparably sized guns. In the twentieth century the trend was toward a larger number of big guns of common size on battleships, growing by steps from 10 inches to 12, 14, 15, 16, and ultimately 18 inches in the Japanese Yamato class. The largest guns on American battleships were 16 inches in diameter with a range of approximately 32 kilometers (20 mi.). With the development of aircraft as a threat, some World War II battleships mounted more than 100 guns each. Some battleships were capable of firing torpedoes, but that weapon was removed prior to World War II.

Armor

Because battleships were designed to contest enemy counterparts, logic dictated the armoring of vulnerable portions of each ship to protect it from enemy gunfire and torpedoes. A rule of thumb was that a given battleship should be able to withstand shells fired by ships with the same size guns. Belt armor at the waterline became a standard defense against torpedoes, as did a system of internal compartmentation and double bottoms. Also heavily armored were turrets, ammunition magazines, and conning towers to protect those who were directing the ship's movements. In the twentieth century, deck armor was strengthened to protect against aerial bombs and the plunging fire of long-range gunnery. (The higher the angle of elevation of the guns, the longer the range, and thus the steeper the angle at which the projectiles approach.) The USS Nevada class, commissioned in 1916, introduced the all-or-nothing armor scheme in which vital parts of the ship were heavily armored and the rest essentially unprotected. The heaviest battleship armor is nearly 20 inches thick.

Propulsion

For much of their history, battleships were slow, ponderously moving ships. In the nineteenth century, they had coal-fired steam engines of the compound reciprocating type and were rated at less than 20 knots. Steam turbines in battleships were introduced early in the twentieth century; they produced higher speed with less noise and vibration than had been experienced with reciprocating engines. The switch from coal to oil as fuel for new battleships took place around the time of World War I; oil permitted greater speed and was also much more convenient to handle. Following the war, several older ships were converted to burn oil. Range was a consideration in battleship propulsion. British, Japanese, and U.S. designs called for much greater endurance than most continental European counterparts because of the need to operate much farther from home.

Fire Control

At the beginning of the twentieth century, battleship gunnery was notorious for its inaccuracy. The effective range was only a few thousand meters or yards. The introduction of optical range finders enabled a more precise approach than the previous method of going close to the enemy and firing at an essentially flat trajectory. Later innovations were gun directors that communicated orders to the guns, plotting rooms for tracking moving targets and providing firing solutions, and stable elements so that guns could remain steadily on target even when the ship was rolling in a seaway. Spotting the fall of shot was accomplished by stationing sailors high in each ship and later by using observation balloons and pontoon-equipped aircraft carried on board ship. The final refinement came around the time of World War II, introduction of fire-control radar to provide target range and bearing electronically.

Russo-Japanese War

One early U.S. battleship, the *Oregon*, had a perfunctory role in the Spanish-American War of 1898; it fired ineffectively at a fleeing cruiser. The real combat debut of the modern battleship took place during the Russo-Japanese War of 1904–1905. In the Battle of Tsushima Strait in late May 1905, six Russian battleships with 10-inch guns opposed four Japanese battleships with 12-inch guns. In the engagement, firing was at relatively close range to allow effective shooting by smaller guns. The Japanese, partly through good fortune, won a decisive victory. Tsushima was the only major naval engagement fought by predreadnought-type battleships.

HMS Dreadnought

In late 1906, the Royal (British) Navy put into service a revolutionary new battleship named HMS *Dreadnought* that simultaneously made all existing battleships obsolete and launched a new arms race among the world's naval powers. Completed in just about a year from the time its keel was laid, the *Dreadnought* was the invention of Britain's First Sea Lord, Admiral John Fisher. The ship carried ten 12-inch guns and was the first all-big-gun battleship, thus moving away from the previous concept of mixing primary and secondary batteries of different sizes. The *Dreadnought* also introduced steam turbine propulsion, enabling it to make a speed of 21 knots. Because of the innovations of the new warship, all succeeding battleships came to be known generically as *dreadnoughts*.

International Naval Competition

In the years leading up to World War I, battleships were viewed as the embodiment of naval power and international prestige. Naval-minded U.S. President Theodore Roosevelt sent a Great White Fleet of sixteen battleships on an around-the-world cruise (1907–1909) to demonstrate national power. During his term of office, the country began construction of seventeen new battleships. Still more were laid down in the years immediately afterward. In Europe, Great Britain and Germany were engaged in an energetic building race that led to bigger and more capable ships. By the end of 1912, Britain had nineteen dreadnought-type battleships completed and another twelve under construction; the comparable figures for Germany were thirteen and ten. Japan and Russia were acquiring battleships, and so were Argentina, Austria-Hungary, Brazil, Chile, France, Greece, Italy, Japan, Russia, and Turkey. On the eve of World War I, Britain had a total of 32 dreadnought-type battleships and battle cruisers; Germany had a total of 22.

Battle Cruisers

Shortly after Admiral Fisher's innovation of the dreadnought battleship, he inaugurated another type of warship that emphasized speed at the expense of armor protection. Armed with the same size guns as battleships, the type of ship that came to be known as the battle cruiser was introduced with HMS *Inflexible*, which went into service in 1908 with eight 12-inch guns, 28 knots of speed, and armor only a little more than half as thick as a battleship's.

The theory was that the battle cruiser could outrun any enemy battleship armed as heavily as it was and outshoot any enemy cruiser that was as lightly protected. In practice, circumstances on a number of occasions compelled use of battle cruisers in fleet engagements against battleships—a role for which they were not intended—and they suffered losses as a result, most notably in the May 1916 Battle of Jutland during World War I.

World War I

The principal irony concerning battleships in what was then the largest war in the history of the world was that their use was largely confined to sitting at anchor or exercising out of harm's way. Both the British Grand Fleet (augmented in 1917 by a squadron of battleships from the U.S. Navy) and the German High Seas Fleet served largely as "fleets in being." This means that, while the war of the trenches fell into stalemate on the western front, the power of the battleships derived mostly from their existence rather than their use in combat. Each was cautiously safeguarded as a counter to the other, and the two fleets tied down enormous amounts of resources that might have been employed elsewhere.

The one notable exception to the pattern was the Battle of Jutland, fought in the North Sea on 31 May 1916. The rival naval commanders were Britain's Admiral John Jellicoe and Germany's Vice Admiral Reinhard Scheer. Each developed a tactical plan that called for sending forth a relatively small contingent of ships to serve as bait and expose the enemy's warships to the fleet's main body. The plans were executed roughly simultaneously and surprised both sides. The British lost the battle cruisers *Invincible*, *Indefatigable*, and *Queen Mary* in the action; the Germans lost the new battle cruiser *Lützow*. Each side lost several smaller cruisers. The battle was a tactical victory for Germany but a strategic victory for Britain. The High Seas Fleet never again came out to challenge the Royal Navy. Both fleets retired to their anchorages, and the British naval blockade of Germany continued as before. The war was decided on the battlefields of France, not at sea. Following the armistice that halted fighting in November 1918, the former High Seas Fleet steamed to Scapa Flow in the Orkney Islands north of Scotland and surrendered. In June 1919, remaining skeleton German crews scuttled the ships that had once been the pride of their nation.

International Disarmament Agreements

In 1921, as a new post–World War I battleship-building race threatened to impose considerable financial burdens on various nations, the United States called for an international naval disarmament conference to be held in Washington. The Washington Treaty, signed in 1922, called for a ten-year moratorium on new battleship construction and imposed tonnage limitations on the battle fleets of various nations: Great Britain, 580,450; United States, 500,650; Japan, 301,320; France, 221,170; Italy, 182,000. Under the terms of the treaty, some new battleships under construction could not be completed, and some older ships were scrapped as well. Ships then in existence were permitted to be replaced after reaching the age of 20; the new ships, however, were to displace no more than 35,000 tons. The only new battleships allowed to be completed under the terms of the treaty were the Japanese *Mutsu*, British *Nelson* and *Rodney*, and the American *Maryland*, *Colorado*, and *West Virginia*.

The moratorium was later extended for five years, but in the mid-1930s the international mood changed. Further negotiations led to some delays in new construction, along with the retention of the limit of 35,000 tons and 14-inch guns. Because the Japanese would not agree to abide by those limits, an escalator clause permitted new limits of 45,000 tons and 16-inch guns. In fact, the Japanese were building the *Yamato* and *Musashi*, each with a displacement of 68,200 tons and armed with 18-inch guns. The other nations adhered to the tonnage limitations in varying degrees.

Between the World Wars

With new battleship construction prohibited by the Washington Treaty, the world's naval powers set out in the 1920s and 1930s to use their existing ships to best advantage. During the course of shipyard modernization periods, ships were made more capable. In a number of instances, oil replaced coal as fuel; armor protection was upgraded because of the recognition of aerial bombs as threats; gun elevation was increased to extend the range for main battery guns; antiaircraft guns were added; protection against torpedoes was increased; and in a few cases speed was enhanced.

During these years, battleships were acknowledged as the primary naval vessels. War plans called for pitting the big guns of each fleet against those of an enemy. Ships such as aircraft carriers, cruisers, destroyers, and submarines were to have supporting roles. Fleet practice was held in the interwar years to provide training and to develop and refine tactics. From the late 1930s onward, as the disarmament treaties were no longer able to prolong the construction moratorium, a new battleship-building race ensued—reminiscent of the one that had preceded World War I (Fig. 1). Germany, vanquished in World War I, began building new dreadnoughts. The other major naval powers—Britain, France, Italy, Japan, and the United States—embarked on building campaigns. The U.S. campaign was the most ambitious. It completed ten fast battleships with the speed of the ill-fated battle cruisers but carrying sufficient armor protection to operate against other battleships.

World War II

Although battleships were overshadowed during the war by other types of ships—principally aircraft carriers and submarines—the vast scope of the global conflict still provided battleships a good deal of action. In the early months of the war, for instance, the German pocket battleship *Admiral Graf Spee*, armed with six 11-inch guns, created havoc in the Atlantic as a surface raider before being brought to bay off Uruguay by three British cruisers. In the spring of 1941, the German *Bismarck*, a far more capable ship mounting eight 15-inch guns, went on another raiding foray in the Atlantic. The *Bismarck* sank the battle cruiser *Hood* with a hit that exploded on the *Hood's* magazine and tied down a considerable number of Royal Navy ships before being disabled by aerial torpedoes and finally sunk by shell fire. The *Bismarck's* sister ship *Tirpitz* served for many months as a one-ship fleet in being in Norway before it, too, was disabled.

Figure 1. The Almirante Latorre, *1921, first dreadnought of the Chilean Navy.* (SOURCE: U.S. Library of Congress)

The French and Italian battleship fleets in the Mediterranean were largely ineffectual. After the fall of France to Germany in the spring of 1940, the Royal Navy shelled French ships at Oran, Algeria, in July 1940, and other French ships were scuttled at Toulon in November 1942. The *Jean Bart* put up token resistance during the Western Allied invasion of Casablanca in November 1942 and was badly damaged; the *Richelieu* was taken over by the Allies. In November 1940, planes from the British aircraft carrier *Illustrious* disabled the Italian battleships *Littorio*, *Caio Duilio*, and *Conte di Cavour* in the port of Taranto, Italy. Other Italian ships were victims of both the British and the Germans at various times.

The Royal Navy used its battleships in a wide variety of roles in the Atlantic, Mediterranean, and Pacific. The *Warspite*, for instance, intimidated the Italians at Cape Matapan in 1940 and bombarded Normandy during the D-Day landings in 1944. The *Prince of Wales*, still brand-new, was involved in the hunt for the *Bismarck* in the spring of 1941 but then succumbed to Japanese aircraft attack on 10 December of that year, along with the battle cruiser *Repulse*. The demise of two British capital ships in the Far East demonstrated a new battleship vulnerability: operating without air cover. British battleships were valuable in convoy escort and later operated as part of the British Pacific Fleet in concert with the Americans.

The Japanese, like the other Axis powers, seldom used their battleships to good advantage—in part because the Japanese aircraft carriers were so effective at the outset of the war. The battleships often served in a supporting role because the American battleships they were intended to fight had been knocked out at Pearl Harbor when the war against the United States began. In late 1942, in a desperate attempt to retake Guadalcanal in the South Pacific, the Japanese used their heavy-gunfire ships to bombard the island. The battle cruisers *Hiei* and *Kirishima* were lost. The latter succumbed to gunfire from the USS *Washington*, flagship of Rear Adm. Willis A. Lee, Jr., in one of the few surface actions between capital ships during the war. The only other one involving American and Japanese battleships occurred at Surigao Strait in the Philippines in October 1944, when Rear Adm. Jesse Oldendorf's old U.S. ships performed the classic "crossing the T" tactical maneuver, which brought their guns to bear in broadside on the advancing Japanese column. Of the two Japanese giants armed with 18-inch guns, the *Musashi* was sunk in the Philippines in 1944, and the *Yamato* was knocked out in a suicide mission aimed at Okinawa in 1945. Other Japanese battleships were similarly squandered in the futile attempt to hold off the U.S. fleet.

The Japanese attack on Pearl Harbor on 7 December 1941 was a stunning blow that at once knocked out the bulk of the American battle fleet and at the same time freed aircraft carriers and submarines for offensive action—unfettered by prewar doctrine concerning their use. Two U.S. battleships, the *Arizona* and *Oklahoma*, were total losses at Pearl. Also sunk but later refloated and returned to service were the *California* and *West Virginia*. Four other battleships suffered varying degrees of damage but also returned to action. Of the older, slower battleships with which the United States began the war, most were employed as shore bombardment ships during the Central Pacific amphibious campaign. The newer, faster battleships—completed during the war or shortly before—were used mostly to provide antiaircraft protection in fast carrier task forces. The Japanese surrender ceremony was signed at Tokyo Bay in September 1945 on board the USS *Missouri*.

Demise of the Battleship

Although they had been supplanted by aircraft carriers as the primary naval combatant ships during World War II, battleships remained in service for another decade before what appeared to be their final retirement in the late 1950s. The United States employed all four Iowa-class battleships for shore bombardment during the Korean War and then used them for midshipman training cruises; as of mid-1992, these ships are decommissioned and in mothballs. The ironically named *Vanguard*, the last in a long, distinguished line of British battleships, went into reserve in 1955 and was sold for scrap in 1960. The French *Jean Bart* and *Richelieu* were used in the 1950s as accommodation ships for sailors undergoing training; they were put into reserve, and eventually scrapped in the late 1960s. The South American dreadnought battleships were disposed of in the 1950s, as was the Turkish battle cruiser *Yavuz*.

Vietnam War

Because of the heavy loss of American aircraft bombing North Vietnam, U.S. politicians decreed the reactivation of the Iowa-class ship *New Jersey*, which had been out of service in the reserve fleet since 1957. The *New Jersey* was recommissioned in April 1968, served one combat tour of shore bombardment and support of ground troops in Vietnam, and was then decommissioned and returned to reserve status in December 1969.

Renaissance in the 1980s

As part of a rebuilding of its conventional military strength, the United States modernized and recommissioned its four remaining battleships—the *New Jersey, Iowa, Missouri,* and *Wisconsin*—between 1981 and 1988. The armament of each ship was strengthened considerably with the addition of antiship and land-attack cruise missiles. The result is the restoration of offensive capability to battleships for the first time since World War II. The only combatant use since the recommissioning of the four battleships was the *New Jersey*'s firing in support of U.S. Marines in Lebanon in 1983–84. For the most part, the ships have been used primarily to show the flag and to train in their new roles. In 1990 the U.S. Department of Defense directed the navy to decommission two of the ships for reasons of economy in the wake of political developments in Europe. How long the other two ships will remain in service is also likely to be more a political question than a military one. Their hulls and machinery are considered sufficient to permit their use into the twenty-first century, and their other systems can be updated periodically.

PAUL STILLWELL

SEE ALSO: Seapower; Ship Design and Construction; Ship Protective Systems.

Bibliography

Breyer, S. 1973. *Battleships and battle cruisers: 1905–1970*. Garden City, N.Y.: Doubleday.

Dulin, R. O., Jr., and W. H. Garzke, Jr. 1985. *Battleships: Axis and neutral battleships in World War II*. Annapolis, Md.: U.S. Naval Institute Press.

———. 1976. *Battleships: United States battleships in World War II*. Annapolis, Md.: U.S. Naval Institute Press.

Friedman, N. 1985. *U.S. battleships: An illustrated design history*. Annapolis, Md.: U.S. Naval Institute Press.

Gibbons, T. 1983. *The complete encyclopedia of battleships*. New York: Crescent Books.

Hough, R. 1964. *Dreadnought: A history of the modern battleship*. New York: Macmillan.

Padfield, P. 1971. *The battleship era*. New York: David McKay.

Parkes, O. 1966. *British battleships*. London: Seeley Service.

Reilly, J. C., Jr., and R. L. Scheina. 1980. *American battleships: 1886–1923*. Annapolis, Md.: U.S. Naval Institute Press.

BELARUS (formerly Byelorussia)

Belarus, one of the fifteen former republics in the Union of Soviet Socialist Republics (USSR), joined ten other Soviet republics in dissolving the Union on 21 December 1991 when they agreed to form the new Commonwealth of Independent States. This dramatic end to the Soviet and Communist state followed several years of dynamic and unprecedented change. For several more years, relations between members of the new Commonwealth and with the rest of the world are likely to continue to change. Over time, new structures and patterns will emerge in economics, trade and commerce, politics and government, finance, manufacturing, religion, and virtually all aspects of human life. New arrangements must be devised for dealing separately as sovereign states and as a Commonwealth with the world outside the boundaries of the former Soviet state. If the history of the Soviet Union since 1985 is any guide, we can expect dramatic surprises and dynamic change.

An important question for the world is how the new states and the Commonwealth will organize and provide for their security. The Soviet Union's armed forces, formerly the largest in the world, are likely to be withdrawn from foreign territory, reduced in size, and divided up between the former republics. Also of great concern is the disposition of the largest arsenal of nuclear weapons, the security of these weapons, the command and control of their potential use, and compliance with arms control agreements entered into by the former Soviet government. The world can only hope these issues are settled amicably.

It will be years before all of these issues are resolved for Belarus and some time before events settle down into more routine and measurable patterns. No accurate description of this new country's policies, defense structure, and military forces was available to be included in this encyclopedia. Only time will reveal the future of Belarus as a separate sovereign state. The reader is thus referred to the historic information contained in the article "Soviet Union," and to the latest annual editions of the *Military Balance*, published by Brassey's (UK) for the International Institute of Strategic Studies; the *Statesman's Year-Book* published by the Macmillan Press Ltd and St. Martin's Press; and the *World Factbook*, developed by the U.S. Central Intelligence Agency and published commercially by Brassey's (US).

F. D. MARGIOTTA
Executive Editor

BELGIUM, KINGDOM OF

A bilingual country (French and Dutch) in northwest Europe, Belgium has been traditionally both a commerical center and a "cockpit of war," particularly between 1500 and 1815.

Power Potential Statistics

Area: 30,510 square kilometers (11,780 sq. mi.)
Population: 9,860,800
Total Active Armed Forces: 85,450 (0.867% of pop.)
Gross Domestic Product: US$144.8 billion (1990 est.)
Annual Defense Expenditure: US$4.8 billion (2.5% of GDP, 1990 est.)
Iron and Steel Production:
  Crude steel: 9.744 million metric tons (1986)
  Pig iron: 8.04 million metric tons (1986)
Fuel Production
  Coal: 1.893 million metric tons (1989)
  Coke: 5.459 million metric tons (1989)
  Petroleum products processed: 29.82 million metric tons (1986)
  Natural gas: 689 million cubic meters (1988)
Electrical Power Output: 62,780 million kwh (1989)
Merchant Marine: 69 vessels; 1,785,066 gross registered tons
Civil Air Fleet: 47 major transport aircraft; 42 usable airfields (24 with permanent-surface runways); none with runways over 3,659 meters (12,000 ft.); 14 with runways 2,440–3,659 meters (8,000–12,000 ft.); 3 with runways 1,220–2,440 meters (4,000–8,000 ft.).

For the most recent information, the reader may refer to the following annual publications:
The Military Balance. International Institute for Strategic Studies. London: Brassey's (UK).
The Statesman's Year-Book. New York: St. Martin's Press.
The World Factbook. Central Intelligence Agency. Washington, D.C.: Brassey's (US.)

History

Belgium owes its name to the *Belgae*, who inhabited it in the time of Julius Caesar. After the fall of the Roman Empire, Belgium fell under Frankish rule, and during most of the Middle Ages was governed by a patchwork of semi-independent city-states closely connected with the Netherlands to the north. In the late 1400s, Belgium was part of Charles the Rash of Burgundy's realm, and afterward passed under Spanish rule. Belgium, which remained Catholic during the Reformation, was closely involved in the Eighty Years' War (1567–1648) for Dutch independence, and suffered greatly. At the Treaty of Utrecht in 1713 it passed into Austrian hands, but was annexed by France in 1794. At the Congress of Vienna in 1815, it was awarded to the Netherlands.

The Belgians were unhappy under Dutch rule, and in September 1830 they revolted, winning their independence after nearly nine years of sporadic warfare, political crisis, and diplomatic maneuver when King William of the Netherlands signed the treaties establishing the Kingdom of Belgium in March 1839. Belgium's sovereignty and "perpetual neutrality" was guaranteed by France, Great Britain, Russia, Austria, and Prussia (later Germany). Over the next 75 years, Belgium maintained strict neutrality in European politics, and gained control of the Congo River Basin in Africa in the 1890s.

The outbreak of World War I, which brought an invasion by German troops, ended Belgium's neutrality and brought it into the war on the side of the Allies. From fall 1914 until September 1918, only the extreme southwest of Belgium remained free of German troops, and the occupied territories suffered under the German administration. When the war ended Belgium resumed its policy of neutrality. Although the worsening European political situation after the mid-1930s led to increased defense preparedness, Belgium declined to ally with either France or the Netherlands out of fear of offending the Germans.

The German invasion, which began on 10 May 1940, triggered an Allied reaction and Belgium once more became a battleground. Within three weeks, however, the Allied forces had been routed, and their remnants withdrawn through Dunkirk or driven into France. For the next four years Belgium was under German administration, and again suffered from confiscation, forced transfer of workers to German factories, and similar hardships. Although a government-in-exile was formed in London, King Leopold III remained in Belgium. Fortunately, most of Belgium was liberated by Allied armies in the space of about a week in early September 1944, and by late January the Germans had been cleared from the country. After the war, Belgium at last abandoned neutrality and embraced collective security by joining with Luxembourg and the Netherlands in the Benelux Customs Union (1947) and joining NATO in 1949.

In 1960 Belgium hurriedly granted independence to its former colony of the Congo; but the shortsighted and selfish Belgian policies there were in large measure responsible for the chaos in the Congo between 1960 and 1965. Belgium retains large-scale commercial interests, especially in Katanga province, and has close political ties not only with Zaïre but also with Rwanda and Burundi (seized from German East Africa in 1918). Belgium's postwar political life has been dominated by arrangements for fair representation of Flemish (Dutch-speaking) and Walloon (French-speaking) elements of the population in government and economic life. Belgium and France sent a troop force to aid Zaïre during an invasion by Katangese mercenaries in mid-May 1978.

Politico-Military Background and Policy

After World War II Belgium abandoned its neutralist policies, as its only real chance for national security lay in an alliance with other Western European states. Belgium's armed forces are closely integrated into the NATO command structure, and two-fifths of the peacetime army are stationed in West Germany. Belgium also provides the sites for NATO headquarters in Brussels and for SHAPE (Supreme Headquarters, Allied Powers Europe) in Mons.

The armed forces are manned by conscription, although there are many long-service volunteers in the armed forces as well. All males reaching age 19 are liable for service, either ten months in Germany or twelve months in Belgium (longer for paratroops and officers), but only about 43 percent of eligible men actually serve. All those who serve have reserve obligations lasting for 8 years.

Strategic Problems

As shown in 1914 and 1940, Belgium is vulnerable to invasion. Although there are some natural barriers (the Ardennes and the river and canal waterways), space is so limited that there is little opportunity to delay an invader. To further complicate matters, Belgium periodically suffers from crises caused by ethno-linguistic disputes between the Flemings (57% of the people) in the north and west and the Walloons (33% of the people) in the south and east; the rest of the population is either officially bilingual (10%), or speaks German as a first language (less than 1%).

Military Assistance

Although Belgium now pays its own way in NATO, in the early years of the alliance it received considerable military aid from the United States, amounting to US$1.24 billion through 1977. Belgian military personnel also receive training and advanced education in the United States. Belgium provides considerable security assistance to Zaïre, Rwanda, and Burundi, all former African colonies; there are small military missions (fewer than 175 officers and men total) in those three countries.

Defense Industry

Belgium relies on foreign sources for heavy equipment such as tanks, aircraft, and artillery, but produces many of its own naval vessels, and provides small arms and small-arms ammunition to many countries. The Belgian firms of FN (*Fabrique Nationale*) and Browning are particularly important in this regard, making small arms for both private and government customers.

Alliances

Belgium is a founding member of NATO, and forms, with Luxembourg and the Netherlands, the Benelux economic union. Belgium is also a member of the Western European Union and of the European Common Market, and is a founding member of the United Nations.

Defense Structure

Constitutionally, the armed forces are commanded by King Baudouin. Responsibility for the formulation of defense policy rests with the prime minister and his cabinet, and specific defense decisions are made by the Ministerial Committee of Defense, chaired by the prime minister. Implementation of defense decisions is the responsibility of the defense minister, assisted by a military staff system under the direction of the chief of the general staff.

There are four armed services: army, navy, air force, and *gendarmerie*. The integrated staff echelon of the armed forces has three elements: (1) the general staff, divided into an integrated general staff and a second echelon of general staffs for the army, navy, and air force; (2) the *gendarmerie* general staff, responsible for internal security; (3) the central administration, which provides administrative support to the operational forces.

Total Armed Forces

Active: 85,450 (3,050 women, 34,100 conscripts). Terms of service: 10 months in Germany or 12 months in Belgium.
Reserves: Total Reserve Status: 234,000. With service in past 3 years: est. 146,400 (Army 147,400; Medical Service 34,400; Navy 11,500; Air Force 40,700).

ARMY: 62,700 (27,850 conscripts). Both figures incl Medical Service.
1 Corps HQ
1 armd bde (2 tk, 2 mech inf, 1 SP arty bn, 1 ATK coy).
3 mech inf bde (each 1 tk, 2 mech inf, 1 SP arty bn, 1 ATK coy).
1 para-cdo regt (3 para-cdo bn, armd recce sqn, ATK coy, arty bty).
Recce Comd (2 recce, 1 tk bn).
1 indep tk bn.
3 SP arty bn.
1 SSM bn: 2 bty, each with 2 Lance.
4 AD bn: 2 HAWK; 2 Gepard AA.
4 engr bn (2 fd, 1 bridge, 1 eqpt).
3 lt avn sqn.
Reserves: some on immediate recall status; 2 mech inf bde; 2 inf, 1 SP arty bn, cbt spt, log spt tp. Territorial defense: 11 mot inf regt, 4 inf bn.
Equipment:
MBT: 334 Leopard 1.
Light tanks: 133 Scorpion (CFE HACV); 25 M-41.
Recce: 153 Scimitar.
AIFV: 514 AIFV-B (236 CFE-countable; remainder are non-countable "look-alikes").
APC: 1,421 (932 CFE-countable; remainder are noncountable "look-alikes"): incl 525 M-113 (CFE: 190), 266 Spartan (CFE: 198), 510 AMX-VCI (CFE: 424), 43 BDX, 77 M-75.
Total arty: 376 (60 in store).
Towed arty: 105mm: 21 M-101.
SP arty: 207: 105mm: 28 M-108; 155mm: 41 M-109A3, 127 M-109A2; 203mm; 11 M-110.
Mortars: 107mm: 130 M-30 (incl some SP); 120mm: 18. Plus 81mm: 285.
SSM: 5 Lance launchers.
ATGW: 420 Milan (325 veh-mounted), 43 Striker AFV with Swingfire (7 in store).
ATK guns: 80 JPK-90mm SP (CFE HACV).
AD guns: 20mm: 36 HS-804, 100 M-167 Vulcan; 35mm: 54 Gepard SP.
SAM: 39 Improved HAWK.
Aircraft: 10 BN-2A Islander.
Helicopters: 51 SA-313/-318 (no attack hel).

NAVY: 4,550 (1,600 conscripts). Bases: Ostend, Zeebrugge, Kallo (to close 31 Dec 1991).
Frigates: 4 Wielingen with 2 × ASTT (Fr L-5 LWT), 1 × 6 ASW mor; plus 4 × MM-38 Exocet SSM, 1 × 100mm gun.
Mine Warfare: 22 MCMV: 6 Van Haverbeke (US Aggressive MSO). 10 Aster (tripartite) MHC. 2 Stavelot (US Adjutant) MSC. 4 Herstal MSI.
Support and Miscellaneous: 3: 2 log spt/comd, 1 research/ survey vessels.
Helicopters: 3 SA-318

AIR FORCE: 18,200 (4,650 conscripts).
FGA: 4 sqn with F-16A/B; 1 sqn with Mirage 5 BA/BD.
Fighter: 2 sqn with F-16A/B.
Recce: 1 sqn with Mirage 5BR.
Transport: 2 sqn: 1 with 12 C-130H; 1 with 2 Boeing 727QC, 3 HS-748, 5 Merlin IIIA, 2 Falcon 20.
Liaison: 1 sqn with CM-170.
Training: 3 sqn: 2 with Alpha Jet; 1 with SF-260.
SAR: 1 sqn with Sea King Mk 48.
Equipment: 144 cbt ac (plus 41 in store), no armed hel.
Aircraft:
Mirage: 36. 5BA: 18 (FGA); 5BR: 18 (recce); plus 29 in store (19-BA, 10-BD).
F-16: 108: A/B: 72 (FGA), 36 (ftr); plus 12 in store. C-130: 12 (tpt).
Boeing 727: 2 (tpt).
HS-748: 3 (tpt).
CM-170: 18 (liaison).
SF-260: 28 (trg).
Alpha Jet: 31 (trg).
Helicopters: 5 Sea King (SAR).
Missiles: AAM: AIM-9 Sidewinder

FORCES ABROAD
FRG: 22,800 (reducing); 1 corps HQ, 1 armd, 1 mech inf bde; COMRECCE; 3 arty, 1 SSM, 2 Gepard AA, 2 SAM, 3 engr bn, 200 MBT; 3 hel sqn.
UN and Peacekeeping:
Middle East (UNTSO): 4 observers.

PARAMILITARY
Gendarmerie: 16,800; 62 FN, 80 BDX, 5 SA-313, 3 Puma hel.

FOREIGN FORCES
NATO: HQ NATO Brussels; HQ SHAPE Mons.
U.S.: 2,700.

Future

Belgium's continued participation in the European Community is virtually assured, for the country has nothing to gain by leaving the alliance. The coming integration of the European economy will, if anything, strengthen ties among NATO's European nations. As the military role of NATO adjusts to meet the changing situation in Eastern Europe, Belgium is almost certain to reduce its armed forces significantly. Internally, the pressures of linguistic and ethnic rivalry are forcing a gradual transition to a federally organized government, with more power held locally. This will, in the long run, improve internal stability, although the transition period may be difficult.

DAVID L. BONGARD
TREVOR N. DUPUY

SEE ALSO: NATO; Western Europe; World War I; World War II.

Bibliography

Cowie, D. 1977. *Belgium: The land and the people.* Cranbury, N.J.: A. S. Barnes.
Fitzmaurice, J. 1983. *The politics of Belgium: Crisis and compromise in a plural society.* London: C. Hurst.
Hunter, B., ed. 1991. *The statesman's year-book, 1991–92.* New York: St. Martin's Press.
International Institute for Strategic Studies. 1991. *The military balance, 1991–1992.* London: Brassey's.

BIOLOGICAL WARFARE

Biological warfare (BW) is the military use of harmful organisms as weapons against man, animals, and plants. Because it includes the use of such organisms as bacteria and germs, BW is often referred to as bacteriological or germ warfare. However, BW is broader than germ warfare alone, encompassing the deliberate and direct use of living organisms (biological pathogens) and their naturally occurring by-products, which are commonly called toxins, for military purposes.

Types

Biological Pathogens

Biological pathogens, disease-producing living organisms, can be divided into four categories: bacterial, fungal, rickettsial, and viral. Many pathogens have been studied for use militarily, and some of the more prominent ones are listed in Table 1.

Because pathogens are living organisms, they are difficult to employ militarily. Conventional delivery systems—air-burst rockets, air-dropped bombs, and tube-fired projectiles—often prove too harsh, destroying the organism before it can be disseminated on the battlefield. To overcome this limitation, special munitions have been developed. For example, ceramic bombs were successfully tested for use with fleas that had been infected with the bacterium *Yessinia pestis*, the causative agent for bubonic plague. Spray disseminators have also proven effective, as a variety of pathogens are readily spread through air. Aerial spraying, however, is notoriously difficult to predict and control.

More often, pathogens have been spread by rather conventional means. For example, in 1763, Sir Jeffrey Amherst, commander in chief of British forces in North America during the French and Indian War, suggested that an attempt be made to spread smallpox among some disaffected Indian tribes. At his suggestion, two blankets and a handkerchief from a smallpox hospital were given to two Indian chiefs; the disease soon broke out among the tribes. Similarly, during World War I, German agents in the United States inoculated horses and mules that were destined for shipment to the Allies overseas with highly infectious bacteria, including those causing glanders, a highly contagious and destructive equine disease. During World War II, the British stockpiled linseed cattlecakes, each of which contained a lethal dose of anthrax spores. The concept was to drop the cattlecakes from bombers onto German pastures where they would be found and eaten by the cattle. The cattlecakes were never used.

Table 1. *Potential BW Agents—Pathogens*

Category	Examples
Bacterial	Anthrax, brucellosis, bubonic plague, cholera, glanders, tularemia, typhoid fever
Fungal	Coccidioidomycosis, agent C (*Sclerotium rolfei;* an antiplant agent)
Rickettsial	Q fever, Rocky Mountain spotted fever
Viral	Dengue fever, encephalitis, influenza, meningitis, psittacosis, Rift Valley fever, smallpox, yellow fever

Table 2. *Potential BW Agents—Toxins*

Name	Source	Effects
Botulinal toxin A	*Clostridium botulinum*	Dizziness, sore throat, and dry mouth followed by paralysis. Death by suffocation (respiratory paralysis) or heart failure.
Ricin	Castor bean plant	Nausea, vomiting, bloody diarrhea, and drowsiness. Death by kidney failure (uremia).
Saxitoxin (shellfish toxin)	Dinoflagellates	Tingling around face, loss of sensation in extremities. Death by paralysis.
Tricothecene mycotoxins	Fungus	Nausea, vomiting, diarrhea. Death by internal hemorrhaging.

Another problem with pathogens is that, once disseminated, they are susceptible to destruction by such natural environmental factors as rain, extreme temperature, and sunlight. However, the extent to which these factors will reduce the BW threat depends on the specific pathogen. For example, Gruinard Island off the northwest coast of Scotland was the site of anthrax testing in 1942 and 1943. As a result of these tests, the island was contaminated with anthrax spores, which are resistant to weathering. Follow-up testing from 1947 to 1968 found no lessening of the contamination. Then, in 1986, active decontamination measures were taken, using herbicides to remove vegetation and a solution of formaldehyde in seawater to destroy the spores. In 1990, more than 45 years after the initial testing, Gruinard Island was finally declared safe and returned to civil ownership.

Research during the 1940s perfected freeze-drying, which is a useful technique for enhancing the durability of pathogens that might otherwise perish during prolonged storage, explosive dissemination, or exposure to the environment. Freeze-drying has been successfully applied to the development of improved pathogen-type BW munitions.

Toxins

Toxins are poisons produced by microorganisms, plants, and animals. The parent organism need not be present for the toxin to be used, although it is required for toxin production. Some toxins associated with military use are listed in Table 2.

Toxins have certain advantages for use as military weapons. First, they occur naturally and, consequently, tend to be easy to manufacture. Second, they are nonliving substances and are more stable than biological pathogens. Third, unlike pathogens, they require no special care or treatment for use as weapons. This allows them to be disseminated in combat through conventional spray and explosive devices. Fourth, and perhaps most significant, is the exceedingly high toxicity of selected toxins, for toxins include the most poisonous substances known.

Because toxins are by-products of living organisms, they are sometimes referred to as agents of biological origin. They fall between the categories of classical biological pathogens, such as anthrax and smallpox, and traditional chemical warfare agents, such as nerve gas and cyanide. Soviet military literature viewed toxins as a "third generation" of chemical warfare weapons, with cyanide and mustard gas being the first generation and nerve gas being the second. However, the USSR was a signatory to the 1972 BW Treaty, which treats toxins as BW materials.

Toxins are a public health menace because they occur naturally. An excellent example is staphylococcus enterotoxin B, the toxin responsible for most cases of ordinary food poisoning. The bacterium *Staphylococcus aureus* grows in many foods. As it grows, it forms the toxin, which is ingested when the food is consumed. In general, staphylococcus enterotoxin B is not lethal, but as little as 50 micrograms causes severe vomiting and diarrhea. Deliberate use of staphylococcus enterotoxin B for military purposes is possible, especially for harassment and in situations where the intent is to weaken the enemy's resistance.

A more potent poison found in foods is botulinal toxin A. It is a neurotoxin that causes the nervous system to accumulate acetylcholine in a manner similar to that produced by chemical warfare nerve agents. Botulinal toxin A is produced by the bacterium *Clostridium botulinum* and is the most poisonous substance known. The bacterium can grow and thrive in prepared foods such as sausage and spiced herring and is associated with improperly preserved food such as canned vegetables. A lethal dose for a human is estimated to be one microgram.

The high toxicity of botulinal toxin A has made it the subject of substantial research, including studies of its use with the military. During World War II, the British made a concerted effort, at their Porton Down laboratories, to isolate and develop strains of *Clostridium botulinum*, along with antidotes and treatments for each. A toxin mix was developed and given the code designation BTX. British MI6 is thought to have used a strain of botulinal toxin for the assassination of Reinhard Heydrich, Hitler's governor of Czechoslovakia and presumed heir.

The alleged use of botulinal toxin in the attack on Heydrich illustrates the role of toxins in limited attacks, rather than as weapons of mass destruction. Ricin, the toxin found in the seeds and leaves of the castor oil plant *Ricinus communis*, provides another example of this type of use. Patented by the United States in 1962 for use as a BW weapon, ricin has been confirmed as the BW agent responsible for the Bulgarian "Umbrella Murders" of the 1970s. In these operations, a ricin-impregnated metal ball was shot out of the tip of an umbrella. Two victims, Bulgarians who had fled that country's Communist regime, were positively identified as having been assaulted in this way.

Public attention to toxin warfare was rekindled during the 1980s when U.S. government sources reported evidence of tricothecene mycotoxins in samples of vegetation (leaves and plant stems) from Southeast Asia. Additional evidence of tricothecenes in alleged victims of BW attacks was also claimed. Reports from refugees spoke of rockets and aerial spraying attacks that released clouds of poisonous vapor over their villages. Because these clouds were often yellow in color and had small rainlike particles, the attacks were popularly dubbed "yellow rain."

Tricothecene mycotoxins develop naturally, owing to *Fusarium*-genera fungal contamination of such grains as wheat and corn. Key tricothecene mycotoxins include nivalenol, deoxynivalenol (also known as vomitoxin), and T-2. These substances were responsible for the Soviet crop blights of the 1930s, which killed thousands of people and tens of thousands of cattle and horses. Tricothecene mycotoxin contamination of grains continues to be a concern in agriculture worldwide.

Critics of the U.S. claims regarding the Southeast Asia yellow rain attacks have suggested that the tricothecenes were the result of a natural occurrence—that is, food contaminated by mold. One explanation, advanced by Matthew Meselson of Harvard and accepted by many, suggests that the yellow spots found in Southeast Asia were the natural excreta of bees, which are known to swarm and defecate in flight. Conclusive evidence of deliberate BW attacks using tricothecene mycotoxins is lacking. The controversy over yellow rain underscores the difficulties associated with BW verification.

Role of BW in Combat

The deliberate use of pathogens and toxins for military purposes is ancient. Poisoning the enemy's drinking water and hurling diseased corpses over the walls of fortified cities were tactics used by such military leaders as Solon and Alexander the Great. It is only in recent times that the use of BW agents has acquired a stigma. No modern nation has admitted employing BW against personnel in combat despite numerous allegations to the contrary.

Effective use of BW in combat is difficult, and results are often unpredictable. Four major factors complicate use of BW:

1. Particulate nature of most BW agents makes controlled delivery on target difficult.
2. Delay between exposure and the onset of disease because of an inherent need for an incubation period ranging from hours to days means too much time is needed before results are seen.

3. Susceptibility to such weathering effects as rain, sunlight, and temperature extremes reduce the virulence of selected BW agents and remove them from the target.
4. Natural and acquired immunity against pathogens make it impossible to predict the exact numbers of casualties from any BW attack.

Consequently, BW today is primarily for harassment and special operations.

There is considerable speculation that covert dissemination of BW agents—as in the poisoning of municipal drinking water or infecting food supplies—might occur as a prelude to large-scale assaults. Such use would weaken the enemy while leaving his physical defenses untouched and, therefore, available for the occupying force. Such covert use accommodates the limitations of BW agents. Delivery is done directly rather than by munitions, and the delay between exposure and onset of symptoms becomes a planning factor for the follow-up attack. Adverse effects from the weather are minimized by direct delivery to a compatible source, such as food or water. And the strategic objective of weakening the enemy rather than total annihilation makes precise predictions of the number of casualties less critical.

Although large-scale use of BW is difficult, it has seen substantial use in modern times for special operations. For instance, the suicide pill carried by Francis Gary Powers, the pilot who flew the secret U-2 plane over the Soviet Union in 1960, contained the toxin-type BW agent saxitoxin, a poison found in shellfish that feed on a particular kind of plankton.

Novel Developments

In the 1980s, biotechnology and genetic engineering became commonplace, gaining public acceptance as methods for bettering mankind. Industry, government, and academic institutions began examining the various ways these new technologies could be used, from developing new crop strains to more effective vaccines. But the same techniques that hold promise for increased food production and improved health are also applicable to BW. For example, genetic engineering might be used to develop not only a new strain of a known biological pathogen, but also a vaccine for it. This would give one nation immunity while leaving a potential adversary open to attack by an agent against which they have no defenses. There is no evidence of such BW research, and the scientific community seems to be united in their opposition to it.

Proliferation

One of the grounds cited for opposing BW is the possibility of the agent getting out of control, as is said to have happened in the most celebrated recorded case of biological warfare. During the siege of the Genoese city Kaffa (now Feodosiya, Ukrainian Soviet Socialist Republic) in the mid-fourteenth century, the Mongols hurled the bodies of bubonic plague victims over the city walls. Genoese ships leaving that city may have carried the plague bacillus to Europe, thereby letting loose the massive epidemic known in history as the Black Death.

BW is, however, not confined to nations; the ability of terrorist groups and individuals to disseminate BW is an issue of considerable concern around the world. An episode in Oregon shows the ease with which the use of biological pathogens can spread. In September 1984, an epidemic of food poisoning was reported in Antelope, Oregon, and it was traced to the bacterium *Salomonella typhimurium,* which had contaminated foods at local restaurants. Sworn testimony by the leader of a religious community that existed near Antelope, the Bhagwan Shree Rajneesh, identified the episode as one of deliberate poisonings committed by one of his aides in retaliation against local residents who thought the religious community members were "different."

The spread of toxin-type BW agents to terrorist groups has been verified. In 1980, French police raided an operation of the German Red Army Faction at 41A Chaillot Street, Paris. What they found at that address was a simple but effective "bathtub" facility producing botulinal toxin A.

In 1972, the Bacteriological and Toxin Weapons Convention was signed by more than 70 nations. It prohibits the production, stockpiling, and development of biological weapons and requires the destruction of existing stockpiles. The overwhelming challenge for full implementation of this or any other BW treaty is a working means for both verifying compliance and punishing noncompliance when it occurs.

BENJAMIN C. GARRETT

SEE ALSO: Biological Warfare Technology; Chemical Warfare; Medical Research and Technology.

Bibliography

Brophy, L. P., W. D. Miles, and R. C. Cochrane. 1959. *The chemical warfare service: From laboratory to field.* Washington, D.C.: Office of the Chief of Military History.

Cole, L. A. 1988. *Clouds of secrecy—The army's germ warfare tests over populated areas.* Totowa, N.J.: Rowman & Littlefield.

Compton, J. A. F. 1987. *Military chemical and biological agents: Chemical and toxicological properties.* Caldwell, N.J.: Telford Press.

Douglass, J. D., and N. C. Livingston. 1987. *America the vulnerable: The threat of chemical/biological warfare.* Lexington, Mass.: Lexington Press.

Gutman, W. E. 1986. Chemical and biological weapons: The silent killers. *Nuclear, Biological, and Chemical Defense and Technology International* 1(1):24–25.

Lundin, S. J., J. P. Perry Robinson, and R. Trapp. 1988. Chemical and biological warfare: Developments in 1987. In *SIPRI yearbook 1988: World armaments and disarmament.* Oxford: Oxford Univ. Press.

McDermott, J. 1987. *The killing winds—The menace of biological warfare.* New York: Arbor House.

Seagrave, S. 1981. *Yellow rain: A journey through the terror of chemical weapons.* New York: M. Evans.
Spiers, E. M. 1986. Following decon, anthrax island up for sale. *Nuclear, Biological, and Chemical Defense and Technology International* 1(4):11.
Taylor, L. B., and C. L. Taylor. 1985. *Chemical and biological warfare.* New York: Franklin Watts.
Williams, P., and D. Wallace. 1989. *Unit 731: Japan's secret biological warfare in World War II.* New York: Free Press.

BIOLOGICAL WARFARE TECHNOLOGY

Biological warfare, which involves the use of living organisms or their products to attack people, animals, crops, or materiel, is probably one of the most controversial areas of military art, with both proponents and opponents among the military, civilian, and scientific communities.

Until the advent of biogenetic engineering, biological agents were usually confined to naturally occurring disease agents, exotic natural toxins, and some lesser-known tropical fevers. In the 1980s, however, biotechnical advances the world over provided the potential for specially tailored, unique, highly toxic, and previously unknown agents. This ability to develop and produce uniquely tailored agents raises considerable concern that biological agents could represent a significant threat in the near future. Whereas biological warfare in the early 1970s may have been considered too unpredictable for military use other than for sabotage or terrorist operations, it may now be possible to produce bioengineered agents that are potentially more effective than natural agents, more easily and inexpensively prepared, extremely difficult to identify, and resistant to known vaccines and medical therapy.

History

One of the earliest reported uses of biological warfare occurred in 1347 when the Tartars were besieging Kaffa, a Genoan trading post in the Crimea. The Tartars, who came from one of the few places infected with the plague, catapulted their dead, plague-infested corpses over the wall into the Genoan fortress. Because of the swiftly spreading deaths, the Genoans evacuated the post and sailed to Genoa. From there the plague spread throughout Europe, becoming known as the black death. In the 1700s, during the French and Indian wars in North America, the British distributed smallpox-infected blankets to the Indians, and as a result, thousands perished. According to Chinese statements, the Japanese used biological bombs during the 1930s. The British have revealed that the Japanese also maintained a biological warfare test station, Unit 731, in northeast China during the early 1940s, and that biological warfare experiments were conducted there on prisoners of war.

The use of "bacteriological methods of warfare" is prohibited by the 1925 Geneva Protocol, which is complemented by the 1972 Convention on Biological and Toxin Weapons that was opened for signature on 10 April 1972, and entered into force on 25 March 1975. In this convention, the 102 state parties agreed

> never to develop, produce, stockpile or otherwise acquire or retain microbial or other biological agents, or toxins, whatever their origin or method of production, of types and in quantities that have no justification for prophylactic, protective or other peaceful purposes and the weapons, equipment or means of delivery designed to use such agents or toxins for hostile purposes or in armed conflict.

After World War II, there were extensive research and development programs that led, most notably, to the development during the 1950s and 1960s of a number of U.S. biological weapons systems involving bacteriological, viral, toxin, and rickettsial antipersonnel, antianimal, and anticrop systems. Table 1 provides a listing of the potential natural biological antipersonnel agents that were considered to be of concern to the United States in 1971, along with some of their characteristics and the availability at that time of vaccines or treatment. The United States unilaterally terminated all efforts toward offensive biological systems in 1969, destroying all of its stockpiles and biological weapons in the early 1970s in anticipation of its ratification of the Convention on Biological and Toxin Weapons in 1975. Since that time, the United States, as well as most of the other 102 signatory nations, have directed their efforts toward the development of only defensive efforts against biological warfare—the development of vaccines, medical prophylaxis, immunization techniques, and detection.

The major current concerns about biological weapons have arisen because of the great advances that have been made in the 1980s in biotechnology worldwide. This activity is leading to new pharmaceuticals, growth regulators, pesticides, and food extenders through advances in the ability to modify genes, to easily fabricate "designer drugs," and to develop synthetic toxins and viruses with specially desired characteristics. In 1975, one could not have predicted or expected the current size, complexity, and success that biotechnology now enjoys in the commercial marketplace. This concern is heightened considerably by the secrecy with which many nations are pursuing their advanced biotechnology programs, the excessively large governmental investments in the area, and, in many cases, the strong military influence and presence that seems to be associated with national biotechnology efforts. These concerns are further exacerbated by various allegations of the existence and use of biological or toxin materials in various combat environments. These have so far been very difficult to prove or disprove inasmuch as the Convention on Biological and Toxin Weapons has no provision for adequate verification or definition of the

TABLE 1. *Potential Biological Antipersonnel Agents*

MICRO-ORGANISM	MODE OF TRANSMISSION[a]	INCUBATION PERIOD[b] (DAYS)	MORTALITY RATE[b] (PERCENT)	VACCINE[c]	TREATMENT[d]
Bacteria					
Bacillus anthracis (anthrax)	A, D, I	1–7	5–100[e]	+	E[f]
Brucella group (brucellosis)	A, D, I	5–21	2–6	+	E
Francisella tularensis (tularemia)	A, D, I, V	1–10	<30	+ +	E
Pasteurella pestis (plague)	A, V	2–6	25–100[g]	+ + +	E[f]
Vibrio comma (cholera)	I	1–5	15–90	+ + +	E
Corynebacterium diphtheriae (diphtheria)	A, D	2–5	5–12	+ + +	E
Salmonella typhosa (typhoid fever)	I	6–21	7–14	+ + +	E
Rickettsiae					
Rickettsia prowazeki (epidemic or louse-borne typhus)	V	6–15	10–40	+ + +	E
Rickettsia mooseri (endemic or flea-borne typhus)	V	6–14	2–5	–	E
Rickettsia rickettsii (Rocky Mountain spotted fever)	V	3–10	30 (approx.)	–	E
Coxiella burneti (Q fever)	A, I	14–21	<1	+ +	E
Viruses					
Group A Arboviruses					
Eastern equine encephalitis (EEE)	V[h]	4–24	60 (approx.)	–	N
Venezuelan equine encephalitis (VEE)	V[h]	4–24	<1	+ +	N
Group B Arboviruses					
St. Louis encephalitis	V (mosquito)	4–24		–	N
Japanese B encephalitis	V (mosquito)	5–15	10–80	+ +	N
Russian spring-summer encephalitis (RSSE)	V (tick)	7–14	3–40	+	N
Yellow fever	V (mosquito)	3–6	5–40	+ + +	N
Dengue fever	V (mosquito)	4–10	<1	+	N
Ungrouped Arbovirus					
Rift Valley fever	V (mosquito)	4–6	<1	–	N
Poxvirus					
Variola virus (smallpox)	A, D	7–16	1–35	+ + +	N
Myxovirus					
Rabies virus	A, D[i]	6–365	100	+ +	E
Fungi					
Coccidioides immitis (coccidioidomycosis)	A, D	10–21	1–50	–	E
Histoplasma capsulatum (histoplasmosis)	A	5–18		–	E

[a] Transmission can be by aerosol—A, direct contact—D, ingestion—I, and vector—V.
[b] Incubation periods and mortality rates vary according to a number of factors (e.g., ability of the host to resist infection, infective dose, portal of entry, and virulence of the microorganism).
[c] + indicates vaccine available but of questionable value; + + indicates vaccine available but mainly used in high-risk individuals; + + + indicates vaccine used extensively; – indicates no vaccine available.
[d] E indicates effective treatment available; N indicates no specific treatment.
[e] The 5 percent represents mortality due to skin form; 100 percent represents mortality due to respiratory form.
[f] Treatment must be initiated in the earliest stage of the pulmonary form to be effective.
[g] The 25 percent represents mortality due to bubonic form; 100 percent represents mortality due to pneumonic form.
[h] Mosquitoes are thought to be the primary vectors, but this has not been proved.
[i] Direct contact refers to being bitten by a rabid animal, which is the usual means of transmission, or coming into contact with a rabid animal.

Source: U.S. Army Training Manual, *TM3-215: Military biology*, April 1962.

amounts that are justifiable, nor did it envision the extent of peaceful biological activity that now exists or the need for differentiating peaceful from offensive activities.

Comparison Between Biological and Chemical Warfare Agents

Biological agents are similar to chemical agents in that both can have hazardous effects on personnel, animals, plants, and materials. Both can be disseminated in the air or carried by prevailing weather, and both can contaminate terrain, equipment, food, and water. In general, individual protection comes from the use of masks and protective clothing. Collective protection of facilities and vehicles with filters and overpressure is also helpful in reducing the hazard.

Since some biological agents can multiply when conditions are favorable, and most multiply once ingested by humans, animals, or plants, only a very few active organisms are needed to create a significant hazard. Thus, relatively small amounts can be effectively disseminated to cover large areas (frequently extending tens to hundreds of miles from the point of dissemination) and much higher efficiency of protection is needed to protect against an attack.

Biological agents can have a delayed action ranging from hours to days; chemical agents are usually effective in minutes or hours. Biological agents have a much more variable and wider range of persistence; some are destroyed very effectively by slight temperature changes, low humidity, or sunlight; others can exist as spores for decades.

Detection of biological agents is usually far more complicated, since it requires laboratory procedures such as growing cultures in special media, examining the effects of agents on laboratory animals, and using some very high-technology gene-mapping systems to identify the specific agent. In addition, the development of appropriate immunization, vaccines, or antibodies is far more complicated and lengthy than the determination of an appropriate neutralization or decontamination procedure for chemical agents. In the case of unknown or modified biological agents, the identification and development of an appropriate response mechanism can take years, as evidenced by efforts in the 1970s to identify the bacteria responsible for Legionnaire's Disease and efforts begun in the 1980s to counter the various viruses involved in the AIDS epidemic. Medical treatment of biologically derived infections is frequently more complicated and more specific in nature than the treatments for chemical agents, an aspect that places considerable stress on medical support facilities and may require quantities of specialized antibiotics, vaccines, and immunization far beyond normal medical requirements.

Military Concerns and Considerations

Biological warfare has not generally been employed by military forces since World War II. Natural diseases, on the other hand, have from time to time caused major disruptions to society, as in the European black plague epidemic, occasional outbreaks of anthrax and hoof-and-mouth disease in animals, various rickettsial and viral infections (usually tropical) that kill large numbers of food animals, the spread of yellow fever by mosquitoes in tropic areas, various isolated deaths due to plant or animal toxins, and the destruction of cereal grains by various rust outbreaks.

By the mid-1970s, when the biological warfare convention came into force, the prevailing wisdom was that biological warfare was so unpredictable, the effects of biological agents so delayed, the requirements for production so complicated and expensive, and the ability to develop the needed defensive vaccines, immunizations, and detection so difficult that, on balance, biological warfare was not likely to be militarily useful.

Based on the then-current state of knowledge, much of this wisdom may have been correct in the early 1970s. Natural biological agents do require an incubation period—usually from two to fourteen days—to cause incapacitation or death. As such, they would not be suited for tactical uses where quicker reaction times are required. Only some toxins and venoms are suitably fast acting—and these could not be extracted or synthesized in quantity at any reasonable cost. Many natural bacterial, rickettsial, and viral disease organisms, when transported away from their natural environments, have extremely low persistence, viability, or effectiveness because they cannot be suitably and easily modified to survive the changes in temperature, humidity, or terrain and weather conditions expected in combat without major modifications to their structure. Although some spore formers such as anthrax have very long storage times and can remain effective for years, others with more desirable characteristics could not be kept for the long periods that would be needed for a military munition stockpile. Some bacteria that have desirable characteristics of being quick acting or very resistant to environment cannot be modified to be sufficiently toxic. Many that are sufficiently virulent require the development of vaccine and immunizations for protection of friendly forces that are far too complicated to fabricate or too expensive to produce with sufficient quality control to be considered reliable. Finally, the techniques needed to develop the ability to detect many infectious agents are extremely limited.

Genetic Engineering

Advances in genetic engineering techniques and recombinant DNA technology, particularly in the 1980s, have led to significant new abilities to manipulate the properties of living organisms and to produce bacteria and viruses in quantity. With genetic engineering it is now possible to modify the genetic characteristics of cells or organisms at the molecular level by using a broad spectrum of advanced research techniques that have evolved from molecular biology, as well as from research in biochemical genetics and cell physiology. In the early 1990s, sophisticated computer-controlled equipment and techniques that assure high output, excellent efficiencies, and purity of products routinely manufacture products that were virtually unknown a decade earlier. As a result of these advances, industry has been able to produce and market new molecular genetic products of a wide variety ranging from growth regulators to new pharmaceuticals, including such items as artificial sweeteners, food extenders, pesticides, fibers, plastics, oil and waste emulsifiers, and vaccines more cheaply and in far greater quantities from smaller production facilities than was previously believed possible.

Most of the advances in bioengineering have resulted from the application of computer-based data banks containing data on the composition of natural protein molecules, genes, and peptides, permitting the concurrent synthesis and screening of hundreds of biologicals in only a few days. Using computer-controlled equipment, synthesis of almost limitless numbers of novel peptides and low molecular weight proteins can be done for immunological evaluation. Similarly, identification can be made of sequential peptides derived from almost any protein sequence. Analysis has been greatly improved by the development of digitally controlled equipment for determining molecular weight and for separating protein fragments. Automated cell harvesters, gene-mapping equipment, and a considerable variety of automated equipment for production is now commercially available. Synthetic genes can be ordered from stock by phone. Tailored genes are available that have enzyme sites built in at convenient intervals to permit alterations of virtually any region of the sequence—a level of flexibility impossible with natural, nonengineered genes. All of this technology is being procured and applied in national laboratories around the world, as is clear from advertisements in almost any technical journal.

Advances in recombinant genetics have made possible the development of many previously unknown biological materials. In recombinant genetics, new genetic material is chemically recombined into a host organism. The transferred genetic material may be taken from another organism or chemically synthesized in the laboratory. The altered organism can then be used as the desired product, cloned (replicated), or cultured from this seed material or in a fermentation system to produce large quantities of the desired biochemical.

In view of these advances, in many parts of the world, as demonstrated commercially and in academic circles, it is not surprising that many military planners are expressing concern that the judgments of the early 1970s with respect to biological warfare may need to be rethought. Adequate defenses and effective international agreements have to exist to prevent technological surprise. Careful monitoring of nations might prevent the development of clandestine biological warfare capability, or the tailored protective capability that would protect a nation's forces from slightly modified natural agents while its enemy faced an agent that it could not identify quickly and against which it could not develop an adequate protective capability in a timely manner.

David W. Einsel, Jr.

See Also: Biological Warfare; Chemical Warfare Technology; Geneva Conventions; Medical Research and Technology.

Bibliography

Broll, C. 1986. Genetic technology aids germ warfare research in spite of treaty. *Suddeutsche Zeitung*, Munich, 7 November.

Levinson, M. 1986. Custom-made biological weapons. *International Defense Review*, no. 11, pp. 1601, 1611.

Tu, A. T. 1986. Snake neuro- and necrotic toxins. *Potential New Agents, Nuclear, Biological and Chemical Defense and Technology International*, vol. 1, no. 2 (May).

U.S. Department of the Army. 1971. *Training manual 3-216: Technical aspects of biological defense*. Washington, D.C.: U.S. Departments of the Army and the Air Force.

BLITZKRIEG

Blitzkrieg ("lightning war"), a German word initially made popular by non-German observers of the Polish campaign of September 1939, has acquired over the years a very wide range of meanings and connotations. A number of historians examining the structure of the Nazi economy have detected the existence of a blitzkrieg strategy in the alleged systematic economic planning for a short war as part of an overall military strategy along the same lines. Disagreement on this point includes such basic issues as whether the Germans had any such intentions and whether they actually had an organized system to prepare for short wars and thus spare the economy the burdens of protracted struggle. Other writers interested in strategy and military operations have argued that the German Army developed a strategy for rapid victories in aggressive wars.

A new version of this argument has sprung up in the recent military literature, primarily in the United States. A number of authors now argue for the existence of a particular system of tactics and operations designed to win battles and campaigns by disrupting and confusing the enemy, rather than by destroying him in traditional battles. (This view, in turn, has provided much of the conceptual framework both for the so-called military reform movement in the United States and for much of the doctrinal thought, both official and unofficial, in the U.S. Army.) Other historians characterize the entire period of mechanized warfare as the "blitzkrieg era," which extends at least to the 1980s and includes the Soviet approach to mobile warfare. Orthodox Marxist historians regard blitzkrieg as a broad set of efforts by the German imperialists of both world wars to achieve quick victory. All these points of view argue or assume that behind blitzkrieg lies some sort of grand design, whether in politics, economic planning, or military doctrine and methods. The reality belies all of these interpretations. Blitzkrieg was neither a policy nor an economic expedient, nor was it a military doctrine.

Nevertheless, the idea is widespread that Heinz Guderian and others created a radically new type of tactical and operational doctrine for the armored forces of the German army. Numerous historians, journalists, political scientists, and, most recently, American officers link this alleged blitzkrieg doctrine with the use of maneuver warfare to paralyze the enemy without fighting major battles. These authors have developed elaborate theories about the purposes and methods of blitzkrieg and have created a broad consensus in support of their conclusions. The pervasiveness of these views and their impact upon current military thought give the issue more than a purely academic significance (Hughes 1986).

Nature of German Doctrine

The most fundamental prerequisite for a proper understanding of blitzkrieg in any military sense is an appreciation of the essentials of German military doctrine in the period 1919–45. (As used here, *doctrine* means the army's philosophy of war and its most basic principles of conducting operations and fighting battles within that framework.) German doctrinal manuals contained broad statements of fundamental concepts for the commander to apply as the circumstances warranted. German doctrine had no universal principles of war, no lists of tenets or imperatives, and few if any stereotyped illustrations with maps, charts, or diagrams (see, e.g., *Truppenführung* 1933). Despite this lack of rigidity and of concrete guidelines, German doctrine consistently established a coherent approach to warfare that was applicable to all units, motorized or otherwise. Thus the 1933 *Truppenführung*, written before the creation of large armored formations, provided a sufficiently flexible concept for the tank forces.

Two Types of War

German theory between 1919 and 1945 distinguished between two types of war, positional and mobile. Despite the experiences of the long positional warfare between 1914 and 1918, the great majority of German theorists consistently rejected this as a model for the future and instead envisioned a return to the traditions of Frederick, Moltke, and Schlieffen. In this view, World War I, with its static fronts, meticulously prepared setpiece attacks, and endless battles without decision was an aberration, an operational perversity (Rabenau 1940). This return to basic theories of mobile warfare became evident immediately after the end of the war. Although Gen. Hans von Seeckt and his colleagues and successors have shared the credit (or blame) for the return to theories of mobile warfare after 1918, the truth is more complex (Wallach 1986; Messenger 1976).

Seeckt and His Antecedents

Seeckt's alleged reinstitution of mobile warfare was not the major innovation that is sometimes pictured. His new basic regulation of 1921, *Führung und Gefecht*, was entirely within the broad framework of traditional German theory. By the time that manual was published, the new German army had long since sought alternatives to the positional warfare of 1914–18.

The German offensive methods of 1918 were above all an effort to restore mobility to the western front. The much-misunderstood assault unit tactics were thus a means to return to the traditional mobile warfare (Jochim 1927). World War I never entirely shook the German army's faith in its fundamental principles. As early as 1920, Wilhelm Balck had noted the basic correctness of German wartime tactics and called for a return to mobile warfare (Balck 1920). That same year, Baron Hugo von Freytag-Loringhoven, a leading prewar theoretician and official historian, noted the return to mobile warfare as the basis of postwar German theory. The leading semiofficial handbook of the immediate postwar period, Rohrbeck's *Taktik* (1922), based its entire discussion on the traditional distinction between mobile and positional warfare and confirmed the superiority of the former, even given the experiences of the past war.

Traditional Prussian Concepts

Seeckt's new manual of 1921, which officially confirmed the continuing dominance of the principle of mobility, thus came to an officer corps that had never strayed far from the Prussian army's traditional emphasis on rapid and decisive offensive action based upon mobility and firepower. This information is absolutely essential to an understanding of the developments between 1919 and 1939. Prussian military leaders had always believed that their military system was uniquely suited to the demands and opportunities of mobile warfare. The Prussian army based its preparations for mobile warfare upon rapid offensive action, swift decisions by commanders, initiative at all levels, independent action by subordinate commanders, risk taking, acceptance of high losses, exploitation of uncertainty, the dominance of moral factors, and improvisation. Through all these ran the absolute belief in the superiority of the German system of education and training and in the ability of the army to execute its theories on the battlefield. Mobile warfare was the integrating centerpiece of the entire Prussian system, both in 1921 when Seeckt took charge of the new *Reichsheer* and in the later years when mechanization provided the army with new means of achieving mobility.

World War II Doctrine

The seeds of the German tank army thus fell upon fertile ground that had been well prepared both by many decades of Prussian military tradition and by the theoretical framework put in place by Seeckt and others after World War I. The German army had no special blitzkrieg theory because it had no need for such a construct. Unlike the situation in France or Britain, establishment of a modern approach to mechanized warfare did not demand a revolution in the army's outlook. Although Guderian and Lutz developed a few broad ideas about the employment of large armored formations, no official theory existed in 1939.

Most of the popular studies of the German army, of blitzkrieg, and of tank warfare in general hold that the German army *did* have such a doctrine or strategy (Murray 1984). Beyond that generalization, however, no consensus exists, even on the most basic issues. Len Deighton's popular and influential study, for example, argued that this method involved attack on narrow fronts and concluded that the famous cauldron battles (*Kesselschlachten*) of World War II were not part of blitzkrieg (Deighton 1979). According to his concept, blitzkrieg occurred only in France in 1940 and applies only to the operations of Guderian's forces. Neither Deighton nor anyone else has offered any evidence that German methods or expectations in 1940 were any different from those of the 1939 campaign; in fact, there is strong evidence to the contrary (Jacobsen 1957). Messenger's book (1976) argues that the Germans accepted Fuller's concept of producing paralysis by attacking the enemy's command apparatus, a point broadly consistent with the views of the influential military reformer William Lind. Some current theorists have used these arguments to link blitzkrieg theory to recent concepts of "operational depths," "centers of gravity," and so forth (Tiberi 1985). None of these authors bases his arguments upon a doctrinal publication or regulation in the traditional sense.

Guderian's Views

Guderian's views, although not decisive for the army's theory as a whole, merit attention in this context. Numerous authors have recorded Guderian's long struggle with what he regarded as excessively conservative superiors who for a number of years prevented him from creating large independent tank units to carry out his grand designs for an armored force (Guderian 1952). Guderian's own memoirs, among the most unreliable sources for the period, railed at length against Gen. Ludwig Beck and other enemies, who apparently included most of the General Staff. Nevertheless, neither Guderian's memoirs nor the considerable literature on the development of the German armored force have offered a clear picture of the goals and methods he envisioned for the armored units.

The Disruption Misinterpretation

Partly as a result of this gap in the scholarly literature, a number of civilian authors and military writers have advanced what might be termed the "disruption theory" of blitzkrieg methods. In this view, the essence of the blitzkrieg operational concept was disruption of the enemy's command and control system and the collapse of his resistance without costly battles or lengthy campaigns. In this view, paralysis replaced destruction of the enemy as the primary goal of military operations. This concept has become the basis of much of the so-called military reform movement in the United States and has become a staple of much of the U.S. Army's official and unofficial views of maneuver warfare (Franz 1983; Tiberi 1985; Higgins 1985). In recent years, political scientists have increasingly based part of their theories on the organizational origins of strategy and military doctrine upon this view of blitzkrieg and maneuver and the contrast between these and the alleged attrition style of warfare.

The Annihilation Principle

For an accurate appraisal of what the German army was really trying to achieve by its battles and operations, one must consider both the army's official regulations (*Truppenführung*) and the writings of the German theorists cited above. The most basic fact of German tactical and operational thought was the continuing emphasis upon annihilation of the enemy (Wallach 1986; Hughes 1986). The German army relied upon its traditional theories of mobile warfare to produce battles of annihilation. The goal of the entire process was the conduct of traditional battles of annihilation under the most favorable circumstances possible, not the avoidance of such battles. Armored formations proved to be a new means of mobility and increased firepower; they did not fundamentally change the German army's approach to warfare.

Guderian's own writings make this point quite clear, despite the very widespread practice of linking his name to the disruption idea. In an article published in the General Staff's journal in 1939, Guderian pointed out that in the attack, the main objective of the armored units must be the destruction of enemy obstacles, antitank defenses, artillery, and tank reserves. After that, the tank echelons that follow should turn their attention to helping to mop up the infantry combat zone (Guderian 1939).

This was a slightly more limited concept than that advanced earlier in an article reprinted in a small booklet in 1938. In the 1938 article, Guderian, again limiting his perspective to the sphere of tactics (the concept of *levels* of war was unknown in the German army prior to 1945), spoke of three echelons (*Treffen*) of friendly tanks in breaking through enemy lines. The first echelon should penetrate and destroy enemy staffs and reserves; the second should destroy enemy artillery; and the third was to attack enemy infantry units (Bradley 1978). These tasks were relevant in breakthrough battles and thus were purely tactical.

Guderian's treatment of the combined arms functions of armored forces in a broader perspective provides an interesting example of how easily armored theories fitted in with the traditional idea of German mobile warfare. In his discussion of combined arms actions, Guderian first quoted the British regulations on freeing tanks from excessively restrictive ties to the infantry, then referred to *Truppenführung* for official German views on the same point. As Guderian thus recognized, this fundamental regulation was and remained the basis of official theory (and doctrine in the German sense) (Guderian 1936, 1938). *Truppenführung* was thus a manual for annihilation using breakthrough. It was the opposite of a manual for armored disruption, especially since—at the time of its writing (1933)—the German army was still forbidden to possess tanks and even heavy weapons in the cavalry divisions.

Truppenführung, 1933

Truppenführung, written under the supervision of Gen. Ludwig Beck in 1931 and 1932, officially appeared in 1933 and remained the basic German regulation throughout World War II. This classic manual provided the fundamental framework for German theories of mobile warfare, tactical concepts, and the conduct of operations. Among the manual's most prominent themes was that of destruction of the enemy as the goal of battles and operations. In particular, *Truppenführung* outlined the major task of tank units as the destruction of enemy artillery and reserve forces to prevent stagnation of the front into positional warfare (Erfurth 1957).

The problems of trying to reconcile the post-1945 evaluations of blitzkrieg with the real principles of German theories of mobile warfare become clear when one compares these later views with Guderian's writings and with other contemporary works of German theory, both official and semiofficial. Jehuda Wallach, for example, has argued convincingly that *Truppenführung* was strictly in the tradition of Schlieffen's emphasis on battles of annihilation and flank attacks (Wallach 1986). East German scholarship on this point is equally solid and convincing, if one can go beyond the Marxist rhetoric. Michael Geyer, on the other hand, argues that the authors of *Truppenführung* had "distanced themselves" from Schlieffen's notions in their concepts of operations and their definition of annihilation. Geyer nevertheless recognizes the importance of mobile warfare as the basis of the manual (Geyer 1986).

Other examples of misunderstandings of basic concepts of mobile operations illustrate the difficulty of defining a blitzkrieg methodology. One recent author advocating the disruption theory of blitzkrieg has stressed that the German offensives called for breakthroughs on narrow fronts, followed by concentration in the enemy's rear, and again dispersion (Tiberi 1985). This view, borrowed from Deighton, has utterly no foundation in German theory. Guderian, in fact, rejected any such notion by logically insisting that breakthroughs must be as wide as possible in order to provide greater security along vulnerable flanks.

In a similar manner, a number of authors have argued that the Polish campaign and the Russian campaign were not examples of blitzkrieg because they relied upon the traditional *Kesselschlacht* born in the days of Moltke and Schlieffen. This notion is also at variance with the alleged psychological dislocation of the enemy, which so many regard as the core of blitzkrieg. Guderian himself always wrote of annihilation of the enemy in battle and, on at least one occasion, clearly rejected the idea of attaining victory through moral effects on the enemy. On the contrary, he said, the enemy resistance must be broken "through annihilation by fire of the enemy encountered in the area of attack" (Guderian 1936).

In any case, the basic methods and theories of the German armored forces underwent no significant changes from Poland through France to the early months of the Russian campaign. Blitzkrieg was a rapid victory of the German system of mobile warfare over some enemies. When that same system failed under the very different circumstances of Eastern Europe, no blitzkrieg occurred. On the battlefield and in the campaigns, blitzkrieg was a result, or perhaps an *ex post facto* description of the result. It was never a tactical or an operational system.

Daniel J. Hughes

See Also: Auftragstaktik; Combined Arms; Firepower; Guderian, Heinz; Initiative in War; Mobility; Principles of War; Strategy; Tactics; Trench Warfare; War of Attrition.

Bibliography

Addington, L. 1971. *The blitzkrieg era and the German general staff 1865–1941*. New Brunswick, N.J.: Rutgers Univ. Press.

Balck, W. 1906. *Taktik*. 6 vols. Berlin: R. Eisenschmidt.

———. 1920. Entwicklung der Taktik der Infanterie. In *Militärische Lehren des Grossen Krieges*, ed. M. Schwarte. Berlin: E. S. Mittler.

Bradley, D. 1978. *Guderian und die Entstehungsgeschichte des modernen Blitzkrieges*. Osnabrück: Biblio. Verlag.

Deighton, L. 1979. *Blitzkrieg: From the rise of Hitler to the fall of Dunkirk*. New York: Ballantine Books.

Doughty, R. 1985. *The seeds of disaster: The development of French army doctrine 1919–1939* Camden, Conn.: Archon Books.

Eimannsberger, L. von. 1938. *Der Kampfwagenkrieg*. 2d ed. Munich: J. F. Lehmans.

Erfurth, W. 1957. *Die Geschichte des deutschen Generalstabes von 1918 bis 1945*. Göttingen: Musterschmidt.

Franz, W. 1983. Maneuver: The dynamic element of combat. *Military Review* 63(5):2–12.

German War Ministry. 1921. *Führung und Gefecht der verbundenen Waffen*. Berlin: E. S. Mittler.

Geyer, M. 1986. German strategy in the age of machine warfare. In *Makers of modern strategy from Machiavelli to the nu-*

clear age, ed. P. Paret, 529–97. Princeton, N.J.: Princeton Univ. Press.
Guderian, H. 1936. Kraftfahrkampftruppen. *Militärwissenschaftliche Rundschau* 1(1).
———. 1938. *Die Panzertruppen und ihr Zusammenwirken mit den anderen Waffen*. Berlin: E. S. Mittler.
———. 1939. Schnelle Truppen einst und jetzt. *Militärwissenschaftliche Rundschau* 4(2).
———. 1952. *Panzer leader*. New York: Dutton.
Higgins, G. A. 1985. German and U.S. operational art: A contrast in maneuver. *Military Review* 65(10):22–29.
Hughes, D. J. 1986. Abuses of German military history. *Military Review* 65(12):66–77.
Jacobsen, H. A. 1957. *Fall Gelb. Der Kampf um den deutschen Operationsplan zur Westoffensive 1940*. Wiesbaden: Franz Steiner.
Jochim, T. 1927. *Die Vorbereitung des deutschen Heers für die grosse Schlacht in Frankreich im Frühjahr 1918*. Vol. 1. Berlin: E. S. Mittler.
Kroener, B. 1985. Squaring the circle: Blitzkrieg strategy and manpower shortage, 1939–1942. In *The German military in the age of total war*, ed. W. Deist, 202–303. Dover, N.H.: Berg Publisher.
Lind, W. 1984. The case for maneuver doctrine. In *The defense reform debate: Issues and analysis*, ed. A. A. Clark IV, P. W. Chiarelli, J. S. McKitrick, and J. W. Reed, 88–100. Baltimore: Johns Hopkins Univ. Press.
Macksey, K. 1976. *Guderian: Creator of the blitzkrieg*. New York: Stein and Day.
Mearsheimer, J. 1983. *Conventional deterrence*. Ithaca, N.Y.: Cornell Univ. Press.
Meckel, J. 1890. *Allgemeine Lehre von der Truppenführung im Kriege*. Berlin: E. S. Mittler.
Miksche, F. O. 1941. *Attack: A study of blitzkrieg tactics*. New York: Random House.
Milward, A. A. 1985. Der Einfluss ökonomischer und nichtökonomischer Faktoren auf die Strategie des Blitzkrieges. In *Wirtschaft und Rüstung am Vorabend des Zweiten Weltkrieges*, ed. F. Forstmeister and H. Volkmann, 189–201. Düsseldorf: Droste.
Murray, W. 1984. *The change in the European balance of power*. Princeton, N.J.: Princeton Univ. Press.
Rabenau, F. von. 1940. *Seeckt: Aus seinem Leben*. Leipzig: Hase and Koehler.
Rohrbeck, Major. 1922. *Entwickelung der Taktik im Weltkriege*. 2d ed. Berlin: E. S. Mittler.
Sternberg, F. 1938. *Germany and a lightning war*. Trans. E. Fitzgerald. London: Faber and Faber.
Tiberi, P. 1985. German versus Soviet blitzkrieg. *Military Review* 65(9):63–71.
Wallach, J. L. 1986 [1967]. *The dogma of the battle of annihilation*. Westport, N.Y.: Greenwood Press.

BLOCKADE AND MARITIME EXCLUSION

In sea warfare the counterpart to a siege operation on land is a blockade. Blockades seek to isolate cities, harbors, or entire coastlines and frontiers of a nation by posting military forces to intercept maritime traffic. Blockades are generally thought of as occurring at sea, but they can be conducted on land or in the air. The focus here is exclusively on blockades in the maritime arena.

Strategic Meaning of Blockade

Blockades are mounted to influence what happens on land. The ultimate effectiveness of a blockade, therefore, is measured by its impact on the political situation in the blockaded country or coalition, or on the course and outcome of a crisis or a war. The extent to which the blockaded state is dependent on materials transported in ships and the ability of the blockader to inderdict the movement of commerce are the major determining factors of the blockade's impact.

Control over land areas differs greatly from control over areas at sea. In the open seas, beyond narrow zones close to shore lines, there are no permanent political boundaries. Control over sea areas depends on the ability to control the activities of opposing forces, not the ability to exercise control over territory. There are no sanctuaries at sea, but ships can seek refuge in friendly ports. Thus, if an enemy cannot be brought to battle and defeated, control of the seas depends upon the ability to blockade.

Types of Blockades

Through the years blockades have taken a variety of forms and have been used for a range of purposes. The simplest distinction is between *naval* and *maritime* blockades. The former takes as its objective the destruction, or at a minimum the immobilization, of the main enemy military fleet. The latter, also called a *commercial* or *economic* blockade, seeks to deprive an adversary of the benefits of oceangoing commerce.

Blockades can also be classified according to the method by which they are imposed or how they are conducted. Recognized categories of blockade include *pacific* and *belligerent*, *close* (or *tactical*) and *distant* (or *strategic*), *defensive* and *offensive*. There are also *quarantines* and *exclusion zones* or *exclusion areas*.

The common misunderstanding is that establishing a blockade at sea is an act of war. The issue, however, is much more complex. The pacific blockade, for example, is internationally recognized as a form of limited hostility short of war. It is employed by one state to prevent another from taking an action that would be contrary to a state of peace. Pacific blockades are generally implemented as "police actions" and frequently involve coalitions as the imposing authority. For example, in 1827 Great Britain, France, and Russia joined forces to blockade a section of the Turkish-occupied Greek coast in an effort to persuade Turkey to grant independence to the Greeks. In contrast to the pacific blockade, the belligerent blockade invokes a state of war by its announcement and establishes rights and obligations under the laws of war on the part both of belligerents and of neutrals.

Close or *tactical* blockades describe the form blockades took from antiquity until the middle nineteenth century. They were so called because the only means of detecting blockaded vessels was visual, so ships were required to be in close proximity to the blockaded area. In essence, close blockade was physical blockade of a port. Such blockades can be traced as far back as the Peloponnesian Wars. Galleys, the primary ships of war until the late fifteenth century, however, were poorly suited to conduct blockade operations. They were not very seaworthy because the ships were required to have low sides to accommodate the oars. Propulsion was provided by sail and by the energy of men pulling the oars; using rowers alone, galleys had a very limited range. In addition, galleys could not carry provisions—especially water for the large crews—sufficient to permit them to spend long periods at sea. Sailing ships, by contrast, were quite independent of logistic support from the shore, and thus could conduct prolonged blockades off the ports of an enemy. A variation of the close blockade was called the *open* blockade, the difference being that in the latter ships returned to home base from time to time to be replenished and to rotate crew members, while in the former those services were provided by other friendly ships at the blockade stations.

In the middle of the nineteenth century, the close blockade was rendered impractical by the appearance of the naval mine, the self-propelled torpedo, and the submarine. Before too long the airplane added to the hazards of approaching an enemy coastline in an effort to establish a close blockade. These technological advances caused ship operations within visual distance of their objects of interest to be too dangerous, so blockading became a more distant or strategic enterprise.

A blockade at an extended distance from the coastline, however, meant longer blockade lines, higher patrol speeds, or more ships for the same coverage. Steamships made their debut during the same time frame that other technologies made close blockade less and less feasible; unlike their wind-propelled predecessors, they required fuel. These factors worked together to necessitate a friendly base for resupply that was not far from the blockade lines. Obviously, moving the blockade line farther out permitted, by default, greater freedom of movement on the part of the blockaded force.

Ships can carry heavy loads and move them much farther and often faster than land transportation. The overall effectiveness of blockades, therefore, was undermined significantly by the appearance of the railroad and subsequently of networks of good roads and motor vehicles. Coastal blockades prior to that time had taken leverage from the fact that waterborne transport was by far the most efficient way for littoral states to trade.

Quarantine describes an operation, limited in scope, that seeks to prevent certain items from passing a line of control. In recent times, quarantines have been established, for example, to interdict the flow of illegal drugs by ship or air. Perhaps the most famous quarantine was the Cuban Missile Crisis of 1962, when the United States sought to prevent Cuba from importing offensive nuclear weapons from the USSR. The quarantine was established for that single, limited purpose. In fact, the quarantine was a form of pacific blockade, but the term *blockade* was avoided deliberately so that the operation would not be taken as connoting a state of war.

Of late in some situations states have created maritime exclusion zones or maritime exclusion areas. The terminology notwithstanding, these have actually been a form of blockade. The British in the 1982 Falklands/Malvinas campaign declared what they called *exclusion zones*. The first was a maritime exclusion zone 200 nautical miles (approx. 325 km) in radius, enforced by submarines. The second was a total exclusion zone, which extended the coverage of the 200-mile zone to aircraft. Finally, the British government stipulated that all Argentine warships and military aircraft beyond 12 miles (approx. 20 km) from the Argentine coast would be considered hostile. If a state of war had been declared between the United Kingdom and Argentina, the maritime exclusion zones established by the British would have qualified as a belligerent blockade of the islands.

Finally, defensive blockades keep enemy ships from leaving port, and offensive blockades prevent ships or contraband from entering port or have the objective of inducing the enemy navy to put to sea and engage in battle. These descriptive terms are rarely used because they tend to be ambiguous.

International Law of Blockades

Owing in large measure to the complexity of the subject, international law on blockades remains fragmented and undeveloped. As noted, no immutable link connects blockades and a state of war. As a practical matter, however, some forms of blockade—a naval blockade as defined in the previous section offering the strongest case—indicate a de facto state of war.

Two issues stand out historically as the most contentious in the realm of international law of blockade: the definition of what constitutes an effective blockade (as opposed to a "paper" blockade) and the question of the rights of neutrals. With regard to effectiveness, by the middle of the eighteenth century most maritime nations had agreed that a legal blockade was one that was in fact enforced by sufficient, on-scene military forces. A declared blockade not implemented by ships on blockade station was deemed an ineffective, paper blockade. A paper blockade did not invoke the rights and responsibilities of neutrals and belligerents and invalidated the concept of contraband.

The rights of neutrals to continue to conduct trade and use the seas without interference or without being attacked by belligerents on the high seas (areas beyond territorial waters) enjoy long-standing legal recognition.

With respect to blockades, the issue for neutral countries has centered mainly on the question of *contraband*, that is, materials carried as cargo deemed important to the war effort of the blockaded state. Contraband labors under a history of controversy and confusion all its own. For example, munitions carried in neutral shipping manifested for delivery to a belligerent are unquestionably contraband, and a neutral ship carrying such contraband could legally be seized by a blockading power. In contrast, the status of food and an endless list of other materials is considerably less obvious. Although food contributes to the ability of the enemy to continue fighting, its effect is indirect. Cotton could be used to manufacture clothing, uniforms, or bandages, which is to say that most materials fall into the indeterminate category. In World War I the British had by 1917 increased the list of contraband to include virtually everything that had any bearing on the German war effort.

Some neutrals were extremely sensitive to the curtailing of their ability to trade, even with belligerents, in time of war. Initially the agreed rule was that neutral goods captured in belligerent ships were to be returned to their owners, and enemy goods in neutral ships would be seized. Neutral goods in neutral ships were exempt from seizure by belligerents. Later, neutrals sought to apply doctrines such as "free ships make free goods" and "the flag covers the cargo," in an effort to exempt their trading activities entirely from blockades or embargoes. Some definitional structure for this subject was imposed by the Declaration of London in 1909, which established distinctions between *absolute* contraband, *conditional* or *relative* contraband, and *free goods*. The controversy was not resolved by that declaration, however, and the same issues could easily arise today because the question revolves around whose interests the definitions are to serve.

Another complication has to do with the transshipment of contraband through neutral countries. In the U.S. Civil War, for example, neutrals would ship contraband items bound for the Confederacy to neutral ports where they would be transferred to fast blockade runners of the southern forces. The Union Navy intercepted some of those neutral ships even before they entered the neutral ports and contended that their actions sought only to interdict the first leg of a single continuous voyage to a blockaded port. The U.S. Supreme Court upheld this so-called doctrine of continuous voyage, but the issue was not new and even today is not free of controversy.

Although blockades have a long, evolving history, the body of law associated with them is neither coherent nor static. The British declaration of a maritime exclusion area in 1983, for example, received no protest from any country. When the boundaries were later extended to include all military ships or aircraft beyond the Argentine 12-mile territorial sea, legal protests were lodged by the Soviet Union, Nicaragua, Panama, and Venezuela. Reluctance in modern times by all states to issue a declaration of war or to establish formal blockades adds additional complexity and confusion to questions of belligerent and neutral rights. These issues will undoubtedly not be resolved in the near future.

Blockades and Naval Operations

One of the first operational uses of blockade in naval warfare was in the Peloponnesian War when in 425 B.C. Athenian galleys blockaded a Spartan garrison on the island of Sphacteria for over two months and eventually forced the Spartans to surrender. For the most part, however, galleys were instruments of battle, not of blockade. Friendly land areas were required in very close proximity to the blockaded zone in order to serve the oarsmen and cohorts in the galleys. Frequently, this was simply not possible.

This early blockade, however, does help illustrate several operational features of sea blockades. First, they usually require superior force if they are to succeed. The Athenian fleet was predominant over the Spartan fleet, helping to ensure the blockade's success. Second, the resemblance to a siege on land is apparent. Third, blockades, like sieges, take time to accomplish their objectives. They are not, as sea battles tend to be, fierce and short in duration. Blockades can in some instances complement battle. The Royal Navy's Lord Horatio Nelson, for example, claimed that his blockades of the French in Toulon harbor were for the "offensive" purpose of encouraging the inferior French fleet to sally forth and give battle, not to isolate it. Finally, maritime blockades are for the most part useful to win campaigns, but they cannot by themselves win wars. Blockades help create the conditions for land forces to prevail over a weakened or immobilized enemy, or they prevent the enemy from using the seas for its own purposes, which include commerce interdiction and attack from the sea. There are literally no examples of a maritime or naval blockade alone acting as a single decisive factor in war.

In the age of sail, blockades were designed to ensure that blockaded ships could not leave port unchallenged. Their effectiveness was amplified by the absence of adequate land transportation. Geographical configuration and weather were also important factors. If a state had only a few usable ports or if the blockading force enjoyed access to bases near the blockaded ports, the effectiveness of the blockade was enhanced. Severe weather could devastate the blockading force by damaging its ships or by rendering its sailors ineffective. Prevailing meteorological conditions could aid a blockade by sailing ships, as in the case of the many blockades of the French by the British, the latter of whom enjoyed the maneuverability afforded by the prevailing westerly winds and the fact that those winds tended to hamper French sorties. Meteorological conditions could also complicate blockades, as in the case of persistent low visibility in the North Sea, which allowed German ships to slip undetected through the British blockades of both world wars.

Although blockade is an indirect, slow-acting strategic instrument, it tends to be adopted and preferred by stronger navies because it is less costly than battle in terms of both personnel and ships. Maintaining blockade stations imposes hardship, however. Long periods at sea wear out the blockading force, and the lack of routine resupply can lead to a high incidence of sickness and low morale. In the time of sailing ships, navies often suffered more casualties from bad diet and unsanitary conditions on blockade station than from battles.

Blockaded navies have claimed that with all the comforts of home, they were better off than the blockaders. For the most part history has proven them wrong, however, because the blockaders benefited from the experience and training of maintaining station at sea while the well-rested blockaded force remained untrained and inexperienced.

Although few blockades were so successful that they suppressed all oceangoing commerce, the weaker blockaded force was invariably compelled to resort to strategies of blockade-running or of commerce raiding. This pattern occurred repeatedly throughout the sailing era, beginning most clearly with the three Anglo-Dutch wars fought from 1652 to 1674. This pattern did not stop with the end of sailing ships, however; it continues into the present.

A nation may have a good reason, in certain instances, for not attempting or maintaining a blockade, but history has recorded some instances where failure to impose a blockade resulted in eventual defeat. In the American Revolutionary War, for example, a concerted effort by the British to blockade either the American seaboard or the French coast might well have quelled the rebellion. As it turned out, the assistance of the French troops and navy to the colonists was instrumental in the success of the Americans.

In the ensuing Napoleonic Wars, on the other hand, the British returned to a blockade strategy and imposed both naval and maritime blockades on French ports in the Atlantic and in the Mediterranean. The French effort to break the blockade and to concentrate French and Spanish forces to invade England brought about the British victory at Trafalgar in 1805.

The American Civil War witnessed a very successful blockade of Confederate commerce and warships by the Federal forces. Nearly all the characteristics of blockade operations were demonstrated in this war. Prior to the beginning of this conflict, the standard argument was that steam-powered ships were independent of the prevailing winds, but they could not conduct a close blockade because of their need to refuel frequently. Northern (Federal) forces solved this problem by conducting military operations to seize and control bases near the main southern (Confederate) ports.

This civil war also typified the necessity for the blockaded party to resort to commerce raiding. Even though Confederate commerce raiders captured or destroyed about 300 Federal ships, and even though the Confederate force of 84 blockade runners caused a measure of concern to the leaders in the North, the blockade was devastatingly effective. It was aided by the fact that few Confederate commercial ports were of appreciable size and by the lack of rail service to those few ports. The Federal blockade succeeded in depriving the Confederacy of guns, ammunition, medical supplies, clothing, and many other needed imports. By the end of the war, export of cotton from the South—its primary export to finance imports—had plummeted to barely 10 percent of prewar levels.

Blockades were used with some success in the Spanish-American War and quite effectively by the Japanese at Port Arthur in the Russo-Japanese War. The latter constituted a milestone in blockade operations because it was the first successful distant blockade—made necessary by the mining of Port Arthur. Adm. Heihachiro Togo of Japan established his fleet at an island some 105 kilometers (65 mi.) from Port Arthur and maintained surveillance on the Russian fleet in the harbor by means of torpedo boats and other light warships. The purpose of Togo's blockade was to prevent the Russian warships from sailing from Port Arthur with the intention of disrupting Japanese traffic across the Yellow Sea.

Both World War I and World War II featured blockades of the German navy and economic blockades of the German nation by the British, with some help from its allies. Geographic positioning was a critical enabling factor for these blockades, for Britain sat firmly astride Germany's access routes to the open sea. In both wars the Germans resorted to commerce raiding, which cannot be called unsuccessful but did not prevent Germany from losing those wars. The blockades were effective and important to the allied efforts against Imperial Germany and the Third Reich.

The World War I German fleet in being did prevent the British main battle fleet from participating effectively elsewhere or in other wartime roles. Submarines, of course, are particularly difficult to blockade, especially from long range. Thus, the Germans resorted to the only course of action they believed open to them, and conducted commerce raiding in an effort to disrupt the war efforts of the Allies.

As a result of the World War I blockade, more than three-quarters of a million German citizens died of starvation, and many others suffered greatly from malnutrition or vitamin deficiencies. The commercial blockade ultimately had severe financial, commercial, industrial, and human effects on Germany, and the prospect of facing the winter of 1918 in such an exhausted condition had a significant impact on the German leadership's decision to end the war.

World War II saw largely a repeat of the successful British blockade strategy of World War I. Initially, the British plan was to mine the coastal waters of Norway to prevent trade—especially iron ore—between Germany and Norway and to seal off that route as a possible bypass of the anticipated blockade. The German invasion of Denmark and Norway in 1940 served as a flanking operation to preempt British intentions, and the subsequent occupation of France provided Germany additional access to the Atlantic. The consequence of these German actions was to offset to a degree the effects of superior British geography, and successful German operations elsewhere in Europe rendered the blockade of Germany in World War II not as effective as in the previous war.

In the Pacific, the United States conducted a successful naval and maritime blockade of the Japanese. Carried out primarily by submarines, the blockade sank more than 1,300 Japanese ships, including eight aircraft carriers, one battleship, and eleven cruisers. By preventing necessary war materials from reaching Japanese industry, the blockade ruined the Japanese war machine and contributed significantly to the ultimate defeat of Japan.

Worthy of note, in neither of the world wars were the blockades actually declared, but the rights of neutrals and contraband became issues nonetheless. The Pacific blockade was an exception; the virtual absence of neutral shipping kept the question of neutrality from arising.

In more recent examples of blockades, the United States imposed a blockade of the coast of South Vietnam between 1965–72, but permitted shipping to enter North Vietnamese ports. Subsequently, the mining of the port of Haiphong in 1972 contibuted to ending those hostilities. For a brief period the Egyptians blockaded the Gulf of Aqaba at the Straits of Tiran in their war with Israel, May–June 1967 (in fact, their announcement of the blockade was a primary reason for Israel to initiate actual hostilities on land); the Indian navy conducted a two-week blockade of East Pakistan in the 1971 war; in the 1973 Arab–Israeli War, Egypt blockaded Israel once again, this time at the Bab el Mandeb (where the Red Sea joins the Indian Ocean); and in 1984 Iraq imposed an air and sea blockade around Kharg Island, triggering a tanker war in which more than 500 ships were attacked by the warring sides. In the Gulf War against Iraq in 1991, a comprehensive blockade against Iraq resulted in 10,600 ships being intercepted, 1,660 boarded, and nearly 100 diverted. The embargo enforced by blockade contributed to Iraq's defeat.

Prospects

The American naval strategist Alfred Thayer Mahan once wrote: "Whatever the number of ships needed to watch those in an enemy's port, they are fewer by far than those that will be required to protect the scattered interests imperiled by an enemy's escape. Whatever the difficulty of compelling the enemy to fight near the port, it is less than that of finding him and bringing him to action when he has got far away. Whatever the force within, it is less than it will be when joined to that which may, at or near the same time, escape from another port (1895, p. 856)." This remains true today, indicating that blockade will continue to be viewed as an option in the event of hostilities. Superior force will continue to be most desirable for the conduct of successful blockade.

Endurance is most often a necessary ingredient to the effectiveness of blockades because they are basically slow-acting. A state imposing a blockade must be willing to endure the corrosive effects the prolongation of time generally has on military operations. The time required pivots primarily on how dependent the blockaded state is on maritime commerce, how dependent the blockading state is on unfettered use of the seas, whether the blockading state has sufficient naval strength to maintain blockading forces on station, the provocation that prompted the blockade in the first place, the level of hostilities resulting from the blockade, the attitudes and actions of third parties, the possibility and risks of escalation, and the availability of other military and nonmilitary options.

Some adjustments will be necessary in blockade techniques, certainly, as the characteristics of modern warfare are taken into account. New technologies permit surveillance over increasingly large areas, and modern missiles and aircraft can cover great distances quickly. The great hitting power and accuracy of modern weapons, moreover, coupled with the high cost of warships give the promise of more widespread use of mines and submarines as instruments of blockade. Certainly, however, the blockade will continue to be considered by seagoing states in the event of hostilities in the future.

Roger W. Barnett

See Also: Convoy and Protection of Shipping; Cuban Missile Crisis; Gunboat Diplomacy; Law of the Sea and Piracy; Mahan, Alfred Thayer; Maritime Strategy; Mine Warfare, Naval; Naval Warfare; Sea Control and Denial; Submarine Warfare.

Bibliography

Corbett, J. S. [1911] 1988. *Some principles of maritime strategy.* Annapolis, Md.: U.S. Naval Institute Press.

Daveluy, R. 1910. *The genius of naval warfare.* Annapolis, Md.: U.S. Naval Institute Press.

Mahan, A. T. [1890] 1957. *The influence of sea power upon history 1660–1783.* New York: Hill and Wang.

———. 1895. Blockade in relation to naval strategy. *U.S. Naval Institute Proceedings* 12 (4).

Medlicott, W. N. 1952. *The economic blockade.* London: His Majesty's Stationery Office.

O'Connell, D. P. 1975. *The influence of law on sea power.* Annapolis, Md.: U.S. Naval Institute Press.

Richmond, H. W. 1932. *Imperial defence and capture at sea in war.* London: Hutchinson.

Roskill, S. W. 1972. *The strategy of sea power: Its development and application.* London: Collins.

BOER WARS

The origins of the Boer Wars—sometimes called the Anglo-Boer or South African wars—can be traced back to the French Revolutionary–Napoleonic Wars. In 1795 a small British force seized the Dutch Cape Colony, which had been established in 1652, at the southern tip of South Africa. This was returned to Dutch control in 1802 under the Treaty of Amiens.

After the renewal of the war between France and England, the British in early 1805 again occupied Capetown and the Cape Colony. In 1814 the Treaty of Paris granted the colony to Britain.

From the beginning of British rule, there was friction between the British administrators and the Dutch colonists, known as Boers (the Dutch word for farmers). Between 1835 and 1837, in a migration known to history as the "Great Trek," some 12,000 Boers migrated northward from the Cape Colony to establish independent states west of Natal, in the fertile valleys of the Vaal and Orange rivers. In 1852 Great Britain renounced its sovereignty over the Transvaal region, which was soon proclaimed the South African Republic. In 1854 Britain also recognized the independence of the neighboring Orange Free State. Over the next 40 years, despite frequent friction with both Zulus and British in Natal, the Boers firmly established themselves in their two new homelands.

The discovery of diamonds (1868) and gold (1888) in and adjacent to the territory of the two Boer states complicated what had become a three-way—British, Boers, Zulus—rivalry over the region. The British reannexed the Transvaal region in 1877. The Boers protested vigorously and began to plan rebellion. In 1879 in a bloody and hard-fought war, the British defeated the Zulus and established a protectorate over Zululand. Then, in late 1880, the Boers of the Transvaal again proclaimed their independence from Britain.

First Boer War, 1880–81

This action by the Boers of the Transvaal precipitated the First Boer War. Although they were undisciplined militiamen, the Boers were superb marksmen, and they operated as highly mobile mounted infantry. Although they had the best of the fighting in several sharp battles with British troops, the most important of which were Laing's Nek (28 January 1881) and Majuba Hill (27 February), they were unable to prevent British reoccupation. On 5 April 1881, in the Treaty of Pretoria, Britain compromised, granting independence to the South African Republic, but under a British protectorate.

Second Boer War, 1899–1902

Friction between British and Boers continued, as much due to the ambitions and machinations of Cecil Rhodes, the governor of the British Cape Colony, as to the obstreperous stubbornness of the Boers. In October 1899, President Paul Kruger of the South African—or Transvaal—Republic became concerned by the arrival of British troops in Natal for what appeared to the Boers to be a British expeditionary force. Kruger issued an ultimatum, giving the British government 48 hours to disband all military preparations. The ultimatum was refused. The Orange Free State announced its alliance with the South African Republic.

Boer Military Organization

The Boer military organization was extremely sketchy, a localized militia system grouped into so-called commandos that varied in strength with the population from which they were recruited. Every individual, however, was a marksman, armed with a modern repeating rifle, and every man was mounted. The riders of the veldt were hunters, trained from childhood to take advantage of cover and terrain. The result was an irregular firepower capability that could pulverize, from concealed positions, the ranks of any close-order formation. These irregulars were also capable of rapidly disappearing from the field when seriously threatened. The Boers also had a small quantity of modern German and French field artillery, on the whole well served. On the other hand, the Boers lacked discipline and control, and few of their leaders had any real concept of tactics or strategy.

Boer Offensive

Beginning on 11 October 1899, fast-moving Boer columns advanced, both east and west from the Transvaal. Two days later, Transvaal general Piet A. Cronje invested Mafeking, which was valiantly defended by a handful of British troops and militia under Col. Robert S. S. Baden-Powell. On 15 October, Free State forces besieged Kimberley.

Meanwhile, on 12 October, the Boer main effort, 15,000 strong, under Transvaal general Jacobus Joubert, pushed through the Natal Defense Force, equal in number, under Gen. Sir George White, at Laing's Nek. After brushes at Talana Hill (20 October), Elandslaagte (21 October), and Nicholson's Nek (30 October), Joubert, on 2 November, bottled up White's troops in Ladysmith.

British relieving forces were unwisely divided by the British commander in South Africa, Gen. Sir Redvers Buller, who tried to check the Boers everywhere at once. Gen. Lord Paul Methuen's column, nearly 10,000 men with sixteen guns, moved to the relief of Kimberley. Transvaal and Free State Boer commandos, about 7,000 strong, under Transvaal generals Cronje and Jacobus H. De La Rey, contested the advance in a series of delaying actions. On 28 November, Methuen won a hard-fought battle to reach the Modder River, after losing 72 men killed and 396 wounded, but his troops were so exhausted that he paused to await reinforcements. Boer casualties were negligible.

The Boers under Cronje near the Modder River, then about 8,000 strong, occupied an entrenched hill near Magersfontein. At dawn on 10 October, in the rain, Methuen attacked frontally in mass formation. He was repulsed in a two-day battle with the loss of 210 men killed (including one general officer), 675 wounded, and 63 missing. Again, Boer casualties were negligible.

Buller himself led 21,000 men of all arms to relieve Ladysmith. Crossing the Tugela River on 15 December, he attempted to turn the left flank of Free State general Louis Botha, entrenched near Colenso with 6,000 men. The British flank attack, entangled in difficult terrain, was decimated by small-arms fire. British batteries, unlimbering to support the frontal attack, found themselves at the mercy of a concealed force of Boer marksmen. The British were driven back with losses of 143 killed, 756 wounded, and 220 men and 11 guns captured. Boer losses in this, the Battle of Colenso, are believed to be not more than 50 men.

On 20 December, a British force under Gen. Sir William Gatacre got lost in a night move against an invading Boer spearhead from the Orange Free State, 112 kilometers (70 mi.) north of Queenstown. The British were ambushed and suffered heavy losses.

Roberts' Reorganization

At the end of Britain's "Black Week," General Buller was so badly beaten that he advocated the surrender of Ladysmith. He was at once relieved of the supreme command and replaced by Field Marshal Frederick Sleigh Roberts, Viscount of Kandahar, with Gen. Horatio Kitchener as his chief of staff.

Realizing at once that mobility was the keynote for success against the Boers, Roberts and Kitchener began revamping British field forces (Fig. 1). To meet the Boer fluidity of fire and movement, a progressive buildup of mounted infantry began around the existing militia units, a long and arduous task against conservative British military opinion. Meanwhile, along the southwest border of the Orange Free State, Brig. Gen. John D. P. French, with two small brigades of cavalry, kept up a spirited campaign against De La Rey and Free State general Christiaan R. De Wet, who were proving themselves to be natural leaders of light cavalry.

Figure 1. Royal Munster Fusiliers fighting behind the redoubt at Honey Nest Kloof, South Africa (ca. 1900). (Source: U.S. Library of Congress)

British Offensive

In late January, General Buller began the first of two successive attempts to cross the Tugela River. He was defeated in his first attempt on 23 January at Spion Kop. He tried again on 5 February and was repulsed at Vaal Kranz. British losses in these battles were 408 killed, 1,390 wounded, and 311 missing. The Boers lost some 40 killed and 50 wounded.

On 15 February, General French reached Kimberley, bringing the Boer siege of that city to an end.

Meanwhile, in late January, Field Marshal Roberts had set out toward Kimberley with 30,000 men. While French was driving directly on Kimberley, the main British force marched past General Cronje's left flank at Magersfontein, threatening his communications. On 6 February, the Boer leader began a slow withdrawal.

On 18 February, near Paardeberg, Cronje's retreat across the Modder River was blocked by French, who had come rushing back from Kimberley. As the main British army approached, Roberts, temporarily sick, turned his command over to Kitchener, who made a tempestuous frontal piecemeal attack on the Boers' fortified laager (wagon train). The British were repulsed with losses of 320 killed and 942 men wounded.

Roberts, recovering, took command again and began a systematic encirclement and bombardment of the Boer laager. Cronje might have broken out with his 4,000 mounted men, but he stubbornly refused to abandon his wounded and his train, and was surrounded and besieged. With his men starving, he finally surrendered on 27 February.

On 17–18 February, General Buller, on the Tugela, made a third attack and finally succeeded. As he advanced toward Ladysmith, the besiegers withdrew and the relieving force made contact with the garrison on 28 February. The tide had turned.

Occupation of the Orange Free State

The British, now heavily reinforced, advanced on all fronts. On 13 March, Roberts took Bloemfontein, capital of the Orange Free State; pushing on, he reached Kroonstad on 12 May. Buller, in Natal on 15 May, swept Boer resistance away at Glencoe and Dundee. Nine days later the Orange Free State was annexed by Britain.

On 17 May, a flying column of cavalry and mounted infantry under Maj. Gen. Bryan T. Mahon relieved the garrison of Mafeking after a siege of more than seven months.

Invasion of the Transvaal

Roberts now pushed into the heart of the Transvaal. Johannesburg fell on 31 May, then Pretoria on 5 June. On 4 July, Roberts and Buller joined forces at Vlakfontein, ending all formal resistance. President Kruger fled to Portuguese Mozambique, and then sought Dutch protection. On 3 September, 1900, Britain formally annexed the Transvaal. In December, Roberts went home, leaving Kitchener in command.

Guerrilla Warfare

De Wet, De La Rey, Botha, and some minor leaders rallied the disbanded burgher forces to their respective commandos. For eighteen months they played havoc with British communications and defied all attempts to corner them. Erection of a line of blockhouses to protect the rail and other communication lines was the first remedial action taken by the British. But the raiders seemed to plunge at will through this cordon defense. Kitchener then turned to a war of attrition. The country was swept by flying columns of British mounted infantry; the farms on which the Boer raiders depended for sustenance were burned, and some 120,000 Boer women and children were herded into concentration camps, where an estimated 20,000 of them died of disease and neglect. Under these harsh measures, all resistance collapsed. In the spring of 1902, the guerrilla leaders capitulated.

On 31 May 1902, in the Treaty of Vereeniging, the Boers accepted British sovereignty. As part of the very lenient terms, Britain granted them £3 million compensation for the destroyed farms.

Total British casualties in the war were 5,774 killed and 22,829 wounded. The Boers lost an estimated 4,000 killed; there is no accurate total of the wounded, but they probably exceeded 10,000. About 40,000 Boer soldiers had been captured.

Assessment

It took the British Empire two years and eight months to subdue a foe whose manpower potential was 83,000 men of fighting age and who never had in the field at one time more than approximately 40,000 men. In the beginning, the number of British forces engaged did not total more than 25,000, but before it was over some 500,000 British troops were in South Africa—drawn from empire resources around the world. For the first time since the War of 1812, the British army met hostile mounted riflemen and small-arms fire. The experience of some 85 years of formal and informal wars in Europe and around the world was of little use, and an entirely new system of tactics and techniques had to be evolved on the battlefield.

TREVOR N. DUPUY

SEE ALSO: South Africa, Republic of; Unconventional Warfare.

Bibliography

Bond, B., ed. 1967. *Victorian military campaigns*. New York: Praeger.
De Wet, C. R. 1902. *Three years' war*. New York: Scribner.
Dupuy, R. E., and T. N. Dupuy. 1986. *The encyclopedia of military history*. 2d rev. ed. New York: Harper and Row.
Farwell, B. 1976. *The great Anglo-Boer war*. New York: Harper and Row.
Hillegas, H. C. 1899. *Oom Paul's people*. New York: Appleton.
Pakenham, T. 1979. *The Boer war*. New York: Random House.
Reitz, D. 1929. *Commando*. London: Faber and Faber.

BOLIVAR, SIMON [1783–1830]

A great South American independence leader, Bolívar is hailed as *El Libertador* (the Liberator) (Fig. 1). A soldier-statesman, his victories over the Spanish in the early 1800s won independence for Venezuela, Colombia, Peru, Ecuador, and Bolivia. Bolívar's life struggle was marked by severe vicissitudes—defeat, victory, adulation, and finally, rejection by the newly liberated states.

Early Years

Bolívar was born in 1783 in Caracas, Venezuela, of wealthy Creole parents, who died when he was young. He was sent to Europe in 1799 by his guardian to complete his education. There he married, but his wife died in Caracas of yellow fever in 1803. Bolívar returned to Europe in 1804 and studied Locke, Rousseau, and Voltaire. His idea

Figure 1. Simón Bolívar. (SOURCE: U.S. Library of Congress)

of independence for Latin America probably originated during that time.

After his return to Venezuela from Europe, the young Bolívar joined a group of Venezuelan patriots who wrested Caracas, the colonial capital, from Spain in 1810. After a third trip to Europe that year—largely to seek aid from England, which agreed only to remain neutral—he returned to Venezuela, where independence was declared in July 1811.

The Fight for Independence

In 1811 Bolívar took command of a liberation force occupying the Venezuelan port of Puerto Cabello. When Spain retook Venezuela in 1812, Bolívar fled to Colombia to join liberation forces there, and returned to Venezuela in 1813 at the head of an expeditionary force. After fighting the Spanish to the gates of Caracas, he entered the city and assumed dictatorial powers. However, he was defeated and driven out in mid-1814 by a band of *llaneros* (plains cowboys) organized by the Spanish.

Bolívar then made his way to New Granada (now Colombia) and then to Jamaica. In 1815 he went to Haiti, where he obtained arms and support from that newly independent country's president. In 1816, after two unsuccessful efforts to invade Venezuela, he decided to penetrate into Colombia, and he set up a base at Angostura, now Ciudad Bolívar. After several indecisive actions, he and his army, reinforced by British and Irish mercenaries, moved against the Spanish in 1819. His army marched over the Andes and attacked and defeated the Spanish army at Boyacá. He entered the capital, Bogotá, a few days later and assumed dictatorial powers. Bolívar returned to Venezuela with an army in 1821 to win the Battle of Carabobo (24 June), thus liberating the country. He quickly sent a trusted general, Antonio José de Sucre, into Ecuador at the head of a liberation force, freeing that territory from the Spanish. The territory of *Gran Colombia* (Colombia, Venezuela, and Ecuador) had now been liberated and was recognized by the United States.

There remained only Peru. The next year (1822) Bolívar met with José de San Martín, an Argentinean, the other great liberation figure of Latin America. San Martín had been instrumental in liberating Argentina and Chile, and then went to Peru to help in the nationalist struggle there. No one knows exactly what occurred in the meeting of San Martín and Bolívar, but apparently they disagreed. San Martín, perhaps wishing to avoid dissension in the liberation forces, returned to Argentina. Bolívar then moved into Peru, entered Lima in September 1823, and became that country's new dictator.

Finally, Bolívar's army (led by General Sucre) defeated the Spanish at the Battle of Ayacucho in Peru in 1824, which effectively ended Spanish power in Latin America. Sucre then marched eastward into the Presidency of Charcas, southeast of Peru, where he established a new republic named Bolivia, in Bolívar's honor, in 1825.

The independent *Gran Colombia* of several sovereign states that Bolívar envisioned did not survive. One by one, the newly liberated states withdrew from the union. By 1828, Bolívar governed only what is now Colombia. Sentiment against Bolívar's dictatorial rule grew stronger; there were insurrections and struggles for power by ambitious local leaders; and Bolívar narrowly escaped assassination at one time. In 1830, shortly before his death, Bolívar resigned as president of Colombia and went into exile.

Bolívar as Soldier and Statesman

As a commander, Bolívar was noted for his swift decisions and rapid reactions. His tactics often featured a strong element of surprise. For example, his victory at Boyacá, which liberated Colombia, was possible because he had led his forces through a difficult area of plains and mountains to attack a surprised Spanish army from an unexpected direction. Bolívar's military successes were enhanced by capable and aggressive subordinates, most particularly Sucre.

Bolívar took advantage of the political climate and condition of the time, which favored Latin American independence. A spirit of freedom and revolt against the old order arose in the Old and New Worlds following the French and American revolutions. Spain, which had been colonial overlord of most of Latin America for three centuries, had been weakened by Napoleon's invasion in 1806 and by internal unrest in the 1820s. The times were ripe for Bolívar and Latin American independence.

Bolívar left several important political statements, largely written in exile, which defined and inspired the Latin American struggle. The most important of these was *La Carta de Jamaica*, which outlined a grand scheme for a free Latin America stretching from Chile to Mexico.

His leadership was marked by a strong authoritarian streak. In devising constitutions for the liberated countries, Bolívar followed a vague Western model: a president for life, who would be, in fact, a dictator, and two legislative houses without any real power. This led to his downfall.

WALTER P. WHITE

SEE ALSO: Colombia; Latin American Wars of Independence; San Martín, José de; South America; Spanish Empire.

Bibliography

Johnson, J. J. 1968. *Simón Bolívar and Latin American independence*. Princeton, N.J.: Van Nostrand.

Lecuna, V. 1950. *Chronica Razonada de las Guerras de Bolívar*. 3 vols. Clinton, Mass.: Colonial Press.

Madariaga, S. de. 1967. *Bolívar*. Coral Gables, Fla.: Univ. of Miami Press.

O'Leary, D. F. 1970. *Bolívar and the war of independence*. Ed. and trans. R. F. McNerney, Jr. Austin, Tex.: Univ. of Texas Press.

BOLIVIA, REPUBLIC OF

Bolivia is the larger of Latin America's two landlocked states, and it is also one of the poorest nations in the Western Hemisphere. Its capital La Paz is the highest capital in the world.

Power Potential Statistics

Area: 1,098,580 square kilometers (424,162 sq. mi.)
Population: 7,435,800
Total Active Armed Forces: 31,000 (0.417% of pop.)
Gross Domestic Product: US$4.85 billion (1990 est.)
Annual Defense Expenditure: US$162 million (4% of GNP, 1988 est.)
Iron and Steel Production: none
Fuel Production:
 Crude oil: 0.900 million metric tons (1989)
 Natural gas: 4,969 million cubic meters (1981)
Electrical Power Output: 1,763 million kwh (1990)
Merchant Marine: 2 vessels; 14,051 gross registered tons
Civil Air Fleet: 56 major transport aircraft; 659 usable airfields (9 with permanent-surface runways); 1 with runways over 3,659 meters (12,000 ft.); 8 with runways 2,440–3,659 meters (8,000–12,000 ft.); 120 with runways 1,220–2,440 meters (4,000–8,000 ft.).

For the most recent information, the reader may refer to the following annual publications:
The Military Balance. International Institute for Strategic Studies. London: Brassey's (UK).
The Statesman's Year-Book. New York: St. Martin's Press.
The World Factbook. Central Intelligence Agency. Washington, D.C.: Brassey's (US).

History

Between 100 B.C. and A.D. 900, the Aymara Indians produced a sophisticated culture, known from the ruins at Tiachuanacu. About 1450, highland Bolivia became part of the Inca Empire, and was conquered by the Spanish between 1535 and 1600. Although landlocked and nearly inaccessible, it provided great wealth to Spain, especially from the immense silver mine at Potosi (which at its height was a town of 160,000 inhabitants), exploited between 1545 and 1700. Bolivia, known as Upper Peru, was governed from the Viceroyalty of Peru. As in the rest of Latin America, by the end of the 1700s the small creole class was unhappy with Spanish government, and in the confusion surrounding Napoleon's invasion of Spain, Bolivia declared its autonomy at Chuquisaca (then the capital) on 25 May 1809.

During the struggle for independence in Latin America, Bolivia long remained a royalist stronghold, and independence was not assured until the victory of Gen. José Antonio de Sucre at Tumusla on 2 April 1825, and the creation of the Republic of Bolivia (named for Simón Bolívar) on 6 August. For the next 60 years Bolivia's history was marked by military coups and short-lived constitutions. The War of the Pacific (1879–84), waged by Chile against Peru and Bolivia, cost the country both its outlet to the sea and the rich nitrate deposits along the Pacific coast. Success in exploiting tin and silver deposits from the 1880s to the 1930s provided a measure of political stability, as the government was dominated by mining interests.

Bolivia, trying to compensate for the loss of the Pacific provinces by expanding into the Chaco region to gain access to the Atlantic via rivers, clashed with Paraguay in the Chaco War of 1932–35. Despite superior numbers and equipment, and the services of former German general Hans Kundt, the Bolivians were defeated, and suffered a further loss of prestige. Sparked by this disaster, political change at last crept into the country, and the National Revolutionary Movement's (MNR) revolution of 7–11 April 1952 brought to power Bolivia's first popular government, but this did not end the internal political turmoil.

A low point in Bolivia's recent political history was the thirteen-month regime of Gen. Luis Garcia Meza Tejada (18 July 1980–4 August 1981), which began when General Meza Tejada overthrew the government of Dr. Lydia Gueiler Tejada. Meza Tejada's regime became notorious for its abolition of political parties, its human rights abuses, its involvement in drug trafficking, and widespread official corruption. Meza Tejada was ousted by a coup, but stable civilian rule was restored only with the election of Dr. Herbert Siles Zuazo as president on 10 October 1982.

Politico-Military Background and Policy

Historically, the army has played a major role in Bolivian politics, and many Bolivian presidents have been generals or colonels. During the 1980s, however, the armed forces have carefully avoided direct political action. Since the creation of the Armed Forces Development Corporation in 1972, the army has played an active role in rural and industrial development, and in the exploitation of natural resources (especially the copper deposits around Oruro). Dr. Victor Paz Esstensoro's government has done a remarkable job in ending Bolivia's raging hyperinflation (from 15,000% or more in 1985 to 14.6% in 1987), but this has been at the cost of high unemployment rates and poor economic growth. If these conditions lead to large-scale political unrest, the army might take control of the government to restore order.

The armed forces are manned by conscription. All able-bodied males reaching age 19 are eligible for twelve months' service, but only about 19,000 (30%) of eligible men are selected for service.

Strategic Problems

Bolivia's greatest strategic problems are related to its poverty. Although richly endowed with natural resources, Bolivia's population is both poor and poorly educated; fewer than half the people even speak Spanish as their first language, and at best 75 percent of the people are literate. These factors limit development and hamper economic expansion, both of which in turn feed political instability. The situation is further complicated by Bolivia's dependence on raw material sales for foreign exchange; any decrease in tin prices (which collapsed in 1952–53 and in 1985), for example, can spell economic and political disaster.

Externally, Bolivia faces no serious threats, as its core regions in the *altiplano* (the central Andean plateau) are militarily inaccessible. Bolivia does have a long-standing dispute with Chile over transit rights to the Pacific, which Bolivia lost in 1884, and there are also dormant disputes over territory lost to Paraguay (after the Chaco War), Brazil, and Peru.

Military Assistance

Bolivia received military aid totaling nearly US$50 million from the United States between 1942 and 1980, when it was interrupted because of the excesses of the Meza Tejada government. Civilian aid during the same period totaled over US$800 million. Further, some 4,400 Bolivian military personnel received training and instruction in the United States over the same period. Brazil provided Bolivia with road construction assistance during the 1970s, and provided eight aircraft for aviation college. Since the end of the Meza Tejada government in 1981, the United States has resumed military aid, although on a smaller scale. U.S. aid in general has in recent years been made dependent on Bolivian cooperation in efforts to halt cocaine trafficking, and in 1988 amounted to some US$5.4 million in grants and loans (over 6% of Bolivia's entire defense expenditure).

Defense Industry

Despite abundant militarily important minerals, Bolivia has little real industry, and relies on imports for its supplies of weapons.

Alliances

Bolivia is a member of the United Nations, the Organization of American States, and the Andean Group. Bolivia has no official defense ties with any of its neighbors, but there are fairly close ties with the United States.

Defense Structure

The president of the republic is captain-general of the armed forces, which consist of the army, air force, and a small inland navy operating on Lake Titicaca and the country's extensive river systems. The president heads a Supreme Council of National Defense that appoints service commanders and the armed forces commander in chief. Administrative responsibility rests with the minister of defense.

(For an explanation of the abbreviations and symbols used in the following section of military statistics, see the list of Abbreviations and Acronyms in each volume.)

Total Armed Forces

Active: 31,000 (some 19,000 conscripts). Terms of service: 12 months, selective.

ARMY: 23,000 (some 15,000 conscripts).
HQ: 6 Military Regions.
Army HQ direct control: 2 armd bn; 1 mech cav regt; 1 Presidential Guard inf regt.
10 'div'; org, composition varies; comprise: 8 cav gp (5 horsed, 2 mot, 1 aslt); 1 mot inf regt with 2 bn. 22 inf bn (incl 5 inf aslt bn); 1 armd bn; 1 arty 'regt' (bn); 5 arty gp (coy); 1 AB 'regt' (bn); 6 engr bn.
Equipment:
Light tanks: 36 SK-105 Kuerassier.
Recce: 24 EE-9 Cascavel.
APC: 113: 50 M-113, 15 V-100 Commando, 24 MOWAG Roland, 24 EE-11 Urutu.
Towed arty: 20: 75mm: 6 M-116 pack, est. 10 Bofors M-1935; 105mm: 4 M-101.
Mortars: 81mm: 250; 107mm: M-30.
RCL: 50: 90mm; 106mm: M-40A1.
Aviation: 2 C-212, 4 Cessna 206, 1 King Air B90, 1 PA-3IT, 1 Super King Air 200 (VIP).

NAVY: 4,000 (incl 1,200 marines) (perhaps 2,000 conscripts); 6 naval districts; covering Lake Titicaca and the rivers; each 1 flotilla. Bases: Riberalta (HQ), Tiquina (HQ), Puerto Busch, Puerto Guayaramerín (HQ), Puerto Villaroel, Trinidad (HQ), Puerto Suárex (HQ) Cobija (HQ).
River Patrol Craft: some 10 (; plus some 6 US Boston whalers.
Support: 1 Libertador Bolivar ocean tpt (uses Arg/Uruguay ports); some 20 riverine craft/boats.

Naval Aviation: 1 Cessna 206, 1 402.

Marines: 1 bn plus 5 coy (coy+ in each District).

AIR FORCE: 4,000 (perhaps 2,000 conscripts); 50 cbt ac, 10 armed hel.
Fighter: 1 sqn with 12 AT-33N, 4 F-86F (ftr/trg).
COIN: 2 AT-6G, 12 PC-7.
Special ops: 1 sqn with 10 Hughes 500M hel.
SAR: 1 hel sqn with 4 HB-315B, 1 SA-315B, 1 UH-1.
Survey: 1 sqn with 1 Cessna 206, 1 210, 1 402, 2 Learjet 25, 1 PA-31.
Transport: 3 sqn: 1 VIP tpt with 1 L-188, 1 Sabreliner, 2 Super King Air; 2 tpt with 9 C-130, 1 Convair 440, 4 F-27-400, 1 IAI-201, 2 King Air.
Liaison:
Aircraft: 1 Cessna 152, 2 -185, 13 -206, 1 -402, 1 Commander 500.
Helicopters: 2 Bell 212, 16 UH-1H.
Training: 1 Cessna 152, 2 172, 11* PC-7, 6 SF-260CB, 15 T-23, 9* T-33A, 3 T-41D.
1 air-base defense regt (Oerlikon twin 20mm, some truck-mounted guns).

PARAMILITARY
National Police: some 13,000.
Narcotics Police: some 850.
Militias: There are also semiarmed militias maintained by the tin-workers' and peasants' unions; that of the tin workers is

well organized. These forces are employed to protect union members from the goons and strong-arm methods of landowners and mining companies.

Future

Bolivia's abundant natural resources, if properly managed, could help domestic development greatly. Continued stability will be essential, and that depends on both preventing a return of the hyperinflation of 1985 and avoiding a severe recession in the process.

DAVID L. BONGARD
TREVOR N. DUPUY

SEE ALSO: Bolívar, Simón; Latin American Wars of Independence; South America.

Bibliography

Alexander, J. 1982. *Bolivia: Past, present, and future of its politics*. New York: Praeger.
Dupuy, T. N., et al. 1980. *The almanac of world military power*. San Rafael, Calif.: Presidio Press.
Dunkerly, J. 1984. *Rebellion in the veins: Political struggle in Bolivia, 1952–1982*. London: Latin American Bureau.
Hunter, B., ed. 1991. *The statesman's year-book, 1991–92*. New York: St. Martin's Press.
International Institute for Strategic Studies. 1991. *The military balance, 1991–1992*. London: Brassey's.
Klein, H. S. 1982. *Bolivia: The evolution of a multiethnic society*. New York: Oxford Univ. Press.

BOMBARDMENT, STRATEGIC

Strategic bombardment is direct attack on the enemy state with the object of depriving it of the means or the will to wage war. The distinction between *strategic* and *tactical* has been muddled from being associated with nuclear versus conventional weapons. The notion of what is strategic and what is tactical is further complicated by differences in doctrinal and geographic perspective, and by the capabilities of modern aircraft. For example, what is tactical to the United States is often strategic to its NATO allies and to the former Soviet Union. A number of modern tactical aircraft (e.g., F-111, F-15E, Tornado, Fencer) have ranges and payloads greater than the heavy bombers of World War II, and are often allocated to what are considered strategic missions. The 1991 Persian Gulf War provided several examples of the blurring of "strategic" and "tactical." During the air campaign, targets for B-52 heavy bombers included Iraqi forces in the field, while "tactical" aircraft such as F-15s and F-117s often engaged in deep-strike "strategic" missions into the interior of Iraq against targets such as power plants, refineries, and transportation nodes.

Nonetheless, strategic and tactical bombardment are separate and distinct concepts. To some the difference is based on distance to target; to others it is the length of time it takes the enemy to recover. The heavy bomber has been the primary instrument of strategic bombardment, and its targets are normally the enemy's homeland factories, resources, and morale, rather than its troops in combat.

Heavy bombers possess three distinguishing characteristics: they are manned, carry large payloads, and have long range. On-board crews provide flexibility to adjust to the unexpected, such as changes in enemy deployment (mobile targets and air defenses). The crew's imagination, judgment, and intelligence help see through the "fog of war" and react to tasking changes and equipment failures. A large payload volume (nuclear or conventional) permits increasing the weapons load by reducing fuel load. External pylons can also be used to carry additional weapons, although the trend toward lower radar cross-section (RCS) tends to discourage external carriage of weapons. Long range eliminates the aircraft's vulnerability at forward staging bases and enables quick response worldwide. The best reason for the heavy bomber's continued use is its inherent flexibility.

Strategic bombardment capabilities can stabilize conventional conflicts and deter nuclear conflict. Bombers typically can react more quickly than tactical airpower or carrier battle groups, and a rapid response may prevent a crisis from becoming a major conflict. The manned bomber can also support nuclear deterrence. Since the bomber flies for hours (instead of minutes, as do missiles) to reach targets, it is not considered a first-strike weapon. The bomber is, however, effective against all nuclear objectives (except those requiring immediate strikes), and is the only delivery system that can be recalled, redirected, and reconstituted after launch.

History

Many individuals contributed to the art and theory of strategic bombardment, but three are generally considered the most important: Col. (later Gen.) Giulio Douhet (Italy), Air Marshal Sir Hugh Trenchard (Britain), and Brig. Gen. Billy Mitchell (United States). Douhet's *Command of the Air*, published in 1921, is still regarded as mandatory reading for military aviators. Douhet advocated bombing aimed at destruction of both the material and psychological means of the enemy to conduct war, thereby making bombardment a decisive method of warfare. He recommended large-scale bombing of population centers to produce mass hysteria.

Sir Hugh Trenchard also advocated strategic bombardment directed against the enemy's morale. Trenchard estimated the psychological yield was twenty times greater than the material damage. He considered cities improper targets, however, and advocated attacking industrial facilities such as factories, rail systems, docks and shipyards, wireless stations, and communications facilities. He also foresaw the need to fight the air battle over enemy territory.

A frequent visitor to Trenchard, Brig. Gen. Billy Mitchell based his call for independent airpower on the potential of strategic bombardment. His long and very public campaign cost him his career, but not before the formation of a "Headquarters Air Force," forerunner of a separate United States Air Force distinct from the ground forces.

Early Aircraft and Weapons

The first aerial bombardment operations were attempted by the Austrians in 1849 from hot air balloons. Powered lighter-than-air craft proved quite versatile and could carry out reconnaissance operations, transport supplies, and bombard enemy locations. The development of the internal combustion engine and the efforts of Germany's Count Ferdinand von Zeppelin made the dirigible airship part of military history, although it was only modestly successful as a bomber in World War I.

The first airplane built under military contract was delivered by the Wright brothers to the U.S. Army in 1908. In World War I, military aircraft and missions developed together rapidly. Aircraft, like balloons, were initially used as reconnaissance platforms. Eventually pilots began dropping projectiles on the enemy. The weapons of early World War I ranged from makeshift petrol bombs to hand grenades. Gradually, bomb sizes increased as the capacity to carry heavier loads increased. In 1918 Germany was dropping bombs weighing over 600 pounds.

The separation of tactical versus strategic roles was soon established. Strategic targets required greater range and larger weapons loads, and a new aircraft type. The Handley Page 0/100 was Britain's first true bomber. France developed the Voisin 3, and Germany the Gotha GIV. Russia, however, developed the first true heavy bomber in 1914: The four-engine Ilya Muromatz, which could carry over a ton of explosives almost 1,000 kilometers (approx. 600 mi.).

Historical Legal Considerations

With the advent of aerial bombardment in the nineteenth century, attempts were made to develop rules for aerial combat. The Hague Conference of 1899 banned aerial bombardment for five years. At the Hague Conference of 1907, the major powers rejected any prohibition against bombing. Instead, modified versions of existing laws for land warfare were applied to aerial combat.

In 1911 during the Italo-Turkish War, the Italians conducted aerial reconnaissance operations. During one mission, aerial bombardment with four bombs was attempted. By some accounts, the bombs landed on the Ain Zara hospital. While the Italians denied the charges, the Ain Zara affair initiated the first major debate on the morality of aerial bombardment.

Controversy over the legitimacy of aerial bombardment continued until 1922. The Commission of Jurists met at The Hague from December 1922 through February 1923 and issued a code of aerial warfare, subsequently known as the Hague Draft Rules. The Rules contained 62 articles; five pertained to aerial bombardment, which was considered legitimate only for military purposes against military targets.

Maturation of Strategic Bombardment: World War II

Strategic bombardment came of age in World War II. From the early attacks by Germany on Poland, to the employment of atomic weapons by the United States, strategic bombardment evolved toward the full capabilities foreseen by the early theorists.

The Luftwaffe entered World War II much better trained and equipped for tactical operations, but nonetheless initiated strategic bombardment early in the war. After failing to obtain Warsaw's early submission, Germany started air bombardment of "military targets" within the city on 13 September 1939. About 5,000 tons of bombs had been dropped when Warsaw surrendered on 29 September.

Likewise, Germany began strategic bombardment in 1940 after its ground forces had already made significant gains in their advance to the West. Rotterdam was attacked, and Operation Paula destroyed airfields and factories and took about 250 lives in and around Paris. Material damage was less important than the psychological intimidation that resulted.

Germany's strategic bombing of Great Britain later in 1940 had only limited success due to Royal Air Force (RAF) defensive capabilities. Daylight bombing during the Battle of Britain was aborted due to heavy losses. The Luftwaffe turned to night bombing raids, which it could not execute with any degree of precision. A raid on 24 August inadvertently dropped bombs on London. Retaliatory raids by the RAF against Berlin and other German cities escalated aerial bombardment to attacks against major population centers. "Blitz" bombing against Great Britain continued through May 1941, but Germany failed either to destroy the RAF or to demoralize the British population.

Britain was initially reluctant to start a strategic campaign on German industries and cities, limiting its early efforts to peripheral, harassing operations. However, the RAF steadily increased its strategic bombing efforts. The British quickly learned that the bomber could not defend itself against fighter attacks during daylight bombing and moved to night attacks by the end of 1940.

Night attacks created as well as solved problems, however. Bombers could strike distant targets, such as Berlin, only in the winter because of the short summer nights, and the accuracy of night bombing, which was initially dependent only on eyesight, produced poor bombing results even under the best conditions. For a time, night raids were abandoned.

In early 1942, the RAF once again began nighttime

raids, shifting targeting from individual installations to entire urban and industrial complexes. The Bomber Command continued to improve its tactics and equipment. Electronic navigation aids and airborne radar helped locate targets. Incendiary weapons increased damage and improved overall accuracy because trailing aircraft in bomber streams could follow the more experienced "pathfinder" crews, and simply bomb the fires. Heavy four-engine bombers came into service: Halifax, Stirling, and Lancaster. Bomber Command mounted thousand-plane raids against Cologne, Bremen, and Hamburg, causing widespread devastation.

In the mid-1930s, the Soviet Union had the largest bomber force in the world, but their lack of speed made those aircraft obsolete at the outbreak of war. The United States started development of several heavy strategic bombers in the 1930s. When war broke out in 1939, the B-17 was approaching operational capability, and the B-24 was approaching test flight. By the end of 1941, design work for the B-29 was complete.

The U.S. Army Air Forces entered the European War in June 1942 with firm views regarding the validity of daylight precision bombing, a doctrine developed in its tactical school. On early daylight attacks, U.S. B-17s undertook precision strikes against targets such as railways, factories, and submarine pens at moderate ranges and often within the cover of friendly fighter aircraft. B-17s flying tight formations for mutual support (see Fig. 1) were capable of fending off the limited attacks of fighters, but bombing accuracy suffered and losses increased under more intense battle conditions. Only 20 percent of the bombs aimed at precision targets hit within the target area.

Bombing accuracy eventually improved to 70 percent and defensive tactics continued to be modified. Nonetheless, raids on Schweinfurt in 1943 showed the vulnerability of daylight bombing formations. In August, 36 of 183 B-17s attacking Schweinfurt were lost. A subsequent raid lost 60 of 229, with an additional 138 damaged. These were losses that could not be sustained. Unescorted daylight bombing was halted. In 1944 the long-range P-51 Mustang proved decisive in restoring bomber penetration capability. P-51s could provide support all the way to and from the primary strategic targets.

Figure 1. U.S. Army Air Forces B-17s forming up for mutual protection. (SOURCE: U.S. National Air and Space Museum)

Assessing the results of the combined bomber offensive is complicated. Almost half the effort was devoted to tactical support (especially the Normandy invasion), and not all target categories proved lucrative. For example, attacks on aircraft plants did not significantly reduce aircraft production. Targeting ball bearing production was potentially significant, but was not pursued extensively because of heavy losses. The electric power system was also potentially significant, but received little emphasis. On the other hand, strikes against synthetic fuels production and rail transport proved significant by late 1944, and had essentially immobilized the German military in early 1945. When considering the direct results of the offensive, plus the diversion of resources for air defense, aerial bombardment was a major, perhaps decisive, part of the Allied victory.

The bomber offensive against Japan was almost entirely an American effort. Weather conditions over Japan limited the effectiveness of B-29s using the precision bombardment tactics employed in the European theater because targets were often cloud-covered and the extreme winds at high altitude often blew the bombs away from the aim points. This caused a change in targets, tactics, and ordnance. Incendiary raids at much lower altitudes struck urban complexes rather than individual installations. The Tokyo raid of March 1945 was the most destructive air attack ever carried out, including even the atomic strikes against Hiroshima and Nagasaki. Incendiary strikes continued, with all Japanese cities (except Kyoto for historical reasons) targeted for destruction. Given estimates that an invasion would entail 1 million Allied casualties, President Truman decided to employ atomic weapons to hasten Japanese surrender. On 6 August 1945 the *Enola Gay* dropped an atomic bomb on Hiroshima; a second bomb followed on 9 August, against Nagasaki. Japan soon surrendered.

Strategic Bombardment After 1945

The United States emerged from World War II as the sole possessor of atomic weapons, which promised a massive strategic capability from a relatively small bomber force. Accordingly, the United States began a significant buildup centered on its Strategic Air Command. With worldwide operational requirements, the USAF also began integrating aerial refueling into its operational repertoire.

The Korean War. The Korean War presented problems for U.S. airpower. The B-29 was the only conventionally capable heavy bomber initially available; however, the crews were not fully proficient in tactical operations. Use of nuclear or incendiary weapons was ruled out for political reasons, and frequent changes in targeting also served to limit effectiveness in early operations. Eventually the B-29s were assigned a limited strategic role against four North Korean industrial centers. The entire set of targets was quickly destroyed, and the B-29 returned to tactical operations.

Following the Korean War, both superpowers continued to develop their nuclear forces with strategic nuclear-capable aircraft. The Soviets developed the Badger, Bison, and Bear. U.S. bombers were the B-36, B-47 Stratojet, and B-52 Stratofortress. The British fielded the V-bombers: Valiant, Victor, and Vulcan. With the advent of ballistic missiles, next-generation bombers were cancelled or limited in production, including the U.S. B-70, Soviet Bounder, and British TSR.2.

The Vietnam conflict. The B-52 was used primarily as a tactical asset in the Vietnam conflict. Strategic targets in North Vietnam were initially struck by tactical fighters. In 1972, however, B-52s undertook strategic missions during the "Linebacker" campaigns. Linebacker I involved 84 strategic missions over North Vietnam. When the Paris peace talks appeared to be leading to an agreement, Linebacker I was halted. On 13 December 1972 the North Vietnamese delegation broke off negotiations. An eleven-day bombing campaign, Linebacker II, began on 18 December.

The first phase was a three-day maximum effort against rail yards, power plants, communication facilities, air defense radars, docks at Haiphong, oil storage, and ammunition supply areas. There were initial bomber losses, largely due to poor planning and tactics, but with improved mission planning, the raids on 22 December resulted in no B-52 losses. Operations ended on 29 December after 729 B-52 sorties had been flown, with fifteen aircraft lost and nine damaged. Linebacker destroyed over 80 percent of North Vietnam's electrical power and 25 percent of its petroleum, oil, and lubricants. It also brought the North Vietnamese back to the negotiating table.

Strategic bombardment forces entering the 1990s. There was renewed interest in strategic bombardment capabilities in the 1980s following an extended period of apparent de-emphasis in favor of ballistic missiles. France programmed the Mirage 2000N to replace the aging Mirage IV. The United States upgraded B-52s to carry cruise missiles, deployed the B-1B, and developed the B-2. The Soviet Union upgraded older Bear aircraft to the Bear G configuration (AS-4 cruise missile carriage), produced a new Bear variant, the Bear H (an AS-15 carrier—Fig. 2), and also began developing the Blackjack.

In addition, the Soviet Union continued to modernize its large contingent of bombers allocated to theater operations. Soviet strategic and naval aviation arms received new Fencers and Backfires. The United States likewise showed increased interest in theater operations for its bombers. The B-52 force significantly increased emphasis on conventional operations. FB-111s were programmed to transfer from the Strategic Air Command to the tactical air forces.

Figure 2. Soviet Bear-H cruise missile carrier. (SOURCE: U.S. Dept. of Defense)

The Falklands/Malvinas campaign of 1982 demonstrated the continued importance of long-range bombardment, and the revolutionary developments in weapons and tactics underway. Using Vulcan bombers carrying twenty-one 1,000-pound gravity bombs, the RAF tried five times to destroy the Port Stanley Airfield, without success. Combat operations around the islands demonstrated the new lethality of air defense weapons (such as new Sidewinder models), which was partially offset by precision-guided stand-off weapons (Exocet). These developments will continue to influence bomber operations in the future.

The strategic air offensive during the 1991 Persian Gulf War had as its objective the strategic paralysis of the Iraqi military machine. The plan employed three phases: strategic attack, attacks to suppress air defenses, and attacks against the Iraqi army. These phases overlapped considerably during the actual execution of the campaign. The strategic plan aimed at disrupting command and control and degrading or destroying electric power generation, the transportation network, refined fuel and lubricants production, and the Iraqi air force. The American portion of the allied air campaign consisted of 44,145 combat sorties and 84,200 tons of bombs dropped (of which 7,400 tons were "smart" munitions). The Gulf conflict provided a clear indication of the greater precision and destructiveness of modern air attack. In World War II, American bombers dropped 185,841 tons of bombs during 50,000 sorties against 69 refineries (an average of nearly 2,700 tons of bombs per refinery), reducing production by 60 percent. Of the total bomb tonnage, only 15 percent—an average of 404 tons per refinery—actually hit within the target area. In contrast, in the Gulf War, strike aircraft flying slightly more than 500 sorties dropped 1,200 tons of bombs on 28 Iraqi refineries (an average of 43 tons per refinery), effectively terminating production. Thus for less than one-half the tonnage dropped on a single German refinery during World War II, allied aircraft destroyed all 28 of the Iraqi refineries targeted for attack.

Future of Strategic Bombardment

The future politico-military environment will very likely increase the importance of strategic bombardment, and increase obstacles and threats to bomber effectiveness. Imposing constraints on flight routing, basing, and overflight restrictions by third-party countries will increase the importance of long-range aviation. The global arms trade will complicate the task of penetrating more sophisticated air defenses. Intelligence data on enemy systems will no longer be sufficient; knowledge of systems made in allied and neutral nations will also be needed to ensure mission success. Low observables (LO, or "stealth" systems) will be the norm for future aircraft and weapons, to help avoid increasingly capable air defense systems.

Given the generally unsatisfactory results from long-term commitments to low-level conflicts (e.g., Afghanistan, Angola, and Vietnam), short-term military operations will be more attractive to the superpowers. Brief commitments of overwhelming force (e.g., Grenada in 1983) or prompt reactions (e.g., Libya in 1986) will become more attractive military options. Accordingly, the bomber's long range and quick response will remain important to military planners. These characteristics were demonstrated duirng the 1991 Gulf War. B-52G bombers flew from bases in the continental United States, Great Britain, Spain, and the Middle East, dropping 25,700 tons of munitions during 1,624 sorties.

Arms reductions efforts will continue, with probable emphasis on ballistic missile reductions to diminish first-strike threats. Heavy bombers equipped with gravity bombs and short-range missiles will likely continue to receive favorable treatment in arms control agreements. With the number of weapons constrained, the manned bomber's ability to perform damage assessment and selective strikes will be especially important to maximize force effectiveness in an arms control regime.

Space-based assets will enhance intelligence support for aircrews. Satellite navigation aids, such as the U.S. Global Positioning System and Russian Glonass, will assist in precise application of force, lessening collateral damage and dependence on mapping data.

Adapting Current Aircraft and Weapons to Future Missions

In the future, long-range bomber systems will undergo major changes in equipment, weapons, and missions—as they have in the past. RAF Victors and Russian Bisons have been converted to aerial tankers. The U.S. B-52 was converted from high-altitude to low-altitude penetration in the 1960s, and to cruise missile carriage in the 1980s. The B-52's large size and payload volume have permitted a number of subsystem modifications and mission changes. Countermeasure improvements have helped overcome the large radar cross-section (RCS) inherent in its design. If current bombers such as the B-1, B-2, and Blackjack adapt as successfully as the B-52, they could still be in service in 2020.

Bomber subsystem modifications and roles will reflect operational requirements and changes in the threat environment. Roles will also change with technological opportunity and deployment of new systems. Changes in U.S. bomber forces are illustrative. With the B-1B assuming the primary penetrating role for the United States in the late 1980s, the B-52 was converted to stand-off cruise missile carriage. Selected B-52Gs were also allocated to conventional theater missions.

The B-1B utilizes a combination of electronic countermeasures (ECM), reduced RCS, plus low-altitude, high-speed tactics to penetrate enemy defenses. The B-1B's ECM suite is the first defensive system designed to be totally integrated. If the B-2 assumes the primary penetration role in the 1990s, B-1B cruise missile carriage becomes an option.

The B-2 design incorporates an extensive array of stealth technologies. Relying on low observable (LO) technology to evade detection, the B-2 can penetrate defenses without resorting to low-altitude, high-speed tactics. Even if detected by early warning or search radar, reduced signatures limit missile and interceptor engagement capabilities. The B-2 with suitable sensors is also very useful for locating and attacking mobile targets.

Short-range missiles—used for attacking heavily defended targets and defense suppression—will continue to improve. Earlier versions include the U.S. Air Force (USAF) Hound Dog and RAF Blue Steel. The USAF SRAM-A (AGM-69) and French ASMP are currently in service. The SRAM-A replacement, SRAM-II, is smaller, but has improved range and offers better employment options. New generation short-range missiles will be particularly useful against mobile targets. In particular, increased range affords more time for aircrew decisions on weapons allocations against suspected targets.

Air-launched cruise missiles (ALCMs) will further enhance bomber versatility. Penetrating bombers employed in conjunction with stand-off ALCMs will greatly complicate air defense problems and inhibit development of defenses tailored to a single threat. The U.S. advanced cruise missile (ACM) incorporates stealth technology plus longer range—making interception after launch very difficult and lessening carrier aircraft exposure to forward-deployed air defenses.

Conventional stand-off munitions—such as the U.S. Tacit Rainbow for defense suppression, and Harpoon

(U.S.) and Exocet (French) for antishipping strikes—are available worldwide in large numbers. Terminal guidance and propulsion have also been added to old-fashioned "iron bombs" to increase their effectiveness (e.g., the U.S. GBU-15 and AGM-130). A number of long-range precision-guided munitions (such as the NATO modular stand-off weapon) are in various stages of development. New generations of munitions will probably end those perceptions that associate strategic bombardment with nuclear weapons, and make limited strategic bombardment with stand-off conventional munitions a feasible option for the foreseeable future.

The Tactics Challenge

As Gen. Henry H. ("Hap") Arnold (commanding general of U.S. Army air forces in World War II) stated: "Any Air Force that does not keep its doctrine ahead of its equipment, and visions far into the future, can only delude the nation into a false sense of security." Keeping doctrine and tactics from falling behind equipment is especially challenging when new technology is incorporated into new systems. Security compartmentalization further serves to limit knowledge of new capabilities, and may slow the development of new tactics.

Recent advances in intelligence collection and data processing will enable aircrews to know more about the current threat, plan more effective missions, and respond to threat changes. Intelligence data relayed directly to a bomber in flight expands the crew's situational awareness and enhances their ability to survive. Such data can be used to perform on-board mission replanning and to reroute bombers for maximum effectiveness. Detailed knowledge of target characteristics will also enable a small number of precision guided weapons to destroy the target while limiting damage elsewhere.

The balance between bomber low observables and air defense capabilities determines the altitude at which bomber operations can be conducted, which in turn influences weapons delivery options. Stealth technology may permit operations at the high altitudes of the 1950s, but advanced sensors and weapons may once again make high-flying aircraft vulnerable. Tactics would then change to reflect systems capabilities and vulnerabilities, just as surface-to-air missiles and improved interceptors forced bombers lower in the 1960s.

Similarly, bomber-bomber and bomber-fighter escort tactics will probably reappear in operational concepts. Possibilities also include greater emphasis on mutual bomber support through combined ECM or active defense suppression and combined bomber-fighter operations.

Future Aircraft and Tactics

Several major issues will confront strategists and designers in the future. The question of whether to procure a penetrating bomber or a stand-off weapons carrier will be a perennial issue. In addition to stealth technologies, automation of crew functions and hypersonic technology will influence the design of future bombers. Weapon guidance and warheads will undergo similar revolutions.

Whether bombers should penetrate, or launch stand-off weapons, or do some of both, will probably continue as a major doctrinal and system design issue. This could be important, for example, during modifications to the U.S. B-2, and development of any new bomber. In 1977, the B-1A was canceled because of lower estimated cost to deliver stand-off cruise missiles from existing B-52s instead of procuring a new penetrator. The B-1B program of the 1980s reflected a reassessment of the value of a modern manned penetrator.

Penetration at high altitude may be possible through a combination of stealth, advanced ECM, and lethal defenses (such as on-board lasers) against enemy missiles. Deployed from high altitude, glide weapons could effectively strike targets a significant distance away. Glide weapons have a number of advantages. When combined with a data link, a crew member can direct the weapon precisely to the target, reducing guidance system complexity and eliminating the need for a propulsion subsystem. Glide weapons are therefore cheap and simple and can be carried in large numbers.

Automation

As of the early 1990s, manned systems are the most flexible in dealing with the unexpected. Advances in data automation and artificial intelligence, however, are increasing autonomous systems' capabilities to deal with unplanned events. If current trends in avionics continue, future bombers will certainly have smaller aircrews.

A single crew member can probably manage a future bomber, if supported by an artificially intelligent associate (in effect, an automated flight engineer) to perform routine tasks. With greater experience in the artificial intelligence field, unmanned variants of future bombers may be developed for special missions. To be affordable in large numbers, however, future bombers must incorporate revolutionary design approaches, such as the modular avionics being developed for the U.S. advanced tactical fighter and advanced tactical aircraft. Future avionics systems will probably be linked to battle management centers to permit near real-time situation updates.

Stealth and Hypersonics

In the more distant future, hypersonic bombers may come into service. Stealth may give way to hypersonics as the key technology in future bomber designs. The trade-off between stealth and hypersonics will be a major design issue. Hypersonic flight promises speed and prompt delivery of ordnance. Advances in stealth technology can also be expected, making it likely that the next generation bomber will incorporate stealth technology and also have hypersonic capability.

A follow-on family of aircraft may result, some cruising within the atmosphere at Mach 8 to 15 and at an altitude of 30 to 100 kilometers (19–62 mi.). High speed will enable global response in under two hours. The system could be designed to maintain ground alert as current bombers do, and during a crisis, additional aircraft could be readied.

FUTURE WEAPONS

As Norman Augustine, American aerospace executive, put it, "Clearly, the solution is not to be found in delivering more ordnance. The leverage is in finding and hitting the target." Continued upgrade from "dumb" to "smart" to "brilliant" weapons is a trend that will continue, and probably accelerate. Autonomous "fire-and-forget" systems incorporating target recognition and possible dual-mode sensors will be fielded. Advanced stand-off weapons will enhance the survivability of the carrier aircraft and reduce the number of sorties required. Although the cost per weapon will increase, the overall cost per kill will, in fact, decrease.

Major upgrades to enable bombers to carry cruise missiles will continue. Low observables and improved terrain-following/obstacle avoidance will counter advanced defenses. Reduction in mission planning time, terminal sensors, and improved navigation systems will increase cruise missile flexibility and effectiveness. "Exotic" warheads such as fuel-air, high-power microwave (HPM), laser, reactive fragments, and electromagnetic pulse (EMP) may be used to attack dispersed targets.

Future cruise missiles may also be employed as decoys and pathfinders. Decoys are designed to look like bombers and to divert attention from the bombers and dilute air defense capabilities. The USAF ADM-20 Quail, in service during the 1960s and 1970s, used radar reflectors to masquerade as a B-52. A pathfinder cruise missile would serve as a scout for the trailing manned bomber and warn against unforeseen enemy defenses. The bomber may even act as a fusion center, taking information from several pathfinders, in order to search large areas for mobile targets, and to avoid or suppress air defenses.

Finally, lethal bomber defenses will be feasible against both missiles and aircraft. Air defense forces will no longer be able to operate freely against attacking bombers. Bombers may once again become their own escorts and directly engage air defenses (as in British and American doctrine before World War II). In any event the future role of manned bombers will depend on innovative developments in both technology and tactics.

THOMAS D. PHILLIPS
WILLIAM G. KULLER
RAYMOND E. FRANCK, JR.
MICHAEL J. KAISER
JEFFREY A. NEAL

SEE ALSO: Aerial Refueling; Airpower; Airpower, Strategic; Aviation, Military; Douhet, Giulio; Hague Conventions; Missile, Air-launched Cruise; Missile, Cruise; Trenchard, Sir Hugh Montague.

Bibliography

Cross, R. 1987. *The bombers.* New York: Macmillan.
Emme, E. M. 1959. *The Impact of air power.* Princeton, N.J.: Van Nostrand.
Kennett, L. B. 1982. *A history of strategic bombardment.* New York: Scribner's.
Knight, M. 1989. *Strategic offensive air operations.* London: Brassey's.
Murphy, P. J. 1984. *The Soviet air forces.* Jefferson, N.C.: McFarland.
Saundby, R. 1961. *Air bombardment—The story of its development.* New York, Harper and Bros.
U.S. Department of Air Force. 1991. *Reaching globally, reaching powerfully: The United States Air Force in the Gulf War.* Washington, D.C.: Government Printing Office.

BORDER GUARD

A state's sovereignty begins at its borders, and is that state's duty to protect. Such boundaries are formed by natural frontiers (seas, oceans, rivers, deserts, mountains), obstacles that can only be overcome with difficulty, or by politically designated lines that are mutually recognized and respected by the adjacent states. It is the duty of the border guards to control their nation's borders.

INCREASING COMPLEXITY OF BORDERS

For centuries, the defense of a nation's borders was a clear-cut endeavor. However, with the advent of airpower and the reconsideration of the maritime jurisdiction of coastal nations in the twentieth century, a nation's borders now not only encompass its land and river boundaries and sea coasts, but they also encompass parts of the adjacent seas, the airspace over the nation, and the airports in its jurisdiction. Today, the jurisdiction of nations partially or completely surrounded by the world's seas or oceans usually does not cease at the shoreline. Rather, under the determinations of the Law of the Sea, a nation's sovereignty may extend several miles outward from the coast, requiring unique methods of control and security. The dispute between the United Kingdom and Iceland (the Cod War), territorial disputes between Greece and Turkey over jurisdiction in the Aegean Sea, the seizure of fishing boats by Latin American nations, Soviet sensitivity to foreign naval intrusions into the Black Sea, and the greater responsibilities that have fallen on the U.S. Coast Guard with the extension of U.S. territorial jurisdiction all reflect the increasing complexity of a nation's responsibilities along its coasts.

Likewise, the need to protect a state from aerial attacks is still not adequately defined under international law. This is especially true when trying to determine national borders in airspace, which in turn determines that country's jurisdiction. Outer space is currently considered international territory.

Duties of Border Guards

As the protectors of a nation's frontiers, border guards carry out the state's policy of enforcing national jurisdiction. The principal, but not sole, object of control along a border is to safeguard a nation's territory from hostile incursions. (Fig. 1). Such threats may come from organized armies that attack across borders in a traditional offensive, such as Iraq's offensive against Kuwait in 1990, or they may be waged by insurgent groups that launch forays into a nation from sanctuaries in an adjacent nation. Palestinian intrusions into Israeli-occupied territory and insurgent operations into El Salvador from Nicaragua are examples of such an unconventional threat, and in the broadest sense, combating it is related largely to police security measures.

Aside from security and military considerations, economic policies may dictate the assignment of inspection duties to a nation's border guards. Each nation's economic policy is designed to compensate for international economic disparities through customs control, which requires a legion of customs inspectors, guards, and accountants at borders and airports. In addition, with the upsurge in drug smuggling and terrorism, border guards must provide added security.

Figure 1. A Jordanian border guard patrols the mountains near the border with Israel. (SOURCE: U.S. Library of Congress)

A nation's immigration policies may also place requirements on its border guards. The stream of Latin Americans into the United States, the movement of Germans from East to West Germany and Turks from Bulgaria to Turkey in 1989, and Kuwaitis into Jordan after the Iraqi invasion of 1990 are examples of mass movements of people from one nation to another. Border guards inevitably will have to carry out state policy—that is, to deny entry, if that is the national policy, or, if the nation's policy is to accept immigrants and refugees, to process and direct them to aid stations, shelters, and transportation networks.

This broad scope of duties often results in the assignment of responsibilities to different government departments or organizations consisting of border troops and militia, customs officials, and passport and police authorities. Sometimes several ministries—for example, interior, finance, and justice—might all have some jurisdiction in border matters.

Influence of a Nation's Political System

A nation's political system and strategic situation have a great influence on the type of border guard it operates. Democratic nations that perceive low threats will usually deploy low- to medium-security forces along their borders. These are considered adequate to accomplish run-of-the-mill security functions and can be augmented by additional personnel should a threat arise.

Totalitarian nations and nations with large, dissatisfied minorities, on the other hand, will, for two reasons, generally seek to establish greater control over their borders. The first is to control the national population, and a primary means of doing this is to restrict freedom of movement. Quite often, people within such a society cannot move about freely within the nation, let alone leave the confines of the nation. The second reason is a fear of external influence. Borders are closely protected to guard against infiltration and exfiltration, and border crossings are generally more heavily guarded in order to scrutinize noncitizens entering and leaving. In addition, such nations often wish to control their citizens' access to foreign information and will check closely the belongings of those entering. Here, decisions must be made concerning the entry of books, magazines, clothing such as blue jeans, money, and a host of other items that reflect the freedom of democratic nations or the opulence of more advanced societies. All this is time consuming and labor intensive, and also influences the demeanor of the border guards, who tend to be guarded and reserved, since the goals are to instill submission and force control. Perhaps the most famous of the border guards of totalitarian nations were the Soviet KGB border guards. Equipped with helicopters, light aircraft, ships, tanks, armored personnel carriers, and other modern weapons, they had their own schools. During World War II they participated in pitched combat; more recently, they were involved in action along the Sino-Soviet border. In 1983, it was estimated that there were 560,000 border guards and internal security, railroad, and construction troops in the Soviet Union.

Influence of the Strategic Situation

A nation's perception of a strategic threat also influences the type of border guard that is established. Along those borders where there is considerable tension, such as the demilitarized zone between North and South Korea, border guards are inadequate, and military forces are deployed to assure adequate security. On the other hand, border relationships can progress to the most friendly situations, such as those between the United States and Canada or among the Scandinavian nations, where border guard operations are very relaxed.

Control Methods

There is no uniform application of international border control. Many nations check individuals entering the nation more closely than those leaving. For example, when one leaves the Netherlands and enters Germany via the Dutch-German border, the checking is done by the Germans—there is no exit control by the Dutch—and vice versa. Likewise, there has been no border control between Belgium, the Netherlands, and Luxembourg for decades.

The border control between two friendly nations may be relaxed or even dropped. Before this point is reached, however, a mutual feeling of confidence must exist, and this is generally enhanced by a treaty. Border controls among the member nations of the European Community were gradually relaxed in the 1970s and 1980s, and their internal borders are scheduled to be totally abolished in 1992. The resulting unrestricted freedom of movement throughout much of Europe could complicate the detection and pursuit of criminals if new methods for checking pedestrian and automobile traffic are not introduced on the administrative borders. This requirement presents both technological and legal problems.

At times, border control is very strong in order to maintain complete control over one's population and to restrict border traffic. Before 1989, the Warsaw Pact nations were excellent examples of this type of control, and Albania still retains some of the older practices. Their borders, including the internal borders with other Warsaw Pact nations, were heavily guarded and established in such a way that it was practically impossible for a citizen to leave freely. Legal exit was dependent on approval.

Such practices, customary in totalitarian nations, are necessary because of the possibility that the stream of émigrés would swell considerably. This was the case in the German Democratic Republic (GDR) from shortly after World War II until 1961, a period when more than 3 million people left. Although this was illegal under East German law, it involved relatively little risk, since the borders between West Berlin and the Federal Republic of Germany were easily penetrated despite the high number of personnel employed for guard duty. This situation was altered in August 1961 by intensified border control (the so-called *Schiessbefehl,* or firing order) and the Berlin Wall. It remained so until the borders between East and West Germany were opened in December 1989.

Border Control by the United Nations

When there is tension between two nations, the rear areas of each nation's frontier district serve as military assembly areas, and these concentrations of troops near the border are likely to increase the chances of conflict. This occurred on the Sino-Soviet border when skirmishes broke out between the marshaled forces of both nations. The same applies to limited "police actions," such as the staging of Chinese troops in areas close to the Chinese-Vietnamese border.

An excellent way to prevent such conflict is to deploy UN forces composed of neutral military units for border control duties. UN forces have been stationed in five crisis regions, including the Syrian-Israeli and the Lebanese-Israeli borders. The UN Peace Corps, which was awarded the Nobel Peace Prize in 1988, constitutes the UN's most effective instrument when it comes to maintaining border security and will most certainly gain in importance in the future.

Electronic Border Control

In the age of satellites and electronic reconnaissance, the ability to control one's borders has improved considerably. Satellite photographs taken at regular intervals permit the comprehensive and continuous monitoring of military developments and other changes. The use of special aircraft—equipped with high-quality electronics apparatus and infrared detection gear that can accurately detect border infiltrations and can "listen" deep into other nations from their own airspace—is also a great advance.

Conclusions

Although border controls around the world were greatly relaxed in the 1980s, there are still many areas where the strategic threat is significant and the need for border guards is evident. Such guards will continue to mirror the character of their respective democratic or totalitarian governments. In addition, as further claims of the world's seas are made by coastal nations, and as air flight becomes more sophisticated, the problems confronting border guard forces will become more complex. Finally, the dissolution of border restrictions in Europe will bring about a major change in border guard operations, one that will require new methods of restricting the movements of the guilty while providing the greatest freedom for the just.

MANFRED OBST

SEE ALSO: Coast Defense; Gendarmerie; Intelligence: Indications and Warning; Internal Security Forces; National Guards: International Concepts; Peacemaking; Territorial Army; United Nations.

Bibliography

Federal Ministry of Defense. 1978. *"Die NVA," Heft 20 der Schriftenreihe Innere Fuehrung.* Bonn: Ministry of Defense.

Forster, T. M. 1983. *Die NVA.* Cologne: Markus Verlag.

Geibel, H., and J. Walter. 1971. *NVA—Sozialistische Armee des Friedens.* East Berlin: Verlag "Aus erster Hand."

Henrich, W. 1983. *Wehrdienst- und Grenzgesetz der DDR.* Bonn: Howacht Verlag.

Lapp, P. J. 1987. *Frontdienst im Frieden.* Munich: Bernard und Graefe.

Military encyclopaedia. 1973. East Berlin: Militaerverlag der DDR.

Nawrocki, J. 1979. *Bewaffnete Organe in der DDR: Nationale Volksarmee und andere militaerische und paramilitaerische Verbaende.* Berlin: Holzapfel.

Scott, H. F., and W. F. Scott. 1984. *The armed forces of the USSR.* 3d ed. Boulder, Colo.: Westview Press.

Shears, D. 1970. *Die haessliche Grenze.* Stuttgart: Seewald.

BOSNIA-HERCEGOVINA

Bosnia-Hercegovina, one of the republics in Yugoslavia (until recently a federation of six republics and two autonomous provinces), declared its independence from Yugoslavia on 29 February 1992 and was recognized in April 1992 as a sovereign state by many other governments. These actions led to heavy fighting as Serbian irregular troops and the Yugoslav army occupied almost two-thirds of the breakaway republic. For several more years, Bosnia-Hercegovina's relations with Yugoslavia and with the rest of the world are likely to continue to change often. Over time, new structures and patterns will emerge in economics, trade and commerce, politics and government, finance, manufacturing, religion, and virtually all aspects of human life. Bosnia-Hercegovina must develop new arrangements for dealing as a sovereign state with the Yugoslavian state (which is itself undergoing change) and with the world outside the boundaries of the former Yugoslavia. If recent history is any guide, change and perhaps even more strife can be expected.

A significant question for the world is how Slovenia and Yugoslavia will organize and provide for their separate security. The world can only hope these issues are settled amicably.

It will be years before the above issues are resolved for Bosnia-Hercegovina and some time before events settle into more routine and measurable patterns. No accurate description of this new country's policies, defense structure, and military forces was available for inclusion in this encyclopedia. Only time will reveal the future of Bosnia-Hercegovina as a separate sovereign state.

For more information the reader is referred to the historic information contained in the article on Yugoslavia and to the latest annual editions of *The Military Balance,* published by Brassey's (UK) for the International Institute for Strategic Studies; *The Statesman's Year-Book,* published by the Macmillan Press Ltd. and St. Martin's Press; and *The World Factbook,* developed by the U.S. Central Intelligence Agency and published commercially by Brassey's (US).

F. D. MARGIOTTA
Executive Editor

BRADLEY, OMAR NELSON [1893–1981]

General of the Army Omar Nelson Bradley (Fig. 1) was one of the most influential American military men of the twentieth century. His military career began when he entered the U.S. Military Academy at West Point in August 1911 and officially ended with his death at age 88 in 1981. Bradley was commissioned a second lieutenant upon graduation from West Point in 1915. He served in a variety of peacetime positions that ultimately prepared him for America's largest field command in history in World War II and subsequently the highest military position in the American defense establishment, the chairman of the Joint Chiefs of Staff.

Early Life and Civilian Career

Bradley was born to a family of limited economic means on 12 February 1893 near Clark, Missouri. As a boy, he excelled in school and became involved in hunting, fish-

Figure 1. Gen. Omar Bradley (left) with Under Secretary of Defense Stephen Early in 1950. (SOURCE: U.S. Library of Congress)

ing, trapping, and other outdoor pursuits, including such sports as football and baseball—interests that would remain with him for the rest of his life. When his mother moved the family to Moberly, Missouri, in 1908, Bradley met his future wife, Mary Quayle. It was also in Moberly where he applied for an appointment to West Point. To his great surprise, Bradley passed the entrance exams with excellent scores (surpassing those of the candidate endorsed by his congressman) and received the appointment. He subsequently entered West Point on 1 August 1911.

Bradley graduated with the class of 1915, later called the "class the stars fell on" for its large number of future general officers. Bradley's classmates included his fellow five-star general Dwight D. Eisenhower and the future four-star general James A. Van Fleet. He was actively involved in sports at West Point, where he played varsity baseball and football. He later wrote that his sports activities hurt his overall academic standing, but he never regretted them. Bradley graduated 44th out of 164 in June 1915 and began his active military career as a second lieutenant in the infantry.

Early Military Career

Bradley's military career after graduation was characterized by vain attempts to be assigned to a unit that was deploying to France. He later wrote that the period of American involvement in World War I was "professionally, the most frustrating of my early army career."

Bradley's career in the period between the two world wars was similar to that of many American officers. In the early 1920s he taught mathematics at West Point. That was a time of agonizingly slow promotions; Bradley was promoted to major in 1924 and remained a major for twelve years. It was at West Point that Bradley's only child, a daughter, was born. It was also during his West Point assignment that Bradley became interested in military history.

Following a school assignment at Fort Benning, Georgia, Bradley and his family traveled to their first overseas tour of duty at Schofield Barracks, Hawaii. He served with the 27th Infantry Regiment for three years before returning to the United States to attend the Command and General Staff College at Fort Leavenworth, Kansas. The year at Fort Leavenworth was followed by another assignment to Fort Benning, this time as an instructor. Bradley was later to call his decision to join the faculty at Fort Benning "the most fortunate decision of my life." It was here that Bradley first caught the eye of the future Chief of Staff of the United States Army, George Catlett Marshall. For the next twenty years Bradley was to serve intermittently with Marshall. Bradley spent four years under Marshall at Benning before he was selected to attend the Army War College in 1933. After his year at the War College, Bradley was again assigned to West Point, this time in the Department of Tactics. Bradley spent four years at West Point and profoundly influenced many of the Academy's outstanding graduates, including William C. Westmoreland and Creighton W. Abrams. Upon the completion of his second tour of duty at West Point, Bradley had spent thirteen years of his 23-year career as an instructor of some sort.

Bradley's final peacetime assignments were as assistant secretary to the General Staff and as commandant of the Infantry School at Fort Benning in February 1941. Bradley owed appointment to both of these important positions to Marshall. The commandant's job brought Bradley promotion to brigadier general. Soon after America's entry into World War II, Bradley was promoted to major general and briefly commanded first the 82d Infantry Division and then the 28th Infantry Division; he was the first man in his class to command a division.

World War II

Bradley's first wartime overseas assignment came early in 1943 when, on Marshall's advice, he was cast in the awkward role of Gen. Dwight D. Eisenhower's personal representative at the front in North Africa. It was as Eisenhower's "eyes in North Africa" that Bradley began his often stormy relationship with Gen. George S. Patton, Jr. Bradley was later elevated to assistant II Corps commander under Patton. He later assumed command of the II Corps and led it successfully until the end of the North African campaign. Promoted to lieutenant general, he also commanded the II Corps during the Sicilian campaign (10 July–17 August 1943).

In October 1943, largely as a result of Patton's much-publicized slapping of several soldiers under his command, Bradley was placed in command of the U.S. First Army, the American ground force for the Normandy invasion. (Bradley's command would ultimately consist of more than 1.3 million men.) Shortly after the "Overlord" landings on 6 June 1944 and immediately after the breakout of his First Army at St. Lô on 26 July, Bradley was named commander of the Twelfth Army Group.

As commander of the Twelfth Army Group, Bradley learned the harsh realities of modern coalition warfare when he experienced several disputes with Britain's Gen. (later Field Marshal) Bernard L. Montgomery. Montgomery and Bradley both opposed General Eisenhower's broad-front strategy approach, but Bradley wished to have the narrow thrust performed by his First or Third Army, while Montgomery wanted it for his British First Army. Both were overruled by Eisenhower. These disputes came to a head during the Battle of the Bulge (16 December 1944–mid-January 1945) when Montgomery claimed much of the credit, at the expense of the American troops, for the ultimate Allied victory.

Despite the setback in the Ardennes Forest, and despite Eisenhower's diversion of resources to Montgomery,

Bradley's forces beat their British counterparts in crossing the Rhine River. Bradley subsequently was promoted to full general (12 March 1945). He was indeed fortunate to have such outstanding subordinates as Patton and Gen. Courtney H. Hodges as army commanders. With those aggressive, offense-minded generals leading the way, Bradley's forces soon linked up with the Russians at the Elbe River in April 1945. By May the war was over. It was during the European campaigns that Bradley earned the nickname, "GI General," for his compassion for the common soldier.

Postwar

Immediately after the war Bradley became veterans administrator. Shortly thereafter, on 7 February 1948, Bradley succeeded Eisenhower as chief of staff of the U.S. Army. Finally, on 16 January 1949, he became the first chairman of the Joint Chiefs of Staff. He was promoted to five-star rank in September 1950. Bradley served in these high positions during some of the most trying days of the early cold war.

Although a five-star general cannot officially "retire," Bradley stepped down from active duty on 15 August 1953. He served in a variety of positions in private industry while still giving military guidance when called upon. Bradley died on 8 April 1981 at age 88. He is buried at Arlington National Cemetery.

SEE ALSO: Eisenhower, Dwight D.; Marshall, George Catlett, Jr.; Montgomery, Bernard Law; Patton, George Smith, Jr.; World War I; World War II.

KEVIN J. WEDDLE

Bibliography

Ambrose, S. 1970. *The supreme commander*. New York: Doubleday.

Bradley, O. 1951. *A soldier's story*. New York: Holt, Rinehart and Winston.

———, and C. Blair. 1983. *A general's life*. New York: Simon and Schuster.

Eisenhower, D. 1948. *Crusade in Europe*. New York: Doubleday.

Pogue, F. 1954. *The supreme command: U.S. Army in World War II*. Washington, D.C.: U.S. Dept. of the Army.

Whiting, C. 1971. *Bradley*. New York: Ballantine.

BRANCHES, MILITARY

The armed forces of most countries are organized into three elements: land (army), sea (navy), and air (air force). The size of these forces and their capabilities in different countries vary significantly and, in many cases, have, in addition to regular active duty units, a territorial or militia organization. A nation's armed forces have identifiable roles and missions to fulfill. Accordingly, various branches, specialties, and skills exist within each of the three elements.

The army provides the capability to conduct ground combat by organized, tactical units at the platoon, company, battalion (squadron), brigade (regiment), and division level. To conduct this mission, an army consists of traditional combat branches—infantry, artillery, and armor (cavalry)—and elite units such as the French Foreign Legion (La Légion Estrangère), British Special Air Services (SAS) regiment, Soviet Spetsnaz (Special Forces), and U.S. Army Rangers. Other branches—intelligence, engineers, signal, medical, and transportation—provide support to combat operations.

The navy's conception of its role is focused on warships and control of the seas, including mine warfare. In some countries (e.g., France, the former Soviet Union, the United Kingdom, and the United States), the navy also has a nuclear deterrence mission. Naval forces accomplish their mission with a mix of seaborne assets that may include surface ships, submarines, and ship-based aircraft.

The intraservice distinctions within a navy, with its various branches, components, or activities, may include carrier-based fighter aviation, submarine, and surface warfare specialties or ratings such as seaman, fireman, missile technician, radioman, or sonar technician. In the U.S. Navy, officers who are eligible to assume command of ships and stations are designated unrestricted line officers; other officers are with a staff corps or are specialists in various fields. (Staff corps includes: medical, supply, chaplain, civil engineer, judge advocate general's, dental, medical service, and nurse.)

The mission of the air force includes the different aspects of aerospace warfare—combat in manned aircraft to gain air superiority over the battlefield by attacking enemy air forces in the air and on the ground, destroying military ground targets, and providing close air support for land forces; strategic bombing; long-range intercontinental ballistic missiles; long-range transport; and space.

In the air force, pilots are quite separate from all others (e.g., flight crew members, ballistic missile officers, communication specialists) and distinguished among themselves by their particular flying skill (i.e., fighter, bomber, or transport).

Armed forces branch distinctions are a source of pride but also have an effect on promotion. In most countries, personnel in the traditional combat branches (army-infantry, artillery, armor [cavalry]; navy-line officer; air force-pilot) have an advantage in promotion to general and flag officer.

Whereas members of sea and air forces may be content to identify themselves by their service alone, members of the land forces, in particular officers, almost always append their branch specialty. For example, when a U.S. Army officer identifies himself as an engineer, he is saying much more about his background and qualifications than he is about his status in the army, since his branch is not one of the traditional combat arms.

In addition to pride, branches also establish a certain brotherhood among members. To a degree, significantly beyond that exhibited by navy and air forces, branches of the army generally acknowledge their interdependency and pay tribute to other army branches. While each branch in the army is proud of its unique skills and contribution, the essential artisans of war—infantry, artillery, and armor (cavalry)—realize that their ability to wage war effectively is dependent upon support from the other branches.

In many countries, the armed forces are powerful institutions. While composed of many ever-changing individuals, the land, sea, and air forces have distinct and enduring personalities, shaped over the years by varying experiences, that govern much of their behavior. These forces will face significant challenges in the years ahead, given the changes underway in the national security environment.

All armed forces make intra- and interservice distinctions between and within their organizations regarding branches, specialties, and skills. These distinctions are important not only for tradition and pride but also because they shape the behavior of the various armed forces, and their respective branches, in their approach to war.

James B. Motley

See Also: Airpower; Armor; Artillery; Cavalry; Combined Arms; Infantry; Land Warfare; Naval Forces; Naval Warfare; Navy; Organization, Air Force; Organization, Army; Organization, Naval; Reserve Components; Seapower; Space Warfare; Territorial Army.

Bibliography

Builder, C. H. 1989. *The masks of war.* Baltimore, Md.: Johns Hopkins Univ. Press.

International Institute for Strategic Studies. 1991. *The military balance 1991–1992.* London: Brassey's.

BRAUCHITSCH, WALTHER VON [1881–1948]

German Field Marshal Walther von Brauchitsch, the future commander-in-chief of the German army (ground forces), was born in Berlin on 4 October 1881. Like many of his now-famous contemporaries (Field Marshals Blomberg, Busch, and Goering) Walther von Brauchitsch graduated from the Hauptkadettenanstalt Gross-Lichterfelde in Berlin. Upon receiving his commission as a lieutenant on 22 March 1900, he was posted to the Third Guard Grenadier Regiment at Berlin-Charlottenburg. One year later, he requested a change in his combat arms' designation and was reassigned to the Third Guard Field Artillery Regiment. On 18 October 1909 he was promoted to the rank of first lieutenant, Field Artillery.

His capabilities in the assessment of situations during tactical exercises brought him to the attention of his superiors. This resulted in his appointment to the German Great General Staff on 18 December 1913, about the same time as his promotion to captain.

Assignment to the Great General Staff included attendance at the Imperial War Academy. The three-year curriculum concentrated primarily on tactics and military history, with secondary emphasis on staff procedures for tactical support. The first year's studies centered on regiment- and division-level operations, while the second year covered supply and special problems, again at the regimental and divisional levels. The third year emphasized military history, tactics and, more special problems, with additional concentration on terrain analysis and studies. The last year's studies, however, were approached from the level of army corps operations.

World War I

At the start of World War I, Brauchitsch was a General Staff officer with the XVI Army Corps at Metz. By 1915, he was posted to the 34th Infantry Regiment, then located in the Argonne Forest, as its General Staff officer. He distinguished himself at Verdun in August 1916 and was awarded the Knight's Cross of the Order of the House of Hohenzollern. This was the second highest award for military valor, surpassed only by the Ordre Pour le Mérite, commonly known as the Blue Max.

Brauchitsch's rapid rise in the Great General Staff was no small feat, given that the selection criteria for training and final appointment were high, and competition was keen. Only the best troop unit officers were appointed to the Great General Staff. There were other general staffs and staff schools in the German Imperial Army, such as the Bavarian, whose members in no way met the selection criteria for the Great General Staff.

At the close of World War I, Brauchitsch was a major on the General Staff of Army Group "German *Kronprinz*."

Interwar Years

In 1921, Brauchitsch returned to troop duty, and commanded the Second Detachment of the Sixth Artillery Regiment in Minden, Westphalia. On 1 July 1923, while at Minden, he was promoted to lieutenant colonel. In November 1927, he was reassigned to the Sixth Infantry Division as its chief of staff. He was selected for promotion to colonel on 1 April 1928, well ahead of his peers. With this promotion, Brauchitsch was posted to the Ministry of Defense as chief of the Army Training Branch. He served in this critical position until his promotion to brigadier general on 1 March 1932. At that time, he became inspector general of Artillery. Thus, he was already a general officer when Adolf Hitler assumed the Chancellorship of Germany.

Drastic changes in the Ministry of Defense, instituted by Hitler, resulted in Blomberg's appointment to the post of Defense Minister. This left vacant the position of commanding general, First Division, located in Koenigsberg, East Prussia. Brauchitsch was given command of the division and was also appointed commanding general of Wehrkreis Kommando I, also located in East Prussia. East Prussia was considered extremely vulnerable because it was separated from Germany proper by the Polish Corridor under the Treaty of Versailles.

Upon Hitler's repudiation of the Treaty of Versailles and the reinstitution of universal military conscription, Major General Brauchitsch was promoted to *general der artillerie* (lieutenant general) and was assigned to command I Army Corps (20 April 1936).

The continuing, rapid expansion of the armed forces did not allow him much time in this command. When the new Fourth Army Group was formed at Leipzig, Brauchitsch was posted there as its commander on 1 April 1937. Almost a year later, 4 March 1938, he was promoted to full general (*generaloberst*).

German troops under Brauchitsch's command entered Austria in March 1938, for the Auschluss. In October 1938, he led his troops in the occupation of the Sudetenland and in March 1939 entered Bohemia and Moravia. He was also responsible for the planning and execution of the army's tactical plan for the occupation of Poland (September 1939). For this, he was awarded the Knight's Cross of the Iron Cross.

World War II

Although Brauchitsch vigorously opposed "Case Yellow," the plan to attack France, he proceeded to build up the divisions required for this plan. Attempts to dissuade Hitler from the attack proved fruitless, and Case Yellow, which began on 10 May 1940, was executed successfully with speed and élan. The outstanding performance of the army earned him promotion to field marshal on 19 July 1940.

In the spring of 1940, German forces under Brauchitsch's operational command, concluded successful operations against Yugoslavia, Greece, and Crete. Upon completion of the Balkan Campaign, he received Directive 21 for Operation "Barbarossa," the German campaign against Russia. The operational planning was carried out under the direction of Gen. Franz Halder, chief of the Army General Staff.

By now, both Brauchitsch and Halder were seriously disillusioned with Hitler's methods. In particular, they were concerned about his approach to command and control as well as his allowing political motives to overshadow sound military considerations in the planning of operations.

The attack on the Soviet Union, which began on 22 June 1941, three months later than originally planned, bogged down by December 1941. Incredibly high casualties were inflicted on the army, which bore the brunt of the campaign. The stresses of the campaign became too much for Brauchitsch, already weakened by severe heart disease, and he requested permission to retire. His request was granted on 19 December 1941.

Shortly after this, the field marshal underwent heart surgery and lived in retirement for the remainder of the war. When World War II ended, he became a British prisoner, confined first in England and later in Munsterlager. He died of a heart attack while still a prisoner of war, on 18 October 1948.

Significance

Walther von Brauchitsch's military significance lies both in his rapid rise in rank and in his competence as a military strategist. By virtue of his talents and abilities, he rose to the rank of brigadier general during the turbulent years of the Weimar Republic before Hitler became chancellor. He later earned his marshal's baton on his own merits, and remained true to the ideals and concepts of the General Staff. Although he disagreed on occasion with Hitler, as was his right, he nevertheless performed his duty to his country and to its highest authority, the Führer. It could be argued that he should have been more forceful in the expression of his disagreements; on the other hand, had he been more forceful, he might have been relieved and thus have lost all influence. Under his leadership, the German army successfully executed all its operations from the prewar annexations of the Sudetenland, Austria, Bohemia, and Moravia, to the invasions of Scandinavia, the Low Countries, France, the Balkans, and Greece. The Russian Campaign, as conceived by Brauchitsch, was a sound tactical plan and could have progressed well had it not been for Hitler's meddling in operational matters. Considerable credit for these accomplishments, particularly the planning, goes to his chief of staff, Franz Halder. Walther von Brauchitsch was one of the last worthy examples of traditional and apolitical general officers produced by the German Great General Staff.

SZABOLCS M. DE GYÜRKY
CHERYL DE GYÜRKY

SEE ALSO: Germany; History, Modern Military.

Bibliography

Department of the Army. 1955. *The German campaign in Russia—Planning and operations (1940–1942)*. Department of the Army Pamphlet no. 20–261a. Washington, D.C.

The German general staff corps: A study of the organization of the German general staff. April 1946, produced at GMDS by a combined British, Canadian, and U.S. Staff.

Goerlitz, W. 1953. *History of the German general staff 1657–1945*. Trans. B. Battershaw. New York: Praeger.

Heuer, G. F., 1978. *Die Deutsche General-Feldmarschalle und Grossadmirale*. Rastatt/Baden, Federal Republic of Germany: Erich Pabel Publishers K. G.

Kennedy, R. W. 1956. *The German campaign in Poland (1939)*. Department of the Army Pamphlet no. 20–255. Washington D.C.: Department of the Army.

BRAZIL, FEDERATIVE REPUBLIC OF

Brazil has the most sophisticated and potentially the most powerful military in Latin America. Following 21 years of parsimonious military rule, civilian authorities are providing money for a period of expansion and modernization.

While Brazil faces no real foreign threat, its people (and government) are striving for great-power trappings and status. This can best be seen in a dramatic and largely successful campaign for strategic self-sufficiency and in long-term plans calling for a space program, full-cycle nuclear technology, a vastly expanded navy, and an enlarged, fully mobile army. Alone among democratic nations, the Brazilian government includes six ministries headed by active-duty military officers, including the Ministry of National Intelligence (SNI).

Brazil, with its large population, sophisticated industry, abundance of raw materials, and sagacious, long-range national and national security planning, is already the "Colossus of the South," while its expanding armaments industry has made a major impact in the international market.

Power Potential Statistics

Area: 8,511,965 square kilometers (3,286,470 sq. mi.)
Population: 153,071,400
Total Active Armed Forces: 296,700 (0.194% of pop.)
Gross Domestic Product: US$388 billion (1990 est.)
Annual Defense Expenditure: US$1.1 billion (2.6% of GDP, 1990 est.)
Iron and Steel Production:
  Crude steel: 25.017 million metric tons (1989)
  Pig iron: 24.381 million metric tons (1989)
Fuel Production:
  Coal: 21.368 million metric tons (1983)
  Crude oil: 30 million metric tons (1989)
  Natural gas: 5.844 million cubic meters (1988)
Electrical Power Output: 214,116 million kwh (1990)
Merchant Marine: 263 vessels; 5,898,838 gross registered tons
Civil Air Fleet: 176 major transport aircraft; 3,078 usable airfields (401 with permanent-surface runways); 2 with runways over 3,659 meters (12,000 ft.); 22 with runways 2,440–3,659 meters (8,000–12,000 ft.); 533 with runways 1,220–2,440 meters (4,000–8,000 ft.).

For the most recent information, the reader may refer to the following annual publications:

The Military Balance. International Institute for Strategic Studies. London: Brassey's (UK).

The Statesman's Year-Book. New York: St. Martin's Press.

The World Factbook. Central Intelligence Agency. Washington, D.C.: Brassey's (US).

History

From the time Brazil gained its independence from Portugal in 1822 until the mid-1840s, the Brazilian military was small, disorganized, and occupied with internal unrest. It lost a short, sharp conflict with Argentina during the Cisplatine War (1825–28), but Emperor Pedro II (1845–89) oversaw its professionalization and modernization. By the time Brazil entered the War of the Triple Alliance (1864–70) against Paraguay, the small Brazilian Army was a highly effective fighting force, fleshed out with volunteer regiments from the various states. Similarly, the navy was a competent, professional, and modern force, which utilized Brazilian-built ironclads to cut Paraguay off from contact with the outside world. Victory in the war greatly boosted the morale and prestige of the armed forces.

The previously apolitical armed forces overthrew Pedro II in 1889, and since that date have had an (usually low profile) influence in the political arena. Brazil was involved in World War I, and while its army did not see any action, naval units patrolled the Atlantic. This minor participation permitted Brazil a major voice in the postwar League of Nations.

In 1942, Dictator-President Getulio Vargas entered Brazil in World War II, partly because of American offers to upgrade and modernize the Brazilian military and to help create a national steel industry. Brazil's contribution was a fairly major one: it included sharing with the United States strategically located air and sea bases and facilities, provision to the Allied effort of strategic raw materials and foodstuffs, the Brazilian Navy patrolling the South Atlantic, and sending a Brazilian Expeditionary Force (FEB) to the Italian campaign where it performed well in combat from 1944–45.

Brazilian FEB veterans were to have an unusually strong role in both the military and political spheres for the next 30 years. Most important, they encouraged close relations with the United States, which resulted in joint military missions (e.g., Dominican intervention in 1965), training of Brazilian forces in the United States, the sale of U.S. arms to Brazil, and similar positions in international affairs (e.g., a strong anticommunist stance); they created the Superior War College (ESG) in 1948, which has been responsible for most of Brazil's long-term national and national security planning; and they developed the ideology of "developmentalism," which fomented the Revolution of 1964 that ousted a chaotic and ineffective civilian regime and encouraged the drive for self-sufficiency in all viable areas.

The five generals who ruled Brazil from 1964–85 were all intimately connected with the ESG—as were many high-ranking civilian technocrats in business and industry—and all supernationalists. Relations with the United States deteriorated in the 1970s over the issue of human rights and the refusal of the United States to provide Brazil with the full-cycle nuclear technology it sought. Since then, Brazil has been increasingly independent of American interests and policies, and, with a protracted "Economic Miracle" pointing the way to eventual self-sufficiency, the generals felt secure enough to permit a gradual phasing in of democracy, permitting the election of a civilian president, José Sarney, in 1985. In their years of national stewardship (1964–85), Brazil's booming economy propelled it into the ranks of other developed nations with the eighth largest GNP, yet military expenditures consistently shrank as a proportion of both the government budget and the GNP. Only since 1986, with civilian leadership, has the Brazilian military been allowed the luxury of planning both expansion and modernization, albeit on a relatively modest scale for a nation so large. Almost as if it were a parallel government, the ESG still wields enormous influence in the field of national security, which it defines in the broadest of terms.

Politico-Military Background

Until the military coup that ousted Pedro II in 1889, the Brazilian armed forces did not concern themselves with politics and did not question the constitutional authority of the emperor. Since that year (when they put the words "Ordem e Progresso," or "Order and Progress," on the Brazilian flag), the military has increasingly assumed a "supervisory" role in politics, always ready to influence or intervene when either order or progress is threatened; they have successfully inserted generals into the electoral process at two critical moments. They helped to elect Getulio Vargas into his first term as president (1930–45), and announced the end of his second term in 1954 (Vargas committed suicide rather than resign). In 1964, the military seized the government openly, holding it until 1985, when they willingly gave it back. Through the ESG, the military has imparted thoughtful nationalism and developmentalism to thousands of Brazilian officers and civilian technocrats—two generations of Brazilian military, political, and business leaders. The existence of six military ministries (Army, Navy, Aeronautics, chief of the Joint Staff, chief of the Military Household, and chief of the National Intelligence Service) and two quasi-military ministries (Science and Technology and Mines and Energy) ensures that military influence will pervade the Brazilian government. The ESG equation of nationalism with development permeates all levels of business and the bureaucracies, both military and civilian.

Politico-Military Policy

Brazil's politico-military policies are disarmingly simple and sweeping. In addition to defending the national borders (which touch French Guiana, Suriname, Guyana, Venezuela, Colombia, Peru, Bolivia, Paraguay, Argentina, and Uruguay), Brazil's military and political leaders seek to maintain an "ideological frontier," free of radical regimes. At various times in the past two decades Brazil has used military influence, military aid, arms sales and credits, and covert action to change the political course of neighboring states (e.g., moderating the left-wing regime in Suriname, helping Bolivian authorities hunt down "Che" Guevera, and aiding the Uruguayan government and military against the Tupamaru guerrillas). Also, the ESG-guided elite believe firmly that national security is synonymous with economic development, and it has consistently done everything in its power to stimulate the economy. In this area, self-sufficiency in arms production, coupled with arms exports, has been a singularly successful specific policy. Today, the Brazilian Army obtains almost 80 percent of its weapons from domestic manufacturers and the air force is approaching that figure, while the navy has plans to do the same. This, and other economic progress, permits Brazil a much wider scope of independence than other regional nations, and in fact allows Brazil a substantial voice in world affairs.

Strategic Problems

In the twentieth century Brazil has had essentially no strategic problems, and its neighbors are much smaller and weaker both militarily and economically. Further, rivalry with Argentina has not only diminished; the countries might soon form an alliance. Accords signed in 1987 pave the way for cooperation in the military sphere, in science and technology, nuclear energy, and manufacturing (coproduction of aircraft has begun). No nation threatens Brazil, and discontent within the country has been of minor significance since the urban guerrilla movement of the late 1960s. Not closely identified with any power bloc, and long at peace, Brazil has no enemies.

Defense Industry

In 1960 Brazil produced fewer weapons than it had in 1860, but today it is one of the top five or six exporters of military hardware, selling sophisticated rocket artillery systems to Iraq, aircraft to Britain, tanks to Saudi Arabia, armored fighting vehicles to Nigeria, and warships to Paraguay.

The spectacular growth of the Brazilian defense industry stems from the "export or die" policy following OPEC's escalation of oil prices, government tax and other incentives, a desire to be independent of the United States for weaponry, government research and development agencies sharing patents and research findings, and a burgeoning industrial base situated upon a cornucopia of strategic raw materials. Early successful performance of Brazilian weapons in Middle Eastern conflicts (including the Iran-Iraq War) boosted sales. Developing nations often buy Brazilian weapons not only because of price, but because Brazil is clearly a nonaligned nation; hence there are no strings attached to Brazilian weapons, and the buyer is not buying a piece of the cold war. This helps explain why

Brazil—which admittedly designs its weapons for developing world conditions: simple, rugged, easy to maintain, and inexpensive—is fast becoming the purveyor of arms to the developing nations.

Among the major Brazilian arms companies is Embraer (which is semiprivate), the world's sixth largest aircraft manufacturer (currently producing a dedicated jet attack craft, the AMX, with Italy). Also on its production lines are the well-known EMB-312 *Tucano* trainer (adopted by England, Egypt, Iraq, France, and a dozen other nations), the EMB-110 *Bandeirante* transport in various configurations, the EMB-120 *Brasilia* transport, and the CBA-123, being coproduced with Argentina's government-controlled arms corps. Also to be noted is Avibras (a private company), an important element of Brazil's space program, which produces a full line of bombs (including cluster bombs) and air-to-ground rockets, but also rocket artillery systems (the ASTROS-II) and specialized armored vehicles. The ASTROS-II has made a big dent in the Middle East, with Iraq and Libya acquiring perhaps a billion dollars worth of the systems in the 1980–88 period. Engesa, another private company, manufactures its own complete line of armored vehicles, most notably the EE-11 *Urutú* amphibious APC, the EE-9 *Cascavel* wheeled armored car with a 90mm main gun, the EE-3 *Jararacá* light scout car, the EE-T4 light tracked scout car, the EE-18 *Sucurí* wheeled tank destroyer with a 105mm gun, and the EE-T1 *Osorio* main battle tank, with a 120mm main gun. All have been exported in large numbers, and Engesa also markets a full line of military trucks, explosives, rockets, and electronic suites. Orbita, founded in 1986 by a number of companies, including Embraer and Engesa, is designed to be a major factor in the Brazilian space program, but already is manufacturing (in some cases in cooperation with Italy's Oto Melara or British Aerospace) sophisticated air-to-air missiles and antitank missiles, as well as defense-related electronics.

There are many other companies manufacturing arms: Bernardini makes tanks; Imbel makes explosives; Tupan produces mines, bombs, and pyrotechnics; Hydroar, flamethrowers; Verolme, warships; CBC, automatic weapons and munitions; CEV, mortars, grenades, and rockets; Rossi, light combat weapons; Siteltra, defense electronics; and some 240 more companies are engaged full- or part-time in defense production. Brazil is far down the road to self-sufficiency in armaments.

Alliances

Brazil has no defense treaties with any nation or bloc, but is a signatory of the Rio Pact for mutual defense against a nonhemispheric power. Also, it has recently signed a number of memoranda with Argentina that together may constitute an embryonic, informal "South Atlantic Treaty."

Defense Structure

Constitutionally, the president is supreme commander of the armed forces. As president, he can declare a state of siege or mobilization, and, if Congress is not in session, he can declare war. Beneath him is the advisory—but extremely important—National Security Council (CNS), of which he is chairperson. The CNS membership includes the six military ministers, the chief of the Civilian Household, chiefs of the three services, and selected military officers, totaling some 20 to 25. While not in the formal chain of command, the CNS is a broad-ranging policy board as well as a crisis management institution and is expected to formulate and execute national security policy, including establishment of "permanent national objectives and the bases for national policy." Strictly within the chain of command under the president is the armed forces' chief of staff (largely an honorary position because of the three service ministers) and the ministers of the army, navy, and aeronautics. Next come the heads of each of the three services and their general staffs.

Brazilian officers of advanced rank are superbly schooled, in the general as well as the technical sense. Each service has its military academy and command and general staff school; there is a naval war college and naval research institute, and the air force trains officers on the graduate level at its Aerospace Technical Center (CTA), one of the finest of its type in the world. Promising senior officers are selected for further education at the ESG, whose curriculum focuses on national security issues and world affairs. ESG graduates—military and civilian—are bonded together by the extremely influential organization of ESG graduates (ADESG), which, in essence, continues the educational process. Many generals and admirals serve (while on active duty) several years as presidents of important industries (usually state-run industries such as Petrobras, Embraer, or Imbel). Also, there are a variety of technical schools for noncommissioned officers of all services.

(For an explanation of the abbreviations and symbols used in the following section of military statistics, see the list of Abbreviations and Acronyms in each volume.)

Total Armed Forces

Active: 296,700 (128,500 conscripts). Terms of service: 12 months (can be extended by 6 months).
Reserves: Trained first-line 1,115,000; 400,000 subject to immediate recall. Second-line 225,000.

ARMY: 196,000; (126,500 conscripts).
HQ: 7 Military Comd, 12 Military Regions;
8 div (3 with Region HQ).
1 armd cav bde (2 mech, 1 armd, 1 arty bn).
3 armd inf bde (each 2 inf, 1 armd, 1 arty bn).
4 mech cav bde, (each 3 inf, 1 arty bn).
12 motor inf bde (26 bn).
1 mtn bde.
2 'jungle' bde (7 bn).
1 frontier bde (6 bn).

1 AB bde (3 AB, 1 SF bn).
2 coast and AD arty bde.
3 cav guard regt.
28 arty gp (4 SP, 6 med, 18 fd).
2 engr gp each 4 bn; 10 bn (incl 2 railway) (to be increased to 34 bn).
Avn: hel bde forming, to comprise 46 hel.
Equipment:
Light tanks: some 520, some 150 M-3, some 80 X-1A, 40 X-1A2 (M-3 mod); 250 M-41C.
Recce: 200 EE-9 Cascavel, 60 EE-3 Jararaca, 30 M-8.
APC: 795: 175 EE-11 Urutu, 20 M-59, 600 M-113.
Towed arty: 570: 105mm: 420 M-101/-102, Model 56 pack; 155mm: 150 M-114.
SP arty: 105mm: 120 M-7/-108.
Coast arty: some 240 57mm, 75mm, 120mm, 150mm, 152mm, 305mm.
MRL: 108mm: SS-06; 180mm: SS-40; 300mm: SS-60 incl SP; 4 ASTROS II.
Mortars: 81mm; 107mm: M-30; 120mm.
ATGW: 300 Cobra.
RCL: 57mm: 240 M-18A1; 75mm: 20; 105mm; 106mm: M-40A1.
AD guns: 20mm; 35mm: 38 GDF-001; 40mm: 60 L-60/-70.
SAM: 4 Roland II, BOFI AD system (40mm L/70 gun with RBS-70 SAM).
Helicopters: 36 SA-365 and 10 HB-350 to be delivered.

NAVY: 50,000 (2,000 conscripts) incl 700 naval air and 15,000 marines. 5 oceanic naval districts plus 1 riverine; 1 comd.
Bases: Ocean: Rio de Janeiro (HQ 1 Naval District), Salvador (HQ II District), Natal (HQ III District), Belém (HQ IV District), Rio Grande do Sul (HQ V District). Riverine: Ladario (HQ VI District), Manaus.
Submarines: 5:
1 Tupi (Ge T-209/1400) with 533mm TT (UK Tigerfish HWT).
3 Humaita (UK Oberon) with 533mm TT (Tigerfish HWT).
1 Goias/Bahia (US Guppy III/II) with 533mm TT.
Principal Surface Combatants: 18:
Carrier: 1 Minas Gerais (UK Colossus) CVS (ASW) (currently non-operational), capacity 20 ac: typically 7–8 S-2E ASW ac, 8 ASH-3H hel.
Destroyers: 6:
2 Marcilio Dias (US Gearing) ASW with 1 Wasp hel (Mk 46 LWT), 1×8 ASROC, 2×3 ASTT; plus 2×2 127mm guns.
4 Mato Grosso (US Sumner) ASW, 4 with 1 Wasp hel, all with 2×3 ASTT; plus 3×2 127mm guns.
Frigates: 11:
4 Para (US Garcia) with 1×8 ASROC, 2×3 ASTT, 1× hel; plus 2×127mm guns.
4 Niteroi ASW with 1 Lynx hel, 2×3 ASTT, Ikara SUGW, 1×2 ASW mor; plus 2×MM-40 Exocet SSM, 1×114mm gun.
2 Niteroi GP; weapons as ASW, except 4×MM-40 Exocet, 2×114mm guns, no Ikara.
1 Inhauma, with 1 Lynx hel, 2×3 ASTT, plus 4×MM-40 Exocet, 1×114mm gun.
Patrol and Coastal Combatants: 30:
9 Imperial Marinheiro PCO.
2 Graúna PCC.
6 Piratini (US PGM) PCI, 3 Aspirante Nascimento PCI (trg).
4 Tracker PCI (.
6 Riverine patrol.
Mine Warfare: 6: 6 Aratü (Ge Schütze) MSI.
Amphibious: 3: 2 Ceara (US Thomaston) LSD capacity 350 tps, 38 tk; 1 Duque de Caxais (US de Soto County LST), capacity 600 tps, 18 tk; plus 20 craft; 3 LCU, 3 LCM, 30 LCVP.
Support and Miscellaneous 20: 1 AOR, 1 repair ship, 1 submarine rescue, 4 tpt, 7 survey/oceanography, 1 mod Niterio FF (trg), 5 ocean tugs.

Naval Air Force: (700); 15 armed hel.
ASW: 1 hel sqn with 7 ASH-3A.
Attack: 1 with 8 Lynx HAS-21.
Utility: 2 sqn with 6 AS-332, 8 AS-350B, 10 AS-355.
Training: 1 hel sqn with 16 TH-57.
ASM: AS-11, AS-12, Sea Skua.

Marines: (15,000).
Fleet Force: 1 amph div (1 comd, 3 inf bn, 1 arty gp).
Reinforcement Comd: 5 bn incl 1 engr, 1 special ops.
Internal Security Force: 6 regional gp.
Equipment:
Recce: 6 EE-9 Mk IV Cascavel.
APC: 30 M-113, 12 LVTP-7A1.
Towed arty: 105mm: 12 M-101; 155mm: 6 M-114.
RL: 89mm: 3.5-in. M-20.
RCL: 106mm: M-40A1.
AD guns: 40mm: 6 L/70 with BOFI.

AIR FORCE: 50,700; 313 cbt ac, 8 armed hel.
AD Command: 1 Gp: Fighter: 2 sqn with 14 F-103E (Mirage IIIEBR), 4 F-103D (Mirage IIIDBR).
Tactical Command: 10 Gp:
FGA: 3 sqn with 49 F-5E, 4 -B, 4 -F, 21 AMX.
COIN: 3 sqn with 48 AT-26.
COIN/Trg: 30 T-27.
Recce: 2 sqn with 8 RC-95, 12 RT-26, 3 Learjet 35.
Liaison/Observation: 7 sqn: 1 ac with 8 T-27; 1 hel with 8 UH-1H (armed), 5 ac/hel with 31 U-7 ac and 30 UH-1H hel.
Maritime Command: 4 Gp.
ASW (afloat): 1 sqn with 11 S-2E.
MR/SAR: 3 sqn with 11 EMB-110B, 10 EMB-111.
Transport Command: 6 Gp (6 sqn), 7 regional indep sqn:
Heavy 2 sqn: 1 with 9 C-130E, 5 -H; 1 with 2 KC-130H, 4 KC-137 tkr/tpt.
Med/Lt: 2 sqn: 1 with 12 C-91; 1 with 23 C-95A/B/C.
Tactical: 1 sqn with 12 C-115.
VIP: 1 sqn with 1 VC-91, 10 VC/VU-93, 2 VC-96, 5 VC-97, 5 VU-9, ac; 3 VH-4 hel.
Regional: 7 sqn with 7 C-115, 82 C-95A/B/C, 6 EC-9 (VU-9).
Helicopters: 9 AS-332, 13 AS-355, 2 Bell 206, 6 SA-330, 30 SA-350, 6 SH-1H.
Liaison: 50 C-42, 3 Cessna 208, 30 U-42.
Training Command:
Aircraft: 50* AT-26, 70 EMB-110, 25 T-23, 98 T-25, 78* T-27.
Helicopters: 4 OH-6A, 25 OH-13.
Calibration: 1 unit with 2 C-95, 1 EC-93, 4 EC-95, 1 U-93.
AAM: AIM-9 Sidewinder, R-530.

FORCES ABROAD
UN and Peacekeeping:
Angola (UNAVEM II): 6 observers.
Central America (ONUCA): 21 observers.

PARAMILITARY
Public Security Forces (R): some 243,000 in state military police org (State Militias) under army control and considered an army reserve.

Space Forces

Brazil has no space forces yet, but its coherent, fast-paced space program promises to produce them. The Brazilian space program, born in 1961 with the launch of the first (of over 100) *Sonda I* research "sounding" rocket (made by Avibras), has been loosely overseen by the Ministry of Aeronautics. The Ministry—headed by an air force general—has created and directed two major government institutions, CTA and INPE (the National Institute for Space Research), and forged important links with private companies such as Avibras and Orbita.

CTA, in the small industrial city of São José dos Campos, in the state of São Paulo, employs 6,500 people (80% of them civilian, and mostly scientists and engineers) in five departments. One of these is the graduate training center, the Aeronautical Technical Institute, which educates space scientists; another is the Institute for Space Activities (IAE). The latter is responsible for designing space launch vehicles and creating launch sites. IAE and other research branches of CTA do no manufacturing themselves, but provide the designs to private industry for actual production, saving the latter the R&D expenses.

INPE, headquartered in the same city, specializes in space engineering and technology and such space applications as satellite imaging. Since 1980 over half of INPE's (classified) budget has been devoted to the complete Brazilian space plan, whose short-term goals (through 1993) include designing and building four satellites (for launches in 1989, 1991, and 1993), and designing aid for the launch vehicle and the satellite tracking system. The launch vehicle is a new generation of the various *Sonda* rockets, with four stages and using solid fuel to boost a 115-kilogram (250 lb.) satellite into a 750-kilometer (465-mi.) orbit. The satellites will be launched from near Alcantara, in Maranhão, where there already is a tracking station. A second tracking station is on the coast at Natal, and a third is being built inland at Cuiabá, in the state of Mato Grosso.

In 1987, the Aeronautics Ministry, through CTA (and perhaps the Ministry of Science and Technology), awarded CTA-developed technology to the Andrade Guttierrez Company (just outside São José dos Campos) to produce ammonium perchlorate, a vital oxidizer for solid fuels. The Brazilian company is now one of only six companies in the world producing the oxidizer, making Brazil self-sufficient and soon an exporter. In addition to the work Avibras has done generating the *Sonda* series and building a series of ground stations for the space program, Orbita is heavily involved as well, although details are lacking. Brazil plans to have a significant presence in space within fifteen years.

Future

The Brazilian military will continue to grow and modernize—increasingly with Brazilian-made armaments—until reaching a level consistent with what the politico-military leadership considers great-power status. This military strength, predicated on self-generating scientific and engineering talent, will make Brazil the dominant (if not actually "dominating") force in South America. This and the economic dynamism shown by Brazil might well result in something of a "Greater Southeast Atlantic Co-prosperity Sphere." Brazil's progress in space activities and its uranium-enrichment breakthrough in 1987 are more than mere matters of prestige for the nationalistic Brazilian people. They have a sense of destiny, and that destiny is to be accorded equality with the most powerful nations on earth. With what is noted above, and with Brazil's abundance of strategic raw materials and burgeoning industrial base, it can be assumed that destiny will be fulfilled.

John Hoyt Williams

See Also: Argentina; Bolivia; Colombia; Paraguay; Uruguay; Venezuela.

Bibliography

Adler, E. 1988. State institutions, ideology, and autonomous technological development: Computers and nuclear energy in Argentina and Brazil. *Latin American Research Review* vol. 23, 2: 59–90.

Brazil's space program remains dynamic despite fiscal woes. 1987. *Aviation Week and Space Technology* (August 24): 75–81.

Culkin, D. 1985. Per ardua as astra for Brazil's space giant. *Defense and Foreign Affairs* (April): 12–15.

English, A. J. 1985. *The armed forces of Latin America.* London: Brassey's.

Hopkins, J. W., ed. Annual. *Latin American and Caribbean contemporary record.* New York: Holmes and Meier.

Perry, W. 1986. Brazil: A local leviathan. In *Emerging powers: Defense and security in the third world,* eds. R. W. Jones and S. A. Hildreth. Washington, D. C.: Georgetown Univ. Press, pp. 307–42.

Williams, J. H. 1986. Brazilian weapons. *National Defense* 419: 53–57 and 420: 57–64.

BRIEFINGS

The object of military briefings and presentations is to establish and foster personal communication between commanders and their staffs, or between different staff sections. The purpose of a briefing is to save time by eliminating the need for a detailed study of the topic being discussed. Allowing questions and discussion both during and following the presentation provides further insights and clarification of the points presented.

Both a briefing and a presentation achieve the same purpose. The term *briefing,* however, is normally used when a small group is involved; a *presentation* implies a more formal setting with a larger group. Most briefings and presentations use visual aids (e.g., maps, transparencies, or slides) to illustrate the topic being discussed.

Briefings and presentations are intended to:

- Provide routine or specific information concerning current developments that may have an impact on decisions and plans
- Review a situation and present different courses of action
- Obtain a decision

Briefings and presentations are intended to save the commander time by presenting him with essential information on which to make a decision. They are normally given orally but on occasion a written brief may be used by the staff, often with flagged references to the original document and/or recommendation, to summarize a complex topic.

SEE ALSO: Directives, Orders, and Instructions.

Bibliography

U.S. Department of Defense, Joint Chiefs of Staff. 1987. *Department of Defense dictionary of military and associated terms.* Washington, D.C.: Government Printing Office.

BROOKE, ALAN FRANCIS (1st Viscount Alanbrooke) [1883–1963]

As chief of the Imperial General Staff (CIGS) December 1941–46, Lord Alanbrooke was commander in chief of Britain's military forces during much of World War II, and was Prime Minister Winston Churchill's key military adviser. In these positions, he played a vital role in developing Allied strategy. His daily diary, which he maintained during the war, has been an important source of historical information.

Early Years

Brooke was born in Bagueres de Bigorre, France, on 23 July 1883. His father, Sir Victor Brooke, was an Irish landowner who moved to France because of a lung infection. Brooke attended a French school but spent his summers in Ireland, where he developed his lifelong love of fishing and ornithology.

His family had a strong military tradition. An older brother had died in service in the First World War, and Churchill had served as assistant adjutant to another brother during the Boer War. Brooke entered the Royal Military Academy at Woolwich and graduated in 1902 with a commission in the Royal Artillery.

World War I and Interwar Years

Brooke began his active service as a subaltern, serving four years in Ireland before being transferred to India, where he remained until the outbreak of World War I. In September 1914 he debarked at Marseilles as captain in an Indian cavalry brigade. By the end of the war, he was chief artillery officer for the British First Army where he adapted the French system of creeping barrages to support and encourage attacking troops.

Between the wars, Brooke attended the Staff College at Camberly and became known as a skilled trainer. Later, he served as director of military training for the War Office, commanded the experimental mobile division, and was in charge of the Anti-Aircraft Command.

In appearance, Brooke was the very model of a British general, with a trim figure, a close-cropped mustache, and a stern military bearing. He was strong willed, highly disciplined, patient, and seemingly without nerves. Some felt his daily diary entries helped him get rid of some of the frustrations of his job. He was criticized by some as remote and aloof, an unsmiling man who expected efficiency and speed from subordinates. Yet, off duty he was relaxed, friendly, and mingled freely with troops of all ranks. His American counterpart, Gen. George C. Marshall, commented that Brooke was "determined in his position, yet amenable to negotiation, generous in his judgments, and delightful in his friendship."

World War II

At the outbreak of the war in 1939, Lieutenant General Brooke was given command of one of the two corps of the British Expeditionary Force (BEF) in France. A stickler for discipline and training, he was upset by the casual attitudes of senior French generals and by the seemingly low morale of their troops.

When the German armies struck through the Low Countries in May 1940, Brooke moved his corps north to reinforce the Belgian army. This began for Brooke what was to be only a nineteen-day campaign, which began to unravel with the sudden surrender of the Belgian army. As the overpowered BEF withdrew toward the English Channel and eventual evacuation, Brooke's corps was called upon to delay the German advance. Communication was difficult, and Brooke relied on daily personal visits to his division commanders to direct overall strategy and to improve morale. His best division commanders were Bernard Montgomery and Harold Alexander, and Brooke became their champion from that time on. To ensure his availability for later assignments, Brooke was ordered back to England on 29 May.

A few days after his return he was ordered to return to France and take command of the 150,000 British troops still with the French army. Once in France, and sensing the growing collapse all around him, Brooke urged that no more British troops be sent to the Continent and, later, received permission to evacuate the remnant of the BEF through Cherbourg. In July 1940, Brooke was given command of the British Home Forces and, with only fourteen weak divisions, he began to rearm, retrain, and reinspire the British army and to prepare defenses against the expected German invasion.

In December 1941, Brooke was appointed chief of the Imperial General Staff, succeeding Sir John Dill, and three months later was also asked to serve as chairman of the Chiefs of Staff Committee.

Once America entered the war, British planners led by Brooke dominated much of the early Anglo-American strategy sessions because of their firsthand experience fighting the Germans, and through superior staff work.

The Americans wanted to attack the European mainland in late 1942 or 1943, but Brooke favored first sapping German strength by blockade and aerial bombing. He was very impressed with the high caliber of the German soldier and wanted to make sure that ample resources were available before any campaign was launched. Brooke was in favor of campaigns in North Africa, Sicily, and Italy, but discouraged efforts by Churchill to expand the war into the Balkans.

Key Relationships

After the war, Brooke wrote, "Churchill is the most wonderful man I have ever met." During the war, however, he wrote, "He is quite the most difficult man to work with I have ever seen." On balance, he and Churchill made a good team, the patient and tireless Brooke listening to Churchill's ideas and exercising a moderating influence. Night after night, after a hard day's work, Brooke would be called in by Churchill for a meeting or conversation, which might be followed by the showing of a new film and a sandwich at 2:30 a.m.

Brooke and the Supreme Allied Commander, Gen. Dwight D. Eisenhower, were never close. Churchill had promised Brooke command of the Allied invasion of Europe, but this was withdrawn when the scope of America's participation became clear. In his diary, Brooke often criticized Eisenhower's grasp of strategy but later admitted that Eisenhower was a good team leader and coordinator. Eisenhower wrote later, "Brooke did not hesitate to differ sharply . . . but this never affected the friendliness of his personal contacts or the unqualified character of his support. He must be classed as a brilliant soldier."

Postwar Years

In January 1944 Brooke was promoted to field marshal and after his retirement from military service in 1946 was made Viscount Alanbrooke.

Brooke married twice. His first wife died at his side in an automobile accident in the 1920s, leaving him with two children. One of them was a son who served in the British army in the war. Brooke later remarried and had two more children.

On his retirement, he spent much of his time studying and talking about nature, presenting numerous illustrated lectures on birds. Like Marshall, he did not write memoirs or seek to capitalize on his reputation.

Brooke died of a heart ailment at Wintney, Hampshire, England, on 17 June 1963, a few days before his 80th birthday.

ROBERT CALVERT, JR.

SEE ALSO: Eisenhower, Dwight D.; Marshall, George C.; Montgomery, Bernard L.; World War II.

Bibliography

Alanbrooke, Lord. 1939–46. Diaries.

Bryant, A. 1957. *Turn of the tide.* Garden City, N.Y.: Doubleday.

———. 1959. *Triumph in the West.* Garden City, N.Y.: Doubleday.

Churchill, W. 1949–51. *The Second World War.* 5 vols. Boston: Houghton Mifflin.

Fraser, D. 1982. *Alanbrooke.* New York: Atheneum.

Irving, D. 1981. *The war between the generals.* New York: Congdon and Lettes.

BUDGET AND FINANCE, MILITARY

Government budgets are plans for revenues and expenditure for a specific period, often a one-year period. Budgets may, however, cover longer periods and vary from one nation to another. Some budgets are planned for two-year periods while others may extend over five-year periods. Whatever the national budgetary cycle, they generally have common stages in their development.

Budgeting in Market Economies

National budgets in Western countries are usually prepared under the supervision of the country's chief executive—the president or prime minister. Once the executive arm of the government has determined its budgetary proposals, the proposals are submitted to the legislative branch, where they are enacted into law to legalize the collection and expenditure of funds. Administrative departments and ministries of governments are authorized to conduct operations in consonance with the budget as approved by the national legislature. Budgetary accounts are maintained by the governmental fiduciary branch, such as a financial ministry, to ensure that expenditures are in accordance with the legislative mandate. Budgetary accounts are audited at the close of each fiscal year, and the records are usually made available to the public. The successive stages of the budgetary process in Western economies are known as the budget cycle, which consists of four elements: (a) preparation and submission, (b) authorization, (c) implementation or execution, and (d) review and audit.

The national budget is usually submitted by the chief executive to the legislature three to six months prior to the onset of the coming fiscal year. In many governments the fiscal year does not coincide with the calendar year. In the United States, for example, the fiscal year commences on 1 October and continues through the following 30 September. Budgetary documents usually cover three years: the prior year's budgetary activities, the year in progress, and predicted requirements for the fiscal year to follow.

National budgets are arranged to show major sources of revenue such as value-added taxes, income taxes, business taxes, sales taxes, tariffs, and fees. The revenues generated by these sources are used to finance the operation of the government. The budget lists expenditures by department or ministry such as defense, national health, education, and social welfare. In many instances, budgets will reflect funds that are programmed for future years in addition to those for the forthcoming fiscal year.

A budget is said to be in surplus if revenues exceed expenditures, in balance if revenues match expenditures, and in deficit if expenditures exceed revenues. Deficits increase public (or national) debt, while surpluses lower it.

The governmental budget procedure is generally complex and lengthy. The process begins as various departments, ministries, and agencies prepare their forecast expenditures for the following year(s). This agency preparation can begin as early as eighteen months prior to the fiscal year toward which funding projections are directed. Guidance is provided to each agency concerning factors such as funding estimates and inflation rates. Proposals are usually reviewed by ministers or department heads or their budget officers prior to submission. They then are presented to a central governmental budget office which is directly responsible to either the chief executive or the minister of finance. The budget office reviews each departmental request for appropriations, and may hold hearings that are attended by departmental heads and ministers or their budget officers. The budget office finalizes the budget for presentation in coordination with the chief executive. It may also relate the budget to a central government development plan. Regardless of exact procedures, the central budget office is responsible for comprehensive examination of a government's activities and relating the departmental or ministerial programs to the plans of the chief executive.

The preparation of the budget is essentially a political and an economic process that reflects the interests of many diverse factions within and outside the government. It is also a reflection of the economic policy of the administration. In this regard, many departments or ministries may compete for resources. The requirements of one part of the government thus must be balanced against those of others, and in many instances compromises are necessary. Such compromises have become an accepted part of the budget process in most countries, and are in many cases politically motivated. Defense budgets have traditionally been the target of cost reductions in peacetime because of public perceptions that military programs are too costly in terms of their overall contribution to the national economy while diverting funds that might be better spent on social needs.

Military Budget

As previously stated, each governmental department or ministry prepares its budgetary input many months prior to the executive submission to the legislative branch, but each has unique procedures for this due to diverse objectives. The defense budget preparation for almost all nations is a compromise between perceived national security interests and perceived national social and cultural objectives. In the preparation of the defense budget, the first step is the identification of national security interests and commitments, which determine the need for military forces. The second, interrelated step in budget formulation is assessing the perceived threat to a country's national security interests and commitments. The intentions and capabilities of potential adversaries are assessed to determine what contingencies might require military forces not only over one year, but usually over a long-term period of five to ten years. The policy judgments that devolve from these processes are translated into specific requirements for forces and equipment to provide a nation with the military capabilities it desires, usually at the lowest cost possible.

The most complex aspect of the defense budgetary process is the determination of actual needs (i.e., choosing among competing programs for funding while maintaining a balance between ground, air, and naval forces). In many cases politics plays a critical role in the purchase of major weapon systems, because millions or billions of dollars (or equivalents) are involved, and hundreds or thousands of contracts and jobs in the national economy may be at stake.

Military Budget Allocations

In most nations, the defense budget is divided into various programs. Estimates are made as to how much will be spent on personnel, equipment, and other areas. Not only must equipment be purchased and personnel salaries be paid, every other aspect of the defense establishment must also be accounted for, from housing for families of military personnel to equipment maintenance, ammunition, and spare parts. The result is the division of the budget into numerous different programs. Typical are those of the U.S. Department of Defense, which divides its programs as follows:

Personnel

There are generally three categories of personnel: (a) active military, (b) reserve military or territorial forces, and (c) civilian employees of the military establishment. In countries such as the United States and Great Britain, which have all-volunteer forces, the salaries of the military must be kept at such a level as to make the services an attractive career alternative to civilian pursuits. Thus, a large portion of the defense budget will be allocated to recruiting and maintaining a quality force. In nations such as the Federal Republic of Germany, which depend on draftees or national service to comprise a large part of their military forces, personnel funding tends to be lower, but still at some point must become competitive with the civilian sector to retain career personnel of desired quality. This usually commences at the noncommissioned officer and commissioned officer levels, where not only salaries, but benefits become more bountiful, ultimately extending to retirement pensions which also are a part of most defense budgets.

Operating Costs

This critical component of the defense budget determines the actual combat capability of the nation's military forces, as it encompasses training of military personnel, fuel and supplies of all types, communications for command and control at all levels, maintenance of weapons systems and their components, and facilities maintenance. Inherent in this portion of the budget, for example, is financing of support activities for combat aircraft based on flying hours and missions; support of naval forces, which determines the operating tempo of ships at sea (such as the number of days that can be spent at sea on operational missions); the number and size of military installations; and the quantity and complexity of equipment to be maintained. The amount of money spent in this area has a direct impact on force readiness. Once programmed and approved, any reduction in allocations of operating costs will have an impact on force readiness and the capability of the military to conduct their missions. In recent years great emphasis has been placed on improving combat capability and reducing the support structure (improving the "tooth-to-tail" ratio) in many military establishments worldwide.

Research, Development, Test, and Evaluation

In major powers, this aspect of the defense budget makes a vital contribution to the mid- and long-term future military capabilities of the nation and its allies. In the West, large dependence has been placed on the technological superiority of weapons and equipment, in theory creating a "force multiplier" effect to enable military forces to fight outnumbered and still emerge victorious. Hence, the importance of research and development of weapons systems of qualitatively improved capabilities has taken on new meaning for Western military establishments. To most it represents an investment in their future military capabilities. Inherent in the research and development process is testing and evaluation of new systems, procedures, and devices. With the cost of military equipment escalating due to its increasing complexity, the use of costly matcrials, and especially the very high cost of contracted labor, military establishments wish to ensure that their developmental systems are delivering required levels of performance. Thus, most have incorporated an elaborate and independent test and evaluation establishment at either the defense ministry or service level, sometimes at both. The role of such organizations is to test developmental systems to ensure that they meet design objectives.

Procurement/Acquisition

The portion of the defense budget that finances the purchase of new weapons and equipment, or "hardware," is the procurement budget. Procurement generally includes determining needs, establishing requirements and specifications, selecting from competing designs, testing, and delivery.

Military Construction

While this element of a defense budget might at first be considered of relatively minor importance, major systems require appropriate facilities for effective operation and maintenance. A good example of system/facility integration is the U.S. Navy's Trident submarine program, which was planned from the outset as an integrated system encompassing not only the Ohio-class ballistic missile submarine as its centerpiece, but also complex, large operating bases tailored to utilize this entirely new class of weapons system effectively.

Military Budgeting in Nonmarket Economies

Budgeting in command economies, such as that of the former Soviet Union, is quite different from the processes followed in the West. In the first place, it must be emphasized that there can be no direct comparison of the budget and financial processes followed in the former USSR, because the budgetary data were derived differently than comparable figures in the West. Also, published Soviet budgetary data tended to be scanty, especially as they pertained to military expenditures.

Annual budget preparation was consummated by the Ministry of Finance. Very little data were released for public information in the Soviet system; in fact, the budget was treated as restricted information. The annual budget, however, was geared toward implementing and fulfilling the goals of the annual plan. The annual plan was a component of the larger five-year plan (itself a component of a long-range forecast) but instead of serving as a guide, the plans, once implemented by the Council of Ministers, had the force of law.

Under the Gorbachev regime, Soviet economic controls were relaxed to a degree, but centralized planning was still the norm in most industries.

The centralized planning of the defense budget was carried out under the aegis of *Gosplan*, the state planning commission. Actual draft planning began two years prior to the upcoming five-year plan, performance concerning achievements of the current plan goals having been provided to the national leadership in order that they might determine changed directions for the economy in "out" years. The Politburo and the Communist Party Central

Committee gave *Gosplan* its directives for the plan year. These were then translated into thousands of control figures or "indicators," which were sent to appropriate ministries for output of major industrial products. The budget was the financial portion of the annual economic plan.

In theory the Soviet budget was a balanced budget; there was no deficit financing and the official figures typically showed a small surplus. In practice the budget usually appeared to be in deficit by 10 to 15 percent. The Soviet budget consisted of three major items: (a) the national economy; (b) social-cultural and scientific projects; and (c) defense. There were other items as well but they composed less than 1 percent of the overall budget. As recently as 1980, finance of the national economy, social-cultural and scientific projects, and defense composed, respectively, 52.5 percent, 34.2 percent, and 6.0 percent of the overall officially published budget. (It should be noted that official Soviet budget figures typically did not sum to totals, thus leaving questions for Western analysts attempting to decipher the true nature of Soviet expenditures by means of so-called "residuals.") The single annual figure for defense was first published in 1963, but this was only the figure for the operating costs of the Soviet armed forces; at least 70 percent of the Soviet defense budget was unpublished or hidden in the other two budget categories, leading to extensive skepticism in the West regarding the total size of the Soviet defense budget.

Noting that Soviet rubles were not convertible and in the USSR measured only costs and not values, the total Soviet defense budget just before the collapse of the Soviet Union was equivalent to about one-third of that of the United States.

It is generally accepted that the published Soviet defense budget covered only salaries, some military construction, and operating costs. In economic practices dating from 1938, Soviet defense expenditures such as military research and development, civil defense, internal security, and all procurement were absorbed in the national accounts in such a way as to be undeterminable. Military research and development, for example, was thought to be included in the social-cultural and science portion of the budget. Exactly how much the Soviet Union and its allies spent on their armed forces was long debated in the West. The Soviet government announced in 1989 that it would fully disclose its defense budget beginning in 1990.

The Soviet state budget was financed primarily by taxes. One major tax on consumer goods was called the "turnover tax." This tax was quite heavy, amounting to 100 percent and more of the wholesale price of some consumer goods. This accounted for some 30 percent of revenues. Another major tax consisted of deductions from enterprise profits; this accounted for another 30 percent of revenues. Income taxes amounted to only about 10 percent of overall revenues to the budget of the USSR. The remainder of budget revenues came from other sources.

Financing of the USSR defense establishment was under the overall control of the Defense Council, which directed and controlled the entire Soviet military establishment. The Defense Council was made up of select members of the Politburo and the military establishment and was chaired by the General Secretary of the Communist Party of the Soviet Union. In terms of financing the overall defense expenditures of the USSR, the Defense Council (through the Military-Industrial Commission) probably controlled and directed the allocation of financial, material, and labor assets for use in meeting the military portion of the annual plan, which was a revision of the ongoing five-year plan that governed the entire economy.

There were several parts of the plan for military development. The Soviet General Staff prepared a requirements plan for development of the armed forces and submitted it through the Ministry of Defense to the Defense Council. The Military-Industrial Commission of the Council of Ministers prepared a plan reflecting current research and production capacity, to provide for the economic support of the armed forces. The plan predicted the industrial resources that were expected to be available to support the armed forces. There also was a plan for involving other state institutions such as civilian and military-patriotic organizations to support military requirements. The Secretariat to the Central Committee resolved the conflicts of interest arising among the military and civilian sectors. The State Social and Economic Plan, including the Defense Council's draft plan called the "*smeta*," documented the entire Soviet economic and social system.

Military Budget and Finance Issues

Regardless of the type of economy, the labels appended to the various budgetary and financial stages, and the fiscal procedures that are invoked, governments must have a carefully considered plan for financing every aspect of their operations. Generally, over a long period of time, the stability of a nation or government may be a reflection of its financial management policy. A nation whose revenues equal or exceed its expenditures may not always be fiscally stable; the manner in which those expenditures are apportioned ultimately determines the rise and fall of nations. Equally as important as the amount of revenues collected and their actual apportionment is the perception of the equity or wisdom of these actions by the citizenry. Nations must maintain a balance between defense, social programs, and the requirements of operating the government. Funds are disbursed not solely by perceived national necessities, but also by political motivations. National budgetary and financial policy can thus provide indications as to the success of a government in managing itself and governing its citizens.

Charles Q. Cutshaw
Dianne M. Cutshaw

SEE ALSO: Budget, Defense; Cost Analysis; Economics, Defense; Procurement, Military; Research and Development Establishments and Policies; Test and Evaluation, Materiel.

Bibliography

Loucks, W. N., and W. G. Whitney. 1980. *Comparative economic systems.* New York: Harper and Row.

Barry, D. D., and C. Barner-Barry. 1982. *Contemporary Soviet politics.* 2d ed. Englewood Cliffs, N.J.: Prentice-Hall.

Hodgman, D. R. 1974. *National monetary policy and international monetary cooperation.* Boston: Little, Brown.

1988 Annual Report of the Secretary of Defense to the Congress, FY 1988/FY 1989 budget and the FY 1988–92 defense programs. Washington, D.C.: Government Printing Office.

U.S. General Accounting Office. 1981. *A glossary of terms used in the federal budget process.* Washington, D.C.: Government Printing Office.

BUDGET, DEFENSE

A country's defense budget, when a matter of public record, is often regarded by observers as a major policy statement of the government and a plan of action for the military establishment. It may be the most tangible manifestation—to some, a symbol—of a country's commitment to a particular national security policy.

The defense budgets of the countries of the world differ dramatically in size and composition, and they are formulated in ways that vary much the same way world political systems vary. Although no generic defense budget process exists worldwide, common elements have evolved in terms of budgetary practices and concepts and with respect to budget composition. These common elements provide a useful framework for the study of national security policy decision making.

Political Context

The defense budget process in countries with liberal, democratic traditions is generally a function of the balance of power between the different branches of government and the separation maintained between military and civilian leadership. It is a part of a larger government-wide budgetary process that establishes relative funding priorities among defense and nondefense social programs (the focus of the so-called guns-versus-butter debate).

In countries with Communist or other authoritarian governments where government institutions make decisions, for example, about the production of consumer goods and investment in agriculture, the defense budget process is inseparable from the larger process that determines the distribution of economic and industrial resources in society.

In some countries, the formulation of the annual defense budget is a relatively open process, influenced both publicly and privately by a large number of civilian and military leaders, including nongovernmental participants. In some other countries, virtually every detail about the defense budget, including the aggregate funding level, is kept as a national secret.

Budget Concepts

International comparisons between levels of defense spending may be deceptive owing to difficulties in establishing currency equivalence, accounting for vast differences in national inflation rates, adjusting for differences in the fiscal year used by countries to report defense spending statistics, and finding a common definition for defense spending. To compensate for differences in the fiscal year, annual spending statistics are sometimes adjusted by analysts when possible to a calendar year basis.

Member countries of the North Atlantic Treaty Organization (NATO) have developed a "standard definition" of defense expenditures that they use to compare defense efforts by alliance members. The NATO definition includes spending for regular military forces, military aid to other countries, pensions paid to retired military personnel, and civilian personnel costs and excludes spending for civil defense, veterans' benefits, and domestic security forces.

The defense budget process may be thought of in terms of four basic phases that vary considerably (and may be virtually nonexistent) depending on the national political system and administrative capacity of the country in question. The phases are budget formulation, presentation and approval, budget execution, and review and audit.

BUDGET FORMULATION

In the budget formulation phase of the defense budget process, governments make defense plans and contemplate alternative resource allocations in support of a set of programmatic choices.

Budget formulation is generally a relatively closed phase of the defense budget process whether or not the military is under civilian control. Intermilitary service and bureaucratic rivalries often influence a government's defense budget. Given outside interest in their decisions, often as a result of the size of the contracts ultimately at stake, governments ordinarily choose to consider their defense budget options in secret.

Most governments do not candidly disclose defense budget information. For example, the former Soviet Union was thought by Western defense analysts to have spent considerably more on national defense than the official 1987 Soviet state budget figure of 20.2 billion rubles (Lee 1977). The United States is unique in the vast amount of unclassified information available on its defense budget.

PRESENTATION AND APPROVAL

The relationship between the budget formulation phase of the process and the presentation and approval phase is a function of a country's political system. In the United

States, for example, with its three separate branches of government, the presentation and approval phase of the process is considerably more important than in the United Kingdom, where the parliamentary system of government assures approval of the defense budget by the political party in power in Parliament.

Although most legislatures, where they play a role in the budget process, agree to a level of defense funding one year at a time, many annual budgets are based on multiyear defense budget plans, some of which assume a considerable amount of importance as statements of future policy. In Japan, for example, the Diet approves a long-range defense plan that serves as a blueprint, and subsequently it approves each annual budget increment.

Budget Execution

During the budget execution phase of the defense budget process, governments award contracts, receive services, and otherwise obligate themselves to expend funds. Depending on national financial controls governing spending, at any given time a government may be executing the most recent budget approved as well as budgets approved in previous years for which funds remain to be obligated and expended.

Review and Audit

For most countries, the review and audit phase of the process is rather undeveloped, but in some a great deal of importance is attached to the findings of contract inspectors and auditors. Perceptions of defense "waste, fraud, and abuse" are influenced by national standards of administrative competence and national cultural attitudes toward the role and prerogatives of governmental officials.

Budget Composition

National defense budgets may be organized in vastly different ways, but they are generally composed of a set of common elements. Spending for defense may logically be divided roughly into four categories: people, equipment, readiness, and research and development.

Defense spending is largely fungible. Defense planners routinely confront the trade-off between the funding of force structure and investment modernization, on the one hand, and military readiness for combat, on the other. However, it is notable that a given level of spending is a measure of input rather than output, and it guarantees neither military readiness nor defense capability.

People

Defense establishments may consist of military and civilian personnel. Active-duty forces are more expensive to maintain than reserve forces, and an all-volunteer force is generally considered to be more expensive than a conscripted force. In addition to salaries and bonuses, governments often provide military personnel nonmonetary benefits, for example, housing, transportation and communication privileges, and health care.

Personnel costs are generally regarded as fixed costs that are not easily cut without reducing the size of the force structure. For many countries, spending on personnel represents the largest category of spending for defense.

Equipment

The military equipment and weapon systems a country buys in peacetime will be in its force structure for many years, largely because of the number of years needed to acquire large systems and the enormous cost involved. A country may rely on its own military-industrial base for the procurement of defense equipment or may choose to import weapons. Only a few countries of the world produce their own high-technology defense equipment as only a few can afford to maintain the industrial complex that would otherwise be required. Naval vessels are produced by a relatively larger number of nations. Small arms and armored vehicles are more widely produced internationally. Predictably, developing countries accounted for about 75 percent of world arms imports in 1985.

State-of-the-art defense equipment and weapon systems are—and always have been—very expensive to buy and operate. Defense planners the world over typically are constrained by limited resources; therefore, some defense analysts seek the flexibility inherent in the acquisition of multimission forces, and others debate the virtues of procuring "quality versus quantity."

The amount and kind of equipment purchased depend on the need to have enough equipment for the force structure and the perceived need to modernize by replacing obsolete older equipment. Most equipment purchased by major nations is for the purpose of modernization.

Readiness

The importance of funding for military readiness is correlated directly with the likelihood of war. Defined in terms of a level of training, unit deployability, and adequate inventories of the right ammunition and spare parts, for example, readiness funding has traditionally been the easiest category of funding for a government to reduce in allocating constrained resources.

The requirement for readiness funding is in direct competition with the need for funding for equipment and modernization. Readiness funding is also driven by the decision to expand and modernize the force structure. However, military readiness generally cannot be purchased and placed on the shelf for later use. Its ephemeral nature makes the measurement of how much readiness a given sum will secure difficult.

Research and Development

Military research, development, and testing is a very expensive function for a defense establishment. Very few governments can afford the luxury of supporting a research and development (R&D) infrastructure. Most countries lack the indigenous resources (skilled personnel and equipment) on which to base a long-term effort.

Funding for defense-related research and development in most developed countries is shared by government and industry. As R&D costs increase, some countries, for example, France and the Federal Republic of Germany, have begun cooperative research and development programs. In addition, efforts to sell weapons abroad are sometimes prompted by interest in recouping the expense of costly R&D.

Budget Size

Taken out of context, a given level of spending for defense indicates relatively little. However, rapid increases or decreases in the size of the defense budget may signify a change in political resolve and intentions. A dramatic increase may be regarded as threatening by other countries.

In both open and closed societies, two factors determine the size of a country's defense budget: (1) perceptions of the military posture (active and reserve forces) needed to implement a grand strategy and attain national security objectives; and (2) overall national budgetary priorities.

Strategy and Objectives

Most analysts agree that national security policy (including, but not limited to, offensive and defensive military strategies) should guide decisions on how much defense spending is enough. From an offensive perspective, however, disagreements always arise over how much force is required to succeed. From a defensive perspective, often wide disagreement exists over the nature and extent of the military threat and objectives and the appropriate balance a country should strike between military and nonmilitary responses to challenges from adversaries. Furthermore, military perceptions may change.

In the case of Egypt, prior to the Egyptian-Israeli Peace Treaty of 1979, Israel was perceived as the primary adversary. Today, Libya poses the primary external threat to Egyptian security. The change in the nature of the threat in the 1980s prompted the Egyptian government to review the size and composition of its defense budget.

In the United States, the Reagan administration was more single-minded than the Carter administration, its predecessor, in terms of both (1) its view of the centrality of the Soviet Union as the major threat facing the United States and (2) U.S. policy on the appropriate response to an adversary's challenge. The Reagan administration made countering the Soviet military threat the centerpiece of its security policy and emphasized initiatives to enhance military capability (such as the deployment of new strategic and conventional weapons systems) as the most effective way to neutralize the threat. The relatively large increases in defense funding proposed annually during the 1980s by the Reagan administration reflected this approach (Fig. 1).

Budgetary Priorities

Defense policymakers the world over are preoccupied with the question of how much military spending is enough, given avowed national security policy and possible alliance or other global defense commitments, on the one hand, and competing domestic spending priorities and, in many cases, the need for economic and industrial growth, on the other. Governments often differ in their willingness to sacrifice particular programs (especially defense programs) in the name of sound fiscal policy or domestic program priorities.

The most common measure of the burden of defense spending on a country's economy is defense spending taken as a percentage of the gross national product (GNP) or gross domestic product (GDP). Some analysts use this measure as evidence of the affordability of a given defense program based on national historic standards or to compare the burden of defense on various national economies. Others have used the measure in an effort to demonstrate that advanced industrial nations that spend a larger share of their GNP on defense generally experience lower economic growth than those that spend less on defense. Such uses of defense spending statistics raise serious questions and are a matter of debate in the literature on defense spending (Kennedy 1987).

World Defense Spending

Although defense budget data for many of the countries of the world are not altogether reliable, world military spending is estimated to have exceeded US$900 billion in 1986. Military spending by the Soviet Union and the United States combined represented an estimated 61 percent of world military spending in 1985 (Gallik 1988).

Table 1 shows for 144 countries the relative burden of

Figure 1. Secretary of Defense Dick Cheney (left) and Deputy Secretary of Defense Donald Atwood conducted a Pentagon press conference on 11 July 1989, on the subject of the defense management review that was directed by President Bush in February 1989. (Source: U.S. Department of Defense)

TABLE 1. *Relative Burden of Military Expenditures, 1985*

	GNP PER CAPITA (1984 U.S. DOLLARS)					
ME/GNP[a] (%)	*Under $200*	*$200–499*	*$500–999*	*$1,000–2,999*	*$3,000–9,999*	*$10,000 and over*
10% and over	Cambodia[b] Laos[b]	Yemen (Aden) Cape Verde[b]	Egypt Yemen (Sanaa)	Iraq[b] Syria Korea, North Jordan Nicaragua Mongolia[b]	Oman Saudia Arabia Libya[b] Israel Soviet Union	Qatar
5–9.99%	Ethiopia Mozambique	Guyana Afghanistan[b] China Mauritania Lesotho[b] Pakistan Zambia[b] Vietnam[b]	Peru Morocco Zimbabwe[b] El Salvador Albania	Lebanon[b] Angola[b] Korea, South Cuba	Bulgaria Taiwan Iran[b] Greece Singapore Poland Czechoslovakia United Kingdom	United States Germany, East Kuwait United Arab Emirates
2–4.99%	Guinea-Bissau[b] Burma Burkina Faso[b] Mali Equatorial Guinea[b]	India Kenya Tanzania Guinea[b] Burundi Togo Senegal Liberia Sri Lanka Indonesia Benin[b] Madagascar	Thailand Honduras Botswana	Turkey South Africa[b] Chile Malaysia Yugoslavia Tunisia Congo Portugal Argentina Uruguay Algeria Suriname Panama	Hungary Romania France Bahrain Netherlands Belgium Italy Trinidad and Tobago[b] Gabon[b] Spain[b] New Zealand	Germany, West Norway Sweden Australia Denmark Canada Switzerland
1–1.99%	Chad Malawi[b] Zaire Bangladesh Nepal	Central African Republic[b] Sudan Somalia[b] Rwanda Sao Tome & Principe[b] Haiti The Gambia[b]	Cameroon Papua New Guinea Swaziland Nigeria Philippines Ivory Coast[b]	Guatemala Bolivia[b] Dominican Republic Ecuador[b] Venezuela Fiji[b] Colombia Paraguay Brazil	Ireland Cyprus Austria[b]	Finland[b]
Under 1%		Uganda[b] Sierra Leone Niger	Ghana Jamaica	Costa Rica Mexico Mauritius	Malta[b] Barbados	Japan Luxembourg Iceland

Source: D. Gallik, ed., *World Military Expenditures and Arms Transfers, 1987*, United States Arms Control and Disarmament Agency (Washington, D.C.: Government Printing Office, 1988).

[a] Countries are listed within blocks in descending order of ME/GNP.

[b] Ranking is based on a rough approximation of one or more variables for which 1985 data or reliable estimates are not available.

defense in 1985 expressed in terms of military expenditures (ME) as a percentage of GNP and organized from left to right in the table in terms of GNP per capita.

ALICE C. MARONI

SEE ALSO: Arms Trade and Military Assistance; Planning, Defense; Policy, Defense.

Bibliography

Gallik, D. 1988. *World military expenditures and arms transfers, 1987*. U.S. Arms Control and Disarmament Agency. Washington, D.C.: Government Printing Office.

Hobkirk, M. D. 1983. *The politics of defense budgeting: A study of organisation and resource allocation in the United Kingdom and the United States*. Washington, D.C.: National Defense Univ. Press.

Kennedy, P. 1987. *The rise and fall of the great powers*. New York: Random House.

Lee, W. T. 1977. *The estimation of Soviet defense expenditures, 1955–75: An unconventional approach*. New York: Praeger.

Maroni, A. C. 1984. The defense budget. In *Presidential leadership and national security: Style, institutions, and politics*, ed. S. C. Sarkesian. Boulder, Colo.: Westview Press.

Poole, J. B., and A. J. F. Brown, 1982. Bibliographic note: A survey of national defense statements. *Survival* 24:220–28.

Sivard, R. L. 1987. *World military and social expenditures 1987–88*. 12th ed. World Prior.

Stockholm International Peace Research Institute. 1986. *World armaments and disarmaments, SIPRI yearbook*. Oxford: Oxford Univ. Press.

BULGARIA, REPUBLIC OF

Bulgaria, a Balkan nation and a member of the former Warsaw Pact, is one of the poorer nations in Europe. Its armed forces are equipped with older materiel than the armed forces of its wealthier former allies to the north.

Power Potential Statistics

Area: 110,910 square kilometers (42,822 sq. mi.)
Population: 9,080,000
Total Active Armed Forces: 107,000 (1.178% of pop.)
Gross National Product: US$47.3 billion (1990 est.)
Annual Defense Expenditure: not available
Iron and Steel Production:
  Crude steel: 3.045 million metric tons (1987)
  Pig iron: 1.652 million metric tons (1987)
Fuel Production:
  Coal: 38.5 million metric tons (1987)
  Coke: 1.087 million metric tons (1986)
  Crude oil: 0.280 million metric tons (1989)
  Natural gas: 190 million cubic meters (1986)
Electrical Power Output: 45,000 million kwh (1990)
Merchant Marine: 112 vessels; 1,227,817 gross registered tons
Civil Air Fleet: 86 major transport aircraft; 380 usable airfields (120 with permanent-surface runways); none with runways over 3,659 meters (12,000 ft.); 20 with runways 2,440–3,659 meters (8,000–12,000 ft.); 20 with runways 1,220–2,440 meters (4,000–8,000 ft).

For the most recent information, the reader may refer to the following annual publications:
The Military Balance. International Institute for Strategic Studies. London: Brassey's (UK).
The Statesman's Year-Book. New York: St. Martin's Press.
The World Factbook. Central Intelligence Agency. Washington, D.C.: Brassey's (US).

History

Although Bulgaria has existed as a state intermittently since the ninth century A.D., modern Bulgaria was carved from the waning Ottoman Empire (largely at the behest of Russia, who wanted an ally in the area) in 1878. Ethnically and linguistically, the Bulgarians are closely related to the Russians, and subsequently, ties between the two nations have been close. Bulgaria joined Serbia, Greece, and Montenegro in the First Balkan War (October 1912–May 1913), but overestimation of their own strength led the Bulgarians to attack their allies in the Second Balkan War. That war, waged between 30 May and 10 August 1913, cost Bulgaria further casualties and most of the territory gained in the previous war. This defeat was in part responsible for Bulgaria's alliance with Germany and Turkey in World War I, which cost the nation more lives and more territory. Bulgaria suffered from periodic political unrest throughout the interwar period, and joined the Axis powers in 1941, helping the Germans to invade Yugoslavia and Greece, and thereby receiving some of the conquered lands. Bulgaria, unlike Hungary and Romania, did not send troops into Russia, but its forces were involved in antipartisan operations in Yugoslavia and Greece. Bulgaria defected to the Allies on 8 September 1944 as Soviet armies swept into the Balkans, and for the last eight months of the war fought against Germany at the side of its Soviet allies. After 1945, Bulgaria remained firmly in the Soviet camp but dissolution of the Warsaw Pact in 1991 has left the Bulgarians on their own.

Politico-Military Background and Policy

The old tradition of Bulgarian-Russian cooperation, rooted in Russia's assistance toward the cause of Bulgarian independence, was strengthened after World War II by the common ties of communism. The Bulgarian Communist Party was founded in 1891 as an opposition party. Bulgaria remained a staunch ally of the USSR, following Moscow's lead in foreign as well as domestic policy. As an example, in 1968 Bulgarian forces joined in the invasion of Czechoslovakia. Since 1985, Bulgaria was at first slow to adopt policies of reform and *perestroika* or "openness," which have arisen elsewhere in Eastern Europe through the example of Mikhail Gorbachev. The Bulgarian government nevertheless made notable moves toward reform in autumn 1989, ousting longtime head of state Todor Zhivkov. The Bulgarian government, bowing to increasing public pressure agreed to free elections, which were held in autumn 1991.

Bulgaria has compulsory military service for all males reaching the age of 19; two years in the army and air force, three years in the navy. Bulgarian security policy may have been affected by Turkish distress over the policy of mandatory Bulgarization (name changes, etc.) forced on Bulgaria's Turkish minority, but this policy was abandoned in November 1989.

Strategic Problems

Like most small countries, Bulgaria suffers from a lack of strategic depth. Coupled with Bulgaria's relative paucity of resources, its capacity to play a major role in a European-wide general war is limited. Romania's often independent foreign policy could pose further difficulties for Bulgaria in the event of war, for if Romania did not side with the rest of the former Warsaw Pact nations at the outset, Bulgaria would be geographically isolated. In addition to Bulgaria's potential problems with Turkey noted above, Bulgaria's historical desire to unite the Greek and Yugoslav portions of Macedonia under its rule could also provide a potential point of conflict. A lesser possibility exists for a quarrel with Romania over Bulgarian claims to the Dobruja region along the lower Danube.

Military Assistance

Bulgaria, in the past, received extensive military aid, equipment (including T-72 tanks and MiG-23 and Su-25 aircraft), and assistance from the Soviet Union, but the scale and scope of this support has declined substantially since the events of the early 1990s. Many of Bulgaria's military officers received part of their education in the Soviet Union.

Defense Industry

Bulgaria's national defense industry is limited. Bulgaria does not have enough spare materiel to export, and produces only ammunition, small weapons, and certain vehicles for its own use. Most of the weapons employed have been supplied by the Soviet Union or Czechoslovakia.

Alliances

Bulgaria's principal military alliance was membership in the Warsaw Treaty Organization (Warsaw Pact—founded on 14 May 1955 and dissolved on 1 April 1991). Bulgaria is a member of the Council of Mutual Economic Assistance (CEMA), and had a bilateral treaty of Friendship and Mutual Assistance with the Soviet Union dating from 1955.

Defense Structure

The Bulgarian Armed Forces are under the direction of the Politburo of the Bulgarian Communist Party, of which the Defense Minister is a member. The Defense Minister is also the commander in chief of the armed forces, which are fully integrated under the Defense Ministry; the Bulgarian air force and navy are subordinated to the army.

In January 1989 Bulgaria announced a forthcoming 12 percent reduction in its defense spending and a 10,000-man reduction in its active armed forces. The Bulgarian defense budget, unpublished since 1978, had been about 10 percent or more of the country's net material product (NMP). In late 1989 and early 1990, Bulgaria was making common cause with Greece in developing anti-Turkish strategies, citing the threat of Muslim fundamentalism.

(For an explanation of the abbreviations and symbols used in the following section of military statistics, see the list of Abbreviations and Acronyms in each volume.)

Total Armed Forces

Active: 107,000 (70,000 conscripts). (Excl some 10,000 construction tps.). Terms of service: 18 months.
Reserves: 472,500. Army 420,000; Navy (to age 55, officers 60 or 65) 7,500; Air (to age 60) 45,000.

ARMY: 75,000 (49,000 conscripts).
3 Military Districts/Army HQ: 1 with 1 tk bde; 1 with 4 MRD, 1 tk bde; 1 with 4 MRD, 2 tk bde; (Cat A/B: 5 MRD, 4 tk bde; Cat C: 3 MRD).
Army tps: 4 Scud, 1 SAM bde, 3 arty, 3 AD arty regt, 1 cdo coy.
1 AB regt (manned by Air Force).
Equipment:
MBT: 2,149 (446 in store): 670 T-34, 1,145 T-55, 334 T-72.
Assault gun: 173 SU-100 (CFE HACV).
Recce: 450 BRDM-1/-2.
AIFV: 29 BMP-1, 114 BMP-23.
APC: 765 BTR-60, 1,123 MT-LB.
Total arty: 2,233 (594 in store).
Towed: 716: 100mm: 15 M-1944 (BS-3); 122mm: 282 M-30, 32 M-1931/37 (A-19); 130mm: 72 M-46; 152mm: 104 M-1937 (ML-20), 211 D-20.
SP: 761: 122mm: 748 2S1; 152mm: 13 2S3.
MRL: 246: 122mm: 222 BM-21; 130mm: 24 RM-130.
Mortars: 510: 107mm: 63 M-1938; 120mm: 359 Tundzha M-1938/43 SP; 160mm: 88 M-160.
SSM: launchers: 28 FROG-7, 36 Scud, 2 SS-23
ATGW: 200 AT-3 Sagger.
ATK guns: 85mm: 150 D-44; 100mm: 200 T-12.
AD guns: 400: 23mm: ZU-23, ZSU-23-4 SP; 57mm: S-60; 85mm: KS-12; 100mm; KS-19.
SAM: 50 SA-4/-6/-13.

NAVY: 10,000 (5,000 conscripts). Bases: coastal: Varna (HQ), Atiya, Sozopol, Balchik. Danube: Vidin (HQ).
Submarines: 3 Pobeda (Sov Romeo) class with 533mm TT (2 probably restricted to alongside trg only).
Frigates: 2:1 Druzki (Sov Riga) with 4 × 5 ASW RL; plus 3 × 533mm TT, 3 × 100mm guns. 1 Smeli (Sov Koni) with 1 × 2 SA-N-4 SAM, 2 × 12 ASW RL; plus 2 × 2 76mm guns.
Patrol and Coastal Combatants: 22:
Corvettes: 5: 2 Poti ASW with 2 × ASW RL, 4 × ASTT; 2 Tarantul I ASUW with 2 × 2 SS-N-2C Styx, 1 × 4 SA-N-5 Grail SAM; plus 1 × 76mm gun; 1 Pauk I with 1 SA-N-5 SAM, 2 × 5 ASW RL; plus 4 × 406mm TT.
Missile Craft: 6 Osa PFM with 4 × SS-N-2A/B Styx SSM.
Torpedo Craft: 4 Shershen PFT with 4 × 533mm TT.
Patrol, Inshore: 7 Zhuk PFI (.
Mine Warfare: 33:
Minelayers: None but SS and FF have capability.
MCMV: 33: 1 Sov T-43 MSC; 4 Sonya MSC; 28 MSI: 6 Vanya, 2 Yevgenya, 2 Olya, 18 (.
Amphibious: 2 Sov Polnocny LSM, capacity 150 tps, 6 tk; Plus craft: 21 Vydra LCM.
Support and Miscellaneous: 9: 2 AOT, 2 AGOR, 1 AGI, 2 trg, 2 AT.

Naval Aviation: 12 armed hel.; 1 SAR/ASW sqn with 12 Mi-14 (ASW), 6 Mi-2, 3 Mi-4, 3 Mi-8.

Coastal arty: 2 regt, 20 bty:
Guns: 100mm: est. 150; 130mm: SM-4-1.
SSM: SS-C-1b Sepal, SSC-3 Styx.

Naval Guard: 3 coy.

AIR FORCE: 22,000 (16,000 conscripts), incl AB regt listed under Army; 266 cbt ac, 44 attack hel; 2 air div, 7 cbt regt.
FGA: 1 regt with 39 Su-25.
Fighter: 4 regt with some 26 MiG-23MF B/G; 105 MiG-21PFM, 20 MiG-29, 2 MiG-29 UB.
Recce: 1 regt with 18 MiG-21, 5 MiG-25, 20 Su-22.

Transport: 1 regt with 4 An-2, 5 An-24, 5 An-26, 1 L-410, 1 Yak-40 (VIP).
Survey: 2 An-30.
Helicopters: 2 regt with 14 Mi-2, 30 Mi-8/17, 44 Mi-24 (attack).
Training: 3 trg regt with 70 L-29, 37 L-39, 15 *MiG-21, 16* MiG-23, 16 Yak-18.
Missiles:
ASM: AS-7 Kerry.
AAM: AA-2 Atoll, AA-7 Apex, AA-8 Aphid.
SAM: SA-2/-3/-5/-10 (30 sites, some 280 launchers).

PARAMILITARY
Border Guards (Ministry of Interior): 12,000; 12 regt.
Security Police: 4,000.
People's Territorial Militia (R): 150,000.

Future

Although the Bulgarian economy has enjoyed relatively good fortune in recent years when compared with those in Romania and Yugoslavia, it still lags far behind the rest of Europe. Until the Bulgarian economy can become more modern and efficient, the armed forces are likely to remain equipped with obsolescent and poorly maintained equipment.

In 1987, after a generation of keeping Bulgaria the most loyal and least troublesome of the nations of the Warsaw Pact alliance, the then Bulgarian leader, Todor Zhivkov, began implementing reforms corresponding to those of the Soviet Union. Those reforms included major reorganizations and personnel replacements in the Communist Party and in the Bulgarian government. On 10 November 1989 the 78-year-old Zhivkov resigned as head of the Bulgarian Communist Party and as President of Bulgaria and was immediately replaced by 53-year-old Petar T. Mladenov, the then foreign minister. On that occasion Mladenov said, "We have to turn Bulgaria into a modern, democratic and lawful country."

DAVID L. BONGARD
TREVOR N. DUPUY

SEE ALSO: Balkan Wars; Eastern Europe; Greece; Soviet Union; Turkey.

Bibliography

American University. 1974. *Area handbook for Bulgaria.* Washington, D.C.: Government Printing Office.
Bell, J. 1985. *The Bulgarian Communist party from Blagoev to Zhivkov.* Stanford, Calif.: Hoover Institute Press.
Constant, S. 1979. *Foxy Ferdinand, Tsar of Bulgaria.* London: Sidgwick and Jackson.
Evans, S. G. 1960. *A short history of Bulgaria.* London: Lawrence and Wishart.
Hunter, B., ed. 1991. *The statesman's year-book, 1991–92.* New York: St. Martin's Press.
International Institute for Strategic Studies. 1991. *The military balance, 1991–1992.* London: Brassey's.
Osborne, R. H. 1973. *Revolution administered: Agrarianism and communism in Bulgaria.* Baltimore: Johns Hopkins Univ. Press.

BURIAL, MILITARY

Throughout history, nations have taken great care to honor their war dead. This article will address the historical background of military burials and discuss in detail U.S. burial customs and the U.S. national cemetery system.

The understanding that war dead would be recovered from the battlefield and given a hero's burial has always been important to maintaining troop morale. Prompt recovery and evacuation of casualties are necessary to prevent the demoralizing sight of a battlefield strewn with corpses. With the advent of photography about 150 years ago, the horrors of war could be captured on film and shown to the civilian population far from the battlefield. This further spurred efforts to assure quick removal of battlefield dead and careful attention to dignified and compassionate disposal of remains.

Military burial may take place in government-maintained cemeteries or in private cemeteries. Many private cemeteries set aside sections for the exclusive use of the veteran and the veteran's spouse. Military honors may be provided at the interment of a veteran if requested by the survivor. In the United States, military honors range from placement of the national colors on the casket to a full honors ceremony involving a military chaplain, color guard, escort platoon, military band, casket team, firing party, bugler, and a flag placed over the coffin. Deceased generals and admirals are also entitled to a caparisoned or riderless horse and a cannon salute.

Those who serve in the military form strong bonds of friendship with their fellow campaigners; this is especially true of warriors who share the danger and the grief of combat. Such comradeship often extends to the grave, with veterans whose military service was performed perhaps 50 years earlier specifying their desire to be buried alongside their comrades-in-arms.

Historical Background

The classic *History of the Peloponnesian War* by the Athenian general and military historian Thucydides reported that fallen soldiers were returned to Athens for burial in a state cemetery and that part of the cortege would be an empty casket to represent those who were missing or whose bodies were not recovered from the battlefield. This same period (fifth century B.C.) produced one of history's great speeches, the immortal funeral oration delivered by the brilliant Athenian statesman Pericles in 431 B.C. as a memorial to the first Athenian soldier who fell in the Peloponnesian War.

The custom of burial of the dead dates at least to the Paleolithic period (Old Stone Age). The general practice calls for in-the-ground interment, placement in a mausoleum, or cremation. Earth burial is the most common practice, but for reasons of economy and scarcity of burial space, cremations are becoming increasingly popular except when cremation violates religious belief.

Some primitive societies placed remains on towers or otherwise exposed the deceased to the elements and wild animals. During the Viking Age, before the introduction of Christianity to Scandinavia, deceased Viking warriors were placed on a warship, the ship then being ignited and set adrift. Hindus rank the funeral as a highly important ritual, the preferred ceremony being cremation at the Ganges or another of India's sacred rivers. With mourners in attendance, the body is immersed in the holy waters and then placed on a pyre and set afire.

Burial at sea of civilians as well as military personnel was more a matter of necessity than of desire in the years before ships' personnel had the means to preserve the remains until land was reached. (A more detailed discussion of sea burial of deceased military is provided later in this article.)

Burial on battlegrounds, at prisoner-of-war camps, at military hospitals, and adjacent to, or within, private cemeteries is accepted as a wartime exigency. However, final disposition of remains of war dead is generally in accordance with the desires of the next of kin and this usually leads to disinterment from the battlefield and reinterment elsewhere.

Recovery and identification of war dead has been greatly enhanced in the twentieth century by the introduction of "dog tags," an identification disk carried by each member of the military. Skillful use of fingerprints and dental records and other scientific advances in the study of the human body have reduced the number of unidentified battlefield casualties.

Pilgrimage to Burial Sites of Military Heroes

An eminent military personage's burial site is likely to become a place of pilgrimage. Many visitors to Paris pay their respects at the Dôme des Invalides where Napoleon I, Marshal Ferdinand Foch (commander of French, British, and U.S. armies in World War I), and other French notables are interred.

Among those entombed in the Kremlin Wall in Moscow's Red Square is Marshal Georgi K. Zhukov (1896–1974). During "The Great Patriotic War," Zhukov defeated the Germans at Stalingrad in 1943 and captured Berlin in 1945. Tamerlane (1336–1405), the Mongol conqueror, lies in a mausoleum in Samarkand (Uzbekistan), which was the capital of his empire.

English tradition generally calls for burial on parish grounds, some soldiers being laid to rest at small country churches, some at great cathedrals alongside nobility and other illustrious citizens. One of London's great cathedrals, St. Paul's, is the final resting place of naval hero Lord Horatio Nelson, renowned for his charge, "England expects that every man will do his duty." St. George's Chapel, Windsor Castle, is the burial place of a select few yeomen and master gunners as well as kings. Among the soldier-heroes buried at St. George's is Lt. Gen. Sir John Elley. Elley's monument notes that he "entered the army in 1790 as a private . . . [and] unaided by dignity of birth or the influence of fortune, he raised himself to the highest rank in the British army by distinguished conduct in the field."

The *Arizona* Memorial is the final resting place for approximately 1,100 U.S. Navy and Marine personnel killed aboard the U.S.S. *Arizona* during an attack by Japanese aircraft on 7 December 1941. The memorial is located within the boundaries of the Pearl Harbor Naval Base on the island of Oahu, Hawaii; it spans the sunken battleship. As a special tribute to the *Arizona* and its lost crew, the ship is still considered to be in commission, and the U.S. flag is flown daily from a flagpole which is attached to the severed mainmast of the sunken battleship.

The National Memorial Cemetery of the Pacific in Honolulu, Hawaii, hosts more than 5 million visitors annually. Great numbers of these visitors pay homage at the gravesite of astronaut Ellison Onizuka. Onizuka and the six others aboard the space shuttle *Challenger* perished on 28 January 1986 when the vehicle exploded 74 seconds after liftoff from Cape Canaveral, Florida.

Pilgrimages to Arlington National Cemetery in the vicinity of Washington, D.C., focus on the Tomb of the Unknown Soldier of World War I and the Tomb of the Unknown Servicemen of World War II, Korea, and Vietnam. Their identities "Known But to God," these fallen veterans represent all members of the U.S. armed forces who fought and sacrificed their lives. The tombs of the unknowns are guarded 24 hours a day by an elite group of soldiers from the 3d Infantry Regiment (the Old Guard of the Army).

Other special points of interest at Arlington are the graves of John Fitzgerald Kennedy (marked by an eternal flame), the 35th president of the United States (1961–63), and General of the Armies John J. Pershing, commander of the American armies in World War I. Although never a member of the U.S. armed forces, British Field Marshal Sir John Dill (1881–1944) was accorded the privilege of burial at Arlington. Dill died while on duty in Washington as the senior British representative on the World War II Allied Combined Chiefs of Staff.

In addition to the wars mentioned earlier, the honored dead at Arlington include veterans from the Revolutionary War, War of 1812, Mexican War, Civil War, the Indian Campaigns, the Spanish-American War, and the Philippine Insurrection.

Military Cemeteries on Foreign Soil

A new U.S. policy for the care of its war dead rose out of the 1846–47 War with Mexico when Congress subsequently acted to establish a cemetery in Mexico City for those U.S. soldiers who had perished in battle at that site.

Today, the American Battle Monuments Commission, an independent agency of the U.S. federal government, administers, operates, and maintains on foreign soil 24 permanent American military burial grounds, primarily for casualties of World Wars I and II.

Currently, 124,910 U.S. war dead are interred in 22 overseas cemeteries; 30,920 of World War I, 93,240 of World War II, and 750 of the Mexican War. In addition, 5,608 American veterans and others are interred in the Mexico City and Corozal (Republic of Panama) American cemeteries. Use of these overseas permanent military burial grounds has been granted in perpetuity by the respective host country free of cost, rent, and taxation.

Every grave in these overseas cemeteries is marked by a headstone of white marble: a Star of David for those of Jewish faith, a Latin Cross for all others (Fig. 1). This standardization of markers conveys a feeling of military precision and implies that all are accounted for.

The Commonwealth War Graves Commission (formerly Imperial War Graves Commission) was founded by Royal Charter in 1917. The funds of the commission are derived from the six governments participating in its work: Australia, Canada, India, New Zealand, South Africa, and the United Kingdom. The commission is responsible for the commemoration of 1,695,000 members of the forces of the Commonwealth who fell in the two world wars. More than 1 million graves are maintained in 23,199 burial grounds throughout the world. Over three-quarters of a million men and women who have no known grave or who were cremated are commemorated by name on memorials built by the commission.

Figure 1. This cemetery in Suresnes, a suburb of Paris, contains the remains of American military from both World Wars. (SOURCE: American Battle Monuments Commission)

U.S. National Cemetery System

The U.S. government established a national cemetery system at the time of the American Civil War (1861–65) when Congress enacted legislation authorizing the president "to purchase cemetery grounds . . . to be used as a National Cemetery for soldiers who shall have died in the service of the country." Originally operated by the army, the system is now under the control of the Department of Veterans Affairs. The director of the National Cemetery System oversees the operation of 113 national cemeteries and 32 burial plots and monument sites located throughout the United States and Puerto Rico. Interment in a U.S. national cemetery is available to veterans discharged under conditions other than dishonorable. Also eligible under certain guidelines are a veteran's spouse and specified dependents.

A government-furnished headstone or marker is placed at each grave in a national cemetery; the government also provides a memorial marker or headstone for veterans whose remains have not been recovered. This includes memorial markers for those who were buried at sea, those whose bodies were donated to science, and those who were cremated with the ashes being scattered. In 1873, the U.S. Congress passed a law requiring that headstones of white marble or granite be used throughout the National Cemetery System. These headstones are routinely replaced by the government before the inscriptions become indecipherable.

A few U.S. veterans, generally found among those who served aboard naval vessels, request sea burial. Their remains are held at a commercial funeral home near a U.S. naval facility until being put aboard a vessel sailing for deep water. A full military funeral is held at sea with the ship's captain or executive officer, a military chaplain, firing party, and bugler in attendance. The U.S. Navy will furnish the next of kin a photostat of the nautical chart showing the exact location of the vessel at the time of burial, a folded American flag, and the three shell casings from the final salute.

The U.S. government provides a burial allowance to certain veterans, and a plot allowance is available if a veteran is not buried in a national or other federal cemetery. The government provides an amount toward the purchase of a private headstone if a government headstone is not requested. It also provides an American flag to drape the casket and issues a memorial certificate bearing the signature of the president, an expression of the nation's recognition of the deceased veteran's service. The flag used to drape the casket is traditionally offered to the next-of-kin at the conclusion of the burial service.

President George Bush, referring to the mission of the National Cemetery System, said at a White House ceremony on 15 March 1989: "There is no power or glamor in such a job. But there is caring and respect—for those who are gone, and for those who grieve."

WILFRED L. EBEL

SEE ALSO: Attrition: Personnel Casualties; Casualties: Evacuation and Treatment; Chaplaincy, Military; Medicine, Military; Morale.

Bibliography

Habenstein, R. W., and W. M. Lamers. 1974. *Funeral customs the world over.* Milwaukee, Wis.: Bulfin Printers.

MacCloskey, M. 1968. *Hallowed ground.* New York: Richards Rosen Press.

Mossman, B. C., and M. W. Stark. 1971. *The last salute: Civil and military funerals 1921–1969.* Washington, D.C.: Department of the Army.

Peters, J. E. 1986. *Arlington National Cemetery, shrine to America's heroes.* Woodbine House.

Steere, E. 1959. *The Graves Registration Service in World War II.* Q.M.C. Historical Studies, no. 21. Washington, D.C.: Government Printing Office.

Steere, E., and T. M. Boardman. 1957. *Final disposition of World War II dead 1945–51.* Q.M.C. Historical Studies, Series II, no. 4. Washington, D.C.: Government Printing Office.

BURMA (Union of Myanmar)

The Socialist Republic of the Union of Myanmar, or Burma, and its capital of Rangoon have experienced military repression, political turmoil, and economic problems since Japanese occupation in World War II. The largest country in Southeast Asia, Burma is rich in natural resources and was once Asia's leading oil exporter and a major exporter of rice. This is no longer true. Burma's major export today is teak, which has supplanted rice in recent years, and the country is one of the poorest in Asia.

Rimmed with steep, rugged mountains descending into the central plain facing the Bay of Bengal and Andaman Sea, Burma has a population of nearly 40 million, with ethnic divisions of 68 percent Burman, 9 percent Shan, 7 percent Karen, 4 percent Rakhine, 3 percent Chinese, 2 percent Indian, 2 percent Mon, and 5 percent other groups. Most live in predominantly rural areas or along major river valleys. Burmese, related to Tibetan, is the official language, and English, now in decline, is the second language; however, many ethnic group languages are used. Religious groups are 85 percent Theravada Buddhists, and the remaining 15 percent hold various indigenous beliefs or are Muslims or Christians.

Burma is subject to earthquakes and cyclones, and flooding and landslides result from tropical southwest monsoons (June to September). Rainfall varies from over 200 inches annually to about 30 inches in the dryer central area. Natural resources include oil, timber, tin, copper, tungsten, lead, coal, marble, limestone, precious stones, and natural gas. However, the country is heavily dependent on the agricultural sector, which accounts for 40 percent of Burma's GNP and employs 65 percent of the work force.

Historically, Burma has been an important nation in the Southeast Asian region. While the potential for participation and important contributions to the region in terms of economic growth and security are substantial, these are overshadowed by internal political, economic, and military problems.

Power Potential Statistics

Area: 678,500 square kilometers (261,969 sq. mi.)
Population: 41,469,800
Total Active Armed Forces: 280,000 (0.675% of pop.)
Gross Domestic Product: US$16.8 billion (1990 est.)
Annual Defense Expenditure: US$315.0 million (3% of GDP, 1988 est.)
Iron and Steel Production: not available
Fuel Production:
  Crude oil: 0.7 million metric tons (1989)
  Natural gas: 1,106 million cubic meters (1989)
Electrical Power Output: 2,900 million kwh (1990)
Merchant Marine: 60 vessels; 968,226 gross registered tons
Civil Air Fleet: 17 major transport aircraft; 79 usable airfields (29 with permanent-surface runways); none with runways over 3,659 meters (12,000 ft.); 3 with runways 2,440–3,659 meters (8,000–12,000 ft.); 37 with runways 1,220–2,440 meters (4,000–8,000 ft.).

For the most recent information, the reader may refer to the following annual publications:
The Military Balance. International Institute for Strategic Studies. London: Brassey's (UK).
The Statesman's Year-Book. New York: St. Martin's Press.
The World Factbook. Central Intelligence Agency. Washington, D.C.: Brassey's (US).

History

In the eleventh century, King Anawrahta unified the people of Burma and brought independence and political order to the country. Although Kublai Khan's invading Mongol hordes in 1287 were eventually repulsed by the Burmese, political order was destroyed and the subsequent dynasty established in 1486 was characterized by internal disarray and influenced by successive wars with Thailand (Siam). Reunited by King Alaungpaya in 1752, Burma repelled a Chinese invasion but in the next centuries was annexed by Britain—then competing with

France for dominion in the area. There were three Anglo-Burmese wars between 1824 and 1886, and the British finally annexed the entire country, exiled the king, and destroyed Burma's monarchial system.

During the ensuing colonial era, intruding British, Indians, and Chinese came to control the country's economy. Although Burma was separated from India in 1937 and granted a constitution and limited self-government, the ethnic minorities were separately administered. The Japanese occupied Burma in World War II, and gave purported independence to an anti-British nationalist group. In late 1944, when it was obvious that Western Allies were defeating the Japanese, the nationalists turned against the Japanese and provided modest assistance to the Allies in retaking the country.

The Anti-Fascist People's Freedom League coalition of nationalists helped form the Union of Burma, which became independent (and outside the Commonwealth of Nations) in 1948. With the assassination of war hero General Aung San in 1947, Prime Minister U Nu became president and used parliamentary democracy to create a socialist welfare state. However, there were revolts by communist and other dissident groups, and separatist movements by minority ethnic groups. A party split in 1958 led to a political crisis in which army chief of staff General Ne Win took over as caretaker/prime minister.

U Nu was reelected in 1960, and though his party took office, they were ineffective. Ne Win again seized power in a military coup in 1962, and held it in one form or another until the 1988 popular revolts. The revolts ousted Ne Win from office, but possibly not from power. The Burmese military, although divided within itself, savagely restored some semblance of order in late 1988, enabling defense minister Saw Mausing to become president—essentially a renewal of the old military dictatorship. In 1989, the government officially changed the country's name from Burma to the Socialist Republic of the Union of Myanmar, though it is still generally referred to as Burma.

The democratic stirrings of the revolt had not been without effect, and the government scheduled and held popular elections. Unexpectedly, an opposition political coalition, under the dynamic leadership of Daw Aung San Sun Kyi, the charismatic daughter of Aung San, won an overwhelming popular election victory early in 1990, suggesting that the nation may soon again become a democracy.

Politico-Military Background and Policy

Burma has been governed in recent years by military officers who moved into various offices with civilian titles, implementing a "Burmese Way to Socialism" with an appearance of democratic socialism under a unicameral single-party system based on the European model.

Burma is ruled by a Council of State, which works through a Council of Ministers. The executive branch includes the President, the Chairman of the Council of State, and a Prime Minister. The National Assembly (People's Congress) purportedly has legislative power under a constitution of 3 January 1974, and constitutes the legislative branch of government. The judicial system consists of a system of People's Courts, and features a Council of People's Judges and a Council of People's Attorneys. There is no Supreme or High Court, these being abolished in 1962. Burma does not accept compulsory International Court of Justice (ICJ) jurisdiction.

Administratively, the nation is organized along ethnic lines, with seven so-called divisions that have a Burmese ethnic majority, and seven so-called states with non-Burmese majorities. Suffrage in the country is universal over age 18, and in 1990 the military government legalized formerly illegal political parties, giving rise to heavy voter support for democratic reforms in the May elections.

In 1988, the constitution was suspended by the military government and martial law has been a feature until the present. Burma's military forces seem to be inextricably linked with political power, deriving their modern beginnings from the chaotic post-World War II era. Military service is voluntary at age 18, though eligibility covers ages 15 to 49, and is open to both sexes. Of the eligible people in this age group, approximately half are considered fit for military service, with something less than 900,000 males and females reaching military age annually.

Approximately 230,000 personnel are actively serving in the Burmese armed forces. Traditionally, their efforts have focused on counterinsurgency, maintaining internal security and assisting the government administration, and providing for territorial defense. Until recently, a key role of government and military has been that of counternarcotics, but the collapse of Rangoon's antidrug programs have resulted in an increase in Burma's production of the opium poppy, and the country continues to be the world's largest producer.

Burma is characterized by independent regional forces, most with loose and shifting alliances, and many involved in the opium trade. Primary among these are the National Democratic Front (NDF) with about 20,000 active fighters, and the Burma Communist Party (BCP) with 10,000 active forces and 8,000–10,000 militia. Other independent forces compose various private armies, most of which are closely linked to the narcotics trade.

Strategic Problems

Burma's size and rugged terrain, featuring surrounding mountain ranges with steep valleys and heavy forests, have contributed to the country's isolation, and to a lack of easy east-west communication within the nation. Rivers provide major, if unidirectional (generally north-south), transportation routes.

Although categorized as part of Southeast Asia, Burma

is a geographic juncture for the overlapping South, Southeast, and East Asia regions. Strategically located near key Indian Ocean shipping lanes and having long land borders with major Asian powers in the north, Burma also comprises a substantial part of the Golden Triangle—source of some of the world's most dangerous narcotics. Once Asia's largest oil exporter and a leading exporter of rice, Burma has immense natural resources, but has become "an economic and political backwater" in the view of visitors. Today, Burma is one of the poorest countries in Asia and in 1987 had to apply to the United Nations for Least Developed Country status.

The most significant strategic problem facing Burma is coming to grips with, and rebuilding, an economy torn apart by World War II and subsequent political turmoil. This is also important to the other states in the region, who stand to benefit through trade and increased commercial contacts should Burma reestablish control of its economic future. This surely poses a difficult challenge as long as Burma remains split by military insurgencies and political divisiveness.

Militarily, Burma was a strategic objective of the Japanese at the outset of World War II, and later provided a strategic base for Allied air and ground forces in their successful campaign against Japan. Today, Burma's strategic importance is diminished due to underdeveloped natural resources, and the lessening of international communism's influence. The country will, however, continue to play an important regional role should conflict between regional nations occur.

Defense Industry and Military Assistance

Though Burma does manufacture some military equipment locally (e.g., armored personnel carriers), most hardware comes from outside the country. Burma's main battle tank, the Comet, is of British design and manufacture; also in inventory are Swedish Carl Gustav antitank guns, French Alouette helicopters, and vintage U.S. and Soviet howitzers.

Since the mid-1970s, Burma has, on average, spent something more than 20 percent of its annual budget on military expenditures, similar to other countries in the region. As a percent of GNP, however, Burma ranks higher than average in the region, at 6.1 percent for 1990. Defense expenditures are perhaps somewhat offset by foreign aid; from 1970 to 1988, the United States supplied US$158 million, other Western nations provided US $3.8 billion, and Communist countries provided US$424 million.

Alliances

Burma joined the United Nations in 1948, and belongs to the ADB, Columbo Plan, ESCAP, FAO, GTT, GATT, IAED, IBRD, ICAF, IDA, IFC, IHO, ILO, IMF, IMO, INTERPOL, IRC, ITU, UNESCO, UPU, WHO, and WMO. Despite many international memberships, Burma maintains an intense neutrality, and was a founder of the nonaligned movement. Burma maintains contact with ASEAN, but has no wish to become a member. Of interest is that Burma maintains good relations with China and Japan; however, relations with North Korea were broken after a North Korean assassination plot against visiting South Korean diplomats in 1988.

Defense Structure

Burma's military consists of Army, Navy, Air Force, and paramilitary units. Organized into nine light infantry divisions and ten regional commands, the Army has 233 infantry battalions, two armored battalions, five artillery battalions, and one antiaircraft artillery battalion. The Navy has 12,000 personnel including one battalion of naval infantry (marines), and has bases at Bassein, Mergui, Moulmein, Seikyi, Rangoon, and Sittwe, where 46 patrol and coastal combat vessels are stationed. The Air Force, with 9,000 members, has a mix of aircraft for various missions. Key among these are one fighter squadron, two counterinsurgency squadrons (COIN), and an assortment of transports, liaisons, and rotor-wing aircraft.

(For an explanation of the abbreviations and symbols used in the following section of military statistics, see the list of Abbreviations and Acronyms in each volume.)

Total Armed Forces

Active: 280,000.

ARMY: 259,000.
9 lt inf div (each 3 Tac op comd [TOC]).
10 Regional Comd (8 with 3 TOC, 2 with 4 TOC). 32 TOC with 124 garrison inf bn.
Summary of cbt units: 223 inf bn; 2 armd bn; 5 arty bn; 1 AA arty bn.
Equipment:†
MBT: 26 Comet.
Recce: 45 Ferret, 30 Mazda (local manufacture).
APC: 40 Humber, Hino (local manufacture).
Towed arty: 76mm: 120 M-1948; 88mm: 50 25-pdr; 105mm: 96 M-101; 140mm: 5.5-in.
MRL: 122mm: Type-63 reported.
Mortars: 120mm: 80
RCL: 84mm: 500 Carl Gustav; 106mm: M40A1.
ATK guns: 60: 57mm: 6-pdr; 76.2mm: 17-pdr.
AD guns: 37mm: 24 Type-74; 40mm: 10 M-1; 57mm: 12 Type-80.

NAVY: † 12,000 incl 800 Naval Infantry. Bases: Bassein, Mergui, Moulmein, Seikyi, Rangoon (Monkey Point), Sittwe.
Patrol and Coastal Combatants: 46:
Corvettes: 2: 1 Yan Taing Aung (US PCE-827); 1 Yan Gyi Aung (US Admirable MSF).
Patrol: 44:
Coastal: 8:2 Nawarat, 6 Yan sit Aung (Ch Hainan).
Inshore: 31: 9 US PGM-401/412, 12 Yug Y-301, 10(.
Riverine: 5(and some 30 boats.
Amphibious: 5 Aiyar Lulin LCT plus craft: 8 LCM.
Support: 3: 1 coastal tpt, 1 AGHS, 1 PC spt.

Marines: (naval infantry): 800: 1 bn.

AIR FORCE: 9,000; 25 cbt ac, no armed hel.†
Fighters: 1 sqn: 12 F-7 (may not yet be op).
COIN: 2 sqn: 15 PC-7, 4 PC-9, 6 Super Galeb.
Transport: 1 F-27, 4 FH-227, 7 PC-6A/-B.
Liaison: 6 Cessna 180, 1 -550.
Helicopters: 4 sqn: 12 Bell 205, 6 -206, 9 SA-316.

PARAMILITARY
People's Police Force: 50,000.
People's Militia: 35,000.
Fishery Dept: est. 250: 12 patrol boats (3 Indaw [Dk Osprey]), 9 inshore(.

OPPOSITION: Numerous rebel groups with loose and varying alliances. Only main groups listed.
Burma Communist Party (BCP): 10,000 active, 8–10,000 militia; disintegrated into ethnic factions incl Wa, Shan, Kokang Chinese and Kachin.
National Democratic Front (NDF): Some 20,000: coalition of numerous ethnic gp, mainly in border areas incl Kachin (8,000), Shan and Karen (5,000) groups.
Private armies (mainly narcotics linked):
Mong Tai Army (formerly Shan United Army)
Chang Shee Fu 'Khun Sa' (narcotics warlord): 2,100
Kan Chit: 450.
United Revolutionary Army: est. 1,000; Kuomintang-linked.
Loi Maw Rebels/Army: est. 3,000.

Future

Until recently, Burma's future seemed murky at best. Today, it remains unclear whether, or how much, the military government will accept the popular expression of democratic hopes of the 1990 election. However, that election demonstrated without question the popular demand for democratic rule, and the willingness of varied segments of the population to risk their all in moving the country toward that objective.

CHARLES F. HAWKINS
DONALD S. MARSHALL

SEE ALSO: India; Slim, William Joseph, Viscount; South and Southeast Asia; Stilwell, Joseph Warren; Thailand; World War II.

Bibliography

Aung, M. H. 1967. *A history of Burma.* New York: Columbia Univ. Press.
Bingham, J. 1966. *U Thant: The search for peace.* New York: Knopf.
Cady, J. F. 1976. *The United States and Burma.* Cambridge, Mass.: Harvard Univ. Press.
Cooper, C. L. 1953. *The strategic importance of Burma to the United States.* Washington, D.C.: National War College.
Gyi, M. M. 1983. *Burmese political values: The socio-political roots of authoritarianism.* New York: Praeger.
International Institute for Strategic Studies. 1991. *The military balance, 1991–1992.* London: Brassey's.
Nu, U. 1975. *U Nu: Saturday's son.* Trans. U Law Yone; ed. U Kyaw Win. New Haven, Conn.: Yale Univ. Press.
Shway, Y. 1981. *The Burman.* New York: Norton.
Spiro, M. E. 1982. *Buddhism and society: A great tradition and its Burmese vicissitudes.* 2d ed. Berkeley: Univ. of California Press.
Steinberg, D. I. 1981. *Burma's road toward development: Growth and ideology under military rule.* Westview Special Studies on South and Southeast Asia. Boulder, Colo.: Westview Press.
——— 1982. *Burma: A socialist nation in Southeast Asia.* Westview Special Studies on South and Southeast Asia. Boulder, Colo.: Westview Press.
Trager, F. 1966. *Burma: From kingdom to republic.* New York: Praeger.
U.S. Central Intelligence Agency. 1991. *The world factbook 1991–92.* Washington, D.C.: Brassey's.
U.S. Department of State. 1986. *Background notes—Burma.* Department of State Publication 7931. Washington, D.C.: Government Printing Office.
Yawnghwe, C. T. (Euggene Thaike). 1987. *The shan of Burma: Memoirs of a shan exile.* Singapore: Institute of Southeast Asian Studies.

BYZANTINE EMPIRE

The Byzantine, or Eastern Roman, Empire fell heir to the heritage of the Roman Empire in A.D. 476. In that year a Gothic general, Odavacer, dethroned Romulus Augustulus, Emperor of the West, and recognized Zeno, Emperor of the East, as the sole ruler of the Roman world. The Byzantine Empire maintained the traditions of Rome, through alternating periods of greatness and decline, until the fall of Constantinople in 1453. The longevity of the empire depended to a large extent on the professionalism and efficiency of its armed forces.

The Byzantine Armed Forces

The Byzantine armed forces exhibited, throughout the existence of the empire, an ability to adapt to changing strategic and tactical situations. Organization, weapons, and tactics changed to meet the threat. "Threat assessment" was a continual process within the Byzantine high command, as the empire's frontiers were rarely free from foreign intrusion, and the threats were usually multiple.

Although elements within the Byzantine defense structure were subject to periodic change, the professionalism and effectiveness of its combat formations—cavalry, infantry, specialist units, naval forces—and Byzantine generalship remained constant.

COMBAT FORMATIONS

The greatest contrast between the Byzantine army and the Roman army of the Republic and Empire was the former's reliance on cavalry. However, the Byzantine army, the heir to the traditions and genius of the army of the Caesars, had inherited its cavalry from the Roman army of A.D. 378, not the army of 33 B.C. After the Gothic victory over the emperor Valens at Adrianople (A.D. 378), the Romans adopted the cavalry organization, weapons, and tactics of the Goths and relegated the infantry, the principle arm of the old army, to a secondary role. The Byzantine cavalry later adopted the arms and tactics of the Persians, the perennial enemy of the empire for its first 159 years.

The cavalry was divided into heavy cavalry and light cavalry. The heavy cavalryman wore personal armor consisting of a helmet, thigh-length mail shirt, mail gauntlets, greaves, and heavy boots with spurs. Weapons included a lance, sword, axe or mace, dagger, and bows and arrows. Heavy cavalry horses were also armored, and the Byzantine saddle was fitted with stirrups. So equipped, the Byzantine *cataphract* resembled his Persian counterpart and prefigured the knight of the European Middle Ages.

The light cavalryman was lightly armored; his armor consisted of a helmet and a waist-length mail shirt. Weapons were either bows and arrows or javelins, as well as a sword.

Although secondary in importance to the cavalry, the Byzantine infantry was not allowed to atrophy. The infantry, like the cavalry, was divided into heavy and light formations. The heavy infantry (*scutati*) were equipped with helmet, waist-length mail shirt, gauntlets, and greaves. Offensive weapons were the lance, sword, or axe. Heavy infantrymen also carried large shields (*scutum*) from which they derived their name.

The light infantry (*psiloi*), like the light cavalry, wore little personal armor. When worn, armor consisted of a helmet and a waist-length mail shirt. Weapons included bows and arrows or javelins. Often the infantryman carried an axe and a small, round shield.

Specialist support units consisted of engineer, transportation, supply, and medical units. Besides constructing and repairing roads and bridges, the engineers conducted siege operations. In the field, transportation, supply, and medical assets were drawn from the civilian population and were paid on commission. These units were under command of a *tuldophylax*.

The Byzantine navy dominated the Mediterranean and faced little opposition until the rise of the Arabs in the seventh century. The backbone of the navy was the *droman*, a lateen-rigged, two-masted galley with two banks of oars. Depending on the size of the ship, it had from 30 to 40 oars per side. Normally, 300 men crewed a *droman*.

Byzantine Generalship

The Byzantine approach to the study and practice of war was both professional and scientific. The strengths and weaknesses of enemies and potential enemies were researched. Enemy tactics were analyzed and countertactics developed.

Byzantine combat studies and threat assessments produced a number of treatises on the art of war. These treatises were the equivalent of modern military field and technical manuals. Surviving examples include *Strategikon*, attributed to the emperor Maurice (582–602); *Tactica*, attributed to the emperor Leo VI, "the Wise" (886–912); and *Nicephorus Praecepta Militaria*, attributed to the emperor Nicephorus II Phocas (963–69) but likely written by a staff officer.

The Byzantine high command and general staff were part of the imperial household. The imperial bodyguard functioned as the training ground for officers destined for the highest levels of command.

Strategy and Tactics

Byzantine strategy has often been characterized as defensive. This generalization, however, is contradicted by the aggressive policies of Justinian I, Heraclius, Nicephorus II, John I, and Basil II. Each of these emperors justified his policy on religious and historical grounds. The Byzantine emperor envisioned himself as the anointed protector of Christianity. As the heir of the Caesars, the emperor felt it his duty to reclaim land once part of the Roman Empire, to restore the unity and greatness of the Roman *imperium*. As the *imperium* and Christendom were considered synonymous, Byzantine expansionism was religiously, politically, economically, and historically justified.

Byzantine conduct of war included not only military operations but also diplomatic maneuvers, as well as such niceties as espionage, sabotage, bribery, psychological warfare, subversion, and so forth. Fifteen hundred years before the term became popular, the Byzantines attempted to destabilize enemy governments, either as a prelude to military action or as its substitute. Belisarius, the great general of the Age of Justinian, echoing the sentiments of the Chinese theoretician Sun Tzu, stated that it is best to force the enemy to abandon his objective without resorting to battle. Any means that accomplished this end were felt to be justified.

The basic tactical formation of the Byzantine army was the *numerus* (*bandon*), equivalent to a modern battalion. The size of the *numerus* varied from province to province, ranging from 300 to 500 men under the command of a count (*comes*) or tribune. From three to eight *numeri* formed a *turma* (*moirach*). The strength of the *turma* ranged from 1,500 to 2,400 men, equivalent to a reinforced regiment or demi-brigade. The *turma* was commanded by a *turmarch*. The largest tactical unit was the *thema* (*meros*) consisting of from two to three *turmae*. Commanded by a *strategos*, the *thema* deployed between 4,500 and 7,200 combat troops. Garrison commands were organized on the basis of a *clissura*, a unit roughly equivalent to a *numerus*, commanded by a *clissurarch*.

The Byzantines deployed for battle according to the nature and size of the enemy forces and the nature and size of the Byzantine forces available. All tactical formations were composed of a center and two wings. The composition of the wings was invariably cavalry; that of the center depended upon the availability of heavy infantry. When present, the heavy infantry formed the center and acted as the tactical pivot of the Byzantine line. After receiving the initial enemy assault, the center would hold the foe while the cavalry counterattacked. When the infantry contingent was small, or none was present, heavy cavalry units formed the center, often dismounting when faced by enemy infantry to receive the enemy assault. The armament of the *cataphract* allowed him to function as infantry when necessary.

Byzantine commanders usually deployed their light cavalry hidden in prepared ambush sites. During the battle, these units would attack the enemy flanks and rear.

Byzantine Expansion during the Age of Justinian

The accession of Justinian I, the Great (527–65), initiated the first phase of Byzantine expansion. Justinian, a native of the Latin-speaking province of Illyria, was conscious of his responsibility, as heir of the heritage of Rome, to restore and strengthen the Roman *imperium*. At the time of Justinian's accession, North Africa was controlled by Vandals, Berbers, and Moors; Spain (Hispania) had been overrun by the Visigoths; Italy had fallen prey to the Ostrogoths. Justinian was determined to win back these lands and restore the Roman Empire.

In 533, Belisarius landed in North Africa with a force of 15,000. Of the troops available to him, Belisarius relied on his 5,000 cavalry, composed of his own bodyguard and Hun mercenaries. At the battles of Ad Decimen and Tricameron, Belisarius was victorious. Gelimer, king of the Vandals, surrendered to Belisarius in 534 and Africa (modern Tunisia, as well as much of Algeria and Morocco), once again became a province of the empire.

Justinian's next target was Italy, then under the control of Ostrogoth King Witiges. The emperor gave Belisarius an army of 10,000 with which he was to reconquer Sicily and Italy from a Gothic army ten times the size of his own. Landing in Sicily, where he was welcomed as a liberator, Belisarius quickly secured the island. Crossing the Straits of Messina, Belisarius rapidly advanced as far as Naples, where he encountered stiff resistance. Naples fell after an intrepid detachment of Byzantines penetrated the city defenses by way of the aqueduct system. Rome was occupied in December 536. After withstanding a year-long siege by the Ostrogoths, Belisarius advanced northward from Rome. Defeated in battle after battle, the Goths surrendered in 537.

In 541, the Byzantine hold on Italy was seriously threatened by Totila, the new Ostrogoth king. Raising the banner of rebellion, Totila advanced as far south as Naples before being stopped. Belisarius was able to reoccupy Rome in 546, but was forced to relinquish control of the Eternal City in 549. Justinian recalled Belisarius in 552 and replaced him with Narses. At the battle of Tagina in A.D. 552, Narses crushed the Ostrogoths. The following year, Narses defeated an army of invading Franks at Casilinum. By 554, all of Italy was secured.

The Byzantine reconquest of Italy proved short-lived. In 568, the Lombards invaded Italy and forced the Byzantines into the southern part of the peninsula. However, southern Italy and Sicily remained Byzantine until the advent of the Normans. The Byzantine reconquest of Spain, completed in 554, was somewhat more successful. The empire held the southern third of the Iberian Peninsula until 616, when the Visigoths reclaimed their lost territories.

The Military Reforms of Maurice (582–602)

The Byzantine army of the Age of Justinian possessed many advantages over its enemies in North Africa and Italy. The tactical skill of Belisarius and Narses, as well as the quality of their troops, enabled the Byzantines to overcome numerically superior enemy forces. The flexibility of the *cataphract*, who could fight on foot as well as on horseback, allowed the Byzantine commanders greater latitude and multiple options in operational planning and execution.

The glaring weakness of the Byzantine army was its reliance on foreign mercenaries. The use of mercenaries, a practice inherited from the later Roman Empire, placed a heavy financial burden on the imperial treasury. More troubling, mercenaries tended to desert when the tide of battle turned against their employer. It was for good reason that Belisarius and Narses took steps to reduce vulnerabilities resulting from doubtful troops. Finally, to the extent they had loyalties, mercenaries were loyal to their generals and not to the *imperium*. The specter of a military coup, another legacy of the Roman Empire, was all too real to Justinian and his successors.

The emperor Maurice, a successful general, ascended the throne in 582. Maurice advocated the reorganization of the Byzantine armed forces. First, he greatly reduced the recruiting of mercenaries. Second, all officers were to be appointed by, and responsible to, the imperial government. Third, all soldiers were required to swear loyalty first and foremost to the government, not to their generals.

Maurice's most important reform was the creation of the *themes*. Each *theme* was, in fact, a territorial defense unit under the command of a *strategos*. Under the *strategos* were a number of *turmae*, each having a strength of 2,000 men or more under the command of a *turmarch*. Each *turma* consisted of from six to eight *numeri* (battalions) or *clissurae* (garrisons). The actual tables of organization varied from *theme* to *theme* and depended on such considerations as population and proximity to the frontier.

The *theme* drew its manpower from the large and small landowners within its borders. Officers were recruited from among the large landowners, while the rank and file were drawn from the small landowners. Both officers and men received pay and tax exemptions for their service. Although used primarily in defense of its own territory, each *theme* provided contingents to the national army in times of crisis.

The *theme* system had much in common with the military system of Persia and the later feudal system of western Europe. All three systems tied military service to landholding. All three supplied a specified type of soldier in exchange for land and other perquisites. The *theme* system differed from the other two in that both large and small landowners formed the fighting force of the *theme*. In many respects the *theme* system married the feudal system of Persia with the ancient military tradition of the Greek city-states and the Roman Republic, the tradition of the citizen-soldier.

The *theme* system, begun under Maurice, was not completed until the reign of Leo III (717–41). In the interim, the Byzantine Empire suffered a series of crises and military defeats that threatened its very existence.

The Slavic War

During the reign of Maurice, the empire faced multiple threats on multiple fronts. To the north the Avars, the Slavs, and the rising power of the Bulgars loomed ominously. To the east, Persian expansionism once again threatened Syria, Palestine, and Asia Minor. The Slavic penetration of the Balkans was countered with a war of annihilation. Maurice entrusted the war to General Priscus. In one year in the late 590s, the Byzantines slaughtered 28,000 Slavs. The next year, Slav casualties amounted to 30,000 slain. Priscus finally crossed the Danube and systematically destroyed Slav settlements and put the inhabitants to the sword. Yet, before the Slav onslaught relented, the provinces of Thrace and Illyria—the two principal Latin-speaking provinces of the empire—lay in ruins.

The Persian War (602–630)

In 602 Maurice was overthrown and slain by one of his generals, Phocas, who assumed the imperial dignity. Chosroes II, king of Persia, used Maurice's murder as an excuse to break his treaty with the empire and invaded Syria. Conquering Syria, the Persians advanced into Asia Minor. By 608, the Persians were within sight of Constantinople. Phocas's misrule led to the rebellion of the province of Africa (northwest Africa). The Byzantine general Heraclius, son of the exarch (military governor) of Carthage, assumed leadership of the rebellion. In 610, Heraclius overthrew Phocas and ascended the throne.

For the first twelve years of his reign, Heraclius fought a defensive war against the Persians. All resources of the empire were concentrated on the defense of Constantinople. Consequently, the Persians succeeded in occupying Damascus and Antioch in 613; Jerusalem in 614; Chalcedon in 615; and Egypt in 619. In the west, the Visigoths recovered southern Spain in 616. The Avars once again besieged Constantinople in 619, but were repulsed.

Heraclius took the offensive in 622. Making a surprise amphibious landing on the coast of Cilicia, Heraclius outflanked the Persians and threatened their lines of communication. The emperor out-maneuvered the Persian forces and cut their lines of communication with Egypt, Palestine, and Syria. He won a decisive victory at the Battle of the Halys. At the end of the campaign season Heraclius withdrew to Byzantine territory, having inflicted severe damage on the enemy.

The following year Heraclius, after a feint toward Syria and Palestine, sailed to Trebizond, then swiftly advanced eastward through Armenia. From Armenia, he penetrated the Persian satrapy of Media. With the Persian homeland in peril, King Chosroes recalled his Persian units from Syria. Hoping to force Heraclius' withdrawal from Media, Chosroes convinced his Avar and Slav allies once again to besiege Constantinople.

Even with Constantinople under siege, however, Heraclius remained in Persia, cutting a destructive path through Media. Chosroes had no option but to return to Persia with all available forces. For four years, Heraclius marched through the western provinces of Persia, winning battle after battle. On 12 December 627, the Byzantines won the decisive battle of the war within sight of the ruins of Nineveh, the ancient Assyrian capital. Forced to seek peace, Chosroes agreed to pay a heavy indemnity and return all territories siezed from the Byzantines.

The Byzantine Empire had emerged from its 28-year-long war with Persia victorious. Heraclius was hailed as both hero and savior and, quite deservedly, took his place among the great generals of Roman and Byzantine history. He did not long enjoy the fruits of victory. The war had drained both the Persian and Byzantine empires. To Persia, postwar weakness proved fatal. A new enemy arose on the southern fringes of civilization that swept away the ancient kingdom of Persia and drove the Byzantine Empire to the brink of destruction.

The Arab Conquests

The Arabs burst upon the war-torn Middle East in 634. Damascus fell in September 635 to the combined forces of Abu Obeida and Khalid ibn al-Walid. In 636, Heraclius arrived at Antioch with a strong force. The bulk of this force, commanded by Theodorus, the emperor's brother, reoccupied Damascus without a fight; Khalid ibn al-Walid had withdrawn southward. The Byzantines pursued the retreating Arabs until, at the confluence of the Jordan and Yarmuk rivers, Khalid turned and offered battle. The Battle of Yarmuk (20 August) ended in an Arab victory. Heraclius, upon learning of the defeat of his army and the death of his brother in battle, returned to Constantinople, leaving Syria and Palestine to the Arabs.

The Arabs next invaded Egypt. With the surrender of

Alexandria in November 641, Egypt was secured. Three of the richest provinces of the Byzantine Empire—Egypt, Palestine, and Syria—were in Arab hands. Arab armies threatened North Africa, Asia Minor, and Constantinople itself. In 649 the newly created Arab navy took Cyprus, and in 655 it defeated the Byzantine fleet at the battle of the Masts (Dhat al-sawaib, off Phoenix, Lycian coast).

The Fight for Survival (642–842)

In the 200 years between the death of Heraclius and the rise of the Macedonian Dynasty, the Byzantine Empire waged a desperate struggle for survival. Four times during this period the Arabs laid siege to Constantinople. The sieges of 673–78 and 717–18 were conducted by both ground and naval forces. Constantinople survived all four sieges through a combination of good fortune, courage, and "Greek Fire." The first siege cost the Arabs 30,000 killed; the second, 70,000 killed.

The reign of Leo III, "the Iconoclast" (717–41), marked the turning point in the empire's struggle with the Arabs. Besides successfully repelling the last Arab siege, Leo completed the reorganization of the empire into *themes*. Army reform progressed slowly, but by the end of Leo's reign the Byzantines were able to take the offensive against the Arabs in Anatolia (Asia Minor), scoring a major victory at Akroinen in 739.

In 745 Leo's successor, Constantine V (741–75), initiated operations against the Arabs in Syria. The Byzantine navy defeated an Arab fleet and retook Cyprus in 746. Imperial campaigns in Armenia (751–52) also were successful. Only the loss of Ravenna to the Lombards in 751 marred the rebirth of Byzantine military prowess.

A new enemy now arose to challenge the empire. In the northeastern part of the Balkans, the Bulgar czars embarked on a program of territorial expansion. Between 755 and 764 the Byzantines campaigned against the Bulgars, gaining victories in 759 and 760. War with the Bulgars broke out again in 772, and the Byzantines again were victorious.

Leo IV (775–80) renewed the war with the Arabs in Anatolia. By 800 the Byzantines and the Arabs had reached parity in Asia Minor. Skirmishing continued between the Arabs and the Byzantines, with the border between the caliphate and the empire solidifying along the line of the Taurus Mountains.

In the Balkans, the Bulgars continued to threaten the empire. Leo V (813–20) stopped a Bulgar advance southward at Mesembria in 817.

The Age of Conquest (842–1050)

The accession of Basil I (867–86), first emperor of the Macedonian Dynasty, ushered in the second great period of Byzantine military glory. Basil launched a series of campaigns against the Arabs between 871 and 879. Samosata, on the upper Euphrates, was occupied in 873. During the campaign of 878–79, both Cappadocia and Cilicia were liberated. In Italy, Basil I regained control of Bari (875), Tarentum (880), Sicily (878), and Calabria (885).

Leo VI, "the Wise" (886–912), warred with the Bulgars and their aggressive czar, Symeon. Leo allied with the Hungarians in his struggles with the Bulgars.

Constantine VII (912–59) suffered a series of reverses in the ongoing struggle with the Bulgars. Although the Byzantines successfully repelled a Bulgar attempt on Constantinople in 913, Adrianople fell to the Bulgars the next year; the Bulgars, however, were not able to hold on to the city. At the battle of Anchialus in 914, the Bulgars were victorious. They once again attempted to take Constantinople in 924, again in vain. The only major victory won by Byzantine arms during this period was at the Garigliano River in southern Italy, in 915, when an Arab attempt to gain a foothold in Italy was repulsed.

In 920, Romanus Lecapenus (920–44) became Constantine's co-emperor. During this joint reign the Byzantines, under the command of John Kurkuas, retook Erzerum (928) and Melitene (934). In 941 the Byzantine fleet soundly trounced a Russian fleet attempting to enter the Bosporus. This was the first intrusion of Russian arms into the empire.

During the short reign of Romanus II (959–63), the Byzantines reoccupied Crete in 960–61. In 963 Romanus died and Nicephorus Phocas, who had commanded the successful operation in Crete, seized the throne and married Romanus' widow, Theophano.

Nicephorus II Phocas (963–69)

Nicephorus ascended the throne as co-emperor with his infant stepsons, Basil II and Constantine. Under Nicephorus, the *theme* system reached fruition, tactics were reformed, and the power and might of the empire reached new heights.

Nicephorus introduced a new tactical formation. Regiments were deployed for battle in a wedge. The front line of the wedge had twenty *cataphracts* abreast; the second line, 24 abreast; the third, 28; the fourth, 32; and so forth—each succeeding line was four men wider than the one to its front until the last (12th) line had 64 *cataphracts* abreast. (In the smaller *cataphract* regiment of 300 men, the formation was nine ranks deep.)

The *cataphracts* of the first four ranks were armed with swords or maces; those from the fifth rank on, with lances. Light cavalry archers were deployed within the wedge from the fifth rank back. A *cataphract* regiment of 500 men contained a detachment of 150 horse-archers; a *cataphract* regiment of 300 men had 80 horse-archers. Nicephorus demanded that the regimental commander lead the regiment from a position in front of the first rank.

Nicephorus initiated operations against the Muslims in

southeastern Asia Minor in 964, occupying Adana. Tarsus fell in 965. The Byzantines retook Cyprus the same year. The emperor invaded Syria in 968, occupying Antioch and Aleppo. Nicephorus' victories so impressed the Muslims that they nicknamed him "The White Death."

When not fighting the Muslims in the east, Nicephorus was fighting the Bulgars in the Balkans. In 966, he formed an alliance with Sviatoslav, king of the Kievan *Russ*, against the Bulgars. By 969, Bulgaria had been overrun and the surviving Bulgars sued for peace.

In late 969, Nicephorus was overthrown and killed by his nephew, John Tzimisces, who as John I became the second co-emperor of Basil II. John I aggressively prosecuted the war against the Muslims. Operations in the east, however, were halted by a Russian invasion led by the empire's erstwhile ally, Sviatoslav. In 969 John defeated Sviatoslav near Adrianople at Arcadropolis. The Byzantines then pursued the Russians to Silistria, where they fought six engagements. During the sixth engagement, the battle of Dorostalon in July 971, John positioned himself before his regiments and personally led the final charge. The Russians wavered before the advancing Byzantines, then broke and ran. The Russians eventually sued for peace in 972.

With the Russian threat ended, John again turned his attention eastward. Edessa and Nezib were occupied in 974. He led the Byzantines into Damascus and Beirut in 976. Reaching the vicinity of Jerusalem in 976, John died suddenly and the Byzantines withdrew to Antioch.

Basil II, "the Bulgarslayer" (976–1025)

Basil II became sole emperor upon the death of John I. Basil's fame and sobriquet resulted from his long and ultimately successful wars against the Bulgars and their czar, Samuel (976–1014). Basil's Bulgar Wars did not begin auspiciously. In 981, at the Battle of Sophia, the Bulgars defeated the Byzantines. Thereafter, the Bulgars penetrated Greece as far as the Peloponnesus. Fifteen years later, Basil launched a series of campaigns against the Bulgars that spanned a period of eighteen years. The emperor's victory at Spercheios in 996 led to the withdrawal of the Bulgars from Greece. In 1002 Basil reconquered Macedonia, only to lose it to Samuel in 1003. Samuel's counteroffensive reached Adrianople, which he sacked. At Balathista, however, Basil destroyed the Bulgar army. Macedonia was once more Byzantine. Basil ordered the 15,000 Bulgar prisoners blinded. One man in 100 was allowed to keep one eye so that he could lead 99 of his totally blinded comrades home. According to tradition, the sight of his blinded soldiers caused Samuel to die of shock. In 1018, the Bulgars submitted to Byzantine suzerainty.

During Basil's reign, the Byzantines first came into contact with the Normans, whom the Byzantines would later contest for control of southern Italy. Their first encounter, at Cannae in 1018, resulted in a Byzantine victory over the Normans and the Lombards.

During the reigns of Basil's immediate successors, Michael IV (1034–41), Michael V (1041–42), and Constantine IX (1042–55), Byzantine arms continued to dominate despite occasional reverses. Campaigns against the Muslims continued.

A Byzantine fleet commanded by Harald Haardrada (future king of Norway and unsuccessful candidate for the English throne in 1066) crushed the Muslim pirates who infested the Aegean (1034–35). A joint operation of the Byzantine army and navy, commanded by Georgios Maniakes and Haardrada, took the Muslim strongholds of Rametta and Dragina in 1038. In 1042, Maniakes defeated the Normans at the Battle of Monopoli. In their first encounter with the Seljuk Turks, at Stragna (1048), the Byzantines were victorious.

Byzantine Decline and the Battle of Manzikert

The reigns of Theodora (1042–56), Michael VI (1056–57), and Isaac I (1057–59) marked the decline of Byzantine power. Under Constantine X (1059–67), the empire lost Calabria to the Normans (1060). In Asia Minor the Seljuks, led by Alp Arslan, raided Armenia and occupied its capital, Ani, in 1064.

Romanus IV Diogenes (1067–71) assumed the imperial dignity upon the death of Constantine. In Italy, the Normans took Otranto (1068) and Bari (1071), ending Byzantine rule in southern Italy. In the east, Seljuk raids increased in both frequency and severity. Convinced that the Seljuks were mounting a full-scale invasion, Romanus in 1068 drove the Turks, under Alp Arslan, from Phrygia and Pontus. He then led an army 60,000 strong into Armenia. In 1069 and 1070, Romanus drove the Turks out of most of the eastern provinces of the empire. Alp Arslan returned to Iraq and raised new forces. Assembling east of Lake Van, the Seljuks in 1071 rapidly advanced westward, skirting the southern shore of the lake. Near Manzikert, the Seljuks surprised the Byzantines and—aided by treachery in Romanus' army—crushed them. Romanus was captured by the Turks. Exploiting their victory, the Seljuks advanced into Anatolia, where Sulaiman Beg established the Sultanate of Rum (Iconium). The loss of Anatolia proved disastrous to the empire. Not only were the rich agricultural lands of the region in enemy hands, but with the loss of Anatolia the empire had lost its prime recruiting ground for the army.

The Comneni, the Crusades, and the Latin Emperors

Following Manzikert, the Byzantine Empire suffered the rule of two incompetent emperors: Michael VII (1071–78) and Nicephorus III (1078–81). Michael neglected the military. His answer to Seljuk aggression was recognition of Seljuk sovereignty over Anatolia. In 1078, Michael was overthrown and murdered by Nicephorus Botaniates. Nichephorus III himself was overthrown in 1081 by General Alexius Comnenus.

Under Alexius I (1081–1118), the Byzantine Empire experienced its penultimate period of greatness. His reign began inauspiciously, however, with a Norman incursion into the Balkans. Robert Guiscard led the Normans to victory at Pharsalus, then occupied Durazzo in Epirus (1082). In 1083, the Normans occupied Macedonia, but a victory of a combined Byzantine-Venetian fleet at Corfu in 1085 turned the tide in the favor of the empire.

The First Crusade provided Alexius the means to retake Nicaea, Dorylaeum, and the Anatolian coast. When Bohemund, son of Robert Guiscard, refused to do homage to Alexius for Antioch, the empire embarked on a new war with the Normans. In 1104, the Byzantines repelled a Norman attempt to retake Durazzo. After four years of inconclusive fighting, Bohemund recognized Byzantine suzerainty.

War resumed between the empire and the Seljuks in 1110. At the Battle of Philomelion, Byzantine arms prevailed. The Peace of Akroinen in 1117 returned western Anatolia to the Byzantines.

John II Comnenus (1118–43) succeeded his father. During his 1120–21 campaign against the Seljuks, John regained southeastern Anatolia. In 1122, he defeated a Patzinak invasion. Between 1122 and 1126, John was at war with Venice over trading rights. He retook Cilicia between 1134 and 1137, and reasserted Byzantine suzerainty over Antioch. John was succeeded by his son, Manuel (Manuel I Comnenus, 1143–80).

War with Roger of Sicily broke out in 1147. The Byzantine fleet, neglected and decayed, was unable to stop the sea-borne Normans. Manuel was forced to hire the Venetian fleet. In 1149 the Venetians took Corfu and, in 1151, Ancona. The war finally ended in 1158, with a return to the *status quo ante*. The bad blood between the Byzantines and the Franks was further exacerbated by the Second Crusade (1147–49).

Between 1152 and 1156, the empire was at war with the Kingdom of Hungary. The first Hungarian war ended in 1156 with Hungarian recognition of Byzantine suzerainty.

Manuel I successfully reimposed Byzantine suzerainty on Antioch in 1159. In 1161, he signed a peace treaty with the sultan of Rum, Kilidj Arslan, who recognized the emperor as his suzerain.

The second Hungarian war ended in 1168. The empire gained control of Dalmatia and part of Croatia. King Bela III of Hungary recognized Manuel I as his suzerain.

Manuel I drifted into war with his erstwhile allies, the Venetians, because of his refusal to renew their trading rights within the empire. In 1171, the Venetians took Ragusa and Chios, but they failed in their attempt to capture Ancona in 1173. The Venetian-Norman alliance of 1175 forced Manuel to seek peace. The empire was forced to renew Venetian trading privileges and pay a heavy indemnity.

The last years of the reign of Manuel I were marked by a new war with the Seljuks of Rum. The stunning Seljuk victory at Myriocephalon in 1176 was partially offset by the Byzantine successes in Bithynia in 1177.

The short reigns of Alexius II Comnenus (1180–83) and Andronicus I Comnenus (1183–85) marked the decline of the Comneni and the empire. In 1185, the Normans captured Durazzo and Thessalonica. Andronicus I was murdered and replaced by Isaac Angelus (1185–95).

With the exception of the victory over the Normans in 1191, the history of the empire continued to be one of decline. In 1185, the Bulgars threw off the Byzantine yoke. The Bulgar war of 1190–94 enlarged the newly independent kingdom at Byzantine expense.

The Fourth Crusade (1202–1204) proved more dangerous to the empire than Bulgar aggression. The crusaders, in alliance with Venice, took Durazzo in 1203. Reaching Constantinople in June 1203, the crusaders forced Alexius III (1195–1203) to flee. The crusaders then installed Alexius IV, son of Isaac Angelus. Alexius was a mere front for the crusaders. On 25 January 1204, the citizens of Constantinople rebelled and deposed Alexius IV. Alexius V Dukas (1204) ascended the throne. On 12 April 1204, the crusaders stormed and sacked the city, while Alexius V fled. (This was the first time Constantinople was ever assaulted successfully.) The crusaders installed one of their own, Baldwin of Flanders, as the first Latin emperor. The Latin emperors ruled a truncated and feudalized empire until 1261.

The Paleologi and the Fall of Constantinople

The rule of the Latin emperors led to the break-up of the empire into feudal domains on the western pattern. Besides his own rowdy, insubordinate vassals, the Latin emperor had to contend with three rival Byzantine successor states: the Despotate of Epirus; the Empire of Trebizond; and the Kingdom of Nicaea. In 1259, Michael Paleologus became king of Nicaea and, upon the recapture of Constantinople in 1261, Emperor Michael VIII (1259–82). Michael reconquered the southeastern Peloponnesus (Morea) in 1261 and the Despotate of Epirus between 1262 and 1265. Victory in a war with the Bulgars (1264–65) returned part of Macedonia to the Byzantine Empire.

The reign of Michael VIII promised a return of the glory days of the empire, but the promise proved illusory. During the reigns of the co-emperors Andronicus II (1282–1328) and Michael IV (1295–1320), Athens was lost to the Catalans, while Brusa and Nicomedia fell to the Ottoman Turks. Although Andronicus III (1328–41) won control of Chios (1329), Thessaly (1334–35), and Lesbos (1336), the victories of Stephen Dushan, king of the

Serbs, threatened the empire. The war against the Serbs was complicated by civil war. For six years, Andronicus III and John V Cantacuzene (1341–76) fought for the throne. Each made use of Serbian and Ottoman troops. The triumph of John V did not bring peace to the empire. The internal power struggles continued throughout the reigns of John V, John VI Cantacuzene (1347–54), Andronicus IV (1376–79), and John VII (1390)—father, sons, and grandson.

The accession of Manuel II (1391–1425) ended the 50-year-long struggle over the throne. The empire had been reduced to Constantinople, Thessalonica, and Morea. Catalans, Venetians, Genoese, Normans, Angevins, and Ottoman Turks had picked the bones of the once mighty Byzantine Empire. The greatest danger to the empire was the growing power of the Ottoman Turks. Three times during the reign of Manuel II the Turks laid siege to Constantinople: 1391–95, 1397, and 1422.

During the reign of John VIII (1425–48), Thessalonica (1430) and Corinth (1446) were lost to the Turks. Constantine XI (1448–53) presided over the final destruction of the empire. In 1453, under Sultan Muhammed II, the Turks captured Constantinople. Morea fell in 1460, and the last remnant of Byzantine power, the Empire of Trebizond, was conquered in 1461.

LAWRENCE D. HIGGINS

SEE ALSO: Arab Conquests; Attila the Hun; Crusades (1097–1291); History, Medieval Military; Khalid ibn al-Walid; Ottoman Empire; Roman Empire; Turkic Empire.

Bibliography

Bivar, A. D. H. 1972. Cavalry equipment and tactics on the Euphrates frontier. *Dumbarton Oaks Papers* 26:273.

Brand, C. M. 1968. *Byzantium confronts the West, 1180–1204.* Cambridge: Harvard Univ. Press.

Browning, R. 1987. *Justinian and Theodora: The Byzantine recovery.* London: Thames and Hudson.

Bury, J. B. 1958. *History of the later Roman Empire.* 2d ed. New York: Dover.

Diehl, C. 1957. *Byzantium: Greatness and decline.* New Brunswick, N.J.: Rutgers Univ. Press.

Isaac, B. 1990. *The limits of empire: The Roman army in the East.* London: Oxford Univ. Press.

Procopius. 1914. *History of the wars.* 6 vols. Trans. H. B. Dewing. London: Heinemann.

Obolensky, D. 1971. *The Byzantine commonwealth: Eastern Europe, 500–1453.* New York: Praeger.

Ostrogorsky, G. 1968. *History of the Byzantine state.* 2d ed. Oxford: Basil Blackwell.

Ure, P. N. 1951. *Justinian and his age.* Harmondsworth, UK: Penguin Books.

Vasiliev, A. A. 1958. *History of the Byzantine Empire, 324–1453.* 2d ed. Madison, Wisc.: Univ. of Wisconsin Press.

Whitting, P., ed. 1972. *Byzantium: An introduction.* New York: Harper and Row.